NEW YORK 1880

ARCHITECTURE AND URBANISM IN THE GILDED AGE

NEW YORK 1880

ARCHITECTURE AND URBANISM IN THE GILDED AGE

ROBERT A. M. STERN, THOMAS MELLINS, AND DAVID FISHMAN

THE MONACELLI PRESS

First published in the United States of America in 1999 by
The Monacelli Press, a division of Random House, Inc.
1745 Broadway, New York, New York 10019.

Library of Congress Cataloging-in-Publication Data
Stern, Robert A. M.
New York 1880 : architecture and urbanism in the gilded age /
Robert A. M. Stern, Thomas Mellins, and David Fishman.
p. cm.
Includes bibliographical references and index.
ISBN 978-1-58093-027-7
1. Eclecticism in architecture—New York (State)—New York.
2. Architecture, Modern—19th century—New York (State)—
New York. 3. City planning—New York (State)—New York—
History—19th century. 4. New York (N.Y.)—Buildings, struc-
tures, etc. I. Mellins, Thomas. II. Fishman, David. III. Title.
NA735.N5S727   1999
720'.9747'109034—dc21   99-17892

Printed and bound in China

10 9 8 7 6 5 4 3 2

Designed by Abigail Sturges
Edited by Jen Bilik

Frontispiece:
View to the northeast, 1894, of the Brooklyn Bridge
(John A. Roebling and Washington Roebling, 1869–83).
The Cotton Exchange (George B. Post, 1883–85), with conical
tower, is on the lower left, with the tracks of the Third Avenue
elevated railroad immediately to the right. The roof of the Fire
Engineer House for Fire Hook & Ladder Company Number 15
(Napolean Le Brun & Sons, 1884), with stepped gables, can be seen
on the lower right. Johnston. MCNY.

❧ Acknowledgments ❧

A book as large and as full of intricate detail as this one would not have been possible without the generous help of many people. Due to space limitations we unfortunately cannot thank by name every individual who assisted us, but we are no less grateful for their input. We express our sincerest thanks to Christopher Gray and Suzanne Braley at the Office for Metropolitan History. Michael Adams provided valuable information. We thank Goteh Nzidee for help with research, and Jennifer Goold, Alexa Pinard, and Erin Rulli for much-appreciated assistance during the book's final stages. The whole staff of the Landmarks Preservation Commission was consistently helpful. As always, the entire staff of Columbia University's Avery Architecture and Fine Arts Library provided help without which this book would truly not have been possible. In particular, we thank Angela Giral, Avery Librarian; Janet Parks, Curator of Drawings; and Katherine Chibnik, Kathe Chipman, Paula Gabbard, Edward Goodman, Daniel R. Kany, Katherine Keller, William O'Malley, Anne-Sophie Roure, Christine Sala, and Barbara Sykes-Austin. We applaud Dwight Primiano's herculean effort in photographing material from Columbia's collections.

We are most grateful to all of the individuals and institutions that assisted us with photographic research and allowed us to use the wonderful images showcased on these pages. Again, it is not possible to thank everyone, but special notice is due to Mary Beth Betts, Nicole Wells, Lisa Berger, Dale Neighbors, Laird Ogden, and Wendy Shadwell of the New-York Historical Society; Sherry C. Birk of The Octagon, the Museum of The American Architectural Foundation; Kenneth R. Cobb of the Municipal Archives; Jonathan Coss of the Equitable Life Assurance Society; Dorothy D'Eletto of the Staten Island Institute of Arts and Sciences; Carlotta DeFillo of the Staten Island Historical Society; Beth Dodd of the Alexander Architectural Archive, at the University of Texas at Austin; William Frost; Michell Hackwelder of the Brooklyn Historical Society; Margot Karp of the Pratt Institute; John Ellis Kordes of the Garden City Archives; Marguerite Lavin, Eileen Kennedy, and Elizabeth Ellis of the Museum of the City of New York; Claire McCurdy of the Union Theological Seminary; Anne Mininberg of the Central Synagogue; Herbert Mitchell; John Pennino of the Metropolitan Opera Archives; Lynne Ranieri and Owen Lampe of the Milburn–Short Hills Historical Society; Victor Remer of the Children's Aid Society; Laura Tosi of the Bronx County Historical Society; and Steve Wheeler of the New York Stock Exchange.

All those involved in the book's production deserve our most heartfelt thanks. Beverly Johnson-Godette accomplished prodigious feats of word processing. Abigail Sturges's wonderfully refined and evocative design adds so much to the book; Steven Tlucek and Thomas A. Perry skillfully helped to realize her scheme. Andrea Monfried, Steve Sears, and Mason White at the Monacelli Press guided the book over the rough spots. We are particularly indebted to our editor, Jen Bilik, who contributed so much to the project. Finally, it was the unfailing support of our publisher, Gianfranco Monacelli, that in the end brought *New York 1880* to life.

❧ Contents ❧

Funeral procession for President Abraham Lincoln, April 24, 1865. View to the northwest of City Hall (Joseph François Mangin and John McComb Jr., 1803–11) draped in black. Gurney. NYHS.

❧ Preface ❧

This book chronologically begins what is intended as a five-part series chronicling the architecture and urbanism of New York City from the Civil War to the end of the twentieth century. Three volumes have already been published: *New York 1900*, *New York 1930*, and *New York 1960*, which together document the story from 1890 to 1976. *New York 2000*, still to be written, will carry the history to the end of the twentieth century. The chronological span of the series was planned to reflect New York's rise to prominence as one of the leading cities of the modern world—some would say *the* leading city—and its success in retaining this status. Though by 1865 New York was the nation's largest city, it was still provincial by international standards. By World War I it was not only America's preeminent metropolis but also a rival to London, Paris, and Berlin, the great capitals of Europe. While New York City retained its international standing in the post–World War II era, the character of American urbanism was changing significantly, rendering New York the most important but not the absolutely dominating force in a new, virtually continuous conurbation along the east coast of the United States. Extending from Washington, D.C., to Boston, Massachusetts, this stretch came to be called Megalopolis.

As with the three previous books in the series, our intention is not to sit in judgment but rather to let the architects and promoters, the planners and the critics of New York's evolving urban culture speak for themselves as much as possible. To this end, we have illustrated our text with period photographs and drawings and, where they were unavailable, with later photographs, which are identified as such. We have also relied extensively on the writing of the period so that readers of this book will be able to appreciate the achievements of the Gilded Age in as direct a manner as possible.

We have learned a great deal since 1979, when work began on *New York 1900*; certain peripheral discussions in that book of ideas and buildings of the 1880s are here

vastly expanded and, in some cases, recast. Those familiar with the key personalities of the years covered in detail in *New York 1900* will be pleased to see these same figures in earlier stages of their careers as they emerged onto the New York scene. This is not only true of architects, such as Charles Follen McKim, J. C. Cady, and R. H. Robertson, to name a few whose practices flourished from the 1870s until the first decade of the twentieth century, but also of important critics, such as the fashionable architect Russell Sturgis, who apprenticed with Leopold Eidlitz but stopped an active practice in the 1870s to devote his energies to writing and lecturing on art and architecture.[1] An ardent follower of the British art and architecture critic John Ruskin, Sturgis would write important articles on George B. Post, McKim, Mead & White, and Bruce Price for *Architectural Record*. Mariana Griswold Van Rensselaer, who was more prolific as an author of poetry, fiction, and art criticism, and who also wrote on history and landscape design, was another influential critic, writing about architecture in the pages of the *American Architect and Building News* and *Century Magazine*.[2] Her most notable work in the field was her 1888 study of H. H. Richardson, the first monograph of an American architect. Whether praising the work of Leopold Eidlitz, delineating the inadequacies of Richard Morris Hunt, or abhorring the advance of the Queen Anne style, the most important voice of the period by far belonged to Montgomery Schuyler, who, ironically enough, began his architectural writing career with a negative assessment of Eidlitz's Temple Emanu-El in 1868 in the *New York World*. Schuyler's early work was mostly published anonymously but, with the help of pioneering analyses of his writing by William H. Jordy, Ralph Coe, and William Thorn, a host of Schuyler's articles for the *World*, the *Real Estate Record and Builders' Guide*, and, after 1883, the *New York Times* has been added to the list of signed and otherwise long-identified Schuyler pieces from such publications as the *American Architect and Building*

View to the northeast, 1883, showing, from left to right, the top of the Western Union Building (George B. Post, 1873–75), steeple of Trinity Church (Richard Upjohn, 1846), Washington Building (Edward H. Kendall, 1882–85), Castle Clinton (John McComb Jr., 1807), and New York Produce Exhange (George B. Post, 1881–84). NYHS.

News, Architectural Record, Scribner's Magazine, Harper's Weekly, and *Harper's New Monthly Magazine*.[3]

New York 1880 documents New York's architectural history from the end of the Civil War, in 1865, to the rise of the Classical Revival—the so-called American Renaissance—in 1890. This period is widely known as the Gilded Age, a term coined by Mark Twain and Charles Dudley Warner in their 1873 novel, *The Gilded Age: A Tale of To-Day*.[4] Though Twain and Warner referred to the freewheeling, corrupt Bonanza economy of the late 1860s and early 1870s in their use of the term, it quickly took on a new meaning. The Gilded Age soon encompassed the opulent post-1880 era of such newly rich families as the Vanderbilts who usurped quiet Knickerbocker society with a life of grand social display and glorious architectural patronage.

We did not lightly arrive at our decision to title the book *New York 1880*. At first glance, the year 1876 might seem to be the more appropriate date on which to focus this discussion. After all, 1876 was the year of the Centennial, a decisive turning point in our national life and thought. This momentous anniversary coincided with a time when America was not only capable of putting the Civil War and the Reconstruction Era behind it but also when, for the first time, the young country was able to face up to its identity as a totality rather than a collection of regions. The Centennial was principally celebrated, however, at a well-attended world's fair in Philadelphia.

More significant, the middle of the 1870s was not a fecund period for building, either in New York or in the nation as a whole, both of which were hit very hard by a financial depression triggered by the collapse of the powerful banking house Jay Cooke & Co.[5] The mid-1870s can actually be seen as a low point between two booms. Prior to the Panic of 1873, New York more than any other city had benefited economically from the Civil War and from the postwar Bonanza economy of cheap money—the notorious "greenbacks"—and rampant inflation, consolidating control not only over the nation's financial markets but over its cultural life as well. After 1873, however, the city's fortunes plummeted. Within a year or so the Panic of 1873 would bring local economic life to a virtual standstill. The depression was felt almost immediately after the crash when, in the winter of 1873–74, nearly twenty-five percent of the city's workforce was idle and the number of families receiving assistance from the New York Association for Improving the Condition of the Poor, a prominent private charity, rose from about 5,000 families to almost 25,000 families. Despite the Centennial's positive effect on the nation as a whole, 1876 marked a low point in New York City's self-confidence. Economic conditions were so bad that foreign immigration declined from 45,000 in 1875 to 11,000 in 1876. Even the "gentlemanly" profession of architecture, filled as it was with practitioners of independent means, was devastated, leading the New York correspon-

dent of the newly founded, Boston-based *American Architect and Building News* to report that though "some of the architects hint at large projects which they hope to carry out during the coming working season . . . it seems that businessmen and corporations are in no haste to put their capital into fine buildings. The city is now suffering under high taxes, and a falling rent-market discourages anything in the way of speculative building . . . everywhere stagnation reigns."[6] The collapse of New York's real estate economy occasioned a great deal of soul-searching.[7] Reverend Dr. Maunsell Van Rensselaer, a philanthropist and old-line New Yorker, put the situation succinctly: Broadway, the city's main commercial street and in the late 1860s and early 1870s the most visible sign of the city's explosive growth, was "to-let—and we live in painful uncertainty."[8]

While 1876 marked a low point in New York's economic situation, 1880 signaled the beginning of sustained prosperity that would last until the depression of 1893. By 1880 or just after, the steam elevator, the telephone, electricity, and an elevated railway system were all in place to help make possible the complete reconfiguration of the historic lower city and the occupation by businesses and residences of virtually all of Manhattan. The public institutions founded amid the optimism of the post–Civil War boom had been only falteringly developed in the economically stagnant 1870s, but by 1880 they were ready to play their rightful roles: the American Museum of Natural History, founded in 1869,

had moved into its West Side home in December 1877, and the Metropolitan Museum of Art, founded in 1869, moved into its first purpose-built facility in 1880. Most significant of all, in 1883 the Brooklyn Bridge, begun in 1869, opened at last, marking the city's first major step toward the space-swallowing scale that would be its most distinguishing characteristic among the world's great metropolises.

The 1870s marked an important time of transition in the city's architecture that was not only made manifest in stylistic shifts but also in the very nature of the buildings. In 1865, the city's skyline was dominated by church spires. After 1876, this hierarchy was challenged by George B. Post's Western Union Building, Richard Morris Hunt's Tribune Building, and the towers of the Brooklyn Bridge, all about the same height as the spire of the city's tallest church, Richard Upjohn's Trinity Church, which had been finished in 1846. After 1880, with the explosive development of office buildings and warehouses of great height and extraordinary bulk, New York's skyline would not only look like that of no other place in the world but would also represent a set of values quite different from that of any other city. New York would be, after 1880, a world capital. Unlike any other, however, its power would not come from the realms of politics or religion but from manufacturing, finance, and culture. In those characteristics, New York was—and remains—unquestionably and uniquely modern among cities.

Madison Square Garden, Fourth to Madison Avenue. East Twenty-sixth to East Twenty-seventh Street. McKim, Mead & White, 1887–90. View to the northeast, c. 1895, showing the Leonard P. Jerome house (Thomas R. Jackson, 1859) on the right. NYHS.

CHAPTER 1

∾ Introduction ∾

New York is a great secret, not only to those who have never seen it, but to the majority of its own citizens.

—James D. McCabe Jr., 1868 [1]

New York is a study of contrasts. It has no virtue without its corresponding sin; no light without its shadow; no beauty without deformity; for it is a little world in itself. . . . New York is the City of the time to come. . . . It is now . . . the Great Metropolis of the Continent, and in the next century will be the Great Metropolis of the World. . . . This City will be a country of itself, a nation for its strength, its resources, its incalculable riches. Broadway will be the great thoroughfare of the World; Fifth Avenue the street of luxury and splendor beyond what history has shown. Our rivers will be spanned with noble bridges, and Babylon, Palmyra, Rome, Athens, in their palmiest days will be re-created here.

—Junius Henri Browne, 1869 [2]

New York is not a picturesque city, like London or Paris. . . . It has no great antiquity, and has, therefore, little regard for what is old. In London or Paris you may see some relics of past centuries; these are reverenced and preserved as long as they endure. But New York is a series of experiments, and every thing which has lived its life and played its part is held to be dead, and is buried, and over it grows a new world.

—Harper's Weekly, 1869 [3]

THE WORLD'S COSMOPOLIS

Post–Civil War New York was the nation's most modern city. Even so, and despite a population of 900,000, it remained a comparatively provincial place, a small town exploding. One observer, James D. Miller, nonetheless wrote in 1866 that it was "justly regarded as the Metropolitan City of the New World."[4] While most pre–Civil War New Yorkers lived below Fourteenth Street, by 1875 more than fifty percent of the population—some 511,021 persons—were living "uptown." Uptown at this time fell below Forty-second Street, which meant that 500,000 people were crowded into the lower city, not including the thousands who poured into its commercial, manufacturing, and warehouse districts each business day. The city was ripe for expansion once the development of rapid transit rendered possible a daily commute to the open land at the north end of the island. In anticipation of this growth, almost two-thirds of the gridiron of streets were laid down as far uptown as Ninety-sixth Street. The blocks they formed were empty except for scattered shanties, a few small inns, and country houses built before the war.

The city, including the business district, crowded onto the island's tip, was made up of low structures. Only church steeples punctuated the skyline; the tallest, climbing 284 feet, belonged to Trinity Church (Richard Upjohn, 1846), at Wall Street and Broadway. Among the most prominent commercial structures were John B. Corlies and James

Bogardus's Harper and Brothers Building (1854), at 331 Pearl Street, facing Franklin Square, and James P. Gaynor's Haughwout Building (1857), at the northeast corner of Broadway and Broome Street. While Harper and Brothers was located in the traditional downtown business district, Haughwout's, a retailer specializing in such goods as cut glass and silverware, was farther north along the city's most fashionable shopping stretch, uptown from Alexander T. Stewart's marble-clad department store (Trench & Snook, 1846), America's preeminent palace of trade.

No sooner had the Civil War ended than New York began to grow quickly, outstripping its rivals Philadelphia and Boston, leading the prolific diarist George Templeton Strong, a lawyer, to record that the city was rapidly expanding above Forty-second Street and that the gentry's shopping strip, along lower Broadway, was being rebuilt as a prime business address. On August 6, 1866, Strong observed "another material change in the aspect of Broadway": "Taylor's showy restaurant" had become the office of the American Express Company, and Chapin's Universalist Church, which had been serving as an art gallery, on the east side of Broadway between Prince and Spring Streets, was demolished. Strong, neither an apologist for the past nor a dedicated futurist, took a fatalist's view: "So things go. Let 'em go!" Fourteen months later, on October 22, 1867, Strong took a trip to Fifty-ninth Street from his house at 74 East Twenty-first Street, "traversing for the first time the newly opened section of

View to the southwest from the Brooklyn tower of the Brooklyn Bridge (John A. Roebling and Washington Roebling, 1869–83), 1876. Beal. NYHS.

View to the west along Wall Street, 1870, with the steps of the United States Custom House (Town & Davis, with John Frazee and Samuel Thompson, 1834–42) on the right and Trinity Church (Richard Upjohn, 1846) in the distance. NYHS.

Madison Avenue between Fortieth Street and the [Columbia] College [at Forty-ninth Street], a rough and ragged track, as yet, and hardly a thoroughfare, rich in mudholes, goats, pigs, geese, and stramonium."[5]

A half century of investment prepared New York for the Civil War and post–Civil War boom. One writer, William R. Martin, an early booster of the West Side, stated in an 1865 pamphlet titled *The Growth of New York*:

> New York stands in relation with the whole country as its commercial and financial capital. During the second period of its growth, from 1820 to 1860, a portion of its wealth was employed in constructing railroads and other works of internal improvement, over the valleys of the Ohio and Mississippi and along the borders of the lakes; an employment of capital that involved great waste and loss, and brought but small returns. The leading lines of railroad across this region, beginning to stretch up the western side of the Mississippi valley, have been so long completed that now the promised results of increase of production and wealth have ripened into a harvest for the city. . . . We are now reaping, without further outlay, all the results of our enterprise and investment. The increasing production and commerce of the great Northwestern country (of which but a small portion is as yet fully occupied) are now flowing upon us through channels established and paid for.[6]

In 1869, New York's critical role in national life was cemented with the completion of the Union Pacific Railroad, making transcontinental rail service possible for the first time. John Augustus Roebling, the designer of the

View to the southwest from the Brooklyn tower of the Brooklyn Bridge (John A. Roebling and Washington Roebling, 1869–83), 1876. The spire of Trinity Church (Richard Upjohn, 1846) is visible on the left, the Western Union Building (George B. Post, 1873–75) is on the right, and the spire of St. Paul's Chapel (Thomas McBean, 1764–66; spire, James Crommelin Lawrence, 1794) is on the extreme right. Beal. NYHS.

Brooklyn Bridge, was quick to sense the importance of this event for the city. In his 1867 report outlining his designs for the new bridge and enumerating its value to the city, Roebling wrote that the "great change" that would inevitably follow the completion of the transcontinental line would have international consequences, at first occurring slowly but increasing

> with every coming year, until at last the city of New York will have become the great commercial emporium, not of this continent only, but of the world. In another half-century, Liverpool and London, as commercial centres, will rank second to New York. This is no futile speculation, but the natural and legitimate result of natural causes. As the great flow of civilization has ever been from East to West, with the same certainty will the greatest commercial emporium be located on this continent, which links the East to the West, and whose mission it is in the history of mankind to blend the most ancient civilization with the most modern. The old and the new are to meet on this continent, and this will be effected through the means of commerce.[7]

In the eyes of the so-called civilized world, and especially those in the major European capitals, post–Civil War New York was only just beginning to come into focus as America's representative city, one that vividly exhibited the nation's strengths and weaknesses. According to the historian Albert Fein, New York embodied "the challenge of a democratic nation's capacity to plan for and maintain an urban environment to meet the needs of a uniquely heterogeneous population."[8] Given that New York was not a

View to the north along Broadway, 1860, with the A. T. Stewart & Co. store (Trench & Snook, 1846) on the right. FLC.

View to the west from the Brooklyn tower of the Brooklyn Bridge (John A. Roebling and Washington Roebling, 1869–83), 1876. To the left of the New York pier of the Brooklyn Bridge in the distance are the United States Courthouse and Post Office (Alfred B. Mullet, 1869–75) and the Tribune Building (Richard Morris Hunt, 1873–75). Beal. NYHS.

state capital, its sense of itself as the representative American city was critical, giving rise to what might be called its metropolitan destiny: New York saw itself as a quasi-independent political and cultural entity that was both a microcosm of and a model for the nation as a whole. The ideal of Metropolitanism, not a fully articulated concept until the 1890s, is discussed in *New York 1900*.[9] By the Civil War's end, diversity and breadth of outlook—the "cosmopolitanism" that was to be a key aspect of Metropolitanism—was widely acknowledged as a uniquely New York phenomenon among American cities. This was sensed by William R. Martin, who wrote in his previously cited pamphlet:

New York is cosmopolitan in feeling. Its increase has been so rapid that of its million inhabitants but few are native born. It has received its accessions from every country of Christendom; from the middle states, the proud-spirited South, the true grit of New England; and these accessions have included the very best elements. All feelings and all opinions are represented here. We are all closely in contact. Nowhere are men more energetically intent on their business. Nowhere are opinions more fixed. Nowhere is discussion more earnest and more sharply to the point. Nowhere has it greater freedom. . . . The news of the country concentrates and emanates from here. The intellectual pulsations throb instantly from Portland to San Francisco, and return instantly. No provincialism or sectionalism can secure a lodgment here. Out of this trial

comes the true spirit of New York. The sympathies of all nations and all classes are fused into one common mould and flow out, corrected and purified, for the whole country, with all its variety of people, interests and climate.[10]

New York's cosmopolitanism was extolled as a defining trait by James D. Miller in 1866:

Society in New York has many phases—it is cosmopolitan—an amalgam, composed of all imaginable varieties and shades of character. It is a confluence of many streams, whose waters are ever turbid and confused in their rushing to this great vortex. What incongruous elements are here commingled,—the rude and the refined, the sordid and the self-sacrificing, the religious and the profane, the learned and the illiterate, the affluent and the destitute, the thinker and the doer, the virtuous and the ignoble, the young and the aged—all nations, dialects, and sympathies—all habits, manners, and customs of the civilized globe.[11]

Henry James also took note of New York's cosmopolitanism. In a letter written in April 1883, when the expatriate writer was revisiting New York after a considerable period of time in Europe, James confessed: "I never return to this wonderful city without being entertained and impressed afresh. New York is full of types and figures and curious social idiosyncrasies. . . . It is altogether an extraordinary growing, swarming, glittering, pushing, chattering, good-natured cosmopolitan place, and perhaps some ways the best imitation of Paris that can be found yet with a great originality of its own."[12]

View to the northwest from the Brooklyn tower of the Brooklyn Bridge (John A. Roebling and Washington Roebling, 1869–83), 1876. Beal. NYHS.

Styles and Stylists

New York's cosmopolitanism was frequently invoked as a justification for the eclectic architecture that characterized the Gilded Age. As the editors of the *Real Estate Record and Builders' Guide* observed: "Importations of domestic styles and features in so great variety gives to New York architecture a Mosaic or composite complexion. Much has been said of the uniformity and monotony of our residence quarters, and yet the scrutiny of skilled persons will detect not only a wonderful variety, but a bewildering exuberance of styles and models."[13] The eclecticism of the Gilded Age also reflected its cultural insecurities. The architecture of postwar New York was dominated by a vigorous to the point of vulgar display of French Second Empire–inspired Classicism. A tonic to this aesthetic, seen especially in the work of Richard Morris Hunt, was a more disciplined, if less easily appreciated, synthesis of the more restrained Neo-Grec of France and its opposite, the Gothic favored by the English critic John Ruskin, but largely freed of its moralizing imperative.

There was a moralizing strain and singularity of stylistic approach in such Gothicist architects as Calvert Vaux, as seen in his buildings for the American Museum of Natural History (1874–77) and the Metropolitan Museum of Art (1874–78) (see chapter 2), and C. C. Haight, evidenced in his campuses for Columbia College (1874–89) and the General Theological Seminary (1883–87) (see chapter 2). But after the late 1870s, New York architects, increasingly

Hamilton Hall, Columbia College, east side of Madison Avenue between East Forty-ninth and East Fiftieth Streets. C. C. Haight, 1880–81. View to the southwest from quadrangle. AR. CU.

General Theological Seminary, Ninth to Tenth Avenue, West Twentieth to West Twenty-first Street. C. C. Haight, 1887. View to the northeast from quadrangle showing the library on the left and the deanery on the right. AR. CU.

View to the northwest from the Brooklyn tower of the Brooklyn Bridge (John A. Roebling and Washington Roebling, 1869–83), 1876. Beal. NYHS.

inspired by the exotic, placed a high valuation on individuality of expression and on a self-conscious search for beauty. Puritanical American culture had rarely, if ever, indulged in such a sybaritic view of form. Mirroring Walt Whitman's most intimate poetry, this stylistic ethos reached its climax in 1891 with the selection of Heins & La Farge's exotic, individualistic proposal for the new Cathedral of St. John the Divine (see chapter 2). Rallying under the banner of art for art's sake, the search for beauty could be seen in the overheated opulence of Richard Morris Hunt's Fifth Avenue palace for William K. Vanderbilt (1878–82) (see chapter 4) and in the great new places of public amusement, especially theaters, reaching its peak with Stanford White's Madison Square Garden (1887–90) (see chapter 5). In the late 1870s, artistic architecture began to be seen as something apart from the specific programmatics of building. The cast-iron commercial blocks and the Brooklyn Bridge (see below), with their combinations of advanced engineering and schematized historical-symbolic form, vividly symbolized the split between construction technique and functional program on the one hand and the issue of style on the other. For this reason, such structures were in many ways the era's most liberating, representative, and disturbing monuments. Similarly, George B. Post's historicizing skyscrapers and the mansions of Hunt and McKim, Mead & White were valued not for their compositional integrity but for the original and skillful way in which schematized historical form mirrored the ambitions of their patrons.

The depression of the 1870s caused a virtual stoppage of construction at the same time that a definite break occurred between the architectural tastes of the 1860s and early 1870s and those that would prevail in the 1880s. During the Civil War and subsequent Bonanza economy, New York's architecture reflected the robust, if somewhat vulgar, character of the local culture. Newly rich New York was rough in its manners and provincial in its outlook. Its most prominent architects were almost exclusively foreign-born and foreign-trained. Some, such as Detlef Lienau and especially Leopold Eidlitz, did their best to provide the city with refined buildings.

Perhaps the city's most fashionable architect in the 1860s and surely one of its most gifted, Detlef Lienau frequently mixed ideas from France with those from Germany. Lienau was a German-Dane trained in Berlin and Munich who worked in Paris for Henri Labrouste and others before coming to New York in 1848. He may have emigrated to New York because of political unrest in Europe, but in all likelihood he also made the trip to join up with his brother, an established wine merchant. A meticulous draftsman with a fine sense of building craft, Lienau took advantage of his brother's connections and of the patronage of a French decorator working in New York, Léon Marcotte; with these boosts, he became one of the city's most prominent architects almost overnight, relying heavily on sophisticated interpretations of prevailing French taste. Lienau is credited with introducing the mansard roof to New York; it was the crowning feature of his first large house (1850–52), built at the southwest corner of Fifth Avenue and Tenth Street for Hart M. Shiff, a French merchant and banker.[14] By 1872 the *New York Times* pronounced that a "Mansard Mania" was engulfing architecture.[15]

Leopold Eidlitz was born in Prague in 1823.[16] At the Vienna Polytechnic, Eidlitz studied to be a land steward. His instruction in the construction and maintenance of utilitarian farm buildings sparked an interest in architecture, though there is no record of where he received specialized training in Europe. In 1843, Eidlitz came to New York, following his brother Marc, who was to become one of the city's most important builders. After working as a draftsman in the office of Richard Upjohn until about 1846, Eidlitz joined with Charles "Otto" Blesch, a Bavarian with the architectural training Eidlitz lacked. The partnership, which lasted until 1852, was formed to fulfill the commission for the new St. George's Church (1846–48), facing Stuyvesant Square, a twin-towered house of worship that for many years boasted the largest interior space in the city. While St. George's reflected Eidlitz's admiration for the Bavarian Romanesque Revival of Friedrich von Gärtner, much that Eidlitz learned in Upjohn's office, where Romanesque and Gothic precedent were almost equally valued, could also be seen in the design. Most important, Eidlitz believed in the tectonic morality of Gothic architecture as it was interpreted by the British architect and author A.W.N. Pugin, by the French architect and theorist

Hart M. Shiff house, southwest corner of Fifth Avenue and West Tenth Street. Detlef Lienau, 1850–52. View to the southwest. Lienau Collection. CU.

Eugène-Emmanuel Viollet-le-Duc, and by John Ruskin. At the core of Eidlitz's belief was a Romantic Medievalism that permitted him to work with Romanesque forms and even, as in Temple Emanu-El (1868) (see chapter 2), with Moorish motives. Most of all, Eidlitz's commitment was to a Gothic Revival approach, decrying the Classical and proclaiming that "in true Gothic, so long as you find two stones together, you find architecture."[17]

In the 1870s and 1880s, Richard Morris Hunt and George B. Post presided over a much more important scene than Lienau and Eidlitz had in the 1860s. Their importance lies not only in their sheer success but also in their polished professionalism. As the anonymous author of *A History of Real Estate, Building and Architecture in New York City During the Last Quarter of a Century* put it in 1898: "It may fairly be said they represent perhaps more notably than any other two individuals the thoroughly trained and technically educated element which, about thirty years ago, commenced to gain an ascendancy in the profession."[18] Hunt and Post and the other important architects of the 1880s, such as Charles Follen McKim and Stanford White, were, as Henry-Russell Hitchcock has pointed out, reacting against the moralistic Gothic and hedonistic Second Empire Baroque of midcentury practice.

Richard Morris Hunt, an architect whose career first took off in the Bonanza economy of the late 1860s and early 1870s and, in dramatically different form, flourished in the boom years of the 1880s and early 1890s, was the most representative architect of the Gilded Age.[19] Hunt's importance had its roots in his talent and education as well as in his ability to move in the highest social circles and his profound understanding of the evolving expectations of those figures who shaped and dominated the culture of the reunited republic. Usurping the positions of Lienau and Eidlitz, Hunt was able to continue in top form for close to two decades, until his death in 1895. Hunt was a completely

Cathedral of St. John the Divine, Morningside Drive to Tenth Avenue, 110th to 113th Street. Heins & La Farge, 1891. Winning competition entry, view to the north. CD. CU.

St. George's Church, northwest corner of Rutherfurd Place and East Sixteenth Street. Blesch & Eidlitz, 1846–48.
View to the northwest from Stuyvesant Square. AR. CU.

Temple Emanu-El, northeast corner of Fifth Avenue and East Forty-third Street. Leopold Eidlitz and Henry Fernbach, 1868. View to the northeast. AR. CU.

Pavillon de la Bibliothèque, Palais du Louvre, Paris. Hector Lefuel, assisted by Richard Morris Hunt, 1854–55. LAD. CU.

new type of American architect. Not only was he native born, he was educated in the modern sense—not by apprenticeship but by formal academic training. Born in 1827 in Brattleboro, Vermont, Hunt had a sketchy early education in America and Europe until he entered the studio of Hector Lefuel in Paris in 1845 and then decided to take the entrance examination for the Ecole des Beaux-Arts. He was admitted the following year, the first of a long line of Americans who would study at what was in the nineteenth and early twentieth centuries the world's most important school of architecture. After his studies at the Ecole, Hunt assisted Lefuel with an expansion of the Louvre, returning to New York in 1855 as a uniquely experienced twenty-seven-year-old, ready to establish an independent architecture practice.

Hunt's synthesis of contemporary English and French styles—in essence Victorian Gothic and, despite his training under Lefuel, not Second Empire Baroque but its astringent antidote, the Neo-Grec—was new to the American scene and in many ways his own invention. Although in some ways the early work was not so different from Lienau's and especially Eidlitz's, Hunt's vividly polychromed and vigorously movemented—some would say restless—compositions were bolder and more individualistic. As a result, Hunt failed to impress the increasingly

influential critic Montgomery Schuyler, who much preferred the work of Eidlitz. Hunt was, after all, a trained Classicist, with a full command of formal composition and a scholar's appreciation for virtually all the historic styles of the Western Humanist tradition. In a sense, then, the styles were merely a way of clothing the plan. Beginning with the Lenox Library (1870–77) (see chapter 2) and continuing with a series of remarkable mansions on Fifth and Madison Avenues (see chapter 4), Hunt turned away from the Medievalism of Ruskin and Viollet-le-Duc, with its moralistic overtones, and began to base his work on specific historical models chosen to celebrate beauty for its own sake. This approach, not coincidentally, also celebrated his frequently crude and tasteless millionaire clients' ambitions toward taste and refinement. Hunt triumphed over his age, producing a series of scholarly works that, though they did not achieve a distinct American architectural language, at least established a distinctly American diction. Hunt's very rich patrons wanted, above all, to convey the impression that they were not parvenus, and they treasured the incontrovertible beauty of these seemingly timeless designs. Hunt established the authority of the past and of the architect as an artist, and in so doing he gave the city's architecture and urbanism a gravitas it had never possessed.

After 1880, under Hunt's leadership New York's rich began to house themselves in urban palaces such as had not been constructed in Europe for a hundred years or more. These grand mansions were not only built to exhibit wealth in the public realm but also to enhance and enrich that realm with recognizable interpretations of exemplary specific monuments or styles from the history of architecture. After 1880, fine architecture became a public responsibility of the rich, to be enacted in the houses they built for themselves and in the charitable institutions they supported. This trend would culminate in the civicism of the City Beautiful movement, which Hunt, McKim, White, and others helped initiate and which would be the dominating ideal of American architecture between 1890 and World War I.

By training, experience, and personal inclination, Hunt, more than any other architect, was prepared to shape the metropolitan city. His abortive plan (1861–63) for gateway plazas leading into Central Park (see below), though brilliant, was ill-timed. But when the boom of the 1880s unleashed itself, he was ready to transform the city from a commercially prosperous but culturally provincial backwater into a world capital. He was the first architect to take up the challenge posed by the *Real Estate Record and Builders' Guide* in 1881: "We ought to pay some attention to architecture. Let our descendants see that we can build noble and beautiful as well as large and elaborate structures."[20]

While Hunt had designed commercial buildings in the 1860s and 1870s, it was George B. Post, Hunt's student, who dominated the city's commercial work in the 1880s.[21] Ten years younger than Hunt, Post was a native New

Lenox Library, east side of Fifth Avenue between East Seventieth and East Seventy-first Streets. Richard Morris Hunt, 1870–77.
View to the northeast, showing part of the Presbyterian Hospital (Richard Morris Hunt, 1868–72) behind the Lenox Library on the right.
Holmes. The Octagon, AAF.

William Kissam Vanderbilt house, northwest corner of Fifth Avenue and West Fifty-second Street. Richard Morris Hunt, 1878–82.
View to the northwest, c. 1895, with St. Thomas Church (Richard Upjohn and Richard M. Upjohn, 1865) on the right. NYHS.

Proposed design for Central Park gateway, Gate of Commerce, Sixth Avenue and West Fifty-ninth Street. Richard Morris Hunt, 1861–63. The Octagon, AAF.

Yorker who had studied civil engineering at New York University before entering Hunt's office as a student draftsman in 1858. He remained there for two years before establishing a partnership with another student of Hunt's, Charles D. Gambrill, a partnership that lasted from 1860 to 1867 and was interrupted by the Civil War, in which Post served, rising to colonel from the rank of captain. Post burst to prominence in 1870 with the completion of the Equitable Life Assurance Society Building, on which he had collaborated. Although he was that building's engineer, his association with the project led to the commission for the Western Union Building (1873–75) (see chapter 3), which was built at the same time as Hunt's Tribune Building (1873–75) and with which it was inevitably compared. Montgomery Schuyler wrote: "The pupil evidently surpassed his master. Because in the original Tribune Building, Mr. Hunt, confronted with a novel problem, was fain to resort to a group of stories, instead of a single story as the new architectural unit, whereas Mr. Post in his first essay, hit upon the arrangement of a triple division into a base, shaft and capital, following Aristotle's require-

View to the southwest along Broadway, c. 1875, showing the Astor House (Isaiah Rogers, 1836) on the right and the Western Union Building (George B. Post, 1873–75) on the left. The spire of St. Paul's Chapel (Thomas McBean, 1764–66; spire, James Crommelin Lawrence, 1794) is visible above the Astor House, and Trinity Church (Richard Upjohn, 1846) is seen at the extreme left. FLC.

Tribune Building, northeast corner of Nassau and Spruce Streets. Richard Morris Hunt, 1873–75; Edward E. Raht, 1881–82. View to the east. Holmes. The Octagon, AAF.

Harper and Brothers Building, 331 Pearl Street. John B. Corlies and James Bogardus, 1854. View to the southwest, c. 1870. MCNY.

ment."[22] Post was the architect who best grasped the aesthetic possibilities of the new skyscraper building type, seeing that its formal possibilities lay not in a direct expression of functional and structural realities but in a purely aesthetic overlay that drew from time-honored principles of Classical tripartite composition.

In the 1870s, Post, like Hunt, gave shape to the newly emerging cultural institutions, including New York Hospital and the Long Island Historical Society. His Renaissance-inspired Williamsburgh Savings Bank (1869–75), in the same manner as Hunt's Lenox Library, turned away from midcentury eclecticism to a purer, more scholarly approach rooted in Classicism. In the boom of the 1880s, Post built at least one grand house, that of Cornelius Vanderbilt II on Fifth Avenue. His design echoed Hunt's for William K. Vanderbilt, leading his client to call Hunt in as a consultant. But in the succession of office buildings Post designed between the Post Building (1880–81) and the World Building (1889–90), he was second to none in his mastery of the so-called skyscraper "problem," establishing a pragmatic Classicism of approach that transformed the banalities of a provincial business district into a bold new urbanism fleshed out with convincing monuments to free enterprise.

Hunt set the standard for professionalism. In his Parmly (1861) and Stevens (1878) lawsuits, Hunt vigorously pursued the legal rights of architects as artists and professionals.[23] He also recognized as a professional obligation the need to educate younger architects, establishing an atelier system that in many ways mirrored the way education and practice were combined at the Ecole des Beaux-Arts.[24] Post, who appears not to have been interested in architectural education, was instrumental in transforming the studio-like character of traditional architectural offices into a new type of organization.[25] Post initiated his designs but, rather than turning them over to an assistant to develop, divided the project into component parts and assigned specific tasks to different assistants, organizing the practice of architecture in efficient ways similar to those pioneered by other American professional and commercial enterprises.

Cast-Iron Aesthetic

Cast-iron buildings were a major feature of the city's complex townscape; the material made it possible to recapitulate past forms in a totally modern way. James Bogardus introduced cast-iron construction in the late 1840s on three different city sites: a four-story row of storehouses for Edgar H. Laing, at the northwest corner of Washington and Murray Streets; a grinding plant at Centre and Duane Streets, for Bogardus's own use; and a drugstore for Dr. John Milhau, at 183 Broadway, between Cortlandt and Dey Streets, which, with its tiers of engaged Roman Doric columns and its cornice frieze, demonstrated how grand effects could be achieved with the material.[26] Another

Bogardus design (1854), for Henry Sperry, a clock dealer, at 338 Broadway, near Worth Street, was a six-story, Venetian-inspired building, the round arches of which culminated in an attic pierced by three rondels.[27] That same year Bogardus, acting as engineer for John B. Corlies's design, completed the grandly scaled, inventively if eccentrically detailed, massive and impressive five-story building for the publishers Harper and Brothers, at 331 Pearl Street, facing Franklin Square, which combined offices, storage space, and a printing plant.[28] By 1857, when the financial panic stopped virtually all construction activity, cast iron had become a more-than-respected building material, valued over wood for its presumed fireproofing advantages and, perhaps more important, for its capacity to incorporate a high degree of architectural detail at a low price. In 1857, James P. Gaynor completed a five-story tour de force of Venetian-inspired Classicism for the retail merchants E. V. Haughwout and Co., at the northeast corner of Broadway and Broome Street.[29] Haughwout's was the first to install Elisha G. Otis's safety elevator for passenger use. The brilliantly detailed walls of Gaynor's building, with regular bays that incorporated a window arch carried in a small order between piers with engaged Corinthian columns, were painted to resemble stone. Gaynor used iron from Daniel D. Badger's Architectural Iron Works of New York, one of a number of companies, including the Cornell Iron Works, that would grow to rival and eventually overtake Bogardus's company.

Cast-iron fronts continued to be used in the post–Civil War era, especially for retail stores, occasionally for office buildings, and, in a great last burst during the boom of the 1880s, for the warehouses that transformed the fading residential quarter along Mercer and Greene Streets from Canal to Houston. In 1876, William Fogarty, an English architect visiting New York, recognized the importance of cast iron to the development of American architecture:

> The warehouses and shops in . . . a commercial community assume colossal proportions. In them more particularly the use of cast iron is general, not alone for internal columns . . . but also for all external architectural features. Facades eight and ten stories high are executed with it, and with an excellence of finish and accuracy of detail that is seldom seen at this side [of the Atlantic]. There are several large foundries called "Architectural Iron Works," in which the stock of models is very extensive, comprising all the best examples of the Greek and Roman orders to almost any diameter. The facility with which these can be put together to form fronts, has had a very decided influence on the street architecture, which exhibits a great tendency to run into columns, and the repetition of the same details through nine or ten stories is very common. Indeed, so prevalent have these characteristics become, that even where cast iron is not used, the influence of the cast iron school in this direction is felt. This is noticeable in some . . . buildings . . . which, although built of cut granite, exhibit one order with little variation used throughout the stories. This must be looked on as a decided element in what may be called the "American Renaissance" style.[30]

58–84 Worth Street, between Church Street and Broadway. Griffith Thomas, 1869. View to the southeast. NM. CU.

Buildings framed and facaded in cast iron did not, however, prove immune to fire. On January 17, 1879, the cast-iron rows along Worth Street burst into flames, with the fire spreading from building to building because the party walls, in part intended as firebreaks, had not been taken all the way to the front, making it possible for the fire to spread both vertically and horizontally.[31] The fourteen Worth Street buildings (Griffith Thomas, 1869), comprising street numbers 58–84, together with 11–37 Thomas Street, between Broadway and Church Street, constituted one of the most coherent neighborhoods of cast-iron buildings, filling almost all of a 200-by-310-foot site.[32] The spread of the fire was partially attributed to the fact that the iron posts had been left hollow and therefore acted as chimneys. In 1885, as a result of the 1879 fire, revisions to building laws required that iron posts be filled with masonry, that enclosed columns be capped with a plate at the top to prevent the passage of fire or smoke, and that metal panels be backed by at least eight inches of brickwork.[33] The new regulations were deemed so restrictive that cast-iron buildings were rarely built thereafter. A notable exception was Richard Berger's six-story, six-bay-wide, Neo-Grec building at 112–114 Prince Street (1889–90), between Greene and Wooster Streets.[34]

Even before the legal changes, fear of fire had thrown doubt on the value of architectural cast iron. Moreover, as the editors of the *Real Estate Record and Builders' Guide* made clear in 1884, cast iron was no longer deemed artistically tolerable:

> It is a matter of unmixed congratulation that the fires of Chicago and Boston showed that this construction was as untrustworthy practically, as it was horrible architecturally. The efforts of a few artistic architects to treat the cast-iron front only served to show how intractable the material was. The substitution of brick for the main structure of members made it impossible to play such pranks as could be played with impunity in cast-iron and compelled a treatment which deferred to the material. If now we could secure the abolition of the monstrous tin cornice and the standing of brick walls upon supports of

masonry our warehouse architecture would still be further improved, since it is almost as difficult to make a building positively offensive out of bricks alone as it is to make an inoffensive building out of cast iron.[35]

Montgomery Schuyler was an early critic of cast-iron architecture, writing in 1871 that "it was a sorry day for the architecture of the city, as a fine art, when we commenced making our store fronts as we do our kitchen ranges."[36] Schuyler in particular objected to using paint to mask cast iron so that it resembled other materials: "Instead of honestly avowing themselves iron—when their very construction and multiplicity of detail proclaimed that they could be nothing else—they have been universally smeared all over with some uniform color, in imitation of marble or stone, often aping even the rustications and the chisel marks of the latter materials." Recognizing the need to protect the cast iron from the weather, Schuyler preferred that it be painted in multiple colors, "in imitation of ancient polychromy, and thereby at once delight the eye without offending the judgment by false pretensions."[37] This approach was taken by Renwick & Sands in the eight-story building the firm designed for Edward Matthews, at 549–551 Broadway (1870–71), between Spring and Prince Streets.[38]

In 1883, according to the *Real Estate Record and Builders' Guide*, it was the proliferation of cast-iron–fronted buildings that gave "foreigners . . . their unique impression that New York is made of pasteboard, and is not a real city, but a set in a theatre. This impression comes partly from the absence of any visible roofs, and partly from the attenuation of the supports of the buildings which is made possible by the use of cast iron along the most characteristic parts" of Broadway, with the metal frequently painted to "imitate marble or sandstone, and used in quantities in which it would be impossible to use building stone—even granite. The 'light and airy' appearance thus obtained has been admired by people who have piously believed that Broadway was one of the finest streets in the world, and has been imitated as far as possible by the designers of buildings made of honest masonry. The result is that from the Battery to Union Square, one can count upon his fingers all the buildings which possess any architectural interest."[39]

Concerning Queen Anne

The search for artistic beauty in the 1880s took a number of forms. Richard Morris Hunt's careful, scholarly invocations of historical precedents, while unquestionably successful as works of architectural art, were, in essence, exercises in established European taste. Another exercise in taste, labeled the Queen Anne, was not only more experimental and less blatantly historical but also more flexible and, indeed, affordable. The Queen Anne could also be defended, at least in part, as an interpretation of the local vernacular—the fast-disappearing architecture of the Colonial and Federal periods, which was slowly finding an appreciative public especially as a result of the celebrations associated with the nation's Centennial, in 1876. The

Bishop Berkeley house (1728), Middletown, Rhode Island. Rear view, 1874. NYSB. CU.

Lowther Lodge, London. Richard Norman Shaw, 1872. Entrance facade. RNS. CU.

Centennial, in addition to fostering a recognition that the American republic was old enough to have a viable history of its own, had also championed an appreciation for the architecture and decorative artifacts of the nation's Colonial past; these were held up as icons of simplicity and honesty in contrast with the gimcrackery of their midcentury equivalents. Although the official Centennial took place in Philadelphia, New York was the center of the rekindled appreciation of the nation's Colonial past, led by the young architect Charles Follen McKim.[40] McKim found an outlet for his passion in 1874 with the appearance of a new architectural journal, the *New-York Sketch-Book of Architecture*. Although H. H. Richardson, for whom McKim had worked as a draftsman from 1870 to 1872, was listed as the editor, the actual work was delegated to McKim, who was not only able to publish outstanding examples of recent projects but also drawings and photographs of Colonial architecture. McKim concentrated on Colonial structures in and around Newport, Rhode Island—he chose a rear view of the tumbledown Bishop Berkeley house (1728), in Middletown, Rhode Island, as the first photograph to be published in an American architectural journal—but very soon interest in the past expanded from consideration of charming rural locales to include the big cities. This attention encompassed New York, where the destruction of the houses of the old city at the tip of Manhattan to make way for new office buildings was rapidly robbing the city of its physical history.[41] Not only did McKim and others inspire a movement to save old houses and collect old furniture, they also began to develop a new, highly inventive and synthetic approach to design in their own work. This style came to be known as the Queen Anne, emerging around 1880 as the dominant trend in the design of single-family wooden houses as well as urban townhouses. It was even used in the design of large-scale buildings, particularly where the designer wanted not only to convey a sense of domesticity—as in apartment houses—but also to connect the new work with distinctly local building traditions.

The coinage *Queen Anne* was first attached to English work with similar intentions in 1871. It came to be used in America because young architects—especially McKim—were inspired by an English architect, Richard Norman Shaw, whose houses were based in part on the Dutch-influenced red brick Classical work of the early eighteenth century, when Queen Anne, who reigned from 1702 to 1714, was on the English throne. From an American perspective, as Vincent Scully has pointed out, the term was "undoubtedly a misnomer . . . but it . . . has the advantage of pointing up the direction the movement took from a late medievalism toward an eventual 18th-century classicism."[42]

At its zenith, the American Queen Anne borrowed elements from the styles of Louis XIII, English Tudor, and the Stuart and William and Mary periods, as well as from Japan, the architecture of which came to be appreciated after a Japanese house was built at the Centennial exhibi-

Washington Building, Battery Place from Broadway to Greenwich Street. Edward H. Kendall, 1882–85; mansard addition, 1887. View to the northeast. NYHS.

tion in Philadelphia. Most important, it married Colonial Late Elizabethan and Georgian precedent with the dynamic asymmetries of midcentury English Gothic design and was an attempt to create a style that, though rich in tradition, was, because of its fundamental eclecticism, inherently free. It featured vividly colored contrasts of red brick, white stone, white painted wood trim, picturesque massing, and elaborately gabled roofscapes, with applied pilasters and foliated friezes frequently realized with molded brick or terra cotta. In addition, typical rowhouses and even apartment houses and office buildings in the style featured three-sided bays, oriel windows, and multipaned sashes as well as ornamental sunflower and sunburst motifs. Elaborate brackets helped ease the transitions between facade elements.

While Vincent Scully proposed the superbly evocative and exact term *Shingle Style* for Queen Anne houses built in resorts and suburbs, the American urban examples of the style, whether rowhouses or commercial office blocks, have not been given so distinct a name and continue to be designated Queen Anne though they, like their more rural counterparts, owe far more to American than to English precedent. The Shingle Style at its peak moved away from the riotous eclecticism of the Queen Anne toward a stylistic synthesis that to some seemed a distinctly modern American locution. The urban Queen Anne, however,

failed to evolve, with only a few exceptions, such as Edward H. Kendall's Washington Building (1882–85) (see chapter 3). The style instead gave way to the almost abstract work of H. H. Richardson and his followers, which, it can be argued, was the urban equivalent of the mature Shingle Style.

The Queen Anne, especially as it was practiced in New York, marked a high point of individualism. As such it was widely criticized. In his address to the tenth annual convention of the American Institute of Architects, held in 1876, Alfred J. Bloor, a British-born, long-established New York architect and the AIA's secretary, attacked the "licentiousness or grotesqueness of the strivings in stone or brick, in wood or iron, of the rising generation of practitioners and present race of students."[43] Ironically, the importance of the new style lay not only in its compositional freedom but also in the incipient conservatism of its nativistic approach. Montgomery Schuyler, by no means an unalloyed enthusiast, wrote that the particular appeal of the Queen Anne to American architects lay in their reaction to "the wild work of Broadway and of Fifth Avenue . . . [which] led architects of sensibility to cast many longing, lingering looks behind at the decorum of the Bowling Green and Washington Square, and to sigh for a return of the times when the common street architecture of New York was sober and respectable, even if it was conventional and stupid." According to Schuyler, however, "This justifiable preference . . . for an architecture confessedly colonial over an architecture aggressively provincial" was more emotional than substantive. As Schuyler saw it, the Queen Anne architects failed to analyze "their own emotions as to discover that the qualities they admired in the older work, or admired by comparison with the newer, were not dependent upon the actual details in which they found them." For Schuyler, the Gothic Revival of A.W.N. Pugin, and especially of John Ruskin, which had formed the core belief behind the work of Schuyler's hero, Leopold Eidlitz, had been a true path, "an architecture which, although starting from formulas and traditions, had attained to principles, and was true, earnest, and alive." Not so the followers of Queen Anne, who, in their preference for "the refinements of a fixed and developed architecture to the rudeness of a living and growing architecture . . . [had] abandoned the attempt at an expression of the things they were doing for the elegant expression in antique architecture of meanings which have grown meaningless to modern man."[44]

With the rebound in construction around 1880, the Queen Anne suddenly seemed to become all but ubiquitous in New York. In September 1883, Schuyler told the readers of *Harper's New Monthly Magazine* about "the new departure . . . an apt name for what some of its conductors describe as the new 'school' in architecture and decoration" which has for ten years enjoyed "almost complete sway among the young architects of England and of the United States." Schuyler remarked that it had "all the signs of a departure—we might say of a hurried departure—and gives no hint of an arrival, or even of a direction. It is, in fact, a general 'breaking up' in building, as the dispersion of Babel was in speech." To Schuyler it was a "'movement' so exclusively centrifugal" that it assumed "rather the character of an explosion than of an evolution." And it was unpromising: "In fact, the 'movement' has not, thus far, either in England or the United States, produced a monument which anybody but its author would venture to pronounce very good."[45]

Schuyler saw the term *Queen Anne* as "a comprehensive name . . . made to cover a multitude of incongruities, including, indeed, the bulk of recent work which otherwise defies classification." But it was not a name arrived at arbitrarily, for much to Schuyler's chagrin, the architects who worked in the Queen Anne style genuinely admired the Jacobean and early Georgian styles of English architecture, as exemplified by the work of the architect Nicholas Hawksmoor, the architect and landscape gardener Capability Brown, and the woodcarver Grinling Gibbons, whose work struck Schuyler as decadent. To celebrate a period "which for years had been regarded by everybody as rather ugly and ridiculous" seems "one of the strangest episodes in the strange history of modern architecture." In particular, it appeared that Schuyler, the student of Eidlitz, could not accept the representationalism of the Queen Anne approach: "Classic detail can not grow out of modern structures faithfully designed for modern purposes, as it grows out of antique structures, or as Gothic ornament grows out of Gothic structures, like an efflorescence. It must be 'adjusted' as visibly an after-thought, and to say this is to say that in all Queen Anne buildings the architecture is *appliqué*." But Schuyler recognized the appeal of the Queen Anne to American architects and their clients: "In this country, which has never been much more architecturally than an English colony, there seemed special reasons for following the new fashion of being old-fashioned. American architects, and American builders before there were any American architects, had been exhorted, as they have lately been exhorted again, to do something distinctly American."[46]

Richardsonian Romanesque

By the mid-1880s the urban Queen Anne had begun to run its course, giving way to a version of the Romanesque based on Henry Hobson Richardson's uniquely inventive interpretation of that style.[47] Richardson was the second American to study architecture at the Ecole des Beaux-Arts, and the first to develop a distinctly personal style. This would not only make him highly influential with his fellow architects in the United States but also would earn him the distinction of being the first American to have an impact in Europe. Born and raised in Louisiana, Richardson graduated from Harvard College in 1859 at the age of twenty-one and went to Paris the following year, enrolling in the atelier of Jules-Louis André. After one failed attempt at admission, he attended the Ecole des Beaux-Arts from the fall of 1860 until 1861, when financial hard-

ship, brought about by the outbreak of the Civil War, forced Richardson briefly to end his studies. After a trip to Boston, he returned to Paris in 1862 and reentered the Ecole, also working in the offices of Théodore Labrouste and Jacques Ignace Hittorff.[48] Richardson returned to the United States in October 1865, settling in New York, where he maintained offices until 1874 while living with his wife on Staten Island. He removed his practice to Boston after winning the competition for that city's Trinity Church. Much of his early work was unexceptional, consisting of typically American essays in the French Second Empire taste. Charles F. McKim, who first studied engineering at Harvard and then briefly worked in the office of Russell Sturgis before attending the Ecole des Beaux-Arts from 1867 to 1870, joined Richardson's staff in 1870. McKim probably introduced his employer to the work of Richard Norman Shaw, which he had seen firsthand during an 1869 trip to England. In any case, stimulated by Shaw's work, Richardson's designs became increasingly antiquarian. He turned to English and American late Medieval forms for his country houses and to the Romanesque architecture of southern France and northern Spain for his urban houses and commercial and public buildings. No building of Richardson's had greater influence on New York's architecture than his R. and F. Cheney Building (1875–76), in Hartford, Connecticut, with its bold and imaginative use of arcades to organize a five-story block into an urban palazzo suitable for street-level retail merchants and upper-floor office tenants.[49] The Cheney block was not only a well-thought-out commercial building but a civic monument, with a corner tower rising to a pyramidal roof to proclaim the structure's individuality and the ambitions of its developers.

Richardson's career was as brilliant as it was brief. A victim of the kidney ailment Bright's disease, he died in 1886 at the age of forty-seven, but his impact was profound. Richardson built comparatively little in New York and nothing in his mature manner. Nonetheless, he influenced a number of important local architects, including McKim, William A. Potter, and R. H. Robertson, such that by 1891 Montgomery Schuyler could devote thirty-one pages of the first issue of *Architectural Record* to a survey of "The Romanesque Revival in New York."[50] As Schuyler pointed out, the Romanesque was not new to New York. For example, the German-born Alexander Saeltzer had based his design for the Astor Library (1854) on Friedrich von Gärtner's Staatsbibliothek (1831–40), in Munich, and Leopold Eidlitz and Charles "Otto" Blesch had also looked to the Romanesque for their St. George's Church (1846–48). But in these works, as in Eidlitz's Produce Exchange (1860) or his Brooklyn Academy of Music (1861), it was the Romanesque of Bavaria. Jacob Wrey Mould's All Souls Unitarian Church (1853–55) was also Romanesque, but the Romanesque of Italy. Notwithstanding these examples and quite a few more like them, the works of the Romanesque Revival of the 1880s were of a very different order, a result of the way Richardson

R. and F. Cheney Building, Hartford, Connecticut. H. H. Richardson, 1875–76. View c. 1880. HLHU.

Astor Library, 425 Lafayette Place. Alexander Saeltzer, 1854. View to the northeast, c. 1865, showing Griffith Thomas's 1859 addition on the left. FLC.

All Souls Unitarian Church, southeast corner of Fourth Avenue and East Twentieth Street. Jacob Wrey Mould, 1853–55. View to the southeast, c. 1855. Prevost. NYHS.

used that historical style rather than deriving from the style itself. As Schuyler put it, in "our own time and country [we] have been witness to the most extraordinary and widespread influence ever exerted in the progress of the building art, unless we except the work of Sir Christopher Wren." For Schuyler, Richardson's focus on the Provençal Romanesque was apt, "precisely that variety of Romanesque, excepting only the Italian, in which the survival of the classic Roman elements unmodified is the most obstinate. In the monuments of Rhenish or of Norman Romanesque the process of de-classicising has been carried so far that it needs historical knowledge to affiliate Worms or Speyer or Bayeux or Caen to the architecture of Imperial Rome." So it was believed that Richardson, via the Romanesque, was approaching the fundamental tectonics of the ancients. Schuyler felt that the Romanesque, taken as a whole in all its northern and southern manifestations, constituted "an architectural language that is applicable to all our needs. . . . It has not been conventionalized or formalized so as no longer to be expressive, but is still free and flexible, and it affords ample opportunity for a designer to manifest his scholarship and his individuality, if he have any. So much cannot be said of any previous style that has come so near to

Post Office, northeast corner of Nassau and Cedar Streets. View to the northeast, c. 1865, of the building that served as the Post Office from 1845 until 1875. Originally built as the Middle Dutch Church (1727–31). NYHS.

establishing itself." Perhaps already aware that without Richardson's living example the tide was turning to an academic Classicism espoused by McKim, Schuyler cautioned: "It is to be hoped that our designers may be content to develop its resources and not be tempted to abandon it, as so many promising beginnings have been abandoned in the history of modern architecture, through an unlucky and disastrous caprice."[51]

A Village No More

Stylistic experiments notwithstanding, the most noticeable characteristic of post–Civil War architecture and urbanism had less to do with aesthetics than with the size and scale of both individual buildings and the city as a whole. Not only was the city rapidly expanding, it was rebuilding itself, with many of its old quarters being pulled down and redeveloped at greater densities than ever before undertaken or even imagined. The tendency to renew the city by tearing down old buildings to make way for bigger ones on the same site was taken in stride even by such fundamentally conservative observers as George Templeton Strong, who in 1866 noted: "A new town has been built on top of the old one, and another excavated under it. The cellars of stores on Broadway and its lower cross streets are two or three stories deep. Tenement houses tower upward, story above story. Hence, more crowding, less air-space, more of whatever fosters pestilence."[52] In 1874 James Richardson reported in *Scribner's Monthly* that "the manifest destiny" of most New York houses "is to be torn down after a limited service . . . to give place to something else, something generally better. Commerce crowds, and fashion shifts her seat from year to year. The mansion house of yesterday is a shop to-day, or has been demolished to make room for one; and the business edifice which was the marvel and boast of the generation just past, has been overtopped or displaced by a structure such as our fathers never dreamed of."[53]

Although the loss of historic landmarks did not go unnoticed, in general the assumption was that the growth of the city was not only a virtually unmitigated benefit but also an inevitable fact of modern life. Given this, it is quite surprising to read the report of the New York correspondent of the *American Architect and Building News* for March 1, 1879, who argued that the new buildings were not always better than those they replaced:

There has been a great deal of clearing out and tearing down in New York property during the present season; the old-fashioned, low, and in general poorly built structures are found expensive when cumbering property in the business portions of the city and liable to heavy assessments. A few historic buildings have come down. The old Gotham on the Bowery and the Park House on Beeckman Street had about them many an interesting bit of history, and the old New Yorkers have been busy telling odd and curious tales of years ago. Many old wooden rookeries have fallen before the wreckers' bars and axes, though the architectural improvement is not very marked. When so much might be done in adding to the beauty of our streets, it is disheartening to see common-place edifices going up one after another on every thoroughfare.[54]

Not only were old houses torn down to make way for commerce but also old churches, although these were sometimes saved and converted to commercial use. In 1876, an article in the *New York Express* stated:

> The number of old churches which have been turned into business houses in this city is quite large. The Post-Office occupied the Middle Dutch Church on Nassau Street for thirty years. The Quaker meeting-house at Hester and Elizabeth Streets erected in 1818, has for a long time been the office of the New York Gas Light Company. The Amity-street Presbyterian Church is used as a stable by A.T. Stewart and Company. A livery-stable occupies the Sixth-street Presbyterian Church near Second Avenue, and there is another stable in a church on Twenty-third Street near Sixth Avenue. The Church of the Messiah, on Broadway opposite the New York Hotel, is a theatre. The Presbyterian Church on Fifteenth Street, near Third Avenue, is known as Nilsson Hall. A Universalist church on Twentieth Street, near Seventh Avenue, is used as a bakery. A mineral-water manufacturing occupies a church on Franklin Street, near West Broadway. Old St. Ann's Church, on Eighth Street, near Fourth Avenue, is being turned into a factory for A.T. Stewart and Company.[55]

In 1880 the loss of the buildings of Dutch New York was so nearly complete that the editors of the *American Architect and Building News* were moved to publish a sketch by the architect Max Schroff illustrating the Rhinelander Sugar House (1763), at the corner of Rose and Duane Streets, one of the few such examples still standing in a recognizable condition.[56]

Occasionally a mild voice of protest was raised, as, for example, when the editors of the *New York Times* observed that "there is in New York one fashion which intelligent travelers [from Europe] have remarked upon, although we believe not yet in any book of American travel. This is the recklessness with which substantial and expensively-built houses are removed, or 'torn down' as the phrase is, to make way for more profitable structures." While fine old buildings were valued in Europe, the *Times* continued, in New York,

> one of the oldest towns in the country, a search through its streets for houses of even . . . very moderate agedness—we cannot say antiquity—would be almost in vain. . . . New York is probably the only place which turns its churches into theatres and circuses; and it is almost as singular among cities of more than two centuries old which "tear down" handsome and substantial houses without compunction or remorse. But it by no means follows that New York is exceptionally sacrilegious or ruthless. The simple truth is that New York has become during the last thirty years merely a place in which to make money. . . . And thus New York—not a capital, not a

Rhinelander Sugar House (1763), southwest corner of Rose and Duane Streets. View to the southeast, c. 1892. NYHS.

Rhinelander Sugar House (1763), southwest corner of Rose and Duane Streets. Sketch by Max Schroff, 1880. AABN. CU.

centre of any interest, intellectual or moral, but that of commerce—becomes year by year more and more a splendid shop and railway station.[57]

Not only did most New Yorkers take the transformation of the historic city pretty much in stride, they seemed to see it as a force of nature. The *Real Estate Record and*

Builders' Guide agreed, stating in 1881: "The growth of a city like New York complies with the law of development as laid down by Herbert Spencer, that is, from the homogeneous to the heterogeneous; from the simple to the complex."[58] As Richard Grant White, the art critic and father of Stanford White, observed in 1883: "New York not only adds to itself, but incessantly rends itself in pieces."[59]

By the mid-1870s virtually all of Manhattan below Fourteenth Street was given over to manufacturing, commerce, and the tenements of the very poorest classes. No street better represented the seemingly endless renewal of building stock than Broadway, the city's great commercial street. According to Junius Henri Browne, Broadway was

New-York intensified,—the reflex of the Republic,—hustling, feverish, crowded, ever changing. Broadway is hardly surpassed by any street in the World. It is cosmoramic and cosmopolitan. In its vast throng, individuality is lost, and the race only is remembered. All nations, all conditions, all phases of life are represented there. Like nature, it never cloys; for it is always varying, always new. A walk through Broadway is like a voyage round the Globe. . . . No thoroughfare in the country completely represents its wealth, its enterprise, its fluctuations, and its progress. Broadway is always being built, but it is never finished.[60]

Even Fifth Avenue, long the patrician residential stronghold, was not immune to change. As commercial, warehouse, and wholesale businesses filled the island below Fourteenth Street, and Broadway between Union and Madison Squares became home to large department stores, a long stretch of Fifth Avenue began to give way to shops. In 1878 the *New York Times* reported: "From Fourteenth-street to Thirty-fourth street there is not to-day a single piece of property that is not more valuable for business than dwelling house purposes. . . . As Fifth-avenue dwellings between Fourteenth and Twenty-third streets give way to stores, this portion of the avenue will become to New-York what the Rue de la Paix is to Paris, and what Regent-street is to London—a fashionable lounge for the wealthy and well-to-do classes."[61] In the same year, Raymond Westbrook wrote in the *Atlantic Monthly*, "as trade advances, private life flees before it. It escapes in two directions: towards the upper end of the island, to the limit to which the lack of transit facilities permits it to be endurable, and up into the air in the new French flats."[62]

Even before the elevated railroads made the upper island convenient, the pressure of downtown commerce forced the development of the area above Forty-second Street, once virtually terra incognita. On July 22, 1871, George Templeton Strong recorded in his diary the account of an evening trip uptown to Central Park: "With the growth of this city, my evening strolls have resumed their northern or uptown direction. In old Greenwich Street days— 1838–1848—they were up to Fourteenth Street. Now they are up to Seventy-ninth and Eightieth streets."[63] Strong reported long walks "systematically exploring the West

View to the northeast along Broadway at Spring Street, c. 1868. Anthony. NYHS.

View to the southwest along Broadway from Chambers Street, c. 1865, taken from the A. T. Stewart & Co. store (Trench & Snook, 1846). Trinity Church (Richard Upjohn, 1846) is seen in the distance and the spire of St. Paul's Chapel (Thomas McBean, 1764–66; spire, James Crommelin Lawrence, 1794) is visible on the right. City Hall Park is in the foreground on the left. Archive Photos.

View to the northwest along Fifth Avenue from Twenty-seventh Street, c. 1865, with the steeple of the Marble Collegiate Church (Samuel A. Warner, 1851–54) in the center. NYHS.

View to the northwest at Twenty-third Street and Madison Square, 1886, with Fifth Avenue on the right and Broadway on the left. The Fifth Avenue Hotel (William Washburn, 1859) is on the left and the obelisk (James G. Batterson, 1857) in honor of General William J. Worth is in the center. Instantaneous Photo Company. NYHS.

View to the southwest along Fifth Avenue from Thirty-fourth Street showing the funeral procession for Ulysses S. Grant, August 8, 1885. Part of the William B. Astor II house (Griffith Thomas, 1856) is on the right and the John Jacob Astor II house (1859) is on the left, separated by a shared garden. The Marble Collegiate Church (Samuel A. Warner, 1851–54) is on the far left. NYHS.

*View to the southwest from Broadway and West Forty-second Street, c. 1894, showing the Hotel St. Cloud (Richard Morris Hunt, 1868)
on the left and the Rossmore Hotel (John B. Snook, 1873–75) on the right. In the distance on the right is the Broadway Theater
(J. B. McElfatrick, 1887–88). NYHS.*

Side Avenues, which have grown up quite out of [my] knowledge. The Eighth, for instance, is now a brilliant shopping street—far more brilliant than Sixth. The Seventh seems all compact of the lowest tenement houses and whiskey mills, an elongated Five Points."[64]

Stimulated by the construction of the Grand Central Depot (John B. Snook, 1869–71), forward-looking entrepreneurs were beginning to develop Forty-second Street and areas to its north. Longacre Square, an area of light industry featuring wagon factories, harness shops, and horse dealers and named after the carriage district in London, was becoming a new hotel district. Buildings in the area included the Hotel St. Cloud (1868), four stories plus a mansard, at the southeast corner of Forty-second Street and Broadway, probably designed by Richard Morris Hunt, and John B. Snook's Rossmore Hotel (1873–75), on the west side of Broadway between Forty-first and Forty-second Streets.[65] Facilities catering to the horse trade continued to be built, however, the most notable of which was the American Horse Exchange (D. & J. Jardine, 1881–83), a two-story brick building developed by William K. Vanderbilt on the east side of Broadway between Fiftieth and Fifty-first Streets.[66] In one of his columns in the *New York World*, Montgomery Schuyler, ever disparaging of Hunt's work, wrote that the St. Cloud

rears its large form among surrounding pigmies of buildings, like Gulliver among the Lilliputians. However convenient and comfortable it may be internally we cannot admire the exterior of this building. It is built of fiery red brick—unrelieved even by white pointed joints—alternating with pieces of Ohio stone spasmodically introduced, producing the same violent contrasts and checker-board appearance which we condemned in the building at the corner of Twenty-seventh Street [Stevens House, Richard Morris Hunt, 1870–72]. We notice here, too, the same narrow openings, the same heavy projections and uncouth ornaments as in that building. Without knowing their authorship, we must say that if both these designs did not emanate from the same pencil we never saw twins so much alike.[67]

One can only imagine what disdain Schuyler would have had for Snook's Rossmore, 250 rooms in five stories with a two-story mansard, the tallest building designed by the architect, with French Second Empire–inspired facades lavishly decorated in the incised Neo-Grec manner. Schuyler was impressed with Philip Kissam's design for William B. Astor's four-story-high, Ohio stone rowhouse development:

Occupying two whole blocks . . . very plain in detail [but producing] a very pleasing effect [the buildings could be] said in themselves to completely form this neighborhood and the boundary of northern improvement, as there is nothing at all to correspond around or above them. From this point—the juncture of Seventh Avenue with Broadway—the change is actually startling. Broadway seems to have been utterly killed by its contact with Seventh Avenue, the streetcars having branched off into the latter, and with it apparently all local improvement. While the Seventh Avenue continues here in fine brown-stone buildings, Broadway at once settles down into the appearance of a quiet country village, with its little one and two story shanties of brick or frame. Scarcely a cartwheel breaks the solitude even at midday, and the roughly-paved streets and dilapidated sidewalks are given up to the goats, chickens, and uncombed little urchins. This goes on increasing in loneliness and dilapidation, and rocks cropping out in bare places, until we suddenly come upon the southwest angle of our glorious Central Park and the terminus of what will soon be our magnificent boulevard. Here the city looks as if it paused to rest before taking another spring northward in its race of improvements.[68]

Less than a decade later, the uptown scene would be very different, as George Augustus Sala, an English writer who visited the city for the first time in 1863, reported in 1879 after a second sojourn. "When I came here first," Sala wrote in his book *America Revisited*,

> Twenty-fifth-street was accounted as being sufficiently far "up town," and Fortieth-street was Ultima Thule. Beyond that the course of town lots planned out and prospected, but structurally yet to come, was only marked by boulders of the living rock having weird *graffiti* eulogistic of the virtues of Drake's Plantation Bitters, the Night Blooming Cereus, the Balm of a Thousand Flowers, and Old Dr. Jacob Townsend's Sarsaparilla. . . . Where I remember wildernesses I behold now terraces after terraces of lordly mansions of brown stone, some "with marble facades," others wholly of pure white marble.

Sala, in contrasting New York's spectacular growth with that of London, which was also exploding at the time, pointed out a big distinction between the two cities: the growth rate of Manhattan was not only faster than that of London, it "is also much more astonishing" than the "metropolitan transformation" of the British capital. "Growing London absorbs suburbs, villages, and towns. Growing New York has had nothing to absorb but the open. Its development almost belies the dictum of the illustrious French chemist" that "nothing is lost, nothing is created." As Sala put it, New York, in its extension, "*does* create."[69]

Edith Wharton, who was born in 1862 at 14 West Twenty-third Street, a three-story brownstone remodeled into a store twenty years later by Henry J. Hardenbergh, recalled the northward move of fashion to Murray Hill and beyond that took place in the 1880s. In *The Age of Innocence*, published in 1920, Wharton's protagonist, Newland Archer, reflects on his prospective father-in-law's journey north: "[Archer] knew that [he] already had his eye on a newly built house in East Thirty-ninth Street. The neighborhood was thought remote, and the house was built in a ghastly greenish-yellow stone that the younger architects

were beginning to employ as a protest against the brownstone of which the uniform hue coated New York like a cold chocolate sauce; but the plumbing was perfect."[70]

The growth of the city and the spread of its population was made possible by the construction and expansion after 1878 of the elevated railroad, the city's first rapid-transit system. The need for a rapid-transit system, which would permit settlement of the upper island with desirable areas as much as ten or eleven miles from the downtown business district, had been recognized since the Civil War. One observer, O. B. Bunce, editor of *Appletons' Journal*, in outlining the "City of the Future" for his readers in 1872, instead argued that the elevator held more promise for the city's logical development by making possible a vertical expansion of the city. According to Bunce, it was "not unsafe to say that in the city of New York all the business could be transacted under better conditions, and all the people domiciled more comfortably and conveniently in one-half the space now occupied" were it to be developed vertically. New York had "built up expansively, with little or no conception of the value of space, or of scientific methods for employing it to the best advantage." The city was so spread out that "domiciles are pushed to localities that are accessible from our offices and warerooms only with difficulty, with fatigue and vexatious delay." Bunce continued, "All the current discussion of rapid transit is of lines of travel on the plane of the horizon. There is no reason why locomotion should not ascend, and, far more swiftly than the most rapid means of level transit, bring us to our homes hung in the pure empyrean above." The age-old order of real estate values would thus be reversed, by "making the topmost floor the choicest suite of them all." The use of rooftop plantings could even "carry into these skyhomes some of the best features of suburban life." Bunce recognized that the principal opponents to his theory of "organized compactness" were those "enamoured of the ideal of a suburban city."[71]

Unlike Bunce, Frederick Law Olmsted was a strong advocate of the suburban ideal. In 1870 he wrote that "the advantages of civilization" were best realized in "suburban neighborhoods where each family abode stands fifty or a hundred feet or more apart from all others, and at some distance from the public road."[72] Olmsted envisioned "not a sacrifice of urban conveniences, but their combination with the special charms and substantial advantages of rural conditions of life."[73] Bunce, however, argued that though the "swift and easy communication between the centres and the outlying suburbs of a city should exist, . . . the very life of a metropolis exists in its compactness and neighborhood." Bunce loved city life for the variety only density could support: "A man who loves the town desires to walk out of his front door into all its activities. . . . The City of the Future may have its outlying villages, but within itself it should illustrate all the advantages that may arise from cooperation and centralization."[74]

Within ten years Bunce's vision of a horizontally and vertically expanded city was a fact. Moreover, the size of the building blocks of the new city were unprecedented, leading the *Real Estate Record and Builders' Guide* to observe in 1881:

> The way things are going on, New York will soon have a greater number of vast buildings than any city in the world. These great structures are not intended for business purposes merely, but are intended for dwelling. Great flats and apartments have become an essential feature of New York City life. . . . It follows that the time is coming when there will be more people to the square foot in this city than in any of the other capitals of the world. Our street population will, as a consequence, become denser than any other city. New York will, in appearance at least, in ten years' time be the most populous city on the globe.[75]

A New Scale

In 1883 the *Real Estate Record and Builders' Guide*'s correspondent, perhaps Montgomery Schuyler, wrote that the construction of such enormous downtown buildings as the Produce Exchange, Washington Building, Cotton Exchange, and Welles Building would "completely revolutionize" the lower end of the "island in less than five years":

> A New Yorker returning now after an absence of over three years would not recognize this approach to the city of his residence. What is more to our immediate purpose, he would not be impressed with anything in these piles beyond their hugeness, in the general view in which he saw them all together. Whatever vigor or refinement their architecture shows is only apprehensible close at hand. From a distance they are mere boxes, and they are boxes without any relation to each other. They do not comprise

Elisha G. Otis demonstrating his elevator safety brake at the New York Crystal Palace Exhibition, 1854. OECHA.

an architectural group. They are merely a fortuitous concourse of big buildings. A few years ago, the view of the lower island from either river was really impressive and picturesque. . . . The salient objects were then the *Tribune* building, the Post Office, St. Paul's spire, the Western Union Building, the Equitable building and Trinity spire. These happened to come together as an artist would have composed them.

Recognizing that the composition was fortuitous, the writer went on to observe that there was

> one thing to be noted about every one of the admirable buildings; they each had a roof, a visible roof, and therefore had some form and outline in spite of itself, and had the possibility of taking its place in a group, and enhancing the effect of a skyline, as it could not otherwise have done. . . . A box can have no outline and no general form in any artistic sense. It can neither have an effective skyline of its own, nor group effectively with anything else. . . . The outline of a towering building is really the most important factor in its success. With a good outline, detail which is only tolerable, may pass very well, while no force or grace of detail can redeem a building which has no general form.

The article concluded with a plea for contextual skyline design: "Architects of towering public buildings, which are to be visible in a general view of the city, ought to take thought for the skyline of their buildings and for the relation of their buildings to buildings around them."[76]

The technology that allowed for this new scale to prosper was the refinement of the elevator.[77] Water- and steam-powered elevators, called *teagles*, had been introduced in British factories in the 1830s, but the first American example, designed by Henry Waterman of New York, was not available until 1850. In 1851, Elisha G. Otis invented the safety brake and two years later was able to showcase a steam-powered passenger elevator in the observation tower of the New York Crystal Palace Exhibition. Otis designed a steam-powered elevator for the Haughwout Building (1857), the first practical use of the passenger elevator. Otis Tufts, a competitor of Otis's who is credited with designing the first closed elevator car, completed the next passenger elevator in New York, for the Fifth Avenue Hotel, in 1859. But it was the decision of Henry Baldwin Hyde, president of the Equitable Life Assurance Society, to include steam-powered elevators in his company's new headquarters, completed in 1870, that did the most to spur the use of elevators in large commercial buildings (see chapter 3). After 1870, the next significant advance in elevator technology was the invention of the vertical hydraulic elevator by Cyrus W. Baldwin of Chicago. This innovation used water acting under the force of gravity to greatly improve speed and safety. By 1880, hydraulic elevators were in widespread use in New York. The electricity-powered elevator, which had been successfully tested in Germany as early as 1880 by Ernst Werner von Siemens and which promised to be a major advance over the hydraulic model, was first used in New

Dakota, west side of Eighth Avenue between West Seventy-second and West Seventy-third Streets. Henry J. Hardenbergh, 1882–84. View to the southwest from Central Park, c. 1890. Johnston. NYHS.

York in Renwick, Aspinwall & Russell's five-story Demarest Carriage Company Building (1889–90), at the northeast corner of Fifth Avenue and Thirty-third Street.[78] That elevator was designed by Otis's company, and an electric model was available for the general market in the early 1890s.

The new commercial buildings were not only taller but bigger than their predecessors, no longer occupying the fifty-by-one-hundred-foot sites that satisfied developers and tenants in the 1860s and 1870s. The new buildings were business blocks, frequently occupying whole block-fronts and even entire city blocks. By 1886 the Equitable Building (1867–70), which had been the world's first office building, was completely rebuilt to take advantage of a much-expanded site covering the entire block except for the two corners facing Nassau Street. Complementing the giantism of the new office blocks were the new apartment houses, many huge as well (see chapter 4). With its 112-foot-wide, five-story facade along East Eighteenth Street, Richard Morris Hunt's Stuyvesant (1869–70), arguably the city's first apartment house, was not much bigger than nor dramatically different in appearance from the four or five rowhouses that might have been built on the site. Ten years later, Henry J. Hardenbergh's six-story Vancorlear (1879) filled an entire Seventh Avenue blockfront between Fifty-fifth and Fifty-sixth Streets, signaling the arrival of a palatial scale of multifamily residence never before seen in America or elsewhere. At its 1884 completion, Hardenbergh's Dakota, occupying an even bigger site—two hundred by two hundred feet—and rising to eight amply proportioned stories, dominated the vast West Side wasteland and loomed over the newly finished Central Park.

Accompanying the superscale apartment houses were other new models of urban living, such as residential hotels, and new ways for financing and operating these huge enterprises, none more ingenious than the Home Club, a cooperative plan initiated by the architect-developers Philip G. Hubert and James W. Pirsson at their Rembrandt (1881), at 152 West Fifty-seventh Street (see chapter 4). Before 1880, the apartment house had been a novelty with an uncertain future. After 1880, apartment houses not only catered to the affluent but, in diminished variations, provided the middle class with a suitable alternative to boardinghouse life, which had blighted non-wealthy urban existence since the housing crisis that arose as part of the Civil War.

Rich and Poor

The depression of the mid-1870s made the economic disparity between the small group of the city's rich, preponderantly native-born elite and the large body of impoverished immigrants and second-generation residents particularly noticeable. Some observers traced the roots of the dramatic split between the rich and the poor to the crash of 1857, which, according to the *New York Times*, had a devastating effect on "so many mechanics and men of small salaries and of moderate business" because it was followed by the wildfire boom of the Civil War with its "monstrous inflation of prices, especially of houses and rent."[79] The gap between the rich and the poor could be seen as an all-pervasive corrosion of city life. In 1868, George T. Fox, an English writer who had last visited the city in the early 1830s, returned for a second look. Fox was so amazed by the city's explosive growth that he felt like

Five Points slum, c. 1875, near the intersection of Worth, Park, and Baxter Streets. FLC.

"poor Rip van Winkle after his 20 years slumber on return-ing to his native village!" Fox found "the general features" of the city as he remembered them: "There was Governor's Island, the Battery, the North River and its wharves, Trin-ity Church, and some other well known features, but the rest was all changed."[80] Fox was appalled by the filthy streets and by Battery Park's decay, a by-product of the uptown migration of fashion that left the historic open space with no constituency. But most of all he was shocked by the extremes of wealth and poverty.

Fox kept his observations to himself—they were recorded in a diary—but in 1869 Junius Henri Browne said pretty much the same thing in public, opening his book *The Great Metropolis; a Mirror of New York* with the observation that "more than in any other American city, there are in New York, two great and distinct classes of people—those who pass their days in trying to make money enough to live; and those who, having more than enough, are troubled about spending it. The former suffer from actual ills; the latter from imaginary ones."[81] For the rich, it was argued, New York was the best place on earth. The *New York Times*, in an 1877 editorial that railed against the tendency to "continually thrust" the example of Paris "in our face as a great city," stated that New York apartments were in fact better than their French counter-parts, which were characterized as lacking water or gas or furnaces, "poorly lighted, ill ventilated, out of repair, and have indeed . . . many deficiencies." For those who had the money and wanted luxury in their surroundings, New York was the place, the *Times* continued. True, it might lack the aesthetic and intellectual subtleties of the older capital, but "in respect to such comforts as the whole-some, beneficial, and stimulating, he who quits Manhat-tan to search for them is like the man that abandoned his waving fields and journeys to the desert in hope of golden harvests." New York "is the chosen home of material lux-ury." For those who can afford it, those "who want luxuri-ous residences and surroundings, luxurious fare and luxu-rious enjoyment generally," New York "is the capital of capitals."[82]

The reason for the dramatic widening of the gap between the city's haves and have-nots after the Civil War can largely be explained by one phenomenon: immigra-tion. The population of postwar New York was substan-tially different from that of the 1850s. It was not that the city's growth was out of proportion to the nation's as a whole—in fact, the two ran pretty much in tandem. The nation's population doubled from 1850 to 1880, as did the city's, which increased from 500,000 to slightly more than 1,200,000. By 1890 it would reach 1,500,000.[83] Of course, as the nation grew it expanded into vast new territories, but New York City's land area hardly grew at all. In keep-ing with its status as the nation's de facto capital—its most worldly city—New York's population growth was not so much the result of rising birth rates as of immigration, leading many native-born Americans to regard it as notably "foreign."

At the time of the Centennial, about 83 percent, or 782,000 people, were either foreign born or the children of foreign-born parents, most of whom came from northern Europe. Of the 446,043 foreign-born New Yorkers in 1875, 199,084 had come from Ireland, 165,021 from Ger-many, and 39,340 from Great Britain. When prosperity returned around 1880, the demography of the city notice-ably changed. After 1880 the "new immigration," as it was dubbed, began to flood the city with Italians, Russians, Poles, and Eastern European Jews. Not only was the city inundated with aliens, it was also very crowded, perhaps the most crowded place in the entire New World. In his prophetic 1865 pamphlet, *The Growth of New York*, William R. Martin observed that "in London the average is not over eight [people] to an inhabited house. In New York in 1855 the average was 15 to a house."[84] By 1880 the Lower East Side began to overflow with people, with an average population density of about 300 per acre and one or two areas housing 400 to the acre. By 1890 virtually the entire neighborhood was filled to the brim with 400 peo-ple per acre, and by 1910 many parts contained between 500 and 800 people per acre.

The city's population was not only growing as a result of foreign immigration and rising birthrates. In 1880 the *Real Estate Record and Builders' Guide* reported that New York was growing because so many Americans were com-ing from the hinterland to work. Not only were poor Midwesterners fleeing the harsh life of the farm for urban opportunities, but rich ones, having made their money in the West, "were quietly dropping their 'specs' here, and, having realized their cash profits," were moving to the city.[85] Between 1880 and the depression of the 1930s, the move to the city by those with wealth and those seeking to obtain wealth was the principal engine of New York's greatness. As Lewis Mumford was to put it in 1922: "The perpetual drag to New York, and the endeavour of less favourably situated cities to imitate the virtues and defects of New York, is explicable as nothing other than the desire to participate in some measure in the benefits of city life. Since we have failed . . . to develop genuine regional cultures, those who do not wish to remain bar-barians must become metropolitans. That means they must come to New York, or ape the ways that are fash-ionable in New York."[86]

Gilding the Age: New-Rich New York

In 1865 New York was growing at a faster rate than any other major city in the world.[87] The conclusion of the Civil War, leaving the country on a paper-money basis for the first time, created an unprecedented boom. New York, which had profited enormously during the war by supply-ing the military and financing the government, embarked during the postwar Bonanza economy on a wave of busi-ness expansion that resulted in the construction of hun-dreds of new office and warehouse buildings as well as rowhouses, apartment houses, and hotels catering to the upper middle class and the truly, and usually newly, rich.

Alexander T. Stewart house, northwest corner of Fifth Avenue and West Thirty-fourth Street. John Kellum, 1864–69. Drawing room. AH. CU.

In 1869, Junius Henri Browne reported: "The new rich are at present stronger and more numerous than ever in New York. They profited by contracts and speculations during the War, and are now a power in the Metropolis,—a power that is satirized and ridiculed, but a power nevertheless. They are exceedingly *prononcé*, *bizarre*, and generally manage to render themselves very absurd; but, inasmuch as they annoy and worry the Knickerbockers, who have less money and are more stupid than they, I presume they have their place and achieve a purpose in the social life of Gotham."[88] Disdained by the established Knickerbocker families, the new rich—who, according to James D. McCabe Jr., were frequently lampooned as the "Shoddyites"—constituted "the majority of the fashionables . . . [occupying] the mansions in fashionable streets," crowding "the public thoroughfares and the Park with their costly and showy equipages" and flaunting "their wealth so coarsely and offensively in the faces of their neighbors, that many good people have come to believe that riches and vulgarity are inseparable."[89]

Some of the new rich were native New Yorkers who prospered. But many came from the West, where great fortunes were to be made in minerals and heavy industry. The new millionaires, dependent on the banks to finance their speculations, came to New York because it was the country's undisputed financial center. Before the war they might have chosen Philadelphia or even Boston, but by 1870 New York was home to fifty-six national banks and thirty-two savings banks, as well as to the Clearing House Association, which facilitated exchanges between the banks and the settlement of balances. In 1868 an average of $100,000,000 was cleared by the association each business day. In addition, the importance of the New York Stock Exchange was greatly enhanced when the opening of the first Atlantic cable linked it to Europe, in 1866, and, in 1876, when the ticker-tape machine was introduced to revolutionize financial reporting. The Panic of 1873 severely curtailed business on Wall Street, forcing many brokers to close up shop, and it was not until after 1880 that the stock market revived. But in times of boom and times of bust, New York was the financial center. By 1880 the new rich had sufficiently regained their self-confidence (and their money) to mount public displays of wealth that raised eyebrows among the city's Knickerbocker establishment, encouraging the *New York Times* to observe: "Old New York was famous for its plain, substantial citizens, the men who earned their own living, spoke their own mind, and brought up their children in sound principles and honest industry." Those who have "traced carefully the social life of New York for the last twenty years cannot but have noted a marked decline in the numbers and influence of the middle class of our people."[90]

A FRAMEWORK FOR GROWTH

New York's physical expansion may have been inevitable, but it could not take place without a workable infrastructure, including adequate water supply, a reasonable system to handle sewage, an efficient harbor, and rapid transit to make it possible for workers, rich and poor alike, to travel the length of a twelve-mile-long island on which most jobs were concentrated at one end. In addition, high-density growth such as O. B. Bunce imagined would unquestionably benefit from other services, notably the telephone and electric lighting. While a model system of water supply as well as a rudimentary sewer system had been in place since the 1840s, it was not until 1868 that Charles T. Harvey successfully tested his elevated train and a decade later when a working system of rapid transit was put in place. Telephone service was introduced in 1877. The following year electric lights were installed in a New York building on an experimental basis, followed two years later by the city's first streetlights.

Water Supply

New York's water came from the Croton watershed in upper Westchester County, carried to the city by a system of aqueducts, tunnels, and holding reservoirs implemented as a result of the great fire of 1835. Among the system's principal features were the graceful, Roman-inspired High Bridge Aqueduct, which carried water across the Harlem River at about 174th Street, and, on Fifth Avenue between Fortieth

High Bridge Aqueduct (1848), spanning Harlem River at about 174th Street. View to the southwest, c. 1895, showing the High Bridge Tower (John B. Jervis, 1872) on the right. Schulz. NYHS.

Croton Reservoir, west side of Fifth Avenue between West Fortieth and West Forty-second Streets. James Renwick Jr., 1842. View to the southwest, c. 1875. Jenkins. NYHS.

Croton Gatehouse, southwest corner of Convent Avenue and West 135th Street. Frederick Cook, 1890. View to the southwest. Powers. WF.

and Forty-second Streets, the twenty-million-gallon, Egyptian-inspired, batter-walled distributing reservoir, possibly designed by James Renwick Jr. Both were in place by July 4, 1842, when the water was turned on. Additional reservoirs were erected in Central Park (completed in 1863) and at Carmansville (1867). A two-hundred-foot-high octagonal tower (1872) to pump water up into the system at the New York side of the High Bridge was designed by John B. Jervis, an engineer who had supervised the construction of the original Croton Aqueduct and the High Bridge.[91] Although the tower appears not to have been intended for public visits, an interestingly decorated interior iron stair climbed past six landings to the top, where a superb view of the surrounding countryside could be had. As part of this improvement, the aboveground sections of the aqueduct were replaced with underground pipes and a series of small, gatehouse-like distribution stations were built along Tenth Avenue to help even out the flow. These rough-hewn granite structures were built in the mid-1870s at the southeast corner of 119th Street, the southwest corner of 113th Street, and the northwest corner of Ninety-second Street.[92]

The exceptional development of the city after the war outstripped the Croton system's capacity, and, after considerable public agitation, a special act of the state legislature in 1883 called for a new supply system that, when it opened in July 1890, carried water in from the Croton Dam down the West Side to Central Park, vastly expanding the flow of water.[93] The new, castellated, rock-faced granite and brownstone Croton Gatehouse, at the southwest corner of 135th Street and Convent Avenue, designed by the engineer Frederick Cook, was far less elegant than the earlier structures. In the late 1870s the utility of the Forty-second Street reservoir came under question and, once the new system was proposed, plans were made to tear it down and replace it with a park, complementing the one already in place on the western half of its double block.[94] But because the 1881 state law calling for the new park imposed levies on abutting property owners, it was declared unconstitutional two years later, and the fate of the reservoir would not be resolved until 1899, when it was torn down to make way for the New York Public Library.[95]

New York's water supply, though overtaxed, was otherwise exemplary; its sewers, however, were a scandal. In 1865 the state legislature gave the Croton Aqueduct Board authority to devise a new sewage and drainage system.[96] But little was done to improve conditions, and the editors of the *American Architect and Building News* focused on the situation in the earliest issues of their magazine. In their issue of January 15, 1876, the column "Sanitary Suggestions for Architects" referred to a recent communication from "the well-known engineer Mr. Charles H. Haswell" to the *New York Herald* in which he called "attention to the fact (which he understates), that, with the best location that a city could have, New York has a death-rate twenty percent higher than London and Paris, which are inland towns with inferior drainage."[97] Three weeks later the same magazine recounted the report of Stevenson Towle, the engineer in charge of sewers in New York, that more than corroborated Haswell's claims: many of the old sewers had sunk in the middle, forming "elongated cesspools" that would not empty, and that, under the influence of a heavy flow of rainwater and the pressure of a high tide, were in danger of overflowing and even of bursting. "In some parts of the city," Towle said, "entire sections on the sites of old ponds and marshes have settled, carrying down the sewers and pavements together."[98] Progress was hampered by the generally poor economic conditions of the 1870s and advances had to wait for the return of prosperity. By 1892, however, New York had 444 miles of sewers and 5,134 receiving basins, more than any European city and exceeded in the United States only by Chicago.[99]

Piers

On August 31, 1865, the *New York Times* bemoaned the state of New York's waterfront:

> If New York, as the great commercial port of the western hemisphere has anything to be ashamed of, it is of the condition of her water front. No seaport city in the world half its size, or one-third its mercantile marine importance, is so illy provided with wharves and piers. . . . While European ports can boast their granite quays . . . New York can only claim a string of rotten, filthy, reeking and ricketty old things which we call piers. . . . It would cost but little, in comparison to the advantages to be realized, to build piers of a style in keeping with her character as the greatest mercantile city of this continent.[100]

The problem was hardly new. Ten years before, in 1855, the engineer Egbert L. Viele, in a report commissioned by the state of New Jersey, had warned that "the great national character of the harbor of New York" was being threatened by the condition of its waterfront facilities.[101]

By the middle of the nineteenth century New York's port had achieved dominance over Boston and Philadelphia and in fact handled more goods and passengers than all the other ports in the country combined. The port also enjoyed international prominence, and New York's economy depended a great deal on foreign commerce. Ever since the Dutch built the first primitive wooden docks in 1624 and the British introduced stone piers some forty years later, New York had depended on private interests for the construction and maintenance of its commercial waterfront. In 1869 the Citizens' Association of New York, consisting of prominent property owners and supported by the Shipowners' Association, the Produce Exchange, and many leading manufacturing firms, had failed in its attempt to convince the state legislature to create the Board of Wharves and Piers to oversee the waterfront.[102] The public was nonetheless becoming increasingly concerned that the prosperity of New York's harbor was threatened by England, which had modernized its port facilities in London and Liverpool to take advantage of steam-powered travel. Pointing to the decrepit condition of the 126 piers on the Hudson and East Rivers as the reason for the harbor's troubles, involved citizens and groups demanded that something be done, realizing that the city could ill afford to lose this valuable resource.

In 1870, in the same legislative act that created the Department of Public Parks, the Department of Docks was established and given "exclusive charge and control" of the waterfront and its slips, bulkheads, and piers.[103] The agency consisted of five commissioners and an administrative staff, and it replaced the myriad competing city and state groups that had previously controlled bits and pieces of the puzzle, including the Bureau of Wharves, Piers and Slips of the City Street Cleaning Department; the State Board of Commissioners of Pilots; the City Inspectors of Incumbrances on the Wharves; the Common Council Committee on Wharves, Piers and Slips; and the Captain of the Port and his eleven Harbor Masters. The Department of Docks was also allowed to issue bonds, but the amount was limited to three million dollars each year and required the approval of the city comptroller. The original commissioners were prominent members of the business community and included Wilson G. Hunt, a dry-goods merchant and financier of the first Atlantic cable; William Wood, a banker; attorney Richard Henry; Hugh Smith of the Madison Avenue Stage Company; and John T. Agnew,

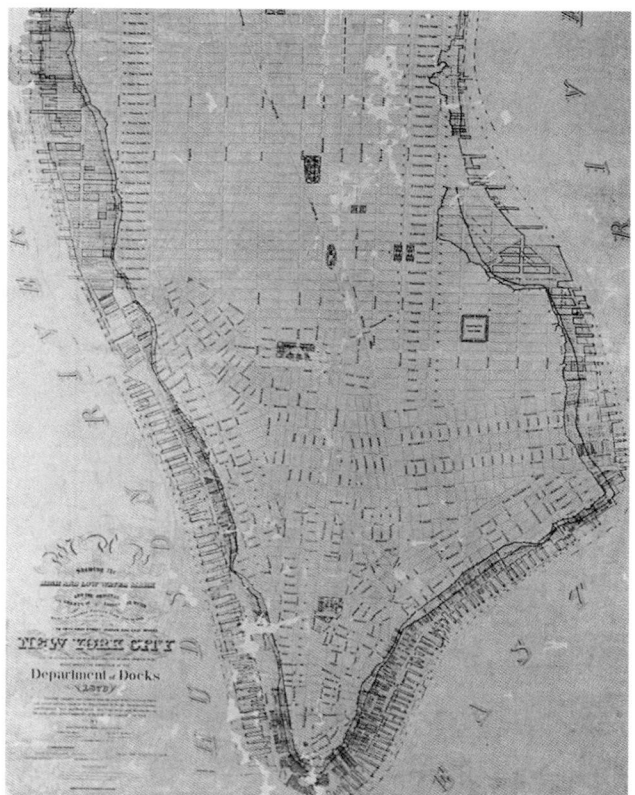

Map showing pier and bulkhead lines, East and Hudson Rivers, the Battery to Fifty-first Street. Department of Docks, 1873. MA.

View to the southwest from the Brooklyn Bridge (John A. Roebling and Washington Roebling, 1869–83) of East River piers, 1892, showing, in the distance, the Union Trust Company Building (George B. Post, 1889–90) on the left, and the steeple of Trinity Church

*(Richard Upjohn, 1846) and the 1892 addition to the Mutual Life Insurance Company of New York Building
(Charles W. Clinton, 1882–84, 1888) on the far right. NYHS.*

Proposed pier design, submitted to the Department of Docks. James C. Nichols, 1870. Perspective. MA.

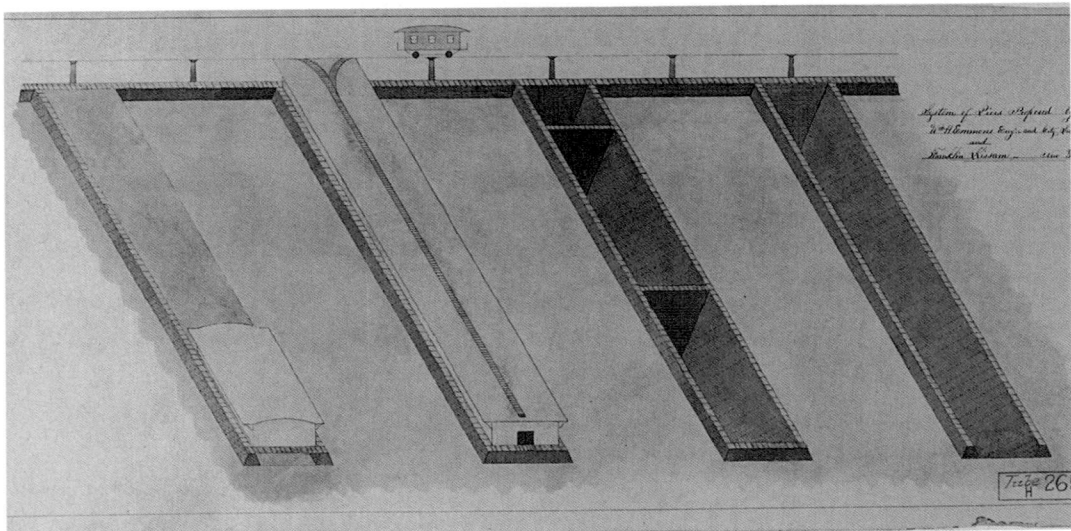

Proposed system of piers, submitted to the Department of Docks. William H. Emmons and Franklin Kissam, 1870. Isometric. MA.

a tobacco exporter, who was president of the board. For their first move, a popular one, the commissioners hired General George Brinton McClellan as Engineer-in-Chief of the Department of Docks.[104] Not only was McClellan more than qualified as an engineer—he had been chief engineer of the Illinois Central Railroad as well as chief surveyor for the Northern Pacific Railroad—he was a national figure, famous for his victory at Antietam and his command of the Union troops around Washington. In 1864, McClellan had been the unsuccessful Democratic candidate against Abraham Lincoln. The *New York Times* professed high hopes for the new group:

The gentlemen who are to direct this Department of

Docks, who are to have such vast power and to wield it so soon, are intrusted with a responsibility of supreme consequence to our future and to that of our children. They may discharge it in a manner to cover themselves with lasting honor—or to share in the unenviable repute which too many of our municipal functionaries have latterly earned. New York has become at her interior a city of palaces, but, at her outskirts and on her superb waterfront she is still a city of hovels. If the improvement of the latter be wrought as it should be, New York may soon and easily surpass every rival in commerce as in beauty; for her advantages in neither will have been equaled even by Venice when she rose from the foam of the Adriatic.[105]

Proposed piers and warehouses for the New York Pier and Warehouse Company, submitted to the Department of Docks. John Burrows Hyde and John Heuvelman, 1870. Street elevation on the left, river elevation on the right. MA.

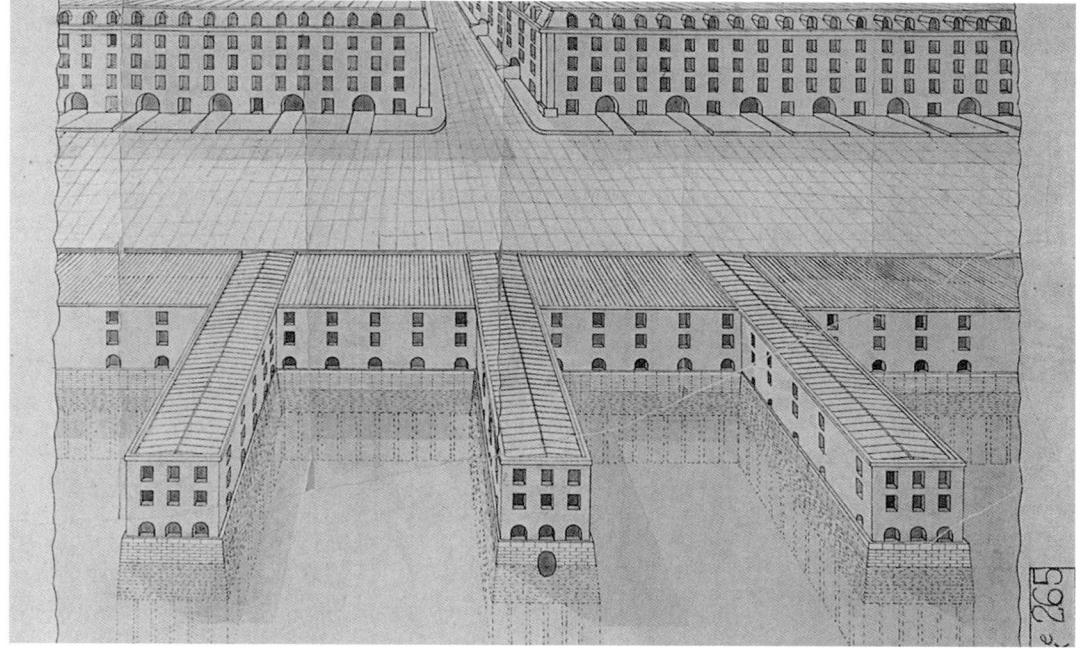

Proposed design of docks and warehouses, submitted to the Department of Docks. Ralph Aston, 1870. Perspective. MA.

In a bold and unusual move, the Department of Docks reached out to the public for waterfront proposals, holding a series of five public hearings and inviting "all persons interested in inaugurating, in the harbor of New York, a proper system of wharves and piers, or who have special plans for the improvement of the waterfront."[106] This was not a competition from which one scheme would be picked and developed but instead an effort to gauge public opinion, stimulate interest in the project, and perhaps solicit a few good ideas. The response was dramatic—some seventy written and oral proposals were received by the department. James C. Nichols, a ship captain, proposed a relatively simple scheme consisting of a stone bulkhead

with iron pier platforms extending over the water. The engineer and city surveyor William H. Emmons, working with draftsman Franklin Kissam, offered a plan of stone piers supporting one-story warehouses with rooftop railroad tracks, while William C. H. Waddell envisioned multistoried warehouses. Working for the New York Pier and Warehouse Company, John Burrows Hyde and John Heuvelman placed a prominent, fully detailed cast-iron warehouse atop an iron pier. Naval engineer Ralph Aston submitted two proposals, the first of which was a modest scheme of multistoried warehouses located on land across the street from the piers. His other proposal was much more innovative, calling for the inclusion of recreational

Blasting of rocks at Hell Gate, September 24, 1876. General John Newton, chief engineer. NYHS.

spaces along the waterfront, with large granite piers placed every mile. The civil engineer Richard Gilpin's submission was one of many that addressed the issue of the unsanitary conditions created by the present system of piers, which tended to inhibit the tide's natural ability to carry sewage out to sea, allowing dangerous conditions of stagnation. Gilpin proposed using triangular piers and devised a sewer system that dumped effluent into the river current.

In April 1871, less than a year after the Department of Docks had received its first proposals, a plan was announced that ignored all of the suggestions. Instead, General McClellan's own ideas would be implemented, including broad riverfront avenues created by landfill, a masonry riverwall, and a series of wood piers at various intervals.[107] The plan called for a solid, cement-block wall, faced in granite, to encircle New York up to Sixty-first Street on the Hudson River side and up to Fifty-first Street on the East River side. Although McClellan's idea for spacious avenues along the river was not realized, work on the riverwall commenced after a detailed survey of conditions was made. The wall was designed to rise six feet above the high-water line and extend twenty feet below. Construction proceeded at a snail's pace due to the difficulties of underwater construction, as with the building of the Brooklyn Bridge, and because of various legal disputes with local property owners. Also, after McClellan's resignation in 1873, his successor, another Civil War general with extensive experience as an engineer, Charles K. Graham, ordered a change in building materials. The bulkhead was now to be constructed of concrete, or béton, block. Construction of the riverwall continued slowly and was not completed until World War I.

Pier construction also progressed slowly. The first undertaking of the Department of Docks, Pier 1, located at the Battery, was not built of wood, the material McClellan preferred, but of concrete faced with granite. Pier 1 proved much more expensive than planned as work dragged on from 1872 to 1877, by which time Graham was out as head of the department, replaced by George Sears Greene Jr. in 1875. Greene was not a military hero (though his father had been a Civil War general), but he was an experienced engineer who had worked on the Croton Aqueduct; unlike his predecessors with their short tenures, he would remain at the head of the department for the next twenty-two years.

The most significant advance in New York's waterways during the 1870s was not the improvement of its piers or the beginning of work on the bulkhead, but the blasting of rocks at Hell Gate in September 1876.[108] Under the direction of General John Newton, the United States Engineer Corps removed rocks from the East River opposite East Eighty-ninth Street, rendering that aptly named notorious stretch of water a little less treacherous. The *New York Daily Tribune* described the scene and noted that the crowd of spectators seemed almost disappointed by the successful results of the massive explosion, as if hoping to witness an even more dramatic and dangerous event:

> The excitement in New York City, opposite Hell Gate was extraordinary and intense before the explosion, and scarcely noticeable a moment afterward. The people of the metropolis are familiar with great multitudes, but such a crowd as gathered opposite the lower part of Ward's Island yesterday afternoon is very rarely seen. Police officers who are frequently called upon to estimate and govern great throngs set the multitude as high as 100,000. One police captain staked his reputation on 250,000. More moderate minds were satisfied to think there were 50,000 persons present. . . . The feeling of the

multitude at 2:51 P.M. might have been well expressed by a universal, "Pshaw!" So high was expectation wrought that the comparatively insignificant results as a spectacle were little more to the crowd than the puncture of a soap bubble. They had congregated by the thousands to witness an awful spectacle. They dispersed, many of them expressing regret that they had come at all, and not a few crying "humbug," as if Gen. Newton, as manager of the great artificial "earthquake" of the age, had failed to keep good faith with the public.[109]

As the 1870s closed with little tangible waterfront progress, Greene did propose an extensive redevelopment of the so-called Chelsea-Gansevoort piers along the Hudson River between Little West Twelfth and West Twenty-third Streets. Work on that project would not begin until after the turn of the century.[110]

A notable exception to the lack of progress was the building of Greene's Pier A (1884–86), at the Battery south of Pier 1.[111] The structure consisted of eight subpiers connected by iron girders and concrete arches. The fireproof, inshore end of the building was built of brick and terra cotta with a tin roof. The offshore end, with its picturesque tower, was separated from the other end by a twenty-inch-thick brick firewall and was built with a conventional wood-frame skeleton and clad with galvanized iron siding. The Department of Docks occupied most of the 45-by-285-foot building. The maritime division of the Police Department had some office space close to where they berthed their steam patrol boat and also used part of the tower as a lookout.

In 1886 the *New York Daily Tribune* was harsh in its assessment of the Department of Docks:

> It has wholly failed to meet the public demand for the proper care and improvement of the water front. . . . Advantages in point of location, means of communication with the interior and along the seaboard, and the excellence and extent of the harbor, should have enabled New York to make a very signal gain in its foreign and domestic trade during the last three decades. But as a matter of fact in comparison with Boston, Philadelphia and Baltimore the city has only maintained its relative position in controlling the foreign commerce of the country, while its position in the domestic trade is less certain. This is largely due to the lack of proper terminal facilities and the excessive cost of handling goods here.[112]

Seven years later, even the booster Moses King was forced to agree: "The piers and wharves are for the most part exceedingly irregular and rather unsightly. . . . Some years ago a well-considered plan was devised and begun . . . but this transformation is a very costly process, and has made but little advance."[113] Progress was undeniably slow, but it would be hard to overestimate the importance of the origi-

Pier A, the Battery south of Pier 1. George Sears Greene Jr., 1884–86. View from land, 1903. NYHS.

nal decision to empower the Department of Docks and the desire of the city's citizens and its leading business interests for the municipal government to take control of what had hitherto been private and create a master plan for the future.

Telephones

On March 10, 1876, just three days after securing a patent, Alexander Graham Bell, a professor of vocal physiology at Boston University, successfully tested the first telephone with a transmission to his assistant, Thomas A. Watson: "Mr. Watson—come here. I want you." Three months later, Bell exhibited the machine at the Centennial Exhibition in Philadelphia. Technical advances in the transmitter by Emile Berliner, and additional refinements by Thomas Alva Edison, quickly followed. Although both Boston and New Haven beat New York to the punch in introducing regular telephone service, it was in New York

Headquarters of the Edison Electric Illuminating Company, 65 Fifth Avenue. View to the east, c. 1888, showing the first electric sign. NYHS.

that the greatest expansion of the new technology occurred.[114] On May 11, 1877, Bell exhibited the telephone at the St. Denis Hotel, and by August of that year five working telephones were in operation in New York. In October 1879 the first directory consisted of 252 subscribers. Arriving on the scene at precisely the same time that the economy was rebounding, the telephone, with its obvious advantages over telegraphic communication, an invention of the 1830s, grew in popularity each year. By the early 1880s, with over 20,000 telephones in operation, the price of a subscription from the Metropolitan Telephone and Telegraph Company, which held a monopoly in New York, had risen from $60 to $120 annually. In 1884 the first long-distance line to Boston was established. Philadelphia was connected the following year, but service to Chicago was not in place until 1892.

Electric Light

Gas lighting, a feature of the city since the 1820s, received its first serious competition in 1878 when the United States Electric Light Company placed, on an experimental basis, electric arc lights in the Park Avenue Hotel, the Equitable Building, and the main Post Office.[115] Electricity came to the city's streets in December 1880, when the Brush Electric Light Company demonstrated its effectiveness on Broadway between Fourteenth and Twenty-sixth Streets.[116] So successful was the new form of illumination that by September 1881 the *Real Estate Record and Builders' Guide* reported: "Electric light is gradually displacing the gas light on our principal thoroughfares. There are no more gas lamps on Fifth Avenue below Thirty-fourth street. Every night the great white light makes its appearance in some new quarter of the city. These are furnished by the Maxim or Brush Company. In the meantime Edison is not idle."[117] Edison was working on a refinement of the arc light, a project he had been involved with since the mid-1870s.[118] Believing that arc lighting had no real future because it was too harsh and expensive for widespread indoor use, Edison concentrated on the development of a practical incandescent lamp. Incandescent lighting consists of current passing through a wire or filament to heat it and thus make it glow, and it dates back to 1802 and the experiments of the British scientist Humphrey Davy. But what had stymied inventors since Davy's time was the creation of a durable filament. During 1879 and 1880 Edison finally solved the problem by using carbon. In March 1881, Edison moved the offices of the Edison Electric Illuminating Company from New Jersey to New York, occupying a double-wide brownstone at 65 Fifth Avenue. Later that year he finished work on his largest generator to date; located in his factory on Goerck Street, the machine was capable of powering over one thousand electric lights. By the end of the year, however, electric power was still not available to individual users even though a significant number of buildings in the heart of the downtown business district had been wired by their owners and Edison's company was busy wiring virtually all the houses in a large section of the city below City Hall Park. The *Real Estate Record and Builders' Guide* reported that the "Edison Company . . . proposes to . . . replace steam engines throughout the city. The coming winter will see the electric lights in private houses. Should all go well an up-town section of the city will next be tested."[119]

On September 4, 1882, the generators were at last started up in the central station, at 257 Pearl Street, which, according to Edison, would go on forever unless stopped by an earthquake. Suddenly, much of the neighborhood bounded by Nassau, Pearl, Spruce, and Wall Streets was ablaze in electric light. Among the first buildings to be electrically lit were the businesses and editorial offices of the *New York Times*, where it met with immediate success: "The light was soft, mellow and grateful to the eye, and it seemed almost like writing by daylight to have a light without a particle of flicker and with scarcely any heat to make the head ache."[120] In addition to the Pearl Street station, which in two years' time was supplying power to over 11,000 lamps in 500 homes, Edison offered his customers the option of having their own individual power plants. In the first six months of its operation, in 1882, these plants provided power to over 10,000 lamps; by 1884 that number had increased by a factor of six. Edison also built his own lamps, dominating the market. Of the 250,000 lamps in use in 1885, some 200,000 were supplied by Edison's company. Unlike the monopolized telephone service, however, the city granted franchises to several companies and by the end of the 1880s, as the demand for electricity continued to grow unabated, power was also provided by the Brush Electric Light Company, the United States Electric Light Company, the Thomson-Houston Electric Light Company, the Mount Morris Electric Light Company, and the Harlem Lighting Company.

Overhead Wires

As early as 1870 the *Real Estate Record and Builders' Guide* had opposed the use of aboveground telegraph lines, the multiplication of which led to "the disfigurement and obstruction of our streets."[121] By 1878 the problem of overhead telegraph wires in the city's business district had grown to such a point that there were calls for laws requiring that they be buried.[122] By the early 1880s, with the widespread use of the telephone, the problem had grown much worse. The *Record and Guide* informed its readers that "the unsightliness of the wires is everybody's business. The whole of lower Broadway is on the way to be rebuilt with finer edifices. . . . Their effect will be greatly injured, as the appearance of the street is almost spoiled as it is, by the hideous poles and the bundles of wires crossing in every direction and at every angle. The wires are an impediment and a source of danger of fires, and are in every way objectionable."[123] So unwelcome were the poles that property owners sometimes came to blows with the workers authorized to set them up, with block associations formed in some cases to fight the municipally authorized private companies doing the installation.[124]

Model of the Edison Electric Illuminating Company's first power station (1882), 257 Pearl Street. MCNY.

In 1883, the New York Board of Aldermen voted to require the burial of wires within two years.[125] Many argued that this process should be part of a larger infrastructure project, the construction of a "subway" in which gas and water mains, steam pipes, pneumatic tubes, and all manner of cabling could be housed. But the new legislation was not vigorously enforced, and when the two years were almost up the *Record and Guide* once again argued for reform: "When we get the telegraph wires down, if we ever do, people who have lived in New York all their lives will rub their eyes and imagine themselves in some strange capital, so spacious will the avenues look and so comparatively respectable even the hum-drum old brown stone fronts. It is the longitudinal streets, naturally, that are chiefly disfigured by poles and wires, that is up-town, for down-town there is little to choose."[126]

By the late 1880s, towering poles of Norway pine dominated the main thoroughfares, some carrying as many as thirty cross arms and three hundred wires. In addition, wires were strung across eleven thousand Manhattan roofs. In winter, ice built up on the wires, frequently causing the towers to collapse from the additional weight. By the mid-1880s a genuine search was on for the best method to consolidate the wires in underground conduits, commonly referred to as subways.[127] In 1884 a commission was appointed to study the problem and devise a specific plan for putting the wires underground. Murky political intrigue surrounded the awarding of the subway contract to the Consolidated Telegraph and Electrical Subway Company. Construction work proceeded slowly, beginning in 1886. Meanwhile, more wires were strung on overhead

View north along Broadway from Cortlandt Street, c. 1890, showing telegraph poles and wires and the Western Union Building (George B. Post, 1873–75) on the left. NYHS.

Blizzard of '88, March 11, 1888. View to the west of Broadway between Liberty and Cortlandt Streets. NYHS.

poles and on the structures of elevated railroads. At last, conduit was laid under a two-mile stretch of Sixth Avenue from Twenty-first to Fifty-ninth Street. Completed in February 1887, the conduit was capable of accommodating 2,500 miles of wire, although only six miles, belonging to the Fire Department, had been installed. By the end of the year, a conduit subway was in operation in the business district, running from Dey Street and Broadway to Park Row and thence to the Brooklyn Bridge. At this time poles were being removed on Sixth Avenue, apparently the first to come down.

On the heels of this preliminary work, the great blizzard of 1888 would unexpectedly intensify the urgency of subway construction.[128] After a wet Sunday evening in the early hours of March 11, 1888, snow began to fall in the city. By the end of the next day, twenty-two inches of snow had fallen and winds of up to eighty-five miles per hour had created drifts as high as twenty feet in some places. The blizzard was not a record snowfall for the city, but the combination of wind and snow was paralyzing. The weather stalled elevated trains, many filled with travelers, some of whom sat out the storm in unheated cars for two days while others climbed down to the street on ladders supplied at

hefty prices by entrepreneurial citizens. The subzero temperatures froze the East River, which was very unusual.

It took almost a year of further discussion and procrastination before Mayor Hugh Grant insisted that no licenses for overhead lines be given where subways were already in place. Grant also refused permission for any further installation of overhead telegraph trunk lines.[129] On April 16, 1889, a crew of workers armed with axes and shears climbed the tall telegraph poles at Fourteenth Street and Broadway and, before crowds of cheering citizens, toppled them to the ground, thereby striking a decisive blow in the long-awaited war against the city's most visible symbol of technological blight.[130]

Surface Transit

Over the course of the nineteenth century, New York's streets became an increasingly unwieldy mess. Clogging the streets were horse-drawn omnibuses, carts, drays, wagons, private carriages, and, after 1832, horse-drawn streetcars. Travel typically entailed long commutes in hideous conditions. Chock-full of conveyances of every kind, Broadway was so difficult to cross by 1866 that Genin the Hatter, with a shop on the southwest corner at Fulton

View to the northwest along Broadway, 1860, showing traffic congestion and the spire of St. Paul's Chapel (Thomas McBean, 1764–66; spire, James Crommelin Lawrence, 1794) on the left. The many American and Japanese flags celebrate Japan's decision to send an ambassador to the United States. FLC.

Loew Bridge, Broadway at Fulton Street. Ritch & Griffiths, 1866–67. View to the northwest showing St. Paul's Chapel (Thomas McBean, 1764–66; spire, James Crommelin Lawrence, 1794) and the Astor House (Isaiah Rogers, 1836). Archive Photos.

Street, persuaded the Common Council to build what would be called the Loew Bridge (Ritch & Griffiths, 1866–67), a cast-iron footbridge over the street.[131] In 1868, after protests by Genin's competition, Knox the Hatter, who claimed that the bridge blocked light to his store and attracted loiterers, it was torn down.

What public transportation existed was vastly overtaxed. The *New York Herald* described the chaos of a typical trip in an omnibus in 1864:

> Modern martyrdom may be succinctly defined as riding in a New York omnibus. The discomforts, inconveniences and annoyances of a trip in one of these vehicles are almost intolerable. . . . Ladies are disgusted, frightened and insulted. Children are alarmed, and lift up their voices and weep. Indignant gentlemen rise to remonstrate with the irate Jehu, and are suddenly bumped back in their seats, twice as indignant as before, besides being involved in supplementary quarrels with those other passengers upon

whose corns they have accidentally trodden. Thus the omnibus rolls along, a perfect Bedlam on wheels.

The *Herald* was just as displeased with any of the twenty-two lines of streetcars, which cost five cents per ride, half the fare of the less popular omnibuses: "The cars are quieter than the omnibuses, but much more crowded. People are packed into them like sardines in a box, with perspiration for oil. The seats being more than filled, the passengers are placed in rows down the middle, where they hang on by the straps, like smoked hams in a corner grocery. To enter or exit is exceedingly difficult. . . . The foul, close, heated air is poisonous. A healthy person cannot ride a dozen blocks without a headache."[132] Two years later, the *New York Daily Tribune* was less melodramatic but just as insistent that something needed to be done to remedy a system that inconvenienced New Yorkers for an average of ninety minutes each day: "Street Railroads and Omnibuses have their uses; but we have reached the end

New York and Harlem Railroad station (1863), Fourth to Madison Avenue, East Twenty-sixth to East Twenty-seventh Street. View to the northwest, c. 1865. FLC.

of them. . . . They are unchangeably too slow; and their capacity is exhausted. To put on more cars or construct more roads is only to monopolize our streets and virtually drive all carriages out of them."[133]

But what was to be done? Surface railroads were clearly undesirable, interrupting the flow of crosstown traffic and, as steam locomotives grew larger and dirtier, blighting wide swaths of land on both sides of their tracks. Since 1832, the New York and Harlem line had run along the surface of Fourth Avenue, with service reaching the Harlem River in 1837, thereby transforming the historic village of Harlem into a suburb. In 1846 the New York and Harlem line was joined by the Hudson River Railroad, which, after five years of construction, connected Albany and New York with track running along the east bank of the Hudson River. In addition to its passenger transport, this was also the first line to carry freight directly into the city. In 1865, after eight years of effort, the seventy-one-year-old Cornelius Vanderbilt—called the Commodore, and perhaps the richest man in New York—finally achieved his goal of controlling the two major railroad lines operating in the city. By accumulation of stock he now could consolidate the New York and Harlem and Hudson River Railroads. The problem he faced with this merger was the inadequate terminal facilities of the various lines, including the Hudson's station (1860–61) at Thirtieth Street and Tenth Avenue and the Harlem's vaguely castellated station (1863) occupying the block bounded by Twenty-sixth and Twenty-seventh Streets and Fourth and Madison Avenues. After addressing the need for a freight terminal for the Hudson line with the construction of St. John's Terminal (John B. Snook, 1867–68) (see chapter 3), Vanderbilt, now working with his son William, turned his attention to passenger service. In a typically bold move, he proposed the construction of America's first significant railroad station, Grand Central Depot.

Grand Central Depot

On May 20, 1869, the state legislature passed a law authorizing Cornelius Vanderbilt to proceed with a station "constructed of the best materials . . . and . . . finished in the best style of architecture."[134] The site selected was in effect a superblock, extending west from the center of Fourth Avenue between Forty-second and Forty-fifth Streets to a new street, Vanderbilt Avenue, created approximately two hundred feet east of Madison Avenue. A much diminished right-of-way carried the traffic of Fourth Avenue along the east side of the terminal. The city had never seen a public facility on the scale of the station, with its train yards and right-of-way; goats were still being raised on the northeast corner of Forty-second Street and Lexington Avenue at its opening. Although the *New York Times* carped that Grand Central Depot could "only by a stretch of courtesy be called either central or grand," it nonetheless propelled the city's expansion northward at a scale and speed hitherto unimaginable.[135] Complaints and witticisms about Grand Central's centrality and grandeur aside, the site was, given the city's decision in the previous decade to ban any surface steam-railroad traffic below Forty-second Street, in fact at the southernmost point possible. The legislation that permitted the station also included a controversial measure that was a testament to Vanderbilt's influence in Albany: the government invoked its power of eminent domain in order to allow Vanderbilt to purchase all the land between Forty-second and Forty-seventh Streets and Fourth and Madison Avenues at "fair market" value.

Vanderbilt chose John B. Snook, the architect of his railroad's St. John's Terminal, to design the new station. Construction began in summer 1869 and the cornerstone was officially laid on September 1. Even under construction, the new terminal was a source of awe: the *Real Estate Record and Builders' Guide* observed that "the scaffolding alone" erected to support the train shed "is worth a visit."[136] In a little more than two years, the massive effort was completed, and the station was officially opened on October 9, 1871. The immense complex, which covered some thirty-seven acres, featured a head house, train shed, track and platform system, coach yard, and engine terminals. Snook's French Second Empire–style, L-shaped head house, inspired by the newly completed portions of the Louvre and by Paris's second Gare du Nord (1861–65), was built of red pressed brick, with cast-iron trim painted to imitate white marble. The 240-foot-long Forty-second Street facade of the head house featured two four-story projecting pavilions at the corners, topped with rounded mansards. In the center, the taller, five-story pavilion was also crowned by a rounded mansard, which was given more detailed treatment, with a clock placed on each of its sides. The tripartite division of the Forty-second Street facade was more than a compositional ploy, reflecting as it did the odd internal division of the terminal. Even though all the lines were owned by the Vanderbilts, each had

Grand Central Depot, Fourth to Vanderbilt Avenue, East Forty-second to East Forty-fifth Street. John B. Snook, 1869–71.
View to the northeast, c. 1872, showing the Forty-second Street facade on the right and the Vanderbilt Avenue facade on the left. NYHS.

Grand Central Depot, Fourth to Vanderbilt Avenue, East Forty-second to East Forty-fifth Street. John B. Snook, 1869–71.
View to the north, c. 1880, of the Forty-second Street facade. NYHS.

Grand Central Depot, Fourth to Vanderbilt Avenue, East Forty-second to East Forty-fifth Street. John B. Snook, 1869–71.
View to the southeast of the train shed on the left and the Vanderbilt Avenue facade on the right. NYHS.

Grand Central Depot, Fourth to Vanderbilt Avenue, East Forty-second to East Forty-fifth Street. John B. Snook, 1869–71. Train shed. NYHS.

Grand Central Depot, Fourth to Vanderbilt Avenue, East Forty-second to East Forty-fifth Street. John B. Snook, 1869–71. Detail of cast-iron bases of train-shed arches. NYHS.

separate waiting, ticket, and baggage areas—so separate, in fact, that people had to leave the building to get from one line's facilities to another's. Small balconies were located below the second-story windows of the three pavilions. Between the third and fourth floors of the center projecting pavilion was a large niche that remained curiously empty, perhaps intended for some decorative work, such as the prominent sculptures added to Snook's St. John's Terminal. The less bombastic, 696-foot Vanderbilt Avenue side of the head house, divided into several sections of various widths, stretched northward until Forty-fifth Street and housed waiting and baggage facilities on its ground floor, with corporate offices above. The head house was serviceable but, as the *Record and Guide* put it, "of no very

novel character in its details" although "massive and commanding in effect, and very appropriately treated."[137]

The real marvel of the complex, the train shed, drew much of the praise. The shed was the creation of Snook, working with his engineer, Isaac C. Buckhout, and Joseph Duclos and R. G. Hatfield of the Architectural Iron Works of New York, the company responsible for the station's cast and wrought iron. Although the immensity of the shed was concealed from outside view by the architecture of the head house and, on the north, by a screen wall that created arcaded portals for the trains and was concluded at the roof by a fussy skyline of gables and pediments, the interior revealed heroic scale and limpid constructional clarity. European stations had served as Snook's inspiration, most notably London's St. Pancras Station (1863–65), but the 652-foot-long, 100-foot-high roof—constructed of equal parts of glass and galvanized corrugated iron and supported by thirty-two forty-ton wrought-iron trusses, connected at their springing points by wrought-iron tie-rods that went under the tracks—was virtually unprecedented in scale. The elaborately stenciled trusses, spanning two hundred feet, covered the largest interior space on the continent, with room for twelve parallel tracks. According to the *Record and Guide*, the shed, with its "immense roof of curved ornamental iron rib and glass which vaults over the huge space in one unbroken span," was "worthy of a visit from a long distance. We question if anything more simple in form and yet effective in arrangement can be found among any of the most vaunted roofs of iron construction to be found in Europe."[138] *Scientific American* noted that previously "the railroad depots are those of which New Yorkers have least cause to be proud," with "discomfort, shabbiness, and dirt, concentrated in ill-ventilated structures." The city could now glory in a building "where space for business, order and discipline in arrangement, ample ingress and egress, and substantial elegance of interior and exterior, are provided."[139]

Despite Grand Central's obvious virtues as a work of architecture and engineering, only five weeks after its official opening the *New York Times* declared the station "a death trap": "One has but to stand a few minutes in Forty-fifth street, where the cars enter and pass out of the depot, to see the peril to which life is daily put, and to wonder that more people are not wounded or killed for their temerity in attempting a crossing." The *Times* was not exaggerating the danger: "Human life is sacrificed at an average of one every other day for want of proper safeguards. Seven persons have been killed between Forty-fifth and Fifty-fourth streets within the last twelve days."[140] It was not until 1875 that bridges were built to carry traffic across the large train yard that filled the area as far north as Forty-eighth Street. Footbridges were built at Forty-sixth and Forty-seventh Streets; vehicular bridges at Forty-fifth and Forty-eighth Streets. Farther uptown there was increasing concern about the disruption and potential danger caused by the frequent steam trains, as many as eighty-five per day, that passed along Fourth Avenue north of the station. One annoyed neighbor was Columbia College, located between Forty-ninth and Fiftieth Streets and Madison and Fourth Avenues, where a professor of astronomy complained that the vibrations caused by the trains made it impossible to take accurate measurements.[141] The developer John McCool organized the 19th Ward Railroad Reform Association, which in late 1871 lobbied to change conditions on what the group labeled the "avenue of death."[142] In 1872, Vanderbilt, reacting to the criticism, authorized work to proceed on the construction of a roofed cut intended to carry Fourth Avenue and the transverse streets on a continuous, iron-framed viaduct that would extend between Fifty-sixth and Ninety-sixth Streets. From Ninety-sixth to 116th Street, where the island's topography dipped into a valley, the railroad tracks were carried above the streets on a massive stone arch viaduct. The work was completed in 1875 at a cost of some $6,000,000, only $500,000 less than the cost of building the Grand Central Depot. But Vanderbilt, ever crafty, was able to convince the city to share the expense on an equal basis.

Rapid Transit

Even through half of Manhattan Island was unsettled, providing convenient homes for New Yorkers posed a serious challenge. Given the geography of the city and the density of traffic already in place, only a system of below-ground or elevated rapid transit could help decant the population crowded onto the island's southern half. As Junius Henri Browne put it in 1869: "New York is much better shaped for a cucumber than a city. It is so long and slender that people who abide here pass a large part of

their lives in getting up and down town."[143] In an editorial of 1866, the *New York Daily Tribune* proposed an answer, even though the solutions were technologically still at the experimental stage, at least for New York: "Gentlemen of the Legislature! give us both the Underground and the Aerial Railway!"[144]

The idea of an aerial railway, or elevated, went back as far as 1832, only two years after the first omnibus had traveled along Broadway from Bowling Green to Bleecker Street. The 1832 scheme was proposed by Colonel John Stevens, an inventor specializing in steam boilers who also helped establish the country's first patent laws, advanced an unrealized proposal in 1807 for floating bridges in the East River, and built an early seagoing steamboat in 1808.[145] Stevens called for a railroad running some ten to twelve feet above the ground, carried on wooden posts. He planned a route that would begin at the Battery and continue north on Greenwich Street to its ultimate destination, the developer's native Hoboken, which it would reach by means of a bridge over the Hudson River. A more realistic and technologically advanced proposal was submitted by John Randel Jr., better known as the secretary and surveyor to the commissioners who laid out the city's streets and therefore generally acknowledged as the author of the so-called Commissioners' Plan of 1811. Randel's idea, debated between 1846 and 1848, was for an elevated train that would run along both sides of Broadway, powered by an endless belt operated by stationary engines.[146] *Scientific American* noted that the cars "do not stop to take in or let down passengers. This is accomplished by means of a tender, which passes along a side track, and by means of a brake pressing upon a brake plate fixed to each car, the speed of the tender is got up to be equal to that of the passenger cars, before they are fastened to each other, for the exchange of passengers."[147] Another innovative feature of this unrealized design, rejected by the Common Council, which feared that its presence and loud operation would depress land values, was the "sofa elevator," or screw shaft, that took passengers from the street to the platform of the elevated.

Twenty years after Randel's proposal, in 1867, the state legislature, after considering more than forty proposals, granted Charles T. Harvey, an inventor, a charter to incorporate the West Side and Yonkers Patent Railway Company and construct an experimental elevated on Greenwich Street between the Battery and Morris Street.[148] Work began in July after Harvey had raised $100,000, and in five months' time the quarter-mile experimental stretch was completed, and Harvey was given the go-ahead to complete the line, running to Twenty-ninth Street and Ninth Avenue. A year after the initial construction had commenced, the half-mile point, at Cortlandt Street, was reached and the line was officially inaugurated on July 3, 1868. The spectacle of the successful opening of the "long-legged railway" or "railway on stilts"—two common descriptions of the day—was considerable, with the governor and the mayor in attendance; the unprecedented operation was certainly a novelty. Nonetheless, the event was

Proposed elevated railway. John Randel Jr., 1846–48. INPS. CU.

Charles T. Harvey testing his elevated railroad on Greenwich Street at Morris Street, c. 1867. NYHS.

Ninth Avenue Elevated Railroad at Little West Twelfth Street, 1869. NYHS.

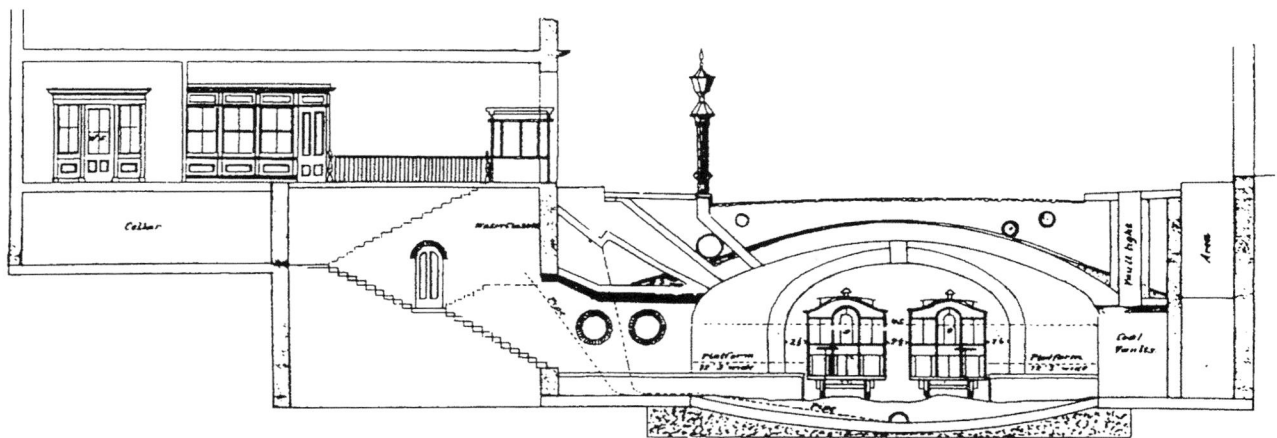

Proposed Metropolitan Railway. Hugh B. Willson and A. P. Robinson, 1864. JBW. CU.

not front-page news in any of the major daily newspapers. *Harper's Weekly* best captured the mood of reserved confidence that an acceptable alternative to the various forms of surface transportation had at last been found: "A trial trip of the new elevated railway in Greenwich Street was had on July 3, and the rapid speed which was attained on that occasion leads the friends of the enterprise to hope that the problem of rapid and safe locomotion throughout the crowded streets of the city has been solved."[149] Harvey's trains, traveling at the rate of fifteen miles per hour, were drawn by three-quarter-inch steel wire cables from John A. Roebling's Sons Company. Power was supplied by subterranean steam engines anchored to bedrock.

Even before Harvey's successful experiment, the other half of that *New York Daily Tribune* editorial cry—"Give us the Underground!"—had unleashed a number of interesting proposals. Although Randel's scheme had complicated features, Harvey showed that the elevateds called for little in the way of technological innovation. The design of underground trains, however, was quite a different matter, especially in an age of steam power, which presented serious environmental challenges. The potential for tunnel fires introduced real concerns for public safety. Nonetheless, the workability of an underground steam railroad was an established fact. London's system, begun in 1853 and operational within a decade, was a compelling inspiration for New York's inventors, engineers, and capitalists.

The first detailed plan for a New York underground belonged to a Michigan railroad man, Hugh B. Willson, who was in London during the construction and opening of its first underground line.[150] In 1864, working with the engineer A. P. Robinson, Willson proposed that his steam-powered Metropolitan Railway run from the Battery to Central Park, traveling under Broadway to Thirty-fourth Street and then continuing under Sixth Avenue to its terminus. Robinson's sixteen-foot-high, twenty-five-and-a-half-foot-wide tunnel could accommodate two tracks, which would serve stations placed at half-mile intervals. The stations, built directly over the tunnel, were to be of iron and glass with glass floors to allow daylight to pass through to the platforms below. Ventilation would be handled by pipes connected to hollow iron gas lampposts placed every one hundred feet along the route. In a report published in January 1865, Robinson described the benefits of the proposed Metropolitan Railway: "There would be no dust. There would be no mud. Passengers . . . have simply to enter a station from the sidewalk and pass down a spacious and well lighted staircase to a dry and roomy platform . . . , be sure of a luxurious seat in a well lighted car, and . . . be carried" to their "destination in one-third the time" it would take to "be carried by any other conveyance. . . . Everything would be out of sight and hearing, and nothing would indicate the great thoroughfare below."[151] The proposal was optimistically greeted by the public but incurred the wrath of Cornelius Vanderbilt, who used his considerable influence to kill the project, first in the state senate and then, after its passage on a second attempt, with Governor Ruben E. Fenton's veto. In addition, the Metropolitan Railway was stymied by Alfred Craven, engineer of the Croton Aqueduct, who believed that its construction would interfere with the city's water pipes.

Egbert L. Viele's Arcade Railway (1866) was the next significant underground scheme to come forward.[152] Viele, a practicing engineer and surveyor who had received his training in the army, was hired by Melville C. Smith to create what was in essence a new street thirty feet below street level, under Broadway. Built for "locomotion and trading, in every respect as accessible and convenient as the present thoroughfare," it would be lit and ventilated by a five-foot-wide areaway cut into each side of the rebuilt upper-level street.[153] Stairs were to connect the two levels at each cross street. The lower street would also be accessible to existing buildings along the right-of-way, through rebuilt cellars. While the upper-level street would continue to serve the usual mix of traffic, the new, lower street would be reserved for fast commuter trains and streetcars serving local stops as well as pedestrian footpaths on either side of the tracks.

Proposed Arcade Railway. Egbert L. Viele, 1866. SA. CU.

The proposed route followed Broadway from the Battery to Sixty-fourth Street and then went beneath Ninth Avenue almost to Fort Washington. *Appletons' Journal* characterized Viele's scheme in 1878 as the "most ambitious" and "most attractive" of all the rapid-transit proposals: "Is it necessary to state the advantages claimed for this fascinating plan by its audacious projectors? It would add a new story to the entire length of Broadway; double the walking capacity of the street; quadruple the carrying capacity. . . . Furthermore, the rental of seventeen hundred stores would be increased at least two thousand dollars each, the aggregate of which amount alone would pay ten per cent interest on a capital three times as great as the calculated cost of the work, which was twenty million dollars."[154] But the project was not universally admired. The *New York Times* editorialized in 1868:

> We are glad to see that the Arcade Railroad project has been defeated in the State Senate. We are sorry to differ so widely as we do on this matter from most of our neighbors of the Press;—but we are utterly unable to see any adequate reason for urging it so strongly as they do. We concede all they say of the necessity for increased transit accommodation through the City, and of the inadequacy of surface-roads to answer the demand; but why Broadway, where the property to be injured is far more valuable than in any other part of the City, should be selected for the most formidable and doubtful of all these experiments, we cannot understand.[155]

It was not the objections of the *Times*, or the protests of the powerful merchant Alexander T. Stewart, who feared for the value of his considerable Broadway holdings, or even the perceived infeasibility of the grand scheme that doomed the project. Like Willson and Robinson's Metropolitan Railway, the Arcade Railway fell victim to politics, in this case the last hurrah of William Marcy "Boss" Tweed. Tweed killed Viele's innovative scheme in favor of his Viaduct Railway, a proposal for an elevated line to be built on solid masonry arches that had more to do with potential graft than with a serious rapid-transit proposal, even though Leopold Eidlitz and the engineer John W. Serrell prepared the original report.[156] In October 1871, only six months after the legislature had voted in favor of the Viaduct over the Arcade, Tweed was removed from power and the Viaduct scheme died with him. Although Melville C. Smith continued to promote the Arcade plan in various forms over the years, it had lost the active support of Viele and never again received serious consideration.[157]

Other underground proposals continued to pour forth, including the New York City Central Underground Company's 1868 scheme to connect City Hall Park and Harlem with a line largely placed beneath Madison Avenue,[158] but only one got beyond the planning stage: Alfred Ely Beach's pneumatic railway of 1870.[159] Beach, a prolific inventor and copublisher of *Scientific American*, had witnessed the failure of previous efforts and was determined that his scheme not be defeated by partisan politics. His idea was to construct an experimental portion of his line in secret and thereby avoid interacting with greedy and vindictive politicians. If his underground was more than just a proposal and could in fact be demonstrated as a built and verifiable success, public enthusiasm, no doubt helped along by his influential publication, would guarantee implementation. Beach was convinced that only pneumatic power was both strong and clean enough to work in a subterranean environment. As early as 1867, he had constructed a model consisting of a six-foot-diameter wooden tube through which a ten-seat car was propelled by a ten-foot-diameter Helix fan that could be reversed when the car reached the end of the miniature tunnel. A year after successfully demonstrating the model at the American Institute Fair, held in the Fourteenth Street Armory, the Beach Pneumatic Transit Company was chartered by the state to construct pneumatic tubes beneath the surface of the streets for the transmission of letters and merchandise; in 1869, the contract was amended to include the transportation of passengers.

Using his own money, Beach was now ready to begin his experiment in earnest. He rented the basement of Devlin's clothing store, at 260 Broadway, and began the surreptitious nighttime construction of a 312-foot-long tunnel beneath Broadway between Warren and Murray Streets. Beach's invention of a flexible hydraulic shield that could tunnel seventeen inches with each press and at the same time guard against cave-ins was crucial to the success of the project. Beach also designed a twenty-two-seat car that neatly fit into the nine-foot-diameter cylindrical tube. Propulsion was supplied by the Roots Patent Force Blast Blower, an immense fan operated by a steam engine. Like the earlier model, this blower, capable of achieving a top speed of ten miles per hour, could be reversed when the car

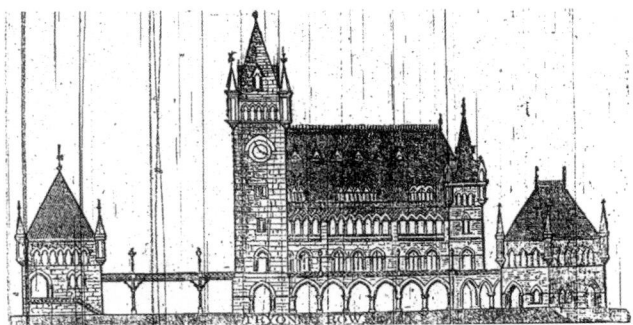

Proposed Viaduct Railway. Leopold Eidlitz and John W. Serrell, 1870. Downtown depot. NYDT. CU.

Proposed Viaduct Railway. Leopold Eidlitz and John W. Serrell, 1870. Bridge over Broadway. NYDT. CU.

reached the end of the tunnel. Beach was also something of a showman, and he spent a great deal of time and money to turn the utilitarian project into an opulent extravaganza, with interior amenities seemingly more appropriate for a luxury hotel or department store, including a grand piano, frescoes, a fountain, and an aquarium.

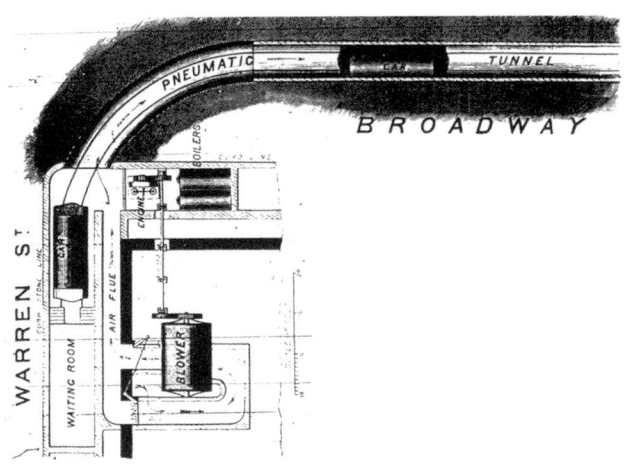

Proposed pneumatic underground railway. Alfred Ely Beach, 1870. BPUR. CU.

Proposed pneumatic elevated railway. Rufus T. Gilbert, 1872. SA. CU.

On February 26, 1870, the tunnel was inaugurated. The *New York Herald* was enthusiastic about the "fashionable reception held in the bowels of the Earth," describing the scene as "a kind of Aladdin's cave opened to view."[160] Not surprisingly, Beach's own *Scientific American* crowed with pleasure: "The whole arrangement is as comfortable and cozy as the front basement dining-room of a first-class city residence. The tunnel . . . is absolutely free from the discomforts of surface car-travel. It is not cold in winter. It will be delightfully cool in summer. The air will be constantly changed in it by the motion of the blowing engine."[161] The *Real Estate Record and Builders' Guide* described the scene after a December 1870 visit: "Descending into the handsomely furnished office, the visitor is conducted by wide folding-doors on the right-hand side to a large and beautiful waiting-room or 'Station,' well furnished with sofas and settees."[162] After the official, invitation-only opening, the curious public, who ultimately numbered 400,000, could take a tour of the operation for a fee of twenty-five cents.

Even though Beach had demonstrated that he could build an underground railway without disrupting the surface street, and that the smooth ride in the pneumatic tube—like a sailboat before the wind, to repeat the most common description of the day—was superior to any other form of transit, skeptics remained. Some argued that Beach's hydraulic shield could not effectively tunnel through

Manhattan's rockier regions, while others discounted the ability of pneumatic power to work on any but the shortest of routes. Still others, most notably John Jacob Astor II, continued to believe that extensive tunneling would weaken the surface street, potentially inflicting untold and unrecoverable damage to property. By 1873, even after Beach was willing to consider both steam power and the traditional cut-and-fill tunneling technique, the inventor was unable to raise sufficient additional funds to continue his dream and Governor John A. Dix was forced to withdraw the Beach Pneumatic Transit Company's charter.

With the failure of all of the underground proposals to go forward in a practical way, it was left to the proponents of various elevated schemes to advance New York's nascent rapid-transit system. In 1873 Alfred Speer, a wealthy wine merchant and amateur inventor from Passaic, New Jersey, came forward with a truly unique idea: an endless traveling train, which he had patented two years earlier.[163] Speer proposed to build an immense loop some fourteen feet above lower Broadway, supported by iron pillars placed along the curbs. Powered by cables driven by steam engines, the perpetually moving trains could be reached by transfer cars boarded at an elevated station. Although Speer's design evoked a fair amount of derision because of its novelty, several engineers vouched for its feasibility, and the inventor and industrialist Peter Cooper offered $100,000 to construct an experimental section. *Appletons' Journal* imagined how the scheme would work:

> Having ascended the stairs at Chambers Street corner, we stand upon a little platform and, looking up Broadway, see an endless flooring, raised on massive pillars, moving down the west side of the thoroughfare and up the east side. It resembles a viaduct, and is traveling at the unvarying speed of ten miles an hour. . . . Some are walking southward and others northward . . . , some are seated on benches and others in cabins, like ordinary railway-cars, erected on the platform. . . . The greatest advantage of the plan is that, as there are no intervals, there is no waiting, and . . . we are almost immediately admitted to the platform-train by one of the transfer-cars, the train never ceasing to move mellifluously or to slacken its speed.[164]

But implementation was blocked by Governor Dix, who vetoed two bills authorizing the plan passed by the legislature.

Another interesting unrealized proposal came from Rufus T. Gilbert, a physician who, after witnessing the terrible conditions of New York's tenements, became convinced that the dispersion of people was a social imperative and that advances in rapid transit were necessary for this population shift.[165] Taking his technological cue from Beach and his aesthetic from Eidlitz, in 1872 Gilbert proposed an ornate, Gothic-inspired, pneumatic elevated railway to run along Sixth and Second Avenues. The Panic of 1873 stopped development, but not before Gilbert was granted a charter from the legislature to build his line.

A number of factors conspired to ensure that elevated rather than underground railroads would be franchised.

For one thing, they could be built quickly and relatively cheaply; this prompted real-estate interests in outlying areas, particularly the undeveloped upper West Side, to push for their construction. The big-money interests saw the elevateds as an inherently better business proposition, with Samuel J. Tilden, Cyrus W. Field, and Andrew Carnegie among the most important and active investors. Unfortunately, Charles T. Harvey's initial success, in the late 1860s, with the West Side and Yonkers Patent Railway had been followed by a series of reversals. The system was forever breaking down and the cables frequently snapped. On September 24, 1869, Harvey was ruined on Black Friday, the stock market collapse created by Jay Gould and Jim Fisk's attempt to corner the gold market. A year later the pioneering venture was sold at a sheriff's auction for less than $1,000.

By this time the issue of rapid transit had become something of a civic obsession, culminating in 1872 with the founding of the New York Rapid Transit Association, which met once a week to discuss the problem. That same year, in October, the outbreak of a severe epidemic of equine distemper reminded New Yorkers yet again of the disadvantages of horsecar travel.[166] The newly formed New York Elevated Railway Company took over Harvey's bank-rupt line. It abandoned the inefficient cable system in favor of dummy steam engines—that is to say, small locomotives camouflaged to appear as cars to avoid frightening the horses below. This proved an immediate success, and by 1873 the line was extended along Ninth Avenue to Thirty-fourth Street.[167] By May and June 1875, when it reached Forty-second Street, the line carried 172,000 passengers; that number doubled during the same two months the following year; and in 1877, 563,000 people traveled in May and June, more than tripling the total in two years.

In 1875, with the passage of the Husted Act, the newly created Rapid Transit Commission was charged with the responsibility of determining future routes as well as deciding which companies would build them. At this time, Rufus T. Gilbert was forced out of power, but his company's charter was still active and the new commission granted it the right to build elevated lines along Sixth and Second Avenues, the same routes originally granted to Gilbert. With Gilbert out of the way, the new directors, who changed the name of the concern from the Gilbert Elevated Railway to the Metropolitan Railway Company in 1878, reverted from the pneumatic technology to the reliable steam model. Reporting on the first trip along the Sixth Avenue line in 1878, which whisked two hundred

Proposed elevated railway. Alfred Speer, 1873. RCR. CU.

Ninth Avenue Elevated Railroad. View to the north from Gansevoort Street, 1876. Powelson. NYHS.

Ninth Avenue Elevated Railroad. View to the north from West Forty-first Street, 1876. Powelson. NYHS.

passengers from Trinity Church to Central Park in seventeen minutes, the *New York Daily Tribune* wrote that not "a jar or jolt was felt by the passengers. . . . Pushing along the avenue at the level of the second-story windows, it was difficult even for persons most familiar with the first-story features of the busy thoroughfare to realize just where they were. It seemed as if one were travelling through some unknown street in a strange city."[168]

The New York Elevated Railway Company, which was so successfully running the Ninth Avenue line, was handed the task of constructing the Third Avenue elevated, which opened on August 26, 1878, running from South Ferry to Sixty-seventh Street. By December 1, it was extended to Eighty-ninth Street, with the expectation that service would reach Harlem by the end of the year, although temporary stations would be used.[169] The trip from Chatham Square to Harlem by streetcar took one hour and twenty minutes; the elevated railroad cut travel time to forty minutes. At Forty-second Street and Third Avenue, a spur line was built connecting it to Grand Central Depot, thereby dramatically shortening the journey of suburban and long-distance travelers alike. *Frank Leslie's Illustrated Newspaper* was enthusiastic about the stations of the new Third Avenue elevated: "The interiors of both the ladies' and gentlemen's waiting rooms are very tastefully furnished throughout, in what is known as the Eastlake style of decoration. . . . The glass ventilators are . . . in var-

Third Avenue Elevated Railroad. View of Forty-second Street spur, c. 1878. NYHS.

iegated colors and ornamental bay windows in the waiting rooms . . . afford a view of the street below."[170]

From this point forward the growth of all the elevated lines was dramatic and swift.[171] New stations opened literally each month from the late 1870s until the early 1880s, when all four lines, now consolidated under the control of the Manhattan Railway Company, ran into the upper part of the island. In May 1886, a new elevated line, the Suburban Rapid Transit Company, organized some six years earlier, began operations to connect New York and the Annexed District.[172] With the intention of linking up with the Second and Third Avenue lines of the Manhattan Railway Company for an additional five-cent fare, the Suburban Rapid Transit Company first constructed a steel drawbridge over the Harlem River. Service commenced from a new station at 129th Street and Second Avenue, jointly built and owned by the two companies, and ended at 133rd Street and Willis Avenue in the Annexed District, the only station of the new line. Within a year, service was extended to 170th Street and Third Avenue. In 1891 the Manhattan Railway Company took over control of the Suburban line, continuing the expansion of the elevated and eliminating the transfer fare after two years.

Though the newly constructed network of elevated lines had at first been advanced as a technological breakthrough in the service of improving people's lives by enabling them to leave the dense central city, it soon became clear that

Ninth Avenue Elevated Railroad. Construction at West Sixty-sixth Street, 1878. NYHS.

Fourteenth Street station of the Sixth Avenue Elevated Railroad. Jasper F. Cropsey, 1878. View to the east, c. 1879. NYHS.

this innovation would not solve New York's housing problem. True, commuting time had on average been cut in half, and whole sections of the city were suddenly rendered convenient such that in 1879, despite the lingering depression, some five hundred houses were built north of Fiftieth Street. But at the same time, as Frederick Law Olmsted wrote: "The elevated roads and the uptown movement lead as yet to nothing better; for even at Yorkville, Harlem and Manhattanville, five or six miles away from the centre of population, there are new houses of the ridiculous jammed-up pattern, as dark and noisome in their middle parts and as inconvenient throughout as if they were parts of a besieged fortress."[173]

In some sense the elevated was a victim of its own success. By 1880 the elevated railroads were carrying 175,000 passengers daily. The Sixth Avenue line ran 420 trains each way between 5:30 A.M. and midnight. In the two-hour-long morning and evening rush hours, 70 trains per hour provided service. Rush-hour service cost a nickel; off-peak travel was twice as expensive. And by the middle of the decade, traffic had increased so enormously that many viewed the elevated lines as no better, and no more comfortable, than horsecar travel. Electrification was seen as a considerable advance over the sooty steam engines and a possible savior, but the successful test run of the Daft motor on the Ninth Avenue line from Fourteenth to Forty-second Street, in 1888, could only offer hope for the future and no present relief.[174]

The environmental issues raised by the elevated lines were considerable. Their design was largely matter-of-fact, although the stations of the Sixth Avenue line, designed by the landscape painter Jasper F. Cropsey, who was given the title of consulting architect, were a notable exception. The Sixth Avenue line's "stations are built of iron in the modern Gothic style," *Appletons' Journal* observed in 1878. "The average length of the platforms is one hundred and thirty feet, the average width eleven feet, and the average height twenty feet. . . . The waiting-rooms are furnished with black-walnut, and finished with yellow-pine, touched and stained with variegated colors; lighted by gas, heated, and provided with separate toilet and retiring rooms. The platform is covered from end to end by a pavilion-roof, the lines of which are . . . broken by wrought-iron crestings and finials, which give the whole structure a graceful and uncommon appearance."[175] While the trains were noisy and the steam and sparks obnoxious, the latticelike structures that carried the tracks were capable of creating highly picturesque effects. At first the elevated lines were built over the sidewalks, leaving roadways unobstructed but rendering adjacent dwellings virtually uninhabitable. This was true of the Ninth Avenue line and portions of the Third Avenue elevated, which were predominantly rebuilt to run in the center of the street beginning in 1879.[176] Whether over the sidewalks or the roadways, the elevated structures had a certain charm, creating a dappled pattern of light and shadow. Junctions, such as the point where the Second

Sixth Avenue Elevated Railroad between West Forty-second and West Forty-third Streets. View showing dappled pattern of light and shadow, c. 1888. NYHS.

Third Avenue Elevated Railroad. View to the east from Pearl Street showing sweep of track through Coenties Slip, c. 1879. NYHS.

Ninth Avenue Elevated Railroad. View showing curving trestle at 110th Street, c. 1889. NYHS.

and Third Avenue lines merged at Chatham Square, were dramatic landmarks on the cityscape. Also impressive were the sweep of track through Coenties Slip and the curving trestle across 110th Street that carried trains between Eighth and Ninth Avenues, which was internationally known and admired by many, including the great French engineer Ferdinand de Lesseps, designer of the Suez Canal.[177]

While most daily commuters tolerated the crowded trains, some people relished elevated-train travel as if they were on an exotic journey. In William Dean Howells's novel of 1890, *A Hazard of New Fortunes*, Mrs. Basil March, recently arrived in New York, "declared" the elevated railroad

> the most ideal way of getting about in the world, and was not ashamed when . . . [her husband] reminded her how she used to say that nothing under the sun could induce her to travel on it. She now said that the night transit was even more interesting than the day, and that the fleeting intimacy you formed with people in second- and third-floor interiors, while all the usual street life went on underneath, had a domestic intensity mixed with a perfect repose that was the last effect of good society with all its security and exclusiveness. He said it was better than the theater, of which it reminded him, to see those people through their windows: a family party of workfolk at a late tea, some of the men in their shirt-sleeves; a woman

sewing by a lamp; a mother laying her child in its cradle; a man with his head fallen on his hands upon a table; a girl and her lover leaning over the windowsill together. What suggestion! What drama! What infinite interest! At the Forty-second Street station they stopped a minute on the bridge that crosses the track to the branch road for the Central Depot, and looked up and down the long stretch of the elevated to north and south. The track that found and lost itself a thousand times in the flare and tremor of the innumerable lights; the moony sheen of the electrics mixing with the reddish points and blots of gas far and near; the architectural shapes of houses and churches and towers, rescued by the obscurity from all that was ignoble in them; and the coming and going of the trains marking the stations with vivider or fainter plumes of flame-shot steam—formed an incomparable perspective.[178]

Henry James saw not the beauty of the trains but their blighting effect. He summed up the view of many when he expressed his horror of the elevated as it "darkened and smothered" the streets below, its superstructure the "immeasurable spinal column and myriad clutching paws of an antediluvian monster."[179] But Moses King, in what seems a near-perfect rejoinder to the expatriate author, declared that "a ride on the London Metropolitan Railway is a depressing necessity; but a flight along the New York elevated rails is a refreshment."[180]

Ferries

Given the island's length and the need to travel some three or four miles between downtown business places and Grand Central Depot, where trains were boarded for such popular Westchester County commuter towns as Irvington-on-Hudson or Larchmont and New Rochelle, both on the Long Island Sound, many middle-class New Yorkers who chose suburban life preferred instead to travel by ferry to Long Island or New Jersey, where they could ride horsecars or railroads for the completion of their daily journeys to and from work. While many could walk between the ferries and their places of business, others had to add a third segment to their trips and take an omnibus or streetcar. Ferry commuters were held in dubious regard by some, such as Junius Henri Browne, who somewhat callously described them as "merely the human overflow of New York's inundation."[181] Their numbers nonetheless swelled so that by 1880 over 200,000 people traveled each business day on the nine ferries serving Brooklyn. In addition, ferries served Hoboken, Jersey City, Fort Lee, Weehawken, Mott Haven, Hunter's Point, and Staten Island. Besides assisting commuters, many ferries, especially those serving New Jersey, were used by long-distance travelers to connect with trunk lines serving the West.

Ferryboat service to New Jersey increased dramatically after 1871 as a result of the takeover of the New Jersey Railroad and Transportation Company by the Pennsylvania Railroad, which was seeking to expand its business between New York and Philadelphia.[182] Soon after, the Pennsylvania Railroad replaced an obsolete terminal in Jersey City with a new building and piers from which boats fanned out to numerous West Side locations and Brooklyn. The Hoboken Ferry Terminal (1883–86),

designed by the architect H. Edwards Ficken, accommodated two lines serving New York. Replacing an outmoded facility that flooded at high tide, the new, 225-foot-wide building contained four slips and a central waiting room. A canopy extended across the entire front to provide a convenient drop-off area. On the land side, the gabled, redwood-shingle-clad, white and yellow pine structure looked similar to McKim, Mead & White's Casino (1879) in Newport, Rhode Island, which also had as its principal feature a large central gable incorporating a Serlian window framed with paneled shutters. On the water side, the building took on a remarkably different appearance, dominated by a bell-tower lighthouse that presided over low gabled roofs carried beyond the structure on boldly projecting brackets. Inside, according to the *American Architect and Building News*, there were long, operable skylights over waiting and smoking rooms finished "in soft wood painted, and hard woods in their natural colors, . . . designed after the manner of old country-house halls."[183]

In 1864 the Staten Island and New York Ferry was purchased by the Staten Island Railroad in an effort to provide integrated passenger service from New York to Tottenville via Clifton. In 1884, a single landing point was established at St. George, which was the closest feasible landing point to New York but which surprisingly had no ferry service at the time. The area was called St. George for no known religious reason but in honor of George Law, a wheeler-dealer who had owned the land. The railroad was extended northward to the new site as well as westward along the shore, where it could connect with various steamboat lines. The new entity, combining rail and ferry service, was called the Staten Island Rapid Transit Railroad Company.[184] In 1886 the new terminal was ready for use.

Hoboken Ferry Terminal, New Jersey. H. Edwards Ficken, 1883–86. View from land. HLT. CU.

TWO DEFINING ACTS OF CIVIC WILL:
CENTRAL PARK AND THE BROOKLYN BRIDGE

Central Park

What may be the two greatest built works in New York City, both completed in the post–Civil War period, are not buildings. One, the Brooklyn Bridge, is a work of engineering; the other, Central Park, though nominally a work of landscape architecture, is equally a work of engineering, the landscape having been so thoroughly transformed as to constitute a product of human invention, not merely an orchestration of preexisting natural elements. Yet Central Park was also a protest against technology—or at least against the consequences of unbridled technology. Designed by Frederick Law Olmsted and Calvert Vaux in 1858, Central Park was completed eighteen years later, during the nation's centennial year.[185] It was originally proposed that the park stretch from Fifty-ninth to 106th Street, between Fifth and Eighth Avenues, covering 760 acres; between 1859 and 1863, the contiguous land extending north to 110th Street was acquired and added to the park, yielding a total of 840 acres. Providing the only significant interruption of Manhattan's insistently regular gridiron plan, Central Park instantly became one of the city's most treasured civic amenities.

The demand for a large-scale public park located near the city's core had its roots, somewhat curiously, in the popularity of the expansive cemeteries that began to be built just outside many American cities during the 1830s. In its synthesis of cultivated beauty and careful planning, Mount Auburn Cemetery, completed in 1831 in Cambridge, Massachusetts, struck a responsive cord in American city dwellers. By 1849, Andrew Jackson Downing, a horticulturalist renowned for his influential *A Treatise on the Theory and Practice of Landscape Gardening* (1841) who would later become an ardent supporter of Central Park, noted that "one of the most remarkable illustrations of popular taste . . . is to be found in the rise and progress of our rural cemeteries. . . . Twenty years ago, nothing better than a common grave-yard, filled with high grass, and a chance sprinkling of weeds and thistles, was to be found in the Union. . . . At the present moment, there is scarcely a city of note in the whole country that has not its rural cemetery." In Brooklyn, the 478-acre Green-Wood Cemetery, established in 1838, contained nearly twenty miles of winding roads laid out by Major David B. Douglass on a picturesque site overlooking Upper New York Bay. The idyllic setting was immediately popular as a park, attracting crowds of pleasure seekers from both Brooklyn and Manhattan. Nearly sixty thousand people visited Green-Wood between April and December of 1848, and Downing, based on personal observation, noted that while some no doubt went "to twine the votive garland," most went simply to enjoy themselves in a natural setting.[186] The desire to escape into nature, or a manicured approximation of it, leaving behind the commercial, social, and aesthetic rigors of the urban gridiron, gave rise to a demand for city parks; not surprisingly this need was nowhere more intensely felt than in Manhattan.

On July 3, 1844, in anticipation of the annual exodus of affluent New Yorkers from the city's heat that occurred every Independence Day, William Cullen Bryant, the poet and editor of the *New York Evening Post*, reportedly sounded the first public call for the creation of a large city park. Bryant emphatically stated: "The heats of summer are upon us, and while some are leaving the town for shady retreats in the country, others refresh themselves with short excursions to Hoboken or New Brighton, or other places among the beautiful environs of our city. If the public authorities, who expend so much of our money on laying out the city, would do what is in their power, they might give our vast population an extensive pleasure ground for shade and recreation in these sultry afternoons, which we might reach without going out of town."[187] Bryant had previously surveyed the city on horseback and proposed that a park be created out of an area known as Jones Wood, a densely grown forest bounded by the East River, Third Avenue, and Sixty-sixth and Seventy-sixth Streets. The property, which previously had served as a country estate for John Jones, a prosperous tavern owner, was far out of town but still within reach of many citizens.

Bryant noted: "All large cities have their extensive public grounds and gardens, Madrid and Mexico their Alamedas, London its Regent's Park, Paris its Champs-Elysées and Vienna its Prater." He urged swift action: "Commerce is devouring inch by inch the coast of the island; and if we would rescue any part of it for health and recreation it must be done now."[188] Municipal action did not come, however, until nearly seven years later, when, on May 5, 1851, the newly elected mayor, Ambrose C. Kingsland, proposed to the city's Common Council the creation of a 160-acre public park. Kingsland had previously argued:

> Such a park, well laid out, would become the favorite resort of all classes. There are thousands who pass the day of rest among the idle and dissolute, in porter houses, or in places more objectionable, who would rejoice in being enabled to breathe the pure air in such a place, while the ride and drive through its avenues, free from the noise, dust and confusion inseparable from all thoroughfares, would hold out strong inducement for the affluent to make it a place of resort. There is no park on the island deserving the name . . . [and] I think that the expenditure of a sum necessary to produce and lay out a park of sufficient magnitude to answer the purposes above noted would be well and wisely appropriated, and would be returned to us fourfold, in the health, happiness and comfort of those whose interests are specifically entrusted to our keeping—the poorer classes.[189]

On June 17, 1851, a bill was unanimously passed by the New York state legislature to acquire through eminent domain the site Kingsland had proposed. One of the appeals of the Jones Wood site was that little would be required to transform it into a park, save the introduction of pathways. Robert Minturn, a wealthy merchant and an early park advocate, circulated a petition to indicate that those citizens who, through taxation, would be called upon to contribute most strongly favored the proposal. Indeed, the city's small but powerful economic elite firmly supported the establishment of a park accessible to all classes.

New York's wealthiest citizens supported a large public park on several grounds. A park would enhance the city's commercial base by reducing the amount of developable land and consequently boosting real estate values. The salubrious effects of fresh air and sunlight would stimulate physical well-being. An environment that promoted constructive group behavior would help to favorably socialize and acculturate an increasingly heterogeneous population. Perhaps most compelling of all was a sense that such a project would constitute a seminal and heroic attempt to refute the accusations of both outsiders and New Yorkers themselves that the city was too young, uncultured, and, above all, too focused on the bottom line to be able to build anything in the public realm that would surpass, or even rival, the grand projects of European urbanism.

By the 1850s, after decades of competition with other American cities, New York had emerged as the nation's commercial capital and a formidable challenge to European cities in terms of trade. Yet when New York shipping mag-

nates and businessmen who traveled to Europe for business as well as leisure compared it to European cities in terms of culture, they found their native city sadly wanting. In 1853 the *New York Times* compared the public parks of London and Paris to those of New York and found the juxtaposition nothing short of "mortifying": "Whether in England or on the continent of Europe, there is no great city so meanly supplied with public grounds as New York; none where the popular welfare has not exacted larger sacrifices of space and capital, than have ever been made in any American city. . . . It is a sorry story that with a boundless continent before us, we are unable to spare more than one acre in ten for public uses."[190] Two years later, in an article of 1855 advocating a public park for New York, the editor of *Harper's New Monthly Magazine*, George W. Curtis, bluntly stated, "We are tired of having everything boorish and coarse and unfeeling called American."[191] The construction of a park would give New Yorkers the opportunity to disprove the criticism of foreigners, assuage their own self-doubts, and in the process not only justify their claim to being a world-class city but, at least in the eyes of some observers, also justify the democratic capitalism of a nation still less than a century old. As early as 1847, the *New York Herald Tribune* published a letter to the editor, signed "Manhattan For Ever!", that advocated the creation of a park, posing the question, "Why should monarchy be allowed to do more . . . for its subjects than republican civic policy can achieve for a City of Sovereigns?"[192]

View to the north from the East River and East Sixtieth Street, c. 1865. Proposed park site at Jones Wood, the East River to Third Avenue, East Sixty-seventh to East Seventy-sixth Street. NYHS.

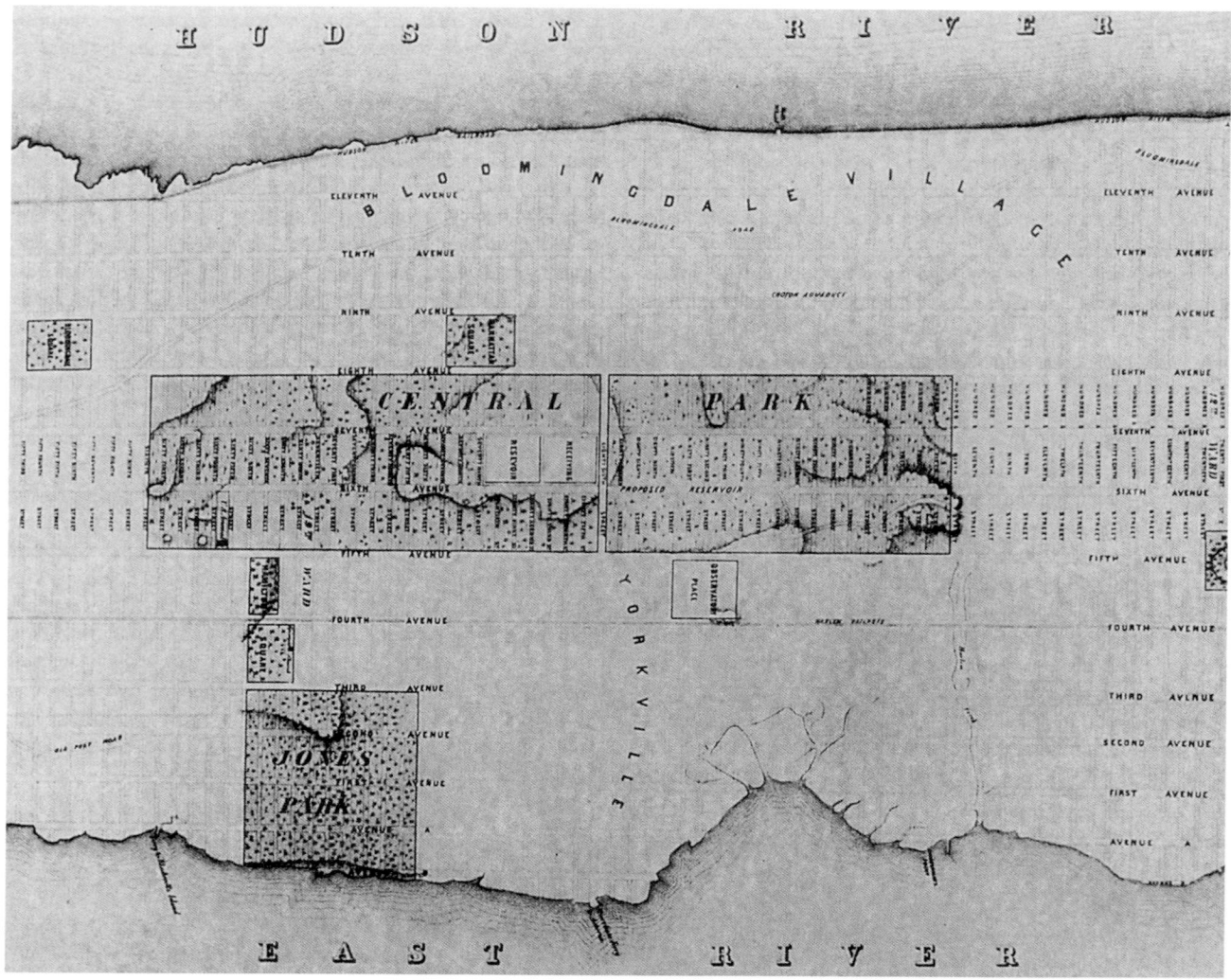

Proposed public parks and squares, the East River to the Hudson River, Fifty-third to 121st Street. Map, c. 1852. NYPL.

While support for a park in general was strong and broadly based, support for a park specifically at Jones Wood was shaky. Some thought the comparative inaccessibility of the proposed East Side location would render the park only a neighborhood improvement rather than a citywide enhancement; others thought the sacrifice of the waterfront's commercial potential was imprudent; and still others thought the proposed park was too large. Andrew Jackson Downing lambasted the notion that the park would be excessive, labeling those who believed so "short-sighted economists!" He charged that the park would be "only a child's playground" and that *"five hundred acres is the smallest area that should be reserved for the future wants of the city, now, while it may be obtained."*[193] Despite the state senate's approval of the Jones Wood site, numerous alternatives were proposed, including a swath stretching from the Hudson to the East River; a curvilinear, northward-winding expanse beginning at Thirty-ninth Street; a site bounded by Fifth and Sixth Avenues,

Thirty-ninth Street, and the Harlem River; and a site bounded by Fifth and Seventh Avenues and Fifty-eighth and 106th Streets.

On January 2, 1852, with the Jones Wood proposal in court over the constitutionality of the city's land-acquisition methods, some of the city's aldermen, organized as the Special Committee on Parks, proposed a site bounded by Fifth and Eighth Avenues and Fifty-ninth and 106th Streets. While its elongated shape was something of an aesthetic handicap, the site, which the aldermen named Central Park, seemed to many observers to possess advantages of size and location that Jones Wood did not. Additionally, as often has been the case in New York's history, idealism was spurred by practical and economic considerations: the site would be highly cost-effective because its irregular and rocky terrain thwarted conventional development and thereby reduced the value of the land. The aldermen estimated the cost of the Central Park site at $1,407,325, approximately $600 less per acre than the cost of Jones Wood. Additionally, as part of the expanding Croton Aqueduct system, the proposed Central Park location already encompassed the designated site of a reservoir and was soon likely to be home to a second one. The incorporation of a new reservoir into a park "would cheapen the cost of both."[194] Yet in terms of scenic beauty, the mid-island site had little to offer. The editors of *Scribner's Monthly* would later state: "When we decided we must have a park, it was in an evil hour that the narrow strip of land out of which we have had to make it was chosen. It may be said, we think, without exaggeration, that it did not have a single natural advantage."[195] In terms of natural features, the site of Central Park, according to Olmsted, was a "very nasty place . . . steeped in the overflow and mush of pigsties, slaughter houses and bone-boiling works [where] the stench was sickening."[196]

To William Cullen Bryant, the choice of which site—Jones Wood or Central Park—was simple: "There is now ample room and verge enough upon the island for two Parks, whereas if the matter is delayed for a few years, there will hardly be space left for one."[197] On July 21, 1853, the New York state legislature authorized the purchase of the Central Park site and it seemed for a brief time that Bryant's hope for two large parks linked by Hamilton Square, one of the small squares initially provided for in the Commissioners' Plan of 1811, would be fulfilled. But

the following year, the act to acquire the Jones Wood site was repealed, and Central Park alone was designated the city's premier open public place.

In May 1856, the two-member Board of Commissioners of Central Park, composed of Mayor Fernando Wood and Street Commissioner Joseph Taylor, hired Egbert L. Viele to conduct a topographical survey of the site. The following month Viele delivered not only an initial survey but also a descriptive report and a proposed design for the park. Viele's plan called for minor alterations of the natural topography, with bogs and depressions transformed into small lakes. He also proposed a system of roads that would loop through the park and connect with principal avenues outside it. Little else in the way of specific development was outlined. Viele was appointed the park's chief engineer and hired to realize his adequate, but fundamentally uninspired, design.

In 1857, the editors of *Harper's Weekly* published Viele's proposal and asserted that by 1862 "New Yorkers may boast of having the finest park in the world. The time is long, one whole fourteenth of a human life, but such works as this can not be done in a day."[198] Not everyone agreed, however, with the journal's positive assessment of Viele's design. Among the dissenters was Calvert Vaux, a thirty-three-year-old English-born and English-trained architect who in 1852 had immigrated to the United States to

View to the east, 1862, of the Willowdell Arch (Calvert Vaux, 1861), East Drive near Fifth Avenue and East Sixty-seventh Street, showing, from left to right, Frederick Law Olmsted, Jacob Wrey Mould, Ignaz Pilat, Calvert Vaux, unidentified man, and Andrew Haswell Green. Prevost. NYPL.

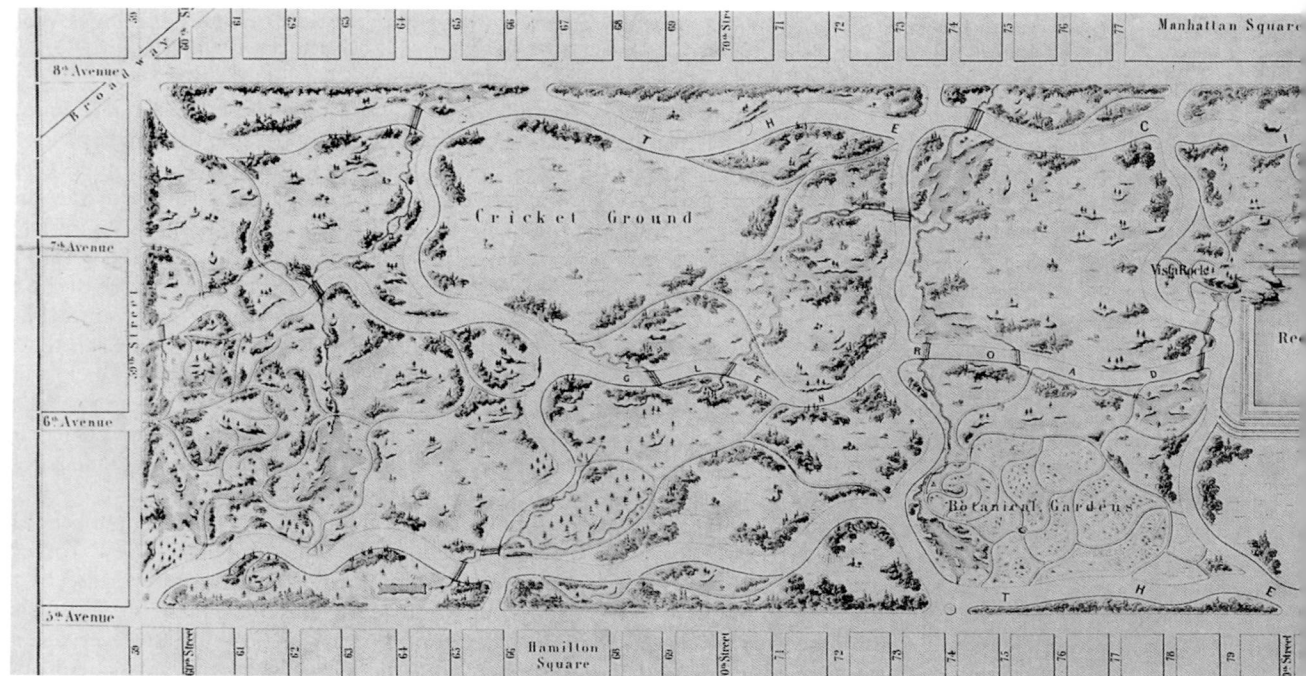

Proposal for Central Park, Fifth to Eighth Avenue, Fifty-ninth to 106th Street. Egbert L. Viele, 1856. Plan. NYPL.

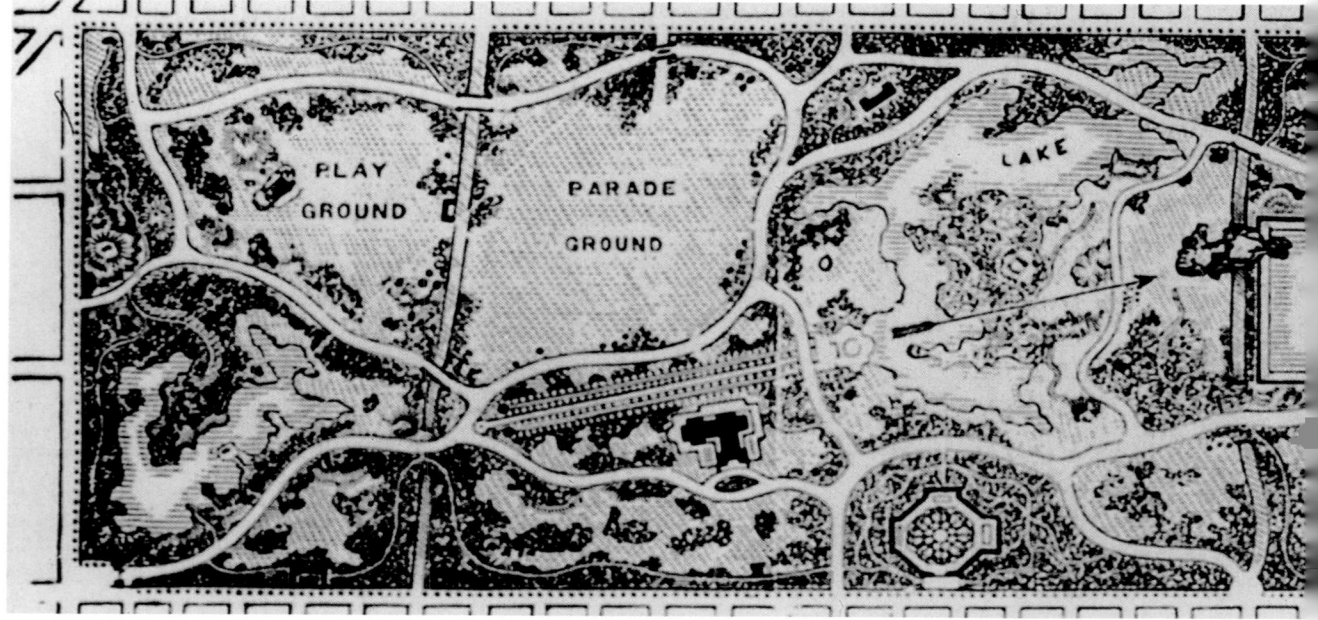

Greensward proposal for Central Park, Fifth to Eighth Avenue, Fifty-ninth to 106th Street. Frederick Law Olmsted and Calvert Vaux, 1858. Plan. DO.

work for Andrew Jackson Downing. In 1853, Vaux had taken over the practice when the thirty-seven-year-old Downing died in a steamboat accident. Vaux would later recall being "thoroughly disgusted with the manifest defects of Viele's design" and feeling that the plan's realization would have been "a disgrace to the city and to the memory of Mr. Downing."[199]

Vaux was not merely opinionated, he was well connected. The Board of Commissioners of Central Park had been expanded to eleven members by October 1857, and Vaux was friendly with two of them. Vaux persuaded the commission to discard Viele's design and initiate a design competition, which was announced in small notices in the city's newspapers. The design guidelines stipulated that

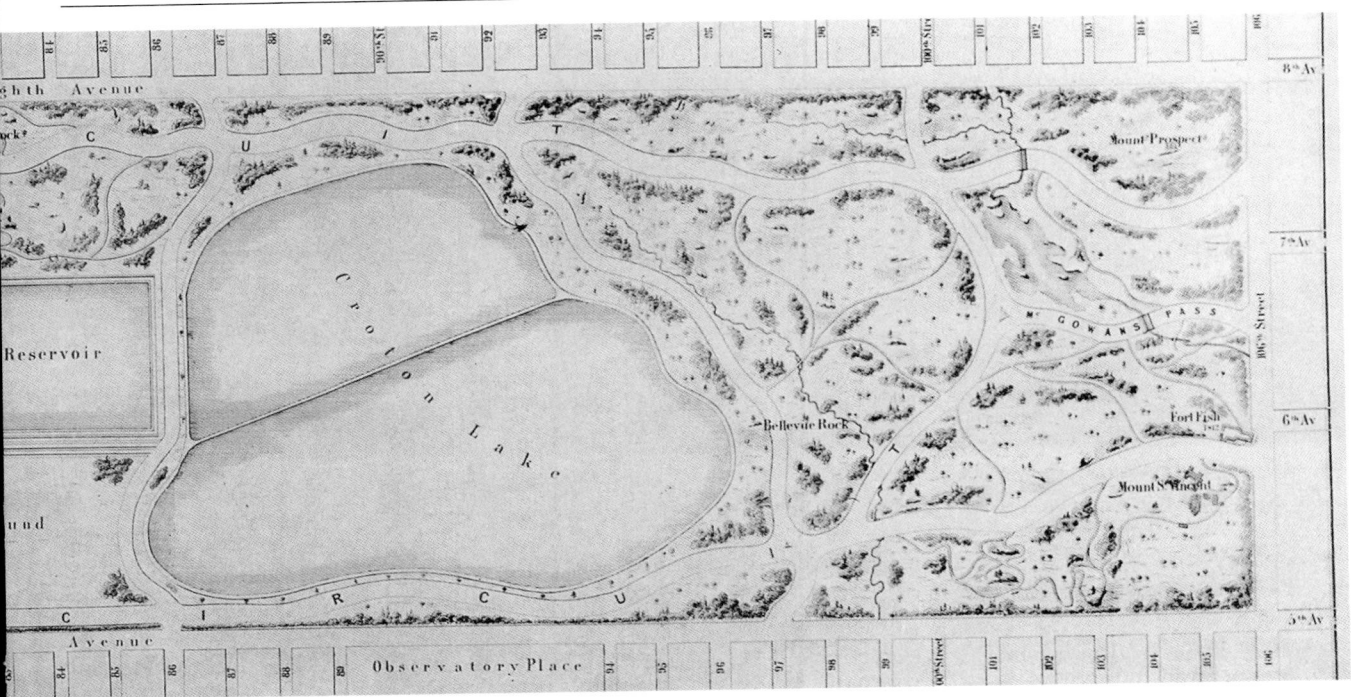

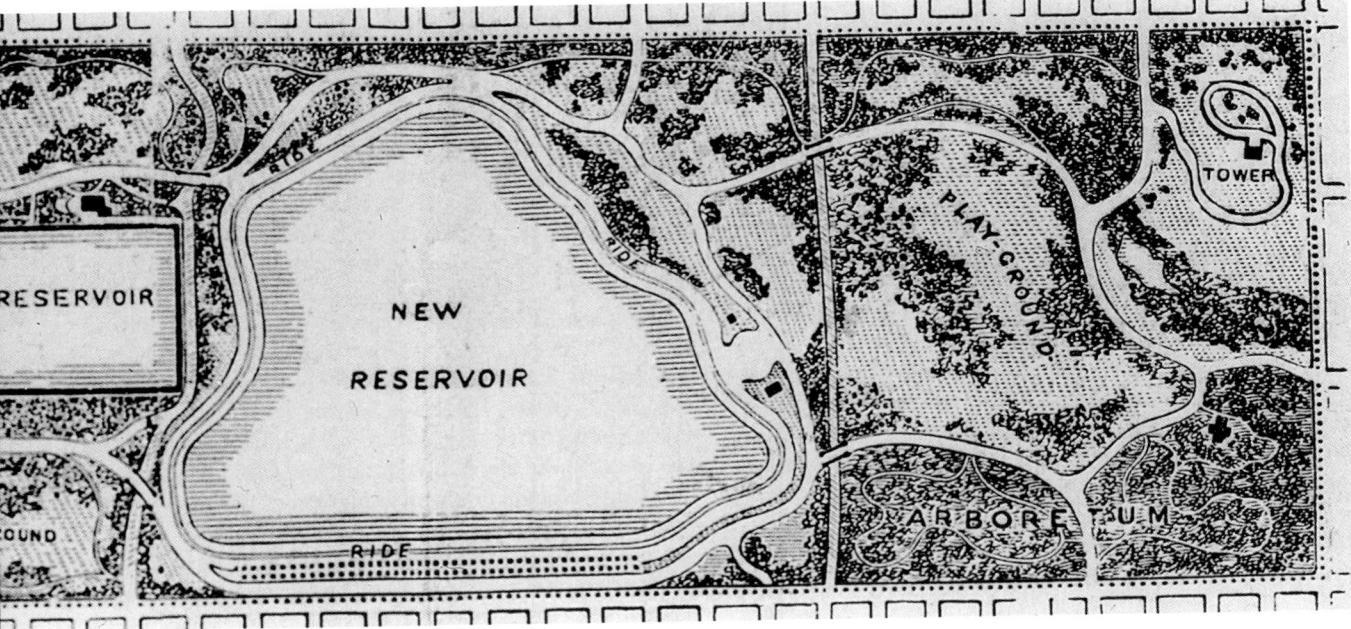

the park incorporate a parade ground, a public exhibition and concert hall, a botanical garden, three playgrounds, a fountain, an observation tower, an ice-skating pond, and a minimum of four roadways latitudinally crossing the park. Split between the winner and the three runners-up would be $4,250 in prize money.

Even after his design was abandoned, Viele remained the park's chief engineer. But a month before the design competition was announced, the park's board hired Frederick Law Olmsted to serve, under Viele, as the superintendent in charge of overseeing the work crews responsible for maintaining the site of the future park.[200] As the art critic and essayist Adam Gopnik has noted: "Olmsted's transition from scribe to landscape architect was

View to the north of Central Park site before 1858, from about Fifth Avenue and West Fifty-ninth Street. MCNY.

improvised. He got himself hired as . . . park superintendent before anybody had any idea what [Central Park]
itself might look like. (He was given the job because he
was seen as being above or outside politics.)"[201] Born in
1822 in Hartford, Connecticut, to wealthy parents, Olmsted grew up in an intellectual and politically involved
environment. By the age of thirty-five, however, he had
been financially unsuccessful and lacked any formal
training in architecture or landscape design, so he seemed
an unlikely choice to oversee the largest public-works
project in the United States. Olmsted's only relevant
vocational experience, a six-year stint as a farmer on
Staten Island, had resulted in a developed intellectual
interest in land management. Extensive travels in the
American South and in England had made him acutely
aware of the environmental consequences of slavery and
industrialization. Under the name "Yeoman" he wrote a
series of letters to the editor of the *New York Times*,
which were collected in a book titled *A Journey in the
Seaboard Slave States in the Years 1853–54.*[202] Olmsted's
observations of England had been recorded in his *Walks
and Talks of an American Farmer in England*, which,
despite its title, was not really much about farming but
instead focused on urbanism and early attempts to
reverse the ill effects of industrialization through enlightened town planning.[203] Olmsted was particularly
impressed by what he saw at Joseph Paxton's Birkenhead
Park (1857), outside of Liverpool, a model suburb with
houses grouped around a collective public space.

At first Olmsted was reluctant to enter the Central
Park design competition, thinking that it might aggravate
his already strained relationship with Viele. He asked
Viele for permission, only to have his chances of winning
ridiculed. Following this rebuff, Olmsted accepted an
invitation from Calvert Vaux, whom he had met previously at Downing's house, to collaborate on an entry.[204]
Olmsted and Vaux made an interestingly complementary
team. As the journalist Francis Morrone has pointed out,
during the 1870s Vaux "was the leading exponent in

America of that decade's bowdlerized Ruskinianism."
Like Olmsted, Vaux was "a man of overflowing gifts, and
a volatile, self-defeating temperament. He was also, as
Olmsted was not, an esthetic ideologue."[205] Olmsted and
Vaux collaborated for several months, working on their
design at night and on weekends. On April 28, 1858, having judged the thirty-three submitted designs, most of
which were entered anonymously, the park commissioners
announced that the $2,000 first prize would go to scheme
number thirty-three, titled Greensward, the nom de plume
adopted by Olmsted and Vaux, who, without question,
had produced the most original proposal. The majority of
the other designs proposed naturalistic landscapes incorporating a variety of architectural features. Number five,
submitted by J. Lauchaume of Yonkers, New York, called
for the inclusion of freely roaming goats, sheep, and oxen
in an effort to give the park "the country-like air of which
we citizens of this great metropolis are so fond and most
of the time deprived."[206] The unidentified designer of
submission number nine proposed a perimeter ring of
buildings housing police and warden facilities, "each one,"
the accompanying text stated, "of a different style. Thus
we would have the Italian lodge, the Chinese lodge, the
Norwegian lodge, the Japanese lodge."[207] The $500 third-
runner-up prize went to the architect Howard Daniels,
whose design synthesized naturalistic and Classical-
inspired elements. The $750 second-runner-up prize was
shared by Lachlan H. McIntosh, the park's property clerk,
and Michael Miller, the park's paymaster. Their entry
called for a generously proportioned saltwater lake. The
$1,000 first-runner-up prize went to Samuel Gustin, the
park's superintendent of planting, whose design—effectively presented in a series of twenty-two-foot-long plaster models depicting "before" and "after" vistas—incorporated several features of Paris's Bois de Boulogne, such as
a deer park, a dairy, a cascade, and several lakes. Gustin's
plan also called for a mock-Greek temple, an amphitheater, restaurants, and a statue of George Washington.

Olmsted and Vaux's winning design, boldly conceived

View of Central Park site before 1858, showing shanties. HM.

and brilliantly presented, called for a romantic landscape of rolling hills, forests, and even a vast lawn trimmed by a flock of sheep administered by a shepherd; it was an idealized slice of nature from preindustrial Manhattan, to be frozen in time and enjoyed as the bustling city grew up around it. As the designers presciently put it in the written description accompanying their competition entry:

> The time will come when New York will be built up, when all the grading and filling will be done, and when the picturesquely-varied, rocky formations of the Island will have been converted into formations for monotonous straight streets, and piles of erect buildings. There will be no suggestion left of its present varied surface, with the single exception of a few acres contained in the Park. Then the priceless value of the present picturesque outlines of the ground will be more fully perceived. . . . It therefore seems desirable to interfere . . . as little as possible, and, on the other hand, to endeavor rapidly, and by every legitimate means, to increase and judiciously develop these particularly individual and characteristic sources of landscape effects.[208]

Despite Olmsted and Vaux's perhaps disingenuous promise to "interfere . . . as little as possible" with the existing landscape, their design for Central Park was a major work of engineering, totally transforming the land to create an easily accessible, inhabitable stage upon which city dwellers could enact an idealized fantasy of life in the open countryside. The park's apparent naturalism was carefully controlled. As the historian J. B. Jackson has pointed out, the park was not about nature, per se, but about scenery.[209] The park thus required the landscape architect's skill, not merely the conservationist's will. But all the effort to create a romantic landscape notwithstanding, Olmsted and Vaux's design proposed that neither art nor nature reign exclusively, but rather envisioned that the two be synthesized in a marriage of naturalistic, picturesque landscaping and rational, technologically advanced planning.

To create the new landscape, five million cubic yards of rock and soil were moved by horse and cart and more than

one hundred miles of drainage pipe were laid. Bedrock was dynamited to create hollows that were in turn filled with rich soil from New Jersey and Long Island so that previously barren ground could be transformed into open meadows and tree-shaded glens. It is estimated that within a three-year period more than a million plants, shrubs, and trees were planted. In 1893 Mariana Van Rensselaer noted: "Prospect Park, Brooklyn . . . may easily be thought more beautiful than Central Park . . . but to an eye which remembers what its site originally was, Central Park will always seem Mr. Olmsted's greatest achievement of the kind."[210]

The creation of the park was not only an engineering challenge but a human one as well. Paying for Olmsted and Vaux's arcadia was a struggle, leading Olmsted to complain bitterly about Andrew Haswell Green, a lawyer who became the park's comptroller in 1859. Said Olmsted, "Not a cent is got from under his paw that is not wet with his blood and sweat. It was slow murder."[211] In addition, approximately 1,600 people were displaced by the park's creation, including 264 residents of a well-established, predominantly African American settlement, Seneca Village, bounded roughly by Seventh and Eighth Avenues and Seventy-ninth and Eighty-sixth Streets.[212] Founded in 1825, Seneca Village was distinguished by the fact that many of its working-class black residents were property owners, something that was rare at the time. When the settlement was destroyed in 1855, it contained multistory wood-frame houses, vegetable gardens, three churches, at least three cemeteries, and one school. The residents were not transient and most paid taxes. Indeed, like many settlements uptown, its residents had anticipated that the northward march of the city would bring such improvements as cobblestone-paved streets. Instead, the city paid the residents the estimated value of their possessions and forced them to move.

Perhaps the most ingenious aspect of Olmsted and Vaux's design was the inclusion of a series of bridges and tunnels that separated traffic into three categories, each of which would have its own independent system of paths or roadways: pedestrians were provided with naturalistically laid-out pathways; carriages on pleasure rides used a gracious, seven-mile-long road that looped through the park; and, most inventively, through traffic was relegated to four transverse roads, located at Sixty-fifth, Seventy-ninth, Eighty-sixth, and Ninety-sixth Streets, that were sunken below grade. The roads were lined with walls of Manhattan schist, cut on the site, with some blocks finely dressed and others left rough-faced. The designers sagaciously hid the transverse roads from recreational view, correctly predicting that they would serve "coal carts and butcher's carts, dust carts and dung carts" and "inevitably . . . be crowded thoroughfares having nothing in common with the park proper."[213]

Olmsted and Vaux's original design did not include provisions for horseback riding, though the designers did not specifically oppose it. One commissioner, Robert Dillon, suggested the addition of bridle paths, and by 1863 six miles of paths, surfaced either with sand or gravel, meandered through the lower portion of the park and around the reservoir.[214] (Sixteen other suggestions made by Dillon, including postponing the establishment of pedestrian pathways until parkgoers had created them through force of habit, and building a suspension bridge over the Lake to connect the Mall to Belvedere Castle, were never adopted.) From the first, active recreation was provided for; the opening of an ice-skating pond in the south-central part of the park in 1858 initiated a fad, drawing legions of skaters on winter afternoons.[215] By the 1870s, all of the park's lakes and ponds were utilized for the sport. So popular—and democratic—was the pastime that private clubs, such as the nearby Manhattan Polo Association at Fifth Avenue and 111th Street and the Manhattan Athletic Club at Eighth Avenue and Fifty-sixth Street, opened skating facilities

Transverse road at Eighty-fifth Street. Frederick Law Olmsted and Calvert Vaux, 1859. View to the east. NYHS.

Greensward proposal. Frederick Law Olmsted and Calvert Vaux, 1858. Detail showing the Mall or Promenade, between transverse road at Sixty-fifth Street and Seventy-second Street cross drive. Plan. NYCPP.

where families such as the Belmonts, Griswolds, and Iselins could avoid mixing with the hoi polloi.

Central Park's northern and southern ends were designed to contrast sharply with each other. The northern end, the last portion of the park to be completed, had the most untamed appearance and was dominated by steep, rocky inclines, briskly running brooks, and a still body of water later known as the Harlem Meer. The lower park was at once more manicured and more varied. The open Sheep Meadow was contrasted by the labyrinthine paths of the densely forested Ramble. The Mall, a Classical-inspired, quarter-mile-long, two-hundred-foot-wide promenade flanked on each side by twin rows of American elms, provided a suitable setting for public strolling. The editors of *Scribner's Monthly* stated: "The Mall—or, as we think it might better be called, the Broad Walk,—is an indispensable provision in any great park, and we know no great park anywhere in which there is a finer promenade, at least as it will be when the elms are fairly grown."[216] The Mall provided the park with a strong axis leading to a defined objective at its north end—the Water Terrace, later known as the Bethesda Terrace, with the Lake and the picturesque, deliberately underscaled Belvedere Castle at its far side. Were it not for this sequence, Olmsted's design might not have survived the barrage of criticism that arose between 1858 and 1861, when the park was in its early stages of construction. Numerous calls were issued to make the overall design more focused, including a suggestion by Robert Dillon that an allée of trees, to be known as Cathedral Avenue, run the full length of the park from Fifty-ninth to 110th Street. Olmsted rejected the idea and successfully prevented its realization, favoring "a series of landscape passages"[217] in which the parkgoer would be "led by . . . what . . . meets the eye, and by the continued discovery of fresh objects."[218]

The Bethesda Terrace was designed by Vaux with stonework detailed by the architect Jacob Wrey Mould.[219] Vaux was directly inspired by designs he had seen in English

Gates opening onto the Mall, south of Seventy-second Street cross drive. Calvert Vaux with Jacob Wrey Mould, 1868–73. View to the southeast. MCNY.

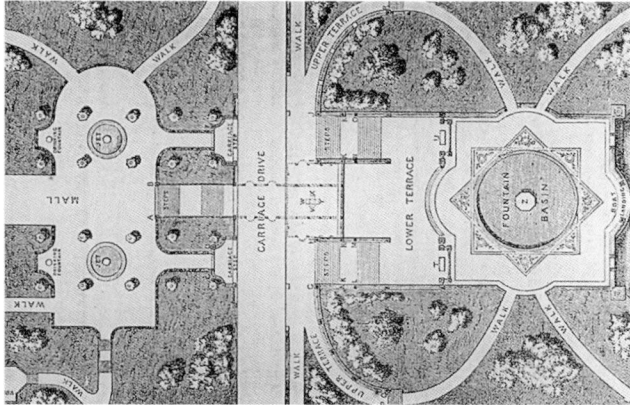

The Mall (left) and the Bethesda Terrace (right), south and north, respectively, of Seventy-second Street cross drive. Frederick Law Olmsted and Calvert Vaux, 1858–73. Plan. NYCPP.

and European gardens in which architectural elements were used to visually and spatially make the transition from the formal to the natural. The Mall's allée was split, with a central portion burrowing underneath the grade-level roadway that wound through the park as an extension of Seventy-second Street, with a grand, vaulted space that opened onto a north-facing arcade looking onto the Bethesda Terrace. The vaults were clad in brilliantly colored tiles imported from England. On either side of the arcade, monumentally scaled staircases incorporated intricately carved railings mixing geometric patterns with scenes depicting the four seasons. To either side of the

stairs, a *rampe douce* scaled the hillside, providing another means of procession. The broad terrace extended to the waterfront of the Lake, a man-made body of water, where it incorporated a boat landing. At the water's edge, two flagpoles supported festive gonfalon pennants. The grand composition, which Vaux considered to be his finest work, clearly suggested that the common people could match in their own "backyard" the splendor of foreign aristocracy.

In the center of the terrace was the three-tiered Bethesda Fountain, twenty-six feet high and ninety-six feet in diameter, designed by Vaux. The fountain was crowned by *Angel of the Waters*, four cherubic figures

Stairs leading from the Mall to the Bethesda Terrace. Calvert Vaux and Jacob Wrey Mould, 1868–73. View to the north. HM.

Bethesda Terrace, north of Seventy-second Street cross drive. Calvert Vaux and Jacob Wrey Mould, 1868–73. View to the southeast, 1894, showing the Bethesda Fountain with Angel of the Waters *(Emma Stebbins, 1873) on the far left. Johnston. MCNY.*

Belvedere Castle, on top of Vista Rock. Calvert Vaux, 1867–71. View to the east. MCNY.

representing Purity, Health, Temperance, and Peace, a sculpture by Emma Stebbins, sister of Henry Stebbins, a member of the park's board of commissioners. Cast in Munich, the bronze sculpture was installed in 1873. The editors of the *New York Daily Graphic* not only praised the fountain and its sculpture on aesthetic grounds, finding the whole composition to be "an ornament of which the city has reason to be proud," but they saw the work's didactic potential as well: "It will teach a love of the beautiful (and of the clean, too, let us hope) to the millions who shall pass in reach of its spray through all the coming summers. . . . Our city needs more of these civilizers of the masses."[220]

The visual focal point of the Mall, seen across a clear expanse provided by the Lake, was the park's highest point, appropriately named Vista Rock. Olmsted and Vaux originally had proposed that the crest be surmounted by a martello tower that would evoke the circular stone fortifications built to defend the English and Irish seacoasts against Napoleon. The design evolved into a more romantic structure, a castle intentionally built small to appear more distant when seen in false perspective through the woods. The designers' point that the park was an artifact of man, not an accident of elapsed time, was lost on the editors of *Scribner's Monthly*, as was the castle's inherent charm: "We confess to but an indifferent interest in the Belvidere [*sic*]. It is a toy-castle, and we are sure it would be improved by a can of nitro-glycerine and a careless Irishman."[221]

Throughout the park, a variety of buildings and structures were built to Vaux's designs. While Olmsted contended that little of the architecture "can be styled grand or magnificent, [its] aim being to harmonize to the character

Dairy, south of transverse road at Sixty-fifth Street, between Center and East Drives. Calvert Vaux, 1869. View to the northwest. HM.

Children's Shelter, south of transverse road at Sixty-fifth Street, east of Center Drive. Calvert Vaux, 1866. HM.

![Mineral Springs Pavilion, northwest of the Sheep Meadow. Calvert Vaux, 1868. View to the northwest. HM.](image)

Mineral Springs Pavilion, northwest of the Sheep Meadow. Calvert Vaux, 1868. View to the northwest. HM.

of the scenery,"[222] and Vaux himself boldly asserted, "The landscape is everything, the architecture nothing,"[223] the designs were nonetheless well considered and charming. Most were inspired by the Gothic: the Dairy, the Children's Cottage, and the Carousel provided refreshment and amusement in the lower park's so-called "children's department."[224] On the lawn in front of these buildings, cows, chickens, and lambs were displayed. Located in the same area, the Children's Shelter was an extraordinary basket weave of naturally twisting twigs and saplings.[225] Standing at the Lake's eastern shore was an elaborately detailed boathouse, designed by Vaux with assistance from Jacob Wrey Mould and from the architect Julius Munckwitz; the roof of the long base building formed an observation terrace shielded by variously designed pavilions.[226] The Ladies' Refreshment Salon, later known as the Casino, stood to the east of the Mall on a site initially intended for a concert hall. The flamboyant exception to these Gothic-inspired designs was the vaguely Moorish, intricately detailed Mineral Springs Pavilion, located just northwest of the Sheep Meadow, where thirty different varieties of water were served.[227]

Forty-six remarkably inventive bridges, most designed

Mineral Springs Pavilion, northwest of the Sheep Meadow. Calvert Vaux, 1868. Interior. HM.

Boathouse, eastern shore of the Lake, west of the East Drive near Fifth Avenue and East Seventy-fifth Street. Calvert Vaux with Jacob Wrey Mould and Julius Munckwitz, 1872–76. View to the northeast. MCNY.

Bow Bridge, spanning the Lake. Calvert Vaux, 1860. View to the northeast. MCNY.

by Vaux or under his guidance, facilitated the efficient flow of all manner of traffic.[228] In general there were three types of bridges: stone-faced bridges adopting a formal, Classical style; cast-iron bridges detailed with fanciful ornament; and wooden bridges that were rustic in construction and aesthetic.[229] In order to further emphasize that the entire park was a synthesis of artifice and nature, not merely part of the latter, the materials used for some of the bridges, Nova Scotia stone and Philadelphia brick, were imported even though equivalent local materials were readily available. Vaux was once again self-effacing regarding the creativity and individuality of his designs, claiming that the bridges were "thoroughly subordinate," that they were "only introduced for convenience," and that if they had not each been different, they would have been "odiously monotonous."[230]

One architectural feature of Olmsted and Vaux's design that did not satisfy the board of commissioners was the treatment of points of entry: simple iron gateways punctuating the low stone wall that enclosed the park. On January 26, 1863, without the approval of Olmsted or Vaux, Andrew H. Green, the park's comptroller, submitted his own design proposal for gateways, to be built along Fifty-ninth Street at Fifth, Sixth, Seventh, and Eighth Avenues. The board turned the designs over to the Committee on Statuary, Fountains, and Architectural Structures with the suggestion that the committee consult with architects about the problem. In June 1863 the committee, apparently having rejected Green's proposal, held a competition for the entrance gateways, once again failing to invite Olmsted and Vaux's participation. Before the competition was announced, Richard Morris Hunt, whose brother-in-law Charles H. Russell was on the committee, had already been approached and indeed submitted sketches.[231] In September 1863 the park's board rejected the ten competition entries it had received (the identities of the designers are not known) in favor of Hunt's proposals, which were exhibited at the National Academy of Design in the spring of 1865. All of Hunt's designs were imposing compositions and directly reflected the great traditions of French civic architecture, particularly the contemporary work being realized in Paris under the guidance of Baron Georges-Eugène Hausmann.

At the park's southeast corner, at Fifth Avenue and Fifty-ninth Street, the Gate of Peace was intended to provide the park with a principal entrance. Hunt placed a fountain near the center of the entrance's four-hundred-square-foot plaza, flanking the semicircular terrace overlooking the park to the west with curving cascades of water emptying into a basin incorporating a sculpture of Neptune and his chariot. A fifty-foot column in the center of the terrace was to support sculptures of a sailor and an Indian holding the municipal seal. Pedestrian and vehicular entrances to the park were to be located at the

Marble Arch, beneath East Drive, near Fifth Avenue and East Sixty-fifth Street. Calvert Vaux, 1861. View to the northeast. HM.

Spur Rock Arch, spanning a bridle path near Seventh Avenue and West Fifty-ninth Street. Calvert Vaux, 1861. MCNY.

Gapstow Bridge, spanning the Pond, west of the East Drive near Fifth Avenue and East Sixty-second Street. Jacob Wrey Mould, 1874. View to the northwest. MCNY.

Proposed design for the Gate of Peace, Central Park, entrance at Fifth Avenue and West Fifty-ninth Street. Richard Morris Hunt, 1861–63. Rendering of view to the northwest. DGCP. CU.

Proposed design for the Warriors' Gate, Central Park, entrance at Eighth Avenue and West Fifty-ninth Street. Richard Morris Hunt, 1861–63. Rendering of view to the northeast. The Octagon, AAF.

Proposed design for the Artists' Gate, Central Park, entrance at Seventh Avenue and West Fifty-ninth Street. Richard Morris Hunt, 1861–63. Rendering of view to the north. The Octagon, AAF.

north end of the plaza. Tall pedestals would carry statues, some depicting horse tamers. For the entrance at Eighth Avenue, to be named the Warriors' Gate, the proposal was the first to suggest that the complex intersection at the park's southwest corner, where Broadway crossed Eighth Avenue, might best be resolved as a circle. Hunt's Warriors' Gate was to incorporate a long, curving stone bench topped by statues of military figures. The roadways leading into the park were to be divided into incoming and outgoing lanes by equestrian statues atop high bases. At Seventh Avenue, the Artists' Gate was to contain two herms supporting an iron gate. Inside the park, a sculpted figure of the "genius of the arts" would stand on a tall column. The Gate of Commerce, at Sixth Avenue, would similarly incorporate stone exedrae flanking iron gates.

The proposed gateways immediately proved controversial, with the strongest opposition coming, not surprisingly, from Olmsted and Vaux. Hunt's gateways celebrated a Classical city and an imperial vision of American urbanism, not the naturalism of the park's design. In a letter to his friend the *New York Daily Tribune* art critic Clarence Cook, Vaux stated: "The park typifies what we have been fighting for and the gates typify what we have been fighting against. . . . The first need of the visitor when he leaves the city sidewalk is a perfectly free and unencumbered drought of 'Park'—The success we have aimed for is to make the change from city to country instantaneous and complete

and in accordance with our theory that the change cannot be too abrupt." To Vaux, Hunt's designs were "Napoleon III in disguise all over."[232] Cook attacked Hunt's plans in the *Tribune*: "We don't like to be reminded of the existence of such rif-raf as the French emperor when we are in our Park . . . nothing [in Hunt's design] springs out of the needs of the place, nor is dictated by conditions that exist and ought to be respected."[233] The editors of *The Nation* were similarly opposed to the gateways:

It is noticeable that Mr. Hunt has almost perfectly well *conceived* his subject. It is evident that he has grasped the whole matter in hand and can handle it. The accessories are all provided and set down as if already "in the form" somewhere. And this fact makes us the more sorry for the unmistakable badness of these designs, matured and thought out and finished and by no means crude and hasty sketches. The architect and the Commissioners know what they are about, it would seem, and are satisfied to go on and add these gateways . . . to the beautiful Central Park. For the community's sake we hope that something will prevent such a misstep as that. The fine arts in New York can hardly bear so severe a chill as that would be; they are not hardy enough yet. The people need no more examples than they already have of bad architecture and misapplied ornament. Let us have gates as plain as those of a farm-yard, unless the ornament shall be appropriate.[234]

Perhaps what struck some observers, including the

park's designers, as most jarring about Hunt's designs, was their blatant rejection of the Ruskinian Gothic vocabulary so closely associated with a moral view of nature. Vaux also feared that Hunt's gateways might "spoil the whole design of the [Bethesda] terrace by weakening the emphasis" on what was surely the most elaborate and formal architectural element of the park.[235] The park's board quickly dropped Hunt's proposals, but thirty years later, in 1895, when the municipal grandeur of the American Renaissance was in full flower, Montgomery Schuyler could clearly see the merits in Hunt's ideas:

> An inspection of these [gateways] makes it evident that they were very carefully thought out from the practical as well as picturesque point of view. Nothing that has since been done, either in the treatment of the park itself or of its bordering buildings, tends to render them obsolete or inapplicable. . . . The designs . . . vindicate themselves as appropriate and decorative entrances to a public pleasure ground, and carry out the suggestion of a *rus in urbe*. Indeed, in studying them, we experience a sensible disappointment that they should not have been executed.[236]

After the rejection of Hunt's designs, Olmsted and Vaux changed their previous stance against architecturally imposing gateways and advocated the redesign of the park's southern entrances. Working with the architect Frederick Clarke Withers, Vaux devised identical gateways for the Sixth and Seventh Avenue entrances, which adopted a picturesque, English-inspired Modern Gothic vocabulary, complete with an arcade of pointed archways, elaborate roofs, and numerous towers.[237] These too were never built.

Olmsted and Vaux, in contrast to other entrants in the park's original design competition, had always been opposed to the proliferation of public sculpture or monuments in the park. Public sculpture had, in fact, been rare in New York—only one sculpture was erected in a public space between 1800 and 1850—but the inception of Central Park stimulated interest, with many New Yorkers anxious to demonstrate their individual wealth, as well as the aesthetic maturity of the nation, by emulating Europe, where statuary was common in public parks. Additionally, ethnically based organizations seized upon public sculpture to legitimize their cultural presence in New York. In 1859 the first sculpture in Central Park, G. L. Richter's bronze bust of the philosopher, poet, and dramatist Johann Christoph Friedrich von Schiller, was erected by the German American community in honor of the centennial of Schiller's birth.[238] Other sculptural tributes to national heroes followed: Sir John Steell's greater-than-life-size figure of the novelist Sir Walter Scott, given by Scottish Americans in 1871;[239] Giovanni Turini's bust of the writer and nationalist Giuseppe Mazzini, given by Italian Americans in 1876;[240] Dennis B. Sheehan's bust of the Irish poet Thomas Moore, given by the Friendly Sons of St. Patrick Society in 1879;[241] and Steell's over-life-size figure of the poet Robert Burns, given by Scottish Americans in 1880.[242]

In 1862 Vaux and Jacob Wrey Mould had suggested that twenty-six statues depicting prominent Americans decorate the Bethesda Terrace, but budget cuts prevented that proposal's realization; when the formally conceived public space, seemingly the most appropriate setting in the park for sculpture, was completed in 1873, it contained only Emma Stebbins's *Angel of the Waters*, topping the fountain. By that time twenty statues had been offered to the park,

Proposed identical Central Park gateways, Sixth and Seventh Avenues and West Fifty-ninth Street. Calvert Vaux and Frederick Clarke Withers, c. 1863. View to the north. Withers Collection. CU.

and the Committee on Statuary, Fountains, and Architectural Structures was established to review all proposals. According to the committee, "There is no class of works of art of which so few are found permanently satisfactory as statues, none which, if awkward, ungraceful or unfitting to the situation in which they are placed, are so obtrusive and unsatisfactory."[243] The committee established a set of guidelines for statuary, emphasizing that all sculpture should take a backseat to the artistically arranged landscape itself: "If a park, as a whole, is to be considered as a work of art, it is in this direction, then, that it needs to be carefully protected; for the demands of the special art of which it is an example must always have the first claim to consideration."[244]

The committee's stipulations were soon put to the test when, in 1874, it was proposed that a thirty-foot-high likeness of the American statesman and orator Daniel Webster, sculpted by Thomas Ball, be erected at the Mall's southern terminus. Olmsted and Vaux vigorously protested, arguing that the sculpture would block vistas, disrupt public congregation, and exist in striking disjunction with the surrounding landscape. The park designers were particularly opposed to the sculpture's proposed south-facing orientation: "The proposition is to place a colossal statue in the middle of the south end of this grand hall of the park *with its back set square to the people*. The impropriety of such an arrangement is plain."[245] Olmsted and Vaux prevailed, but a fourteen-foot-high version of the rather stilted and prosaic sculpture, placed upon a twenty-four-foot-high granite pedestal, was realized in 1876 on the park's West Drive near Seventy-second Street.[246] Among the park's more distinguished sculptures were four by John Quincy Adams Ward: *Indian Hunter*, installed in 1869, southwest of the Mall;[247] *William Shakespeare*, installed in 1872, near the Mall's southern end;[248] *Seventh Regiment Memorial*, with a base by Richard Morris Hunt, completed in 1874, near West Sixty-seventh Street;[249] and *The Pilgrim*, installed in 1884, on the East Drive near Seventy-second Street.[250]

Without question the most colorful and publicized episode regarding sculpture in Central Park involved not the completion of a new work of art but the installation of an ancient artifact: the 3,400-year-old obelisk known as Cleopatra's Needle, which had once stood before the Temple of the Sun in Heliopolis and in the first century B.C. had been moved to Alexandria.[251] In the 1870s, New Yorkers, eager to establish their hometown as a world-class city, looked to the example of Paris, which in 1836 had transported an obelisk from Luxor to the Place de la Concorde. The dream of acquiring an obelisk for Central Park was had first by Henry Honeychurch Gorringer, a lieutenant commander in the United States Navy who had distinguished himself as a Civil War hero. Gorringer got the attention of William Hurlbert, editor of the *New York World*, who in turn succeeded in convincing William H. Vanderbilt to pledge $75,000 for the delivery of an obelisk. The United States State Department then persuaded

Statue of Daniel Webster, West Drive near West Seventy-second Street. Thomas Ball, 1876. View to the northwest. Hepp. MCNY.

Ismail, Khedive of Egypt, to give Cleopatra's Needle to the United States as a gift. The rose gray granite obelisk climbed approximately sixty-seven feet from an eight-foot-square base to a five-foot-square top and was covered with hieroglyphs describing the reign of Thothmes III. John A. Roebling's Sons Company constructed a framework that was sent to Alexandria to lift the obelisk, turn it to a horizontal position, and load it onto the steamship *Dessoug*, which transported it to America. After a treacherous Atlantic Ocean crossing, Cleopatra's Needle was taken to its final destination, a knoll southwest of the Metropolitan Museum of Art, traveling the last leg of the trip, from a wharf at the Hudson River and Twenty-third Street, via a railroad track specially engineered by Gorringer for the purpose. Observing the scene along the Eighty-sixth Street transverse road, the editors of the *New York Daily Graphic* stated that "the obelisk drags like a wounded snake its slow length along."[252] The structural framework used to take down the obelisk in Alexandria had been dismantled and shipped back to New York to be employed to re-erect the antiquity in the park.

Cleopatra's Needle, fifteenth century B.C. View of obelisk being installed in Central Park, 1881. MMA.

Central Park had been the obelisk's intended site since the monument's acquisition was first contemplated, but once it arrived in New York, public debate raged concerning its location. The *New York Times* flatly stated: "The Central Park is no place for it. . . . As an architectural form, [the obelisk] needs a frame of buildings, giving it a background on all sides."[253] The *New York World* advocated placing the monument in Reservoir Square, along Forty-second Street between Fifth and Sixth Avenues, and the *American Architect and Building News* agreed:

> As for a background, the reservoir itself happens to be the only Egyptian building in New York, except the Tombs, and therefore might furnish the nearest approach to an appropriate background that we are likely to see. It is not very good Egyptian, certainly, and might seem to its aristocratic kinsman but a poor country cousin; but still it is Egyptian in intention, and . . . it would at least give the kind of architectural contrast which the Egyptians took care to provide for their obelisks, and would come as near as anything could to making Cleopatra's Needle look at home in New York.[254]

Despite the objections, however, the obelisk was dedicated in Central Park on January 22, 1881, arguably functioning as an appropriate outdoor complement to the ancient arti-facts housed nearby within the walls of the Metropolitan Museum of Art.

The gargantuan task of creating Central Park's *rus in urbe* was not completed until 1876, but as early as December 1858 large numbers of New Yorkers began to use the new pleasure ground. Two and one-half million people visited the park in 1860, and the following year the number exceeded four million. During the 1860s the number of visitors to the park grew fifteen times as fast as the city's population. Journalists were quick to note the park's positive effects on daily city life. In 1860 the *Architects' and Mechanics' Journal* stated: "The humanizing influence of beauty has been, we believe, nowhere more eloquently set forth than in Central Park. . . . In the presence of its artful elegance, [the visitor] sees that, somehow or other, the wildest passions and the most reckless rowdyism are restrained into an inevitable harmony with the repose and decorum of the place. . . . It is a reassuring thing to see."[255] Although the park attracted citizens of all classes, to some observers it seemed a perfect pleasure ground for the well-to-do, establishing a new level of sophistication and civility for New York. In 1865 William R. Martin noted: "We are now able to take pride in the park as a beautiful place to drive, or to ramble in, at a half-hour's distance from our

View to the east, c. 1881, showing Cleopatra's Needle, fifteenth century B.C., *west of East Drive near East Eighty-first Street, and the Metropolitan Museum of Art (Calvert Vaux, 1874–78). MCNY.*

homes. This alone has given a new phase of life in New York. When we begin to live in the midst of beauty, to see it on spring mornings from our windows, to be there without effort in the spare half-hours of an afternoon, metropolitan life will commence. It will be for the autumn and winter what Newport is for the midsummer."[256] For other commentators, such as the *New York Times*, the park symbolized the vitality of the American polity: "There is great hope for a city with the good taste and liberality to create the Central Park. This beautiful place of public enjoyment is not the result of the exceptional refinement of a few nobles or aristocrats, but it was the expression of a wish of a democracy."[257]

While Olmsted's vision of the park and its constituency was essentially inclusive, as early as 1857 he expressed concern regarding public behavior and the need to educate parkgoers about the appropriate uses of the new civic amenity. Olmsted wrote to the park's commissioners:

It is desirable that visitors to the Park, should be led to feel as soon as possible, that wide distinction exists between it and the general suburban country, in which it is the prevalent impression of a certain class that all trees, shrubs, fruit and flowers, are common property. So strong is this conviction with our gamin that the teachers of our ragged schools, when taking their pupils for a holiday into the country, have found it quite impossible to prevail upon them to refrain from completely ravishing the private gardens of the benevolent gentlemen who have offered them entertainment. This suggests what will probably be found a most delicate and difficult duty of the Commission and its officers. A large part of the people of New York are ignorant of a park, properly so-called. They will need to be trained to the proper use of it, to be restrained in the abuse of it, and this can be best done gradually, even while the Park is yet in process of construction, and before it shall be thronged with crowds of unmanageable multitudes of visitors.[258]

On March 16, 1858, the commissioners published the park's first set of ordinances, expanding them on September 23, 1859. Among the regulations were prohibitions against peddling or hawking, as well as against bringing cattle, horses, or pigs into the park. One ordinance read, "No person shall be allowed to tell fortunes, or play at any game of chance, at or with any table or instrument of gaming, nor to do any obscene or indecent act whatever in the Central Park."[259]

As soon as Central Park opened, it fulfilled its promise as a public space worthy of a great capital. The *New York Times* noted in 1861, "The parks of St. Petersburg, which are famous the world over as models of order and neatness, can scarcely excel the Central [Park] in this respect."[260] In his book of 1869, *The Great Metropolis; a Mirror of New York*, Junius Henri Browne asserted: "Many of New York's pretensions are absurd, as every sensible person knows; but it has a right to boast of Central Park, (and it does, too,) for it is indeed an honor and a glory. It is hardly surpassed by any of the old world, and will in

time surpass the celebrated Hyde Park of London and the Bois de Boulogne of Paris."[261]

Despite the park's initial popularity and the highly positive critical responses, conditions began to deteriorate in 1870 when the so-called Tweed Charter, named after the Tammany Hall boss, William Marcy Tweed, turned it into a political football by transferring control of the newly formed Department of Public Parks from the state to the mayor, who was granted the power to appoint park commissioners.[262] When the Tammany Hall politician Peter B. Sweeny was appointed chief park commissioner in 1870, the *Times* bluntly stated, "The Central Park is doomed, and the people will soon discover the fact for themselves."[263] Two years later, after the Tweed Ring had been repudiated, the *Times* summarized the changes made by Tweed's appointments: "Demagogues that they were, they claimed a right for every house-owner on the borders of the Park to 'have his view uninterrupted;' they broke through the invaluable screen on the edges; they began to break up the only bits of pastoral landscape into vulgar 'Zoological Gardens;' they put their rude fingers into the lovely, picturesque scenes, tore up the vines, stripped the rocks, and changed the effect."[264] Following letters from Olmsted and Vaux protesting plans to alter their original design, the newspaper responded: "We need not be informed by these distinguished 'landscape-painters' that the Park was a picture, a work of art, with a purpose, a unity, and with every accessory carefully designed and inserted—the whole public felt that instinctively." The *Times* went on to state that "one has somewhat of the feeling which all lovers of beauty would have if the Commissioners of the Metropolitan Museum of Art announced their purposes to 'improve and correct' their glorious picture of Rubens."[265]

Olmsted and Vaux had been fired by the Tweed administration, but in 1871 they were returned to supervisory jobs at the park. The following year they dissolved their partnership. In 1878 Olmsted, exhausted and plagued by personal problems, was forced to take a leave; four years later, significantly demoralized after years of battling with the park's board, he left New York for Brookline, Massachusetts. His concern for the park nonetheless remained undiminished. The year he left New York, he issued what would become the most important protest against the park's deterioration, a pamphlet titled *The Spoils of the Park, with a Few Leaves from the Deep-Laden Note-Books of 'A Wholly Unpractical Man.'* Bemoaning the "slovenliness and neglect . . . that had befallen the Park," Olmsted held responsible "that form of tyranny known as influence and advice and that form of bribery known as patronage."[266] Conditions at the park subsequently improved. Vaux served as landscape architect for the Department of Public Parks from 1881 to 1883, and, after a five-year hiatus, served again until his death in 1895. Under his guidance, the park once again became a metropolitan treasure.

Central Park was not merely a grace note in the rapidly expanding postwar city: it also helped to shape the course of that growth, immediately and profoundly affecting the real estate market. From the time construction commenced to the Panic of 1873, real-estate speculators bought the vast majority of the approximately 1,100 lots surrounding the park, causing prices to soar. Most lots were kept empty with the expectation that values would escalate further. The Panic of 1873 dashed those hopes. In 1876, the *Real Estate Record and Builders' Guide* traced the collapse of the market in park frontage neither to broad economic forces nor to the failure of the real estate community to accurately read and predict trends but instead to the residential preferences of the rich. The *Record and Guide* somewhat defensively argued:

> It is an open and debatable question to-day whether residences facing such an immense area of unbroken tract of land, as Central Park, affording no opposite neighbors, will ever be satisfactory to persons of wealth, culture and social proclivities under the separated dwelling-house system. . . . Thus, Mr. and Mrs. McElimsey and their daughters desire above all things, in connection with their magnificent establishment, that they shall be permitted to enjoy as a vis-à-vis the spectacle of Mr. and Mrs. Shoddy and family, as they disport themselves in their palatial mansion, along with the parade of an elegant equipage, and the display of costly garments in their ingress and egress. This craving of exhibitory display, and counter display which the lack of opposite neighbors would wholly thwart, underlies and permeates the whole fabric of our fashionable social life.[267]

So opposed to the park was the *Record and Guide* that in 1878 it proposed that the park's acreage be reduced and that its southern boundary be moved uptown to Seventy-second Street, thereby increasing the opportunity for residential development in the city's most fashionable areas.[268] Needless to say, the proposal was never taken up, and the fears of the alternately prophetic and myopic journal that the park would hinder development proved unwarranted. With the upturn of the real estate market in the 1880s, the streets surrounding Central Park—particularly Fifth Avenue, which lay farthest away from the sights, sounds, and smells of the city's working, industrial rivers—began to emerge as a residential magnet for the city's wealthiest residents.

By the mid-1880s, the still-immature park's enduring virtues and its contribution to the daily lives of the city's residents were abundantly clear. Henry James stated in his 1886 novel, *The Bostonians*: "In spite of . . . its pavilions and statues, its too numerous paths and pavements, lakes too big for the landscape and bridges too big for the lakes, [Central Park] expressed all the fragrance and freshness of the most charming moment of an April afternoon."[269] Ten years later, tastes had shifted to Classical design and planning, and the author William Dean Howells, in his book *Impressions and Experiences*, leveled charges against the park's design. He nonetheless gratefully acknowledged the gift to the city that the park most certainly was:

> Some of the decorative features here are bad, the sculp-

ture is often foolish or worse, and the architecture is the outgrowth of a mood, where it is not merely puerile . . . but the whole design, and much of the detail in the treatment of the landscape, bears the stamp of a kindly and poetic genius. The Park is in no wise taken away from nature, but is rendered back to her, when all has been done to beautify the American woodland, breaking into meadows, here and there, and brightened with pools and ponds lurking among rude masses of rock and gleaming between leafy knolls and grassy levels. It stretches and widens away, mile after mile, in the heart of the city, a memory of the land as it was before the havoc of the city began, giving to the city-prisoned poor an image of what the free country still is, everywhere.[270]

As brilliant as the park's design was as a built arcadia—a tour de force of the scenographer's art in an outdoor theater of metropolitan scale—it was also the way in which the park functioned as a democratic gathering space that ultimately defined the breadth of Olmsted and Vaux's vision and the significance of their achievement. Writing in 1893, Mariana Van Rensselaer focused on the park's civic dimension:

> Seeing the decorous, law-abiding, rule-respecting throngs which now fill Central Park of a Sunday afternoon in spring,—throngs much larger and of much more motley composition than were anticipated in the fifties,—it is amusing to know that, when the plan of Messrs. Olmsted and Vaux was accepted, some of our influential citizens cried: "Such a park is too aristocratic to be sanctioned in America, too artistic to be respected by the American populace. It would be an unrepublican waste of money to make it, for only the rich would use it; or, if the poor used it, they would quickly destroy its beauty." One well-known architect declared in a newspaper letter that our people should have a rustic pleasure-ground, not an elegant park; that the thing to do was to fence in the area, introduce cows and geese, let them make the paths, and let the public enjoy the result with perfect freedom. And another prominent person said that the place should be turned into a forest,—planted preferably with Ontario poplars alone, as they grow very quickly,—and then given over to the unaided ministrations of Nature. I fancy that these gentlemen now realize they were mistaken; but their mistakes excellently explain the great responsibility which rested upon Mr. Olmsted and Mr. Vaux. Had their park been a failure, artistically or practically, the making of public parks in America would have been retarded during many years—during years each of which would have rendered the acquisition of suitable lands more difficult and costly. But their success was quickly achieved, was as triumphantly apparent on the side of utility as on the side of beauty, and was welcomed with pride and respect by all the people of New York. Indeed, the whole country soon learned to feel a pride in Central Park, and a respect for the ideas upon which its formation had been based; and the result shows today in the scores of public parks possessed by American cities large and small.[271]

Brooklyn Bridge

On April 16, 1867, the New York state legislature passed a bill authorizing the New York Bridge Company, a private concern, to build the world's longest suspension bridge—stretching 1,616 feet between two towers with its roadway 135 feet above the water—across the turbulent East River, connecting the cities of New York and Brooklyn.[272] Not only was the bridge the world's longest but its cables were to be spun out of strands of steel, the first construction use of the relatively new material. Although $4.5 million in actual funds had already been set aside for the bridge ($3 million of which was provided by the city of Brooklyn, the municipality assumed to be the greater beneficiary of the two it would connect), there was still an air of disbelief that the risky and massive project would actually get built. Even in the optimistic mood of the post–Civil War years, the citizens of the two cities were distrustful of the politicians who would oversee the effort. There was also concern about the feasibility of the project itself; though there had been successful suspension bridge projects internationally to date, there had also been some failures. Amid this mix of emotions, one voice was clear: that of John Augustus Roebling, the bridge's designer and so much more. In his 1867 report to the New York Bridge Company, Roebling immodestly described his brainchild: "The contemplated work, when constructed in accordance with my design, will not only be the greatest bridge in existence, but it will be the greatest engineering work of this continent, and of the age. Its most conspicuous features, the towers, will serve as landmarks to the adjoining cities, and they will be entitled to be ranked as national monuments."[273]

The idea of spanning the East River between New York and Brooklyn dated to 1802, when a petition was presented to the state legislature to consider the proposal. Two schemes followed: the first, presented in 1807 by Colonel John Stevens, called for floating bridges; the second, prepared between 1809 and 1811 by the architect Thomas Pope, proposed a "Flying Pendant Lever Bridge," a single 1,800-foot-long span connecting Fulton Street in Brooklyn with Fulton Street in Manhattan.[274] A six-lane tunnel was also proposed, in the 1830s, by Major David B. Douglass. But the first proposal that was accompanied by the possibility of practical success, presented in 1857, belonged to Roebling.

Roebling was born in 1806 in Mühlhausen, Germany, in the province of Saxony. Although his father drew only a modest income from running a small tobacco shop, the family saved and was able to send John, at the insistence of his ambitious mother, to the famed Polytechnic Institute in Berlin, where he studied architecture, engineering, bridge construction, and hydraulics. He also came under the influence of the philosopher Georg Wilhelm Friedrich Hegel, who apparently instilled in the student a belief in the power of self-realization and the supremacy of reason. Hegel convinced Roebling to leave old, tired Europe for the new world of America, where he would be free to achieve his own destiny. Roebling arrived in the United States in 1831 with his brother Karl and settled first in Pennsylvania, some twenty-five miles from Pittsburgh. There the two laid out the town of Saxonburg, where they hoped to establish a farming colony with other German immigrants. After six years, Roebling, who was now an American citizen and the father of three, decided to pursue other ends. Working as an engineer and surveyor on construction projects for the Pennsylvania canal system and for the Pennsylvania Railroad, he observed numerous failures of the hemp rope used to haul canal boats up and down the mountain chains of western Pennsylvania on the new portage railroads. In 1841, recalling an article he had read in a German periodical, Roebling began manufactur-

Proposed Flying Pendant Lever Bridge. Thomas Pope, 1809–11. LHL.

Brooklyn Bridge. John A. Roebling and Washington Roebling, 1869–83. View of Brooklyn caisson before launching, 1870. MCNY.

ing wire rope in Saxonburg, the first time this material was made in America. The product was an immediate success and Roebling prospered, ultimately moving his business and home to Trenton, New Jersey.

Roebling also began to turn his attention to bridge building, attracted by the activities of Charles Ellet, an American engineer trained in Europe who was boldly proposing the construction of suspension bridges, first advocating an unrealized span across the Potomac and then a bridge that was built over Philadelphia's Schuylkill River. Although developed in Europe, the modern suspension bridge, consisting of two rigid towers with cables slung between the towers and anchored into the ground beyond and a stiff, level deck hung from the cables, was invented in the United States in 1801 by James Finley, who built a modest bridge over Jacob's Creek near Uniontown, Pennsylvania.[275] At first, Roebling had to content himself with building aqueducts over the Allegheny River. But these projects, along with the success of his wire-cable manufactory, soon made his reputation. After Charles Ellet had a falling-out with his employers, Roebling was given the job of designing the 821-foot-long, double-deck Niagara Railway Suspension Bridge over the famous Niagara Falls. Completed in 1855, one year after one of Ellet's bridges had failed, Roebling was now considered the most important and competent bridge designer in America.

In the winter of 1852, during the Niagara bridge's construction, while attempting to visit a cousin in Brooklyn, Roebling was stuck for several hours on the East River in a ferryboat blocked by ice floes. It was during this inconvenient voyage that the idea of an East River bridge first occurred to him. Originally thinking that the bridge should cross the river uptown at Blackwell's Island, in 1857 he instead proposed a suspension bridge that would soar above the route of the Fulton Ferry. Although the scheme did not go forward, no doubt hampered by the crash of 1857, it

again brought the idea of a bridge to the public's attention and connected Roebling's name with the project. In 1860 Roebling tried to revive interest in the undertaking, writing a letter to the *Architects' and Mechanics' Journal*, which had recently advocated a New York–to–Brooklyn bridge, pointing out the advantages of a suspension bridge: "The navigation of the East River will ... become so crowded ... that no obstruction whatever in the form of piers, low superstructure, or draws can be tolerated."[276]

The Civil War further delayed Roebling's dream, but the winter of 1866 and 1867 provided him with two needed catalysts.[277] For one thing, New York and Brooklyn were prospering as never before. For another, the brutal weather grievously disrupted ferry service—harking back to Roebling's own ferry experience fourteen years earlier—and it was commonly lamented, sometimes with barely an exaggeration, that the 142-mile trip to Albany aboard Commodore Vanderbilt's Hudson River Railroad was quicker than the ferry trip between New York and Brooklyn. At the same time, Roebling changed tactics and directly approached Brooklyn businessmen with his $4 million suspension bridge proposal. With the success of another suspension bridge behind him, the 1,057-foot-long Cincinnati-Covington Bridge spanning the Ohio River, Roebling was able to enlist the support of thirty-four-year-old William S. Kingsley, Brooklyn's leading contractor and the publisher of the important newspaper the *Brooklyn Daily Eagle*. Kingsley brought in the former congressman and mayor of Brooklyn Henry Murphy, who was now an influential state senator. It was Murphy who pushed through the enabling legislation incorporating the New York Bridge Company, which Murphy and Kingsley essentially controlled. Although the two cities subscribed to most of the capital stock, the private company was given control over the design of the bridge and allowed to fix tolls, although its profit was limited to fifteen percent. On

Brooklyn Bridge. John A. Roebling and Washington Roebling, 1869–83. View of Brooklyn tower under construction, c. 1875. MCNY.

Brooklyn Bridge. John A. Roebling and Washington Roebling, 1869–83. View of cable spinning from New York side, c. 1877. MCNY.

Brooklyn Bridge. John A. Roebling and Washington Roebling, 1869–83. View of Brooklyn side under construction, c. 1874. BHS.

May 23, 1867, a little more than a month after the enabling bill had been passed, the New York Bridge Company officially named John Roebling chief engineer in charge of construction, to no one's surprise.

Roebling proposed a five-lane bridge to accommodate what he estimated as forty million crossings a year. The two outer lanes would serve horsecars and a cable train would use two more lanes. The fifth lane, elevated eighteen feet above traffic, would serve pedestrians. The pioneering use of steel was emphasized, as was a system of iron trusses and inclined stays running diagonally down-

ward from the towers. Until Roebling's proposal, iron had been the material of choice in suspension bridge cables. Many contemporary engineers distrusted steel, which had only been rendered free of impurities in 1857, by the English inventor Henry Bessemer, and which had only been manufactured in the United States since 1864.

Everything about the new bridge was large. At 1,616 feet, its free span across the river was rivaled by the length of its approaches—on the Brooklyn side estimated at nearly 1,000 feet and on the New York side slightly more than 1,500 feet. John W. Kennion

Brooklyn Bridge. John A. Roebling and Washington Roebling, 1869–83. View to the east, c. 1890, from the Tribune Building (Richard Morris Hunt, 1873–75; Edward E. Raht, 1881–82). MCNY.

Brooklyn Bridge. John A. Roebling and Washington Roebling, 1869–83. View from Brooklyn side, c. 1885, with the Fulton Ferry Terminal (1865) on the left. FLC.

described the complicated route the bridge would take from shore to shore:

> [Roebling] selects the terminus at the City Hall Park. . . . It is proposed to have the bridge to enter Chatham street, opposite the Registrar's office. . . . Leaving this point the bridge then crosses North William, Rose, Vandewater, Cliff, Franklin-Square, Cherry, Water, Front

and South; thence to the end of the Old Pier No. 29, now broken down; the line continues in a straight course across the river and then passes on the Brooklyn shore nearly through the centre of the spare slip of the Fulton Ferry Company; thence passing over Water, Dock and Front. A part of James street, near Garrison, will be occupied by the Brooklyn anchorage. Leaving the anchorage, the line continues to pass over James, and then crossing York and Main streets, obliquely, deflects toward Fulton; after crossing Prospect near its intersection with Fulton, it terminates finally in the block which is bounded by Fulton, Prospect, Sands and Washington streets.[278]

In short, as the *New York Times* put it: "It is not only a bridge across the river, but almost equivalent to a bridge from City Hall to City Hall."[279]

A commission to study the feasibility of Roebling's proposal was soon created, and the United States Secretary of War appointed a three-member engineering task force to determine whether the bridge would block navigation. At the same time, the politically savvy directors of the New York Bridge Company greased Boss Tweed's political machine in order to avoid the project's delay or cancellation. The summer of 1869, when both the federal government and the local panel of experts cleared the bridge for construction, promised to be the high point of Roebling's career and the beginning of the fulfillment of a long-cherished dream. Roebling had by now taken up residence in Brooklyn Heights, at 37 Hicks Street. The project was estimated to take five years to complete, at a cost of eight million dollars.

On June 28, 1869, while trying to determine the exact location for the Brooklyn tower, Roebling was gravely injured by a ferry that haphazardly entered its slip, knocking down pilings that crushed his right foot. Several toes were amputated, and Roebling insisted on his own treatment regimen of dousing the wound with cold water. But

a few weeks later, on July 22, Roebling died from the resulting tetanus infection. Fortunately for the project, Roebling's son Washington, a trained engineer educated at the Rensselaer Polytechnic Institute, had been working with his father for some time and was able to take over. In addition, John Roebling had left a multitude of notes for his son to follow and Washington Roebling had recently returned from Europe, where he had studied firsthand the ingenious method by which the towers of the bridge would be constructed.

In January 1870, work finally started, beginning with the caissons that needed to be built beneath the river's surface to support the towers.[280] The construction technique Washington Roebling observed overseas involved the use of pneumatic caissons, which were immense, hollow, bottomless boxes built of solid timber. The Brooklyn caisson was 168 by 102 feet and the New York caisson 172 by 102 feet; both measured some twenty feet thick on top, with V-shaped sides that were eight feet at their thickest but tapered to an eight-inch-thick, iron-sheathed cutting edge. They were essentially airtight cages that allowed workers to dig into the riverbed while the eighty-ton towers were built overhead. Constructed partially on land, the caissons were launched into position and the first courses of stone were then laid on top. When the box hit bottom, compressed air was pumped in to force the water out of the work area. A system of air locks prevented the compressed air from escaping, and debris was removed with a clamshell scoop through specially constructed water shafts.

Brooklyn Bridge. John A. Roebling and Washington Roebling, 1869–83. View of the pedestrian promenade, 1894. Johnston. MCNY.

Brooklyn Bridge. John A. Roebling and Washington Roebling, 1869–83. View of cable cars, c. 1890. BHS.

Conditions for the caisson workers, called "sand hogs," were predictably difficult. Water often accidentally entered the chamber, and the only means of illumination were gas and calcium lamps that made the threat of fire in the predominantly wood environment a real concern. Blowouts—loud explosions caused by changes in air pressure—were also a factor in the decisions of some one hundred workers to quit each week. But the biggest danger inside the caissons, not properly understood at the time, was caisson disease, or the bends, a malady induced by a too-rapid decrease in air pressure after an extended stay in a compressed atmosphere, which caused nitrogen bubbles to form in blood and tissue. The results of the disease ranged from cramps to paralysis to death. The bends, combined with the other difficulties of the work site, conspired to slow construction almost exponentially as the caissons got deeper. Eight-hour shifts were reduced to two hours when, on the Brooklyn side, the first of the two caissons to be built, huge boulders were reached. Washington Roebling had the idea to use blasting powder but was unsure as to its interaction with compressed air. After experimenting by shooting a gun in the caisson, blasting powder was eventually used to good effect and, after one and a half years, bedrock was hit on the Brooklyn side at forty-four and a half feet below the water's surface. The caisson's work area and shafts were then filled with concrete and permanently sealed.

The New York caisson was to prove an even more difficult challenge and one with far deadlier results. Conditions beneath the riverbed required heavy blasting, and a proper surface of tightly packed sand was not reached until seventy-eight and a half feet. During the three years of work, three men died of the bends and 110 were injured, as opposed to only six injuries from caisson disease on the Brooklyn side. One of the injured was Washington Roebling. Stricken during the summer of 1872, Roebling recuperated first in Trenton and then in Wiesbaden but returned in 1873 to his Brooklyn home, at 110 Columbia Heights, to supervise construction. Although an invalid, Roebling kept in contact with his engineers and workers through his wife, Emily, who attended meetings and relayed messages.

Other parts of the bridge's construction proceeded with much less incident.[281] The New York anchorage was built between May 1875 and July 1876, and the Brooklyn anchorage between February 1873 and November 1875. The Brooklyn tower was completed in June 1875, while the New York side was finished in July 1876. To celebrate the completion of the massive structures, which rose to a height of 271 and a half feet above mean high-water, one of the engineers, E. F. Farrington, traveled in August 1876 from Brooklyn to New York in a boatswain's chair attached to a three-quarter-inch wire rope stretched between the two towers. An estimated ten thousand people enjoyed the spectacle.

But all was not entirely well. In 1874, with cost overruns a continuous problem, the state legislature passed an act allowing the two cities to take control of the project provided the original investors were repaid with interest. Control of the now-public work was placed under the management of a board of trustees comprising ten members from each city, including both mayors and comptrollers. This arrangement would prove unwieldy, to say the least.

After the towers and anchorages were completed, the next job was the spinning of the cables. In order to avoid a conflict of interest, Roebling resigned from the family wire manufactory and assumed that his former company would get the commission to provide the material. Even though Boss Tweed was no longer on the scene, corruption remained a problem, however, and the contract was instead awarded to J. Lloyd Haigh, an acquaintance of Congressman Abram Hewitt, a member of the board of trustees hitherto regarded as a crusading reform Democrat. Hewitt, a son-in-law of Peter Cooper as well as Cooper's partner in an iron plant, held a mortgage on Haigh's ironworks and promised not to foreclose on his business in exchange for a ten percent kickback on Haigh's bridge contract. Roebling was not surprised when alert workers noticed that Haigh was supplying some defective wire. Roebling had specified wire six times stronger than necessary and was confident that the bridge was safe despite the faulty wire, but he nonetheless decided to add additional wire to the cables, using wire from the family business to wrap the four main cables. On October 5, 1878, the last wire of the great catenary arches, shaped by the elemental force of gravity itself, was drawn across the river as the bridge, so much the product of individual will, more and more seemed a force of nature.

The "wire fraud," combined with additional cost overruns—a total of $13.5 million had now been spent—sapped some public support for the project, and in November 1878 work was briefly stopped due to a lack of funds. In 1879 the *New York Daily Graphic*, which, like most publications of the day, had viewed the project in a predominantly favorable light, succumbed to cynicism: "The profoundest conundrum . . . connected with the bridge is, what under the sun will it be good for when it is done? The answer to this 'no fellah' has yet been smart enough to suggest."[282] For the next four years, construction on the bridge and its approaches continued in an atmosphere of tension, including a failed attempt to fire Washington Roebling, and apprehension as to when it would all truly be done.[283]

On May 24, 1883, in a celebration the likes of which New York and Brooklyn had never seen, the bridge was opened.[284] Like the opening of the Erie Canal, in 1825, and the Croton Aqueduct, in 1842, both events that also marked the expansion of New York's power through the conquest of vast space, the celebration of the bridge's completion was a milestone that transcended local interest to become a national event. President Chester A. Arthur and his entire cabinet, as well as every prominent local politician, shared in the glory with a promenade across the span from New York to Brooklyn, where the ceremonies and speeches took place. Brooklyn's businesses and schools were closed for the entire day, while a comparatively blasé New York took only a half day. Emily Roebling represented her husband. At the end of the festivities both the president

Brooklyn Bridge. John A. Roebling and Washington Roebling, 1869–83. View of the Brooklyn terminal under construction, c. 1881. MA.

and New York's governor, Grover Cleveland, personally congratulated the bridge builder at his Brooklyn Heights sickbed. The evening ended with a fireworks display that culminated in a grand finale consisting of some five hundred rockets. The *New York Times* headlined the event as "Two Great Cities United," but observed that "the opening of the bridge was decidedly Brooklyn's celebration."[285]

A spectacular feat of engineering and a beautiful object to contemplate, the new bridge was an icon of the new age. Along with the Western Union and Tribune Buildings, the bridge, by dwarfing the hitherto dominant church towers, symbolized the triumph of modern secularism over an outmoded spiritualism. Yet in the soaring verticality of the towers, with their Gothic-inspired pointed arches, and in the diagonal cable webbing that rendered the roadway a bounded street hurling across space, the bridge itself seemed to possess an extra, almost spiritual dimension, which Abram Hewitt caught in his opening address: "It stands before us today as the sum and epitome of human knowledge; the very heir to the ages."[286]

Blue-white electric arc lamps had been selected by Roebling, who believed them superior to Edison's incandescent bulbs, to illuminate the bridge. These were lit just a few days before the dedication. At either end, but not quite finished at the time of the bridge's inauguration, were terminal buildings designed to handle the 37,000 daily commuters who, beginning in September, made the five-minute trip on the cable-powered trains that crossed the bridge between the two cities. The Brooklyn terminal was a cavernous, extensively glazed, iron-paneled structure painted dark red, while the facility on the New York side was comparatively modest, about half the size.

On the first full day of operations, May 25, 1883, 150,300 people crossed the bridge by foot, joined by 1,800 vehicles. Then, a week after the opening, on Decoration Day, twelve people were killed in a stampede when a woman's screams after tripping were misinterpreted by the crowd as a signal of the bridge's impending collapse.[287] And only five months after its completion, the herculean project of fourteen years, sixteen million dollars, and twenty-seven lives lost, including that of its brilliant creator, was subject to a taunting editorial in the *New York Times* titled "Our Impending Ruin," which blamed the bridge for beginning the depopulation of New York.[288] The *Times*'s fears proved ungrounded. While Brooklyn's population swelled from 599,495 in 1880 to 838,547 in 1890, New York's also grew during the same period, from 1,164,673 to 1,441,216.

Montgomery Schuyler, in a review published in *Harper's Weekly* at the time of the opening, acknowledged the bridge's overwhelming scale and technical prowess: "The Brooklyn Bridge is . . . one of the mechanical wonders of the world, one of the greatest and most characteristic of the monuments of the nineteenth century." Schuyler was also able to find merit in some of the details: "The approaches themselves are greatly impressive. . . . The street bridges are uniformly imposing by size and span,

and especially attractive also by reason of the fact that through them we get what is to be got nowhere else in our rectangular city, glimpses and 'bits' of buildings." But for the most part Schuyler's critique was filled with disappointments, although he noted that he was not "so much criticising the crowning work of a great engineer's career as noting the spirit of our age." Convinced that the bridge constituted "not a work of architecture," Schuyler paid particular attention to the detailing of the towers, which held the key to his problem with the work as a whole. His argument was somewhat tortured, but his point was that the piers failed to "assert themselves starkly and unmistakably as the bones of the structure. . . . A drawing of one of the towers . . . without its cables would tell the spectator nothing. . . . With its flat top and its level coping, indicating that the whole was meant to be evenly loaded, it would seem to be the base of a missing super-structure rather than what it is." In short, Schuyler regretted that the towers were not more directly expressive of their structural role, visibly cradling the cables. The very abstraction of the towers, however, with their almost impassive aloofness, may have rendered them the exalted monuments John Roebling had promised they would become. According to Schuyler, "It so happens that the work which is likely to be our most durable monument, and to convey some knowledge of us to the most remote posterity, is a work of bare utility; not a shrine, not a fortress, not a palace, but a bridge."[289] Twenty-five years after the bridge's completion, in his obituary tribute to his friend and mentor Leopold Eidlitz, Schuyler reported that the architect "through a common friend, [was] endeavored to transmit to . . . Roebling an offer to model, gratuitously and out of pure interest in the great work, the towers of that structure. The friend declined to convey the proposal, fearing to wound the susceptibilities of the engineer. It was a great pity," Schuyler opined, "for the work the architect volunteered to do was work he was pre-eminently qualified to do. If he had done it, the towers would not now stand as disgraces to the airy fabric that swings between them."[290]

But Schuyler's critical analysis was, at the time, something of an anomaly. Most observers were impressed that a mere bridge could be so inspiring. The towers, by virtue of their Gothic references, were exactly right, symbolizing a synthesis between spiritualism and secularism just as the latter threatened to overwhelm the former. Even though the imposing towers had reached their apex in 1876, and the bridge's completion seven years later was accompanied by the predictable mix of delays, cost overruns, and corruption, the majority of New Yorkers and Brooklynites were enchanted and entranced by the bridge's poetic and mechanical virtuosity. Perhaps Brooklyn mayor Seth Low best captured their mood: "The beautiful and stately structure fulfills the fondest hope. . . . The impression upon the visitor is one of astonishment that grows with every visit. No one who has been upon it can ever forget it. . . . Not one shall see it and not feel prouder to be a man."[291]

In 1884, just one year after the opening of the Brooklyn

Proposed Hudson River suspension bridge. Gustav Lindenthal, 1884. Rendering of view to the southeast. SA. CU.

Bridge, a little-known, Moravian-born engineer, Gustav Lindenthal, proposed an all-steel, triple-deck suspension bridge for the Pennsylvania Railroad to span the Hudson River either between Desbrosses Street in New York and Pavonia Avenue in Jersey City or between Twenty-third Street in New York and Twelfth Street in Hoboken.[292] Lindenthal's bridge, designed to accommodate railroad lines, vehicles, and pedestrians, would have dwarfed the Roeblings' bridge, with 625-foot towers and a span of 2,850 feet. Even though the proposal was sponsored by the powerful railroad company, which desperately wanted a direct connection to New York (its passengers now had to take a ferry from its last stop in Jersey City) and which had recently rejected building a tunnel, the project was stalled through the rest of the decade because of its great cost. And Lindenthal, who would go on to become one of New York's most prominent bridge designers in the next century, was reported to have remained bitter for the rest of his life over its eventual defeat.

Another major bridge-building project, one that did go forward in the 1880s, was the Washington Bridge (1886–89), spanning the Harlem River between 181st Street at Tenth Avenue in New York and University and Ogden Avenues in the Annexed District.[293] Charles Conrad Schneider won the competition for the bridge, judged by the newly created Harlem River Bridge Commission, with a design consisting of a pair of steel arches, each spanning 510 feet—one crossing the river, the other the tracks of the New York Central Railroad—and supported by masonry piers. Schneider's elaborate design was soon deemed too expensive, and the Union Bridge Company was given the task of altering the proposal by combining it with the simpler, second-prize scheme of William Hildenbrand. The prominent engineer William R. Hutton was appointed chief engineer in charge of construction, Edward H. Kendall served as consulting architect, and DeLemos & Cordes was hired to produce a decorative cast-iron cornice and balustrade. The bridge, whose 80-foot-wide roadway soared 135 feet above mean high-water, was completed in less than three years and named in conjunction with the centennial celebration of the first president's inauguration. Besides its orderly construction schedule, the Washington Bridge differed from the Brooklyn Bridge in another notable way: it received the almost unstinting praise of Montgomery Schuyler. In 1900, in the pages of *Century Magazine*, Schuyler described it as "an admirable and exemplary work, perhaps the most conspicuously successful monument that American engineering has produced." Although he had some objections to the arcaded masonry approaches—"[though] doubtless adequate structurally, are less than adequate architecturally for want of the emphasis, of the exaggeration if you please, which is needed to certify their sufficiency, and which an architectural artist would have known how to supply"— Schuyler deemed "the bridge proper . . . difficult to overpraise. The completed work so perfectly and evidently fulfills its function and fills its place that the general scheme seems to the spectator a matter of course."[294]

Washington Bridge. Charles Conrad Schneider, William Hildenbrand, and William R. Hutton, 1886–89. View to the north, 1894. Johnston. MCNY.

Third Judicial District Courthouse, site bounded by Sixth and Greenwich Avenues and West Tenth Street. Calvert Vaux and Frederick Clarke Withers, 1874–77. View to the southwest, c. 1885, showing the Sixth Avenue elevated railroad in the foreground. AABN. CU.

CHAPTER 2

❧ Representative Places ❧

Since I came back [from Europe] I have liked New York decidedly less—so little in fact that *hideous* is the most amiable word I can find to apply to it. If one could only get over the trick of judging things aesthetically!

—Henry James to Sarah Butler Wister, January 23, 1875

New York seems to me very brilliant and beautiful, and the streets amuse me as much as if I had come from Hartford, Conn.—or Harrisburg, Penn.—instead of from London and Paris—and Boston!

—Henry James to Isabella Stewart Gardner, December 7, 1881[1]

GOVERNMENT BUILDINGS

During the post–Civil War period, buildings for government at every level, municipal, state, and federal, began for the first time to challenge the scale of those for religion and commerce, reflecting the explosive growth of political bureaucracies as well as of the city itself. The early-nineteenth-century City Hall, designed by Joseph François Mangin and John McComb Jr., was an elegant, small-scale, English- and French-inspired Classical building that had been completed in 1811, when its location in a triangular park bounded by Chambers Street, Broadway, and Park Row marked the city's northern boundary.[2] By midcentury, it was suggested that the city's government move to significantly expanded headquarters at Madison Square, which could then be argued to constitute the new northern limit. New York's officialdom chose to expand but stay put, however, remaining close to the city's financial center. In 1855 plans were developed by Arthur Gilbert, Thomas R. Jackson, and Henry L. Stuart for a three-story, U-shaped annex to the existing City Hall, extending 520 feet along Chambers Street with 365-foot wings running south along Broadway and Centre Street, thereby forming a quadrangle with Mangin and McComb's building providing the fourth side.[3] This plan went unrealized, and in 1857 Mayor Fernando Wood revived the idea of a new City Hall, establishing a municipal commission to oversee the project. There was still strong sentiment in some quarters for a new building, with the *New York Herald* suggesting that the existing City Hall be renovated as the mayor's residence and that the Five Points slum area, east of City Hall Park, be cleared to form a new public square surrounded by a city hall, a post office, and other municipal buildings.[4] Still nothing was done. Thirty years later, in 1888, during the administration of Mayor Hugh Grant, a design competition was held for a municipal building intended to flank both City Hall and the so-called Tweed Courthouse (see below). The winning entry, submitted by Charles B. Atwood, who employed the young architect Willis B. Polk as his delineator, called for seven-story pavilions to be placed on either side of the existing City Hall.[5] The proposal picked up on Mangin and McComb's vocabulary but expanded it to create a bold yet compatible design. A towering campanile on axis with the original building's cupola was intended to represent the city at its new skyscraping scale. Once again, the plan was not realized and the city's government made due with its architecturally charming but functionally outmoded facility.

Mirroring the rampant individualism of the Gilded Age as a whole, grand civic ensembles were not the mode of the day. There were instead large, grandiloquent, individualistic buildings, of which three left an indelible mark on the city scene: the New York County Courthouse, the Third Judicial District Courthouse, and the United States Courthouse and Post Office. In 1858 widespread attention was focused on the city's lack of courtrooms, a problem

Proposed municipal buildings flanking City Hall, City Hall Park, bounded by Park Row, Centre Street, Broadway, and Chambers Street.
Charles B. Atwood, 1888. Rendering of view to the northeast. BLDG. CU.

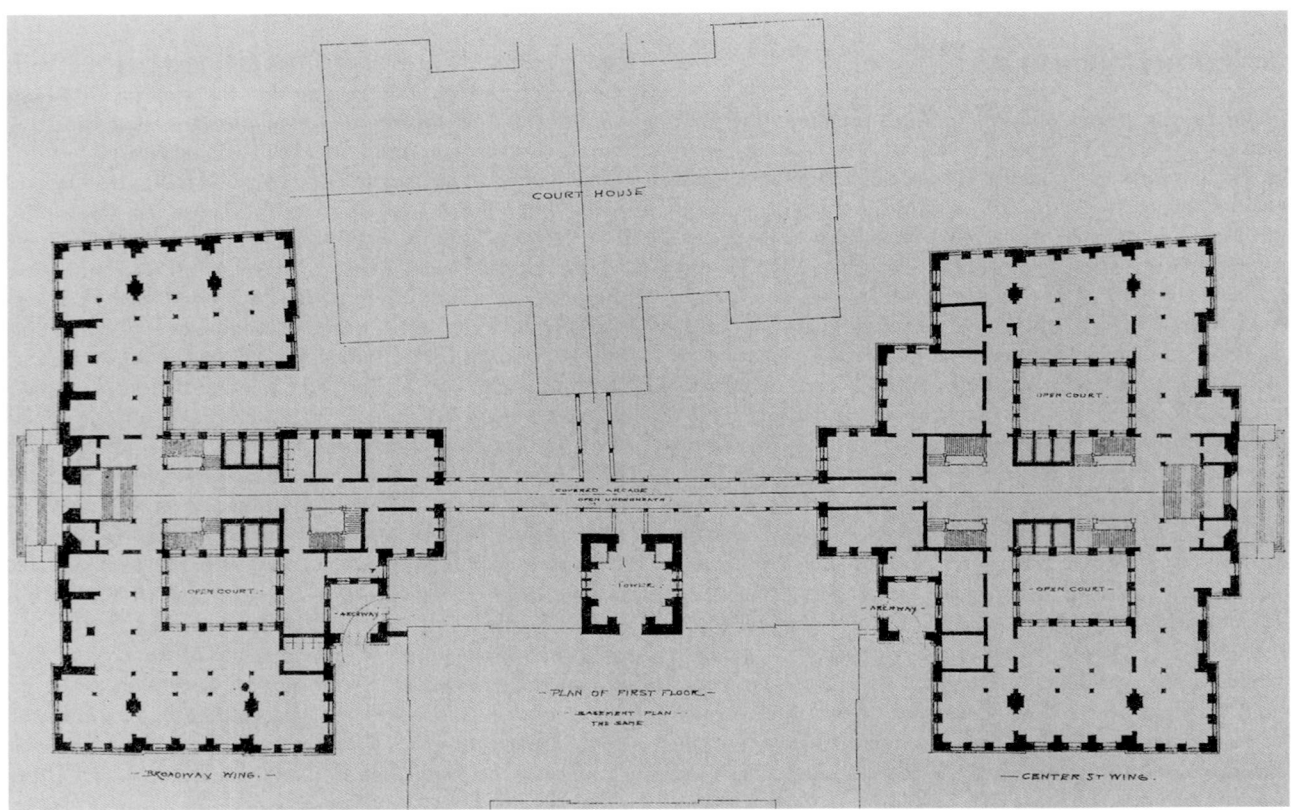

Proposed municipal buildings flanking City Hall, City Hall Park, bounded by Park Row, Centre Street, Broadway, and Chambers Street.
Charles B. Atwood, 1888. First-floor plan. BLDG. CU.

caused in part by an 1854 fire that destroyed several courts. As a result, the city's Board of Supervisors appointed a County Courthouse Committee, which in turn selected the architect John Kellum to design a new courthouse.[6] Kellum completed plans within a year, but progress was impeded by a political battle over whether the city's Board of Supervisors or the state's Board of Commissioners should oversee the appropriation of funds for the new building. William Marcy "Boss" Tweed artfully argued the city's case and won, quickly becoming the president of the Board of Supervisors.

Ground was broken for the new courthouse in 1862 on a site just north of City Hall, facing Chambers Street. The loss of a portion of City Hall Park, increasingly valued as a green oasis in a densely developed part of the city, to Kellum's Anglo-Italianate, gray Massachusetts marble, four-story, 246-by-49-foot building did not go unnoticed, but the courthouse was desperately needed. Taking a cue from the Capitol Building in Washington, D.C., where, despite the Civil War, work was proceeding on Thomas U. Walter's iconic dome, the construction of the new courthouse continued during the war. Ambitions for the building were high. It was to rival, if not exceed, the domed Kings County Courthouse then under construction in the neighboring city of Brooklyn (see chapter 7).

Kellum's plan entailed a flight of steps leading up from Chambers Street past the rusticated base to a pedimented,

Proposed tower adjacent to City Hall, City Hall Park, bounded by Park Row, Centre Street, Broadway, and Chambers Street. Charles B. Atwood, 1888. Rendering by Willis B. Polk showing the top of the tower. BLDG. CU.

Proposed New York County Courthouse, south side of Chambers Street between Broadway and Centre Street. John Kellum, 1862. View to the southeast. NYHS.

New York County Courthouse, south side of Chambers Street between Broadway and Centre Street. John Kellum and Leopold Eidlitz, 1862–76. View to the southeast. NYHS.

tetrastyle, Corinthian portico framing the principal entrance. At a time when Gothic-inspired work held sway even in the realm of civic buildings, Kellum stuck to the more typically governmental Classical approach, with a design combining pilasters, foliated brackets, and windows surrounded by sills resting on corbels, as well as consoles supported by paneled pilasters. Though Kellum's original design had called for a high, ribbed dome carried on a polygonal base, an element that would have dwarfed the delicate cupola of the adjacent City Hall, this feature was not built. Inside, Kellum's use of cast-iron framing, intended as a fire-fighting precaution, had the happy side effect of producing large, well-lighted, column-free rooms that also enjoyed excellent acoustics thanks to the use of an early form of soundproofing consisting of lime mortar placed between joists and masonry vaults.

Despite the building's architectural merits, the public came to be blinded to the virtues of Kellum's grand design by the corrupt circumstances that surrounded the building's long process of construction. Early on, when things were going well, the building was well received. In 1865 enough progress had been made to impress a reporter from the *New York Times*: "High up in the air, bright and clean as a mirror, rose the polished wall of the marble structure,

its many doors and countless windows, its cast iron girders, and its beautifully carved cappings, speaking eloquently on behalf of the busy, dust-grimed men at its base."[7] The reporter nonetheless expressed concern about the building's construction schedule and mounting costs. The following year, when the *New York Times* called attention to the scheme of graft that plagued the courthouse's construction, the public's affection for the structure itself soured. Corrupt practices were being enforced at the direction of Tweed, who saw to it that close to $9 million in cash found its way from the building's construction budget into the pockets of various Democratic Party political cronies from Tammany Hall, a group coming to be known as the "Tweed Ring."[8] As a result, the building came to be called the Tweed Courthouse in tribute to the corrupt political boss whose shenanigans led to a construction cost more than four times that of Sir Charles Barry's Houses of Parliament (1836–68), in London, and more than twice the purchase price of the entire territory of Alaska. The Tweed Ring's audaciousness knew virtually no bounds. For three tables and forty chairs the city was charged $179,729.60. A New York State Republican leader, Roscoe Conkling, asserted that the building's furnishings cost more money than was spent to run the entire United

States Postal Service and nearly three times the amount spent to execute the nation's total diplomatic activities for two years.

The *New York Times* continued its anticorruption campaign for five years. At the same time, it opposed the *New York Daily Tribune*'s call for a work stoppage, arguing instead that the Board of Supervisors, consisting of Tweed and his cronies, be abolished. In 1870 the board was replaced by a new commission, authorized by the state legislature, that bizarrely but perhaps not altogether surprisingly, given Tammany Hall's power, consisted of members appointed by Mayor A. Oakey Hall, a Tweed stalwart. The commission used $600,000 worth of new funding from Albany for patronage and tried to repudiate all outstanding bills on the courthouse. The board members also attempted to update Kellum's design by contemplating the replacement of the proposed iron dome with a slated mansard, which they argued would be both more stylish and cheaper. Fortunately, the *New York Times* pointed out that the slate for the roof was to be purchased from a quarry owned by Tweed.

In 1867, the still-incomplete courthouse accepted its first tenant, the Court of Appeals of New York State, which occupied a first-floor room. When other rooms were opened in 1868, observers were pleasantly surprised by the quality of the workmanship. John W. Kennion regarded the work to be "most thoroughly done . . . for the vast outlay of money, there is an abundant, if not wholly satisfactory exhibit."[9] But the building's architecture remained overshadowed by politics. The adoption of a new city charter in April 1870 served to solidify Tweed's stronghold by investing more power in the mayor, who appointed Tweed Commissioner of Public Works and installed Tweed's sidekicks Richard B. Connolly and Peter B. Sweeny as Controller and head of the Department of Public Parks, respectively. By then, however, the jig was nearly up, and the following year the *New York Times* exposed the courthouse scandal in its entirety in a series of articles beginning on July 8, 1871.[10] The series was based on the transcripts of accounts obtained from the controller's office, which revealed that the building had cost $11 million more than the original estimate of $800,000. G. S. Miller, a carpenter, had received more than $350,000 for a month's work, making him, as the *New York Times* wryly observed, "the luckiest carpenter in the world," while Andrew Garvey, "clearly the prince of plasterers," had been paid almost $3 million in 1869 and 1870 for work on city buildings.[11] The *New York Times*'s attack would not necessarily have felled Tweed had not the editorial cartoonist Thomas Nast mounted a parallel campaign in *Harper's Weekly*.[12] Many of Tweed's rank-and-file constituents were illiterate, but they could easily understand the scathing cartoons that soon motivated the corrupt politician to offer Nast $500,000 if he would cease his attacks and go to Europe to study art. Nast refused, and the combined force of the two editorial campaigns finally rallied the city's business community. Under the leadership of Henry

Claus, a prominent stockbroker, Tweed's regime was toppled. Convicted of both civil and criminal charges, Tweed, after several trials and appeals, fled the city under the alias John Secor. He went first to Florida, then to Cuba, and finally to Spain. American authorities demanded his return, and Tweed died in jail in New York on April 12, 1878.

Just as Tweed was tumbling from his throne, John Kellum died, on July 24, 1871, and the new commissioners hired Leopold Eidlitz to finish the building. Eidlitz enclosed the rotunda with polychromatic brickwork topped by a low polygonal glass skylight, clearly contradicting Kellum's design. Eidlitz also introduced a Moorish sensibility similar to that of his and Henry Fernbach's Temple Emanu-El (see below) in the rotunda and in one courtroom, the latter compartmentalized by arches into nine square, flat-ceilinged bays. In 1876, just as the courthouse was at last being finished, fourteen years after construction had begun, serious problems in its ventilation system were uncovered that were attributed to Kellum, who by then had become a favorite object of professional scorn, leading the *American Architect and Building News* to blame him for "blunders of construction which should disgrace the merest tyro in an architect's office."[13] Kellum was redeemed when further inspection revealed that many of the problems were the result of the poor maintenance and shoddy workmanship that went hand in hand with corruption. Sadly, it was ultimately the building's politics and not its architecture that became its principal legacy, memorialized in verse by an anonymous poet:

> This is
> BOSS TWEED . . .
> Who *controll'd* the plastering laid on so thick
> By the comptroller's plasterer, Garvey by name,
> The Garvey whose fame is the little game
> Of laying on plaster and knowing the trick
> Of charging as if he himself were a brick
> Of the well-plaster'd House
> That TWEED built.[14]

The Tweed Courthouse's aesthetic achievement may have been obscured by corruption, but Calvert Vaux and Frederick Clarke Withers's Third Judicial District Courthouse, more commonly known as the Jefferson Market Courthouse, was undisputably a bravura architectural statement.[15] Combining a minor prison for temporary detention with a police court, Vaux and Withers's complex occupied a triangular block at the northwest corner of Sixth and Greenwich Avenues, with West Tenth Street forming the third side. The site had previously been occupied by an outmoded prison and the Jefferson Market, a one- and two-story facility established in 1833, to which had been added an eight-story wooden fire watchtower, one of the city's tallest and a bold landmark in its low-scaled neighborhood. While the new building group included a rebuilt market at the corner of Sixth and Greenwich Avenues, its principal feature was the courthouse and jail (1874–77) that occupied the northern portion of the site.

New York County Courthouse, south side of Chambers Street between Broadway and Centre Street. John Kellum and Leopold Eidlitz, 1862–76. View to the southeast, c. 1888. NYHS.

View to the northwest from Sixth Avenue between West Eighth and West Ninth Streets, showing the first Jefferson Market (1833) with its fire watchtower. NYHS.

The idea for the new complex grew out of a Tweed-sponsored pork-barrel bill passed in the state legislature in 1870. The bill led to the appropriation of $150,000, which by 1873 had been more or less squandered so that there was nothing to show for it but a pile of rotting building materials. In 1874 Withers and Vaux were hired to draw up a plan. (Although both men are usually listed as the project's architects, Withers's biographer Francis Kowsky contends that Vaux was only marginally involved.[16]) Construction began in 1875 amid contractor disputes, investigations into wrongdoing by public watchdog groups, and protests by individual citizens. In addition to the general cynicism about municipal projects that prevailed in the city even after the Tweed Ring was disbanded, there were other objections to the plan, mostly arising from the fact that taxpayers resented so large an expenditure of public funds in one of the city's poorest neighborhoods. The old Jefferson Market, which had included a police court located where a saloon once had been, was not held in high regard by "nice" New Yorkers, who associated it with "everything that is bad, mean and unsavory."[17] Some of the public's resistance was perhaps also due to the proposed building's richly polychromed exuberance. The civic-minded Municipal Society criticized the work on the

grounds that it would give "to the criminal brought to it a suggestion of the gaudy vulgarity connected with gilded dens of infamy."[18] Additionally, the juxtaposition of courthouse and market was deemed by many to be less than ideal. Though the editors of the *New York Times* liked the building's design, they deemed it "a jewel in a swine's snout."[19]

Making excellent use of a difficult site, Withers devised a geometrically ingenious plan that divided the project into four parts: the courthouse, facing Sixth Avenue; a five-story prison set behind a high wall, running along West Tenth Street and Greenwich Avenue; a fire and bell tower to replace the outmoded wooden landmark, placed at the exact corner of Sixth Avenue and West Tenth Street; and the market, occupying the corner of Sixth and Greenwich Avenues, designed by Douglas Smyth and completed in 1883. The prison, which provided space for sixty men and thirty women, included an exercise area in the attic. A small service yard separated the prison from the courthouse, which functioned as both a police and district court.

Withers's design was one of New York's first examples of the robust, variegated Gothic that had been introduced in England around 1860. Especially influential, as Kowsky has pointed out, was the example of William Burges, whose inventive use of medieval precedent belonged as much to the architecture illustrated in the books of the Middle Ages as to the actual buildings of that period. The influence of Burges in the completed complex was less pronounced, however, than it had been in an initial scheme published in the *New-York Sketch-Book of Architecture* in April 1874.[20] As built, the boldly striped Ohio sandstone–trimmed, red pressed brick design was vivacious yet dignified. Ornament was concentrated on the courthouse, which was distinguished by a slender tower that began as a piece of the building's curved corner, emerged as a cylinder, and then carried a square, Venetian-inspired campanile to a pyramidal roof. The jailhouse was simpler, with tall arches that evoked lancets. Here the walls were somewhat severe, forming an almost skinlike wrap that was particularly effective in the curved bay of the male prisoners' wing. The *New York Daily Tribune* noted that "some of our art critics declare [the building complex] to be the only piece of architecture with brain in it which our city can show, and which everybody agrees in declaring is a gem in our street architecture: standing at the junction of several streets, it may be studied from ever so many points. . . . It is 'Englishy' throughout, and shows that Messrs. Withers and Vaux have kept pace with the creators of Victorian Gothic across the sea."[21]

Withers prepared a scheme for a new market as part of his courthouse design, but, as the *Real Estate Record and Builders' Guide* put it:

> In a community in which there was any real regard for architecture or any standard of professional comity, the architect who was recognized to have done so successful a piece of work as the courthouse and jail would have been selected, as a matter of course, to complete his own work, or, if it were desirable to give "the job" to some other architect, the architect so chosen would have felt bound to carry out the design of his predecessor. In the present case the new architect has carried out an entirely different design of his own, and there is no evidence in the architecture of the market that the original architect had been consulted at all. This is not only a violation of professional comity; it is, in this case, a distinct architectural misfortune.

Withers had proposed a polygonal iron and glass dome that would have perfectly mediated the strong contrast between the differing scales and characters of the courthouse and jail. Smyth's market consisted of a glass-roofed shed, which the editors of the *Record and Guide* believed to have been "designed without any visible reference to the buildings it adjoins, of which it forms part, except in the adoption of what the designer supposes to be the same style. The new work is Gothic, if Gothic be held to reside in pointed arches, and that is all. The material is not even the same. The old work is bright with wrought work of Ohio sandstone, the new of red brick and red terra cotta, with sparing use of brown stone." The editors conceded that "judged by itself, the new Jefferson Market is not a bad piece of work," but they would praise it only "up to a certain point."[22] In the final analysis the editors found that

Smyth's Jefferson Market "does nothing towards completing what should have been an artistic group, and . . . in itself shows a thoughtless notion that Gothic architecture consists in a certain set of forms, applied with or without meaning, [showing] a real acquaintance with the forms of a workmanlike facility of design."[23]

Of all the government buildings constructed in New York during the Gilded Age, Alfred B. Mullett's United States Courthouse and Post Office (1869–75), at the southern tip of City Hall Park, bounded by Broadway and Park Row, perhaps most vividly expressed the period's bombastic self-confidence.[24] From 1845 until 1875, the city's only post office had been located in the former Middle Dutch Church (1727–31), on Nassau Street (see chapter 1). By 1870, with over one hundred tons of mail being processed each business day, the makeshift facility was hopelessly overtaxed. After the new post office was opened, the former church was demolished to make way for Charles W. Clinton's building for the Mutual Life Insurance Company of New York (see chapter 3).

In January 1866 a bill was introduced into the House of Representatives calling for a commission to select a site for the new post office. City Hall Park was an obvious choice, but some observers saw drawbacks to the proposed location and in April 1866 the editors of the *Real Estate Record and Builders' Guide* deemed the site "inappropriate not only for the requirements of the building itself, but for its destructive effects upon the commerce, convenience, and even health of our city." With the surrounding streets clogged with traffic, and City Hall Park one of the city's few oases, the editors asked, "Why willfully and gratuitously select the most inconveniently located piece of ground that could possibly have been found on the whole island—like a sugarloaf laid broadside—and this too, in one of the very few miserable little holes misnamed 'parks,' that in spite of former miscalculations, are still left the city

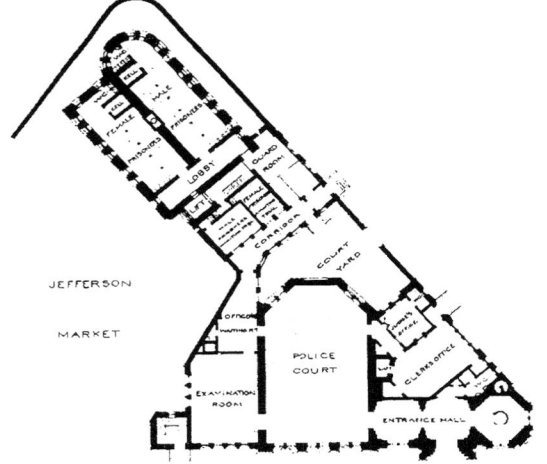

Third Judicial District Courthouse, site bounded by Sixth and Greenwich Avenues and West Tenth Street. Calvert Vaux and Frederick Clarke Withers, 1874–77. First-floor plan. NYDG. CU.

Proposed Third Judicial District Courthouse, site bounded by Sixth and Greenwich Avenues and West Tenth Street. Calvert Vaux and Frederick Clarke Withers, 1874. Rendering of view to the southwest. NYSB. CU.

Third Judicial District Courthouse, site bounded by Sixth and Greenwich Avenues and West Tenth Street. Calvert Vaux and Frederick Clarke Withers, 1874–77. View to the northwest showing the first Jefferson Market (1833) in the foreground. NYHS.

for breathing?" All in all, the editors deemed the project "a huge blunder, from beginning to end."[25] Three months later, however, the journal's editors began to come around, advocating the construction of the post office in the park, but only after all the existing buildings, including City Hall, were removed and the post office incorporated into a new complex of buildings specifically designed to capitalize on the site. The editors stated: "The City Hall Park, as it at present exists . . . looks as if a park, a fountain, and half a dozen public buildings had been shaken together in a huge dice-box, thrown out promiscuously, and left as chance located them."[26] Public protest notwithstanding, in December 1866 the city's Common Council agreed to sell 62,000 square feet of the lower end of City Hall Park to the federal government for $500,000, a transaction effected the following April. *Harper's Weekly* bemoaned the loss "of the fine open space at its most crowded point" while asking for the introduction of branch post offices to help speed up the mails.[27]

An open competition for the new building resulted in fifty-two submissions, which were put on pubic display in June 1867. The *New York Times* found the "majority of the designs . . . wanting in originality and appositeness" and suggested that "a result quite as satisfactory would have been reached at less expense, had an architect of standing been employed to select from among the public buildings

Proposed New York City Post Office, southern tip of City Hall Park, bounded by Park Row and Broadway. Alexander Jackson Davis, 1867. Competition-entry rendering showing view to the north. MMA.

of the world several of the most elegant, and combine their most excellent points."[28] Among the competition entries was a startlingly bold design by Alexander Jackson Davis that called for a circular, three-tiered, stone and glass building articulated with Roman orders.[29] Davis, who initially had objected to the proposed City Hall Park site, instead advocating one on the north side of Chambers Street between Broadway and Centre Street, resigned himself to the city's choice. Dismissing the competition's stipulation that the new building fill its site, Davis suggested a circular building that would leave room for landscaped plazas as well as more open sight lines to and from City Hall. The proposed building's geometry also held spiritual meaning for Davis: "The circle is . . . the most proper figure to show the unity, infinite essence, the uniformity and justice of God."[30] Synthesizing Classical elements with steel construction and extensive glazing, Davis piled atop a rusticated base two arcades and an attic, incorporating setbacks to achieve a memorable building profile. The building was to be crowned with a glass dome protecting a central courtyard below from the elements.

On December 28, 1867, the commissioners appointed to select a site and an architect for the new building announced that they were unable to make a single choice and submitted to the federal authorities a list of fifteen architects whose schemes they most admired. The com-

mission awarded the fifteen winners cash prizes, giving $2,000 each to John Correja, Richard Morris Hunt, Napoleon Le Brun, Schulze & Schoen, and Renwick & Sands. Prizes of $500 went to William Field & Son, Duncan J. MacRae, Potter & Clinton, Alexander Saeltzer, and James H. Giles. Prizes of $300 were given to Walter Dickson, Hammatt Billings, King & Wilcox, Louis Burger, and E.J.M. Derrick. The commission also announced its intention to have the five winners of the $2,000 prize collaborate on a design. Hunt was selected to be chairman of the resulting committee, which submitted a report in February 1868 that was forwarded on to Washington, D.C., where it was quickly approved. The *New York Daily Tribune* found the process repugnant and saw in it a metaphor for the building that would no doubt result from it: "The new Post-Office is to add another monster of ugliness to those we already have, and, what is worse, it has chosen at the same time the most inconvenient and the most conspicuous place in the whole city to air its ugliness in. Situated at the end of the City Hall Park, it will be like a boil on the end of a man's nose."[31]

Alfred B. Mullett, supervising architect of the Treasury Department, modified the collaborative design and was ultimately credited with it. Reflecting French Classical taste in the manner of the Palais des Tuileries and the Hôtel de Ville, in Paris, the three-story, pavilionated, gran-

United States Courthouse and Post Office, southern tip of City Hall Park, bounded by Park Row and Broadway. Alfred B. Mullett, 1869–75. View to the north. NYHS.

ite and white marble building rose to a mansard and, at its center, to a dome, while the south end facing down Broadway culminated in a cupola. The stone building incorporated cast-iron columns and wrought-iron girders that carried the interior loads. The building's ground floor was given over to the post office; the second and third floors along the north end of the building were intended for federal courts.

Ground was broken for the new building on August 9, 1869, in the presence of Mullett, who, according to the *New York Times*, had taken rooms across the street in the Astor House hotel to be near the scene of operations. The lawyer and prolific diarist George Templeton Strong noted:

> Yesterday they broke ground for the new Post Office at the south end of the City Hall Park, and today a great wooden enclosure is going up around its site. This will destroy the best-known and most characteristic street view in New York, viz., looking up from Fulton Street and Broadway across the Park to the South front of the old City Hall. "The Park" will be destroyed, but it has long survived its usefulness, except as a place for blackguard boys to pitch coppers in all day, and for thieves and ruffians to meander through all night.[32]

Given the time needed to excavate the 100,000 cubic yards of dirt to create the foundations and basements, and

because Congress was slow to authorize money for construction, the work dragged on fitfully. The superstructure began to take shape by spring 1871. At this time, with over $1,500,000 invested in the project, what remained of City Hall Park was being relandscaped, and as Mullett's design revealed itself, the once controversial project began to be more and more appreciated. In 1872 the formerly hostile editors of the *Real Estate Record and Builders' Guide* stated: "Since we were destined apparently to have the Post Office located where it is—a choice of location which to this day appears a very serious blunder—it is a matter of congratulations that the unwelcome intruder promises to be a building worthy of this great metropolis. Whether judged by its internal arrangement, its solidity of construction, or its effect externally, no public building hitherto erected in New York was ever more adapted to the purpose intended, or proved a greater ornament to the city than this will be when completed." The editors praised Mullett's use of rustication and careful stone modeling to enhance the building's inherent bulk. But it was the sheer mass that was its most impressive feature: here was a new scale of urban development. "When completed," the editors contended, "the Post Office will completely dwarf all other objects in the immediate neighborhood. The Astor House and *Herald* office will look as if they could be stowed away in some corner of its basement, and even the venerable City

Hall will shrink into the dimensions of some old-fashioned toy." On a related issue, the *Record and Guide*'s editors warned against the ill-conceived plan to add a new story crowned by a mansard roof to City Hall: "They had much better leave such a notion alone. Instead of thereby adding anything to the dignity or beauty of the City Hall, they would only be converting that old structure, with which nobody at present finds fault, and for which every one feels a sort of local veneration, into a pitiful object of architectural pretension and absurdity."[33] The mansard addition was never realized.

In 1872 Mullett revised the Post Office design, adding a fourth story and making the building, which was then estimated to cost $5,000,000, "larger than any granite or marble building yet completed by the Government outside the District of Columbia, and . . . not only the largest post-office building in the world" but one unequaled in its facilities.[34] By February 24, 1874, Strong recorded in his diary that the "skeleton of a great dome is slowly developing above the north front."[35] Because of the tight site and the congestion of the bounding streets, new techniques for coordinating the construction were developed involving

unusual amounts of off-site work. In May Strong returned to the subject, remarking that "no great building has ever grown so silently. . . . All hewing and stonecutting has been done miles away at the quarry, and it's strange how seldom one sees any workmen."[36]

At last, on August 25, 1875, the Post Office could be occupied, although construction on the upper portions of the building was abandoned until August 1876, when work began on the stairs, elevators, and attic. By the time the building was completed, in 1878, Mullett had quit and been replaced by William A. Potter, though Potter made no significant changes to the design. Nine years had gone by since construction began and eleven years since the site had been purchased by the federal government. As built, the trapezoidal building included a frontage of 240 feet facing what remained of City Hall Park, 340 feet on Broadway, 320 feet on Park Row, and 130 feet facing south toward the apex of the triangular site. The building rose 195 feet to a lantern on the south, 182 feet to a central dome, and 140 feet to corner pavilions. Inside, the floors were unusually spacious, with high ceilings: the first story was twenty-nine feet high and the floors above each

View to the northwest along Broadway from Ann Street, c. 1888, showing the Astor House (Isaiah Rogers, 1836) on the left and the United States Courthouse and Post Office (Alfred B. Mullet, 1869–75) on the right. NYHS.

twenty-two feet, except in the case of the courtrooms, which rose almost sixty feet from the second to the fourth floor. At the building's center, above the first floor, an open court brought light to inner offices. Ten freight and four passenger elevators, as well as seven spiral iron staircases, provided access to the upper floors. In the wake of the Draft Riots of 1863, the building may well have been designed as much with defense in mind as with justice or communication. The building's walls were ten and a half feet thick, built of iron-reinforced brick and Maine granite. In addition to the iron reinforcement, cement was used extensively to bind the structure together as a solid mass. Window frames were made of plate armor similar to that specified for battleships. The dome was birdcage-like in its construction but at a giant scale, with interlacing wrought-iron beams carrying the slate roof.

Montgomery Schuyler lambasted the Post Office as no small offense wrought upon the city by a self-trained architect. In 1874 the critic applauded the state senate's refusal to increase the budget for the project, arguing that the decision,

> whatever its motive, will have the good result of curbing the ambition of the uninstructed and incompetent Mr. Mullett and hinder him from making the Post Office still more ridiculous than it is. Mr. Mullett has already piled incongruous dormers on his pediments, and crowned his dormers with irrelevant fowls, and reared pavilions above his eagles, and crowned his pavilions with iron crests, and culminated his crests with domes, and surmounted his domes with cupolas; and now he wants $356,000 more to complete the heterogeneousness of his work by putting further nondescripts over his cupolas. . . . When we consider that with much less money, though to be sure much more brains, than he has spent on this building, Mullett might have produced instead of this incongruous jumble four respectable walls, pierced with respectable openings and covered with a respectable roof, the thirst of every cultivated spectator of his work for his blood is not appreciably allayed by the reflection that he will not get $356,000 to play more monkeyshines with.[37]

Schuyler, in a detailed review of the building, first put forward what would forever be the mixed reputation of Mullett's achievement: "The new Post-Office is the largest, the most conspicuous, many times the costliest and one of the most admired buildings in New York. It is also, we are sorry to have to say, one of the worst buildings in New York as a work of architectural art." Attacking Mullett's design from a point of view highly biased in favor of Gothic-inspired expressiveness, Schuyler faulted the design on virtually every possible count, including its failure to express on its exterior elements such as the high-ceilinged courtrooms or the dramatically spiraling stairs, charging that "evidently we have got rid of expression completely in this building, which means that we have got rid of architecture. For this is really the point. The artist exhibits; the sham artist conceals. Architecture is a face which reveals the idea behind it; sham architecture is a mask which reveals nothing."[38]

Police Stations and Firehouses

Until the passage of a new city charter in 1870, the police operated independently from city officials and therefore were beyond local politics. There was actually no city police force as such, but instead a "metropolitan police district" that incorporated the cities of New York and Brooklyn as well as Richmond, Westchester, and parts of Queens Counties.[39] After 1870 New York City had its own force, divided into two inspection districts, which by 1890 were subdivided into thirty-eight precincts, each with its own police station. As a result of this reorganization, a program of station-house construction was undertaken to supplement the existing stations, which fell far short of the number the new precincts required. Additionally, because the city lacked a municipally run system of social services, the police also provided temporary accommodation for homeless or inebriated New Yorkers; every precinct house was equipped with a jail.

In the early 1860s, the police department hired Nathanial D. Bush as its full-time architect in charge of designing new precinct houses and renovating existing ones. In 1869 Bush expanded the Police Headquarters Building at 300 Mulberry Street, between Bleecker and Houston Streets, adding to its north side a wing that maintained the

Police Headquarters Building, 300 Mulberry Street. Addition, Nathaniel D. Bush, 1869. View to the southeast. King, 1893. CU.

Italianate vocabulary of the older building in an extended, ninety-foot principal facade of white marble.[40] In an economizing measure, the Mott Street side was rendered in pressed brick, trimmed in marble. As the *New York Times* noted, "there is little or nothing about the building that strikes the observer as evidence of undue lavishness in the use of public money."[41] Bush's 14th Precinct House (c. 1870), at 205 Mulberry Street, between Kenmare and Spring Streets, mixed an Italianate vocabulary with a mansard roof.[42] His French Second Empire–style building for the 32nd Precinct, completed in 1872 at 1854 Tenth Avenue, on the southwest corner of 152nd Street (see chapter 6), was more interesting. When Bush returned to the Italianate style in his 6th Precinct House (1881), at 19–21 Elizabeth Street, between Bayard and Canal Streets, the *Real Estate Record and Builders' Guide* found the design "architecturally nothing but tenement house fronts, with no attempt towards a characteristic or expressive treatment."[43] Bush's 25th Precinct House (1887), at 153 East Sixty-seventh Street, represented a higher level of design, emulating a Florentine palazzo; the effect was nonetheless quite dull.[44] The police station shared a party wall with the New York City Fire Department Headquarters (see below).

Despite the fact that by the advent of the Civil War, fire had ravaged New York City seven times, most devastatingly in 1835 and 1845, firefighting was in the hands of volunteers until March 1865, when the state legislature created the Metropolitan Fire Department.[45] Telegraphy was used to alert station houses from manned fire towers and pull boxes were installed throughout the city, facilities that, together with the professionalism of the new department and its systems, quickly made New York's the nation's model fire department. The pattern of firehouse design that would prevail for a generation was set in 1878 with the introduction of the sliding pole, a Chicago invention, which permitted firemen to bunk on the second floor away from the smell of horses, whose hay, raised and lowered by iron jib hoists mounted to the facade, was stored on a higher floor still. With this new pattern in place, a significant building campaign got under way, with Napoleon Le Brun & Sons hired to design all of the firehouses constructed between 1878 and 1894.

Le Brun's Engine Company Number 13 (1881), at 99 Wooster Street, between Prince and Spring Streets, was a three-story building with masonry upper floors carried on an expressed cast-iron ground floor that was flanked by piers decorated with shields containing the engine company's insignia.[46] More exceptional was Le Brun's Fire Engineer House for Fire Hook & Ladder Company Number 15, at Old Slip, completed in 1884.[47] The freestanding building, unusual for its type, consisted of a two-story-high, one-hundred-by-twenty-five-foot main structure, with a twenty-five-by-twenty-five-foot one-story extension. The editors of the *Real Estate Record and Builders' Guide*, who characterized the building as "a refreshing novelty in municipal architecture," found "the

use of red and black brick in its walls . . . laid up in 'Flemish Bond'" the building's "most striking peculiarity." The handling of the walls was, they contended, "appropriate to the style of the building, which is apparently intended to recall the Dutch architecture of the seventeenth century at the time of the settlement of New Amsterdam, which was the primitive architecture of Old Slip." But, the editors noted, "In that case its use was founded upon a historical error, since the bond called 'Flemish' was not and is not used in Flanders or the Low Countries at all, but is almost exclusively English in spite of its name." Overlooking the fine points of historical scholarship, however, the editors acknowledged:

> Upon the whole, the new engine house is quaint and attractive and decidedly gives appropriate local color to the neighborhood. The alternation of red and black in the brickwork is so simple as to become monotonous when spread over so large a surface. If it had been confined to the lower story and a larger pattern used above the walls [it] would have been more effective. A good deal of quarreling might be done with the detail, but that would be unprofitable, considering how much better the building is than anything that could reasonably be expected of our municipal departments.[48]

Fire Engineer House for Fire Hook & Ladder Company Number 15, Front to Water Street, Old Slip to Gouverneur Lane. Napoleon Le Brun & Sons, 1884. View to the northeast. AR. CU.

Fire Engineer House for Fire Hook & Ladder Company Number 15, Front to Water Street, Old Slip to Gouverneur Lane. Napoleon Le Brun & Sons, 1884. View to the northeast. Bracklow. NYHS.

Montgomery Schuyler, writing in 1910, looked back on the station as "the most satisfactory" of the architect's buildings for the fire department, arguing that it was "an unpretentious piece of Dutch Renaissance, appropriate to a site within the confines of the Dutch settlement of Manhattan."[49]

Le Brun's Fire Engine Number 27 (1881–82), at 173 Franklin Street, between Hudson and Greenwich Streets, was a three-story, cast-iron and brick building combining elements of the Queen Anne and Neo-Grec styles, its uppermost story terminating in a foliated frieze and a pressed-metal cornice.[50] Also noteworthy were Le Brun's buildings for Fire Hook & Ladder Company Number 14, at 120 East 125th Street (see chapter 6), which adopted a Romanesque vocabulary, and Fire Engine Company Number 47 (1889–90), at 500 West 113th Street, between Broadway and Amsterdam Avenue, which synthesized Romanesque and Classical elements.[51] The three-story building was distinguished by a rusticated stone base, terra cotta quoining, and a richly decorated entablature surmounted by a dominant cornice.

As the city grew northward, a fire department with operations located at the southern tip of Manhattan made increasingly less sense. In 1887 the department moved its headquarters from what had been known as Firemen's Hall, on Mercer Street, to a new building designed by Le Brun, at 157 East Sixty-seventh Street, between Lexington and Third Avenues.[52] The New York City Fire Department Headquarters Building constituted much more than a typical station. It contained room for an engine and a new truck company, all the department's offices, and the complicated telegraph apparatus that made the system work. In a departure from his typical firehouse, Le Brun designed a six-story, mansarded, brownstone and brick, Romanesque-inspired building that filled every square foot of its fifty-by-one-hundred-foot lot. A lookout tower was included that, given its fifty-foot height and the natural elevation of the site, on clear days afforded watchmen the ability to observe all of Manhattan south to the Battery. The *Real Estate Record and Builders' Guide* greeted the building with almost unalloyed praise:

It is always a matter for public congratulation when the city of New York puts up a decent-looking building for any municipal purpose. The Fire Department was as bad as the rest [of the city's departments] until the Commissioners had the good sense to employ architects of repute to design new buildings, and selected Messrs. N. Le Brun & Sons for that purpose. The first good result of this retainer was an engine-house in Old Slip, which people who cared for architecture actually found themselves studying with interest. . . . The Department has now erected, from the designs of the same architects, a much more extensive and more interesting building, for its general headquarters on 67th Street, near Third Avenue. This is a five story building, or six counting the roof story, of 50 feet frontage. These dimensions seem unnecessarily large but, besides the headquarters proper, the building contains an engine-house, a hook-and-ladder house, the

Firemen's Hall, 157 East Sixty-seventh Street. Napoleon Le Brun & Sons, 1887. View to the north. AR. CU.

PLACES OF LEARNING

Throughout the post–Civil War period, Columbia College constituted New York's most respected institution of higher learning; founded in 1754 as King's College, it was also the city's oldest.[1] Colonial New York, in contrast to other American provinces, was neither a center of learning nor a center of learned people: in the 1740s, when a New York college was first seriously contemplated, the province numbered only fifteen college-educated men, exclusive of clergymen. After King's College had been instituted, the so-called Great Awakening, which had already had a significant impact on life in New England, began to affect the middle colonies. In 1784 the college was renamed Columbia, an eponym invented to describe the North American continent in commemoration of Christopher Columbus, and the school grew in both size and prestige. Between 1754 and 1857, the college occupied four locations. Initially classes, consisting of eight students taught by Professor Samuel Johnson, the first non-clergyman in the English-speaking world to serve as a college president, met in the vestry room of the Trinity Church schoolhouse. The college's first purpose-built home was completed in 1760 on Park Place, renamed College Place, occupying part of a parcel of land extending from the west side of Broadway between Murray and Barclay Streets westward to the Hudson River. The site was donated by the church, which had previously utilized it as King's Farm. The Reverend Andrew Burnaby, visiting from England before the college building's completion, somewhat hyperbolically characterized King's College as "the most beautifully situated of any college, I believe, in the world."[2] The four-story, approximately 40-by-150-foot brick and stucco building combined classrooms and dormitory space and faced south on the tree-shaded, fence-enclosed property. It was surmounted by a gracefully detailed, open cupola, which in turn supported a crown, a feature that was removed following national independence. Despite the college's ties to the Anglican Church, the long, relatively low silhouette of its new building established a distinctly secular and civic presence in a skyline still dominated by church spires.

During the Revolutionary War, classes were held at King's College's third venue, Leonard Lispenard's house on Wall Street. After the war, the school returned to College Place, but soon contemplated moving again, not so much because it had outgrown its facilities—the pattern of growth and subsequent overcrowding that would become a hallmark of the college's history had not yet begun—but to escape Lower Manhattan's increasingly dense and noisy environment. Moreover, the area adjacent to the college was turning into a red-light district. Columbia contemplated consolidating with Washington College on Staten Island and moving to that location, but the proposal was rejected and plans were drawn up in 1813 by the architect and Columbia professor James Renwick Sr. to expand and

gymnasium and "school of probation" of the department, and a watch-tower. These several uses the new building fulfills amply and comfortably, but with no apparent waste of room. The architectural basement is of two stories in rough brownstone, the superstructure in red brick relieved with the same material, except the upper stage or observatory of the tower, which is in metal.[53] Looking back from the vantage point of 1910, Montgomery Schuyler found the building "not a bigoted example" of the Richardsonian Romanesque, with a somewhat confused handling of the elements of the facade redeemed by the tower, which was "a practical as well as a picturesque feature, being both a belfry and a watch-tower," and particularly useful in its neighborhood of four-story brownstones.[54]

renovate the college's existing building. Renwick proposed an ambitious but ultimately unrealized Gothic-style library to which two symmetrically arranged classroom wings were to be added when required.[3] Instead, following a design by the architect James O'Donnell, the existing school building was expanded and reconfigured to incorporate two new wings, each fifty feet square. The original building's gables and cupola were removed and the facades reworked to adopt a simple Greek Revival style rendered in stucco. C. C. Haight, a Columbia graduate who later became the principal architect of its East Side campus (see below), would later recall, "How grand, how grand everything about the college seemed!—the stately sycamores on the green, venerable from age, overshadowing the edifice, the old building, the great staircase, the chapel with its strange hanging gallery, the dais at the east end."[4]

In 1814 the college petitioned the state legislature for a large, uptown site and that same year was given a property extending from Middle Road, later Fifth Avenue, to a point one hundred feet east of Sixth Avenue, and from the north side of Forty-seventh Street to the south side of Fifty-first Street. The site had been maintained by the Columbia professor of botany David Hosack as the Elgin Botanical Garden and was sold by him to the state in 1810. Approximately three miles north of the heart of the city, the location was considered by some to be too remote and rural (Madison Avenue was not open for use above Forty-ninth Street or paved above Forty-second Street).[5] In 1849 Columbia nonetheless began to consider the uptown move, in 1855 going so far as to hire Richard Upjohn to develop a comprehensive design for the land; Upjohn's plans are lost. Columbia concurrently rejected a plan to buy and remodel Cozzen's Hotel at West Point as well as a proposal to purchase a one-thousand-acre site in Westchester, where a complete university town was proposed.[6] Though college coffers were enhanced by the sale of the very valuable downtown campus, the school still lacked the funds sufficient for a full-scale building program. Thus Columbia remained downtown until May 1857, when it moved to its fourth location, a block-long site bounded by Madison and Fourth Avenues and Forty-ninth and Fiftieth Streets, occupying buildings formerly owned and used by the New York State Institution for Deaf Mutes.[7] That institution, opened in 1830, had selected its site because at that time the city, which owned much of the land in the area, sought to develop it as a district of charitable and publicly oriented organizations and offered sites to such groups at favorable prices.[8] By the 1880s Columbia could afford to undertake a major campus-building project but remained on its cramped block and did not utilize the larger botanical garden site nearby; leased to developers, that parcel was well on its way to becoming one of the college's most lucrative investments.

From the first, Columbia had envisioned the economically motivated move to the former asylum to be strictly temporary in nature. The editors of *Harper's New Monthly Magazine* would recall in 1884 that the college had been reluctant to move uptown, after nearly a hundred years, from "its home in that fine 'limehouse' with the cupola which the trustees had proudly completed in 1760. There had been extensions and additions, and the college was proud of its site, its grounds, and that umbrageous and delightful College Place . . . but now commerce was crowding it."[9] Columbia's College Place building was demolished in 1857 and replaced with commercial structures.[10]

The decision to leave the historic campus was masterminded by Columbia's president, Charles King, the editor of the *New York Courier and Enquirer*. Though himself not a college graduate, King had a broad vision not only for Columbia's future—which, in a characteristically pragmatic New York manner, he saw partially in terms of real estate considerations—but also for the expanding character of American higher education in general. Under his administration, a law school was founded in 1858, located on Great Jones Street, and the following year the College of Physicians and Surgeons was united with Columbia.

The *New York Evening Post* found the uptown setting most agreeable:

> The new location of the College is a delightful one, and undesirable only on account of the distance uptown—an objection which, by the tendency of population, will be in a few years obviated. The old Asylum buildings have been altered somewhat, repaired, and greatly improved. . . . A beautiful lawn slopes from the College southward down to 49th Street, and is ornamented by some fine old trees. This will be for the present the main entrance to the College, but as soon as the more extensive grounds northward to 50th Street can be graded, laid out, and properly embellished, the principal entrance will be in that direction. The site is on a commanding eminence, affording an extensive and pleasant view. That part of the city is still quite new, and the hand of improvement is visible in all directions.[11]

In reality, the setting was not quite so bucolic or even advantageous: to the east lay the tracks of the New York Central Railroad. Though the college saw this as a convenience and tried unsuccessfully to negotiate a deal for the construction of a new station nearby and a reduced-fare arrangement for commuting students and professors, with the increasing size of rail equipment and the number of daily trains the railroad would soon prove to be a problem neighbor. Another problem neighbor to the southwest, near Fifth Avenue and Forty-fifth Street, were the noisy and malodorous Bull's Head cattle yards. In 1871 a college commission looked into acquiring other sites, including nearby lots, with the hope that the city might authorize street closures, allowing for the creation of a larger campus within the street grid. The city refused. Nine years later Columbia would fail in its efforts to purchase all or part of the block bounded by Madison and Fourth Avenues and Fiftieth and Fifty-first Streets, the Madison Avenue frontage of which became the site of the Villard Houses (see chapter 4).

Before erecting any buildings on its Forty-ninth Street site, Columbia renovated the existing asylum building,

Columbia College, Fourth to Madison Avenue, East Forty-ninth to East Fiftieth Street. Rendering, c. 1890, showing view to the northwest with St. Patrick's Cathedral (James Renwick Jr., 1850–79, 1888) on the upper left. Columbiana. CU.

adding to it a long Ionic portico facing Forty-ninth Street. To its west, a circular building, nicknamed by undergraduates the Cow House, was made to serve as an astronomy observatory, and to the east a two-story wing was fitted out with a chapel below and a library above. So decrepit was the former asylum building that even following renovation large flakes frequently fell off its exterior walls. Located close to the depressed but open New York Central Railroad tracks that were traveled by coal-fired steam engines, the building was filled with smoke similar to that produced by a "punk," a smoky and slow-burning type of match. Later on, when the building was home to engineering and architecture students, it was irreverently referred to as the "Maison de Punk."[12] In 1862 an architecturally straightforward, mansarded president's house was completed on the campus's southeast corner. After the Civil War, as the college began to grow rapidly, transforming itself into a university, new buildings were required to house its different programs. In 1874 the college completed the first section of its building for the School of Mines, founded ten years earlier as the nation's first such school.[13] The new building, fronting Fiftieth Street on the northeast corner of the campus, replaced the School of Mines's first home, a run-down building on the same site that had been a window-blind factory, leading waggish observers to quip that Columbia was home to the deaf, dumb, and blind. To design its new School of Mines the college turned to C. C. Haight, who produced a Ruskin-inspired, four-story brick and Belleville sandstone Gothic composition. In 1884 the School of Mines completed the second, six-story portion of its building, also designed by Haight, connected to the existing building and fronting Fourth Avenue; at the same time, Haight added two stories on to the previously completed wing. The newer portion of the building housed, on its fourth floor, the city's first academic program in architecture, founded in 1881 as part of the School of Mines by William R. Ware.[14] University president Frederick A. P. Barnard, who had succeeded Charles King in 1864, had called Ware to Columbia from Boston; Ware had founded the School of Architecture at the Massachusetts Institute of Technology twenty years earlier. Ware had been lured to Columbia not only by the promise of a doubled salary but also by Barnard's assurance that he would have a free hand in shaping the new school.

Despite the superior accommodations in the School of Mines's new building, students continued to call it the Maison de Punk. Occupying a prominent corner site at a time when the neighborhood was still largely undeveloped, Haight's building could, according to Montgomery Schuyler, "be best seen . . . from the track and the trains, from which it remained a welcome sight to the approaching visitor or returning wayfarer . . . , a nearly cubical mass, with a steep roof, and some peculiarity of the plan [that] allowed it an unusual and very grateful expanse of blank wall, punctuated in the second story with double windows, embraced under pointed arches, with the tympana left solid." Schuyler considered the design "fairly successful" and

a very straightforward piece of work, which relied for its effect upon the disposition of its masses, and in which the decoration was the mere expression of the construction. The fragment of two bays, with two arched openings in the second story, an arcade of single arches in the third, and a pair of dormers breaking the expanse of the roof, was in itself very good. So was the homely little staircase tower at the inner corner. But the things did not go together very well, and in the principal mass of the building the things were not very good in themselves. . . . What remained admirable in the work was the straightforward and simple handling of detail; but this straightforwardness, though it lies at the base of artistic success, is scarcely itself an artistic quality.[15]

Inside, where the brickwork was left exposed so that only the ceilings were plastered, there were lecture rooms large enough to seat one hundred students and laboratories sufficient for eighty, as well as a library and various rooms to house specimen collections. According to the *New-York Sketch-Book of Architecture*, the "furniture and fittings were made expressly for the school and are the result of careful observation and experiment."[16]

In 1880, the college trustees closed in the west end of the campus with a fifty-five-foot-wide, two-hundred-foot-long, brick and sandstone building, Hamilton Hall, designed by Haight to complement his School of Mines.[17] The new building replaced an old house on the southeast corner of Fiftieth Street and Madison Avenue as well as the west wing of the original Maison de Punk. Whereas all of Columbia's previous buildings had faced the street, Hamilton Hall faced the interior of the block, where a quadrangle was being formed, creating, despite the unwillingness of the city to close intervening streets, that feeling of cloistered campus enclosure already characteristic of Columbia's leading urban rivals, Harvard and Yale. Inside the building there were four large classrooms as well as recitation rooms, faculty offices, and, over the entrance, the president's room, lit by an oriel window that commanded a view of the quadrangle. Significantly—or perhaps ironically—the trustees' room faced Madison Avenue. In his 1881 survey of public buildings in New York, written before the building's completion, Montgomery Schuyler stated that its

style might be called the Oxford mode, or very late Gothic, best seen in much of the collegiate architecture of the English university towns. The building will be low and long, having above a high basement, three stories and an attic. The western flank will have no entrance, but opens upon the inner or quadrangle face, in the center of which is a broad, projecting porch with groined ceiling, while over it is an oriel window, corbeled out with a

Columbia School of Mines, southwest corner of Fourth Avenue and East Fiftieth Street. C. C. Haight, 1874, 1884. View to the southwest. Columbiana. CU.

Hamilton Hall, Columbia College, east side of Madison Avenue, East Forty-ninth to East Fiftieth Street. C. C. Haight, 1880. View to northeast showing the Villard Houses (McKim, Mead & White, 1882–85) on the left. NYHS.

conspicuous feature, and rising above the attic story. . . .
Within, the halls and classrooms will be finished in brick of
a light tint with a strongly contrasted pointing. . . . The heating will be indirect radiation, though heat by direct radiation
will be gained by two fireplaces in each classroom.[18]

Schuyler applauded Hamilton Hall as "perhaps the most
important, and pretty certainly the most interesting of all
the recent buildings" in New York, finding in Haight's
design the balance between stylistic coherence and invention that he so often sought but found wanting in the work
of other New York architects: "The 'features' of the design,
a rich oriel, an angle turret, and groups of tall chimney-
stacks, are very cleverly introduced so as to relieve what
would otherwise be a tame composition, without disturbing the quiet and cloistral aspect of the building. . . . This
is the most scholarly and best studied of Mr. Haight's
work." Schuyler, ever campaigning against the Queen
Anne, particularly liked the building because "it makes no
attempt at novelty, but only at excellence, and might furnish a text on the disadvantages of eclecticism."[19]

In 1884, *Harper's New Monthly Magazine* praised both
Haight's Hamilton Hall and his overall campus planning:

> Columbia has found her permanent home and her archi-
> tect has had to meet the difficult problem of housing a
> great and growing university within the contracted limits
> of a city block. The difficulty has been very well met by
> planning a double quadrangle. . . . Mr. C. C. Haight has
> had the good sense to plan from within outward, instead
> of cramping interior accommodations to provide for
> architectural effects, and the result of "decorating con-
> struction and not constructing decoration" has been as
> happy as it is honestly reached. The general style of the
> new buildings is the English collegiate—of whose early
> examples at the English universities Mr. Haight has been
> a careful student—worked out in red brick and Potsdam
> sandstone. . . . In planning [Hamilton Hall], each profes-
> sor was given an opportunity to state his needs, and the
> windows, and consequently the entire facade, were
> worked accordingly. A graceful and slender bastion tower
> at the upper corner and a hanging bay give variety of
> effect to this front, and make it, although there are no
> doorways to provide striking features, an architectural
> adornment of Madison Avenue.[20]

So highly regarded was the design of Hamilton Hall that
in an 1885 poll of the best buildings in the United States,
the *American Architect and Building News* reported, the
building ranked as number fifteen.[21]

Montgomery Schuyler returned to the subject of
Haight's Columbia work in his 1899 monograph on the
architect. According to Schuyler, Haight "had studied"
his School of Mines "with greater care than any other
critic, and had extracted from it whatever lessons it had
to teach. . . . It is very rare indeed that such a progress can
be discerned in the work of an architect within six years."
For Schuyler, Hamilton Hall was a

> distinct and unqualified success. There are very few
> buildings in New York that have worn so well and been

Hamilton Hall, Columbia College, east side of Madison Avenue, East Forty-ninth to East Fiftieth Street. C. C. Haight, 1880. View to the southeast. NYHS.

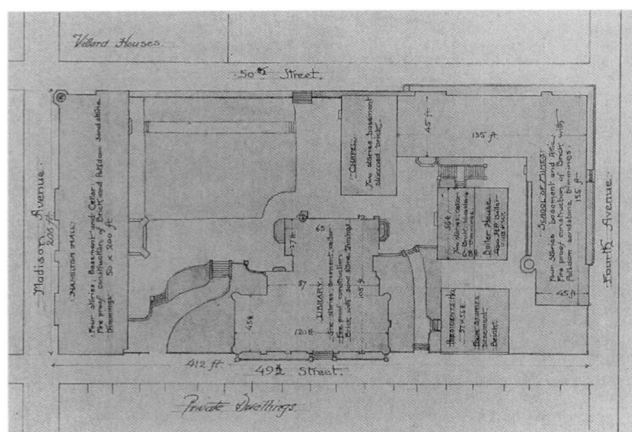

Library, Columbia College, East Forty-ninth Street between Fourth and Madison Avenues. C. C. Haight, 1882–83.
View to the southeast showing the Columbia College quadrangle in the foreground. Columbiana. CU.

Columbia College, Fourth to Madison Avenue, East Forty-ninth
to East Fiftieth Street. Map drawn for property sale, c. 1897.
Drawings Collection. CU.

regarded by people who care about architecture with such repeated pleasure. . . . The enormous advance it marks upon its predecessor seems to preach a sermon upon the disadvantages of eclecticism. . . . It is one of the lessons of the building how fully the requirements of a modern college can be met without transcending the limits of historical Gothic. The building is not, and indeed if it were faithfully designed for its purpose could not be, a mere reproduction of an old work. And yet it would take its place in the High Street of Oxford, or among the "backs" of Cambridge, without a jar, much less of incongruity, indeed, than almost any of the modern additions to those ancient seats of learning. . . . The air of seclusion and repose has been as completely attained on a bustling New York avenue as in the sleepiest of old college towns, and is almost more grateful, by reasons of its unexpectedness.[22]

Haight followed Hamilton Hall with a mixed-use building (1882–83) housing both the Law School and the

![Library, Columbia College]

Library, Columbia College, East Forty-ninth Street between Fourth and Madison Avenues. C. C. Haight, 1882–83. View to the northwest showing Hamilton Hall (C.C. Haight, 1880) on the far left. AR. CU.

School of Arts as well as a chapel and library, the latter having 120 feet of frontage on Forty-ninth Street and 100 feet of depth.[23] The five-story basement and subcellar brick structure, known only as the Library, adopted the "English Collegiate Style," with interior walls of pressed white and red brick and floors of iron carried on brick arches. The lower stories of the building were occupied by the Law School, but the upper portion was dominated by one large room, 120 feet long, 40 feet wide, and 75 feet high, that served as the main hall of the library, with a triple-arch wood and iron ceiling, scrollwork spandrels, iron tension rods emanating from the mouths of grotesques, and massive twin fireplaces. The room's truss-work eliminated the need for any divisions at floor level. "Here, of course," Russell Sturgis wrote in 1883, "there is no sham construction at all, nor any concealing of the construction. Here the stone and brick wall surface without and the brick wall surface within are merely the two faces of the massive wall with which, indeed, there is a narrow

Library, Columbia College, East Forty-ninth Street between Fourth and Madison Avenues. C. C. Haight, 1882–83. View to the southwest showing a corner of the original classroom building on the far right. AR. CU.

Library, Columbia College, East Forty-ninth Street between Fourth and Madison Avenues. C. C. Haight, 1882–83. Reading room. Columbiana. CU.

open space kept for dryness, but which is otherwise a solid piece of masonry. Upon this the roof of wood and iron rests in the most simple and obvious way. . . . This is a really beautiful design, one of the finest things New York contains."[24] The editors of *Harper's New Monthly Magazine* were also enthusiastic, characterizing the whole building as "one of the chief architectural features of this notable group of buildings" and its interior "altogether a most honest and noble piece of work. . . . The most important interior feature of the new building is the noble library hall, a room of grand proportions." The editors went on to note that the building was placed so close to the original classroom building to the north—only inches away—that students had nicknamed the space in between "the Pass of Thermopylae."[25]

Mariana Van Rensselaer was taken with the library's reading room, finding in its combination of "large windows above, and small ones, rather widely spaced, below" an arrangement that provided "the best illumination while avoiding the shut-up feeling that comes when all the openings are above the level of the eye." She admired the ceiling as well as the general finish of the room, with its pale yellow brick walls "diversified by bands of dull red . . . [a] sort of interior finish, [that] though common in England, is a novelty with us, and worthy of remark since it offers a fortunate way of securing color in the fabric itself—color that is absolutely permanent as well as satisfactory." Van Rensselaer contended, however, that "the great feature of the room" was the square-sectioned red brick arch flanked by the stairways that led to the upper shelves:

> Its beauty of form and great size—thirty-four by thirty-six feet—gives dignity and distinction to the whole composition, and turns what might have been merely excellent into an extremely imposing apartment. Meeting a structural necessity—that of really uniting the two rooms—in the frankest and the simplest way it gives us a touch of freedom, originality, and grandeur that we should never have got from an architect to whom his craft was a formulated thing of laws and precedents, and not a practical and vital art. . . . I do not know of any recent interior which surpasses this in showing how true and impressive architectural beauty may be produced in the most simple structural way. . . . It is as *natural* a piece of work as one could well imagine, and as beautiful in its severely simple way.[26]

Despite the abundant praise from other critics, Montgomery Schuyler was rather cool to Haight's design. "Not by any means that the library was architecturally a failure," he wrote in 1899, "but it would have required a very brilliant success indeed not to be an anti-climax after Hamilton Hall. The library is merely a correct and rather common-place piece of Gothic, the kind of competent and not inspired performance, which, if it were German music, would be known in the land of its birth as 'kapellmeistermusik.'" Haight's composition reminded Schuyler of the Free Academy (which had become the College of the City of New York on March 30, 1866), on the southeast corner of Twenty-third Street and Lexington Avenue, completed in 1849, a building he felt to be "in general composition . . . not at all bad," but not one that worked well for a library. Like Sturgis and Van Rensselaer, Schuyler found Haight's interior "a very notable success," though he did not like the exterior: "The relation of the two virtually equal lower stories, either to each other or to the tall upper story, is not fortunate, nor is the sub-division of the wall throughout the whole height by buttresses, nor the treatment of these."[27]

Whatever the attributes of the college's individual buildings, it was the campus as a whole that made Haight's work so outstanding. The *Real Estate Record and Builders' Guide* asserted:

> The new buildings of Columbia College . . . taken together, constitute by far the most important piece of public architecture now under construction in New York. Even more undisputably they constitute the best. . . . Nothing about the work is more noteworthy than the advance shown by the later work upon the earlier. The architecture is throughout Gothic, but the earlier buildings are in a free and "eclectic" version of Gothic, while the later are much more historically and academically correct. In the earlier building it is also evident, the architect was more straitened for money than in the later.

The earlier buildings were flatter, with much more emphasis on pattern, achieved through the use of blackened brick, giving a restless effect different from the "quietness and force of composition . . . as well as . . . effectiveness of detail" in the newer work. The Madison Avenue front "is known to lovers of architecture as one of the best things in New York," but the Fourth Avenue frontage, which incorporated older work, "is not so elaborate or successful a composition." In conclusion, the *Record and Guide*, voicing the claim that the best architecture faithfully expressed the requirements of a building, saw Columbia's success as the product of "that process, and not to a straining after originality and individuality."[28]

Perhaps Van Rensselaer best summed up Haight's contribution to Columbia and to the rapidly evolving movement toward quadrangular campus planning that was shared by other colleges, particularly Yale and Harvard, finding his plan "an extremely effective and picturesque group resulting from the intelligent and artistic resolution of a difficult problem." Van Rensselaer stated:

> It was not an easy task to take such a site—one single city block—and yet secure such ample accommodation and illumination with so much external variety and charm— so much diversity, and, at the same time so much harmony. The little college yard, too, has been preserved— fortunately for practical reasons, and also for the sake of exceptional interest. The style chosen for the work—a late type of English Gothic—is appropriate here at least, and is used with great intelligence and taste, though with a freedom which is a different thing from mere grammatical precision.[29]

In his 1926 history of Columbia, Robert Arrowsmith

would similarly comment on the effectiveness of the early quadrangle plan: "Although confined to the narrow limits of a city block, the old College managed to retain an effect of spaciousness and remoteness not warranted by its actual dimensions."[30]

Even as Frederick A. P. Barnard was reshaping Columbia from a provincial college into a cosmopolitan university, most of its students continued to come from New York's traditional elite. The majority of the students lived at home. Some lived near the campus in rented rooms or in college clubs such as the chapter house of Delta Psi (see below), but none lived on campus. Columbia lacked not only the space for residence halls such as were then being built at Harvard and Yale but, given the school's lingering provincialism, the administration also neglected to understand the role on-campus living accommodations played in transforming the college into a national institution. Columbia also lacked substantial athletic facilities. In 1887, the class of 1886 started a fund for the purpose of building a gymnasium, and additional money was contributed by older alumni.[31] The head of the architecture program, William R. Ware, assisted by the firm of Little &

Connor, drew up plans for a T-shaped building of three stories and a basement to contain a wide array of facilities including bowling alleys, a baseball cage, billiards tables, and a running track. Because no site had been procured, the project advanced slowly. In 1890 a renewed effort was made to create the facilities as a membership club along the lines of the Manhattan or New York Athletic Clubs, but by then Columbia was arranging to relocate from midtown Manhattan to the rural isolation of Morningside Heights so the project was never realized.

The decision to move far uptown was being made even as the college planned to continue its expansion at the midtown location. As late as 1888 plans were under way for a seven-story, forty-by-one-hundred-foot, red brick and Potsdam redstone, Collegiate Gothic building designed by C. C. Haight, intended to replace the former asylum building, which was ultimately demolished in 1891.[32] Haight's building was never realized. The last construction on the midtown campus was completed in 1889, the extension of a two-story, fifty-six-by-fifty-six-foot boiler house, built ten years earlier, into a four-story building to house the electrical-engineering faculty on its upper floors.[33]

College of Physicians and Surgeons, 437 West Fifty-ninth Street. W. Wheeler Smith, 1886. View to the northwest. CUHSD.

In 1884 the editors of *Harper's New Monthly Magazine* asserted: "After many false starts, Columbia College has at last physically and intellectually begun to build thoroughly the foundation of a true metropolitan university." The editors further stated: "The progress of the last ten years points to the possibility of a university in this great commercial city which, like the great city universities of the Renaissance, shall attract thousands of students by the facilities for study which only a great centre of civilized activity can supply."[34] While the journal's optimism would prove justified in terms of Columbia's academic quality, by the late 1880s it was clear that the college could no longer be accommodated on its limited campus. When Barnard College was established in 1889 for the education of women, it had to content itself with facilities in a former townhouse at 343 Madison Avenue, between Forty-fourth and Forty-fifth Streets.[35] This was understandable given the fledgling nature of the enterprise. But one of Columbia's most important colleges, the College of Physicians and Surgeons, had gone unhoused on the campus for more than twenty-five years. King's College had founded a medical school in 1767, the second such school in the Western Hemisphere (the first, the College of Philadelphia's medical school, had been founded two years earlier), but six years later the College of Physicians and Surgeons opened and immediately established itself as a more prestigious institution. The Columbia school closed, and its entire faculty joined its rival. The College of Physicians and Surgeons was located on Park Place from its founding until 1837, when it moved to Crosby Street. In 1855 the College of Physicians and Surgeons moved to the southeast corner of Fourth Avenue and Twenty-third Street, and four years later the expanded facility became part of Columbia.[36] But by this time the medical school's independence was so entrenched that when, in 1884, it announced that it had retained W. Wheeler Smith to prepare plans for a new home, the site was about as far across Manhattan from Columbia's campus as it could be, adjoining the newly organized Roosevelt Hospital on the east side of Tenth Avenue between Sixtieth and Sixty-first Streets.[37] The project did not get under way in earnest until late 1885, when a substantial gift from William H. Vanderbilt made it possible to acquire a site, a midblock parcel running from Fifty-ninth to Sixtieth Street between Ninth and Tenth Avenues, with the Roosevelt and Sloan Maternity Hospitals (see chapter 6) to the west and the Church of St. Paul the Apostle (see chapter 6) to the northeast. Here Smith designed a rather severely articulated, H-shaped, red brick, terra cotta–trimmed, three-story-and-basement building (1886) surmounted by a series of low hipped roofs and a cupola that complemented the lively profiles of the adjacent hospitals. The medical school's principal entrance, at 437 West Fifty-ninth Street, was enhanced by a monumental semicircular archway.

In 1888, the Bloomingdale Insane Asylum decided to leave its campus on Morningside Heights for a new start well beyond the city line in White Plains, the seat of Westchester County.[38] According to the *New York Times*, local community groups had been actively protesting the asylum's presence and, the newspaper predicted, the institution's move would have positive benefits for the development of upper Manhattan: "While the wonderful transformation of the west side from a succession of rocky hills into a beautiful residential district has been in progress, this refuge for maniacs has remained a barrier and an obstacle to the onward march of population." By February 1892 the trustees of Columbia had determined to acquire the Bloomingdale Insane Asylum's land and move the college to Morningside Heights. The *New York Times* applauded Columbia's decision to move far uptown:

> The trouble with the present site of Columbia is twofold. It is overcrowded and it is swamped. . . . When Columbia removed from College Place to its present site, the site was much more remote from the activities of the city than the proposed site near Morningside Park is now. Since that time the college has been surrounded and overwhelmed by the march of improvements. . . . No expansion is possible on this site. Even if it were possible it would not be desirable, for a college community can no more be maintained in a quarter so busy than it could be maintained in the heart of the commercial quarter. . . . An undergraduate of Columbia, while it remains between Madison Avenue and the "yard" of the Grand Central Station, can no more be a member of a scholastic community than he was a member of such a community at the day school at which he fitted for college, and the dust of which he gladly shook from his feet at the close of recitation hours. What the college needs is a place that is not only sufficiently spacious, but also that is sequestered; a place that shall substitute the atmosphere of learning and science for the atmosphere of business and society.

The *Times* also conjectured that the decision of the college to join the Protestant cathedral on Morningside Heights "will attract to their neighborhood not only the men charged with the working of both of them, but a community of quiet and scholarly people, who will convert the neighborhood into a 'close,' to adopt the expressive English term, into an academic quarter such as New York does not now possess, and as Columbia cannot possess while it remains where it is now."[39] The student newspaper, the *Columbia Spectator*, advocated the move to Morningside Heights, succinctly stating, "It is safe to say that the advantages of the [new] grounds have, if anything, been underrated."[40]

While Columbia was far and away the most important institution of higher learning in New York to undertake significant building during the post–Civil War era, in 1873 another noteworthy school, the Normal and High School for the Female Grammar Schools of the City of New York, found in 1869 and renamed the Normal College of the City of New York one year later, abandoned a rented space at Fourth Street and Broadway and moved into a large, purpose-built facility occupying a full-block, campuslike site bounded by Fourth and Lexington Avenues and Sixty-eighth and Sixty-ninth Streets.[41] The college, which incorporated a model kindergarten and grammar school staffed by college students, served as a principal training ground for the city's public-school teachers. As designed by the architect David I. Stagg, working closely with the college's first president, Thomas Hunter, the college's grand, cathedral-like building, housing a spacious main hall, three lecture rooms, and thirty recitation rooms, was set back from the surrounding streets on landscaped grounds. The building's richly Gothic vocabulary, complete with pointed-arch windows and a dominant, square entrance tower terminating in corner pinnacles, made it a crown jewel in a neighborhood of institutional facilities, including the Union Theological Seminary (see below), the Lenox Library (see below), and the Presbyterian, German, and Mount Sinai Hospitals (see below).

Seminaries

To educate the Protestant clergy, the city supported two leading seminaries. Four years after its founding in 1817 by the General Convention of the Episcopal Church, the General Theological Seminary, which began with a class of six students taught in St. Paul's Chapel and ultimately became the largest seminary under the jurisdiction of the Protestant Episcopal Church, acquired the entire block between Twentieth and Twenty-first Streets and Ninth and Tenth Avenues.[42] The generously scaled site, known as Chelsea Square, had been given to the seminary by Clement Clarke

Moore, a Chelsea landowner who later would write the classic children's poem "A Visit from St. Nicholas." Montgomery Schuyler noted the site's highly favorable qualities: "Chelsea Square is that region in that settled and crowded part of New York, which an architect would be apt to select for the creation of a cloistral quarter, even if the whole island had been before him."[43] The seminary's first building was opened in 1826 and ten years later a near twin followed on what remained for several decades, until rowhouses began to surround it, little more than a clearing in an undeveloped outpost of the city. Both buildings, early examples in New York of the Gothic Revival, here rendered in gray stone, set the stylistic tone for the seminary's later developments. In the 1880s, under the direction of its well-heeled, well-connected, Harvard-educated dean, Eugene Augustus Hoffman, who also contributed significant sums of money to the effort, the seminary, after considering a move to a site at Seventy-ninth Street and the East River, expanded in its Chelsea Square location.

Hoffman retained C. C. Haight for the project. Haight's father had taught at the seminary in the 1840s and 1850s, and the junior Haight had in 1872 helped with renovations to one of the seminary's original buildings. Haight was a logical choice as the campus's architect given his work for Columbia College and also because his stylistic speciality, the Collegiate Gothic, fit in perfectly with the seminary's self-conception. Between 1884 and 1904

Normal College of the City of New York, Lexington to Fourth Avenue, East Sixty-eighth to East Sixty-ninth Street. David I. Stagg, 1873. View to the northeast. NYHS.

General Theological Seminary, Ninth to Tenth Avenue, West Twentieth to West Twenty-first Street. C. C. Haight, 1884–1904. View to the east, c. 1919, of buildings lining the East Quadrangle. GTS.

Haight completed sixteen buildings for the seminary in fulfillment of his master plan, which called for a continuous line of four- and six-story buildings along Twenty-first Street and Ninth and Tenth Avenues as well as two three-story buildings along Twentieth Street. Together these buildings defined the periphery of a large greensward internally interrupted only by the Memorial Chapel of the Good Shepherd, the presence of which divided the overall space into two quadrangles. Hoffman noted that "the function of the grounds as a private park is interfered with as little as possible."[44] In some ways Haight surpassed his success at Columbia, creating one of the most visually harmonious groupings realized in New York in the post–Civil War era. Reviewing the architect's work in 1899, Montgomery Schuyler praised the General Theological Seminary's campus as "the most complete and most homogeneous collegiate 'plant'" he knew of, with the exception of the University of Chicago, with its 1893 master plan by Henry Ives Cobb.[45] Close inspection revealed, however, that Haight's design, rendered in red brick and brownstone, also encompassed a subtle melding of architectural characteristics; as *The Churchman* stated, the structures "carry out admirably the idea of a range of buildings half monumental and half domestic in character, which marks the collegiate architecture of Oxford and Cambridge."[46]

Haight had an advantage at the seminary that he lacked at Columbia: space. The Columbia campus was two hundred by four hundred feet; the Chelsea site was two hun-

dred by eight hundred feet. Additionally, unlike Columbia, the seminary incorporated dormitory space and thus constituted the most fully realized academic campus—a largely self-contained community dedicated to scholarship—in New York. The *Real Estate Record and Builders' Guide* made the telling point that Haight's plan for the development of the grounds was

> one of the most complete plans for a collegiate establishment in the country, more complete than that at Columbia, where the students do not reside and where the chief element of collegiate architecture, the cloistral life which gives the chief charm to the buildings of Oxford and Cambridge, is thus perforce lacking. . . . Moreover, the frontage is half as long again as that of the buildings at Columbia, while the depth is the same, and length is a great advantage in carrying out the idea of a "range" of buildings . . . which is also characteristic of collegiate architecture.[47]

Sherred Hall (1883–84), a brick and Belleville stone, slate-roofed, three-story, eighty-by-thirty-foot classroom building, was Haight's first seminary building to be completed. Located on the north side of the East Quadrangle, the hall set the tone for the complex with its simple, gently modeled silhouettes and massing as well as impressed the editors of the *Real Estate Record and Builders' Guide*, who found that "in a time when architecture is running so much to 'palatial magnificence,' and the distinction between art and luxury is so extensively lost sight of, that it is especially interesting to see an artistic use made of simple materials and a plain treatment."[48]

General Theological Seminary, Ninth to Tenth Avenue, West Twentieth to West Twenty-first Street. C. C. Haight, 1884–1904.
View to the northeast, c. 1910, showing the Chapel of the Good Shepherd (C. C. Haight, 1886) on the left. GTS.

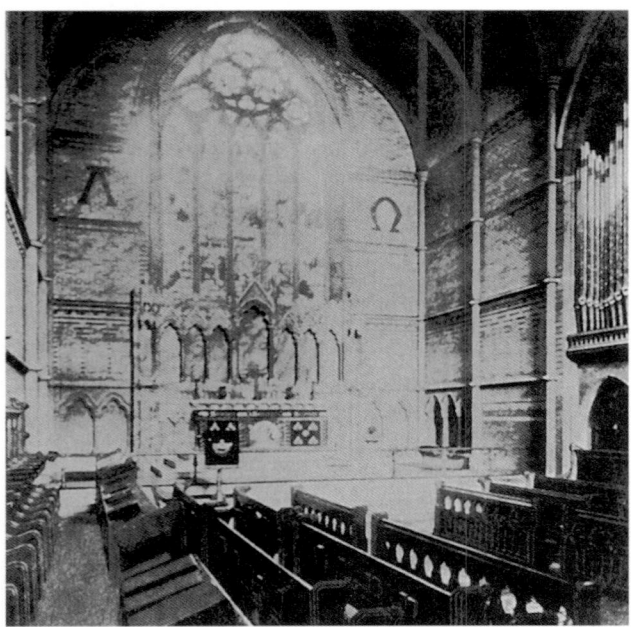

Chapel of the Good Shepherd, General Theological Seminary,
south side of West Twentieth Street between Ninth and Tenth
Avenues. C. C. Haight, 1886. View toward the altar. AR. CU.

Except for Sherred Hall, most of the buildings undertaken according to Haight's plan were paid for fully or in
part by Eugene Augustus Hoffman or a member of his
family. These included dormitories, which Schuyler characterized as "mere curtain walls, so to say, between the central
pavilion of the recitation building [Sherred Hall] and the
end pavilion of the library and chapel";[49] the Chapel of the
Good Shepherd (1886), the bell tower of which was modeled on the tower of Magdalen College, Oxford; the
administration building, deanery, and library (all 1887),
facing Ninth Avenue; and Hoffman Hall (1900), at the
northwest corner of the quadrangle. The chapel, arguably
the most elegant of Haight's designs for the seminary, was
distinguished by a towering, square campanile and a double
main entrance enclosed by a pointed arch. Inside, the sanctuary, reminiscent of those at Oxford and Cambridge, was
simply articulated, with walls incorporating decorative patterns rendered in contrasting red and yellow Roman brick,
punctuated by stained-glass windows made by the studio of
Lavers & Westlake, in London. Hoffman Hall, distinguished on the exterior by an octagonal staircase tower terminating in an ogee turret, housed a gymnasium below and
a refectory above. The gloriously articulated, notably vast,
oak-paneled dining room incorporated a triple-arch cof-

General Theological Seminary, Ninth to Tenth Avenue, West Twentieth to West Twenty-first Street. C. C. Haight, 1884–1904. View to the southwest from Ninth Avenue. AR. CU.

Hoffman Hall, General Theological Seminary, southwest corner of Ninth Avenue and West Twenty-first Street. C. C. Haight, 1900. View to the northeast from the East Quadrangle. GTS.

Hoffman Hall, General Theological Seminary, southwest corner of Ninth Avenue and West Twenty-first Street. C. C. Haight, 1900. Rendering of the refectory. Haight Collection. CU.

Rendering of proposed Union Theological Seminary, St. Nicholas Avenue between West 130th and West 134th Streets. Richard Morris Hunt, 1873. The Octagon, AAF.

Union Theological Seminary, west side of Fourth Avenue, East Sixty-ninth to East Seventieth Street. William A. Potter, assisted by James Brown Lord, 1884. View to the west. UTS.

Union Theological Seminary, west side of Fourth Avenue, East Sixty-ninth to East Seventieth Street. William A. Potter, assisted by James Brown Lord, 1884. View to the northwest. UTS.

fered ceiling supported by cast-iron beams covered by carved oak, and also contained, at its east end, a musicians' gallery decorated with carved oak lions playing viols.

Montgomery Schuyler was lavish in his praise of Haight's seminary campus:

> If the result be "a Tudor-chimneyed bulk of mellow brickwork on an isle of bowers," and we find it charming, its charm is not of the scenic kind, but the real thing, and has been obtained, not by any denial or suppression of the actual conditions, but only by the artistic affirmation and expression of them. . . . It seems to me to be its author's masterpiece, and as exemplary as it is beautiful. It is a public benefaction as well as an artistic achievement thus to create an oasis of beauty and repose in the "fumum et opes strepitumque" of our modern Rome, to bring back to a happily passed-over and neglected and rather shabby quarter of New York, as it were, "The sound of doves in quiet neighborhoods."[50]

Union Theological Seminary, founded by nine Presbyterians in 1835, opened for instruction in 1836, by which time it had already secured eight lots to be purchased from the Sailor's Snug Harbor.[51] Four lots, intended for school buildings, fronted Jackson Avenue (later known as University Place) between Seventh and Eighth Streets, while the other four were located directly to the east facing Greene Street. A rather undistinguished three-story building facing Jackson Avenue containing classrooms, a library, and a chapel was completed in 1838; two upper stories were added in 1852. In 1875 an addition to the main seminary building, in part accommodating an enlarged library, was completed to the designs of J. C. Cady. The existing building was also renovated at that time. Two years earlier the seminary had contemplated a move to St. Nicholas Avenue between 130th and 134th Streets, but the Panic of 1873 made it difficult to collect on the pledges needed to complete the land purchase. In the meantime, the seminary's board of directors had hired Richard Morris Hunt to draw up plans for the new campus.[52] As designed by Hunt, the seminary was to be housed in a 550-foot-long building incorporating T-shaped wings at the north and south ends and a tower containing the main entrance. The four-story, brick and stone-trimmed building was to contain classrooms, dormitory accommodations, and a refectory. Two chapels, one seventy-two by forty feet and the other seventy-five by forty-eight feet, were to be built of stone. Hunt also drew up plans for professors' houses to be located on the seminary site's northern section. Hunt's proposal was never realized.

As a result of a gift from Governor Edgar D. Morgan, the seminary instead moved to a block-long site on the west side of Fourth Avenue between Sixty-ninth and Seventieth Streets, a location selected in part because of its proximity to the Lenox Library. The site had a frontage of 200 feet along the avenue and extended 125 feet deep. In 1884 the president of the seminary, Roswell Dwight Hitchcock, asserted: "The present location is apparently for many decades, if not for all time. This commanding

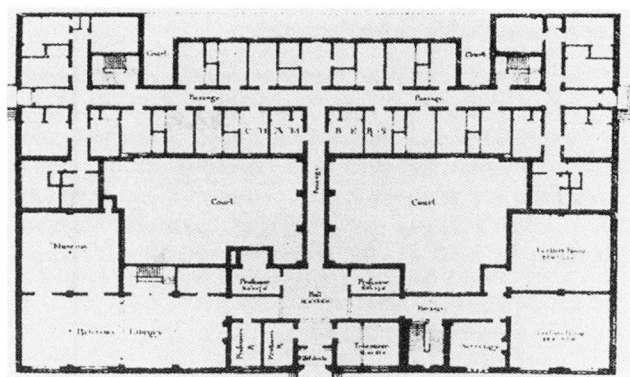

Union Theological Seminary, west side of Fourth Avenue, East Sixty-ninth to East Seventieth Street. William A. Potter, assisted by James Brown Lord, 1884. First-floor plan. UTS.

site, so near the center of the island, is in little danger of losing its advantages. Right behind us is the grand Central Park; close around us are hospitals, schools, and galleries of art—the trophies and adornments of an advancing Christian civilization."[53] Moses King similarly noted in his popular guidebook that the "velvety green lawns and the groups of shrubbery between the buildings . . . and the quiet dignity of the seminary buildings make a charming oasis of verdure and peace in the vast whirl of the city's secular life."[54]

William A. Potter and his young assistant James Brown Lord were hired to design what the *Real Estate Record and Builders' Guide* praised in 1883 as the "most brilliantly successful piece of architecture under construction in New York."[55] The seminary's trustees desired a campus setting but feared the spread of fire, and asked the architects to form a quadrangle out of what appeared to be five separate buildings but which were in fact just two red brick and Longmeadow stone Gothic-style buildings, one a two-story building named Jessup Hall, the other a five-story dormitory. Jessup Hall was organized as three distinct but joined parts: a library and museum along Sixty-ninth Street, lecture rooms along Seventieth Street, and, between the two, an entrance hall, above which was a chapel. The dormitory was placed parallel to Jessup Hall at the back of the site. A passageway connecting the two buildings was flanked by courtyards. In each building the upper stories and roofs were treated to provide a varied skyline, including a contrast between a steep gable roof over the library, a more gently sloped hipped roof over the lecture hall, and a tower located next to the north end of the chapel. The chapel incorporated five bays, each containing pointed and traceried windows and separated from each other by shallow piers. Schuyler praised the composition: "The success of the work comes in great part from the straightforward, expressive and purposeful character of the general scheme, during the arrival at which it is pretty plain the designer was not thinking about 'style' at all."[56]

Parish and Public Schools

The post–Civil War period's most architecturally important elementary school was the parish school run by Trinity Church.[57] In 1871 the school hired the aging Richard Upjohn, architect of the church itself, to prepare plans for a site across from the churchyard. On April 21, 1871, after a vestry meeting that approved Upjohn's plans, to be built on the southwest corner of Thames Street and Lumber Street (later known as New Church Street), the diarist George Templeton Strong noted: "The elevations are well enough but are marked by Upjohn's poverty of invention. Pursuant to instructions, he has given the interior plenty of light through a score or two of windows, but they are all exactly alike in dimensions and in outline; so the building will look like Alexander T. Stewart's big iron store, or a factory, or an ecclesiastical penitentiary. I begged the committee on Supplies and Repairs in charge of the matter to get this monotony relieved."[58] The building, as redesigned by Upjohn's son, Richard M. Upjohn was completed in 1873. The younger Upjohn's design called for a four-story building, on each story of which was a twenty-five-by-sixty-foot classroom. The principal feature of the Gothic design was the crocketed and gargoyled tower that rose above the stair hall to form an interesting skyline element visible from Trinity Churchyard. The *American Architect and Building News* reported: "As seen from Broadway, it forms a prominent architectural feature. Trinity Square has in this building an exponent of thirteenth century Gothic, in the monument an exponent of the fourteenth century, and in the church of the fifteenth century Gothic. It is rare in this country that we see so preeminent examples of the three styles at one glance one might say."[59]

Trinity Parish School, southwest corner of Thames and Lumber Streets. Richard M. Upjohn, 1873. First-floor plan and rendering showing view to the northwest from the churchyard. AABN. CU.

Another privately funded school of architectural note was the Italian School, on the south side of Leonard Street between Centre and Baxter Streets, in the heart of the notorious Five Points slums. As designed by J. C. Cady and completed in the 1870s, the building incorporated a brownstone basement articulated with flat arches, above which red brick walls were visually relieved with buff brick. Montgomery Schuyler praised the design as "the straightforward fulfillment of practical requirements and [the] expression of the structure," realized in such a way as to constitute "a very agreeable object."[60]

Given the rather dismal state of higher education in New York City during the eighteenth and early nineteenth centuries, it was not surprising that elementary and high school education programs in the city also lagged behind those of other American cities and even other parts of New York State.[61] In the early 1800s school attendance in the city was still not universal, though it was in small towns upstate. By 1809, the Free School Society, later known as the Public School Society, used both private and public funding to build and run nondenominational elementary schools, particularly for the poor. The school system expanded rapidly and was de facto the city's public elementary school system. In 1842 the state legislature created an officially sanctioned public school system and nine years later it absorbed the Public School Society's operations. In 1872 elementary school attendance became compulsory statewide. Throughout the nineteenth century, however, New York, in contrast to most cities in the northeastern United States, still lacked a public high school program.

Public School 84, south side of Fiftieth Street between Ninth and Tenth Avenues. David I. Stagg, 1885. View to the southeast. TC.

Grammar School 8, 29–55 King Street. G. W. Debevoise, 1887. View to the northeast. TC.

While numerous public school buildings were erected in New York during the post–Civil War period, very few could be said to be architecturally distinguished, or even notable. As the editors of the *Real Estate Record and Builders' Guide* harshly stated in 1884, the school board lacked the ability to "perceive the difference between the work of an educated architect and the work of a speculative builder's draughtsmen." The editors further charged that "there is not a public school in New York . . . which is even a decently creditable piece of architecture."[62] Among the exceptions to this were five buildings designed by the architect David I. Stagg, who served as the Superintendent of Public School Buildings. Stagg's Primary School 6 (c. 1875), at 15 East Third Street, between the Bowery and Second Avenue,[63] Public School 107 (1885), at 272 West Tenth Street, between Greenwich and Washington Streets,[64] Public School 84 (1885), on the south side of Fiftieth Street between Ninth and Tenth Avenues,[65] and Public School 79 (c. 1886), at 38 First Street, between First and Second Avenues,[66] were all rather lively Neo-Grec designs that ornamented their densely developed, predominantly working-class neighborhoods. More imposing in scale was Stagg's Public School 72, in Harlem (see chapter 6). Also noteworthy were G. W. Debevoise's two

similarly articulated, four-story, brick and stone buildings, Grammar School Number 2[67] and Grammar School Number 8,[68] each completed in 1887 and located, respectively, at 116 Henry Street, between Pike and Rutgers Streets, and 29–55 King Street, between MacDougal and Varick Streets. Both buildings, incorporating rusticated bases, quoining, and pedimented rooftop silhouettes, were a cut above the more standard brick-box schoolhouse. But the widespread construction of architecturally significant public schools would have to wait until after 1890, when the architect C.B.J. Snyder became Superintendent of Public School Buildings.[69]

MUSEUMS

New-York Historical Society

In 1860, the New-York Historical Society, founded fifty-six years earlier, constituted the city's most significant publicly accessible collection modeled along the lines of Europe's great museums, presenting a grand survey of culture through art, antiquities, manuscripts, and maps as well as through objects of historic and scientific value. Despite

New-York Historical Society, southeast corner of Second Avenue and East Eleventh Street. Mettam & Burke. View to the southeast showing the Baptist Tabernacle (c. 1850) on the right. Bracklow. NYHS.

Rendering of proposed renovation of the State Arsenal (Martin Thompson, 1851) for the New-York Historical Society, Central Park near Fifth Avenue and East Sixty-fourth Street. Richard Morris Hunt, 1865. View to the northwest. The Octagon, AAF.

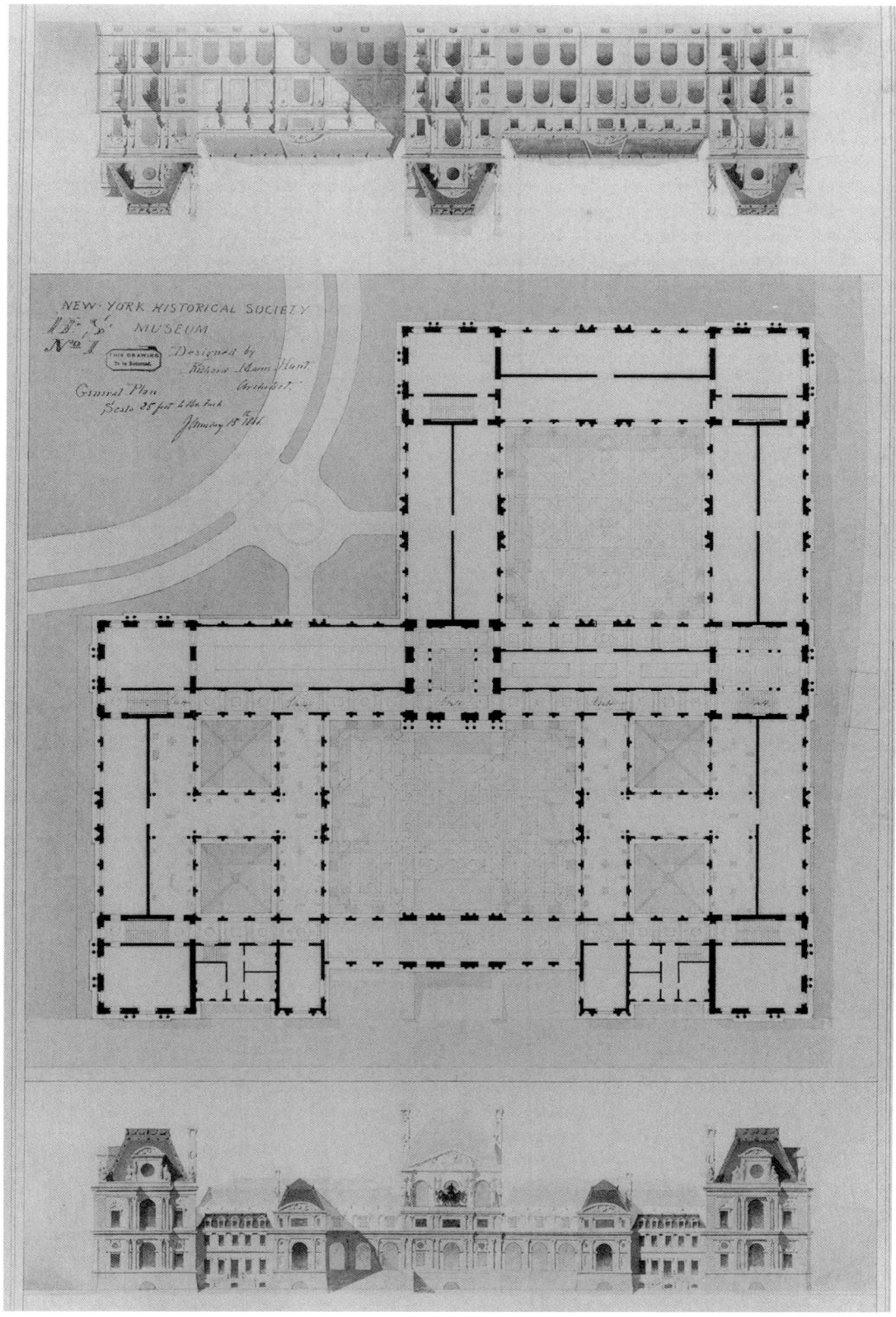

West elevation (top), first-floor plan (middle), and east elevation (bottom) of second proposed renovation of the State Arsenal (Martin Thompson, 1851) for the New-York Historical Society, Central Park near Fifth Avenue and East Sixty-fourth Street. Richard Morris Hunt, 1865. The Octagon, AAF.

the sweep of its presentation, the randomness of the society's acquisition policies and its extremely inadequate physical conditions dramatically reflected the fact that New York had a very long way to go in terms of being a culturally important city. Until 1857 the society had occupied rooms at New York University, which had been spatially adequate for an institution founded "to collect and preserve whatever may relate to the natural, civil or ecclesiastical history of the United States in general and this state in particular." But because New York lacked a comprehensive general museum, the society had deviated from its original mission and expanded its scope to accept much of what institutions, art dealers, and private dealers had to offer. In 1857, when its collection was enriched by the addition of 79 paintings and 250 engravings inherited from the bankrupt New York Gallery of Fine Arts, the New-York Historical Society moved into a home of its own at the southeast corner of Second Avenue and Eleventh Street.[1] Designed by Mettam & Burke, the new two-story-and-basement, sandstone-clad Italianate building incorporated a forty-seven-foot-high dome capping the principal room on the second floor. The building was intended to be as fireproof as possible, with hollow walls and wrought-iron beams, among the first such measures employed in New York. A Roman Doric porch marked the main entrance facing Second Avenue. The New-York Historical Society's new home was quickly outmoded and overcrowded, however, in part because its very completion stimulated new bequests from donors, most notably thirteen large stone bas-reliefs from Nineveh that were the 1858 gift of James Lenox. In 1860, with the purchase of a 1,127-object collection of Egyptology, the society began to rethink its mission in earnest. No longer just a repository of local history, it was on its way to becoming an encyclopedic museum.

Given the New-York Historical Society's evolving nature, in the early 1860s its trustees began to contemplate building a new facility that would better represent its enhanced status as New York's first "grand museum of antiquities, science and art."[2] In 1862, under the authorization of the Board of Commissioners of Central Park and the state legislature, the society was permitted to take over the State Arsenal (Martin Thompson, 1851) in Central Park, facing Fifth Avenue at Sixty-fourth Street, a battlemented Gothic building built as a munitions warehouse but believed by the park's designers, Frederick Law Olmsted and Calvert Vaux, to be an ideal home for a museum. In 1865 Richard Morris Hunt was commissioned to prepare plans for the State Arsenal's transformation into a museum.[3] Hunt boldly proposed a sweeping renovation entailing only a modest expansion, calling for the replacement of the four crenellated corner towers with mansarded pavilions and the elimination of four other towers. According to Hunt's design, the State Arsenal would have become a striped, polychromed monument suggesting the Gothic work of Eugène-Emmanuel Viollet-le-Duc in France or of George Edmund Street and William Butter-

field in England. Because the size of the building was not to be significantly increased, however, the Board of Commissioners of Central Park, which was legally responsible for the building, requested that Hunt "prepare other plans for buildings of more extensive scope and with ample requirements of this proposed great and noble undertaking."[4] In response Hunt created an elaborate design arranged around two courts that was quite brilliantly adapted to the tight site. Similar in its massing and details to the wing Hector Lefuel had added on to the Louvre (1854–55), a project on which Hunt had worked while in Paris, the composition was nonetheless utterly fresh and ingenious, with a *cour d'honneur* facing east, screened from Fifth Avenue by an arcade, and a second court, off-axis and completely surrounded by galleries.

The society's building committee approved the plan in January 1866 amid high praise from the editors of the *New York Times*, who saw in Hunt's design the makings of "an appropriate and beautiful edifice" that could be "indefinitely enlarged and extended, without the least detriment to its symmetry."[5] But once again the Board of Commissioners of Central Park demurred on the basis of limited size, determining that the site was inadequate, and urged the New-York Historical Society to build farther uptown in the park, between the hulking Croton Reservoir and Fifth Avenue at the latitude of Eightieth and Eighty-first Streets, a site Olmsted and Vaux's Greensward design reserved for a playground but which had since been considered for a casino or a deer park. At first the society's trustees fought for the State Arsenal site but by 1868 their battle was lost and the uptown locale, equivalent in size to approximately six square blocks, was designated by the state legislature as the New-York Historical Society's new home. While it is not clear that the trustees intended to build Hunt's design uptown, they did proceed with fundraising, which unfortunately did not go well. The site remained assigned to the society in April 1871, when the state legislature designated Manhattan Square on the West Side as home to both the newly founded Metropolitan Museum of Art and the American Museum of Natural History. But by the spring of 1872, the New-York Historical Society was willing to admit defeat and abandon its ambitious plans so that the site could be turned over to the trustees of the Metropolitan Museum of Art, who, though they preferred to be farther downtown, in Reservoir Square, agreed to build on upper Fifth Avenue (see below).

National Academy of Design

The National Academy of Design, founded on January 19, 1826, by a group of artists led by Samuel F. B. Morse, was midcentury New York's leading institution dedicated exclusively to art education and the display of contemporary fine art; it was also the city's only rival to the prestigious Pennsylvania Academy of the Fine Arts, in Philadelphia.[6] Without a building of its own, the academy met in various locations, including, between 1850 and 1855, the

View to the northeast from the roof of the Young Men's Christian Association headquarters (Renwick & Sands, 1869) showing the National Academy of Design (Peter B. Wight, 1863–65), northwest corner of Fourth Avenue and East Twenty-third Street, in the foreground. NYHS.

former Bowers' Stables, at 663 Broadway, which John B. Snook and Joseph Trench had renovated for the academy's use in 1849–50.[7] In 1854 the members began to look for a building site, considering the prominent south end of the block bounded by Broadway, Fifth Avenue, and Twenty-fifth Street. Two years later another site was considered, at Fifth Avenue and Twenty-third Street. In November 1860, having sold 663 Broadway, the academy purchased a one-hundred-by-eighty-foot site at the northwest corner of Twenty-third Street and Fourth Avenue, on which it constructed a vigorously patterned and polychromed, gray and white Tuckahoe marble and North River bluestone,

Ruskin-inspired, Venetian Gothic building (1863–65) that instantly became one of the city's most remarkable sights.[8] Seen from its inception as "an important addition to the street architecture" of the city, the academy's new home, designed by a young and until then unknown architect, Peter B. Wight, was valued as much for its inherent quality as for the fact that though the Gothic Revival had been in full swing for almost a generation, the academy was "the only Gothic building of any importance, other than a Church, yet erected within the city limits," and one that was "more richly decorated by sculpture than the exterior of any building in America."[9] In 1861, the twenty-three-

National Academy of Design, northwest corner of Fourth Avenue and East Twenty-third Street. Peter B. Wight, 1863–65. View to the northwest. NYHS.

Proposed National Academy of Design, northwest corner of Fourth Avenue and East Twenty-third Street. Richard Morris Hunt, 1861. Rendering showing the south facade (left) and the east facade (right). The Octagon, AAF.

year-old Wight had only six years earlier graduated from the Free Academy (later City College). He spent an additional year there studying drawing before working in the New York offices of Thomas R. Jackson and Isaac G. Perry as well as in the Chicago firm of Carter & Bauer. Wight was chosen in a competition that initially included only Leopold Eidlitz, Jacob Wrey Mould, and Richard Morris Hunt. At his own request, Henry Van Brunt was added to the list. Soon after, Wight, who learned of the competition from a friend then studying at the academy, was permitted to join the contest over the objections of the other competing architects, who eventually also included John B. Snook.[10] All in all, fourteen proposals were submitted. Eidlitz's scheme is lost, as are Mould's, Van Brunt's, and Snook's. A diptychlike drawing of Richard Morris Hunt's entry survives, however, showing both street facades of his remarkably rigorous, battlemented, Gothic design.[11] Hunt's proposal was, somewhat surprisingly, more commercial than institutional in character, perhaps because of a misreading of the program's call for ground-level shops, which Hunt included behind a glassy, arcadelike treatment.

Wight's original design was Romanesque but it proved too expensive, and after wrangling with the trustees he revised it, keeping the round arches but simplifying the details and reducing the colors from the initial proposal, which had called for alternately coursed Philadelphia brick and Dorchester stone. This palette was a reflection of Jacob Wrey Mould's much-admired insistently striped, bright red brick and white Caen stone, Pisa- and Sienna-inspired All Souls Unitarian Church (1853–55), at the southeast corner of Fourth Avenue and Twentieth Street, widely known as the Church of the Holy Zebra. Wight's first design did not please the academy's trustees, who were also apprehensive about turning the project over to a relative beginner. Instead they chose the proposal of John B. Snook, who had helped renovate the academy's Broadway building. But the academy's council held firm on Wight's behalf and, after two years of bickering and redesign, on April 29, 1863, they forced the trustees to adopt his third scheme, prepared with the assistance of Russell Sturgis. Approval was given with some contingencies, including a requirement that the ornamental program be simplified, leading to the omission of statues of Michelangelo and Raphael that had been planned for pedestals at either side of the south-facing gable crowning the monumental split entrance stairs, as well as the elimination of bas-relief heads of academicians to have been set in roundels on the Fourth Avenue side. The cornerstone was laid on October 21, 1863, and after two years of construction, Wight's building—draped in mourning for President Abraham Lincoln, who had been assassinated two weeks before—opened on April 27, 1865. Despite all efforts at economy, the new building cost three times the original estimate.

In the final design the ground floor was reserved for a studio containing plaster casts of works from antiquity.

National Academy of Design, northwest corner of Fourth Avenue and East Twenty-third Street. Peter B. Wight, 1863–65. View of stairs from the lobby. Stadtfeld. NAD. CU.

The second floor housed the council room, library, and reading room. The windowless, skylighted third floor, given over to the exhibition galleries, was made legible on the building's exterior through the use of a diaper pattern of white and gray marble covering the big surfaces, occasionally interspersed with glazed, roundel-like ventilators. The building's nickname—the Doge's Palace—was not undeserved. Although Wight claimed Veronese and Florentine inspirations, the building's connection to the famous Venetian palace at San Marco was inescapable. Sturgis, in an unsigned article, tried to deflect attention away from the search for specific stylistic sources, praising the new building as an example of direct problem-solving, "such . . . as a Gothic artist of the thirteenth century might well build, should he live now in New York, study our customs and needs, and become familiar with our materials and our workmen and their ways."[12] Insofar as Wight's design represented a conscious effort to translate the ideas of the English art critic and philosopher John Ruskin into a specific design—that is, to make a modern Gothic building—Sturgis was right, but the arguments he offered in defense of the highly stylized decoration were nonetheless exaggerated. True, the polychrome patterning grew out of

the use of natural materials logically handled, and the decoration, much of it not completed, put art in the service of architecture. But the carving of the column capitals was poor: Wight, in deference to Ruskin's belief in nature as the proper source for ornamental detail and his belief that ordinary workmen could be trained in the field to perform at the level of medieval craftsmen, as demonstrated in the construction of Thomas Deane and Benjamin Woodward's University Museum (1855–59) at Oxford, had supplied largely unskilled workmen with drawings and photographs of plants to inspire their work. Wight's hopes for a revival of artisanal creativity went largely unfulfilled, but many of his fellow Ruskinians were willing to overlook the poor quality of the work, arguing that the nobility of the intention was what mattered.

The murder of President Lincoln, whose body lay in state at City Hall for twenty-three hours beginning on April 24, 1865, after an early morning funeral procession starting on Desbrosses Street, and the news of the shooting and death of John Wilkes Booth on the very day of the academy's opening, on April 27, distracted the press so that despite its inherent newsworthiness, the building was not immediately discussed. It was almost a month before the

New York Times got around to considering Wight's design in any detail, offering ambiguous praise by observing that the "impression" of the building was "fresh and novel . . . we can easily imagine that an untraveled stranger must experience a warm and comfortable sensation of something new in examining this courageous copy of what is old."[13]

Metropolitan Museum of Art

The National Academy of Design was an important art school and a showcase for the work of living artists, but it was not a museum. While the New-York Historical Society functioned in part as a museum, its art collections were in reality a distraction from its main purpose as a center of historical and genealogical research. The lawyer John Jay, grandson of the famous jurist, president of the Union League Club, and the man who is usually credited with first conceiving the idea of a national art museum in New York, urged the publisher George P. Putnam to support the concept. On October 14, 1869, in a speech delivered at the Union League Club, Putnam called for the establishment of "a permanent gallery and museum of Art, which . . . shall be worthy of the great city of a great nation," advocating a national institution "in a building spacious in its dimensions, and thoroughly fire-proof."[14] So convincing was he that many in the audience gathered a month later, on November 23, at the same club to participate in an evening of further discussion, moderated by William Cullen Bryant. In his address to the group, Bryant went to some lengths to make sure the audience understood that the new museum would not conflict with the New-York Historical Society's plans for its own building in Central Park or with the work of the National Academy of Design. In outlining the purposes of the new museum—to educate the public, establish levels of taste, and provide examples for beginning artists to study—he did imply, however, that the National Academy of Design was somehow deficient because it was unwilling or unable to impose sufficiently rigorous standards in its annual exhibitions. At the same meeting, Richard Morris Hunt, who was to become a founding trustee of the new museum, claimed that the American Institute of Architects, of which he was New York chapter president, had for ten years advocated establishing a "National Museum . . . similar to the Kensington Museum in London. . . . But," the architect not surprisingly argued, "there is one thing that we must have first, and that is the building itself; because, when you catch a bird you need a cage for it."[15]

Montgomery Schuyler lost no time in commenting on the potential new art museum. In an editorial published in the *New York World* on November 25, 1869, two days after the meeting at the Union League Club, he cautioned that "the architectural botches, in the way of public buildings, which abound in New York, although New York has architects of real genius, and the pictorial botches which they enclose, while we have painters of real genius, sufficiently show that there will be an attempt made to degrade this newest institution into an instrument of jobbery or of puffery."[16]

In January 1870, an association was formed under the name "Metropolitan Museum of Art" with the ambitious goal of establishing "an institution in which our whole people shall be freely provided with ample facilities for the study of select examples in every department of the fine arts, and for the cultivation of pure taste in the application of art to manufactures and to practical life."[17] Financial support for the new institution, incorporated on April 13, 1870, was slow in coming, although John T. Johnston, a railroad tycoon and the association's first president, was notably generous.[18] According to the museum's enabling legislation, the city would own the new building and be obliged to maintain it. From the first there was pressure to open the galleries in the evenings with no admission charge so as to facilitate visits by working people; at least part of this request was satisfied in the museum's agreement with the city to keep the museum open to the public for free four days a week.[19]

Preceding any plans for the Metropolitan Museum of Art was a proposal prepared in 1868 by the popular painter of animals William H. Beard for a museum to be located in Manhattan Square.[20] Beard's Gothic Byzantine–inspired design, developed for Henry Keep, a Wall Street businessman who pledged $1.5 million to build it and create an art collection, was to lead from a domed entrance pavilion in Central Park to Manhattan Square via a tunnel under Eighth Avenue. The tunnel was to be enriched by sculpture depicting man's awakening consciousness of art and history. Keep died in 1869 before his and Beard's plan could be realized.

On May 5, 1869, the state legislature authorized the construction in the park of buildings for a Meteorological and Astronomical Observatory, a Museum of Natural History, and a "Gallery of Art."[21] On January 1, 1870, on the orders of Andrew Haswell Green, the comptroller of Central Park, a new map of the park was published showing a museum at Eighty-second Street and Fifth Avenue, fulfilling Green's decade-old dream of locating key cultural institutions within the park. Just as the Metropolitan Museum Association was organized, plans for the new museum building were curtailed when Boss Tweed's hand-picked mayor, A. Oakey Hall, folded Green's Board of Commissioners of Central Park into the New York City Department of Public Parks. The Tweed-dependent commissioners of the department deliberately set out to trash the Greensward park plan, firing Frederick Law Olmsted and Calvert Vaux in November 1870 but retaining their assistant, Jacob Wrey Mould, in the role of chief architect. The Tweed regime's decision to combine the art and natural history museums on Manhattan Square in order not to "obstruct too much of the Park surface with buildings" was opposed in a petition signed by forty thousand New Yorkers that led the state legislature to agree on April 5, 1871, to equally divide the $1 million allocated to the two museums so that each could build on a different site.[22] A special subcommittee on buildings was formed to represent both the Metropolitan and Natural History Muse-

Metropolitan Museum of Art, formerly the Douglas house, 126 West Fourteenth Street. James Renwick Jr., 1853–54. View to the southwest. HMMA. CU.

ums: members of the group included the architects Russell Sturgis, Richard Morris Hunt, and James Renwick Jr., the engineer Theodore Weston, and a number of leading citizens. The group drafted a list of design recommendations that, in recognition of the inherently different purposes of the two institutions, called for two separate buildings, neither more than two stories high but with high basements, and each planned "as to enclose ultimately a court or courts which may be roofed with glass."[23] Meanwhile, the Metropolitan's trustees continued in their effort to secure a more centrally located site, at Reservoir Square. But in November, after Boss Tweed's cronies were toppled from their perches, Green recaptured his power, reinstating Olmsted and Vaux, and in March 1872 the museum was told that it was to have the Eighty-second Street site, across from the Croton Reservoir, a site that Olmsted had designated as the Deer Park.[24]

Pending the construction of a permanent home, the Metropolitan Museum was first located at 681 Fifth Avenue, between Fifty-third and Fifty-fourth Streets, formerly Allen Dodworth's Dancing Academy.[25] The building was surprisingly well suited to its new purpose, with a top-floor, skylit ballroom, previously the place "where the poetry of motion had been taught to so many of the young men and maidens of New York," that could be easily made to serve as a picture gallery.[26] In 1873, after one year's occupancy, the museum, needing more space for its expanding collections, moved to the Douglas mansion (1853–54), at 126 West Fourteenth Street, one of the city's grandest houses, designed by James Renwick Jr.[27] The house was already large, and its 225-foot-wide lot was believed big enough to allow for the construction of future galleries.

Given the new mandate to build in Central Park, and the acquisition of Louis Palma di Cesnola's large collection

of Classical art from Cyprus, the urgency to build a large, proper museum building increased. The park commissioners were authorized to select the architects as well as the site, so the job of designing the new museum and master plan was almost inevitably Vaux and Mould's. The two architects were sometimes less than friendly to each other: not only did Mould have a very difficult personality (George Templeton Strong described him as "ugly and uncouth"), he was also in with the Tweed crowd, while Vaux enjoyed Green's support.[28]

Vaux and Mould both resigned as architects for Central Park in order to take on the commission for the new art museum and, virtually simultaneously, for the American Museum of Natural History (see below). Even before quitting their jobs, at Green's behest they had prepared plans for a museum building to be constructed and equipped by the Board of Commissioners of Central Park.[29] Vaux and Mould's first design after receiving the commission was nonetheless rejected by the special committee of architects appointed by the museum to superintend construction. Given that the committee included the rival architects Renwick and Sturgis as well as Hunt, whose proposal for the Central Park gates Vaux had opposed (see chapter 1), this probably came less as a surprise than as an irritant to Vaux and Mould. The criticism appears to have been leveled against the proposed

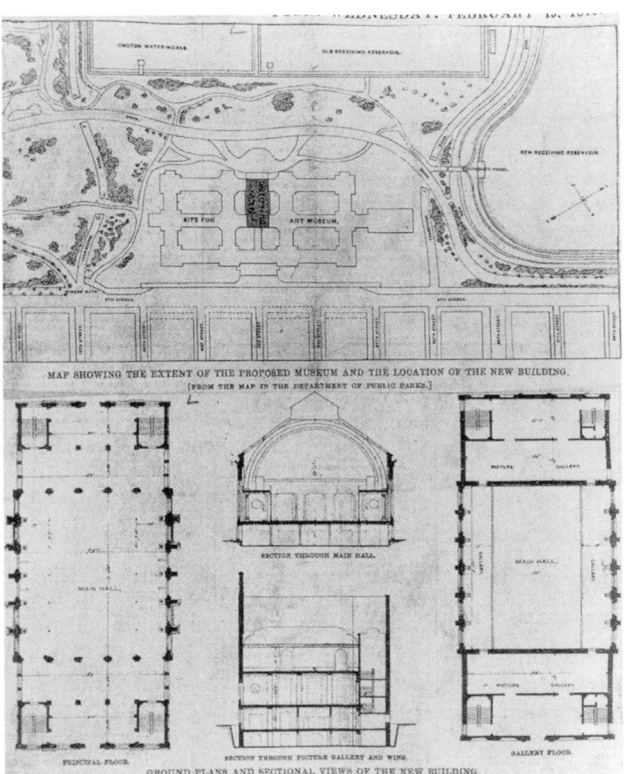

Metropolitan Museum of Art, Central Park at Fifth Avenue and East Eighty-third Street. Calvert Vaux and Jacob Wrey Mould, c. 1872. Sections and plans. NYDG. CU.

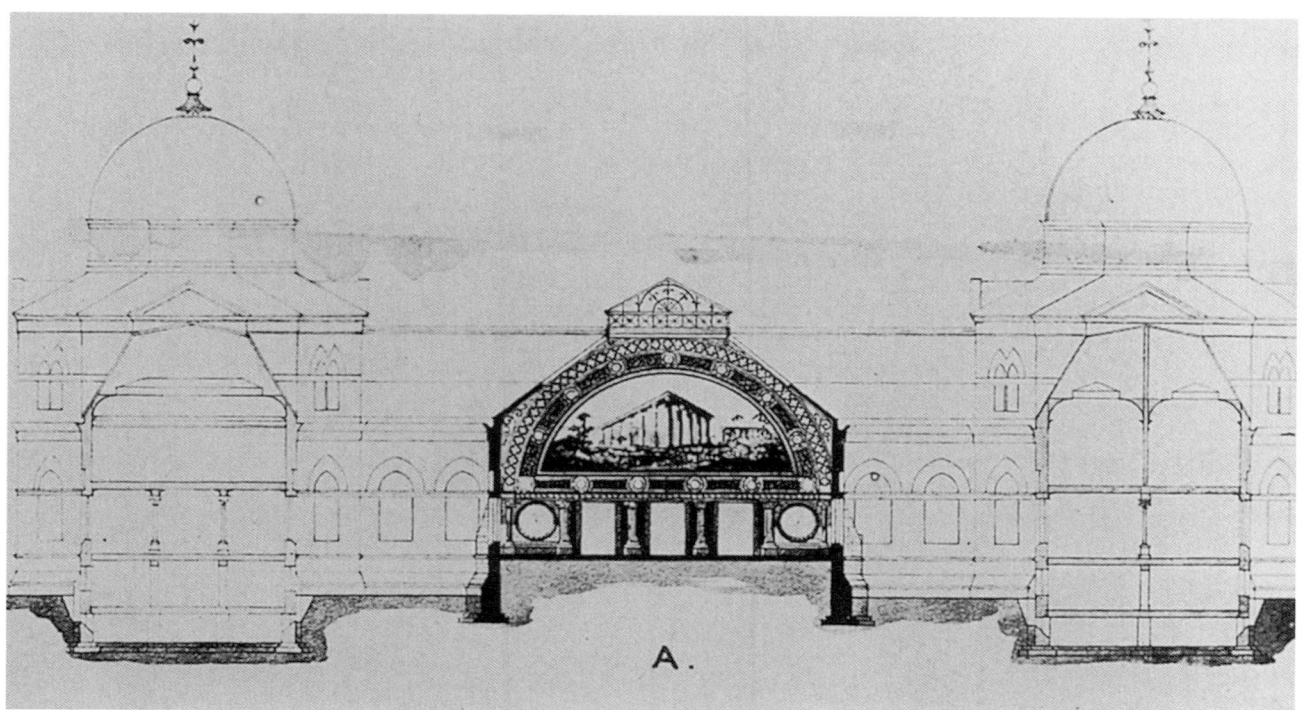

Proposed master plan for the Metropolitan Museum of Art, Central Park at Fifth Avenue and East Eighty-third Street. Calvert Vaux and Jacob Wrey Mould, c. 1872. Section. MUS. CU.

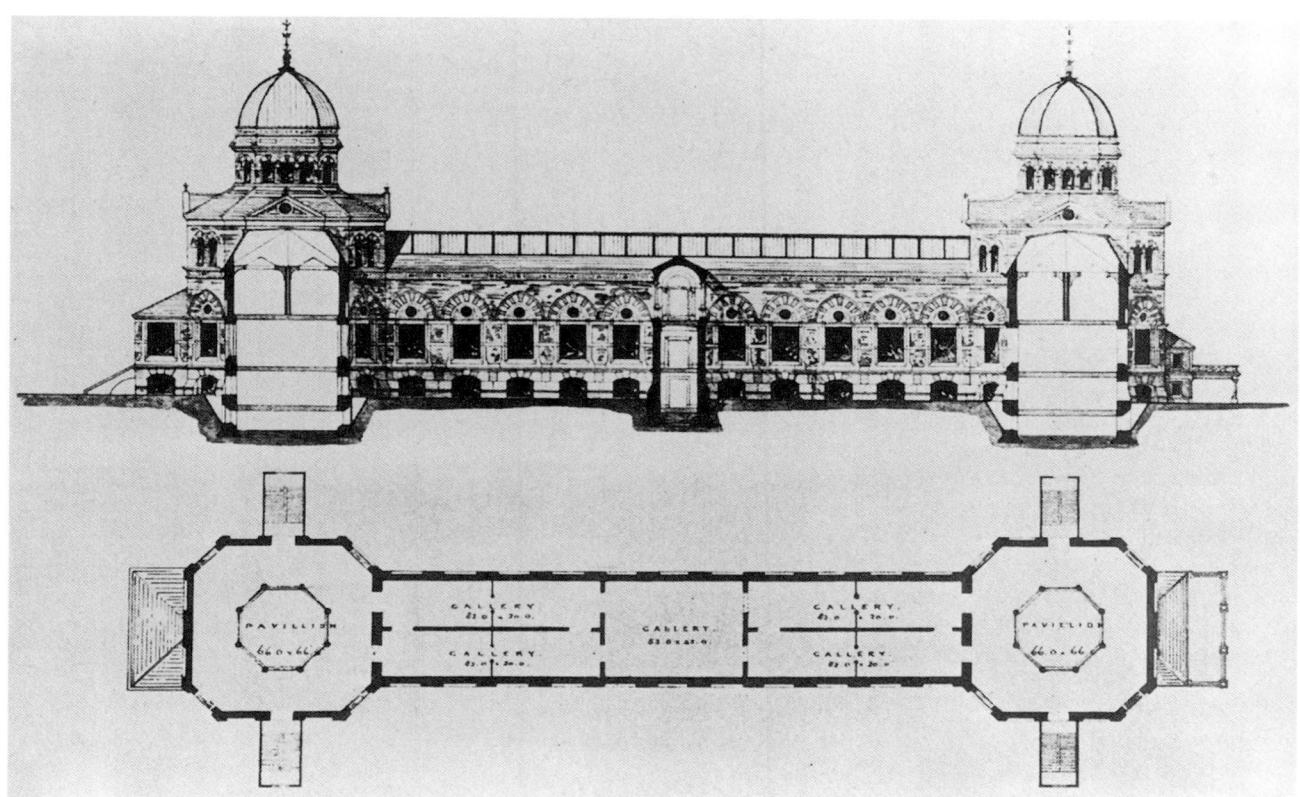

Proposed master plan for the Metropolitan Museum of Art, Central Park at Fifth Avenue and East Eighty-third Street. Calvert Vaux and Jacob Wrey Mould, c. 1872. South elevation and first-floor plan. MUS. CU.

Metropolitan Museum of Art, Central Park at Fifth Avenue and East Eighty-third Street. Calvert Vaux and Jacob Wrey Mould, 1874–80. View to the southeast. MMA.

building's plans, which seem not to have suited the museum's management. According to Winifred E. Howe, author of a 1913 history of the museum, "When Mr. Vaux had changed his plans, the shell of the building was constructed. Even then, the Trustees were compelled to ask for important changes in the interior. Their criticism was not against the building as such, but against its adaptability for the exhibition of their collections."[30]

Vaux and Mould's building (1874–80) for the Metropolitan Museum of Art was designed as the central element of a much larger composition.[31] Although Olmsted and Vaux were generally opposed to the construction of large buildings in Central Park, the pressure from Green and other commissioners to locate one or two museums there led them in 1872 to suggest that such buildings could be considered in areas that did "not precisely coincide with the desirable limits of the Park as a work of art." According to Olmsted and Vaux, "A large range of buildings" at Eighty-second Street and Fifth Avenue "would be seen from no other point of the Park, the locality being bounded on two sides by the reservoir walks, on a third by

a rocky ridge, and on the fourth by exterior buildings, while the whole of the territory thus enclosed was too small for the formation of pastoral grounds."[32]

Vaux and Mould's master plan, which was never implemented, grew out of the plot plan they prepared as part of the revised map of Central Park showing the "proposed Art Museum and Hall" as three large quadrangles made up of individual narrow wings connected at their intersections by projecting square pavilions, with a larger domed entrance pavilion centered on the Fifth Avenue facade. In a scheme of around 1872 Vaux and Mould showed how the museum's typical wings would be connected to the octagonal pavilions, which had double-height openings on their centers. But the domed pavilions seemed a bit rich for the tastes of the fledgling museum's trustees, and the master plan was immediately compromised by a decision to locate the first wing on the east-west axis in the center of what was to have been one of the quadrangles.

The first wing was initially proposed as a two-story unit, with top-lit galleries above a lower floor holding bays of glass cabinets for the display of objects. In keeping with

Metropolitan Museum of Art, Central Park at Fifth Avenue and East Eighty-third Street. Calvert Vaux and Jacob Wrey Mould, 1874–80. View to the northeast. MMA.

Metropolitan Museum of Art, Central Park at Fifth Avenue and East Eighty-third Street. Calvert Vaux and Jacob Wrey Mould, 1874–80. Rendering of view from the sculpture gallery toward the main hall. HW. MMA.

the architects' Ruskinian tastes, the Gothic-inspired exterior was finished with a rich palette of stones to yield a polychromatic effect that included tans, greens, reds, and blues. Acting on the recommendations of the committee of architects that the new building "include . . . some picture gallery, some glass-roofed court, and some . . . cloister or side-lighted gallery surrounding the court," Vaux and Mould developed a new design, wider than the wings they had originally proposed, incorporating an imposing, double-height, glass-and-steel-roofed hall.[33] The room, inspired by the south court of London's South Kensington Museum (Thomas Cubitt, 1856), was to function as a hall of plaster casts set between the picture galleries that were to be located at either end.

The project was delayed by various local political crises and then by the Panic of 1873, but in the summer of 1874 construction began on the new building. Although the building's design should be credited to Vaux and Mould,

the assistance of the engineer George K. Radford was no doubt very important.[34] Progress was slow and the building was not enclosed until 1876, in part because the trustees were not happy with the design and required that a partial basement be blasted out under the half-built main hall. In 1877 the decision was made to connect the second-floor picture galleries, hitherto isolated from each other by the great hall, with cast-iron "galleries of communication" built at either side.[35] In March and April 1879 the collections were at last moved from Fourteenth Street. With its almost houselike, temporary, two-story wooden porch serving as the principal entrance, the new museum, which was not opened until March 30, 1880, seemed at best a fragment of some much larger complex that was by no means certain to be built.

The public was not exactly enthralled by what it saw, especially the exterior brickwork of the cross gables, left unfinished in anticipation of future connections. Yet the new building had its charms. Even though it was intended to be a part of a grand ensemble, as realized it seemed almost casual, a pavilion-like complement to the park's rustic- and Gothic-inspired architecture, as if attempting to suggest that art was born not of abstract ideals but out of natural circumstances. Moreover, at a time when the wretched excesses of the Tweed Ring's construction program were a fresh memory, many found the very modesty of Vaux and Mould's building appealing. The *New York Times* regarded this architectural reserve as "a guarantee to the public—who will have to pay, in the long run, for future additions—that the money has been so far carefully spent. It has gained, then, the confidence of the New Yorker of today, especially since he has been witness of so much rascality in the way of public expenditure in other places."[36]

Despite its modesty and modest charms, the building was by no means a popular favorite. Its location was found wanting, but complaints were not from park preservationists. The *New York Daily Tribune*, hoping that the museum would become more than "an exclusive social toy," complained of the long distance to the nearest elevated station, at Third Avenue and Eighty-fourth Street. But the paper acknowledged that the almost suburban location might in the long run prove an advantage: "Our New York civilization is a tornado that spins along with a center that keeps steady to one track, and as things are with us, 'tis no doubt better to have the Museum where it can be caught up with than to have left it where it must soon have been passed by."[37] Even those sympathetic to the Ruskinian approach denounced the exterior of Vaux and Mould's design. The critic James Jackson Jarves called it "a forcible example of architectural ugliness, out of harmony and keeping with its avowed purpose."[38] So vociferous were the objections to the museum's first permanent home that the trustees, in their annual report for 1879, felt obliged to tell members that although "the exterior of the building has been much criticized, . . . it must be borne in mind that it is part of a larger structure, and that every addition will tend to harmonize the whole edifice."[39]

While the exterior of the museum was generally deemed problematic, the main hall, containing the Cesnola collection of antiquities in specially built glass cases, was certainly impressive. The 109-foot-long, 92-foot-wide, 85-foot-high room, supported on iron arches springing from large iron columns, was flanked by subsidiary pavilions, each about 130 by 60 feet. Though separated from the big room by large brick columns, the space of the ground floor of the end pavilions and that of the hall flowed together to provide a spectacular vista of the park from the entrance. Broad, gentle staircases led up to the second-floor painting galleries in the end pavilions, glimpsed through large circular windows as one ascended. The painting galleries were top-lit, thereby initiating what was to be the museum's lasting hierarchical programmatic strategy: the arts of the ancient world were housed on the ground floor, figuratively supporting those of the modern world above. The size and constructional frankness of the big room pre-

sented a challenge. As *Harper's New Monthly Magazine* put it: "To rescue from its nakedness a vast hall of iron columns and arches supporting a glass roof eighty-five feet from the floor, and make it a really attractive museum of art, was no easy undertaking. It seems to have been accomplished. The general effect of the vast room is warm, and the eye is satisfied. Under the north gallery runs a continuous line of wall cases, passing in front of the useless side windows, and sweeping around and hiding the iron columns which sustain the roof." In the center, more cases held loan collections. *Harper's* found the "galleries . . . an immense relief to the appearance of the large hall," but did not say why.[40]

Unhappy though the editors of the *New York Daily Tribune* were with the museum's location, they did have nice things to say about the building's interior, which they praised as "temporary and economic," not to mention "spacious, well planned, comfortable and cheerful," to a degree equal to or even greater than that of "Old World Museums." "We must not be deceived," the editors continued, "by the appearance of the exterior, nor forget that the building as we see it is only a small part of the immense structure that coming generations will see standing on this spot. . . . As it stands at present the architect's part in the building has been confined to the planning and the proportions; of architecture, properly speaking, there is nothing."[41]

Barely had the new building opened before the trustees realized its inadequacy. In December 1880 they decided to expand, choosing not to return to Vaux but instead commissioning Theodore Weston, a civil engineer and a museum trustee. It was Weston who had called the museum's attention to the Dodworth dance school, with its top-lit ballroom, when they were searching for its first home ten years earlier. Vaux was fired because the museum's trustees found fault with his design even though many of the problems arose over last-minute changes they themselves had imposed. Also, the trustees felt that Vaux was too closely connected with the Department of Public Parks, a body from which they had somewhat detached the museum with the passage of enabling legislation on May 20, 1881; responsibility for the development of the museum's plans was turned over to the trustees, subject to the approval of the department's board of commissioners.

Having chosen Weston, the museum's trustees again set out to undermine their architect's authority by appointing a "special Committee of Advisory Architects" intended to "decide about the plan for the new addition."[42] James Renwick Jr. and Richard Morris Hunt were asked to be Weston's advisers. Given that Renwick had designed the Smithsonian Institution (1848–49) in Washington, D.C., and that Hunt was America's best-trained architect, one can only imagine how Weston, an engineer, must have felt. Surely Renwick and Hunt must also have each wanted to be the museum's architect. Hunt's Lenox Library (see below) had demonstrated just how much clear planning and scholarly details could contribute toward creating an

Metropolitan Museum of Art, Central Park at Fifth Avenue and East Eighty-third Street. Calvert Vaux and Jacob Wrey Mould, 1874–80; south wing, Theodore Weston, 1888. View to the northeast of the south wing. NYHS.

impressive yet functional institutional facility. Though Hunt was a founding trustee, his professionalism probably worked against him, as did his reputation as an artistic architect fond of grand projects. More than ever the trustees wanted a no-frills building that worked. Moreover, trustee Louis Palma di Cesnola, a warm, outgoing Italian, found Hunt's New England reserve uncongenial. Fifteen years later, after Hunt died while at last working on a Metropolitan Museum project, Cesnola confessed that he "personally . . . did not care much" for him "but for his architectural ability . . . always had the highest esteem."[43] By contrast, Cesnola and Weston got on famously.

Money for the new building, initially requested from the state legislature in 1880, did not get authorized until 1884, but in August 1883 Weston was officially hired.[44] The project dragged on, and the new 230-by-112-foot wing was not completed until 1888. Weston turned out not to be quite the functionalist that the trustees may have hoped for. The new wing fronted the south with a two-story, Philadelphia brick, granite, and terra cotta facade topped by a complicated array of steep gabled and hipped roofs holding skylights. Before construction started, the *Real Estate Record and Builders' Guide* found the design not only "more suitable for the users of a museum" but also "happier in its exterior achievement" than its predecessor.[45] Hunt surely did not share this view. During the course of design, he became so incensed over Weston's scheme that he threatened to withdraw from the building committee. In 1884, in response to a letter from John T. Johnston

attempting to mollify Hunt, who was vacationing in Newport, the architect bared his soul, protesting Weston's appointment: had Weston not been "a member of the Board . . . I could not have objected however much my professional pride might have been wounded at being ignored after a professional career of forty years, & being one of the original trustees."[46] Hunt went on to say that it was he alone among those who reviewed Vaux and Mould's designs for the original building who had protested their deficiencies. Johnston passed Hunt's letter on to Cesnola, commenting that "Our first building was a mistake, there must be none about the second."[47] Rather indiscreetly, Cesnola shared the letter with Weston, who chalked up Hunt's remarks to "pique and jealousy that . . . is entirely unworthy [of] the man. . . . I propose that we have a sensible, simple as well as artistic building, thoroughly correct architecturally. I do not believe that Mr. H is the only man in the country who is capable of carrying it out."[48]

Weston's assertions notwithstanding, he was no doubt helped by Hunt in simplifying his original design with its complex roof, as well as aided by an assistant, Arthur Tuckerman. *Art Age* reported that the facade treatment "is simple and classic, in the modern French school, suggesting the Prix de Rome contests in the Ecole des Beaux-Arts."[49] But *Harper's Weekly*, which regretted the abandonment of Vaux and Mould's master plan, was not pleased with Weston's design, finding it "squat and heavy."[50] Nonetheless, Weston's switch from a Gothic-inspired design to one that was Classical was to prove decisive for the museum's future development. At its core, however, the new wing was not really different from the one that preceded it: by location and orientation it continued the fiction that the museum was nothing more than an enlarged park pavilion.

American Museum of Natural History

When the first building of the American Museum of Natural History, designed by Calvert Vaux and Jacob Wrey Mould, was completed, in 1877, it was far and away the most prominent building on the West Side.[51] The idea for the museum was conceived by Albert Smith Bickmore in 1860 while a student of Louis Agassiz at Harvard's Museum of Contemporary Zoology, at the time the nation's foremost such institution. After the Civil War, Bickmore began to approach rich New Yorkers about his idea, and in December 1868 eighteen men signed a letter to the Commissioner of Central Park requesting a building site. Also in 1868, an abortive attempt was made to create a Paleozoic Museum on the west side of the park near Sixty-third Street.[52] Intended as an exhibit of full-scale restorations of extinct creatures similar to one the painter and sculptor Benjamin Waterhouse Hawkins had undertaken in London's Crystal Palace for Sir Richard Owen, the English paleontologist who had coined the word *dinosauria*, the New York version, as conceived by Andrew Haswell Green, was to be based on prehistoric American subjects. But Green's enthusiasm for the project was not matched by one scientist, who denounced the plan as a "gloomy and half subterranean receptacle for restorations, a sort of fossil catacombs wherein the visitor, suppressing his dismay and encouraging his understanding, would wander about through shapes of pre-Adamite existence, and escape again into the light of day like Marcellus and Bernardo, 'distilled almost to jelly with the act of fear.'"[53] But according to the historian Douglas J. Preston, the plan for a giant, iron, vine-covered framework carried on iron Classical columns "would have been rather spectacular, an extravagance appropriate for New York."[54]

Proposed Paleozoic Museum (1868), Central Park near Eighth Avenue and West Sixty-third Street. Rendering of exhibition hall. AMNH.

Hawkins came to the United States and began a search for fossils. Delighted to learn that a mold of the *Hadrosaurus*, which had been dug up in Haddonfield, New Jersey, in 1858, had already been cast, he decided to make it the centerpiece of the museum, showing it being attacked by a carnivorous dinosaur, *Laelaps*, while nearby two others of the same species feasted on the corps of another *Hadrosaurus*. Foundations for the museum were laid, but Boss Tweed, unable to find a way to profit from the new venture, made it a political target and halted construction in 1870, plowing over the substructure and then arranging for the vandalization of Hawkins's studio.

Plans for Bickmore's natural history museum solidified in 1869, when, joining forces with the newly founded Metropolitan Museum Association, the trustees of what had recently been formally organized as the American Museum of Natural History successfully petitioned the state legislature to authorize the construction in the park of homes for the Meteorological and Astronomical Observatory, the American Museum of Natural History, and an art museum. Amazingly, at the age of thirty, Bickmore found himself superintendent of a new museum that promised to rival, if not exceed, Harvard's zoology museum.

Once established, the new museum contented itself beginning in 1870 with a home in the State Arsenal, still the designated site of a relocated New-York Historical Society (see above).[55] There was some ironic justification to this: once home to part of the park's menagerie, the State Arsenal's halls remained filled with scents of living nature. But historical association was not strong enough to overcome the building's limitations, and in 1871 the new museum secured the Manhattan Square site for itself after separating its government funding from that of the Metropolitan Museum of Art (see above). One of the few open spaces provided for in the Commissioners' Plan of 1811, Manhattan Square was added to Central Park's lands in 1864, when it was slated to be home to the zoo. The site was isolated and, as Bickmore later recalled, "most desolate and forbidding. There was a high hill at the north east corner . . . and in the north west corner another hill of solid rock rose much higher than the elevated railroad station. . . . In the southern and central part of the square, just where the first section of our building was to be erected, was a third hill, whose crest rose as high as the ceiling of our present Hall of Birds. As I sat on top of this rock, the surrounding view was dreary and my only companions were scores of goats."[56]

Vaux and Mould's Ruskin-inspired Gothic design, no doubt intended to complement and balance their Metropolitan Museum across the park, was, like their design for that institution, conceived on a grand scale. The master plan proposed four quadrangles bounded by galleries linked at their intersections by pavilions. All in all, the museum would be 850 feet in its north-south dimension and 650 feet running east-west, covering an area of some eighteen acres, an expanse two-thirds larger than that enjoyed by the British Museum. In fact, as planned, the

American Museum of Natural History would have been the world's largest museum and the largest building on the North American continent.

While the first gallery constructed at the Metropolitan Museum of Art essentially torpedoed the master plan, at the American Museum of Natural History the plan was followed to the letter. The new, 112-foot-tall, 200-foot-long gallery, located in the plan's center, ran north from Seventy-seventh Street. The master plan called for a main entrance facing Seventy-seventh Street. Eight lofty towers were to mark the intersecting pavilions, and a 120-foot-diameter dome was to crown the central intersection, high enough to be seen from Central Park. The new building, consisting of three stories, a high basement, and a dormered attic, sparkled with polychromed detail, its deep red brick walls rising past Venetian Gothic arches in two shades of granite to a patterned slate roof.

The cornerstone ceremony for the first gallery took place on June 3, 1874, with President Ulysses S. Grant and many other dignitaries in attendance. The museum opened on December 22, 1877, with President Rutherford B. Hayes on hand. Even before the building was finished the popularity of the new enterprise had more than proved itself, with 856,773 visitors to the State Arsenal in the first nine months of 1876, over 250,000 more than attended the British Museum in all of 1874 and over 17,000 more than the South Kensington Museum attracted in 1875. Inside the American Museum of Natural History, each floor consisted of one gallery devoted to a single subject.

On the ground floor were mammals; on the first floor, birds; on the mezzanine, which overlooked it, anthropological exhibits; and on top, fossils. Most of the displays were placed in special wood and glass cabinets designed by George K. Radford. One unusual feature concerned the use of natural daylight to illuminate the display cases. According to the *American Architect and Building News*, in "each of the cases for the exhibition of specimens, on the two principal floors, the usually dark end close to the wall is to be glazed with ground glass, and lighted through a comparatively small slit, left for the purpose in the pier between the windows."[57] The galleries themselves were notable for the presence of evenly distributed daylight. This was the by-product of Bickmore's decision to orient the first building along the north-south axis so that there would be east or west light all day long, a decision that soon proved itself misguided when the sun's rays began to fade and dry out the specimens on display. The iron structure, which was imaginatively worked with floral forms, carried low brick arches that formed the ceiling. The floors were finely finished, with Minton tiles.

The new museum stood in stark contrast not only to the still-underdeveloped Manhattan Square, but also to the surrounding West Side neighborhood, which, as a writer in *Harper's New Monthly Magazine* reported in 1880, could not

be precisely described as city, nor as suburb, nor as the unsettled but broken territory that outlies most cities while waiting to be absorbed in their advance. The anticipations that led to the grading and paving of the streets

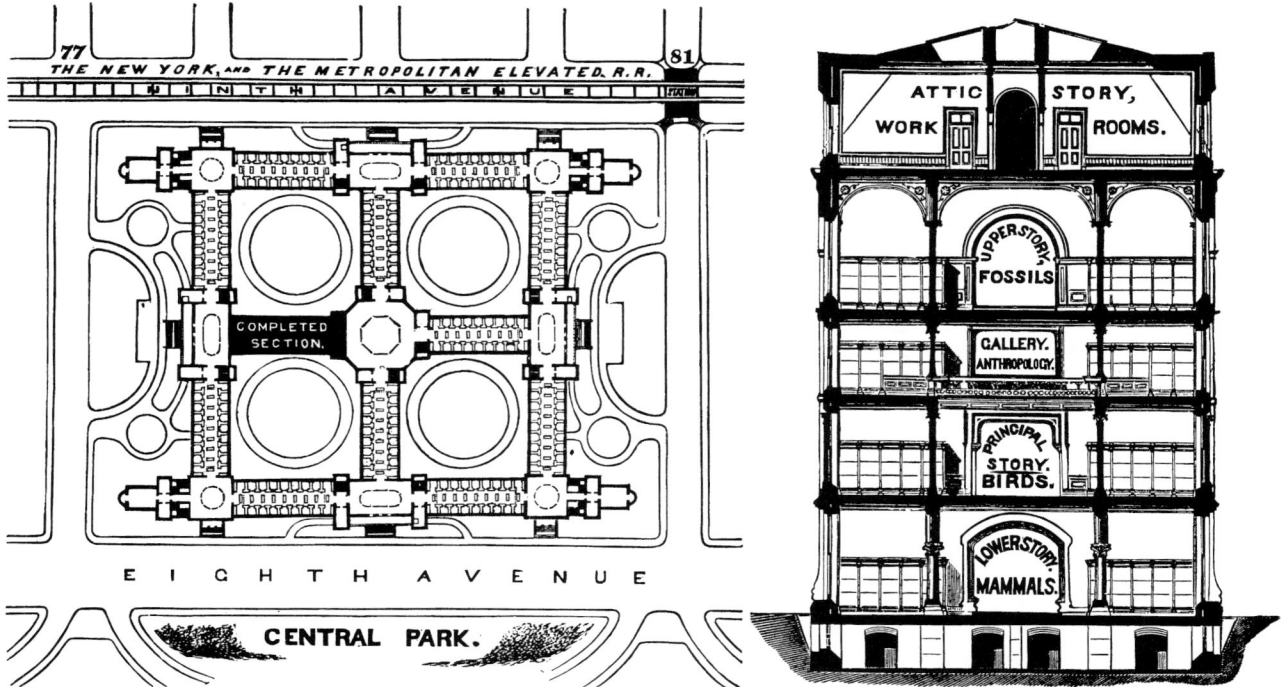

American Museum of Natural History, Eighth to Ninth Avenue, West Seventy-seventh to West Eighty-first Street. Calvert Vaux and Jacob Wrey Mould, 1874–77. Master plan and section. AMNH.

American Museum of Natural History, Eighth to Ninth Avenue, West Seventy-seventh to West Eighty-first Street. Calvert Vaux and Jacob Wrey Mould, 1874–77. View to the southwest. MCNY.

American Museum of Natural History, Eighth to Ninth Avenue, West Seventy-seventh to West Eighty-first Street. Calvert Vaux and Jacob Wrey Mould, 1874–77. View of gallery exhibiting birds. AMNH.

have had a very limited fruition in isolated rows of pretentious "brown-stone fronts," which seem oddly out of place. Here and there a vestige of old times remains in a pre-metropolitan homestead, with an improved orchard around it, or in a grand mansion with a classical front of Doric columns. . . . But it is not the new buildings, premonitory of the city's advance, nor the old ones reflecting the past, nor those two in contrast, that give the region its characteristics and peculiar interest. All down the hollows between the graded streets, and in spaces where no streets have been opened, the gray Laurentian rock stands with but a superficial layer of soil upon it, thousands of acres under cultivation by squatters, and without other inclosure to the land than the embankments formed around the hollows by trap-rock foundations of the streets.[58]

Despite the many niceties of Vaux and Mould's design, the disintegration of their partnership led the trustees to hold a competition (1888) for a revised master plan, leading to the construction of the principal entrance pavilion facing Seventy-seventh Street. Competing were R. H. Robertson and J. C. Cady; Cady was selected. Robertson's Romanesque-inspired scheme honored the master plan.[59] Cady's design was bolder and simpler, but it too followed the master plan.[60] The decision to expand the museum had been made as early as 1881, when it was decided to build the south central section of the master plan. Political machinations in city hall and Albany held up appropriations for years, but by 1888, when Cady's design was selected, the museum was ready to build, despite the criticism of Samuel Parsons Jr., Superintendent of Parks, who thought the new design contradicted the master plan.

Excavation for the central portion of the Seventy-seventh Street front was completed in the fall of 1888. Cady's rock-faced granite, Richardsonian-inspired Romanesque design, with its multiple turrets punctuating what would be upon its completion New York's longest continuous facade, was technologically notable—twenty-eight sixty-two-foot-long box girders, the largest ever used, made column-free floors possible. The size of the forty-thousand-pound girders made for considerable challenges, not the least of which was the difficulty in trucking them to the site from the Hudson River docks at Fiftieth Street: "One truck collapsed in Fifty-seventh street near Tenth-avenue," the *New York Times* reported, "another at Seventy-seventh street and Ninth-avenue, while a third, which was fortunate enough to reach the square without mishap, buried its wheels to their hubs and stuck fast, as soon as it left the pavement of the street."[61]

When the building opened in 1892 it was, according to the *New York Times*, "a museum worth seeing."[62] The principal feature of the new 60-by-110-foot, 92-foot-high wing was its glorious rock-faced red granite entrance facing Seventy-seventh Street, where a broad drive swept up from the sidewalk to an entrance arcade set between two turrets. Inside, a grand stairway covered in slate with iron railings ran from the basement to the third floor. The decision to face the building on Seventy-seventh Street and not on Eighth Avenue was justified by the proximity of the crosstown street to the station of the Ninth Avenue elevated railroad, half a block away. The new building contained gallery spaces for the museum's ever-expanding collections as well as a reference library.

American Museum of Natural History, Eighth to Ninth Avenue, West Seventy-seventh to West Eighty-first Street.
Calvert Vaux and Jacob Wrey Mould, 1874–77. View to the northwest. NYHS.

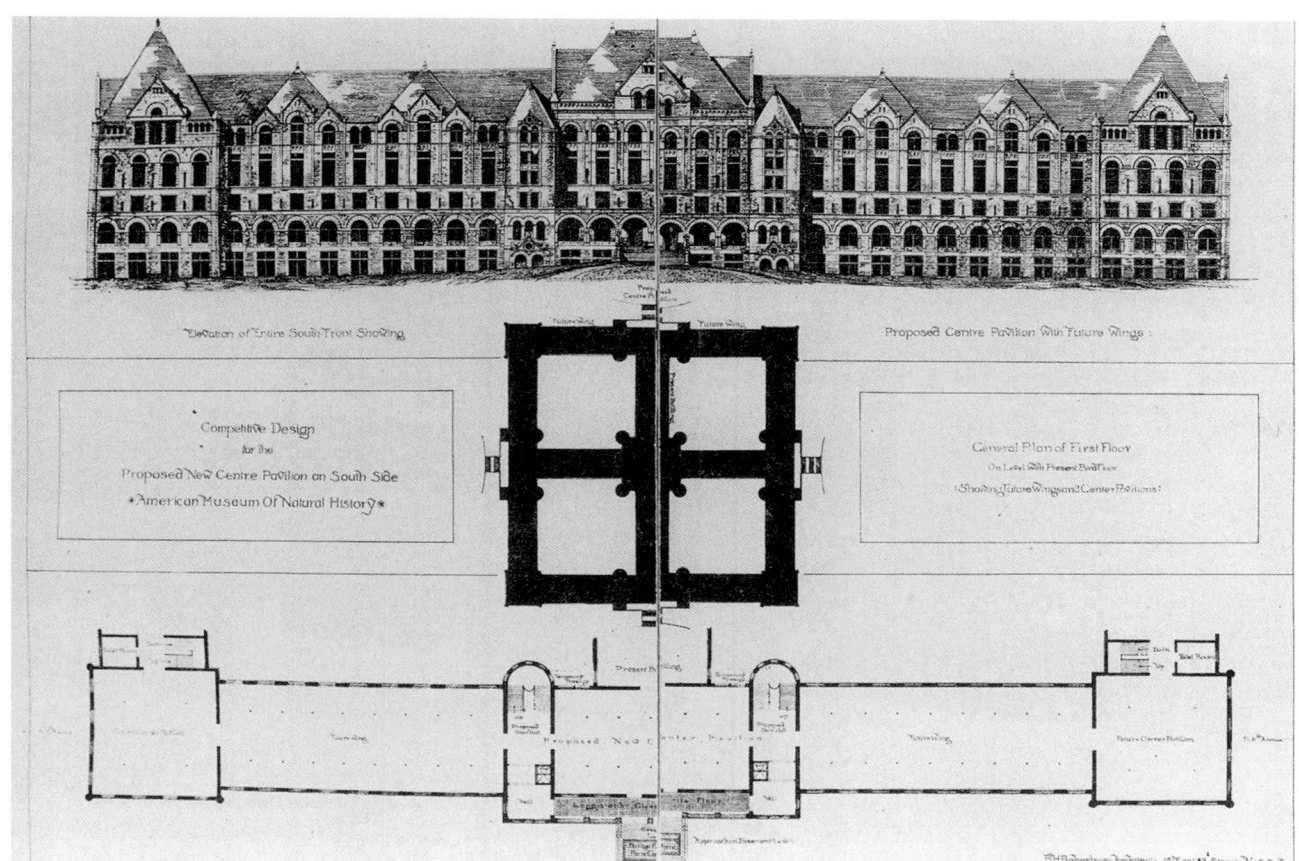

Proposed American Museum of Natural History, Eighth to Ninth Avenue, West Seventy-seventh to West Eighty-first Street.
R. H. Robertson, 1888. Competition-entry south elevation and plans. AABN. CU.

View to the northeast of the American Museum of Natural History, Eighth to Ninth Avenue, West Seventy-seventh to West Eighty-first Street, showing the original building (Calvert Vaux and Jacob Wrey Mould, 1874–77) on the left and the addition (J. C. Cady, 1892) on the right. NYHS.

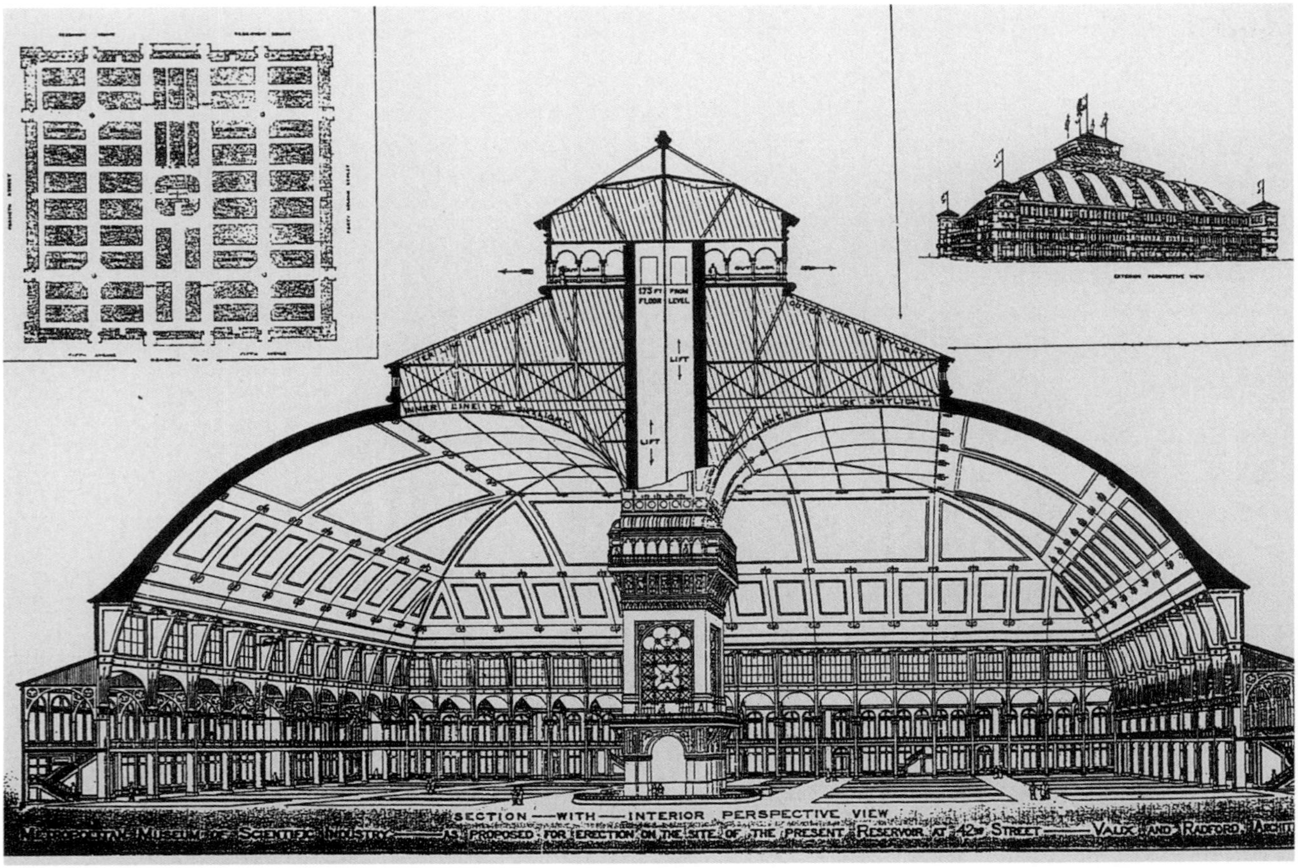

Proposed Metropolitan Museum of Scientific Industry, west side of Fifth Avenue, West Fortieth to West Forty-second Street. Vaux & Radford, 1877. Site plan (left), section with interior perspective (center), and exterior perspective (right). AABN. CU.

Eden Musée, 55 West Twenty-third Street. Henry Fernbach and Theodore DeLemos, 1884. View to the northwest showing the museum on the left and the William C. Schermerhorn house (Detlef Lienau, c. 1858) on the right. NYHS.

Metropolitan Museum of Scientific Industry

With institutions for art and natural history, as far as New York museums were concerned the modern world itself remained unaddressed. To that end, in 1877, a Metropolitan Museum of Scientific Industry was proposed for Reservoir Square, where the holding tank of the Croton water system was no longer required.[63] The unrealized idea was Vaux & Radford's, who proposed a vast, 390-foot-square, 175-foot-tall, glass and iron, pavilion-like shed with an arched roof carried on outer walls and a central column, all in all covering five and a half acres. In some ways the design recalled George Carstenson and Charles Geldemeister's Crystal Palace, which had occupied the same site in 1853.[64]

Eden Musée

One other of the city's museums bears noting, the Eden Musée, a New York version of Madame Tussaud's Wax Museum, in London.[65] Located at 55 West Twenty-third Street, between Fifth and Sixth Avenues, the museum, which was built for a French company, opened on May 29, 1884, six months after the death of its architect, Henry Fernbach. The work was completed by Theodore DeLe-

Eden Musée, 55 West Twenty-third Street. Henry Fernbach and Theodore DeLemos, 1884. View to the north, c. 1900. Hall. NYHS.

Eden Musée, 55 West Twenty-third Street. Henry Fernbach and Theodore DeLemos, 1884. Second-floor galleries. NYHS.

mos. The Eden Musée housed a collection of wax-figure tableaux displayed in an elaborate setting filled with tropical plants. The chamber of horrors, featuring versions of well-known crimes, was particularly popular. At the rear of the second floor there was a large music hall called the Winter Garden, surrounded by a gallery. Music was supplied by a small group of musicians and refreshments were served in the manner of a tearoom at a hotel or resort. Fernbach and DeLemos's building ran through the block to Twenty-fourth Street and had as its principal facade a vigorously modeled, pavilionated version of the French Renaissance with a high, steeply pitched, crocketed, slate-covered mansard. Mariana Van Rensselaer was decidedly unimpressed, charging that the composition incorporated "a showy accumulation of superficial details, mechanical in spirit, and thrice too plentiful in the size of its facade."[66]

LIBRARIES

Before the Civil War, New York had significant private subscription libraries, most notably the New York Society Library, the city's oldest institutional library, which opened in City Hall in 1754 and after 1856 was housed in Griffith Thomas's brick and stone-trimmed building at 109 University Place.[1] But the establishment in 1848 of the Astor Library, New York's first library open to the public without the requirement of a paid subscription, marked a watershed in the city's developing cultural life.[2] The New York Society Library had long been a gathering place for New York's most elite families. The Astor Library served the scholarly needs of a much broader clientele, reflecting the era's growing democracy as well as the conviction that the bottom-line-oriented city, no longer content to be merely prosperous, was intent on usurping the distinction of being the country's intellectual capital from Philadelphia and Boston, hitherto rival claimants. In keeping with New York's unabashedly commercial orientation, however, the Astor Library was, though public, privately funded; it was in fact the nation's first public library to be funded exclusively through private philanthropy.

In the late 1830s, John Jacob Astor, the western fur trader turned New York real estate entrepreneur (by 1840 he was reported to be the richest man in America), began to contemplate establishing a public cultural institution. Guided by his friend Joseph Green Cogswell, the editor of the *New York Review* as well as a pioneering librarian and bibliographer whose indexing systems would serve as the foundation of the modern card catalogue, Astor decided to endow a library. The library was founded after Astor's death in 1848, at which time his son William B. Astor used a $400,000 bequest from his father's will to send Cogswell on European buying trips, during which he ransacked book markets to put together the country's finest reference collection. Within a twenty-year period, the Astor Library would become the nation's premier reference library and an important addition to the city's intellectual life. Writing in 1886, the journalist and historian Martha J. Lamb observed: "Although in name a city institution [the Astor Library] was soon found to be more truly national than any other library in the country."[3]

To house the expanding collection and accommodate its burgeoning readership, a 65-foot-wide, 120-foot-deep site was acquired at 425 Lafayette Place. At the end of the

New York Society Library, 109 University Place. Griffith Thomas, 1856. View to the northeast. Bracklow. NYHS.

Astor Library, east side of Lafayette Place between East Fourth and East Eighth Streets. Alexander Saeltzer, 1854. Rendering of view to the east. HNYC. CU.

eighteenth century the site had been part of a popular outdoor space that contained a monumental equestrian statue of George Washington. The Astor Library's board of trustees organized a design competition for its new building. Thirty drawings were submitted, and while, according to I. N. Phelps Stokes, "none was wholly satisfactory," first prize was awarded to the German-born architect Alexander Saeltzer, who had an active practice in New York.[4] Saeltzer had completed a Gothic-style synagogue for Congregation Anshe Slonim (1849) and would later design an Italian Renaissance palazzo-like building (1855–56) for the private banking concern Duncan, Sherman & Co. Second prize in the library building competition went to James Renwick Jr.

Opened in 1854, Saeltzer's three-story Astor Library building incorporated a principal facade divided into three bays, the outer ones projecting forward slightly. Above a rusticated brownstone base, the red brick facade was punctuated by arched windows typical of the nineteenth-century German Rundbogenstil, or "round-arched style." Often used for civic buildings in Germany, here the style was articulated with details inspired by early Renaissance forms. The stylistically eclectic composition was crowned by a strapwork cornice and Ionic frieze, which were in turn surmounted by a solid parapet decorated with finials.

Despite the collection's major intellectual contribution to the city, the building itself was judged to be less than entirely successful. The author of an unsigned article pub-

Astor Library, east side of Lafayette Place between East Fourth and East Eighth Streets. Alexander Saeltzer, 1854; addition to the north, Griffith Thomas, 1859. View to the southeast. NYHS.

lished in the *New York Quarterly* in 1855 assailed Saeltzer's design as "not a good specimen of a bad school of architecture," finding fault with the facade but praising the "fine, handsome" reading room "divided into alcoves by a series of lofty arches," although these were "subdivided in their height by galleries of iron, the castings of which are of fanciful but not very successful design."[5]

While the Astor Library's initial collection of twenty thousand books was substantial, the city's overall library resources were meager compared with those of European cities. In 1853, five years after the opening of the Astor Library, even a second-tier city such as Lyons, France, could boast that its public libraries contained nine times as many books as those of New York; indeed, Lyons's public libraries had nearly as many books as possessed by all of the public libraries in the United States.[6] But this was to change dramatically with the rapid expansion of the Astor collection. Between 1856 and 1859 the size of the building tripled with the addition of an extension to the north. Surprisingly, in light of the decidedly lukewarm reception given the design of the original building, the architect of the new wing, Griffith Thomas, carefully maintained the composition of the original facade. Thomas, who was well known for his structurally innovative cast-iron loft buildings, eschewed making an individual statement in favor of designing a wing that so exactly matched the original building as to seem an integral part of it.

In 1879, by which time the library housed 150,000 volumes, making it the biggest book collection in America, William B. Astor's sons, John Jacob Astor II and William B. Astor II, hired the architect Thomas Stent to complete the complex with another wing, again extending the building to the north, so that up to 500,000 books ultimately could be housed.[7] It was not just that the book collection was growing: the library itself was immensely popular as a place to visit. In 1882, 51,856 patrons were reported to have used it, an average of approximately 200 per day. With the completion in 1881 of Stent's sixty-five-foot-wide-by-twenty-foot-deep wing, which was built as a memorial to William B. Astor, the library occupied two hundred feet of street frontage. Remarkably, Saeltzer's original round-arched, red brick and brownstone design was followed once again. Fortifying the building's visual coherence Stent added an attic story to Thomas's annex, giving a strong central focus to the long facade. Inside, three double-height, colonnaded, skylit rooms served as the principal reading rooms. In 1887, more than thirty years after the original building's completion, the valuation of Saeltzer's original design had so vastly increased that the *Real Estate Record and Builders' Guide* claimed it "a new departure, being about the first specimen seen here of the revival of Romanesque architecture after the example of Gärtner in Munich. The library looks tame enough now, and indeed was at all times a demure and well-behaved

Astor Library, east side of Lafayette Place between East Fourth and East Eighth Streets. Alexander Saeltzer, 1854; addition to the north, Griffith Thomas, 1859; fourth floor and second addition to the north, Thomas Stent, 1879. View to the southeast. HNYPL. CU.

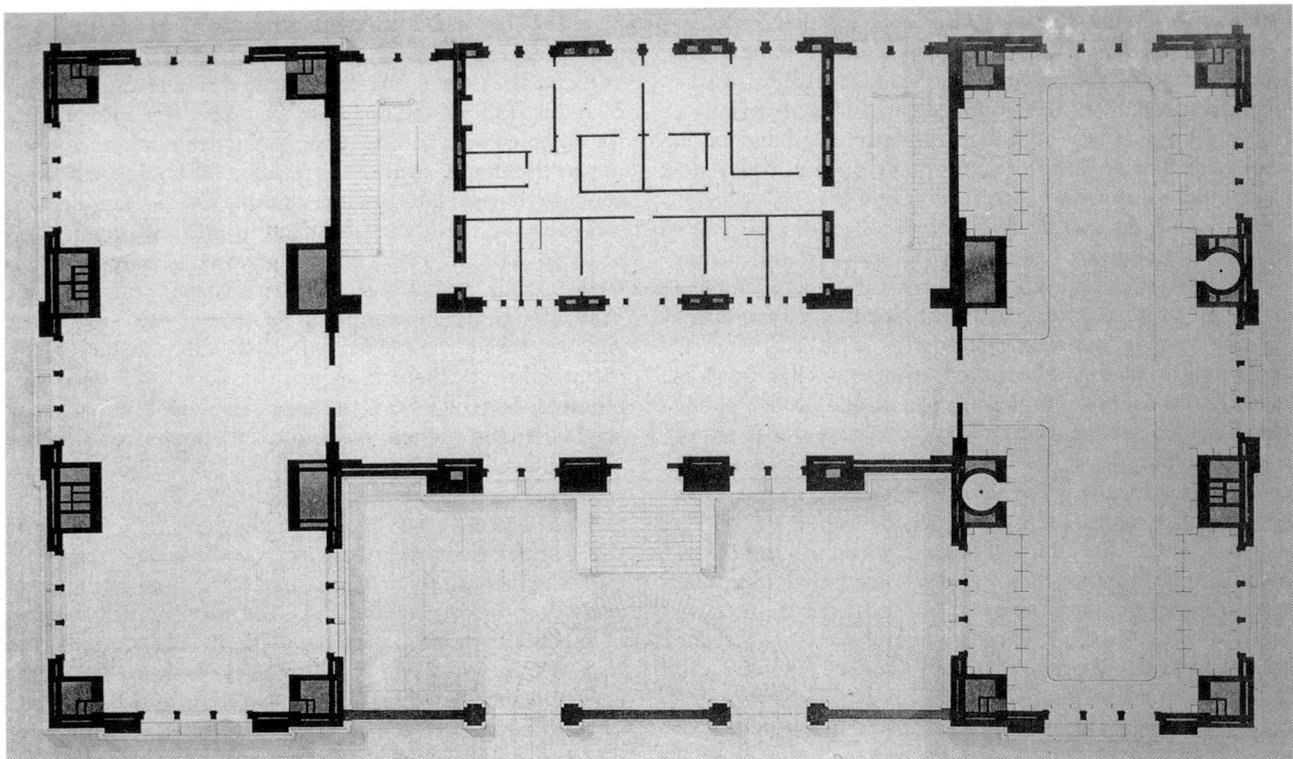

Lenox Library, east side of Fifth Avenue, East Seventieth to East Seventy-first Street. Richard Morris Hunt, 1870–77. First-floor plan. The Octagon, AAF.

Lenox Library, east side of Fifth Avenue, East Seventieth to East Seventy-first Street. Richard Morris Hunt, 1870–77. Section. The Octagon, AAF.

edifice, though its modeling and detail were unfamiliar when they were erected in a city that has now many better examples of the German Romanesque."[8]

Far uptown, on a prime Fifth Avenue block-long site, facing Central Park between Seventieth and Seventy-first Streets, Richard Morris Hunt's Lenox Library (1870–77) was without question the city's most architecturally significant library and one of its great buildings.[9] James Lenox, the son of a wealthy Scots-born merchant, was the owner of about twenty thousand mostly rare books and manuscripts that competed with his fine collection of paintings for virtually every available surface of his large townhouse at 53 Fifth Avenue, on the northeast corner of Twelfth Street. In 1870 Lenox incorporated and endowed a library that would make his collections available to a select segment of the public. In contrast with the democratic Astor Library, access to Lenox's rare and esoteric collection was confined to scholars. It was, as Moses King put it, "a curiosity of the world . . . [a] library of a bibliophilist, made public."[10] The restricted use was not universally admired; *The Nation* urged "that [the collection] be called a museum rather than a library."[11] Among the nine trustees Lenox appointed to oversee the new library was William H. Aspinwall, former guardian of Richard Morris Hunt's wife, Catherine. The library was Hunt's second commission from Lenox, who had hired the architect to design the Presbyterian Hospital (see below). Hunt's scheme for the

library would be an early landmark of the Classical revival of the late nineteenth and early twentieth centuries that would come to be called the American Renaissance.

The site for the Lenox Library constituted a significant portion, but not all that remained, of the Five Mile Stone Farm Lenox had inherited from his father and sold off in the 1860s as the northward growth of the city began to invade the lower environs of Central Park. The entire site was still relatively rural; in fact, for quite some time after the Lenox Library was completed, cows were pastured behind the building and market gardening was conducted across the street. Construction of the library began in May 1871 but proceeded slowly so that work on the interiors did not take place until 1874–75, with collections moved in during 1876. On January 15, 1877, the first rooms were opened, for an exhibition of paintings and statues, with the manuscript and rare-book rooms opening at the end of the same year. The south reading room was not open until 1880, and then only for exhibits; it was not until 1882 that the book collection itself was made available to scholars, who had to obtain admission cards.

The library's plan was the essence of clarity. The 192-by-114-foot, U-shaped building nearly filled its site except for a centrally located, 100-foot-wide-by-42-foot-deep courtyard facing Fifth Avenue. Entering across the courtyard, visitors were received in a 24-foot-wide-by-96-foot-long hall that connected the two wings, each containing a

*Lenox Library, east side of Fifth Avenue, East Seventieth to East Seventy-first Street. Richard Morris Hunt, 1870–77.
View to the northeast. AABN. CU.*

Lenox Library, east side of Fifth Avenue, East Seventieth to East Seventy-first Street. Richard Morris Hunt, 1870–77. View to the southeast. AABN. CU.

Mercantile Library (1855), former Astor Place Opera House (1848), west side of Lafayette Place, East Eighth to East Ninth Street. View to the northwest. MCNY.

24-foot-high, 108-foot-long, 30-foot-wide reading room. Offices and other service spaces were compactly located in the center of the building, behind the entry hall. Above the entry hall, on the second floor, a picture gallery overlooking the courtyard and Central Park beyond contained works by Thomas Gainsborough, Albert Bierstadt, Joseph Turner, Jacob van Ruisdael, Gilbert Stuart, and Sir Joshua Reynolds. Behind the picture gallery lay a top-lit gallery, while at each end there was a reading room, sized as the ones below but incorporating vaulted ceilings that rose to a height of forty feet. On the partial third floor, which formed an attic story over the central portion of the building, there was yet another twenty-four-by-ninety-six-foot gallery.

The library's gray Lockport limestone facade was simply worked with flat rustication to mark the ground floor and plain surfaces above. The building was surmounted by copper roofs. Pink granite Ionic columns carried the triple arches that gave the central, second-floor gallery a loggia-like effect. Large arched windows provided light to the second-story reading rooms, while the reading rooms on the ground floor had to rely on smaller segmental lunettes. The north wing contained a pediment carrying a representation of Apollo, and the south wing was similarly decorated with a bust of Minerva. The simplified detail of the building's fluted pilasters hinted at the Neo-Grec basis for the design, but, as the *New York Times* pointed out when the building was still under construction, Hunt's design was not so much Neo-Grec as "modern classic. . . . [While

the] French apartment building of the Stevens estate [see chapter 4] . . . is pure Neo-Grec, and contains many other things which are Gothic in character," the Lenox Library has "a much greater feeling of classicism," which was "somewhat to be deplored."[12] The specific source of the design, as the *New York Daily Tribune* pointed out, was widely held to be Jacques-Félix Duban's building for the Ecole Nationale Supérieure des Beaux-Arts in Paris, designed in 1858 but not completed until 1864.[13] Another possible inspiration was Charles Questel's Musée-Bibliotheque (1862–75), in Grenoble, France. But, as the architectural historian David Van Zanten has recently pointed out, Questel's building, so like Hunt's in its program if not its organization, may not have been the source of the Lenox design so much as a remarkably parallel effort, revealing just how thoroughly French · Hunt's approach was.[14] Behind all three designs lay Henri Labrouste's Bibliotheque Ste-Geneviève (1844–50), in Paris, in which, as was the case of Hunt's design for the wings of the Lenox Library, the stone was treated almost as though it were a skeleton of piers joined by arches with screen walls stretched between.

Hunt's design was far more self-consciously articulated than Labrouste's, more Renaissance in its approach than Neo-Grec, the latter a direction that by the early 1870s Hunt no doubt saw as stylistically passé. It was the connection between Hunt's library and Renaissance design that identified the building as a first step in a new direction and not a provincial reflection of an established French trend. At the time of their completion, Hunt's Classical Lenox Library and his Gothic Presbyterian Hospital, both built with the same client's money and located only a block away from each other, were completely visible in a single glance. To Alfred J. Bloor, addressing the annual convention of the American Institute of Architects in 1876, "the restless aspiring vitality, the picturesque massing, and the bright double-tinted surface of [Hunt's] Presbyterian Hospital, with the low horizontal lines, the single subdued tint, the thoroughly expressed repose, and the quiet but elegant simplicity of its immediate neighbor, the Lenox Library," testified to "the versatility of their architect."[15] Yet, the fact that the two buildings varied so radically in stylistic vocabulary did not so much reveal eclecticism as a dramatic shift in architectural taste. In each case, it would appear, Hunt was struggling to make a modern building, not to revive but to exploit inherited forms while saying something wholly new. It was not only the detail of the library's design but its very French plan, with projecting wings and a central courtyard, that was completely new to the city. In 1898 the anonymous author of *A History of Real Estate, Building and Architecture in New York City During the Last Quarter of a Century* stated: "It is a cold and stark building, but it possesses a stately and monumental character, which was a new element in American architecture at the time [of its completion]. Its good qualities are French."[16] In his postmortem on Hunt, Montgomery Schuyler praised the library as "almost alone among Mr. Hunt's buildings of this period in presenting a situation of an important architectural problem, which is at once academic and individual, and which combines animation with dignity. . . . The net result of the designer's dispositions is to give the building an impression of 'scale,' in which it was almost alone in New York or in the country at the time of its erection, and has had very few successful rivals since."[17]

The Mercantile Library, founded in 1820, was one of the city's most important subscription libraries, notable not only for its size—by 1871 it was the largest lending library in the country and the fourth largest of any kind, exceeded only by the Astor Library, the Public Library of Boston, and the Library of Congress—but also for the profile of its readers. As the journalist John Rose Greene Hassard, writing in *Scribner's Monthly*, put it, the library "is the creation of merchants' clerks, who can spare only a few hours in the week from their desks and counters, and have never had much leisure to devote to any kind of books except day-books and ledgers."[18] The library was first housed in an upper-story room at 49 Fulton Street. Between 1855 and 1889 the library was located in the former Astor Place Opera House, renamed Clinton Hall. The library shared the three-story, templelike building with Leavitt, Strebeigh & Co., an auction house for books. Inside, a reading room dominated the second floor, while the book stacks were located on the third floor surrounding a rotunda with fluted columns and a skylit dome. Has-

sard noted that the room "seems to be well enough adapted to its special purpose,—the reception and delivery of books,—but it has no beauty, either of ornament or architectural design; it is rather cramped, and it lacks even the elegance which rows of neatly-bound books generally confer upon a library, for all the volumes here are covered with brown paper, and the shelves, though neatly kept, present a decidedly dingy aspect. In fact it is not a lounging-place for readers, but a depot where business is transacted with mercantile dispatch and regularity." One of the library's most distinguishing features, however, was related neither to its building nor its collection; unlike the Astor Library, the Mercantile was open late and thus easily accessible to working people. As Hassard noted:

> It is not until six or seven o'clock in the evening that the class of young men for which the institution is chiefly designed are found here in great numbers. As soon as the dinner or tea hour has passed the clerks begin to drop in, and until the room closes for the night at ten o'clock, the desks and tables are well filled. . . . This is the time when the reading room fulfills the noblest of its functions,— when it not merely serves for the amusement of the curious and idle, and the convenience of the studious, but draws away from the worst temptations of the great city those who are most accessible to its seductions and least able to guard against them.[19]

In 1890 the library's headquarters was demolished and a new, seven-story building, also known as Clinton Hall,

Mercantile Library, west side of Lafayette Place, East Eighth to East Ninth Street. George E. Harney, 1890. View to the northwest. King, 1893. CU.

was erected on the same site by the library and its trustees.[20] As designed by George E. Harney, the buff brick and red sandstone building was distinguished by a two-story rusticated base incorporating double-height arched windows. The building's top two floors, which housed the library, were articulated with similar fenestration. Writing in 1896, the historian Charles H. Haswell regretted the passing of the old Clinton Hall, "its graceful proportions giving way to a new structure, larger and more convenient no doubt, but in point of architecture showing a mournful decline of taste as compared with its predecessor."[21]

With only the Astor Library available to those who could not afford a library subscription fee, the need for more free libraries was acute. Especially in demand were free neighborhood reading rooms or libraries. By the late 1860s such facilities were being run in various impoverished districts by the City Mission and the Children's Aid Society, but the creation and operation of these libraries were dependent on charity and, in the case of the City Mission libraries, religious agendas compromised utility for a wide segment of the population.[22] Although there were libraries that were free in name, such as the New York Free Circulating Library, which was founded in 1878, initially occupying space at 36 Bond Street, these were in fact private charities operating with the express purpose of providing moral and intellectual elevation for the masses.[23] As the *New York Daily Graphic* stated in 1888, "it is true that we have books enough on the shelves of our so-called 'free' libraries, but there it ends. They are not accessible to the public as they would be in a large library which is public property." According to the *Daily Graphic*, "The New York Free Library, formerly called the Printers' Free Library, is anything but 'free,' as its name would indicate."[24] The *Daily Graphic* resented the requirement that borrowers submit references. By the mid-1880s the lack of free libraries was seen as a serious municipal problem. The *New York Times*, which had in the past occasionally editorialized for a nonsectarian public library like Boston's, strongly asserted in 1884 that it was "not too much to say that next to a clean administration of its affairs a great free circulating library is the city's chief lack."[25]

In 1880 the New York Free Circulating Library embarked on a plan to "establish small libraries . . . in the centers of the poorest and most thickly settled districts of the city."[26] The first of these, the Ottendorfer Branch (1884), at 135 Second Avenue, between St. Mark's Place and Ninth Street, was designed by William Schickel.[27] The library was paid for by Oswald and Anna Ottendorfer, themselves immigrants, to serve a thriving community of German immigrants. Oswald Ottendorfer was publisher of the *New Yorker Staats-Zeitung*, the city's leading German-language newspaper. Over the door, an inscription proclaimed in German that the building was a Free Library and Reading Room ("Freie Bibliothek und Lesehalle"). The shelves were stocked equally with English- and German-language books initially selected by the donors.

The library branch was built at the same time as the adjacent German Dispensary (see below), also a gift of the Ottendorfers. The choice of Schickel as the library's architect reflected the Ottendorfers' interest in the German community; personally chosen by Anna Ottendorfer, Schickel had been born and trained in Germany before immigrating to the United States in 1870, and he was new to independent practice. He had worked for a number of local firms, including Richard Morris Hunt's, before establishing his own practice. His design, like that of his fellow countryman Alexander Saeltzer, the architect of the Astor Library, reflected the Rundbogenstil, although the flattened arch that formed the entrance seemed more late-Georgian via the Queen Anne style than it did German. The ornamental terra cotta that framed the friezes and outlined the arches of the red Philadelphia pressed brick building was notable for its programmatic symbolism: spandrels were filled with books and urns, and the frieze was made up of owls and globes, respectively representing wisdom and knowledge. The *New York Times* was quick to sense that the work of the New York Free Circulating Library was a distinct improvement over previous efforts, seeing its "substantial growth . . . since its modest beginning" as a "cornerstone of the city's future great free library."[28]

Other branches soon followed. George E. Harney's George Bruce Memorial Library (1888), at 226 West Forty-second Street, between Seventh and Eighth Avenues, was deemed by the *Real Estate Record and Builders' Guide* "a creditable and tasteful performance even if it fails of being completely artistic."[29] The picturesque Jackson Free Library (1888), at 251 West Thirteenth

Ottendorfer Branch of the New York Free Circulating Library, 135 Second Avenue. William Schickel, 1884. View to the west showing part of the German Dispensary (William Schickel, 1883–84) on the right. HNYPL. CU.

George Bruce Memorial Library, 226 West Forty-second Street. George E. Harney, 1888. View to the south showing the Central Baptist Church (c. 1863) on the left. NYHS.

Jackson Free Library, 251 West Thirteenth Street. Richard Morris Hunt, 1888. View to the north. HNYPL. CU.

Street, between Greenwich and Seventh Avenues, near Jackson Square, was designed by Richard Morris Hunt and paid for with funds donated by the scholarly youngest child of William Henry Vanderbilt, George Washington Vanderbilt, then twenty-six years old.[30] Appropriately, given the library's location at the edge of one of New York's most historic neighborhoods, Hunt elected to house it in a version of a crow-gabled Dutch guildhall. The principal facade of the three-story building contained a main entrance and seven windows, each surmounted by a blind arch decorated with a trefoil. Iron strapwork articulated top-floor windows and the gable. Leaded glass gave the domestically scaled building an even more intimate sense of scale.

In 1887 the New York State Legislature passed a bill granting public funding to augment the private monies that supported the New York Free Circulating Library system, making the libraries public property for the first time. The infusion of public tax revenues further stimulated private philanthropy, leading to a period of tremendous growth, especially after 1901, when the system merged with a few other smaller free circulating libraries to become the circulation department of the newly created New York Public Library. The following year, as a result of the generosity of Andrew Carnegie, branch libraries began to be built throughout Manhattan, the Bronx, and Staten Island. Carnegie also provided funds for the branch systems of the Brooklyn Public Library and the Queens Borough Public Library.

CLUBS

By the Civil War, New York's clubs were a fixture on the local social scene. Very much versions of clubs in London, the organizations catered almost exclusively to men, especially young bachelors who perhaps took furnished rooms in the neighborhood but ate their breakfasts and dinners at a clubhouse, where, as a writer in the *Galaxy* put it in 1876, they could "always command agreeable society" and "a greater degree of liberty in living" than it was otherwise possible to achieve.[1] While many clubs were organized along purely social lines, some catered to a particular ethnic group or were united by a common business purpose, trade, or even political affiliation.

Social Clubs

The Union League Club, founded in 1863 by prominent Republicans in order to aid the Union cause, was first headquartered in the Henry Parish residence at 26 East Seventeenth Street. In 1867 the club commissioned designs for a large new clubhouse from Richard Morris Hunt for a location at Fourth Avenue and Twenty-third Street; Hunt's proposal distinctly recalled Hector Lefuel's extension to the Louvre (1854–55).[2] The club chose not to proceed with the plan, however, and in 1868 relocated to the former home of Leonard P. Jerome (Thomas R. Jackson, 1859), at the southeast corner of Twenty-sixth Street and Madison Avenue.[3] It remained there until a fire destroyed much of the building's interiors on April 25, 1875. In 1881 the Union League Club moved to its first purpose-built clubhouse, at the northeast corner of Fifth Avenue and Thirty-ninth Street, formerly the site of Dickel's Riding Academy.[4] The new clubhouse, far and away the city's grandest as well as comparable in scale and facilities to the most lavish of London's clubhouses, was designed by the Boston-based firm of Peabody & Stearns, which had secured the commission two years earlier through a competition. The other competitors, an interesting mix of the city's top firms and some promising newcomers, were McKim, Mead & Bigelow, Edward E. Raht, Gambrill & Ficken, George E. Harney, Richard Morris Hunt, Stephen D. Hatch, Thorp & Price, Potter & Robertson, West & Anderson, and James Renwick Jr., who submitted two designs. Despite its comparative youth, the Union League had become one of the city's most important, if not truly fashionable, clubs, so the decision to build a lavish clubhouse on Fifth Avenue may have marked a bid to change its image. Indeed, as the *New York Times* observed, the choice of a Fifth Avenue location was "natural and proper. For it is not a conservative club, nor one that can afford to shrug its shoulders at wealth which is not supported by brains or birth. It is a progressive, alert club, a young man's club. . . . In moving to a building on Fifth-avenue it may really express a desire on the part of the members who accomplished the move to make it a fashionable club." But the chances of accomplishing that would

Proposed Union League Club, Fourth Avenue and East Twenty-third Street. Richard Morris Hunt, 1867. Elevation. The Octagon, AAF.

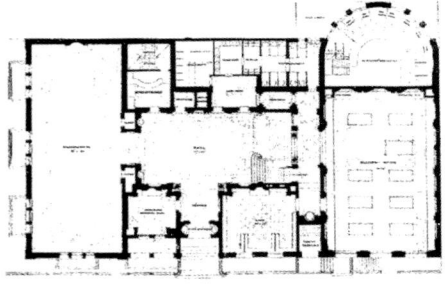

Proposed Union League Club, northeast corner of Fifth Avenue and East Thirty-ninth Street. McKim, Mead & Bigelow, 1879. Competition-entry perspective showing view to the northeast and first-floor plan. AABN. CU.

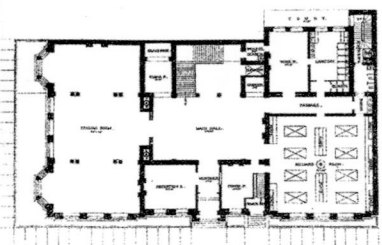

Proposed Union League Club, northeast corner of Fifth Avenue and East Thirty-ninth Street. Edward E. Raht, 1879. Competition-entry south elevation and first-floor plan. AABN. CU.

Proposed Union League Club, northeast corner of Fifth Avenue and East Thirty-ninth Street. Gambrill & Ficken, 1879. Competition-entry south elevation and second-floor plan. AABN. CU.

Proposed Union League Club, northeast corner of Fifth Avenue and East Thirty-ninth Street. George E. Harney, 1879.
Competition-entry perspective showing view to the northeast and first-floor plan. AABN. CU.

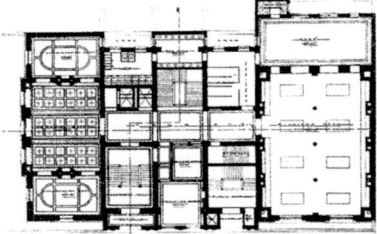

Proposed Union League Club, northeast corner of Fifth Avenue and East Thirty-ninth Street. Richard Morris Hunt, 1879.
Competition-entry perspective showing view to the northeast and first-floor plan. The Octagon, AAF.

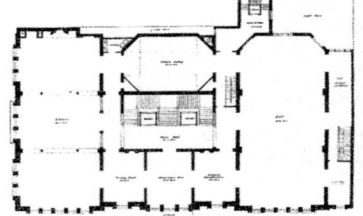

Proposed Union League Club, northeast corner of Fifth Avenue and East Thirty-ninth Street. Stephen D. Hatch, 1879. Competition-entry perspective showing view to the northeast and second-floor plan. AABN. CU.

Proposed Union League Club, northeast corner of Fifth Avenue and East Thirty-ninth Street. Thorp & Price, 1879. Competition-entry south elevation and first-floor plan. AABN. CU.

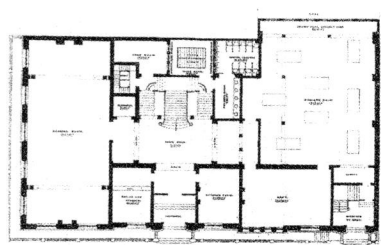

Proposed Union League Club, northeast corner of Fifth Avenue and East Thirty-ninth Street. Potter & Robertson, 1879. Competition-entry perspective showing view to the northeast and first-floor plan. AABN. CU.

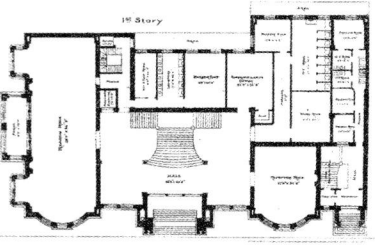

Proposed Union League Club, northeast corner of Fifth Avenue and East Thirty-ninth Street. West & Anderson, 1879. Competition-entry perspective showing view to the northeast and first-floor plan. AABN. CU.

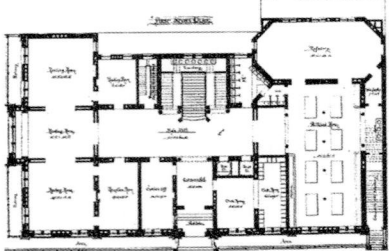

Proposed Union League Club, northeast corner of Fifth Avenue and East Thirty-ninth Street. James Renwick Jr., 1879.
Competition-entry perspective showing view to the northeast and first-floor plan. AABN. CU.

Proposed Union League Club, northeast corner of Fifth Avenue and East Thirty-ninth Street. James Renwick Jr., 1879.
Alternate competition-entry perspective showing view to the northeast and first-floor plan. AABN. CU.

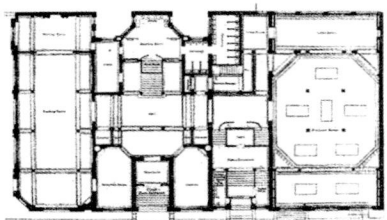

Proposed Union League Club, northeast corner of Fifth Avenue and East Thirty-ninth Street. Peabody & Stearns, 1879. Competition-entry south elevation (left), west elevation (right), and first-floor plan. AABN. CU.

inevitably be halted by the political nature of the institution, the *Times* argued, and by the changing nature of Fifth Avenue itself, which was "no longer that name of awe as the exclusive resort of fashion which it once appeared to be. Tailors, harness-makers, and grocers of a genteel variety have already invaded it above Madison-square, and the days of its lofty exclusiveness are numbered."[5]

The program called for a large building to house many more elements than had been accommodated in the Jerome mansion, including a variety of rooms for socializing, dining, reading, and games, as well as bedrooms. The work of all the competitors was published, constituting in its totality a revealing overview of contemporary practice. According to the New York correspondent of the *American Architect and Building News*, Richard Morris Hunt's palazzo-like design was "in the severe style which served well in the Lenox Library" and here "introduced with a few concessions toward club life," while Potter & Robertson's cozy Queen Anne proposal was "as precise and attentive to detail as though it were a gate-lodge or a college memorial hall," projects that the firm currently had under way at Princeton. The correspondent would have been more impressed with Gambrill & Ficken's austere, French Renaissance–inspired

scheme had the architects "paid more attention to the plan." The writer somewhat sarcastically characterized George E. Harney's innovative proposal as "an out-and-out Queen Anne design, which would suit to a nicety some wealthy Knickerbocker club, anxious to keep up the memory of their Dutch ancestors. It is the most homelike structure of any on the walls, and not withstanding its size has a real cozy look and feeling." Edward E. Raht's mansarded design was dismissed as "precise," while Stephen D. Hatch's rhythmically fenestrated proposal, which owed much to the Neo-Grec, was castigated as "meagre," with "a pinched look [that] does not fairly present the possibilities of the problem." McKim, Mead & Bigelow's light-hearted Italianate design, the most stylistically innovative of the submissions, was notable for its use of pergola-shaded roof terraces, arched windows, some arranged in the Serlian manner, and a rooftop loggia, which was deemed "very peculiar," manifesting "a curious notion of club life in New York. There might have been good reason for such contrivance had the club been situated in an Italian city, but such a hanging garden would be a deserted domain for ten months of the year and during the other two the club men are not in town." There was not much said in favor of the unsolicited designs

Union League Club, northeast corner of Fifth Avenue and East Thirty-ninth Street. Peabody & Stearns, 1881. View to the northeast. Byron. MCNY.

of Alfred H. Thorp and Bruce Price and West & Anderson: "Mr. Thorp in his Racket Club did honest work with a legitimate building material, but his club-house seems designed on the conventional model for an English town warehouse or store, and the club members embodied this verdict in very direct language." West & Anderson's scheme possessed "a combination of coarse emphatic features, which would possibly suit the building committee in a Western town." Regarding James Renwick Jr.'s two entries, the correspondent noted only that the architect had "tried a Gothic treatment, as well as something more formal, but they were rather irreverently criticised by many of the laity press." All in all, the *American Architect and Building News*'s correspondent noted, Gambrill & Ficken and Potter & Robertson represented "the best of the New York plans":

Both indicate an appreciation of what a club-house should be, and show that mixture of publicity and the privacy and comfort of home with somewhat of pretentious show. It is not to be repellant or cold; conspicuous enough to invite public attention and criticism, while it does not seem to extend an invitation to the casual stroller to walk in, as a museum, a church, a library, or a theatre might; it is to be something more than a grand private house, which a certain number of individuals propose to hold with common privileges.[6]

Peabody & Stearns's Queen Anne–inspired design, emphasizing the baroque aspects of the early Georgian, was considerably changed after the competition. As the *American Architect and Building News*'s correspondent observed about the original design, it "could hardly be styled a homelike structure, and though the club is an active political body at times [and] makes itself very prominent in the public eye, there is a retiring side to the life of the club, which will hardly find this exterior a congenial one. In their Queen Anne outlines the architects get what no formal style would permit—a freedom to arrange the elevation to meet the exigencies of the plan [which] has dominated over the exterior."[7] The club was to be entered beneath a slightly projecting porch rising to a tower on the Thirty-ninth Street side. The ground floor was treated as a rusticated basement with bands of Belleville stone, used there and throughout, alternating with brick. The principal social room on this floor, extending the entire length of the Fifth Avenue facade, was the "reading-room, or ogling apartment, whence the club men can observe, through its broad windows, the fair promenaders on the Avenue."[8] Also on this floor were the billiards and smoking rooms; the bowling alleys were in the basement, which was lit via windows opening onto a sunken moat that lined both street frontages. An art gallery was located at the rear of the second floor, where it was lit from above by a skylight. Also on the second floor was the library, facing Fifth Avenue, and a large meeting hall along the lot line. The third floor contained guest rooms, while the main dining room, one and a half stories tall, stretched along Fifth Avenue on the fourth floor, which also contained smaller dining rooms. Three floors of bedrooms piled above the assembly room formed a separate wing.

Between the competition and construction, Peabody & Stearns's design was altered. Many of the boldest features of the original were dropped, including the bronze dome and the clock tower, which Montgomery Schuyler had deemed a "conspicuous irrelevancy." Even after the revisions, Schuyler reported that the club's exterior had "not made a popular success" for reasons that "are sufficiently evident. The chief of these is that the building is a collection, rather than a union, of parts." Schuyler noted, however, that the amended design showed more unity than the competition version. The design "is gathered under one roof, and this roof is simple, of steep pitch, and in itself an agreeable object, both in form and color." Nonetheless, "the building still 'scatters,'" with "very little relation" between its two facades.[9] The *New York Times* was slyly dismissive: "The Union League has planted itself in a big handsome structure, on a gay thoroughfare, where it can see and be seen. No more noticeable building exists on Fifth-avenue, and, though the want of an organic construction in the building may offend a few of the critical, the picturesqueness of its chimneys and rooflines, together with the size and weight of its two faces, will be sure to make a favorable impression upon nine passers out of ten."[10]

After the club opened, an occasion marked by a ceremonial breakfast on March 5, 1881, Schuyler congratulated the association "on having started a new era in the history of New York clubs, and on having a house which is not only . . . splendid in its appointments but most comfortable." Touring the newly opened clubhouse, Schuyler remarked to his friend the architect Leopold Eidlitz that

the treatment "as columns with capitals and bases complete" of king posts in the ceiling of the dining room seemed "somehow wrong," to which Eidlitz, ever the rationalist, replied: "To appreciate the entire iniquity of the arrangement, you are to bear in mind that that member is not a compression-piece but a tension-piece."[11] Though Schuyler found John La Farge's work in the gabled dining room deficient, he applauded the interior decorations, citing the "Moresque manner" of using stucco, "the lavish employment of Louis C. Tiffany's glass," the "most judicious and happy selection of woods, and [the] bold and original treatment of all the brass-work connected with illuminating purposes." Schuyler also called attention to the provision of a separate entrance to the picture gallery and members' hall so that "visitors on festive occasions" might gain access without disturbing the members.[12] In contrast, the *New York Times* found the decorating troublesome, citing a lack of coordination among the gifted interior decorators and artists: "One decorator should have been chosen and liberally dealt with. As it is, the dining-room takes the color out of the halls and the halls out of the theatre [*sic*—actually, the members' hall]." The *Times* nonetheless concluded: "The Union League can comfort itself with the reflection that it has taken the lead before all the other clubs in trying to arrange for itself a habitation beautiful within and without, and will not fail to get the credit of being the first to encourage American painters in the treatment of decoration on the highest planes of art."[13] Five years after the clubhouse's completion, Mariana Van Rensselaer, reflecting a widespread repudiation of the Queen Anne style, faulted Peabody & Stearns's picturesque approach as "an unworthy aim in a building of this size, in this position and devoted to this purpose." Moreover, the critic contended, the search for picturesqueness had gone unfulfilled and the design offered "instead a restlessness, a want of unity, an unmotived variety," which struck her as "irrational."[14]

Knickerbocker Club, 319 Fifth Avenue. Former Moller house; expansion and renovation, R. H. Robertson, 1882. View to the northeast. King, 1893. CU.

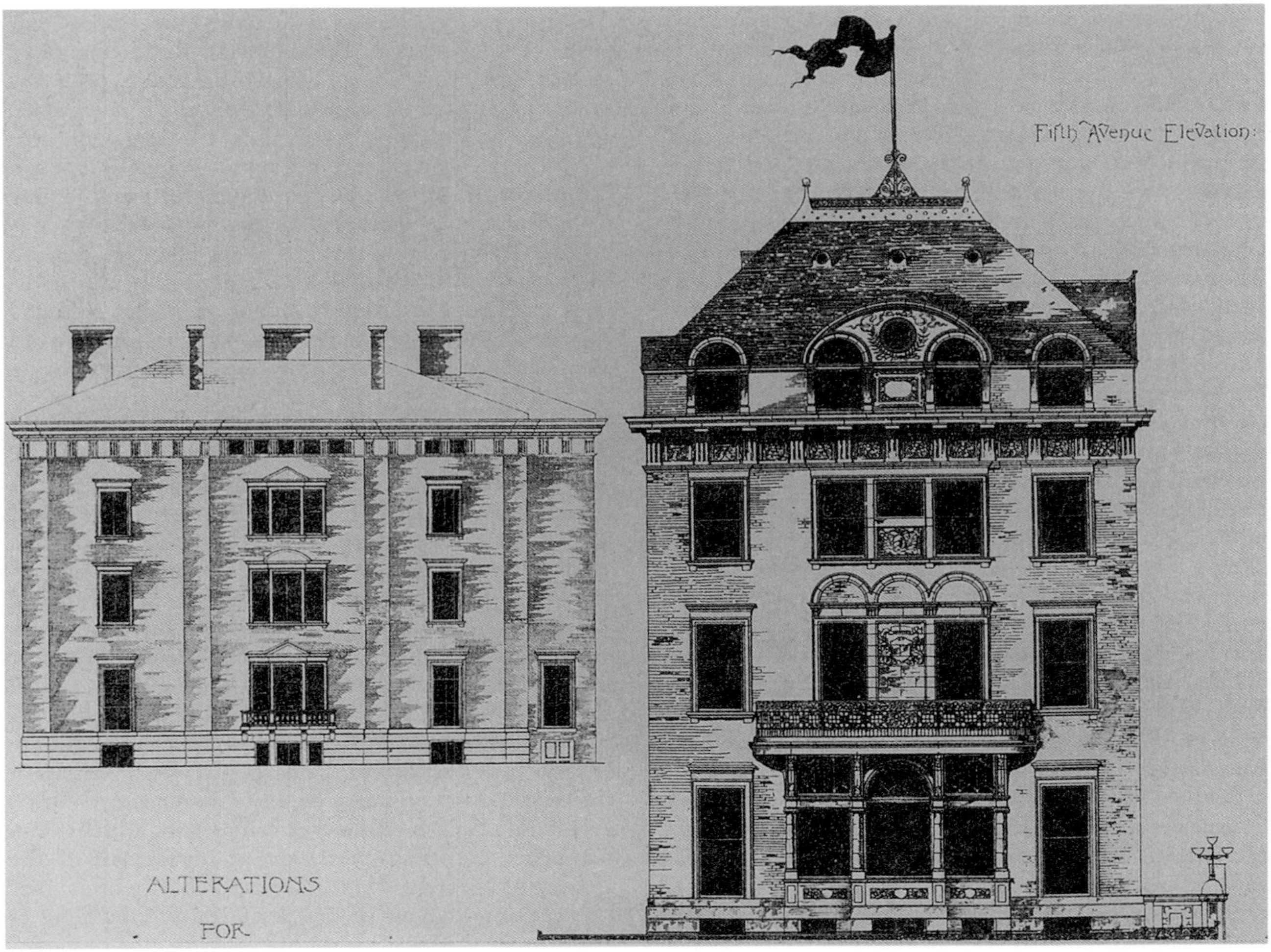

New-York Club, 370 Fifth Avenue. Former Caswell house; expansion and renovation, R. H. Robertson and A. J. Manning, 1888. North (left) and east (right) elevations. AABN. CU.

New-York Club, 370 Fifth Avenue. Former Caswell house; expansion and renovation, R. H. Robertson and A. J. Manning, 1888. View to the southwest. King, 1893. CU.

The example of the Union League's new clubhouse was not lost on the much more self-consciously social members of the Knickerbocker Club.[15] Organized in 1871 by descendants of the original settlers of New York, the club occupied the former William Butler Duncan house, at 249 Fifth Avenue, on the southeast corner of Twenty-eighth Street, for ten years beginning in 1872. In 1882 the club moved to 319 Fifth Avenue, on the northeast corner of Thirty-second Street, taking over the former Moller house, an Italianate building of brick and brownstone that had recently been home to Cornelius Vanderbilt; the club occupied it after completing additions and extensive renovations by R. H. Robertson. Ironically, the Knickerbocker's new clubhouse featured a long, awning-covered balcony that was similar in some ways to the loggia McKim and his partners had been criticized for in their Union League Club project: presumably more old-line Knickerbocker men stayed in New York during the summer than did new-rich Union League members.

Founded in 1846, the New-York Club, one of the city's

oldest, moved frequently as it prospered and followed fashion uptown. In 1888 it moved to 370 Fifth Avenue, on the southwest corner of Thirty-fifth Street, where it took over the Caswell residence, which had previously served as headquarters for the University Club.[16] R. H. Robertson and A. J. Manning were selected in a competition to remodel the club, rendering the Italianate mansion's exterior "scarcely recognizable" by transforming it into a stylistically eclectic, red brick and sandstone version of the Queen Anne.[17] As the *New York Daily Tribune* observed, "little of the old building was used, and that little was radically remodelled. . . . The interior of the whole house was

also subjected to an entire renovation."[18] The new clubhouse had to live up to the standards of the previous, outgrown clubhouse, at 1 West Twenty-fifth Street, facing the General William J. Worth monument (James G. Batterson, 1857), where, according to the *New York Daily Graphic*, the "sunlight streamed in through . . . wide windows all the wintry days, and there were cozy, quiet corners and cool nooks for the men in town during the summer solstice."[19] Inside Robertson and Manning's building, specially designed English-inspired furniture, including versions of fashionable work associated with William Morris and his group, filled two floors of public rooms that

Century Association, 7 West Forty-third Street, McKim, Mead & White, 1889–91. View to the northeast. CA.

Century Association, 7 West Forty-third Street. McKim, Mead &
White, 1889–91. View to the northwest along West Forty-third
Street showing, from right to left, the Century Association,
the New York Academy of Medicine (R. H. Robertson, 1889),
and the Racquet and Tennis Club (Cyrus L. W. Eidlitz, 1890).
Underhill. CA.

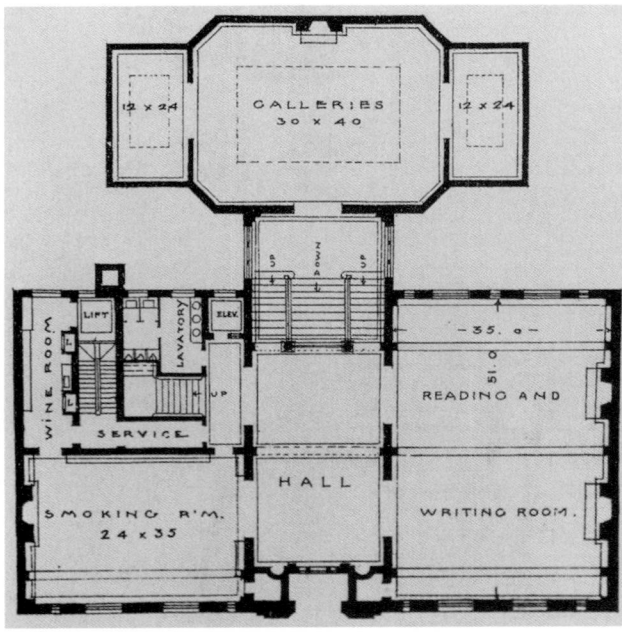

Century Association, 7 West Forty-third Street. McKim, Mead &
White, 1889–91. Second-floor plan. AABN. CU.

included the usual lounges, dining, and game rooms.

Created to "form an association of gentlemen of the city of New York and its vicinity, engaged or interested in literature and the fine arts, with a view to their advancement, as well as the promotion of social intercourse," the Century Association was organized in 1847.[20] It first occupied rooms at 495 Broadway, and twice moved farther up that thoroughfare before residing for a short time on Clinton Place near Greene Street. In 1857, it relocated to a modest, houselike building at 109 East Fifteenth Street, between Union Square and Irving Place, where it would settle for over thirty years. In 1869 that building was remodeled, perhaps by H. H. Richardson, into a structure consisting of two stories plus a mansard, of red brick trimmed in limestone, in the Neo-Grec style. In 1889 the club again decided to move northward. After considering the site of the First Baptist Church, at the northwest corner of Thirty-ninth Street and Park Avenue, the club purchased a one-hundred-by-one-hundred-foot site at 7 West Forty-third Street, replacing in 1889–91 the stables of the Fifth Avenue stage line with a palatial, Veneto-inspired, brick and terra cotta clubhouse designed by McKim, Mead & White.[21] The new clubhouse, a realization of the idea first proposed by the firm ten years earlier for the Union League Club and explored in somewhat timid fashion at the Freundschaft Club (see below), would prove to have a decisive influence over the architectural taste of the decade to come. Distinctly a palazzo, the building's cubic massing may have been similar to that of London clubs of the 1830s and 1840s; the scholarly interpretation of Italian precedent for the facade, however, principally based on Michele Sanmicheli's sixteenth-century Palazzo Canossa, in Verona, and the decided horizontality of the massing, with its sixty-foot height made to read as two stories, marked a new sensibility that led the architect and critic Russell Sturgis to praise it, noting:

> The first thing that strikes the observer after a pleasant feeling of graceful proportions and a pleasant creamy-white color is the frank way in which the facade is treated as a facade, and the fact dwelt upon—insisted on—that this architectural frontage is one thing and the other three walls of the building plain and bare. Those are the conditions of almost all our city buildings which are wedged in by others, and are either divided by party walls, or crowded close together, wall touching wall. Those are not often acknowledged in the design of the front. It is one merit, and a rare one, that this assertion is made here and made gracefully.

Sturgis went on to assert that the building constituted "an excellent design of its kind; perhaps the most pleasing front in New York; at least it is not easy to think of another which it is so worth while going to see or so agreeable to see often."[22] Inside, though the plan exhibited a rigorous columnar order, the decor added to the building's Italianisms in the comfortable character of the Century's former home on Fifteenth Street, although all the furniture and cabinetwork, much of it designed by the architects, was new.

Century Association, 7 West Forty-third Street. McKim, Mead & White, 1889–91. View of the library toward the private dining room. CA.

Century Association, 7 West Forty-third Street. McKim, Mead & White, 1889–91. Smoking room. CA.

The Down-Town Association was not quite in the same category or class as the grand uptown clubs. Organized in 1860 to provide "facilities and accommodations for social intercourse, dining and meeting during intervals of business," it occupied various locations until 1885–87, when it built a brick and stone, Romanesque-inspired permanent headquarters designed by C. C. Haight on a 44-by-134-foot site at 60 Pine Street running through to Cedar Street.[23] The luncheon club was especially suited to New York City, as the *Real Estate Record and Builders' Guide* observed: "Luncheon clubs are not peculiar to New York among great commercial cities, but for several reasons they attain their highest development here. In no other American city are the distances between residence and business so great, and in no other is it so inevitable that the man who goes to business in the morning goes 'to make a day of it.'" The new clubhouse was extravagant by comparison with its purpose, a symbol of the "amount of money that is to spare in New York. . . . Here is a big house, ornate outside and sumptuous within, of which practically the sole function is to enable some hundreds of busy men to take one hurried meal a day, six days in the week."[24] Haight piled three brick-faced stories above a two-story brownstone base, announcing the location of the principal dining room with three large arches. Though Romanesque designs were not typical of Haight's work, Montgomery Schuyler included the club in his comprehensive article on the Romanesque Revival in New York, stating: "The building constitutes a refreshing oasis in a neighborhood that is nearly blank of architectural interest, being both rational and rhythmical in general composition, especially well studied detail and fortunate in color."[25]

Sports Clubs

While the city's most important clubs were typically organized on the basis of shared social values, there were also many clubs formed around a distinct area of interest in sports, such as the American Jockey Club, founded in 1866. The club occupied a building designed for it in 1871 by Detlef Lienau, the second floor of which was given over to the New York Yacht Club, which maintained its own clubhouse on Staten Island.[26] Except for a chamfered corner, the four-story building was unremarkable. Located at the southwest corner of Twenty-seventh Street and Madison Avenue, it combined many aspects typical of earlier Italianate brick and brownstone townhouses by Lienau and others.

Unlike the American Jockey Club, most of the athletics clubs were founded by men interested in participating in the sports themselves. Informally existing as a club since about 1784 but organized only in 1875, the Racquet Court Club moved into 55 West Twenty-sixth Street, on the northeast corner of Sixth Avenue, in May 1876, occupying the top three floors of a building designed by Alfred Thorp, the sixth American to attend the Ecole des Beaux-Arts, in Paris, here assisted by William A. Potter.[27] Innovative in many ways, the clubhouse marked, as Augustus

Down-Town Association, 60 Pine Street. C. C. Haight, 1885–87. View to the northwest. King, 1893. CU.

Down-Town Association, 60 Pine Street. C. C. Haight, 1885–87. Main entrance. AR. CU.

Stonehouse wrote in 1887, the "complete emancipation of club life from the tradition of the private dwelling."[28] Certainly it looked like no other club, more closely resembling an office building. But there were notable features, including the arcaded handling of the brick facades above the one-story base and the remarkable friezelike attic carrying a cornice on metal brackets, a strategy devised to allow the top-floor courts to be naturally ventilated while shaded from direct light, rain, and snow. Thorp, not a particularly prolific architect, was given the commission by his brother, who was developing the building as an investment. The architect gave it his all, providing one of the most sophisticated expressions of the volumetric character of a cast-iron structural cage encased in a masonry bearing wall.

Possibly the first building to house indoor racquet courts in America, the clubhouse contained two racquet courts painted differently, red for daytime and white for nighttime play, a gymnasium, a running track, and bowling alleys as well as lounge space and dressing rooms. The ground floor was leased as shops and the second floor as a place "for persons desiring to make their residence in the building." The *New York Times* regarded the building to be "of a decidedly peculiar style of architecture," but failed to explain its determination.[29] Montgomery Schuyler found it "remarkable for the frankness with which its architect accepted his not very attractive conditions, not less than for the skill with which he treated them."[30] Over thirty years later Schuyler would recall the building, praising its "straight-forward and vernacular" expression.[31]

The commercial character of both the clubhouse and its setting, combined with the club's reorganization in 1890 as the Racquet and Tennis Club, led to the construction of a new facility on a 142-foot-wide site at 27 West Forty-third Street, designed by Cyrus L. W. Eidlitz.[32] The four-story brick and Longmeadow stone building consisted of two slightly projecting end pavilions and a five-bay center, the second and third floors of which were recessed behind an arcade. The fourth floor housed the tennis courts and so was almost completely without windows, making for a bold attic facade. Racquet courts were on the second floor and the gymnasium on the third, with each set to the rear of the building so that a regular pattern of windows lit supporting rooms facing the street. In his article on the Romanesque Revival in New York, Schuyler found little to fault in Eidlitz's design, deeming the building "very interesting and impressive . . . a piece of quite free and modern architecture, for which the architect has taken whatever suggestions seemed to be suitable for his purpose from whatever source he could find them without troubling himself about incongruities that were only scholastic and aesthetic incongruities, and it exhibits also an individual inventiveness." Schuyler was particularly taken with "the large and powerful arcade of the centre," Romanesque in inspiration, "with its great depth of reveals, enclosed and abutted by the simple and solid frame of the wings."[33]

The New York Athletic Club was founded in 1868 in the back room of the so-called Knickerbocker Cottage, on

Racquet and Tennis Club, 27 West Forty-third Street. Cyrus L. W. Eidlitz, 1890. View to the northeast. NYHS.

Racquet and Tennis Club, 27 West Forty-third Street. Cyrus L. W. Eidlitz, 1890. Detail of fenestration. AR. CU.

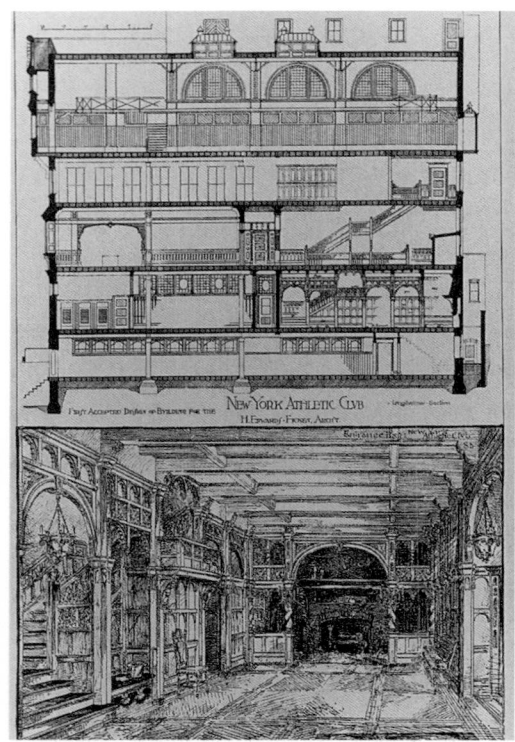

Proposed New York Athletic Club, southwest corner of Sixth Avenue and West Fifty-fifth Street. H. Edwards Ficken, 1886. Section and perspective of the entrance hall. AABN. CU.

Sixth Avenue between Twenty-seventh and Twenty-eighth Streets, for "the promotion of amateur athletics, physical culture and the encouragement of all manner of sport."[34] In 1886 the club moved into a grandly scaled headquarters, as much warehouse as palace, designed by Charles W. Clinton on a seventy-five-by-one-hundred-foot site at the southwest corner of Sixth Avenue and Fifty-fifth Street.[35] For its new building the club first turned to H. Edwards Ficken, who designed a six-story, brick and stone building containing bowling alleys, shooting galleries, and a basement laundry, encapsulated in a medieval fantasy based on the half-timbered architecture of Alsace, with beautifully detailed interiors. But when the bids came in high Ficken's services were terminated, even though he offered the guaranteed bid of a "responsible builder" to construct his design for the amount budgeted.[36] Instead, the club's building committee turned to Charles W. Clinton, while Ficken tried the matter in the press and in the courts, which decided in the plaintiff's behalf regarding fees owed to him.

A rather crude interpretation of sources similar to those that inspired Eidlitz's Racquet and Tennis Club, Clinton's five-story, red brick and terra cotta clubhouse incorporated six bowling alleys, a shooting gallery, a swimming pool, Turkish and Russian baths, a sparring room, and, on the fourth floor, a fifty-nine-by-ninety-two-foot gymnasium around which a one-twentieth-of-a-mile running track

was suspended from the roof. The *Real Estate Record and Builders' Guide* found Clinton's arcaded design "sober, scholarly and dignified," with "good" detail, "though perhaps nowhere exquisite. At least the architect has not been betrayed by the often fatal facility of terra-cotta."[37]

Not quite as old as the New York Athletic Club and much less well-heeled, the Manhattan Athletic Club was organized in 1877. With a strong emphasis on track and field, the club maintained grounds first on West Fifty-seventh Street and then, after 1883, on the entire block bounded by Eighth and Ninth Avenues and Eighty-sixth and Eighty-seventh Streets.[38] At the same time the club sought to build an indoor facility for gymnastics and socializing, beginning in 1885 with an unrealized plan to build a clubhouse designed by M.I.B. Ferdon on the northeast corner of Madison Avenue and Fifty-ninth Street. As an interim measure the double house at 524 Fifth Avenue, just south of Forty-fourth Street, was renovated as a clubhouse. In 1888 the club announced plans to build a new clubhouse, on a 125-by-125-foot site on the southeast corner of Madison Avenue and Forty-fifth Street.[39] A limited competition among six architects was organized, with the participants asked to concentrate on the design of the proposed building's exterior. Henry J. Hardenbergh, J. C. Cady, W. Wheeler Smith, John R. Thomas, Francis H. Kimball, and Thayer & Robinson were invited to compete, while other architects submitted unsolicited entries, including P. J. Lauritzen, a Philadelphia architect, who captured the contest with a somewhat heavy-handed six-story design notable for its corbeled circular mastlike corner towers, one of which formed the base of the club's flagstaff. Lauritzen crowned his brick and

New York Athletic Club, southwest corner of Sixth Avenue and West Fifty-fifth Street. Charles W. Clinton, 1886. View to the southwest. King, 1893. CU.

Manhattan Athletic Club, southeast corner of Madison Avenue and East Forty-fifth Street. P. J. Lauritzen, 1890. View to the southeast. King, 1893. CU.

stone design with a steeply pitched, hipped, Spanish tile–covered roof carried on columns that created a covered roof garden, possibly intended for winter use as a skating rink. The clubhouse had a twenty-one-foot-wide, one-hundred-foot-long swimming pool in the basement, the water of which could be heated during the winter, as well as a shooting gallery and bowling alleys. The rest of the plan incorporated the predictable facilities, with the notable exception that the gymnasium, at 92 by 107 feet, was very large, interrupted only by two structural columns. While the building was blocky in its mass, it nonetheless worked well with R. H. Robertson's YMCA Railroad Branch across the street (see below), forming what the *Real Estate Record and Builders' Guide* deemed a "picturesque" response, with "the repetitions in the roof of the Manhattan of the pyramid of the older roof, on a larger scale and at a greater altitude, [making] an effective whole and in a comprehensive view combines the two masses into one pile, different as they are in all details."[40] In 1892–93, with the collapse of the economy, the club became, as Moses King put it, "financially embarrassed," and closed the clubhouse, auctioning off its contents.[41] The building was taken over by a new group, headed by a brewer named Ballantine, and thereafter functioned as the Knickerbocker Athletic Club.

Bradford Lee Gilbert's Riding Club (1886), located on the north side of Fifty-eighth Street between Fifth and Madison Avenues, consisted of a four-story clubhouse attached to a one-hundred-by-one-hundred-foot riding ring and stable for three hundred horses.[42] The largest such club in the United States, and the only one with equal privileges for men and women, it was organized in 1883 as an outgrowth of the earlier Gentlemen's Riding Club. Gilbert's design, consisting of renovation as well as new construction, combined red brick, tile, and terra cotta in a pavilionated and slightly episodic Queen Anne composition that brought the huge facility into scale with its residential context.

Ethnic and Religious Clubs

While it can be argued that such clubs as the Union and the Knickerbocker, or even the Century Association, were in effect ethnically based insofar as they were pretty much the exclusive purview of the white Anglo-Saxon Protestant establishment, there were other clubs that catered specifically to defined groups with distinct European or religious ties. Foreign-born New Yorkers established a number of important clubs; among these, the clubs founded by German immigrants were the most prominent.

The Freundschaft Society built a grand clubhouse (1885–89), the first realized by McKim, Mead & White in New York, on the southeast corner of Park Avenue and Seventy-second Street.[43] When the club opened in 1889, the *Real Estate Record and Builders' Guide* found itself pleased with the bold scale and sheer size of the three-story palazzo. Most impressive was "the choice and treatment of the material. In color and in treatment of surface it is extremely agreeable. The designer [Stanford White] apparently had in mind the massiveness and breadth of the

Riding Club, north side of East Fifty-eighth Street between Madison and Fifth Avenues. Bradford Lee Gilbert, 1886. View to the northeast. King, 1893. CU.

Freundschaft Society, southeast corner of Park Avenue and East Seventy-second Street. McKim, Mead & White, 1885–89. View to the southeast. NYHS.

Florentine palaces as an expression desirable to attain in so large a building, though in detail the work owes nothing to them."[44] Above a rusticated base, there were two superimposed floors, the windows of which were grouped into tall arcades cut by a prominent stringcourse indicating the floor of the all-white ballroom, the most famous room in the clubhouse. Scotch sandstone and speckled Roman brick were used for the base, while the sandstone gave way to matching terra cotta trim above. Below the prominent tile roof, a frieze of swags suggested late Georgian work—an odd note in the otherwise Italianate design. Russell Sturgis found the Freundschaft to be "an unclassable modern design." While it was "rather featureless, rather devoid of decisive character," he admired it nonetheless: "It is too full of windows; yes! And on a corner where a hundred-foot street meets a still wider avenue, some of these openings might have been spared or made smaller. But the proportions of its walls taken vertically are peculiarly good. There is not a building in town in which that difficult problem has been solved in a better way."[45]

Though much less affluent than the Freundschaft Society, the Central Turn-Verein, organized in 1886, nonetheless undertook in 1887–89 to build an imposing, six-story, 104-by-175-foot clubhouse at 211 East Sixty-seventh Street, between Second and Third Avenues.[46] Five architects were asked to compete for the commission. The building committee, which included the architect Alfred Zucker, chose Albert Wagner, whose plans called for a 110-by-50-foot gymnasium, a 20-by-48-foot swimming pool, a restaurant, and a billiards room, all on the first floor, a large assembly hall on the second, and more dining space and guest rooms above. According to the *Real Estate Record and Builders' Guide*'s reporter, the buff brick and Longmeadow stone facade possessed "considerable architectural pretensions and some architectural interest." But it was the ballroom, "which occupies as nearly as large a floor space as that of the Metropolitan Opera [and] . . . in its appointments . . . [is] the equal of any room of similar character in the metropolis," that was the building's most notable feature.[47] The 75-by-150-foot, white and gold room was ringed by a mezzanine gallery so that about 2,500 people could be seated and as many as 200 couples could dance. The club faltered in the 1892–93 depression and, after defaulting on mortgage payments, the building was taken over by the brewer Jacob H. Ruppert, a large landholder in the area, who rented it back to them.[48]

Another German club of note was William C. Frohne's appropriately German Renaissance–style Deutsch-Amerikanische Schuetzen Gesellschaft (1888–89), at 12 St. Mark's Place, east of Third Avenue, which served as the principal clubhouse for a group of German shooting clubs based in New York and adjacent cities.[49]

In 1891, the Deutscher Verein, founded in 1842, moved from its location in a building at 13 West Twenty-fourth Street to purpose-built headquarters at 112 West Fifty-ninth Street (1889–91) designed by McKim, Mead & White.[50] By comparison with the similarly sized Century

Association, the new midblock building was rather severe in its expression. The principal facade of the five-story, limestone-faced, Italian Renaissance–inspired, palazzo-like clubhouse was dominated by a regular pattern of large double-hung windows; a second-floor loggia and third-floor escutcheons, together with an arched entrance, enlivened the composition.

The Progress Club, organized in 1864, was the first club founded by assimilating German Jewish businessmen.[51] In January 1883 Emil Gruwé was reported to be at work on a Moorish-inspired clubhouse, but a year later Rafael Guastavino was "superintending [its] construction."[52] According to the historian George Collins, Guastavino was working with Henry Fernbach, a member of the selection committee, but Fernbach died in 1883, a year before the building was completed on its fifty-by-one-hundred-

Central Turn-Verein, 211 East Sixty-seventh Street. Albert Wagner, 1887–89. View to the northeast. King, 1893. CU.

foot site on the south side of Fifty-ninth Street between Fourth and Lexington Avenues. The details of the three-story design, with its central, minaret-inspired tower, corner minarets, and ogive arches, certainly suggested Fernbach's nearby Central Synagogue (see below), which no doubt served the religious needs of many club members.

In 1887 the Progress Club announced its intention to hold a competition to select an architect for the new clubhouse it proposed to build on an even more prominent site, at the northeast corner of Fifth Avenue and Sixty-third Street.[53] McKim, Mead & White, George B. Post, Alfred Zucker, and DeLemos & Cordes participated in the competition, which was judged by Professor William R. Ware of Columbia and a committee of club members. Zucker was selected, and in late 1888 construction was under way for the five-story building, which had one hundred feet of frontage on Fifth Avenue and ninety-two feet facing Sixty-third Street. The untutored Classicism of the facade of fawn-colored brick trimmed with terra cotta in a deeper shade and Belleville gray stone was clearly inspired by Florentine Renaissance work, although its *parti*, consisting of three principal stories and two mezzanines, probably pointed to more immediate sources, such as the club work of McKim, Mead & White, including that firm's unrealized scheme for the Union League Club and its design for the Freundschaft Society. The importance of the design, however awkward and even gauche, did not go unnoticed, with the *Real Estate Record and Builders' Guide* commenting that the new clubhouse

represents a tendency that . . . in the future will be more pronounced. Hitherto, in the design of similar structures, the needs and comforts of the members as individuals have been mainly kept in mind with the result that the private or shall we say the "homelike" characteristics of club life have received most consideration in the internal arrangements of buildings. Consequently the clubs of New York may be described with sufficient accuracy as private dwellings of large dimensions. This, however, would not be true of the Progress Club. It is this very fact that gives it its exceptional character. The architect . . . has worked upon unusual if not actually novel lines, and has planned his building so that, though the conveniences and requirements of the members as individuals are not disregarded or even slurred, particular emphasis and consideration has been given to the collective or social phase of club life. As a result, the new club-house is more strictly palatial in character than perhaps any building yet erected in this country. This fact stated, the building is at once half described. Expectation looks immediately for large approaches, wide staircases and corridors, apartments of noble dimensions, sumptuous decoration, color, light, brilliancy—in a word splendor, a striking richness of effect. That this has been attained at the Progress Club there can be no doubt. . . . [It is] one of the "show-places" of the city.[54]

The Progress Club's interiors were equally impressive to the *Record and Guide*:

*Deutscher Verein, 112 West Fifty-ninth Street. McKim, Mead &
White, 1889–91. View to the south. AR. CU.*

*Deutsch–Amerikanische Schuetzen Gesellschaft, 12 St. Mark's
Place. William C. Frohne, 1888–89. View to the south.
King, 1893. CU.*

This ballroom is without doubt a truly remarkable success. It is a great artistic conception, royally executed. . . .
The imperial dimensions of the room are noteworthy. . . .
It is 90 feet long, 65 feet wide and 35 feet high. . . . The
prevailing color is old ivory. . . . The ceiling . . . is coved
several feet in depth and divided by means of heavy ornamental groins into six recessed panels, the centre of each
panel being formed into a dome, in each of which is a
cluster of electric lamps representing the descending stars
of a rocket. This idea is ingenious, and the result excellent—with electric light, illumination is at last becoming
a part of decorations.[55]

The Catholic Club of New York, organized in 1871,
occupied an artistically ambitious, five-story, seventy-
eight-foot-wide, reddish yellow Roman brick and terra
cotta, Italian Renaissance–style clubhouse (1891–92) at
120 West Fifty-ninth Street, designed by William
Schickel & Co.[56] The fourth and fifth floors were given
over to apartments, with dining rooms and a loggia overlooking Central Park also on the fifth floor, but it was the
decoration of the public rooms, lavish to the point of
excess, especially the assembly hall and parlor, that was
certainly notable if not exceptionally fine.

Napoleon Le Brun's Masonic Temple (1871), at the
northeast corner of Twenty-third Street and Sixth Avenue,
was the city's first postwar purpose-built clubhouse.[57]
Occupying a frontage of 141 feet on Twenty-third Street

Progress Club, northeast corner of Fifth Avenue and East Sixty-third Street. Alfred Zucker, 1887–90. View to the northeast showing the Jabez A. Bostwick house (D. & J. Jardine, 1877–78) on the left. AABN. CU.

Catholic Club, 120 West Fifty-ninth Street. William Schickel & Co., 1891–92. Rendering of view to the southeast. AABN. CU.

and almost 100 feet on Sixth Avenue, the four-story-tall, boldly modeled, mansard-crowned building was entered from Twenty-third Street, where a Doric portico led initiates up a grand staircase to the second floor and the 80-by-90-foot Grand Lodge Room and other lodge and banqueting rooms on upper floors, culminating on the fourth floor with the Chapter Room and above, in the mansard, the apartments for Knights Templars and Grand Commandery.

The Young Men's Christian Association

Not all clubs were built for the very rich: the Young Men's Christian Association was organized in 1852 to help with the mental, spiritual, social, and physical well-being of average citizens.[58] The association's headquarters was located on the southwest corner of Fourth Avenue and Twenty-third Street in a French Second Empire–style building (1869) of four stories plus an inhabited mansard designed by Renwick & Sands.[59] The building faced Peter B. Wight's National Academy of Design (see above) across Twenty-third Street. Upon entering at the center of the 175-foot-long Twenty-third Street facade, association members found reception rooms, reading rooms, parlors, and dressing rooms. A two-story lecture room, big enough to accommodate 1,640 persons, as well as smaller lecture rooms, a twelve-thousand-volume, triple-height, seventy-

Masonic Temple, northeast corner of Sixth Avenue and West Twenty-third Street. Napoleon Le Brun, 1871. View to the northeast along West Twenty-third Street. NYTN. CU.

Young Men's Christian Association headquarters, southwest corner of Fourth Avenue and East Twenty-third Street. Renwick & Sands, 1869. View to the southwest, c. 1900, showing the Fourth Avenue Presbyterian Church (1854) on the left. Bracklow. NYHS.

two-by-thirty-one-foot library, a gymnasium, bowling alleys, baths, a concert hall, artist studios, and a gallery rounded out a facility that combined the sociability of a club with the educational ambitions of a lyceum. One of the YMCA's early tenants was Louis Comfort Tiffany, who rented his first studio there despite the fact that he was hardly economically challenged.

Branch YMCAs soon followed, including the Young Men's Institute (1885), at 222 Bowery, between Spring and Prince Streets.[60] Designed by Bradford Lee Gilbert, the four-story building of Philadelphia brick trimmed with terra cotta and Nova Scotia sandstone rose to a gabled mansard atop which a floor was constructed for summer meetings and parties. Gilbert's English Renaissance–inspired design, with its shallow-vaulted arcade at the base and Corinthian pilasters that tied together the second and third floors, achieved a welcome balance between monumentality and domesticity on a street where fifty-year-old houses were being overwhelmed by new construction and by the soaring tracks of the elevated railway. Other branches of the YMCA catered to specific groups: the German Branch, organized in 1881, at 140–142 Second Avenue,[61] the French Branch, formed in 1889, at 114 West Twenty-first Street,[62] and the Railroad Branch, founded in 1875, which in 1887 moved into a purpose-built clubhouse at the northeast corner of Madison Avenue and Forty-fifth Street, designed by R. H. Robertson.[63] Paid for by Cornelius Vanderbilt II, the Railroad Branch was

intended for the exclusive use of employees of the railroads serving Grand Central Depot. The three-story building, red brick trimmed in Scotch sandstone, terra cotta, and tawny brown brick, rose to a corrugated-tile-covered hipped roof. Though the editors of the *Real Estate Record and Builders' Guide* praised the design as "interesting and picturesque" and "a welcome addition to our street architecture," they did not find it to be as successful as Robertson's Mott Haven Station (see chapter 8).[64] In his monograph on Robertson, Montgomery Schuyler asserted that the building owed "its effect, which is very good, to its general disposition and picturesque outline, next to the successful adjustment of its voids and solids, and then to its effective combination of color. . . . Ornament is sparingly introduced, but always at the right place, in the right quantities, and of notably good design. Mr. Robertson has done nothing better in its kind than the canopied doorway with its rich reeded pier and decoration in terra cotta, and the equally rich and spirited carving of the stone buttresses of the 'stoop.'"[65]

The Young Women's Christian Association was founded in 1870 to assist young women who were alone in the city, a decision stemming from the realization that the 185,000 single working men in the city were served by numerous clubs, athletic associations, and private libraries while the city's 100,000 working women were served not at all. In 1884 the organization tore down the midblock double townhouse it had occupied at 7 East Fifteenth

Young Men's Institute, 222 Bowery. Bradford Lee Gilbert, 1885. View to the northwest. YMCA.

View to the northeast along Madison Avenue from near East Forty-fourth Street, showing the New York Central Railroad's freight and express service offices in the center and the Railroad Branch of the Young Men's Christian Association (R. H. Robertson, 1887) on the right. NYHS.

Railroad Branch of the Young Men's Christian Association, northeast corner of Madison Avenue and East Forty-fifth Street. R. H. Robertson, 1887. View to the northwest. YMCA.

Young Women's Christian Association, 7 East Fifteenth Street. R.H. Robertson, 1885–87. View to the northwest. AR. CU.

Margaret Louisa Home, 14–16 East Sixteenth Street. R. H. Robertson, 1889–91. View to the south. Byron. MCNY.

Street to erect R. H. Robertson's seventy-five-foot-wide, five-story, Romanesque Revival facility (1885–87), designed under the direction of Margaret Louisa Shephard, daughter of William H. Vanderbilt and wife of Elliott Fitch Shephard.[66] Among the project's programmatic features, its twenty-thousand-volume circulating library, the first open to women, was the most notable. The ground floor contained parlors, offices, and a seven-hundred-seat auditorium. The second floor housed the library. Classrooms were located on the third, fourth, and fifth floors. No provision was made for athletics. The dark, wood-paneled interiors were well appointed, with furniture supplied by Herter Brothers as well as stained glass and oriental porcelains. The front of the new building displayed a subtle triple division consisting of an arcuated basement, a three-story middle section combined to suggest an arcade, and an attic story of regular windows set between paired corner pilasters. A three-sided bay window over the projecting entrance and a raised portion of the attic enlivened the composition, which terminated in a steeply pitched, hipped, tile-covered roof.

In describing the opening-night preview, the *New York Times* reported on the architecture of the new YWCA: "Towering considerably above its neighbors and having a style of substantial elegance quite worthy of the architectural opportunity furnished by an ample frontage, the building is by far the most imposing in that immediate vicinity."[67] Montgomery Schuyler, who was troubled by Robertson's stylistic eclecticism, observed that the architect faced the typical condition of New York's urbanism—its seemingly endless evolution: "One of the things to be kept mainly in view in a situation in which the architect cannot command his surroundings, is the desirableness of conformity, and in the shiftings of New York this involves conformity not only to what exists, but to what may probably come to pass. This is a duty of what may be called artistic civics. . . . In European cities it is enforced by public authority, but in American cities there is no compulsion to it except what the designer voluntarily imposes on himself." Robertson seemed to Schuyler "noteworthy and laudable" for his commitment to artistic civics. The facade "'will go' with anything that a civilized designer is likely to adjoin it. It is a symmetrical, decorous and well-behaved composition."[68]

In 1889–91 Robertson added the Margaret Louisa Home, at 14–16 East Sixteenth Street, to the YWCA complex.[69] The severe, flat, six-story, Romanesque-inspired dormitory and dining hall, intended as "a temporary home for Protestant women seeking employment," was donated by Shephard, after whom it was named.[70] Containing 78 furnished bedrooms to accommodate 104 women, it also housed parlor and reception rooms, private dining rooms, and a public restaurant. A high, one-story annex linked the building to the older facility, with a large room used as a studio and for occasional meetings. Of this building, which had been originally designed with a seventh story under a peaked roof that was not permitted

Lower East Side Branch of the Young Men's Hebrew Association, southeast corner of East Broadway and Jefferson Street. Brunner & Tryon, 1889–91. View to the southeast. King, 1893. CU.

Choral Clubs

Music was an important part of post–Civil War New York's cultural and social life, especially among German American citizens, giving rise to the formation of choral clubs, the earliest and perhaps most famous of which was the Deutscher Liederkranz, organized in 1847.[74] While the Deutscher Liederkranz was located in a purpose-built, German Renaissance–inspired brownstone building (1863) on the north side of Fifty-eighth Street between Fourth and Lexington Avenues, designed by the firm of Weber & Drosser, it was the Arion Society, a group that broke away from it, that had the more prominent home.[75] The three-story, 125-by-90-foot building (1885–87), located on the southeast corner of Fourth Avenue and Fifty-ninth Street, was designed by DeLemos & Cordes, which won the commission in a competition against six other firms, including Weber & Drosser, which took second prize, and Schwarzmann & Buchman, which came in

Deutscher Liederkranz, north side of East Fifty-eighth Street between Lexington and Fourth Avenues. Weber & Drosser, 1863. View to the northeast. NYHS.

under building regulations governing lodging houses, Schuyler wrote that it was "properly, less institutional and more domestic of aspect."[71] The rock-faced brownstone structure was in effect two buildings, each entered through a pedimented porch at the extreme ends of the lot. The ground floor was set behind large triple windows. Above an entresol, three floors were combined in five Romanesque-inspired arcades. A cornice carried twice the number of windows set between short Corinthian pilasters, and in place of a gable, which Robertson was denied by the Building Department, an openwork arcade formed a parapet rail. Somewhat more domestic in character than Robertson's main YWCA building, the Margaret Louisa Home was also rather more crude. Montgomery Schuyler noted the "emphatic triple division" of the facade relieved from the "commonplace" with a picturesque colonnade at the top and "well-detailed porches."[72]

The Young Men's Hebrew Association, founded in 1873, was first headquartered at 110 West Forty-second Street, and then at 721 Lexington Avenue; its Lower East Side Branch (1889–91), at East Broadway and Jefferson Street, also known as the Hebrew Institute, was for decades an important force in immigrant life. The institute was housed in an imposing five-story, Romanesque-inspired block designed by Brunner & Tryon that included a 710-seat auditorium, kindergarten and industrial schoolrooms, classrooms, and the Aguilar Free Library, as well as a top-floor gymnasium and baths, cooking room, and manual training workshop.[73] The roof was paved to function as a summer garden.

Arion Society, southeast corner of Fourth Avenue and East Fifty-ninth Street. DeLemos & Cordes, 1885–87. View to the southeast. King, 1893. CU.

Mendelssohn Glee Club, 113–119 West Fortieth Street. R. H. Robertson, 1891–93. View to the northeast. AABN. CU.

third. DeLemos & Cordes's palazzo-like building was faced in Berea sandstone, buff brick, and terra cotta. Above a cornice, a balustrade made of metal—a surprisingly utilitarian material in an otherwise sumptuous building—featured, on the Fourth Avenue side, sculptural groups illustrating the Ancient Greek poet Arion, mythologized by Herodotus, on a huge shell borne by dolphins accompanied by Tritons, and on the other side, Prince Carnival with Terpsichore and the Genius of Music. Combining a club and a concert hall, the ground floor contained two large rehearsal rooms and a billiards room. Bowling alleys filled up much of the basement while the second floor was given over to a social hall and the third to a large combination ballroom and concert hall.

In 1885 the Mendelssohn Glee Club, organized in 1866, moved into its own studio building, at 108 West Fifty-fifth Street, west of Sixth Avenue.[76] The fifty-foot-

wide building, arguably one of the most unusual in the city, was designed by R. H. Robertson, a member of the club, who piled two floors of north-facing studios rented to artists atop two floors of offices used by the group. The Philadelphia brick, terra cotta, and Belleville stone facade was divided in two, with separate, low-stooped entrances for the club and its tenants. The *Real Estate Record and Builders' Guide* marveled at the design: "It is only a fifty-foot front, or rather the front of two buildings of twenty-five feet, and it is to be set down to the credit of the architect that it is about the longest looking fifty-foot front in New York, although it is divided by a strong vertical line in the centre." Robertson eschewed a bombastic solution in favor of one that was "nothing more monumental than a dwelling," one that was "quaint, attractive and individual."[77] But the Fifty-fifth Street building did not satisfy the club's pressing need for a concert hall, which was met in 1891–93 with the construction of a clubhouse on an eighty-foot-wide lot at 113–119 West Fortieth Street, also designed by Robertson, who was now the club's president.[78] The location, just down the block from the Metropolitan Opera House (see chapter 5), was very nearly ideal. The new clubhouse, a gift of Alfred Corning Clark, had as its main feature an eighty-by-one-hundred-foot, white and gold Empire-style concert hall seating 1,100 people, almost as many as could be accommodated in Chickering Hall (see chapter 5). The Roman brick and brownstone facade reflected the new taste for Renaissance Classicism, although the triple pediments above the fifth-floor attic seemed almost Georgian.

Special-Interest Clubs

The Tammany Society, also known as the Columbian Order, or, most commonly, by the name of the building that housed it, Tammany Hall, was a club that functioned as the city's most powerful and efficient political organization. Founded in 1789 as a benevolent civic group, by the mid–nineteenth century Tammany Hall was synonymous with Democratic Party "machine" politics and in particular with the corrupt administration of Boss Tweed. In 1868 the society moved from its headquarters on Nassau Street to a new building, designed by Thomas R. Jackson and located next to the Academy of Music (see chapter 5) on the north side of Fourteenth Street between Third Avenue and Irving Place.[79] The four-story, red brick and marble-trimmed building was distinguished by prominently framed arched windows and a principal entrance enclosed by double arches and surmounted by a balcony of appearances. Urns decorated the parapet, while a centrally located rooftop projection bore the society's name and incorporated a niche containing a sculpture of an Indian. Inside, a second-floor assembly hall could accommodate 4,500 people.

Bibliophiles gathered together in the Grolier Club, organized in 1884, which six years later moved into a three-story clubhouse designed by Charles W. Romeyn and Arthur J. Stever for a midblock site at 29 East Thirty-

Tammany Hall, north side of East Fourteenth Street between Third Avenue and Irving Place. Thomas R. Jackson, 1868. View to the northeast. NYHS.

View to the west along East Fourteenth Street from near Third Avenue, 1893, showing the Lincoln Building (R. H. Robertson, 1885) on the far left, the Academy of Music (Alexander Saeltzer, 1854; renovation, Thomas R. Jackson, 1868) in the center, and Tammany Hall (Thomas R. Jackson, 1868) on the right. NYTN. CU.

Tammany Hall, north side of East Fourteenth Street between Third Avenue and Irving Place. Thomas R. Jackson, 1868. View of the auditorium toward the stage. NYHS.

second Street, between Madison and Park Avenues.[80] Using stone and light Roman brick in a composition that drew inspiration from both the Romanesque and the Classical, Romeyn and Stever concocted an imaginative facade consisting of two linked arches at the ground floor, a suggestion of a Serlian window above, and a row of four windows separated by small half-columns, beautifully embellished with carved stone ornament. Inside, everything was much plainer, with a ground-floor skylit lecture and exhibition room filling the entire site while the second and third floors, extending only part of the way back, contained meeting rooms and a library.

The Delta Psi Chapter House, completed in 1884, was designed by Renwick, Aspinwall & Russell.[81] William Russell, a graduate of Columbia College, was a member of the fraternity. Located at 29 East Twenty-eighth Street, the four-story houselike building of red and yellow brick was essentially Queen Anne, with a stoop, leaded windows, and a distinctive profile composed of a steeply pitched pyramidal roof surmounted by a finial and flanked by a chimney. Though the editors of the *Real Estate Record and Builders' Guide* asserted that the building was "not without good points of design," they quarreled with "the color treatment," which was for them "exactly and exquis-

Grolier Club, 29 East Thirty-second Street. Charles W. Romeyn and Arthur J. Stever, 1890. View to the north. AABN. CU.

Delta Psi Chapter House, 29 East Twenty-eighth Street.
Renwick, Aspinwall & Russell, 1884. Rendering of view
to the northeast. AABN. CU.

itely wrong, the two colors being transposed, so that it is a negative of a much better building than itself."[82]

The Players, made up of actors and others in the arts, was founded in 1887. A year later, the eminent actor Edwin Booth purchased the Valentine G. Hall house (1845), at 16 Gramercy Park South, for the club and commissioned Stanford White to transform it into a clubhouse.[83] White replaced the stoop and cast-iron veranda of the Gothic Revival house with a two-story Tuscan Doric loggia, flanking the entrance with flamboyantly bracketed gas lanterns and enhancing the interior with details appropriate to a club devoted to the theater, while avoiding any suggestion of grandiosity that might confirm the public's deepest suspicions about the acting profession's tastes.

ARMORIES

The armory building type is a phenomenon virtually unique to the United States, specifically designed to provide local militia companies with enclosed drill rooms as well as meeting space for administrative and social functions. As early as 1835, the word "armory," originally used to describe a place of arms manufacturing, began to denote a militia headquarters; by 1843, New York's Twenty-seventh Regiment had adopted for its headquarters the changed meaning of the term. The new building type powerfully reflected innovations in industrialized construction methods and evolving tastes in architectural style, particularly the narrative use of style to communicate to a broad public audience. In a time of rapid and sometimes tumultuous social, political, and economic change, the armory was a symbolically rich building type, pioneered in New York and more visible there than in any other American city.[1]

Given the American republic's early distrust of standing armies, militia companies were from the first an important part of national life. Initially many states implemented compulsory service in the militia, but this was abandoned by the 1850s in favor of volunteer arrangements, which appealed, as the historian Robert Fogelson has written, "to young men with an interest in martial arts, a passion for pomp and circumstance, and a desire to socialize with individuals of their own class."[2] In effect, the militia was a series of social clubs dedicated to the martial arts. While most towns had only one such group, large cities like New York had many. Pre–Civil War militia typically drilled and paraded in public places such as the Washington Square Parade Ground, and in bad weather contented themselves with so-called long rooms in local taverns and indoor riding academies. New York came to rely, as did other states, on these militia groups to help with natural disasters and outbursts of public disorder. The states supplied the volunteers with weapons and thereby fostered a movement to build armories that would be appropriately secure for equipment as well as suitable to practice drills.

When the Twenty-seventh Regiment petitioned New York for an armory in 1843, the city awarded it, together with some other local regiments, the use of three large rooms on the second floor of the newly completed Centre Street public market. Ten years later the Seventh Regiment began to use the State Arsenal (1851), built primarily for use as an arms storage facility by the State of New York, on the west side of Fifth Avenue at Sixty-fourth Street.[3] As designed by Martin Thompson, the five-story building, with orange brick facades above a rough-hewn granite base, adopted an appropriately militaristic appearance, evoking a Tudor castle, with crenellated, octagonal towers. Given its placement in a hollow below Fifth Avenue, the State Arsenal did not exert a widely visible architectural presence.

The Players, 16 Gramercy Park South. Former Valentine G. Hall house (1845); renovation, Stanford White, 1888. View to the southeast showing part of the Samuel J. Tilden house (Vaux & Radford, 1881–84) on the right. NYHS.

State Arsenal, west of Fifth Avenue near East Sixty-fourth Street. Martin Thompson, 1851. View to the west. MCNY.

In 1855 the Seventh Regiment signed an agreement with a group of butchers to share a new facility, the Tompkins Market Armory (1856–60), on a site on the east side of Third Avenue between Sixth and Seventh Streets that formerly had been occupied by a wooden market structure completed in 1830. As designed by James Bogardus and Colonel Marshall Lefferts, the new building was the city's first purpose-built regimental armory, although the three-story, cast-iron-fronted Italianate palazzo housed the butchers on the ground floor.[4] The building provided two large drill halls and eleven company meeting or squad drill rooms, planned by a member of the regiment's Company K, the architect Charles W. Clinton. On the third floor was a single, undivided, 100-by-181-foot column-free regimental drill room, also planned by

Clinton, that rose to thirty feet at the center, making it, according to the *New York Times*, "the handsomest and largest drill-room in the United States."[5] The officers' rooms were lavishly furnished with "elegant works of art" and a "black-walnut desk, tables and chairs, with a wealth of carving about the wood-work."[6] As well there was a library devoted to military science. While the building was well appointed, however, it was not so well engineered. Soon after opening it was discovered that the cast-iron structure was not capable of handling the physical effects of hundreds of men marching in time.

In 1863 the Twenty-second Regiment built its own armory on a site on the north side of Fourteenth Street between Sixth and Seventh Avenues, running through to Fifteenth Street, that was leased to it by the city.[7] Even

Tompkins Market Armory, east side of Third Avenue, East Sixth to East Seventh Street. James Bogardus and Colonel Marshall Lefferts, 1856–60. View to the northeast. FLC.

View to the north along Park Avenue from East Sixty-fifth Street, 1888, showing, from left to right, the tower of the Union Theological Seminary (William A. Potter, assisted by James Brown Lord, 1884), the pinnacled tower of the Normal College of the City of New York (David I. Stagg, 1873), the Hahnemann Hospital (Alfred B. Ogden, 1878), and the Seventh Regiment Armory (Charles W. Clinton, 1880). NYHS.

though it was New York's first armory to be exclusively devoted to a regiment, the two-story, French Second Empire–style design, providing for company rooms and regimental headquarters, did not seem to stylistically express the client's distinct mission, a situation that would be corrected by the new building for the Seventh Regiment.

By 1880, when the Seventh Regiment built its new headquarters on the block bounded by Fourth and Lexington Avenues and Sixty-sixth and Sixty-seventh Streets, the social structure of the city, and of the nation as a whole, was significantly different from what it had been during the pre–Civil War era, and this shift would be directly reflected in the perceived role of militia companies and the architectural expression of armories.[8] Rapid industrialization had dramatically increased the gulf between rich and poor; at the same time, massive waves of immigrants from eastern and southern Europe, mostly poor and uneducated, and consequently widely seen as easy targets for the proponents of anarchism and organized labor, created a jittery, xenophobic mood among many upper-middle- and upper-class New Yorkers. Local militia units were no longer seen as merely battling uncontrolled forces of nature or the rare civil disturbance, but also as potentially protecting their members against full-scale class conflict. The armory building type therefore needed not only to accommodate troops and their military needs, as well as serve as a safe upper-class haven in an increasingly socially stratified city, but also to serve as a powerful symbol of law and order, communicating more effectively than any speech or treatise to the masses of new arrivals who could neither read nor speak English.

Formed in 1806, the Seventh Regiment was the city's most elite militia company. The first to adopt the term "national guard," it saw distinguished service in the War of 1812. It also had been active in maintaining order during the Election Riot of 1834 and the Astor Place Riot of 1849. The silk-stocking character of the regiment notwithstanding, it was one of the first to reach Washington, D.C., after President Abraham Lincoln's call for volunteers on April 15, 1861, and it subsequently acquitted itself with honor in many Civil War battles, returning to New York in 1863 to help suppress the Draft Riots. It lost fifty-eight members in the Civil War, a record of service memorialized by a statue (1874) on the west side of Central Park, designed by John Quincy Adams Ward with a base by Richard Morris Hunt (see below).

Though the Seventh Regiment had been headquartered in the Tompkins Market Armory, a number of its companies were scattered around the city, and in 1873 the regiment attempted to obtain a site on Reservoir Square as a new home. A Romanesque-inspired building was proposed to go immediately to the west of the holding tank, extending from Fortieth to Forty-second Street but leaving a substantial part of the block along Sixth Avenue open to be used as a park.[9] Nothing came of this idea, although in 1878 the reservoir itself, by then deemed superfluous, was considered as a site for another armory, as

Seventh Regiment Armory, Lexington to Fourth Avenue, East Sixty-sixth to East Sixty-seventh Street. Charles W. Clinton, 1880. View to the southeast. NYHS.

was Washington Square, an idea that met with angry protests from members of the scientific and medical community, who argued for the preservation of the open space on the basis of public health.[10] By 1880, it had been resolved that the Seventh Regiment's new armory—New York's only one to be built and furnished entirely with private funds—would be constructed on land that was originally part of Hamilton Square, bounded by Third and Fifth Avenues and Sixty-sixth and Sixty-eighth Streets, to be leased from the city for an initial period of twenty-one years. The square, intended as a public park, had been laid out in 1807 but was eliminated from the city plan with the creation of Central Park.

The regiment selected as architect one of its members, Charles W. Clinton, who had helped with the design of its previous headquarters. Although the choice of Clinton was logical, and indeed nearly inevitable, there may have been a competition for the commission. At least one other proposal is known, that of Henry D. Casey, whose design for a two-story administration building, with its turret-flanked massive center tower rising to a pyramidal mansard, suggested the Romanesque, although the handling of the arched windows surely owed something to Richard Morris Hunt's nearby Lenox Library (see above).

Over the years of its design and construction, Clinton's original 1875 proposal was modified so that the continuous crested mansard was eliminated, the projecting corner sections raised and castellated to make them more like tower fortifications, and its central tower heightened and simplified, all in all making the building less fashionably French and more specifically medieval and fortresslike. A massive parapet, like "the machicolated cornices of the middle ages," as Colonel Emmons Clark put it in his history of the regiment, crowned the composition.[11] A bronze gate, a bronze portcullis, and a six-inch-thick oak door defended the main entrance.

The Seventh Regiment Armory was opened to the public on September 30, 1880, and visited by 38,000 people on December 15, 1880, for the New Armory Inauguration Ball. Though hardly as interesting as Frank Furness's Armory for the First Troop (1874) in Philadelphia,[12] the building set the standard for what was to become a nearly commonplace type in the city and across the country. It established the basic arrangement of the parts, adopting the composition of large railroad termini by locating a vast, shedlike drill hall—in this case, at nearly two hundred by three hundred feet, three times the size of its downtown predecessor—behind an elaborately articulated head house. Beyond its planning innovations, the armory was also a stylistic trendsetter, adopting the architectural imagery that would henceforth be almost exclusively employed by armory designers. Clinton's armory was a medieval fortification replete with slender towers, crenellated parapets, slit windows protected by iron grilles, and massive entrance doors. Going well beyond the rather modest architecture of Martin Thompson's medieval-inspired State Arsenal, completed twenty-nine years earlier, Clinton's was a massive,

picturesque building, the towers of which were not only practical for long-distance signaling but which also added dramatically to the building's power as a symbol.

The Seventh Regiment Armory set a standard of quality in the care taken with the building itself and especially in the lavish appointments on the interior that was never achieved elsewhere. The regiment had begun to exhibit an exemplary concern for such luxury in its Tompkins Square home, but at the new armory the regiment carried it much further, employing a number of other architects, including Stanford White and Sidney V. Stratton, as well as a raft of artists, artisans, and decorators: Louis Comfort Tiffany, Pottier & Stymus, Kimbel & Cabus, Alexander Roux & Co., George C. Flint & Co., and Herter Brothers. The effect of their collective work was nothing short of remarkable.

The commencement of the new armory's construction was spurred on in considerable measure by the regiment members' memories of the armory on East Twenty-first Street, which had been destroyed during the Draft Riots of 1863. Another, more immediate inducement was the far-reaching railroad strike of 1877, which, though it did not have any effect on New York, renewed fears of urban mob uprisings. Not simply a matter of artistic taste, the conception of the armory as a fortress reflected a real sense of fear on the part of the volunteer soldiers, who, in an earlier and presumably less violent time, had been content to practice and store their weapons over a butcher's market but now required a virtually impregnable redoubt. In effect, the northward move from the edge of the Lower East Side's tenement district to the developing upper-class neighborhood reflected a concern for safety; in less dramatic terms, the regiment, as much as anything a social club built on the theme of manliness, needed to be located near the women and children it was dedicated to protect.

At first the regiment sought the city's help in paying for the building, but in 1876, after putting aside a preliminary scheme of Clinton's that called for a two-story administration building surmounted by an occupiable mansard, efforts were made to raise the money privately. The officers recognized the general depression in business as well as the city's precarious financial condition in the wake of the Tweed Ring's plundering and quickly attracted contributions from leading families and businesses; a very impressive $237,000 was raised by 1880. Nonetheless, despite cost-cutting measures undertaken by Clinton, who substituted brick for the granite he had originally proposed, the regiment had to borrow $150,000 in the form of bonds authorized by the state legislature in 1879. In the same year, with the building fully enclosed, heated, and gaslit, and with floors in and the main stair built but no decor yet under contract, the regiment held a three-week-long New Armory Fair. Opened by President Rutherford B. Hayes on November 17, 1879, the fair brought in $140,550. All in all, $589,000 was raised by the regiment for its new home, about twice the amount raised for the Statue of Liberty. On April 26, 1880, the regiment, in what was

Seventh Regiment Armory, Lexington to Fourth Avenue, East Sixty-sixth to East Sixty-seventh Street. Charles W. Clinton, 1880. View of the Veterans' Room, designed by Associated Artists. Pach. NYHS.

deemed the city's most spectacular parade to date, marched from the old Tompkins Market Armory to its new building. Because so much money had been raised at the fair, Colonel Emmons Clark, who worked closely with Clinton, authorized the interior decoration program. When the lavish interiors drew criticism, Clark replied that "it was thought that nothing better could be done with it [the money raised at the fair] than to accomplish the perfection of the armory."[13] After all, as a member of the regiment noted in a letter published in the *Seventh Regiment Gazette* in February 1890, "It is as much to its social attractions as to its military renown that the regiment owes its popularity among a class of

young men who are desirable as recruits. . . . The regiment, the veterans and the generous citizens who subscribed the vast amount required to build the Armory, did so with the idea it was to be a club house as well as an Armory."[14]

The Veterans' Room was perhaps the armory's most notable interior, with a profusion of stenciling, ironwork, and other decoration designed by Associated Artists, the short-lived collaboration of artists and architects headed by Louis Comfort Tiffany and by Stanford White, who was responsible for the room's architectural details. Tiffany, the master decorator, designed the stained glass; Francis D. Millet and

Seventh Regiment Armory, Lexington to Fourth Avenue, East Sixty-sixth to East Sixty-seventh Street. Charles W. Clinton, 1880. View of the library, designed by Associated Artists. Waks. RK. CU.

George H. Yewell painted the frieze; and Samuel Colman established the color scheme and painted the decorative stenciling. Candace Wheeler provided elaborately embroidered and appliquéd hangings, and Lockwood de Forest is said to have been responsible for some of the carving. The room's military theme—two columns partially wound with chains carrying a broad structural beam covered in bronze plates—was counterbalanced, indeed nearly overwhelmed, by the impressionistic handling of colors and materials, especially those on the north wall, where an elaborate fireplace and inglenook were furnished with turquoise blue glass tile, marble and brick, carved wood, painted plaster, embossed iron, and opalescent stained glass. While a frieze that ran around the room depicted shields and battle scenes, the silvery arabesques virtually robbed them of any bellicosity. The blue gray metallic tone of the rough wallpaper, stenciled in silver and copper to resemble chain mail, and the oak wainscoting inset with rusted iron and silvered bolts, furthered the impression of war as a grand parlor game in some fabulous sultanic palace. Tiffany and White also collaborated on the Library, which was in every way a fit complement to the Veterans' Room. Here a barrel-vaulted ceiling, ornamented with a salmon-colored basket weave and silver disk pattern, crowned a galleried room lit by two Tiffany-designed stained-glass windows.

The editors of the *Decorator and Furnisher*, in a specially issued pamphlet published in 1885, characterized the Veterans' Room's astonishingly skillful eclecticism: "The preponderant styles appear to be the Greek, Moresque and Celtic, with a dash of the Egyptian, the Persian and the Japanese in the appropriate places."[15] The brilliance of the effect was not lost on the veterans themselves, whose membership organization, in a privately printed booklet published in 1881, wrote: "What most impresses, and what is most worthy to impress, in the artistic treatment of this Veterans' Room is the positive, practical and yet poetic adaptation of decorative material to the purposes in hand . . . by the very noticeable accordant chime of all side decorations; the clamp and clang of iron, the metallic lustres, the ponderous soffit beams . . . are all clearly and undeniably assimilable and matchable with the huge, hard, clanging ponderosities of wars and tramping regiments and armories."[16] But William C. Brownell, reviewing both the

Seventh Regiment Armory, Lexington to Fourth Avenue, East Sixty-sixth to East Sixty-seventh Street. Charles W. Clinton, 1880.
View of the Drill Room, designed by Charles W. Clinton with R. G. Hatfield. NYHS.

Veterans' Room and the Library, seemed to suggest that the rooms' eclecticism bordered on sensory overload, or at the least cacophony: "Until Mr. Tiffany becomes convinced that the planning of a work of monumental dignity demands more of him—or of some single mind, whoever it may be—than the preparation of a general sketch, the selection of specialists to advise as to the details, as well as to execute them, and the confining of his further effort to a mere harmonizing of possible discords, we may be sure the work of the 'Associated Artists' will not differ substantially from this decoration."[17]

No other room in the armory matched the sumptuousness bordering on hedonism that was the particular pleasure of the Veterans' Room and the Library. In fact, of all the other spaces, only the very different, one-hundred-foot-high Drill Room was as memorable. It was designed by Clinton with the assistance of the architect R. G. Hatfield, an expert on the use of structural iron who had helped with the design of the train shed at Grand Central, and Charles MacDonald, a consulting engineer who was president of the Delaware Bridge Company, a subsidiary of Cooper, Hewitt & Co., leading producers of architectural iron and steel. The eleven arch trusses of the Drill Room, manufactured by the Danforth Locomotive and Machine Co. and each spanning over 187 feet, were notable early examples of "balloon shed" framing, wherein a barrel-vaulted roof was supported on visible arch trusses or ribs acting as lateral braces. The design of the trusses marked an improvement over the earlier use of the same system at Grand Central because the armory's elliptical trusses had intrados and extrados springing from different points to create greater strength at the haunches while the span between the top and bottom chords of the trusses used at Grand Central were uniform. As if the magnitude of the space and the drama of its exposed structural system were not enough, the artist Jasper F. Cropsey was hired to create a decorating scheme using red, white, and blue. Cropsey's ornamental painting could be seen on the

Twelfth Regiment Armory, west side of Ninth Avenue between West Sixty-first and West Sixty-second Streets. James E. Ware, 1884–87. View to the northwest. King, 1893. CU.

trusses and galleries, the walls, the national emblem on the buttresses, and on the ceiling. This room proved successful not only as a drill hall but as the scene of large dances and as the home of an indoor tennis club; the Seventh Regiment Tennis Club, one of the nation's first, was founded in 1881. The drill room's structurally elegant ironwork was contrasted by the masonry arches of the three-hundred-foot-long rifle range, which was located directly below and contained six targets.

In 1884 the Armory Board of the City of New York was created to solve the housing problems of the various guard units that did not have the Seventh's resources. Six regiments requested assistance in the board's first year, and in 1886 the Sixty-ninth Regiment, the "Fighting Irish," joined the list; in the meantime it had been enjoying the use of the Seventh Regiment's former home, the Tompkins Market Armory. In each case the regiments requested a two-hundred-foot-square drill room, large enough to handle a battery of Gatling guns.[18] By the end of 1884 three sites had been purchased, plans for two new armories had been accepted, and a two-million-dollar bond issue had been floated to fund the new buildings.

The first of the armories built by the Armory Board was the new home of the Twelfth Regiment (1884–87), on the west side of Ninth Avenue between Sixty-first and Sixty-second Streets.[19] James E. Ware, a member of the Seventh Regiment, won the commission in competition, besting McKim, Mead & White, C. C. Haight, Douglas Smyth, and Theodore Weston. Because the site was L-shaped, the usual hierarchy had to be reversed, with the drill hall facing the principal street, Ninth Avenue, and the administration building located in the ell, where its elaborately iconographic mass rose to a tall, square, battlemented tower that surely lorded over Sixty-second Street. The *Real Estate Record and Builders' Guide* appreciated the difficulties posed by the site: "The disadvantage of the arrangement . . . is that the more important building, in height and architectural elaboration, occupies the rear of the group, while the principal front is taken by what must look like the back of the building, being the long and comparatively low side of an enormous shed."[20] For the Twelfth Regiment, Ware was able to draw upon his new-found expertise in paramilitary articulation, which he had gained in the construction of a massive storage facility in 1882–85 for the Manhattan Storage and Warehouse Company (see chapter 3). His design for the armory was much more literal, a "castellated structure in the Norman style" with a "solid fortress-like character, with its mediaeval bastions, machicolations and narrow slits in corbelled galleries, and grille-work at the windows."[21] At each corner, flanking towers held loopholes and arrangements for howitzers or Gatling guns, and the entire roof was a paved exercise area, protected by a parapet with many loopholes from which to defend the premises.

On April 11, 1887, the regiment moved from its old home on Forty-fifth Street and marched up Broadway to its new quarters. A little more than a week later, on April 21,

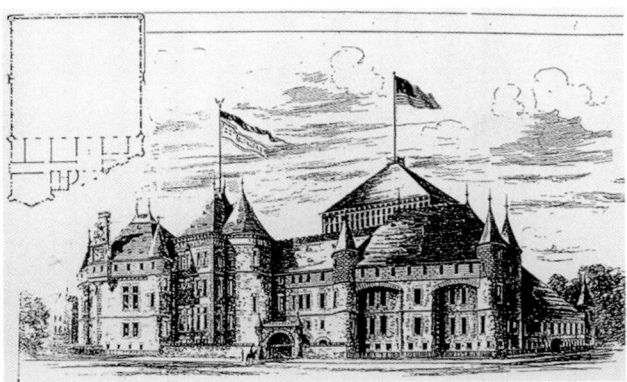

Proposed Twenty-second Regiment Armory, Ninth Avenue to the Boulevard, West Sixty-seventh to West Sixty-eighth Street. George B. Post, 1885. First-floor plan and rendering of view to the northeast. NYDG. CU.

the new armory was dedicated with a grand review before General William T. Sherman and others. But too many invitations were sent out and near riot conditions prevailed, causing one of the regiment to charge with his bayonet, which sent a wave of fear surging through the crowd. After a seeming return to order, an altercation between a soldier and a stockbroker grew ugly and the crowd went wild. The police were called to restore order and the regiment was publicly embarrassed.

Nearby, the Twenty-second Regiment occupied the site bounded by the Boulevard, Ninth Avenue, and Sixty-seventh and Sixty-eighth Streets.[22] George B. Post, a colonel and former commander of the regiment, was originally selected in 1885 as the architect of the new armory, built to replace the company's Fourteenth Street facility (1863). Post's design was a splendid essay in the Norman French style, less an armory than a whole fortified town, with numerous turrets of various sizes and, over the two-hundred-by-two-hundred-foot drill room, a lantern surmounted by a steeply pitched pyramidal roof. But when Post's building came in over budget, the Armory Board invited John R. Thomas, John P. Leo, Henry F. Kilburn, James E. Ware, Theodore Weston, and Post to make new plans. Later George E. Harding & Co. and Napoleon Le Brun & Sons were also invited to compete. In July 1888, Leo's design was selected, a building, according to the *New York Times*, that was "something on the mediaeval style, but modernized in accordance with the ideas of engineer officers for buildings of this character."[23] Moses King described Leo's granite-trimmed fortress as "to an exceptional degree, a defensive structure, with re-entering angles, loop-holes for cannon and musketry, a bastion for heavy guns on the northwest corner, a machicolated parapet, and a sally-port and portcullis."[24] The main entrance was on the Boulevard at the south corner of the building, where a six-sided turret accommodated wide portals spanned by flat arches. The building was designed and built very quickly, leading to problems for its relatively

inexperienced architect. The cornerstone was laid less than a year after the competition, and Leo, the commander of Company I in the regiment, was clearly in shaky command of the situation on the construction site. Accusations were made and refuted about the armory's structural soundness, and disputes with subcontractors led to flare-ups reported in the *New York Times*. The building was nonetheless completed in under two years' time. Even as the armory opened in February 1891, Leo, no longer an officer in the regiment, was charged with malicious mischief after having broken down the door of his office in the armory to gain entrance and help solve problems of vandalism that were plaguing the building.

The Eighth Regiment acquired a new building designed by John R. Thomas in 1888–90.[25] It too faced Park Avenue but was far uptown from the Seventh's home, on the west side of the avenue between Ninety-fourth and Ninety-fifth Streets. Thomas had been chosen in a competition held in 1884. Other participating architects included Charles W. Clinton, Hugo Kafka & Co., Lamb & Rich, and A. B. Jones. According to the *Real Estate Record and Builders' Guide*, the winning scheme showed "a free treatment of the style that flourished in Scotland in the twelfth and thirteenth centuries, giving means of offence and defense, as well as habitation."[26] The plans originally called for an armory filling the entire block west to Madison Avenue. The design was scaled back, however, and in 1887 Thomas had to replan the building to fit only that part of the block extending three hundred feet west of Park Avenue, leaving room for a future armory on the west end of the site, which Thomas would design for Cavalry Squadron A in 1894–95. A 180-by-300-foot drill room built in the first wave of construction served both units and lay between the two administration buildings; because it served a cavalry unit, this room provided stables and had a dirt floor. The cornerstone of the Eighth Regiment Armory was laid in October 1888, with the regiment marching to the construction site of its new home from its

Twenty-second Regiment Armory, Ninth Avenue to the Boulevard, West Sixty-seventh to West Sixty-eighth Street. John P. Leo, 1891. View to the northeast. King, 1893. CU.

old armory on Twenty-third Street, which had been ravaged by fire on February 17, 1878.[27] Like the construction of the Twenty-second Regiment's armory, that of the Eighth was plagued with problems, not the least of which was the destruction by gale-force winds of a high wall in November 1888.

The editors of the *Real Estate Record and Builders' Guide* deemed Thomas's design the best of the batch of armories following that of the Seventh Regiment, all of which they deemed superior to Clinton's, "the front of which already looks antiquated, though in fact it is so nearly new." While they found fault with Thomas's drill hall, which they believed, as in all other similar cases, to suffer from being too low for its size, they took pleasure in the overall exterior effect: "The material is baked clay, and is almost entirely common bricks, selected for their color, which is excellent and deep. Terra cotta is used in the crenellated copings that crown walls and towers, while a brown sandstone is introduced very sparingly indeed, the sills of the openings and the water-table being composed of it."[28] The *New York Times* went on to praise it as a model public building: "To the citizen and taxpayer it possesses an interest beyond its commanding position, its formidable proportions, its strategic importance, and its evident adaptability to the purposes for which it is designed. For it is that rara avis on these days of official shortsightedness and shortcomings in high places, an 'honest' building, a structure built within the amount of the original appropriation and pronounced by experts, after painstaking critical inspection, to be complete and substantial as a whole and in detail."[29] With its massive crenellated round towers at the two Park Avenue corners, its smaller turrets, its flights of stairs leading to the elevated main floor, its altogether articulated composition, and the predominance of wall over window, Thomas's design unquestionably ushered in a new phase of armory design: bold massing and simplicity replaced the sketchily picturesque effects of the Gilded Age, reflecting the calm authority of a new era dedicated to scholarly composition and monumental civicism.

HOSPITALS AND CHARITIES

Despite the arrival of massive waves of poor immigrants during the post–Civil War era and the subsequent proliferation of overcrowded tenement slums, by the end of the Gilded Age sanitary and public health conditions in New York, judged by both American and European standards, were quite good. Reflecting a broad public mandate, the New York City Board of Health was established in 1873 to oversee public health issues.[1] The mayor appointed members of the board, which consisted of the Health Officer of the Port, the President of the Board of Police, and two other commissioners, one of whom was required to be a practicing physician. The board hired an extensive corps of inspectors to visit individual houses and commercial establishments in order to enforce sanitary codes and

Eighth Regiment Armory, west side of Park Avenue, East Ninety-fourth to East Ninety-fifth Street. John R. Thomas, 1888–90. View to the northwest. NYHS.

Proposed New York Hospital, West Fifteenth to West Sixteenth Street between Fifth and Sixth Avenues. J. C. Cady, 1876. Competition-entry rendering showing view to the northwest. NYSB. CU.

Proposed New York Hospital, West Fifteenth to West Sixteenth Street between Fifth and Sixth Avenues. R. H. Robertson, 1876. Competition-entry south elevation. AABN. CU.

New York Hospital, West Fifteenth to West Sixteenth Street between Fifth and Sixth Avenues. George B. Post, 1877.
View to the north. NYHC.

health laws; additionally, separate corps were dedicated to overseeing disinfection and vaccination. The most significant, and certainly the most visible, reflection of New York's emerging role as a leader in health-care provisions, however, was its large number of hospitals—the number skyrocketed from around a dozen at the beginning of the Civil War to nearly eighty by 1890—constituting, not surprisingly, the largest number in any North American city.

Reflecting a commitment not only to medical science but also to the general welfare of the common person, the city's hospitals did not cater to wealthy citizens, most of whom were treated at home by private doctors. Instead, hospitals treated about 100,000 patients annually, more than seventy-five percent of whom were tended to free of charge. During the mid–nineteenth century, hospitals in New York, like those in most American cities, typically fell into two categories: institutions, which were supported by individual bequests and were intended for the use of the poor; and public hospitals, which cared for those with chronic problems and communicable diseases or for the insane.

New York Hospital, founded in 1771 through a charter granted by King George III and located on Broadway between Anthony and Catherine Streets (later Duane and Worth Streets, respectively), was the city's oldest hospital.[2] The hospital was in charge of the medical faculty of the University of the City of New York and operated as a branch of the Bloomingdale Insane Asylum, which after 1821 was located on twenty-six acres on Morningside Heights, along the Bloomingdale Road and what would become 116th Street.[3] New York Hospital's original building had grown overcrowded and obsolete by 1870, and the hospital, newly rich from selling its land to make way for the expanding district of cast-iron commercial buildings, moved uptown. On a site between Fifth and Sixth Avenues, running through the block from Fifteenth to Sixteenth Street, it began to build a new facility, designed by George B. Post, that was completed in 1877.[4] While the new building was under construction, the hospital ran the Chambers Street House of Relief, which in 1884 moved to Hudson Street, dropping its geographical

Bellevue Hospital, the East River to First Avenue, East Twenty-sixth to East Twenty-eighth Street. View to the northwest, 1879, showing the East River in the foreground. NYHS.

nomenclature. Post's building was to be linked to the Thorne mansion, at 8 West Sixteenth Street, which remained on the site to function as a business office and a library to house fifteen thousand volumes for the hospital. Post had won the commission in a competition with entrants including J. C. Cady, whose pavilionated proposal included a Viollet-le-Duc–inspired, boldly cantilevered, oriel-like tower that rose from the fourth floor well past the steep mansard roof, and R. H. Robertson, who submitted an accomplished, well-planned design calling for a New Jersey stone base supporting a brown sandstone–trimmed, brick superstructure, the lively principal facade of which was distinguished by both arched and dormer windows. Post and his partner at the time, F. Carles Merry, offered a design calling for a seven-story,

mansarded, strictly symmetrical, iron-structured, red brick and brown sandstone building, with strongly emphasized horizontal bands of windows terminated by bold pierlike masses, and elaborately patterned brickwork. The building, intended to serve two hundred paying patients as well as to provide wards for the poor, was remarkably palatial— Moses King declared that it was "said to be one of the most luxuriously appointed hospitals in the world"—but it was also practical, with every effort made to eliminate the possibility of fire. Wood was used only for doors and windows. Floors consisted of tile set in cement on iron girders; the wainscoting was marble. Two elevators were included in the design, as was a glass-roofed "solarium," described by King as a "large room . . . covered with a canopy of translucent glass, filled with plants and flowers,

Bellevue Hospital, the East River to First Avenue, East Twenty-sixth to East Twenty-eighth Street. View to the southeast, c. 1880. NYHS.

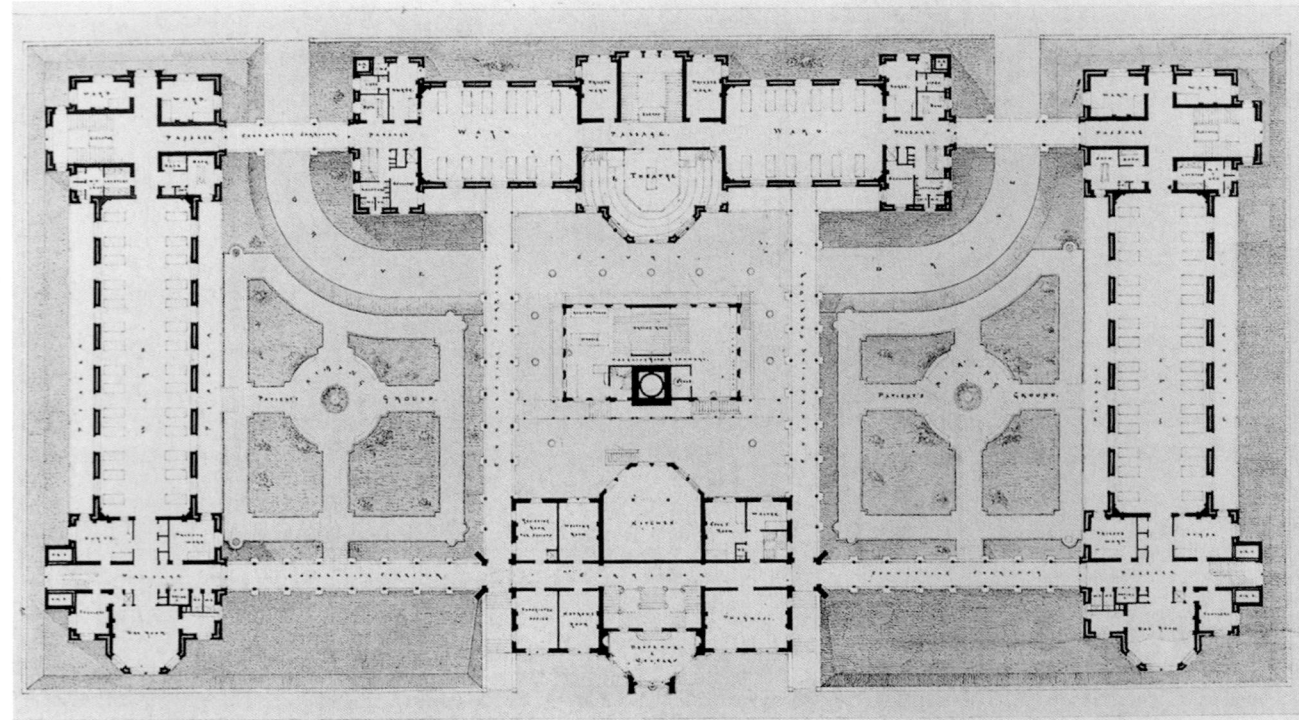

Presbyterian Hospital, Fourth to Madison Avenue, East Seventieth to East Seventy-first Street. Richard Morris Hunt, 1868–72. Plan. The Octagon, AAF.

fountains and aquaria, a sunny and healthful resting-place for convalescents."[5]

The architect and critic Russell Sturgis succinctly stated, "The New York Hospital is certainly a building of design appropriate to its function; a structure suggesting utility and intelligent planning."[6] But the architect Alfred J. Bloor, while praising the building's street facade as a "deliberately designed . . . piece of art-work, and . . . one of the most striking fronts in the city," claimed that the "general execution" did "not give with customary emphasis that impression of specially studied construction usual in [Post's] work," although "the effects, both of form and tint, around the archway, in the brick and stone work, in the polished granites of blue and red, and in the white marble caps and bases, are extremely pleasing. The party-colored mosaic work of the wings in brick and tile is well designed; and the lines and decorations of the roof are much quieter than usual, and thus harmonize well with the small scaling of the facade design."[7]

New York's premier charity hospital, to be named Bellevue after its future site, originated as a municipal infirmary in 1736 and was first housed in a building on lower Broadway on a site later occupied by City Hall.[8] In 1794 the city acquired Belle Vue, five acres at First Avenue and Twenty-sixth Street; the site contained a house and had originally been part of the Kips Bay Farm. Seventeen years later the city acquired a nearby site, bounded by Second Avenue and the East River and Twenty-third and Twenty-eighth

Streets, to house an almshouse and penitentiary known as the Bellevue Establishment. All three facilities were operated by the Common Council. In 1826 the hospital was separated from the penitentiary and almshouse, with the latter two moving into new facilities on Blackwell's Island (see below); a portion of the riverfront site was sold to private developers, and the remaining four-and-a-half-acre parcel, between First Avenue and the East River at Twenty-sixth Street, became the hospital campus. In 1860, the still-independent hospital was taken over by the Commissioners of Public Charities and Corrections, but its historical associations with the prison and almshouse hampered its ability to attract a middle-class clientele.[9] With the rapid growth of the population of the city's poor, the hospital's beds were quickly filled, however, and the institution expanded: by the early 1890s, it contained 40 wards and 768 beds, making it one of the world's largest charity hospitals. The complex was entered through a gateway arch built in 1885 and located at the foot of Twenty-sixth Street. In the center of the campus, the austere, prisonlike stone building built in 1816 to serve as the almshouse was enlarged, ultimately attaining a length of 350 feet; it was transformed into the hospital's main facility, containing, in addition to patient rooms, a library and, at one thousand seats, the nation's largest surgical theater. The building's severe external appearance was somewhat ameliorated by the construction of its northeast wing, completed in 1855, which included continuous balconies, used by patients for

Presbyterian Hospital, Fourth to Madison Avenue, East Seventieth to East Seventy-first Street. Richard Morris Hunt, 1868–72. View to the northeast from East Seventieth Street between Fourth and Madison Avenues. NYHS.

outdoor exercise. The one-story, brick Marquand Pavilion (1877) for women and children was located immediately to the north of the complex's entrance gate, while to the south, the one-story, brick Sturgis Surgical Pavilion, completed two years later, was distinguished by an entrance portico and a pitched roof with cupola-like projections that gave it both a distinctive silhouette and character that was well suited in scale and expression to its almost bucolic setting. Along First Avenue were a chapel and library as well as the Townsend Cottage, which in its first year of operation (1888) was the site of the first cesarean section performed in a hospital in the United States.

Hospitals in post–Civil War New York were often founded and operated by religious institutions or groups defined by particular ethnic identities. Foremost among these was the Presbyterian Hospital, founded in 1868 at the instigation of the prominent landowner and philanthropist James Lenox.[10] In early 1868 Lenox wrote to several prominent Presbyterian laymen, asking them to join him as managers of a new church-affiliated hospital. Lenox offered the gift of a valuable site, on the south side of Seventy-first Street between Fourth and Madison Avenues, as well as $100,000 toward the cost of construction. By June the state legislature had incorporated the hospital, Lenox had been elected its president, and more land had been made available; the hospital's site now encompassed the full block bounded by Madison and Fourth Avenues and Seventieth and Seventy-first Streets.

Richard Morris Hunt, who had cultivated a friendship with the famously dour Lenox, was asked to design the new building. Construction began in 1869, and the hospital was opened in October 1872 after Lenox contributed $250,000 more. Like most hospitals sponsored by religious groups in New York, the Presbyterian Hospital was operated on a nonsectarian basis.

Hunt's design was as notable for its innovative grafting of Gothic and Neo-Grec details onto a French Second Empire mass as it was for its sophisticated plan, probably based on the Hôpital Lariboisière (1846–54), in Paris: in keeping with the widely held theory that infectious disease was spread by miasmas (an idea later superseded by the germ theory), both hospitals segregated patients according to types of illness and were organized into open, well-lit and well-ventilated wards in detached pavilions interconnected by passages. Hunt's plan called for an administration building on Seventieth Street, a northward pavilion facing Seventy-first Street, and a combined boiler house and laundry between the two. Later, additional pavilions were added on the east and west sides of the original complex, forming a fully defined campus group. The pavilions were connected at the basement and ground-floor levels as well as at the second floor, where an open-air walkway surmounting a single-story section of the complex also provided access. The administration building had a grand entrance with a carriage portico; upstairs was a chapel.

The Presbyterian Hospital was one of Hunt's boldest

Presbyterian Hospital, Fourth to Madison Avenue, East Seventieth to East Seventy-first Street. Richard Morris Hunt, 1868–72. View to the northwest from East Seventieth Street and Fourth Avenue. The Octagon, AAF.

View to the northeast from East Seventieth Street between Madison and Fifth Avenues, c. 1892, showing the Presbyterian Hospital's north pavilion (J. C. Cady, 1889) on the left, the hospital's power plant with ventilating tower (J. C. Cady, 1889) in the center, and the hospital's main building (Richard Morris Hunt, 1868–72) on the right. NYHS.

and most inventive designs, contrasting red, smooth-faced Philadelphia brick with Lockport limestone extensively used for lintels, trim, and banding at the base such that, according to Alfred J. Bloor, "the top and bottom jamb-stones of the windows" suggested "so many little white flags being distractedly waved."[11] In the first of a number of assessments he made of Hunt's design, Montgomery Schuyler wrote, as the building was nearing completion:

> It is a very large, irregular building in plan, with a projecting portion in front and wings at the rear, in the center of the mass of which rises a lofty and massive chimney. The general effect is very picturesque when seen in perspective, the masses being well distributed and the general proportions good—especially in the treatment of the roof and the ornamental dormers with which it is perforated. The entrance porch is ingeniously contrived and very novel in arrangement, being three open sides of an octagon, spanned over by segmental arches resting on richly carved attached columns.

Though impressed with the composition, Schuyler was troubled by its stylistic expression:

> The building is of Gothic design with very red brick, and very irregular stone dressings which, it must be confessed regretfully, are not pleasing to the eye. The architect of this building, a man evidently replete with artistic ingenuity and invention, seems nonetheless to have the most

extraordinary fancy for these excessive violent contrasts of materials, and also for openings altogether disproportioned in width to their height.... From a short distance the eye takes in the whole general outline, which . . . is very pleasing, but it is utterly impossible to form any idea of the proportions of the openings or indeed to see anything but a huge red surface checkered all over with irregular small patches of light-colored stone.[12]

Schuyler reassessed the hospital's design shortly after Hunt's death in 1895, still finding it wanting:

> The administration building of the Presbyterian hospital [is] a vigorously-grouped, picturesquely-outlined and aspiring mass, crowned with a flèche, and also showing here and there a Gothic detail, but of which the predominant expression is Parisian *chic*. The merits of the design are more or less obscured in execution by the color-treatment. Not only is the contrast between the red brick and the white stone glaring, but it is rendered more vivid by the manner in which the stone-work is employed.... This disposition . . . gives to the front . . . a confused and spotty aspect which is unfavorable to repose, and which the vigor of detail and the undeniable spirit and success of the composition do not succeed in redeeming.[13]

A fire swept through the north pavilion in 1889, and J. C. Cady was asked to design its replacement. Cady's

Lombardic Romanesque–inspired design, the most prominent feature of which was a red brick and terra cotta ventilating tower that rose, campanile-like, from a new power plant, departed from Hunt's work. Schuyler, no fan of Hunt's architecture, justified Cady's decisions:

> Even if Mr. Hunt himself had been called in to do over again his own work, it is highly unlikely that he would have recurred to the phase of his professional development which these buildings indicated, and through which he had long passed. Indeed, the administration building which was spared by the fire, was that part of his design which was best worth saving. While the talent it shows is undeniable, the vivacity imparted to it in the first place by its design, and in the second by the startling contrast of color, was so excessive as to render it ineligible as a model for the group of new buildings that was to adjoin and surround it.

Despite Cady's considerable ingenuity in adapting this stylistic precedent to the needs of a modern hospital, Schuyler found that this particular work lacked "architectural effect . . . words cannot aspire to any higher praise than that of inoffensiveness." He did, however, find the two-story square building housing the operating room "a very agreeable object in spite of its limited dimensions and in spite or because of its simplicity of treatment." Schuyler best liked the dispensary, which "worked out naturally into a church-like structure of which the nave was the waiting room, and the bays of the aisles . . . became private consulting rooms, while the nave was continued to an apsidal termination. It is this apse that combines so happily with the tower. . . . There are few more welcome examples in our street architecture of thoroughly studied and artistic design."[14]

In 1882, the Roman Catholic order of the Sisters of Charity of St. Vincent de Paul, which ran St. Vincent's Hospital, built a new facility for the institution, which had since its founding in 1849 been housed in a series of renovated townhouses in Greenwich Village.[15] Located on the south side of Twelfth Street between Sixth and Seventh Avenues, the five-story, red brick building was designed by William Schickel, who adopted a Georgian vocabulary, complete with hipped roofs and cupolas.

By 1852 the city's Jewish population was large enough to support its own Jews' Hospital, originally intended to be called the Hebrew Asylum and Hospital, a modest, four-story, sixty-five-bed brick building on Twenty-eighth Street, extending through to Twenty-seventh Street, between Seventh and Eighth Avenues.[16] The hospital had been founded by a group led by Sampson Simon, a lawyer who, in 1800, was among the first Jews to graduate from Columbia College, and who later became the first Jew admitted to the New York State Bar. Soon after the beginning of the Civil War the hospital's overseers decided to receive Gentiles as well as Jews, quickly overtaxing the building and motivating the search for a new location. The surrounding neighborhood was becoming increasingly industrial and was thus considered hazardous and ill-suited to a health-care facility; the final blow came when a

Mount Sinai Hospital (1870), east side of Lexington Avenue, East Sixty-sixth to East Sixty-seventh Street. View to the southeast. MSMC.

German Hospital and Dispensary, south side of East Seventy-seventh Street between Fourth and Lexington Avenues. Carl Pfeiffer, 1869; DeLemos & Cordes, 1888. View to the southeast. King, 1893. CU.

German Dispensary, 137 Second Avenue. William Schickel, 1883–84. View to the west showing the Ottendorfer Branch of the New York Free Circulating Library (William Schickel, 1884) on the left. King, 1893. CU.

Woman's Hospital, south side of East Fiftieth Street, Lexington to Fourth Avenue. Henry G. Harrison, 1867. View to the northeast from Fourth Avenue. Bracklow. NYHS.

nearby boiler explosion came close to damaging the hospital. In 1870, the hospital, since 1866 known as Mount Sinai, moved into a new, four-story, brick and marble, mansarded building on a site leased from the city for ninety-nine years at one dollar per year, extending from Sixty-sixth to Sixty-seventh Street on the east side of Lexington Avenue.[17] The pavilionated hospital consisted of three structures running parallel along Lexington Avenue: two sixty-foot-long wings flanking a central sixty-by-sixty-foot administration block, all connected by corridors. Mount Sinai, which was the first hospital in New York to admit women to its house staff, continued to grow, and in 1876 Henry Fernbach added a boiler house and a mortuary. In 1888–90 Buchman & Deisler and Brunner & Tryon collaborated on a new dispensary, at 151 East Sixty-seventh Street, which was connected to the main building via a tunnel.[18] The Italian Renaissance styling of the new building, which was six stories high with a first story of stone giving way to a light brown brick and terra cotta superstructure, reflected the prevailing trend of the late 1880s toward Classicism.

Some hospitals were organized to cater to specific groups; like the religiously affiliated institutions, however, these typically accepted all types of patients. The German Hospital was founded in 1861 and became the German Hospital and Dispensary in 1884, and occupied a four-story building (1869) on the south side of Seventy-seventh Street between Fourth and Lexington Avenues.[19] The two-story building consisted of a 33-by-167-foot central portion flanked by 52-foot-wide wings. As designed by Carl Pfeiffer, the building adopted a Rhenish style appropriate to the institution's ethnic identity. The Philadelphia brick walls, accented with cornices and window frames of cream-colored stone, were surmounted by a slate mansard roof and, over the central pavilion, a high dome that helped to give the building a strong civic presence. By 1888 DeLemos & Cordes was at work on extensive additions, which included a wing fronting Fourth Avenue with two imposing mansarded towers.[20]

In effect an outpatient clinic, William Schickel's palazzo-like, Philadelphia pressed brick, stone and terra cotta, Italian Renaissance–style German Dispensary (1883–84), at 137 Second Avenue, between St. Mark's Place and Ninth Street, incorporated niches containing portrait busts of famous ancient and modern physicians and scientists.[21] The building was surmounted by a frieze that also was decorated with likenesses of people in medicine. Like the branch of the New York Free Circulating Library located next door (see above), the dispensary was a gift of Oswald and Anna Ottendorfer.

As medical practice progressed, hospitals catering to special categories of diseases or patient groups became more common. The Woman's Hospital, the only one of its kind in the country, was founded in 1855 as the result of the efforts of J. Marion Sims, who was widely considered to be the world's leading authority on women's health.[22] In 1867 the hospital occupied its first purpose-built structures, on

Fiftieth Street between Fourth and Lexington Avenues. The site, formerly a potter's field, was given to the institution by the city and provided a generously scaled, nearly campuslike setting. As designed by Henry G. Harrison, two connected Philadelphia brick buildings, each seventy-five feet high and consisting of four stories with a high basement and a mansard roof, were constructed on the French pavilion plan. Five buildings were intended to fill the entire block, all similar in design and linked together, but three were never realized, leaving temporary, one-story wooden pavilions to occupy the open portions of the site.

In 1855 a 60-by-119-foot brick building with two wings was built on the southeast corner of Lexington Avenue and Fifty-first Street to house the Child's Nursery, originally located on St. Mark's Place, where it had been founded the year before by Mrs. Cornelius Dubois. In 1856 a hospital was added to the facility to serve the needs of the children of working women, and the name of the institution was changed to the Nursery and Child's Hospital in the City of New York.[23] The nursery subsequently grew to include a foundling asylum, a soldier's home, and a lying-in hospital, which, after 1888, were housed on an adjacent site in a vaguely Georgian, four-story red brick building, crowned by a central pediment and

distinguished by a grid of round-arched windows flanked by dark-painted wooden shutters.

In 1890 the New York Infirmary for Women and Children, founded in 1854 by Drs. Elizabeth and Emily Blackwell, moved into a purpose-built structure at Stuyvesant Square East and Fifteenth Street.[24] The four-story building, set back from the street behind a metal-fence-enclosed garden, took on the appearance of a commodious house, with arched single as well as tripartite windows and a mansard roof pierced by dormers.

The highly polychromed, vaguely militaristic building that housed the New York Society for the Relief of the Ruptured, Lame and Crippled (Edward T. Potter, 1870), at the northwest corner of Lexington Avenue and Forty-second Street, incorporated facades of brick and stone arranged in decorative, syncopated patterns.[25] One contemporary observer praised the hospital's location for its "pleasant and salubrious site and its easy access by rail in all directions.[26] The five-story building's principal entrance was centrally located along the Forty-second Street facade; to the east and west, semicircular bays swelled forward. Dr. James Knight, who had founded the society in 1863 and who reputedly had a major role in designing the building's interior, described the exotic stylish blend of the hospital's

New York Society for the Relief of the Ruptured, Lame and Crippled, northwest corner of Lexington Avenue and East Forty-second Street. Edward T. Potter, 1870. View to the northwest. NYHS.

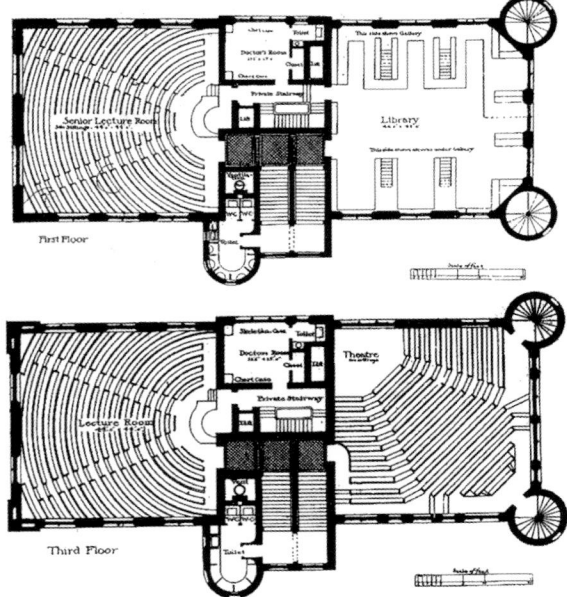

New York Homeopathic College and Hospital, west side of Avenue A, East Sixty-third to East Sixty-fourth Street. Russell Sturgis and George Keister, c. 1888. Rendering of view to the northwest, first-floor plan (top), and third-floor plan (bottom). NYDG. CU.

exterior as being "in the 'pointed style' of architecture. The alternate voussoirs in the arches of the windows and doors are of a light olive-colored Ohio freestone and of Connecticut brown stone. A light balcony, with an ornamental iron railing, is carried all around the building on the level of the winter garden that crowns it. The garden is furnished with domical roofs, above a clear story, for the purpose of thorough ventilation, and is decorated with ornamental cresting."[27] Montgomery Schuyler deemed it "a strange-looking checkered building with an extraordinarily shaped roof, but very conveniently arranged internally."[28] The *Real Estate Record and Builders' Guide* agreed, asserting that it was a "peculiar looking structure, of far less pretension to architectural beauty than of judicious arrangements internally for the use of the occupants."[29]

The New York Eye and Ear Infirmary, the first such hospital in the United States, founded in 1820, was initially located in two rooms in a building on Chatham Street.[30] Four years later the highly successful operation leased the former Marine Hospital, a part of New York Hospital, and subsequently occupied a house on Mercer Street. In 1854, having appealed to the state legislature for a public grant, the hospital completed its first purpose-built structure, located on the northeast corner of Second Avenue and Thirteenth Street; in 1890 it erected a larger facility on the same site. The new building, four stories of brick with stone trim, contained a mansard roof punctuated by dormer windows and chimneys. In 1891, the hospital added a seventy-bed in-patient wing.

Founded in 1869, the Manhattan Eye and Ear Hospital soon grew larger than its predecessor, and in 1880 completed a sixty-by-one-hundred-foot, four-story building

New York Academy of Medicine, 17–23 West Forty-third Street. R. H. Robertson, 1889. View to the northwest. AR. CU.

on the southeast corner of Forty-first Street and Fourth Avenue, at the edge of Murray Hill.[31] As designed by C. C. Haight, the mansionesque building took its stylistic cues from the homes of its well-heeled neighbors, incorporating Croton brick and Belleville sandstone facades in a Jacobean-inspired design. A central entrance court dominated by an imposing staircase was flanked by wings that projected out to the lot line.

In 1878 the Hahnemann Hospital, established in 1875 with the merger of the New York Homeopathic Hospital and the New York Homeopathic Hospital for Women and Children, completed a four-story, mansarded, brick and stone-trimmed building on the east side of Fourth Avenue between Sixty-seventh and Sixty-eighth Streets.[32] The building, designed by Alfred B. Ogden, was distinguished by its rooftop silhouette with its four corner towers. The building's realized design was not the first to be contemplated. The *American Architect and Building News* noted: "The new structure will not be erected from the designs of Mr. George Hathorne, prepared several years since, and awaiting of the proper funds before operations were commenced. . . . As far back as 1871 there was a society of the Hahnemann Hospital, who had secured from the city a grant of a tract of land a hundred and twenty-five by two hundred feet on the easterly line of Fourth Avenue, extending from Sixty-seventh to Sixty-eighth Street." Hathorne's original design had been deemed "too expensive for these days of economy and retrenchment and in a stroke of building-committee management a new architect was called in to turn out a cheaper design."[33] Even Ogden's design proved too ambitious; two pavilions to the north and south of the main building, each to be thirty by one hundred feet, were never built. In 1887, however, a house-like, two-story building known as the Ovariotomy Cottage was added to the complex directly to the south of the hospital but deeply set back from Fourth Avenue on the institution's large site.

One of the most architecturally interesting health-care facility designs of the 1880s, Russell Sturgis and George Keister's proposal for the New York Homeopathic College and Hospital, was to occupy an approximately two-hundred-by-two-hundred-foot site between Sixty-third and Sixty-fourth Streets along the west side of Avenue A.[34] The complex was to consist of a six-story classroom building flanked by two hospital pavilions housing medical and surgical facilities, connected to each other by means of one-story corridors. The three buildings were to be set back from the avenue, with the classroom building the most deeply recessed and approached by a semicircular driveway. To the west a separate building adjacent to Sixty-third Street was to house a nursing school, while a fifth building, fronting Sixty-fourth Street, was to serve as a maternity hospital. The *New York Daily Graphic* somewhat grandly described the campuslike arrangement as consisting of "four corner pavilions and a central corps-de-Logis."[35] Sturgis and Keister adopted a fifteenth-century French Gothic style, with circular corner staircase towers

and ogee-arch window enframements. Only three of the warm, rosy gray, terra cotta–trimmed brick buildings, the central classroom building and the two along Sixty-third Street, were ultimately built.

In 1875, the New York Academy of Medicine, a professional group organized in 1847 to elevate medical practice and education and promote public health standards, bought a large building at Thirty-first Street near Broadway.[36] In 1889, to meet the academy's growth, Dr. Alfred Loomis, its president, began negotiations for the purchase of 17–23 West Forty-third Street, hitherto the stables of the Fifth Avenue Stage Line. R. H. Robertson received the commission for a new building on the site, designing a vigorously detailed, five-story, red sandstone and brick, Romanesque-style building, known as Hosack Hall, that located an assembly hall, smoking room, and double-height banqueting room on the ground floor, with the third and fourth floors given over to stack rooms for the academy's huge book collection; the library was big enough to accommodate 200,000 volumes. Montgomery Schuyler found the design more interesting in its "parts rather than in the whole," pointing out "that the features, interesting as they are in themselves, do not make up a physiognomy." He objected to the front, which, though it had one entrance, suggested two buildings, a situation further exacerbated by the conclusion of only a portion of the facade with a pedimented gable. Taking exception to various details, Schuyler went on to find the "main defect" of the design to be "a defect of unity. The front is neither single nor twofold," and as such "a mere caprice."[37]

By the mid–nineteenth century New York City was nationally recognized for the number and scale of its reformatory, correctional, and charitable institutions. The New York City Department of Public Charities and Corrections was established in 1860 to serve the needs of the poor and the insane as well as to punish and incarcerate those convicted of crimes. The creation of the department, which ran municipally sponsored institutions and supervised privately run charities, reflected a rapid increase in the ranks of New York's poor and criminal elements, both resulting in part from massive waves of immigration and a particularly vicissitudinous economy. The department's organization was based on a widespread belief that illness, poverty, and criminality were inextricably linked and that often both a soft heart and a strong hand—charity and punishment—were called for. In 1828 the city had purchased the 120-acre, one-and-a-half-mile-long Blackwell's Island in the East River, extending from the latitude of approximately Fiftieth Street to that of Eighty-fourth Street in Manhattan, to house municipally run institutions. By 1860 it had erected a group of buildings on the island: a gray stone penitentiary built in 1832 and expanded in 1858; an almshouse consisting of two buildings, one for men and one for women, built with convict labor in 1846 of granite quarried on the island; a 600-foot-long, 221-cell, three-story granite workhouse, built in 1852; and James Renwick Jr.'s Smallpox Hospital (1854–56), a three-story,

New York City Asylum for the Insane, Blackwell's Island. Alexander Jackson Davis, 1839, 1847–48; Joseph M. Dunn, 1879. View to the west, 1914. NYHS.

Charity Hospital, Blackwell's Island. Renwick & Auchmuty, 1861. View to the southeast. NYHS.

Department of Public Charities and Corrections, 66 Third Avenue. James Renwick Jr., 1869. View to the southwest. King, 1893. CU.

U-shaped building of rough-hewn stone adopting a Gothic vocabulary, complete with pointed arches, corbels, and crenellated bays and towers.[38] In the post–Civil War period the almshouse added a hospital for incurables (1866), a hospital for women (1881), and two brick buildings (1888–91) containing the almshouse proper. By the early 1890s, the almshouse and related facilities, constituting a kind of city for the poor, received and accommodated more than three thousand men and women annually. Moses King described it, perhaps overenthusiastically, as a "pleasant island home" where the poor "are more comfortably situated than are thousands of dwellers in the crowded tenement-houses of the city."[39]

The New York City Asylum for the Insane (1839; 1847–48; 1879) was also located on Blackwell's Island; it likewise fell under the jurisdiction of the new department.[40] Alexander Jackson Davis designed the asylum, which was constructed in stages. Davis's building incorporated an octagonal tower containing a dramatic, soaring entrance rotunda. Built of gray gneiss quarried on the site, the building's facades contained crisp, spare, Neo-Grec details. Davis had originally envisaged an elaborate scheme calling for a U-shaped plan with two octagonal towers, but the plan was only partially realized. When, in 1879,

Joseph M. Dunn was commissioned to expand the complex, he added a story, but in order to maintain the visual dominance of Davis's tower, he heightened it with a convex mansard roof that provided a domelike addition to the building's silhouette. In 1881 a stone building was completed to house those with acute cases of mental disturbance, and in 1892 a brick building serving chronic cases was completed. Charles Dickens had visited the hospital in 1840, finding "a lounging, listless, madhouse air, which was very painful. . . . It was badly ventilated, and badly lighted; was not too clean; and impressed me, on the whole, very uncomfortably. But it must be remembered that New York, as a great emporium of commerce, and as a place of general resort, not only from all parts of the States, but from most parts of the world, has always a large pauper population to provide for."[41] Treatment improved during the ensuing decades, and by 1893 Moses King stated: "The patients are kept without restraints, and every passable effort is made to ameliorate their condition, by allotting them some occupation to employ their minds."[42] Nonetheless, in 1887, the pioneering journalist Nellie Bly (Elizabeth Cochrane) had shocked readers of the *New York World* with her hair-raising account of ten days she spent, under false pretext, as a patient in the asylum.[43]

In 1852, the municipal Charity Hospital opened on Blackwell's Island. Six years later the wooden building was destroyed by fire, and in 1861 it was replaced by a stone building designed by Renwick & Auchmuty in the French Second Empire style.[44] The hospital's board of governors boasted of its new building, "Its truly magnificent structure presents the appearance of a stately palace. The scale upon which it is built is far beyond the requirements of the class of people that have heretofore occupied the Institution it was built to replace."[45] In 1892 a new facility for the Charity Hospital's Stecker Laboratory was completed, designed by Frederick Clarke Withers.[46] The small, two-story, T-shaped stone building was a particularly fine example of the Romanesque Revival style it adopted. The Department of Public Charities and Corrections was also responsible for the House of Refuge (1868), an Italianate pile designed by R. G. Hatfield for a site nearby on Randall's Island.[47]

To meet its growing administration needs, in 1869 the Department of Public Charities and Corrections, which had occupied rented quarters at 1 Bond Street, moved a short distance away to a new, two-story, pavilion-like building at 66 Third Avenue, designed by James Renwick Jr.[48] At the rear, a stable served the city's first ambulance corps. Renwick's design, as with so many contemporaneous buildings, owed its overall appearance to the French Second Empire version of the French Renaissance, but had about it the alternately restless and massive detailing of the Neo-Grec. All in all it did not please an anonymous *New York Times* writer, who found little to admire in the "cumbrous style of the roof. With one or two more stories, it would be a handsome structure instead of the costly looking barn one might mistake it for at first sight."[49]

East Side Boys' Lodging House and Industrial School, south side of East Broadway between Gouverneur and Montgomery Streets. Vaux & Radford, 1879. View to the southwest. CAS.

Proposed West Side Lodging House for Boys and Industrial School, northwest corner of Seventh Avenue and West Thirty-second Street. R. H. Robertson, 1882. Competition-entry south elevation. AABN. CU.

*West Side Lodging House for Boys and Industrial School, northwest corner of Seventh Avenue and West Thirty-second Street.
Vaux & Radford, 1882. View to the northwest, 1903. Pelletreau. NYHS.*

*Tompkins Square
Lodging House for Boys
and Industrial School,
127 Avenue B.
Vaux & Radford, 1887.
View to the northeast.
MCNY.*

Like medical care, most charity in New York was either church-sponsored or in the hands of private agencies. Foremost among these was the Children's Aid Society, founded in 1853 by Charles Loring Brace, who was devoted to caring for the city's abused and abandoned children.[50] Brace was a friend of Frederick Law Olmsted's brother John, who introduced Brace to Frederick in the late 1840s. In 1851 the Olmsted brothers and Brace took a walking tour through England which would have a decisive impact on the future landscape architect's career.[51] Beginning in the 1860s, the society embarked on a plan to build shelters in various city neighborhoods. Not surprisingly, given his friendship with Olmsted, Brace retained Olmsted's partner Calvert Vaux as architect. Vaux had already built a house for Brace in Dobbs Ferry. Between 1879 and 1892, the firm of Vaux & Radford designed nine facilities for the society.[52]

Vaux & Radford's first building for the society, the East Side Boys' Lodging House and Industrial School (1879), on the south side of East Broadway between Gouverneur and Montgomery Streets, was funded by Catherine Wolfe, although the society paid for the site.[53] Vaux & Radford's straightforwardly Gothic, five-story, Nova Scotia sandstone–trimmed, Philadelphia pressed brick building contained a gymnasium, library, and conservatory, as well as a wardlike dormitory for three hundred boys. The *New York*

Daily Graphic praised it as "an example of Christianity solidified in brick and mortar, and managed by a charity which 'seeketh not her own.'" Though simple in construction, the building was sophisticated in its massing, with tall towers rising to hipped roofs creating a memorable skyline. The *Daily Graphic* contended that the richness of the building's architecture and its array of facilities might give rise to questions about "whether the boys are to have all these comforts and luxuries for nothing. The answer is both yes and no. When they knock at the doors of the Lodging House in a condition of absolute destitution they will be fed and lodged free of charge. But when the boys have money they will be charged six cents for a night's sleep."[54]

Vaux & Radford had to compete against R. H. Robertson for the commission to design the society's next facility, the West Side Lodging House for Boys and Industrial School (1882), also known as the Newsboys' Lodging House, on the northwest corner of Seventh Avenue and Thirty-second Street.[55] Robertson's unrealized proposal for the four-story building was notable for its bold scale and for the ingenious handling of the roofs, which broke up the essentially boxlike mass to suggest a cross-axial plan. A lovely bay window would have graced the second-floor schoolroom. In any case, Vaux & Radford's five-story design was more than satisfactory, although the multiple towers and turrets and many-dormered mansard gave it a spiky verticality that

Sixth Street Industrial School, 630 East Sixth Street. Vaux & Radford, 1891. View to the south. CAS.

Rhinelander Industrial School, 350 East Eighty-eighth Street. Vaux & Radford, 1891. View to the south. CAS.

Jones Memorial Industrial School, north side of East Seventy-third Street between Avenue A and First Avenue. Vaux & Radford, 1890. View to the north. AB. CU.

Mott Street Industrial School, east side of Mott Street between Prince and East Houston Streets. Vaux & Radford, 1890. View to the east. CAS.

Forty-fourth Street Lodging House and Industrial School, northwest corner of Second Avenue and East Forty-fourth Street. Vaux & Radford, 1888–89. View to the northeast. CAS.

House of Reception, 106 West Twenty-seventh Street. Vaux & Radford, 1890. View to the southwest. NYJA. CU.

must have seemed fussy and old-fashioned compared with Robertson's suave simplicity.

Five years later, Vaux & Radford's Tompkins Square Lodging House for Boys and Industrial School opened, a gift of Mrs. Robert L. Stuart.[56] Facing Tompkins Square at 127 Avenue B, on the northeast corner of Eighth Street, the home provided double bunks at six cents per night and, as an incentive to self-improvement, single beds at ten cents. The four-story design was a simple version of the firm's previous work, and its articulated composition, Venetian Gothic windows, and strong square corner tower rising to a steep hipped roof crested in iron, was very well suited to the neighborhood's townhouse scale. Nearby, Vaux & Radford's Sixth Street Industrial School (1891), paid for by Mrs. William Douglas Sloane, located at 630 East Sixth Street, between Avenues B and C, looked more like a luxurious townhouse than a charitable school with its asymmetrical facade, four-story bay window, and steep crowstepped gable.[57] The design echoed Vaux & Radford's eight-classroom Rhinelander Industrial School (1891), at 350 East Eighty-eighth Street, between First and Second Avenues, which the Children's Aid Society built with a gift from Julia and Serena Rhinelander.[58] Both of these

designs, in turn, had behind them Vaux & Radford's Jones Memorial Industrial School (1890), which, together with a playground, occupied a spacious lot on the north side of Seventy-third Street east of First Avenue.[59] Here the crowstepped gable was complemented by a side bay that rose past swooping roofs to a belfry. A building of similar design was realized for the society's Henrietta School (1889), at 215–217 East Twenty-first Street, between Second and Third Avenues.[60] Another essay using the crowstepped gable was the Mott Street or 14th Ward Industrial School (1890).[61] A gift of John Jacob Astor III in memory of his wife, Charlotte, it served a neighborhood of Italian immigrants, undertaking to teach the children sewing, drawing, and kitchen gardening.

In discussing Vaux & Radford's design for the Forty-fourth Street Lodging House and Industrial School (1888–89), on the northwest corner of Second Avenue, the *Real Estate Record and Builders' Guide* made the essential point that the decision to switch from a conventionalized Gothic to the more specific work of German- and Dutch-inspired crowstepped gables recalled

the earliest European architecture of Manhattan Island, and [added] a touch of quaintness to the architecture entirely in keeping with its character. That character, partly "institutional" and partly domestic, is entirely appropriate to the purpose of the building, which forms an ornament to a part of the city the ugliness of which is particularly in need of some relief. It is a fortunate circumstance that the objects of the Children's Aid Society require it to undertake its building operations in quarters where, but for its efforts, it is unlikely that there would be any architecture worth looking at or discussing.[62]

The society's House of Reception (1890), at 106 West Twenty-seventh Street, west of Sixth Avenue, also employing a crowstepped gable, had a somewhat different purpose from the lodging houses: here wayward children were received and temporarily detained until they could be returned to friends or family or alternate arrangements made.[63] The building also housed some of the society's administrative functions. The society's Elizabeth Home for Girls[64] and the Sullivan Street Industrial School,[65] both realized in 1892, adopted a similar stylistic palette as the organization's previous efforts but were attributed to Nicholas Gillesheimer, who was a partner of Calvert Vaux's son Downing Vaux.

In addition to those for children, there were almshouses dedicated to virtually every specific ethnic, racial, and age group. Few were as architecturally distinguished as those of the Children's Aid Society, although Sidney V. Stratton's House and School of Industry (1878), at 120 West Sixteenth Street, between Sixth and Seventh Avenues, was an especially fine red brick essay in the Queen Anne style, incorporating a two-story-high wooden bay with elaborately muntined windows.[66] Emlen T. Littel's Gothic-style St. John the Baptist House (1877), on the north side of Seventh Street between Second and Third Avenues, was also architecturally distinguished, as was C. C. Haight's western addition (1883) to the building.[67]

J. C. Cady's Sailors' Home (1878–79), at 190 Cherry Street, caught the attention of Montgomery Schuyler, who described it as "a reminiscence of colonial work":

> It is only a street front, though an ample one. A red brick wall, divided by piers into a centre and wings, stands upon a Doric colonnade in gray granite, which forms a recessed veranda along the whole front. The central division is crowned by a curvilinear Dutch gable, and an emphatic belt of brickwork converts the upper story into an attic. The treatment of the openings is very simple and the expression attained is one of homely comfort. It is necessary, however, to look at the front elevation in order to get its effect, which is disturbed in the view from either side by the circumstances that the roof of the building is flat, and that the gable appears as a mere excrescence with a relation of lines which is rather disturbing.[68]

One of the most prominently located orphanages, Renwick & Sands's Catholic Male Asylum (c. 1870), stood just to the north of the same firm's St. Patrick's Cathedral (see below), occupying a one-hundred-by-two-hundred-foot plot on the west side of Madison Avenue, filling the blockfront from Fifty-first to Fifty-second Street.[69] The Gothic-style brick and stone-trimmed building was deemed by the *Real Estate Record and Builders' Guide* "one of the most perfect and satisfactory buildings in this style of architecture, that has ever been erected in New York,"[70] and the young Montgomery Schuyler praised it as "a simple but charming Gothic edifice of brick with stone dressings—in its outline and details one of the best in the city."[71]

PLACES OF WORSHIP

Despite New York City's characteristic materialism, during the Gilded Age New Yorkers exhibited a spiritual fervor that was reflected not only in the number but also in the size of the churches and synagogues that were built. While some observers questioned the depth and sincerity of the public's devotion, houses of worship were nonetheless built in abundance, with many new parishes opening throughout the city. In addition to the new organizations, there was also much movement within the city as numerous established congregations sold their buildings to follow the northward migration of their parishioners to more fashionable and convenient sites uptown. The vacated downtown sites were increasingly engulfed by commercial development.

The narrative aspect of architecture is perhaps nowhere more evident than in religious programs. For some congregations, the desire to return to the principles of the early Christian church led to an adoption of the Romanesque style, while others continued to mine the Gothic for inspiration. Jewish congregations were faced with more complex stylistic questions, as they sought to retain a distinct religious identity despite a dominant trend toward secularization. No matter the faith, however, it was not simply the issue of the style for the creed, as it were, but also the problem presented by the context—the city's unprecedentedly large-scale, high-density urbanism—which challenged architects and their religious clients as never before. Additionally, because many churches and synagogues embraced both religious reforms and a greater involvement in contemporary social issues, preaching was emphasized over ritual such that congregations required auditorium-like spaces conducive not only to individual devotion but also to social assembly. Programs for religious buildings were thus fertile ground for both aesthetic exploration and imaginative problem-solving.

In 1872, James D. McCabe Jr. stated in his guidebook *Lights and Shadows of New York Life* that "In some respects New York may be called the City of Churches." With 430 Protestant churches and chapels, 40 Roman Catholic churches, one Greek church, and 27 synagogues, there were almost 500 places to worship in public. Despite this great opportunity, however, McCabe reported: "New Yorkers can hardly be said to be a church-going people. . . . It is astonishing to see the widespread carelessness which prevails here on the subject of church-going. There are thousands of respectable people in the great city who never see

*Church of the Covenant, northwest corner of Fourth Avenue and East Thirty-fifth Street. James Renwick Jr., 1863–65.
View to the northwest showing the Church of the Incarnation (Emlen T. Littel, 1865) on the left. NYHS.*

Fifth Avenue Baptist Church, south side of West Forty-sixth Street between Fifth and Sixth Avenues. D. & J. Jardine, 1865. View to the southwest, c. 1892. NYHS.

the inside of a church, unless drawn there by some special attraction." Supported by comparatively few people, religious life was inextricably bound up with distinctions in social status, which, as McCabe noted, "prevail in the city churches. Fashion and wealth rule here with an iron hand. The fashionable churches, with the exception of Grace Church, are now located high uptown. They are large and handsome, and the congregations are wealthy and exclusive. Forms are rigidly insisted upon, and the reputation of the church for exclusiveness is so well known that those in the humbler walks of life shrink from entering its doors."[1]

While examples of religious architecture were conventionally considered among the city's glories, the quality of ecclesiastical buildings did not strike Montgomery Schuyler with the same force as those devoted to business and government. In 1871 he observed:

> It is very remarkable that in a great city like this, where so many religious edifices exist, upon many of which large sums of money have been expended, that so very few should be found which can even remotely pretend to be worthy representatives of ecclesiastical architecture. It is not so in our civic architecture. In this branch of art we can readily trace our rapid developments from mere shanties of ordinary brick work to palatial structures . . . that can take rank among the noblest edifices of any age or country. But in ecclesiastical architecture it seems to be quite different. A perfect incapacity for evolving new forms of grandeur or beauty in this direction seems to have taken possession of our architects; and this is the more remarkable when we consider how much wider a field there is for the development of artistic talent in this direction than is ordinarily found in the practice of civic architecture.[2]

Since the 1840s, as Schuyler pointed out, the Gothic was "the most available, and consequently most frequently adopted style for ecclesiastical architecture—the Gothic, in one or other of its varied forms—is more capable of diversified treatment, and richer in endless combinations than any other style of architecture ever invented by man."[3] Nonetheless, despite this unifying stylistic tendency, aesthetic experimentation could be seen in the use of Romanesque, Moorish, and Byzantine styles, as well as, on occasion, post-Medieval Classical models, with many new houses of worship mixing the styles in an effort to evolve, by a process of eclectic hybridization, a distinctly modern expression.

A Boom in Church Building

From 1863 to 1874, the city, flush with a wartime and postwar boom economy, experienced a spate of church building. Coincident with the rapid expansion uptown, much, but not all, of the new church construction was concentrated in the Thirties and Forties between Third and Ninth Avenues. James Renwick Jr.'s Presbyterian Church of the Covenant (1863–65) was an early example of the era's penchant for stylistic hybrids.[4] Located on the northwest corner of Fourth Avenue and Thirty-fifth Street, the church was said by *Appletons' Journal* to have adopted a

Church of the Divine Paternity, southwest corner of Fifth Avenue and West Forty-fifth Street. John Correja, 1865–66. View to the southwest, c. 1895. NYHS.

Lombardo Gothic style, but it struck other observers differently.[5] As an article in the *Real Estate Record and Builders' Guide*, perhaps written by Montgomery Schuyler, noted, the "handsome new Byzantine church and dwelling houses" made of Ohio stone adopted a "very peculiar French style" and were finally "not quite so pleasing as curious to the spectator."[6]

In 1865 the Church of the Incarnation was completed at 205 Madison Avenue, on the northeast corner of Thirty-fifth Street, by Grace Church, which built it as a satellite chapel in the increasingly fashionable Murray Hill district.[7] As designed by the architect Emlen T. Littel, who ran a successful practice specializing in churches in New York, New Jersey, and Pennsylvania, the brownstone ashlar building, with trim and coping of a lighter-hued sandstone, adopted the thirteenth-century style English Decorated Gothic. Inside, the church was distinguished by the quality of its furnishings: over a period of time Edward Burne-Jones, John La Farge, Louis Comfort Tiffany, and William Morris designed stained-glass windows; Daniel Chester French designed a carved oak communion rail; Heins & La Farge designed a reredos; and John La Farge created a chancel mural depicting the Adoration of the Magi. Located just to the north of the church, at 209

Church of the Messiah, 61 East Thirty-fourth Street. Carl Pfeiffer, 1867. View to the northwest, c. 1900. Bracklow. NYHS.

Church of the Heavenly Rest, 551 Fifth Avenue. Edward T. Potter, 1868–71. View to the northeast. NYHS.

Madison Avenue, the townhouselike rectory, also designed by Littel, adopted a Renaissance vocabulary. In 1882 the church's east end, as well as portions of its south and west facades, were destroyed by fire; that same year the building was restored and enlarged by David Jardine of the firm D. & J. Jardine, with the church's nave lengthened and a shallow transept containing pews added to the north. It was not until 1896 that the church's distinctive broached, early English Gothic–style spire, located at the street intersection and designed by Littel as part of his original scheme, was finally completed, becoming not only an important part of the overall composition but a widely visible neighborhood landmark as well.

Located on the south side of Forty-sixth Street west of Fifth Avenue, D. & J. Jardine's Gothic-style Fifth Avenue Baptist Church (1865) filled most of its narrow midblock site.[8] Atypically, the fifty-foot-wide, ninety-foot-deep, fifty-foot-high interior lacked a gallery. Around the corner

was John Correja's 1,800-seat Universalist Church of the Divine Paternity (1865–66), built for E. H. Chapin.[9] Occupying the southwest corner of Forty-fifth Street and Fifth Avenue, the church presented a rather unscholarly version of the Perpendicular Gothic. It extended ninety-five feet along the avenue and included two towers of unequal height, the tallest of which, at the corner, rose about two hundred feet to the top of the spire.

Carl Pfeiffer's round-arched German Gothic, or Rhenish Gothic, Unitarian Church of the Messiah (1867), at 61 East Thirty-fourth Street, on the northwest corner of Fourth Avenue, was also a stylistic mix, described by Montgomery Schuyler as "a beautiful Byzantine edifice, of brown and Ohio stone. It is a very interesting building, both in outline and detail, the only objection being the too common pretense of making tracery to the windows out of wood instead of iron."[10] The year 1868 saw the completion of C. C. Haight's Church of the Resurrection, at the north-

Church of St. Benedict the Moor, 342 West Fifty-third Street. R. C. McLane & Sons, 1869. View to the southeast, 1936. NYHS.

Church of the Holy Trinity, northeast corner of Madison Avenue and East Forty-second Street. Leopold Eidlitz, 1871–74. View to the northwest showing the steeple of St. Bartholomew's Episcopal Church (Renwick & Sands, 1872–76) on the far left. NYSB. CU.

View to the north along Madison Avenue from East Forty-first Street showing the steeple of St. Bartholomew's Episcopal Church (Renwick & Sands, 1872–76) on the left and the Church of the Holy Trinity (Leopold Eidlitz, 1871–74) on the right. NYHS.

east corner of Madison Avenue and Forty-seventh Street.[11] The building was one of the architect's first essays in the Gothic vocabulary that was to become his signature.

Edward T. Potter's Church of the Heavenly Rest (1868–71), at 551 Fifth Avenue, was built, in conjunction with a pair of flanking brownstones also designed by Potter on the east blockfront just north of Forty-fifth street, for Dr. Robert S. Howland, at the time the rector of the Church of the Holy Apostles.[12] The Church of the Heavenly Rest had been founded in 1865. With only thirty-one and a half feet of frontage on Fifth Avenue for the church, Potter inventively treated the front of his building as a tower rising not to a spire but to a steep, iron-crested mansard. Trumpeting angels at the tower's corners, combined with the cresting and the flamboyant tracery of the pointed-arched, west-facing window, conspired to make the building seem at once modern and medieval, and dis-

tinctly French. Inside, where polished marble columns carried the elaborately carved woodwork of the nave arcade and trusses, the treatment seemed more traditionally Gothic. Comparing it to W. Wheeler Smith's Collegiate Dutch Reformed Church (see below), Schuyler found the design to be "outrageous" in its "rage for unmeasuring novelty."[13] One passing observer was said to have remarked: "I can perceive the Heavenly, but where is the Rest?"[14] Schuyler was particularly dismayed by the "incomprehensible Episcopal tower, cut off at the top, on purpose to receive a colossal bronzed angel at each corner blowing [Dr. Howland's] fame to the four quarters of the world."[15] Despite his frequent pleas for invention, Schuyler had very clear ideas about the boundaries within which artists should work; he was nonetheless honest enough to admit that the times permitted, even encouraged, a wide variety of tastes: "In an age where the chignon is conceived more

All Souls Unitarian Church, southeast corner of Fourth Avenue and East Twentieth Street. Jacob Wrey Mould, 1853–55. View to the southeast. NYHS.

beautiful than nature's adornment and when Walt Whitman's poetry is placed alongside Byron's, it is to be presumed that even such ravings as Dr. Howland's Church will find those who understand and admire them."[16] Four years later, however, in 1875, writing on the occasion of Potter's appointment as the architect of the United States Treasury Department, succeeding Alfred B. Mullett, Schuyler confessed to not knowing "what the inside of [the church] is made of," though he now admired the facade, which, he asserted, "in spite of its unfavorable position and its cramped dimensions . . . shows much ingenuity and elegance of detail, and if we miss from it the repose which it is supposed particularly to typify, and which—the crowning excellence of any art—is the first aesthetic essential in the art of architecture, we certainly hope to find it in Mr. Potter's work hereafter."[17]

Not all the churches built during the postwar building boom were located in fashionable neighborhoods. The Church of St. Benedict the Moor (1869) was completed for a congregation of black Protestant Evangelicals at 342 West Fifty-third Street, between Eighth and Ninth

Avenues, just to the north of the densest concentration of churches built during the church-building boom of the 1860s.[18] As designed by the firm of R. C. McLane & Sons, the building adopted a rather understated Italianate style. Edward D. Lindsey's West Presbyterian Church's Faith Chapel (1870), at 423 West Forty-third Street, between Ninth and Tenth Avenues, served a largely working-class population.[19] The Gothic church had a lively principal facade, with pointed-arch windows punctuating a decorative-brickwork wall. The pitched roof was clad in slate shingles set in a fish-scale pattern. As designed by William T. Hallet, the Episcopal Church of St. Mary the Virgin (1871), at 145 West Forty-sixth Street, was distinguished less by its Gothic style than by its coloration: red sandstone walls were trimmed with buff-colored sandstone.[20] Inside, the sanctuary could accommodate five hundred worshipers. J. C. Cady's United Presbyterian Church of the Covenant (1871), at 310 East Forty-second Street, between First and Second Avenues, was a skillful essay in the Tudor Gothic style.[21] In an effort to maximize the constricted midblock site, Cady designed the church, of which he was a lifelong member, so that classrooms and lecture rooms surrounded the main sanctuary.

The Church of the Holy Trinity (1871–74), on the northeast corner of Madison Avenue and Forty-second Street, was built to serve the parish of Dr. Stephen Tyng Jr., an evangelical minister and son of Dr. Stephen Tyng Sr., the presiding divine at St. George's Church (Blesch & Eidlitz, 1846–48); the Madison Avenue congregation was housed in a rock-faced brownstone building designed by Leopold Eidlitz.[22] While the senior Dr. Tyng's parish, in Stuyvesant Square, was a fashionable one, that of his son was, as Schuyler put it, a "working church for working people." Located only a stone's throw from the new Grand Central Depot (see chapter 1), the new building replaced a smaller church by Jacob Wrey Mould that Schuyler characterized as "a cottage ornée," which had served the same congregation.[23] For Schuyler, Holy Trinity's severely detailed, Gothic-inspired design, with its blocky massing incorporating an asymmetrically located 185-foot-tall tower, held "a place midway between the harsh cutting loose from the past that distinguishes Puritanism, and the tender yearnings after art and nature worship which cling around the Catholic cultus. The working church remembers the past, but it belongs to the present."[24] The modernity of the design could be seen in the flat facades of Philadelphia brick, relieved by elaborate pale yellow and blue brick diaper work, "less an ornament than a relief to the eye," that gave rise to the nickname "The Church of the Holy Zebra," a phrase perhaps more aptly applied a generation before to Jacob Wrey Mould's insistently striped All Souls Unitarian Church (1853–55). To help with acoustics, the space inside the Church of the Holy Trinity formed an ellipse. The *New York Daily Graphic* found the shape "by no means suggestive of a church, but rather resembles a concert-room or theatre,"[25] an assessment confirmed by Schuyler, who wrote that Eidlitz had conceived of the church as "a theatre with ecclesiastical details."[26]

Faith Follows Fashion

It was not just newly established congregations that built in the increasingly dense uptown section of the city but also long-established, well-heeled congregations decamping from locations in lower Manhattan. The desire, indeed the symbolic necessity, of following fashion uptown was perhaps most strongly and urgently felt by religious minorities eager to prove they were a formidable presence in the city by occupying a prominent Fifth Avenue house of worship. It is not surprising then, that the two most prominent ecclesiastical buildings erected during the Gilded Age were built on Fifth Avenue by religious minorities: St. Patrick's Roman Catholic Cathedral (see below) and Temple Emanu-El (see below).

In 1865 St. Thomas Church became the first Protestant congregation to follow its parishioners uptown, relocating from its forty-four-year-old building at Broadway and Houston Street into a spacious brownstone Gothic church designed by Richard Upjohn, working with his son Richard M. Upjohn, for a 100-by-235-foot site at the northwest corner of Fifth Avenue and Fifty-third Street.[27] While some of the spacious site was left open, later to be occupied by C. C. Haight's three-story parish house (1882),[28] Upjohn was able to fill most of the real estate with a spectacular, rubble-stone, freestone-trimmed cruciform in the English Decorated Gothic style. The composition culminated in a 260-foot-tall tower, rising from a square base past a belfry and lantern to a soaring spire that dramatically marked the Fifth Avenue corner. As many as 1,600 worshipers could sit under an open-timbered roof washed in light from stained-glass clerestory windows. The plan was unusual in one key aspect: instead of being a single intersection of nave and transepts, the crossing was widened to form an octagon on one side of which was a polygonal apse flanked on either side by a Roosevelt organ.

The prolific diarist George Templeton Strong found "the interior peculiar but effective—the stained glass is very good."[29] Schuyler, who ranked St. Thomas "among the finest specimens of the post–Civil War churches," was nonetheless troubled by the location of the altar at the western end of the church, a decision forced upon the congregation by the church's location on the west side of Fifth Avenue. Schuyler also criticized the use of brownstone, which he described as a "dingy, funereal stone [that] has done more to disfigure New York than anything else," and he argued that the dark material minimized the potentially poetic play of shadows across the Gothic forms.[30] Later he was to praise the treatment of the crossing, which he felt Upjohn had adopted "on the ground that a congregation, or rather an audience could be better 'accommodated' in that form than in the long drawn aisle."[31] The church's interior was embellished with Augustus Saint-Gaudens's reredos representing the Adoration of the Cross by Angels, which was flanked by two murals depicting scenes of the Resurrection painted by John La Farge, collectively constituting what was perhaps the first collaboration between a distinguished architect, sculptor, and artist in the design of an American church.

Built for Manhattan's oldest church congregation, dating back to 1628, W. Wheeler Smith's Collegiate Dutch Reformed Church (1872), on the northwest corner of Fifth Avenue and Forty-eighth Street, was a Gothic-style brownstone building distinguished by an elegantly tapered, 270-foot-high, crocketed spire located at the corner.[32] Installed in the the tower was a bell cast in Amsterdam in 1731 which had first hung in the Middle Dutch Church on Nassau Street but was taken down and secreted when the British took over New York. On May 25, 1869, the congregation celebrated one hundred years of worship at the corner of Fulton and William Streets, and then traveled uptown to lay the foundation stone for its new building. Writing about the building as it rose, Montgomery Schuyler described the church as an "extraordinary and incomprehensible conglomeration of Gothic curiosities."[33] Three weeks later Schuyler returned to the subject,

St. Thomas Church, northwest corner of Fifth Avenue and West Fifty-third Street. Richard Upjohn and Richard M. Upjohn, 1865.
View to the north along Fifth Avenue showing the Fifth Avenue Presbyterian Church (Carl Pfeiffer, 1875) in the background. NYHS.

St. Thomas Church, northwest corner of Fifth Avenue and West Fifty-third Street. Richard Upjohn and Richard M. Upjohn, 1865.
View toward the polygonal apse, c. 1895. MCNY.

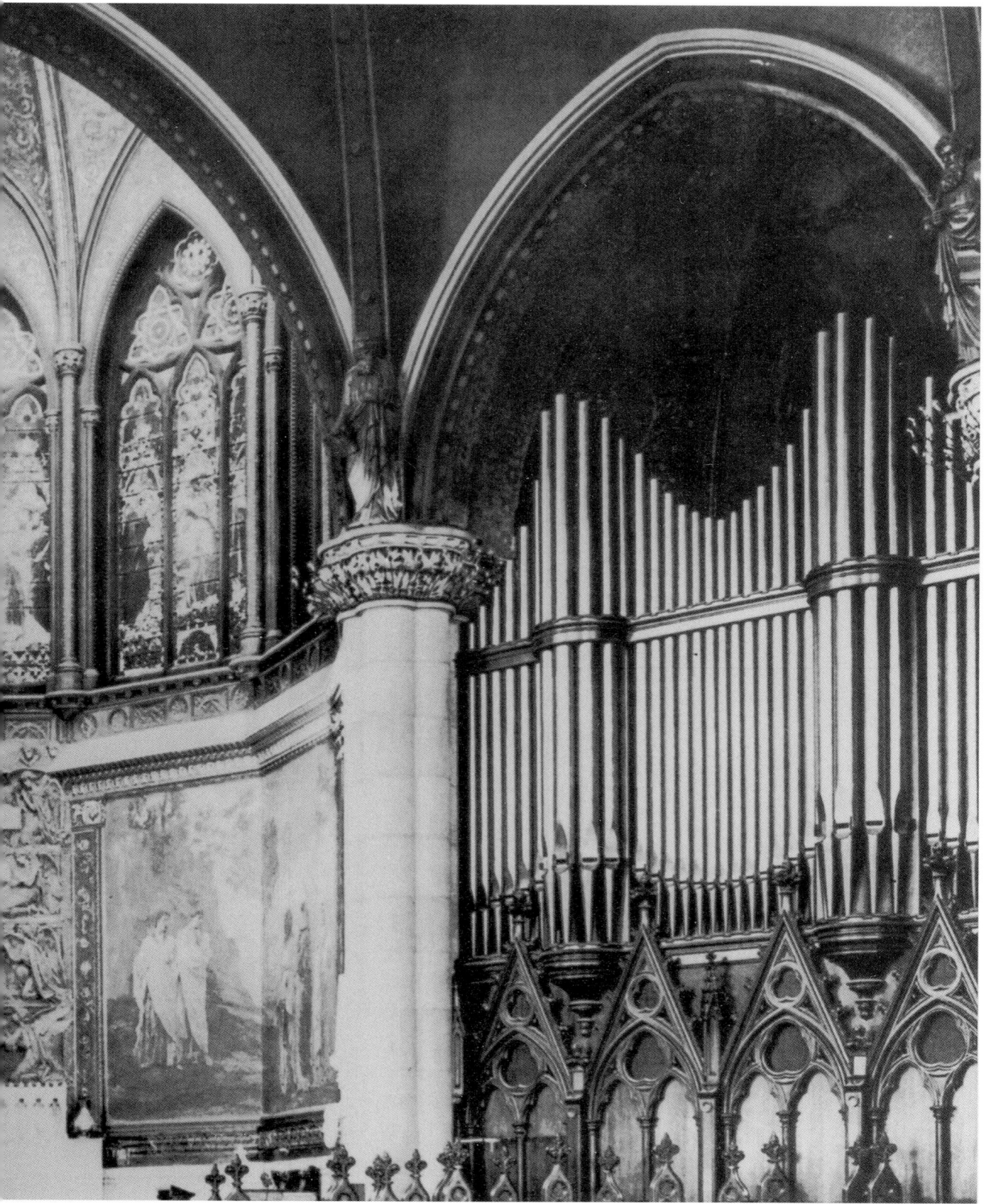

Collegiate Dutch Reformed Church, northwest corner of Fifth Avenue and West Forty-eighth Street. W. Wheeler Smith, 1872. View to the northwest. NYHS.

Fifth Avenue Presbyterian Church, northwest corner of Fifth Avenue and West Fifty-fifth Street. Carl Pfeiffer, 1875.
View to the northwest along Fifth Avenue showing the church under construction. NYHS.

Fifth Avenue Presbyterian Church, northwest corner of Fifth Avenue and West Fifty-fifth Street. Carl Pfeiffer, 1875. View to the northwest, c. 1890. NYHS.

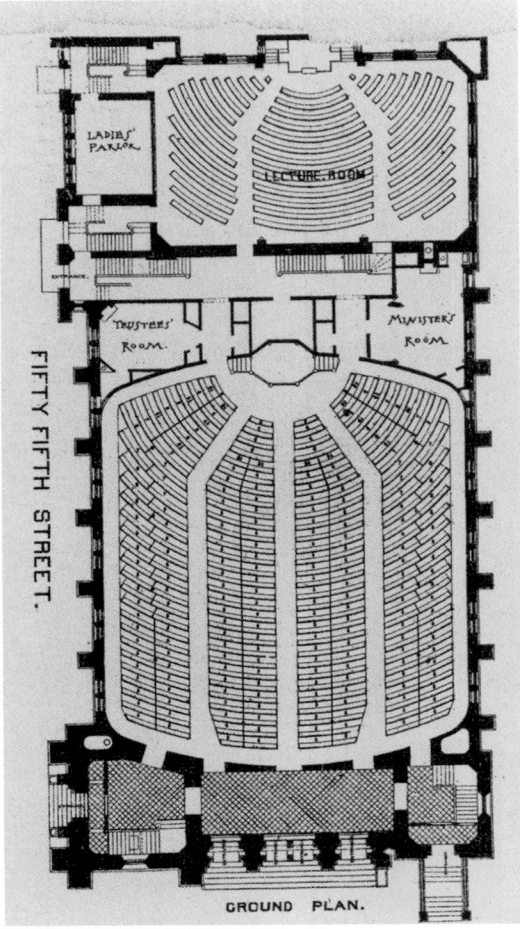
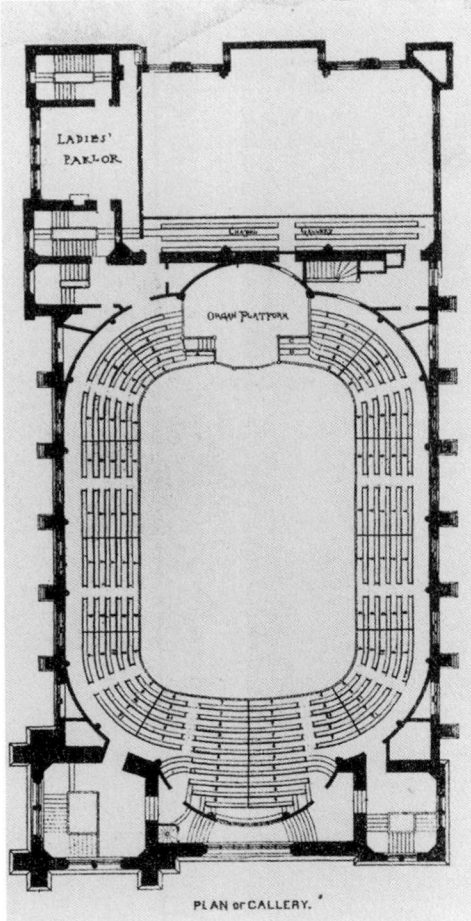

Fifth Avenue Presbyterian Church, northwest corner of Fifth Avenue and West Fifty-fifth Street. Carl Pfeiffer, 1875.
First-floor plan (left) and gallery-level plan (right). AABN. CU.

appalled by a design he found "scarcely possible to criticize . . . by any known rule . . . it is simply Gothic gone roaring mad. . . . In short, it is one unintelligible jumble of Gothic forms, adopted to all sorts of purposes for which Gothic architecture never intended them."[34]

Carl Pfeiffer's twin-towered, early English Gothic building for Reverend John Hall's Fifth Avenue Presbyterian Church (1875), occupying a one-hundred-by-two-hundred-foot site on the northwest corner of Fifth Avenue and Fifty-fifth Street, was scholarly, if somewhat understated.[35] Founded in 1808, the church's first home was on Cedar Street. It was later housed in a Greek Revival temple on Duane Street, and in 1852 it moved to a Belleville stone church at Broadway and Nineteenth Street, which at 1,020 seats proved too small to accommodate the crowds that the charismatic Dr. Hall, who was appointed in 1867, drew every Sunday. Faced with a fourth move in sixty-four years, the trustees decided to relocate far uptown, to Fifty-fifth Street, this time erecting an auditorium that could seat 2,000 people. When it came

time to move, some of the trustees contributed funds to buy the old building and give it to the Central Presbyterian Church, which had it taken down to be reerected on Fifty-seventh Street between Broadway and Seventh Avenue. The Nineteenth Street lot was sold to Arnold Constable for its new store (see chapter 5).

At the Fifty-fifth Street church, two towers of unequal height—the taller, thirty-foot-square one at the corner being, at three hundred feet, the highest in the city—lent the church a high degree of visual interest. A projecting porch might have enhanced this appeal had not an objecting neighbor forced Pfeiffer to abandon this feature. The lesser tower, rising to a height of 160 feet, contained air intakes powered by a seven-foot-diameter fan; the air filling the interior of the church could be renewed every fifteen minutes. Dr. Hall, said to be indifferent to the church's outward appearance, was, however, very interested in the interior of what would often be called "The Cathedral Church of Presbyterianism." Primarily interested in getting the word to his parishioners, he called for an audi-

St. Bartholomew's Episcopal Church, southwest corner of Madison Avenue and East Forty-fourth Street. Renwick & Sands, 1872–76. View to the southwest, c. 1892. NYHS.

torium without central aisles. The one-hundred-by-eighty-five-foot, sixty-foot-tall sanctuary was treated as a scientific problem in acoustics, with the aim, as the *New York World* put it, "to produce a building which should first be a perfect auditorium . . . and second, one which should be thoroughly substantial, distinguished and ecclesiastical in its architecture."[36] The auditorium had no sharp corners or angles; its semicircular ends were joined to the walls by elliptical curves, all intended to achieve good sight and sound communication with the pulpit.

Mariana Van Rensselaer was not impressed, cataloging Pfeiffer's among the first of those "churches which are still more unlike all past examples of ecclesiastical architecture—which, in truth, have been inspired by the secular lecture-room or concert-hall. . . . We can hardly be surprised if the architect, who essayed to treat so immense an interior on so novel a scheme, has failed to satisfy the eye. Convenience he has secured, but no particle of beauty can be found in his vast, bare galleried room—no expression of structure, and no more ecclesiastical effect than Steinway Hall [see chapter 5] exhibits, unless, indeed, we are to find this lost in the Gothic detail of his woodwork."[37]

Renwick & Sands's St. Bartholomew's Episcopal Church (1872–76) was located on the southwest corner of Madison Avenue and Forty-fourth Street.[38] The congregation was organized in 1835 and for many years worshiped in a church on Lafayette Place and Great Jones Street. The new building complex consisted of a church and a rectory, which together sat on a site running 100 feet along Madison Avenue and 145 feet on Forty-fourth Street. Renwick & Sands's Lombardic Gothic–inspired design, with its judicious use of polychromy, suggested influences from Byzantine architecture as well as that of Pisa. Little arcaded recesses and windows and small columns crowned with floreated capitals enlivened the pedimented Madison Avenue facade, which also incorporated a lofty, two-hundred-foot-high campanile rising to an open belfry. The *Real Estate Record and Builders' Guide* praised the "palatial" principal facade facing Madison Avenue but found the termination of the bell tower inferior to the geometry at Temple Emanu-El, which was just around the corner.[39] Inside, St. Bartholomew's nave and side aisles were finished with lavishly carved, polychromed and polished surfaces, including those of a triforium gallery carried on Scotch granite columns, gathered together under a vaulted roof. Moses King noted that "all the appointments bespeak the wealth of the congregation."[40] The *New York Times* pointed out, however, that while the congregation may have been well-heeled, it was also fiscally prudent: "The entire cost of the building and its surroundings was $100,000, and when the congregation moved into it there was a debt upon it of $175,000. This was a heavy burden, but it has now been paid off. St. Bartholomew's is the first church Bishop Potter has consecrated during his Episcopacy, it being a custom, if not a law, of the Episcopal Church, that no edifice can be consecrated until it is wholly out of debt."[41]

Park Avenue Methodist Episcopal Church, southeast corner of Fourth Avenue and East Eighty-sixth Street. J. C. Cady, 1882–84. View to the southeast. NYHS.

J. C. Cady's English Gothic, brick and Connecticut brownstone Park Avenue Methodist Episcopal Church (1882–84), on the southeast corner of Fourth Avenue and Eighty-sixth Street, represented in even more exaggerated form than Pfeiffer's church for Dr. Hall the new, so-called "auditorium" church type that was being built to reflect the increasingly important role of sermons in worship services.[42] The congregation, the nation's first Methodist Episcopal church, initially worshiped in a church built on John Street in 1708 and later, beginning in 1818, in a small wooden chapel at Third Avenue and Ninth Street that incorporated a single beam from the original church. In 1837 it moved far uptown to a brick building on Eighty-sixth Street that was later sold to the Jewish congregation Gates of Hope. As designed by Cady, the new church incorporated a principal entrance facing Fourth Avenue that consisted of two double doorways enclosed by archways. Above, a large rondel surrounded by a dozen small, circular windows was set in a smooth-faced square frame. A 150-foot-high corner tower carried a steeply pitched roof of red tile. Inside, the one-thousand-seat sanctuary was finished in cherry wood. The wooden beam from the John Street church was placed beneath the pulpit. The editors of the *New York Times* described the interior as giving "an effect of lightness and cheerfulness, to which the pale-blue-stained glass windows contribute to a considerable

Calvary Baptist Church, north side of West Fifty-seventh Street between Sixth and Seventh Avenues. John R. Thomas, 1883. View to the northeast, c. 1894. NYHS.

extent." They praised the building in general, stating that "its solid gray stone exterior is very imposing" and that the church was "handsome in every respect." The editors also noted that the Reverend Dr. A. D. Vail, speaking at a dedicatory service,

> alluded to the seeming departure from Methodist principles in the architecture of the church of to-day. He asked whether the old severe Methodism, which gained success by its plainness, was the same as that of the present time. He answered the question by stating that to-day was the age of progress and the Methodism of to-day was simply the result of progress. "Architecture is a power," he said, "which is even greater than the moral power which is in a church. Architecture dominates church life. Social life must dominate architecture." The speaker thought that the church platforms were nowadays too large. They afforded ground for non-religious discussion. He stated that the new church preferred the little pulpit, as being restricted to religious matters.[43]

Mariana Van Rensselaer saw the interior of Cady's church as an example of the fact that "much greater novelty than any Episcopal interior shows" had been achieved in recent Baptist, Methodist, Congregationalist, and Presbyterian churches, where "the 'long-drawn aisle' and the cruciform plan" were abandoned "and a simple rectangle frankly utilized." According to Van Rensselaer, Cady provided

> a square interior with deep galleries, running around three sides. At each corner of the inner square . . . stands a column. Round arches connect these columns, and are thrown from them to the outer walls. Above the inner rectangle thus formed, the ceiling rises higher than it does above the galleries. At the east side (one can no longer say east *end*) is the large pulpit platform, behind it are the seats for the choir, and behind these, again, the tall organ pipes. Unfortunately the columns and the arches which are painted throughout, appear to be of iron, and the spandrels above are filled in with an open network of turned wood [creating an effect] too fragile to be architecturally fine. It is not a very beautiful interior, but it is very convenient, and I do not think its purpose could be mistaken. It looks certainly not like an ancient church, but still not unlike a place for religious use.[44]

John R. Thomas's Calvary Baptist Church (1883), on the north blockfront of Fifty-seventh Street between Sixth and Seventh Avenues, was built for a congregation founded in 1846 which had originally worshiped in a chapel on lower Broadway, and, beginning in 1854, in a brownstone church on Twenty-third Street.[45] The new church on Fifty-seventh Street was less interesting for its spikily Gothic, triple-towered, five-porched, stone exterior that sprawled along an exceptionally generous, 160-foot street frontage than it was for its interior planning. In an attempt to come to terms with the problem of the modern Protestant church—namely, the need "to make an audience room which has very little affinity with any past type of church, and to make it look like a church"—Thomas provided a one-hundred-by-one-hundred-foot principal worship room accommodating an "amphitheatrical arrangement of seats."[46] Light poured in through a south-facing rose window as well as through an opening in the west wall and a clerestory above. According to Van Rensselaer, "the room was given an amphitheatrical effect by slanting the floor somewhat steeply, curving the rows of seats, and also giving a curvilinear form to the face of the shallow gallery which runs around three sides and even along a portion of the fourth." While she did not find the "deep-toned" decoration of the room "artistically remarkable," the light-bathed, low-ceilinged room conveyed a religious feeling "in spite of its analogy in plan to a secular interior for public use."[47] In 1883 the *Real Estate Record and Builders' Guide* praised the design for its "expressive and well balanced" composition but asserted that it derived its "somewhat hidebound look from the fact that so many and various masses [were] all faced by one plane . . . which shows but little skill in the treatment of detail."[48] As development along Fifty-seventh Street increased, however, Thomas's composition seemed better and better. In 1885 the *Record and Guide* reported: "Flanked by newer buildings it is impressive by reason mainly of its unusual extent of frontage and of the good judgment of the architect in securing ample masses of wall. The spire, too, is graceful and well studied, more so indeed than most of the detail in the building proper, which can claim no higher praise than ineffectiveness."[49]

In addition to the dominant trend of long-established congregations following their affluent members uptown, the rapidly developing and tony East Side, particularly in the Sixties and Seventies between Fifth and Fourth Avenues, was also attracting newly formed churches. Completed in 1869, Renwick & Sands's Episcopal Church of the Holy Sepulchre, located on the north side of Seventy-fourth Street between Fourth and Lexington Avenues, presented a random ashlar bluestone facade to the street and incorporated a steeply pitched, polychromed slate roof, a tower punctuated by pointed-arch windows, and tripartite window groupings with curved quatrefoils.[50] Despite the visual interest of this Gothic essay, it nonetheless constituted an appropriately understated presence on the largely residential side street. Inside, the church's nave was illuminated by a pointed arch divided into three cusped lancets, which was in turn surmounted by a rondel. As designed by William A. Potter, the St. James Lutheran Church (1889), on the southwest corner of Madison Avenue and Seventy-third Street, took McKim, Mead & White's adjacent Tiffany mansion (see chapter 4) into account, repeating the height of its base to mark the separation between the gable-fronted rectory, which adjoined the Tiffany house, and the church proper.[51] The church itself adopted a gabled cruciform entered at the corner through a fussily detailed porch facing Madison Avenue. Echoing typical Romanesque-inspired practice, Potter used alternating narrow and wide courses of rock-faced pink Milford granite for the church walls, complementing the overall tawny color of the Tiffany house without repeating its bluestone basement story.

St. James Lutheran Church, southwest corner of Madison Avenue and East Seventy-third Street. William A. Potter, 1889. View to the southwest showing the Charles L. Tiffany house (McKim, Mead & White, 1882–85) on the left. AABN. CU.

In the 1870s and 1880s, Madison Avenue between Six-tieth and Seventy-third Streets became the site of four new churches by R. H. Robertson. Robertson was one of the leading ecclesiastical architects of Gilded Age New York; in addition to his work on the East Side, he also built churches on the upper West Side and in Harlem (see chapter 6). The first of Robertson's Madison Avenue churches constituted an immature though very interesting work, Dr. Phillips's Presbyterian Church (1873), at the northeast corner of Seventy-third Street.[52] Montgomery Schuyler, writing more than twenty years after the build-ing's completion, called it "a free and rather individual ver-sion of Victorian Gothic":

> It is Victorian Gothic, there is no doubt about that, and it exhibits the indifference to academical correctness which was especially the characteristic of Victorian Gothic, as it was practiced on this side of the Atlantic, but it shows the individuality which in some cases was a compensation for this indifference and in others an aggravation of it. The general scheme is very successful. There is an effective bal-ance, without any attempt at formal symmetry, between the two sides and they are effectively reconciled and dom-inated by the central feature, the big angle-tower of which the central third is a square and solid shaft. . . . The tower with its saddle-backed roof is very good indeed.[53]

Robertson's Church of the Holy Spirit (1881–83), at the northeast corner of Madison Avenue and Sixty-sixth Street, was far more representative of the tectonic solidity of the architect's mature work.[54] The seventy-five-by-one-hundred-foot brownstone building was visually dominated by an octagonal tower, located at the street corner, which supported a circular, pavilion-like structure that was in turn surmounted by a conical roof. When, in 1881, the *American Architect and Building News* published Robert-son's preliminary sketches for the church, which the con-gregation had just accepted, it was noted: "The small amount of money at the disposal of the congregation as well as their desire demanded a cheap and picturesque treatment which would not in any way compete with the more formal and pretentious church architecture in the vicinity."[55] The *New York Daily Graphic* stated, "The order of the architecture may be termed the Queen Anne," and described the church's appearance within the context of its increasingly urban surroundings: "Great changes have taken place in this neighborhood in the past few years, which aptly illustrate the marvelous growth of the metrop-olis. Where ten years ago were vacant lots surrendered without remonstrance to the rude occupancy of the prim-itive 'squatter' are now to be seen block upon block of costly mansions. . . . Such is the Lenox Hill of to-day, and

Dr. Phillips's Presbyterian Church, northeast corner of Madison Avenue and East Seventy-third Street. R. H. Robertson, 1873. View to the northeast. NYSB. CU.

Church of the Holy Spirit, northeast corner of Madison Avenue and East Sixty-sixth Street. R. H. Robertson, 1881–83. View to the northeast. NYHS.

in the midst of the palatial environment which surrounds it stands the Church of the Holy Spirit, challenging the attention of the passer-by by its picturesque simplicity." The *Daily Graphic* described the building's facades as "treated with almost Quaker like plainness," suggesting that the architect had been "urged" by the congregation's building committee "to avoid the merely conventional in ecclesiastical construction and the result is a structure unique but harmonious. The impression conveyed is that while no proper outlay has been avoided, there has been no attempt to vie with the lavish expenditure of money visible everywhere in the vicinity. Indeed the interior of the church is more like that of the sanctuary to which one is accustomed when residing in the country. There is nothing

of the modern city church about it. The ceiling is low, the general appearance cozy: a building where worship is not of fashion, but of reality."[56] The editors of the *Real Estate Record and Builders' Guide* were considerably less impressed, finding the church's architectural detail "much more domestic than ecclesiastical in character, and . . . moreover, somewhat incongruous by its minuteness as well as by its classicism, with the simple, rugged and romantic treatment of the masses."[57]

The Madison Avenue Methodist Episcopal Church (1881–84), at the northeast corner of Madison Avenue and East Sixtieth Street, was a mature Robertson work.[58] According to Montgomery Schuyler, it "was rather loosely Romanesque, and not at all Richardsonian."[59] The congregation was new, "formed to supply a place of worship where it was thought a church was greatly needed."[60] Robertson's design for the 100-foot-wide-by-89-foot-deep site included the main church, which seated 750 worshipers, facing Madison Avenue, and a Sunday school to the side. In his continuation of James Fergusson's history of architecture, Robert Kerr discussed this building and Robertson's St. James (see below), farther up on Madison Avenue, at Seventy-first Street, as illustrations of the freedom American architects exhibited in church design. Kerr went as far as to call the style "round arched Gothic."[61] The basilica-like sanctuary was lit via clerestory windows. To the north of the church was the 32-by-89-foot Sunday school, but the most memorable feature of the freestone church, aside from what Schuyler called "the plainness and amplitude of the rough-faced wall," was the 175-foot-tall bell tower that rose over the main entrance, on Madison Avenue, culminating in four turretlike finials and a steeply pitched roof. Schuyler thought "the tower . . . too important to serve merely as the apex of the pyramid" of the facade, noting its "watch tower" appearance.[62]

The most inventive of Robertson's churches was St. James Protestant Episcopal Church (1883–84), at the northeast corner of Madison Avenue and Seventy-first Street, which Montgomery Schuyler struggled to classify stylistically, finding it "scarcely Romanesque at all in detailing, being, so far as it need be classified, in an early, indeed the earliest, phase of the French Gothic."[63] St. James, since its founding in 1810 as a summer church, had always been located on Lenox Hill, occupying its first building, a wooden structure at Lexington Avenue and Sixty-ninth Street, from 1810 until 1869; it then relocated to a new, polychromed Gothic church at 153 East Seventy-second Street, between Fourth and Lexington Avenues, designed by James Renwick Jr.[64] In 1883 the vestry bought the site at Madison Avenue and Seventy-first Street and, impressed with the Methodist Episcopal church at Sixtieth Street, especially its tower, hired Robertson, whose plan unconventionally located the altar at the west end of the church, facing Madison Avenue. While the altar's location had the disadvantage of blocking the logical point of entrance from Madison Avenue, it did assure unobstructed sunlight from the west. A never-finished tower at the corner served as a secondary entrance to the side of the chancel, but the principal doors, located at the east end, were entered from Seventy-first Street. The *Real Estate Record and Builders' Guide*'s correspondent, probably Montgomery Schuyler, immediately took notice of the unusual plan: Saint James "had advanced far enough to show an unusual arrangement. What seems to be an apsidal chancel occupies the avenue front, with an entrance at the corner, but the main entrance is apparently at the other end of the church. This reversal is not unusual where the purpose in 'advanced' churches [is] to preserve 'orientation,' that is to say, to keep the altar at the east end. But in this case it seems to have been resorted to purely for

picturesque purposes, since the cathedral orientation is exactly reversed."[65] A few months later, the *Record and Guide*'s critic, again probably Schuyler, assessed the composition overall:

> The highest success of the work is not in detail but in mass. The flank of the church, with the terminal masses of the tower and the transept balancing each other, is a sober, scholarly and effective composition, while the arrangement of masses at the east end is full of poignancy and picturesqueness and fully justifies the unusual disposition. From any point of view, the relation of the projecting apse with the gabled wall to which it is attached, and to the higher gable which rises behind the first, and to the flanking members, the tower and the turret, forms a harmonious composition, the life and spirit of which in no way derogates from its sobriety and repose. We do not know a more successful and attractive parish church among the hundreds in New York.[66]

Oddly enough, given that it was the Madison Avenue Methodist Episcopal Church's tower that attracted the St. James vestry to Robertson in the first place, only the first stage of the tower was completed. Nonetheless, as Schuyler put it: "In spite of the incompleteness of the tower, which is an integral part of the composition, the building is one of the most interesting churches of New York."[67]

Madison Avenue Methodist Episcopal Church, northeast corner of Madison Avenue and East Sixtieth Street. R. H. Robertson, 1881–84. View to the northeast. AR. CU.

Proposed St. James Protestant Episcopal Church, northeast corner of Madison Avenue and East Seventy-first Street. R. H. Robertson, 1883. Rendering showing view to the northeast and ground-floor plan. AABN. CU.

Neighborhood Churches

In addition to the churches built by affluent congregations in fashionable locations, churches were constructed at out-of-the-way sites by poorer congregations whose members lived nearby. In 1875 the Madison Square Presbyterian Church completed a branch facility occupying a one-hundred-by-one-hundred-foot site on the north side of Thirtieth Street east of Third Avenue.[68] As designed by J. C. Cady, the church, which could seat 1,100 people, adopted a French Gothic style realized in Philadelphia pressed brick and trimmed in buff brick and Nova Scotia sandstone. A three-story structure housing a Sunday school faced Thirtieth Street, while the sanctuary was placed at the rear of the site. A campanile completed the composition. Despite its tight, forty-seven-by-eighty-two-foot site at 151–153 East Twenty-second Street, on the north side of the block between Lexington and Third Avenues, Cady's Gustus Adolphus Swedish Lutheran Church (1887–88) presented an imposing Gothic exterior built of brownstone from Amherst, Ohio, and dominated by a 155-foot-high steeple.[69] Inside, the church's main sanctuary, which could accommodate one thousand worshipers, was placed on the second floor, elevated above a gymnasium.

Cady's Forsyth Street Church (1890), at the southeast corner of Forsyth and Delancey Streets, was more noteworthy for its ingenious urbanism than for its exterior architectural expression.[70] Built for the congregation formerly known as the Allen Street Presbyterian Church, the

St. James Protestant Episcopal Church, northeast corner of Madison Avenue and East Seventy-first Street. R. H. Robertson, 1883–84. View to the northeast. AR. CU.

Catholic Apostolic Church, north side of West Fifty-seventh Street between Ninth and Tenth Avenues. Francis H. Kimball, 1886–87. View to the north. NYHS.

building, constructed of Kentucky limestone and brick, faced Forsyth Street with a four-story facade surmounted by an imposing cornice above which there was a hipped roof. The building's principal entrance was enclosed by three arches and elevated a full story above the street; reached by means of a grand double staircase, the building's entrance was clearly separated from the bustling street activity that was a hallmark of the densely populated neighborhood, largely composed of poor immigrants. Above the entrance a central expanse of wall was outlined by an arch and punctuated with an oculus; to either side, arches enclosed three-story-high vertical stacks of win-

dows. Along the Delancey Street frontage, most of the building consisted of three stories and was dominated, above the first story, by four double-height arches filled in with windows. The first floor was depressed several feet below street level and visually treated as a base upon which the rather imposing upper floors sat. Inside, the first floor contained a Sunday school, while the second story was exclusively occupied by a five-hundred-seat auditorium. In the front of the building, the third and fourth floors contained a ten-room suite for the church's pastor and his family. The *New York Times* praised the building's "handsome appearance," remarking that in light of the church's poor constituency it was "noticeable for its economical construction" and that it was "a substantial structure that will stand hard usage and require few repairs."[71]

Built by a group sometimes known as the Irvingites, a London sect following the "gifted and unhappy" Reverend Edward Irving, "some of whose story is known to all readers of Carlyle," as Moses King put it, Francis H. Kimball's masterly Catholic Apostolic Church (1886–87), said to be the only worship center for the faith in the United States, was obscurely located on the north side of Fifty-seventh Street between Ninth and Tenth Avenues.[72] The congregation was organized in 1850, meeting in rooms at the University of the City of New York until 1855, when it purchased a church on West Sixteenth Street before leaving that building in 1886 in favor of a

purpose-built home farther uptown. (The former Catholic Apostolic Church became home to the French Evangelical Church, and in 1886 Alfred D. F. Hamlin redesigned the principal facade.[73]) According to the *Real Estate Record and Builders' Guide*'s commentator, probably Montgomery Schuyler, Kimball's church was "a very pretty and effective bit of street architecture, [presenting] a solution of a problem that most architects who have attempted it have found very untractable. The problem is that of a city church on an inside lot; that is to say, in such a situation that it can be lighted only from the ends, or even from one end, and from a clerestory so arranged as not to be deprived of its light by towering alongside."[74] For a fifty-foot-wide site, Kimball designed a truncated cross with a short transept. While the aisles were kept low and narrow, the thirty-foot-wide space in the center was allowed to soar over the nave, creating the possibility for clerestory windows conducting both east and west light. The impact of the building on the street was enhanced by its dense detail, rendered even more dense by the exclusive use of red brick and, in only a slightly different tint, terra cotta roughened in the mold to give the effect of stonework. Ten years after the building's completion, Montgomery Schuyler, assessing Kimball's career, wrote: "There is no more scholarly Gothic work in New York. The charm of it is heightened by the fact that although the ornament is in terra-cotta, and is or might be for the most part a substitute for stone-carving, there is yet in some of it, as in the main offset of the front and the gabled offsets of the buttresses, a recognition in design of the material which adds the raciness of idiom to scholarly diction."[75]

Mission Churches

Reflecting an increased public concern for the welfare of the city's poorer residents, the 1870s and 1880s saw the completion of a number of so-called mission churches. In 1876 Grace Church replaced its red and yellow brick Gothic Grace Chapel (James Renwick Jr., 1860), which had been destroyed by a fire four years earlier,[76] with a new building on the same site, on the south side of Fourteenth Street between Third Avenue and Irving Place, nearly opposite the Academy of Music and a few blocks from its home church.[77] As designed by Potter & Robertson, the new Grace Chapel, which occupied a 60-foot-wide, 141-foot-deep lot, contained a 50-foot-wide-by-80-foot-deep octagonal chapel that sat 250 people under an open-timbered roof.

In 1883, the venerable St. Mark's Church, organized in 1791, completed a chapel, built by Rutherfurd B. Stuyvesant as a memorial to his wife, Mary, at 288 East Tenth Street, on the southwest corner of Avenue A.[78] James Renwick Jr. and William Russell's lively design in red brick with matching terra cotta trim synthesized Gothic and Renaissance elements. Complexly massed, the building confronted Tenth Street with a 106-foot-long principal facade containing an asymmetrically placed entrance porch flanked to the west by the 450-seat sanctu-

Grace Chapel, south side of East Fourteenth Street between Third Avenue and Irving Place. Potter & Robertson, 1876. Rendering of view to the southeast. AABN. CU.

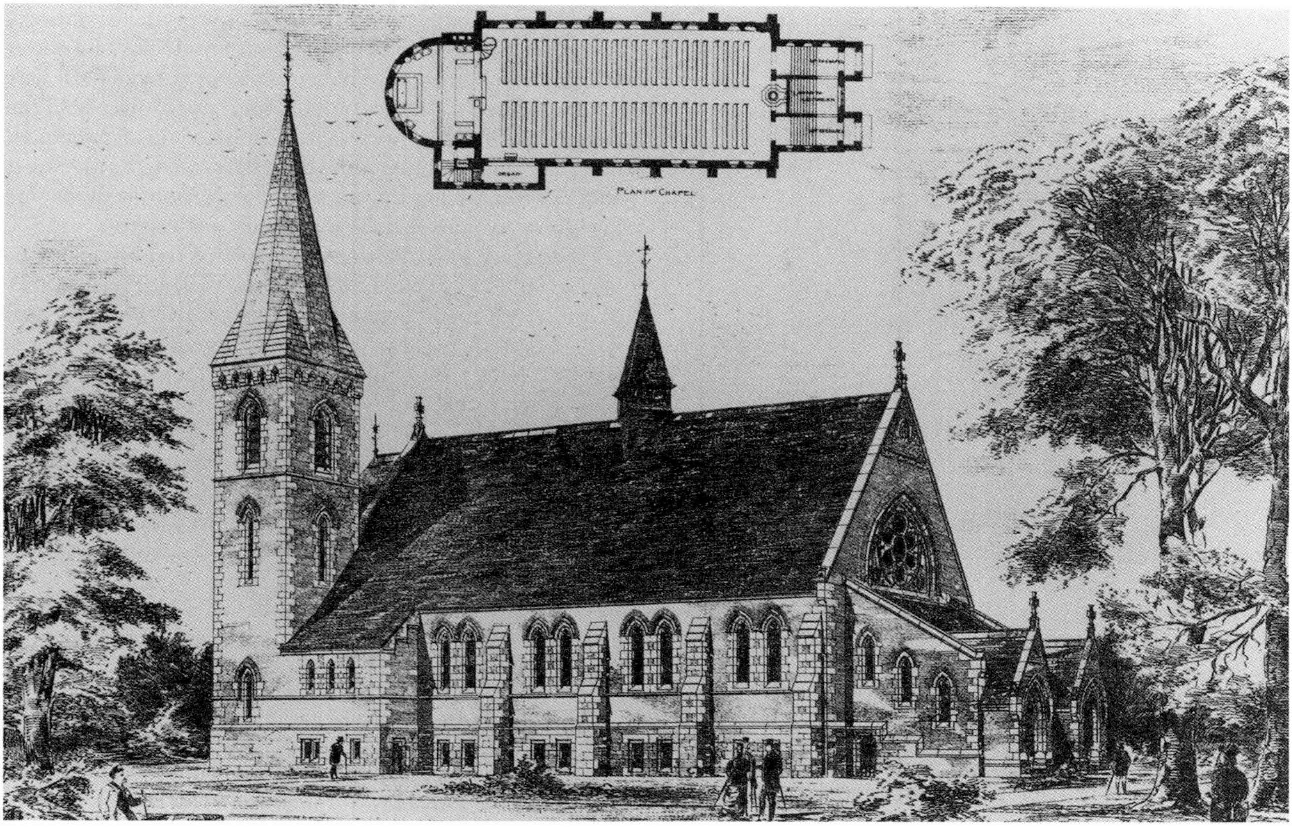

Chapel of the Good Shepherd, Blackwell's Island. Frederick Clarke Withers, 1888–89. First-floor plan and rendering of view to the northwest. AABN. CU.

Episcopal Church of the Beloved Disciple, 65 East Eighty-ninth Street. Hubert, Pirsson & Co., 1870. View to the northeast. STM.

Broome Street Tabernacle, south side of Broome Street, Centre Market Place to Centre Street. J. C. Cady, 1885. View to the southwest. King, 1893. CU.

ary and immediately to the east by a tower incorporating a syncopated pattern of pointed-arch windows. The tower terminated in an arcaded belfry with a pyramidal roof. Farther to the west, a lower, bulkier, four-story tower held the corner; the lower tower also terminated in a pyramidal roof, this one punctuated by chimneys along Tenth Street and a dormer along the avenue. The portion of the building along Avenue A housed a library and school.

Frederick Clarke Withers's Chapel of the Good Shepherd (1888–89), located on Blackwell's Island, was another of the city's mission churches.[79] Built by the Episcopal City Mission Society with funds provided by George Bliss, a Grace Church parishioner, the rock-faced granite, Croton red brick, and Belleville stone chapel, intended to serve residents of the city's almshouse, contained a four-hundred-seat, open-timbered, eighty-foot-long, twenty-four-foot-wide chapel, raised a half level so that a combined lecture and reading room, as well as a room for women's events to be staffed by the Mission Society, could be housed in an airy basement.

The Episcopal Church of the Beloved Disciple (1870), at 65 East Eighty-ninth Street, between Madison and

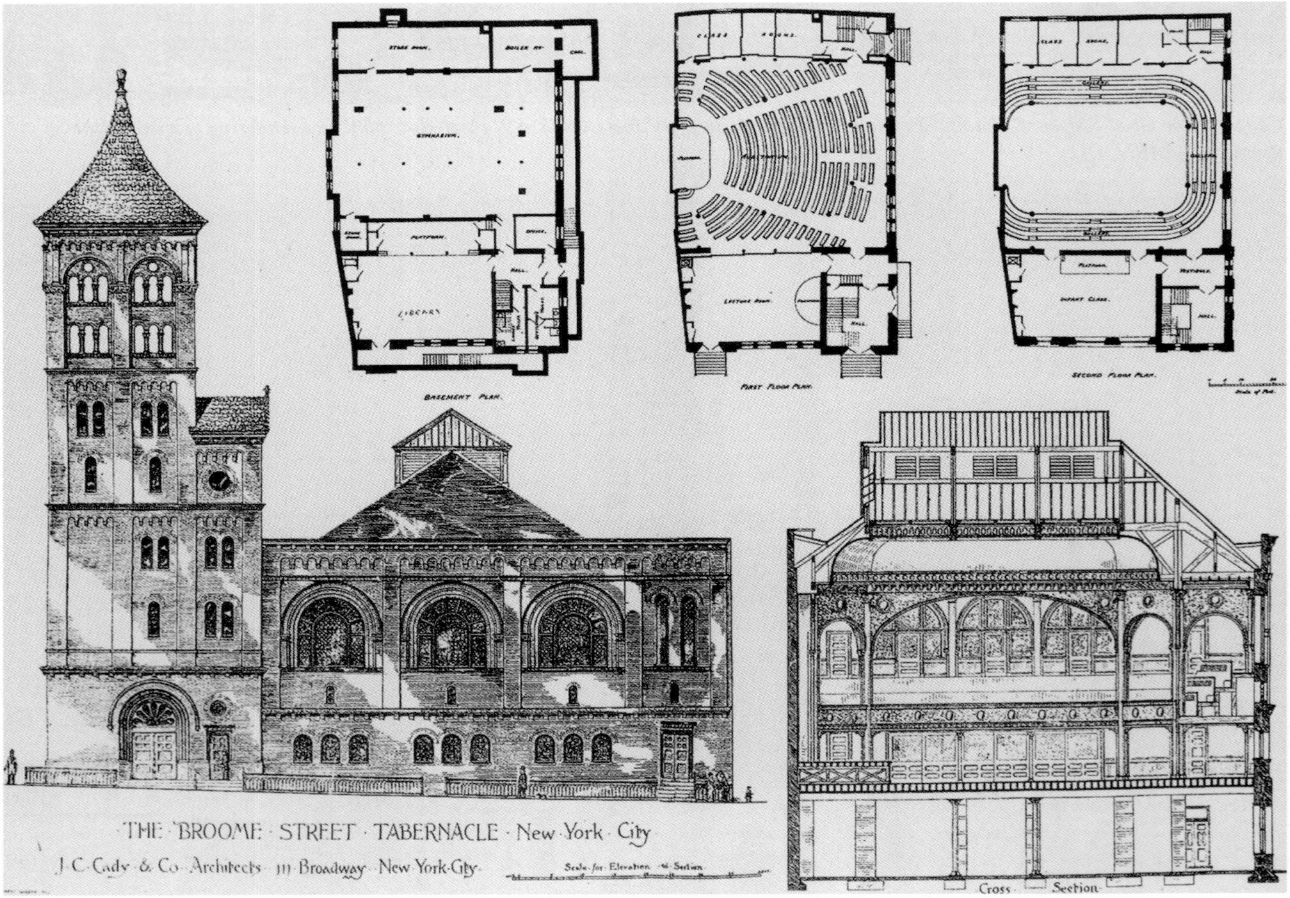

Broome Street Tabernacle, south side of Broome Street, Centre Market Place to Centre Street. J. C. Cady, 1885. Basement plan (top left), first-floor plan (top center), second-floor plan (top right), south elevation (bottom left), and section (bottom right). BLDG. CU.

Trinity Church, west side of Broadway at Wall Street. Richard Upjohn, 1846. View of nave, c. 1900, showing the Astor Memorial (Frederick Clarke Withers, 1877). NYHS.

Fourth Avenues, was established in conjunction with the Home for Indigent Christian Females, founded by St. Luke's Episcopal Church in Greenwich Village; when, in the 1860s, the home moved uptown to the northeast corner of Madison Avenue and Eighty-ninth Street, a chapel was built for the women who could not make the long journey.[80] Modeled after Edward B. Lamb's Church of St. Martin's (1865), in Gospel Oak, London, the restlessly massed, olive gray Nova Scotia sandstone building was designed by the firm of Hubert, Pirsson & Co., which would later specialize in the design and syndication of cooperative apartment houses (see chapter 4). To the east of the entrance porch was a soaring square tower capped by a rakishly asymmetrical crown.

J. C. Cady's Lombardic Romanesque–inspired Broome Street Tabernacle (1885) was built by the New York City Mission and Tract Society on a seventy-by-one-hundred-foot lot that had once been the site of a celebrated dog pit owned by Harry Jennings, an Englishman.[81] The two-level, square auditorium had amphitheater seating and a three-sided gallery that was lit from windows facing Centre and Broome Streets as well as from a roof monitor. There were also classrooms, a pastor's apartment located in a monumental tower, and, in the basement, a gymnasium, a Sunday-school room, and a 2,600-volume library.

Trinity Church Parish and Its Missions

Trinity was New York's first Episcopal parish, founded in 1705 on land granted to the church by Queen Anne. The parish had its principal place of worship in one of the most significant ecclesiastical buildings in the United States, a church (1846) designed by Richard Upjohn that

Trinity Parish vestry office and clergy house, east side of Church Street between Fulton and Vesey Streets. C. C. Haight, 1887.
View to the northwest showing the St. Paul's Chapel cemetery in the foreground. PTC.

commanded a vista down Wall Street from Broadway. The parish had outlying chapels, including St. Paul's a few blocks up Broadway and St. Luke's in Greenwich Village. In the post–Civil War era, the parish added buildings to its Wall Street campus while also building branch chapels, including a schoolhouse designed by Richard M. Upjohn (see above) as well as the St. Agnes chapel complex and the Trinity School, the latter two located on the West Side (see chapter 6).

In 1877 the interior of Upjohn's church was enhanced by a new reredos, a gift from John Jacob Astor II and his brother William in memory of their father, William B. Astor, who had died two years earlier.[82] The eleven-foot-wide white marble altar and nearly thirty-five-foot-wide, elaborately carved Caen stone, Perpendicular Gothic–style reredos were designed by Frederick Clarke Withers. Known collectively as the Astor Memorial, these elements provided Trinity Church with a focus on a scale of magnificence hitherto absent in any American church. Trinity's rector, the Reverend Dr. Morgan Dix, who

selected Withers as the project's architect, quickly determined that the church needed to be expanded to accommodate the new altar and hired Withers to redesign the chancel as well as to add a one-story sacristy to the building's west end. Intended to harmonize with Upjohn's original building, these projects were realized in reddish brown sandstone and completed in the same year as the interior alterations. To design the altar and reredos, Withers, the author of a scholarly treatise, *Church Architecture*, published in 1873, which heavily contributed to rekindling the popular interest in Gothic-inspired ecclesiastical architecture, followed English precedent, combining a Gothic structure with pictorial elements borrowed from Renaissance art, particularly Leonardo Da Vinci's *The Last Supper*. The reredos further incorporated additional carved scenes and decorative diaper work and was crowned by four fully sculpted angels holding musical instruments. The entire composition was based on spatial divisions of three, a symbolic reference that would not have been lost on Trinity churchgoers. While the altar and reredos established a new benchmark for American church decoration and constituted the most prestigious commission of Withers's career, the project largely escaped critical assessment. An anonymous reporter for the *American Architect and Building News* paid the work a somewhat left-handed compliment, stating that "the execution is magnificent as a specimen of workmanship . . . almost too good, leading one to feel like tasting it, as a richly ornamented bit of confectionary."[83]

In 1887 Trinity Parish completed a new vestry office and clergy house, designed by C. C. Haight. The three- and four-story, multigabled red brick and brown sandstone building, referred to as the Trinity offices, was built on Church Street between Fulton and Vesey Streets, overlooking St. Paul's Chapel and its graveyard. Combining church offices with living space for the unmarried clergy of Trinity Church and St. Paul's Chapel, the thirty-foot-wide building turned its back on Church Street, where the elevated railroad had a blighting effect. The decision to build something so low at a time when real estate interests were developing twelve-story cliffs on surrounding properties was remarkable. As Montgomery Schuyler pointed out, Haight's Gothic scheme, "of that half-churchly and half-domestic design" that "has . . . come to be known as 'collegiate,'" was similar to the architect's buildings for Columbia College (see above).[84]

The project of Richard M. Upjohn's Chapel of St. Chrysostum (1868–78) was prompted by the Trinity clergy's concern for the spiritual needs of the rapidly growing working-class section of the city farther uptown on the

west side.[85] A small, temporary mission for the poor was established on Thirty-second Street near Sixth Avenue in 1865; the following year it moved to larger quarters, on West Thirty-fourth Street. In 1868 Richard M. Upjohn was called upon to design a permanent chapel for a one-hundred-by-one-hundred-foot site at the northwest corner of Seventh Avenue and Thirty-ninth Street, which opened for worship in November 1869 though it was not completed for another nine years. Incorporating an eight-hundred-seat chapel as well as a schoolhouse and mission rooms, the stone-trimmed brownstone chapel was, according to Montgomery Schuyler, "a corner church which occupies merely the ground it stands on; in effect, a square, abutting at each of its ends on the adjoining secular buildings and so compelling a rather unusual arrangement, especially as orientation is preserved, and the chancel occupies the street front. The result is an effective exterior, in which the low mass of masonry, stopping at the springing of the large pointed windows that occupy the flanking gables, is crowned with a steep hood which serves almost as well as a lofty spire would do." Schuyler also admired the interior, noting "a particularly interesting solution of the chronic and crucial problem of a transeptual church with an open-timbered roof, the expressive and appropriate framing of the 'crossing.'"[86]

Potter & Robertson's St. Augustine's Mission House and Chapel (1876–77), built on the site of the Quaker burial ground at 107 East Houston Street, between Second Avenue and the Bowery, went far beyond St. Chrysostum in representing on a grand scale the city's most estab-

Chapel of St. Chrysostum, northwest corner of Seventh Avenue and West Thirty-ninth Street. Richard M. Upjohn, 1868–78. View to the northwest, c. 1900. Bracklow. NYHS.

St. Augustine's Mission House and Chapel, 107 East Houston Street. Potter & Robertson, 1876–77. View to the southeast. PTC.

St. Augustine's Mission House and Chapel, 107 East Houston Street. Potter & Robertson, 1876–77. View toward the altar. PTC.

lished parish, and in a neighborhood that was home to the city's highest concentration of the poor.[87] St. Augustine's was to be as impressive as Trinity Church itself. Incorporating a free chapel that, in contrast to most established New York churches and synagogues, did not rent out its pews but rather offered entrance free of charge, as well as a Sunday school and parish day-school, the building replaced a smaller chapel that had been constructed in 1869 at 262 Bowery. The importance of the church's decision to build so elaborate a structure in so poor a neighborhood was not lost on the *New York Daily Graphic*, which reported on the dedication ceremony, held when only the foundations had been laid, in September 1876: "It was a novel sight to see the foundation laid for such a building in the lower part of the city" at a time when it "was customary . . . to see religious societies tearing down their churches down-town and rebuilding them up-town."[88]

The new, asymmetrically massed, five-story, ashlar Longmeadow stone Gothic chapel and mission occupied a 225-foot-deep site with 86 feet of frontage on Houston Street widening to 150 feet at the rear of the lot; the remaining bits of land were laid out with grass and flower beds. The street facade consisted of a 207-foot-high tower terminating in arched windows that lit a 20-foot-high, 79-by-56-foot lecture hall. The building boldly and colorfully confronted the street. The plan seemed to emphasize education over worship; to reach the dark-red-and-green-

painted, openwork-timber-framed, 805-seat chapel, parishioners entered from Houston Street under an archway, passed through the school building along a broad tile-lined, timber-vaulted brick hall, and then moved up a short flight of stairs and through a vestibule. Massive, black-ornamented mahogany roof timbers sheltered the nave, which was ringed by dark red, eight-foot-high wainscoting separated from a dull green painted wall by wide bands of elaborate relief. The buff-colored choir and sanctuary were stenciled in gold and yellow. Between the school and the chapel was a light court, the boundary walls of which were faced with red and white brick trimmed in Dorchester stone.

Schuyler did not get around to writing about St. Augustine's until 1909. Although he failed to see the wisdom in locating the chapel behind the mission, he admired Potter & Robertson's handling of the approach: "The corridor itself . . . [was] an interesting piece of design, with mouldings and cut bricks, which were a novel means of expression and decoration in 1877 . . . [and] the vista furnished by its own length much enhances the effect of a well-designed, well constructed and distinctly 'churchly' interior, which would be impressive even if it had not such a forecourt, and in which the animation by no means destroys nor even disturbs the repose. It is, in fact, in many respects a model for a church interior which is relegated, not merely to an 'inside lot' but to the back of the lot."[89]

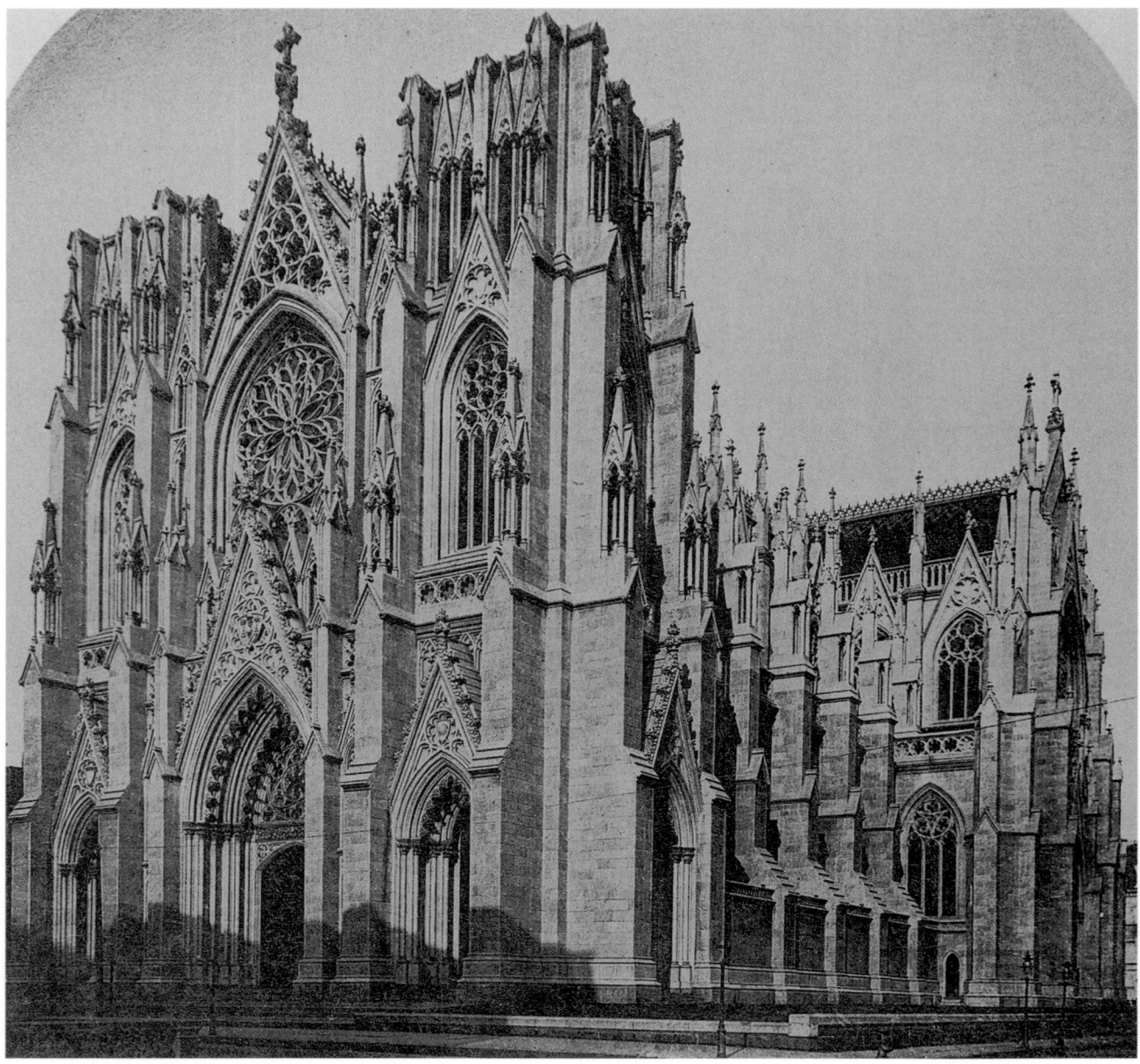

St. Patrick's Cathedral, Madison to Fifth Avenue, East Fiftieth to East Fifty-first Street. James Renwick Jr., 1850–79, 1888. View to the northeast, c. 1886. AABN. CU.

Roman Catholic Churches

Between 1840 and 1865 the number of Roman Catholics in New York skyrocketed from 200,000 to 400,000; in the process Roman Catholicism became the single largest religious denomination in New York City, commanding the loyalty of nearly half of the city's population.[90] In 1880 the political clout of the city's Catholic community was indisputably demonstrated when William R. Grace was elected mayor, the first Catholic to hold that office in New York. The clearest architectural expression of the Catholic community's enhanced role in New York was,

without question, James Renwick Jr.'s St. Patrick's Cathedral (1850–79, 1888), occupying most of the block bounded by Fifth and Madison Avenues and Fiftieth and Fifty-first Streets.[91] Since 1815 the congregation had resided in a church designed by Joseph François Mangin, on the east side of Mulberry Street between Prince and East Houston Streets, a synthesis of a Georgian vocabulary with Gothic elements that was not fully resolved.[92] Plans for the new cathedral were begun in 1850, and the cornerstone was laid before a crowd estimated at 100,000 people on August 10, 1858. Originally intended to take eight years to complete, the Civil War halted construction after only two years of work had been performed, just as the foundation was completed. Construction was not resumed until 1869. On November 29, 1877, the new cathedral was open to visitors. A little over a year later it was complete with the exception of the spires, which had to await additional funds and were not finished until 1888. The construction of the cathedral thus anticipated and then paralleled the dramatic development of its Fifth Avenue neighborhood.

From the very first New York was amazed and enthralled by the project. While the church was still in construction, a reporter for the *Real Estate Record and Builders' Guide*, possibly Montgomery Schuyler, praised it as "perhaps the most gorgeous ecclesiastical edifice on this continent," although he felt the composition was marred by the "unusual and altogether unnecessary projection" of the unrelieved side buttresses on the north and south, which he contended completely blocked out the view of the side elevations, especially when viewed diagonally from Fifth Avenue. "There is consequently no point of view," the reporter argued, "from which a spectator can take in at a glance the detached beauties of any two fronts together."[93] In an article in the *New York World*, a writer, again probably Schuyler, stated that St. Patrick's "will unquestionably when completed be not only the grandest

building on this continent, but one of the leading ecclesiastical structures of the world."[94]

To prepare for his work, Renwick, who hitherto had specialized in central-steepled churches typical of American Protestant practice, traveled in Europe for more than three years, from 1853 to 1857, finding in the incomplete Cologne Cathedral, begun in 1248, the inspiration he sought. Ultimately Renwick's twin-towered design synthesized aspects of German, French, and English Gothic work. His heavily buttressed design, intended to be built entirely of stone, with some iron reinforcing, had to be revised for financial reasons; the cost of masonry made it necessary to substitute plaster vaulting. As a result, the buttresses, which would have created unresisted thrust against the superstructure, were eliminated, resulting in a sleeker but arguably duller design. The interior was English in character and illuminated in part by a large stained-glass rose window, designed by Charles Connick, that punctuated the cathedral's principal facade.

The challenge St. Patrick's posed to New York's Protestant establishment was loud and clear. When the all-but-spired cathedral was opened for public view during a fair held in 1878, many observers saw the Catholic community's achievement through the narrow lens of reli-

St. Patrick's Cathedral, Madison to Fifth Avenue, East Fiftieth to East Fifty-first Street. James Renwick Jr., 1850–79, 1888. View to the southwest, c. 1875, showing the cathedral under construction. NYHS.

St. Patrick's Cathedral, Madison to Fifth Avenue, East Fiftieth to East Fifty-first Street. James Renwick Jr., 1850–79, 1888. View to the northeast, 1876, showing the cathedral under construction. NYSB. CU.

gious prejudice. The journalist Clarence Cook was moved to write a near-libelous attack on Renwick as part of a virulently negative assessment of the design which was underpinned with religious and ethnic bigotry. St. Patrick's was partially paid for by wealthy parishioners, but mostly it was the nickels and dimes of Irish immigrants, the majority of whom worked as domestics in the homes of the Protestant rich, that made the new cathedral's construction possible. An editorial that appeared in the *New York World* in 1873 had characterized the situation succinctly: "Certainly as matters stand the Roman cathedral is a reproach to Protestant bodies. For the Roman cathedral will be built not of the superfluity of wealth, but for the most part out of the offerings of poverty."[95] This situation created no end of feelings of bias and snobbery that were only mildly hidden in much of the discussion in the public press. It also in part motivated Henry C. Potter to initiate a movement that would lead to the construction of the Protestant Cathedral of St. John the Divine (see below).

Writing in 1878, the editors of the *New York Daily Tribune* were quite harsh in their assessment of Renwick's design:

> In the interior proportions of the building the architect has been happiest, for the effect is light and elegant, but the exterior is unfortunately heavy, ill-digested, and made ineffective by the multiplication of petty parts. . . . We hesitate as to whether to speak of the principal doorway as it deserves, or to pass it by in silence, but let those who wish to judge it compare it with the door, we will not say of any one of the great cathedrals for that would be superfluous malice but with the door of almost any parish church in England. . . . We do not mean that it is not large enough . . . but what could be more trivial than the sculpture about it, what more unfortunate than the distribution of the mouldings of the splay, while all depth and suggestion of thickness in the wall is recklessly thrown away. . . . The material of which the Cathedral is built is a very mistaken one to have employed for a style that depends so much as this on sculpture, and tracery, and delicate mouldings. This so-called marble is really not a marble at all, but only a very coarse limestone, and it utterly refuses to be carved or moulded with delicacy or take kindly to shadow. . . . It seems to us a pity to use any material that is very pronounced in color for use in so large a building. If a neutral-tinted stone cannot be found, then the material should be varied in tone, in order that the eye may not take up all at once, as it most certainly does in the present building. . . . But, it is urged, there was a want of money to do more. Very well, then those in authority should have waited until there was money enough. As a very good Catholic, second to none in his desire to see his church take her position at the head of the arts and culture of our time, has said: "Why build the Cathedral before we were ready? There was no necessity for being in such a hurry!"[96]

In 1866, as the congregation was indeed hurrying to build its monument, its former church, completed in 1815, was

St. Patrick's Cathedral, Madison to Fifth Avenue, East Fiftieth to East Fifty-first Street. James Renwick Jr., 1850–79, 1888. View to the southeast. AABN. CU.

St. Patrick's Cathedral, Madison to Fifth Avenue, East Fiftieth to East Fifty-first Street. James Renwick Jr., 1850–79, 1888.
Nave. NYHS.

St. Patrick's Cathedral, Madison to Fifth Avenue, East Fiftieth to East Fifty-first Street. James Renwick Jr., 1850–79, 1888. View to the southwest showing the vicar's residence (James Renwick Jr., 1882) on the left. NYHS.

heavily damaged by fire.[97] In 1868 the old church was restored by Henry Engelbert.

In 1880 plans were announced for a vicar's residence, completed according to Renwick's designs two years later on the southwest corner of Madison Avenue and Fifty-first Street.[98] The *Real Estate Record and Builders' Guide* more or less approved, stating that "the architecture conforms to that of the Cathedral, and would not be noticeable except for the absurd way in which all grace of outline is destroyed by clapping on over the gables of the building a great black pan of a mansard roof."[99] At last, in 1888, the cathedral was finished, complete with its two spires articulated with foliated tracery, and critical assessment, though not unqualified, was positive. The *Record and Guide* asserted: "The Cathedral . . . might doubtless be a good deal better, but it is respectable in design, and highly impressive by dint of magnitude, detachment and materials, when its dependencies group with it picturesquely, and it is evident that the spires, now nearing completion, will add greatly to its effect."[100]

The completion of St. Patrick's was merely the most dramatic architectural reflection of the expanding role of Roman Catholics in New York; throughout the city the construction of parish churches as well as schools, hospitals, and other institutions met the Catholic community's needs and showed its strength. A few architects dominated the design of Catholic parish churches: Patrick C. Keely, whose practice was national but who built more in Brooklyn than in New York (see chapter 7), Henry Engelbert, Laurence I. O'Connor, Arthur Crooks, and Napoleon Le Brun & Sons. An early Roman Catholic church on the East Side, Keely's Gothic St. Vincent Ferrer (1869), at 869 Lexington Avenue, on the southeast corner of Sixty-fifth Street, occupied a site purchased two years earlier by the order of Dominican fathers.[101] In 1881 a five-story priory joined the church on the south half of the block.[102] Designed by William Schickel, the priory exhibited a Gothic style that integrated Neo-Grec detailing, a synthesis pioneered by Richard Morris Hunt two decades earlier. Keely's Church of the Holy Innocents (1870), at 128 West Thirty-seventh Street, between Broadway and Seventh Avenue, built to serve a lower-middle-class neighborhood, was a typical Gothic-inspired brownstone design.[103] In 1875 Keely completed the Church of St. Bernard, at 330 West Fourteenth Street, between Eighth and Ninth Avenues, a skillful essay in Ruskinian Gothic, incorporating two tones of brownstone and a dominant rondel.[104]

Henry Engelbert designed the Holy Cross Church (1870), at 333 West Forty-second Street, between Eighth and Ninth Avenues.[105] Built on an 80-by-100-foot midblock site, the church confronted the street with a comparatively modest red brick and Belleville brownstone facade which gave no hint that inside was to be found a richly orchestrated composition including barrel-vaulted transepts, a 35-foot-diameter dome lifted 130 feet above the nave's floor, and a 100-foot-high belfry. Laurence I. O'Connor's 1,530-seat Church of St. Agnes (1873–77), on the north side of Forty-

Holy Cross Church, 333 West Forty-second Street. Henry Engelbert, 1870. View to the northwest. King, 1893. CU.

Church of St. Anthony of Padua, Sullivan to Thompson Street, between Prince and West Houston Streets. Arthur Crooks, 1886. Rendering of view to the northeast. BLDG. CU.

third Street between Lexington and Third Avenues, was built on a 105-by-100-foot site between high brick buildings that blocked out all side light.[106] Using what was becoming a common strategy, O'Connor designed twin towers to flank the entrance to the sixty-foot-high nave, which grabbed light from clerestory windows.

Arthur Crooks brought to the problem of Catholic church design the more scholarly approach that was to be characteristic of design after 1890. His Church of St. John the Evangelist (1887), on the northwest corner of Fifty-fifth Street and First Avenue, adopted the Perpendicular Gothic vocabulary of fourteenth-century England. The church was, as the *New York Times* put it, a "gem" that was "architecturally, an important accession to the Roman Catholic churches of New York, most of which are old-fashioned in style."[107] Crooks's building complex for the Church of St. Anthony of Padua (1886), on the east side of Sullivan Street between Houston and Prince Streets, running through to Thompson Street, was a grandly conceived essay in Lombardic Gothic, with a 1,500-seat, 75-foot-wide church rising to 100 feet at the peak of its gable, as well as a four-story monastery facing Thompson Street.[108] At the sanctuary end of the church, a 220-foot-high granite campanile celebrated the design, the style of which was appropriate, if not necessarily familiar, to the congregation's Italian-born parishioners, most of whom came from Sicily and the south.

In addition to dominating the New York City Fire Department's building program during the Gilded Age (see above), Napoleon Le Brun also excelled in the design of Roman Catholic churches. In 1868, the Philadelphia-based Le Brun, fresh from the success of designing that city's Academy of Music and completing its Cathedral of St. Peter and Paul, moved his twenty-year-old practice to New York. Not surprisingly given his experience, one of his earliest commissions in his new home city was for a Catholic church, the Italian Romanesque Church of the Epiphany (1870), which occupied a midblock site on the west side of Second Avenue between Twenty-first and Twenty-second Streets.[109] Le Brun took as his main motive a Ruskin favorite, the facade of the twelfth-century Church of San Zeno, in Verona. Le Brun followed with the beautifully crafted brownstone Gothic Church of St. John the Baptist (1872), at 211 West Thirtieth Street, between Seventh and Eighth Avenues; this building rose to a central spire with splendid disdain for its midblock site.[110] In 1885, Le Brun realized his design for the French Canadian Catholic Church on the north side of Seventy-sixth Street between Lexington and Third Avenues.[111] Adopting a plain Gothic design, Le Brun placed the parsonage toward the street to serve as an entry to the 1,500-seat church. Le Brun's 81-by-100-foot, 1,600-seat Church of the Sacred Heart of Jesus (1884), at 457 West Fifty-first Street, between Ninth and Tenth Avenues, replaced a Baptist chapel on the site.[112] The new, Romanesque-inspired church was built with deep red brick, matching terra cotta, and contrasting light-colored stone trimmings.

Temple Emanu-El, northeast corner of Fifth Avenue and East Forty-third Street. Leopold Eidlitz and Henry Fernbach, 1868. View to the northeast. NYHS.

Synagogues

The massive influx of Jewish immigrants that would become a defining phenomenon of fin de siècle New York, with 1,100,000 Jews forming nearly a quarter of the city's population by 1910, did not commence until the latter half of the Gilded Age.[113] The post–Civil War era nonetheless saw the city's Jewish population grow in both size and importance, and by the late 1860s architecturally signifi-cant synagogues were taking their place among the city's ecclesiastical buildings. During this time, synagogue architecture began to take on a unique identity. Before the Civil War, New York's Jewish congregations had tended to occupy churches, but after the war many began to build for themselves, adopting an architectural exoticism based on the forms of Byzantine and Moorish Spain. These trends reflected a greater sense of self-confidence and pride as well as increased societal acceptance. Like their Christian counterparts, many Jewish congregations followed fashion

north, leaving buildings in lower Manhattan. Leopold Eidlitz and Henry Fernbach's Saracenic-Moorish–inspired Temple Emanu-El, on the northeast corner of Fifth Avenue and Forty-third Street, dedicated on Sep-tember 11, 1868, was America's largest and most promi-nently located Jewish house of worship.[114] It was also, as Montgomery Schuyler put it in his first signed work of architectural criticism, published on the day after the building's dedication, "the new church of a faithful but advanced people: no longer refugees, no longer shut in by a form and fashion from the outer world, but equal with it—part of it."[115] The German-speaking congregation was founded in 1845 by thirty-three immigrants as an out-growth of a *Cultus Verein* (culture society) that met in a rented parlor on the Lower East Side at Grand and Clin-ton Streets, and was the city's first to espouse the new, sec-ularizing principles of Reform Judaism. These had initially been articulated in Germany, most significantly by Rabbi Abraham Geiger.[116] The congregation was first housed in

Temple Emanu-El, northeast corner of Fifth Avenue and East Forty-third Street. Leopold Eidlitz and Henry Fernbach, 1868. View to the northeast. NYHS.

View to the north along Fifth Avenue showing, from left to right, the steeple of the Church of the Divine Paternity
(John Correja, 1865–66), the steeple of the Collegiate Dutch Reformed Church (W. Wheeler Smith, 1872), and Temple Emanu-El
(Leopold Eidlitz and Henry Fernbach, 1868). NYHS.

a former Methodist church at 56 Chrystie Street, which Leopold Eidlitz helped to renovate and furnish in 1848. The congregation subsequently moved to a former Baptist church (c. 1847), at 120 East Twelfth Street, between Third and Fourth Avenues, which quickly became overcrowded, leading it to purchase a site at Fifth Avenue and Forty-third Street in May 1867 and commission the Vienna-trained, forty-four-year-old Eidlitz, together with the Berlin-trained Henry Fernbach, six years younger, to design a house of worship large enough to last for generations and important enough to take its place on the city's most fashionable street, where many churches were locating and where, seven blocks farther uptown, a vast Roman Catholic cathedral was under construction.

When Montgomery Schuyler reviewed the building in 1908 as part of his memorial tribute to Eidlitz, who over the years had become a close friend, he neglected to credit Fernbach, who died in 1883, as co-designer. This was somewhat understandable given that virtually all publications in the intervening years only named Eidlitz. Yet Fernbach retained a close association with the congregation, preparing designs in 1877 for a pastoral residence intended to be built next door to the temple on Forty-third Street, an ultimately unrealized work as notable for its sympa-

Proposed Temple Emanu-El pastoral residence, north side of East Forty-third Street between Madison and Fifth Avenues. Henry Fernbach, 1877. Rendering of view to the northwest. AABN. CU.

thetic contextualism as for its artistic inventiveness.[117]

The decision to use Saracenic and Moorish motifs for the synagogue had precedent. In 1865, after six years of design and construction, the synagogue on Oranienburgerstrasse in Berlin, designed by Eduard Knoblauch but finished after his mental incapacitation in 1862 by August Stüler and Gustav Knoblauch, opened to wide acclaim not only among Reform Jewry but also among Berlin's intelligentsia, who regarded it as Eduard Knoblauch's best building.[118] The Berlin Synagogue, as it was known, was imitated in a number of Central European cities as well as in San Francisco and in Cincinnati, where James Keys Wilson's Plum Street Temple for Congregation B'nai Jeshurun, one of America's leading Reform congregations, was completed in 1866.[119] The Berlin Synagogue's design was arguably well suited to the belief widely held among both Christians and Jews that Jews were exotic, Oriental, and other. The preference for Moorish exoticism was, however, at its core odd, particularly due to the assimilationist goals of the Reform movement, and because, as the architect Arnold Brunner, an American-born Jew who himself designed a number of synagogues, including the exotic Temple Beth-El (see below), pointed out in 1908, "it strengthened the impression that the Jew was necessarily an alien, and did not wish to be regarded as an American."[120]

There was another oddity about Temple Emanu-El's Moorish design: it may have been instigated by Fernbach rather than by Eidlitz. Eidlitz's previous synagogue, designed in 1847 with his Bavarian-born partner, Charles Blesch, for Congregation Shaaray Tefila on Wooster Street, was in the round-arched Romanesque style, as were many buildings from the 1850s to the 1870s designed by Eidlitz, whose religious origins remain unknown. As a Jew and a former student at the Berlin Building Academy, Fernbach was probably more familiar with current trends in synagogue design, and he may have suggested the Moorish approach. If that is the case, Eidlitz—who, as Schuyler stressed, had never designed anything like Emanu-El—was somewhat unjustly castigated for the design by his young critic friend and may have been too much the gentleman to implicate Fernbach.

The 2,300-seat Emanu-El was built in less than two years, although it was not quite finished at its dedication, lacking the Shields of David that topped the two open minaret-like towers flanking the main entrance. The synagogue's profusely decorated facade enclosed a 130-foot-long, 78-foot-wide, 68-foot-tall interior resembling in plan and section that of a Christian church. Schuyler, who attended the opening, professed dismay at this arrangement, although it in fact worked well for Reform Jewish worship, which, unlike more traditional services, incorporated sermons and organ as well as choral music, and substituted forward-facing fixed seating for the older arrangement of grouping chairs around a central bimah. Schuyler's objections were based on symbolic rather than practical considerations. He asked why "of all forms in the world" did the architect select "the cruciform for the temple of the

Temple Emanu-El, northeast corner of Fifth Avenue and East Forty-third Street. Leopold Eidlitz and Henry Fernbach, 1868. View to the northeast showing the steeple of the Church of the Divine Paternity (John Correja, 1865–66) on the left. NYHS.

Jews . . . a form hallowed by associations, intrinsic and derived to all Christendom, but by the self-same associations hateful to all Judaism." Ignorant of the Reform movement's efforts to break with traditional Jewish practice, Schuyler blamed the use of the cruciform plan on Eidlitz's lack of direct understanding of Judaism: "We do not know, indeed, but that the present architect is one of the ancient race and religion; but if he be, he certainly builds synagogues in a most heterodox and scandalously Christian manner."[121] In 1908, looking back on his review of forty years earlier, the mature critic wryly observed: "My obvious point of attack was the solecism of the cruciform plan for a synagogue, and I worked that for much more than it was worth. But I am glad to observe that the 'effort' attested the hearty admiration for other and earlier works by the same author which the jaunty young critic felt."[122]

Notwithstanding his reservations about issues of symbolic propriety, on the whole Schuyler assessed the synagogue's architecture on its own terms. The main sanctuary, which seated 1,800 worshipers on the ground floor and 500 in the balconies, was, he observed, "almost all Saracenic in detail, and almost all Gothic in arrangement. The nave, the

choir, the aisles, the triforium, are all here, but they have all suffered a sea-change into something rich and strange," creating an impressive effect but not quite "a harmonious whole." Schuyler concluded his rather harsh assessment by noting an irony. He regretted the building's construction

on the artist's account and on the public's, because we foresee that it will be applauded and admired, and we fear that it may seduce a builder, who has done much better work many times before, from doing that better work again. The synagogue is most honestly and faithfully built, as far as building goes, from top to bottom, and that is a great comfort at any rate. But it is not in Mr. Eidlitz's style; and when that is said, all is said. . . . If we ever get an American architecture, [we shall not get it by] procreating hybrids of Saracen or Goth. As a commodious place of worship the new temple is a success; as an honest building it is a success; but as a religious monument it is a failure, and as a work of art commensurate with the ability of its designer, or of good augury for American architecture, it is *nicht*.[123]

Three years later, reviewing the city's new ecclesiastical buildings and finding himself appalled by such "monsters

Temple Emanu-El, northeast corner of Fifth Avenue and East Forty-third Street. Leopold Eidlitz and Henry Fernbach, 1868. View of the sanctuary toward the bimah. AR. CU.

Shaaray Tefila, 127 West Forty-fourth Street. Henry Fernbach, 1868–69. Rendering of view to the northeast. ST. CU.

of art" as W. Wheeler Smith's Collegiate Dutch Reformed Church (see above) and Edward T. Potter's Church of the Heavenly Rest (see above), both located just blocks from Emanu-El, Schuyler began to see Eidlitz and Fernbach's design in a different light:

> Without any excepting, this is the finest ecclesiastical building which has ever been erected in New York. Built in a style with which our people are but little acquainted . . . it pleases at once by its great novelty and by the exceeding beauty of its treatment. . . . The variety of design, richness of ornamentation, and beautiful treatment of material in this building are surprising, and both externally and internally—the interior being frescoed in the most gorgeous manner—the lover of art can find hours of pleasing entertainment. If such artistic elements as are embodied in this building could only be a little more diffused, there would be little to fear for the future of ecclesiastical architecture in our city.[124]

The construction of a new kind of synagogue designed by a top architect was a major event in a city that took its religion seriously, if not necessarily deeply, and it attracted curiosity-seekers from outside the faith, including the prominent lawyer and prolific diarist George Templeton Strong, who, accompanied by his wife and some friends,

Central Synagogue, southwest corner of Lexington Avenue and East Fifty-fifth Street.
Henry Fernbach, 1872. View to the southwest. CS.

attended a "Sunset Service" on Friday, November 3, 1869, in the building, which he referred to as "the grand new Synagogue of the Reformed—Porkophagous, or porcivorous—Jews, on Fifth Avenue." Strong reported an interior "glowing and gorgeous with gold and color, arabesque wood carvings, and columns of polished syenite."[125]

Henry Fernbach designed two other architecturally significant synagogues in New York during the post–Civil War period. His exotic Shaaray Tefila (1868–69), built for an Orthodox congregation on a midblock site at 127 West Forty-fourth Street, between Sixth and Seventh Avenues, incorporated a gilded dome, perhaps reflecting the influence of Knoblauch's Oranienburgerstrasse synagogue, above a central entrance pavilion.[126] Fernbach received the commission despite the fact that Blesch & Eidlitz had designed the congregation's previous home (1847), on Wooster Street; the change of architect may be attributable to the modest size of the project, which included only 400 seats, and the low construction budget, $150,000, but it may also have reflected the congregation's greater comfort with a Jewish architect. Fernbach's design mixed a variety of themes, leading *Occident* magazine to label it "Byzantine Moresque."[127] The sanctuary, described by Moses King as "richly decorated" and "costly," was illumi-

Central Synagogue, southwest corner of Lexington Avenue
and East Fifty-fifth Street. Henry Fernbach, 1872.
View of the sanctuary toward the main entrance. CS.

nated by a large rose window over the ark, which, following tradition, was located on the east wall, oriented toward Jerusalem, despite the fact that this placement was awkward in a south-facing building.[128] The open space of the sanctuary was interrupted by four slender iron columns supporting the roof and a separate gallery for women, in keeping with Orthodox tradition.

Central Synagogue (1872), on the southwest corner of Lexington Avenue and Fifty-fifth Street, was home to Congregation Ahawath Chesed, which had been formed in 1846 by immigrants from Bohemia.[129] In 1864 the Reform congregation took over a church at Avenue C and Fourth Street, but in 1869, perhaps inspired by the construction of Temple Emanu-El, it decided to move uptown, choosing a location that was becoming a popular residential area for upper-middle-class Jews. As designed by Fernbach, Central Synagogue was Moorish in theme, but it owed less to his Shaaray Tefila than to Temple Emanu-El. According to Fernbach, the 140-by-93-foot Central Synagogue, with an extreme interior height of 62 feet, was "divided by pillars into bays, of which one is the organ loft, another the choir, and the others the naves. The windows are filled with rich glass, and the east end is ornamented with a beautiful rose window. The interiors are profusely decorated in polychrome, applied in geometric patterns. The style is mainly Moorish, although the arrangement is Gothic."[130] Smaller than Emanu-El, the interior sat 1,500 people and the building was constructed for $300,000, half the cost of the Fifth Avenue temple. Some members of the

Anshe Chesed, southeast corner of Lexington Avenue and East Sixty-third Street. D. & J. Jardine, 1872–73. View to the southeast. King, 1893. CU.

congregation's board were nervous about making a splash, arguing: "Excess promotes envy, grudges and hate on the part of our enemies. . . . We need neither towers nor architectural scrolls on the outside, nor interior ornaments that are overloaded with gold and multi-colored splendor."[131]

Nonetheless, in many respects Central Synagogue resembled Emanu-El, though it lacked a transept. It had turrets and domes, but their design seemed to be based on features of Ludwig von Forster's Dohany Street Synagogue (1854–59), in Budapest.[132] The composition of the New Jersey brownstone and Ohio stone mass was skillfully handled, with wings extending the full width of the Lexington Avenue frontage to house the balcony stairs and visually support the precisely modeled minarets with their onion-shaped domes. To create a distinct setting, the congregation installed specially designed street lamps. Because the site faced east, Fernbach chose to place the ark on the west end of the sanctuary, a logical if not traditional arrangement. The rich interior stencilwork, in coral, brown, and two shades of blue on deep tan walls, combined with the extensive use of gilding, which caught the light from the clerestory windows, counterbalanced the black walnut woodwork that was trimmed with white oak, creating at considerably less cost an interior that was as vivid if not as lavish as Emanu-El's.

D. & J. Jardine's Anshe Chesed (1872–73), also known as Ahavath Chesed, on the southeast corner of Lexington Avenue and Sixty-third Street, was another Moorish-influenced synagogue.[133] A year after the building's completion, the congregation, possessing a fine home but in need of a rabbi, merged with Adas Jeshurun, whose rabbi, Aaron Wise, was a renowned Talmudic scholar but whose building on West Thirty-ninth Street was overcrowded. The merged congregations changed the name of the new building to Temple Beth-El, which Moses King described as "a lofty stone building in Spanish-Moresque style" with an interior "elaborately decorated in the Oriental manner."[134] The Jardines' design was distinguished by twin 122-foot-high towers that were transformed, bottom to top, from square to octagon, terminating in gilded cupolas. Inside, a 70-foot-high, domed and vaulted, 1,400-seat sanctuary incorporated side balconies carried on slender columns.

In 1885, B'nai Jeshurun, the city's second oldest congregation, completed a new synagogue, on the southwest corner of Madison Avenue and Sixty-fifth Street, designed by Rafael Guastavino working with Schwarzmann & Buchman.[135] The congregation had previously occupied a Gothic-style synagogue, on Greene Street, designed by Field & Correja in 1851, and in 1864 a 650-seat, vaguely Romanesque-style, 75-by-98-foot building on Thirty-fourth Street between Broadway and Seventh Avenue. Field & Correja's rather crude Spanish-Moorish design featured pilaster-like buttresses with superimposed globes each surmounted by a Shield of David. A rose window brought south light inside. A triple-arched porch enclosed the principal entrance, while a minaret-like cupola crowned the composition. The stone and brick of the

B'nai Jeshurun, southwest corner of Madison Avenue and East Sixty-fifth Street. Rafael Guastavino and Schwarzmann & Buchman, 1885. View to the northwest. NYHS.

*Zichron Ephraim, 163 East Sixty-seventh Street. Schneider &
Herter, 1889–90. View to the northwest. PES.*

Thirty-fourth Street synagogue were used in the construction of the building on Madison Avenue. The 1,100-seat,
white and gold interior of the new building was modeled
after a synagogue in Toledo, Spain.

Zichron Ephraim was a new Orthodox congregation
founded by Bavarian Jews in 1888. Moses King described
its one-thousand-seat building (1889–90), at 163 East
Sixty-seventh Street, between Lexington and Third
Avenues, designed by Schneider & Herter, as a "handsome
piece of Saracenic architecture, with a North-African sentiment."[136] Its boldly composed exterior featured two towers of unequal height. An elaborately carved Moorish
arcade was reached by two broad flights of stairs. A rose
window fit into the chamfered gable; atop the window was
a domed, pavilion-like structure. As the synagogue neared
completion, the *Real Estate Record and Builders' Guide*
stated: "While the exterior to a large extent displays uni-

formity of design, the architecture is not entirely what one
might expect a place of worship to be, the religion of
whose devotees had its origin in the Orient."[137]

The rapid rise of Jewish immigration in the post–Civil
War era meant that the Lower East Side synagogues abandoned by the established Jewish congregations that moved
to fashionable uptown locations did not stand empty, but
were reused by newly arrived Jews, who were mostly from
Eastern Europe. Yet the new arrivals far outnumbered
those migrating uptown and, despite the poverty of the
newcomers, additional synagogues were soon built. Congregation Kahal Adath Jeshurun was the first congregation
of Eastern European Jews to erect its own building in the
United States, the so-called Eldridge Street Synagogue
(Herter Brothers, 1886–87), at 12–16 Eldridge Street,
between Forsyth and Canal Streets.[138] The congregation
was founded in 1856 by a group of Polish Jews and grew
to such a size that in 1872 it could hire its own full-time
rabbi, Isaac Gellis, perhaps better remembered for his deli-
catessen on Essex Street than for his religious work. The
synagogue constituted a late example of the eclectic blend
of Romanesque, Gothic, and Moorish elements that
Eidlitz and Fernbach had introduced twenty years earlier.
Inside what was the largest synagogue on the Lower East
Side, the main sanctuary was lit by an elaborate glass-
shaded brass chandelier that, complementing the rose window which was the principal feature of the brick and terra
cotta facade, cast a glow over the barrel-vaulted room.

At the close of the Gilded Age, in 1891, Temple Beth-
El sold its Lexington Avenue synagogue (see above) to
Rodelph Sholem, moving into what was, with the excep-
tion of Emanu-El, the city's grandest synagogue and surely
its most splendidly situated.[139] Its new location, on the
southeast corner of Fifth Avenue and Seventy-sixth Street,
made it the only house of worship to face Central Park.
Constituting one of the first important works of the firm
Brunner & Tryon, which was to become a leader in the
Classical revival of the 1890s and early 1900s, the design
seemed to get to the Moorish world of Spain by way of
H. H. Richardson's work. Also echoing Henry Fernbach's
Shaaray Tefila and Eduard Knoblauch's Berlin synagogue,
Arnold Brunner called for a prominent central dome as
well as for curving auditorium-type seating within, features
that did almost as much to define contemporary synagogue
architecture as Eidlitz and Fernbach's marriage of exotic
form and Christian plan had in the 1870s and 1880s.
Above a rock-faced Indiana limestone superstructure that
virtually filled the 102-by-150-foot site sat an overscaled
hipped dome, ribbed in a traditional Moorish pattern blown
up to enormous size. Entered through a low-springing
Saracenic arch, the sanctuary revealed itself as an almost
square room, with galleries on three sides and a second
gallery above the entrance, seating 2,900 people in all. The
arched ceiling was decorated in gold tracery using a mixture
of Byzantine, Romanesque, and Gothic motifs beneath a
skylight. The synagogue was also illuminated by light blazing from one thousand incandescent bulbs.

Zichron Ephraim, 163 East Sixty-seventh Street. Schneider & Herter, 1889–90. View of the sanctuary toward the bimah. PES.

Kahal Adath Jeshurun, 12–16 Eldridge Street. Herter Brothers, 1886–87. Rendering of view to the east. MCNY.

Temple Beth-El, southeast corner of Fifth Avenue and East Seventy-sixth Street. Brunner & Tryon, 1891. View to the northeast. NYHS.

St. John the Divine

On June 1, 1887, Henry C. Potter, Episcopal Bishop of New York, released a letter "to the Citizens of New York" in which he called for the construction of the largest religious building in the country. To be called the Cathedral of St. John the Divine, Potter envisioned the church as a tangible symbol of the city's cosmopolitanism. He wrote in his letter, which was widely published in the daily press, "More and more are the faces of men and women all over this and other lands turned to it [New York] as a city of pre-eminent interest and influence, the dwelling place of culture, wealth, and of a nation's best thought. Never before in its history was there so cordial an interest in its prosperity and greatness, and recent benefactions to literature and art have shown, what earlier and scarcely less princely benefactions to science and humanity have proclaimed, that its citizens are determined to make it more and more worthy of that foremost place and that large influence which it is destined to hold and exert."[140]

Potter's call was much more than an attempt to celebrate New York's prominence. He believed that only the construction of a massive monument could effectively raise and promote the issue of human spirituality in the commercial capital: "Great moral and spiritual ideas need to find expression and embodiment in visible institutions and structures, and it is these which have been in all ages the nurseries of faith and of reverence for the unseen." In contrast to the large Roman Catholic cathedral, St. Patrick's, then nearing completion after close to three decades of construction, Potter promised a "people's church" serving the entire city and appealed especially to the ideal of unifying a population made remarkably diverse through years of immigration.[141]

Although the construction of the new cathedral was not begun until 1893—and has not yet been completed—the two-and-a-half-year competition to select a design serves as a brilliant mirror of dramatically shifting tastes in architecture in the late 1880s. And the selection of Heins & La Farge's eclectic design, given the fact that it was so radically altered during the building process, serves as an appropriate cap to an era of exemplary individualism.[142]

The idea for an Episcopal cathedral in New York dated back to 1828, when Bishop John Henry Hobart broached the subject with Mayor Philip Hone, a practicing Episcopalian. Hone convinced Hobart that the time was not quite right and that the Revolutionary War and the War of 1812 were still too deep in the American psyche to attempt what might be perceived as creating a link to the Anglican Church in England. The issue lay dormant until 1872, when it was raised by Bishop Horatio Potter, who, within a year's time, convinced the state legislature to incorporate the "Cathedral Church of St. John the Divine."[143] Three pledges of $100,000 each were quickly secured and a group of trustees was selected. But before any meetings could be held, the Panic of 1873 forced the withdrawal of two of the three pledges and the project was again abandoned. The

return of prosperity at the end of the decade failed to revive the project, although in 1882 Joshua Jones, a developer, offered a parcel on Eighth Avenue between Seventy-fourth and Seventy-fifth Streets for the undertaking.[144] But Jones's price proved too high, especially after Horatio Potter failed in his attempt to persuade St. Luke's Hospital and the General Theological Seminary to share the site. The basic problem in reviving the project was Bishop Potter's health, which so deteriorated in 1883 that his nephew, Henry C. Potter, the assistant bishop, took over effective control of the New York Episcopal Church. The forty-eight-year-old Henry C. Potter had already established his reputation as both a liberal thinker and a dynamic, active clergyman with stints as an assistant minister in Boston's Trinity Church and rector of Grace Church in New York.[145] Although the younger Potter was anxious to resume the project for a cathedral, he had to wait until his uncle's death, in January 1887, and his appointment as Bishop of New York before he could proceed in earnest.

Within a week of Bishop Henry C. Potter's June 1887 letter proposing the cathedral more than $500,000 had been pledged. The trustees of the church then appointed an architecture committee, which included William Waldorf Astor, the real estate developer and son of John Jacob Astor II; Morgan Dix, the rector of Trinity Church, who served as the group's chairman; the thirty-three-year-old James Alfred Roosevelt, the youngest member of the trustees and a cousin of Astor's after his marriage to Helen Schermerhorn Astor; and Philander Kinney Cady, a rector in Roosevelt's Hyde Park parish who was distantly related to the architect and competitor J. C. Cady. The committee also included Richard T. Auchmuty, the only architect among the trustees, who in the 1850s had been a partner of James Renwick Jr. before retiring from active practice to devote his energies to philanthropic concerns. Other notable trustees who did not serve on the architecture committee included Hamilton Fish, the former governor and senator as well as a descendant of Peter Stuyvesant, and J. Pierpont Morgan, the financier, who served as treasurer. The trustees were ultimately aided by three professional advisers who were to play active roles in the architect selection process: William R. Ware, a former student of Richard Morris Hunt who in 1865 went on to found America's first architecture school, at the Massachusetts Institute of Technology, and in 1881 started Columbia's architecture school; Charles Babcock, a founding member of the American Institute of Architects who taught at Cornell University and was also an ordained Episcopal priest; and John Bogart, a prominent engineer.

The first order of business for the trustees was the acquisition of a suitable site. In 1828, when the cathedral project had initially been broached, Washington Square was the intended location. In 1873 attention focused on a site below Central Park bounded by Fifty-seventh and Fifty-ninth Streets and Sixth and Seventh Avenues. At the time they were proposed each of these locations was at the northern end of the city's developed area. In keeping

Proposed Cathedral of St. John the Divine, Morningside Drive to Tenth Avenue, West 110th to West 113th Street. J. C. Cady & Co., 1889. Competition-entry perspective showing view to the northwest. Drawings Collection. CU.

with that tradition, which had the advantage of more easily yielding a large site, trustee George MacCulloch Miller, a lawyer, working with the Reverend R. J. Nevin, recommended a thirteen-and-a-half-acre parcel bounded by 110th and 113th Streets and Morningside Drive and Tenth Avenue, owned and occupied by the Leake and Watts Orphan Asylum.[146] In November 1887, after considering and rejecting because of cost the nearby site of the Bloomingdale Insane Asylum, bounded by 117th and 120th Streets and the Boulevard and Tenth Avenue, the trustees of the church purchased the high, prominent ground for a considerable $850,000, enabling Leake and Watts, which had occupied it since 1843, to acquire a new location just north of the city in Yonkers as well as to fund an endowment with the remaining dollars.[147] The *New York Daily Tribune* was pleased with the selection: "No better site could be found in the city, perhaps, than the three city blocks which the Orphan House owns. . . . From the top of the knob, where the Asylum stands, there is a broad view in every direction. All of Harlem is spread below to the north and east. Beyond the house-tops due

east across the thin strip of river the hills of the north shore of Long Island can be seen. . . . The Park and the city lie to the south and on the west are the Hudson and the high bluffs, which stretch from Weehawken up to where the Palisades begin."[148] In 1891, in official recognition of the project's significance, the city would rename 110th Street between Seventh Avenue and Riverside Park Cathedral Parkway.[149]

From the very beginning church officials tried to emphasize that such a mammoth undertaking, if it was to be realized properly, would take time. "Now, of course, it is but natural to the people of our go-ahead country that they should be eager to have the work get underway," an unidentified trustee told the *New York Times*. "But in that matter they will have to exercise a little old-world patience. You know, Rome was not built in a day, and even some of the European cathedrals were several centuries in building, and it is hoped that the American cathedral shall, when completed, be second to no other in the world. But that does not mean that it will be several centuries in building. American patience will not endure that."[150]

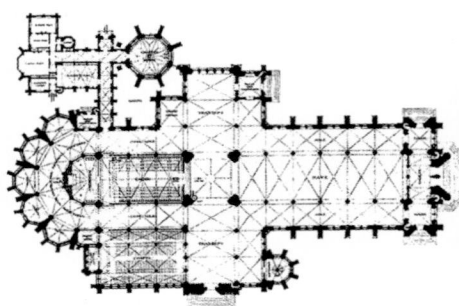

Proposed Cathedral of St. John the Divine, Morningside Drive to Tenth Avenue, West 110th to West 113th Street. Frederick Clarke Withers, 1889. Competition-entry perspective showing view to the northwest, south elevation, and ground-floor plan. CD. CU.

The architectural press was quick to react to the proposed cathedral and called for a design that would express Potter's ideals and anticipate the aesthetics of the twentieth century. The *Real Estate Record and Builders' Guide* editorialized, "Doesn't the age require something different from what has come down to us from the past? The religious conceptions of the nineteenth century require a different expression from what they had in the tenth or twelfth centuries."[151] The idea of an open competition was particularly appealing, especially given the slump in the building industry that left many architects idle.[152] One correspondent to the *Record and Guide* argued:

> Many people doubt the pressing necessity for the Cathedral from a religious point of view, but very few from an architectural point of view, and it was because . . . Potter dwelt so strongly on this dual value of the building that his appeal was so well received by all denominations. . . . In an age of doubt and ceaseless inquiry into the names of things, may we not think that possibly it will be archi-

tecture that will give the building its widest and deepest power for good, if by a wise choice of an architect each stone of the structure is made to hold before the eyes of men something of that spirit-form which we call Beauty, and under whose power the hearts of all generations, Pagan or Christian, has been softened and ennobled.[153]

Speculation on the cathedral project continued well into 1888. In an editorial the *New York Times* touched on many aspects, not the least of which was the "staggering" cost of the site and the public's misguided expectation that the building could be realized with the "swiftness of Eiffel's tower on the Champs de Mars. The Parisian tower waxes so fast because the workmen are ordered to send back to the shops of the contractors any piece of iron which does not fit accurately in its place. A building of stone and brick cannot be treated in such a dogmatic mood. The size and complexity of a great cathedral are such that haste makes waste. It will not do to expect of the best architects, supplied unstintingly with funds, that dispatch which we observe in the erection of our great apartment and ware

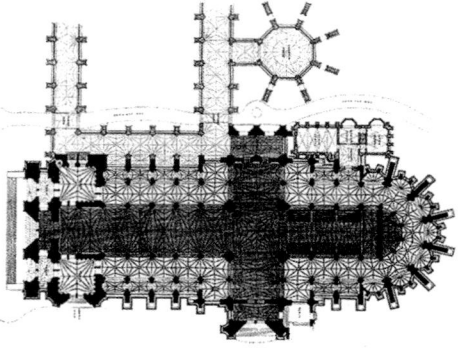

Proposed Cathedral of St. John the Divine, Morningside Drive to Tenth Avenue, West 110th to West 113th Street. Robert W. Gibson, 1889. Competition-entry perspective showing view to the northwest, longitudinal section showing view to the west, and ground-floor plan. CD. CU.

houses." It may not have been possible for architects to realize, the *Times* continued, what

> for convenience we . . . call the laymen's view . . . [that] the architect should evolve on new soil a new kind of cathedral. Much sarcasm is expended on this view by many worthy and worshipful critics. But in truth what more honorable, what more natural, than this very desire? Americans would not be worth much if they did not aspire to a national expression in the fine arts, of which architecture is a good branch. Possibly a good imitation like St. Patrick's is better than a wild, crude piece of originality. Yet imitation always produces a thing so smooth, sapless, and weak that perhaps it is no worse to make a big failure, if it be a failure on original lines.[154]

After securing the site, the trustees turned to the issue of selecting an architect, which was to occur through a competition consisting of both invited entries and unsolicited submissions. To foster diversity in keeping with Potter's hope for a unique architectural statement, the terms of the competition were remarkably open-ended. The two pages of instructions included no mention of cost, seating capacity, liturgical requirements, or ancillary buildings to be included. In addition to placing no limits on an entry's style, there was no specific indication that the building would serve only the Episcopal Church; it was, in fact, promoted as the Protestant Cathedral. Competitors were asked to include a general plan, front and side elevations, a longitudinal section, and a pen-and-ink perspective. Furnished with a map of the site, they were required, in a break with medieval tradition, to orient the building on a north-south basis, with the front of the cathedral facing south, toward 110th Street, where it could presumably take better advantage of the prominent site. The anonymously submitted designs were to be fireproof, feature an exterior of granite, marble, or other durable stone, and be no longer than four hundred feet, which still allowed for an enormous building exceeding the size of St. Patrick's. An additional rule, which the trustees would later regret, required the approval of the competitors before their designs could be publicly exhibited.

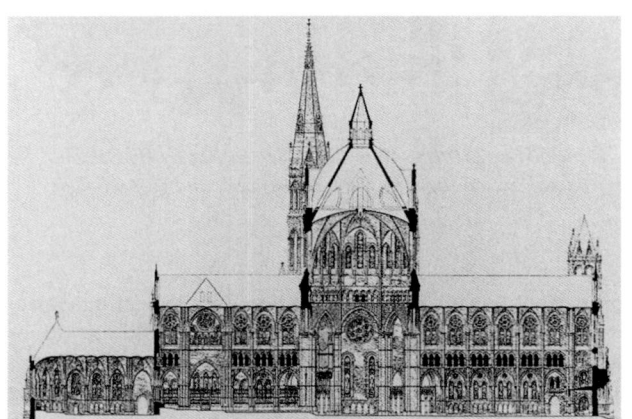
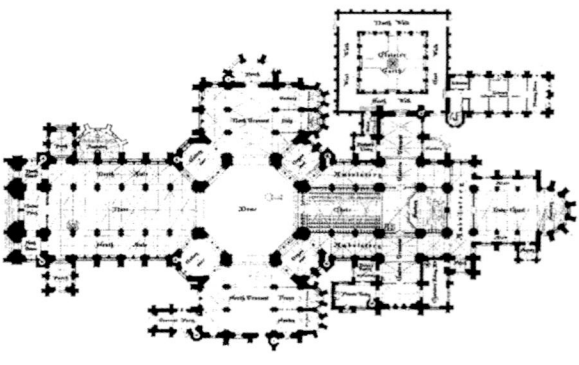

Proposed Cathedral of St. John the Divine, Morningside Drive to Tenth Avenue, West 110th to West 113th Street. Henry M. Congdon, 1889. Competition-entry perspective showing view to the southwest, longitudinal section showing view to the east, and ground-floor plan. CD. CU.

By the spring of 1888 the trustees were ready to mail invitations to fourteen firms, which were each paid a modest honorarium of five hundred dollars. The list of invited architects was mostly drawn from the establishment: J. C. Cady & Co.; C. C. Haight; Frederick Clarke Withers; Robert W. Gibson; Henry M. Congdon; Richard Morris Hunt; Renwick, Aspinwall & Russell; McKim, Mead & White; Potter & Robertson; Henry Vaughan; Van Brunt & Howe; W. Halsey Wood; and Frank Furness.[155] Only the invitation of Carrère & Hastings, a new partnership,

suggested an effort to reach out to the younger generation.[156] In June the trustees opened the competition to the profession at large. Although the competition program created a fair amount of confusion over what the trustees really desired, the response from "volunteers" was large and swift. Over one hundred letters of interest were received by the trustees in July. An initial deadline of December 15, 1888, was extended by a month, and forty-one submissions were received by January 15, 1889. A week later an additional twenty-seven proposals were received, making

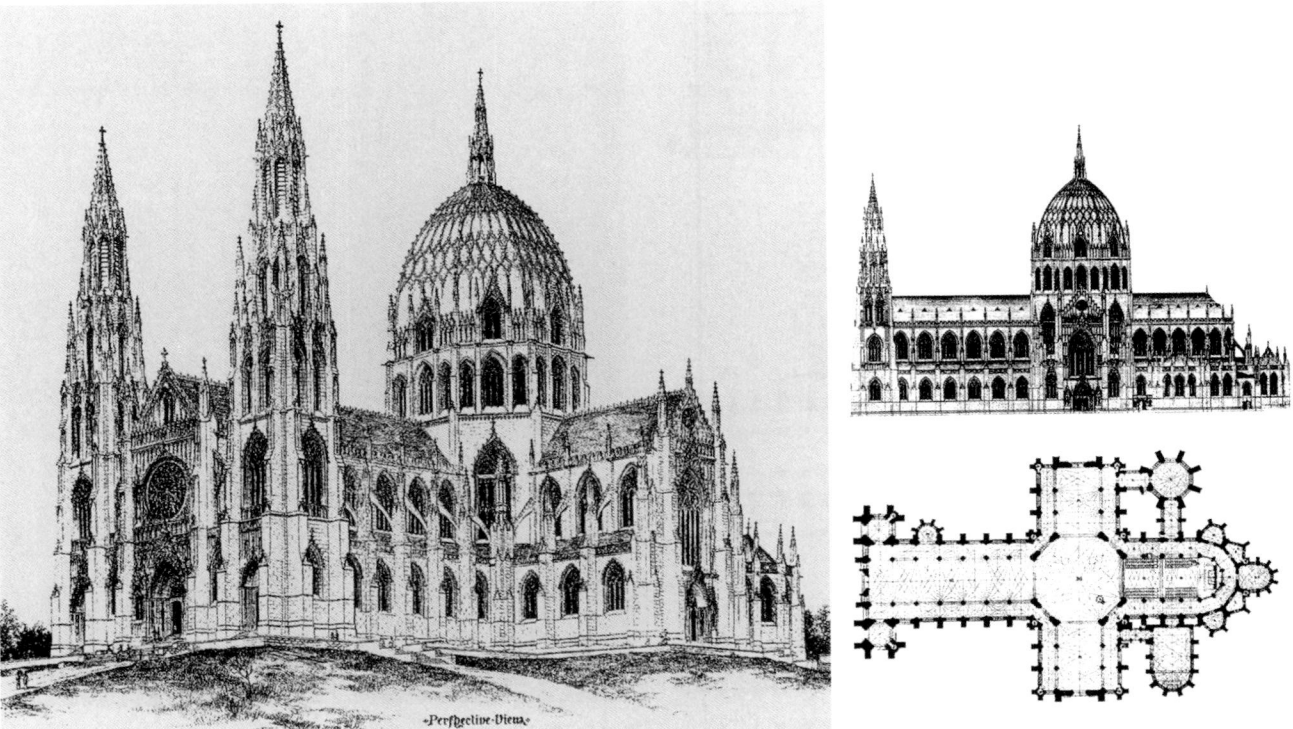

Proposed Cathedral of St. John the Divine, Morningside Drive to Tenth Avenue, West 110th to West 113th Street. Richard Morris Hunt, 1889. Competition-entry perspective showing view to the northwest. The Octagon, AAF.

Proposed Cathedral of St. John the Divine, Morningside Drive to Tenth Avenue, West 110th to West 113th Street. Renwick, Aspinwall & Russell, 1889. Competition-entry perspective showing view to the northwest, east elevation, and ground-floor plan. CD. CU.

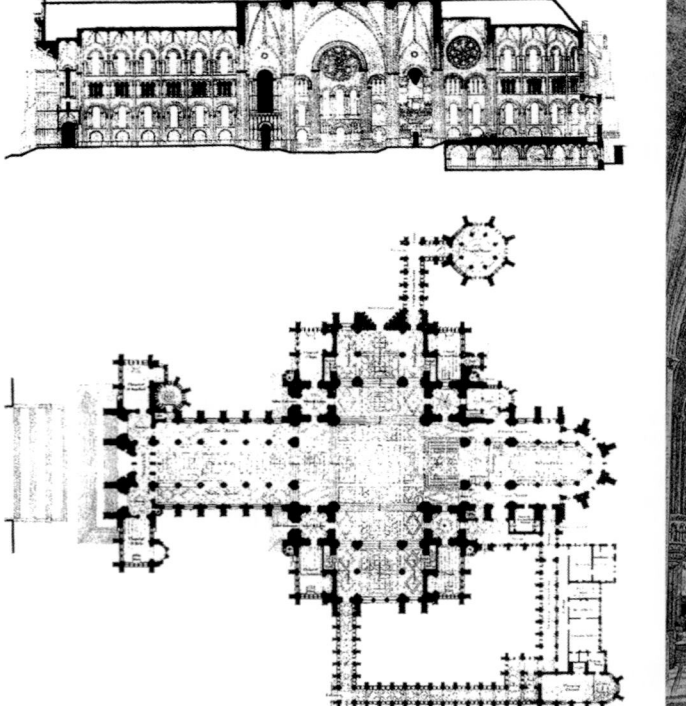

Proposed Cathedral of St. John the Divine, Morningside Drive to Tenth Avenue, West 110th to West 113th Street. Potter & Robertson, 1889. Competition-entry perspective showing view to the southeast, longitudinal section showing view to the west, ground-floor plan, and interior perspective showing pulpit. CD. CU.

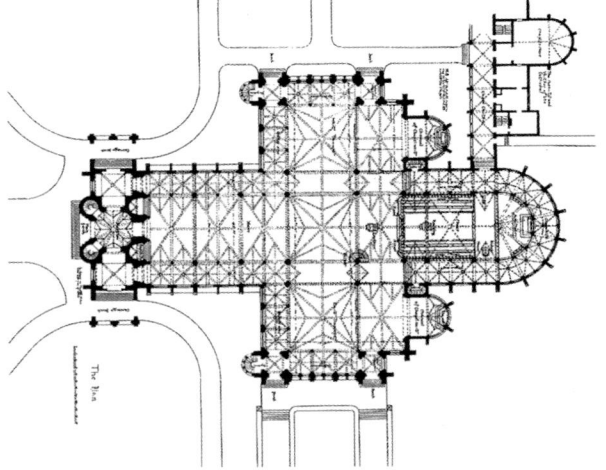

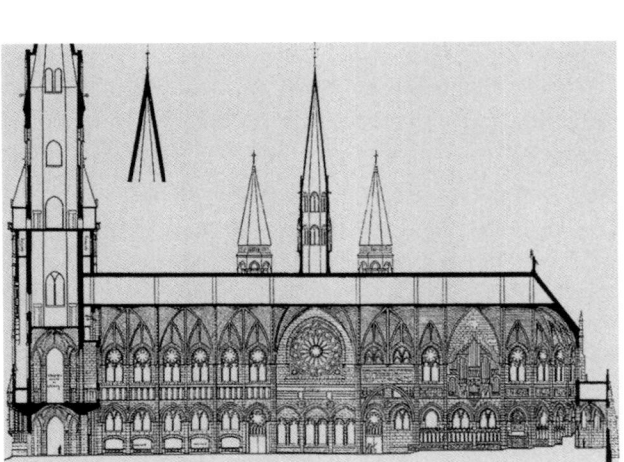

Proposed Cathedral of St. John the Divine, Morningside Drive to Tenth Avenue, West 110th to West 113th Street. Van Brunt & Howe, 1889. Competition-entry perspective showing view to the northwest, longitudinal section showing view to the west, and ground-floor plan. CD. CU.

Proposed Cathedral of St. John the Divine, Morningside Drive to Tenth Avenue, West 110th to West 113th Street. W. Halsey Wood, 1889. Competition-entry ground-floor plan, perspective showing view to the southeast, perspective showing view to the northwest, and rendering of nave. CD. CU.

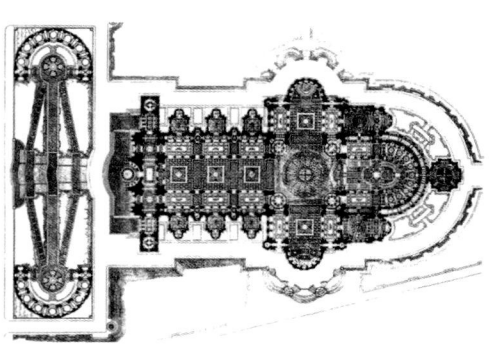

Proposed Cathedral of St. John the Divine, Morningside Drive to Tenth Avenue, West 110th to West 113th Street. Carrère & Hastings, 1889. Competition-entry perspective showing view to the northwest, longitudinal section showing view to the west, and ground-floor plan. CD. CU.

Proposed Cathedral of St. John the Divine, Morningside Drive to Tenth Avenue, West 110th to West 113th Street. Herter Brothers, 1889. Competition-entry perspective showing view to the northwest. RERG. CU.

for a total of sixty-eight, including, according to how one looks at it, twelve or thirteen submissions from the fourteen invited competitors (Henry Vaughan dropped out of the running due to pressure from other work and Frank Furness's scheme was submitted by Baker & Dallett, the partners of which had been junior partners in Furness's firm). The majority of the open entries were from Americans, although architects from England, France, and Italy sent schemes. Only four of the competitors had extensive experience with a cathedral commission and three of those were British. The lone American with experience was the seventy-year-old James Renwick Jr., whose advanced age made it unlikely that his firm would be chosen for a project that promised to be of such long duration. Once the competition was opened up, it took on a youthful cast, with the average age of the competitors thirty-eight.

Among the volunteers to prepare designs were many from New York, including Herter Brothers; George Martin

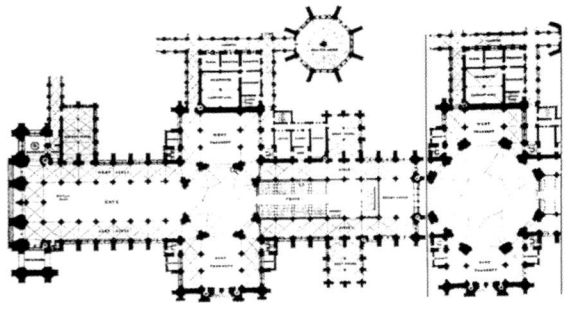

Proposed Cathedral of St. John the Divine, Morningside Drive to Tenth Avenue, West 110th to West 113th Street. George Martin Huss and John H. Buck, 1889. Perspective showing view to the northwest, longitudinal section showing view to the west, section beneath central tower, and ground-floor plan. CD. CU.

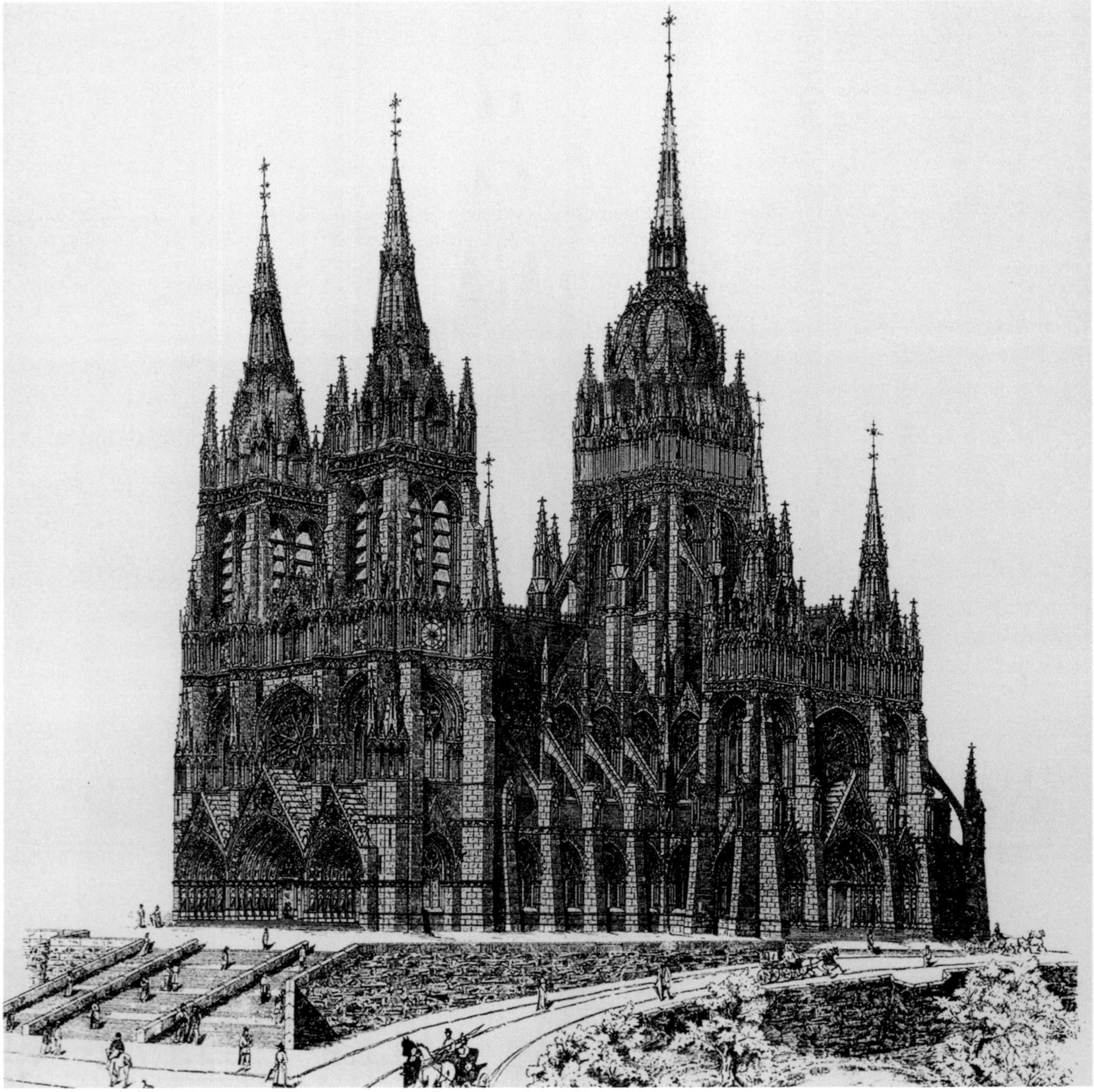

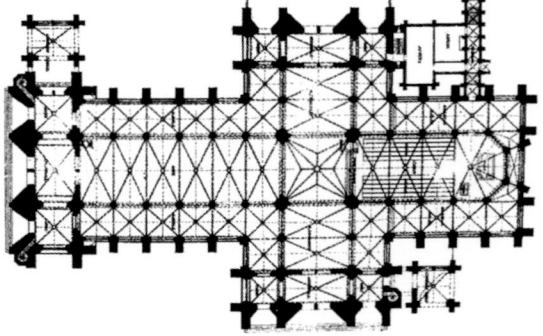

Proposed Cathedral of St. John the Divine, Morningside Drive to Tenth Avenue, West 110th to West 113th Street. James Roth, 1889. Competition-entry perspective showing view to the northwest and ground-floor plan. BLDG. CU.

Huss, who was associated with John H. Buck; James Roth; Edward Pearce Casey; Arthur B. Jennings; Mellen, Westell & Kirby; Richard M. Upjohn; F. W. Winterburn; the nineteen-year-old Bertram Grosvenor Goodhue; Parfitt Brothers, of Brooklyn; and William H. Cusack, of Poughkeepsie.[157] The Boston architects Peabody & Stearns, John Lyman Faxon, Rotch & Tilden, Sturgis & Cabot, and H. Langford Warren, as well as Alexander Hay of Lowell and Stephen C. Earle of Worcester, sent submissions, as did the Philadelphia architects Theophilus P. Chandler, Cope & Stewardson, and John J. Deery.[158] Other volunteers from around the country were L. S. Buffington of Minneapolis; Glenn Brown of Washington, D.C.; W. S. Fraser of Pittsburgh; Daniel H. Gorsuch of Baltimore; and George Keller of Hartford.[159] Foreign competitors included Carpenter & Ingelow, Henry Dudley, and William Emerson, all from England; Malcolm Stark from Scotland; Charles Boesch, Pierre Bossan, Alphonse Gosset, and Jules-Leon Kin from France; and James R. Rhind, a Scottish architect practicing in Montreal.[160]

The American Ralph Adams Cram, who would become a thorn in the side of the winning architects and ultimately the consulting architect of St. John the Divine, submitted two schemes, one Gothic and the other Romanesque, with his partner Charles Wentworth.[161] Another of the volunteers was the relatively unknown firm of Heins, La Farge & Kent, whose third partner, William W. Kent, left the

firm after its preliminary design was completed.[162] The most unusual of the uninvited entries belonged to Carlo Sada, a Sicilian architect whose flamboyant scheme, seeking to exploit the possibilities of a skyscraper church, called for a tower of nearly 1,200 feet, an unprecedented height for a building in New York and indeed the world.[163] Even more surprising than the audacity of Sada's proposal was the initial support it received from trustees Morgan Dix and Richard T. Auchmuty. All in all the stylistic range of the schemes was broad, reflecting the free spirit of the era, which at the time was viewed by many as anarchic. Gothic proposals predictably dominated. Also not surpris-

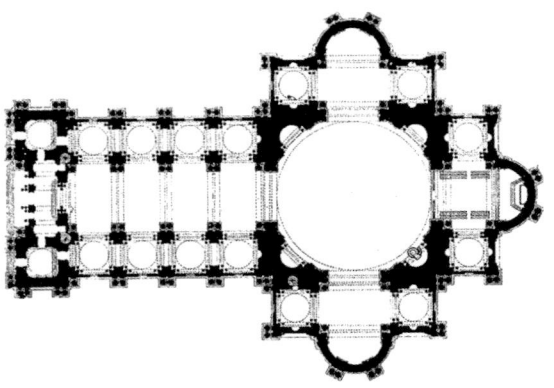

Proposed Cathedral of St. John the Divine, Morningside Drive to Tenth Avenue, West 110th to West 113th Street. Edward Pearce Casey, 1889. Competition-entry perspective showing view to the northwest and ground-floor plan. CD. CU.

Proposed Cathedral of St. John the Divine, Morningside Drive to Tenth Avenue, West 110th to West 113th Street. Richard M. Upjohn, 1889. Competition-entry perspective showing view to the northwest, west elevation, and ground-floor plan. Upjohn Collection. CU.

ing was the strong preference for Byzantine and Romanesque schemes—H. H. Richardson, only recently deceased, was far and away the nation's most admired architect, and his Trinity Church in Boston and his unrealized design for the Albany Cathedral exerted considerable influence. What was unusual was the number of schemes derived from Classical precedent, including submissions from Carrère & Hastings, Malcolm Stark, Alphonse Gosset, and James R. Rhind.

In keeping with the theme of patience that the trustees hoped to instill in the restless public, and in response to the sheer volume of the submissions, the trustees proceeded carefully, working with the help of their professional advisers in near secrecy over the next four months to whittle down the possibilities under consideration in a series of votes.[164] On May 17, 1889, they were ready to release their decision. The submissions of Potter & Robertson, Huss & Buck, W. Halsey Wood, and Heins &

Proposed Cathedral of St. John the Divine, Morningside Drive to Tenth Avenue, West 110th to West 113th Street. F. W. Winterburn, 1889. Competition-entry perspective showing view to the northwest and ground-floor plan. BLDG. CU.

La Farge were picked as finalists, with the ultimate selection to be made after a runoff competition. The reaction to the announcement was almost universally negative. The *New York Times* captured the cynical mood in an editorial published soon after the decision: "There is no denying that the results of the competition for the design of the cathedral thus far has not been such as to encourage the belief of the better-informed part of the public in the final success of the project. By that we mean the production of

a building that shall be fairly comparable to the medieval cathedrals, and that shall give New York an architectural monument worthy of a capital."[165] In a field which included such luminaries as Richard Morris Hunt and McKim, Mead & White, the public was skeptical about the committee's choices, which included three relatively unknown firms. And the firm that was prominent, Potter & Robertson, carried non-architectural baggage as well. The architect William A. Potter was a half-brother of

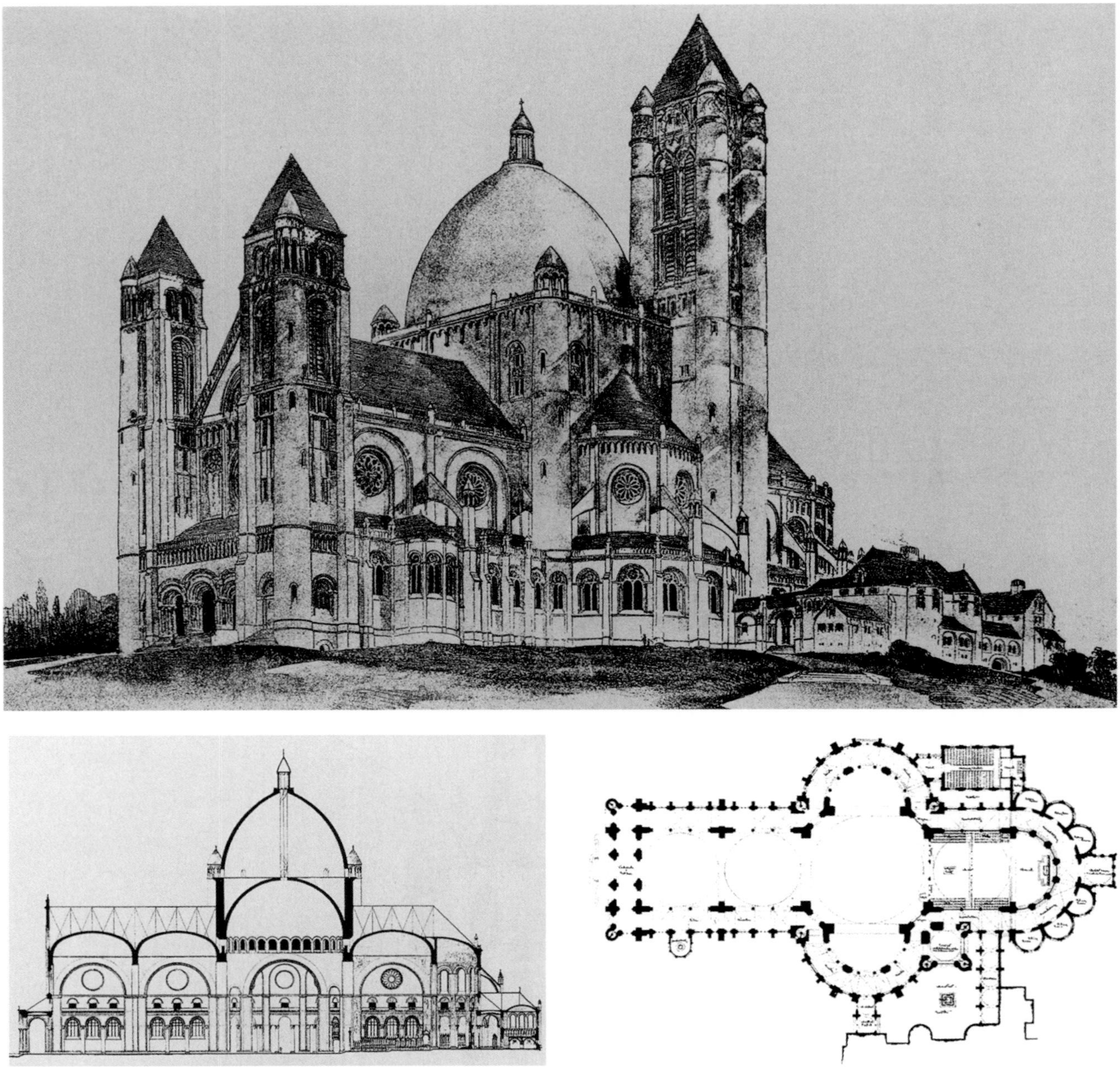

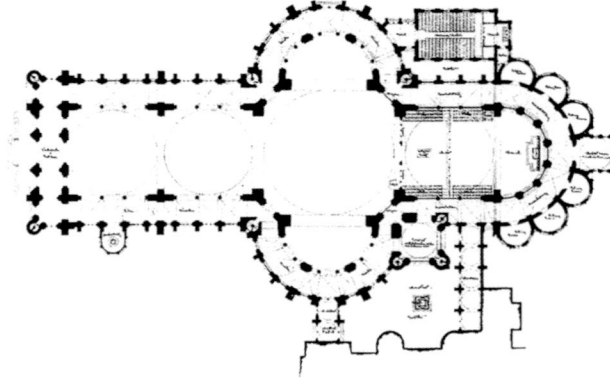

Proposed Cathedral of St. John the Divine, Morningside Drive to Tenth Avenue, West 110th to West 113th Street. Bertram Grosvenor Goodhue, 1889. Competition-entry perspective showing view to the northwest, longitudinal section showing view to the west, and ground-floor plan. CD. CU.

Bishop Potter, raising the ugly issue of nepotism, which was particularly vexing given that neither of the selected designs, nor those of the other contestants, had been publicly exhibited, due to the original competition regulations requiring the approval of the participants. Adding pressure to this situation of perceived favoritism was the Episcopal Diocese's decision to award to William A. Potter the commission for the St. Agnes Chapel, on West Ninety-second Street, just two months before the St. John's competition results were released (see chapter 6). Bishop Potter was particularly sensitive to this issue because he had reached his present position by replacing his uncle. Another factor contributing to the negative mood was the realization by the public that despite Bishop Potter's liberalism and idealistic goals, St. John the Divine would definitely be an Episcopalian cathedral and not some sort of interdenominational or nondenominational national church. Tension was eased somewhat by the publication of a number of schemes in the architectural press and by an exhibition, mounted independently of the trustees, of thirty-seven

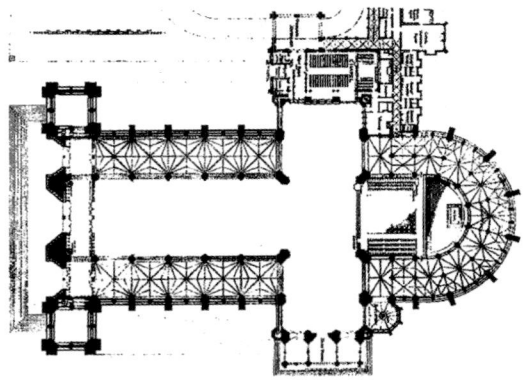

Proposed Cathedral of St. John the Divine, Morningside Drive to Tenth Avenue, West 110th to West 113th Street. Parfitt Brothers, 1889.
Competition-entry perspective showing view to the northwest, longitudinal section showing view to the west, and ground-floor plan. CD. CU.

designs at the Architectural League between December 27, 1889, and January 11, 1890.[166] The result of the exhibition was the partial vindication of the trustees—no one came forward clamoring that a brilliant design had been missed.

The second phase of the competition was similar to the first except that three additional views were requested.[167] In addition, in order to achieve a greater consistency among the entries, Hughson Hawley's renderings for Richardson's unrealized Albany Cathedral proposal were recommended as a model. The initial deadline of February 1, 1890, was

extended when the Morningside Heights site was proposed as a possible location for a world's fair, which New York later lost to Chicago (see below). The trustees had learned at least one lesson from the first phase and got the approval of the participating architects to display their schemes. A new deadline of March 2, 1891, was set and the exhibition of the entries was held at the National Academy of Design between March 24 and May 17, 1891. The trustees also added two new finalists to the mix. In recognition of Richardson's influence, his proposal for the

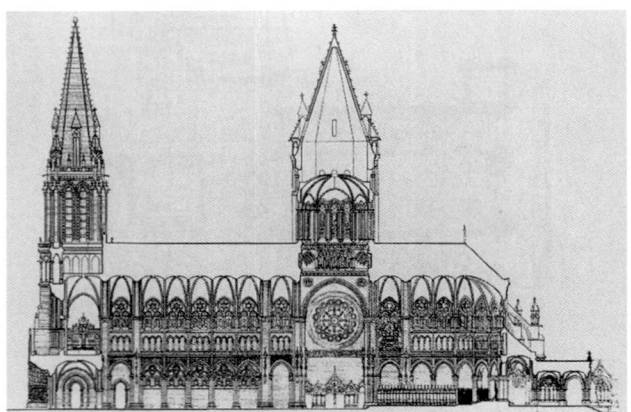

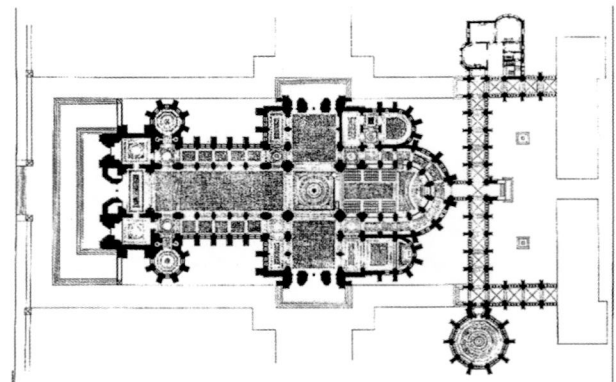

Proposed Cathedral of St. John the Divine, Morningside Drive to Tenth Avenue, West 110th to West 113th Street. Peabody & Stearns, 1889. Competition-entry perspective showing view to the northwest, longitudinal section showing view to the west, and ground-floor plan. CD. CU.

Albany Cathedral was put forward for consideration.[168] Its prospects for success were deemed doubtful given the comparatively small size of the Albany project, not to mention the fact that all the reworking would be done not by the late master himself but by his successor firm. The severe, almost cubic, Romanesque proposal of L. S. Buffington, the Minneapolis architect who had one of the largest practices in the Midwest, was also raised to the finals, although it too was considered an unlikely choice.[169]

Bishop Potter tried to convince his half-brother to withdraw his proposal but the architect refused. When Potter & Robertson missed the March 2 deadline, only the bishop voted against giving them a brief extension. Although Potter & Robertson's scheme was thus allowed to go forward, the circumspect clergyman had probably cinched its defeat by his outspoken actions; it is not known whether he actually liked the design or not. Inspired by the fourteenth-century Cathedral at Gerona,

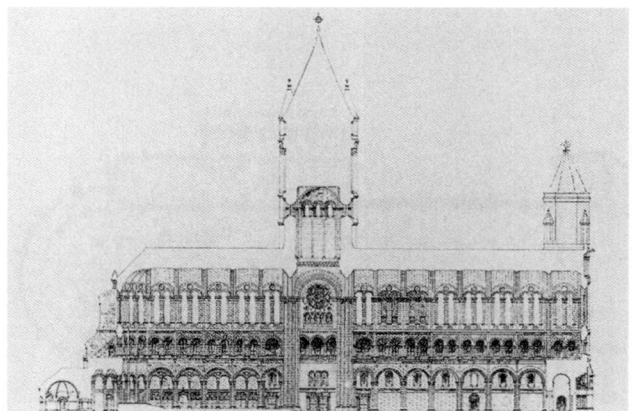

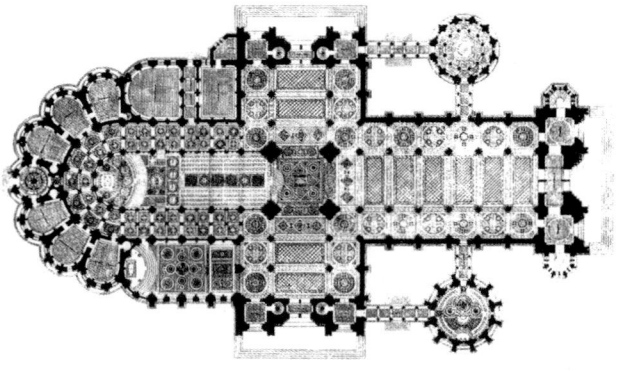

Proposed Cathedral of St. John the Divine, Morningside Drive to Tenth Avenue, West 110th to West 113th Street. John Lyman Faxon, 1889. Competition-entry perspective showing view to the northwest, longitudinal section showing view to the east, and ground-floor plan. CD. CU.

Spain, Potter & Robertson's entry was Gothic in spirit although it featured Romanesque details, most notably its monumentally scaled, triple-arched portal. The architects emphasized how their plan especially suited the trustees' desire for a grand cathedral that also contained an effective preaching space:

> The scheme . . . which is based upon the conjunction of a single-span nave with a choir of the usual arrangement of naves and aisles . . . consists of a central space 86 feet square with four lesser spaces placed at the four faces of the central square, forming a space, cruciform in plan and unobstructed by columns, containing 21,000 square feet of floor space, an achievement which, it is believed, is unprecedented in the whole range of the Gothic style. To be able to seat nearly three thousand people within radius of not more than 115 feet of the preacher has never been accomplished in any cathedral of the usual type, certainly not in any building of the Gothic style.[170]

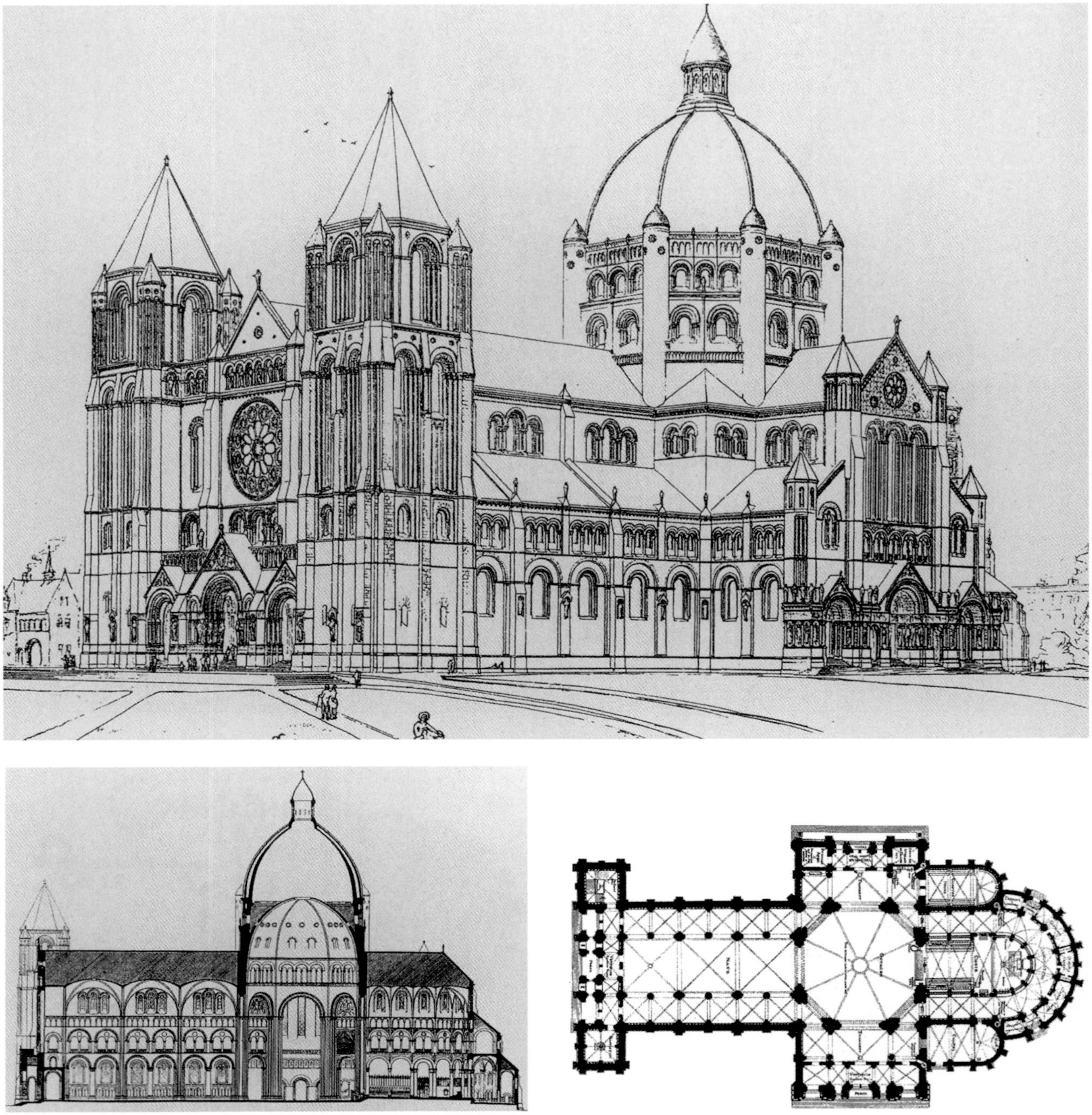

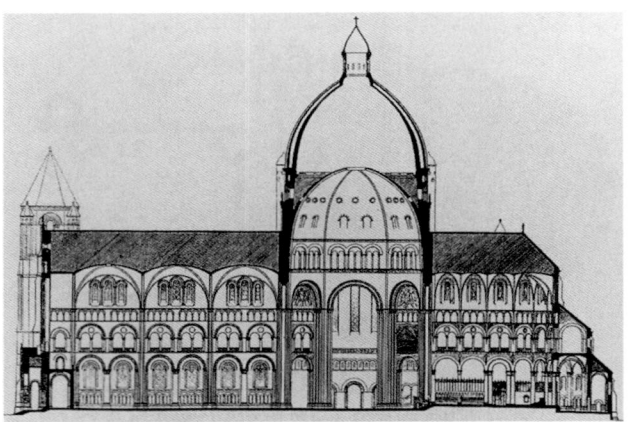

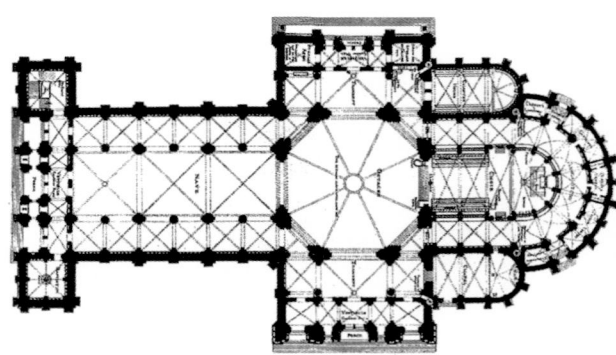

Proposed Cathedral of St. John the Divine, Morningside Drive to Tenth Avenue, West 110th to West 113th Street. H. Langford Warren, 1889. Competition-entry perspective showing view to the northwest, longitudinal section showing view to the west, and ground-floor plan. AABN. CU.

But the *New York Times* noted that the advantages achieved by the interior were at the expense of the exterior: "The need of a very large auditorium had induced the architects to sacrifice the exterior in several respects. At a distance the four spires look like several churches, one behind the other; the facade looks meagre, and the dome of the big vault between the four spires has a depressed appearance from outside. . . . Singularly lacking in imagi-

nation is the repetition of the same spire four times."[171] Montgomery Schuyler, writing in 1909, disagreed: "That quartet of spires would have crowned Morningside Heights very grandly. The spirit of the design is equally remote from fettered and 'puristic' imitation and from any straining after difference and 'originality.'"[172]

George Martin Huss and John H. Buck produced an English Gothic scheme, which, though it included some

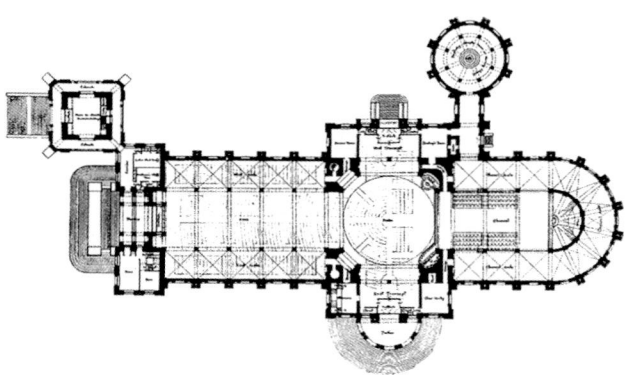

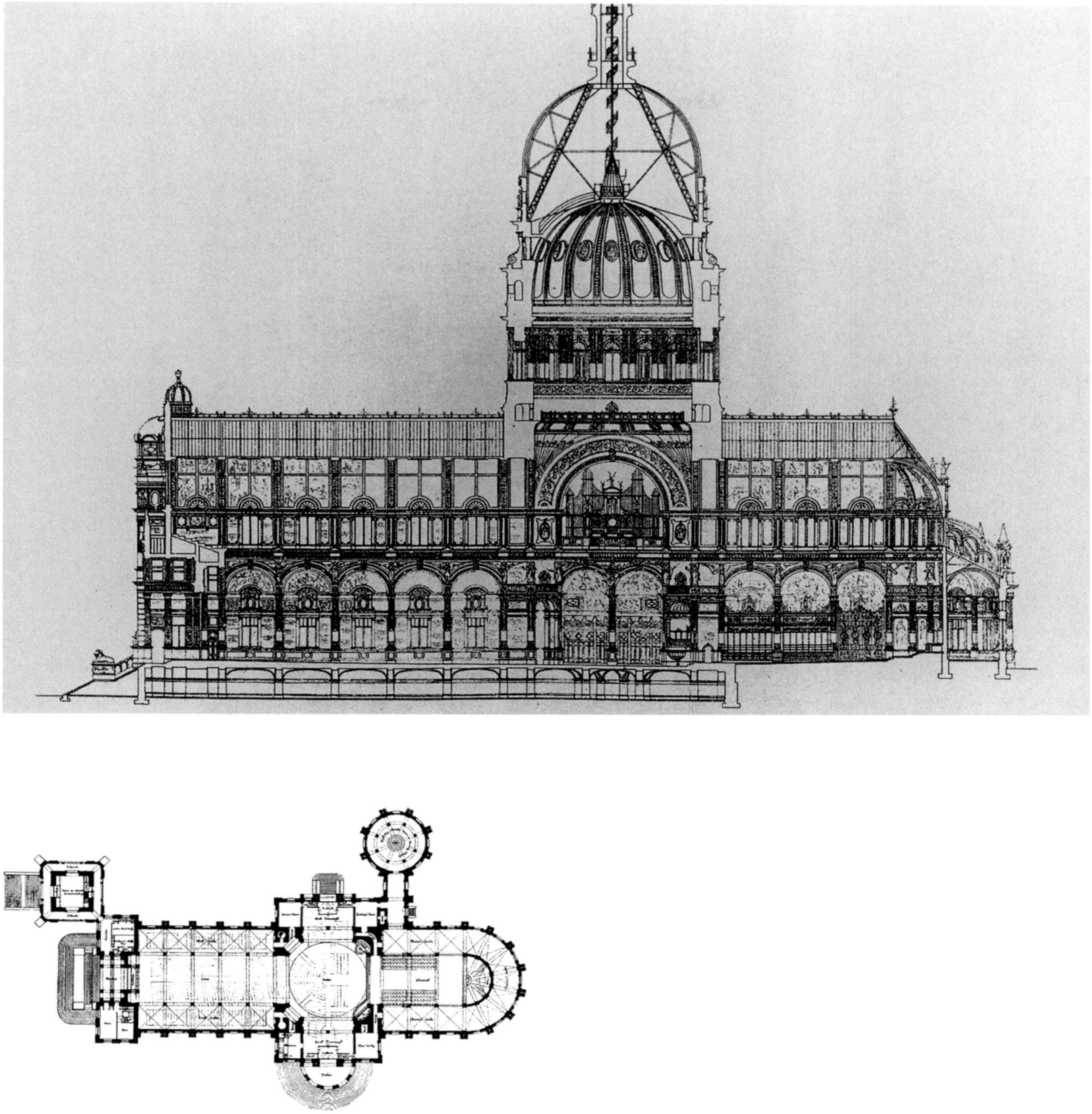

Proposed Cathedral of St. John the Divine, Morningside Drive to Tenth Avenue, West 110th to West 113th Street. Alexander Hay, 1889. Competition-entry longitudinal section showing view to the west and ground-floor plan. AABN. CU.

French details and an enormous central tower, was widely viewed as an uninspired design with little chance of winning. The *New York Sun* summed up the view of many, labeling it

the most conventional of the four submitted designs. . . . In plan the church is thoroughly English, with nave and choir of equal length, a flat east end, a central octagon evidently inspired by Alan of Walsingham's work at Ely,

and a minor transept half way between the great transept and the east end. But if we look at the section we see French influence in the lofty roof, in the space thus afforded for a small gallery above the triforium, and in the fact that the vaulting shafts spring from the piers of the floor arcade instead of from corbels above them, as was the typical English way. . . . In short, much good sense has been shown . . . in their effort to adapt the typical old

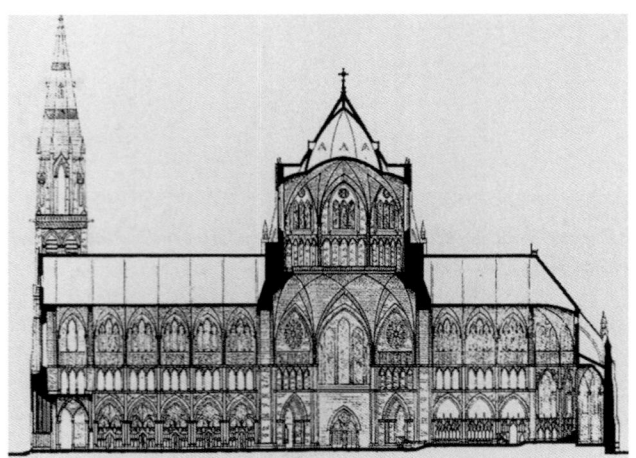

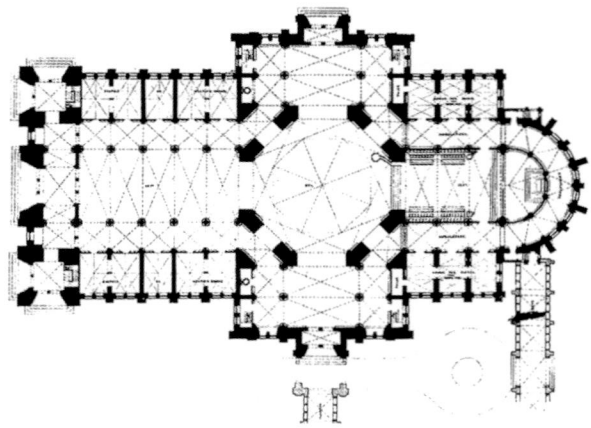

Proposed Cathedral of St. John the Divine, Morningside Drive to Tenth Avenue, West 110th to West 113th Street. Stephen C. Earle, 1889. Competition-entry perspective showing view to the northwest, longitudinal section showing view to the west, and ground-floor plan. CD. CU.

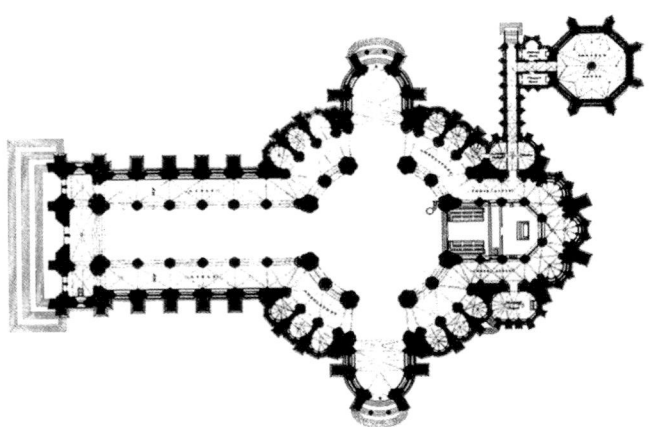

Proposed Cathedral of St. John the Divine, Morningside Drive to Tenth Avenue, West 110th to West 113th Street. Theophilus P. Chandler, 1889. Competition-entry perspective showing view to the northwest, longitudinal sectional showing view to the west, and ground-floor plan. CD. CU.

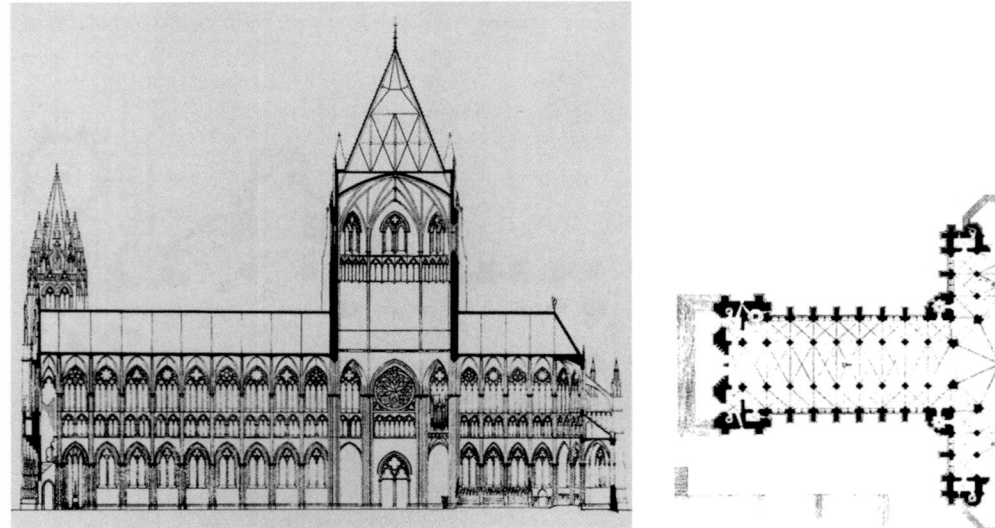

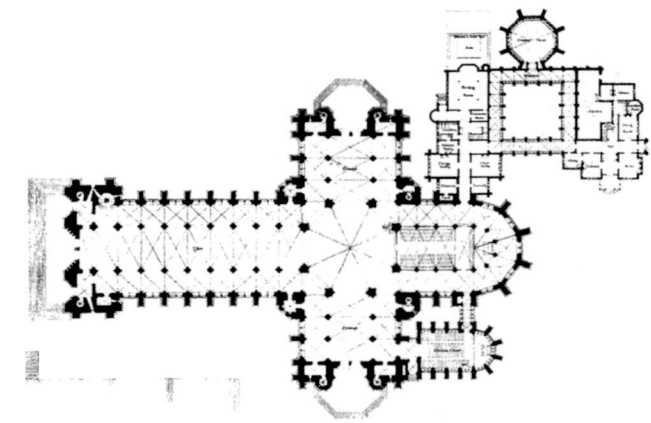

Proposed Cathedral of St. John the Divine, Morningside Drive to Tenth Avenue, West 110th to West 113th Street. Cope & Stewardson, 1889. Competition-entry perspective showing view to the northwest, longitudinal section showing view to the west, and ground-floor plan. CD. CU.

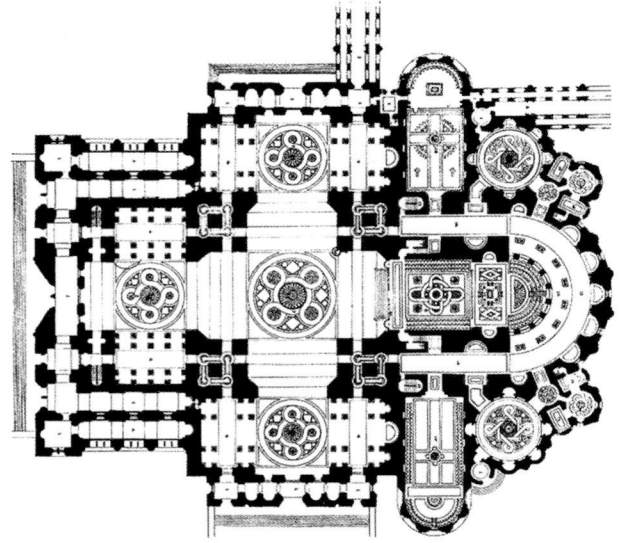

cathedral form to the needs of modern worship. . . . But their result must be called intelligent rather than highly artistic, and cannot be pronounced successful from either the modern or the traditional, the practical or the aesthetic point of view. . . . If it were well built and beautifully ornamented this church would not disgrace New York: but it certainly would not prove that cathedrals to rival the old ones can be built to-day.[173]

At the other end of the spectrum was the breathtakingly eclectic submission of an obscure architect, W. Halsey Wood of Newark, New Jersey, a deeply religious Episcopalian whose romantic scheme appealed to Bishop Potter and other members of the clergy while drawing the enmity of the profession and the press. Wood had apprenticed in the New York office of John F. Miller and studied in England with the church architects Bodley & Garner before opening his own practice. The predominant style of Wood's highly original scheme, which featured an enormous, eight-hundred-foot-tall, Byzantine-inspired, domed crossing tower and a symbolic program unprecedented in scope, was largely Early English Gothic. He claimed his design constituted a new ecclesiastical style, which he labeled American Gothic, arguing that it responded to the increasing verticality of New York's skyline and the ecumenical

Proposed Cathedral of St. John the Divine, Morningside Drive to Tenth Avenue, West 110th to West 113th Street. L. S. Buffington, 1889. Competition-entry perspective showing view to the northwest and ground-floor plan. CD. CU.

Proposed Cathedral of St. John the Divine, Morningside Drive to Tenth Avenue, West 110th to West 113th Street. Glenn Brown, 1889. Competition-entry perspective showing view to the northwest, longitudinal section showing view to the west, and ground-floor plan. CD. CU.

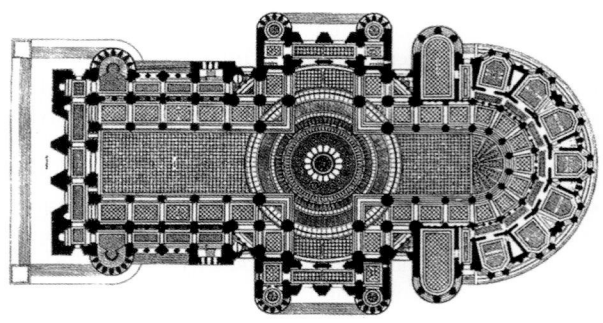

Proposed Cathedral of
St. John the Divine,
Morningside Drive to
Tenth Avenue, West
110th to West 113th
Street. W. S. Fraser,
1889. Competition–
entry perspective
showing view to the
northwest, east
elevation, and ground-
floor plan. CD. CU.

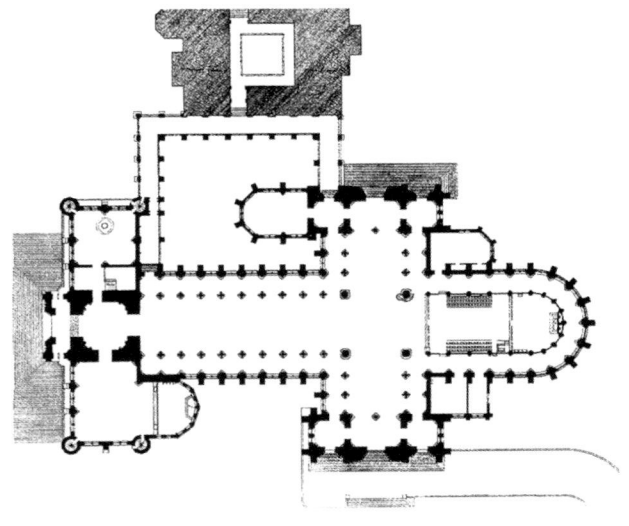

Proposed Cathedral of St. John the Divine, Morningside Drive to Tenth Avenue, West 110th to West 113th Street. Malcolm Stark, 1889. Competition-entry south elevation. CD. CU.

Proposed Cathedral of St. John the Divine, Morningside Drive to Tenth Avenue, West 110th to West 113th Street. Alphonse Gosset, 1889. Competition-entry south elevation (left), ground-floor plan (center), and east elevation. AABN. CU.

Proposed Cathedral of St. John the Divine, Morningside Drive to Tenth Avenue, West 110th to West 113th Street. James R. Rhind, 1889. Competition-entry perspective showing view to the northwest. CAB. CU.

Proposed Cathedral of St. John the Divine, Morningside Drive to Tenth Avenue, West 110th to West 113th Street. Cram & Wentworth, 1889. Competition-entry perspective showing view to the northwest, longitudinal section showing view to the east, and ground-floor plan. CD. CU.

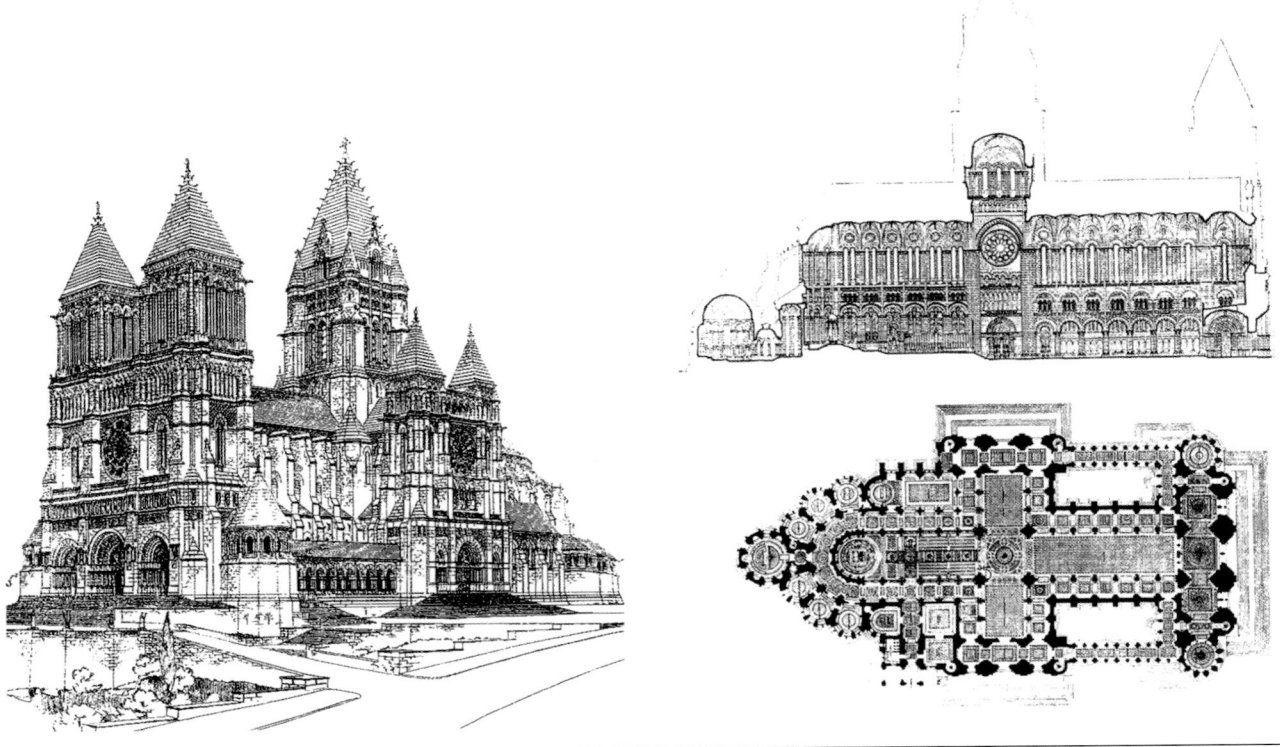

Proposed Cathedral of St. John the Divine, Morningside Drive to Tenth Avenue, West 110th to West 113th Street. Heins & La Farge, 1889. Competition-entry interior perspective of space beneath central tower (above) and perspective showing view to the northwest (right). CD. CU.

spirit of the program. But he failed to win over the *New York Times*, which launched a strong attack: "The weakness of Mr. Wood's design is conspicuous in the lines of his 'tower-dome-spire' which are heavy and betray the inorganic mixture of styles hunted out of any and every quarter of the world. . . . [The interior] is Gothic badly carried out, or else Romanesque with Gothic adaptations. . . . If it is to be accepted, it will have to be revised in a way that must change it, within and without, that another structure will be the result."[174] The *Real Estate Record and Builders' Guide* was even more dismissive: "It is very far from flattering to the architectural knowledge and taste of the cathedral trustees that they should have deliberately introduced such a design into the final competition."[175]

Heins & La Farge's design fell somewhere between Huss & Buck's conservatism and Wood's adventurous eclecticism; as such, it was given front-runner status along with Potter & Robertson's submission. George Lewis Heins, who came from a privileged background and was educated in his teens in Paris, Heidelberg, and Italy, attended architecture school at the Massachusetts Institute of Technology, where he became friendly with William R. Ware, the most important of the professional advisers. Grant La Farge also briefly attended MIT. He was the son of the painter John La Farge, who was responsible for the interior decoration of Richardson's Trinity Church, in Boston. Grant La Farge subsequently worked in Richardson's

gg

office, so it is not surprising that the firm's eclectic design owed so much to Trinity Church. After Wood's design, Heins & La Farge's scheme featured the most prominent crossing tower. Their plan for the cathedral was a blend of Gothic and Byzantine sources and took its inspiration from Hagia Sophia in Istanbul, St. Mark's in Venice, and St. Front in Périgueux. Although they renounced the use of iron, the architects were hardly backward-looking, proposing to construct their domes and vaults with Rafael Guastavino's innovative tile-arch system.[176] Heins & La Farge's scheme also featured the most extensive program of interior wall decoration, which was again not surprising given La Farge's family ties. Reaction to the proposal was generally positive, with most critics emphasizing their admiration for the interior design. The *New York Sun* observed: "Seen in the beautifully executed water-color perspective, where all the eventual color decoration is carefully indicated, this interior strikes one as beautiful and as more appropriate to the needs of to-day than either of its rivals."[177] But some critics were bothered by the design's freewheeling eclecticism. The *Real Estate Record and Builders' Guide* noted:

> The round arch has been used throughout and a general appearance of Gothic given to the exterior, but the building is in no sense Gothic. Within the style is totally different from what it is without. It is neither Romanesque nor Gothic, Byzantine nor Renaissance. . . . Though considerable variety is given to the centre of the church by the main tower and four lower square ones, two on each side of the transepts, the body of the church suffers from the plainness of the sky line. . . . The central lantern . . . is so very large and heavy as to be out of proportion to the whole building.[178]

The *New York Times*, which also had trouble with parts of the design, nonetheless preferred it to the other finalists: "If one must be chosen, that of Messrs. Heins and La Farge, shorn of its superficial Gothicism, commends itself as the most likely to stand apart as a building meant for worship, yet unlike the ordinary church, and one in which beauty is allied to no little originality in design."[179]

In June 1891 the trustees, in a decision that can only be regarded as a compromise and not an enthusiastic endorsement, picked Heins & La Farge as the architects for the proposed cathedral. A small article announcing the decision in the *New York Times* in July intimated that there was less than complete faith in the winning design, stating "that in general the plans submitted by this firm will be followed" but adding the coda that "large modifications, however, are quite likely."[180] Even before the cornerstone ceremony, on St. John's Day, December 27, 1892, just how extensive the modifications could be was made apparent to Heins & La Farge when the trustees ordered that the cathedral be reoriented on the more traditional east-west basis, with the front now to face Tenth Avenue.[181] This was but the first of a series of drastic reconsiderations to which the cathedral project would be subjected before Heins & La Farge was replaced by Ralph Adams Cram in 1911. That story, and the ups and downs of a cathedral that is not yet complete as of this writing, is told in other volumes in this series.[182]

MEMORIALS AND MONUMENTS

Despite the Civil War's enormous impact on New York, from the dramatic expression of extreme antiwar sentiment in the Draft Riots of 1863 to the prosperity the war fostered, the postwar city initiated surprisingly few commemorations of battles fought and lives lost. The first of New York's memorials was designed by Richard Morris Hunt toward the end of 1865.[1] Commissioned by Alexander Hamilton Jr. and John Jacob Astor II, the modestly scaled monument, placed inside Trinity Church, was dedicated to Captain Percival Drayton, chief of the Naval Bureau of Navigation, who had distinguished himself in battle during the war and died on August 5, 1865. As designed by Hunt and executed by the sculptor Leo J. Larmande, the approximately fourteen-foot-high, six-foot-wide, and two-foot-deep bluestone monument, located on the church's east interior wall, next to the main entrance, consisted of an iron gate flanked by piers that in turn were

Proposed Seventh Regiment Memorial, Central Park near Eighth Avenue and West Sixty-ninth Street. Richard Morris Hunt and John Quincy Adams Ward, 1870. Rendering of view to the west and aerial view. The Octagon, AAF.

Proposed Seventh Regiment Memorial, Central Park near Eighth Avenue and West Sixty-ninth Street. Richard Morris Hunt and John Quincy Adams Ward, c. 1873. Rendering of view to the west. The Octagon, AAF.

surmounted by a horizontal form evocative of a sarcophagus, marked with the letters alpha and omega. The piers were decorated with scenes of the battles of Port Royal, Fort Sumter, and Mobile Bay, in which Drayton had served. Above the piers, two pink marble columns flanked a black marble slab marked with Drayton's name and a list of his principal accomplishments. The slab supported a pediment decorated with a shield.

Hunt's far more significant and visible Seventh Regi-

ment Memorial (1874), conceived and executed in collaboration with the sculptor John Quincy Adams Ward, honored the regiment's fifty-eight men who died in the war.[2] The idea of depicting a solitary soldier was suggested to the sculptor by Frederick Law Olmsted and Calvert Vaux, who were consulted when a site was selected for the memorial on the west side of Central Park near Sixty-ninth Street. Hunt's elegant and understated, nearly fifteen-foot-high granite base, in effect a short obelisk, carried

Seventh Regiment Memorial, Central Park near Eighth Avenue and West Sixty-ninth Street. Richard Morris Hunt and John Quincy Adams Ward, 1874. View to the southwest. The Octagon, AAF.

Admiral David Glasgow Farragut Monument, Madison Square Park at the southeast corner of Fifth Avenue and East Twenty-sixth Street. Augustus Saint-Gaudens and Stanford White, 1881. View to the east. AABN. CU.

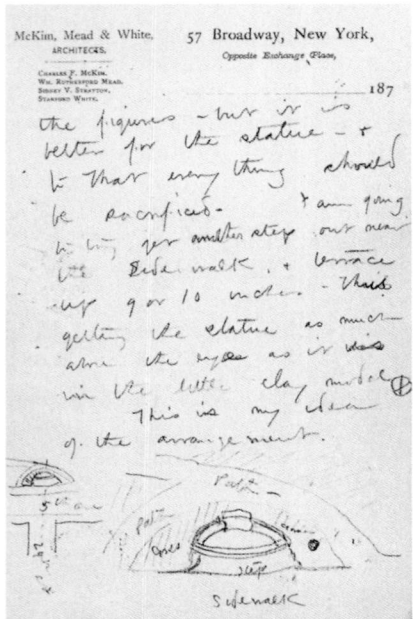

Letter from Stanford White to Augustus Saint-Gaudens, December 27, 1879, with sketch showing proposed site of Admiral David Glasgow Farragut Monument, Madison Square Park on the east side of Fifth Avenue at East Twenty-fourth Street. DC.

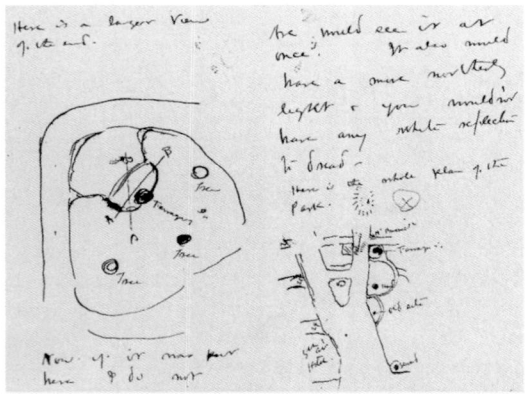

Letter from Stanford White to Augustus Saint-Gaudens, February 24, 1880, with sketch showing proposed site of Admiral David Glasgow Farragut Monument, Madison Square Park at the southeast corner of Fifth Avenue and East Twenty-sixth Street. DC.

Ward's ten-foot-high depiction of a private dressed in the heavy overcoat of the Union army uniform and resting on his rifle. Effective though the monument was, the base had in fact been designed in 1868 for a different sculpture and offered little in terms of environmental presence and architectural complexity, especially in comparison to previously conceived but ultimately unrealized proposals by Hunt, who had originally intended for the memorial to be part of his monumental, unbuilt Warriors' Gate for Central Park (see chapter 1). Another unrealized proposal of

Hunt's for the memorial, issued in 1870, called for an elevated circular platform reached by three staircases, each to be flanked at both top and bottom by bronze eagles. A graduated pedestal was to stand in the center of the platform and support Ward's soldier. Perhaps in deference to Olmsted and Vaux's fundamental antipathy toward including monuments in their park, Hunt and Ward redesigned the memorial so that a central pedestal carrying the sculpture was flanked by lower bases, each supporting a sculptural group: one was to depict soldiers at rest, the other a soldier treating an injured comrade. This proposal also seems to have met opposition from the park's designers and officials and was rejected in favor of the far simpler design ultimately installed in 1874.

While the impact Hunt's and Ward's unrealized designs had on the architecturally ambitious monuments built during the so-called City Beautiful movement of the 1890s and early 1900s is difficult to assess, Augustus Saint-Gaudens and Stanford White's Admiral David Glasgow Farragut Monument (1881), installed at the northwest corner of Madison Square Park, clearly set the standard by which all such work in that movement would be measured.[3] The Farragut Monument marked a high point in the history of American public sculpture, constituting the most complete integration of a fully modeled figure, relief sculpture, base, lettering, and siting—with each element contributing to both the work's formal and thematic totality—ever achieved at the time of its completion. Born in Dublin in 1848, the son of a French-born shoemaker and an Irish working-class woman, Saint-Gaudens moved to New York during infancy. At thirteen he apprenticed with a cameo cutter, and at nineteen he became one of the first Americans to study sculpture at the Ecole des Beaux-Arts, in Paris. Saint-Gaudens was not only highly talented and ambitious but also very charismatic and moved easily in high social circles. It was not until he was thirty-nine years old, however, that he won his first public commission—the memorial to Farragut, commander of the Union fleet during the Civil War, who is remembered for his command, "Damn the torpedoes! Full speed ahead!" To get the commission, Saint-Gaudens had directly approached not only Farragut's widow but also the well-known jurist Edwin Stoughton and other members of the Farragut Monument committee, as well as the forty-nine-year-old John Quincy Adams Ward. Ward had been given the commission but declined so that the project could go to the younger, up-and-coming artist.

Saint-Gaudens depicted Farragut in an assertive posture, with feet apart and coat opened by the oncoming wind. Working closely with White, Saint-Gaudens placed the bronze statue on a bluestone pedestal that was part of an exedra, the curved flanking portions of which contained stylized relief sculptures, also by Saint-Gaudens, depicting idealized female figures representing loyalty and courage. A sword superimposed on a background of waves filled the center. The exedra also contained an inscription, carved with highly stylized lettering, describing Farragut's achievements. At either end the exedra terminated in sculpted dolphins. During the course of design White had written to Saint-Gaudens: "All I have to say is if any Greek temple had any more parabolic, bucolic or any other olic kind of curves about it than this [monument] has, or if the architect had to draw them out full size, a lunatic asylum or a hospital must have been an addenda to an architect's office. I hope you will not go into a hospital trying to understand them, old boy."[4]

The Farragut Monument catapulted Saint-Gaudens into the highest rank of American sculptors. The journalist Richard Watson Gilder, writing in *Scribner's Magazine*, favorably compared him to Donatello, seeing the Farragut as a worthy descendant of the Renaissance master's statue of Saint George (1416–20). Gilder found Saint-Gaudens's sculpture to be "in modeling, severe, broad, yet minute in finish and modern in expression—in character, alert, eager . . . full of dignity and reserved force."[5] Mariana Van Rensselaer stated, "It may, I think, be claimed without hesitation for Mr. Saint-Gaudens's statue of Admiral Farragut . . . , that it is the best monument of the kind the city has to show." Van Rensselaer was particularly impressed with the base, on which sculptor and architect had closely collaborated to create a powerful representation of liquidity, one worthy of the movemented surfaces of the typically French and Belgian Art Nouveau designs of the 1890s with which it is frequently compared: "The outline of the substructure has been well calculated, running neither into a conventional rigidity, nor into an evident effort to escape therefrom. Its decorations combine 'representative' with more 'decorative' work,—a difficult problem, but one which has been cleverly met. . . . The modeling of the low-relief figures is especially to be praised."[6]

While the sculpture and its base were widely admired, the choice of a site within Madison Square Park seemed more problematic; the *American Architect and Building News* argued that the memorial "suffers lamentably in dignity from the continual passing of persons behind it."[7] The sculpture's placement had, in fact, been decided after considerable thought and debate. The committee had originally proposed that the monument be erected facing Fifth Avenue opposite its intersection with Twenty-fourth Street, thus serving as a termination for the cross street. Frederick Law Olmsted told White that he disliked the Madison Square Park site. As White would recount in a letter to Saint-Gaudens, Olmsted found the site "a sort of shiftless place, which would give the statue no prominence whatever," favoring a location in front of James G. Batterson's Worth Monument (1857), on the triangular traffic island formed by the crossing of Broadway and Fifth Avenue just below Twenty-fourth Street.[8] Olmsted also suggested alternative sites at the triangle formed by the intersection of Broadway and Sixth Avenue below Thirty-fifth Street; at an unspecified entrance to Central Park; and at Union Square. But White favored Madison Square Park, and when members of the committee suggested a

site at the southeast corner of Fifth Avenue and Twenty-sixth Street, after much deliberation he endorsed the suggestion, writing to Saint-Gaudens:

> I have been to the site for the Farragut at least fifty times, sometimes I think it is a bully site and sometimes I think a better one might be found. I have gone there with lots of people, and their opinions vary as much as mine do. . . . I have come to the almost decided conclusion that the 26th Street corner of Madison [Square] Park and 5th Avenue is a better place. It is more removed from the other statues and is altogether a more select, quiet and distinguished place, if it is not quite so public. It is in a sweller part of the Park, just where the aristocratic part of the Avenue begins and right opposite both Delmonico's and the Hotel Brunswick and the stream of people walking down Fifth Avenue would see it at once. It also would have a more northerly light and you wouldn't have any white reflections to dread.[9]

Ultimately the monument was placed at the park's northwest corner, though despite White's preference for placing it on a northeast-southwest axis, facing the intersection, it was placed on a north-south axis, directly facing the avenue.

Whatever the virtues or shortcomings of its siting, the *New York Times* correctly stated that the memorial would establish a new standard for American public art:

> In this country we can never be accused of hiding our lights under a bushel. The Farragut monument is incontestably the handsomest in or about New York City. . . . The importance of its erection will not be misunderstood when it is remembered how almost without a statue of a high degree of artistic value we have been. Our citizens have had no standard to judge by. With the Farragut [Monument] begins the era when criticism of sculpture for civic decorations will be as sharp and exacting as it now is in painting. We can never afford to put up public statues hereafter which are inferior to the Farragut.[10]

While the memorial was undoubtedly the post–Civil War era's most artistically challenging public sculpture and in many ways its most influential, without question the most commanding monument erected in New York during that time—or at any other in New York's history, and in fact the most commanding since ancient times—was the Statue of Liberty.[11] In the summer of 1865, at a dinner party held at the French historian Edouard-René Lefebvre de Laboulaye's estate in Glatigny, near Versailles, the idea of some sort of tribute or memorial to America's independence was reportedly raised by the evening's host. The Union army had only recently secured victory, and the assassination of Abraham Lincoln, an event that touched France greatly, contributed to a mood particularly hospitable to a gesture celebrating American liberty. The French were especially moved by the theme, taking pride in their critical role in recognizing the emerging nation ninety years earlier, highlighted by the contribution of General Lafayette in the Revolutionary War. Laboulaye, the author of a three-volume history of the United States and the most prominent French expert on American his-

Proposed lighthouse, entrance to the Suez Canal, Egypt.
Frédéric-Auguste Bartholdi, 1867–69. MB.

tory after the death of Alexis de Tocqueville, in 1859, was a vocal supporter of the Union cause. But Laboulaye's interest in the memorial was not purely idealistic; a crafty politician, intent on removing Napoleon III from power and instituting a republican government, he saw the provocative power of such a project at home. When a modest medal in honor of Lincoln that was intended for the president's widow received the simultaneous praise of the French people and ire of the reigning government, Laboulaye knew that his idea of a grand monument built by both nations would serve as a brilliant propaganda tool for the cause of French liberty. Notwithstanding these motivations as well as the initial apathy of Americans living outside of New York, what was begun by Laboulaye would ultimately result in the most important emblem of liberty and American democracy ever realized.

One of Laboulaye's dinner guests on that fateful summer evening was the thirty-one-year-old Frédéric-Auguste Bartholdi, a fashionable painter and sculptor who shared Laboulaye's republican sentiments. Born in Colmar, a city in Alsace, Bartholdi was raised in a middle-class family and studied with the society portraitist Ary Scheffer and the sculptors J. F. Soitoux and Antoine Etex. From the beginning Laboulaye viewed Bartholdi as the sculptor who would carry out his wishes, trusting his artistic sense completely, but nothing much happened for some five years as Bartholdi worked on other projects and Laboulaye pushed for political reform within France. The Franco-Prussian War (1870–71), in which Bartholdi fought and during which time his house was occupied by Prussian soldiers, shattered France, and the Alsace region was ceded to the Germans in the ignominious defeat. The idea of a monument jointly erected by France and the United States in celebration of freedom, though never entirely dropped, was taken up after the war with renewed enthusiasm, and Bartholdi made plans, in consultation with Laboulaye, to visit the United States. On June 10, 1871, he set sail already having developed the idea for a statue of a female figure, draped in classical garb, holding a torch aloft in her right hand, a proposal that was remarkably similar to his unrealized scheme (1867–69) for a lighthouse to be built at the entrance to the Suez Canal for Ismail Pasha, the ruler of Egypt.[12]

For five months Bartholdi traveled extensively in the United States, meeting a wide array of influential Americans, including President Ulysses S. Grant in Long Branch, New Jersey, Senator Charles Sumner of Massachusetts in Washington, D.C., the poet Henry Wadsworth Longfellow in Boston, and the religious leader Brigham Young in Salt Lake City, Utah. He received a mixed reception for his monument, although the project was more enthusiastically greeted when he emphasized that it would be a gift from the French people that could be used to help celebrate the Centennial, in 1876, and would involve only a relatively modest American contribution, that of the site and pedestal. He also used his visit to solicit private commissions for other work; the most notable among these to be realized was a frieze for H. H. Richardson's Brattle Street Church, on Boston's Commonwealth Avenue.[13] In Philadelphia Bartholdi was graciously welcomed by members of that city's Union League Club, who greatly respected Laboulaye. Members of New York's Union League Club would later prove invaluable in promoting the monument. Bartholdi also visited Newport, Rhode Island, where he met Richard Morris Hunt, who would have so much to do with the project.

The main purpose of the visit, however, was to pick an appropriate site, which apparently was accomplished within Bartholdi's first few days in New York. Although he considered Central Park and the Battery, Bartholdi focused on the various islands in New York Harbor, picking out Bedloe's Island, near the mouth of the Hudson River, because of its visibility from both the city and the harbor approach. In 1885, in a pamphlet produced for a fund-raising effort, Bartholdi was understandably dramatic in describing his epiphany regarding the location of the statue:

In the course of the voyage I formed some conception of a plan of a monument, but I can say that at the view of the harbor of New York the definite plan was first clear to my eyes. The picture that is presented to the view when one arrives at New York is marvelous; when, after some days of voyaging, in the pearly radiance of a beautiful morning is revealed the magnificent spectacle of those immense cities, of those rivers extending as far as the eye can reach, festooned with masts and flags; when one awakes, so to speak, in the midst of that interior sea covered with vessels, some giant in size, some dwarfs, which swarm about, puffing, whistling, swinging, the great arms of their uncovered walking-beams, moving to and fro like a crowd upon a public place. It is thrilling. It is, indeed, the New World, which appears in its majestic expanse, with the ardor of its glowing life. Was it not wholly natural that the artist was inspired by this spectacle? Yes, in this very place shall be raised the Statue of Liberty, grand as the idea which it embodies, radiant upon the two worlds.[14]

Originally called Minnissais (lesser island) by the Mohegan Indians, the twelve-acre island Bartholdi selected for his statue had been renamed for Isaack Bedloo (Bedloe being an anglicized form of the name, also often spelled Bedlow), an owner of the island in the mid–seventeenth century. Variously used as a quarantine station and a refuge for Tory sympathizers during the Revolutionary War, in 1806–11, in anticipation of hostilities, it became home to a fort in the shape of an eleven-point star. After the War of 1812, the fort was named after a hero of the conflict, Colonel Eleazer D. Wood. Although officially located within New Jersey territorial waters, Bedloe's Island had been considered part of New York since the late seventeenth century. In 1834 an agreement was reached between the two states: above the mean low-water mark the island was considered in New York, and below that point it belonged to New Jersey. In addition to the island's advantageous location, Bartholdi was assured in his meeting with President Grant that it could easily be made available for the proposed monument.

After Bartholdi returned to France, in the fall of 1871, he continued to refine his ideas for the project, but the bulk of his time was spent pursuing other work. Once Napoleon III was exiled to England, Laboulaye also turned his attentions away from the project, concentrating his energies on securing a republican government for France. In 1873, Bartholdi began another work destined for American soil, the statue of General Lafayette that had been commissioned by the French government in recognition of the assistance to Parisians provided by New Yorkers during the Franco-Prussian War.[15] The oversized bronze statue, which was to be placed in New York in time for the Centennial celebrations, represented Lafayette at the age of twenty, when he first came to America. Placed on a granite pedestal designed by H. W. DeStuckle that was paid for by French residents in New York, the statue was unveiled in Union Square on September 6, 1876, in a ceremony attended by Bartholdi.

Practical progress toward the construction of Bartholdi's *Liberty* statue did not take place until 1875, when the Franco-American Union was founded in Paris. This organization, not surprisingly headed by Laboulaye, was charged with promoting the statue project and overseeing all fund-raising. Laboulaye insisted that no financial help come from the national French government, instead soliciting funds from individual cities, with Paris and Le Havre making large contributions. Official fund-raising activities began with a banquet at the Hôtel du Louvre and included a benefit performance at the Paris Opera for which Charles-François Gounod composed a special cantata. A lottery was also instituted, and the Free Masons contributed to what was quickly viewed as a successful effort.

At this time Bartholdi was finalizing his thoughts on the design, which was to embody the theme "Liberty Enlightening the World." Since 1865 and the early days of Laboulaye and Bartholdi's ideas about the project, it was understood that exceptional size was a critical component of the design. Bartholdi had experience with oversized statues, but *Liberty* promised to explode the scale in which he and virtually all other sculptors worked. Not counting the pedestal, the figure of *Liberty* was planned to rise 151 feet from its base to the top of the torch. From the first she was to be dressed in Roman-style robes and sandals, wearing a crown with seven spikes representing the seven seas and seven continents, with her outstretched right hand holding a torch and her left hand clasping a tablet inscribed with the date of July 4, 1776. A broken chain, symbolizing the triumph of freedom, rested at her feet. Bartholdi used his mother as the model for *Liberty*'s face, and his mistress and future wife for her arms. Everything about the figure's design was colossal, from her four-foot-six-inch nose to her thirty-five-foot-thick waist to her sixteen-foot-five-inch hands.

The immense size of the statue posed problems for construction, but its intended site in Upper New York Bay, where the unprotected monument would be subjected to great temperature changes and high, salt-laden winds, provided even greater challenges.[16] Bartholdi chose copper for the statue because of its lightness, using more than three hundred separate sheets of three-thirty-seconds-of-an-inch-thick copper that in combination weighed in excess of one hundred tons. Although Bartholdi originally turned for engineering advice to his former teacher, the architect and theorist Eugène-Emmanuel Viollet-le-Duc, who suggested an ironwork armature above a system of compartments filled with sand, it was the engineer Gustave Eiffel, after Viollet-le-Duc's death, who perfected the structural system that was used. Eiffel designed a system around a central wrought-iron pylon running from the base of the statue with a separate girder attached to the main pylon to support the upthrust arm. Each section of the copper statue was supported independently, with no copper plate placing weight upon another. In order to avoid the phenomenon of galvanic action—the generation of an electric current if the copper of the statue and the iron of the

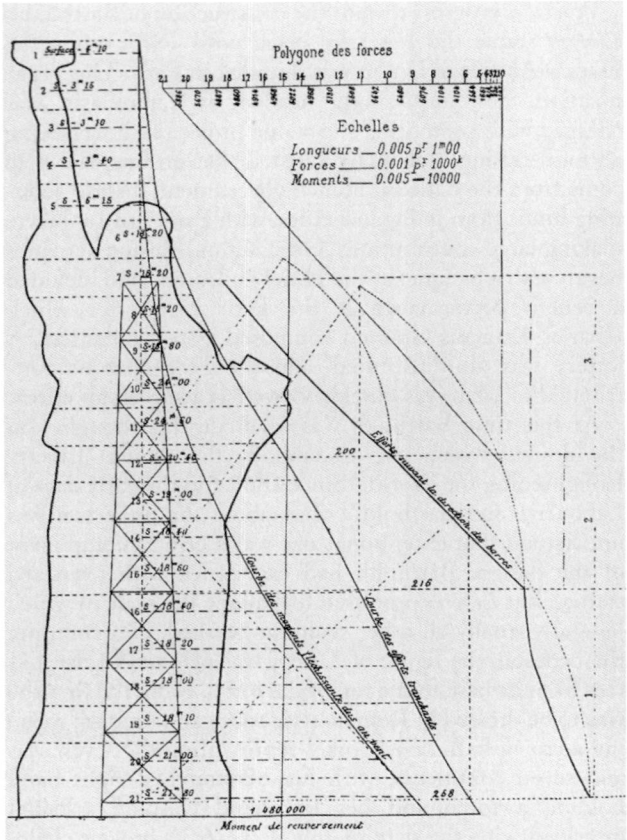

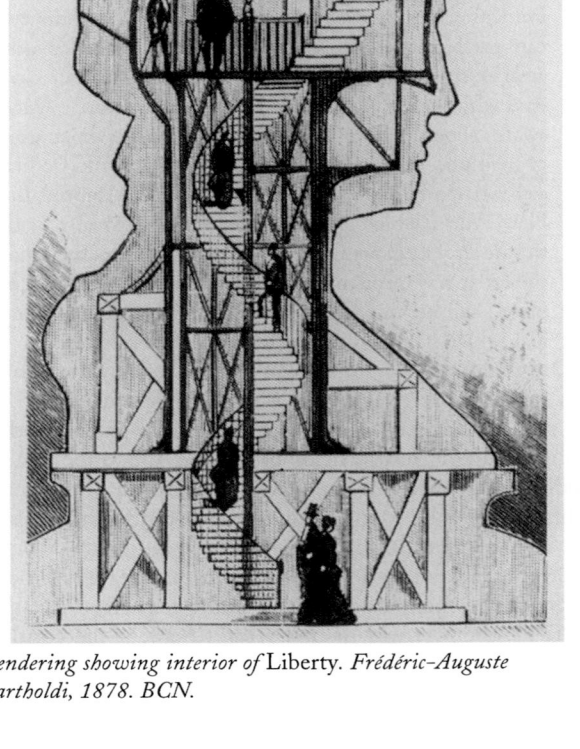

Diagram of Liberty *showing the stresses on the armature.*
Gustave Eiffel, 1883. BF.

Rendering showing interior of Liberty. *Frédéric-Auguste*
Bartholdi, 1878. BCN.

framework came in contact—Eiffel specified insulation of
asbestos impregnated with shellac. He also designed the
168-step staircase leading to *Liberty*'s head as well as a
smaller stairway in the arm supporting the torch.

Bartholdi's work, conducted in the Paris workshop of
Gaget, Gauthier & Co., proceeded rapidly. Beginning
with an approximately four-foot-tall model, he enlarged
the scale four times until he had made a plaster model
thirty-six feet in height, almost one-quarter the size of the
finished work. From this point on the model was enlarged
section by section until it reached full scale. Carpenters
created massive wooden molds and the thin sheets of copper were hammered inside the molds into the correct
shape in an ancient process known as repoussé, a technique
that Bartholdi had used with previous copper work.

To boost American fund-raising efforts, the completed
hand holding the torch was shipped to America in time for
display at the Centennial Exhibition, in Philadelphia, and
was later placed in Madison Square Park, in New York.[17]
While great progress on *Liberty* was achieved by the
French in both the fund-raising and construction arenas,
the situation in America in the mid-1870s was almost
exactly the opposite. Sentiment was noticeably lukewarm,
driven in part by local economic conditions but more by

the fact that the gift had never been formally accepted by
the federal government, nor had the donation of the site
and the promise to construct a pedestal been officially confirmed. By the late 1870s, however, the tide of public opinion began to turn in the project's favor. In an article chronicling Bartholdi's life, published in *Scribner's Monthly* in
1877, Charles de Kay offered an explanation for America's
apparent indifference to the undertaking:

> [Bartholdi's] statue of Liberty is not such as an American
> artist would be likely to erect. . . . Even if we can feel some
> pride as being a model to republics, we could hardly go so
> far as to erect a statue looking over toward Europe and call
> it "Liberty Enlightening the World." But when another
> nation puts it up for us, we cannot afford to refuse the honor
> with hypocritical disclaimers. For with individuals an exces-
> sive sensitiveness to a compliment is apt to argue some form
> of egotism,—self depreciation, let us say. Yet for all that, one
> would not hazard much to say that the general run of
> Americans are not as enthusiastic about this statue as they
> would have been; were its size smaller and its name more
> modest. Familiarity with republicanism or liberty of the
> American type breeds contempt, and Americans at home
> cannot be expected to regard their liberties with the same
> admiration as Americans and their foreign friends abroad.[18]

Sketch of proposed pedestal for Liberty. *Frédéric–Auguste Bartholdi, 1880. MB.*

Sketch of proposed pedestal for Liberty. *Attributed to Frédéric–Auguste Bartholdi, 1882. The Octagon, AAF.*

Sketch of proposed pedestal for Liberty. *Richard Morris Hunt, c. 1883. The Octagon, AAF.*

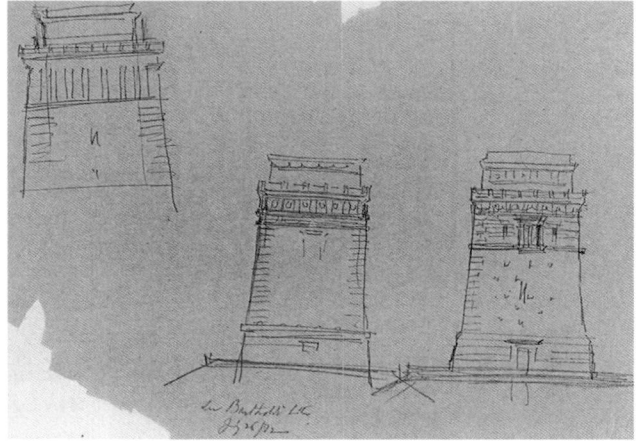

Sketches of proposed pedestal for Liberty. *Attributed to Frédéric–Auguste Bartholdi, 1882. The Octagon, AAF.*

Rendering of proposed pedestal for Liberty. *Richard Morris Hunt, c. 1883. The Octagon, AAF.*

A less high-minded explanation of American indifference was the fact that most citizens tended to view the statue as something for New York—it was often derisively described as "New York's lighthouse"—and not a truly national monument, no matter what the French envisioned. In addition, there was widespread distrust as to whether the French would live up to their side of the bargain and finish the statue.

In order to get the project moving on the American side, a parallel organization to Laboulaye's Franco-American Union was needed. This was provided early in 1877 with the establishment of the American Committee for the Statue, which assumed the duties of securing the site, raising funds, and choosing the architect and engineer for the pedestal as well as overseeing its construction.[19] The group was largely composed of members of New York's Union League Club, which essentially shared Laboulaye's political vision. The key members of the American Committee were the lawyer and Union League Club president John Jay; Richard Butler, a wealthy merchant; and the committee's chairman, William Maxwell Evarts, a prominent lawyer and future secretary of state as well as senator from New York. With the existence of an influential committee, originally composed of twenty members, the United States Congress was now ready to accept the gift as well as pledge to building an appropriate pedestal. As with the French effort, the national government authorized no funds to pay for the statue, relying on the American Committee to raise the money. General William T. Sherman was authorized by Congress to formally select the site and he quickly acceded to Bartholdi's wishes for Bedloe's Island.

From 1877 to 1881, the American Committee tried both to raise money for the pedestal as well as to stimulate national interest in the project. Their work was largely unsuccessful, with the largest donations coming from members of the American Committee itself or other Union League Club members. In contrast to the general inertia of the American Committee's early efforts was the

Sketch of Liberty *showing proposed base. Richard Morris Hunt, 1883. The Octagon, AAF.*

Model of Pharos I. *Richard Morris Hunt, 1883. The Octagon, AAF.*

Head of Liberty *(Frédéric-Auguste Bartholdi, 1875–78), displayed on the Champ de Mars, Paris, at the Exposition Universelle of 1878. SMB.*

Hand and torch of Liberty *(Frédéric-Auguste Bartholdi, 1875–76), displayed in Madison Square Park, 1876. NYHS.*

decision in 1881 to appoint Richard Morris Hunt as designer of the pedestal.[20] The prominent architect, who donated his one-thousand-dollar fee to the building effort, was a logical choice because of his impeccable connections in French and American artistic and social circles. Hunt's record of successful collaboration with sculptors, most notably his work with John Quincy Adams Ward, was very much in his favor. In addition, he was a long-standing member of the Union League Club and an intimate of the principal players on the American Committee. The committee also selected General Charles Stone as chief engineer.

Hunt's first step was to contact Bartholdi, who shared with the architect his thoughts on the pedestal, including preliminary designs the sculptor had made for a Doric pedestal placed on a stepped pyramid. But the design was left up to Hunt, who was guided by Stone's opinion that the existing star-shaped fort was the best spot for the pedestal's foundation. Hunt's basic challenge was to provide an appropriate backdrop for the sculpture that would not dominate Bartholdi's composition but would at the same time provide the necessary structural support and ensure the prominence that everyone desired for the

statue. Hunt's initial designs, which included a domed pedestal, date from 1882, at which time he was assisted in his office by Henry Ogden Avery, a young architect recently trained at the Ecole des Beaux-Arts, who prepared more alternate designs. By 1883 Hunt's first detailed model for a 114-foot-high version was ready. Dubbed *Pharos I* because of its resemblance to the ancient lighthouse in Alexandria, the gradually tapering, heavily rusticated mass, studded with projecting blocks, sat on a low plinth decorated with a Doric frieze. A triple loggia was set high on all four sides of the pedestal's shaft. A second version, which eliminated the Doric frieze and integrated the loggia with a heavy cornice located directly above, was produced in 1883–84. Objection to these designs was focused on their height, and later in 1884 Hunt settled on a final, eighty-nine-foot-high version.

One of the heaviest pieces of masonry every built, Hunt's truncated pyramid, ninety-one feet square at the base, had thick concrete walls and an exterior facing of granite from Leete's Island, Connecticut. Each side was treated identically and consisted of a deeply recessed loggia set above stone panels and flanked by heavily rusticated walls at the corners. The Neo-Grec details included a frieze of forty shields, representing the forty states in the Union, encircling the base. An observation platform set behind a bold parapet crowned the composition. Construction of the pedestal's foundation proceeded slowly as Fort Wood proved to be more solidly built than had been believed. In order to firmly anchor the statue, four steel girders were built into the walls twenty-nine feet above the base of the pedestal to form a square across the inside; this same arrangement of girders was repeated fifty-five feet higher, only a few feet from the top of the pedestal. The two sets were then connected by wrought-iron tie beams that continued beyond the pedestal to become part of the framework of the statue itself.

Montgomery Schuyler was impressed with Hunt's pedestal, believing that the architect had successfully walked a delicate design tightrope by not overpowering Bartholdi's statue but still producing his own monumental work:

> It is impossible to overlook, or to avoid looking at, the huge mass of masonry which serves as a substructure for the huge figure. In this instance not alone the architect, but the untrained observer, must take notice of the pedestal as something more than an accessory of the figure, so great and lofty is the mass required to give to the statue, as was the sculptor's evident intention, the same dominating relation to the upper bay of New York that is borne by a statue of merely heroic size to the plaza in which it stands. This has been so successfully done that one is apt not to think of the difficulties until they are brought to his attention, but these were in fact very considerable. To avoid on the one hand making the pedestal a mere brute mass and to avoid on the other such an elaboration as should make it appear an independent work to be looked at for its own sake—these were respectively the Scylla and Charybdis between which and clear of which the designer had to steer. It was fortunate that the island was already occupied by a fortification which might serve as an ample base for the pedestal, but it was not luck that gave the architect the perception of the value of this base and enabled him to make it an integral part of the composition. In fact it is the plinth of a structure of which the whole pedestal is the die and the statue the capital, while the pedestal has also its own triple division, and well avoids the extremes of crudity and of over-elaboration. Its proportions are not without felicity; its ornament, sparing as it is, yet suffices to emphasize the structure. It is in the right place and it helps to give the scale.[21]

While Hunt was designing the pedestal, the American Committee tried to revive its fund-raising efforts.[22] On November 28, 1882, they sponsored a meeting held at the National Academy of Design which attracted over six hundred prominent citizens. They also began to increase the size of the committee itself, ultimately naming about four hundred members. Although some progress was made, most Americans remained uninterested and clung

Liberty, *Bedloe's Island. Frédéric-Auguste Bartholdi, Gustave Eiffel, and Richard Morris Hunt, 1875–86. View to the north of the monument under construction. The Octagon, AAF.*

Liberty, *Bedloe's Island. Frédéric-Auguste Bartholdi, Gustave Eiffel, and Richard Morris Hunt, 1875–86. View to the northwest. The Octagon, AAF.*

Liberty, *Bedloe's Island. Frédéric-Auguste Bartholdi, Gustave Eiffel, and Richard Morris Hunt, 1875–86. View to the northwest during the inauguration ceremony, October 28, 1886. O'Neil. NYHS.*

to the view that the project was mostly for New York. The fund-raising activities sponsored and encouraged by the American Committee included art auctions, raffles, banquets, and benefit balls, which served to reinforce the notion that the whole enterprise was just another high-society plaything rather than a celebration of liberty and friendship. This impression was exemplified by the photograph of Mrs. Cornelius Vanderbilt holding a torch aloft in her guise as "The Electric Light," the costume she wore to the famous fancy-dress ball given by her sister-in-law Mrs. William K. Vanderbilt in honor of the completion of her new Fifth Avenue mansion, designed by Richard Morris Hunt (see chapter 4). In connection with an 1883 fund-raising event, Emma Lazarus, a thirty-four-year-old poet active in relief efforts for immigrants, who had been published in *Scribner's Monthly* and *Lippincott's Magazine,* composed a poem, "The New Colossus," which, in twenty years' time, would be inscribed on a tablet and placed on the pedestal.[23] Even as construction was under way, the Franco-American Union, in an effort to prod the American Committee to action, went so far as to suggest that an alternate site be chosen if not enough funds could be raised to complete the pedestal on Bedloe's Island.[24]

In the fall of 1884 lack of funds forced the temporary

suspension of work on the pedestal, which had only reached fifteen feet. American Committee members contributed more of their own funds but something else needed to be done to raise the additional $100,000 deemed necessary for completion. The French were growing impatient and the statue itself was ready, having been officially presented to Levi P. Morton, the American ambassador to France, on July 4, 1884, in a ceremony in Paris.[25]

In 1885, in a brilliant scheme that not only raised the necessary funds but also increased his own empire and standing, Joseph B. Pulitzer, publisher of the *New York World,* aggressively solicited money for the pedestal, in effect turning the table on the country's indifference by reminding New Yorkers that their responsibility was to achieve a project of national importance. Pulitzer printed the names of all contributors in the *World* and circulation on his paper soared. In less than five months over 121,000 donors, the majority of them New Yorkers, contributed more than $100,000. Besides raising money, Pulitzer was also able to remove the stigma that the statue was only a project of the very rich and, in so doing, remind the country of the sculpture's idealistic roots and potential symbolic power. An editorial in the *World* on August 11, 1885, the day that Pulitzer

Liberty, *Bedloe's Island. Frédéric-Auguste Bartholdi, Gustave Eiffel, and Richard Morris Hunt, 1875–86. Night view to the northwest. Stoddard. NYHS.*

announced that the $100,000 goal had been reached, was clear:

> The great bulk of this money is out of the hard-earned savings of the poor. It was the love of Liberty that broke into the box of pennies and brought the earnings from the widow's home and the children's little bank. . . . The magnificent lesson of this now completed work lies here in the hearts of the people, which turned instinctively to the idea of Liberty and responded promptly to a call that involved National Honor. The Statue itself gains an inestimable value from this fact. It is not only an ideal of Liberty, but an attestation of Liberty in every stone.[26]

With American efforts at last up to speed the French began dismantling *Liberty* for its voyage to America. Each piece was carefully marked for reassembly and placed in one of 214 specially designed crates ranging in weight from 150 pounds to over three tons. Traveling by train to Rouen the boxes were placed aboard the frigate *Isère*, donated by the French government, which set sail on May 21, 1885, arriving in Sandy Hook almost a month later, at which time the crates were transferred to Bedloe's Island, where work was still under way on the pedestal.[27] On April 22, 1886, the pedestal was finished and the reassembly of the statue began.[28] Due to the awkward size of the base, workers hung from the armature itself during this operation and no scaffolding was used. Work proceeded relatively smoothly and only the issue of lighting the statue remained. This was resolved to no one's satisfaction with arc lamps placed inside the torch after circular holes had been cut and covered with glass. Besides providing an inadequate supply of light, especially for a monument charged with "enlightening the world," this solution, donated by Edward Goff of the American Electric Manufacturing Company, also compromised the statue's structural integrity. The lighting of the statue was not changed until 1916.

The official inauguration of *Liberty* was set for October 28, 1886.[29] France was represented by Bartholdi, who was pleased with the reassembly work, and Ferdinand de Lesseps, the well-known designer of the Suez Canal, who had become head of the Franco-American Union after Laboulaye's death, in 1883. Unable to see the statue completed, Laboulaye at least lived long enough to see a republican government in France. The day of the statue's inauguration was declared a public holiday. Unfortunately it was foggy and a fine drizzle fell over the parade, which proceeded down Broadway to the Battery and was estimated to have drawn a crowd of close to one million. A flotilla of ships carried invited guests to Bedloe's Island for the festivities. Bartholdi was given a position of honor, stationed in *Liberty*'s crown and charged with the responsibility of removing the French flag that covered the statue's face, at the end of President Grover Cleveland's speech. The sculptor inadvertently missed his cue and dropped the flag during William Maxwell Evarts's speech but decorum was eventually restored and Cleveland gave his talk. Due to the inclement weather, a fireworks display was postponed, as was the lighting of the torch.

Reaction to the completed *Liberty* was overwhelmingly favorable. Even more than that of the Brooklyn Bridge, the dedication of *Liberty* was a national occasion, putting a lie to the cynicism of its original detractors. It was evident to all that, though inspired by French partisan politics, the statue was less a symbol of Franco-American amity than of American freedom. The *New York World*, which had done so much to see to the completion of *Liberty*, got it just right in an editorial, "The Lesson of the Statue," written to commemorate the opening:

> Yesterday's impressive demonstration has a significance beyond a successful celebration of a public event. It marks an era in the history of republican government. It was the recognition of the romance of the century. . . . From the moment this proof of the patriotism of the masses was given [in the *World*'s successful fund-raising campaign] the real interest in the French gift dates its birth. People began to appreciate for the first time the noble sentiment embodied in the offering. They recognized in the mighty Statue an emblem of the growing strength of the cause of freedom among the peoples of the earth. . . . For the torch of the great Statue is not illumined by the glare of Error but by the blaze of Truth; not by a fire to destroy but by a flame to lighten—a flame that will reach across the ocean and, penetrating the darkness of oppression, will enable the people of all nations to see how to build such an edifice of Liberty as that which the France of Lafayette's day helped so much to erect.[30]

WORLD'S FAIR

Between the Civil War and World War I, world's fairs exerted a tremendous influence on the United States, principally in regard to the country's economic power, its international status, and its restless popular imagination.[1] World's fairs gave American business an opportunity to show new wares and mechanical innovations as well as to establish markets for those goods and services; fairs equally provided a showcase for new artistic, architectural, and urbanistic forms. During a time in the nation's history marked by convulsive boom-and-bust economic cycles, national soul-searching, and the perceived threat of large-scale, organized class conflict, fairs also constituted temporary model communities in which socioeconomically diverse segments of the nation could learn about—and act out—acceptable modes of social conduct. Beyond all of these goals and repercussions, ranging from the frankly bottom-line-oriented to the supremely utopian, world's fairs were a very big draw. In the forty years following the nation's Centennial, in 1876, almost one hundred million people attended world's fairs held in a dozen American cities.

The Centennial Exhibition, in Philadelphia, which opened on May 10, 1876, was both quantitatively and qualitatively different from the American fairs that preceded it, including the New York World's Fair of 1853, most memorable for its Crystal Palace, an interpretation

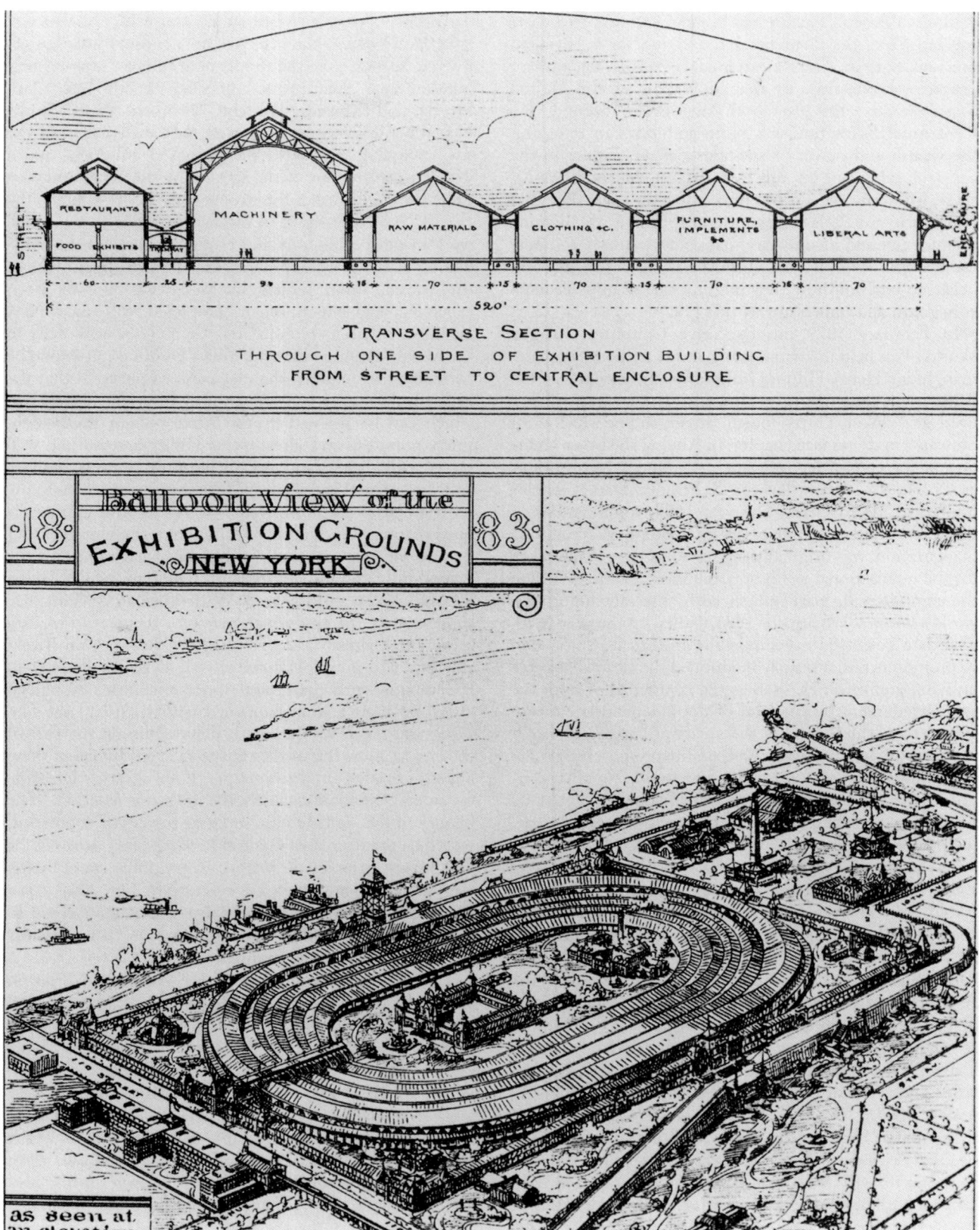

STREET · RESTAURANTS · FOOD EXHIBITS · TRAMWAY · MACHINERY · RAW MATERIALS · CLOTHING &C. · FURNITURE, IMPLEMENTS &C. · LIBERAL ARTS · ENCLOSURE

60 · 15 · 90 · 15 · 70 · 15 · 70 · 15 · 70 · 15 · 70

520'

TRANSVERSE SECTION
THROUGH ONE SIDE OF EXHIBITION BUILDING
FROM STREET TO CENTRAL ENCLOSURE

·18· Balloon View of the EXHIBITION GROUNDS NEW YORK ·83·

as seen at an elevation

*Proposed New York World's Fair of 1883, Morningside, Tenth, and Manhattan Avenues to Riverside Drive, West 110th to West 127th
Street. William G. Preston, 1880. Section of main exhibition building and aerial perspective showing view to the northwest. AABN. CU.*

of the one Joseph Paxton had built in London two years earlier.[2] First, the Centennial Exhibition far outstripped previous fairs in terms of attendance: nearly ten million people—or one-fifth of the population of the United States—visited the six-month-long event. Second, the Centennial Exhibition was more ambitious in reflecting the wealth and power of an industrialized nation on the verge of exhibiting its full maturity on the international stage. Ironically, the fair was held at just the same time that New York, not Philadelphia, was emerging as the nation's premier city and its only city that could seriously compete for the title "world class." Influential New Yorkers soon began to envision how they might stage an unprecedentedly grand and impressive world's fair.

In February 1879 the Executive Committee of the World's Fair held its first meeting, at the home of its chairman, Judge Henry Hilton.[3] Hilton was the executor of the department store magnate Alexander T. Stewart's will and lived at 7 West Thirty-fourth Street, in the shadow of Stewart's mansion (see chapter 4). Among the other members of the committee were such prominent New Yorkers as Charles L. Tiffany, Jackson S. Schultz, Daniel Appleton, and Edward Clark. The year 1889, commemorating the one-hundredth anniversary of George Washington's inauguration, was originally suggested as the possible date for the international exhibition, but within a month's time the committee, in part influenced by the scheduling of a world's fair in Germany for 1885, settled on the year 1883. The date possessed no compelling historical justification so promoters rather quietly mentioned the various possible unifying anniversaries, such as the centennial of both the acknowledgment by England of the independence of the colonies and the signing of the Treaty of Paris. But historical memory was not really high on the promoters' agenda: their motivation was primarily economic. New Yorkers, influenced by the success of Philadelphia's Centennial Exhibition, wished to take advantage of the nation's growing prosperity.

The first order of business was the selection of a site. Early proposals included the "sloping point" of Staten Island between New Brighton and West New Brighton, championed for its easy access from a variety of different locations and its "magnificent water front" setting;[4] Manhattan Square, which was advocated by the director of the American Museum of Natural History; Washington Heights; lands adjoining Brooklyn's Prospect Park as well as portions of that park itself;[5] and Port Morris, which Calvert Vaux and George K. Radford recommended in a letter published in the *New York Daily Tribune*, a largely undeveloped, 170-acre tract in the southeastern corner of the Annexed District. According to Vaux and Radford the site was "especially desirable" because its situation could "minister directly to that need for a change of air in connection with agreeable scenery which is so widely felt in the United States during our hot weather."[6] But the initial favorite of Judge Hilton's committee would prove to be the most controversial: Central Park.[7]

Another possible Manhattan site, which *Demorest's Monthly Magazine* characterized as "almost as little known to New Yorkers as to the residents of Illinois," was a three-hundred-acre tract located between 110th and 125th Streets and Morningside and Riverside Parks. In its November 1879 issue, *Demorest's* published a map of the site, including a view of the proposed buildings, and a detailed explanation of the locale's presumed advantages: "The site . . . furnishes the strongest motive possible to the city of New York itself, in the fact that the plan . . . will work in most admirably and economically with the completion of the great improvements upon the upper part of the island, upon which so much has already been expended, and which, when completed, will make New York more than a second Paris, the most beautiful city in the world." Arguing that the "finest buildings . . . would be permanent structures," the magazine emphasized that the centrally located site, "seven miles from the City Hall, which can be reached by the Metropolitan Railroad in thirty minutes," was already thoroughly drained and well served with "water and gas for lighting, heating, sanitary and ornamental purposes." Most important, considering its Manhattan location, was the site's relatively undeveloped nature: "The buildings at present occupying that section of the city are small, and of little account, with the exception of the Lunatic Asylum buildings, which can be used as offices, and Leake & Watts Orphan Asylum, also supported by the city, which may be left intact." Property owners had already been assessed for the work on Riverside and Morningside Parks as well as the roads built in conjunction with them, and those alterations would go ahead no matter what happened with regard to the fair. *Demorest's* felt it would be a brilliant coup on the part of the city to allow the world's fair to take advantage of these already funded improvements. Even given the still-considerable remaining costs, the magazine asserted: "The history of the World's Fair, so far as the city is concerned, would be the history of Central Park repeated. It would be like bread cast upon the waters. Every dollar spent by the city would meet with a large return."[8] The *Real Estate Record and Builders' Guide* was also favorably disposed to the Morningside site, observing that it "has certainly strong claims for consideration."[9]

The prominent Boston architect William G. Preston also took up the cause of the upper Manhattan site, designing a version of the heavily engineered glass-and-metal oval that had been built for the Exposition Universelle of 1867, in Paris, for the same location described in *Demorest's*.[10] Preston, who probably visited the Paris fair while a student at the Ecole des Beaux-Arts, called for a hippodrome plan of heavily glazed sheds, half of which would house the American exhibit with the remainder given over to foreign countries. At the hollow center of the hippodrome would be a freestanding art gallery set in a park. At the four corners of the site small individual pavilions would represent America, Asia, Europe, and, combined in one, Africa and Australia. North of 121st Street, where the site narrowed, individual buildings set in greenery would be devoted to agriculture and horticulture; also in this area an iron foundry, cotton factory, and glass factory would be grouped around a music pavilion. Preston's plan included the construction of a spur leading from the Ninth Avenue elevated to a fair terminal at Tenth Avenue and 110th Street.

Adding to the confusion over site selection was bickering over who would organize the fair, with a second group formed to challenge Judge Hilton's committee, started by the United States Board of Trade and headed by Ellwood E. Thorne.[11] A third group, the West Side Association, which had been founded a few years earlier by Dwight H. Olmstead to aid local property owners, also decided to devote its energies to picking a world's fair site.[12] Even within Hilton's executive committee there was disagreement over the locale, with Hilton favoring Central Park and the group's subcommittee on sites, which included Jackson S. Schultz and Charles L. Tiffany, leaning toward Port Morris.[13] Except for innumerable meetings of all three organizations between May 1879 and the end of the year, and a public meeting at Chickering Hall in January 1880 (poorly attended according to the *New York Times* but well attended according to the *New York Daily Tribune*), nothing much was accomplished and certainly no consensus was reached in regard to a possible site by the new year.[14]

While the *Times* was cool to the fair, the *Tribune* was optimistic about its chances: "There seems to be no reason now why the project for a World's Fair in New York in 1883 should not be pressed forward to a successful result," the paper editorialized in January 1880. But, the *Tribune* warned, "Three years are long enough to organize an International Exhibition if the time is zealously employed, but not a week can safely be lost after the Spring opens."[15]

On March 31, 1880, the United States Senate passed a bill authorizing the formation of a corporation to develop a world's fair in New York; the House passed the measure three weeks later and President Hayes signed it in May.[16] Although the bill was the one pushed by the Board of Trade's committee, an amendment to the original bill, intended to prevent any future squabbling, placed all members of Hilton's committee on the one-hundred-member New York delegation to the commission created to oversee the fair. The commission, authorized to raise twelve million dollars through the issue of capital stock and bonds, also included two members from each state and one representative from each territory and the District of Columbia.

Even after the commissioners had their first organizational meeting, in August 1880, the process of site selection dragged on, in large part because no funds had been raised.[17] The northern end of Central Park continued to be a favorite proposed site. About this choice the *New York Times* rather cynically editorialized: "It is quite true that six months of a great Exhibition might do no more injuring to the Park than has been done by three or four years of the neglect and mismanagement of the incapable and unscrupulous set of tricksters who by the grace of [city comptroller and Tammany Hall head] John Kelly, control

the Department of Parks. But," the *Times* thundered on, "the people will never deliberately decree the ruin of Central Park, were the necessity ten times more pressing than that involved in providing a site for a World's Fair."[18] In fact, the *Times* argued, the fair should not be located on Manhattan Island at all but in some part of the newly annexed territories. The *Tribune* agreed with the *Times*, declaring that "there must be no desecration of [Central] Park," and urged the selection of Port Morris, "which is not only good by comparison with others now offered, but it is positively an improvement upon any and all of those where the great Fairs of the world have been held."[19]

Meanwhile, the *Real Estate Record and Builders' Guide* began to conceptualize the fair: "Let the buildings be entirely unlike any other International Fair ever held. Why not have the several edifices represent distinct types of architecture, Egyptian, Doric, Corinthian, Gothic, Moorish and Modern, so that the inspection of the various structures would in itself be an art education?"[20] Others argued that the fair not be housed in temporary buildings but, as with the permanent reconstruction of Paxton's Crystal Palace in Sydenham, near London, have structures built "to serve admirably as a grand series of winter gardens."[21] This was an idea that appealed to the prominent journalist David G. Croly, who proposed in a letter to the Executive Committee of the World's Fair that the exhibition buildings be designed so that they could be converted to use as a sanatorium, or "Hygiearium," the term he preferred. Such a building, featuring special microclimates suited to curing various diseases, "could be used not only for health but pleasure. It could be a resort. . . . It would involve grounds and walks, room for bicycle contests, cricket, ball, athletic exercises, croquet parties and lawn tennis. . . . The amusements from the outside world would help to enliven the invalids."[22]

On December 1, 1880, the United States International Commission bowed to public pressure and removed the Central Park site from consideration.[23] A week later the commission proposed that the fair be located on a 250-acre tract in Inwood, at the northern tip of Manhattan Island, with one mile of frontage on King's Bridge Road.[24] But this prospect also met with objections and the long-awaited decision did little to move matters along. "The choice of the Inwood Hollow has certainly not called forth any enthusiastic indorsement from the people or the press," the *New York Daily Tribune* noted on December 26, 1880. "It may have merits, but they are unobtrusive, and a common-sense community has the right to demand common-sense reasons for its selection." The *Tribune* began to wonder, given the return of prosperity, whether the fair, in part conceived as a stimulus to economic activity, would take place at all:

> Two years ago there was a genuine popular interest in the project for a World's Fair. Since then Congress has been induced to pass an elaborate act creating a Commission which was supposed to be a conglomerate of two separate efforts to enunciate the fact that New York needed and

demanded an exhibition. The business prosperity which was only promised then has actually come, and the arguments to prove the advantages which the city would reap from the enterprise are as forcible now as they were when the Commission was appointed. And yet, to-day, the public interest in the undertaking is apparently dying or dead. In view of this patent fact, it is possible that the Fair may be postponed or abandoned.[25]

Absent any strong leadership, General Ulysses S. Grant's name began to emerge as one who might give the fair a more positive direction.[26] Grant, who was president from 1869 to 1877 and had spent the two years after leaving office on a world tour, had just failed in an attempt to secure the Republican nomination for a third, nonconsecutive term, losing on the thirty-sixth ballot. He came to New York late in 1880, ostensibly to make money, setting up residence in a brownstone at 3 East Sixty-sixth Street purchased for him by friends. At the time he was appointed president of the world's fair commission, in January 1881, he was a partner in the ultimately disastrous brokerage firm of Grant & Ward.[27] Grant's brief tenure in the role—he resigned three months later, on March 24, 1881—was symptomatic of the organization as a whole, which quickly fell apart.[28] Only one month after Grant's resignation, the New York Times gloatingly editorialized that the world's fair "project is apparently on its death bed."[29] This failure could not only be attributed to the lack of a clear national purpose, such as the Centennial Exhibition in Philadelphia had possessed, or a clear consensus on the site. Given the high tariffs charged on foreign goods, foreign manufacturers could see no purpose in spending money to introduce their wares to a public that could not afford them, and the prosperity the fair might bring to the city was not now needed with the booming economy. The New York Daily Tribune was even more glib in its assessment of events but was at least genuinely disappointed: "'Now you see it and now you don't,' describes pretty accurately the condition of the New York World's Fair project. . . . If the Fair is not dead it is plainly in a moribund condition. A change of doctors and of medicines might possibly save it, but we fear there is no hope."[30] The Tribune's editors proved correct and an attempt in late summer and fall of 1881 to revive interest in the fair also failed.[31]

In rejoicing over the collapse of plans for an 1883 fair, the New York Times suggested that 1887, the centennial of the ratification of the Constitution, might be a more appropriate year.[32] While this idea did not appear to inspire the citizenry, in 1887 plans began to percolate for a fair to be held in 1890, with many arguing for permanent exhibition grounds that would attract tourists. As Building magazine put it: "New York . . . has but little really to attract visitors. New Orleans, St. Louis, and Montreal have all drawn largely on our sightseers by special attractions. . . . Singers, actors, lecturers can be heard anywhere, and the great Sullivan [the pugilist] does not confine himself to Madison Square Garden."[33] But plans for an international exhibition in 1890 did not materialize. It was not

until the successful celebration in the city in 1889 of the centenary of George Washington's inauguration as the nation's first president—ironically the original motivating idea of the first world's fair committee, in 1879—that interest was stimulated for a world's fair to be held in 1892 to celebrate the four-hundredth anniversary of Christopher Columbus's arrival in the Americas.[34] Also, the huge success of Paris's Exposition Universelle of 1889 spurred interest in an American world's fair. This time real estate interests and public watchdogs were in agreement that Central Park was not an appropriate site, although the newly acquired parklands in the Annexed District, especially Van Cortlandt and Pelham Bay Parks, were both deemed quite suitable.[35] Barretto Point, just north of Port Morris, was also considered.[36] A committee was soon formed to spearhead the fair and Mayor Hugh Grant was besieged with proposals.[37]

The kinds of problems that plagued preparations for the 1883 fair soon surfaced but with one notable difference: now there was serious competition from several cities interested in hosting the fair. In fact, as early as 1887 the National Board of Trade had proposed a world exposition to be held in Washington, D.C., to celebrate Columbus's voyage.[38] Other cities with designs on the fair included Minneapolis, St. Louis, and Chicago. The contest quickly narrowed to New York and Chicago. Confident of its city's victory, the New York Times was dismissive of the challenge: "Such an attempt to seize and appropriate the project after it had been started in New York was hardly dignified in the metropolis of the West, and it has met with very little sympathy elsewhere. It was the offspring of that civic pride and ambition which are so characteristic of Chicago, but any persistency in it will put that noble city in a ridiculous attitude."[39] The New York Daily Tribune agreed and the debate between the two cities became ugly: "New York will derive a direct and practical advantage from the attempt to prove that the Western metropolis is the proper place for the fair, inasmuch as it will certainly result in convincing the world that the pretence is ridiculous. Outside of that city it doesn't seem to have occurred to a single human being that Chicago is qualified for the undertaking. . . . A varied and instructive exhibition of hog products might unquestionably be held in Chicago, but it would be absurd upon the face of it to establish a World's Fair a thousand miles from the seaboard."[40] The mudslinging boosterism continued and the description of Chicago as "the windy city" was born of the contentious competition.[41]

The issue of site selection was again the most hotly debated point in New York, with many of the locales suggested for the 1883 fair endorsed a second time.[42] At a September 20, 1889, meeting of the Committee on Site and Buildings, one of four committees set up by the mayor—the others being finance, legislation, and permanent organization—a resolution was passed recommending that a site "be selected from the lands between Ninety-seventh and One Hundred and Twenty-seventh streets, Fourth-avenue, and the North River, comprising Morningside and Riverside Parks and the intermediate lands, and, if necessary, Central Park north of the large reservoir and the lands adjacent to those of Central Park."[43] The mention of Central Park again created a controversy, drawing the opposition of many, including Andrew Haswell Green and William Waldorf Astor, but not Richard Morris Hunt. When Hunt argued that Paris typically used its parks for its expositions, Astor countered: "The case is different. Paris is a city of parks, New York has really only one park."[44] But Hunt had a cautious ally whose point of view could not be ignored. This was Frederick Law Olmsted, the park's designer along with Calvert Vaux. In a letter to the *New York Times*, Olmsted flatly rejected any serious rebuilding of the park or disruption of the North Meadows but did allow for some encroachment: "If the fair is to centre on a plot connecting Riverside and Morningside Parks, the Central Park will be a fine attachment to it, and it is probable that localities could be found in the Park for the exhibition of objects not required to stand in systematic connection with any of the classified exhibits. Buildings of moderate size for temporary use might be placed in it."[45]

Like the December 1880 decision to hold the 1883 fair in Inwood, this choice for a Manhattan site did little to settle the issue and did almost nothing to unite the city, which was experiencing political problems owing to division in Republican ranks compounded by conflicts with Tammany Hall.[46] While debate raged over the site and some progress was made in the raising of funds,[47] the Architectural League held its third annual drawing competition for draftsmen under the age of twenty-five, assigning as the subject an "Entrance for a World's Fair."[48] Julius Harder won the gold medal, with the silver going to Claude Bragdon. The *Real Estate Record and Builders' Guide* admired the entry of Charles H. Israels, the youngest competitor.

Meanwhile, the city of Chicago, in the final stages of recovering from the disastrous fire of 1871 and anxious to thrust itself onto the larger public stage, made great strides in its attempt to impress the federal government and win the right to host the fair. Not only had Chicago issued over five million dollars in bonds by the middle of August 1889, but that city's delegation also began lobbying Congress a full five weeks before the New York group arrived. Still, New Yorkers and New York institutions remained supremely confident in their city's prospects, perhaps because they were unable to conceive of defeat at the hands of what they considered a backwater and perhaps because of the public involvement of so many of New York's most prominent citizens, including Chauncey Depew, president of the New York Central Railroad, William Waldorf Astor, J. Pierpont Morgan, Cornelius Vanderbilt II, William Rockefeller, Jay Gould, Elihu Root, and August Belmont. Chicago, though a provincial city, nonetheless boasted a stable of influential millionaires who were dedicated to bringing the fair to the Midwest, including Philip Armour, Gustavus Swift, Cyrus McCormick, George Pullman, and Marshall Field.

"There is very little doubt now that the World's Fair will be held in New York City," the *Real Estate Record and Builders' Guide* declared on February 22, 1890. "Apart from the geographical, social and mercantile advantages which the metropolis possesses over rival cities, the fact that she alone does not appeal to Congress as a beggar for national assistance to carry out the World's Fair project gives her request a weight that is in all human probability irresistible."[49] The magazine was almost right and New York came within a hair of getting the exhibition. After initially rejecting Chicago's proposal, the congressional committee in charge of the decision appeared to be on the verge of selecting New York. But they gave the Chicago delegation a second chance, with the proviso that it raise another five million dollars in twenty-four hours. Lyman Gage, president of the First National Bank and head of Chicago's lobbying effort, was able to get the necessary pledges, and on February 24, on the eighth ballot, Chicago was declared the winner in the House of Representatives.[50] One month later President Benjamin Harrison signed the exposition bill into law.

Reaction in New York was swift and angry but it was the previously confident editors of the *Record and Guide* who seemed most shaken, taking the occasion of the defeat to reassess a city they usually viewed through boosters' eyes:

> After this New York should learn the lesson, or rather the lessons, which her defeat teaches. No matter what some of the causes that led to her defeat may have been, the fact that New York *could* be defeated, and defeated easily too, could be deliberately passed by, shows that her importance in national affairs is relatively not by any means as great as it was. She now has rivals who, no matter how extravagant their claims may be, can dispute, and in this case did dispute successfully, her position as the chief city of the country. . . . Is she pre-eminently the centre of the intelligence and culture of the nation? Are her streets the most magnificent, her public works the most complete, her museums and libraries and schools the finest? Let anyone who thinks so turn to our poverty-stricken municipal buildings, monuments of steals and jobs; our dark, filthy, badly-paved streets; our imperfect rapid transit, the general inadequacy of nearly everything municipal, and then point out what we have that is truly worthy of a city that aspires to be the metropolis of the country. But then we have the money, and, let it be added, a stupendous indifference to defects and evils which should not be tolerated for an instant by a civilized community, a fatuous self-satisfaction, a marvelous lack of real public-spiritedness, and a government which, considered as a whole, produces less for a given amount than any other under the sun.[51]

A new attitude toward the public realm was called for, and in the decades ahead, New York would develop an enlightened civicism, unparalleled and unprecedented in the United States, elevating itself into what was without question the country's most important metropolis—in many ways, its de facto capital.

New York Life Insurance Company Building, 346 Broadway. Griffith Thomas, 1868–70. View to the southeast. MCNY.

CHAPTER 3

❧ Workplaces ❧

In New York, closed in by rivers, pressing desperately toward the business center at its southern end, and characterized by an unparalleled fierceness in money-chasing, land is dear. This of course makes the possession of it a basis for an increased ostentation of it; for the greater a thing is, the more pride in showing it, and wonder in staring at it.

—Walt Whitman, 1856[1]

The old policy of conducting business in a rookery is dying out, and New York is building up a series of business palaces which will be without a rival in any city on the globe. Once it was thought that money spent in such improvements was wasted, but experience has shown that a liberal expenditure in architecture is a good investment. In view of this change of public opinion, our businessmen are building up to the clouds, and covering the ground with blocks that are a city in themselves. In time we shall have markets, depots, and warehouses that will absorb trade to themselves, and drive out of sight the low and unsightly piles that so long have disgraced our streets.

—*New York Daily Graphic*, 1873[2]

THE RISE OF THE OFFICE BUILDING

Despite almost a century of historical discussion intended to establish the modern office building as the virtually inevitable result of technological innovation, the fact remains that the elevator and the metal structural frame had been developed before the Civil War but no one had thought to put them together in a building of unusual height.[3] Two impulses more than any other led to the development of the tall building: the drive to maximize the return on land and the desire to symbolically represent the essentially abstract activities of corporate enterprise. Before the Civil War, businesses and professionals contented themselves with quarters in converted residences along lower Broadway or Wall Street that were frequently referred to as rookeries.[4] After the war, the explosion of white-collar business activities created a need for increasingly large amounts of centrally located work space to house lawyers, accountants, realtors, and their increasingly immense armies of support staff—clerks, secretaries, office boys, and messengers. This shift was amplified by the almost compulsive desire to use architecture to impress the public with the vitality, stability, and even the permanence and civic value of large businesses. Motivated by these two ends, architects pushed to create ever more individualistic designs despite the fact that at its most basic the commercial building was little more than an undifferentiated loft or warehouse. Russell Sturgis was moved to claim that the

"'Office Building' and the private office are to us what the church was to medieval Europe, the typical buildings from which our modern architecture must shape itself, if, indeed, it is capable of taking any shape."[5] Taken together, the new world of office work, the drive to make a statement, and the increasing rise of land values pushed architects to take advantage of hitherto untapped technologies, imaginatively combining them to form a new building type—the tall office building, with its crowning subset, the skyscraper.

Post–Civil War New Yorkers, their pockets swelled with the cheap money of the Bonanza economy, set out to make a splash with architecture. That they built lavish houses and hotels was not unusual. What was surprising, given the hitherto tightfisted utilitarianism of American businessmen, was the construction of grand buildings that monumentalized the workplace and celebrated commerce. The office building was a new type. Though it had regularity and flexibility in common with the loft or warehouse, or their consumer-oriented offshoot, the department store, the office building required far more access to natural light. While the department store needed daylight to favorably display goods, its large floors were unpartitioned and interrupted only by structural columns. If department stores were of exceptional size, such as Alexander T. Stewart's cast-iron building (John Kellum, 1862–70) (see chapter 5), they featured glazed rotundas to bring light into the center. The office building, on the other hand, needed to provide light and ventilation to individuals, usually working singly or in small groups in cubicles. Office workers relied on daylight also to facilitate their principal business activities—meeting each other and writing and rewriting by hand the endless documents that were the essential instruments of business exchange.

Insurance Headquarters

Insurance companies, along with newspaper and communications companies, the representative city-based businesses of the dramatically expansive postwar economy, pioneered the modern office building type. No business, except perhaps banking, had more need to convince the public of its stability. Because it drew so much of its capital from average people, the insurance industry used every means available to reassure the public that their investments would be honored in the future. Enjoying spectacular growth in the 1860s, the insurance business, as Henry-Russell Hitchcock observed, was "the first to seek dignity and architectural display by employing architects of established reputation."[6] With their great pools of capital, insurance companies could afford to build well, and, with their need to reach out to sell their product to as many Americans as possible, they were receptive to the idea that architecture could contribute to marketing and public relations. As a result, throughout the Gilded Age insurance company headquarters dominated the city's skyline, leading M. F. Sweetser, author of an 1894 guidebook, to glowingly claim that "beside their benevolent work, these life corporations have been among the prime causes of the city's architectural growth, for the life insurance buildings of New York surpass the office structures of any

Proposed Mutual Life Insurance Company Building, 140 Broadway. Russell Sturgis and Peter B. Wight, c. 1863. Elevation. AIC.

city in the world. Life insurance is indeed one of the vital features of modern life, in which New York City alone leads any nation on the face of the earth."[7]

John B. Snook's grandly scaled Manhattan Life Insurance Company Building (1865), at 156–158 Broadway, developed by the hotelier David H. Haight, was the first of the postwar insurance buildings.[8] With four stories and a basement, it was very much in keeping with the kind of business environment that had suited New York for so long. At first glance the building was residential in character, although the palatial scale of its imposing, Italianate, white marble Broadway facade, with its regular fenestration and elevated entrance, also suggested that the structure's principal tenant was an economic force to be reckoned with. The front office spaces were in fact reserved for small tenants, with Manhattan Life thriftily accommodated in the less desirable rear, where a grand, twenty-six-foot-tall, sixty-by-forty-foot domed room, embellished with pilasters, pedestals, and entablature in the Corinthian order, echoed the typical arrangement of a bank—for example, the Bank of New York (Vaux & Withers, 1856–58) (see below)—more than compensating for the inconspicuous location. At the end of this room, the company president surveyed the entire operation from an elevated dais surrounded by an ornamental enclosure.

While the character and spatial organization of Manhattan Life's headquarters were virtually interchangeable with those of a bank, John Kellum's Mutual Life Insurance Company (1863–65), at 140 Broadway, provided a more distinctly commercial design.[9] The building established a standard for large office blocks that would prevail until the emergence of the mature skyscraper type in the late 1880s. Kellum's four-story, lushly detailed, marble-faced building piled floor upon floor of closely spaced arcaded windows until it reached a bracketed galvanized-iron cornice ninety-two feet above ground. Kellum accommodated the needs of a bureaucratic enterprise with a design that gave his clients, the nation's oldest operating and largest mutual company, a specifically "businesslike" corporate identity. Mutual Life occupied only two floors; the American Bank Note Company was a principal tenant, occupying more than a quarter of the building's available space. Extant records of preconstruction negotiations between Mutual Life and American Bank Note suggest that this may have been the earliest example of a process that has since become all but typical in developing new commercial office space.

In addition to Kellum, four architects were invited to compete for the job, with each offered one hundred dollars for his trouble. The proposals of Leopold Eidlitz, Griffith Thomas, Samuel A. Warner, and R. G. Hatfield have disappeared. A number of other architects and firms also submitted unsolicited designs for what was clearly a highly coveted prize: Henry Hudson Holly, Diaper & Dudley, Richard Upjohn & Son, Richard Morris Hunt, and the partnership of Russell Sturgis and Peter B. Wight. Sturgis and Wight adapted the firm's preferred Ruskin-inspired polychromed Venetian Gothic to a five-story building,

Manhattan Life Insurance Company Building, 156–158 Broadway. John B. Snook, 1865. View to the east. IBB. CU.

which, though handsome, seemed interchangeable with the kind of building that might be undertaken by an educational or charitable institution.[10] Kellum, himself unsure about which language most suited his client, submitted Classical and Italianate designs for the Broadway facade as well as a so-called Norman, or round-arched, scheme. Though deemed the most expensive, the latter plan was selected because the client believed Kellum's claim that it would admit more light.

Griffith Thomas's New York Life Insurance Company Building (1868–70), clad in white Tuckahoe marble, pushed the new building type even further.[11] New York Life was located on an irregularly shaped site bounded by Broadway, Leonard Street, and Catherine Lane, an early intrusion on a residential neighborhood that was becoming home to the wholesale dry-goods trade. Thomas's building replaced what until 1856 had been the home of the Society Library (Frederic Diaper, 1838–40), after which it served as headquarters of the publishers D. Appleton & Co. until it was severely damaged by fire in 1867.[12] Founded in 1845, New York Life had since 1856 occupied the Bowen & McNamee Silk Warehouse (Joseph Wells, 1849), at 112–114 Broadway.

Thomas had won a paid design competition, held in late 1867, beating Bryant & Gilman, James Renwick Jr., and Leopold Eidlitz with a design that responded to the site's awkward configuration by breaking the mass into a long three-story middle section flanked by four-story pavilion-

like elements. In addition, the sloping grade of the site made the basement a full floor at the rear, intended for use as retail stores. An elaborately framed, twenty-foot-wide, split-pedimented portal, similar to that of Thomas's National Park Bank (1866–68) (see below), incorporated John M. Moffitt's sculpture of the insurance company's insignia, an eagle's nest with an eagle feeding its young. The entrance led to a twelve-foot-wide central corridor that ran the building's length, with the principal staircase off to one side. The central hall, flanked by two large rooms, one twenty by eighty feet, the other twenty by sixty feet, led to the owner's principal office via a twenty-by-twenty-foot vestibule. Thomas's plans innovatively called for a steam elevator in the well-hole of the stairs, extending from the basement through the upper stories, a factor that surely must have motivated Henry Baldwin Hyde to stipulate that elevators be included in the Equitable Building (see below). But for reasons that are not clear, perhaps financial, the elevator remained uninstalled until after the 1870 completion of the Equitable Building. Cost had become a political issue: the lavishly detailed building drew unwanted attention to New York Life from the House of Representatives, which was debating the insurance industry, and one commentator felt obliged to reassure readers that they "need not be alarmed at the report of the millions lavished by the managers of these [life insurance] companies on imposing business temples."[13]

Precisely to the degree that Thomas's design reflected the requirements of corporate clients for flexible, well-lit interior space, it caused the fledgling architecture critic Montgomery Schuyler to find fault with the building. Schuyler might have forgiven Thomas, who piled the Tuscan and Doric orders of the third and fourth floors atop two stories of Ionic columns at the base, for violating "all the classic rules" had he not visited other "graver" blemishes on the design. Schuyler railed against the building's lack of "that solidity which we look for imperatively in a building of this class," a lack caused by "the large number and size of the openings, making the voids far more than proportionate to the solid masses of the building. The sides are painfully cut up with chimneys, and the details, too, are very commonplace. . . . If this building claims, as we believe it does, the same authorship as the Park Bank, the architect was certainly not in his best mood when he designed it." Despite this invective, Schuyler went on to admit that "compared with many others, however, it may be considered one of the leading buildings of the city."[14]

While New York Life's new building was big and lavish, and so glassy as to make its function as an office block absolutely clear, its slightly out-of-the-way location somewhat diminished its impact on office building practice. Quite the opposite was true of Arthur Gilman and Edward H. Kendall's centrally located Equitable Life Assurance Society Building (1867–70), at 120 Broadway.[15] Completed with the assistance of George B. Post, the Equitable can be said to be the world's first modern office building. This was partially due to the prominence of the

Proposed Equitable Life Assurance Society Building, 120 Broadway. Richard Morris Hunt, 1867. Perspective. The Octagon, AAF.

phenomenally successful company that owned the building, but mostly it was due to the clearly thought-out design. Founded in 1859 by Henry Baldwin Hyde, Equitable had quickly become the second-largest life insurance company in America. In 1865, after having outgrown quarters at two Broadway locations, the company purchased 116–120 Broadway as well as lots facing Cedar

Street. Plans for a new building were not begun until 1867, after the site had been further expanded to include a number of substantial if not necessarily venerable buildings, among them the headquarters of the American Express Company. Although Hyde's would be the decisive voice in directing the architects, a building committee was formed, chaired by William G. Lambert, a merchant, and, in addition to Hyde, consisting of Henry G. Marquand, William T. Blodgett, and John Auchincloss. After preparing a building program, the committee conducted a design competition. There is some confusion over how many architects were invited to compete, with figures ranging from five to eleven. In addition to that of the competition winners, Gilman and Kendall, designs were also prepared by Richard Morris Hunt and the recently formed partnership of Charles D. Gambrill and H. H. Richardson as well as by George B. Post, who had terminated a partnership with Gambrill in 1867. The Equitable Building represented the first partnership between Gilman, Boston's leading architect, who had just relocated to New York, and the much younger Kendall, who had been the third American to study architecture at the Ecole des Beaux-Arts in Paris and who was also new to New York from Boston. Although the program document has not survived, competition drawings suggest that a six- or seven-story building was specified, with the basement and first floor suitable for rental to banks, the second and third floors to be used by Equitable, and the rest for commercial tenants. In addition to a main staircase there was to be a passenger elevator, a feature probably suggested by Hyde. Although an elevator had been already planned for New York Life, the Equitable Building was the first office building to have

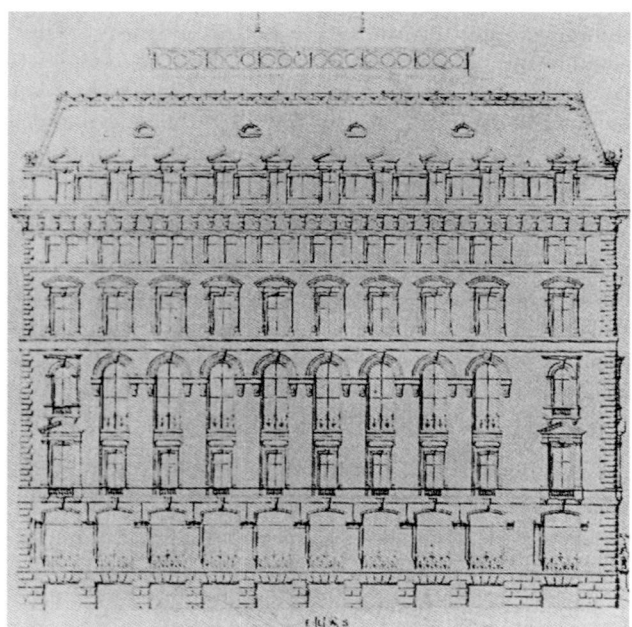

Proposed Equitable Life Assurance Society Building, 120 Broadway. Gambrill & Richardson, 1867. Elevation. HHR. CU.

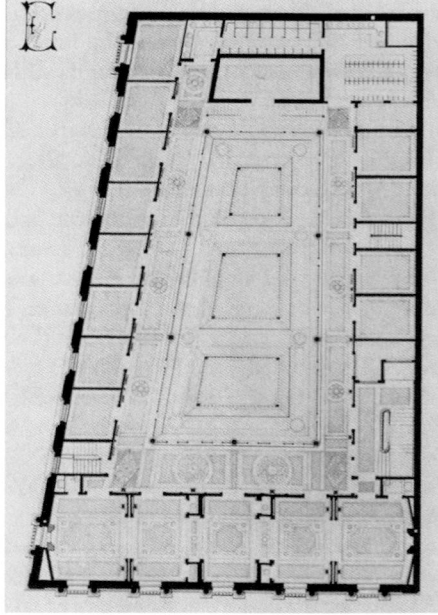

Proposed Equitable Life Assurance Society Building, 120 Broadway. Gambrill & Richardson, 1867. Main-floor plan. HLHU.

Proposed Equitable Life Assurance Society Building, 120 Broadway. George B. Post, 1867. Preliminary study. NYHS.

Proposed Equitable Life Assurance Society Building, 120 Broadway. George B. Post, 1867. Competition drawing. NYHS.

an elevator installed. Post and Hyde especially recognized the value of this investment: it would render all floors in the building equally desirable. While the Equitable's passenger elevator was the first in an office building, it was not the first to be installed in New York. There were passenger elevators in the Haughwout store (James P. Gaynor, 1857) and in the Fifth Avenue Hotel (William Washburn, 1859).

Richard Morris Hunt had just returned to New York from a summer in Paris, where as a commissioner and juror on the Committee of Fine Arts he had explored the Exposition Universelle. Hunt was intent on winning the Equitable competition, producing twenty-two presentation drawings documenting three different schemes.[16] Though each of Hunt's schemes sought to provide light along the party wall, each located the clerking hall differently, alternately opening it to Cedar Street or Broadway, or containing it within the building in a grand room with apsidal ends off which the gallery and offices radiated. Hunt also provided a variety of elevations and perspective drawings to illustrate how the building would look, including a compactly massed, rhythmically fenestrated, Gothic version.

In contrast to Hunt's geometrically shaped central space, Gambrill & Richardson gave the site precedence and made no provision for lot-line illumination, thereby resulting in an irregular quadrilateral clerking hall and many unlit offices.[17] In addition, Richardson's plan suggested that the central hall would be lit by three skylights, which, in penetrating the rental floors above, would compromise those floors' flexibility. Richardson's elevations vertically grouped the windows under arches and between piers, and his mass was concluded with a mansard roof.

Though the organization of the facades was imaginative, the design, like George B. Post's rather carefully composed pavilionated scheme (for which the plans are lost), lacked the bravura of Gilman and Kendall's superscaled design. Another Post design proposed a corner entrance guarded by a statuary group not unlike the one eventually placed in the final building's pediment, which would become a symbol of the company. On the basis of these two design contributions, Post's role in the building's design was securely established. But it was Gilman and Kendall, not Post, who notably departed from a flat architecture of walls to one that emphasized the structural frame through the use of large glazed openings articulated by vigorously modeled paired pilasters combining multiple stories to give the impression of fewer floors and colossal height.

At its annual meeting in January 1868, Equitable announced that Arthur Gilman and Edward H. Kendall had been selected to design the new headquarters, and that George B. Post had been named assisting architect. Meanwhile, Gilman and Kendall's partnership seemed to be collapsing, and in October 1869 the *New York Herald* stated that Kendall was in charge of the building, which was to be his "first great work."[18] Adding to the confusion over authorship of this landmark design was the role of Post, who is generally credited as the building's co-designer because of his work in reconfiguring the building's structural system to achieve better space utilization on the office floors. Post's prior training as a civil engineer and his two years in Hunt's atelier had clearly impressed Hyde, who later described him as an "expert builder" complementing Gilman and Kendall.[19] Post changed the building's proposed structure and its materials, using stone only

Equitable Life Assurance Society Building, 120 Broadway. Arthur Gilman and Edward H. Kendall, 1867–70. View to the southeast showing the Bowen & McNamee Silk Warehouse (Joseph Wells, 1849; mansard addition, c. 1870) next to the Equitable Building. MIT.

on the ground-floor walls, with brick and terra cotta above, and substituting iron columns and beams for internal load-bearing walls. Together with Hyde, Post is also credited with insisting on the installation of an elevator. According to Montgomery Schuyler, although Hyde "foresaw the prospects of the higher vertical extension of his building" it was Post who seized on them and, to demonstrate his confidence in height, made an offer on one of the top-floor suites, "an offer based on and equalling the highest rent then paid on Broadway for the like accommodations." Post made this offer only to have Hyde counter with twice the amount, to which Post "acquiesced, retaining the offices until he sold out his lease for a substantial advance even upon the unprecedented rental he had agreed to pay. Of course, such an object-lesson as this in the advantages of elevator buildings was not thrown away upon the commercial community."[20] Despite Post's very important role in realizing the Equitable Building, there seems no evidence that he had anything significant to do with the building's aesthetics.

No doubt Gilman and Kendall's design was selected for its superior logic as well as for its artistic bravura. The top two of its seven stories were incorporated in a high mansard, and there was limited additional space in the pavilions marking the centers of the building's two street facades. While there is some disagreement about the building's height, with estimates ranging from 125 to 172 feet, convincing analysis by Lee Edward Gray suggests that it was probably 130 feet tall and as such was the second-tallest construction in New York, exceeded only by the 284-foot-tall spire of Trinity Church (Richard Upjohn, 1846). Above a base of darkish Quincy granite, the boldly scaled building was composed of fine-grained white granite from Concord, New Hampshire, introduced to New York by Gilman, who had frequently used it in his Boston buildings. The granite was backed by a layer of hard-burnt North River brick, which was laid up so as to provide chases for pipes and ducts. The same brick was used for the party walls and for interior load-bearing partitions, although Post had replaced many of these with a framework of twelve cast-iron columns filled with concrete and covered with cement. Iron studs infilled with brick were used to form the non–load-bearing partitions, an effective response to Hyde's request for a fire-resistant interior; fire damage had nearly crippled the company in the mid-1860s. The floor system consisted of rolled-iron girders spanned by brick arches topped by a layer of concrete.

Gilman and Kendall's plan took wonderful advantage of the site, giving preference to Cedar Street so as to create a long rectangular hall surrounded by an enfilade of offices that got light from the street and from a single light court between the building and its neighbor. Executive offices faced Broadway, with agent offices wrapping a double-height hall in which Equitable's 120 clerks worked. The clerking hall was subdivided into work areas three feet in length by six feet nine inches in depth, big enough for the desk and standing room appropriate to each clerk. The main stair and the elevator were both located at the midpoint of the long axis of the hall.

Viewed from the street, the new Equitable Building seemed even bigger than its considerable actual size because of Gilman and Kendall's decision to visually bind pairs of floors; at first glance, the building seemed composed of only three colossally tall stories. This strategy, combined with the use of a steep mansard, associated the building with the monuments of Baron Georges-Eugène Haussmann's Paris, a connection particularly welcomed by the editors of the *New York Herald,* who felt that the Equitable was "a public benefit . . . decisive of the new school and points to what must follow—that companies whose resources are so enormous . . . must make some outlay of their immense incomes, which come directly from the people, in the interest of those people—that is, in the construction of palaces and which the public purse, in the hands of derelict officials, has failed to provide. This not only ornaments the city, but it provides labor with a wide field and stimulates all departments of mechanical industry."[21]

Gilman and Kendall's Equitable Building was the city's, and therefore the world's, first modern office building. This distinction was owed to many factors: the building's size and height, especially in the context of the four- and five-story world of post–Civil War New York; its rational plan; its technological features, including superior heating and ventilation and the inclusion of a passenger elevator; and its timing, given that it preceded by five years any other construction of similar height and prominence. A place of work, the Equitable Building was also a symbolic representation of the eponymous company that built it and called it home. Efficient and well lighted, the Equitable gave the impression of a building uniquely designed for the modern world of office work and for the emerging world of self-promotion, advertising, and public relations. It did not merely accommodate corporate activity, it celebrated corporate enterprise. As the *Real Estate Record and Builders' Guide* put it:

> By the prevailing characteristic of overpowering proportions, it dwarfs all surrounding objects—a feature in itself sufficient to impart a certain majesty, for the absence of which no amount of mere decoration can compensate in civic architecture. Precisely as the previously much lauded *Herald* Building [see below] was, on the erection of the Park Bank, by the force of contrast instantaneously transformed into a dull conglomeration of little marble pigeonholes, so this granite giant of the Equitable Insurance Company has made the adjoining New York Life Insurance Building [the former Bowen & McNamee Silk Warehouse, Joseph Wells, 1849], with its infinity of vertical lines and invisible narrow little openings, so utterly insignificant that, from a short distance up or down [the] street, it presents no more artistic appearance than a blank sheet of ruled foolscap paper.[22]

While not a skyscraper—that is, not a building massed to form a sky-piercing tower that would remain forever free of other buildings—by virtue of its unique bulk and height the

Mutual Life Insurance Company Building, 140 Broadway.
John Kellum, 1863–65. View to the southeast showing the 1871
mansard addition by Kellum. NYHS.

Equitable was a critical stepping-stone to the skyscraper type. As the *New York Sun* observed, it was the first building to rise above "the brown roofs of the buildings of the city [that] extend over the island like a vast table land."[23]

The Equitable's impact on the real estate market was dramatic. New York Life moved into its home, the first owned by the company, on May 1, 1870, the same day that Equitable opened its building. But the Equitable's owner and architects had seen the future more clearly, and within a few years New York Life's palatial design was modified by the addition of a reasonably sympathetic, if florid, inhabited mansard (Henry Fernbach, 1879), imitative of the Equitable's. In 1871, one year after the Equitable's completion, John Kellum also added a large mansard and an elevator to his Mutual Life Building, and a few years later, Metropolitan Life hired Napoleon Le Brun to renovate its plain, five-story-tall, Italianate block at 32 Park Place, adding in 1874–75 a stylistically improbable two-story mansard, an enhanced street-level treatment, and an elevator.[24] In addition, in 1876, the Germania Life Insurance Company, a neighbor of Equitable's at 20 Nassau Street, added an elaborate mansard to its Italianate building.[25]

According to an 1899 survey of city architecture, "The Equitable Life Assurance Company was the first corporation bold enough to undertake a great office building in connec-

tion with its own necessary place of business."[26] The new structure was also the first building the ten-year-old company had owned and was consequently deemed an important statement of its success and that of its founder, who took great pride in the building, especially in its height. While vacationing in the Sierras after the building's completion, Hyde wrote: "I got my head at the base of a perpendicular rock six thousand feet high, and looked over so far into the clouds; but somehow the sight did not impress me as when I saw the last cornice of the Equitable Building put in its place."[27] Some twenty-three years after its completion, the value of Gilman, Kendall, and Post's building continued to impress Hyde, who wrote in a letter to Post: "Without the Equitable Building as a fulcrum from which to move the insurance world, the unparalleled results attained by the Equitable Life Assurance Society of the United States could never have been accomplished. . . . It is manifest that the Equitable is destined to tower above all the institutions of a similar character in the civilized world."[28]

The Equitable proved the market for tall buildings. Within five years of its completion, its 130-foot height was close to doubled by George B. Post's ten-story Western Union Building (230 feet) and exactly doubled by Richard Morris Hunt's ten-story Tribune Building, the slender campanile of which pierced the sky 260 feet above the street. These two subsequent buildings defined the skyscraper type as the Equitable Building did not quite do: each was a functionally determined, logically organized and constructed, cubically massed building articulated into a base, midsection, and strongly profiled roof capped by an individualistic sky-piercing tower. Though the tower of Post's design was more like an appended finial, Hunt's tower constituted a much more definitive skyline feature, a slender campanile that seemed not so much to have been planted on top of the building as to have grown out of it, rising uninterrupted from the ground, functioning as the pivot of a complex composition and as the representative embodiment of the complex as a whole.

Western Union Building

When it was completed in 1875, George B. Post's Western Union Building, at the northwest corner of Broadway and Dey Street, was the city's tallest commercial building.[29] It was also a grand corporate monument, one of a handful of important office buildings that would be initiated on the strength of the Equitable Building's success, during a boom that lasted until 1873. The site, selected after a failed attempt to buy the more strategically located Astor House across from the new United States Courthouse and Post Office, spanned 75 feet on Broadway and 150 feet on Dey Street. The commission, decisive in the formulation of Post's reputation as an architect, was won in 1872 in an invited competition with a design for a ten-story building of which the communications company expected to occupy only three floors. Aside from its value as a source of revenue for the corporation, the new building appears to have been intended as

Western Union Building, northwest corner of Broadway and Dey Street. George B. Post, 1873–75. View to the northwest showing the spire of St. Paul's Chapel (Thomas McBean, 1764–66; spire, James Crommelin Lawrence, 1794) on the right. NYHS.

a visible representation of Western Union's virtual hegemony in its field and of the solidity of its leadership under William Orion, its president, and Cornelius Vanderbilt II, its principal stockholder.

Post bested Richard Morris Hunt, Russell Sturgis, Napoleon Le Brun, George Hathorne, and Arthur Gilman in a competition that seems to have been held in two stages, with initial sketches requested from five architects and then more detailed designs from three (in the first stage, the drawings appear to have been submitted without designer identification). Three architects, R. G. Hatfield, Leopold Eidlitz, and Griffith Thomas, had refused to enter the competition because the offered fee would not cover the cost of preparing a design and because the company would not agree to compensate the winning architects at recognized fees. As Post put it in a letter to Orion, written after being selected when he was struggling to establish an adequate fee structure for the project, "it was supposed that the competition would not be decided upon the merits of designs."[30] The dispute was resolved to Post's satisfaction and he was compensated at an appropriate level. The job was not only critical for Post's reputation, it was a lifesaver for his career. His office was not prospering; in fact, he was in arrears on his rent for the office he occupied in the Equitable Building. He was further burdened by a loan he had taken to tide the business over.

Despite the fact that the building was initially intended to be only partially occupied by the rapidly expanding communications company, it functioned more as a corporate headquarters than did the Equitable Building, housing both clerical functions and operations. While much of Western Union's own space was devoted to fairly conventional office uses, the sixth floor housed the battery room that powered the telegraphs and served as the point of entry for the company's wires, and the seventh floor housed the 23-foot-high, 45-by-145-foot operating room. The plan of the operating room was interrupted only by four columns at the east end; these supported the clock tower. The room housed the ten-foot-high, twenty-six-by-five-and-a-half-foot switchboard and the pneumatic-tube reception and dispatch area that together formed the system's heart. The operators—290 in all, comprising 215 men and 75 women, the sexes segregated by an eight-foot-high partition—were stationed in groups of four at seven work tables, all gathered beneath a ceiling "handsomely frescoed as the sky."[31] Inside the mansard, the eighth floor contained the offices of the New York Associated Press and a five-thousand-gallon water tank; the ninth floor held various services, including a company kitchen and employee dining room; and the tenth floor housed an auxiliary water tank and storage.

At 230 feet, about four times the average height of New York buildings, the Western Union Building dwarfed its neighbors. At the time of its completion, only Trinity Church, the Tribune Building, and the towers of the Brooklyn Bridge were taller. A technical tour de force, it was most awkward at the top, where the tower sat uncomfortably at the eastern end of the flamboyantly modeled roof, which incorporated a profusion of oeil-de-beouf windows, pedimented dormers, and ironwork crocketing. Post's design, influenced by the Equitable, used piers and a regular pattern of windows to create a unified effect. The facades were vividly articulated with a rusticated gray Quincy granite base, above which alternating bands of granite and red Baltimore brick wrapped the four typical office floors. The facade was not intended as a schematic representation of internal functional arrangements, but instead represented an attempt to organize the building into a coherent Classical composition of base, shaft, and crown that began with the cornicelike sixth floor, continued with the high seventh floor and the dormered mansard, and culminated in the singular clock tower, an arrangement that, when seen in perspective from Broadway, can be said to have brought the tall building to the threshold of the mature skyscraper type.

The prominent flight of stairs that projected onto the sidewalk at the center of the Broadway facade marked the building's principal entrance, although the gently sloping site allowed the public to enter the basement at grade on the corner. In the basement a number of company divisions could conduct business, including the cable message department, which was housed in a nineteen-by-eighty-foot room stretching along Dey Street, the company's principal public face. With a structural system similar to that of the Equitable, the Western Union incorporated a number of technical advances, including an elaborate system of plumbing and gas lighting, the wiring and pneumatic tubes needed for telegraphy, and two eighteen-passenger steam-powered elevators for public use. A fourteen-passenger elevator reserved for staff, supplied by Cyrus W. Baldwin of Chicago, was of the "water balance" type, which used gravity for its operation. There was also a service elevator, supplied by Otis.

Western Union was quick to see the publicity value of its building. A magazine devoted to the study of nature, literature, and the arts, *The Aldine*, pointed out the analogy between the urbanistic role of the new headquarters and that traditionally played by the great cathedrals: "There is really something almost oppressive in the effect produced by its height, forcibly reminding the traveler of Strasbourg Cathedral as seen at the distance of many miles, lifting its spire into the upper air and even its very body above the tops of the ordinary steeples."[32] Clearly, Post's clients were happy with the building; in 1878 Cornelius Vanderbilt II would hire Post to design his mansion on Fifth Avenue, even though the architect had hitherto designed few residences (see chapter 4).

The bravura of Post's design and the logic of his composition were widely appreciated. The *New York Daily Tribune*, itself embarking on the construction of an even purer exemplar of the new skyscraper type, greeted Post's achievement as a sign that "the short-sighted utilitarianism which has filled the city with low and unsightly markets, depots, warehouses, and business blocks, is fast dying out."[33] Despite some reservations, the architect Alfred J. Bloor was also impressed with the building. In his 1876 address to the tenth annual convention of the American Institute of Architects, Bloor stated:

> The enterprise which harnesses the modern Puck to its triumphal car, and literally puts a girdle round about the earth in much less than forty minutes, has been most notably illustrated in architecture, by Post's Western Union Telegraph Building, a bold and towering performance in Renaissance of the modern type, which he has done so much to extend, and of the sub-type partially suggestive of an engineering standpoint, which has become peculiar to him. While the great cleverness of the whole design will be generally acknowledged by experts, objection may be made by some that the superstructure is not so refined as the basement and first story; while the roof is rendered picturesque at the cost of repose, and in some of its ornamentation, and in its sky-lines, is not without a suspicion of coarseness. It is to be regretted too, that the quieter-tone stone selected by the architect for the banding should have been replaced, for economical reasons, by that which has been used.[34]

Looking back with thirty years' perspective, Montgomery Schuyler saw Post's building as the prototypical skyscraper, "a much more radical solution of the novel problem" than even Hunt's Tribune Building:

> Above the basement and below the cornice, which indeed was crowned with a steep roof containing additional stories, the included stories repeated one another with similarity amounting almost to identity of treatment, and this was the recognition in the new architecture of the Aristotelian requirement in every work of art of a beginning, a middle and an end. Speaking the language of architecture, it was a division into base, shaft, and capital. The pioneer thus arrived at once at the scheme of composition . . . which has "imposed itself" . . . as the fundamental design of the "skyscraper."[35]

Newspaper Headquarters

Telegraphy allowed newspapers to revolutionize communication during the Civil War, connecting battlefields with political centers and the population at large as never before. With improvements in printing and increased literacy, newspapers were becoming big business, rivaling insurance companies as pioneering patrons of the new office building type.[36] In 1873 the *American Builder* observed: "Probably in no direction is the progress and improvement of architecture in this country more obvious than in the magnificent buildings—veritable palaces— which are so rapidly taking the place of the old, dingy newspaper offices of our principal cities."[37] The newspapers required highly specific facilities tailored to the complex process of quickly editing, printing, and distributing their daily product. Because they needed central locations to effectively gather and distribute the news, and because their entrepreneurial and highly competitive publishers were anxious to impress the public with the civic spirit of their offerings, newspapers were typically headquartered at prominent locations. Many of them chose Park Row, where, in an effort to communicate their self-image as quasi-public institutions serving the people, they could literally confront City Hall—this stretch would come to be called Newspaper Row. Like insurance companies, newspapers were keen to make strong architectural statements but were also concerned with the bottom line, seeking ways to realize rental income from their buildings. But they were different from the insurance companies in that only part of their business was white-collar. Another major component distinctly involved manufacturing—the actual printing of the newspapers. For this reason, the newspaper building type mixed uses to a degree hitherto unknown, reaching its highest expression in the post–Civil War years with Richard Morris Hunt's building for the *New York Daily Tribune* (1873–75) (see below).

The *New York Times* was the first to commission a structure specifically designed for the needs of a newspaper; the *Times*'s building, completed in 1857, was designed by Thomas R. Jackson (see below). The next important newspaper headquarters to go forward was built for the *New York Herald*. Constructed from 1865 to 1867, John Kellum's white marble–fronted Herald Building consisted of four stories plus an occupiable dormered mansard and was prominently located on the key corner opposite St. Paul's Chapel where Park Row, Broadway, and Ann Street meet.[38] Following the example of the *Times*, this was the second newspaper to establish an imposing headquarters facing City Hall Park. The *Herald* had been founded in 1835 by James Gordon Bennett and was the most successful of the city's dozen newspapers, with a daily circulation of 77,000, the nation's largest. In the 1860s, Bennett's flamboyant son took control of the paper. To celebrate his own status and that of his newspaper, in 1865 James Bennett Jr. took over the prominent site that had been home to P. T. Barnum's American Museum until its destruction by fire and chose John Kellum to design the new building. George Templeton Strong did not mourn the museum's closing, complaining in his diary about the "horrible little brass band . . . always tooting in its balcony . . . tormenting all passengers at the very junction of our two most crowded thoroughfares."[39]

Kellum's building, a mansarded, vertically expanded version of the typical commercial palace, placed newspaper and rental offices above a deep basement housing the press room. It was intended as a personal statement of the publisher, whose initials were carved on a shield placed in the tympanum above the main entrance. Kellum's first use of a mansard roof in a commercial building, the new Herald Building set a fashion. With its cast-iron cresting and imposing masonry facades, the structure came close to contemporary French work, a fact that was commented on by John W. Kennion.[40] Compositors were put on the top floor, in the mansard, where they could get the best light for their work with thousands of pieces of small type. The building failed to please Montgomery Schuyler, however; writing for the *Herald*'s rival newspaper the *New York*

World, Schuyler's somewhat prejudiced review deemed the building an opportunity lost:

> The conspicuousness of its position, its size, the liberality in its expenditure, the fact of its occupying a corner lot, by which all the advantages of perspective could be obtained, all contributed to give the designer a chance for erecting an edifice that could have been a pride and ornament to the city. Look at it, study it from foundation to roof, with its great array of little pigeon-hole windows, commonplace architraves, window and door heads, and show us one original or inventive thought in the whole composition—any ornament, any suggestion that we have not seen repeated everywhere, *ad nauseum*.[41]

Charles A. Dana's *New York Sun* also moved into new headquarters, a renovated Tammany Hall, on Nassau and Frankfort Streets. In 1872, Oswald Ottendorfer's German-language *New Yorker Staats-Zeitung* constructed another prominent facility facing City Hall, this time from the northeast.[42] Located on an irregular site bounded by Tryon Row (Chambers Street) and Chatham and Centre Streets, Henry Fernbach's design, five stories plus an inhabited mansard, was praised by the *Real Estate Record and Builders' Guide* as one likely "to set the example of . . . a building really worthy of the press of this great metropolis."[43] The city's oldest newspaper, the *New York Evening Post*, founded by Alexander Hamilton in 1801, followed in 1875 with a new headquarters at the southeast corner of Broadway and Fulton Street—just out of view of City Hall—which, when completed to the designs of Thomas Stent, the last of three architects to work on the building (Stent's predecessors were George Hathorne and the somewhat shadowy Charles F. Mengelson), was a towering mass rising 115 feet above the street.[44] Though a writer for the *Record and Guide* found the Evening Post Building "piteously and helplessly feeble,"[45] in fact the ten-story, pressed-brick and stone-trimmed building was notably straightforward in design, especially after Hathorne's mansard was removed over that architect's protest. The mansard was replaced by Mengelson with two more stories, yielding a strictly utilitarian mass embellished at the top only by an octagonal cupola which itself contained a room. So straightforward was the design, with continuous piers emphasizing the vertical, that the *Post*'s editors, no doubt chiding their rivals at the *Tribune*, whose new headquarters was finished at about the same time (see below), praised their building as "simple in style" and one that "will be admired more for its massiveness and substantiality, and for its complete adaptation to the uses for which it was constructed, than for anything peculiar or striking in its outlines or extravagant in the treatment of its interior."[46]

After constructing the Herald Building, James Gordon Bennett Jr. caught the real estate bug and decided to finance the purely speculative Bennett Building (1872–73) for the block-long site on the west side of Nassau Street between Ann and Fulton Streets that had previously housed the *New York Herald*.[47] Despite the architect's apparent return to Boston at this time, Bennett hired

View to the northeast showing, from left to right, City Hall (Joseph François Mangin and John McComb Jr., 1803–11), Brooklyn Bridge Terminal (1883), World Building (George B. Post, 1889–90), Tribune Building (Richard Morris Hunt, 1873–75; Edward E. Raht, 1881–82), Times Building (George B. Post, 1887–89), and part of the Potter Building (Norris Gibson Starkweather, 1883–85). The American Tract Society Building (R. H. Robertson, 1894–95) is visible above the Times Building. NYHS.

Evening Post Building, southeast corner of Broadway and Fulton Street. Thomas Stent, 1875. View to the southeast. King, 1893. CU.

Bennett Building, Nassau Street between Ann and Fulton Streets. Arthur Gilman, 1872–73. View to the northwest. King, 1893. CU.

Arthur Gilman for the commission. To attract tenants, Bennett not only promoted the building in his own newspaper during construction but also extensively advertised it in those of his competitors, publishing floor plans to demonstrate that the design was "well adapted for professional men."[48] Gilman's building was promoted as "entirely fireproof," a significant point given that two disastrous fires—in Chicago in October 1871, and in Boston in November 1872—were very much on everyone's mind. To this end, the design called for wrought-iron beams supporting an infill of lightweight gypsum which in turn carried the finished floor. Hollow gypsum-block partitions were provided by the Fireproof Building Company of New York, reducing the weight carried by the load-bearing walls. Surprisingly, given the concern about fire, the building was clad in cast iron. Despite the incorporation of two passenger elevators, the top floors were leased at dramatically lower rates than those nearer the street, suggesting that the market was slow to realize the benefits of light and view which height afforded, Post's experience at the Equitable Building notwithstanding.

With its combination of printing plant, editorial offices, and rental offices in a structure that took advantage of a prominent location with a sky-scraping campanile nearly twice the height of the building itself, Richard Morris Hunt's Tribune Building (1873–75), at the northeast corner of Nassau and Spruce Streets, was not only a pioneer of the skyscraper type but also a complex functional hybrid.[49] Appropriating the campanile of the late-thirteenth-century Palazzo Vecchio, in Florence, the Tribune Building was a bold usurpation of civic imagery that deliberately confronted New York's diminutive, corruption-plagued City Hall with a powerhouse of industry and ideas. The building embodied in three dimensions the paper pulpit that the *Tribune*'s founding publisher and editor, Horace Greeley, had occupied for over thirty years.

The *Tribune* had prospered quickly after its 1841 inception. In 1843 the paper moved into buildings at 158 and 160 Nassau Street, which, after burning in February 1845, were rebuilt as one unit that also incorporated the lot at the corner of Spruce and Nassau Streets. In the late 1860s, when Greeley began to accumulate capital to build a "new printing palace" for the *Tribune* that was intended to "surpass any newspaper building in America," he assembled properties adjacent to his headquarters so that he could create an imposing building in two stages without interfering with his newspaper's operations.[50] But plans for the project, which was to combine space for newspaper operations along with income-producing rental offices, were temporarily shelved when Greeley decided to oppose President Ulysses S. Grant in his November 1872 bid for reelection. Greeley died shortly after admitting defeat, but he had already turned over control of the paper to his managing editor, Whitelaw Reid, a thirty-five-year-old Ohio-born journalist. Soon after surviving a power struggle from which he emerged as both the newspaper's editor and owner, Reid announced his decision to carry out Greeley's plans for a new headquarters.

When completed, the new Tribune Building would be the city's tallest occupied structure, exceeded in height only by the steeple of Trinity Church and the towers of the as-yet-incomplete Brooklyn Bridge. It replaced three separate structures: the original newspaper headquarters, at the northeast corner of Spruce and Nassau Streets; the so-called "iron building" addition, which faced Spruce Street; and a building on Nassau Street that had been purchased in the 1860s. Early in 1873, Reid succeeded in buying the Lawrence Bank Building, which was located between the *Tribune* structures and the *New York Sun*'s building. Reid also purchased a parcel that ran behind the *Sun*. Put together, these acquisitions created a U-shaped plot that ran along Nassau Street for 93 feet, along Spruce Street for 100 feet, and along Frankfort Street for 27 feet. On March 17, 1873, possibly with the assistance of J. C. Cady, Reid prepared a fifteen-point architectural program for the new building, outlining requirements for the newspaper's own space as well as for extensive commercial rental space, with separate entrances and circulation systems serving each. Reid also specified a stone-trimmed brick building of no fewer than eight stories topped by a tower with an illuminated clock. As Greeley had planned, the building was to be constructed in two stages in order not to interrupt the newspaper's operations.

By spring, Cady and Richard Morris Hunt were each at work on designs, along with about six other architects, including Henry Hudson Holly. Cady's scheme, notable for its Siennese corner tower and for the arcading that combined three floors and was repeated as an occupiable attic below the mansard, was not selected, but it was published in the short-lived, influential *New-York Sketch-Book of Architecture*. For this reason, the architectural historians Sarah Bradford Landau and Carl W. Condit have suggested that Cady's design "may actually have had even more influence on the developing design scheme of the tall commercial building than did Hunt's. . . . The rhythms, round-arched form, and bichromatic banding" of the arcades Cady used to organize his design were surely an influence on the work of H. H. Richardson, the titular editor of the *Sketch-Book*, while the corner campanile, "generally prophetic of the tower-skyscrapers of the future," was closely echoed by Napoleon Le Brun's Metropolitan Life Tower (1909).[51] Hunt was ultimately selected in May 1873, despite misgivings by some at the *Tribune*, especially Bayard Taylor, who warned Reid to take care not to "let Dick Hunt, who is great in decorations, overlook the practical part of the arrangement."[52]

Throughout the summer, while demolition was proceeding on the site, Hunt developed his design, rearranging the elements of the scheme, sometimes locating the tower at the corner of Nassau and Spruce Streets as Cady had proposed. With its centrally placed tower—perhaps inspired by H. H. Richardson's Hampden County Courthouse (1871–74), in Springfield, Massachusetts—the final

design separated the two phases of the building and acted as a transitional element so that the building could easily respond to the slight bend in the site along Nassau Street. Phase one, delayed by problems with the granite supplier and by labor difficulties, was completed in April 1875, a year behind schedule; economic conditions delayed phase two until 1881 and 1882. The impression of the building burned into the public's mind was thus that of a nearly cubical base pinned in place by a slender campanile. Hunt had put Edward E. Raht in charge of the project, a decision with which Reid was initially uncomfortable. Reid nonetheless began to trust Raht, perhaps more than he did Hunt; when Hunt sought to combat illness with a trip to Europe in 1874 while the building was under construction, Reid turned to Raht to increase the building's height. Raht obliged by adding a floor between the cornice and the mansard, engaging the 260-foot-tall campanile-like tower into the mass more than Hunt had intended and thus diminishing the impression of its height.

Hunt's building proclaimed the *Tribune*'s presence to all New Yorkers by virtue of its height and visibility across City Hall Park. The ground floor housed the newspaper's counting house (business office), decorated by the Herter Brothers; the middle floors were leased to tenants; and the top two floors were also used by the newspaper, with Whitelaw Reid holding forth from the tower. Hunt's design was a remarkably straightforward expression of the building's structure, graced by a felicitous play of contrasting materials, including black brick used for ornamental accents. After the tower, the entrance was the building's most memorable feature. Located at the bottom of the tower, the entrance was flanked by two polished granite columns carrying a carved, abstract pediment. It led to an entry hall crowned by a groin vault formed by granite ribs and red brick set in black mortar. The windows were set back about one foot from the face of the intermediate piers, which in turn were set back from the structural piers by an almost equal amount, enhancing the building's impression of rugged strength.

Despite quarrels with Hunt over fees and delays (when it came time to build phase two, Raht was put in charge), Reid was very happy with his building and set out to make sure that the *Tribune*'s new home would be the most famous commercial building in the country. In addition to its publication in the *Tribune*, Hunt's building was depicted and discussed in a host of other newspapers and journals. The design was clearly newsworthy, not only for its height and the challenge it posed to Trinity Church or for its use of iron columns and beams to support the structure, but especially for the sheer boldness of Hunt's concept, which seemed to illustrate the June 1873 observation made by the *New York Daily Graphic* that business was "building up to the clouds, and covering the ground with blocks that are a city in themselves."[53] Hunt's building introduced the idea that not merely height, but height somehow projected so that the upper reaches of the building would remain forever free of encroaching development

Proposed Tribune Building, northeast corner of Nassau and Spruce Streets. J. C. Cady, 1873. Competition entry. NYSB. CU.

that might compromise its value as an icon—or an advertisement—was the best way to imbue an ordinary commercial building with the aspirational dignity of a church. Like the steeple of a church, Hunt's tower was the representation of the building it served, growing out of its mass. Though the specific form of Hunt's tower was secular in origin, the design as a whole can be characterized as the world's first "cathedral of commerce," a phrase later coined to describe Cass Gilbert's Woolworth Building (1910–13), which would occupy a site across City Hall Park from the Tribune Building.

Montgomery Schuyler was impressed with the sincerity of Hunt's effort but cool to the design: "The architecture of the *Tribune* building may be ugly, nay it is, but it is not altogether meaningless. It is an attempt to express construction." Schuyler had few kind words for its color, "a glaring collocation of red and white and black, which time can never mellow," but he went on to say "that it would be extremely ugly [even] in monochrome." Despite the expression of structure on the facade, Schuyler found that the building conveyed a sense of "insecurity," enhanced in his view by the "irrelevant and ugly nuisance" of the tower. The tower, when seen "directly in front . . . is very bad. It is built wrong side up and wrong side out. That is to say, instead of being solid at the bottom and growing lighter and more open as it rises, it is open at the bottom, and the only part of it which is virtually solid is the part above the cornice and just under the clock. Moreover, it is gradually detached from the face of the wall by successive corbellings

Proposed Tribune Building, northeast corner of Nassau and Spruce Streets. Richard Morris Hunt, 1873. Pencil drawing of unbuilt scheme. The Octagon, AAF.

Tribune Building, northeast corner of Nassau and Spruce Streets. Richard Morris Hunt, 1873–75. View to the northeast, c. 1875, showing the Times Building (Thomas R. Jackson, 1857) on the right. To the left of the Tribune Building are the headquarters of the New York Sun and French's Hotel. On the west side of Park Row is a corner of City Hall (Joseph François Mangin and John McComb Jr., 1803–11) on the left and the top of the New Yorker Staats-Zeitung Building (Henry Fernbach, 1872). NYHS.

until the top nods from high and totters to its fall." Schuyler's complaint with Hunt's work was by no means confined to the Tribune Building:

> With Mr. Hunt's gifts it seems to be impossible for him to be quiet, and repose being the very first of qualities in architecture, this is the worst of all signs for his work. To some extent this is true of the whole *néo-grecque* attempt to express, in the architectural vernacular in which the eternal peace and victory of Pallas were glorified, the weariness, the fever and the fret of modern French life. In any hands such an attempt must fail, and when an architect like Mr. Hunt adds his own fitfulness and eccentricity to this essentially fitful and eccentric style, we need not wonder that the result should be even so discouraging as the new *Tribune* building.[54]

Twenty years after publishing his first review of the Tribune Building, in 1895 Schuyler dramatically reversed his earlier assessment in his memorial tribute to Hunt. Schuyler better appreciated Hunt's achievement, although he mistakenly claimed it to be "the first of the elevator buildings":

> When we consider that . . . it was literally unprecedented, and an initial attack upon a problem at which a whole generation of designers have been working for the twenty intervening years, it is clear that every needful allowance must be made for its shortcomings. Indeed, the allowances that need to be made are surprisingly few. . . . The contrast between the granite and the brick is so vivid, and the granite is so applied in patches rather than in accentuation of the main lines and features of construction as in a great degree to obscure the design . . . and to concentrate attention upon what in the design is a very minor matter. . . . The design . . . remains very interesting.[55]

Taking yet another look at the building in the context of the evolving skyscraper type, in 1903 Schuyler at last came round to a full appreciation of the architect's accomplishment: Hunt "made groups of stories with piers and arches, so as to simulate the division of a lower building and to make the group of stories fulfil the same function of an organic member of the composition that the single story had previously performed."[56] With the Tribune Building, Hunt broke the prevailing paradigm of commercial architecture. It was, as Winston Weisman has written, "an antipalace": "The total effect of the design is not elegant. It is structural. Sensuousness gives way to logic. Magnificence is replaced by massiveness. Brick is substituted for marble and iron. Color turns from white and gold to bright red."[57]

Given Reid's feelings that Hunt had not followed through, it was not surprising that Reid turned to Raht to help in completing the building when stories were added to the Nassau Street side in 1881–82, almost doubling its height and thereby robbing the tower of some of its bold, self-declarative qualities. These extra floors may well have been part of Hunt's original plan, although the flat-roofed block massing of Raht's extension surely was not what the master had in mind.

With the completion of the Western Union and Tribune Buildings, the skyline of New York began to look like that of no other city. When the English scientist Thomas Henry Huxley sailed into New York Harbor in 1876 to begin a lecture tour, he asked about the two buildings. The London correspondent of the *Tribune*, who happened to be on board, identified the structures for him. Huxley approvingly observed: "Ah, that is interesting; that is America. In the Old World the first things you see as you approach a great city are steeples; here you see, first, centres of intelligence."[58]

The Standard Office Block

Post's Western Union Building and Hunt's Tribune Building laid the groundwork for the skyscraper type, but the economic depression that followed the Panic of 1873 temporarily arrested its further development. The few office buildings realized during the remainder of the decade eschewed the self-proclaiming, quasi-institutional statements of the insurance and newspaper buildings in favor of far more modest designs. The typical office blocks of the 1870s and early 1880s were more akin to traditional town buildings, filling up sites and honoring street walls. Some were not even particularly tall. For example, Detlef Lienau's forty-six-foot-wide, seventy-two-foot-high, five-story office building at 62–64 Cedar Street (1876), commissioned by the De Lancey Kane estate, was a throwback to the residential scale of pre–Civil War downtown office building construction, reflecting the doldrums of the late 1870s.[59] The timidity of Lienau's design may be only in part attributable to the prevailing economic insecurity; its Italianate design, with rhythmically grouped windows, was the product of an architect whose sensibility had been shaped a generation before. Five years later, for Henry Parish, Lienau designed a seven-story building at 67 Wall Street that was also old-fashioned in its domestic scale. Seeming more like a French apartment house of the Second Empire than an office building, this design even more clearly suggested that Lienau had failed to grasp—or had rejected—the spirit and the magnitude of the new urban order.[60]

In key ways the typical office blocks of the 1870s and early 1880s were radically different from traditional town buildings, however: they were bigger than any before, and, released from the strictures of bearing-wall construction by the introduction of metal structural frames, they were taller, with glassier facades. Reflecting their internal organization, they were also more repetitious in design than had been typical with most previous city buildings. For these reasons the standard office block, as opposed to the skyscraper, was and was not traditional. For example, Arthur Gilman's Drexel Building (1872–73), at the southeast corner of Broad and Wall Streets, built for Drexel, Morgan & Co., though probably a bearing-wall structure, was one of the first large postwar office blocks, consisting of a five-story Italianate design set on a high basement and crowned by an occupied mansard.[61] But because the floors were higher than usual and the building occupied a very

62–64 Cedar Street. Detlef Lienau, 1876. View to the southeast. Lienau Collection. CU.

67 Wall Street. Detlef Lienau, 1881. View to the southwest. Lienau Collection. CU.

big site, it swamped the scale of its setting.

Richard Morris Hunt's much more daring, threatening, and inventive Coal and Iron Exchange (1873–76), at 17–21 Cortlandt Street, on the southeast corner of Church Street, shot up nine stories from its diminutive streetscape.[62] An exchange in name only, the building was developed by the Delaware and Hudson Canal Company as a home office and as a business center for companies dealing in coal and iron. It also housed Hunt's practice between 1877 and 1881. As with the Tribune Building, working with Hunt on the project was Edward E. Raht, who was named supervising architect. Setting triple windows between masonry piers, the Coal and Iron Exchange consisted of a below-grade cellar, a sidewalk-level basement, five full floors, and a tall, slate-covered mansard incorporating two more usable floors. At the corner and at the building's eastern end, Hunt, like Gilman with the Drexel Building, raised his mansard a full story higher to suggest rectangular pavilions. Above a battered-granite basement, the building was carried on exterior bearing walls of light red Baltimore pressed brick trimmed in light green Nova Scotia sandstone. Inside, masonry load-bearing piers and walls, the latter also serving as firebreaks, were supplemented with wrought-iron floor beams spanned by flat arches topped with concrete. Though Hunt's design was rooted in practical problem-solving, it nonetheless reflected a serious effort to discover an appropriate vocabulary with which simultaneously to express and transcend the repetitious nature of the tall commercial office building type. Hunt's attempt was not entirely successful, according to Mariana Van Rensselaer. Although she characterized the building as "rich, dignified, and pleasantly effective," she held back "unqualified praise, since it is hardly a piece of true architectural composition. Its beauty comes from the polished columns which flank every window, and is *applied* beauty, though honest and elegant in its own way."[63] But Montgomery Schuyler found the structure "more successful" than the architect's Tribune Building, though "less interesting and less successful" than his Guernsey Building (see below). Notwithstanding the incised lines of the Neo-Grec decoration emulating molded Classical forms, which made the building seem heavy and stark, Schuyler deemed the Coal and Iron Exchange "a sober, dignified performance."[64]

Hunt's career was taking him away from the commercial work his Paris training had caused him to disdain. His final commercial project, the Guernsey Building (1881–82), at 160–164 Broadway, between Liberty Street and Maiden Lane, was in many ways his best—and as such, was one of the city's finest office blocks.[65] Commissioned by Henry G. Marquand, for whom Hunt was designing a townhouse (see chapter 4), the seven-story

Drexel Building, southeast corner of Broad and Wall Streets. Arthur Gilman, 1872–73. View to the southeast. NYHS.

Coal and Iron Exchange, 17–21 Cortlandt Street. Richard Morris Hunt, 1873–76. View to the southeast. King, 1895. CU.

Coal and Iron Exchange, 17–21 Cortlandt Street. Richard Morris Hunt, 1873–76. Elevation. The Octagon, AAF.

Guernsey Building was a model of urban decorum. Confined by its midblock location to a single facade, the building consisted of a two-story stone base supporting upper floors finished in brick and trimmed with stone, culminating in an attic-like top floor crowned with a bracketed cornice. The elevation was divided horizontally into three bays, two of which were equal. The third, to the south, was narrower, marking the building's entrance and rising above the cornice to form a tower capped by a steep, pyramidal roof, an echo of the architect's Tribune scheme but so locked into the building's street wall as to seem perfectly natural to the building's midblock situation. Finely detailed colonnettes framed the windows, combining with the stone banding to give the facade a distinctly horizontal emphasis. Montgomery Schuyler found the Guernsey to be "the most successful . . . of Mr. Hunt's commercial buildings. . . . Here the unit of design is the story and not a multiple or combination of stories. . . . There is no lack of animation in the design, but there is also no lack of repose. The detail is vigorous and telling without excess in quantity or scale."[66]

The Coal and Iron Exchange anticipated the future direction of office building design but was a product of the Bonanza economy. Stephen D. Hatch's 100-by-146-foot Boreel Building (1878–79), at 113–119 Broadway, occupying the entire blockfront between Thames and Cedar Streets, was the city's first large office block to be built after the Panic of 1873.[67] Greeted as a sign of renewed economic activity, the prospect of its construction was widely

Guernsey Building, 160–164 Broadway. Richard Morris Hunt, 1881–82. View to the southeast. The Octagon, AAF.

Boreel Building, 113–119 Broadway. Stephen D. Hatch, 1878–79. View to the northwest. HRE. CU.

Morse Building, northeast corner of Nassau and Beekman Streets. Silliman & Farnsworth, 1879. View to the northeast. King, 1893. CU.

reported. With none of the artistic aspirations of its across-the-street neighbor the Equitable Building, the Boreel Building exemplified the no-nonsense materialism that was to dominate much of the commercial construction of the 1880s. Hatch, selected from a competition that included entries by George B. Post and Charles F. McKim, created a highly utilitarian, flat-roofed office block, with straightforward Philadelphia brick and Ohio stone elevations that recalled the Evening Post Building. Hatch piled six floors above a two-story base incorporating street-level shops, differentiating only the top floor, as an attic set above a projecting cornice. The design had one notable feature: at the center of the Broadway facade, a tall, Classical arched entry led to a "great court fifty square feet in the center . . . supplied with an enormous skylight, throwing an immense flood of light upon what is really the principal entrance to the numerous offices."[68] Four elevators served the building, giving access to the galleries that ran along the north and south sides of the court. But even this important feature was compromised in the name of profit. The New York correspondent of the Boston-based *American Architect and Building News*, who was also "extremely negative" about the exterior, wrote: "The chance to make the large

glass-covered court . . . on which many of the offices open, an ornamental and attractive feature, seems to have been sacrificed to get a few more offices, which are, after all, but inside staterooms, depending for light and air upon the court."[69] The building's very straightforwardness and size was nonetheless admired as such. As one observer put it: "The architect . . . did not hide his poverty of means by meretricious devices, to make the whole look like a palace. It catches the eye of the multitude—as the New York Post Office does—by its size alone."[70]

Hatch followed the Boreel Building with an eight-story, midblock, dark brick and dark brownstone building (1880–81) for the Liverpool, London & Globe Insurance Company, at 45–49 William Street and 41–43 Pine Street.[71] Montgomery Schuyler deemed this structure "less conspicuous" than the Boreel, "mainly through its color. . . . But for its quieter color, it would not deserve to be distinguished from the Boreel Building." All in all, Schuyler was not taken with Hatch's work, which he not only compared with Silliman & Farnsworth's Morse Building (see below) but also with Richard Upjohn's Trinity Building (1851–53), a structure that "was always, in spite of some degree of baldness, a respectable edifice. Since it has had the good fortune

View to the northeast along Broadway showing the Welles Building (G. R. Shaw and R. G. Shaw, 1882) on the right and the Standard Oil Building (E. L. Roberts, 1884–86) on the left. AABN. MMA.

to stand next to the Boreel Building, it has gained an air of absolute distinction. The companion serves to show, both what progress New York has made within a generation in architectural knowledge, and how wide the difference is between an earnest and artistic architect and a projector of cheap commercial palaces."[72]

The 1879 completion of Silliman & Farnsworth's Morse Building, at the northeast corner of Nassau and Beekman Streets, was seen by real estate interests as a positive sign that though the city's business district was expanding northward, "the hard, solid work which gives the metropolis its character of pre-eminence and true worth will always remain in that section which has its terminus at Chambers Street."[73] Replacing the Park Hotel, which "had run its course," the Morse Building was located on the very site where the developer's ancestor Samuel F. B. Morse had made his first experiments in telegraphy.[74] Notwithstanding the small site, the building rose 145 feet, presenting the city with its tallest unbroken wall and representing as no other except perhaps the Boreel Building a class of tall, large, fundamentally utilitarian office blocks with no aspiration to make a skyline statement. In comparison to the Boreel, however, the Morse Building was more self-

consciously architectural, although Montgomery Schuyler deemed both of them "probably for their size the cheapest office buildings that have been put up in New York since 1861."[75] Whereas the Boreel Building had a comparatively spacious setting, the Morse Building faced two narrow streets, robbing it of a perspective. It in no way could be deemed iconic—though it was of an unprecedented height it was merely a bit of infill in the city's fabric. Schuyler was nonetheless pleased with the results: "To put up a parallelepiped of such dimensions under such circumstances so that it should not be a monument of ugliness was a hard problem [which] . . . the architects . . . have solved . . . so successfully that their work is impressive and dignified in the mass, and in many places exceedingly agreeable in detail." Schuyler was impressed with the way the young team of architects used the building's construction for decorative advantage, especially the use of molded bricks in the lower floors, which he found "positively delightful," and the use of black bricks to highlight important structural elements such as an arch, "or to add vigor to a springer." Above the two-story base there was much less modeling, which also pleased Schuyler, who observed that "it behooves us to remember how much better monotony is than miscellany."

Royal Phelps Building, 25 Union Square West. Richard Morris Hunt, 1872. View to the west. The Octagon, AAF.

Schuyler disapproved of the building's great height—he would have preferred five rather than eight stories—and he would have been happier had the composition been crowned with a steep roof rather than the flat one Silliman & Farnsworth designed. But he praised the building as "one of the most interesting pieces of brickwork in New York, and [a] really needed demonstration, that an elevator building half as high again as its width need not be either a miracle of ugliness or a monument of vulgarity."[76]

Given the narrow streets flanking its site, the Morse Building's height was all the more startling. The New York correspondent of the *American Architect and Building News* reported that "many who watched the uprising walls wondered whether they would ever cease growing skywards."[77] Intriguing also was the extensive use of architectural terra cotta—New York's first demonstration of that material's value in commercial construction. (George B. Post had experimented with it in a house [1877] for Henry M. Braem at 15 East Thirty-seventh Street [see chapter 4].) Schuyler, characterizing the Morse Building as the "first of the noteworthy attempts to build in brick alone, and to discard stone, even in the positions in which stone had been accepted as indispensable," found the brickwork exemplary.[78] Looking back on the Morse Building with twenty years' hindsight, he deemed it

> one of the last and one of the best works of the Gothic revival in New York, of that true Gothic revival which consisted not in the reproduction of Gothic forms but in the application of the Gothic principle of functional expression. The piers and pinnacles of the main entrance were perhaps a little clumsy. Perhaps the vigor of handling degenerated into "brutality." But the entrance was none the less a considered and artistic piece of design, and a grateful object. Better yet, in fact one of the most interesting pieces of commercial architecture in New York, was the two-story basement itself, the tall principal story with its round arches of red brickwork, with a temperate use of black and of moulded brick, admirably expressing the construction, over the segmental arches of the sunken story, turned between springers of black brick.[79]

Silliman & Farnsworth followed this success with the Temple Court (1881–83), diagonally across from the Morse Building at 7 Beekman Street, at the southwest corner of Nassau Street.[80] The Temple Court, a vigorously detailed, ten-story design, though in essence a commercial block sought to break with the type by incorporating twin towers, which gave it some of the presence of a true skyscraper. Inside, the Temple Court featured a generous, 212-foot-square light court topped by a pyramidal skylight and ringed by elaborately ornamented balustrades.

Sometimes the new sobriety of approach proved too much, either for the architects or their clients, and a splash of ornament was slapped on to gussy up the final effect. Such seems to have been the case with the Boston architects G. R. Shaw and R. G. Shaw's nine-story, steeply mansarded Welles Building (1882), on the east side of Broadway facing Bowling Green, which the *Real Estate*

Record and Builders' Guide dismissed as a building that its "architect, having assayed to build . . . [in] plain granite . . . , had feared that it would be too plain, and added the orders as an afterthought, thereby spending the money of his clients unnecessarily and confusing the character of his building by adding trivialities to its plainness."[81] Next door, E. L. Roberts's Standard Oil Building (1884–86), built to house the newly prosperous oil company, was more commanding because of its clifflike granite street wall.[82] Despite an attempt to suggest a campanile at the midpoint of the facade, as the *Record and Guide* observed, "nothing can be simpler than the composition nor plainer than the treatment."[83] Taken as a pair, the two buildings exploded the scale of lower Broadway and historic Bowling Green, signaling a new order of urbanism.

No office building of the 1880s was more reviled for its directness than Alfred J. Bloor's seven-story Bryant Building (1882), erected on the site of the old offices of the *New York Evening Post*, at the northwest corner of Nassau and Liberty Streets. Attacked by the *Record and Guide* for "plainness . . . near to baldness and . . . simplicity [that] becomes monotonous," Bloor's design, with its "unmodelled and undecorated brick piers" and identical, repeated rectangular windows, suggested that "no attempt has been made at architecture. . . . Nobody is likely to admire this building, perhaps, but on the other hand, nobody can be offended or disgusted by it, and if its architect has missed professional fame, he has escaped professional reproach."[84]

The Artistic Office Building

While sobersided utilitarianism marked many of the largest office blocks, there was, beginning around 1880, a growing tendency, mostly manifested in smaller infill buildings, to experiment with new forms and unusual compositions in an effort to take advantage of emerging building technologies and provide efficient space to commercial tenants. This trend toward self-consciously artistic design was initiated by Richard Morris Hunt with his Royal Phelps Building (1872), which occupied a twenty-five-foot-wide site at 25 Union Square West, south of Sixteenth Street.[85] The building combined cast iron and stone in a glassy, rhythmically disposed tripartite scheme with an arcaded midsection. As Sarah Bradford Landau has pointed out, the design probably had a decisive influence on the young architect Louis Sullivan, who, after visiting New York and Hunt's office in the early 1870s, made it the basis for his and Dankmar Adler's Jewelers' (1881–82) and Troescher (1884) Buildings, in Chicago.[86]

On the so-called Jauncey Court plot on Wall Street, Alfred Thorp's seven-story home for the Orient Insurance Company (1876–77), at 41–43 Wall Street,[87] and Clinton & Pirsson's six-story Queens Insurance Company Building (1877), at 37–39 Wall Street,[88] were notably artistic midblock office buildings. They suggested a new scale and reflected a new sense of efficiency while somehow managing to connect with pre–Civil War scale. While Detlef Lienau's Cedar and Wall Street buildings seemed only to

View to the southeast along Wall Street showing the Orient Insurance Company Building (Alfred Thorp, 1876–77) on the left and the Queens Insurance Company Building (Clinton & Pirsson, 1877) on the right. Part of the Mills Building (George B. Post, 1880–82) is visible on the extreme right. LAA. CU.

55 Broadway, southwest corner of Exchange Place. Babb & Cook, 1880–81. Rendering of view to the southwest. CM. CU.

Corbin Building, northeast corner of Broadway and John Street. Francis H. Kimball, 1888–89. View to the northeast, c. 1920. NYHS.

Potter Building, 36 Park Row. Norris Gibson Starkweather, 1883–85. View to the northeast showing, from right to left, the Potter Building, Times Building (George B. Post, 1887–89), and World Building (George B. Post, 1889–90). King, 1893. CU.

look back, the Jauncey Court buildings managed to refer both back and forward. At first the two companies intended to construct a single building, but when they could not agree on certain issues each proceeded independently. According to the *American Architect and Building News*, the "two designs [were] . . . as far apart as Gaul from Briton."[89] Thorp's design, developed with his assistant Henry Rutgers Marshall, was French in inspiration, much like a Paris apartment house. Not only did the white marble–clad exterior with its continuous ironwork railings at the attic story seem French, so too did the interior planning, where an irregular lot gave rise to unequal front and rear offices separated by an open staircase wrapping two elevators. The Queens Insurance Company Building seemed more modern, more structurally expressive in a Viollet-le-Duc–inspired, English Gothic sort of way. Clinton & Pirsson's design was vividly polychromed, combining red and black brick for the walls with ordinary brownstone and Wyoming bluestone for the voussoirs of the vaguely pointed window embrasures. Wyoming blue-

stone was a new material on the New York scene, but one whose "excellence must bring it into general use."[90] While Thorp's horizontal organization was regular, Clinton & Pirsson's was asymmetrical, with a narrow bay adjacent to its neighbor rising above the dormered mansard to a steep pyramidal roof, a strategy that would be similarly employed by Richard Morris Hunt in his Guernsey Building. Montgomery Schuyler was not impressed with the buildings either as an ensemble or taken individually. Of Thorp's building he wryly observed: "It is not an easy thing to make a seven-story building thirty feet wide by eighty high look respectable." He dismissed Clinton & Pirsson's work as a "'fancy building' . . . of the deepest dye, [which] has the appearance of having been done by an 'architect.'"[91]

Babb & Cook's 55 Broadway (1880–81), at the southwest corner of Exchange Alley, was another artistically noteworthy building.[92] Although it was only twenty-six feet four inches wide, the building climbed a full six stories. The design was highly inventive, an early example of the influence of the Queen Anne style, with a narrow bay and wide bay facing Broadway, the latter featuring Serlian windows on the first and fourth floors. Beautifully detailed, the building lacked a sense of structural urgency, what Mariana Van Rensselaer called "the finest sort of structural composition." But, as Van Rensselaer put it, the overall effect was handsome: "Unity is not lost in variety, and yet the variety is great enough to hide from the eye the preposterous proportions of the wall."[93] George E. Harney's five-story building (1883) for the Commercial Union Insurance Company, at 46 Pine Street, on the northwest corner of William Street, was another tall, narrow corner building, occupying an exceptionally slim site, just twenty by seventy-five feet.[94] The red brick and Carlisle stone building with red terra cotta trim displayed "a . . . liberal use of sheet metal," which caused the *Real Estate Record and Builders' Guide* to wonder whether Harney "would have preferred it if he had had his own way." With its pyramidally capped corner tower and street-level arcade, the composition was nonetheless inventive "while stopping short of the point at which variety in a building of these dimensions becomes restless or ridiculous."[95] Francis H. Kimball adapted Harney's *parti* to the taller and longer Corbin Building (1888–89), an eight-story effort that rose along John Street between Broadway and Nassau Street.[96] Kimball's clifflike, 20-foot-wide, 161-foot-long design consisted of a long wall divided into two equal parts, set between two pyramidally roofed corner "towers." The arcaded ground floor contained bay-windowed storefronts and carried a two-story base punctuated with triple windows and an "attic" of arched windows, which also served as a "base" for triple-height arcades filled with bay windows, supporting a two-story-high attic and a rooftop balustrade. The tawny brick and dark terra cotta of the upper stories sat upon a dark brownstone base. Schuyler found that in spite of the "drawback" of the compositional superimposition of one building on the other, the "work is of a very high interest. . . . We can scarcely see elsewhere in New York, except in Mr. Kimball's own work, so idiomatic and characteristic a treatment of terra cotta on so elaborate a scale." In addition, Schuyler observed that "at the Broadway end, the pavilion works out naturally and effectively into a tower, and the tall arcade is an impressive feature."[97] The design departed from the usual stylistic precedents to suggest the French Renaissance of Francis I, which enabled Kimball to reveal a virtuoso command of terra cotta, combining round arches with Gothic detail.

Four years after the completion of the Morse Building, Norris Gibson Starkweather's elaborately ornamented, Queen Anne–style Potter Building (1883–85), at 36 Park Row, carried forward the experimental use of terra cotta in a rich design that managed to combine a highly efficient, superscaled infill block with a remarkable yet not overweening individuality.[98] The developer of the building was Orlando B. Potter, a prominent lawyer, businessman, and former congressman who had been pilloried for a tragic fire killing several people at the building that had previously stood on the site, which was also known as the Pot-

ter Building. The new building was thus intended as a textbook case for fire retardation. The developer and architects chose to clad the structural iron and masonry in hollow brick, making it the first fireproof tall building in New York. As Andrew Dolkart has recently pointed out, while the Potter Building was a fireproofing pioneer, it was also rather backward; despite the structural use of iron, it had the distinction of being the city's last major building to be built entirely with load-bearing walls. Terra cotta had only been available from a Boston company, and Potter became so interested in the material that in 1886 he established the New York Architectural Terra-Cotta Company, with headquarters in the Potter Building.

At its completion, the Potter Building was the tallest in the area, with exceptionally detailed street facades that offered a bravura show of craftsmanship, especially above the eighth floor, where flamboyant Composite capitals, broken pediments, urns, buttress caps, and other details demonstrated terra cotta's decorative possibilities. The *Real Estate Record and Builders' Guide* failed to appreciate

Western Union Building, 16–18 Broad Street. Henry J. Hardenbergh, 1882–83. View to the northwest showing part of the New York Stock Exchange (James Renwick Jr., 1879–82) on the right. HRE. CU.

Washington Building, Battery Place from Broadway to Greenwich Street. Edward H. Kendall, 1882–85. View to the east from West Street showing the Washington Building on the left and the New York Produce Exchange (George B. Post, 1881–84) on the right.

In the distance, to the left of the Washington Building, are the Welles Building (G. R. Shaw and R. G. Shaw, 1882) and the Standard Oil Building (E. L. Roberts, 1884–86). NYHS.

the elaborate facades, and when the building was completed stated:

> At least there will be no more of it. It is a long time since it became artistically possible to put on anything more. It is now mechanically impossible to pile any more bricks over the pediments and pinnacles without taking them down. Two stories ago the architect seemed to have discharged his function of design. But then, apparently at the instigation of the owner, who had discovered the walls could carry more weight . . . the luckless designer seems to have braced himself and taken a fresh start . . . relieving the strain of his professional feelings with a wild orgy of pediments and pinnacles. . . . All the good work that has been done in recent architecture has been thrown away on the designer of the Potter building, which is coarse, pretentious, overloaded and intensely vulgar.[99]

Potter and Starkweather also collaborated on the seven-story Astor Place Building (1881–83), at 746–750 Broadway, on the northeast corner of Astor Place, combining an entirely cast-iron, Neo-Grec–inspired first floor with an elaborately detailed superstructure of brick and terra cotta.[100] Originally intended as a mixed-use building combining hotel and mercantile facilities, it was instead occupied by clothing manufacturers.

Henry J. Hardenbergh's Western Union Building (1882–83), at 16–18 Broad Street, housing a branch office of the company, was the first of the architect's commercial structures.[101] A synthesis of the ideas of Richard Morris Hunt and Detlef Lienau, with whom Hardenbergh had apprenticed, the commission for the eight-story building was won in competition. Its height was conspicuous among Broad Street's still residential scale, although its neighbor to the north, James Renwick Jr.'s New York Stock Exchange (see below), with four stories and an attic, was just as high. Montgomery Schuyler was troubled by the vertical composition of the brick building; he liked the design of the one-story stone basement floor but found it too low, and praised the building's "crowning member, including the double square-headed openings of the seventh story, the cornice and the range of dormers."[102] The following year, Hardenbergh completed another branch office for the rapidly expanding company, at Fifth Avenue and Twenty-third Street (see chapter 5).

Edward H. Kendall's Washington Building (1882–85) was the most spectacularly sited as well as one of the largest and most memorable of the artistic office buildings of the early 1880s.[103] The Queen Anne–inspired building was commissioned by Cyrus W. Field, a self-made man whose company laid the first cable under the Atlantic, in the 1860s, and who had gone on to invest in New York's elevated railroads. Kendall won a six-firm competition to replace the Kennedy Mansion (1761), which had long since been converted to use as the Washington Hotel. The new building would be set on a spacious, exceptionally prominent corner site extending 172 feet along Battery Place from Broadway to Greenwich Street. The competitors included J. C. Cady, George B. Post, Richard M.

Upjohn, Thomas Stent, Silliman & Farnsworth, and Charles B. Atwood. Atwood's glassy, boldly articulated design featured a crowstepped gable incorporating a clock and carrying a Georgianesque tower as well as a tenth-floor restaurant and a flexible arrangement of office partitions that could be changed to suit the needs of tenants. Kendall's romantic design was at once simpler than Atwood's but blocky, until 1886–87, when the architect, asked to increase the building's height from ten to twelve stories, added a high-dormered mansard and a bold tower adapted from a lighthouse to enable the building to more appropriately celebrate its dramatic site.

The *Real Estate Record and Builders' Guide*'s critic, probably Montgomery Schuyler, reviewed the building before the mansard was added, finding little to like. The critic objected to its fantastic ornament, which included the depiction of a dragon as well as festoons and cornucopias, proclaiming that "there is more satisfaction to be got out of a twenty-foot house that shows straightforward purpose and virility in its design than out of a mile of this insipid, ineffectual, namby-pamby stuff which the public is expected to accept as artistic architecture."[104] Mariana Van Rensselaer, also writing before the mansard was added, was likewise unimpressed, although she admired the handling of the stone with its "profusion of delicately carved decoration." But she noted that composition, though "attempted, . . . can hardly be said to be achieved; for the tall pilasters which run up the cornice and are crowned with capitals do not compose the wall and unite its features, as do true piers with arches thrown between them. And the elaborate detail is wasted; for it is too delicate and too small in scale, and is distributed too impartially."[105] Problematic though these buildings may have seemed to the critics, they nonetheless established the design of the standard office building as a worthy pursuit for artistically ambitious architects and not merely an exercise in functionally and financially dictated urban infill.

The Influence of Henry Hobson Richardson

By the mid-1880s, the impact of the artistic but fundamentally domestic Queen Anne style had run its course, replaced by a Romanesque-inspired approach that explored the potential of the arcade to organize the increasingly vertical walls of the proliferating office blocks. While the Romanesque, or round-arch, style had been the basis of a number of important pre–Civil War efforts to find an appropriate expression for the tall building, it was not until Henry Hobson Richardson interpreted the Romanesque—highlighting its bold scale, heavy massing, and, above all, rigorous, Classical-inspired compositional clarity—that it set the agenda for the work of the 1880s and beyond.[106]

Possibly the earliest design to apply the lessons of the Romanesque arcade to the tall building was that of the United Bank Building (1880–81), at the northeast corner of Wall Street and Broadway, designed by the Boston firm of Peabody & Stearns, which had opened an office in New York as a result of being selected to design the Union

United Bank Building, northeast corner of Wall Street and Broadway. Peabody & Stearns, 1880–81. View to the northeast. King, 1893. CU.

League Club (see chapter 2).[107] Replacing Hurry & Rogers's Bank of the Republic (1851–52), a pioneering five-story commercial palazzo, the methodically composed, flat-roofed design of the United Bank took its cues from Richardson's R. and F. Cheney Building (1875–76), in Hartford, Connecticut, perhaps the first significant arcaded office block to be realized and surely the most influential.[108] Framed by strong corner piers and a trabeated attic crowned by a corbeled cornice, the United Bank also included Neo-Grec and Ruskinian Gothic details. Punctuated by significant portals at each street, the building consisted of a two-story base carrying two intermediate floors, four floors treated as an arcade of closely spaced pilasters, and an attic cornice, all combining to create a remarkably unified effect. The design was important not only for its composition but also because it broke with the previous model for bank architecture: whereas Griffith Thomas's National Park Bank (1866–68) (see below), for example, had been conceived as a civic monument, with an elaborate sculpture program on the facade and a spectacular banking room, the United Bank was simply an office

building, with a not unusually high main floor providing banking space for United as well as for the First National Bank, which was given pride of place at the corner. Critics found the building's character off-putting; according to Montgomery Schuyler, during the early stages of its design development, the scheme raised an "active animosity [among those] interested in architecture."[109] The critic of the *Real Estate Record and Builders' Guide*, possibly Schuyler as well, was scathing in his assessment:

> It used to be a favorite theory [that the two partners] were doing a "limited competition" against each other. . . . There are more outrageous and more vulgar and even more ignorant pieces of architecture in New York, but it is questionable whether there is one more silly. In the first place, there was that robustious foundation and then there were those incredibly helpless and foolish looking pilasters and then there were the iron mullions in the windows in Wall Street, which seemed to be put in only to show that iron could be so used as to take up as much room as stone and then there were the fraudulent entrance arches, which are not entrances at all.[110]

Youngs & Cable's Aldrich Court (1886–87), at 41–45 Broadway, running through to 17–21 Trinity Place, was the first tall building to interrupt the five-story-high wall of buildings between the Washington Building and Trinity Church.[111] Though eclectic in detail, the design was fundamentally Richardsonian Romanesque, especially at the base, where a bold, low-sprung arch formed the main entrance. Though the vertical integration of the middle floors, effected by an alternating rhythm of paired arcades rising to steeply raked, dormerlike pediments, was a decided step forward from Peabody & Stearns's United Bank, the design failed to please the *Record and Guide*:

> There is no pretense in the design of adherence to any known style, nor is there any reason shown for the departure. An intelligent eclecticism is one thing, a thoughtless hodge-podge is quite another. An architect is entitled to take what he needs wherever he can find it, if the result is unity, but his artistic responsibilities and difficulties are increased by that course. In this case we have Gothic gables and finials, Rococo balusters, pediments of the Dutch Renaissance, and carving that is rather more Romanesque than it is anything else. The scheme of composition by which the horizontal lines were effaced and the vertical lines emphasized and multiplied, doomed a front of these dimensions to look weak and monotonous, and there is nothing in the detail to redeem this impression. Except the basement there is nothing to call for admiration. We do not know who the architect is, but we regret to say that his work betrays both want of training and want of thinking, and furnishes a solemn warning against intrusting a work so important to an untrained and unthinking designer.[112]

Robert W. Gibson's United States Trust Company (1888–89), at 45–47 Wall Street, replacing a modest three-story building, was the period's last consequential highrise, midblock infill and was the most literal reflection of

Aldrich Court, 41–45 Broadway. Youngs & Cable, 1886–87. View to the south showing Aldrich Court in the middle and the Washington Building (Edward H. Kendall, 1882–85; mansard addition, 1887) on the extreme left. MCNY.

Richardson's ideas.[113] Gibson beat Babb, Cook & Willard as well as Charles W. Clinton, George B. Post, and J. C. Cady in a competition for the building, which would vastly overpower its near neighbors, including Alfred Thorp's Orient Building (see above), at number 41. Anticipating the trend of the next decade, Babb, Cook & Willard's rejected scheme was more restrained and Classical than Gibson's design, which Montgomery Schuyler deemed Richardsonian to the point of embarrassment. Schuyler nonetheless found pleasure in "the parts rather than in the whole," and praised it "as one of the most picturesque 'bits' in our street architecture."[114] The *Record and Guide* found Gibson's brownstone-trimmed granite building

> impossible to ignore. The designer has attained one requisite of commercial art in making it extremely conspicuous. . . . [Even given the cacophony of Wall Street's architecture] the effect of the new building . . . is more than commonly self-assertive. It adjoins on one side a prim, white marble building, characterized by much precision and delicacy of detail, and on the other a decorous and respectable four-story building in brown stone. This last is so evidently obsolete and doomed that it need not in any case have been considered by the designer of the new building; but the combination of materials he has chosen, admirable in itself and for a detached building, greatly sharpens the contrast with its neighbors that is created by its treatment. . . . The fault one finds with the architect of the United States Trust Company is that his work does not betray a purpose. That is to say, it has no character, unless obstreperousness may be so considered. The impression it makes is not single, but multiplex, and even miscellaneous. It is here meagre and rude and there barbarically rich, without harmonious relations. It is an assemblage of "features" that does not form a countenance. The features must be taken by themselves, and it is noteworthy that in the best of them, in the doorway, in spite of the drawbacks noted, and in the colonnade of the second story he owes his exemplar little or nothing. For these we are sincerely obliged to him, but a building for which its parts may be taken without injury to them, as these may, is not an architectural composition.[115]

Another significant Romanesque-inspired building of the late 1880s was William B. Tubby's seven-story, red brick and brownstone Market and Fulton National Bank (1888–89), at 81–83 Fulton Street and 55–59 Gold Street, with thirty-eight feet of frontage on Ann Street as well.[116] Notable for its battlemented corner rising above the building for a half story to form "a rudimentary and roofless tower," the *Record and Guide* saw this "most ambitious feature" as the "great mistake in the composition," creating a jarring interruption of the otherwise accomplished arcaded walls.[117] Schuyler also faulted the corner tower, which he deemed "distinctly injurious" to the building's narrow front, but praised the building's details, many of which— including the tall arcaded base, the arcaded treatment of the walls tying together floors four through seven, and the elaborate handling of the entrance—were based on

United States Trust Company Building, 45–47 Wall Street. Robert W. Gibson, 1888–89. View to the south showing the Orient Insurance Company Building (Alfred Thorp, 1876–77) on the right. King, 1893. CU.

Proposed United States Trust Company Building, 45–47 Wall Street. Babb, Cook & Willard, 1888. Elevation. AABN. CU.

Market and Fulton National Bank Building, northwest corner of Fulton and Gold Streets. William B. Tubby, 1888–89. View to the northwest. King, 1893. CU.

Richardson's view of the Romanesque.[118]

Charles W. Clinton's intermittently arcaded building for the Mutual Life Insurance Company of New York (1882–84), at 34 Nassau Street, with additional frontages on both Liberty and Cedar Streets, replaced a former post office that had been built as the Middle Dutch Church.[119] The design embodied the principles of the Romanesque but expressed them in a distinctly Classical way, anticipating the work of the 1890s. Clinton was awarded the commission for the eight-story, 161-foot-high building after an invited competition that also included entries from Edward H. Kendall, J. Morgan Slade, Napoleon Le Brun & Sons, John Correja, George B. Post, and W. Wheeler Smith. Clinton's design called for a lavishly detailed, Classical-inspired building that filled its lot except for a slight recess of the middle portion along Nassau Street. The design was notable for its handling of the broad pilasters and numerous other details, as well as for its overall pavilionated composition: a rusticated two-story base rising through a two-story intermediate zone to four floors combined between giant orders, culminating in an elaborate cornice and an arcaded attic. Despite these attributes, it was the building's bulk and its lavish interiors that drew the most attention. Mariana Van Rensselaer declared the light-colored limestone building "sumptuous," suggesting "a certain elegance" that one finds along the streets of Paris: "Its rather elaborate detail is sufficiently well distributed, and its mass has some excellence (though not striking excellence) of composition. . . . [It] is attractive in many ways, and is neither vulgar nor commonplace."[120] But while the building was still under construction, the *Real Estate Record and Builders' Guide*, in one of the earliest discussions of the urbanistic issues raised by tall buildings, argued that it was "a mistake . . . to set a building of the dimension and proportions of this on an alley, and Nassau Street is little more than an alley." It was not the

Mutual Life Insurance Company of New York Building, 34 Nassau Street. Charles W. Clinton, 1882–84. Entrance. MONY.

Mutual Life Insurance Company of New York Building, 34 Nassau Street. Charles W. Clinton, 1882–84. Perspective. NYHS.

height in and of itself that was troubling to the *Record and Guide*'s editors but the implications such great height would have on the future development of the city's oldest neighborhood: "If the owner opposite chooses to put up another ten-story building, he will, of course, make the fifth story of the Mutual building nearly as dark as the ground floor of the ordinary Nassau street building, and the stories beneath it will get still less light." The *Record and Guide* went on to suggest that the Mutual Life Insurance Company could have "protected itself by setting back its building with a plaza in front of it . . . and would probably have found this sacrifice paid in the increased attractiveness of its building to tenants, even if the city had not assumed and assessed upon the adjoining property some portion of the cost of the improvement."[121] In a subsequent article, the *Record and Guide*'s editors repeated their criticism and went on to say that "architecturally there is probably nothing so absurd as the relation of the new building to its surrounding to be seen in any other city in the world."[122]

The interior of the Mutual Life Building was particularly ornate. According to *Building* magazine, it seemed "to contain a quarry-full of marble. . . . In going from the portico, on Nassau street, to the top story, the visitor finds marble beneath his feet all around him; the main stairway is marble. The corridor presents marble arches in relief, together with marble pillars. The room of the corporation within the counter is floored with marble." But the "light and elegant" molding of the principal suite of offices was made of cement.[123] The interior also contained large amounts of scagliola and gilding. Four years after the Mutual Life Building's completion, Clinton added an eight-story addition.

George B. Post

George B. Post was the architect who dominated commercial office building construction in the 1880s. Capitalizing on his success at the Equitable and Western Union Buildings, Post designed numerous major office buildings during the decade, which, taken as a group, were regarded, as Russell Sturgis put it, "to be among the best built, best planned, most useful and most truly economical of our modern structures."[124] Post's gray limestone Smith Building (1879–80), at 3–7 Cortlandt Street, was one of the early important exercises in straightforward commercial design.[125] Like Hunt's Coal and Iron Exchange (1873–76) (see above), a neighbor, the Smith Building was, as Montgomery Schuyler put it, "only a street front" but "crowned with gabled dormers which are the only features of architectural interest, and they not of much; but if it be not interesting, it is at least an entirely inoffensive piece of prosaic work."[126] Despite Schuyler's harsh judgment, the Smith Building had rather more to offer. As Winston Weisman has written, it was "a masterpiece of functional, commercial design. The bones of the building stand out clear and strong with the leaded glass, terra-cotta, and classical features giving great visual appeal to a facade so intelligently articulated."[127]

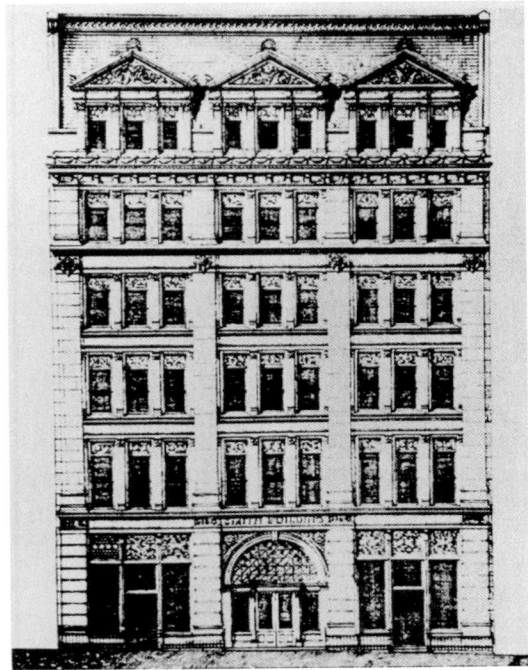

Smith Building, 3–7 Cortlandt Street. George B. Post, 1879–80. Elevation. NYHS.

Post Building, site bounded by Exchange Place and Beaver and Hanover Streets. George B. Post, 1880–81. View to the northwest. AR. CU.

Mills Building, northeast corner of Broad Street and Exchange Place. George B. Post, 1880–82. View to the northeast. NYHS.

Post's first office building in the 1880s and, according to Sturgis, one deemed by many to be "the best" of his office buildings, "at least in New York City," was the seven-story Post Building (1880–81), financed by the architect's father and uncle, occupying half a block bounded by Exchange Place and Beaver and Hanover Streets.[128] The site was triangular, with light on three sides, and Post had the smart idea to carve out a large court above the second floor along the Beaver Street side of the building, thereby guaranteeing an outside exposure to every room. This resulted in an arrangement that Schuyler praised, even though he quarreled with details of the design, not the least of which was the "huge and swaggering entrance arch" which he felt revealed Post's unregenerate desire to "'collar the eye' at all hazards." Schuyler nonetheless pronounced the building "a piece of cultivated architecture, and a real addition to the short list of artistic business buildings in New York."[129] The *Real Estate Record and Builders' Guide*'s critic, who may have been Schuyler, praised the building as well, comparing it favorably to Vaux & Withers's handling of a triangular site at the Jefferson Market Courthouse (see chapter 2), noting that the use of external courts gave "an opportunity for a striking architectural treatment . . . leaving boldly projecting wings, and forming a very effective composition." The *Record and Guide*'s critic nonetheless decried the absence of expression of the elevator penthouse, making an interesting point: "The elevator itself, which necessarily rises above the inhabited parts of the building, and requires a tower-like enclosure seems to offer a very suggestive motive for architectural treatment. Even the grain elevators of the lare [*sic*] cities, none of which have ever been taken in hand by an architectural artist, have a character and a polychromy of their own . . . and it is the mark of bad architecture that it conceals things, and of good architecture that it expresses things."[130]

The use of the court, creating unequal wings facing Beaver Street, marked a breakthrough in planning, providing for evenly lighted offices on all floors above the base. The western wing needed to be half the width of the other because it sat along the lot line, necessitating a windowless party wall. The daylighting conditions, combined with the regularity of Post's fenestration, made each floor far more uniform, and therefore more suitable for the typical cubicle office arrangements of the day than virtually any building preceding it, defining perhaps even more decisively than any feature of technology the unique nature of the office building type. Post's pale yellow brick and terra cotta facades combined stacked window arcades suggestive of the Romanesque with colossal Classical pilasters that bound together four of the building's eight stories. The building's principal corners were rounded, with the pilasters held back to form an implied tourelle pierced by a window on each floor, yielding an exceptionally glassy effect that was also a characteristic of the two-story base, where windows were set into elaborately crafted ironwork.

Post's Mills Building (1880–82), at the northeast corner of Broad Street and Exchange Place, with an ell running

Mills Building, northeast corner of Broad Street and Exchange Place. George B. Post, 1880. Preliminary scheme. NYHS.

through to Wall Street, financed by Darius O. Mills, went much further in the direction of straightforward utilitarianism.[131] While the Smith Building had been notably rational in its structural expression and the Post Building introduced a level of accommodation that would become standard for first-class office buildings, the ten-story, 156-foot-tall, red brick and New Jersey brownstone Mills Building, occupying a half-acre site, has been acclaimed by Winston Weisman as the world's "first modern office building."[132] It was certainly the largest, housing 800 tenants with a daily resident population of 1,500 workers who, together with visitors, were said to make 11,000 trips on the building's ten elevators. The Mills Building was the first to have its own electricity-generating plant, with sufficient capacity to light 5,588 Edison lamps, supplementing the daylighting provided by the U-shaped plan surrounding an open court facing Broad Street. A grand, skylit lobby rotunda was served by passageways leading from entrances on Broad and Wall Streets and Exchange Place, thereby providing through-block passageways, initiating a trend that would in essence render ground-floor lobby space an extension of the public realm. The individual entrances to the Mills Building were connected to the sidewalk over areaways that sent light down to leasable cellar spaces.

Post's facade consisted of a two-story base topped by a two-three-two pattern of piled Classical piers and entablatures. A projecting cornice crowned by a balustrade concluded the composition. A secondary system of recessed intermediate piers and terra cotta spandrels—one of the earliest architectural uses of this material—heightened the compositional clarity of a remarkably straightforward design. While at first glance the building seemed a flat-roofed, palazzo-inspired design, in fact a mansarded penthouse set well behind the parapet provided an additional leasable floor. An earlier version without a courtyard was more eloquent in its expression of verticality, as well as more picturesque, with a dormered mansard that reflected Post's previous work.

Mortimer Building, southwest corner of Wall and New Streets. George B. Post, 1884. Perspective view to the south. AABN. MMA.

Equitable Life Assurance Society Building, 120 Broadway. Edward H. Kendall and Theodore Weston, 1875–76. View to the east. NYHS.

Apart from its design, the Mills Building was something of a construction marvel, with the flow of materials scientifically organized in advance and laborers working at night under calcium lights. As a result, by the time the building was completed in 1882 it had, according to the critic for the *Real Estate Record and Builders' Guide*, "probably been more talked about than any other building lately put up in New York." Not everyone appreciated Post's straightforward utilitarianism. But the project's fame in part rested with what this critic described as its "misfortunes." These included its size—it was just about the largest building in New York—and the problems faced during construction, most of them attributable to the fact that "the building was built too fast," a condition the *Record and Guide*'s critic also felt plagued the building's architecture, which he claimed "suffered" from having "been done in a hurry." The *Record and Guide*'s critic found the Mills Building's light court "so deep for its width that it has the appearance from within and without of a mere slit rather than of a recess capable of a dignified architectural treatment." The critic went on to dismiss the almost

neutral grid of the elevations as virtually random:

> That is to say, there is no reason why the building should end where it does rather than at any other place. . . . In fact, it does not end, but merely gives out. . . . And saying this is saying that the Mills Building is not a work of architecture. . . . No building, even if it had great merit otherwise, could be successful if it had, like the Mills Building, two middles. . . . In mass and detail, the Mills Building is an architectural failure. It is remarkable that so large and important a building should be erected from the designs of a man of ability, which should be so stupid and tiresome to look at, and which can scarcely be said to have an interesting feature.[133]

Mariana Van Rensselaer found the Mills Building "bad in many ways, but good in the bold disposition of its masses, which has been effected by recessing the central portion, and thus putting the courtyard outside."[134] Perhaps Russell Sturgis, writing in 1898, put the problem of the Mills Building best: "[It] is one of those structures about which the traditional critic and the realistic critic can never agree." But, Sturgis continued, the building had

Equitable Life Assurance Society Building, 120 Broadway. George B. Post, 1886–89. View to the east. ELAS.

Equitable Life Assurance Society Building, 120 Broadway. George B. Post, 1886–89. Lobby arcade. ELAS.

Equitable Life Assurance Society Building, 120 Broadway. George B. Post, 1886–89. Lawyers Club. NYHS.

Equitable Life Assurance Society Building, 120 Broadway. George B. Post, 1886–89. Business hall. ELAS.

virtues: "There is no building in town which seems to serve its purpose better, and which makes less pretense of being something else than what it really is—a pile of nine superincumbent stories of precisely similar offices."[135]

Given the evidence of many of Post's typical office buildings, which were far more picturesque, it can be argued that the severity of the Mills Building was probably imposed on the architect. Post returned to the aesthetic compositional strategies of his early work, especially to pavilionated massing and prominent mansarded roofs, in his Mortimer Building (1884), at the southwest corner of Wall and New Streets.[136] The limestone and yellow brick and terra cotta building replaced a previous building of the same name built fifty years before. Again, the editors of the *Real Estate Record and Builders' Guide* lambasted Post's design as "monotonous," in part because they were still unprepared, it would appear, for the repetitive realities of the increasingly standardized office building type. The *Record and Guide* writers were so put out by the design that they editorialized against it, claiming that it belittled the neighboring Stock Exchange. They found the building's deeply recessed Wall Street entrance, incorporating a stairway that wound its way up to the main floor, particularly egregious, "enough to make the Exchange a laughing stock. Better no entrance at all than the pretentious but shabby little front on the little street."[137]

By the mid-1880s, with business booming and many new downtown buildings being constructed, Arthur Gilman and Edward H. Kendall's once pioneering Equitable Building (1867–70) (see above) was fast becoming out of date. In 1875–76 Kendall, assisted by Theodore Weston, had already extended the building east along its Cedar Street side, raising the mansard on the original portion one more story. In 1886, after Richard Morris Hunt declined the job, Post, who had worked on the original building with Gilman and Kendall but had not been its designer, was called on to help with its reconstruction and expansion. This renovation, completed three years later, was made possible by the acquisition of all the property on the block except for the two corners facing Nassau Street.[138] The 1886 expansion was in part a response to the growing appetite of the Equitable Life Assurance Society for office space, but it also offered an opportunity to reconfigure the building, electrify it, make it fully fireproof, and improve its public lobbies, creating a clear three-hundred-foot-long passage connecting Broadway and Nassau Street as well as a forty-four-by-one-hundred-foot central court. As the renovation was under way, the *Real Estate Record and Builders' Guide* reported that the passages "will practically form beautiful streets running through the block" that would "open into a great number of little shops and booths between the columns. They will be comparable to the arcades of Paris and other European cities, but will surpass them."[139] The *New York Times* observed that the presence of so many arcade shops and services made the remodeled Equitable Building "a little city within four walls."[140] The new Equitable also contained space for the recently formed Lawyers Club, which first met on February 8, 1887, in quarters designed by Post.[141]

Post's new headquarters for the *New York Times* (1887–89), at 41 Park Row, revealed just how capable he was of harnessing managerial sophistication to realize artistic goals.[142] Founded in 1851, the *Times* was first headquartered in a converted house at 151 Nassau Street and then in a larger converted house at Nassau and Beekman Streets. Younger than most of its rivals, it nonetheless was the first among them to abandon rookery-like quarters for its own purpose-built home. The paper held a limited competition for a headquarters building that was won by Thomas R. Jackson, whose five-story, round-arched, arcaded design (1857) rose on the site bounded by Park Row and Spruce and Nassau Streets, previously home to the Brick Church. For the first time a newspaper used architecture to proclaim its institutional identity. Jackson's stylistically eclectic composition was praised by its owner as "singularly bold and striking . . . designed with a total disregard of classical models and artistic rules," displaying "great inventive genius and a most harmonious combination of apparently incongruous elements."[143] The building provided for a huge vaulted basement housing the presses, with broad arches thirty feet overhead. Augustus Maverick, biographer of the *Times*'s founder, Henry J. Raymond, was dazzled by the room: "But for the vast piece of complicated machinery . . . which fills so much of the space," a visitor "might fancy himself under the dome of some huge cathedral rather than in the crypt of a newspaper office."[144]

By 1885 Jackson's building was overshadowed by its next-door neighbor, Norris Gibson Starkweather's Potter Building (see above). With their home no longer a commanding presence, the publishers felt the need to rebuild, hiring Post in 1887 to design a new structure to be built while maintaining uninterrupted operations. *Building* magazine reported that Post's approach to the problem, developed in association with the builder David H. King Jr., was "a novel feat of engineering": after shoring up the walls of the existing building, new foundations were laid for the new building.[145] Floors were supported on a temporary basis while the old foundations were stiffened and new foundations laid; once new wrought-iron columns and beams were set in place, the old walls were taken down and new ones locked into the new structural system. So well was the job done that the old brick-arched floors showed no sign of cracking nor did any of the plasterwork. After about nine months' labor, conducted in two shifts per day, six days a week, Post's new limestone walls rose from a granite base to not only envelop Jackson's building but to virtually reach the end of their twelve-story skyward climb and conclude with an attic floor and a dormered mansard. The *New York Herald* characterized the results as "the old *Times* Building with a new stone overcoat on, a mansard roof for a high hat and a practically new interior."[146] With continuous piers and windows vertically grouped in three-, four-, and three-floor units above a two-story base, the Times Building did not exactly repre-

Times Building, 41 Park Row. Thomas R. Jackson, 1857.
View to the south, c. 1874. Bill. NYHS.

sent a breakthrough to a more coherent expression of verticality in the tall building, but more than any other tall structure, with the possible exception of Hunt's Tribune Building across the street, it approached that goal.

The Times Building was not only an impressive feat of engineering and constructional ingenuity, it was also "a remarkable popular success," according to the *Real Estate Record and Builders' Guide*, "being generally esteemed the finest commercial building in New York."[147] Even the normally critical Montgomery Schuyler held it in high regard as "a very noteworthy adaptation of the Romanesque to commercial uses" and "a new departure for its architect, whose work before it had virtually been confined to one and another phase of the Renaissance."[148] Russell Sturgis was not quite so enthralled, finding fault with "the attempt to give a more varied skyline . . . by means of a mansard roof rising from a low attic in which the lofty dormers are inserted." Given the height of the building, the roof was not, in Sturgis's opinion, tall enough to count from a pedestrian's point of view, even when seen from the vantage point of City Hall Park. More importantly, he objected to the grouping of the floors, though he admired "the great piers which rise from sidewalk to cornice almost unbroken, and which lack only a more fortunate combination with the cornice and its superincumbent attic to give in themselves great character to the building."[149]

For the eleven-story, midblock Union Trust Company Building (1889–90), at 80 Broadway, between Wall Street and Exchange Place, Post was able to refine the approach he had taken in the Times Building.[150] Freed of the problems posed by the need to maintain the newspaper's operation during construction, he also achieved a far better-integrated design, with the three-bay-wide facade organized as a three-story base, an entresol, and five-story arcades carrying an attic and a boldly dormered, promi-

nently proportioned mansard. Post's Union Trust design brought the tall office building to the brink of the skyscraper type—not in terms of its iconic role as an emblematic object in space but in terms of its compositional organization, establishing the governing clarity of base, middle, and top that he had first devised as a way to resolve the problem of the tall building in his Western Union Building. Using a richly orchestrated blend of elements inspired by the Romanesque and French Renaissance, Post achieved one of the most satisfying solutions to date of the aesthetic challenges of the tall building. Schuyler considered this treatment an improvement over the north facade of the Times Building, "a success which was only partial by reason of the indistinctness and confusion of the primary divisions, when he perceived, from a contemplation of the executed work, what was the matter with it, and proceeded . . . to remedy those defects."[151]

The narrow, 72-foot-wide, midblock Union Trust was only 196 feet tall on its Broadway side, but when viewed from a distance across the Trinity Church graveyard, which it faced, it was highly visible as a composition. For the Broadway facade, Post used granite for the piers and painted iron for the spandrels and window frames; on New Street, the narrow passage at the rear of the building, the granite gave way to buff brick and terra cotta. The bank reserved the second floor for its own use, where a twenty-eight-and-a-half-foot-high banking hall opened to a fourteen-and-a-half-foot-high gallery, which was toplit by a skylight at the bottom of a court that separated the building into two sections.

Shortly after the Union Trust's completion, the *Real Estate Record and Builders' Guide* reported that it was "common to hear the new building . . . spoken of as 'a slice of the Times building.'" Although the motifs were similar, argued the *Record and Guide*, the scale was "somewhat smaller," and in any case it was only the north facade of the Times Building that was being adapted, "which is the most successful in the building." The *Record and Guide* found the Union Trust's New Street front

> even more picturesque than that on Broadway, in as much as we can get a "glimpse" of it, as one can do of so few buildings in the rectangular and regular parts of town. There is nothing more inspiring in its way than the view north from the corner of New Street and Exchange Place, with the Union Trust Company on the left, nothing more paintable and nothing that gives a more favorable notion of our commercial architecture. If anyone suggests that the Union Trust Company is the very best specimen of that architecture yet produced we shall not quarrel with him.[152]

Schuyler, who may have written the *Record and Guide*'s piece, agreed about the New Street side, which, because of the steep decline from Broadway, made the first view of the Union Trust's back facade "a glad surprise." Moreover, he shared the *Record and Guide*'s appreciation of Post's achievement, but in a kind of backhanded way, saying that it "is questionable whether the Union Trust Company be not the very best commercial building to which the eleva-

Times Building, 41 Park Row. George B. Post, 1887–89. View to the south showing the Potter Building (Norris Gibson Starkweather, 1883–85) to the right of the Times Building. NYHS.

Union Trust Company Building, 80 Broadway. George B. Post, 1889–90. View to the east. AR. CU.

tor has given use in New York; and it is not questionable that it is an admirable piece of design which fully indicates the applicability of Romanesque to commercial uses."[153]

Eight years later, in 1899, when the skyscraper type had become very nearly commonplace, Schuyler reasserted and expanded upon his conviction that Post had played a critical role in its development. With the Western Union Building, Post "first impressed upon his contemporaries" the Aristotelian concept "that a work of art must have a beginning, middle and an end," a concept Schuyler deemed central to architecture and the only acceptable way to resolve the formal problems of the tall building. For so doing, Post "was a public benefactor. It was from his inculcation of a forgotten truth that the consensus in the design of tall buildings began. . . . Confusion became order in his path." While Schuyler was not willing to absolutely credit Post with first adopting the Aristotelian approach—after all, Richard Morris Hunt's Tribune Building was also so organized—he was moved to "say that the designer who enforced it most powerfully was the architect of the Union Trust."[154]

One other building in the Romanesque manner by Post

is worth noting: the eight-story Schermerhorn Building (1890), built on the site once home to Vauxhall Gardens, at 696–702 Broadway, on the northeast corner of Fourth Street.[155] Even though it was a building that was economically constrained given its marginal location far north of the choice office neighborhood, Russell Sturgis considered it "the best exemplar" of Post's use of the style, exhibiting "unusual power of design, combined with very unusual sense of proportion," although it constituted "no real architectural advance."[156]

At the time of its completion, Post's 309-foot-high, twenty-six-story building for the *New York World* (1889–90), at the northeast corner of Park Row and Frankfort Street, commissioned by Joseph B. Pulitzer, the newspaper's publisher, was the world's tallest and, along with the Western Union and Tribune Buildings, a true skyscraper.[157] The World Building, though a full-fledged representative of the skyscraper type, was, in terms of composition, something of a misstep for Post, lacking as it did the integrative clarity of the tripartite organization that the architect had years before introduced in the Western Union Building. But Post's design made up what it lacked in compositional clarity with stylistic bravura. A complete about-face from the Romanesque-inspired Times and Union Trust Buildings, this design was a skillful essay in Renaissance Classicism, with three two-story-high tiers of windows grouped together as columnar arcades and a three-bay temple front that formed a transition to the crowning feature, a magnificently modeled cupola-crowned dome set on a high drum recalling Michelangelo's dome for St. Peter's (1546–64). As it loomed over Park Row, the World Building was not only the city's grandest celebration of the business of communication but also newspaperdom's boldest architectural confrontation with City Hall. With its high-shouldered, towerlike massing crowned by a domed cupola—in its way an homage to, or upstaging of, City Hall's cupola—the World Building sacrificed usable floor area to a celebratory gesture. Post's inhabited icon, in which six floors of offices, including Pulitzer's, were located in the drum below the dome, set the standard for the fully realized skyscraper type that would for the following thirty years be the singular hallmark of New York's architecture.

In 1881, the *New York World* left its headquarters in the original Potter Building, relocating nearby to 32 Park Row (1881), a five-story building of no particular consequence developed by Jay Gould.[158] On January 31, 1882, shortly after its move, the *World*'s former home was destroyed in a fire that the *Real Estate Record and Builders' Guide* characterized as doing "two good things for architecture": "It took that building out of the way and it left Messrs. Silliman & Farnsworth's solid, impressive and artistic Morse building [see above] clearly visible."[159] At the time of the fire, the nearly defunct *World* was respected but unread. The Hungarian-born Joseph B. Pulitzer had made his name and fortune as publisher of the *St. Louis Post-Dispatch*, and when he purchased the *New York World* in 1883, he turned the

Schermerhorn Building, northeast corner of Broadway and East Fourth Street. George B. Post, 1890. View to the northeast. Parshley. NYHS.

Proposed World Building, northeast corner of Park Row and Frankfort Street. R. H. Robertson, 1889. Park Row elevation. AABN. CU.

World Building, northeast corner of Park Row and Frankfort Street. George B. Post, 1889–90. View to the east. NYHS.

paper into a liberal, mass-market publication.[160] The *World* was so successful by the fall of 1888 that Pulitzer was ready to build a new headquarters, on the site of French's Hotel, at the northeast corner of Park Row and Frankfort Street, which many thought should have been kept clear as an approach to the Brooklyn Bridge. Pulitzer held a competition for the building, supervised by Richard Morris Hunt. Post's entry was selected over one by R. H. Robertson, who, presumably inspired by J. C. Cady's unsuccessful scheme for the Tribune Building ten years earlier, proposed a romantic, Romanesque-inspired, asymmetrically massed design with a curved corner—from which a figure carrying a globe was to be mounted on the eleventh floor—rising to a slender, sky-piercing, beehive-roofed tourelle.

In March 1889 Post was summoned to Europe by Pulitzer to discuss the new building, the plans for which were already under way. Possibly at this time Pulitzer was inspired to add a dome to the top of the building—an idea he always claimed as his own, as he did the decision to create a grand, three-story-high entry portal leading into the seventeen-foot-high rotunda. Pulitzer's role in the design should not be underestimated. The relationship between the driven publisher and the equally determined architect was highly charged, especially after Post refused to guarantee Pulitzer that his building would not cost more than one million dollars, but instead bet his client twenty thousand dollars to Pulitzer's ten thousand dollars that it would not exceed that figure; in the end the building probably cost two million dollars.

As the World Building neared completion, the *Real Estate Record and Builders' Guide* reported that it had

> grown to be one of the most conspicuous objects downtown. It shares with its neighbors, the Tribune building and the Times building, the advantage of a visibility that is not secured in the same degree for any other edifice below Union Square. . . . But the size and shape of the World building make it stand out even more strikingly than the other tall structures that border Printing House square. The site affords an area quite ample for even an eight-story building, being about 100 feet on Park row by about 125 on Frankfort street. But a thirteen-story building is a different matter. . . . Here . . . there have been no pains at all taken to keep the building down . . . and its height is increased by the super-addition of a dome of apparent stories in addition to the cupola. . . . No architect of any sensitiveness ever gave a domical termination to a tower, and a building as tall as the new World building, even with its considerable area, is virtually a tower.[161]

The decision to put the dome on the top of the tower did not grow out of a concern for the subtleties of architectural history but out of a desire to overwhelm the competition, in this case Hunt's Tribune Building, next door, and to elevate a popular newspaper into the realm of a public institution by appropriating one of the world's great symbols and thereby advertise the product. As expressed by an 1890 history of the *New York World*, published in celebration of the new building, the World Building "well deserves to be

known as the People's Palace."[162] It was the dome that galvanized opinion, becoming for many "the obstacle to the architectural success of the World building. That fact," argued the *Record and Guide*, "'jumps to the eyes' . . . and it is fair to suppose that the client has imposed it."[163] The problem lay in the unprecedented placement of a dome on what appeared to be, at least pending the development of the remaining buildings on the block, a freestanding tower. Moreover, the dome seemed merely placed atop the building—not integrated with it.

In some ways the World Building may seem a repudiation of all of Post's efforts to rationalize the design of the tall building, in its bold public scale, both as seen in the dome and in the handling of the ground-floor spaces. It was, however, very much the culmination of an almost two-decade-long development of the modern office block as a new building type which, though commercial, was mindful that corporations had a responsibility to make a contribution to city life. The World Building's provocative, iconic silhouette was the important thing—surely not its composition or its structural system, which was a rather ad hoc combination of wrought-iron columns, steel beams, and girders. In these respects, the structure was a far cry from the technological innovations of a much smaller building being completed as Post's building was being designed: Bradford Lee Gilbert's Tower Building.

The Tower Building and the Emergence of Skyscraper Construction

Bradford Lee Gilbert's Romanesque-inspired Tower Building (1888–89), at 50 Broadway, between Beaver Street and Exchange Place, was the first skeletally structured tall building in New York.[164] An improbable sliver of a building designed for the silk manufacturer J. Noble Stearns, it had only 21 and a half feet of frontage on Broadway, widening to 39 and a half feet at the rear of its 108-foot-deep site. Because the long sides of the 129-foot-tall, eleven-story, slablike structure were only partially visible from Broadway, Gilbert concentrated his architectural embellishments at one end, creating the illusion of a square, battlemented tower rising above the street. The scarcely sensible building, with its potentially compromised lot-line windows, would hardly have been economically feasible were it not for the use of a cast- and wrought-iron frame, the slender columns of which only minimally interrupted the available floor area. Gilbert's structural design met with initial opposition from the New York Board of Examiners, and its construction was only possible after the architect succeeded in having the building code revised to permit the use of skeleton framing. The controversial nature of the structural design affected leasing prospects, so Gilbert felt obliged to occupy the top-floor office—much as George B. Post had taken space at the top of the Equitable Building—to demonstrate his faith in his own ideas. Compositionally, the slender, five-story arcade of the Tower Building's midsection not only greatly enhanced the sense of height but also helped push

Tower Building, 50 Broadway. Bradford Lee Gilbert, 1888–89. View to the southeast. MCNY.

Lancashire Insurance Company Building, 25 Pine Street. J. C. Cady & Co., 1889–90. View to the southeast showing part of the United States Custom House (Town & Davis, with John Frazee and Samuel Thompson, 1834–42) on the right. HRE. CU.

the design toward the columnar model that would thereafter exemplify the tall building type.

Just as the Tower Building was nearing completion, plans were filed by J. C. Cady & Co. for the Lancashire Insurance Company's new home at 25 Pine Street (1889–90).[165] The design provided for an artistically undistinguished, ten-story skeleton structure on a twenty-four-foot-wide, seventy-four-foot-deep lot that took from the structural lessons of the Tower Building but advanced the engineering by introducing steel Z-bar columns. According to one of the architects in the Cady firm, Louis De Coppet Berg, writing in 1892, the Lancashire scheme was the first "in which all the walls are built with skeleton wrought iron construction."[166]

Though the two key technical components of tall building design—the elevator and a structural frame that would carry the building's load without any bearing walls—were

well understood by the end of the 1880s, architects had only just begun to grasp the artistic possibilities that accompanied exceptional height. Bruce Price's unrealized design for the *New York Sun* (1890) was perhaps the first to articulate the tall building as a pure tower.[167] In 1894, the *New York Daily Tribune* reported Price's assertion that when a skyscraper could be constructed on a square lot, and it was possible to have four fronts, it might be a fine addition to the city.[168] But Thomas Hastings, among others, felt that the pure skyscraper had its drawbacks. In the same article in the *Tribune*, Hastings observed:

From the artistic point of view, it is admitted by almost everyone who has tried to solve the problem that the limitations are almost insurmountable. The extreme height, tending to the treatment of every building as a tower, on the one hand; the exaggerated demand for light, which destroys all possibility of wall surfaces which are requisite

View to the northwest along Wall Street showing, from left to right, the Gallatin Bank Building (J. C. Cady, 1886), Thompson Building (DeLemos & Cordes, 1886), Manhattan Company and Merchants' Bank Building (W. Wheeler Smith, 1883–85), and part of the Bank of America Building (Charles W. Clinton, 1888–89). King, 1893. CU.

to the design of a beautiful tower and the impossibility, owing to fire laws and other regulations, of using even the structural features of the building to accentuate the design, have resolved the problem into vain attempts, resulting either in absolute monotony, expressive only by its size, or absolute decoration of wall surfaces.[169]

Rebuilding Wall Street

Stretching for less than half a mile from Broadway to the East River, Wall Street took its name from the rampart constructed in 1653 by the Dutch to protect themselves from an invasion of hostile New Englanders, which never materialized.[170] Some thirty years later, Thomas Dongan, appointed Royal Governor by the Duke of York, officially mapped the first portion of the street, a thirty-six-foot-wide section running from New to Pearl Street, which was soon lined with houses. In 1696, at the head of the street, the first Trinity Church was constructed, followed three years later by the city's second City Hall, at the northeast

corner of Nassau Street, which was remodeled and enlarged almost a century later by Pierre L'Enfant to serve as the nation's capitol for just one year. The prosperous decades of the late eighteenth century brought increased commercial activity for the street, especially near the river, where stores and various exchanges were established, most notably the Tontine Coffee House (1792), at the northwest corner of Water Street. The Bank of New York, which built the street's first banking facility, in 1798 at the northeast corner of William Street, was quickly followed by the Bank of the Manhattan Company, the First Bank of the United States, and many others. Despite the fact that the street was almost exclusively devoted to financial and commercial interests, Wall Street still looked and felt residential well into the nineteenth century. The scale and character of the street began to change significantly in the 1850s with the construction of a series of palazzo-like banking buildings, including new facilities for the Bank of the Manhattan Company (1848), the Bank of the Republic (Hurry & Rogers, 1851–52), and the Brown Brothers Bank (Edward T. Potter, 1864–65). By the late 1860s, Wall Street was synonymous with banking and finance, despite the fact that the nation's main trading vehicle, the New York Stock Exchange, was located around the corner on Broad Street.

In the 1870s, Wall Street began to take on a strictly commercial character, becoming the city's principal setting for large-scale office buildings. Previously discussed early efforts included Arthur Gilman's Drexel Building, at the southeast corner of Broad Street, Alfred Thorp's and Clinton & Pirsson's buildings for the rebuilt Jauncey Court, and Detlef Lienau's building at number 67. George E. Harney's seven-story 14–18 Wall Street (1879–81), with its triple-width, L-shaped lot running through to Nassau Street, was a Queen Anne–inspired design of considerable subtlety, notable for a crowstepped central gable, which Montgomery Schuyler deemed a detail "small to minuteness," multipaned transoms, and two Georgian-inspired entryways.[171] Harney's structure at last brought the new scale of office building to the heart of the financial district while maintaining the domestic character of the seventeenth- and eighteenth-century development. The history of the site was indicative of Wall Street's evolution. It had originally been home to the Presbyterian Church (1719), the first in the city, which, after being rebuilt in 1785, relocated to Eleventh Street and Fifth Avenue in 1846.[172] Two sets of business houses were subsequently built and demolished on the site. As plans for Harney's building were announced, the *American Architect and Building News* predicted that the locale was now "to suffer, or enjoy, another transformation and become a veritable temple of Mammon for money-changers."[173] Harney's client was Frederick W. Stevens, who had retained the architect to design his house (1875–76), on the southwest corner of Fifty-seventh Street and Fifth Avenue (see chapter 4), as well as another building (1873–74), on the northeast corner of Broadway

Astor Building, 10 Wall Street. Henry J. Hardenbergh, 1885–86. Rendering by Henry S. Ihnen. AR. CU.

Astor Building, 10 Wall Street. Henry J. Hardenbergh, 1885–86. View to the northwest showing, from right to left, part of 14–18 Wall Street (George E. Harney, 1879–81), the Astor Building, and the United Bank Building (Peabody & Stearns, 1880–81). BLDG. CU.

and Bond Street, which housed the clothiers Brooks Brothers from 1874 to 1884 (see chapter 5).

Harney's 14–18 Wall Street may have been the city's first office building in the new Queen Anne style. According to the *American Architect and Buildings News*: "There is Queen Anne enough about it to indicate that it was done in the season of the fever of that pseudo-style, but much moderation has been exercised and the building is a natural one and excellently composed" in Baltimore brick and Belleville, New Jersey, brownstone.[174] Yet Harney's deliberate recollection of Colonial American precedent should not be easily dismissed. It was not a piece of wild work, according to another article in the *American Architect*, but one of a handful of new buildings "in which the architect has made so evident and strenuous an effort to be in the style of his great-grandfathers, that one would think the highest art was to be reached by reproducing what was never more than picturesque, and then only in its surroundings, and for the society and people occupying the structure. Mr. Harney may fairly be said to have gone, in

Astor Building, 10 Wall Street. Henry J. Hardenbergh, 1885–86. Detail of entrance. AR. CU.

View to the southwest along Wall Street, 1888, showing, from
left to right, the Assay Office (Martin Thompson, 1823), Gallatin
Bank Building (J. C. Cady, 1886), Thompson Building (DeLemos
& Cordes, 1886), and Manhattan Company and Merchants' Bank
Building (W. Wheeler Smith, 1883–85). BLDG. CU.

Bank of America Building, northwest corner of Wall and William
Streets. Charles W. Clinton, 1888–89. View to the northwest. King,
1893. CU.

the Wall Street building, as near to a picturesque treatment
of Queen Anne [that] will bear for city use."[175] Harney's
building was quickly overshadowed by Peabody &
Stearns's Romanesque United Bank Building, at 2–4 Wall
Street, on the northeast corner of Broadway, also completed in 1881 (see above), which led Montgomery
Schuyler to observe that "though not small" it had been
"inconspicuous . . . even before [it was] overpowered."[176] In
1886, Harney completed a seven-story building for the
Eagle Insurance Company on an irregular plot at the junction of Wall, Pearl, and Beaver Streets, a far more subdued
affair that fit very well into the city fabric.[177]

The domestic character of Wall Street was further shattered with the construction of two buildings by George B.
Post: the Mills Building (1880–82) (see above), which,
although located on the northeast corner of Broad Street
and Exchange Place, contained a Wall Street entrance in
the ell that ran back to the street; and the more picturesque
Mortimer Building (1884) (see above), at the southwest
corner of New Street. W. Wheeler Smith's 40–42 Wall
Street (1883–85), replacing buildings that had individually
served the Merchants' National Bank and the Manhattan

Company State Bank, represented a larger scale than had
hitherto been seen along the street but was in keeping with
what was shortly to come, including J. C. Cady's Gallatin
Bank Building and Charles W. Clinton's Bank of America
Building (see below).[178] Smith's new Manhattan Company
and Merchants' Bank Building, which ran through to Pine
Street, had seventy feet of frontage on each street. According to the *Real Estate Record and Builders' Guide*, the Pine
Street facade was straightforward, "like what it is—the
back of a building," rendered in red brick and gray granite,
"very plainly treated." But the Wall Street facade was composed "of granite of different tints, much of it polished,
and with an unusual amount of rich carving" and was
complexly articulated, synthesizing structural expression
with a Classical vocabulary in a remarkably convincing and
wholly original way.[179]

The next large building to be erected on Wall Street was
Henry J. Hardenbergh's eight-story-high, sixty-five-foot-
wide Astor Building (1885–86), at 10 Wall Street, in
which, according to Schuyler, "the designer profits by his
own mistakes."[180] Separated by one narrow building from
the United Bank on the west and sharing a party wall with

Harney's 14–18 Wall Street on the east, Hardenbergh produced one of the decade's freshest designs for a tall office building, perhaps a result of the contribution of Henry S. Ihnen, whose rendering suggests a lightness of detail somewhat absent from the finished building. Ihnen would go on to be Francis H. Kimball's partner for one year, during which time Kimball produced one of his finest works, a warehouse building at the northwest corner of Hudson and Beach Streets (see below). Combining lessons from the Richardsonian Romanesque and the Queen Anne, Hardenbergh interrupted the smooth wall of his red brick superstructure with a four-story-high triple arcade, the lower three floors of which were filled in with bay windows. Above an attic, a prominent gable, diaper-patterned in terra cotta, intersected the high-dormered mansard. At the two-story dark brownstone base the arcade piers rested on squat Byzantine polished granite columns that announced the entrance, a strategy Montgomery Schuyler found weak, certainly so in contrast with the way it had been handled in the original design, in which the enclosing wall had been deeply recessed to form a loggia.

J. C. Cady's fifty-eight-foot-wide, nine-story Gallatin Bank Building (1886), at 34–36 Wall Street, rose clifflike between its two neighbors, the two-story, late-Georgian Assay Office (Martin Thompson, 1823) and DeLemos & Cordes's comparatively diminutive, six-story, brick-and-stone-clad Thompson Building (1886), at 38 Wall Street.[181] Even though Wall Street was wider than Nassau, the *Real Estate Record and Builders' Guide*, which did not like the vaguely Classical, layered organization of the Gallatin's facade, complained that the attic-like uppermost floor of the building was "virtually invisible from any point of view at the street level." Moreover, the facade was "not so much 'free classic' as a combination of classical features and features non-classical. It is not even a combination but merely a juxtaposition—the satirical might say a jumble."[182] More noteworthy than its aesthetics was the Gallatin Building's use of a forced system of ventilation, the first of its kind in an office building, with air heated in a cellar-level plenum and conveyed by a system of fans to individual offices via flues. A separate set of flues placed under the floors returned the air to the basement for reheating.

Charles W. Clinton's Bank of America Building (1888–89), at 44–46 Wall Street, on the northwest corner of William Street, was one of four by the architect that, along with Robert W. Gibson's Richardsonian Romanesque United States Trust (see above) across the street, culminated Wall Street's reconstruction in the 1880s.[183] The *Record and Guide* offered a form of backhanded praise for the vaguely Romanesque design of the nine-story block, deeming it "strictly business-like," which is to say that its utilitarianism was a bit out of place on a street that was otherwise a corporate showplace. The Bank of America's design was notable for its contextualism, carrying through the key horizontal bands of W. Wheeler Smith's earlier 40–42 Wall Street next door, "a proceeding

quite as uncommon in Wall Street as the erection of a business building instead of a commercial palace."[184] Clinton's 31–33 Wall Street, between Broad and William Streets, a nine-story, forty-two-foot-wide building undertaken for the Mechanics' National Bank (1888–89) on the site of its previous headquarters, was also Romanesque in inspiration and, like his Mutual Life Building, Classical in detail.[185] His nine-story Central Trust Company of New York Building (1886–87), at 54 Wall Street, with its flat pilaster order, went even further in the direction of 1890s Classicism.[186] Clinton's ten-story Wilks Building (1889–90), at 15 Wall Street, on the southwest corner of Broad Street, was his most vivacious, even dynamic, Wall Street design, combining arcades that tied together the basement and first two floors, and the sixth and seventh floors, with a three-story pilaster order and multidormered mansard as well as a curved corner.[187]

Uptown Office Buildings

While the concentration of office buildings was definitely below City Hall, the rapid commercial growth of Broadway above Canal Street, combined with the transformation of Union Square to commerce, resulted in the construction of a few notable office buildings uptown. In

Domestic Sewing Machine Company Building, southwest corner of Broadway and East Fourteenth Street. Griffith Thomas, 1872–73. View to the west. NYHS.

Century Company Building, 33 East Seventeenth Street. William Schickel, 1880–81. View to the northeast showing, from left to right, the Parish Building (Detlef Lienau, 1883–84), Century Company Building, and Everett House (1854). NYHS.

753 Broadway, southwest corner of East Eighth Street. J. Morgan Slade, 1880. View to the southwest. LAA. CU.

fact, architects seemed to have been pushed to a higher level of creativity than was typical in downtown buildings, perhaps because of the need for these new structures to fit in with a still fashionable residential neighborhood that was also home to the city's most exclusive shops. At the time of its completion, Griffith Thomas's Domestic Sewing Machine Company Building (1872–73), at the southwest corner of Broadway and Fourteenth Street, was the city's tallest, at 110 feet.[188] Given its prominent location in a still mostly residential area, it stood out as a monument. Thomas's design, consisting of five stories plus an inhabited mansard, was very Parisian, with its pronounced corner tower rising to a steep segmented dome. In contrast, J. Morgan Slade's five-story 753 Broadway (1880), at the southwest corner of Eighth Street, was a severely detailed three-by-five-bay brick and iron cube.[189] William Schickel's Century Company Building (1880–81), facing Union Square at 33 East Seventeenth Street, between Broadway and Fourth Avenue, developed as a speculative venture by the dry-goods company Arnold Constable, was principally leased by the company that gave the building its name, the publishers of the popular *Century Magazine* as well as *St. Nicholas Magazine*, which was written for children.[190] The Century Building was also home to

Lincoln Building, northwest corner of Broadway and East Fourteenth Street. R. H. Robertson, 1885. View to the northwest. AR. CU.

McIntyre Building, northeast corner of Broadway and East Eighteenth Street. R. H. Robertson, 1890–92. View to the northeast. King, 1893. CU.

Johnson and Faulkner, upholsterers, and, after 1890, to the architect George B. Post. The charming, Queen Anne–inspired, three-bay-wide, seven-story, red brick building, trimmed in white stone, rose on its Union Square side to a high, fish-scale-slated mansard relieved by pedimented dormers and framed by massive chimneys, a brick and terra cotta balustrade, and a terra cotta cresting of sunflowers. A two-story-high, oriel-like pedimented bay window, placed in the center on the third and fourth floors, combined with small-paned leaded-glass windows, conspired to give the building a surprisingly domestic character, as if to help ameliorate the large building's impact on the residential character of the neighborhood. The Century Building ran through the block to confront Eighteenth Street with a far more severe facade. Despite its overall vivacity, the critic for the *Real Estate Record and Builders' Guide* was not impressed, dismissing it as "respectable, moderate, straightforward and massive looking, even if it be prosaic and without any felicity in general disposition or in detail, so that its magnitude at least does not make it an offence."[191]

R. H. Robertson's Lincoln Building (1885), at the northwest corner of Fourteenth Street and Broadway (Union Square West), was as substantial as any office building downtown.[192] A not-quite-resolved essay in the

Romanesque, with many layers of motifs rather than a dominant arcade, Robertson's first tall building was said to possess, according to the *Record and Guide*, "a wandering, hesitating air about it as though the architect could not hit upon the right word for his idea and took refuge in redundancy."[193] Five years later, Robertson designed the McIntyre Building (1890–92), at 874 Broadway, on the northeast corner of Eighteenth Street, which displayed a much clearer composition.[194] Built by a prominent pharmacist, Ewen McIntyre, whose shop had been located on the site before construction, the narrow, steel-framed building, clad in limestone, brick, and terra cotta, stretched along Eighteenth Street and extended in an ell to Nineteenth Street. Its bold tripartite composition, with a five-story midsection articulated by four-story giant Doric brick columns rising to a dramatic arch, as well as a one-and-a-half-story tower, made it, as Montgomery Schuyler observed, a building "every New Yorker knows by sight."[195] Renwick, Aspinwall & Russell's six-story, 40-by-105-foot, Gothic-inspired office building at 808 Broadway (1888), adjoining the Grace Church parsonage opposite East Eleventh Street, was as notable for its contextualism as for its sophisticated skyline of buttresses and pointed arcades.[196] The *Record and Guide* noted that "as far as we are aware," the building "is the first Gothic store

808 Broadway, opposite East Eleventh Street. Renwick, Aspinwall & Russell, 1888. View to the northeast showing Grace Church parsonage (James Renwick Jr., 1846) on the right. AR. CU.

Methodist Book Concern, southwest corner of Fifth Avenue and West Twentieth Street. Edward H. Kendall, 1888–90. View to the southwest. AABN. CU.

building of any size or importance that has been erected in this city."[197]

Edward H. Kendall's Methodist Book Concern (1888–90), at 148–152 Fifth Avenue, on the southwest corner of Twentieth Street, stood in contrast to Renwick, Aspinwall & Russell's stylistic specificity and to the typical unresolved attempts to organize a tall building by piling up motifs.[198] Kendall's design was a remarkable example of a free eclecticism of form combined with a sure sense of organization, resulting in a nine-story building that at once suggested a palazzo and an office block. Kendall was given the job through competition, winning over entries from George B. Post, Babb, Cook & Willard, Charles W. Clinton, and D. & J. Jardine. The building combined offices for bishops; the Missionary Society; the *Christian Advocate*, the official organ of the Methodist Episcopal Church; and the church's board of education and other departments. It also included a printing house at the rear of the upper floors, a daily service chapel on the third floor, a library, and reception rooms. Located only one block from Chickering Hall (see chapter 5), the Methodist building was also home to William Knabe, a rival piano manufacturer to Chickering, who leased one of the shops facing Fifth Avenue. With the Methodist Book Concern, Kendall once again demonstrated his command of the tall-building problem, setting four-story arcades containing three floors of three-sided bay windows on top of a two-story, heavily rusticated, dark red granite base. Above was an attic story and bracketed cornice at the seventh floor, then two floors set back to form an attic. Though Kendall employed Serlian windows, and his use of arcades could be seen as somehow related to H. H. Richardson's work, the design was in fact remarkably fresh, although the *Record and Guide* claimed that the pinkish red brick was laid up with joints that gave the building "a prim and old-fashioned aspect that most designers of late have carefully avoided."[199]

A few blocks downtown, replacing three masonry structures that had been home to Knabe's piano showroom and Martinelli's restaurant, McKim, Mead & White's Judge Building (1888–90), at 110–112 Fifth Avenue, on the northwest corner of Sixteenth Street, combining office and manufacturing space, was developed by Robert and Ogden Goelet.[200] The eight-story, arcaded building, clad in bluish gray granite, buff brick, and terra cotta, echoed Babb, Cook & Willard's De Vinne Press Building (1885–86) (see below)—before entering into his partnership, George Babb had been one of the McKim firm's bright young talents—but was grander and slightly more Classical, with segmentally arched storefront windows flanking an Ionic portico. The second and third floors were united by arches resting on piers, as were the fifth, sixth, and seventh floors, where, in the middle of the Fifth Avenue facade, the word "Judge" was inscribed in honor of the principal tenant, the humor magazine. A band of arched win-

Judge Building, northwest corner of Fifth Avenue and West Sixteenth Street. McKim, Mead & White, 1888–90. View to the northwest. AR. CU.

dows and a lion's-head cornice supporting an arcaded parapet concluded the composition.

The *Record and Guide* greeted the building as

> one of the most noteworthy of recent additions to our commercial architecture. As it stands it is a fragment only, though a fragment comprising somewhat more than half of the projected whole. . . . That which remains to be executed is the northern part of the avenue front. . . . The executed part of the front on the avenue is some 50 feet, and the whole of this part is to be nearly 100. The street front has a total length of 150 feet nearly, though the westernmost 25 feet are decisively refined so as not to count in any general view of the building.[201]

This last point referred to the fact that this part of the facade was set back from the building line to conform with the townhouse row to the west and to enable the building to be read as a two-by-three block. Except for the Classical porches and some decorative details, Russell Sturgis found "nothing, or nothing but the profiles of some mouldings . . . to help the would-be classifier. It is a modern business building, and a downright sensible one." Noting the sources of the building's design in the work of Babb and his partners, Sturgis went on to say that "its treatment with a much more decorative system of design" separated it from a warehouse and placed it "much closer . . . to the

Goelet Building, southeast corner of Broadway and East Twentieth Street. McKim, Mead & White, 1886–87. View to the southeast. BLDG. CU.

modern office building."[202] In fact, it could not be considered a warehouse because it was

> too "architectural." The very unexpected and effective round corners when the two principal facades meet; the repetition of the treatment of those very large and highly developed quoins on the two other corners, especially that treatment which is to be seen at the extreme western edge where there is a large offset in the wall, and where the mass which is in retreat comes into sight beyond the main corner, as to emphasize effectively the *chainage* of the main structure; the refined group of mouldings like a classical entablature which marks the springing line of the arches below, these, and more especially the wall cornice with the heads which pass for gargoyles, whether they serve as such or not, are all of them claims upon our attention as taking the building out of the Factory-Warehouse group into a more generally recognized class of architectural design. The pilasters and even the columns of the entrance front are of less consequence.[203]

McKim, Mead & White's six-story Goelet Building (1886–87), at the southeast corner of Broadway and Twentieth Street, marked an important step in the development of the tall building and especially in the application of H. H. Richardson's use of the arcade to that building type.[204] The design was remarkably sleek, with smooth brick and terra cotta walls organized to convey the impression of a single unit of enclosure sweeping around the corner. The *New York Daily Tribune* reported that the "round corner . . . was extremely difficult to mould. The Cornells, who furnished the iron, were obliged to make a special moulding for all the metal employed on this corner. No two inches of space in the curve are alike."[205] Vertically organized in a two-three-one composition, the most obviously traditional aspects of the design were the details of the two-story arcaded base, where two Ionic columns, with drums composed of polished granite shafts banded in terra cotta, marked the corner entrance. Three floors of windows were framed together and piled on top of the base, all crowned by a full-story attic, ornamented frieze, and projecting cornice.

The *Tribune* characterized the design as "a sort of Italian Renaissance style of architecture, though carefully preserving at the same time" the "individuality" of McKim, Mead & White's approach.[206] Russell Sturgis praised the building as a superb exemplar of the modern office building type and was particularly impressed with the building's columnar order: "Especially successful is the arrangement of the three stories of windows above the great arches. Always, in these big buildings, with so many stories all alike, is the designer trying to bring two or three stories into one. Almost always does he fail." But in the Goelet Building, Sturgis observed, "there is no pretense at the three windows being one. . . . It does seem a masterly solu-

Goelet family headquarters, 9 West Seventeenth Street. McKim, Mead & White, 1885. View to the northwest. AR. CU.

tion of a very troublesome problem."[207] While Sarah Bradford Landau has proposed that Hurry & Rogers's Bank of the Republic (1851–52), at the northeast corner of Broadway and Wall Street, may have inspired the McKim firm's design, it is clear that the Goelet Building, which surely took lessons from Richardson's arcaded commercial blocks, broke new ground.

At a very different scale, but also worth noting, was McKim, Mead & White's office building at 9 West Seventeenth Street (1885), which was designed for the Goelet family's own use as a business headquarters.[208] The polychromed, Dutch-inspired design, with its high-rising dormer and stepped gables, was surely intended to reify the family's role among the Knickerbocker elite. The triple-arched arcade carried on Ionic columns forming the ground floor, however, pointed to the Classicism that the firm would so passionately advocate in the years to come. The *Real Estate Record and Builders' Guide* found it "very amusing. . . . It is only two stories and a half in height, though the wall is tall enough for three stories."[209]

View to the northeast along Wall Street, c. 1867, showing, from left to right, the Manhattan Bank Building (1848), Merchants' Bank (1840), 44 Wall Street (c. 1848), Bank of America (1835), and Bank of New York (Vaux & Withers, 1856–58). MCNY.

BANKS AND EXCHANGES

Banking was the most established and most important business in the downtown area, rapidly growing in the 1850s in the aftermath of Jacksonian economics.[1] Given the increasing value of New York real estate, many banks followed the Bank of the Manhattan Company's 1848 lead in departing from the Greek Revival model of a banking temple, housing themselves in more spatially efficient rowhouse- and soon thereafter palazzo-like buildings. These accommodations also included offices that could be leased to tenants, leading the *New York Times* to report in 1858 that though the

> commercial metropolis of the New World is indebted to the banking interests for some of its finest examples of architectural effect and improvements in construction, [there] is no one banking-house in the whole city that can be taken as a perfect specimen of any particular style in architecture, nor of construction, because there is not one that has the advantage of exhibiting more than two

sides, and the greater number of these have but one front. Costly and magnificent as some of these temples of mammon are, they are still only parts of buildings, architecturally considered. Land is too valuable in the business part of the city to admit of a building for business purposes being considered so that all parts of it can be seen, or to afford an architect an opportunity of exhibiting his talent for design.[2]

Though it appeared hardly more than an imposing rowhouse of three stories and an attic, the Bank of the Manhattan Company's new building, fronting on Wall Street, was in fact leased to an insurance company, private bankers, lawyers, and a banknote engraver, while at the rear, a thirty-four-by-fifty-two-foot, two-story extension housed a domed banking room.[3] The bank's identity was second to that of the enterprise as a whole, which was called the Manhattan Bank Building.

The Phenix Bank (c. 1849), attributed to Frederic Diaper, was the first to adopt the Italian palazzo as a model,[4] a stylistic trend reinforced by Hurry & Rogers's

Nassau Bank Building, northeast corner of Nassau and Beekman Streets. Samuel A. Warner, 1854–55. View to the northeast, c. 1890. Beal. NYHS.

Mechanics' Bank Building, 31–33 Wall Street. Richard Upjohn, 1855–56. Elevation. Upjohn Collection. CU.

influential five-story brownstone Italianate palazzo Bank of the Republic (1851–52), at the northeast corner of Wall Street and Broadway.[5] Samuel A. Warner's Nassau Bank Building (1854–55), a five-story brownstone palazzo located on a prime fifty-by-forty-seven-foot corner site bounded by Nassau and Beekman Streets, had separate entrances for the offices and for the bank, which was not housed in a grand room at the back but prominently, if less nobly, on the ground floor overlooking the street.[6] The Mechanics' Bank Building (1855–56), at 31–33 Wall Street, by Richard Upjohn, was another example of the new integrated bank-office type,[7] as was Vaux & Withers's Bank of New York (1856–58), at 48 Wall Street, on the northeast corner of William Street, constructed on the site of Wall Street's oldest bank building, which had been built for the same institution in 1798.[8] The exterior consisted of a stylistically ambiguous but nonetheless imposing application of gridded dark red Philadelphia brick and brownstone. The Bank of New York occupied the rear of the ground

floor so that the front could be leased, diminishing the bank almost to tenant status. At this rear facade, however, opening onto William Street, the bank was celebrated with tall windows and a double-height banking room. Finally, a central flight of steps led to a prominent portal emblazoned with the bank's name. The building had been originally constructed as a four-story palazzo rising to a projecting cornice, but in 1879 Calvert Vaux, working with George K. Radford, lifted the cornice to make way for one additional floor. Above that was added an inhabited, copper-clad mansard crowned by iron crocketing. The architectural design of the facade recalled Renaissance prototypes favored by Georgian designers, effectively identifying the enterprise both with banking's historic past in Florence and with the Bank of New York's own venerable traditions. At the same time, the grandeur of the design, and what was to a limited extent its abstraction, made it clear that the new structure was something more than just an office building. Edward T. Potter's four-story Brown Brothers

*Bank of New York, 48 Wall Street. Vaux & Withers, 1856–58.
View to the northeast showing the 1879 mansard addition by
Vaux & Radford. BNY.*

*Proposed National Park Bank Building, 214–218 Broadway.
Peter B. Wight, c. 1866. Competition-entry elevation. AIC.*

*Brown Brothers Bank Building, 59 Wall Street. Edward T. Potter,
1864–65. View to the southeast. MCNY.*

Bank Building (1864–65), at 59 Wall Street, was the last and grandest of the banking palazzos, and was styled rather like a London club.[9]

In 1866, Griffith Thomas's National Park Bank Building (1866–68) initiated a new era in bank construction.[10] Thomas won the commission for the building in competition, beating Peter B. Wight, who proposed a restrained Italian Gothic–inspired design with two separate entrances and, at the roof, two small equilateral triangular pediments flanking a much larger version of the same. The National Park Bank site had a 59-foot frontage on the east side of Broadway between Fulton and Ann Streets, and penetrated 140 feet into the block. A narrow, nine-foot-six-inch-wide extension forming an ell faced Ann Street. Thomas's palazzo, clad in white Tuckahoe marble, provided a high basement that could be rented as offices and four full stories below a steep, inhabited mansard, boldly demonstrating the practical utility of contemporary French Classicism. While not the first building to use the style associated with Napoleon III for commercial purposes—it was preceded by Griffith Thomas's Continental Insurance Company Building (1862–63), at 100–102 Broadway,[11] as well as by John Kellum's Herald Building (1865–67) (see above), which stood next door to the National Park

National Park Bank Building, 214–218 Broadway. Griffith Thomas, 1866–68. View to the east showing the Herald Building (John Kellum, 1865–67) on the left. MCNY.

Bank—this was the first to capture the bold scale and vivid articulations of the most representative Parisian example, Hector Lefuel's New Louvre (1852). So bold was the conception that *D. Appleton's New York Illustrated* reported "crowds of people [pausing] by the railing of St. Paul's to stare up at the elaborate and massive . . . front."[12] The building was entered via a central flight of stairs that led through a hall to the building's principal internal feature, a soaring banking room in the form of an elongated octagon, rising almost fifty feet to an

iron and glass dome. This room was ringed by a second-floor gallery, which provided access to the two-story block at the rear of the site that accommodated the bank's offices as well as to the narrow extension used by the bank as a book room. Both the Broadway facade, which exploded the scale of the street, and the banking room were glorious. The *New York Daily Tribune* described the "beautiful effect of the Pompeian decoration of the walls and ceiling" of the banking room, whose "warm tints are almost intoxicating . . . the effect

German Savings Bank, southeast corner of Fourth Avenue and East Fourteenth Street. Henry Fernbach, 1870–72. View to the southeast. MCNY.

of the color [which] is that of the light, by which the color is, if the expression be allowed, warmed into life. The mellow light streams through the plate-glass, which is so amply woven into the iron dome that on the cloudiest days no gas-light will be required."[13] The bold handling of the basement and two lower floors facing Broadway was further embellished by statuary and by pairs of Corinthian columns. The columns flanking the entrance were pushed forward for full effect and carried a broken pediment ornamented with sculpture by a Russian artist, R. E. Launitz, deemed by the *Real Estate Record and Builders' Guide* "a new and most important work of art in this metropolis." Most significantly, as the *Record and Guide* observed, the National Park Bank stamped "a palatial character on the city's civic architecture."[14] In 1876, in his address for the tenth annual convention of the American Institute of Architects, Alfred J. Bloor noted that Thomas's design "probably finds little favor with purists of the modern school; but it only follows abundant precedents in famous examples of its type, for such solecisms as trussed keystones, and pediments broken into and deeply disembowelled as it were, for the deposit of consoles, vases, statuary, etc.; and it is, notwithstanding them, a rich and spirited production in French Renaissance—one of the best examples of its florid phase to be found among us."[15]

Flying against the prevailing financial wisdom that as much building as possible should be piled onto down-

Dry Dock Savings Bank, southeast corner of Bowery and East Third Street. Leopold Eidlitz, 1875. Banking room. AR. CU.

Dry Dock Savings Bank, southeast corner of Bowery and East Third Street. Leopold Eidlitz, 1875. View to the east. NYHS.

Union Dime Savings Bank, West Thirty-second Street between Sixth Avenue and Broadway. Stephen D. Hatch, 1875–76. View to the south, c. 1883, showing Sixth Avenue elevated station on the right. NYHS.

town sites, the Farmer's Loan and Trust Company commissioned a two-story building (Thomas Stent, 1883) on South William Street near Beaver Street, but hedged its decision by preparing it for the addition of eight more floors.[16] The principal feature of the design was a monumentally scaled porch, which the *Record and Guide* deemed unnecessarily self-important, suggesting the work of Frank Furness in Philadelphia. By 1890 Stent's building was torn down and replaced.

While most commercial banking was concentrated downtown, by the 1870s savings banks began to proliferate in uptown locations, where they could serve residents as well as businesses. Like commercial banks downtown, the typical savings bank was an office building with a first-floor banking hall. Carl Pfeiffer's Metropolitan Savings Bank (1867), at 1–3 Third Avenue, on the northeast corner of Seventh Street, opposite Cooper Union, was an iron-framed building clad in white marble.[17] With three stories plus an inhabited mansard, the building lifted the main-floor banking room above a high basement and incorporated space for leased offices. Nearby, Henry Engelbert's Bond Street Savings Bank (1874) was a narrow, five-story, cast-iron-clad, French Empire–style office slab on the northwest corner of Bowery and Bond Street.[18] Henry Fernbach's Parisian inspiration for the four-story cast-iron German Savings Bank (1870–72) might have seemed improbable given the nationality of his client, but the use of a round entrance porch and a high ribbed dome were very appropriate responses to the acute angle of the building's site, on the southeast corner of Fourth Avenue and Fourteenth Street.[19] Much farther uptown, Stephen D. Hatch's Union Dime Savings Bank (1875–76), at the northern end of the block facing Greeley Square, bounded by Broadway, Sixth Avenue, and Thirty-second Street, consisted of five stories and a mansard.[20] Hatch took advantage of the building's visibility from and location adjacent to a station of the not-quite-completed elevated railway by mounting the bank's name on a cornice-height panel with a high, flagstaff-bearing cupola above.

Leopold Eidlitz's Dry Dock Savings Bank (1875), at the southeast corner of Bowery and Third Street, was the most interesting of all the neighborhood banks.[21] Far more like a public building than a commercial enterprise, it was one of the finest buildings of the era. Eidlitz won the commission in competition. George B. Post was among the entrants, and his Classical design was cool and cubic, a dense, compact mass that recalled the Classicism of late-eighteenth-century France. Post clearly believed in the Classical at a time when few shared his vision: his unrealized design for the Marine National Bank (c. 1870), intended for 78 Wall Street, at the northwest corner of Pearl Street, was an exceptionally suave interpretation of the Neo-Grec.[22] Eidlitz's proposal was a picturesque, Ruskinian Gothic design that surrounded a central hip-roofed pavilion with a movemented composition of towers and porches, each

Proposed Dry Dock Savings Bank, southeast corner of Bowery and East Third Street. George B. Post, 1873. Competition entry. NYHS.

Marine National Bank, 78 Wall Street. George B. Post, c. 1870. Drawing for unrealized design. NYHS.

with its own steep, crocketed roof. With its transeptual plan, it could have been a church, though the approach taken was freely eclectic, with the spacious banking room carried on four polished granite columns that rose past elaborate Romanesque-inspired capitals to a pointed vaulted ceiling. For Montgomery Schuyler, the stylistic specificity was surprising: "The wayfaring man could not be prevented from perceiving that the Dry Dock Bank was 'high Gothic,' and the ready nomenclator found it quite feasible to dismiss it with the ready criticism that it 'looked like a church.'"[23] Alfred J. Bloor found Eidlitz's design

> perhaps the most pleasing example of its author's characteristic manner of interpreting German Gothic to modern eyes, and along with his usual apt appropriation of good but somewhat monotonous detail, shows more mastery of outline and cosmopolitan feeling than have hitherto distinguished his generally interesting and clever but somewhat stiff and unequal work. The squaring of the plan on the site (which is considerably off the square) seems to indicate a facile building-committee, and cleverly cuts a Gordian knot with the least expenditure of trouble to the designer; while at the same time the unusual arrangement calls attention to the building.[24]

Another highly memorable uptown bank, the slender, seven-story American Safe Deposit Company and Columbia Bank (McKim, Mead & White, 1882–84), at the southeast corner of Fifth Avenue and Forty-second Street, consisted of a slablike mass crowned by a boldly projected cornice.[25] One of the early monuments of the Classical Revival, it confronted Forty-second Street with two wide rectangular bays, each equal to the building's Fifth Avenue frontage and each topped by balconies covered by flat roofs carried on paired Ionic columns. The bays were projected from the Forty-second Street facade to transform a typical New York corner into a boldly articulated, Italianate version of the cubic geometry of Jean-Nicolas-Louis Durand. Charles W. Baldwin said the McKim firm's design "gave an impression of 'walliness,' which was further enhanced by the texture of the stone and by the emphasis given to the masonic substructure."[26] Above the rusticated base, a panelized treatment of the grouped windows that comprised the four floors of the midsection was comparable in its abstraction and order to the handling of similar elements in the firm's house for Phillips and Lloyd Phoenix (see chapter 4). The Classical treatment of the balconies, suggestive of devices seen in Pompeian wall paintings, together with the building's light brick and terra cotta ornament, did much to convey a sense of lightness, even gaiety, to a building type that was typically monumental and even pompous. Perhaps this character can be in part explained by the building's location in a top residential neighborhood, but surely it also reflected Stanford White's particular sensibility and does much to explain the hold his work had over the young Frank Lloyd Wright.

American Safe Deposit Company and Columbia Bank Building, southeast corner of Fifth Avenue and East Forty-second Street. McKim, Mead & White, 1882–84. View to the southeast. AABN. CU.

Exchanges

Founded in 1792, by the time of the Civil War the New York Stock Exchange was central to the city's financial life. It occupied rented quarters in various downtown business locations until 1863, when it undertook to build its own home on an irregularly shaped lot fronting Broad Street and extending through to New Street with a small connection to Wall Street.[27] John Kellum quickly produced plans for a marble-faced, iron-framed, four-story Tuscan palazzo (1865), which *Frank Leslie's Illustrated Newspaper* deemed an appropriate "temple for the worship of Mammon."[28] Though the stylistic reference to the era of the Medici family was appropriate, the design was in fact a near reproduction of Kellum's store for the jeweler Ball, Black & Co., at 550 Broadway, which he had completed only five years before.[29] The design tellingly departed from the civic monumentality of other New York exchanges of the previous generation, such as Isaiah Rogers's Mercantile Exchange (1842), located farther east along Wall Street, which occupied a full block and was accommodated in a grand Classical temple. Inside Kellum's Stock Exchange the so-called "Long Room" on the first floor was immense, a 22-foot-high, 40-by-145-foot marble-tiled hall that was leased to George W. McLean Associates, whose trading business replaced the street-market-like activities of the "curbstone" brokers. But it was the fifty-three-by-seventy-five-foot Board Room on the second floor that was the building's most important space, an "interior temple of the money-changers," where the exchange's 225 members traded in securities.[30]

In 1879, the board of the Stock Exchange acquired

New York Stock Exchange, 12 Broad Street. John Kellum, 1865. View to the southwest, c. 1868. Archive Photos.

more land next door and commissioned James Renwick Jr. to expand and remodel Kellum's building.[31] Renwick's plan, completed three years later, also replaced the facade, resulting in a five-story building facing Broad Street with a passageway running through to New Street. Renwick's Renaissance-inspired Broad Street front, combining distinctly Venetian and Parisian motifs, was grand to the

New York Stock Exchange, 12 Broad Street. James Renwick Jr., 1879–82. Trading room, 1883. NYSEA.

New York Stock Exchange, 12 Broad Street. James Renwick Jr., 1879–82. View to the southwest. NYSEA.

New York Produce Exchange, Moore to Whitehall Street, Water to Pearl Street. Leopold Eidlitz, 1860. View to the northeast. AR. CU.

point of being bombastic, with tiers of paired pilasters culminating, above an attic story, in an elaborately decorated, high, truncated pyramidal mansard. At the street, a portico of eight banded columns of polished Nova Scotia granite carried on pedestals marked the entrance. Montgomery Schuyler greeted Renwick's work with tepid enthusiasm: "His street front . . . is a piece of very florid Renaissance, executed in a coarse white marble. It contains a great many things, and they are not ill combined, but the design does not go beyond pretentious commonplace, and is everywhere overloaded. The general character attained is a certain ostentation of costliness, which very possibly expresses well enough the temper of the body for which the place is built."[32] Inside, on the second floor, the fourteen-thousand-square-foot, T-shaped trading room was a lushly modeled, elaborately stenciled, three-story, eighty-foot-high skylit chamber ringed by a visitors gallery. With its combination of Gothic vaulting and Classical detail, the trading room was surely one of the city's great rooms, suggesting a lavish hall in a hotel, though the purpose was anything but social.

George B. Post's New York Produce Exchange (1881–84), at 2 Broadway, was one of the most accomplished buildings of the Gilded Age, exemplifying the nineteenth-century ability to adapt traditional forms to new programs and building technologies.[33] The Produce Exchange, an outgrowth of the Corn Exchange, which was organized in 1853, was by 1860 sufficiently important that it had commissioned Leopold Eidlitz to design a building for its exclusive use on a trapezoidal site bounded by Moore Street on the east, Water Street on the south, Pearl Street on the north, and Whitehall Street on the west. Eidlitz, who had been selected through competition, designed a building that Montgomery Schuyler preferred to Post's replacement as "a proof of its author's studies in German Romanesque."[34]

With a "very effective transeptual arrangement, with the arcaded attic in each of the faces . . . evidently a reminiscence of the works of that style as it was evidently an improvement upon them," Eidlitz lifted the trading area to the second floor.[35] Schuyler praised the design of the trading room as one of Eidlitz's best, a "great hall, abundantly lighted from the sides and the transeptual clerestories, . . . entirely unobstructed except for the four brownstone piers at the inner angles, sustaining [an] open-timber roof, and modelled with reference to its framing. The clerestory walls were carried upon iron bowstring girders introduced and shown with perfect frankness."[36]

In 1879 the Produce Exchange, having outgrown Eidlitz's building, purchased a new site facing Bowling Green. In October 1880 invitations to enter a paid competition were sent to ten architects. Seven more designs were submitted on speculation. The exchange's building committee narrowed the field to four entries, which, without architect identification, were then "nailed up in the grand hall of the Exchange, with an accompanying placard notifying the members that they are to cast ballots."[37] A little more than a week before the vote, the members of the exchange requested additional guidance. The eight-member building committee replied that "your best interests will be conserved by the adoption of the design named *In me mea spes omnis*"; although anonymity was still officially maintained, the *New York Times* was confident enough to state that this design belonged to George B. Post.[38] Post, who prepared three alternate designs, was given the commission for a mansarded scheme. In the course of development, this design was modified: more floors and a 224-foot clock tower housing a stair and two elevators incorporated on the New Street side were added. The runner-up was E. T. Mix of Milwaukee. Other known competitors were Frederick Clarke Withers, Leopold Eidlitz, Richard M. Upjohn, and Charles B. Atwood.

The program called for leasable offices housed in a continuous superstructure wrapping a fifty-foot-wide light court that would be formed in the space above the center of the trading room, located on the second floor. The inner walls of the four floors of offices were to be carried on iron columns that would form the only interruptions in the otherwise unencumbered 215-by-134-foot, 64-foot-high trading room. Skylit by stained glass, the room was more than twice the size of that of the Stock Exchange. Post's arcaded red brick and terra cotta design was entered on three sides through triple arches framed by paired columns. The suppressed base, which accommodated retail shops, carried two superimposed arcades: the lower, more monumental arcade extended through four floors to express but not reveal the height of the trading room; the other was doubled in its rhythm to include two floors of offices; and just below the cornice rectangular openings doubled the rhythm once again. An attic story concluded the composition, with a terra cotta frieze above the main arcade illustrating the animals traded on the exchange. The overall effect was of a massive masonry envelope encapsulating a cage of space—not exactly a curtain or skin, but more a hard shell. The result was unquestionably powerful. Post himself claimed that "with its long, simple, and strongly marked cornices and unbroken rows of arches," the building was "in marked contrast to the prevalent fashion of minute moldings, small window panes, and irregularly broken sky lines. What is lost in picturesque effect is certainly gained in dignity and repose."[39]

Compared with the Stock Exchange's lavishly decorated trading room, the almost Roman Classical skylit hall of the Produce Exchange was austere, with the walls formed by the four-story arcade and the inner court carried on widely spaced square Corinthian columns supporting shallow arches. But the room was not entirely undecorated: the spandrels of its arches were filled with symbolic ornaments in terra cotta. Nonetheless, Schuyler deplored the room, writing that "no effort . . . has been made to design a monumental interior." He regretted the falsework of plaster that concealed the actual structure: "The 'finish' of the room is thus merely an envelope . . . devoid of an interest properly architectural."[40]

The Produce Exchange was quite important from a technical point of view, with a speaking-tube system and an electrically illuminated tower "forming a blazing beacon visible miles away."[41] But its structural system was most significant of all: though the exterior walls were load bearing, changing in size in relation to the weight they carried, so that they were eleven feet thick at the base but only four feet at the top, the inner-court walls exhibited skeleton or skyscraper construction. As Post was later to state, these walls were the "first adopting a metal cage for exterior wall construction," anticipating by a year or more similar methods used by William LeBaron Jenney in the construction of the Home Insurance Building (1882–85), in Chicago, which is generally held to be the first example of a fully consistent use of modern metal-frame construction.[42] According to Carl W. Condit, Post revealed his engineering skills by using an iron frame that, though not quite a fully formed structural skeleton, was surely a breakthrough, fulfilling "the primary requirement which was to support the floor, roof and wind loads entirely . . . thus freeing the partitions and walls from any bearing function and reducing the latter to protective screens."[43] Post compromised the purity of his iron skeleton by placing his wall columns inside the exterior brick piers, which also carried a small portion of the peripheral load by supporting the ends of the spandrel girder. But, as Winston Weisman has suggested, it was not that Post failed to understand the implications of skeleton framing but that he mistrusted it, preferring instead "cage construction," in which the outer walls are self-supporting.[44]

The selection of Post's Renaissance-inspired scheme over the Gothic-inspired proposals of Withers, Upjohn, and Eidlitz signaled an important shift in taste, one with

Proposed New York Produce Exchange, 2 Broadway. Frederick Clarke Withers, 1881. Competition-entry elevation. AABN. CU.

Proposed New York Produce Exchange, 2 Broadway. Richard M. Upjohn, 1881. Competition-entry elevation and plan. AABN. CU.

which leading critics were not comfortable. Both Montgomery Schuyler and Clarence Cook faulted the decision-making process, which left the selection in the hands of the exchange members without professional guidance. Cook's anger over the competition results can, however, be in part attributed to his Gothicist biases:

A carefully thought-out design, like that, for instance, sent in for our Produce Exchange by Mr. Withers, had no chance whatever—the drawings not even taken out of their portfolio, simply because the staircases were put in the only place fit for the staircases of such a large building, namely, at the angles. And a design that met with great favor was one in which the water-closets of the whole upper building were discharged through one of the iron columns that support the great main hall intended to accommodate the whole membership of the society! I could fill my paper with anecdotes of mismanagement like this, and the exposure might do some good. The builders of old time never made such blunders as these. They looked to the main things first—to light and air,

New York Produce Exchange, 2 Broadway. George B. Post, 1881–84. View to the southeast. NYHS.

New York Produce Exchange, 2 Broadway. George B. Post, 1881–84. Interior court. AR. CU.

comfort and convenience and hospitality. Too many of our architects look to all these essentials last.[45]

As Schuyler emphasized, the very program for the exchange—combining trading room and related facilities with leasable office space—compromised the building's monumental potential: "The requirements of the Exchange were subordinated to the 'investment' in fact, but that the committee insisted that the subordination should be conspicuous, and that the Exchange should be visibly mutilated for the sake of the shops under it and the offices over it. Those architects, who, while satisfying the commercial needs of the building, studied to keep those from ruining the building as a monument, simply threw their labor away."[46] Schuyler expounded on the selection process, remonstrating the exchange's building committee for shirking its responsibilities, and suggested calling in professional advisers, proposing of all architects Richard Morris Hunt, whose work he had for so long disparaged.[47]

In an assessment of the completed building published in the *Real Estate Record and Builders' Guide*, the critic, probably Schuyler, could not even begrudge Post the charm of his tower, which he felt was wasted on the rear, where a paved plaza and a broad flight of granite steps led up from the alley:

This might constitute a dignified approach if it were at the principal front of the building, or even faced a broad street.

New York Produce Exchange, 2 Broadway. George B. Post, 1881–84. Trading room. AR. CU.

But it can be gained or even seen only after a low vaulted passage at the end or an alley at the other, so that it is amusingly incongruous with the plainness of the entrances of the principal fronts; as if one were to lavish all the decoration of his house upon the kitchen door. The tower seems to be purely monumental, since an edifice of this kind, considered merely as a dwelling for a janitor, must be admitted to be extravagant. It contains a clock to be sure.[48]

Mariana Van Rensselaer tried to offer a more balanced view, calling it "the most conspicuous of all the new commercial buildings of New York." She went on to state:

There is no recent work of which it is so difficult to speak with fairness,—so great are its defects, and yet so great in some respects its excellence. I may as well confess at once that its ornamental details are as bad as bad can be. Also,—and this is a more important point,—that it is an extremely untruthful structure, so far as expressiveness is concerned, its exterior being quite unrelated to the disposition of its interior parts. The problem was not an easy one, I know—to build an immense hall for public use, and to put small offices beneath and around and above it in every inch of space it left unfilled. But a better solution, if not a perfectly true one, might well have been secured; and knowing Mr. Post's ability, we may believe he would have found it but for the feverish haste with which the work was pushed—a haste that is likely to do us ill service very often in the

future, as it has done in the past in more instances than this. But, after all possible deficiencies are noted, it remains true that the Produce Exchange, superficially considered for beauty only, is one of the most imposing monuments we have. I have often spoken of the sort of composition which results from the harmonious disposition of diverse masses and features; but there is another sort which comes through the emphatic repetition of a few well-chosen motives. This is the kind Mr. Post has used in a broad, powerful, and singularly effective fashion. Take away in imagination the story above the cornice, which was, I believe, an addition to the original design; suppress the utterly superfluous and disturbing tower; forget the unfortunate porches and the crude ornamentation, and we have a structure which is very fine in general proportion, and in the shape, sequence, and contrast of strong and even noble features. The good qualities of the Produce Exchange must be good indeed, since they so easily persuade us to shut our eyes to so many and so grave defects.[49]

Karl Hinckeldeyn, the former technical attaché to the German legation at Washington, D.C., offered a less partisan view in the pages of the *American Architect and Building News*:

I believe comparison be admissible between the proud Palazzo Farnese, towering with its grand horizontal lines above the multitude of houses of Rome, and the Produce Exchange dominating in the picture of lower New York.

United States Army Building, Moore to Whitehall Street, Water to Pearl Street. Stephen D. Hatch, 1888. View to the northeast, c. 1905. Ingalls. NYHS.

Nay, more, the latter appears to me even more impressive than the first named, through the addition of the proud tower, which, with its calm and beautiful contour and its effective composition, forms a far-visible characteristic feature of New York. The architect, Mr. Post, a most gifted master, in this building has shown the meaning of true and genuine effects in architecture. In this simple work you do not find any weak results, no playful divisions, no meaningless ornaments; but you find grave and grand wall-spaces in noble proportions, and decisive contrasts to the various stories, everything true, natural, practical and perfect in its entirety—with perhaps the single exception that the main entrances are not sufficiently characterized, and that the form and color of the small projecting granite supports, in a measure, disturb the harmony of the lower portion.[50]

All through the early 1880s, the *Real Estate Record and Builders' Guide* never ceased to admonish the developers of the Produce Exchange and Post for "being really greedy in a building of monumental pretensions" by requiring "half a dozen stories, more or less of rentable offices, over the monumental part of the building," and thereby creating "a failure as a monument, even if the architect had taken

more intelligent pains than he has put himself to to redeem it."[51] Despite the reservations of New York's leading critics, Post's design was widely appreciated, particularly as a response to an emerging trend that combined commercial uses with institutional programs in an effort to underwrite costs. The design itself was certainly very influential. For example, it was the Produce Exchange, and not H. H. Richardson's Marshall Field Warehouse (Chicago, 1885–87), as some have claimed, that was the specific model for Adler & Sullivan's Auditorium Building (Chicago, 1887–89), a key monument in the trend toward commercial and institutional hybridization.[52] As Post had done with the Produce Exchange, Adler & Sullivan wrapped a public facility—an opera house—with a revenue-generating hotel and an office building.

Influential or not, New York writers continued to fret about the Produce Exchange for a generation or more. In his 1898 monograph on Post's work, Russell Sturgis struggled to come to terms with the design: "The building is without special charm of proportion or of detail. It is a big, burly, manly, solid, impressive structure which no one can love very heartily but which everyone must respect. The same words may be used almost in the same sense for the great meeting room. Here, also, the sense of great space and of good construction pervades the whole, and no one can disregard the dignified look of the huge room, although, again, it is not especially attractive or fascinating."[53]

With the completion of Post's building, Eidlitz's much-admired old exchange was demolished to make way for Stephen D. Hatch's United States Army Building (1888), at 39 Whitehall Street, between Water and Pearl Streets.[54] Hatch's design resulted in a blocky structure that failed to please. Atop a heavily rusticated two-story, pink granite base Hatch piled six stories of red brick and reddish sandstone. In keeping with its appropriately castellated appearance, the two-story, fortresslike basement was lit only through narrow slits, interrupted by an overly flat arch forming the main entrance. The *Real Estate Record and Builders' Guide*, which characterized the building as "modern in design and somewhat composite in character," reported that the entrance had "already become the theme of the scoffers, and in fact . . . is a most ridiculous performance."[55] Inside, a central court rising from the fourth floor guaranteed light and air to the offices that filled the upper building.

The Cotton Exchange, though not so important as those devoted to stocks and produce, nonetheless housed itself in an imposing building (1883–85), also designed by Post, who came up with an inventive solution for an irregular downtown site, as at his earlier Post Building (1880–81) (see above), this one a trapezoid bounded by William and Beaver Streets and Hanover Square.[56] Filling the site with a three-story base that housed the thirty-five-foot-high principal exchange room and related clubhouse, Post broke the upper building, containing offices, into two parts, a rounded section at the corner of Beaver and

Cotton Exchange, site bounded by William and Beaver Streets and Hanover Square. George B. Post, 1883–85. View to the east. NYHS.

Mercantile Exchange, northwest corner of Harrison and Hudson Streets. Thomas R. Jackson, 1883–86. View to the northwest. Gubelman. NYHS.

William Streets and a rectangular block at the rear, separating the two with a court that provided natural light to all the offices. The building was entered at the bottom of the tower, at the corner of William and Beaver Streets—an odd choice given that the Hanover Square frontage was far and away more prominent. But the tower form at this corner gave the building prominence while helping to take up the geometric oddities of the site. With its high conical roof, the tower created an interesting silhouette and also helped visually to transform the French Renaissance–inspired design from an exchange into a club through the aggrandizing reference to the Château Chambord (1519–47), resulting in one of the earliest demonstrations of the referential eclecticism that would soon constitute the dominant trend in residential, institutional, and commercial design.

At the same time that Post's Cotton Exchange was under way, Thomas R. Jackson's Mercantile Exchange (1883–86) was being planned for the northwest corner of Harrison and Hudson Streets.[57] Jackson competed for the project against Carl Pfeiffer, James E. Ware, and Henry P. Gilvarry, with the results put on display for the members to review and vote on. In July 1884 the *Real Estate Record and Builders' Guide*, blaming the choice in part on the absence from the selection process of a professional adviser, found Jackson's vigorously articulate Queen Anne design "the least respectable of the four," damning it as "the worst kind of current architecture, crude, obstreperous and vulgar, and with nothing in it for all its swagger."[58] The same issue of the magazine carried a letter from an anonymous draftsman complaining that the choice of Jackson's scheme was largely based on cost.[59] The Mercantile Exchange was a new organization, begun in 1872 as the Butter and Cheese Exchange of New York and renamed in 1882 because the scope of its activities had grown to include the pricing, selling, and distribution of groceries, dried fruits, canned goods, and poultry. Jackson's six-story, brick and granite building, with its deep-set round-arched windows, paired columns, and corbeled brickwork, was a far cry from the regularity of Post's Produce Exchange or the stylistic suavity of the same architect's Cotton Exchange. Divided into two elements, the Mercantile Exchange faced Hudson Street with a gabled and pedimented block that suggested Georgian public architecture. Facing Harrison Street, piled arcades provided a more neutral midblock reading, only to be interrupted at the west end, where, above a columned portico, the building rose to form a tower culminating in a dormered pyramid. The second-floor trading room, located on the Hudson Street facade, could be easily identified by passersby, who surely would not fail to notice the broad central bay extending through the second and third floors, crowned with an exaggerated, overscaled, wide swan's-neck pediment.

In 1888 the Consolidated Stock and Petroleum Exchange, a group formed in 1875 by the union of a number of small exchanges, occupied its new building,

Consolidated Stock and Petroleum Exchange, northeast corner of Broadway and Exchange Place. Edward D. Lindsey, 1888. View to the northeast. Bogart. MCNY.

designed by Edward D. Lindsey.[60] Located on a ten-thousand-square-foot, highly visible site, at the northeast corner of Broadway and Exchange Place, the building ran through to New Street. The lower floors of the seven-story building were given over to the exchange, with offices above. The massive structure was Romanesque in inspiration, with Corse Hill Scotch red sandstone used for the base. Enormous windows along Exchange Place lit the ground-floor trading room, and Philadelphia pressed brick formed the four upper stories, which were leased as offices. The column-free trading room, a significant bit of engineering at the time, was spanned by deep trusses carrying the upper floors and resting on the outside bearing walls and heavy Byzantine columns of chocolate granite. The *Record and Guide* reported: "The interior is also noteworthy as exhibiting the most ambitious attempt that the city has to show in any of its exchanges of an architectural organism. The Exchange itself occupies [virtually] the whole main floor."[61]

WAREHOUSES

Even more than the office building, the warehouse was a prominent feature of the city's commercial landscape. While the terms *store* and *storehouse* were often used before the Civil War, by the 1870s they began to give way to *warehouse*, which by about 1880 became the universally recognized designation for a building type defined by big, minimally interrupted floors and straightforward—even stripped-down—facades. Warehouses were distinct from office buildings, which required much more perimeter in order to provide air and light for the numerous workers. The New York City Building Department, which was founded in 1860 and began to issue permits four years later, only started to recognize the "office building" as a classification in 1875, and did not designate the "warehouse" as a distinct type for another seven years.

Before the Civil War, warehouses were mostly located along South Street near the East River piers. With the rise of railroads serving the West via New Jersey ferries and the introduction by Cornelius "Commodore" Vanderbilt of freight service along the west side of Manhattan Island, however, activity dramatically shifted to the West Side. While most of the East River warehouses, like the one occupied by Reed & Sturges on the east side

Reed & Sturges Building, Front Street between Wall and Pine Streets. View to the east, c. 1855. Prevost. NYHS.

View to the southwest along Broadway showing, from right to left, the St. Nicholas Hotel (1853–54) and 503–511 Broadway (John B. Snook, 1878–79). NYHS.

of Front Street between Wall and Pine Streets, were built to a townhouse scale, the development of cast iron in the late 1840s combined with the expanding economy resulted in the wider and taller buildings characteristic of the West Side warehouse district, as well as that which developed in the area above Chambers Street, just north of the city's business district, catering to the wholesale dry-goods business.[1]

Cast-Iron Warehouses

Griffith Thomas was the architect of the rows of fourteen buildings (1869) at 58–84 Worth Street and 11–37 Thomas Street, between Broadway and Church Street, that were damaged in an 1879 fire which ultimately resulted in the 1885 changes to the building laws regarding cast-iron construction (see chapter 1). From 1860 until his death in 1878, Thomas was one of the city's most prolific practitioners working with cast iron, designing over twenty cast-iron–fronted buildings in the wholesale dry-goods district that faithfully mirrored the prevailing stylistic trends.[2] One of Thomas's best buildings was the towering cast-iron Domestic Sewing Machine Company Building (1872–73), at the southwest corner of Broadway and Fourteenth Street, which incorporated a retail showroom (see above). Isaac F. Duckworth, another important architect specializing in cast iron, tended to favor the French Second Empire style, employing some version of it in at least six buildings in the wholesale district between 1868 and 1873, including 72–76 Greene Street (1873), between Broome and Spring Streets, an expansive, vigorously modeled, five-story, ten-bay-wide building.[3] Duckworth also built extensively in the warehouse district near St. John's Terminal, which was located on a site bounded by Laight, Varick, Beach, and Hudson Streets (see below).[4] The prefabricated, cut-and-paste nature of cast-iron design made it possible for a firm like David and John Jardine's, whose work in other materials was generally mundane, to produce buildings nearly as excellent as those of their rivals. The Jardines' pair of mirror-image, five-story, Venetian-inspired buildings (1869–70) designed for the Civil War hero and Croton Aqueduct engineer General Thomas A. Davies formed a noble gateway to Thomas Street at Broadway, with buildings on the southwest and northwest corners.[5] The Jardines built a number of other cast-iron buildings in the St. John's Terminal area before abandoning metal for masonry.

Before the Civil War, John B. Snook, perhaps the most prolific commercial architect of the day, also experimented with cast iron for warehouse construction. He occasionally returned to it in some of the dry-goods warehouses he designed in the 1870s, producing such admirably straightforward buildings as 446–450 Broadway (1876–77)[6] and 503–511 Broadway (1878–79).[7] John Kellum was another leading designer of cast-iron buildings. Best known for his store (1862–70) for Alexander T. Stewart (see chapter 5), Kellum also designed a number of important warehouse-type buildings, including the Cary Building (1857), at 105–107 Chambers Street, west of Church Street, an Anglo-Italianate palazzo with iron fabricated by Daniel D. Badger.[8] Kellum's 502 Broadway (1860), painted white, featured slender arches grouping two stories.[9] His seventy-three-foot-wide, five-story-high 55 White Street (1861), commissioned by the saddlers John Eliot and Samuel Condict and fabricated by Badger, explored the "sperm candle" motif, employing tall, gracefully shaped columns that resembled the then-ubiquitous candles made from whale oil.[10] Although this slender effect could easily be achieved in cast iron, any number of marble-faced buildings were also of the sperm-candle type, suggesting that architects, if they liked a form created as the result of a new technology, were perfectly content to imitate it with traditional building methods. James H. Giles was another architect specializing in cast iron. His Lord & Taylor store (1869–70) was a key monument of the new uptown shopping district (see chapter 5). In the downtown business district, Giles's five-story 80–82 Leonard Street (1860–61), developed by Henry Young and longtime home to William Zinn's dry-goods company, piled two ranges of double-story arcades above a base.[11]

Frederick Clarke Withers, Russell Sturgis, and Richard Morris Hunt were the most prominent architects to experiment with cast iron. Withers's four-bay-wide, five-story-high warehouse at 448 Broome Street

Condict Building, 55 White Street. John Kellum, 1861. Elevation. DDB. CU.

(1871–72), between Broadway and Mercer Street, was built for Mrs. A. G. Ullman.[12] Ever the Gothic Revival structuralist, Withers reduced the cast iron to little more than a beautifully decorated frame for an exceptionally glassy facade. As Montgomery Schuyler put it some thirty years later, Withers's "application of Gothic principles resulted in a wide departure from Gothic forms."[13] Both Richard Morris Hunt's Roosevelt Building (1873–74), at 478–482 Broadway, between Grand and Broome Streets,[14] and his building (1871–72) for his brother-in-law, Alexander Van Rensselaer, next door at 474–476 Broadway,[15] used cast iron to great effect. If the fifty-foot-wide Van Rensselaer building, with its Moorish lattice of iron painted black, yellow, white, blue, and red—"the colors of the rainbow, startlingly and yet not unpleasingly blended"[16]—was slightly trivial, the three-bay-wide, five-story-high Roosevelt Building, constructed for investment purposes by the trustees of Roosevelt Hospital, was not. In his address for the 1876 convention of the American Institute of Architects, Alfred J. Bloor stated that Hunt's two facades

> at once exemplify perhaps the maximum of success that
> has so far been attained in such expression, and the versa-
> tility of their architect. . . . Even with the depreciation of
> their original polychromatic surface, by which the con-
> structional ironwork of a facade is so much heightened,
> the two store fronts just mentioned express their material
> at a glance; yet nearly all the lines of one of them are gen-
> uinely Moorish, which, of established architectural forms,
> is decidedly the best, perhaps the only fitting one for such
> work, while the other is motived on the Ionic column of
> the Scamozzian-capped type, and all its lines of solid and
> void, from water-table to crown mould of cornice, are as
> different as possible from those of the other.

Bloor emphasized the innovative potential of cast-iron construction: "After all, it will probably take a generation to decide fully whether iron on artistic grounds is to be relegated, as Ruskin and Seddon would have it, to the simple duty of constructive skeleton-work, or to take rank with stone for purposes of exterior expression deeper than mere surface-rendering."[17]

Montgomery Schuyler also praised the Roosevelt Building, describing it in 1881 as "a very free classic" design.[18] In his memorial to Hunt, published in 1895, he recalled that each of the two buildings

> had the fundamental merit of being designed for its mate-
> rial. . . . [The Roosevelt] was a series of openings three
> high and three wide. . . . It is this building which Profes-
> sor Kerr has done the honor of choosing as a most favor-
> able example of the iron storefront, for his continuation of
> Fergusson, and of it he remarks that the architect has "pro-
> duced a composition which is decidedly unobjectionable
> and not inartistic." In the other [the Van Rensselaer build-
> ing] the designer has employed Moorish motives, and
> especially the horse-shoe arch, as congruous with the
> nature of the material, and indeed . . . [promoting] the
> impression the whole front makes of being unmistakably

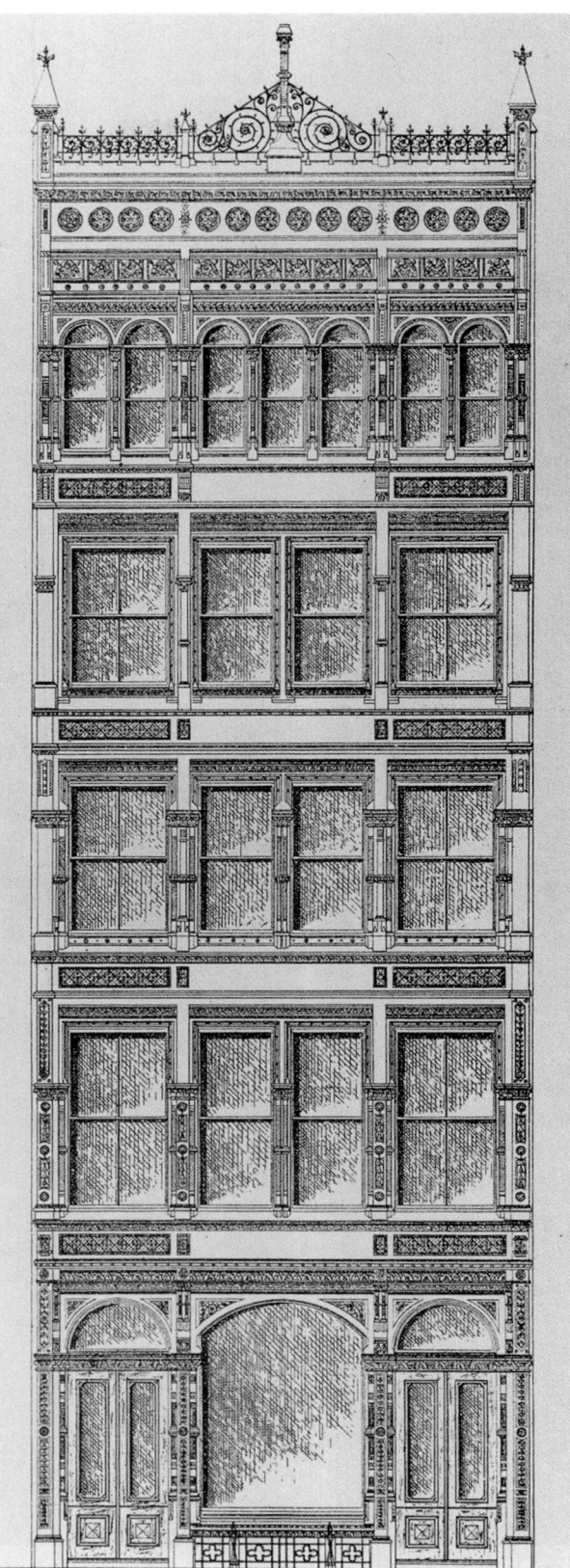

Ullman Building, 448 Broome Street. Frederick Clarke Withers, 1871–72. Elevation. AJB. CU.

View to the northeast along Broadway, 1877, showing in the center the Roosevelt Building (Richard Morris Hunt, 1873–74), to its right the Van Rensselaer Building (Richard Morris Hunt, 1871–72), and to its left across the street the Haughwout Building (James P. Gaynor, 1857). NYHS.

Van Rensselaer Building, 474–476 Broadway. Richard Morris Hunt, 1871–72. View to the east. The Octagon, AAF.

metallic, and excluding any other material than metal. . . . The "iron age" in commercial building produced nothing better than these two fronts and very few things as good.[19]

Hunt understood the problem of the warehouse and the possibilities of iron construction from early on in his career. In an 1859 discussion of architectural cast iron, he was quoted as saying, "Where land is exceedingly valuable, the whole lot is often built over for economy of space, and in the absence of interior courts and areas, it is necessary that the facade should become, as it were, one immense window for the sake of light. . . . Iron, requiring the protection of color, thus offers to us an opportunity of developing one of the greatest beauties of architecture."[20] Hunt completed a second warehouse building for the trustees of Roosevelt Hospital, in 1873 near the East River waterfront at 21–23 Peck Slip, on the northeast corner of Water Street.[21] This was not a midblock facade but a solid, six-story, brick and stone block, which Hunt superbly modeled and decorated so that it fit in with its pre–Civil War rowhouselike neighborhood despite being twice as wide and almost twice as tall as most of the surrounding buildings.

According to the New York correspondent of the Boston-based *American Architect and Building News*, Russell Sturgis's severely rectilinear, very glassy, five-story Austin Building (1876), at the southwest corner of Houston Street and Broadway, "used iron in such a way that nobody could doubt that it was an iron and not a stone structure." But the writer went on to say that "showing the bolt-heads was not, however, creating an iron architecture." Moreover, that same correspondent continued, the year 1879 "shows more than ever the returning feeling against this work [cast iron], and brick and stone are used in the majority."[22]

Edward H. Kendall was also a leading architect of both cast-iron and masonry (see below) warehouses, frequently attracting high-profile clients who built in still-fashionable residential areas in the early stages of commercial transformation. Kendall's 51 Lafayette Place (1870), built for Charles Wood, was a five-story cast-iron building adjoining La Grange Terrace (Alexander Jackson Davis, 1832–33), which was also known as Colonnade Row.[23] Mrs. Walter Langdon, a daughter of John Jacob Astor, had in the 1840s developed the area as a fashionable neighborhood, and the building replaced her garden and riding ring, running through the block to Broadway. Kendall's gridded facade exemplified the Neo-Grec severity that was his heritage from time spent at the Ecole des Beaux-Arts. His 378–380 South Fifth Avenue (West Broadway) (1873), between Spring and Broome Streets, was a straightforward effort manufactured by the J. L. Jackson Brothers' Foundry.[24] Kendall's 425–427 Broome Street (1874), at the southeast corner of Crosby Street, was a five-story warehouse built for William Bloodgood and the Reverend James McElroy, neighbors who, seeing that the tide of commerce was rolling north, replaced their houses with new construction.[25] Like Kendall, George W. DaCunha was an active architect of masonry buildings (see below) who also designed some interesting cast-iron work, including his highly ornate, five-story, three-bay-wide, Neo-Grec 31 Greene Street (1876), between Canal and Grand Streets, built for Ambrose C. Kingsland.[26] The building may have been designed by the twenty-four-year-old Charles W. Romeyn, who took credit for it in the *American Architect and Building News*, but the Building Department as well as a report in the *Real Estate Record and Builders' Guide* identify DaCunha as the architect. Some ten years later, also for Kingsland, DaCunha designed a building with an identical cast-iron facade at 74 Grand Street (1885–86), between Wooster and Greene Streets.[27]

John Correja designed a massive, six-story, double-width building at 462–468 Broadway (1879–80), at the northeast corner of Grand Street, running through to Crosby Street, for George Bliss and F. H. Cossitt, who leased it to the prominent dry-goods firm of Mills & Gibb.[28] Brooks Brothers had occupied the site's previous

Austin Building, southwest corner of Broadway and West Houston Street. Russell Sturgis, 1876. View to the southwest. NYHS.

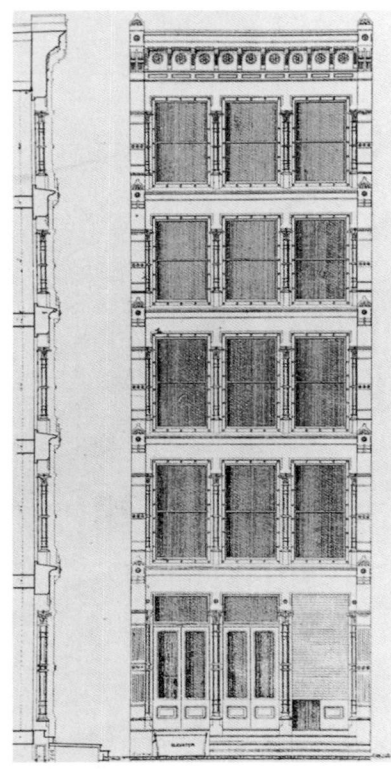

31 Greene Street, between Canal and Grand Streets. George W. DaCunha, 1876. Section and elevation. AABN. CU.

Mills & Gibb Building, northeast corner of Broadway and Grand Street. John Correja, 1879–80. View to the northeast. NYHS.

building, which was destroyed by fire. The *Record and Guide* praised Correja's exceptionally glassy, tectonically straightforward design: "The exterior of the building is a plain iron facade, on all three streets painted white. It is very high and it impresses the spectator with its solidity."[29] By contrast, Stephen D. Hatch chose the voluptuous language of France's Second Empire for his 1–5 Bond Street (1879–80), at the southeast corner of Jones Alley, built for Henry Robbins and Daniel Appleton, who used the five-story and mansard building as a factory for their American Waltham Watch Company while leasing some of the space to their publishing concern, D. Appleton & Co.[30] It replaced a similar cast-iron building (1870–71), also constructed for Robbins and Appleton and designed by Hatch, which had been destroyed by fire in 1877.[31]

Henry Fernbach, who was born in Prussian Silesia and educated at the Berlin Building Academy before establishing himself in New York in the mid-1850s, was a prolific and inventive designer who produced an astonishing body of cast-iron work along Greene Street between Canal and Houston Streets, with over twenty buildings constructed along that stretch in the 1870s and 1880s. Prior to his domination of Greene Street, Fernbach designed four adjacent five- and six-story buildings combining aspects of the Italianate and French Second Empire styles at 79, 81, 83, and 85 Walker Street (1868–69), but the similar buildings were all constructed for different owners.[32] Fernbach designed another version of this type at 8–10 White Street (1869–70), but this five-story, forty-foot-wide building enjoyed more elaborate detailing on the cast-iron facade, including unusual rusticated arches and acanthus-leaf keystones over the windows.[33] One of his earliest and best Greene Street buildings was the five-story, six-bay-wide 62–64 Greene Street (1872–73), between Broome and Spring Streets.[34] The French-inspired composition avoided monotony with a variety of carefully composed facade details, including projecting side bays, square and circular fluted engaged columns, and a cornice crowned by a curved pediment. On the east side of the block bounded by Spring and Prince Streets, Fernbach completed the six-story, ten-bay-wide, double-front 114–120 Greene Street (1881–82), which was distinguished by intricately detailed ground-floor piers and an elaborate treatment of the cornice and entablature, a signature feature of Fernbach's cast-iron work.[35] His six-story, six-bay-wide 121–123 Greene Street (1882–83), between Prince and Houston Streets, was a particularly ornate affair, with intricate detailing on the cast-iron facade, including bays separated by fluted columns with elaborate, almost Corinthian capitals topped by an Ionic scroll.[36] After his unexpected death at the height of his powers in 1883 when he was only fifty-five, Fernbach's practice was taken over by Alfred Zucker, also born in Prussian Silesia and educated in Germany. Although the majority of Zucker's warehouse work was executed in masonry (see below), he did follow Fernbach's example along Greene Street, completing in 1884 three adjacent six-story cast-iron buildings at numbers 126–134.[37]

Masonry Warehouses

John B. Snook's St. John's Terminal (1867–68), a combined freight and passenger station bounded by Laight, Varick, Beach, and Hudson Streets, was an early and exceptionally large exemplar of the warehouse type and a remarkable landmark that by virtue of its design and purpose was critical to the redevelopment of the city's West Side.[38] Commissioned by Commodore Vanderbilt, the straightforward, fifty-foot-high, boxlike building, constructed of red brick with a cast-iron frame and trimmed in granite, confronted the street with a loading platform designed to facilitate the transfer of goods between trains and wagons. The upper floors were devoted to storage. To break down the scale of this enormous block, which measured 405 by 439 feet, Snook articulated his design to suggest individual buildings. Virtually without precedent, the center of the building was opened up to form a 120-by-100-foot courtyard. In addition, eight twenty-four-by-twenty-six-foot skylights illuminated the interior. At the midpoint of the Hudson Street facade, where the masonry was organized to suggest a pediment, Ernest Plassman was commissioned to create a 150-foot-long, 31-foot-high monumental bronze sculptural group celebrating Vanderbilt's achievements. The group's subjects included classical river gods, Vanderbilt's first small boat, his larger steamships, a train, and a miniature version of the depot itself, flanking a giant figure of the Commodore set into a central niche.

St. John's Terminal not only brought a new building type to a high degree of resolution, it also marked the opening for redevelopment of a once fashionable and still respectable residential neighborhood as a warehouse district. Snook's warehouse sat on land that had been St. John's Park until 1866, when, two years after gaining control of the Hudson River Railroad, Commodore Vanderbilt bought it from the trustees of Trinity Church in order to provide warehouse facilities for the train line. The line's Manhattan tracks ran south along the Hudson River from Spuyten Duyvil to Sixty-first Street, where they followed Eleventh Avenue to Thirty-third Street and then proceeded one block east to follow Tenth Avenue and then West Street to Canal Street, where they again went east until Hudson Street.[39] Trains entered the building on Hudson Street between Laight and Beach. The passing of the park, though not unnoticed, was not exactly lamented either. The *New York Times* editorialized that it fell to "the omnivorous appetite of improvement." Acknowledging that the park was "never the property of the public," the *Times*'s editors did observe that it had been created for the benefit of those who lived "around its borders," even if the church held the title. Nonetheless, the "destruction of a public square is not a matter for light consideration."[40]

St. John's Terminal, Varick to Hudson Street, Beach to Laight Street. John B. Snook, 1867–68. View to the northeast, c. 1871. FLC.

St. John's Terminal, Varick to Hudson Street, Beach to Laight Street. John B. Snook, 1867–68. Detail of Ernest Plassman's sculptural group, c. 1871. FLC.

The completion of Snook's massive terminal, coinciding as it did with the postwar building boom, resulted in the construction of a number of large new warehouses in the area around it, many designed by George W. DaCunha. DaCunha, born in Funchal, the capital of Portugal's Madeira Islands, had only just established his architectural practice in New York after service in the Union army. Although DaCunha was sometimes the architect of buildings with cast-iron facades (see above), the bulk of his work was in masonry, even though, as with most warehouses of the period, much if not all of the structural framing was executed in cast iron. One of DaCunha's earliest efforts was a five-story, sixty-two-foot-wide, brick warehouse at 41–45 Vestry Street (1867), between Hudson and Greenwich Streets.[41] The design of this building, using arches, may have been influenced by the German Rundbogenstil. It was soon joined by other five-story brick warehouses, similarly designed, including DaCunha's pedimented 54–56 Laight Street (1870), 39 Vestry Street (1872–73), and 437–441 Greenwich Street (1875), also known as 47 Vestry Street, all built for Henry J. Meyer.[42] DaCunha continued the theme of his earlier buildings, this time for William Menck, with the six-story, twenty-foot-wide, red brick 37 Vestry Street (1882–83).[43] DaCunha also designed the six-story, red brick and stone, round-arched building at 461–469 Greenwich Street (1884–85), between Desbrosses and Watts Streets, a warehouse with a 175-foot facade on Greenwich, a 100-foot facade on Desbrosses, and a 75-foot facade on Watts.[44] Erected in six units, with three thirty-three-foot sections facing Desbrosses Street and three narrower sections perpendicular to Greenwich Street, its relatively unusual arrangement was expressed on the exterior, where pilasters divided the facades into four-bay-wide sections. DaCunha's other warehouses in the area included the French Second Empire–style, six-story 131–137 Franklin Street (1879–80), at the southwest corner of West Broadway, supported with cast iron and faced in brick and granite, an imposing block designed for the grocer Henry Welsh.[45] DaCunha's severe, six-story, Neo-Grec 157–159 Franklin Street (1881–82), between West Broadway and Hudson Street, was designed for Augustus C. Bechstein, a meat packer and real estate developer.[46] Replacing eight separate structures was the much taller, more elaborately composed and detailed, Queen Anne–style 126–128 Franklin Street (1881–82), between West Broadway and Varick Street, designed for Francis H. Leggett, a leading grocery, tea, and coffee importer.[47] The *Real Estate Record and Builders' Guide* praised DaCunha's five-story brick and limestone warehouse (1880) for Morris L. Herrman, at 18 White Street, on the northwest corner of Sixth Avenue, for its quiet character: "It is by the construction of buildings like these in a section of the city now fixed for a permanent business centre, that character is given to the warehouse district, where there has been heretofore too much ornamentation, and too little solid, honest work."[48]

While Edward H. Kendall's warehouse work in still fashionable residential neighborhoods primarily used cast iron for the facades (see above), his buildings on the West Side were faced in masonry. Early among these was his six-story, Philadelphia brick and Dorchester stone building (1876–77) for E. Oelbermann & Co., wool importers, at 57 Greene Street, replacing the Greene Street Methodist Church.[49] Built after the example of George B. Post's recently completed Western Union Building (see above), with the external wall frankly expressing the building's structural system, the Oelbermann building pleased the New York correspondent of the *American Architect and Building News*, who believed it showed the superiority of masonry construction:

> The style is of the Greek-Renaissance [Neo-Grec] now so generally employed by the best French architects in designs for town buildings. The effect of the whole front is that of substantial honesty in construction, and modest power in design. . . . Iron has been used in the designs very sparingly and very properly. . . . Light cast-iron gutter cornices are . . . used; but everywhere the metal is in entire subordination to the general design. . . . The work will show to business men and capitalists that a building including all possible conveniences can be put up within reasonable bounds, and that in place of employing second or third rate architects to put up

Francis H. Leggett Building, 126–128 Franklin Street. George W. DaCunha, 1881–82. View to the northeast. King, 1895. CU.

one of the commonplace stock structures selected from the price-list of the iron works, money may be saved by hiring brains to prepare the plans and supervise the erection.[50]

Commissioned by Robert and Ogden Goelet, Kendall's 84–94 Hudson Street (1881–82), between Worth and Leonard Streets, a massive, seven-story structure of red brick with stone and terra cotta trim, displayed an uneasy aesthetic tension between vertical piers that rose almost uninterrupted to seventh-floor arcaded windows and continuous horizontal stone bands.[51] In a fifty-foot-wide, seven-story warehouse at 10–12 Leonard Street (1884–85), between West Broadway and Hudson Street, Kendall suppressed the spandrels of every other floor above the base to create a tripartite reading that more effectively balanced the horizontal and vertical elements of the composition.[52] His 103-by-97-foot American Express Building (1890–91), at 55–61 Hudson Street, on the southwest corner of Jay Street, one of the most imposing Romanesque-inspired warehouses in the city, replaced a freight depot and stable that the company had built on the site in 1867 (Ritch & Griffiths).[53] Kendall was at the peak of his form here, deftly organizing the ten-story block into a tripartite arrangement that was in many ways even more skillful than his design for the Methodist Book Concern (see above). The principal features were a two-story rusticated base and a rhythmic arrangement of arcades that tied together four floors in the middle of the building. Above an intervening floor of mostly square windows, a paired arcade combined the top two floors to form an attic, above which an arcaded parapet decisively concluded the design.

Thomas R. Jackson, architect of the pioneering 1857 building for the *New York Times* (see above), was a fairly prolific designer of masonry warehouses in the St. John's Terminal area but, like Kendall, he also designed a number of cast-iron buildings. Most notable among his cast-iron work were the highly elaborate, five-story warehouse for A. J. Dittenhoffer, at 427–429 Broadway (1870–71), on the southwest corner of Howard Street,[54] and the modest, five-story, French Second Empire–style 82 Franklin Street (1871), between Franklin Place and Church Street.[55] In 1882 Jackson designed an austere, five-story, red brick building for Isaac Odell at 416–424 Washington Street, between Laight and Vestry Streets, which was enlivened by Romanesque Revival elements.[56] Divided into sections according to prevailing building laws, the Odell warehouse had a 125-foot facade on Washington and a 118-foot facade on Vestry. Jackson designed a number of buildings for the soap manufacturer James Pyle in the 1880s, including 430–436 Greenwich Street (1883), a seven-story, red brick warehouse with a cast-iron first floor,[57] and 428 Greenwich Street (1883–84), a narrow, five-story building that repeated the Romanesque Revival detailing of its larger neighbor.[58] He also completed two additional brick warehouses for Pyle in 1885–86: a seven-story building at 415–419 Washington Street, which replaced a portion of the

E. Oelbermann & Co. Building, 57 Greene Street. Edward H. Kendall, 1876–77. View to the northwest. King, 1893. CU.

William T. Wilcox & Co. lard refinery,[59] and the five-story, forty-two-foot-wide, red brick 70–72 Laight Street, between Greenwich and Washington Streets.[60] In the neighborhood of his far more prominent Mercantile Exchange (see above), at the northwest corner of Harrison and Hudson Streets, Jackson designed three buildings on Harrison Street: the five-story, twenty-five-foot-wide 8 Harrison Street (1885), and two identical six-story, three-bay-wide buildings at numbers 12 (1885) and 10 (1889).[61] On the southwest corner of Hudson and North Moore Streets, Jackson designed a six-story warehouse (1888–89) for John Castree intended for the storage of perishable foodstuffs.[62] Stretching fifty feet on Hudson Street and one hundred feet on North Moore Street, the first floor of the Romanesque Revival building was cast iron, topped by red brick floors trimmed with terra cotta and granite sills and lintels.

486 Broadway, southeast corner of Broome Street. Lamb & Rich, 1882–83. Drawing of facade for New York City Building Department. NYHS.

While the *Real Estate Record and Builders' Guide* did not exactly admire Lamb & Rich's Queen Anne–style, six-story, Philadelphia brick warehouse designed for William H. De Forest at 486 Broadway (1882–83), on the southeast corner of Broome Street, the magazine did acknowledge that it showed "serious study on the part of the designers."[63] With only a twenty-five-foot frontage on Broadway but with nine bays fronting Broome Street, the principal design idea of the facade was the articulation of the end bays to suggest towerlike corner pavilions between which, along Broome Street, an iron screen-wall painted dark green created an impression of exemplary lightness. The *Record and Guide* was impressed with the use of metal: "If we are to use iron as a building material at all, except to tie other materials together, it is evident that this is a much more rational use of it than any other." While much of the detailing of the metal imitated construction in wood and

149–151 Franklin Street, between West Broadway and Hudson Street. C. C. Haight, 1888–89. View to the south. AR. CU.

55–57 North Moore Street, between Hudson and Greenwich Streets. C. C. Haight, 1890. View to the northeast. AR. CU.

stone, the magazine was pleased by "the scattering over the plates between two windows of what look like imitations of bolt-heads," noting that this was done in a place where "the actual use of bolt-heads would be meaningless."[64] Mariana Van Rensselaer was of two minds about the building, writing that it "can hardly be called a successful work of art. But below the infelicities of its execution we perceive a general idea which seems deserving of much praise. This is the idea of treating the central portion of the long wall in a somewhat screen-like fashion, subordinating it to bays which project at its extremities. These bays correspond in width to the narrower facade, and the corner, of course, is treated as a whole." She also praised "the attempt . . . to bring the signboards which so disfigure our business structures into harmony among themselves, and to render them as little hurtful as possible to their architectural background."[65] In 1885, two years after its completion, the building was leased to the Mechanics and Traders Bank.

C. C. Haight, remembered primarily for his institutional buildings, also built a number of warehouses that were in keeping with his sober approach to architectural form. Two moderately interesting efforts of 1881 were the five-story, brick, Romanesque Revival 81 White Street, between Cortlandt Alley and Elm Street, and the six-story, brick and Belleville stone 106 Grand Street, at the northeast corner of Mercer Street.[66] For one of his principal clients, the Trinity Church Corporation, Haight designed a number of warehouses near St. John's Terminal, including 12–16 Vestry Street (1882–83), also known as 440–444 Canal Street, a seven-story warehouse that extended through the block, with seventy-five-foot facades on Canal and Vestry Streets.[67] Projecting piers, dividing the red brick facade into bays, were broken into one- and two-story pilasters by terra cotta plaques substituted for capitals. Haight's 443–453 Greenwich Street (1883–84), also commissioned by Trinity, was much more prominent, with 175 feet of frontage on Greenwich Street and 125 feet on Vestry and Desbrosses Streets.[68] In 1884, Haight added 34–38 Vestry Street, next door.[69] Together, the buildings enclosed a large courtyard entered through passageways in the Vestry Street building. Using orange bricks trimmed with sandstone, Haight was able to render the massive block subtle through the manipulation of the facade, where colossal pilasters crowned by corbeled brick capitals were extended to form a corbeled stringcourse. The Vestry Street addition, though similar, was tectonically purer, with stacked, two-story-high piers punctuated by corbeled brick courses.

While Haight's work for the Trinity Church Corporation had the virtue of being absolutely straightforward, for other clients he became more self-consciously architectural. His rigorously framed and crafted six-story warehouse at 149–151 Franklin Street (1888–89), between West Broadway and Hudson Street, did not please Montgomery Schuyler, who denigrated its front as "a huge sash-frame . . . [but] not a satisfactory sash-frame."[70] The critic

found fault with Haight's use of superimposed colossal Doric pilasters to band pairs of floors, which he felt introduced a concern for "classical proportions" out of place in a strictly utilitarian building. Schuyler also disliked Haight's arched doorway, which echoed a much smaller one on the two-and-a-half-story Federal house next door: "Let the tenants upstairs go in through a square undecorated hole. And quite good enough for the likes of them."[71] The composition of Haight's fifty-foot-wide, six-story 55–57 North Moore Street (1890), between Hudson and Greenwich Streets, was more decisively vertical, with a two-bay arcade rising through four floors above a utilitarian base and a strong attic of square windows alternating with terra cotta plaques.[72]

The warehouse work of Babb, Cook & Willard was far and away the high point of Romanesque-inspired utilitarianism in all the United States during the 1880s. The firm was begun when George Fletcher Babb, who had worked for Thomas R. Jackson, Peter B. Wight, Russell Sturgis, and Charles F. McKim, joined Walter Cook in 1877. Cook, the firm's lead designer, had studied in Paris and in Munich, where he was exposed to the round-arched work of Leo von Klenze and Friedrich von Gärtner. Daniel Wheelock Willard entered the partnership in 1884. According to

173–175 Duane Street, between Staple and Greenwich Streets. Babb & Cook, 1879–80. View to the north. AR. CU.

Hanan Building, southeast corner of White and Centre Streets. Babb, Cook & Willard, 1884–85. View to the southeast. AR. CU.

Russell Sturgis, looking back from 1904 on the evolution of the warehouse type, Babb, Cook & Willard

> were the first to present the character which we wish to insist upon . . . as being the most marked among all . . . warehouse buildings. The massive structure of rough brickwork with no high-priced material—no face brick of any sort used anywhere about the building (except where actual castings in terra cotta are the order), the effect produced by very deep reveals, a natural result, by the way, of that relegation of the lower stories to mere groups of piers with larger openings between them; the absence of a projecting cornice, indeed of any wall cornice whatsoever and the substitution for it of a parapet of one kind or another, very often a mere brick wall pierced with open arches.[73]

De Vinne Press Building, 27 Lafayette Place. Babb, Cook & Willard, 1885–86. View to the northeast showing 1891 addition by Babb, Cook & Willard on the right. AR. CU.

De Vinne Press Building, 27 Lafayette Place. Babb, Cook & Willard, 1885–86. Detail of Lafayette Place entrance. AR. CU.

Babb & Cook's 173–175 Duane Street (1879–80), between Staple and Greenwich Streets, was built as two buildings for Cook's mother, Catherine, and was one of the first in the new St. John's Terminal warehouse district to introduce arcading as a design strategy to help visually unify tall buildings.[74] The exceptionally stylish, six-story, load-bearing, red brick building, trimmed in stone and terra cotta, featured two explosively scaled, three-story-tall, Serlian-like arches that rose from a two-story-high base. For this feature alone, which makes the design an early exemplar of the Classical Revival, which was not to become a widespread movement for another five or six years, the building was very important. Overall its composition was sophisticated, with a seven-window arcade at the top floor and an openwork arcade above forming the parapet. The warehouse was widely admired. Schuyler felt it was best seen from the Greenwich Street elevated railway, and Mariana Van Rensselaer deemed it a triumph over adversity: "There was little to work with here: cheap materials, scanty ornament, and not even a corner site; only one of those high narrow facades that go so far to discourage effort. But effort, intelligent effort, has been brought to bear, and the result is fine in the first and chief essential of good architecture—fine in composition. . . . Such a building . . . is an architectural growth, an entity, an organism."[75] Russell Sturgis acknowledged the building's "simple character," but quarreled with some elements of the design.[76] He nonetheless found the open arcade at

the roof, a quintessentially modern device he credited the firm with introducing, positively inspirational.

The Hanan Building (1884–85), at the southeast corner of White and Centre Streets, designed after the partnership had expanded to include Daniel Willard, reversed the arrangement of arcaded buildings, screening the four lower floors with an arcade that carried the upper three floors, which were organized in bays separated by structural piers.[77] An arcaded openwork parapet rose gently toward the midpoint, suggesting a pediment on the Centre Street facade, even though the building was entered at the midpoint of the longer facade on White Street, where an alternating rhythm of wide and narrow bays sacrificed structural rationality for compositional finesse. Sturgis praised the big-boned shoe factory, especially its Centre Street front, which he believed to be "one of the most striking . . . and one of the most sincerely designed of all the warehouse buildings." He also admired the way the structural frame was articulated, with "the great uprights [taking] precedence even of the most important—the largest—the most significant arches of the exterior. The piers, three feet square and from that to four feet on the face, are carried up in unbroken line from sidewalk to skyline. They grow thinner, of course, as they ascend, but they keep what may be called their 'face value.'"[78] To the *Real Estate Record and Builders' Guide*, the Hanan Building was "another indication that capitalists are appreciating the value of New York City as a

Tarrant Building, 278–282 Greenwich Street. Henry Rutgers Marshall, 1892. Perspective view to the northwest. AR. CU.

135 Hudson Street, northwest corner of Beach Street. Kimball & Ihnen, 1886–87. View to the northwest. AR. CU.

manufacturing centre. This is no longer a ship-building port, and we have lost a good deal of our jobbing trade to the interior cities, but the census shows that this city has grown to be the most important and the largest manufacturing centre in the country."[79]

Babb, Cook & Willard's De Vinne Press Building (1885–86), at 27 Lafayette Place, on the northeast corner of Fourth Street, was a climactic work and a marvel of compositional invention, a building "so clean-cut and essentially American as to win instant respect," as Homer Saint-Gaudens put it.[80] The design was at once straightforward, even utilitarian, yet remarkably monumental in scale and surprisingly and memorably figural. Commissioned by Theodore Low De Vinne, a printer and publisher as well as a scholar of the printing arts, the building, more printing plant than warehouse, was one of the grand undertakings of the mid-1880s. The principal features of a design that was also delicate in detail were the massive scale of the brick facades, emphasized by the deep reveals of the triple arcade connecting the fourth, fifth, and sixth floors facing Lafayette Place, and the attic story of regular arcaded openings culminating in a subtly pedimented gable facing Lafayette Place that gathered the elements of the design into a striking unity.

The building was entered up a short flight of steps set between elaborate patent lights that illuminated the cellar, where the biggest presses were housed. Massive though it was, the De Vinne Building, viewed close up, managed to appear almost domestic in character, a helpful attribute given its location amid the early-nineteenth-century houses of its once fashionable neighborhood. The domestic scale was in part the result of the mullioning of the sash and in part the result of the beautiful entry arch combining fancy but delicately detailed work in stone and iron, which Russell Sturgis deemed "an almost perfect example of how ornament may be concentrated at one point, while still serving well the general purpose of the building as a whole."[81] The *Real Estate Record and Builders' Guide* was not so moved, finding the "big bald brick printing house . . . affectedly bold and quaint, and not successful as a harmonious composition."[82]

The architect and prestidigitator Oscar S. Teale's fussily decorated Marvin Safe Company (1885–86), at 468–472 South Fifth Avenue (West Broadway), between Prince and West Houston Streets, clearly derived from Babb, Cook & Willard's Hanan Building.[83] It confronted the avenue with a deep, three-story, triple arcade at the base, a two-story, six-bay arcade above, and an arcade of rhythmically grouped windows at the top that formed a veritable Roman aqueduct in brick. The building ran through the block to 138–144 Thompson Street, where its back facade restated themes from the front but in much blunter terms. Teale's six-story brick warehouse at 53–55 Beach Street (1885), between Collister and Greenwich Streets, originally used as a factory, was much less interesting.[84] Henry Rutgers Marshall's Tarrant Building (1892), at 278–282 Greenwich Street, on the northwest corner of Warren Street, a seven-story building of brick and stone trimmed in terra cotta, was a version of the De Vinne Building.[85] A warehouse in character, the Tarrant Building served that function as well as providing the headquarters for an established pharmaceuticals company until October 29, 1900, when a fire set off a massive explosion in one of the laboratories, destroying the building and eight adjacent ones as well as the Ninth Avenue elevated station.

William A. Potter's 186 Grand Street (1882–83), at the northwest corner of Mulberry Street, a narrow, six-story brick building, was one of the most resolved examples of the arcaded type, with a delicately modeled five-story arcade resting on an arcade base.[86] William B. Tubby's five-story, brick building (1883–84) for G. B. Horton, at 19–23 Jacob Street with an ell running back to Frankfort Street, was rather less resolved, yet the *Real Estate Record and Builders' Guide* lavished praise on the leather warehouse: "It is not only excellent as a building, but it shows an unusual self-restraint in keeping so clearly within the line of what is appropriate to a merely utilitarian building. . . . Its respectability comes solely from a careful adjustment of parts, and a straightforward and expressive use of common materials."[87] George B. Post, who rarely designed warehouses, created a modest, five-story, Romanesque-inspired, red brick example (1885) for Ellen Auchmuty, a member of the Schermerhorn family, near the East River waterfront on the northeast corner of Beekman and Front Streets.[88] The building featured appropriately themed terra cotta ornamental details, including starfish and cockleshells. In the same year, Post completed an even more austere, four-story, red brick warehouse next door at 146–148 Beekman Street.[89] Like Hunt, Post saw to it that his buildings fit in with the older, houselike warehouses of the neighborhood. As a result, they seemed almost tenement-like and a far cry from the vigorous overstatement of the much larger examples of such warehouse specialists as Babb, Cook & Willard.

For Montgomery Schuyler, "by dint of the sheer power of [its] flanking piers," there were "few street fronts of the same dimension" so impressive as the narrow front of Kimball & Ihnen's 135 Hudson Street (1886–87), at the northwest corner of Beach Street, occupied by the interior woodworking firm of Charles H. O'Neill & Co.[90] Aside from Hunt's 474–476 Broadway (see above), 135 Hudson Street was surely the most self-consciously artistic of the city's warehouses, though there it did not exhibit decorative excess. In fact, seen from afar, the six-story building

was severe to the point of bleakness, although when viewed from a closer distance, it revealed a wealth of interesting details, including exposed iron impost plates serving as bases for the first-story piers, an iron plate at the foot of the entire building, and tie-rod ends as well as exposed "anchor strips" at the corners. Though Schuyler did not admire it, the pseudo-gabling of the parapet did much to relieve the severity of the design, particularly when viewed along Beach Street. In addition to the variable parapet, the windows were interestingly grouped to reflect structural forces in the bearing wall. Terra cotta corner plaques indicating the street names were styled in a fashion almost Art Nouveau, suggesting that Francis H. Kimball's partner, Henry S. Ihnen, a talented draftsman whose rendering of Henry J. Hardenbergh's Astor Building (1885–86) (see above) was one of the period's most inventive and unusual, may have had a strong role in this building's design. Despite his reservations about the parapet, Schuyler felt that Kimball "confined himself absolutely to the structural necessities and made his effect by his abstinence. The thickening of the lower walls in pilaster-buttresses is plainly reasonable." All in all, wrote Schuyler, "the beholder has to say that here is a building of no style which yet has style, and he may very well reflect that if our buildings of bare utility were all as good as this, and were confined as closely to bare utility, our architecture of ornament would soon grow itself, and be as plainly indigenous as it is now plainly exotic."[91]

Albert Wagner's Puck Building (1885–86, 1892–93) was realized in two stages.[92] The first building replaced St. Catherine's Convent, at the southwest corner of Houston and Mulberry Streets, and later was expanded westward to fill the full block of Lafayette Street, between Jersey and Houston Streets. It was constructed as the printing plant of a satirical magazine published in both German- and English-language editions. A colossal gilded statue of Puck held forth from a third-floor perch at the corner of Mulberry and Houston; when the addition was built, a smaller version was made to greet those entering from Lafayette. In 1887–88 Wagner designed a six-story warehouse for the D. S. Walton Company, America's largest manufacturer of printed wrapping paper, at 1–9 Varick Street, between Franklin and North Moore Streets, but with a second facade on Franklin Street, a Romanesque-inspired design that boldly orchestrated scales of arcades to create a powerful composition in brick and terra cotta graced by a crenellated clock tower. The *Real Estate Record and Builders' Guide*, finding Wagner's design "simple and effective," went on to describe its composition in minute detail, suggesting so many shortcomings that its initial praise was cast in doubt.[93]

William Schickel & Co.'s six-story, brick and stone warehouse for John Jacob Astor II at 93–99 Prince Street (1887–88), on the northwest corner of Mercer Street, carried the arcaded building type to its logical conclusion, with full-height arcades comprising broad bays.[94] With this underappreciated building, the arcade had

1 Lafayette Place, northwest corner of Great Jones Street. Henry J. Hardenbergh, 1888. View to the northwest. AR. CU.

203–213 West Fifty-first Street, between Seventh Avenue and Broadway. Henry J. Hardenbergh, 1892. View to the northwest. AR. CU.

gone about as far as possible toward an expression of the tall building as a singular thing, one comprehensive idea rather than a mixture of various elements. His success in creating so consistent a design for a tall building, with what Sarah Bradford Landau has described as its "strikingly skeletal" arcades, carved for Schickel, an otherwise merely competent practitioner, a place at the forefront of the search for an appropriate expression of great height—ahead, in fact, of such Chicago pioneers as Adler & Sullivan, whose Walker Warehouse of the same year was notably less well advanced, a point made by Winston Weisman.[95]

Henry J. Hardenbergh's 1 Lafayette Place (1888), on the northwest corner of Great Jones Street, in some ways a bony structure like Babb, Cook & Willard's Hanan Building, rivaled its near neighbor, the De Vinne Press Building, in mass and sculptural presence if not in unity of effect.[96] Schuyler felt that in this warehouse Hardenbergh carried "the peculiarity of design" of his Astor Building on Wall Street "very much further," which is to say perhaps too far. Bracketed at each property line by two towerlike masses containing the stairs and elevators and crowned by singular roof features, Hardenbergh's building was organized as a series of regular arcaded bays. These were set on a complexly articulated base that incorporated dwarf, Romanesque-inspired columns rising from high plinths as at the entrance to his Astor Building but, as Schuyler put it, "more squat."[97] Above these, buttresslike piers articulated the second floor and then, reduced in size, formed flat piers rising through two floors to the flattened arcade.

Paired windows on the fifth floor and a regular rhythm of round-headed windows on the sixth culminated the structurally expressive and highly inventive scheme. The *parti* was rendered exceptionally vivid by using dark brown brick for the lower four floors and light buff brick for the top two. Hardenbergh's much less complicated arcaded warehouse (1892) on the blockfront of Fifty-first Street between Broadway and Seventh Avenue pleased Schuyler more: "The design resides purely in the disposition of the masses. . . . By mere force of this disposition, the factory becomes a work of art. . . . This work is especially exemplary because of its perfect plainness."[98]

Alfred Zucker, after his education in Germany and brief service as assistant superintendent for the State Railways Service at Hanover, immigrated to the United States in 1872 at the age of twenty.[99] He worked first in New York as a bricklayer before heading to Washington, D.C., where he was a draftsman in the Office of the Supervising Architect of the United States. After a brief stop in Galveston, Texas, where he designed the Galveston Cotton Exchange in collaboration with John Moser, Zucker became the consulting architect for the Vicksburg & Meridian Railroad, a job he held from 1876 to 1882, during which time he was also the architect in charge of all public buildings in Mississippi. After returning to New York and taking over the late Henry Fernbach's practice in 1883, Zucker completed some cast-iron work along Greene Street (see above) before coming into his own as a designer, producing an impressive array of stylistically diverse, large-scale

Cohnfeld Building, southeast corner of Greene and Bleecker Streets. Alfred Zucker, 1884–85. View to the southeast. UT-AAA.

92–96 Bleecker Street, southwest corner of Mercer Street. Alfred Zucker, 1890. View to the southwest. Parshley. UT-AAA.

484–490 Broome Street, northwest corner of Wooster Street. Alfred Zucker, 1890–91. View to the northwest. UT-AAA.

Rouss Building, 549–553 Broadway, between Spring and Prince Streets. Alfred Zucker, 1889–90. View to the west. UT-AAA.

masonry warehouses. His first building of note, the nine-story, 140-foot Cohnfeld Building (1884–85), at the southeast corner of Greene and Bleecker Streets, built for Isidor Cohnfeld, a prominent manufacturer and ostrich and fancy-feather importer, was perhaps more important for its location, which was selected by Zucker, than for its architecture.[100] The *Real Estate Record and Builders' Guide* heralded the massive stone, brick, and iron, terra cotta–trimmed building as a "pioneer" for its location north of the established dry-goods district.[101] The *Record and Guide* stated: "The appearance from the outside is imposing, and the structure towers high and above all the surrounding buildings, looking like a giant in the midst of dwarfs. It has added to the importance of Bleecker street as one of the great cross-town routes, and has greatly improved the neighborhood, having resulted in a considerable increase in the value of property in the immediate vicinity." The otherwise straightforward design was highlighted by an elaborate, two-story, French Second Empire–style mansard, which contained rooms for dyeing and drying feathers. The *Record and Guide* was also impressed by the warehouse's interiors, which were "furnished in a much superior style to the manner in which warerooms are usually fitted up. There is hardwood trim on most of the floors. The staircases are wide and spacious . . . and that on the first floor is elegantly carved in ash, the newel being of handsome design and carved by hand. . . . In the southwest wing . . . there is also an elegant staircase . . . which has highly polished marble stairs and wainscoting."[102]

Zucker changed stylistic direction with his ten-story building (1890) of brick, stone, and terra cotta for Rachel Cohnfeld, on the southwest corner of Bleecker and Mercer Streets, which featured multistory arcades grouping triple windows in the manner of H. H. Richardson.[103] At the corner a conical tourelle rose above the cornice, a conceit Zucker repeated on his six-story, brick, iron, and stone warehouse for Charles Wise, at 3–5 Washington Place, on the northeast corner of Mercer Street, which was also designed in 1890.[104] A much more literal interpretation of Richardsonian Romanesque was Zucker's six-story 484–490 Broome Street (1890–91), on the northwest corner of Wooster Street, built for Simon Goldenberg, which featured an inventive and complex arrangement of parts, especially along its ten-bay-wide Broome Street facade, where a deeply recessed, rusticated stone base was dominated by twin, three-story, round-arched, three-bay-wide groupings in the center.[105] The top three floors of the building were also grouped as a unit, with towerlike masses on the center of the Broome Street facade and at the corners, although the effect of this arrangement did little to alter the horizontal emphasis established by the powerful base, which appeared capable of carrying a much taller load. Zucker provided witty and elaborate detailing on the facades, including carved impost blocks depicting the medieval motif of a dragon biting his own tail.

In contrast to the exuberant detailing of the Broome Street warehouse was Zucker's straightforward, ten-story, 130-foot-high Rouss Building (1889–90), at 549–553 Broadway, between Spring and Prince Streets, running through to Mercer Street, which replaced another notable tall building, Renwick & Sands's eight-story cast-iron building of 1870–71.[106] It was built for Charles Broadway Rouss, a colorful Southerner who came to New York heavily in debt after the Civil War and celebrated his financial recovery by erecting at the building's construction site a sign that read, "He who builds, owns and will occupy this marvel of brick, iron and granite, thirteen years ago walked these streets penniless and $50,000 in debt." Rouss also monumentalized his achievement on the completed structure, with his name spelled out in large letters across the entablature atop the two-story granite base and again at the top in the central pediment. The main feature of the Broadway facade were the pilasters that ran the full length of the building and divided the front into three three-bay-wide sections, which were further divided by thin cast-iron colonnettes between the windows. The two-story pilasters were heavily banded for the first eight stories, while the top group was fluted. With the structurally articulate Rouss Building, Zucker offered an alternative to the arcading of H. H. Richardson as a method of expressing great height.

Household Storage Warehouses

Warehouses devoted to the storage of household goods represented a particular type especially designed to suit the needs of rich New Yorkers who found the largely windowless facilities particularly useful during the summer months. Having given up a house or apartment while vacationing in the country, at the shore, or abroad, they needed to park their chattel until taking new quarters in the fall. John B. Snook's seven-story, Belleville stone, brick, and terra cotta Lincoln Safe Deposit Building (1882–83), at 32 East Forty-second Street, located near the head of Vanderbilt Avenue, was, according to the *New York Times*, an "imposing" building of "massive proportions," with one hundred feet of frontage on Forty-second Street and fifty feet on Forty-first Street.[107] The first floor was devoted to business offices and elaborate reception areas used by the Lincoln Bank, with separate coupon rooms for men and women, while the six windowless floors above contained fireproof space for the storage of furniture, works of art, and other household merchandise.

James E. Ware, best known for his tenement-house designs and as the architect of one of the city's most luxurious apartment houses, the Osborne (1883) (see chapter 4), produced two massive storage facilities for the Manhattan Storage and Warehouse Company. His first building (1882–85) for the company was located on the southwest corner of Lexington Avenue and Forty-second Street.[108] Ware emerged victorious in competition with a design consisting of ten separate buildings grouped together in two blocks bisected by a thirty-foot-wide pas-

Manhattan Storage and Warehouse Company Building, southwest corner of Lexington Avenue and East Forty-second Street. James E. Ware, 1882–85. View to the northwest. AABN. MMA.

Manhattan Storage and Warehouse Company Building, east side of Seventh Avenue between West Fifty-second and West Fifty-third Streets. James E. Ware, 1890–92. View to the northeast. King, 1893. CU.

sage leading from the center of the Lexington Avenue frontage to a central eighty-by-eighty-foot light court. Clad in brown brick, the essentially blank-faced design, possibly inspired by the Castle at Carcassonne, was relieved by "a heavy and powerfully machicolated cornice" and by corner towers rising above the cornice to red-tile-covered pinnacles.[109] *Builder* magazine thought Ware's crenellated brick keep constituted a building that "in structure and design, leaves the beholder free from doubt as to its intention. . . . Massive in structure, it combines breadth of treatment with depth. . . . The round towers with which it is flanked, rising boldly above the roof, aid the sense of solidity. Instead of duplication of details extending along each story in monotonous uniformity, we have entrance arches of different dimensions, disposed according to convenience, leaving wide interspaces of solid brick, suggestive of massiveness."[110]

Mariana Van Rensselaer was equally enthusiastic: "No architect of the day deserves more hearty congratulation than does Mr. Ware for the truthful, rational, strictly architectural way in which he achieved his design." She admired his handling of the walls, stating that he had redeemed "them from barrenness, emphasized their scale, and turned his building into an imposing work of architectural art. Purpose and interior disposition could not be more truthfully explained. . . . Everywhere we see evidence of original and happy inspiration. And it *is* original and happy, because entirely based on practical necessities, which are turned (not forced) into artistic opportunities."[111] Ware's second building (1890–92) for the company, on the east side of Seventh Avenue from Fifty-second to Fifty-third Street, was a nine-story brick warehouse that replaced a row of wooden shanties.[112] An equally imposing Italianate design, it had been inspired by the Palazzo Vecchio, in Florence, with bold towers rising above the massive building at each corner.

Power Plants and Factory Blocks

The shift from gas to electric illumination, beginning in the 1880s, also stimulated the growth of a new building type, the power substation. Because these structures were frequently located in residential neighborhoods, they were styled like civic buildings rather than like factories. In 1882, one year after Thomas Alva Edison moved his electric-light company from Menlo Park, New Jersey, to New York, the first massive dynamos were started at his facility at 257 Pearl Street. Later in the decade, Albert Buchman and his partner, Benjamin Deisler, became the Edison Electric Illuminating Company's architects. For their first assignments they designed substations at 47–51 West Twenty-sixth Street (1887) and 117–119 West Thirty-ninth Street (1887).[113] The five-story, brick and stone designs, with their boldly striped bases and play of big and conventional windows, were stylistically advanced, eschewing the individualistic Romanesque of the 1880s for the Classicism that would be a hallmark of the civic architecture of the 1890s. Another

Western Electric Company Building, 125–131 Greenwich Street. Cyrus L. W. Eidlitz, 1888–89. View to the southeast. King, 1893. CU.

Edison Electric Illuminating Company Substation, 117–119 West Thirty-ninth Street. Buchman & Deisler, 1887. View to the northwest. BLDG. CU.

substation of note, William G. Grinnell's red brick, Romanesque-inspired Excelsior Power Company (1887–88), at 33–43 Gold Street, was actually a renovation of an existing four-story plant originally designed by Grinnell for the American Heating and Power Company in 1882.[114]

In the late 1880s, Leopold Eidlitz's son, Cyrus L. W. Eidlitz, began his association with the recently founded Western Electric Company with the design of a ten-story-high, brick and terra cotta office and factory (1888–89), at 125–131 Greenwich Street, on the southeast corner of Thames Street.[115] The *Real Estate Record and Builders' Guide* saw the design as a breakthrough:

> A factory has lately been put up . . . that is so interesting and appropriate a piece of architecture it is a pity its site prevents it from being better seen. It stands at the corner of Thames and Greenwich streets. The former is little more than an alley and the latter is occupied by the elevated railroad, which not only cuts the building in two

on the side and conceals its basement, but prevents any general view from being had from the opposite sidewalk. In fact, it is only from the roof or upper windows of the building opposite that the factory can be fairly seen or judged. . . . The main peculiarity of the design, and a very successful peculiarity it is, is the treatment of the corners, which are conceived as buttresses and left very much more solid than the intermediate wall.

All in all, the magazine concluded, "The effect of the building, badly as it is placed, is extremely good, and a great part is due to the plainness which proclaims it a work of bare utility. There is no ornament apart from the expression of structure, and this is confined, except in the upper story, to the simple moulding at the arris of the arches."[116] Montgomery Schuyler was equally pleased with Eidlitz's design, which he deemed "an exemplary specimen of a class of buildings which not only owners, but even many architects, do not seem to consider to belong to architecture at all."[117]

View to the north, c. 1870, along Mulberry Street between Park and Bayard Streets. NYHS.

CHAPTER 4

Places Called Home

Tenements, Hotels, Apartment Houses, and Houses

There is probably no great city in the world which needs a reform in domestic architecture more urgently than New York, as there is none which contains such a preponderance of dwellings unsuited to the wants of the people who inhabit them.

—James Richardson, 1874[1]

In no considerable, thoroughly settled city on the civilized globe is material living attended with so many difficulties as in New York.

—*Harper's New Monthly Magazine*, 1882[2]

Even though New York had attained its position as America's premier metropolis by the middle of the nineteenth century, it was hardly as built up as Paris or London. Above Forty-second Street there was plenty of open land. But below Fourteenth Street, the island was packed to the gills. While the poor were crowded into what would come to be known as the Lower East Side, the city was losing its middle class to suburbs beyond its political jurisdiction. New York's logical northward expansion was limited by available transportation. It was difficult to get to the upper island on a daily basis; for many middle-class citizens, it was easier to travel by boat to Brooklyn or to various riverfront towns in New Jersey than to travel from business places to potential homesites in Harlem or Washington Heights. Meanwhile, the upper class could settle just above Fourteenth Street, where, because of its comparative convenience, the price of land was well out of reach for most other people.

Even before the Civil War, the city's population had been growing dramatically, increasing by almost 700,000 between 1820 and 1860, when it stood at 814,000.[3] Much of New York's growth was the result of immigration. New Yorkers had tended to regard their city as untainted by the problems of European urbanism, but by the 1850s it was becoming clear that Old World problems were also cropping up in the New World. In 1847 Philip Hone, mayor in 1826 for a one-year term, recorded in his diary: "Our good city of New York has already arrived at the state of society

found in the large cities of Europe; overburdened with population, and where the two extremes of costly luxury in living . . . are presented in daily and hourly contrast with squalid misery and destitution."[4]

The crowding of the poor was worst in the Lower East Side, especially in the so-called Five Points area, at the intersection of Worth, Park, and Baxter Streets, just a few blocks north of City Hall, and in Mulberry Bend, a block bounded by Bayard, Baxter, Park, and Mulberry Streets. In these neighborhoods, hundreds of people—families and unrelated adults alike—were jammed together in old houses converted to tenement use; these were popularly known as rookeries. Also filled with people were purpose-built tenements. A four-floor, four-family tenement built in 1833 by James Allaire to house the employees of his engine works, at the eastern end of Water Street near Corlears Hook, was said to be the city's first purpose-built dwelling of its kind, and numerous jerry-built structures followed, virtually filling their lots and providing almost no fresh air or sunlight to the innumerable cubicles within.[5] The Five Points slum was not new to post–Civil War New York. It grew up with the republican city and as early as 1829 was targeted for clearance. But by the 1870s little had been done and its conditions were truly scandalous. James D. McCabe Jr. described a typical Five Points tenement in his guidebook of 1872: "The stairways are rickety and groan and tremble beneath your tread. The entries are dark and foul. . . . Every room is crowded with people. Sometimes as many as a

Mulberry Bend slum dwelling, northeast corner of Baxter and Park Streets, 1872. Riis. MCNY.

Mulberry Bend slum dwelling, northeast corner of Baxter and Park Streets, 1872. Rear view. Riis. MCNY.

dozen are packed into a single apartment."[6] In 1884, the State Tenement House Committee, headed by Felix Adler, a social reformer and founder of the Ethical Culture movement, studied the Five Points area and recommended that all its slum buildings be demolished.[7] But it was not until Jacob A. Riis, the Danish-born journalist, dedicated an entire chapter of his 1890 book, *How the Other Half Lives,* to the conditions of this notorious area that action was finally taken, leading to the construction of Columbus Park on the site of Mulberry Bend in 1894–96.[8]

The slums, no less subject to expansion than any other aspect of post–Civil War city life, spilled out beyond the Five Points, covering virtually all of the Fourth and Seventh Wards (which comprised the Lower East Side) and even taking over long-established neighborhoods that had once been fashionable. No area of the old city was sacred, including St. John's Park, in the 1820s the city's choicest residential area, which was developed after 1802 by Trinity Church when it built a chapel (John and Isaac McComb, 1803–07) on the site. The area around St. John's Park began to degenerate in the late 1840s, becoming run-down, if not exactly a slum. H. C. Bunner's 1887 novel, *The Story of a New York House,* one of many works of the period looking back, with only partial nostalgia, to the simpler days of the pre–Civil War city, characterizes a St. John's Park house as it evolves from a single-family residence to a boardinghouse to a tenement, until it is finally destroyed to make way for an eight-story factory building.[9] In 1867, after a decade or so in which local families "fought the tide of trade," the square, which had been consigned to its neighbors as a park, was redeveloped as St. John's Terminal (see chapter 3), although the chapel was spared.[10]

When the twenty-eight-year-old Charles Dickens vis-

ited New York in 1840, the slums were a public scandal and embarrassment. "What place is this," Dickens wrote in *American Notes,*

> to which the squalid street conducts us? A kind of square of leprous houses, some of which are attainable only by crazy wooden stairs without. What lies beyond this tottering flight of steps, that creak beneath our tread?—A miserable room, lighted by one dim candle, and destitute of all comfort, save that which may be hidden in a wretched bed. Beside it, sits a man: his elbows on his knees: his forehead hidden in his hands. "What ails that man?" asks the foremost officer. "Fever," he sullenly replies, without looking up. Conceive the fancies of a feverish brain, in such a place as this![11]

Conditions in the city's slum districts were hardly better thirty years later, when Edward Crapsey took readers through *The Nether Side of New York.* Though conditions at the Five Points had improved, Crapsey reported, the worst slum conditions seemed to have emerged at the edges of Greenwich Village, where the Arch Block, a group of connected tenements on Thompson and Sullivan Streets between Broome and Grand, presented "the most striking view which can be obtained of the vile and squalor of the city." The slums, though changing and moving around, had become a fact of city life. According to Crapsey, "There seems to have always been in the city, between where reputable people live and where they do business, a region where only crime and poverty find refuge. This territory has shifted with the changes of the city."[12]

More squalid even than life in the slums was a semi-rural existence in shantytowns, which, according to the *New York Times,* in 1864 provided for the needs of twenty thousand people who "comprise that portion of the population known as squatters."[13] While many squatters were truly destitute, others had the means to rent the land on which they built their hovel-like accommodations. That rent went to speculators who had purchased land in outlying areas in anticipation of the city's expansion but in the meantime leased it to the squatters, who paid enough to cover original capital investment and annual taxes. While most of the squatters were located in the farthest reaches of the as-yet-undeveloped West Side—three hundred shacks having been removed from the site of Central Park in 1857—some were in more central locations. As late as 1864, the *Times* bemoaned the squatters still housed in the middle of Fifth Avenue, "that high ground which promises to be in a few years the most magnificent terrace on the continent."[14]

In 1865, the *Times* reported that in the 19th police precinct alone, ten thousand people—a low estimate—were living in "not fewer than eight hundred shanties or cabins, each one containing from one to six prolific families" along with their cows, goats, pigs, geese, and chickens. Though overcrowded and unsanitary, the settlements, "which have been growing over the years, were not without their charms, with" some of the antiquated cabins "now possessing quite a moss-grown and picturesque appearance from the passing years," in part because the "squatters have evinced no little judgment and taste in the selection of sites for building," choosing shady rock outcroppings to "pitch their shanties together, in irregular groups, forming miniature villages, in which [to] . . . bid defiance to the advance of city civilization." According to the *Times*, the shanties were inhabited by Irish ruffians, "indolent, desolate, boiling over with the instincts of robbery, arson, murder and riot," who terrorized the neighborhood at night "by their yells, their rows, and their scenes of violence and debauchery." Because of the corrupt nature of city politics, the squatters "rule the ward and no man who owns property in the neighborhood dares to make a complaint against them." The *Times* claimed that the squatters were behind the burning of the Colored Orphan Asylum, in 1863, and the attempt to burn the entire city in the same year, when passions were high as a result of the military draft and the Civil War as a whole.[15]

The shanty problem persisted well into the 1880s, when, according to the *Times*, about ten thousand Irish and Germans had "built villages in the midst of the City," forming "communities of their own" on land they had taken possession of without permission. The largest and most prominent of the impromptu shanty communities was located on East Forty-third Street between Second and Third Avenues, near Grand Central Depot. "Did it ever occur to you," the *Times*'s writer inquired, "that within plain sight of that big building, . . . there was a settlement as completely isolated from the big City as if it stood in the middle of the Jersey meadows. . . . A settlement where the people, though they have no more right to the land than they have to the City Hall Park, drive the landlords and

their agents off with clubs and dogs and sometimes with guns, and fight the Police, and refuse to leave their houses till the roofs are thrown off and the walls torn away?"[16] Another large shantytown existed near the site of the new Mount Sinai Hospital, at Sixty-fifth Street and Lexington Avenue. But the most entrenched shantytowns were two on the West Side, one bounded by Sixty-fifth and Eighty-fifth Streets and Central Park and Ninth Avenue, and the other, estimated to be as dense as any neighborhood in the developed part of the city, occupying the area bounded by Fifty-eighth and Sixty-eighth Streets and Tenth Avenue and the Hudson River. Amazingly, parts of the shantytowns survived as permanent development came. Moreover, they still possessed a certain appeal to those not forced to live in them, as the *American Architect and Building News* reported:

> It may seem hardly becoming a journal which upholds a high sanitary ideal to regret the disappearance of these filthy dens, but we confess that we never pass a village of them without being irresistibly attracted by their picturesqueness. Less gloomy and vicious-looking than the city rookeries, the habitations of the squatters, with their whitewashed walls of rough boards leaning in all directions, their roofs of rusty tin, torn in a crumpled sheet from some demolished warehouse, their dilapidated stovepipes projecting unexpectedly through roof or walls, and their groups of goats and children climbing about in the sunshine through the circuitous paths among the rocks, have a naive charm peculiar to themselves. Now and then one can see among them dwellings of larger size, with porches and wings of the same general style of architecture, exhibiting a variety of outline and shadow, a breadth of effect, and unconscious simplicity, which would make them admirable objects for the background of a picture. Before they have been entirely improved out of existence, we would suggest that an enterprising sketcher might find among them many a motive which he could use to advantage in work of a much higher class.[17]

Shantytown, Fifth Avenue near Ninetieth Street, c. 1880. MCNY.

TENEMENTS

> As New York lies, it would probably be impossible to invent
> a system of tenement-houses, unless built with no windows
> at all, more perfectly adapted than is the present to deprive
> the homes of the poor of light, air, sunshine, and ventilation.
> —Edward T. Potter, 1878[18]

At first the cheapest, most substandard housing was to
be found in once-respectable, shamelessly subdivided rowhouses. But by the 1840s it had become common for
entrepreneurs to meet the insatiable demand for cheap
accommodation with purpose-built slum houses, soon
called tenements. These were the city's first form of multiple dwelling, a form so horrific that for at least a generation it stigmatized for the middle and upper classes all
efforts to build multiple dwellings. The very name can be
traced to the Latin word *tenere*, meaning "to hold," and it
was, as Amy Kallman Epstein has pointed out, an apt
locution, precisely suggesting "the level of domestic comfort aimed for by the real estate speculators who built
them." The tenement was "a structure intended 'to hold'
rather than 'to house' a number of families."[19]

Gotham Court (1851), at 36–38 Cherry Street, was the
most notorious of all slum buildings at the time.[20] Ironically,
this complex of twelve six-story houses, the brainchild of
Silas Wood, built in two rows along two narrow alleys
extending from Cherry Street deep into the block also
bounded by New Bowery, Oak, and Roosevelt Streets, was
not only intended as a model tenement but was also initially
so regarded. Gotham Court originally housed 140 families,
but by 1879, when it was purchased by a group of philanthropists who repaired the structure and placed its management in the charge of two women previously associated with
the City Mission, it was said to house 240 families. After
about fifteen years as a respectable tenement, Gotham
Court was condemned by the city and torn down, in 1896.

Despite the fact that crime and disease accompanied the
growth of tenement neighborhoods, they were at first characterized by comparatively little social unrest. But riots in
1849 and 1857 called attention to tenement conditions,
motivating the New York State Assembly to investigate the
housing problem. In 1857 the assembly issued a report of
the "Select Committee Appointed to Examine into the
Condition of Tenant Houses in New York and Brooklyn,"
which outlined the pattern of real estate transactions that
had turned the oldest parts of both cities into slums:

> As a city grows in commerce, and demands new localities
> for traffic and manufacture, the store and workshop
> encroach upon the dwelling house and dispossess its
> occupants. At first the habitations of citizens are removed
> to a limited distance, because, with an industrious popu-
> lation, time is money, and neighborhood of residence and
> business secures both economy and convenience. The
> merchant and master, then, find it for their interest to
> dwell in the vicinity of their active operations; and so,
> likewise, do the mechanic, laborer, and all dependent on
> business life. . . . [Later] as our wharves became crowded
> with warehouses and encompassed with bustle and noise,
> the wealthier citizens, who peopled old "Knickerbocker"
> mansions, near the bay, transferred their residence to
> streets beyond the din; compensating for remoteness
> from their counting houses, by the advantages of
> increased quiet and luxury. Their habitations then passed
> into the hands, on the one side, of boarding house keep-
> ers, on the other, of real estate agents; and here, in its
> beginning, the tenant house became a real blessing to
> that class of industrious poor whose small earnings lim-
> ited their expenses and whose employment in work-
> shops, stores, or about the wharves and thoroughfares,
> rendered a near residence of much importance. At this
> period, rents were moderate, and a mechanic with family
> could hire two or more comfortable and even commodi-
> ous apartments, in a house once occupied by wealthy
> people. . . . This state of tenantry comfort did not, how-
> ever, continue long; for the rapid march of improvement
> speedily enhanced the value of property in the lower
> wards of the city, and as this took place, rents rose, and
> accommodations decreased in the same proportion. At
> first the better class of tenants submitted to retain their

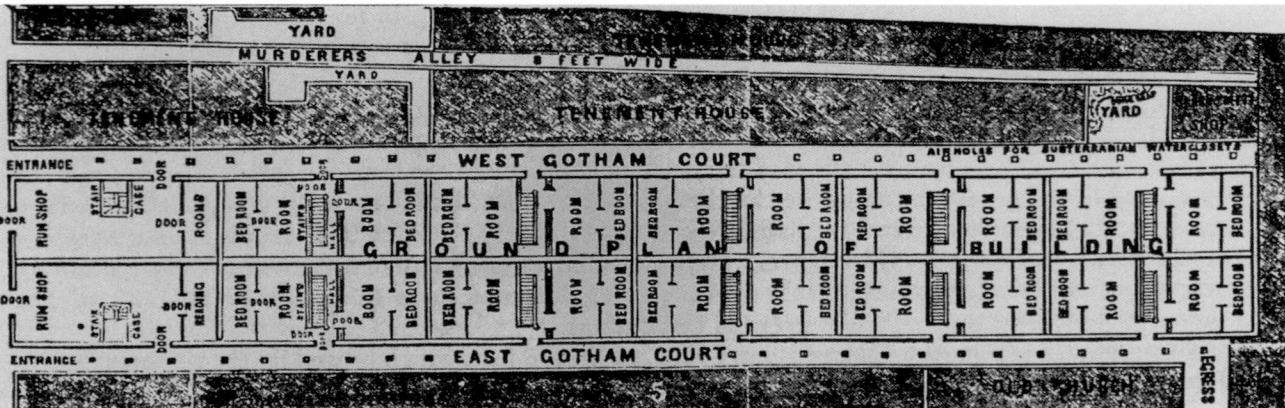

Gotham Court (1851), 36–38 Cherry Street. Plan. SAH. CU.

Gotham Court (1851), 36–38 Cherry Street. View c. 1890. Riis. MCNY.

single floors, or two and three rooms, at the onerous rates, but this rendered them poorer, and those who were able to do so, followed the example of former proprietors, and emigrated to the upper wards. . . . It was soon perceived, by astute owners or agents of property, that a greater percentage of profit would be realized by the conversion of houses and blocks into barracks, and dividing their space into the smallest proportions capable of containing human life within four walls. . . . Blocks were rented of real-estate owners, or purchased on time, or taken in charge at a percentage, and held for underletting to applicants with no ready money and precarious means of livelihood. . . . To this class, then, entire blocks of buildings, worn out in other service, were let in hundreds of sub-divided apartments . . . and they soon became filled, from cellar to garret, with a class of tenantry living from hand to mouth, loose in morals, improvident in habits, degraded or squalid as beggary itself.[21]

No improvements resulted from the assembly's report and local laws provided only minimum standards for sanitation and structural safety—and even these were often indifferently enforced.

In 1863, despite the raging Civil War, 156,844 people immigrated to New York from abroad, joining countless other poor foreign- and native-born Americans in the city's 15,369 tenement houses, more than half of which were located on the Lower East Side.[22] More and more tenements were built to satisfy the burgeoning market. Typical among these, now preserved as the Lower East Side Tenement Museum, was 97 Orchard Street (1863), between Delancey and Broome Streets, with its basement shop, leased as a saloon in 1870, and five floors of four apartments per floor, with only one window in each apartment.[23]

The Draft Riots of 1863 played a part in the growing movement toward tenement reform. While the riots were triggered by an issue having to do with military conscription, the anger of the crowds, especially the resentment of whites against blacks, was in part attributable to the disastrous living and working conditions in the Sixth Ward. A dense slum populated by poor white workers, the Sixth Ward saw the most pronounced rioting; poor whites feared that the extended franchise would only further shrivel their opportunities for economic advancement. As a prominent journalist, Nathaniel P. Willis, put it:

The high brick blocks of closely packed houses where the mobs originated seemed to be literally hives of sickness and vice. It was wonderful to see and difficult to believe that so much misery, disease, and wretchedness could be huddled together and hidden by high walls, unvisited and unthought of so near our own abodes. Lewd but pale and sickly young women, scarcely decent in their ragged attire, were impudent, and scattered everywhere in the courts. But what numbers of these poor classes are deformed, what numbers are made hideous by self-neglect and infirmity! Alas, human faces look so hideous with hope and self-respect all gone, and female forms and features are made so frightful by sin, squalor, and debase-

ment! To walk the streets as we walked them in those hours of conflagration and riot was like witnessing the day of judgment, with every wicked thing revealed, every sin and sorrow blazingly glared upon, every hidden abomination laid before hell's expectant fire.[24]

In 1865, the Citizens' Association of New York, formed in the spring of 1864 as a result of the Draft Riots, issued a detailed report surveying slum conditions. Prepared by an association subcommittee, the Council of Hygiene and Public Health, which included many of the city's leading physicians, the report shocked the public with the revelation that over 480,000 people, almost half the city's population, lived in substandard tenement houses, a fact that was confirmed a year later by the report of the state legislature's committee on tenement houses. In the council's report, the consequences of laissez-faire development were clearly outlined: "The plans, construction and management" of tenement houses "had been left almost exclusively to the caprice and inordinate selfishness of men whose sole object has been to make small investments and a borrowed capital pay enormous advances without regard to the poor tenants' welfare or the public safety."[25]

An epidemic of cholera broke out in the summer of 1866, eventually costing the city 1,200 lives. At the heart of the problem, as the prolific diarist George Templeton Strong, a lawyer who was the head of the United States Sanitary Commission during the Civil War, pointed out, were the dreadful living conditions of the poor, especially the overcrowded tenements with inadequate sewerage systems that cradled typhoid. On August 6, Strong recorded the epidemic in his diary:

Cases are confined as yet to our disgraceful tenement houses and foul side streets—filthy as pigsties and even less wholesome. The epidemic is God's judgment on the poor for neglecting His sanitary laws. It will soon appear as His judgment on the rich for tolerating the neglect—on landlords for poisoning the tenants of their unventilated, undrained, sunless rookeries, poisoning them as directly as if the landlord had put a little ratsbane into the daily bread of each of the hundred families crowded within the four walls of his pest-house. And the judgment will not be on the owners of the tenement houses alone, but on the whole community. It is shameful that men, women, and children should be permitted to live in such holes as thousands of them occupy this night in this city. We are letting them perish of cholera and then . . . they will prove their brotherhood and communal humanity by killing us with the same disease—that capacity for infection being the only tie between us that we could not protest against and decline to recognize.[26]

In 1866, the state legislature at last took action, passing a comprehensive law creating a Metropolitan Sanitary District, co-equal with the Metropolitan Police District, including in its area of operation the counties of New York, Westchester, Kings, Queens, and Richmond, "the sanitary affairs of which were to be regulated by the Metropolitan Board of Health."[27] While this law was relatively

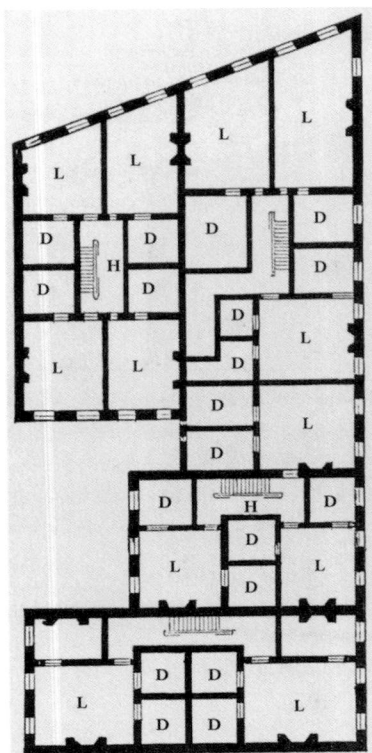

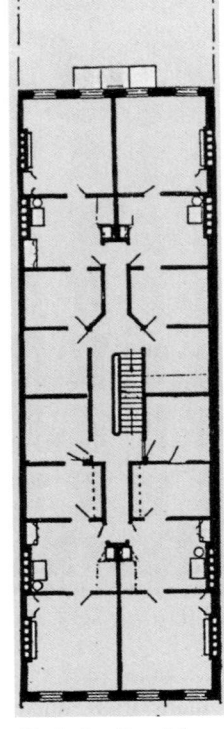

Typical tenement of 1863, noted by the Council of Hygiene and Public Health of the Citizens' Association of New York. Plan showing dark (D) and light (L) rooms and halls (H). HOHL. CU.

Typical railroad flat, c. 1855. Plan. SAH. CU.

weak, a year later the legislature passed a law specifically controlling the construction of new tenement houses, requiring some provisions for escape in the event of fire, for the ventilation of inner bedrooms through outer living rooms and ventilated halls, for the maintenance of roofs and stairs, and for reasonable sanitation. The Tenement House Law of 1867 did not directly address many issues of tenement design, but its call for fire escapes dramatically altered the city's street architecture and to an extent its street life, especially during the hot summer months, when families would use the escapes as balconies for socializing and even sleeping. The provision for fire escapes applied only to those buildings that were over three stories in height and accommodated four or more families. In 1871 the law was amended, requiring fire escapes in all buildings over two stories that housed two or more families above the ground floor and for those buildings over three stories that contained three or more families above the first floor. The 1867 law also required at least a ten-foot-wide rear yard and an even wider space between a new front building and an existing back building on the same lot. Minimum ceiling heights of eight feet were established for all habitable rooms except those in attics.

Despite the introduction of these features and standards, the new law was essentially weak. For example, a bedroom, if it did not directly face the outside, was merely required to be ventilated by a transom window opening onto a neighboring room or hall. This mild stipulation perpetuated the so-called railroad flats, prevalent since the 1850s, in which numerous interior bedrooms opened only to halls.[28] The Tenement House Law of 1867 was significant, however, in providing a legal definition of the tenement as a building type: "Any house, building, or portion thereof which is rented, leased, let, or hired out to be occupied, as the home or residence of more than three families living independently of one another, and doing their own cooking upon the premises, or by more than two families upon a floor, so living and cooking and having a common right in the halls, stairways, yards, water-closets, or privies, or some of them."[29]

By establishing a definition of the tenement as a type and imposing a few standards on new construction, the new law was a breakthrough, but its work was seriously compromised by the fact that it was written as a health ordinance: as such, it had no jurisdiction over the New York City Building Department, which ignored the law's provisions in its preconstruction review of drawings. As a result, inspections by health officials, which uncovered enormous abuses, were laughably confined to post-construction, when little could be done. Moreover, given the nature of city and state politics at the time, conditions in the Building Department, led by Superintendent of Buildings James MacGregor, were notoriously corrupt. On April 3, 1870, the *New York Sun* characterized MacGregor's performance:

> He has connived for a long time at the grossest violations of the law providing for the safety of buildings in this city. We . . . allege . . . that for the last three years not one tenement house has been built in the city of New York in conformity with the law. That nearly every man building a tenement house within that time has paid from one hundred to five hundred dollars a house for the privilege of violating the law. That within the past three years over 5,000 [1,107 according to Building Department records] tenement houses have been built, and that for the unlawful privileges accorded the builders over one million two hundred and fifty thousand dollars have been paid. And we cite, as an example, a case in which Andrew J. Kerwin was made to pay $1,400 for permission to build thirteen tenement houses in Thirty-ninth street otherwise than as the law required. . . . In the face of all these reasons for sternly inquiring into Mr. MacGregor's fitness for his position, Mayor Hall gives him a new lease of power! The general supposition is that he has done so to oblige Taxpayer Tweed, who is said to share in Mr. MacGregor's illegal emoluments to the extent of $100,000 per annum.[30]

In defining the tenement house, the legislature not only specifically separated this type from the rowhouse occupied by a family or an extended family but also from a rowhouse occupied as a boardinghouse, which, by the 1860s, was the principal form of housing for the middle classes, accommodating both single people and entire families.

Workmen's Home, Mott and Elizabeth Streets north of Canal Street. John W. Ritch, 1855. Perspective. SAH. CU.

The new tenement law thus seemed only to establish standards for the housing of the very poor. By excluding boardinghouses as well as hotels—which, though generally perceived as catering to travelers, were increasingly becoming the refuge of the "homeless" lesser rich—it established the two-tier structure for multifamily housing that would prevail until the passage by the state legislature of the Multiple Dwelling Law in 1929.

Although tenement reform did not begin in earnest until after the Civil War, a model tenement was built in 1855 by the New York Association for Improving the Condition of the Poor. The twelve-year-old organization had in 1847 first tried to interest builders in a radical reworking of the city's typical development pattern.[31] Its unrealized 1847 proposal called for a twenty-foot-wide passage running in one direction and three other passages, two twenty feet wide and one ten feet wide, running in the other, that would divide a two-hundred-by-two-hundred-foot site into eight building lots, upon each of which would be built a four-story block, further divided into three separately entered eight-family houses, with each unit containing its own sink and water closet.

In 1854 the association set about to build a model tenement, rejecting a now-lost scheme by Richard Upjohn in favor of a proposal from John W. Ritch, who would become a founding member and the first secretary of the American Institute of Architects.[32] The association's project was the city's second model tenement, and the first in the country intended specifically for blacks. Called the Workmen's Home (1855), it was located on a midblock, six-lot site between Mott and Elizabeth Streets, north of Canal.[33] Similar to but larger than Gotham Court, which its basic

organization mirrored, the Workmen's Home housed eighty-seven families in a 53-foot-wide, 188-foot-deep, six-story-high building facing a 22-foot-wide flagged alleylike courtyard that extended through the block. Ritch's design was admired for its use of wide, streetlike exterior circulation galleries, for its pioneering use of fireproof construction in a residential building (brick arches spanning iron beams), and for its provision of water in each tenant's three-room apartment. Toilets and water taps were located in the public hall on each floor. Shops occupied the ground-floor street frontage at each end and two rooms were reserved on the sixth floor for uplifting social and religious meetings as well as occasional concerts. Given the fact that the project was conceived as a model, it was amazing that Ritch not only copied the ground plan of Gotham Court, he also emulated that undertaking in a shoddy way, in some respects failing to match even its dubious standards. As at Gotham Court, many rooms received no natural light, although at least one room in every apartment had an outside exposure. Lawrence Veiller, an early-twentieth-century housing reformer, was the first to point out just how retrogressive the project was:

> In "Gotham Court" the apartments were but two rooms deep, and each room opened on the outer air. In this Mott Street building the apartments were practically four rooms deep and only one in each suite opened on a public hallway 9 feet wide, which hallway opened upon a court. Of course, the many bad features of "Gotham Court," as to lack of plumbing and the sewers running under each courtyard or alley, were absent; but, on the whole, the plan of the "Gotham Court" building was far superior to the Mott Street so called "model" tenements.[34]

Even the more enlightened features of the Workmen's Home did not prove beneficial. For example, the decision to connect the two streets by means of a single hall proved to be a bad idea, with the double-ended streets compromising building security and degenerating into hangouts for disorderly outsiders. The tenants were not quite as genteel as Robert M. Hartley, the association's founder and secretary, had hoped, especially after the end of the Civil War, when the most affluent members of the black community migrated farther uptown and prejudice prevented whites of the same class from taking their place. In 1867, the association sold the building to the trustees of the Five Points House of Industry for $100,000. Renaming the building the Workingmen's Home, the new owners invested an additional $40,000 to refurbish the property and run it as a boardinghouse. Between four hundred and five hundred residents would be housed in sixty dormitories and twenty apartments on the five upper floors, with the ground floor reserved for a dining room, parlor, sewing room, and administrative offices. The experiment was not a success. In 1872 the trustees sold the building for what they had paid for it. The new owners reverted the building more or less to its original plan but packed more families into it. Sloppy maintenance on the new management's part and ignorant tenant behavior combined with the inherent limitations of the building's design to create a notorious slum, now nicknamed the "Big Flat." The building changed hands a few more times before being demolished, around 1888, to be replaced by a carriage factory. Upon the tenement's demise, Jacob A. Riis exulted that "Business had done more than all other agencies together to wipe out the worst tenements."[35]

The Panic of 1873 and the depression that followed slowed down tenement construction, but as things picked up after the Centennial journalists turned their attention to the sorry conditions of slum life and architects began to agitate for tighter controls governing tenement design.[36]

Edward T. Potter was the most prominent to devote his attention to the city's housing problem. In 1866, working for the department store mogul Alexander T. Stewart, Potter offered the first of a series of model tenement schemes that he would design over the following twenty-five years.[37] Potter's proposals were probably stimulated by the report of the Council of Hygiene and Public Health of the Citizens' Association of New York, which included a discussion of two important model tenement projects in London, George F. Peabody's Model Dwelling Improvements and Alderman Sidney Waterlow's Finsbury Square tenements. Potter called for the typical narrow, deep New York lot to be developed with two separate tenement buildings. In the new, unbuilt areas of the city, where larger sites could easily be assembled, Potter suggested that alleylike air passageways run between the houses, in effect subdividing the standard New York block. At the core of Stewart and Potter's approach was the belief that in order to effect genuine reform in the marketplace, model tenements had to be designed with typical densities and prevailing construction costs in mind. Overcrowding was not seen as the fault of unscrupulous landlords but as a direct consequence of "the natural desire of those whose work is in the City, to live as near their work as possible." Moreover, "an improved tenement house must, to be any benefit, be one that pays, otherwise it will not be followed."[38]

Potter was the first to link the typical size of a New York building lot, twenty-five by one hundred feet, to the inability to produce a satisfactory product, arguing that it required houses too big for middle-class purposes and too small for well-designed multiple dwellings. From 1876 to 1878 Potter updated his decade-old design, proposing that the typical east-west gridiron block be modified by the inclusion of sixteen-foot-wide north-south mews, thereby creating small lots for which he planned new, twenty-five-by-thirty-two-foot multi-unit houses, bachelor-apartment buildings that would achieve population densities compa-

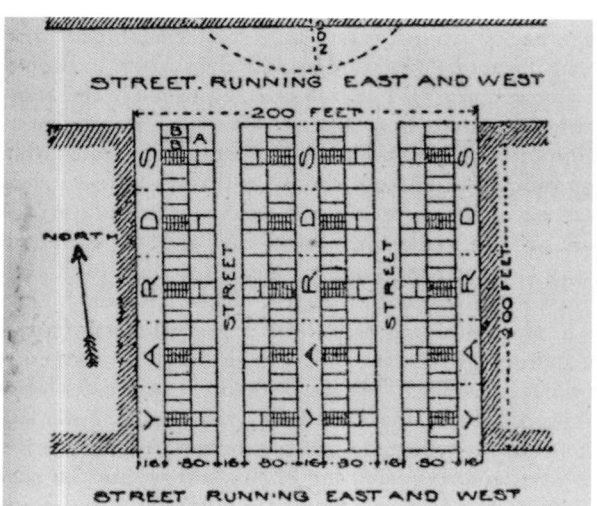
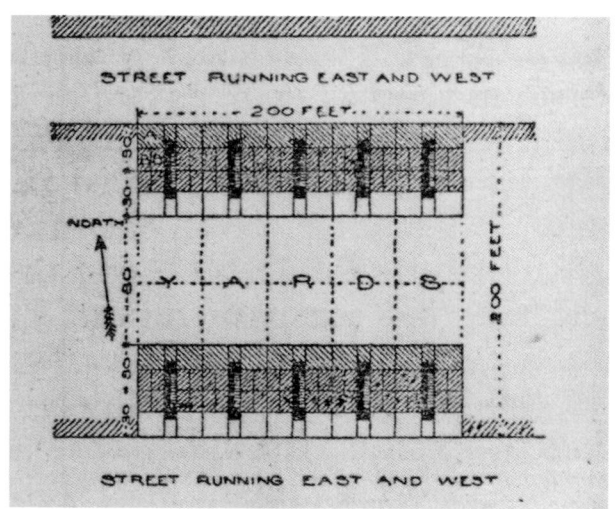

Diagrams comparing Edward T. Potter's 1878 proposal for tenements (left) with the existing system (right). AABN. CU.

rable to those prevailing in tenements.[39] Potter's plan, which he circulated in a privately printed pamphlet dated December 20, 1876, and which he presented in a paper read before the Congress of the American Social Science Association in 1877 and the annual meeting of the American Institute of Architects in 1880, owed quite a lot to the alley arrangement of the notorious Gotham Court and to Ritch's Workmen's Home. It also grew out of his apprenticeship in Richard Upjohn's office, during which time Upjohn was struggling with the design of a model tenement for the New York Association for Improving the Condition of the Poor. Breaking with many reformers who wanted wider lots in order to allow for internal courtyards, Potter, in a sense rationalizing the random pattern of front and back houses that had grown up in the most crowded parts of the city, called for smaller buildings facing existing streets and newly created mews. According to Potter,

The peculiar evils of the tenement-house system of the upper part of New York are not due to the limited size or

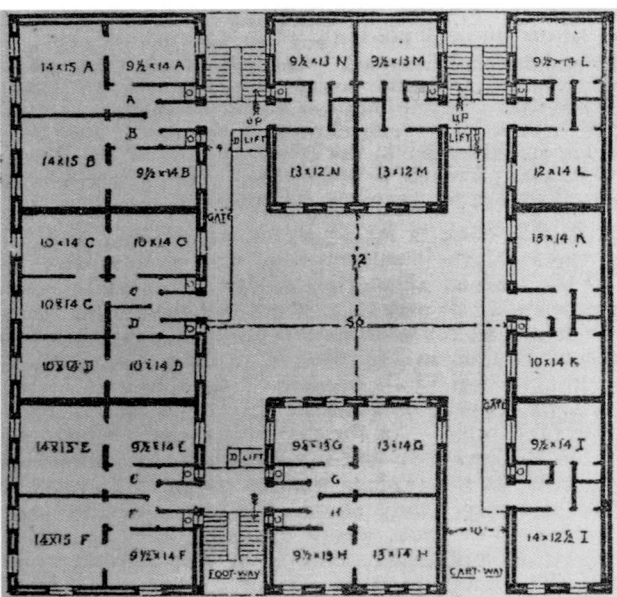

Proposed tenement. Nelson L. Derby, 1877. Plan. AABN. CU.

Proposed tenement. George B. Post and George Dresser, 1879. Elevation. PSE. CU.

narrow width of the island on which New York is built, as is generally supposed, nor are they due to overcrowding, but to the inflexible depth of 100 feet each of the uptown lots [which] is much larger than persons of moderate means can afford to build on. . . . By consequence, only very deep houses are built, in which only the rich can afford to live with comfort; in which people of moderate means cannot live with economy; and which, for the very poor, and even for mechanics and artisans, become tenement-houses of a sort which can be lived in with neither comfort, true economy, nor decency.[40]

Potter's plan was supported by Frederick Law Olmsted, who in 1879 observed that the tenement situation was "a calamity more to be deplored than the yellow fever at New Orleans because [it is] more impregnable; more than the fogs of London, the cold of St. Petersburg or the malaria of Rome because [it is] more constant in its tyranny." On the other hand, Olmsted continued, the "first-class brownstone, high-stoop, fashionable modern dwelling house is really a confession that it is impossible to build a convenient and tasteful residence in New York, adapted to the ordinary civilized requirements of a single family, except at a cost which even rich men find generally prohibitive."[41] A number of other architects shared Potter's view, including George B. Post, who, with George Dresser, an engineer, proposed a remarkably well-thought-out mews scheme (1879),[42] and Nelson L. Derby, whose proposal, published in 1877, called for an asymmetrical arrangement of four buildings around a central court on a one-hundred-by-one-hundred-foot lot.[43] Ultimately, however, no actual tenements would be built along the lines of Potter's suggestions.

In 1878 the *Plumber and Sanitary Engineer*, a journal founded in the previous year by Henry Meyer, who owned a water, gas, and steam supply fittings company, countered the radical proposals of Potter, Post, and Derby with a competition calling for a model tenement that could be economically developed on the typical twenty-five-by-one-hundred-foot lot.[44] The decision to focus on a narrow lot was in part based on Meyer's belief that the possibilities for large-lot development had already been demonstrated by Alfred T. White in Brooklyn (see chapter 7). The jury selected to judge the competition consisted of Charles F. Chandler, a professor at Columbia College and an active housing reformer who, as president of the New York City Board of Health, had at last succeeded in seeing to the enforcement of the provisions of the Tenement House Law of 1867; Reverend Henry C. Potter of Grace Church; Reverend John Hall of the Fifth Avenue Presbyterian Church; Robert J. Hoe, the head of a leading pressworks and machine shop; and the architect R. G. Hatfield, who also drew up the terms of the competition but died before the results were announced. From the outset, the *American Architect and Building News* reported, "many architects declare that the idea of attempting anything of this sort within the narrow limits of a city lot is sure to end in failure, and point to the blocks built for Alfred T. White in Hicks Street,

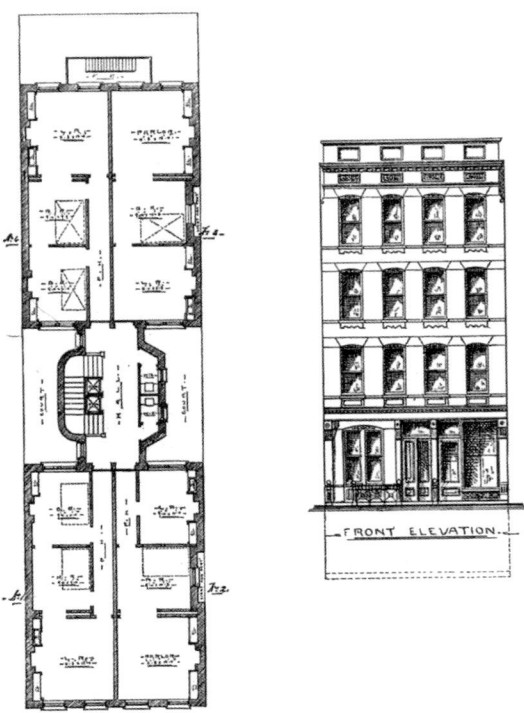

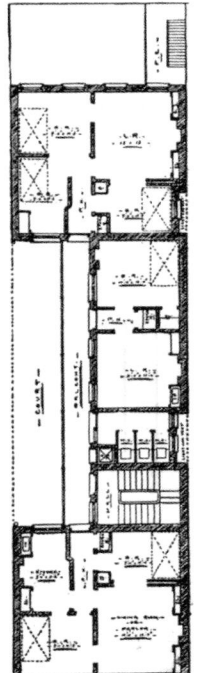

Plumber and Sanitary Engineer's *model tenement competition, 1878. James E. Ware, winning entry. Second-floor plan and elevation. PSE. CU.*

Plumber and Sanitary Engineer's *model tenement competition, 1878. James E. Ware, alternate entry. Second-floor plan and elevation. PSE. CU.*

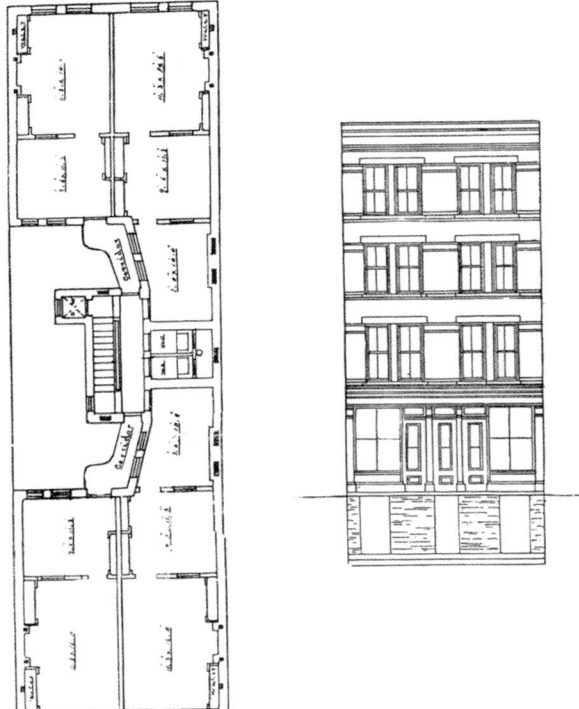

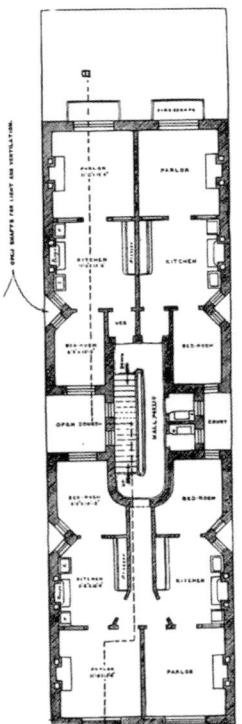

Plumber and Sanitary Engineer's *model tenement competition, 1878. George W. DaCunha. Second-floor plan and elevation. PSE. CU.*

Plumber and Sanitary Engineer's *model tenement competition, 1878. Henry F. Kilburn. Second-floor plan and elevation. PSE. CU.*

Brooklyn, as meeting the problem of a model tenement."[45] Before the jury reviewed all 190 competition entries, mostly from architects but also including some from builders and civil engineers, they were put on public display for ten days in the Leavitt Art Rooms, on Broadway. At about the same time, on February 23, 1879, several churches focused attention on the housing problem by organizing a Tenement House Sunday, and soon thereafter Mayor Edward Cooper appointed a nine-person investigative committee that included William Waldorf Astor, the city's most important landlord, whose portfolio contained numerous tenements.[46] Given the practical-mindedness of the competition program, it was not surprising that the winning scheme, by James E. Ware, as well as many other of the entries, conventionally filled the lot, although George W. DaCunha and, in a second entry, Ware himself, had attempted to break out of the confines of the narrow lot by using U-shaped plans and larger interior courtyards.[47] The prominent architect Henry F. Kilburn produced a stylish, if less enlightened, design. Among the other top-prize winners were Henry Palmer, D. & J. Jardine, and William Kuhles.

According to Lawrence Veiller, writing in 1903, Ware's plan introduced "into the tenement house system of New York City . . . what is known as the 'double-decker' dumbbell tenement, so called because of the shape of the outline of the building."[48] Ware's plan, along with a number of others, was arranged like a dumbbell, with wide portions extending across the lot in front and back connected by a narrower element in the center containing a stairway and water closet. Although ninety percent of the lot was covered, small courts and an areaway guaranteed that at least a modicum of light and air would reach every room of the four apartments that were accommodated on each floor. If more than one tenement were built in a row, the courts and areaways of neighboring buildings could be combined, further improving conditions in the individual apartments. Though criticized by reformers, Ware's practical scheme was widely adopted by developers: by 1900, as Veiller pointed out, the design was not only ubiquitous but also "the curse of our city."[49]

The committee judging the competition deemed the problem it posed to be virtually impossible to solve in a high-minded way. In the March 1879 issue of the *Plumber and Sanitary Engineer*, the committee stated that "the object of the competition was to demonstrate if it is possible to build a model house for workingmen on the existing city lot [twenty-five by one hundred feet]. . . . [The] committee emphatically declare that in their view it is impossible to secure the requirements of physical and moral health within these narrow and arbitrary limits."[50] The press was even more critical, with the *New York Times* stating that although the three top schemes "offer a slightly better arrangement than hundreds of tenement-houses now do . . . [they] are simply 'double houses' front and rear, with the space between occupied by halls and water closets. . . . The only advantages offered, apparently,

over the old system, are in fireproof stairways, more privacy of halls, and the ventilation of the water closets." The *Times*, which supported Edward T. Potter's proposal for "short lots" and Alfred T. White's work in Brooklyn, was blunt: "The limitations of the designs . . . were the shape of the lots, and cheapness of construction. . . . If the prize plans are the best offered, which we hardly believe, they merely demonstrate that the problem is insoluble."[51] Edward E. Raht, an architect closely associated with Richard Morris Hunt, felt the plans made no advance over prevailing conditions, a point with which Hunt agreed. Hunt argued that one large court would have been better than the rear yard and pocket-sized side courts, an idea Hunt had previously explored in his unrealized design for the Stuyvesant Apartments (1869–70) (see below). Contrary to prevailing thought, John B. Snook, whose practice included tenement design, saw the proposals as too idealistic and doubted that the market could justify the improvements.[52]

The competition influenced the Tenement House Act of 1879, which pretty much institutionalized the dumbbell type by restricting lot coverage to sixty-five percent, requiring open space at least ten feet deep at the rear of each building and six hundred cubic feet of air space per person per apartment—a stipulation that was virtually meaningless, since most tenements housed far more people than their plans originally specified.[53] Enforcement of the new law's area requirements, which marked the first time the usable amount of a lot was specified, was compromised by a clause granting the Board of Health the ability to modify the provision. As Veiller has noted, this stipulation practically nullified the whole effect of the law, with the result that in some cases as much as ninety percent of the lot was covered. But the provision that the Board of Health as well as the Building Department had to approve plans before construction was a move in the right direction, inspiring further calls for reform and culminating in the establishment of a second legislative commission, led by Felix Adler, that in turn led to the Tenement House Law of 1887.[54] The new law, which was surprisingly well received by builders and owners engaged in tenement construction, required fireproof construction of air and light shafts and mandated one water closet for every two families (revised the following year to stipulate one for every fifteen occupants but no fewer than one per floor). These changes led to reduced site coverage (typically about seventy-eight percent) and better lit and ventilated stairs and rooms.

Regrettably but not surprisingly, the building boom of the early 1880s brought on an explosion of tenement construction. On July 2, 1883, a writer for the *New York Times*, most likely Montgomery Schuyler, who had just joined the newspaper, reported: "Everywhere the old rookeries of the past half-century are disappearing." Some were succeeded by comfortable flats but "now and then," continued the writer with remarkable understatement, by "what is less desirable, by some high tenement house, with a capacity to stew, broil, and otherwise discomfort untold, and as yet unborn, hundreds. It is a matter of deep regret that in spite of all sorts of schemes for model apartment houses for the poor, the average structure now building for them is but little in advance, in point of comfort, of the old time stew pens." The writer also pointed out that even some of the lesser-quality French flats were being run as tenement houses:

> Under an impulse to do something for the cause of humanity many builders during the past few years built on a cheap plan "through" apartments, so that the occupants should have both front and rear exposures, and by this means secure wholesome and cooling draughts. But not a few have found to their cost that the number of working people who can afford the additional expense involved in providing them with such reasonable, not to say necessary, accommodations, is much smaller than was supposed, and during the present season several owners have felt compelled to remodel buildings originally built on the more generous plan. To build a house on a 25 feet [*sic*] lot, five stories high, with accommodations for four families on each floor, from a purely business point of view, is a very safe and remunerative investment in an average tenement locality. To depart from the rule involves risks. The trouble is that in tenement districts an owner is necessarily dependent on what may be called a tenement population. To give them improved accommodations, unless it can be done at the old rental, is to pass beyond their capacity to meet the expense, and those who can afford to pay the extra charge will object to the locality.[55]

Three days later the *Times* editorialized: "The tenement consists of a long narrow box, three times as long as it is broad, of which at least the middle third is unfit to live in." The *Times*'s editorial, also probably written by Schuyler, called for tighter laws, recognizing that the "real difficulty" lay in the fact that "the speculative builder is apt to be a creature of routine, as uninventive as he is greedy, and that he will take no care for the health and comfort of the persons to whom he proposes to let his dwellings until he is coerced into doing so by a stringent building law, the passage of which he will oppose."[56]

James E. Ware's 186 Hester Street (1879), between Mulberry and Centre Streets, was deemed a model tenement by the *Real Estate Record and Builders' Guide*, which extolled it as "a vast improvement on the old style of barracks," not only offering "a pleasant domicile to ordinary people" but also constituting "an ornament to the street." Ware's building, which occupied a typical twenty-five-by-one-hundred-foot lot, benefited from the fact that its neighbors did not quite fill out their sites, creating a wider than usual side yard that helped relieve potential gloom for the ten apartments that were packed on each of the building's six floors. Helpful also was the twenty-by-twenty-five-foot rear yard. Though tightly packed, the apartments were an improvement over the typical product in many ways. Each suite, for example, had its own sink, and, the *Record and Guide* reported, "in fact, the plumbing arrangements" were such "that even if everything else was not looked at this feature alone would mark" the building as an "extraordinary tenement" in the context of its neighborhood, as water closets on each floor had been substituted for the usual yard privies. Fire escapes were provided at the rear, while the street facade was relieved by iron balconies. The apartments also featured "nicely carved slate mantels of the latest ornamental design," plaster cornices, and black walnut shutters.[57]

Occasionally, an individual developer was moved to exceed the standard. In 1879 William Field & Son, which had just completed Alfred T. White's model tenements in Brooklyn, was commissioned by Jackson S. Schultz, a well-known leather merchant, philanthropist, and leader in the movement for sanitary reform, along with R. M. Strebeigh and T. B. Thomas, to design the Monroe, a version of the Brooklyn project, for an eighty-eight-by-seventy-foot plot at the angle of Corlears and Monroe Streets.[58] Not intended as a charitable scheme, but as a limited-profit venture along the lines pioneered by White, the Monroe was seen by the *New York Evening Post* as a demonstration of putting "theory into practice."[59] The six-story structure housed forty apartments and six stores. Each apartment had its own toilet, but no gas or stoves were supplied. The red brick building, trimmed with polished bluestone and slate, was similar in some ways to Field's work for White in Brooklyn. It was capped by two towers: one contained the stair and led to open balconies and was placed in the center of the Monroe Street front, while the other tower was at the building's corner. The *American Architect and Building News* admired the direct approach the architects took in designing the Monroe "because here the elevation in most respects grew out of the construction of the plan, and the finish was honest and direct, without pretension and with no intention to make things appear other than they are."[60]

Nicholas Gillesheimer's tenement at 181 Mott Street (1885) for Edward and James Murphy was representative of the new dumbbell type but superior in the handling of the facade, with elegant Queen Anne–style details.[61] E. W. Gandolfo's six-story, thirty-three-family tenement house (1887), at the northwest corner of Hubert and Greenwich Streets, for W. S. Livingston, was palatial in appearance and offered a high level of accommodation with all but two rooms on each floor ventilated by street- or yard-facing windows.[62] Richard Morris Hunt also built a number of tenements. For Frederic Bronson, Hunt designed 140 and 142 Tenth Avenue (1886–87), between Eighteenth and Nineteenth Streets, the former housing only nine families but the latter intended for twice that number; for Peter T. O'Brien, Hunt designed 226 and 228 East Thirty-sixth Street (1887), each accommodating twenty families; and for Thomas Riley he designed an eleven-family building (1888–89) on the north side of East Seventy-eighth Street west of Avenue A.[63]

The Tenement House Building Company was headed by Joseph Drexel, the banker, and Oswald Ottendorfer, the proprietor of the *New Yorker Staats-Zeitung*, and numbered Felix Adler among its directors. This interest commissioned William Schickel & Co. to design a 108-family model ten-

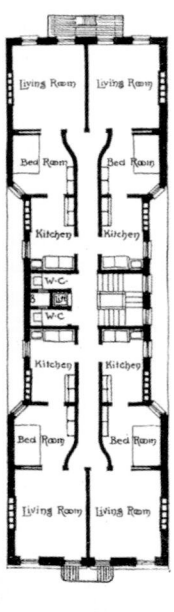

181 Mott Street, between Broome and Kenmare Streets. Nicholas Gillesheimer, 1885. Elevation and plan. BLDG. CU.

Tenement House Building Company model tenement, 338–344 Cherry Street. William Schickel & Co., 1887. View to the northeast, 1929. Wurts. MCNY.

ement (1887) on a 117-by-85-foot lot at 338–344 Cherry Street, near Montgomery Street.[64] The complex consisted of four six-story houses. Between the two pairs there was a deep, slotlike light court opening to the rear, paved to serve as a play space but barely able to light and ventilate the rows of rooms that lined them. The plan was only a cut above normal tenement practice. Families lived in three- and four-room suites, with a heated water closet for every two families. The roof, fenced and paved to serve in part as a playground, was connected by dumbwaiter to the basement laundry room to provide easy transport for clothes to dry upstairs in the open air. A ground-floor kindergarten, reserved for resident children, was a significant innovation.

Meager though this design was, the *Real Estate Record and Builders' Guide* predicted that as an investment the building would "probably prove a failure as, with all the improvements, the rent will be no higher than the ordinary rent of tenement houses in the district. The company, however, is largely composed of men of benevolent purposes, and in the erection of this building they hope to institute a movement for the erection of clean and wholesome tenement houses."[65] The Cherry Street tenements grew out of ideas advanced by Felix Adler, who argued for cooperative living arrangements consisting of shared kitchens, art rooms, and playgrounds, and believed that

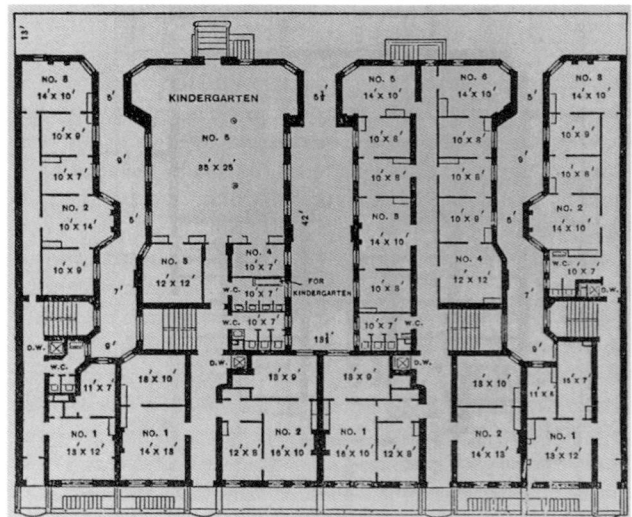

Tenement House Building Company model tenement, 338–344 Cherry Street. William Schickel & Co., 1887. Ground-floor plan. SAH. CU.

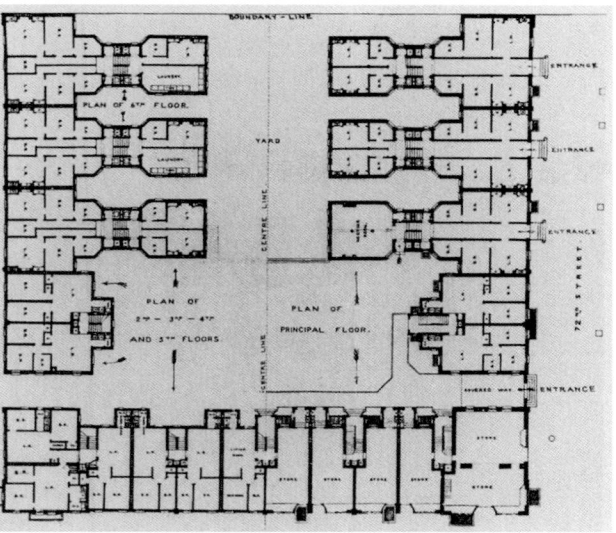

Improved Dwellings Association model tenement, west side of First Avenue between East Seventy-first and East Seventy-second Streets. Vaux & Radford, 1880–81. Perspective view to the southwest. SAH. CU.

"squalid houses . . . make the squalid people."[66] But when the original Cherry Street tenement dwellers were replaced by newly arrived Russian Jews, the condition of the buildings declined dramatically as the tenants set up stoves in the halls, used the living rooms as sweatshops, and brought in lodgers to sleep on bedroom floors.

To some citizens, concerned that the individual tenement house was inherently flawed as a building type, the only way to reform was through large-scale development, which was occasionally undertaken by philanthropic enterprises. In 1879 the *Record and Guide* reported that the "prevailing fancy of fashionable philanthropy is tenement house reform. . . . This subject has been constantly agitated for the past ten years and the discussion is only now beginning to bear practical fruit."[67] Among those who undertook the cause of reform, the "sanitarians" were the most outspoken, inveighing against the system as a whole and recommending the abolition of the building type. More practical philanthropists, such as Alfred T. White, working in Brooklyn, sponsored large-scale model tenements to test new ideas and, by example, combat the worst features of the traditional type.

In 1879 William A. Potter, half-brother of Edward T. Potter, the longstanding proponent of tenement-house reform, was hired by Catherine L. Van Rensselaer Cruger

Improved Dwellings Association model tenement, west side of First Avenue between East Seventy-first and East Seventy-second Streets. Vaux & Radford, 1880–81. Plan. SAH. CU.

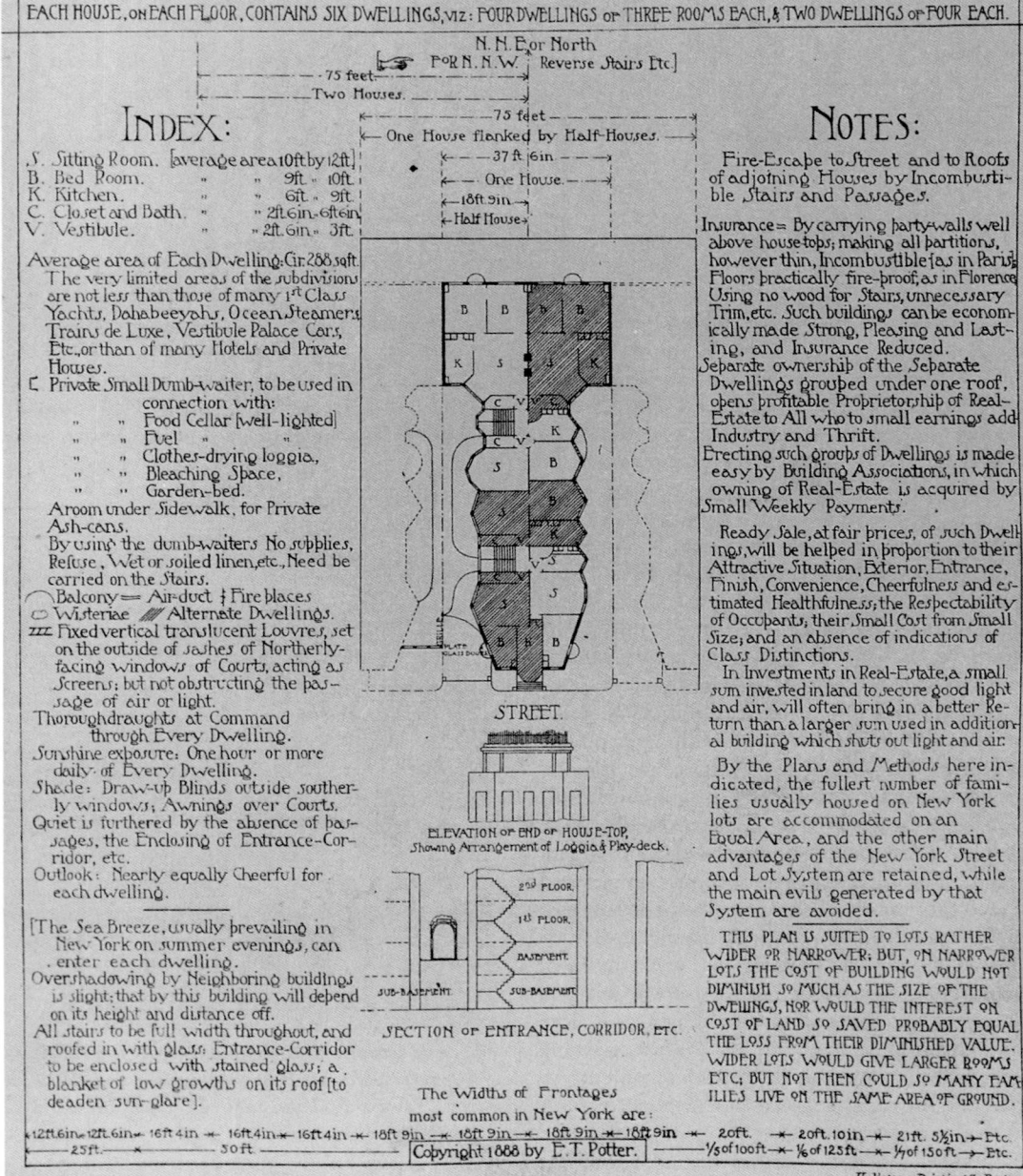

Proposed tenement scheme. Edward T. Potter, 1888. Plan. AABN. CU.

to design a model tenement at 203 Grand Street, on the southwest corner at Mott Street.[68] The seven-story-high building—one floor higher than most tenements at the time—contained ground-floor stores and five apartments per residential floor. The large lot allowed for some features usually associated with higher-class apartments, not the least of which was the elaborate, Classicizing organization of the exterior with entresol, paired floors, attic story, and bold cornice, all probably the design contribution of William A. Potter's sometime partner, R. H. Robertson.

In 1880, one year after the passage of the Tenement House Act of 1879, several trustees of the Children's Aid Society joined others to form the Improved Dwellings Association, with the express purpose of sponsoring a model tenement house.[69] W. Bayard Cutting was president of the newly formed association and Cornelius Vanderbilt II and Henry H. Babcock were among the investors, who expected a five percent return on their capital. George W. DaCunha developed plans for a portion of the project before the association turned over all design responsibility to Vaux & Radford, which had done previous work for the Children's Aid Society. The six-story, fireproof building, capable of housing eight hundred people in three- and four-room apartments on a two-hundred-by-two-hundred-foot lot, occupied the west blockfront of First Avenue from Seventy-first to Seventy-second Street, in the heart of the Upper East Side, one of the city's fast-growing working-class districts. The plan was made up of two distinct sections: facing First Avenue was an admirably shallow wall of apartments, each unit with a rear extension containing toilet and washing facilities, while facing each of the side streets were three houses planned by DaCunha as modified versions of the dumbbell type, arranged to permit side courts that opened to the rear. Rooms either faced the street or the shallow courts that opened to the large, paved central court, which was entered through arched gateways on both side streets and guarded by a night watchman. Twelve stores faced First Avenue. In a significant innovation, the rooftop housed a common laundry, with each tenant entitled to the use of a certain number of tubs one day per week.

The architectural detail of the Improved Dwellings Association's project was quite stylish, especially the rooftop shelters, which were similar to shelters designed by Calvert Vaux for Central Park. As a business proposition the complex was also a success, with a very low vacancy rate and a rent roll that yielded a steady return of five percent per annum. So successful was the project that in 1886 a second model tenement was undertaken by the association, on a 114-by-88-foot site at the southwest corner of Avenue C and Fourteenth Street.[70] This tenement was realized as a six-story brick building with stores, designed by C. C. Haight.

In 1884, H. W. Fabian, perhaps influenced by Henry J. Hardenbergh's Dakota apartments (1882–84) (see below), developed a forward-looking tenement scheme: a single building constructed on four lots, with a central courtyard as well as two fairly wide side yards to ensure light and air

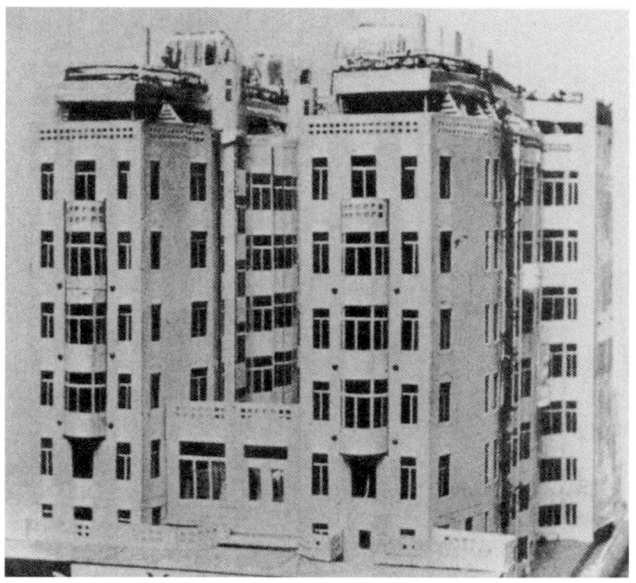

Proposed tenement scheme. Edward T. Potter, 1890. Model. Edward T. Potter Papers. CU.

to all rooms as well as to the public halls and stairs.[71] Meanwhile, Edward T. Potter, assisted by an anonymous engineer, continued his studies of ways to maximize sunlight in tenements. In 1888 he published a drawing showing that architects could, while working completely within existing codes, create better-ventilated units with T-shaped buildings, placing the widest portions toward the rear of the lot so that air spaces were not just enclosed air shafts but reasonably wide cuts opening to the streets between buildings.[72] Although his plan was based on twenty-five-foot-wide lots, the buildings would have to be developed three at a time. As part of his system, he proposed that the side walls of the buildings consist of prowlike shallow bays, intended to increase privacy while maximizing sunlight in the rooms behind them. In effect, Potter was proposing to reverse the normal urban order, opening up courtyards to the street above the first floor and creating narrow alleyways behind. Potter's design, for which he prepared plans and a model for a nine-story version (1890), incorporated such features as rooftop clothes-drying facilities as well as a garden and children's playground; called for only two or three apartments per floor; and left room for the possibility of installing elevators. He also proposed the exclusive use of steel, glass, and masonry as well as fairly elaborate sun-shading devices. Potter's ideas were not realized until 1900, and then only partially, when the Charity Organization Society commissioned Andres & Withers of Newport, Rhode Island, to design a pair of six-story tenements at 326–330 East Thirty-fifth Street. This project turned the deep courtyards to the rear in accordance with more conventional practice, and was in other minor ways modified from Potter's model to meet the requirements of the Tenement

Typical tenement–house yard, c. 1890. Riis. MCNY.

Bottle Alley, Mulberry Bend, c. 1890. Riis. MCNY.

Law of 1901 (the so-called New Law), which Potter's ideas helped shape.

By the late 1880s, despite all attempts at reform, to many the situation seemed really to be no better than it had been a generation before. As the *Real Estate Record and Builders' Guide* put it in 1887:

Within the last quarter of a century the population of New York City and its suburbs has considerably more than doubled. . . . But with all these changes in the population . . . and the enormous increase in the number of buildings of the city, the tenement house district proper is practically unchanged as to its location and boundaries, and in a general way, one might say that the only result of the increase in wealth and population has been the . . . denser crowding of the districts already overflowing with unfortunate humanity. To be sure many tenement and cheap apartment houses have been erected along the upper portion of the extreme east and west side avenues, and not far south of the Harlem on the east side of the city certain elements of the foreign population are gradu-

ally forming an up-town colony; but, even taking these facts into consideration, our main proposition stands unchallenged, and any well-informed person will readily concede that the vast majority of the working population and the poorer classes of the city reside in the densely crowded tenements of the lower portion of the city.[73]

The 1890 publication of Jacob A. Riis's book *How the Other Half Lives* publicized the disastrous state of New York's slum housing and amplified the call for reform.[74] Riis was a Danish-born carpenter who came to America in 1870, when he was twenty-one years old. After an impoverished period of travel and odd jobs, Riis found work as the city editor of the *Review*, a Long Island City weekly newspaper. In 1878 he became a police reporter, first with the *New York Daily Tribune* and then with the *Evening Sun*, a journalism career that lasted twenty-one years and put him in intimate touch with slum life. As a result, Riis expanded his beat to include housing affairs. He reported on the 1884 meeting of the Tenement House Commission, where he first encountered Felix Adler. In 1888 Riis attended a meeting at Chickering Hall at which Alfred T. White urged the assembled ministers to support the cause of housing reform: "How are these men and women to understand the love of God you speak of, when they see only the greed of men?"[75] White's powerful talk spurred Riis on to the serious investigations that resulted in his influential book.

Riis saw the dimensions of the tenement problem as moral as well as economic: "It was just a question whether a man would take seven per cent and save his soul, or twenty-five and lose it."[76] While awaiting a publisher, Riis offered to lecture on the problem at various churches, only to be turned down over and over again, including by his own congregation. On February 22, 1888, he was finally offered the opportunity to present an illustrated talk at the Broadway Tabernacle Church, which was followed by a series of talks that captured the interest of one of the editors of *Scribner's Magazine*. The periodical commissioned an article for the December 1889 issue, inspiring Jeannette Gilder, editor of the *Critic*, to arrange for the book's publication.[77] Riis's book lifted the tenement-house issue out of the technical pages of trade journals, the occasional sermonizing of press and church, and the slightly condescending sentimentalizing of the rich, bringing into the popular conversation the everyday life of the slums. As Anthony Jackson put it: "For the first time the reformer appeared as a human being among others, neither compromised by excess money or conscience nor impersonalized within a philanthropic organization."[78] Riis did not call for commissions or legislative action—on the whole he distrusted government—but in fact placed his faith in the power of physical form, calling for the rehabilitation of old buildings and the construction of new model tenements, arguing that "such is the leavening influence of a good deed in that dreary desert of sin and suffering, that the erection of a single good tenement has the power to change . . . the character of a whole block."[79]

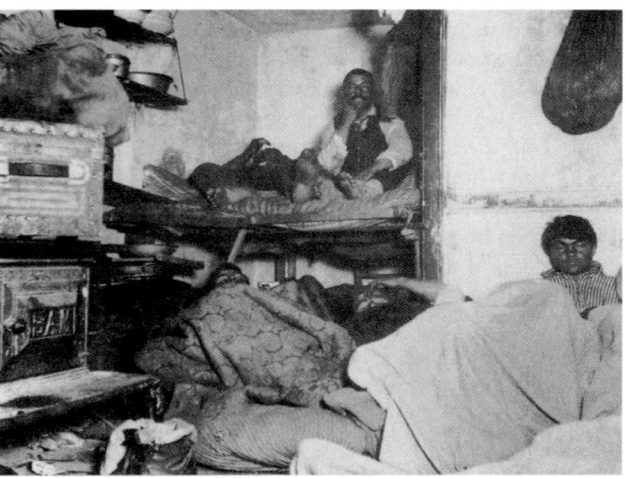

Lodgers in a Bayard Street tenement, c. 1889. Riis. MCNY.

HOTELS

New York is the paradise of hotels. In no other city do they flourish in such numbers, and nowhere else do they attain such a degree of excellence. The hotels of New York naturally take the lead of all others in America, and are regarded by all who have visited them as models of their kind.
—James D. McCabe Jr., 1872[80]

In October 1866, the *New York Times* reported that though most middle-class families—that is, the families of "professional men, clergymen, artists, college professors, shop-keepers, and upper mechanics"—were too affluent for the tenement house, they were increasingly unable to afford to lease an entire rowhouse for their own use and therefore were either forced to take in boarders, become boarders themselves, or flee to the suburbs.[81] The city's rapid population growth had created serious housing problems for the middle class. Skyrocketing land costs combined with the expansion of the commercial district made it difficult for artisans, clerks, and professionals, accustomed to living in single-occupancy rowhouses, to find affordable accommodations convenient to their workplaces. Although boardinghouse life was at best a mixed blessing, compromising privacy, it also liberated the middle-class woman from many chores that might have kept her otherwise housebound. As such, it opened up the way for "respectable" women to enter the workplace. It also led to the acceptance of apartment living, which became increasingly widespread among middle-class families starting in the late 1870s. Some boardinghouses, if not quite top-drawer, were nonetheless reasonably fashionable and well located, near Union and Madison Squares, where the city's premier hotels were also located. But the upper-middle-class boardinghouse was not in the majority; typically, boardinghouse life was the best hope of the lower middle class, a last resort of "doom and distress. . . . Men are born to it, and, through narrow circumstances, compelled to continue it when every instinct and taste revolt at it."[82]

Though top society looked down on hotel living, it did not have the stigma of boardinghouse life. It was, of course, much more expensive. Hotel living was quite popular with families, and a number of reform-minded writers saw the hotel, or some version of it, as a form of cooperative housing, an idealistic concept first developed in France. The residential hotel, which in the United States had its origins in Boston in the 1850s and was coming to be called the "apartment hotel," was seen as a way to resolve the middle-class housing dilemma and to advance the cause of women's liberation. By 1869 it was claimed that there were between two hundred and eight hundred hotels catering, at least in part, to long-term residents, but only twenty-five or thirty of these were really "first class."[83] None, however, had been purpose-built for long-term residency by families.

In 1870, less than a year after the completion of Richard Morris Hunt's Stuyvesant Apartments (see below), the brothers David H. Haight and Richard K. Haight commissioned Stephen D. Hatch to help rebuild Richard K. Haight's former mansion (Trench & Snook, 1848–49), at the northeast corner of Fifth Avenue and Fifteenth Street.[84] The building had just been vacated by the New-York Club, which had been headquartered there since 1861, and Hatch converted it into a five-story, mansarded multiple dwelling, with five apartments per floor. While the Stuyvesant Apartments, long considered the city's first apartment house, was a walk-up supplemented by a dumbwaiter, Haight House included an Otis safety elevator. According to James Richardson, writing in *Scribner's Monthly*, this feature gave Haight House "a position midway between an apartment house proper and a family hotel." There was a common dining room, but each apartment also had its own kitchen and dining room. Residents could "order their own marketing through the steward, have the food cooked in the common kitchen, and served in their own rooms."[85] Besides the central kitchen, which was located in the basement, Haight House provided other services to its residents that the Stuyvesant Apartments did not, including a central steam laundry and, stationed in a lobby-level lodge tucked under the imposing black walnut staircase, a porter who monitored the comings and goings of tenants and their guests. Bells and speaking tubes connected the lodge and the central kitchen to individual apartments. The apartments themselves were more luxurious than those at the Stuyvesant Apartments, with dining rooms large enough to seat eighteen people, and lavishly appointed master bathrooms. On the top floor, bachelors were accommodated in two- and three-room apartments.

Haight House quickly took on its own identity as "the chosen refuge of artistic and literary people," giving social cachet to a new housing type.[86] As a renovated existing house it had a distinct advantage in the struggle for social acceptance over any new, self-conscious statement: "Nobody passing along Fifth Avenue on Fifteenth Street would imagine that it was anything else than the private residence of some private individual."[87] Haight House was interesting to James Richardson as much for its sociology as for its architectural arrangements, "neatly" illustrating "what promises to be a characteristic feature of New York life under the coming *régime*,—that is, the clustering of particular social sets about particular centers."[88] Twelve years after Haight House's completion, a writer in *Harper's New Monthly Magazine* remembered it as "small, inconvenient, and very expensive [but] leased long before completion by persons delighted with the novelty."[89]

While Haight House combined features of the apartment house with those of the hotel, Detlef Lienau's Grosvenor House (1871–72), at the northeast corner of Tenth Street and Fifth Avenue, was arguably New York's first purpose-built apartment hotel.[90] Francis Cottenet, a well-to-do, French-born importer, had developed the dwelling on the site of his own townhouse. Richardson reported that the building, "a success from the start," was

Haight House, northeast corner of Fifth Avenue and East Fifteenth Street. Originally the Richard K. Haight house (Trench & Snook, 1848–49). Renovated by Stephen D. Hatch, 1870. View to the northeast, 1893. NYHS.

Grosvenor House, northeast corner of Fifth Avenue and East Tenth Street. Detlef Lienau, 1871–72. View to the northeast. Lienau Collection. CU.

Stevens House, south side of West Twenty-seventh Street between Fifth Avenue and Broadway. Richard Morris Hunt, 1870–72.
View to the southwest. The Octagon, AAF.

"a type unique. Starting with a singularly clear conception of the wants of a particular class of New York families—a class possessing wealth, culture, refinement, and love of ease," the Grosvenor might "well be considered a model, since it secures the economy of multiple tenancy and co-operative living, with the atmosphere of home, and combines all the advantages of English exclusiveness . . . with the utmost independence in all that pertains to individual life. It is, in fact, a nest of elegant homes, each distinct and thoroughly secluded, yet all provided for with the elaborate machinery and systematic service of a first-rate hotel."[91] The Grosvenor was an L-shaped structure wrapped around a forty-foot courtyard, an unusually open arrangement. Its restrained French Second Empire design, with a low mansard roof, stone balconies, and plain segmental leaded windows, echoing townhouse design, was a far cry from the flamboyant expressionism of Richard Morris Hunt's Stevens House or Stephen D. Hatch's Gilsey House (see below), two recently completed rivals for top-class tenants.

Richard Morris Hunt's luxurious, six-story Stevens House (1870–72), on the south side of Twenty-seventh Street from Fifth Avenue to Broadway, was a troubled venture but a superb work of architecture, with a bold mansard containing two additional floors of living space, a continuous, bracketed railing forming a cornice at the first floor, and a magnificently detailed shopfront facing Fifth Avenue.[92] Slender in mass and wrapped around a shallow courtyard, it ran 254 feet along Twenty-seventh Street and 105 feet along Broadway but only 28 feet on Fifth Avenue. As originally built, Stevens House included eighteen apartments, the larger ones arranged three to a floor. Served by an elevator, the ninety-six-foot-tall building's mansard was the design's particular joy—a picturesque assemblage of finial-topped, hipped pavilions, two rows of dormers of descending size and various shapes, and prominent chimneys. Announced as an apartment house "on the French plan of 'flats' and rented in suites of apartments," it became an apartment hotel two years after its completion.[93] Coming on the heels of the Stuyvesant Apartments, which established the apartment house as a desirable building type socially and physically distinct from the tenement, Stevens House appears to have been commissioned as a luxury apartment building by Paran Stevens, the "Napoleon of Hotel Keepers," who ran a number of hotels in various cities, including the Fifth Avenue Hotel in New York.[94] Stevens House was "designed on the European plan for families to live separately in their different suites of apartments."[95] Like Hunt's Stuyvesant Apartments, Stevens House was described by the Building Department as a "first class dwelling," a category typically reserved for single-family houses. The building inspector went on to classify Stevens House as a "Parisian Dwelling Building," a tacit tribute not only to its functional type but also to Hunt's design.

Hunt had designed one of the city's most stylish buildings, although Stevens, who died in 1872, had little time

Stevens House, south side of West Twenty-seventh Street between Fifth Avenue and Broadway. Richard Morris Hunt, 1870–72. View to the southeast. The Octagon, AAF.

to appreciate it. Nor did many others—Stevens's formidable widow, perhaps because apartment living had not really caught on yet, or perhaps because of the Panic of 1873, immediately had it renovated by Arthur D. Gilman, the designer of what many consider the first apartment hotel, Boston's Hotel Pelham (1857),[96] and an architect who had already bested Hunt in the 1867 competition for the Equitable Building. Gilman was hired to add thirty-four more feet to the Fifth Avenue side of the building. He also seems to have remodeled the building's interior, eliminating the individual apartment kitchens in favor of a restaurant-type dining room catering exclusively to residents and thereby establishing it as an apartment hotel. In 1874, James Richardson reported that "as an investment it has not been fortunate, its great height, ornate front, and extravagant internal decoration, making it far more impressive to the beholder than profitable to the owner. While it splendidly illustrates one phase of the new order of domestic architecture, its influence on the reform has hardly been favorable."[97] As an apartment hotel, Stevens House never caught on as a place for families, and in 1879 it was renovated again, emerging as the Victoria Hotel, with five hundred rooms available to the traveling public.

The replacement of Hunt by Gilman was particularly awkward because Hunt was in the midst of trying to collect fees owed him by the deceased Stevens, whose estate Hunt would sue in 1873. His claim was complicated by problems with the building's performance, not the least of which was the fact that the water pipes had frozen during the winter of 1871–72 because almost all the pipes had been placed in the exterior walls and some of the heating equipment had failed to function. Settling had caused the street-level arches to bulge, requiring new supports, a condition that became very serious after Gilman used Hunt's party wall to support the floors of his addition. Though attempts were made to blame Hunt for these problems, at the January 1878 trial the architect was able to show that he had been paid only a three percent fee to design the building, with two percent more going to a party charged with superintending construction. After ten minutes' deliberation, the jury found in Hunt's favor, thereby not only satisfying the architect's claims and reaffirming his professional competence but also validating the fee schedule and guidelines for the responsibilities of clients, architects, and contractors that had been only recently established by the American Institute of Architects. In any case, Gilman's addition was very sympathetic to Hunt's design, and may have followed plans already prepared by him. After Gilman finished his work, he too was not paid and had to sue Stevens's widow, making the same claim of neglect in superintendence and also capturing the sympathy of the jury.

A bad situation that could have seriously injured his reputation, Stevens House proved to be a professional triumph for Hunt, not only because of the lawsuit's outcome and the building's aesthetics but also because of the structure's inventive functionalism. With Stevens House Hunt brought to New York a building that not only looked French but also worked in a Parisian manner, with an especially deft handling of the site's complex geometry and a sophisticated treatment of the street floor, with shops located all around, even on the Fifth Avenue side, when that street was still almost exclusively residential. Stevens House made its mark on New York's imagination as a new type, a kind of super–apartment house that provided the services of a hotel but did not cater to a transient clientele, setting the standard for the "cooperative" apartments of the 1880s. O. B. Bunce, writing in *Appletons' Journal*, implied that it was representative of the "City of the Future."[98] Lewis Leeds, also in *Appletons'*, deemed it "a splendid edifice" with a facade that was "one of the most striking in the city; the design is bold and unique . . . ; and, lifting to its great height, it presents a striking picture, which would be greatly enhanced if located on a wider street or upon an open square."[99] But Montgomery Schuyler, in one of his early articles of criticism, decried Hunt's design as "certainly no welcome addition to New York," dismissing it for the same reason he dismissed Hunt's Presbyterian Hospital (1868–72) (see chapter 2).[100] Schuyler characterized Hunt as having "the most extraordinary fancy for . . . excessively violent contrasts of materials, but also for openings altogether disproportioned in

width to their height."[101] Hunt's blend of French Second Empire massing with Neo-Grec– and Ruskin Gothic–inspired details—especially the polychromy of the facades—set Schuyler off:

> We deprecate those violent contrasts between large surfaces of glaring red brick and spasmodic patches of stone, making a building look, at a short distance, like a huge checkerboard. We dislike also those heavy projections of carved stone and exhibition of strength where no strength is required—the sudden and unmeaning introduction of courses of gaudy encaustic tiling for no purpose whatever—the narrow, disproportioned windows—the hieroglyphic flourishes incised into every little innocent piece of plain surface, and the thousand undone *fantaisies* of this new Frenchified style now coming so much into vogue. It is not so much art as legerdemain, and the absence of true beauty, and it cannot be compensated for by the introduction of mere novelties, no matter how curious or extravagant.[102]

Twenty-four years later, when Schuyler reassessed Hunt's work a few months after the architect's death, on July 31, 1895, he softened his criticism, praising Stevens House for its "regular and grandiose . . . composition, ingenious and clever . . . detail, especially . . . in the iron-work and masonry in the basement, and perhaps the most Parisian in effect of any thing of its period or of its author, so Parisian indeed that it is difficult to characterize it without resorting to French and pointing out how it has *chic* and how it has *élan*."[103]

The fashion for purpose-built apartment hotels was short-lived, yielding to the boom in luxury apartment-house construction that began in the late 1870s. But the popularity of hotel living for families continued to grow and, together with the increase of business and pleasure travel and New York's status as the country's most popular destination, fostered a boom in hotel building. While pre–Civil War New York was home to many hotels, few were architecturally distinguished. New York's most famous old hotel was the Greek Revival–style Astor House (Isaiah Rogers, 1836), on Broadway facing City Hall Park, at the time of the building's construction a location convenient to every aspect of city life, including the most fashionable residential neighborhoods. As such it was for a long time a stylish rendezvous. But with the northward expansion of the city after the Civil War, the Astor House became almost exclusively a businessman's stopping place, its more cosmopolitan role assumed by the fashionable hotels that clustered on or near Ladies' Mile, where travelers could easily journey to downtown appointments in the morning and return to a neighborhood of shops, restaurants, and theaters in the evening.

The fashion for living in hotels began developing in the 1850s. *Putnam's Magazine* reported: "Society is rapidly tending towards hotel life and the advantages of a cluster of families living together under one roof, are everyday more apparent."[104] Recognizing the city's uptown trend

Fifth Avenue Hotel, northwest corner of Fifth Avenue and West Twenty-third Street. William Washburn, 1859.
View to the northwest, c. 1887. FLC.

and the increasing taste for luxury on the part of locals and visitors alike, Amos R. Eno set a new standard for socially acceptable hotels with his five-hundred-room, six-story, white marble Fifth Avenue Hotel (William Washburn, 1859), at the northwest corner of Fifth Avenue and Twenty-third Street, extending along Broadway to Twenty-fourth Street.[105] At first known as "Eno's Folly," the location was mocked as too far uptown—according to one observer, stopping there would be like "living . . . among the goats"—but the Fifth Avenue Hotel quickly

became a keystone in the structure of New York social life, especially after the Prince of Wales chose to stay in it on his celebrated visit to the city in 1860.[106] Eno's folly had been carefully planned to meet the needs of demanding travelers and was served by one of the city's earliest passenger elevators.

The Fifth Avenue Hotel was followed by the elegantly detailed, mansard-roofed Albemarle (Renwick & Auchmuty, 1860),[107] at the northwest corner of Twenty-fourth Street and Broadway, and in 1864 by John B. Snook's

View to the northwest along Broadway between West Twenty-fourth and West Twenty-fifth Streets, c. 1887, showing the Albemarle Hotel (Renwick & Auchmuty, 1860) on the left and Hoffman House (John B. Snook, 1864) on the right. NYHS.

Grand Hotel, southeast corner of Broadway and West Thirty-first Street. Henry Engelbert, 1868. View to the southeast, c. 1877, showing Gilsey House (Stephen D. Hatch, 1869–71) in the distance. NYHS.

Hoffman House, at the southwest corner of Twenty-fifth Street and Broadway. Hoffman House became popular with the fast crowd of promoters and agents and "other bits of flotsam and jetsam from the pavement of Broadway."[108] Montgomery Schuyler found the ensemble of hotels "a combination of marble palaces rarely seen, and the result is consequently splendid, without any individual building claiming especial architectural merit."[109]

Next came the Grand Hotel (Henry Engelbert, 1868), far uptown at 1232–1238 Broadway, on the southeast corner of Thirty-first Street.[110] Built for Elias S. Higgins, a manufacturer and importer of carpets, the Grand Hotel marked the beginning of upper Broadway's transformation into a glamorous thoroughfare. The marble-faced, seven-story pile was a close interpretation of recent work in Second Empire Paris, with a slightly pavilionated massing culminating in a bold, two-story dormered mansard roof above a heavily bracketed cornice. At the skyline, towers made explicit the pavilionization that was modestly suggested in the plan below. The Parisian source was here and elsewhere along Broadway perfectly appropriate, given that the condition raised by the diagonal geometry of this exceptional street was so much like the one typically confronted by architects along Baron Georges-Eugène Haussmann's newly laid-out boulevards. In 1871 Montgomery Schuyler noted that the Grand "loomed up with immense proportions in [its] neighborhood until its larger rival—the Gilsey—came to overtop it . . . [forming] the present northern boundary of colossal hotels, almost of architectural improvements."[111]

Gilsey House, northeast corner of Broadway and West Twenty-ninth Street. Stephen D. Hatch, 1869–71. View to the northeast, 1885, showing the Marble Collegiate Church (Samuel A. Warner, 1851–54) on the right. NYHS.

Stephen D. Hatch's Gilsey House (1869–71), at the northeast corner of Twenty-ninth Street and Broadway, replaced a building that had over time housed a number of popular amusements, including Daly's Theater and Bauvard's Museum and Theater.[112] Built by Peter Gilsey, a Danish-born real estate developer and politician, the 125-foot-high, three-hundred-room hotel also replaced the last surviving farmhouse in midtown. Hatch's boldly massed design, painted white to suggest marble, was rendered in cast iron produced in the works of Daniel D. Badger. A tour de force of urbanism, with 60 feet of frontage along Broadway and 128 feet along Twenty-ninth Street, it piled a two-and-a-half-story billowing mansard atop five stories of nearly identical height. The composition was restless, punctuated by two-story pavilions and, at the diagonal corner, by a sweepingly scaled mansard clock tower that rose above the rest. Closely spaced pedimented windows were typical in the building except near the corner, where wide glass openings flooded rooms with light and views of the passing throngs. Where there was no glass, marble panels were inset between the rhythmically arranged pilasters that ringed the building separating each carefully expressed floor. Montgomery Schuyler admired

> the treatment of the angle of the building, which was cut off octagonally, making a handsome frontispiece, entrance, and tower, with illuminated clock. The frontage on Twenty-ninth Street is also agreeably broken, and the roof, which from its enormous depth would have been otherwise painfully prominent, has been so skillfully diversified in its treatment that the result is satisfactory and picturesque. While open to the objections that all iron buildings . . . profess an imitation of stone worksmanship, it is certainly one of the finest of this class in the city.[113]

The next great hotel, the Grand Central (Henry Engelbert, 1870), at 673 Broadway, between Bleecker and West Third Streets, also built by Elias S. Higgins, bridged the downtown and uptown crowds with a location near the beginning of Ladies' Mile, where Alexander T. Stewart's new store was the principal drawing card. Intended by its developer to be the "most palatial hotel in America" and "one of the most conspicuous objects on the street," the seven-story building, crowned by a mansard, was a force to be reckoned with.[114] It was the three slightly projecting pavilions, with a regular pattern of windows, crowned by mansarded towers supporting flagpoles that gave this six-hundred-room palace, the largest in America, its memorable profile. Inside, there were six parlors and six dining rooms, enough to feed six hundred people at a time, while seven acres of carpets, presumably supplied by Higgins, paved the guests' way to a range of rooms tailored to business travelers as well as to single gentlemen and family residents. Suites consisting of a parlor, bedroom, and closet could be combined with others to make even larger apartments. In 1872

Grand Central Hotel, 673 Broadway, between Bleecker and West Third Streets. Henry Engelbert, 1870. View to the northwest, c. 1870. Anthony. MCNY.

Working Women's Hotel, west side of Fourth Avenue between East Thirty-second and East Thirty-third Streets. John Kellum, 1869–78. View to the southwest. FLC.

the Grand Central became notorious as the setting for Edward S. Stokes's murder of James "Jubilee Jim" Fisk, a partner of Jay Gould who also shared Stokes's mistress.[115]

Hotel life was not only seen as a solution to the problems of the vagabond rich but also to those of working women. In 1857 a writer in *Harper's Weekly* proposed that flats be constructed for single women so they could escape the indignities of boardinghouse life.[116] In the 1860s, the Working Women's Home, created in a rehabilitated tenement building at 45 Elizabeth Street, provided five hundred beds in curtained alcoves as well as parlors, a reading room, a laundry, and a common dining room.[117] But this was hardly what was needed to accommodate the rapidly increasing number of middle-class single women who were working at jobs in the city. Alexander T. Stewart, who employed many single women in his wholesale and retail stores, knew about this prob-

lem from firsthand experience, leading him to build a "hotel for women of modest means" on the west side of Fourth Avenue between Thirty-second and Thirty-third Streets.[118] As designed by John Kellum, Stewart's Working Women's Hotel, which began construction in 1869 but was not completed until 1878, grouped five hundred generously sized, well-furnished bedrooms, either sixteen-by-eighteen-foot rooms to be shared by two women or eight-by-nine-foot rooms for single occupancy, around a large interior courtyard. According to the *American Architect and Building News*, each bedroom was "finished in good style, and each room has hot and cold water-taps, gas, and electric bell communication with the office. Bathrooms and water closets are provided in abundance."[119] The street level was lined with shops while the upper floors were fitted out with many of the features of a first-class hotel, including parlors, reading rooms, a six-hundred-seat dining room, and a concert and assembly room. Elevators rendered all seven floors easily accessible.

As a work of architecture, Stewart's hotel failed to please the critics, who were, in any case, almost to a man hostile to both the philanthropist and his architect. The boldly scaled cast-iron design, with the first story painted dark brown and upper floors painted a light drab, surrounded a one-hundred-by-one-hundred-foot courtyard graced with a fountain and plantings. Peter B. Wight dismissed the design as "three immense fronts, each at least two hundred feet in length, all of heavy cast-iron, and suggesting the form of a type of Italian Renaissance architecture which has come in vogue within a few years past in connection with some great insurance buildings and a host of whole-sale stores."[120] In essence, Wight seemed to find the hotel commercial rather than residential in character. Part of the problem, as the *American Architect and Building News* somewhat cynically reported in December 1877, lay in the shift of taste that had taken place during the building's prolonged period of gestation:

> It would require a middle-aged New Yorker to recall the date of the beginning of work on Stewart's Working-Women's Hotel. Records show that it was started between ten and twenty years ago, and has been crawling to completion ever since. . . . There are no changes of plan from the original design prepared by the late John Kellum, whose inflictions upon New York in the several Stewart piles and the County Court House recall Shakespeare's lines upon the evil which is not interred with

men's bones. . . . Stewart too has gone, and among the many *quasi* successes of his life, those connected with matters architectonic find a type in this Women's Hotel. Everybody has seen it, as it stands in all its iron rendering of Italian Renaissance, frowning down upon the thousands of travellers from the north and east, as they emerge into the lower section of the city from the Fourth Avenue tunnel. Of all the innumerable examples of this common style of the use of iron in street fronts, it is the worst, because it is the largest and the most pretentious. It is well built, well furnished, substantial, and in its purpose and interest of providing an eating and sleeping place for a thousand working-women, should in all material aspects serve admirably; but artistically it is a magnificent failure, a two-million-dollar example of what New York does not want if she is ever to show a decent architectural face along her principal thoroughfare.[121]

Stewart intended to build a similar facility for men, but as the women's project dragged on he did not get around to it. By the time the Working Women's Hotel opened on April 2, 1878, two years after Stewart's death and seven years after Kellum's, its purposes were compromised. Fifty-three days after opening, on May 23, Stewart's executor, Judge Henry Hilton, pronounced the experimental enterprise a failure and closed the building down, instituting minor renovations and reopening it as the Park Avenue Hotel in June of the same year. The new name was something of a reach. Although the stretch of Fourth Avenue between Thirty-fourth and Thirty-sixth Streets had been listed in city directories as Park Avenue since 1860, and the portion continuing to Forty-second Street was called Park Avenue by 1867, the site of Stewart's building, between Thirty-second and Thirty-third Streets, was officially Fourth Avenue until 1928 (in 1888, the length above Forty-second Street was changed to Park Avenue). High rents and overly strict codes of behavior imposed on the guests had combined to doom the project. According to the darkly sarcastic magazine *Puck*, "The Late A. T. Stewart was a man of cold disposition and frigid manners. . . . Stewart and Vanderbilt are both dead . . . but in one thing the dry-goods man has the advantage of the Commodore. His executors are men after his own heart. If the old Philistine were alive to-day, he couldn't suggest one additional item of meanness and petty tyranny in the arrangements of the 'Woman's Home.'"[122]

After the Panic of 1873, smaller, more modest hotels became popular. William Field's seven-story Buckingham (1876), at the southeast corner of Fifth Avenue and Fiftieth Street, with its flat north-facing facade overlooking the new Catholic cathedral across Fiftieth Street, was articulated with a central and two corner pavilions.[123] At midblock, the hotel extended to Forty-ninth Street. Henry J. Hardenbergh's compact, seven-story, wrought-iron-trimmed, Queen Anne–style, red brick Hotel Albert (1881–83), at the southeast corner of Eleventh Street and University Place, was no rival for the apartment palaces

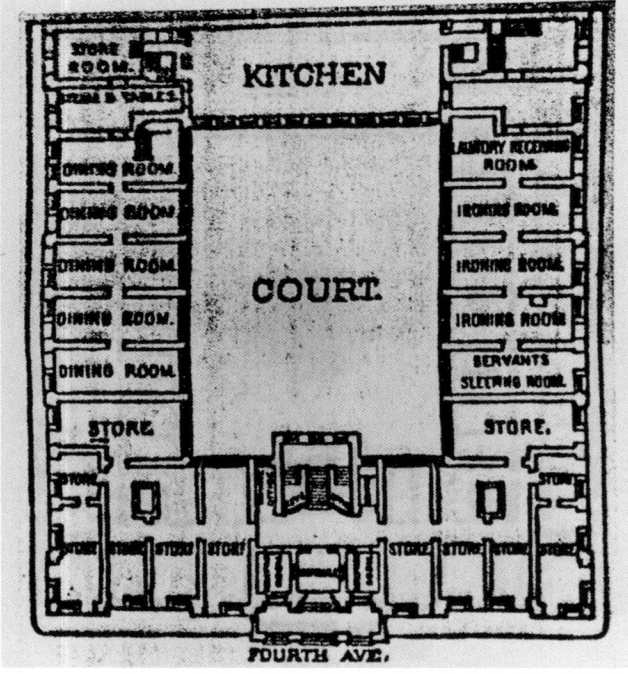

Working Women's Hotel, west side of Fourth Avenue between East Thirty-second and East Thirty-third Streets. John Kellum, 1869–78. First-floor plan. HW. CU.

Buckingham Hotel, southeast corner of Fifth Avenue and East Fiftieth Street. William Field, 1876. View to the southeast, c. 1877, showing St. Patrick's Cathedral (James Renwick Jr., 1850–79, 1888) under construction on the left. NYHS.

Hotel Albert, southeast corner of Eleventh Street and University Place. Henry J. Hardenbergh, 1881–83. View to the southeast. AR. CU.

Hardenbergh had designed for the West Side.[124] Stephen D. Hatch's Murray Hill Hotel (1884), on the west side of Park Avenue between Fortieth and Forty-first Streets, complemented the Working Women's Hotel a few blocks away and marked a return to the grand ambitions of the hotels of the post–Civil War boom years.[125] Developed by Hugh Smith, a broker and sportsman, the eight-story, red brick, six-hundred-room hotel, arranged around two courtyards, commanded its site and, together with the far less distinguished Grand Union Hotel (Edward Schott, 1872), at the southeast corner of Forty-second Street and Park Avenue,[126] formed a gateway to Grand Central Depot. The site of the Murray Hill Hotel, formerly home to the stables and carbarns of the Madison Avenue stagecoach line, was exceptionally large, extending from Park Avenue 230 feet west along Fortieth Street and 130 feet west along Forty-first Street. At each corner the building's mass was broken by pavilions rising to towers, identical except at the site's northeast corner, facing Grand Central, where a higher tower took advantage of the downward slope of the land to create a memorable, easily identified landmark for travelers exiting the terminal. The main entrance, and one of the chief features of the design, was a colonnaded portico above which the building rose to a clearly articulated gable. The *Real Estate Record and Builders' Guide* pronounced the elevations "not bad," noting that "the fronts are not 'pestered' with multiple features." But "in avoiding restlessness . . . the architect has not escaped monotony."[127]

Murray Hill Hotel, west side of Park Avenue between East Fortieth and East Forty-first Streets. Stephen D. Hatch, 1884. View to the northwest, c. 1890, showing Grand Central Depot (John B. Snook, 1869–71) on the right. NYHS.

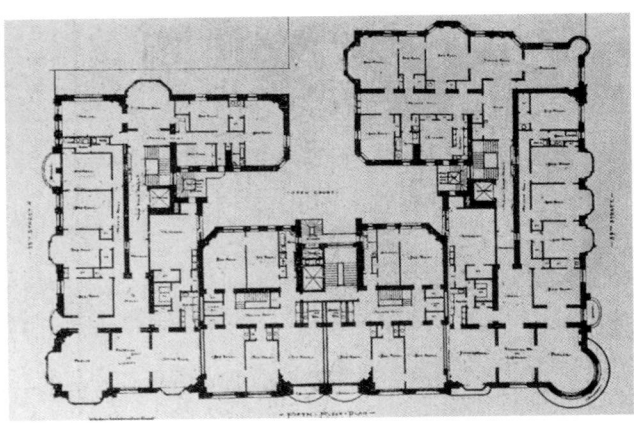

Proposed Plaza Apartments, west side of Fifth Avenue between West Fifty-eighth and West Fifty-ninth Streets. Carl Pfeiffer, 1883. Perspective rendering by E. Eldon Deane. AABN. CU.

In 1882 a bold project was proposed for a grand hotel to occupy the entire west blockfront facing the Fifth Avenue Plaza, between Fifty-eighth and Fifty-ninth Streets.[128] The neighborhood was exclusive: to the south lay George B. Post's house for Cornelius Vanderbilt II (1878–82) (see below), while behind the hotel, and extending almost as far west as Eighth Avenue, a string of luxury apartment houses were being constructed. In December 1882, Jared Flagg acquired the site for $850,000. Extending back 125 feet on Fifty-eighth Street but 200 feet on Fifty-ninth Street, the plot was one of the most advantageous for a high building in the city. Flagg entrusted the building's interior layout to his son Ernest, working with William A. Potter, who was to be the building's overall architect. The Plaza Apartments was to be a twelve-story building, with the top three floors housed in a mansard roof except at the central pavilion of each front. The massive building was to

Proposed Plaza Apartments, west side of Fifth Avenue between West Fifty-eighth and West Fifty-ninth Streets. Carl Pfeiffer, 1883. Fifth-floor plan. AABN. CU.

wrap around a generous, six-thousand-square-foot central court. Flagg's plans called for fifty-two individual apartments, with twenty-three duplexes and nine triplexes to be cooperatively owned and twenty simplex units to be rented. The apartments were to be grouped by type, each served by a separate street entrance.

Jared Flagg was unable to raise funds for the building, however, and in 1883 James Campbell and John Duncan Phyfe, who had just sold their interest in another project, the Gramercy Family Hotel (see below), took over as developers, hiring the architect Carl Pfeiffer, whose Berkshire apartment house (1883) was highly regarded. As depicted by a superb delineator, the English-born architect E. Eldon Deane, Pfeiffer's elaborately detailed and turreted Queen Anne design would have brilliantly commanded the site. It called for a twelve-foot-wide driveway leading from Fifty-ninth Street into a ninety-by-twenty-two-foot court, a space significantly smaller than the one Flagg had proposed. A combination of sim-

plex and duplex apartments were planned for eight of the nine floors, with servant rooms as well as a restaurant located in the top floor overlooking the park. Though room service was to be available, each apartment was also to have its own kitchen. Ground was broken in late 1883, but construction was halted the next year when the foundation walls had been built to the level of the sidewalk.

In 1884 the New York Life Insurance Company, which held the mortgage, took over and hired McKim, Mead & White to replan the project. As completed by that firm, the eight-story Plaza (1889), advertised as "the Model Hotel of the World," was a relatively undistinguished, if compactly massed, brick and brownstone palazzo, principally notable for the regularity of its fenestration and the bold double-loggia porch facing Fifth Avenue. Inside there were elaborate public rooms, including the Pink Parlor and the Blue Parlor, each facing Fifth Avenue on the second floor and furnished in the eighteenth-century French taste the firm was doing so much to promote.

Plaza Hotel, west side of Fifth Avenue between West Fifty-eighth and West Fifty-ninth Streets. McKim, Mead & White, 1889. View to the southwest, c. 1897, showing the eight-story Dalhousie (John Correja, 1884) on the far right; to the left of the Dalhousie are 36 West Fifty-ninth Street (William Kuhles, 1878) and the Bradley (John G. Prague, 1877), at 30 West Fifty-ninth Street. NYHS.

APARTMENT HOUSES

Within a few years a change in the way of living has been made here, but the change has been so quiet and gradual as to excite little notice and almost no public attention. In a very short time, indeed, this City may be said to have entered on what may be called a domiciliary revolution. The revolution has no more than fairly begun, but it is rapidly spreading, and will, before long, become complete. It has already been of much benefit to the community, and the benefit will continually increase, since it adds materially to the convenience, comfort, and wholesomeness of our homes. The desirable change is in the substitution of flats or apartment-houses, as they are generally named here, for boarding-houses, and the entire or partial occupation of dwellings.
                    —*New York Times*, 1878[129]

The apartment house was not a New York invention.[130] The Romans built multiple-unit dwellings and that tradition was carried on in Italy during the Renaissance. During the Second Empire in France, the apartment house reached a high degree of refinement in design and appealed to all but the very richest members of French society.[131] The French established two types of apartment house. One, the courtyard apartment house, was based on a socially cooperative idea of collective habitation, with the apartments gathered together in a continuous wall but functioning as individual stacked houses around an interior courtyard, in effect a private street or square shared by all the residents and exclusive to them. The second type, the *maison à loyer*, was collective but not cooperative in its implications. The common courtyard was replaced by a building that externally conveyed the impression of a single large house. The hierarchy among the residents was represented by their placement in the building, with the tenants of the highest class on the lower floors and lesser tenants above. A concierge oversaw the comings and goings of the *maison à loyer*, which featured elaborate lobbies, stair halls, and corridors that were viewed as extensions of the street. The example of Paris was critical to New York's adoption of apartment-house living.

As early as 1854, *Putnam's Magazine* argued for apartment houses modeled on hotels.[132] Having recently moved to the city from Newburgh, New York, Calvert Vaux had experienced difficulty in finding suitable housing for his family. In a talk delivered before the American Institute of Architects on June 2, 1857, Vaux advocated the apartment house as a solution to the housing problem plaguing middle-class New Yorkers, proposing "separate suites of rooms under the same roof" on the European plan, as distinguished from what came to be known as the American plan, in which meals were included with the daily or weekly tariff as was also typical in hotels and boarding-houses.[133] Vaux accompanied his talk with a perspective drawing and plans of his "Parisian Building," a four-story-high structure on a fifty-foot-wide site that would accommodate two semiduplex units per floor. Each unit included a parlor, dining room, and kitchen on one level and three

Proposed Parisian Dwelling. Calvert Vaux, 1857. Elevation. HW. CU.

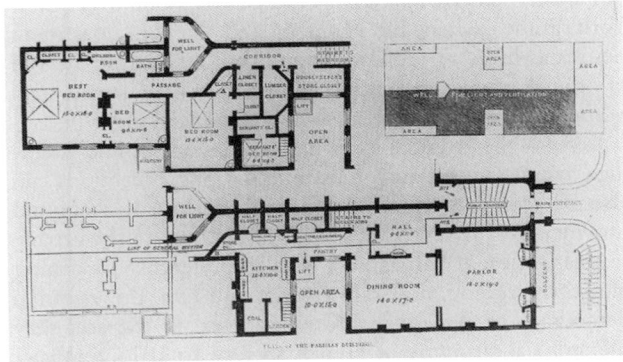

Proposed Parisian Dwelling. Calvert Vaux, 1857. Plans. HW. CU.

family bedrooms and one servant's room on a half level above, an arrangement that permitted high ceilings in the principal rooms while stacking the servant's room and some storage over the kitchen. Outside, the design was stylishly French, with the stair hall expressed by an almost continuous window rising from the street to above the cornice, and living rooms leading through large triple-hung windows to small iron balconies carried on brackets. For all its Frenchness, the facade terminated with an elaborate, surprising, vaguely Tudorbethan pediment. Vaux saw the apartment house not only as a way to solve a pressing housing problem but also as a way to satisfy the rising expectations of an increasingly affluent and extensive middle class: "The mechanic, now-a-days, shares with the millionaire his taste for the luxuries of privacy, fresh air, water and light, and the wish to occupy . . . a commodious residence, is widely spread amongst all classes."[134]

Although the apartment house model continued to intrigue American architects and the editors of the *Real Estate Record and Builders' Guide* lobbied for it heavily, it was clear that substantial changes would have to be made in the prototype to render it acceptable for the American market. As Peter B. Wight put it: "An apartment house must be built to accommodate a class of tenants who are in a nearly uniform scale," as distinguished from the hierarchical scale of tenants in the *maison à loyer*, which was the type most easily adapted to New York's narrow lots.[135] Influential New Yorkers resisted the apartment house for some basic reasons, generally attributed to the differences assumed to exist between Anglo-Saxon and French social practice and culture. In 1878 the *New York Times* noted that when apartment houses were first advocated, there "was a strong prejudice against them . . . —a prejudice natural to Anglo-Saxons, who are instinctively opposed to living under the same roof with other people."[136] In *The Age of Innocence* Edith Wharton, writing in 1920 about city life in the 1870s, described proper society's negative reaction to Mrs. Manson Mingott's living accommodations, a perfect depiction of New York's reluctance to live in French flats.[137] James D. McCabe Jr. had spelled out this attitude in 1869 in *Paris by Sunlight and Gaslight*, the companion to his New York guide, when he characterized French apartment houses as little more than "magnificent tenements" devoid of "the privacy and tender influences which surround a home organized on the English or American plan."[138]

Besides the Anglo-Saxon native Puritanism and prejudice against multifamily accommodations, objections can also be traced to two other areas: one, the homebound provinciality of New York society as opposed to the urbane sophistication of Parisian life with its preference for dining out, theatergoing, and café sitting; and two, the essential democracy of American life as opposed to the still very hierarchical structure of French society. In 1873 *Scribner's Monthly* reported: "We sometimes hear it said that the American people are different from Europeans; that they are a home-loving race; whereas the Europeans, especially the French, have no homes, have no word for 'home' in their language, and are forever gadding about: whereas the Americans do not care for pleasures that are only to be had in public; hence, for them, no need of squares, 'piazzas,' 'places,' public gardens, parks, etc."[139]

Efforts to explain the differences between the two cultures were a staple of any discussion of the apartment house, from Calvert Vaux's lecture introducing the idea before the American Institute of Architects to Sarah Gilman Young's book *European Modes of Living; or the Question of Apartment Houses*, published in 1881 but based on ideas she had written about as early as 1872, just as the trend toward apartment-house living was establishing itself in New York. In her book, Young summed up the arguments against apartment-house living:

> There are no objections to apartment houses in American cities, except prejudice. . . . To Americans it is a question of rank. Anything that resembles what we term a tenement house is tabooed. There being no fixed caste in America, as in foreign states, we have established a certain style of living and expenditure, as a distinctive mark of social position. . . . Especially do we seek an exterior of respectability and wealth in our homes. The desire to live in a fine house is particularly American. Europeans of distinction, of all countries, think much less of the exterior of their residences.

Young recognized that part of the prejudice against apartment houses could be traced to the shoddiness of tenements, which were the principal example of the multiple-dwelling type, and to poor management. Her principal proposed remedy to the situation was to have the new apartment houses designed by architects trained in France, "where this system has reached its greatest perfection."[140]

No building type was more dramatically affected by the introduction of the elevator than the multiple dwelling. In a *New York Times* editorial about the role apartment-house construction was playing in insuring that the city would be home only to the poor and the very rich, it was noted that the spread of the passenger elevator would have an extraordinary impact on the city: "Time only can determine what kind of people will be developed from a population living in towers and castles twelve and fifteen stories high."[141] The elevator also played a role in solidifying the distinctions between Parisian and New York apartment-house design. In his essay "The Cliff-Dwellers of New York," Everett N. Blanke, a journalist, summed up the distinctions between the two that were firmly established by 1890:

> In Europe, Paris and London not excepted, the steam elevator is uncommon, and as a result the upper stories of an apartment-house not supplied with this substitute for stairways, diminishes in rental value as the top of the building is approached. The apartment-house in Paris, therefore, differs from that in New York in the peculiarity of giving shelter to representatives of every grade of society, the weightier and wealthier members of each community, making as it were, the foundation of the social structure, while those of diminishing responsibility and resources climb laboriously toward the roof. The elevator, being democratic, had done much to do away with an aristocracy of wealth in the American apartment-house, by performing, unwittingly, for tenants, the duties of a board of equalization, both in the matter of rent and of self-respect.[142]

The *Real Estate Record and Builders' Guide* began to campaign for apartment houses right after the Civil War, when the city's growth spiraled upward: "Were one such building erected in New York . . . , whole streets of them would be built before the supply could meet the demand. It is idle to say that people would reject what they have never seen. To compare a building so designed and constructed with a 'tenement house,' is to confound things utterly dissimilar in conception; to see no difference between a public exchange and a private mansion on Fifth Avenue; between a Bowery groggery and the Astor House."[143]

As if in response to the *Record and Guide*'s editorial, the completion in 1870 of Richard Morris Hunt's Stuyvesant Apartments at last introduced what Peter B. Wight happily reported "was intended for a first-class house, and would rank as such according to César Daly's classification, so far as space and convenience are concerned." Wight characterized the Stuyvesant Apartments as "superior in many respects to any house of its kind in the city of Paris, and altogether better adapted to the necessities of New York life. As compared with its manifest advantages, its shortcomings are slight."[144] In 1867 Rutherfurd B. Stuyvesant, a twenty-nine-year-old lateral descendant of the New Amsterdam governor, had commissioned Richard Morris Hunt to design the Stuyvesant Apartments, New York's first apartment house, at 142 East Eighteenth Street. He may have been inspired by his time spent in Paris (where he first met Hunt) or by the *Record and Guide*'s campaign, or he may have been moved by his own business instinct. Stuyvesant was the son of Lewis Rutherfurd, an astronomer, but his mother was a Stuyvesant; in keeping with the requirements of the family estate, he had reversed his name in order to be eligible for a vast inheritance.

Though Stuyvesant's apartment house was undoubtedly the pioneer of its kind, in the 1850s, according to James Richardson, Hunt was said to have built "a small but handsome apartment house . . . on Wooster Street. . . . About the same time, perhaps a little earlier, a similar house in Hudson Street [by an unknown designer] offered complete facilities for modest housekeeping on separate floors."[145] Also preceding Hunt's Stuyvesant Apartments was Stuyvesant House (c. 1855), built by Dr. Valentine Mott on Bleecker Street, which Lewis Leeds described in 1874 as "the first fabric, built upon a Parisian model, in this city. It was on a large scale, with porte cochères, porters' lodges, court-yards, and a suspended veranda, which ran along the whole front of the building. But it was divided into separate houses, each of which must be occupied by a family."[146] Another progenitor of Hunt's Stuyvesant Apartments may have been the model houses (1852) built by Richard K. Haight, developer of Haight House (see above), at 256–258 West Thirty-seventh Street.[147] Though Haight's units were self-sufficient, thereby qualifying as apartments, they were intended for working-class families, which made them highly unusual. There is one more candidate for the distinction of first apartment house. In 1902 Thomas Kilpatrick was credited by the editors of the *New York Times* as the builder of the first apartment house (1853), on Thirtieth Street near Lexington Avenue, which contained several family units, each with a bath and other conveniences.[148]

Hunt was also responsible for another precursor to the apartment house. Shortly after his arrival in New York from

Studio Building, 15 West Tenth Street. Richard Morris Hunt, 1857. View to the northeast, c. 1858. The Octagon, AAF.

Paris in 1855, Hunt was commissioned by two brothers, James B. Johnston and John T. Johnston, leading art patrons, to design what was for New York a dramatically different type of building combining artist studios and an art gallery.[149] New York's artists had mostly been scattered around town, many working in attic studios while living in boardinghouses. Hunt's Studio Building (1857), at 15 West Tenth Street, in many ways a development of his Rossiter-Parmly house (1855–57) (see below), was also based on examples Hunt knew from Paris, including the converted *hôtel particulier* at 1 Rue Jacob in which he had lived and in which the orientation was to a courtyard rather than to the street. Around a skylit two-story exhibition room Hunt wrapped three floors of individual high-ceilinged studios; off many of the studios were bedrooms at half-levels. The Studio Building's facade of dark red brick with brown sandstone trim, ornamented in accordance with the severe, Neo-Grec taste Hunt preferred at the time, consisted principally of large studio windows and French-style balconies that lent scale to the front. The Studio was the first building in America designed to provide gallery and work space specifically for artists, housing in its early years such painters as Worthington Whittredge, Sanford R. Gifford, John La Farge, Frederic Church, Albert Bierstadt, Eastman Johnson, William Merritt Chase, and Winslow Homer. Even more important, as Sarah Bradford Landau has written, "Here, all in one building, were precedents for the New York apartment house, apartment hotel, duplex apartment, and courtyard apartment house."[150] A year after the building's com-

Studio Building, 15 West Tenth Street. Richard Morris Hunt, 1857. View of Hunt's studio, c. 1859. Beer. The Octagon, AAF.

Studio Building, 15 West Tenth Street. Richard Morris Hunt, 1857. View of William Merritt Chase's studio, c. 1879. Cox. MCNY.

pletion, Hunt took over one of the studios for the architectural atelier he had previously conducted in New York University's University Building. Hunt's pupils at the Studio included George B. Post, Charles D. Gambrill, Henry Van Brunt, William R. Ware, and the Philadelphian Frank Furness. The students, as Van Brunt was to recall, worked surrounded by "cartoons in colors and . . . casts of architectural and decorative detail . . . [in] the midst of a congenial and sympathetic brotherhood of painters and sculptors from the neighboring studios."[151] In 1879 early Studio tenant Frederic Church convinced the banker, insurance executive, and art collector John H. Sherwood to develop the first apartment house designed specifically for artists and their families providing both studio and living space.[152] Located far uptown on the southeast corner of Sixth Avenue and Fifty-seventh Street, the seven-story, red brick and stone Sherwood Studios (1880) consisted of forty-four three- and four-room suites and was apparently designed by Sherwood himself. Large windows that provided abundant light to the fifteen-foot-high studio spaces constituted the building's most notable feature.

Despite the many precedents, it was Hunt's Stuyvesant Apartments that formed the foundation stone upon which the entire tradition of New York apartment-house design rests: not only did it constitute the foundation of a critically important building tradition but, at the time when the apartment house was struggling for acceptance as a building type in New York, it was the standard-bearer as well.[153] From the first the Stuyvesant was regarded as distinct from the tenement house as a type. In the annual report of the Building Department's activities, James MacGregor, superintendent of buildings, justified his decision to rank the structure as a "first-class dwelling" despite the fact that it was a multiple dwelling, because of "its vast dimensions, the novelty of its construction, its elaborate finish and great cost."[154] The *Real Estate Record and Builders' Guide* argued that the key factor in separating the Stuyvesant from the typical tenement was the introduction of the "private hall door on each landing."[155] But Amy Kallman Epstein has recently pointed out that this claim does not really seem justified given that most tenements were divided into "apartments," usually two to a floor, even though these apartments more often than not were occupied by numerous families, with one family squeezed into each windowless bedroom in the worst cases.[156]

Hunt treated all apartments in the Stuyvesant virtually alike, although the apartments on the second floor, with their taller ceilings, taller windows, and iron balconies, commanded the building's highest rents. To minimize odors in the individual apartments and to guard against the transmission of those odors from one apartment to another, Hunt located the kitchens at the rear of the building, separated from the dining rooms by a small bedroom and a servant's bedroom, an awkward arrangement. In a time before mechanical ventilation the problem was no small one. As the *Record and Guide* put it: "Should the first floor have corned beef and cabbage for dinner, while the

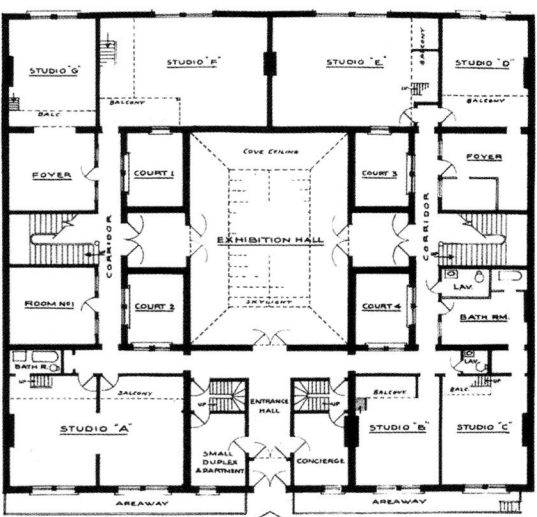

Studio Building, 15 West Tenth Street. Richard Morris Hunt, 1857. Plan drawn by Alan Burnham. TSSB. CU.

second floor content themselves with fried fish and beefsteak, and should the third floor be partial to onions and garlic, it is very easy to imagine the effect which the combined effluvia arising from these various dishes would have on a delicate and sensitive stomach."[157]

Though it had dumbwaiters, the Stuyvesant lacked passenger elevators, but this did not seem a problem given that upper-class New Yorkers were used to climbing flights of rowhouse stairs. In his 1857 paper advocating the apartment-house type, Calvert Vaux had suggested that apartments on higher floors might even be more desirable than those near the street, given New York's conditions: "Two or three flights of easy stairs may be readily surmounted and the freedom from dust and noise obtained by those who might live in the third or fourth stories would be found to compensate, in a great measure, for the troubling of traversing an extra flight or two of stairs; and thus people of the same standing in society could, in all probability, be readily induced to occupy comfortable apartments as high as the fourth floor." Above that, inconvenience would demand cheaper apartments, which would attract a lower class of tenant, a situation which "in all probability [would] be thought very disagreeable in an American city."[158]

The editors of the *Record and Guide* followed the Stuyvesant project very closely. On July 17, 1869, two months after construction had begun, they wrote:

> The apartment house, after the Paris plan, in Irving Place, built by Mr. Stuyvesant, is naturally attracting some attention. . . . We have always been inclined to doubt the feasibility of the Paris flats transferred to New York. Our people, we are afraid, would not take kindly to it. It is not and never has been fashionable here to rent apartments, and the American middle-class head of family . . . prefers to spend a couple of hours a day in going to and from a suburban village, rather than put up with apartments in the great city;

Stuyvesant Apartments, 142 East Eighteenth Street. Richard Morris Hunt, 1869–70. View to the southwest. The Octagon, AAF.

hence we shall observe with a great deal of interest the progress of Mr. Stuyvesant's experiment. There is no doubt but that four times the number of people could live in New York on the same space that is now occupied.[159]

On November 6, 1869, the editors of the *Record and Guide* noted that they saw Hunt's plan of apartments as a fulfillment of the goals of Vaux, doing away "entirely" with "all the well-founded prejudices against ordinary tenement houses, as a family thus situated is quite as private as in the

finest residence on Fifth Avenue." While the editors believed that the lessons of the Stuyvesant's plan would trickle down to the middle classes, they recognized that "it is altogether too costly in scope for that far larger class of our citizens, of equal respectability but smaller incomes, who may be counted by hundreds where such as those who are to inhabit this building may be counted by tens."[160] On March 26, 1870, with the building largely occupied, the *Record and Guide*'s editors crowed that in erecting the fine new block . . . Mr. Stuyvesant has done a large amount of public good. He has proved . . . the universal demand that exists for such houses in New York, by the simple fact that every room in his structures was bespoken before they were completed, and that over a hundred disappointed applicants have since been sent away. The class of tenants, too, he has secured will go far towards destroying that narrow prejudice which never until now could comprehend—what has all along been understood in all the crowded capitals of Europe—how it is possible for several families to live under one roof just as separately, privately, and respectably as if each occupied a separate house on the same street.[161]

Though the *Record and Guide*'s editors were pleased by the Stuyvesant's arrangements, they quarreled with Hunt's treatment of its 112-foot-long pressed brick and Ohio sandstone facade, which they deemed "rambling and incoherent in general effect [making] an impression . . . of a public building."[162] This judgment seems rather surprising given that the facade was not so very different from that of a typical mansarded rowhouse of the 1860s, no doubt a conscious strategy of Stuyvesant's or Hunt's to make the new building type appear as familiar as possible to conservative New Yorkers. In any case, the facade's conservatism was a far cry from the iconoclastic individuality of Hunt's first and very specifically French New York townhouse, the Rossiter-Parmly house

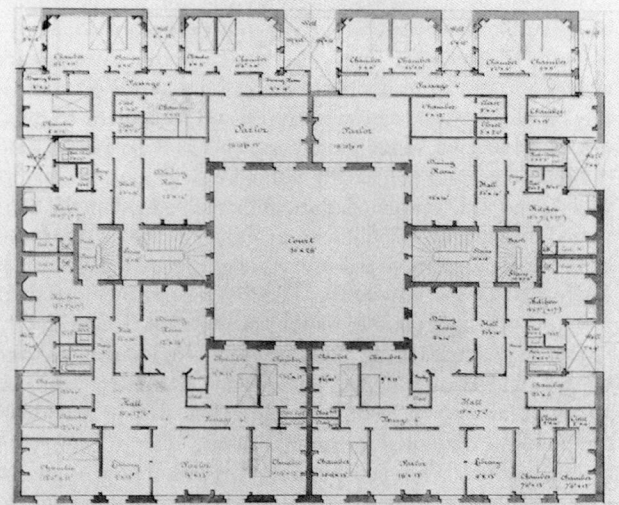

Proposed courtyard scheme. Richard Morris Hunt, c. 1869. Unidentified plan, most likely for the Stuyvesant Apartments. The Octagon, AAF.

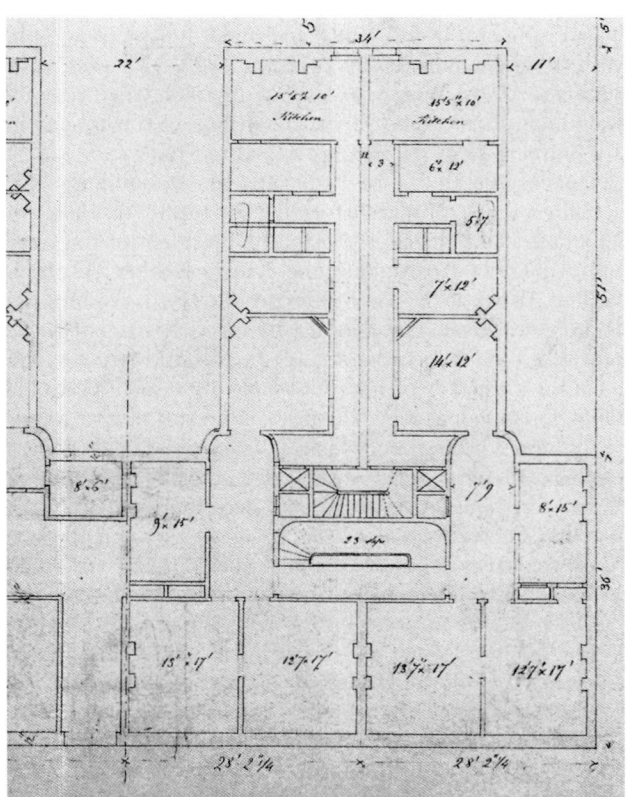

Stuyvesant Apartments, 142 East Eighteenth Street. Richard Morris Hunt, 1869–70. First-floor plan. The Octagon, AAF.

(see below). And it was less daring than the rationally articulate brick and glass expanse that his Studio Building had presented to the street thirteen years before. Nonetheless, the Stuyvesant's facade was not without interest or distinction, with polychromy and ornament, hard surfaces, and severe carving that achieved a synthesis between the Neo-Grec and the Neo-Gothic. According to Sarah Bradford Landau, this style combination was probably inspired by a block of flats in Paris at 28 Rue de Liège (1846–48), designed by Eugène-Emmanuel Viollet-le-Duc, especially "by its polychrome brick and stone-trimmed courtyard walls."[163]

The resemblance of the facade to a row of houses extended to the organization of the apartments themselves. The building was divided into two identical units, with two floor-through apartments per floor in each unit, arrayed in a way that married the en suite plans of Paris, opening to a hallway typical of a New York rowhouse, with a corridor system that, in recognition of the fact that all rooms were on a single floor, ensured greater separation of the various functions. Given that there was not to be an interior or central courtyard such as was typical in Paris, the front and back units of the French model were abandoned in favor of a rowhouselike arrangement of "floor-throughs." Hunt may actually have considered a courtyard plan. Though it might be for a second, unrealized project intended by Rutherfurd B. Stuyvesant, a drawing in the Hunt archives for an unidentified apartment house designed for a lot of exactly the same dimensions as the one occupied by the Stuyvesant shows a thirty-six-by-twenty-eight-foot central light court, as well as smaller courts—air shafts, really—along the side and rear lot lines. In this scheme there would have been front and back apartments, a feature Vaux had warned against in 1857: "American ladies . . . think it far more lively and cheerful to look out on a busy thoroughfare than on a monotonous quadrangle, however elegantly it may be decorated."[164]

New Yorkers were quick to recognize the Stuyvesant's virtues and it was immediately successful as a real estate venture. It was luxurious—each seven-room apartment featured not one but two water closets as well as a bathroom and dumbwaiter—and generously planned as well as reasonably well-lit and well-ventilated, though that depended on the continued low height of buildings to the south on Seventeenth Street. Each apartment was twenty-eight feet wide, three feet wider than a typical rowhouse. The first tenants included widows, one of whom was the mother of the actor Edwin Booth. After the disaster at Little Bighorn in 1876, General George Custer's widow moved into the building. The Stuyvesant also attracted fashionable young people. After visiting friends in the building, the noted lawyer and diarist George Templeton Strong wrote: "This substitute for householding seems to work well, and Rutherfurd is a public benefactor, especially to young people who want to marry on moderate means. Nothing could be brighter, more comfortable, or more refined-looking than these tiny, cosy drawing rooms."[165] One such young couple was Burton and Constance Gray Harrison. In her memoirs, Constance Gray Harrison, who would co-author an important history of New York, recalled that the

Proposed apartment house, northwest corner of Broadway and West Fifty-sixth Street. Potter & Robertson, 1875. Broadway elevation. NYSB. CU.

building was largely filled with the owner's friends, creating "a very old Knickerbocker sort of effect upon the outside mind."[166] The Stuyvesant also attracted artists and writers, including the painter Worthington Whittredge (who had previously rented in Hunt's Studio Building); the travel writer Bayard Taylor; Colonel W. C. Church, editor of the *Galaxy*; and even Calvert Vaux, Hunt's nemesis in the matter of the Central Park gateways (see chapter 1) but a fellow proponent of apartment-house living. W. C. Church was so impressed with the Stuyvesant that he wrote a passionately argued article promoting apartment living in his magazine and published an article on the same subject by Sarah Gilman Young.[167]

That the importance of the success of the city's first apartment houses—the Stuyvesant Apartments, Haight House, Grosvenor House, and Stevens House—was critical to the future success of the new building type was not lost on contemporary observers. As James Richardson observed in 1874: "The successful establishment of a few elegant apartment houses for the rich demonstrated to those of moderate means the possibility of multiple tenancy without the risk of social debasement."[168] Despite the Stuyvesant's success, the Panic of 1873 effectively curtailed further development of apartment houses. Potter & Robertson's mansarded and crocketed apartment house (1875) for a twenty-five-by-one-hundred-foot lot on the northwest corner of Broadway and Fifty-sixth Street was not built, a possible victim of the poor economy.[169] But when the economy began to improve after 1876, construction of French flats began to boom. In 1875, 112 apartment houses were built, with a similar number in 1876. In 1877, 157 were constructed. After a temporary decline in 1878, when only 99 were built, there were 253 apartment houses constructed in 1879, and in 1880 the number soared to 516.[170]

One of the first post-Panic apartment buildings was actually a renovation, transforming the former residence of Myndert Van Schaick, for years the president of the Croton Aqueduct Board, into the Knickerbocker (D. & J. Jardine, 1876), at the southwest corner of Fifth Avenue and Fourteenth Street. The resulting five-story apartment house provided nine two-bedroom apartments for families and included a number of important amenities, such as double floors for soundproofing, laundries, and extra servant rooms in the attic. The location, which it shared with Haight House (see above), was excellent. Its proximity to Washington Square Park was an advantage, but even more important, as the *Real Estate Record and Builders' Guide* pointed out, it was "most convenient to those who prefer healthful exercise when going downtown to being crammed in a horse-car."[171]

Much farther uptown, on the east side of Fifth Avenue between Fifty-second and Fifty-third Streets, Duggin & Crossman's Osborne (1876), an elevator building consisting of two apartments per floor separated by a stair core toward the front and an open court near the rear, provided remarkably well-zoned apartments that challenged those at the Stuyvesant, Haight, and Knickerbocker by offering an external window in each room and a separate service entrance.[172] The Osborne was owned by Dr. Lohman, the

Osborne, 667 Fifth Avenue, between East Fifty-second and East Fifty-third Streets. Duggin & Crossman, 1876. View to the northeast, c. 1879, showing Dr. Lohman and Madame Restell's four-story house on the corner. NYPL.

husband of the infamous abortionist Madame Restell, who lived next door in an imposing mansion until 1878, when the very bluestockinged Anthony Comstock hounded her to suicide. As a result, Restell's house was combined with the Osborne; the complex was renamed the Langham and converted to use as a hotel.

Besides a handful of top-class apartments, the recovering economy resulted in the construction of a large number of buildings catering to a middle-class clientele. These were significantly less luxurious and frequently less well laid out than the Stuyvesant, which had quickly become the standard of excellence. The *Real Estate Record and Builders' Guide* noted that "for the most part" the new apartment houses, "although calling themselves 'French flats' are so badly planned, and bring the different families into such unpleasant contact with each other (sometimes two on one floor) that it is difficult to see in what they differ from the old 'tenement house,' except in increase of charges."[173] If most of the new construction did not exactly address the self-image of the middle class, which continued to prefer to live in individual houses, at least it met their pocketbooks. Nonetheless, knowledgeable observers were increasingly concerned about the low standards. Even as early as 1876, when there were comparatively few apartment houses, the *Record and Guide* took to calling apartment houses the "tenement houses of the rich."[174] Yet despite their flaws, the French flats were seen by the *Record and Guide* as "a fresh demonstration of the latent mechanical skill and architectural ingenuity that exist among us, and an exhibition of the promptness with which capital is supplied for the elaboration of all really deserving and

2133–2137 Third Avenue, northeast corner of East Seventy-first Street. Detlef Lienau, 1870–71. Elevation. Lienau Collection. CU.

meritorious new ideas."[175] But when the rising economy brought with it an explosion in apartment-house construction, standards became a matter of great concern. According to a correspondent to the *American Architect and Building News*, writing in 1879, "It does not seem improbable that, thanks to bad planning and defective arrangements of light and ventilation, a great number of these houses will sooner or later become utterly useless for the class of tenants for whom they were intended, and either will have to be rebuilt or lapse into commoner uses with necessarily much lower rents."[176] By 1880 the French flat, catering to the middle class, was a fixture of the city's architecture, a "revolution in living," as the *New York Times* editorialized in 1878.[177]

Most of the early French flats could be found on the Upper East Side, east of Third Avenue, an area pioneered as a middle-class neighborhood by the Schermerhorn family, which in 1870 commissioned from Detlef Lienau a four-building, five-story row, at 2131–2137 Third Avenue, on the northeast corner of Seventy-first Street.[178] Lienau's quietly detailed facades complemented an especially lucid plan that introduced comparatively generous, thirty-one-by-twenty-foot light courts between each house, echoing Hunt's unrealized plan. Lienau's apartments, completed in 1871, were followed by John G. Prague's nearby group, at 2139–2143 Third Avenue (1873), which was less well planned, with narrow light shafts between houses and busily detailed facades.[179] In 1877, the *American Architect and Building News* reported that Thom & Wilson's Madison, comprising five

buildings, each with a store below and three stories of flats above, at the southwest corner of Third Avenue and Seventy-second Street, added "to the large number of this class of dwellings which fill the upper part of the island."[180] George B. Post, better known for his commercial work, also built a few French flats. For William Black, Post designed a seven-story building (1872–74) on the northeast corner of Fifth Avenue and Twenty-eighth Street; for Charles E. Rhinelander, he completed two five-story brick buildings (1883–84) at 1578–1580 Third Avenue, south of Eighty-ninth Street, two four-story brick and Wyoming stone flats (1883–84) at 178–180 East Eighty-ninth Street, west of Third Avenue, and eight twenty-five-foot-wide, five-story, brick buildings (1886–87) that filled the west blockfront of First Avenue from Eighty-ninth to Ninetieth Street; and for James Thomson, Post designed a five-story, brick and terra cotta, eleven-family flat (1885–86) at 206–208 East Ninth

Louis Comfort Tiffany apartment in the Bella (William Schickel, 1878), southwest corner of Fourth Avenue and East Twenty-sixth Street. Louis Comfort Tiffany, c. 1880. Hall. AH. CU.

Louis Comfort Tiffany apartment in the Bella (William Schickel, 1878), southwest corner of Fourth Avenue and East Twenty-sixth Street. Louis Comfort Tiffany, c. 1880. Drawing room. AH. CU.

Street, east of Third Avenue.[181] McKim, Mead & White also built one modest French flat. Set within the West Side tenement-house district, the Wanaque (1886–87), at 359 West Forty-seventh Street, was a ten-family unit built for James C. Miller, a contractor who had occupied a small house on the site before moving to his McKim, Mead & White–designed rowhouse in Harlem.[182]

The rapid acceptance of the French flat by the middle class was an early, even perhaps the first, demonstration of what has come to be described as the trickle-down effect in consumerism. As the *New York Times* observed: "Poor Americans are apt to be over-sensitive, and, having associated apartment-houses with tenement-houses, were afraid that the former might be confounded with the latter. But when the well-to-do and the rich consented to occupy flats, and really liked them, the poor, or at least the not-rich felt that they could afford to occupy and like them also. Hence, flats became popular," leading to the construction of apartment houses catering to a variety of pocketbooks and offering the middle class a viable alternative to suburban living.[183]

With the prosperity of the late 1870s came a new wave of luxury-apartment-house construction, as well as some renewed interest in the apartment hotel. An apartment house that may well have functioned better as a hotel was Emile Gruwé's Florence (1878), at the northeast corner of Fourth Avenue and Eighteenth Street. The forty-two-unit building was, according to the *American Architect and Building News*, "superior to the usual run of such buildings. A frontage of 200 feet on the street, and a flank of 53 feet on the avenue, with six stories in height, gives opportunity for some good grouping of parts. There is an L running back 92 feet also." The brick and Nova Scotia stone facades wrapped a plan of awkwardly organized but well-lit apartments with "long narrow passages so frequent and so objectionable in flat-houses."[184] The Florence was planned for three kinds of people: "First, for the family, that adheres to the old style of housekeeping, next, for the young married, who desire to keep house without being burdened with any of its cares and troubles, and last but not least, for the old bachelor class."[185] Thus on a typical floor there were at least two bachelor suites, consisting of a bedroom, parlor, and dressing room, as well as suites with kitchens and suites without for those who preferred to take their meals in the tenant restaurant located on the ground floor.

Perhaps because of its excellent location, William Schickel's brick and stone-trimmed Bella (1878), at the southwest corner of Twenty-sixth Street and Fourth Avenue, enjoyed a great success despite its ordinary architecture.[186] Developed by Oswald Ottendorfer, the Bella was divided into two separate five-story sections, one facing Twenty-sixth Street and the other facing Fourth Avenue, with two apartments per floor in each section. The Bella's most notable tenant was Louis Comfort Tiffany, who transformed a top-floor apartment into an elaborate, unique baronial environment combining objets d'art and artifacts from Eastern and Western cultures.[187] In so doing he created a pioneering and astonishing exemplar of the "artistic" taste of the 1870s, the new aestheticism shared by some of the most talented American, English, and Continental architects. In presenting Tiffany's apartment to the readers of the *Art Journal*, John Moran wrote that "some might think that Mr. Tiffany pushes his decorative ideas to an extreme."[188] But the eclecticism of taste and mixture of objects—Tiffany's "finds"—though provocative was controlled. Visitors entered through a foyer illuminated by a sinuously patterned stained-glass window, said to have been inspired by the daubing residue of Tiffany's palette knife. In 1903 Charles de Kay recalled the entrance:

> As you entered . . . you found yourself in a lobby, lighted with stained glass, which reached high up into the peak of the gable where the beams themselves showed in a rich dull color-scheme lighted here and there with plates and studs of bronze, the broad surfaces of the beams showing the knots and grain of the wood. The roof-slopes were set with thick glass tiles to aid the light from the windows, and the windows themselves were made up of rounds of glass of uneven thickness. What with staining and carving and inlays of metal and glass, the dark, brown-beamed ceiling made a foil to the warm India-red walls and trim.[189]

The stained-glass sashes were operated by pulleys, with a large wooden wheel and chain exposed to view, transforming a practical situation into a work of decorative art. The drawing room was Moorish but, as George W. Sheldon noted, "by Moorish decoration the reader is to understand, not a copy of anything that ever existed or still exists, but only a general feeling of particular type." The Moorish element was undercut, as Sheldon put it, "with a dash of East Indian, and the wall-papers and ceiling-papers are Japanese, but there is a unity that binds everything into an *ensemble*, and the spirit of that unity is delicacy."[190] The Japanese ceiling paper was flecked with mica. Another notable feature in this intensely decorated treasury was the library cabinet, which combined space for books and curios in an asymmetrically massed design surrounding a fireplace. All in all, as Donald G. Mitchell, using the pseudonym Ik Marvel, wrote in his series of eleven articles devoted to Tiffany's apartment, the artist had shown how the "extreme East and the extreme West may be married together, and wisely, in the offices of decorative art."[191]

The area around Washington Square was also home to apartment houses, including Ralph Townsend's Portsmouth Apartments (1882), at 38–44 West Ninth Street, and his Hampshire Apartments (1883), next door at 46–50 West Ninth Street, between Fifth and Sixth Avenues.[192] Both buildings were six stories tall and built of brick and terra cotta. McKim, Mead & Bigelow's Benedick (1879), at 80 Washington Square East, between West Fourth Street and Washington Place, a six-story apartment house intended for bachelors, was developed by

Benedick, 80 Washington Square East. McKim, Mead & Bigelow, 1879. View to the east, c. 1916. NYUA.

Lucius Tuckerman, a prosperous iron merchant.[193] With only fifty-six feet of frontage on Washington Square, the H-shaped plan of the one-hundred-foot-deep building contained thirty-three apartments on the first five floors with four artist studios on the sixth. The apartments consisted of a sixteen-by-eighteen-foot parlor, a thirteen-by-fifteen-foot bedroom, either two or three large closets, and in most cases a private bath. The framelike handling of the Philadelphia red brick and Nova Scotia stone facade was relieved by two iron-clad oriel-like bay windows running through three stories. In a report on the city's building activities, the New York correspondent of the Boston-based *American Architect and Building News* characterized the Benedick as "a quaint structure, made such by special design, but having a very modern purpose."[194] From its very beginning the building attracted an artistic crowd, including Olin Levi Warner, Winslow Homer, J. Alden Weir, John La Farge, and the architect William Rutherford Mead, a partner in the firm, among its early tenants. The *New York Times* was also impressed: "A new order of domestic architecture has grown out of the demands of modern society, or of that portion of it which seeks either to escape the high rents of the conventional three or four story brown-stone front house, or to find something less rigidly commonplace and gloomy. Of this variety of architecture Mr. Tuckerman's building will be a pleasing specimen."[195] Three years later, in 1882, the firm, now known as McKim, Mead & White, designed another bachelor apartment house, the Percival, at 230 West Forty-second Street, between Seventh and Eighth Avenues.[196] Built on the site of an 1872 Roman Catholic school for boys, the six-story brick building, nearly square in plan, featured balconies with intricate ironwork. Renwick, Aspinwall & Russell's Washington Apartments (1885), at 29 Washington Square West, on the southwest corner of Waverly Place, was an imposing seven-story, brick and terra cotta, Queen Anne–style building with only two apartments on each of six floors, the seventh being home to servant bedrooms and a drying yard.[197] The same firm's five-story Lancaster (1887), at 39–41 East Tenth Street, between Broadway and University Place, also featured beautiful brick and terra cotta work orchestrated in the fashionable Queen Anne taste.[198] Renwick, Aspinwall & Russell was also responsible for the five-story brick apartment house at 9 East Tenth Street (1888), which took its stylistic cues from its next-door neighbor, Van Campen Taylor's highly unusual, Indian-inspired house for Lockwood de Forest (see below).[199]

The recovering economy and the opening up of elevated railways on Second and Third Avenues further stimulated the construction of middle-class apartments in the hitherto remote reaches of the Upper East Side, such as the Rhinelander family's Manhattan (1879–80), at the southwest corner of Second Avenue and Eighty-sixth Street, designed by Charles W. Clinton, a severe six-story red brick box trimmed with bands of granite.[200] While designing the Manhattan, Clinton was also at work on the Seventh Regiment Armory on Fourth Avenue (see chapter 2), which may help to explain the apartment building's militaristic demeanor. By 1883 the editors of the *Real Estate Record and Builders' Guide* were disheartened by the quality of the apartments in Yorkville and other Upper East Side locations:

> It is curious and discouraging to see how little influence the advances in the planning and architecture, especially of apartment houses, have had upon the common run of these edifices. The vernacular building of contract builders seems to have been no more affected by the labors of a few educated architects than the vernacular speech is affected by the studies of learned men. . . . Anybody, who will take the trouble to look at a series of new tenements, of the "French flats" class, within a square or two of Ninety-first Street and Fourth Avenue, some lately finished and some now building, will see that most of them show no improvement over the type in vogue ten years ago. And the same may be said of most of the run of new flats in Harlem.

Among the buildings in this group were the five-story brick Atlantic and Pacific flats (Alfred B. Ogden, 1882), at 108–110 East Ninety-first Street, between Fourth and Lexington Avenues, and the row of four four-story brick flats (1881), also by Ogden, on the southeast corner of Ninety-first Street and Fourth Avenue, all of which were said to exhibit overly fussy, bombastic facades. "The only front among the new flats in Yorkville, which looks as if an architect could have had anything to do with it," reported the *Record and Guide*, "is the one on the north side of Eighty-ninth Street, near Lexington Avenue [Cleverdon & Putzel], a plain brick wall, deep in color, over a rusticated basement of red sand-stone, with two broad arches, giving access to open vestibules finished in oak. The arrangement looks liberal and hospitable, and the treatment of detail is not bad, although the rustication is much exaggerated, and the detail is taken from the corrupted period of the Rococo."[201]

By the 1880s virtually all classes of New Yorkers were living in multiple-unit dwellings, and fairly precise terms had been developed to describe and define the various and subtle architectural and social distinctions in what was essentially one building type. For example, if no central "hotel-type" services were provided, such as meals centrally prepared and served in a private flat or in a common dining room, a multifamily residence was either a tenement, a flat house or French flat, or an apartment house. If a building was a walk-up of five stories or more and contained small rooms and shared toilets and bathing facilities, it was a tenement. If a building was a walk-up but with larger rooms arranged in fully self-contained suites, it was a flat house or French flat. Finally, an apartment house had four or more stories and contained generously sized and luxuriously appointed self-contained suites, usually augmented by separate servant rooms in the attic. But apartment houses were even more complicated, because many, like apartment hotels, contained central dining rooms, but also always had full kitchens within each individual apartment. Thus the Dakota (1882–84) (see below), which had a dining room, might have been considered an apartment hotel but was not because with cooperatively owned apartments there was no expectation of transience. Terminology was quite important. For example, in 1878 a property owner sued her neighbor for building on an adjoining lot what she deemed a tenement—a use that was expressly forbidden by a deed restriction. The enterprising neighbor argued that his building was not a tenement house at all but an apartment house because it had a dining room, a position supported by the courts.[202] This was a slightly odd ruling because the generally accepted wisdom held that a building providing apartments with full toilet and bathing facilities within the units but only a pantry instead of a kitchen, or no pantry or kitchen at all, substituting instead a group dining room for residents, was an apartment hotel.

By 1883, the peak of the post-Panic boom, 10,174 dwelling units were under construction in the city, with 200 of these being luxurious single-family houses, 600 middle-class single-family houses, 5,700 middle-class apartments, and 3,674 tenements.[203] As a result, for the first time more New Yorkers lived in either apartment houses or tenements than in rowhouses. For all but the very rich, the stigma of living "over a store, especially on an avenue . . . [had] passed away."[204] In what the editors of the *Record and Guide* characterized as "an Oscar Wildian flavor," a writer in the *New York Sun* exulted that the apartment house might give rise to a new social order:

> If anything is proven by the success of the apartment house system it is that we are becoming more capable of organization, more sociable, more gregarious than ever before. It is doubtful whether there is any other feeling so peculiar to our modern life that offers as fair a field for artistic expression as this. The very fact that a dozen to one hundred families can dwell together in harmony under one roof should be inspiring to the architect. He should seize the idea of their unity, or their solidarity, and express it in stone and bricks and iron. . . . The system will engender a new sentiment—the apartment house sentiment, which will take the place of civic pride, of family feeling, perhaps even of patriotism. Is not this what architecture has been looking for, this material and spiritual need for a new kind of building?[205]

The opening of Central Park established Fifty-ninth Street as a desirable residential location. Although the park had been a fact of New York life since the 1860s, lack of adequate transportation retarded the development even of the land around its southern edge. By the late 1860s, with only horse-drawn omnibuses and streetcars to connect the area to downtown, the only structure that had been built close to the park was a small frame store with a few hotel rooms above, on the southwest corner of Fifty-ninth Street and Seventh Avenue. In the 1870s a few rowhouses were built between Seventh and Eighth Avenues, but soon the construction of the Sixth Avenue elevated railroad made Fifty-ninth Street, with its virtually unlimited north-facing views, an obvious location for apartment houses. John G. Prague's brick and stone Bradley (1877), just west of Fifth Avenue, opened up this advantageously situated street to high-density apartment-house development, long before the blocks south of it were filled in.[206] A simple, regular design of red brick and Nova Scotia stone,

Bradley, 30 West Fifty-ninth Street. John G. Prague, 1877. Rendering of view to the east. MCNY.

Proposed family hotel, Trinity College, Hartford, Connecticut. Henry Hudson Holly, 1874. Rendering by J. Minton. SM. CU.

the six-story Bradley, like the Stuyvesant, was entered up a low stoop. The building introduced a number of features to the luxury-apartment-house category, including separate passenger and service elevators, water hydrants on each floor, ash chutes, and electric bells. Pioneering large-scale investment in the area, the Bradley called attention, as no building before had, to the value of a Central Park frontage, causing the *Real Estate Record and Builders' Guide*'s editors to crow that "finally, the lonesomeness, which a large unoccupied space naturally suggests is entirely overcome by the congregating of a number of families under one roof. . . . No grander field can be imagined for the expatiation of the apartment house idea than the margin of the Park."[207] William Kuhles's fifty-foot-wide, six-story-high apartment house for C. Robert Peters, a wholesale cutlery merchant, at 36 West Fifty-ninth Street, between Fifth and Sixth Avenues, followed the Bradley the next year.[208] The design, executed in Philadelphia brick combined with Nova Scotia stone up to the second story, incorporated special sgrafitto work imported from Berlin.

The grandest of the Fifty-ninth Street apartments, and the most ambitious undertaking in the category ever, were the Central Park Apartments (1883, 1885) (see below), a collaboration of the developer José F. de Navarro and the entrepreneur Philip G. Hubert and his architect-partner, James W. Pirsson. In 1879 Hubert, a French-born inventor and promoter and son of an architect, entered into partnership with Pirsson, who in midcareer had abandoned music

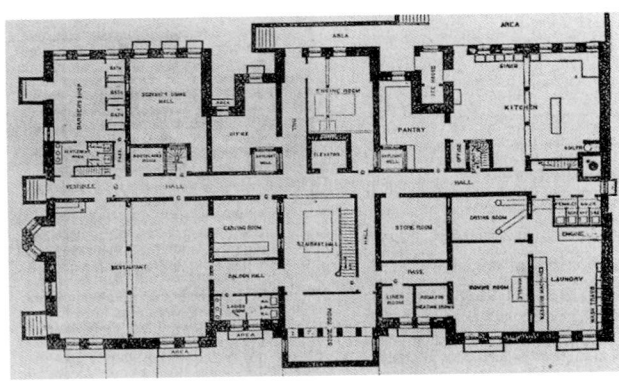

Proposed family hotel, Trinity College, Hartford, Connecticut. Henry Hudson Holly, 1874. Basement plan. SM. CU.

and art for architecture. Their purpose was to rethink the physical organization of apartment houses and the techniques used to finance their construction. Calling their enterprise Hubert Home Clubs, they first set out to demonstrate their approach in the rapidly developing apartment-house district south of Central Park, beginning with the Rembrandt (1881), at 152 West Fifty-seventh Street, just east of Seventh Avenue, and followed with the Hawthorne (1883), at 128 West Fifty-ninth Street, between Sixth and Seventh Avenues. From the point of view of architecture, as opposed to real estate development, the firm's special contribution was the duplex type of apartment, which they may have based on Henry Hudson Holly's proposed family hotel, prepared for Trinity College, in Hartford, Connecticut, first published in *Scribner's Monthly* in 1874.[209] Holly's plan called for a self-sufficient entity, with a centralized laundry and kitchen connected by elevators to the individual duplex apartments above. The Rembrandt was developed for artists by a syndicate headed by the clergyman-capitalist Jared Flagg, who often took credit for the cooperative idea despite Hubert's claims to it. It was heralded as "a studio-building which proclaims its purpose with distinctness in the large north windows, and is a moderate and well-behaved piece of Gothic."[210] According to *Harper's New Monthly Magazine*, the Rembrandt contained "studios and apartments, common property, whose rents go toward defraying the current expenses of the building. . . . It stands on two lots, 25 x 100 feet each; contains ten apartments and eight studios, the larger apartments having eleven rooms, counting the bathroom, and the smaller apartments, with the bath, eight and nine rooms."[211] The Hawthorne was an eight-story building located on a wider, seventy-five-foot-wide site, which led the designers to achieve what the *Real Estate Record and Builders' Guide* praised as an "economy of space through the adoption of an entirely new scheme. . . . The main peculiarity of the plan is that a sixth of the space at each end is reserved for a small three-story house, which runs back only about half the depth of the lot . . . the remaining space becoming an open court . . . on each side of the apartments, which widen again towards the rear but not to the full width of the lot." As a result all rooms in the building were guaranteed light and air, except for the public staircase. The Hawthorne's principal facade was "Gothic, and in that modern version of it which is readily recognized as 'Victorian Gothic,' of which the inspiration has come from the monuments of North Italy, so fervently celebrated by Mr. Ruskin." Exhibiting the characteristic "restlessness" of this approach, the Hawthorne's facade, which was finished with "many materials, red brick, red terra cotta, brown and gray sandstone, and polished black granite in the columns at the entrance," was powerfully massed, but not powerful enough for the editors of the *Record and Guide*, who complained of "'too many things' taking variations of form and color together." Nonetheless, they found the Hawthorne to be "one of the most interesting results yet reached in the development, which has really only begun, either of 'associated dwellings' or of many storied apartment houses."[212] The logic of the Hawthorne's plan was not lost on the developers of the eight-story, mansard-roofed Dalhousie (John Correja, 1884), at 40–48 West Fifty-ninth Street, which provided each apartment with four large windows overlooking Central Park by alternating simplex and duplex floor-through apartments, combining fifteen-and-a-half-foot ceilings for important rooms on the park side with bedrooms, baths, and kitchens grouped at the rear under ten-foot ceilings.[213]

To the enhanced domesticity of the duplex and the idea of cooperative living, Hubert and Pirsson added a third feature, the strategy of cooperative ownership, creating

121 Madison Avenue, northeast corner of East Thirtieth Street. Hubert, Pirsson & Co., 1883. View to the north, 1885. MCNY.

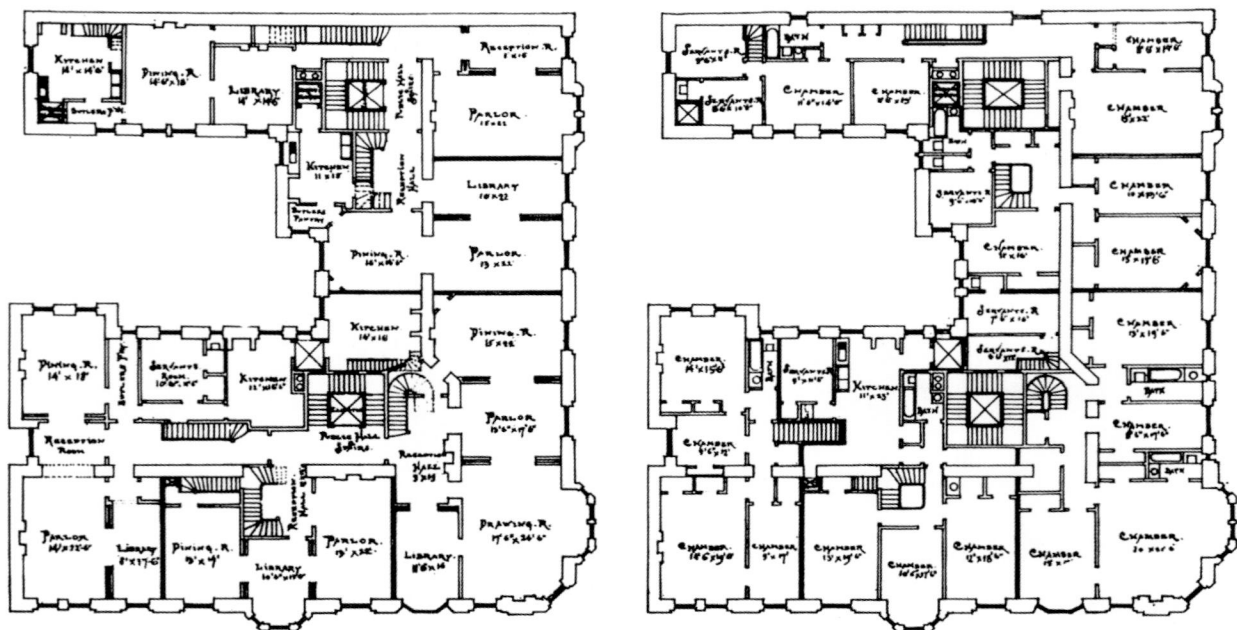

121 Madison Avenue, northeast corner of East Thirtieth Street. Hubert, Pirsson & Co., 1883. Plan for duplex apartment. NYF. CU.

what they called the Home Club, a venture wherein like-minded people could form a joint stock company to undertake the development of an apartment building on a shareholder basis. Each investor, in proportion to his or her share, would receive a lease on an apartment where it was expected he or she would live, although the apartment could be subleased out to others. Additional units in the building were to be held by the Home Club as a whole and rented out to help retire the mortgage and provide operating funds for the building. Hubert was a promoter, inspired to create the Home Clubs as the result of his first experience as a developer: after building an apartment house in a modest neighborhood, he soon found it filled with well-to-do businesspeople.[214] But Hubert was also something of an idealist, possibly influenced by the French utopian Charles Fourier, whose ideas, especially those calling for the reorganization of society into "phalansteries," or small communities, were given architectural expression as self-contained courtyard-bounding apartment houses.

The purest expression of the Home Club type was Hubert and Pirsson's 121 Madison Avenue (1883), at the northeast corner of Thirtieth Street, built in collaboration with Jared Flagg, whose son Ernest, though not yet trained as an architect, made important contributions to the Home Club duplex type.[215] Consisting of five generously sized duplex apartments for each two floors of the twelve-story building, 121 Madison Avenue, which was developed on land owned by Flagg, enjoyed "two obvious distinctions among all apartment houses: it is the tallest one yet built, and it is anonymous," by which the writer meant that it did not bear a pretentious name but was con-

tent to be known by its street address. Reflecting on the trend to ever taller apartment houses, the *Record and Guide*'s critic observed that when "two fifteen-story buildings confront each other across a sixty-foot street, we may begin to have trouble."[216] The massive red brick pile with its intricately gabled roofs loomed over the neighborhood of brownstone rowhouses. While the Rembrandt's duplex plan, based on an interlocking system of staggered floor heights to create the tall studio spaces, was ingenious, it was also awkward. For 121 Madison Avenue, Ernest Flagg, who would later study architecture at the Ecole des Beaux-Arts and rise to prominence, worked out a variation of the duplex scheme that, though more conventional, provided some apartments with bedrooms located above the main rooms. The plans provided for two to five bedrooms over a living room, dining room, drawing room, and library arranged en suite.

While praising the duplex plan and the use of "plank partitions with laths nailed upon them like battens, in such fashion that the key of the plaster fills up the space between the laths, and leaves, if the work is accurately done, no air spaces whatsoever, and no surfaces exposed to fire," the *Record and Guide* was not so impressed with the building's architecture, which "not only proceeds from its practical arrangements, but has evidently been frankly sacrificed to it, when any collision arose, both in composition and details." The building's mass, clad in brick and brownstone, was almost without articulation, breaking only for two projecting bays and two large gabled dormers, one of each on each front. The extensive use of sheet metal for exterior detailing was also noted with displeasure: "It is a pity that any sham should have been permitted in so large and costly a building. Sheet metal is scarcely a building material." The *Record and Guide* continued with its negative assessment: "Of the two temptations of architects of many-storied buildings—the Scylla of monotony and the Charybdis of miscellany—the architects have steered clear of the latter." Principally vexing was the misreading of the building's internal organization, with stories of different heights on the alternately but regularly banded facade—a less honest treatment than "in a narrow apartment house on Fifty-ninth Street [the Hawthorne], arranged on the same system and designed by the same architects, by a balcony under the lower floor, grouping the two stories which belong to each apartment."[217]

Not only did the *Record and Guide* find 121 Madison Avenue wanting in its architecture, but less satisfying even than that of the Knickerbocker (1883), at 245 Fifth Avenue, two blocks south at the southeast corner of Twenty-eighth Street, also developed by Hubert, Pirsson & Co. with Jared Flagg, but designed by Charles W. Clinton.[218] Montgomery Schuyler took note of the massive, brick, stone, and terra cotta Knickerbocker: "And finally there is a notable 'Home Club' building, twelve stories high, on Fifth Avenue and Twenty-eighth Street, which,

owing to its central situation, is attracting a great deal of attention."[219] Early Knickerbocker residents included the merchant-politician Isaac H. Bell and James T. Woodward, a banker. An application for an injunction against the Knickerbocker, deemed too high by neighbors, aroused the press to the injuries tall buildings could inflict on the monetary value of neighboring structures. In his decision, Judge Charles H. Van Brunt declared that he could do nothing for the situation, referring the aggrieved parties to the state legislature. As the *Record and Guide* pointed out, the sixty-foot width of New York's typical streets was very well suited to the heights of traditional walk-up structures, but with the coming of metal-frame construction and elevators the balance had dramatically been shifted so that either the "height of houses must be restricted or the streets be widened."[220]

In the first Home Club buildings, a booming real estate market enabled some investors to resell their apartments for substantial profits, and the cost of running the property had been exceeded by the rents so as to produce a return on investments. Buoyed up by these successes, Hubert conceived of more elaborate projects, the first of which was the eleven-story, red brick, Ruskinian Gothic Chelsea (1883), at 222 West Twenty-third Street, west of Seventh

Knickerbocker, southeast corner of Fifth Avenue and East Twenty-eighth Street. Charles W. Clinton, 1883. View to the southeast, c. 1925. NYPL.

Chelsea, 222 West Twenty-third Street. Hubert, Pirsson & Co., 1883. View to the southwest, c. 1915. Day. NYHS.

Avenue.[221] The Chelsea proved the most popular and profitable of the Home Clubs. Its relatively long stretches of regularly fenestrated wall were brought to life by continuous filigreed cast-iron balconies that stretched between three projecting full-height bays. Inside, a lavish palette of materials, including marble, onyx, and polished hardwoods, enlivened the lobby, which led to a sweeping cast-iron staircase and an elevator, as well as individual apartments. A private ballroom under the roof, just above the duplex artist studios that took up the north-facing portion of the tenth and eleventh floors, and a private restaurant staffed by a French chef and a French maître d'hôtel, catered exclusively to the building's ninety families, who lived in apartments that varied in size from three to twelve rooms. There was also a roof garden where residents could enjoy concerts on summer evenings. A president of one of the Home Clubs observed that the Chelsea "has proved the most profitable and popular of this firm's enterprises. All the apartments were purchased soon after the building was underway, and every suite of rooms is at a large premium over the original cost. The public have little idea of the magnificence of the interior of the 'Chelsea.' The dining room is the finest of its kind of any in New York. The owners of the various apartments do not think that running expenses will cost them anything, as the stores on the ground floor and the two upper stories are retained for tenants, so as to bring in an income."[222]

Hubert, Pirsson & Co.'s eight-building Central Park Apartments (1883, 1885) for the developer José F. de Navarro, the city's—and probably the world's—largest apartment-house complex, was the climax of the Home Club movement.[223] Navarro named each of the ten-story buildings in the group after a town in Spain, giving rise to the nickname for the group, the Spanish Flats, that belied its extensive number of duplex units. The nickname was probably coined by Montgomery Schuyler in an article in the *New York Times*: "This pile is a group of eight buildings, but so constructed that the exterior gives the impression that it is a single structure. The far-famed Chateau d'Espagne is here fully realized. Castles they are in very truth, and is named after some Spanish or Portuguese city. . . . In time, to distinguish them from other Central Park apartments, they will probably become known as the 'Spanish Flats.'"[224]

Taken as a whole, the development was one of New York's landmarks, especially when viewed from Central Park, where its rooftop landscape of gables and chimneys, combined with the tall bay windows and the shadowy bridges that connected the buildings, presented an unforgettable picture. Fronting Central Park on a 200-by-425-foot site running east from the Seventh Avenue blockfront between Fifty-eighth and Fifty-ninth Streets, the buildings were arranged around a narrow, 40-foot-wide, 300-foot-long courtyard that was planted and included a fountain. Open spaces between each building providing cross-ventilation in the courtyard were bridged by arched balconies on every other floor. All services were located beneath the

Central Park Apartments, 150–180 West Fifty-ninth Street and 145–175 West Fifty-eighth Street. Hubert, Pirsson & Co., 1883, 1885. View from Central Park, c. 1886. NYHS.

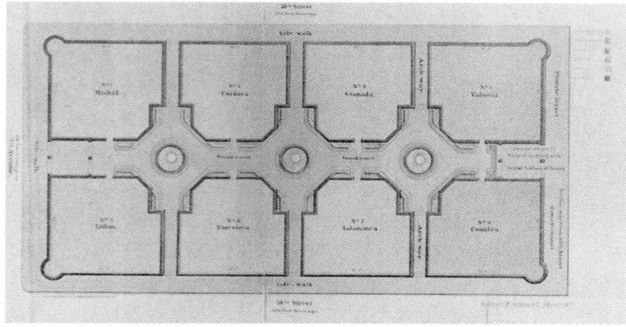

Central Park Apartments, 150–180 West Fifty-ninth Street and 145–175 West Fifty-eighth Street. Hubert, Pirsson & Co., 1883, 1885. View to the southeast, 1889, showing the Central Park Hotel (c. 1865) on the right. NYHS.

Central Park Apartments, 150–180 West Fifty-ninth Street and 145–175 West Fifty-eighth Street. Hubert, Pirsson & Co., 1883, 1885. Plan. CPA. CU.

courtyard in a basement reached by a ramp to provide access to wagons. The building complex generated its own electricity, pumped its own water from its own artesian well, and created its own steam for heat. Each building in the group held twelve enormous apartments, the largest of which included a twenty-three-by-twenty-nine-foot drawing room, a fourteen-by-twenty-nine-foot reception room, a fourteen-by-twenty-nine-foot library, and a twenty-by-twenty-three-foot dining room, as well as a kitchen, several pantries, and six bedrooms, the smallest of which was fourteen by eighteen feet. It also included three servant rooms and three full bathrooms. All in all, this particular apartment offered more space, was better lit, and was certainly more easily managed than any typical rowhouse. Not only did the complex include the simplex and duplex apartment suites found in previous Home Clubs, there were also triplex units, a newly devised type that Hubert and Pirsson adroitly arranged in interlocking fashion so that they presented two stories to the front of the building, where the principal rooms could enjoy the park vista, while the kitchens and bedrooms overlooked the courtyard.

Composed of granite, brownstone, Ohio stone, and Milwaukee and Philadelphia red brick, the buildings were essentially Queen Anne in style but overlaid with wisps of Moorish detail to reflect their developer's native culture and to help pay more than lip service to the names he had selected for them. The Madrid, Lisbon, Barcelona, and Cordova were the first to be completed, in 1883, facing Central Park, and the Valencia, Granada, Salamanca, and Tolosa were realized in the second wave of construction, in 1885. The complex attracted a gilt-edged list of investors. Oswald Ottendorfer, owner of the *New Yorker Staats-Zeitung*, who had developed the Bella (see above), lived in the Valencia. Episcopal Bishop Henry Codman Potter, the brother of the architect Edward T. Potter and half-brother of the architect William A. Potter, lived in the Granada, and Mary Mapes Dodge, author of *Hans Brinker, or the Silver Skates*, lived in the Cordova, while the lawyer Frederic Coudert hung his hat in the Madrid.

The Spanish Flats culminated a decade of experimentation in the field of multiple-unit dwellings. But they did not have much influence on the future, in part because the so-called Daly Law, passed by the state legislature in 1885, limited the height of dwelling houses to eighty feet on avenues and seventy feet on side streets, in part because of the overbuilding of flats in midtown above Forty-second Street, and in part because the Navarro enterprise itself "came to grief" and had to be sold at auction.[225] According to the *American Architect and Building News*, Navarro intended to build the complex of eight buildings four at a time using his own money and sell the apartments absolutely by means of trust deeds and perpetual leases, with owners becoming members of the Home Club. Unfortunately, construction costs far exceeded the original estimates. When Navarro ran out of money long before the shell of the first building had been completed, he was forced to take out a first and a second mortgage against the project. But even this infusion of capital was not enough to finish the building and, with no more individual lenders to be found, the second mortgagee was forced to advance more money to complete the building. When the first buildings proved popular, investors decided to go forward with the second half, facing Fifty-eighth Street, which also were sought after. But the general decline in the value of apartment-house property in 1886 proved the development's undoing. Rents failed to cover mortgage costs and the property was sold at auction to the second mortgagee, who was faced with the problem that individual cooperators had paid for their apartments as members of the Home Club. The mortgagee disregarded the certificates of perpetual tenancy and sought to impose rents, "just as if

Central Park Apartments, 150–180 West Fifty-ninth Street and 145–175 West Fifty-eighth Street. Hubert, Pirsson & Co., 1883, 1885. Rendering of courtyard by Harry Fenn. CO. CU.

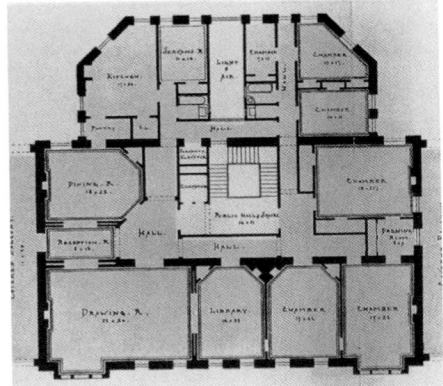

Central Park Apartments, 150–180 West Fifty-ninth Street and 145–175 West Fifty-eighth Street. Hubert, Pirsson & Co., 1883, 1885. Plan. CPA. CU.

they [the tenants] had no money invested in the building."[226] *Building* magazine assessed the situation rather bluntly: "The sale of the eight Navarro apartments . . . at only $200,000 over the mortgage price seems to indicate that the enterprise in this direction of a year or two back was untimely and that the principle of home clubs on which these speculations are based is scarcely consistent with American ideas of house ownership . . . [and] it is probable that those who bought their apartments will lose their investments." The collapse of the Navarro enterprise "also, probably, marks for some time, at least, a halt in building of such costly apartments."[227]

The failure of the Spanish Flats symbolized for some observers that the majority of upper-middle- and upper-class people still preferred houses over apartments. The long-anticipated development with rowhouses of the East Side park blocks, of the West Side, and of Harlem was already testifying to the depth of that desire and reflected the widely held feeling that no matter how luxurious, apartment-house living was invariably impersonal and inferior to life in a house of one's own. As *Building* put it: "A noble mansion affords the owner a gratification of that justifiable pride which a well-filled purse and a competent architect alone can afford him when built as a single dwelling. When grouped together, as in these monstrous apartment houses, these homes of taste and luxury are merged in a building of, it may be, fine architectural effect, but the individual is lost."[228]

Before the collapse of the Central Park Apartments enterprise, Hubert, Pirsson & Co., in 1883–84, took on an even more ambitious scheme, a thirteen-story courtyard apartment building to be erected on the site of Madison Square Garden, from Madison to Fourth Avenue and Twenty-sixth to Twenty-seventh Street.[229] The site was owned by William H. Vanderbilt, who granted Hubert an option on it in 1884, and it housed an antiquated passenger station (1863) that had originally served the New York, New Haven, and Harlem Railroad and had also been leased, starting in 1873, to the impresario P. T. Barnum (see chapter 5). Hubert, Pirsson & Co.'s scheme for the full-block site proposed to pile six tiers of houselike duplexes atop a street-level floor that covered the entire block and contained stores. Each 22-foot-wide, 50-foot-deep house—there would be 40 per tier, 240 in all—would be accessed by an open-air balcony that would ring the central, 80-foot-wide courtyard on alternate floors. Elevators would link the aerial walkways to the ground. Sadly, the plan was thwarted by the passage of the Daly Law. Had it been realized, it would have been the Home Club closest to Fourier's vision of the phalanstery. As its designers put it: "This aerial sidewalk arrangement, by making the public access to the houses absolutely open and free, carries out to the utmost the French idea, that the public halls and stairs are a mere continuation of the public street, and that each apartment is in all its essentials, a separate and individual house."[230] The Madison Square Garden design resolved, as no other New York apartment-house design did, the two givens of the city's housing problem—the need to develop at the highest possible density, and the desire to live in separate houses. But the critical innovation of the plan was not its connec-

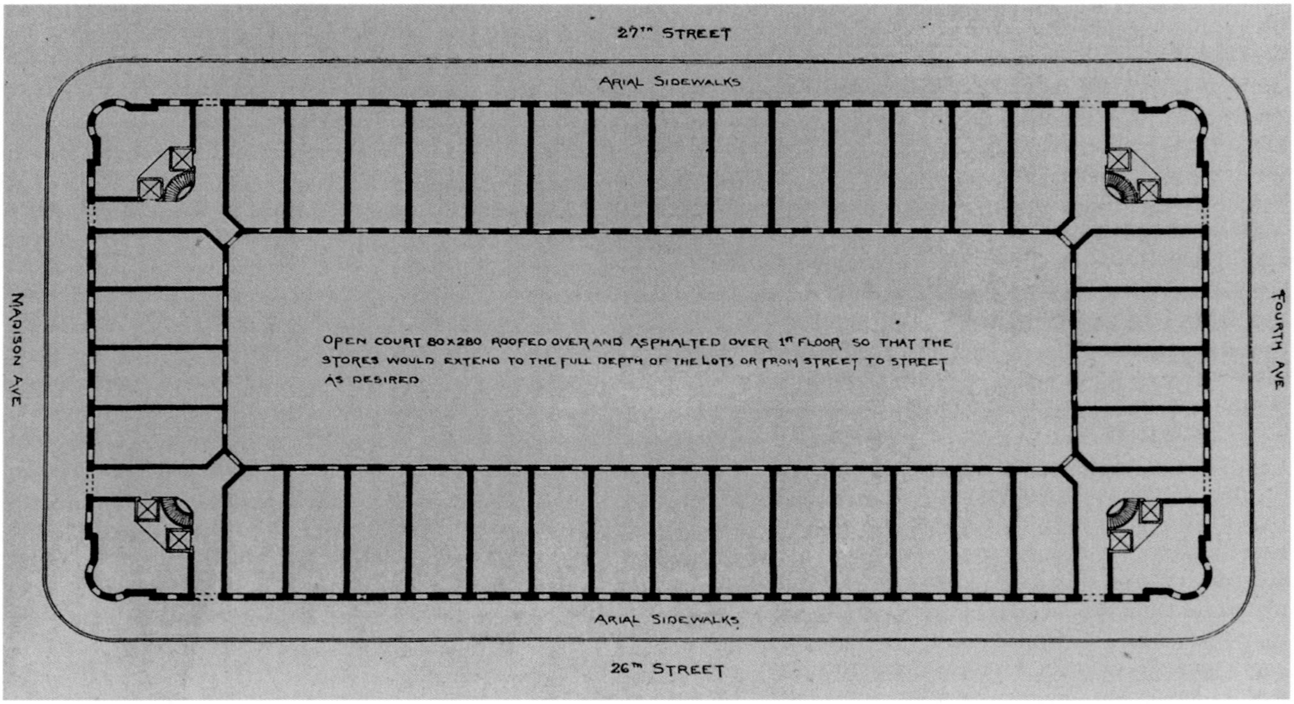

Proposed apartment house, Fourth to Madison Avenue, East Twenty-sixth to East Twenty-seventh Street. Hubert, Pirsson & Co., 1883–84. Plan. AR. CU.

Albany, west side of Broadway between West Fifty-first and West Fifty-second Streets. John C. Babcock, 1874. View to the northwest, c. 1921. Wurts. NYPL.

tion to the utopian social engineering of Fourier, but its clever way of coping with the realities of New York life. Its very ingenuity in adjusting the gridiron plan and the desire of New Yorkers for single-family houses to the economic necessity for high-density construction was distinctly pragmatic rather than ideal. Piling individual houses atop each other was, as Elizabeth Hawes has recently pointed out, "merely a geometric rearrangement of reality."[231]

Though the Home Clubs failed, their effect on top-class apartment-house design was profound, demonstrating what Edward T. Potter and others had stressed as a solution to the shortage of working-class housing: only large-scale development could effectively and humanely satisfy the city's seemingly insatiable demand for new housing. This had been demonstrated by William Field & Son's work for Alfred T. White in Brooklyn and by John C. Babcock's four-story Albany apartments (1874), which filled the entire west blockfront of Broadway between Fifty-first and Fifty-second Streets in an area—but hardly a neighborhood—well beyond fashion or even ordinary development.[232] The size of the site enabled Babcock to take advantage of extensive street frontages to plan for thirty-two suites of generally well-lighted rooms, creating at the rear a generous light court as well as larger-than-usual light wells, none smaller than eight feet on a side and some, called "open courts," measuring twelve by forty-one feet. Originally planned as ten individual buildings but

realized as a single block, the Albany was the first of the city's apartment-house palaces. With eight ground-floor shops along Broadway, the Albany was entered from the side streets, where the absence of shops only slightly helped to convey a sense of domesticity.

The Albany was but one of a number of medium- and large-sized apartments built in the 1870s and 1880s on the fringes of fashion south of Central Park, principally along Seventh Avenue and Broadway above Longacre Square. These included James H. Giles's Windsor Apartment House (1879), at the southeast corner of Broadway and Fifty-fourth Street, which consisted of six stories and an attic and contained twelve suites and featured an elaborately shaped towerlike corner bay window.[233] The stone-trimmed brick building, extending one hundred feet along Broadway and twenty-three feet along Fifty-fourth Street, was divided into two parts by a twenty-three-by-forty-foot courtyard. Stephen D. Hatch's six-story Sonoma (1875) and Thom & Wilson's nine-story brick and Dorchester stone Rockingham (1883) shared the east blockfront of Broadway between Fifty-fifth and Fifty-sixth Streets.[234] Other buildings in the area included John C. Babcock's seven-story brick and brownstone apartment house (1875) on the northeast corner of Broadway and Fifty-sixth Street,[235] and D. & J. Jardine's Clermont (1878), at the northeast corner of Broadway and Fifty-fourth Street.[236] Slightly to the west

Berkshire, northwest corner of Madison Avenue and East Fifty-second Street. Carl Pfeiffer, 1883. View to the northwest showing St. Thomas Church (Richard and Richard M. Upjohn, 1865) on the far left. Levy. AIC.

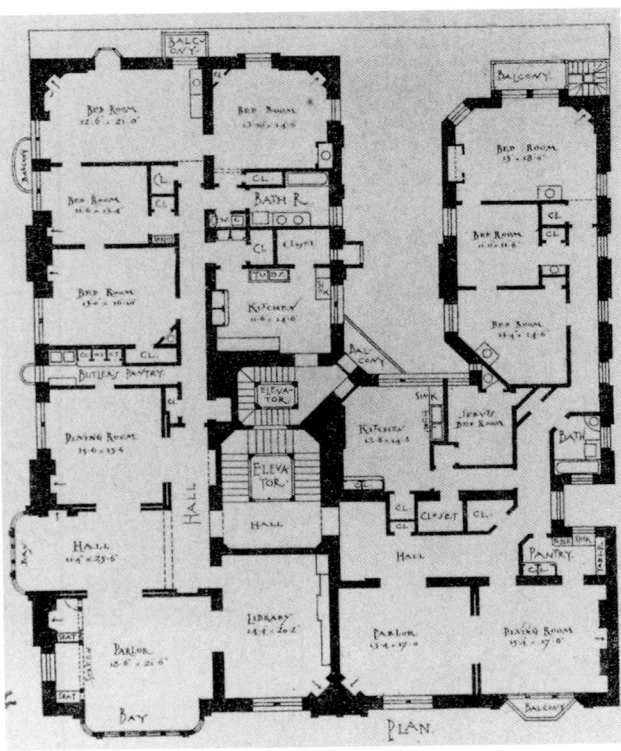

Berkshire, northwest corner of Madison Avenue and East Fifty-second Street. Carl Pfeiffer, 1883. Drawing of typical interior. AABN. CU.

was William F. Burrough's seven-story-high, three-house Windermere Apartments (1881), at the southwest corner of Ninth Avenue and Fifty-seventh Street, developed by N. A. McBride and Theophilus G. Smith.[237] The complex wrapped thirty-eight suites of seven- to nine-room apartments around a thirty-foot-square central court. Though the apartments were comparatively large with lots of exterior exposure, the Ohio stone and red, black, and buff brick exteriors were overly fragmented into narrow, pedimented bays.

The boom in the mid-1880s saw the construction of a number of notable luxury apartment houses. The Berkshire (Carl Pfeiffer, 1883), at the northwest corner of Madison Avenue and Fifty-second Street, piled two floors in the mansard atop seven stories. Lively facades punctuated with bays and oriels were wrapped around a plan that the *American Architect and Building News* found "somewhat less successful" than that of the Dakota (see below).[238] Hugo Kafka's eight-story St. Catherine (1883), on the southeast corner of Madison Avenue and Fifty-third Street, boasted a notably luxurious entrance lobby and filled all of its forty-seven-by-one-hundred-foot site with a single apartment per floor.[239] Downtown, only a few blocks from Hunt's Stuyvesant Apartments, George W. DaCunha's nine-story Gramercy (1883), at 34 Gramercy Park East, on the northeast corner of Twentieth Street, jolted the scale of the townhouses that other-

Berkshire, northwest corner of Madison Avenue and East Fifty-second Street. Carl Pfeiffer, 1883. Plan. AABN. CU.

Gramercy, 34 Gramercy Park East. George DaCunha, 1883. View to the east, c. 1890. NYHS.

wise ringed the private park, which had been created as the centerpiece of Samuel B. Ruggles's fifty-year-old real estate development.[240] Ruggles had placed restrictions on properties facing the square, specifying materials and establishing a minimum height for houses at a time when five stories was the maximum imaginable. Replacing a five-story hotel, Gramercy Park House, DaCunha's red brick interloper was broken into two wings flanking a narrow court facing the square. Despite its height, the building was not perceived as being overwhelmingly intrusive. In fact, the newly founded *Building* magazine admired the "bold and conspicuous" design with "its first and second stories of stone, rock faced, imparting to the edifice a massive appearance at the base." The magazine also admired the two angled towers that united the two wings separated by the center court, "a special feature . . . giving air and light, providing a good opportunity for architectural display, such as could not be obtained from an unbroken front."[241] In addition to conventional foliage, the richly molded terra cotta bands that marked the upper floors were ornamented with heads of squaws and domestic and wild American animals. Inside, a beautifully tiled lobby led to a caged elevator and beyond to the apartments. An eighth-floor restaurant was run for the residents by Louis Sherry, who guaranteed the standards of Delmonico's. The original idea for the development, to be called the Gramercy Family Hotel, was the brainchild of the developers James Campbell and John Duncan Phyfe, who early on in the building's construction sold out their interest and moved on to promote the Plaza Hotel (see above). The project was purchased by a group of investors headed by Judge William H. Arnoux and including William Duncan Phyfe, Harley Fiske, and Charles A. Gerlach. Despite the fact that Gerlach was a hotel entrepreneur, the new investors changed the building's plans and opened the building as an apartment house, with twenty-seven simplex apartments, as well as bachelor and studio accommodations and servant quarters on the roof. The Sherry restaurant proved a failure and was closed within a year.

James E. Ware's Osborne (1883), at the northwest corner of Fifty-seventh Street and Seventh Avenue, was the grandest of the apartment buildings in the area south of Central Park and one of the city's incomparable monuments to shared domesticity.[242] The building was developed by Thomas Osborne, an overreaching stone contractor who was forced into bankruptcy before the building was completed. With defensible immodesty, Osborne advertised his building in boldface type in the city's newspapers as "the most magnificently finished and decorated apartment house in the world."[243]

Osborne selected Ware in a competition—an odd choice given that he was an experienced architect known for his working-class tenements. Ware rose to the occasion with an eleven-story fireproof building of stone, composed of two T-shaped wings sharing a single lobby. The massive facades, suggesting a cross between the architecture of Italian Renaissance palazzi and the Richardsonian Romanesque, were, given Osborne's principal business, probably intended to convey a sense of the power of stone. The building's rock-solid exterior enclosed four lavishly decorated apartments per floor except on the second, where there was a banquet room, and the eleventh, where there were rooms for servants. Echoing the Hubert Home Clubs, the apartments were ingeniously arranged so that the rooms for entertaining enjoyed fifteen-foot-tall ceilings while the more private rooms, stacked in a semiduplex arrangement, were only eight feet tall. The Osborne's magnificent apartments paled before the splendors of the building's public spaces, including an elaborate front porch, entry vestibule, and lobby, the latter an overwhelmingly embellished room framed by arches, furnished with two ample staircases, and colored in jewel tones of red, blue, green, and gold. The lobby was the work of Jacob Holzer, a Swiss-born sculptor and painter who worked with Louis Comfort Tiffany to create a common reception room like that of no other apartment house. Details included a carved Renaissance ceiling, an inlaid marble floor, elaborate friezes and dadoes, bas-relief tondi, and foil-backed mosaics, the first use of this Byzantine-inspired technique outside churches.

Osborne aimed at self-sufficiency, intending to provide residents not only with communal dining but also with a florist, doctor, and pharmacy. A year-round croquet court on the roof was one unrealized idea. When Ware's plans were filed with New York's superintendent of buildings, Osborne proclaimed that his project would be not only the city's tallest building but probably the tallest in the country as a whole, rising two hundred feet from the ground to the tower. As built, there were eleven floors facing the street and fourteen lower floors at the rear. To help relieve the sense of mass, Ware punctuated the facade with bay windows as well as small balconies and continuous balconies at the third, seventh, and tenth floors. Many windows featured varicolored and patterned stained-glass transom lights, probably designed by Holzer and possibly made by the Tiffany Studios. The editors of the *Real Estate Record and Builders' Guide* were not very impressed with the Osborne, observing that "the material, a rough brownstone, used with wrought work and belting of light olive, is attractive, but it is not well used, the weak color being used for emphasis. The vertical division of four parts . . . would be effective if better managed. In fact it is crude and unskillful. The doorway . . . is . . . very pretentious, being a round arch of unusual height, space and depth. . . . In fact there is nothing architecturally interesting about the Osborne, except the grouping of the stories, and here and there some carving that is good in execution."[244]

Thomas Osborne's vanity was such that he insisted on using his own name even though it had been used earlier for an apartment house on Fifth Avenue between Fifty-second and Fifty-third Streets (see above). Despite its developer's financial problems, the Osborne was a success from the start, attracting returning suburbanites as well as

Osborne, northwest corner of Seventh Avenue and West Fifty-seventh Street. James E. Ware, 1883. View to the northwest, c. 1886. NYHS.

Vancorlear, west side of Seventh Avenue between West Fifty-fifth and West Fifty-sixth Streets. Henry J. Hardenbergh, 1879. Elevation. AABN. CU.

New Yorkers, including the pioneering advertising mogul J. Walter Thompson. In 1889 plans were announced but not executed to make the "sky-scraping 'Osborne' flat . . . still higher by the addition of four stories on the front and one story on the rear."[245]

Unquestionably, the greatest contributions made to apartment-house design after Hunt and Hubert were those of Henry Janeway Hardenbergh, an architect trained in the office of Detlef Lienau. Hardenbergh's first important apartment house, the six-story, thirty-six-suite Vancorlear (1879), occupying the west blockfront of Seventh Avenue between Fifty-fifth and Fifty-sixth Streets, was commissioned by Edward Clark, president of the Singer Sewing Machine Company.[246] With a full blockfront to work with, Hardenbergh was able to surpass what Hunt had first proposed: the Vancorlear was the first apartment house to have, in the opinion of the editors of the *Record and Guide*, "a courtyard worthy of the name and such as the Parisians understand it. True," they continued, "there is not yet the *porte cochere*, but, nevertheless, all the other appurtenances are there, and the court extends over 3,500 square feet and an entrance is provided for wagons that can find access to the place by a roadway especially constructed for that purpose."[247] To maximize the frontage along Seventh Avenue, the building was split in two, with entrances off the side streets. The courtyard ensured brightly lit, well-ventilated apartments that provided tenants with both the vitality of a street view and the serenity of a courtyard exposure. Hardenbergh described his design as "pure Renaissance with considerable of the

Queen Anne features about it." But the *Record and Guide* found the uniformity of the building's Philadelphia brick and Dorchester stone facades, particularly the one along Seventh Avenue, an "unbroken barrack looking line."[248] The interior fittings were lavish, with marble, mosaics, and fine woodwork extensively used in each of the spacious nine- or ten-room apartments. Wine cellars and laundry and drying rooms were in the basement. The New York correspondent of the *American Architect and Building News* had nothing but praise for Hardenbergh's plan: "Instead of being strung along a passage, like cells on a corridor, the rooms are grouped, the social or guest room about an ante-room, or lobby, while the family or private rooms are placed in more retired situations."[249] For Hardenbergh, who would become New York's undisputed master of apartment-house and hotel design, the Vancorlear was an important first step. Reviewing Hardenbergh's work in 1897, Montgomery Schuyler praised it for revealing "in some of its details the efforts of his special studies [with Lienau]. Much more than in detail it reveals them in what I am compelled, for want of a better word, to call the spottiness of effect which seems to belong to all the neo-grec work done on this side of the water, at least. Nothing could be more remote from the quietness which the architect has cultivated and attained in his riper work than this jerky and detonating style."[250]

Hardenbergh and Clark next collaborated on a development incorporating an eighty-five-unit, eight-story apartment house called the Dakota (1882–84), which occupied a two-hundred-by-two-hundred-foot site along

Dakota, west side of Eighth Avenue between West Seventy-second and West Seventy-third Streets. Henry J. Hardenbergh, 1882–84. View to the northwest, c. 1890. MCNY.

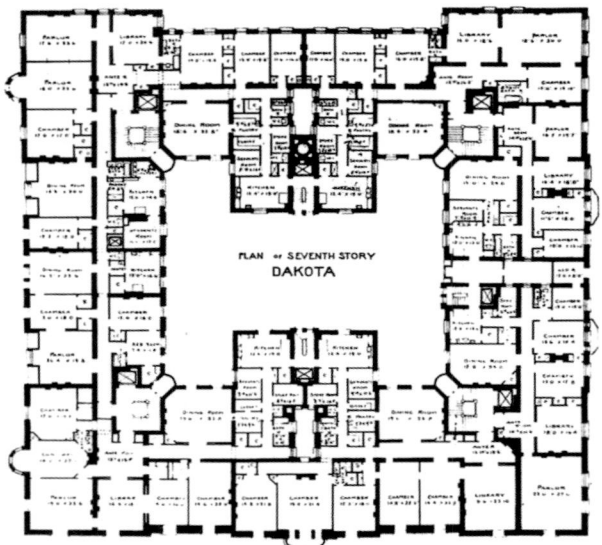

Dakota, west side of Eighth Avenue between West Seventy-second and West Seventy-third Streets. Henry J. Hardenbergh, 1882–84. Seventh-floor plan. NYF. CU.

the west blockfront of Eighth Avenue between Seventy-second and Seventy-third Streets, and a continuous row of twenty-seven houses that ran along the north side of West Seventy-third Street from Eighth to Ninth Avenue (see chapter 6).[251] The Dakota was an undisputed masterpiece, far and away the grandest apartment house of the Gilded Age in New York and rivaling, if not exceeding, in logic and luxury any comparable building in Paris or London. The building received its name as part of Clark's strategy to promote the West Side, an area he believed would come into its own as a result of the exten-

sion in 1879 of elevated train service along Ninth Avenue. The previous terminus had been Fifty-third Street, and the line was continued northward to 110th Street and then via Eighth Avenue to 155th Street. Clark named his apartment house the Dakota—a name not given in jest, as recent myth would have it, but in keeping with his idea that the important streets of this new area of town should bear distinctly American names. Clark saw the West Side as an upper-middle-class neighborhood, with top people choosing between row-houses and apartment houses. In 1879 he outlined his vision for members of the West Side Association: "There are but few persons who are princely enough to wish to occupy an entire palace, but there are many who would like to occupy a portion of a great building, which would be more perfect in its arrangement than any palace in Europe."[252]

When the Dakota was completed in September 1884, it was widely heralded. The *New York Daily Graphic*'s headline claimed that it was "one of the most perfect apartment houses in the world."[253] The Dakota propelled the New York apartment house into a new category of prominence and luxury, leaving behind the side-street townhouselike modesty of Richard Morris Hunt's Stuyvesant Apartments as well as the comparative architectural anonymity bordering on banality of such other large examples as the Albany, the Bradley, or even Clark and Hardenbergh's own palatial Vancorlear. Its siting alone guaranteed the building perennial prominence, clearly reinforced by commanding height and a vigorously articulated skyline of turrets, gables, dormers, chimneys, finials, and flagpoles. The châteauesque mass of the salmon-colored brick building trimmed in olive-colored Nova Scotia sandstone, surrounding a fifty-five-by-ninety-foot interior carriage court, was broken into four separate units, each entered from the court at a corner. The courtyard itself was entered through a tall archway leading off Seventy-second Street. Another, less grandly scaled opening led to Seventy-third Street but was not used on a regular basis. A gently sloped service alley along the building's west side led down to the basement level beneath the courtyard, where there was a "sub-court of precisely the same dimensions, lighted by two large openings" where "are received all the commodities of housekeeping and all supplies for the tenants or house proper."[254]

At ground level, facing Seventy-second Street and Central Park, there was a dining room reserved for the use of residents, although the original plans called for a more elaborate suite of a café, restaurant, and private dining rooms that would be accessible to the public from a separate entrance. Deemed "the handsomest dining room in Manhattan," it was only a bit more splendid than the principal rooms of the individual four- to twenty-room apartments.[255] Hardenbergh had originally planned six roughly equal apartments on each of the seven main floors, but as the building was being designed and constructed Clark

Dakota, west side of Eighth Avenue between West Seventy-second and West Seventy-third Streets. Henry J. Hardenbergh, 1882–84. View from Central Park, c. 1884. Anthony. FLC.

Ontiora, southwest corner of Seventh Avenue and West Fifty-fifth Street. Henry J. Hardenbergh, 1885. View to the southwest, 1922. Underhill. MCNY.

Imperial, 55 East Seventy-sixth Street. Frederick T. Camp, 1883. Rendering of view to the north. NYHS.

began to tailor the plans to the requirements of individual tenants and the building emerged a much more complex organism. Clark's own apartment, an eighteen-room, seventeen-fireplace suite, was located on the sixth floor in order to dramatize the value of height to a still cautious, townhouse-loving market. It contained a ballroomlike drawing room, second in scale and magnificence only to the common ballroom that was on the ground floor next to the dining room.

The Dakota was one of the grand monuments of the Gilded Age. Seven years after its completion, the *American Architect and Building News* was still enthusiastic: "In this beautiful house the entrances to the suites are all in the court-yard, just as they would be in a Paris house, and the court-yard is symmetrically and handsomely shaped."[256] Though intended as a money-making proposition undertaken by a shrewd businessman, it was clearly more than that. No expense was spared in its construction. Ceilings were fifteen feet high. While the building's walls were load-bearing, the thick floor slabs were carried on rolled-steel beams set three to four feet apart and infilled with masonry arches. A passenger and a service elevator served each quadrant. Four thousand electric lights and three hundred electric bells were installed, powered by the building's own 120-horsepower dynamos, the excess capacity of which powered Clark's nearby rowhouse development. Six rooftop tanks supplied two million gallons of water per day running through two hundred miles of piping. The building was connected via private wires to a nearby fire station. There were offices to send telegraphs and to hire messengers, as well as a florist.

Clark died at the age of seventy-one, in 1882, before his masterwork had been completed and proven to be a success. The property was left to his twelve-year-old grandson, Edward Severin Clark, casting some doubt over its future. In 1883 Montgomery Schuyler, writing in the *New York Times*, reported that the impact of Clark's development "remains to be seen. At present it is too isolated to come to anything like an immediate favor with the wealthy classes, but, when by slow and judicious accretions this drawback shall be measurably overcome, fashion may by any caprice turn in that direction, and then there is no telling what will happen."[257] When the Dakota opened, however, it was fully rented, to such noteworthy New York businessmen with an interest in the arts as Gustav Schirmer, the music publisher, Theodore Steinway, the piano manufacturer, as well as John Browning, an educator. Schirmer was particularly prominent, hosting innumerable parties in his apartment, with such guests as the writers William Dean Howells and Stephen Crane as well as the Russian composer Peter Ilich Tchaikovsky, who dined there during his stay in the city in April and May 1891 when he came to celebrate the opening of Carnegie Hall by conducting several of his own compositions.[258] These tenants were culturally but not socially prominent, and an address at the Dakota, though more revered than any other on the West Side as a whole, failed nonetheless to become as acceptable as one on or near Fifth Avenue.

Looking back on Hardenbergh's work, Montgomery Schuyler wrote in 1897:

> The architectural results were so successful that it is a very considerable distinction to have designed the best apartment house in New York. The Dakota was acclaimed upon its completion of having attained that distinction, which after thirteen years it continues to hold. . . . Central Park is the one municipal possession of which we have a clear right to be proud, and to erect what was in 1883 a towering building of eight stories fronting it, and visible from a great part of it, was for an architect, artistically speaking, to take his life in his hand. . . . That an eight-story apartment house could become a positive addition to the attractiveness of the Park was an attainment which the architect could scarcely have ventured to promise to himself. Yet in the Dakota this complete success has been attained. The building actually helps the Park. Its picturesqueness of outline and effect is attained without any sacrifice of unity, or even of formal symmetry, for each front is laterally, as well as vertically, a triple composition, which in both cases is carefully studied in mass and carefully carried out in detail.[259]

The Dakota set a new standard of quality and scale for apartment houses. But the 1885 passage of the Daly Law and the reluctance of investors to take on large projects in the wake of the problems at the Osborne and at the Central Park Apartments curtailed luxury-apartment-house construction. In 1885, one year after the opening of the Dakota, Hardenbergh completed work on the six-story, twenty-five-by-ninety-six-foot, brick and stone, Queen Anne–inspired Ontiora, at the southwest corner of Fifty-fifth Street and Seventh Avenue, a much more modest apartment house developed by the Clark estate and the last project initiated by Edward Clark.[260]

Most new apartment-house development occurred on the East Side, and was very definitely intended for a middle-class clientele. A stretch of Fourth Avenue in the upper fifties and lower sixties and farther uptown in Lenox Hill became home to a number of substantial developments, including Thom & Wilson's South Kensington Apartments (1880), at the northeast corner of Fourth Avenue and Fifty-sixth Street, six stories in brick with light freestone trim;[261] Frederick T. Camp's seven-story, Connecticut brownstone, Neo-Grec Imperial (1883), at 55 East Seventy-sixth Street, a midblock building with three small two- and three-bedroom apartments per floor;[262] William B. Franke's six-story, twelve-unit, brick and Belleville stone Lenox Hill Apartments (1886), at the southeast corner of Madison Avenue and Seventy-seventh Street;[263] Henry J. Hardenbergh's Adelaide (1887), at the southeast corner of Fourth Avenue and Sixty-sixth Street, six stories in brick with stone trim;[264] and Julius Munckwitz's seven-story, brick, stone-trimmed, Romanesque apartment house, at the north-

Adelaide, southeast corner of Fourth Avenue and East Sixty-sixth Street. Henry J. Hardenbergh, 1887. View to the southeast. AR. CU.

west corner of Park Avenue and Fifty-sixth Street, completed in 1888, the same year that the avenue's name was changed for the stretch above Forty-second Street.[265] McKim, Mead & White's Yosemite (1888–90), at the southwest corner of Park Avenue and Sixty-second Street, was the Dakota's closest new rival, not only in name but in architectural distinction.[266] Built by the New York Life Insurance Company, the Yosemite echoed the firm's less distinguished Plaza Hotel (see above) and in some ways anticipated the firm's Century Club (see chapter 2). Ornamental bands and terra cotta voussoirs were used to visually transform the lower four floors of the seven-story palazzo into a high basement and to close the corners of the upper floors, which, according to Russell Sturgis, who disapproved of the *parti*, were "treated as the principal story in the architectural sense."[267]

Despite the success of the apartment-house movement, there remained in the minds of many New Yorkers a strong lingering prejudice in favor of living in a house. For some, a house in the suburbs was the solution; for others who could afford it, only one on Fifth Avenue or the blocks immediately in its environs would do; and for those less well-heeled, a small house in Harlem or on the West Side was acceptable. But for those who preferred a central location but weren't really rich, an apartment was the best solution. While larger and larger apartment buildings seemed the trend, at least one architect, Bruce Price, succeeded in offering an alternative, a five-unit apartment house that conveyed in its appearance if not its internal organization the feeling of a charming townhouse, indi-

Yosemite, southwest corner of Park Avenue and East Sixty-second Street. McKim, Mead & White, 1888–90. View to the west. AABN. CU.

Yosemite, southwest corner of Park Avenue and East Sixty-second Street. McKim, Mead & White, 1888–90. Entrance. AR. CU.

vidual to the point of idiosyncracy. Occupying a twenty-five-foot-wide lot, similar to that of nearby single-family houses, Price's 21 East Twenty-first Street (1878), developed by David H. King Jr., was a five-and-one-half-story building containing five floors of flats, with servant rooms on the roof and basement accommodations for the janitor.[268] Its facade suggested the cozy domesticity of a Queen Anne townhouse—it was one of the city's earliest examples of that style applied to a house, coming at about the same time as McKim, Mead & Bigelow's Dickerson house (see below). Montgomery Schuyler praised Price's design as "the most successful of all the new twenty-five-foot houses" of the individualistic type, a "tall, gabled, Gothic house" the "whole arrangement" of which "has great spirit and picturesqueness, as the details also have. . . . This frank and spirited design is of quite another order from that which models large doorways with microscopic moldings and twists constructive features into forms irrelevant to their functions. This has life, the first condition of progress."[269] But Price's facade concealed an awkward plan of apartments that placed bedrooms in a row between the kitchen at the rear and the principal social rooms in the front—an arrangement not so different from the one described by William Dean Howells in his 1890 novel, *A Hazard of New Fortunes*: "The New York ideal of a flat . . . was inflexibly seven rooms and a bath. One or two rooms might be at the front, the rest crooked and cornered backward through increasing and then decreasing darkness til they reached a light bedroom or kitchen at the rear."[270]

Howells was writing from firsthand experience. In 1888 the author and his wife, Elinor Mead Howells, sister of William Rutherford Mead of McKim, Mead & White and herself an architect manqué, settled in New York after spending twenty-two years of married life elsewhere, mostly in Boston.[271] The Howellses looked at nearly one hundred apartments and houses in a six-day period before settling on a fourteen-room flat at the Chelsea. In *A Hazard of New Fortunes*, deemed by many to be the first novel written about the modern city, Howells recorded his experience of house-hunting through his protagonists, the March family, who leave a comfortable townhouse in Boston to settle in New York, inspecting prospective apartment-house residences named the Wigwam, the Esmeralda, the Jacinty, the Helena, the Asteroid, and the Xenophon. Before embarking on the search, Isabel March muses to Basil March:

> "We must not forget just what kind of flat we are going to look for. The sine qua nons are an elevator and steam-heat, not above the third floor, to begin with. Then we must each have a room, and you must have your study and I must have my parlours; and the two girls must each have a room. With the kitchen and dining room, how many does that make?"
>
> "Ten."
>
> "I thought eight. Well, no matter. You can work in the parlours, and run into your bedroom when anyone comes; and I can sit in mine, and the girls must put up with one, if it's large and sunny, though I've always given them two at home. And the kitchen must be sunny, so they can sit in it. And the rooms must all have outside light."[272]

As the March family's search revealed, the New York standard was a seven-room flat with one bath and not much else to commend it. For the Marches, an apartment seemed just plain unsuitable as a residence type:

> Think of a baby in a flat! It's a contradiction in terms; the flat is the negation of motherhood. The flat means society life; that is, the pretense of social life. It's made to give artificial people a society basis on a little money,—too much money, of course, for what they get. So the cost of the building is put into marble halls and idiotic decoration of all kinds. . . . It's confinement without coziness; it's cluttered without being snug. You couldn't keep a self-respecting cat in the flat; you couldn't go down to the cellar to get cider. No; the Anglo-Saxon house is simply impossible in the Franco-American flat, not because it's humble, but because it's false.[273]

21 East Twenty-first Street. Bruce Price, 1878. Rendering of view to the north. AABN. CU.

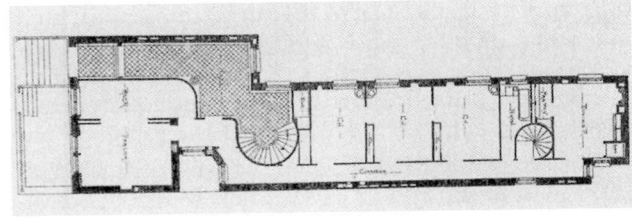

21 East Twenty-first Street. Bruce Price, 1878. Plan. AABN. CU.

Apartment-house life, as Howells understood directly, no matter what its proponents might claim for it, was hardly ideal. Even in first-class buildings, the problems of poor construction resulted in unwanted noise transmission from unit to unit. Maintenance of public halls was often problematic. And in the summer, the street teemed with the activities of children and there was a "tendency of many of the tenants to make parlors of, and hold receptions on, the stoops."[274] For those of some means, this was not such a problem, as it was typical to close up one's flat for the summer months and decamp to the country. Others who also wanted to go away but had less money simply moved out in May, skipping out on the summer's rent and resettling in another flat in September, creating a degree of transience that hardly fostered a sense of community.

Despite these drawbacks, by 1892 Moses King, the guidebook writer, could report that apartment houses held more than half the middle-class population of Manhattan Island:

> Real estate is so valuable and consequently rents so high that to occupy a house is quite beyond the reach of a family of ordinary means, and the suburbs on account of their inaccessibility are out of the question. Consequently apartments and flats have become a necessity, and a system of living, originally adopted for that reason, has now become very much a virtue. Apartment-life is popular and to a certain extent fashionable. Even society countenances it, and a brownstone front is no longer indispensable to at least moderate social standing. And as for wealthy folk who are not in society, they are taking more and more to apartments.[275]

But perhaps *Harper's New Monthly Magazine* had put it best a decade earlier, in 1882: "As a generalization, it may be said that reasonable apartments are not good, and that good apartments are not reasonable."[276]

THE ARTISTIC HOUSE

> Never was a grander field open to artistic developments than is now presented to our architects in Domestic Architecture.
> —*Real Estate Record and Builders' Guide*, 1868[277]

Between the city's founding and the Gilded Age the typical dwelling unit of all but New York's very poorest and very richest citizens was the rowhouse. Most of these were between eighteen and twenty-five feet wide and, over the course of the first half of the nineteenth century, grew in height from three to five stories. Usually these were relatively anonymous in design, with brick facades trimmed in stone and painted wood. In the 1840s, however, both style-setting architects, who designed comparatively few rowhouses, and designer-builders, who initiated and executed most of this type of construction, turned to brownstone, hitherto used as a cheap substitute for marble, as the facade material of choice. Brownstone was a generic term

for various types of sandstone or freestone principally quarried in Portland, Connecticut, and Little Falls, New Jersey, nearby locations with easy transportation to the city. A comparatively soft, friable stone, for use only as facing—rowhouses almost uniformly being framed in wood carried on load-bearing walls of brick—brownstone first came to prominence in Gothic Revival churches, beginning with Trinity Church (Richard Upjohn, 1846).[278] Though some houses were designed with brownstone in mind, most frequently in a Gothic Revival, villa-like style, they were usually constructed in suburban communities. In the city it was church rectories that introduced New Yorkers to the material's residential possibilities. Some brownstone rowhouses in the Gothic Revival style were built in the early 1840s, and by the 1850s brownstone had become "the favorite building material for shops, churches and residences. . . . The prevailing tint of New York is fixed."[279] In 1854 a guidebook to the city published in England reported: "Wherever any of [the] older brick edifices have been removed, their place has been supplied by tenements built of brown sandstone; and it may be said that at present New York is in process of being renewed by this species of structure."[280]

By the Civil War, rows of brownstone-faced houses were ubiquitous in every fashionable and nearly fashionable quarter, leading Montgomery Schuyler to bemoan the exclusive use of brownstone in so many buildings. While he felt it worked well in combination with other materials, used by itself it was "dingy" and "funereal," its dark color robbing buildings of shadow play and "doing more to disfigure New York than anything else."[281] By the 1870s the term "brownstone" began to become interchangeable with "townhouse" as a term used to describe the basic rowhouse unit that, grouped together, formed street upon street of repetitious building fabric. Some would say that the brownstone was so generic that it worked well for no one. In 1874, James Richardson characterized the typical New York rowhouse as "not made for any one in particular, or in case they happen to have been so constructed, they are rarely occupied by the people, or even the same class they were originally intended for." New York's rowhouses, Richardson argued, were too big: "It is safe to say, that there are in the city ten times as many houses, three, four and five stories high, planned,—so far as they are planned at all,—for the accommodation of but one family each, as there are families, large enough to fill them or rich enough to support them."[282]

The typical rowhouses of the Civil War period sat on a high basement, with the front door accessible by a wide, steep flight of steps called the stoop—from the Dutch word *stoep*. They were serviced at the basement level, a few feet below the sidewalk. Usually eighteen to twenty feet wide, with some as narrow as twelve feet and many as wide as twenty-five feet, whether three, four, or five stories, the typical rowhouse was, by world standards, commodious.[283] The raised stoop led to the parlor floor, where there were either two parlors or one parlor and a formal dining room. Below, in the high base-

View to the west from Madison Avenue along East Twenty-sixth Street, c. 1868, showing brownstone row facing Madison Square Park. Anthony. FLC.

ment, were the kitchen and larders and the family dining room. Bedrooms were located on the upper floors, where there might be small sitting rooms, while servants were housed in the garret. This arrangement by no means pleased all. Particularly irksome to many was the parlor floor, a socially required space that was seldom used. Because it separated the below-stairs family functions from the bedroom floors, where the informal sitting spaces were located, it not only condemned residents to endless stair-climbing but also contributed an abandoned look to the streetscape, particularly at night, when the parlor floors were frequently dark.

Given the obsessive individualism of most Americans, the brownstone was surprisingly uniform. While this could be justified as a logical reflection of democratic life in an increasingly mass society, it was more likely a by-product of the city's high real estate values, which turned most middle- and upper-middle-class families into renters. In order to get the best rates, these families moved each year from one house to another, with minimal disruption because all houses pretty much not only looked alike but were also planned alike.

In the 1870s the brownstone type began to change, with

the high-stooped English basement houses being replaced by lower-stooped designs that placed parlors and dining rooms on the same floor, with pantries located in rear extensions or in ells connecting to basement kitchens.[284] But by the late 1870s the fashion for brownstone, and for living in rows of identical houses, was over, replaced by an emphasis on individual, "artistic" houses. With the exception of a relative handful of palaces commissioned by the city's richest families, over the course of the next decade these individualized houses were very often built according to the freewheeling principles of the Queen Anne style. Montgomery Schuyler was of a mixed mind about the new fashion among the rich for commissioning their own houses rather than renting ones built by speculating developers: "Each man, in a certain circle, at least, tries now to get a house built for himself—with the inevitable result that sometimes you wish he wouldn't. But even crude vivacity is better than death, and of course the city is a great gainer by the process upon the whole."[285]

Brownstone's descent from fashion was not uniformly applauded. Though Mariana Van Rensselear, writing in 1886, found brownstone "cold and unattractive in color, and too poor in substance to receive carving well, or to stand well enough when not carved at all," she still refused to completely dismiss the brownstone era. The "'brownstone' front was as barren of true architectural ideas as the older brick box, but it sought stateliness by the aid of pedimented windows, of columned porticoes, and of heavy, overhanging cornices of zinc." It was, after all, a distinctly New York building type, "'a poor thing, but mine own,' a style—or, much more properly, a *pattern*—that we did not borrow ready-made, but formed by retaining the Dutch high-stoop, joining it to a provincial translation of Italian Renaissance ornament, and executing the result in a local material. The type has spread far and wide. . . . But *we* are responsible for it."[286]

Palaces on Parade

In April 1868, the recently founded *Real Estate Record and Builders' Guide* argued with only little exaggeration that post–Civil War New York was history's first great opportunity for "rich merchants and capitalists" to house themselves in splendid houses of a kind hitherto reserved for royalty. According to the magazine's editors, "by taking many an expensive house on Fifth Avenue, for instance, and contrasting them (artistically and inventively) with those of similar cost in the streets of Genoa; or by placing one of our any [*sic*] latest and most auspicious specimens of domestic architecture," such as Alexander T. Stewart's mansion at the corner of Thirty-fourth Street and Fifth Avenue (see below), "alongside of any of the thousand marble palaces of Venice, that probably never cost any-

William B. Astor II house, southwest corner of Fifth Avenue and West Thirty-fourth Street. Griffith Thomas, 1856. View to the northwest, 1893, showing the Alexander T. Stewart house (John Kellum, 1864–69) on the right. MCNY.

William B. Astor II house, southwest corner of Fifth Avenue and West Thirty-fourth Street. Griffith Thomas, 1856. View of ballroom, added by Thomas in 1875. NYHS.

thing near its outlay," there was much to be learned about "the tasteful appreciation and knowledge of the Fine Arts." But, the editors continued, "we have all the elements in our favor. . . . We have abundant evidence, from many a genuine work of art among us, as well as the boundless future before us, that the Fine Arts generally—and Architecture especially—are about to start . . . on a career unparalleled in the annals of the past."[287]

Although Fifth Avenue came into its own as a street of millionaires' palaces with the 1869 completion of Stewart's house, it had begun to reveal its destiny quite a bit earlier. Knickerbocker society lived downtown near City Hall, or around Washington Square, Union Square, and especially Gramercy Park. But Fifth Avenue attracted the big—that is to say, the "new"—money. The English novelist Anthony Trollope, who visited New York in 1861, felt that the city's rich were justified in flaunting their wealth along Fifth Avenue, although he snobbishly regretted that "no great man, no celebrated statesman, no philanthropist of

peculiar note" lived there: "The gentleman on the right made a million of dollars by inventing a shirt collar; this one on the left electrified the world by a lotion; as to the gentleman at the corner there,—there are rumours about him and the Cuban slave trade; but my informant by no means knows that they are true. Such are the aristocracy of Fifth Avenue."[288]

Knickerbocker society was basically a euphemism for pre–Revolutionary War rich. By this standard even the Astors were nouveau riche although they had so much money that their position among the top class was quickly established. The Astors were further able to enter the ranks of top society because they married well. William B. Astor II's wife was Caroline Schermerhorn, whose inherited position combined with her inherited and acquired wealth enabled her to rule New York society and limit its number to the four hundred people she could fit in her perfectly cubical thirty-five-by-thirty-five-foot ballroom. In 1875 Griffith Thomas had added this room to the

Alexander T. Stewart house, northwest corner of Fifth Avenue and West Thirty-fourth Street. John Kellum, 1864–69. View to the northwest, c. 1883. Rockwood. NYHS.

house he had designed nineteen years earlier, at the southwest corner of Fifth Avenue and Thirty-fourth Street.[289] Though paid for with new money, the Astors' generously proportioned, Italianate house, four stories plus a basement, was the last bastion of dull respectability for Old New York society. At the south end of the same Fifth Avenue block, William B. Astor II's older brother, John Jacob Astor II, occupied an equally conventional house (1859) built to a somewhat grander scale, with three high floors capped by a mansard. Between the Astor houses the remaining lots were kept open as a walled garden shared by the two families.

Prosperous and presentable though post–Civil War Fifth Avenue was, some found it wanting in charm. In his guidebook of 1869, *The Great Metropolis; a Mirror of New York,* Junius Henri Browne wrote:

> It is the habit of New Yorkers to style Fifth Avenue the first street in America. . . . The architecture is not only impressive, it is oppressive. Its great defect is in its monotony. . . . A variation, a contrast—would be a relief. . . . Block after block, mile upon mile, of the same lofty brown-stone, high stoop, broad-staired fronts wearies the eye. . . . One longs in the Avenue for more mar-

ble, more brick, more iron, more wood even—some change in the style and aspect of these sombre-seeming houses. . . . The stately mansions give the impression that they have all dreamed the same dream of beauty the same night, and in the morning have found it realized; so they frown sternly upon one another, for each has what the other wished, and should have had alone. It is a grievous pity that there is so much money there and so little taste.[290]

Ushering in a new, ostentatious era dominated by private house-building, Alexander T. Stewart's five-story-tall, blazingly white, marble-clad house (John Kellum, 1864–69), at the northwest corner of Fifth Avenue and Thirty-fourth Street, was the city's first residential showplace and a resounding response to Junius Henri Browne's call for architectural boldness.[291] The house was from the first known as the Marble Palace and, according to Mariana Van Rensselaer, was the first home in America "to suggest to the reportorial pen . . . [the] epithet 'palatial.'"[292] The Stewart mansion was built on the site of a mansion that had belonged to the late Dr. Samuel P. "Sarsaparilla" Townsend, who, upon making his fortune in the soda business, had built a four-story cubical freestanding brown-stone house (1854–55) that, though the city's largest pri-

View to the southwest along Fifth Avenue from Thirty-sixth Street, 1879, showing the Alexander T. Stewart house (John Kellum, 1864–69) in the center, and the William B. Astor II house (Griffith Thomas, 1856) and the John Jacob Astor II house (1859) directly south of Stewart's house. The Marble Collegiate Church (Samuel A. Warner, 1851–54) is on the far left. NYHS.

Dr. Samuel P. "Sarsaparilla" Townsend house (1854–55), northwest corner of Fifth Avenue and West Thirty-fourth Street. View to the northwest, c. 1860. MCNY.

vate dwelling, was of no particular artistic value.[293] In the late 1850s, after the sarsaparilla king lost his money and died, the property passed via Dr. G. D. Abbott to Stewart, who originally intended to renovate the house, tearing out the interior except for the floor joists. Stewart then changed his mind and tore the house entirely down, including the foundations, and commissioned a design for a new house from John Kellum, who had recently designed Stewart's dry-goods palace on Broadway and Tenth Street (see chapter 5). The prospect of Stewart's new mansion filled the Knickerbocker diarist George Templeton Strong with something akin to terror. In his diary entry for March 21, 1864, Strong recorded going "up Fifth Avenue this morning to call on Mrs. William Astor, and get instructions for drawing her will," only to find that the "great, hideous one hundred-thousand dollar Townsend-Sarsparilla-Springer house on the other side of Thirty-fourth Street has just been bought by A. T. Stewart, who has razed it to the ground and tells William Astor he is going to lay out one million on a new white marble palazzo. I suppose it will be just ten times as ugly and barbaric as its predecessor, if that be conceivable."[294]

Technically speaking, Stewart's was not New York's first palazzo. That distinction belongs to the John T. Johnston house (1856), designed by Alfred J. Bloor, at the southeast corner of Fifth Avenue and Eighth Street. Faced with slate-gray quarry stone from Lee, Massachusetts, which whitens over time, Bloor's Renaissance-inspired design broke with the prevailing rowhouse pattern of its neighborhood but was a fundamentally subdued statement that grew bolder as the Lee stone weathered. As Mosette Broderick has suggested, this perhaps inspired Stewart to choose a white marble that would be bright from the first.[295]

Stewart was not only an important merchant but, after John Jacob Astor II, also the city's largest private landholder. Though he was rich and educated—he had begun life as a schoolteacher—and he and his family were widely traveled in Europe, Stewart, a Scotch-Irish immigrant rising to riches in trade, was not treated as an equal by members of established Knickerbocker society. A shrewd businessman with a reputation for being tight with his money, Stewart was surprisingly casual about the construction of his own house, which took the better part of five years, beginning in 1864, to reach completion. Said to have required the labor of five hundred workers, construction progressed rapidly at times but often ground to a halt. The stop-and-go progress of the job contributed to the public's fascination with the project, stimulating, according to Peter B. Wight, "more surmise and gossip than any other house ever erected in America. It became, in the public mind, another Fonthill Abbey, though unlike that structure, it was never in any danger of falling down."[296]

Kellum's floridly detailed, freestanding palazzo was in the view of many just about as bad as George Templeton Strong had feared it would be. Its whiteness—not to mention its size, its imposing monumentality, and detailing of equal richness on all four facades—made the neighboring brownstone houses, even Caroline Astor's across Thirty-fourth Street, seem modest and dowdy by comparison. This incongruence was exacerbated by that fact that it was separated from its neighbors and the two streets it faced by a deep moat surrounded by a stone balustrade. Beyond its obvious Classicism and a vague Frenchness, the building's style was elusive. Some called it pure Corinthian, and in later life Catherine Howland Hunt, the architect's widow, recalled Stewart having once described the house as Greek, causing Richard Morris Hunt to reply: "Well Mr. Stewart, it may be Greek to you, I assure you it is 'Greek to me' but I don't think it would deceive the smallest little yellow dog that runs down the street."[297]

If not exactly a design breakthrough, the house was at least grand and well built. A 120-by-72-and-a-half-foot structure, it was compact in mass and clear in composition, factors that further separated it from the rather more casually conceived brownstone rank and file that characterized the city's Civil War–era mansions. The pavilionated composition of the six-bay-wide principal facades, though awkwardly detailed, was an impressive prelude to the fifty-five lavishly furnished rooms inside, many appointed with Carrara marble or painted panels. Steps led up from Thirty-fourth Street to the principal rooms on the raised ground floor, including the hall, reception, dining, and drawing rooms as well as an art gallery, which was housed in an almost two-story-high lower wing that extended from the northwest corner of the main mass. The second floor of the house contained the principal bedrooms as well as a sitting room and a billiards room, all enjoying the benefit of eighteen-foot-nine-inch ceilings. The third floor also contained well-proportioned bedrooms and sitting rooms, while above a six-foot-high entresol contained eight rooms. Two more floors of rooms, with higher ceilings, were housed in the mansard. To contemporary observers, such as the editors of *Harper's Weekly*, the house seemed decidedly undomestic: "Everyone who looks upon the result must feel that this splendid palace was never designed primarily for a private dwelling. It is a temple rather than a mansion." They argued that the "building, with scarcely an alteration of its rooms, could be transformed into a magnificent art gallery. It almost astonishes us to hear the architect speak of this as a reception room, of that as a breakfast room, and of another as the parlor. The beautiful wardrobe and bath rooms are the only portions of the house which distinctly suggest the idea of a private residence."[298]

The house was indeed filled with art, some of it of quite high quality. Rooms opened off the main hall, articulated by Corinthian columns and lined with sculpture by contemporary Europeans as well as the Americans Thomas Crawford and Harriet Hosmer. The main hall led to the seventy-foot-long, thirty-foot-wide, fifty-foot-tall picture gallery, windowless but with a glass and iron skylight, where about 150 works were displayed, including three paintings by Jean-Léon Gérôme, three by A. D. Bougereau, and four by J. L.

Alexander T. Stewart house, northwest corner of Fifth Avenue and West Thirty-fourth Street. John Kellum, 1864–69. Hall. AH. CU.

Meissonier. Also displayed were Rosa Bonheur's *The Horse Fair* (1853) and Frederic Church's *Niagara from the American Side* (1867), an enormous, eight-by-five-foot environmental canvas, as well as examples of work by other Americans, including Albert Bierstadt, and sculpture including two works by Hiram Powers.

In part, perhaps, because of a prejudice against its owner, in part because its self-trained architect was not respected, the Stewart house was the focus of widespread contempt among the architectural cognoscenti. The *Real Estate Record and Builders' Guide* denounced it as an "architectural abortion,"[299] and Peter B. Wight wondered how "anyone surrounded by works of art . . . could have . . . so little understanding of what constituted a work of architecture."[300] Long after it was completed it continued to fascinate—or perhaps repel—critics. Mariana Van Rensselaer's assessment of 1886 was perhaps the fairest:

> The great marble house . . . was one of our earliest attempts at novelty, and in ambition it has certainly not since been surpassed. But it was not really a new depar-

ture—it was merely an effort to glorify the "vernacular" by increase of size, by isolation, and by change of materials. In the last-named respect the effort was commendable . . . [but] here we have no good proportioning and no skillfull composition either with masses or with features. Beauty has been sought only in the applied columnar decoration, and this is not architecturally valuable because it has been used without moderation, without care for contrast or relief or structural or artistic grace in execution. We can only call it a very showy house, and add that to some eyes it may seem imposing.[301]

Stewart's marble home set the standard for rich men's houses in the Gilded Age. By the very nature of its size, position, and publicity, it also became New York's most visible symbol of the growing split between the extreme wealth of a few and the extreme poverty of very many. Matthew Hale Smith contrasted Stewart's house with the squalor of the Five Points slums by using images of each to render vivid the title of his popular guidebook of 1868, *Sunshine and Shadow in New York*.[302] The house's construc-

Alexander T. Stewart house, northwest corner of Fifth Avenue and West Thirty-fourth Street. John Kellum, 1864–69. Picture gallery. AH. CU.

tion was celebrated as a kind of force majeure. *Appleton's New York Illustrated* gushed that "of all the famous buildings on Fifth Avenue, none will ever be so famous. . . . Words are absolutely inadequate to describe its beauty and unique grandeur," while the *New York Sun* saw Stewart's private investment as a significant public gesture.[303] The editors of *Harper's Weekly* hailed the Stewart house as a work far and away more remarkable than any other in New York, "one edifice in New York that if not swallowed by an earthquake, will stand as long as the city remains."[304] But they were wrong. Stewart got only seven years of pleasure from his palace before dying, in 1876. His widow survived him for another ten years, whereupon the house was leased to the Manhattan Club, which after eight years' use found it too expensive to maintain and decamped. In 1901 Stewart's palace was demolished to make way for McKim, Mead & White's Knickerbocker Trust Company.[305]

Different as its design was from the characteristic brownstone houses of its day, Stewart's Marble Palace was safely located in the "heart of uptown" and well within the boundaries of fashion, which extended along Fifth Avenue as far north as the lower Forties, at the top of Murray Hill. Much farther uptown, two sisters, Mary and Rebecca Mason, married to and widowed by two Knickerbocker cousins, Colford and Isaac Jones, were pioneering new ground on Fifth Avenue just below Central Park. Taking advantage of inherited farmland that had been purchased in 1823 by their father, John Mason, one of the founders of Chemical Bank, the two sisters decided to develop two block-long rows of near-mansion-sized houses and each live in one of the houses themselves. Mary Mason Jones commissioned Robert Mook to design a row of houses on the east blockfront between Fifty-seventh and Fifty-eighth Streets and Rebecca Colford Jones hired Detlef Lienau for a row on the east blockfront between Fifty-fifth and Fifty-sixth Streets. In each case, in a departure from typical practice whereby identical units were built to form brownstone rows, the rowhouses were built with the intention of creating the impression of an aggregated or collective dwelling, such as had been developed only a few

Frontispiece from Matthew Hale Smith's Sunshine and Shadow in New York *(1868), contrasting the Alexander T. Stewart house (John Kellum, 1864–69) with a view of the Five Points slums. SSNY. CU.*

times before in New York. Predecessors included Alexander Jackson Davis's La Grange Terrace (1832–33), also known as Colonnade Row, commissioned by Seth Geer, on the west side of Lafayette Place between East Fourth Street and Astor Place, and Davis's Gothic-style House of Mansions (1856), commissioned by George Higgins, on the east side of Fifth Avenue between Forty-first and Forty-second Streets, consisting of eleven attached houses that formed an overall composition.[306]

Mary Mason Jones, recently widowed and just returned from Paris, took the lead with Mook's design for a seven-unit, white-marble-clad row (1867–69), at 734–745 Fifth Avenue, that would soon be called Marble Row.[307] The development consisted of boldly mansarded houses in a version of the French Renaissance–inspired style that had recently been used for the new pavilions at the Louvre. The first of the houses in the development to be built, on the northeast corner of Fifth Avenue and Fifty-seventh Street, was reserved for Mary Mason Jones's own use. Jones was an aunt of Edith Wharton and the basis for

Wharton's character Mrs. Manson Mingott, who sat in the isolated splendor of her new house far above the developed part of the city, "watching calmly for life and fashion to flow northward to her solitary doors."[308] Jones set the fashion for building up near Central Park and made it acceptable for even Knickerbocker families to live in a conspicuously lavish way; it is said that the phrase "keeping up with the Joneses" was coined about her. In 1870, just to the east of her house, Jones sold a parcel of land to the iron merchant Sidney W. Hopkins, who commissioned a three-house, red brick and Ohio stone row (1871), at 13–17 East Fifty-seventh Street, from Arthur D. Gilman.[309] Hopkins occupied the center, forty-three-foot-wide house at number 15 and sold the sixteen-foot-wide houses at numbers 13 and 17 to the flour merchant George Hollister and the iron dealer William Atwater respectively. Detlef Lienau's eight-house row (1869–70) at 705–719 Fifth Avenue, for Rebecca Colford Jones, kept pace with French fashion like Mook's row, though it was compositionally less bold, shifting the emphasis away from the corners, reserving the two tallest units for the third points of the avenue facades.[310] The elegantly articulated row was clad in light Ohio stone, making it seem quite grand, an impression enhanced by the use of a colossal order of Corinthian pilasters that visually tied together the two principal bedroom floors.

The Marble Palace and the two Jones developments marked the end points of the stretch of Fifth Avenue that would in the 1880s be transformed from a virtually featureless wasteland into the most desirable stretch of the nation's most famous residential street and the preeminent monument to the opulence of the Gilded Age. Though houses of worship, including St. Patrick's Cathedral (1850–79, 1888) and Temple Emanu-El (1868), as well as a few hotels, notably the Buckingham (1876), were first to come, the stretch of Fifth Avenue between Thirty-fourth Street and the Plaza was to become a parade ground of private residential palaces set out for public review. At the head of the parade, and by sheer number dominating the scene, were the six houses built by members of the Vanderbilt family between 1878 and 1882, beginning with the matched pair of houses built by William Henry Vanderbilt.[311] The southern one, at 640 Fifth Avenue, was created for Vanderbilt's own use, and the northern one, a double unit on the same block, was to be shared by his daughters Mrs. William Douglas Sloane, at 642 Fifth Avenue, and Mrs. Elliot Fitch Shephard, at 2 West Fifty-second Street.

In 1877, William H. Vanderbilt had inherited about ninety million dollars from his late father, Cornelius, and became president of the New York Central Railroad. Now arguably the richest man in America, perhaps in the world, Vanderbilt wanted to build a new house, although his wife, Maria Louisa Kissam, the daughter of a Brooklyn minister, was quite content to remain at 459 Fifth Avenue, on the southeast corner of Fortieth Street, where they had been living since 1867. As the couple's children were grown, Mrs. Vanderbilt proposed instead that a new wing

House of Mansions, east side of Fifth Avenue between East Forty-first and East Forty-second Streets. Alexander Jackson Davis, 1856. View to the northeast, c. 1875, showing Temple Emanu-El (Leopold Eidlitz and Henry Fernbach, 1868) on the left. NYHS.

Marble Row, east side of Fifth Avenue between East Fifty-seventh and East Fifty-eighth Streets. Robert Mook, 1867–69. View to the northeast, 1875. MCNY.

View to the northwest from East Fifty-fourth Street between Madison and Fourth Avenues, 1871, showing the Mary Mason Jones house, part of Marble Row (Robert Mook, 1867–69), on the left; the mansarded 13–17 East Fifty-seventh Street (Arthur Gilman, 1871) in the center; and the Madison Avenue Reformed Church (E. L. Roberts, 1869–71) on the right. MCNY.

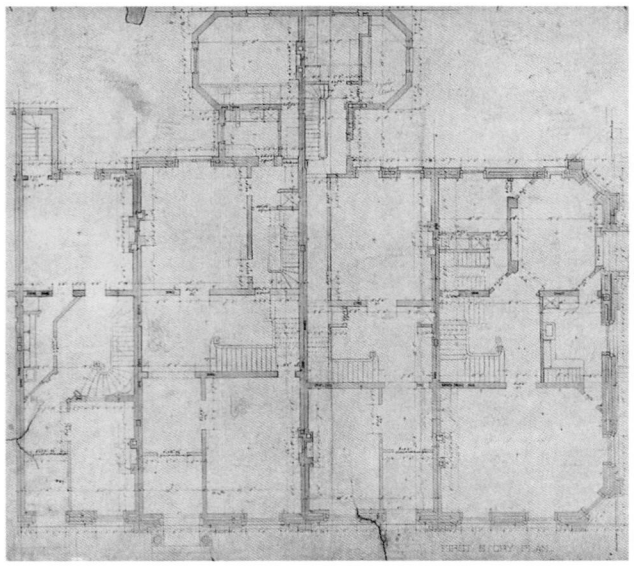

Rebecca Colford Jones row, east side of Fifth Avenue between East Fifty-fifth and East Fifty-sixth Streets. Detlef Lienau, 1869–70. View to the southeast. Lienau Collection. CU.

Rebecca Colford Jones row, east side of Fifth Avenue between East Fifty-fifth and East Fifty-sixth Streets. Detlef Lienau, 1869–70. First-floor plan. Lienau Collection. CU.

be added on to the house to provide hanging space for her husband's rapidly expanding collection of paintings. But Mr. Vanderbilt had bigger plans and the Fortieth Street house was ultimately given to his son Frederick. In January 1879, after arguments over his father's will had been resolved, William H. Vanderbilt purchased a one-hundred-foot-deep blockfront of vacant land on the west side of Fifth Avenue between Fifty-first and Fifty-second Streets, thereby setting in motion the family's spree of home building along Fifth Avenue that would soon transform the stretch between Fifty-first and Fifty-seventh Streets into Vanderbilt Row. At the same time, William H. Vanderbilt's second son, William Kissam, announced that he would build a house on a one-hundred-foot-wide lot on the northwest corner of Fifth Avenue and Fifty-second Street, and it was rumored that the eldest son, Cornelius II, was purchasing land facing Fifth Avenue at the northwest corner of Fifty-seventh Street.

The Vanderbilts did not choose to settle a bit farther uptown where they could easily have occupied spacious lots facing Central Park, surely a decision not made because of the inadequacy of public transit. Probably, as the *Real Estate Record and Builders' Guide* suggested, the park-facing blocks of Fifth Avenue lacked appeal because "as fastidious as we know our wealthy people to be, they are also gregarious and social beings, and pre-eminently of all classes are dependent on daily, even though dumb intercourse with their neighbors. . . . To our minds it is questionable, whether a really fashionable quarter could be established without opposite neighbors or without at least, the intervening space being so small as to admit of visual contact."[312] The Vanderbilts' uptown move stimulated others to follow, abandoning Fifth Avenue between Madison Square and Thirty-fourth Street to the exclusive shops that quickly occupied converted ground-floor space in the houses that had until recently housed the rich.[313]

Vanderbilt purchased the blockfront for $500,000—a drastic reduction from the asking price of $800,000 before the Panic of 1873, which Vanderbilt, alone among the big tycoons, had weathered with virtually no loss of capital. Stock-market economics may have reduced the land's value, but also to be considered was the weekly arrival for St. Patrick's Sunday masses of hordes of Irish immigrants and the scandalous presence across the street of the society abortionist Madame Restell, who died just as Vanderbilt was buying his land.

Virtually identical, William H. Vanderbilt's two brownstone houses quickly came to be known alternately as the "Vanderbilt Twins" or the "Triple Palace," given the fact that the northernmost house was actually a double unit. By undertaking to build for his own use a house that closely mirrored his personal taste and showcased his art collection, Vanderbilt was intent on outshining the recently deceased Alexander T. Stewart. More importantly, he was committed to making a name for himself independent of his father's and to smoothing out the rough edges on his family's reputation that had been created by the Commodore's blustery nature.

In 1883, to celebrate the completion of the house, Vanderbilt authorized, and probably paid for, a lavish two-volume work written by Earl Shinn, using the pseudonym Edward Strahan, entitled *Mr. Vanderbilt's House and Collection*, which opens with a clear declaration of the railroad king's ambitions for the project:

> In these volumes we are permitted to make a revelation of a private home which better than any other possible selection may stand as a representative of the new impulse now felt in the national life. Like a more perfect Pompeii, the work will be the vision and image of a typical American residence, seized at the moment when the nation begins to have a taste of its own. . . . The country, at this moment, is just beginning to be astonishing. Re-cemented by the fortunate result of a civil war, endowed as with a diploma of rank by the promulgation of its centenary, it has begun to re-invent everything and especially the House.[314]

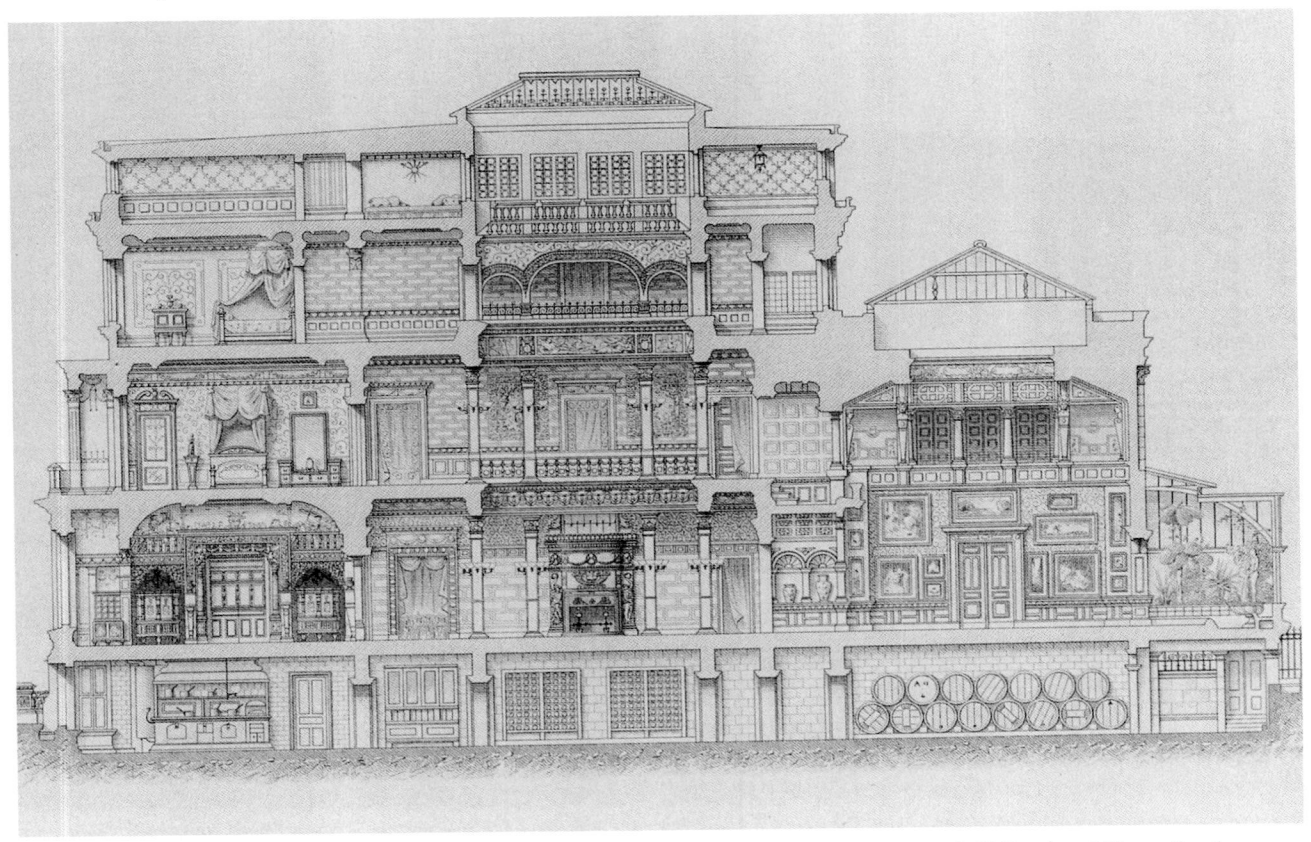

William Henry Vanderbilt house, northwest corner of Fifth Avenue and West Fifty-first Street. Trench & Snook and Herter Brothers, 1879–82. Section. MVHC. CU.

View to the northwest along Fifth Avenue from Fifty-first Street, 1894, showing, from left to right, the William Henry Vanderbilt Triple Palace (Trench & Snook and Herter Brothers, 1879–82), the William Kissam Vanderbilt house (Richard Morris Hunt, 1878–82), St. Thomas Church (Richard and Richard M. Upjohn, 1865), and the Fifth Avenue Presbyterian Church (Carl Pfeiffer, 1875). Johnston. MCNY.

Vanderbilt's desire to set an example was not merely lip service. When the house was completed, by invitation on Thursdays from 11:00 A.M. to 4:00 P.M., members of the public could enter the galleries through a special door on Fifty-first Street to experience the art and its setting and, presumably, come away with a heightened ambition for their own collections and building projects. On December 20, 1883, after Vanderbilt had added on to his gallery and built a new glassed-in winter garden, he invited 3,000 business associates, out-of-town visitors, and most of the city's art community to an "art levee." The invitation was accepted by 2,500, and they were admitted through the front door, where Vanderbilt greeted them and attempted to expound on the collection. But many of the guests were more interested in the house. According to the *New York Times*, "Young men in dress suits, business suits, and threadbare Prince Alberts roamed all over. . . . They took down the books from the shelves of the elegant library, poked the blazing logs on the andirons in the private parlors, and wandered at will into the richly furnished bed-chambers."[315]

To supervise the construction of the Triple Palace, Vanderbilt turned to the established but plodding firm of Trench & Snook, which had worked for him on two business projects, St. John's Terminal (1867–68) (see chapter 3) and Grand Central Depot (1869–71) (see chapter 1). The firm had also designed Commodore Vanderbilt's house at 10 Washington Place (1845).[316] John B. Snook often took more claim for William H. Vanderbilt's project than he deserved, introducing himself as the building's architect when he escorted the press through the house during construction. In point of fact, Vanderbilt hired the firm of Herter Brothers, one of New York's leading cabinetmakers and decorators, to design the house. Herter Brothers had on their payroll the architect Charles B. Atwood, who was put in charge of the architectural aspects of the interiors and who may well have been given full responsibility for the overall design of the buildings themselves, with Snook seeing to the technical side. Atwood, educated at Harvard University's Lawrence Scientific School, was a key member of the firm, which, since the return to Europe of Gustave Herter in 1870, was led by Christian Herter, his younger and more gifted stepbrother. Christian Herter died in 1883 at the age of forty-four, marking the end of the firm's importance, but Atwood would go on to serve as the architect of the Peristyle and the Art Building at the World's Columbian Exposition of 1893, in Chicago, and to work in the office of Daniel Burnham, where Atwood was credited with a number of important buildings.[317]

Vanderbilt's Triple Palace was completed in 1882, taking dramatically less time than Stewart's house but using an army of labor estimated at between 600 and 700 workers, 250 of whom were solely occupied with the interior carving. Vanderbilt was intimately involved in every detail of the construction, visiting the site or the Herter Brothers shops on a daily basis. Two-thirds of the two million dollars spent on the construction and decoration of the pair went to his own house, which had fifty-eight rooms. In 1885 William Baumgarten, the Herter Brothers general management assistant at the time of the Vanderbilt commission, recalled to a reporter: "We have rarely had a customer who took such a personal interest in the work during its progress. All the designs were submitted to him from the first stone to the last piece of decoration or furniture. Mr. Vanderbilt was at our warerooms or at our shops almost every day for a year. He spent hours in the designing rooms, and often looked on while the workmen were busy in the shops."[318]

Although Snook and Atwood preferred light-colored Ohio limestone trimmed in red and black marble, Vanderbilt, perhaps in reaction to the blazing whiteness of Stewart's palace, insisted on brownstone, which was not only humbler because it was familiar but also cheaper and quicker to erect. This caused Montgomery Schuyler to wonder "how so much good work . . . can be so ineffective. The material, a very dark, almost black Connecticut brownstone, which has been almost discarded for many years by reason of its friableness and tendency to rapid decay, is against the effect of the buildings, but the design is still more unfavorable." Stewart had been fighting his reputation as a tightwad by splurging on white marble, but Vanderbilt, not burdened with this particular reputation, chose to be quiet and thrifty, leading Schuyler to observe that in "size and cost, these Vanderbilt houses are the most 'important' dwellings which have been built in New York since the 'palatial mansion' in white marble of Mr. Stewart, which probably cost more than any two of the Vanderbilt houses, and possibly as much as all four."[319]

Brownstone it was, but as Mariana Van Rensselaer observed, pointedly correcting her friend Schuyler, it was

> not of the old poor quality, and used in a very different manner. They are not ostentatious or vulgar or distressingly ugly houses, but neither are they really good or beautiful. In their quieter way they are great architectural sinners too. Stripped of their carving, they would be, as I have heard it expressed, merely "brown-stone packing-boxes." And their carving does not help them save to a superficial eye. We know that decoration is not *architectural* decoration unless it emphasizes construction. I may add that it is not architectural decoration unless it is *itself constructed*. Here neither requirement is fulfilled. The carving—one must not call it by any nobler name—is applied in just those places where it does not belong, and where it hurts, not helps, the structural expression. And it is not itself in any sense constructed. It consists simply of broad bands (of naturalistic foliage for the most part) which have no beginnings or endings, no moldings or framings, nothing to prove that they were designed for the role which they attempt, much less for the places that they fill. Their relief, moreover, is so low and uniform that they suffer doubly from want of proper setting, and utterly fail to perform not only the first purpose of orna-

ment, structural emphasis, but the second also, the creation of effects of light and shadow. Abstractly considered, the carving is pretty enough in design and quite charming in execution; but in both respects it is carving such as a cabinet-maker might use in wood, not such as an architect should use in stone. And, I repeat, it is displayed for its own sake only. It is an interesting testimony to the fact that these dwellings were built, in truth, not by an architect, but by a clever decorator of interiors.[320]

Montgomery Schuyler disliked the Free Classical approach Atwood's design represented, objecting to the use of the orders as representations of structure but not as the structure themselves. Nonetheless he praised the work as being the best of its kind: Free Classicism "is seldom done with the winning candor with which it has been done in the house of Mr. W. H. Vanderbilt . . . which is officially described as a specimen of the 'Greek Renaissance,' possibly because its details are all Roman." Schuyler objected to the "two kinds of exquisite carving [that] girdle the building . . . at levels where they are quite meaningless . . . , where, consequently, they would not help the expression of the building, if the building can be said to have any expression beyond that of settled gloom." In sum, Schuyler dismissed the houses as "those boxes of brown stone with architecture appliqué,"[321] laying responsibility on Atwood: "If these Vanderbilt houses are the result of intrusting architectural design to decorators, it is to be hoped the experiment may not be repeated."[322]

The Vanderbilt Twins were virtually identical cubic pavilions set back and separated from the sidewalks by a shallow moat bounded by a low iron balustrade punctuated by stone piers. From the street the houses appeared to have only three floors above a basement, but a fourth floor was tucked away at the top behind a stone balustrade. The two principal floors were sixteen and a half feet high and the third floor fifteen feet. The houses were each approximately 80 by 115 feet, leaving little space around them and thereby compromising their status as urban villas. The press frequently rumored that to provide breathing room, Vanderbilt had it in mind to buy the Roman Catholic orphanage across Fifth Avenue and create a garden forecourt.

On January 17, 1882, two thousand people came to the opening reception, where they were greeted by interiors of stupendous opulence that revealed a higher level of taste and connoisseurship than had ever been seen in New York. Entering from the north side, where a lobby connected the two houses, visitors found themselves in a spectacular, indeed virtually overwhelming Pompeian room with marble walls and marble mosaic on both the ceiling and the floor; it was said that this was the first use of marble mosaic in America. At the center a nearly six-foot-tall Russian malachite vase with French gilt-bronze mounts, made in approximately 1819, was elevated on a pedestal. Visitors were then escorted past gilt-bronze copies of Lorenzo Ghiberti's *Gates of Paradise* doors, cast in Paris in 1878, into a grand sixty-by-forty-foot atrium-

William Henry Vanderbilt house, northwest corner of Fifth Avenue and West Fifty-first Street. Trench & Snook and Herter Brothers, 1879–82. Drawing room. AH. CU.

like hall punctuated by eight square columns of dark red African marble with bronze capitals, carrying galleries and rising through the full height of the house to a leaded-glass skylight. To one side a grand staircase was illuminated by nine stained-glass windows designed by John La Farge, depicting such appropriate allegorical figures as Prosperitas, Hospitalitas, and Commerce. The interiors were not merely lavish: they were vivid. George W. Sheldon wrote that "everything sparkles and flashes with gold and color—with mother of pearl, with marbles, with jewel-effects in glass—almost every surface is covered, one might say weighted, with ornament." Beyond the hall lay the thirty-one-by-twenty-five-foot drawing room, with its extensive use of mother-of-pearl and gilt and a remarkable mural for the ceiling cove by Pierre-Victor Galland. The mural and the rest of the room were extraordinary when illuminated, with light reflected from the mother-of-pearl butterflies and the cut crystal sewn on the red velvet walls, transforming the room, according to Sheldon, into "an illustration to some of the most opulent pages of the 'Thousand and One Nights.'"[323] The library, also with glittering and shimmering mother-of-pearl surfaces, was Vanderbilt's favorite room. The forty-

eight-by-thirty-two-foot picture gallery was more conventional, but the Japanese parlor, designed to show off Vanderbilt's collection of blue, brown, and yellow porcelain, was a tour de force comparable in its way to the drawing room, with a network of delicate split-bamboo nailed to the ceiling contrasting with rafters that were stained and enameled to simulate red lacquer.[324]

At the same time he was working on the Vanderbilt Twins, Snook also helped to construct another pair of houses, presumably also designed by Charles B. Atwood, for Vanderbilt's other two married daughters, Mrs. William Seward Webb, at 680 Fifth Avenue, and Mrs. Hamilton McKown Twombly, at 684 Fifth Avenue, on the southwest corner of Fifty-fourth Street.[325] The houses did not take their cue from the Twins but from the house designed by Richard Morris Hunt for William K. Vanderbilt and the house designed by George B. Post for Cornelius Vanderbilt II (see below), leading the *Real Estate Record and Builders' Guide*'s critic, surely Montgomery Schuyler, to proclaim them a summary "on two lots [of] all the features of all the other Vanderbilt houses. . . . The featureless houses built for Mr. Vanderbilt himself are succeeded here by fronts which have features so multiplied

William Henry Vanderbilt house, northwest corner of Fifth Avenue and West Fifty-first Street. Trench & Snook and Herter Brothers, 1879–82. Hall. AH. CU.

William Henry Vanderbilt house, northwest corner of Fifth Avenue and West Fifty-first Street. Trench & Snook and Herter Brothers, 1879–82. Library. AH. CU.

William Henry Vanderbilt house, northwest corner of Fifth Avenue and West Fifty-first Street. Trench & Snook and Herter Brothers, 1879–82. Japanese parlor. AH. CU.

William Henry Vanderbilt house, northwest corner of Fifth Avenue and West Fifty-first Street. Trench & Snook and Herter Brothers, 1879–82. Picture gallery. AH. CU.

Mrs. Hamilton McKown Twombly house, 684 Fifth Avenue, southwest corner of West Fifty-fourth Street, on the right, and Mrs. William Seward Webb house, 680 Fifth Avenue, on the left. Trench & Snook and Herter Brothers, 1882–84. View to the southwest, c. 1885, also showing St. Thomas Church (Richard and Richard M. Upjohn, 1865). LAA. CU.

William Kissam Vanderbilt house, northwest corner of Fifth Avenue and West Fifty-second Street. Richard Morris Hunt, 1878–82. View to the northwest. MCNY.

that the effect is much as if one should come upon a countenance furnished with five eyes and three noses." The Webb and Twombly houses, he continued,

> are perhaps the thingiest edifices in New York. . . . The one glimmering of purpose that can be made out is the purpose of making two French Renaissance houses, the southern inclining most to the Gothic, and the northern to the classic. . . . The highest architectural skill could not work in so many things in a building of this size so as to secure a harmonious and reposeful result, and there does not seem to have been any effort here either at harmony or repose. The architect seems to have been penetrated by the consciousness that he had a great deal of money to spend, and the only way in which it occurred to him to spend it was to make many things. The money was evidently not spent in order to carry out a design, but the design was made in order to spend the money. The things look as if they had been thrown at the building rather than grown out of it, and as many seem to have been thrown as would stick. The result is ostentation and variety of a kind, but where there is no general motive, by which unity in variety is obtained, variety is miscellany, and these houses are not works of architecture, but collections of objects of architecture.[326]

Soon after William H. Vanderbilt acquired his block-front, the city was electrified by the news that his son

William Kissam Vanderbilt house, northwest corner of Fifth Avenue and West Fifty-second Street. Richard Morris Hunt, 1878–82. Oriel. WKV. CU.

William Kissam Vanderbilt had bought the next site up the avenue, at the northwest corner of Fifty-second Street, where he proposed to build a house designed by Richard Morris Hunt.[327] Hunt began work in 1878, and 660 Fifth Avenue was completed four years later. Like his father, young William was able to take on a major building project as a result of the settlement of the Commodore's estate. It was logical that the thirty-nine-year-old Vanderbilt should turn to Hunt, who had designed an earlier project for him, a Queen Anne–style country house in Oakdale, Long Island.[328] Vanderbilt requested a house "with air and breathing space around it," but Hunt argued, to no avail, that the 100-by-125-foot lot was not big enough, and that his client should buy the rest of the Fifth Avenue blockfront, a suggestion Vanderbilt later regretted not taking.[329] After sketches for a number of alternate designs had been prepared, Vanderbilt and Hunt settled on one in the French Renaissance style of Francis I. Construction began at the end of 1879, and though the house was basically finished in 1882, some interior details were lacking until 1883. With the William K. Vanderbilt house Hunt was able to come to terms with the struggle between Classical planning and Gothic form that had characterized his early career by adopting what Sarah Bradford Landau has described as "a legitimately composite style," that of the French Renaissance, which combined the two.[330] Hunt's design carried further ideas he

had first explored in 1870–71 in his unrealized design for a residence for Jim Fisk, which was to have been built on Fifth Avenue and Seventieth Street.[331] But Hunt's scheme for Vanderbilt was a fresh composition and much more assured in massing and detail than the one he had drawn for Fisk, although both owed a great deal to a number of French prototypes, especially the château at Blois. The telling source of inspiration, however, may have been the mansion built in the heart of Bourges by a fourteenth-century Vanderbilt-like businessman, Jacques Coeur.

William K. Vanderbilt—or Willie, as he was known—was affable and well educated, unlike his Vanderbilt forebears. As he was very busy with his business interests, responsibility for the project fell to his twenty-five-year-old wife of three years, Alva Smith Vanderbilt, a headstrong woman who ruled the roost in most matters. The Southern-born daughter of a Mobile, Alabama, cotton merchant, Alva grew up in New York but lived briefly in Paris after the Civil War. While stories about Alva are frequently unreliable, it does seem that she had a real flair for architecture. According to Catherine Howland Hunt, Richard Morris Hunt "had the greatest admiration for [her] intellect and broad grasp of architecture and often said: 'She's a wonder.'"[332] Even more than the construction of the Stewart mansion or the other Vanderbilt homes, the construction of Hunt's château took New York by storm. Set behind a shallow grassy moat, the light gray Indiana limestone house seemed distinctly at odds with its context, not because it was as big or bright as Stewart's had been but because it was complex and subtle. Broken into elements, the house was further articulated by bay windows, oriels, elaborately pedimented dormers, and balconies. A slender corbelled tourelle, the most memorable feature, emerged from the Fifth Avenue facade to one side of the front door and rose to a conical roof. Despite the richness of the detail and the complexity of the massing, the design seemed calm, in part because of the broad expanses of unbroken wall Hunt used to counterbalance the ornament.

Though he was not totally comfortable with Hunt's stylistic specificity, Montgomery Schuyler in 1881 praised the still incomplete house for making "the greatful impression of being emphatically a building. In spite of all the richness . . . the main impression is of weight and mass."[333] In 1882 Schuyler amplified his views: "In this a design intrinsically interesting has been carried out with an amplitude of means of all kinds which yet nowhere degenerates into profusion or mere ostentation."[334] Schuyler was impressed with the decision to use "soft gray" Indiana limestone and with the quality of the decoration and its "exquisite execution." But "above all" he found the house "quiet and dignified."[335] Compared to William H. Vanderbilt's Triple Palace, Mariana Van Rensselaer proclaimed that Hunt's design for William K. Vanderbilt

is a house and not a carver's chest. I think, too, that it is the most beautiful house in New York. . . . We may pick

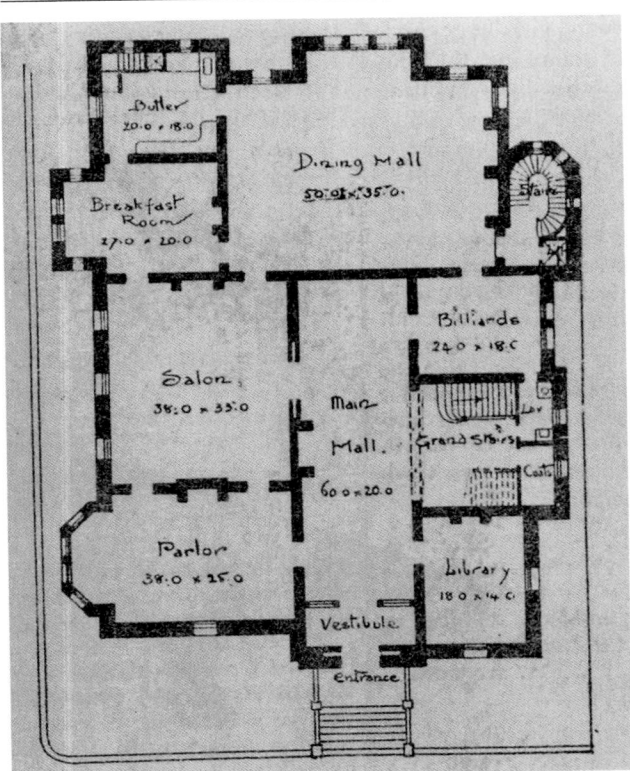
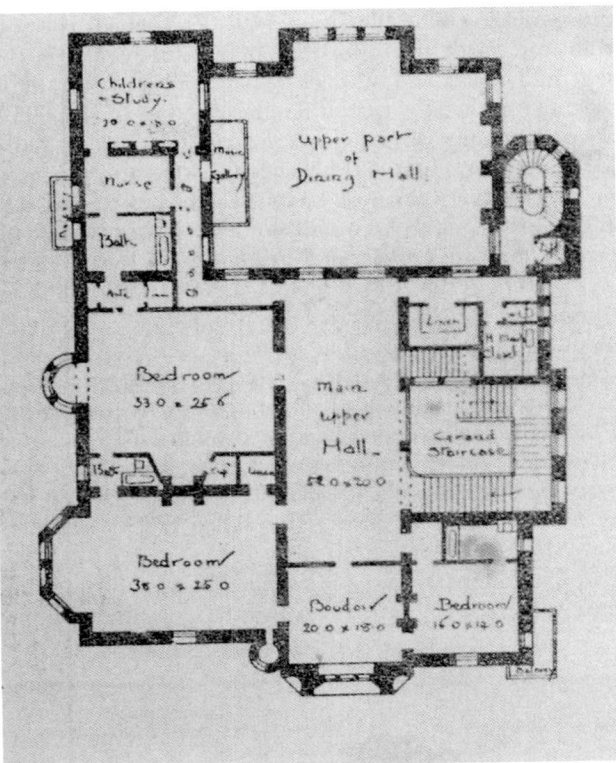

William Kissam Vanderbilt house, northwest corner of Fifth Avenue and West Fifty-second Street. Richard Morris Hunt, 1878–82. Plans. AABN. CU.

little faults in his building if we will. We may say—and the more we admire it the more apt we are to say, I think—that it would be better as a country than as a city house. We may think, too, that it has an overabundance of features; yet unity of effect has not been sacrificed to them—unless, perhaps, in the treatment of the roof. We may feel, again, that since it *is* a city house its ornamentation is rather too profuse and delicate. But it is so skillfully applied and so charmingly executed, is so *architectural* in spite of its delicacy, that we have not the heart to wish it altered. . . . If we examine his decoration closely, moreover, we shall see how great an improvement we have made in manual skill. What would have been the use had Mr. Hunt designed such work even a dozen years ago? Can we think with tolerance of how it would then have been translated into stone?[336]

Most American architects agreed with Schuyler and Van Rensselaer. In a survey of seventy-five of the country's leading practitioners taken in 1885, just two years after its completion, Vanderbilt's was the only house singled out for praise in a list of the ten best buildings in the United States. Voted number three, it was exceeded in esteem only by the United States Capitol, which was number two, and H. H. Richardson's Trinity Church, in Boston, which was number one. So extraordinary was the design that, as Henry Van Brunt recalled in 1895, the year of Hunt's death, in completing the house, "that delicate casket of precious architec-

ture, the workmen, using a wisely given liberty of design in carving the finial of the highest gable, placed there the life-sized portrait figure of the architect in the garb of a fellow-workman with mallet and chisel in hand."[337]

Hunt's miniature château startled and inspired New York with its color, style, scholarship, and individuality. It transformed the thinking not only of architects but also of

Proposed Jim Fisk house, Fifth Avenue and East Seventieth Street. Richard Morris Hunt, 1870–71. Elevation. The Octagon, AAF.

the governing blue bloods of New York's high society, who were made to realize that architecture could represent individuals and advance social ambitions. In a city where even the very richest families lived in the comparative anonymity of rowhouses virtually identical in both look and plan, Hunt and his client charted a new course in which the rivalries of established hostesses and the ambitions of parvenus would not only be played out in private drawing rooms and ballrooms but also in the architecture of the city's principal streets. It would not be completely accurate to attribute this dramatic development in the social role of architecture merely to the success of Hunt's design: Alva Vanderbilt played no small part when she decided to inaugurate her new house with a big party, reviving an abandoned tradition by holding New York's first costume ball in a generation. Until this party, held on March 26, 1883, the social kingdom ruled by Mrs. William B. Astor II excluded the Vanderbilts. But Mrs. Astor somehow allowed her young daughter Caroline to rehearse for a quadrille that would be part of the evening's festivities. Alva conspired in this, getting the

young girl's hopes up for the party and then dashing them by telling her that she, Alva, couldn't invite a girl whose mother had snubbed her by not including her in the annual January cotillion held in Mrs. Astor's ballroom, the most important social event of any given year. Alva had deliberately invited virtually anyone to her housewarming who had or could get a costume, but not Mrs. Astor. Caroline Astor made such a fuss that the concerned mother, accepting social defeat, made her way up the avenue to call on Mrs. Vanderbilt and subsequently receive her invitation.

Eight hundred guests swarmed the mansion on party night, arriving at 11:00 P.M., moving along a red carpet specially laid for the occasion to help them find their way through a series of rooms that outshone the party itself. First of these was a sixty-foot-long, twenty-foot-wide hall, wrapped in Caen stone to the height of seven feet and warmed by a huge stone fireplace. From a dais in the French salon, guests were greeted by Vanderbilt, dressed as the Duc de Guise, and his wife, dressed as a Venetian princess. Most of the guests were marvelously decked out.

Mrs. Cornelius Vanderbilt as "The Electric Light" for the housewarming costume ball at the William Kissam Vanderbilt house (Richard Morris Hunt, 1878–82), March 26, 1883. Mora. NYHS.

Richard Morris Hunt as Cimabue for the housewarming costume ball at the William Kissam Vanderbilt house (Richard Morris Hunt, 1878–82), March 26, 1883. RMH. CU.

William Kissam Vanderbilt house, northwest corner of Fifth Avenue and West Fifty-second Street. Richard Morris Hunt, 1878–82. Hall. ARCH. CU.

Mrs. Cornelius Vanderbilt, alluding to the still-to-be-completed Statue of Liberty, came in white satin and called herself "The Electric Light." Catherine Howland Hunt dressed as a courtier from the time of Francis I, while her husband, with a sly nod to history, came as Cimabue, the painter Dante selected to symbolize the transience of fame. To one side of the hall rose a carved Caen stone fireplace, flanked by the entrances to the French Renaissance library and to the tiled Moorish billiards room, the latter more a gesture to prevailing taste than contributing to a sense of stylistic coherence. The dark parlor, paneled in French walnut, was more in keeping, while the white paneled salon, combining Régence and Louis XV motifs, brought the his-

tory of French taste nearly up to date. The tapestry-hung, twin-fireplaced, Henry II–style dining room, far and away the biggest and most imposing room, fifty feet by thirty feet and rising through two stories, was located at the rear. Dancing took place after midnight in the lightly waxed, oak-paneled dining room, with several quadrilles, including a Hobby Horse Quadrille in which dancers were costumed to look as if they were mounted on real horses. At 1:00 A.M. guests were invited to the rose-bedecked top-floor gymnasium, where they supped under the strong white calcium light of the new electric bulbs, which Alva's house was the first to have installed.

The Vanderbilt house set new standards for architecture

and interior decoration, adding to the sheer opulence of Alexander T. Stewart's mansion a very high level of artistic scholarship and taste. Much more than a rich man's townhouse, 660 Fifth Avenue was the first New York address to earn a place on the world's roster of representative places—the first built symbol of America's arrival on the international stage of world financial and cultural power. The house initiated a new era of luxury and ostentation but it also initiated, in its own un-ironic way, a new era of public responsibility—the homes of the rich, in emulation of William K. Vanderbilt's, would henceforward each have to play a role on New York's public stage. The anonymity of brownstone life would subsequently be deemed antediluvian; brownstone residents were coming to be called "cave-dwellers."

"No house is more deservedly known in all the length and breadth of the country," the *Real Estate Record and Builders' Guide* observed. "It is numbered among the sights of Fifth Avenue, and part of the pleasure and duty of the stranger within the gates is to walk slowly up and down admiring its detail, and to view it from every point of vantage."[338] Charles F. McKim took great satisfaction in Hunt's design. Late in life he remarked that he enjoyed

strolling past the house in the evening, refreshed by its very presence.[339] The critic Barr Ferree would be similarly extravagant in his praise, writing in 1895:

This sumptuous and exquisite design—for it is difficult to speak of it in moderate language—has fortunately become sufficiently well known to the lovers of the fine arts in America to need no description at this time. It unites, in a singularly happy manner, many diverse elements of the artistic and the beautiful. It is picturesque, varied and unsymmetrical; it is beautiful, stately and harmonious. The detail is rich and abundant, yet it is so well used, and is so admirably distributed and concentrated—the doorway being especially notable and successful in this respect—that while the building as a whole is eminently rich in effect, it is so without a sense of overloading. The design of a master, it is almost his master work.[340]

At about the same time that William K. Vanderbilt decided to build his Fifth Avenue château, his older brother, Cornelius Vanderbilt II, decided on a more or less similar course of action, acquiring a site farther uptown at the northwest corner of Fifth Avenue and Fifty-seventh Street.[341] On the site stood two houses, 742 and 744

William Kissam Vanderbilt house, northwest corner of Fifth Avenue and West Fifty-second Street. Richard Morris Hunt, 1878–82. Dining room. ARCH. CU.

Cornelius Vanderbilt II house, northwest corner of Fifth Avenue and West Fifty-seventh Street. George B. Post, 1879–82. View to the northwest, c. 1891. MCNY.

Fifth Avenue. Rather than simply destroy them, Vanderbilt's architect, George B. Post, had them taken down piece by piece and rebuilt on a site Vanderbilt had acquired for them on the west side of Madison Avenue at Fifty-seventh Street. Post, who had been a student in Hunt's atelier and was typically an architect of commercial buildings, had received the commission in a competition with entrants including George E. Harney, Charles W. Clinton, John B. Snook, and Stephen D. Hatch. Whether plans for this competition were submitted anonymously is not clear. If not, Post may have gotten the job in part because he was a member of the social set Vanderbilt sought to conquer: he was the only architect included in Ward McAllister's list of the Four Hundred.

Post's design, which was completed in 1882, mirrored its down-the-street neighbor by Hunt in its French Renaissance styling. But it was stiffer in composition and far more Classical than Gothic in detail. It was also much more vivid in color, combining red pressed brick with trim of gray Bedford limestone. Each floor was strongly expressed and the composition was crowned by a large hipped roof covered in brick and tile. In comparing the two designs, Montgomery Schuyler suggested that the Vanderbilts were intent on establishing a natural history for their family by building two important houses, one "in the earliest French Renaissance," the other "in the French Gothic." But he went on to say that despite its Gothic aspirations, Post's design was "classic throughout."[342] All in all, Schuyler was disappointed in Post's performance. Writing much later in *Architectural Record*, he found that the "admixture of materials makes the color effect noticeably unfortunate, while the skyline seems out of harmony and very ill proportioned." In sum, the house was a "sad botch, incident to a reaching desire for imposing effect."[343] But Post's design was in some ways more interesting than Hunt's. For one thing, it was less a copy of French work and more an invention. To Russell Sturgis it was "a concentrated, energetic expression of an idea . . . and . . . as good a piece of French Renaissance modified to meet New York requirements as we are likely to see."[344]

Cornelius Vanderbilt II house, northwest corner of Fifth Avenue and West Fifty-seventh Street. George B. Post, 1879–82. Smoking room. NYHS.

Disappointing though the exterior massing and detail of Post's house may have been, the interiors were by and large widely admired, representing, as Mary Gay Humphreys wrote in 1883, "the most important example of decorative work yet attempted in this country, in respect both to the scale on which it is employed and to its artistic intentions."[345] Post's most notable contributions to the interior were the spectacularly carved Caen white marble staircase, which spiraled up from the entrance to the principal rooms on the second floor, and the Moorish octagonal smoking room. The domed ceiling of the smoking room was ornamented with iridescent metallic tints of blue that complemented geometrically laid panels of opalescent blue tiles on the walls, all brilliantly illuminated by an antique chandelier brought from the East by Lockwood de Forest. In the dining room between the oak beams of the coffered ceiling were six opalescent glass panels by John La Farge and fourteen panels in carved mahogany by La Farge and Augustus Saint-Gaudens. The *New York Sun*'s correspondent pronounced the ceiling a trendsetter, by far "the most ambitious which has yet been attempted in America," calling attention to special techniques used in the wood carving as well as to the sumptuous palette of supplementing inlay materials, including marble, ivory, and coral, as well as hammered bronze that had been permanently tinted by a secret process of oxidation. Waxing at once poetic and sarcastic, the *Sun*'s writer pictured

> Mr. Vanderbilt and his confrères leaning back in their chairs after dinner, and, in that enviable frame of mind in which a man can take pleasure in being more than ordinarily obtuse, looking up at this miraculous ceiling impending over them, weighted with stone and metal, fretted with carving, and glittering with mother-of-pearl, and wondering how it is held aloft, and what in thunder it all means. And we may imagine Mr. Gould, whose classical acquirements are well known (if he should be of the guests), explaining that yonder panel represents the triumph of Diana . . . and that the companion one displays Bacchus and his vintagers. . . . Mr. Gould, being a man of few words, may omit the adjectives; but it would be excusable in him if he should use them, for nowhere will he see a finer piece of work, or one, it is likely, more to his taste.[346]

When Cornelius II's father, William H. Vanderbilt, died in 1885, his will, reflecting in part the English tradition of primogeniture, made Cornelius, as the eldest, heir to the largest portion of his fortune, sixty-seven million dollars (William K. got sixty-five million dollars, but the daughters and the two other sons, Frederick and George, received only ten million dollars each). The bequest of the extra two million dollars and of a portrait and marble bust of his father were clear signals to Cornelius that he was now the head of the family. In keeping with this responsibility, Cornelius felt he would need a larger and improved house and acquired the remaining brownstone houses to the north of his site along Fifth Avenue, demolished them, and, from 1892 to 1894, expanded and completely rebuilt

Cornelius Vanderbilt II house, northwest corner of Fifth Avenue and West Fifty-seventh Street. George B. Post, 1879–82. Detail of main staircase. NYHS.

Cornelius Vanderbilt II house, northwest corner of Fifth Avenue and West Fifty-seventh Street. George B. Post, 1879–82. Hall. MCNY.

Cornelius Vanderbilt II house, west side of Fifth Avenue between West Fifty-seventh and West Fifty-eighth Streets. George B. Post, 1879–82, 1892–94. View to the southwest, 1895, showing the William J. Hutchinson house (George B. Post, 1882) on the right and the Frederick W. Stevens house (George E. Harney, 1875–76) on the far left across Fifty-seventh Street. Bogart. MCNY.

Cornelius Vanderbilt II house, west side of Fifth Avenue between West Fifty-seventh and West Fifty-eighth Streets. George B. Post, 1879–82, 1892–94. Porte cochere. NYHS.

his house. Disappointed in Post's work, Cornelius had first asked Ernest Flagg, his cousin by marriage, for advice in reconfiguring the house only a few years after its 1882 completion.[347] When Vanderbilt was ready to expand in earnest he asked Richard Morris Hunt to design the extension, which was to present a grand face to the Fifth Avenue Plaza. Hunt was reluctant to poach on the territory of his student and friend, however, and Post was retained as the architect for the work, which included the addition of a ceremonial entrance facing north toward the plaza and a porte cochere set back from the plaza in a landscaped court, the first significant formal garden to be part of a New York townhouse.[348] The front door remained on Fifty-seventh Street, where the conservatory on the west side was replaced by a three-story wing that only served to increase the bulk of Post's design. Hunt's hand was felt in aspects of the exterior, for which he proposed a tower on the new wing facing the plaza and elaborately decorated the gables of the dormers on the original house. The commentator for the *Illustrated American* found "the huge house . . . by no means remarkable for beauty, grace or sympathy. It strikes the observer simply as a very, very large structure, and suggests rather a pretentious family hotel than a luxurious and elegant home."[349]

The addition was set well back from Fifty-eighth Street,

where at the west end of Vanderbilt's new property, Post had designed a French Renaissance house (1882) for William J. Hutchinson, at 4 West Fifty-eighth Street. Sturgis found the Hutchinson house deficient in the same way as the Vanderbilt house: "With all its merit as an elaborate piece of linear design, and as showing in the exterior a great deal of careful thought for comfort and elegance of the arrangements within, [it] is yet open to unfavorable criticism in the matter of contrast of color. . . . Emphasis is, perhaps, what the exterior of the house lacks. The only thing about it which seems to be fearlessly carried out is the design of the great chimneys."[350] Post's house for Hutchinson complemented the one he designed for Vanderbilt, but the two had been separated by a row of Italianate brownstones. With Vanderbilt's expansion, however, the two were now visually united to form so impressive an ensemble that observers assumed that the Hutchinson house was part of the expanded Vanderbilt château.

Between the Vanderbilts and the Joneses and various religious institutions there was little land left on the avenue's fashionable stretch for any other rich families. As a result the side streets were built up with imposing houses (see below), and to an extent Madison Avenue, where one notable house project was built, the coordinated group of six houses (1882–85) that Henry G. Villard commissioned from McKim, Mead & White, on the east side of Madison between Fiftieth and Fifty-first Streets.[351] Family friendships probably led Villard to the young firm— Charles F. McKim's father, Miller McKim, was one of a group of abolitionists with whom Villard associated. Villard's wife, Frances, the daughter of another in that group, William Lloyd Garrison, had a brother who was married to Charles F. McKim's sister, Lucy. In 1865 Villard, together with Miller McKim and Stanford White's father, Richard Grant White, had founded the liberal magazine *The Nation*. Villard's patronage of the McKim firm extended beyond the house to buildings for his railroad, including a hotel, a hospital, and a proposed terminal in Portland, Oregon.

In some ways, the site Villard chose was an odd one. Madison Avenue was not nearly so fashionable as Fifth Avenue and the immediate environs were occupied by a number of institutions and manufactories, further compromising the location. To the south lay the Columbia College campus, to the north the women's section of the Roman Catholic Orphan Asylum, and to the east Fourth Avenue with its open cut of railway tracks, on the far side of which was the F. & M. Schaefer Brewery. But across Madison to the west, the apse of the new Roman Catholic cathedral, flanked by two ecclesiastical residences, left a green lawn that was visually incorporated into the Villard scheme, creating a commanding foreground of open space and guaranteeing abundant light.

Villard, born in Germany as Ferdinand Heinrich Gustav Hilgard, arrived in the United States in 1853 and soon became publisher of the *New York Post*. He was also active

William J. Hutchinson house, 4 West Fifty-eighth Street. George B. Post, 1882. View to the south. AR. CU.

in the railroad business; at the time he undertook to build on Madison Avenue, he was attempting to create a consolidated transcontinental railroad. The idea of the six-unit palazzo was Villard's own, as was the desire to see it realized in brownstone and not in the limestone favored by the architects. The sources for Villard's idea of grouping the houses together around a courtyard have never been precisely determined, but the planning strategy resembles houses in parts of Villard's native town of Zweibrücken, buildings at the University of Munich, where he had been a student in the early 1850s, as well as some of his favorite places in Frankfurt.

Although Classical motifs had been a part of McKim, Mead & White's work from the firm's founding in 1879, the Villard Houses constituted the partners' first scholarly essay in the Classical architecture of the Italian Renaissance. This style would soon become their hallmark and would have enormous influence over American architecture for the next thirty years or more. McKim and White developed Villard's U-shaped plan, possibly turning to Baldassare Peruzzi's Villa Farnesina (1509–11), in Rome, or François-Alexandre Duquesney's Gare de l'Est (1847–52), in Paris, for inspiration. But the busy partners of the fledgling firm rested responsibility for the project in the hands of Joseph

Villard Houses, east side of Madison Avenue between East Fiftieth and East Fifty-first Streets. McKim, Mead & White, 1882–85. View to the east of the entrance court, 1885. MCNY.

Morrill Wells, who played a decisive part in creating the severely detailed facades, derived from those of the Palazzo della Cancelleria (c. 1485), in Rome, then believed to have been a work of Donato Bramante. The Cancelleria was one of Wells's two favorite works of Renaissance architecture, the other being the sixteenth-century Palazzo Farnese in Rome.

The houses were built over the course of six years, with Villard's, at 451 Madison Avenue, on the southwest corner of the site, completed first. Villard instructed his architects to design the group as one coordinated ensemble even though he recognized that the families that would occupy the houses would each want individualized interiors. To ensure the same high artistic level as in his own house, he required that McKim, Mead & White be retained by each homeowner, although Artemas H. Holmes, a lawyer, refused. The wish to have the architects involved in the interior design marked a break from the typical practice of the day, which left most residential interior design in the hands of decorators and cabinetmakers such as Herter Brothers and Pottier & Stymus. Stanford White was responsible for the interior decoration of Villard's house, developing a lavish suite of rooms that were not fully realized until the house's second owners, Whitelaw and Elisabeth Mills Reid, took possession in 1886. In the spring of 1884, when Villard had only been living in his still incomplete house for about three months, his plans for railroad consolidation failed. Angry crowds, thinking the entire mansion-block was his, came to the courtyard to protest. Villard fled to his country house and turned the entire complex over to trustees, who completed the project and handled its eventual sale.

Villard's house contained a dozen rooms on four floors. In the basement were a kitchen, a laundry, a wine room, a dining room for the servants, and a billiards room. White had almost unlimited funds at his disposal. Working with artists who were also friends, including Augustus and Louis Saint-Gaudens, Francis Lathrop, and

Villard Houses, east side of Madison Avenue between East Fiftieth and East Fifty-first Streets. McKim, Mead & White, 1882–85. View to the northeast, c. 1901. Byron. MCNY.

Henry G. Villard house, northeast corner of Madison Avenue and East Fiftieth Street. McKim, Mead & White, 1882–85. Music room. AH. CU.

Henry G. Villard house, northeast corner of Madison Avenue and East Fiftieth Street. McKim, Mead & White, 1882–85. Drawing room. NYHS.

Henry G. Villard house, northeast corner of Madison Avenue and East Fiftieth Street. McKim, Mead & White, 1882–85. Entrance hall. MMW. CU.

Henry G. Villard house, northeast corner of Madison Avenue and East Fiftieth Street. McKim, Mead & White, 1882–85. Library. MCNY.

Henry G. Villard house, northeast corner of Madison Avenue and East Fiftieth Street. McKim, Mead & White, 1882–85. Dining room. MMW. CU.

David Maitland Armstrong, as well as with other decorators and craftspeople, White created a suite of interiors as sumptuous as any in New York, but stylistically more coherent and infinitely more restrained than what was typical in the precincts of the very rich. Entered from the courtyard, a short flight of marble steps led to a vaulted hall off of which opened a magnificently appointed music room, dining and breakfast rooms, and a drawing room. The hall incorporated a marble fireplace and ornamental sculpture carved by Augustus Saint-Gaudens. The two-story, barrel-vaulted music room was one of the city's grandest salons. For the Reids, White added a paneled ceiling and commissioned John La Farge to paint biblical panels adapted from Luca della Robbia's Cantoria (1431–38), in Florence. Grand also was the elaborately paneled and plastered drawing room facing Madison Avenue, really a suite of two drawing rooms that could be combined into a spacious entertaining space. White reconfigured these rooms for the Reids, combining them with the reception room to form one large, grandly Classical room replete with gilded marble Corinthian columns. White also convinced the Reids to further embellish their house with art by his friends, including a panel over the dining fireplace, *A Pavanne*, by the painter Edwin Austin Abbey. The twelve-foot-wide yellow marble stair leading to the second floor was graced by a zodiac clock designed by White and Augustus Saint-Gaudens. The stair was located in its own room, an urban version of the living halls of the resort and suburban villas the McKim firm specialized in.

White was immensely proud of the project, recalling it in 1896 as "the beginning of any good work that we may have done . . . designed on simple and dignified classic lines, which we have ever since endeavored to follow."[352] But the critics, though impressed by the overall urban strategy of the Villard Houses, were, at least initially, less favorably disposed to the architectural language chosen by Wells. This failure to appreciate the self-assured command of Renaissance-inspired Classicism that the design surely exhibited can be attributed to the prevailing predisposition to picturesque compositions shared by most critics. Coming at the apogee of the Queen Anne style, the Villard Houses were seen as aesthetically dry and academic, which they were. But in their formal purity and urbanistic ambition they were just short of revolutionary—in most ways unlike anything New York had ever seen before.

The startling unconventionality of the group caught critics by surprise, sometimes leading them to dismissive observations. When the complex was only partly complete, the *Real Estate Record and Builders' Guide*'s critic found it deficient:

> There are apparently to be ultimately three houses surrounding a quadrangle, and even the one already built looks more like an "institution" than a dwelling . . . being an undissembled box, with a conspicuous tiled roof on it. . . . There is no composition attempted, no grouping of the openings, which are aligned over each

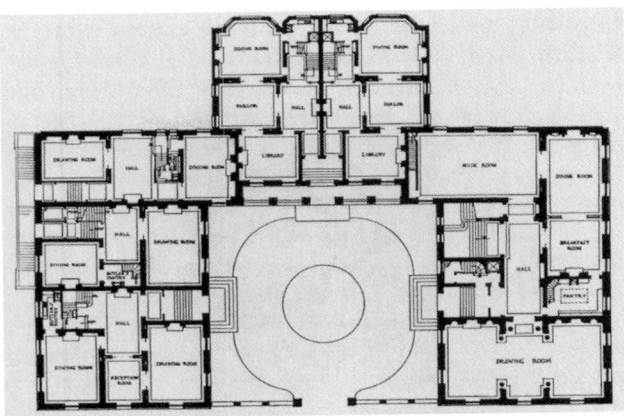

Villard Houses, east side of Madison Avenue between East Fiftieth and East Fifty-first Streets. McKim, Mead & White, 1882–85. First-floor plan. MMW. CU.

other at regular intervals, no effort to express the interior, nothing indeed, to indicate architecture except the delicacy of some of the detail, as in the cornice, the delicacy which is lost by a misjudgment of its distance from the eye. This detail is all in correct Italian Renaissance, very unexceptionable and very unnoticeable. The building recalls an Italian monastery, or an Italian barrack, rather than the Italian palaces which probably suggested it.[353]

The *Record and Guide* would warm up to the design, however, and in a subsequent article, in 1884, noted:

> It is difficult to talk about Mr. Villard's house without going into reflections, which may be highly moral and instructive, but are irrelevant to architecture. . . . The scheme is of an unusual amplitude and liberality and is very liberally carried out. The giving up of a whole block to three houses in the fashionable quarter of the city, is unexampled except in the [William H.] Vanderbilt houses, where the three houses appear architecturally as two. The arrangement of the Villard houses is much better—a deep court with a house at the back and one on each flank—much more expressive, since the architecture distinctly explains the relations of the buildings, and abstractly more artistic since a proportion cannot exist with less than three terms or a group with less than three members. Another advantage of the Villard houses over the Vanderbilt houses is that they have roofs, and although without roofs they would be as merely boxes as the others, the tiled roofs, although only of moderate pitch, give each of the three buildings some form and connect the three into a composition. Except in this general grouping, however, there is no more composition than in the Vanderbilt houses. . . . The general effect of the houses thus is that they are big and tiresome and as unnoticeable as so big a pile can be. But they are in no way offensive and can never come to look trivial or vulgar, and thus, with the gratifying liberality of the plan and its execution, must be scored as a mild success.[354]

In an 1885 review, the *Record and Guide* saw the virtues in McKim, Mead & White's approach: "The Villard house is, in fact, the only example of consistent adherence to one style, and, as yet, it remains the most noteworthy house in town. . . . It is significant that the calmness of the architecture, its symmetry and straight lines is a source of much disappointment to the wayfaring man and stranger, accustomed as he is to regard the word architecture as a term that came in with Queen Anne and to be indissolubly associated with gables and other rampant forms."[355]

Mariana Van Rensselaer was more open to the group's virtues, finding the Villard design a "happy variation on our usual arrangement":

> The external treatment is throughout very simple, after an Italian Renaissance fashion which wins a local flavor from the use of "brown-stone,"—better, however, than the average, both in quality and in color. The broad plain walls and regularly spaced and delicately ornamented windows are enlivened by the introduction of a *loggia* in the central portion, and are *composed*, moreover, by intelligent proportioning. The effect is very quiet, a little cold, perhaps a little tame; but it is extremely refined, and affords an interesting contrast to the effect of those "vernacular" examples whose inspiration was drawn from similar sources. . . . As in their [Tiffany] house [see below] . . . , so here as well, though in a very different language, these artists seem to be protesting against frivolity, tawdriness, unrest, and ostentation.[356]

Henry G. Villard house, northeast corner of Madison Avenue and East Fiftieth Street. McKim, Mead & White, 1882–85. Zodiac clock designed by Augustus Saint-Gaudens and Stanford White for the first landing of the main stair. NYHS.

The Art Gallery of the Streets

While for the Civil War–era generation the identical brownstone house had seemed to meet the requirements of both the more affluent members of the middle class as well as all but a handful of the really rich, it no longer seemed enough for those setting out to buy or build a house once prosperity returned in the late 1870s. To commission a house was to commission a work of art. A house was no longer merely a home, or even an investment; it was a public act of art patronage. For the first time in New York's history the very rich, led by the Vanderbilts, and even the merely rich, set out to build houses that were individual in character. In contrast to most of their predecessors they turned not to builders or builder-architects but to some of the country's best architects, a majority of them New Yorkers, many trained in Europe, who were more than happy to create designs that were unique and "artistic," to use a term that was becoming increasingly popular.

The artistic houses of the Gilded Age fell into two distinct groups. In one category were those that set out to emulate great moments in architectural history, best exemplified by Richard Morris Hunt's and George B. Post's Vanderbilt palaces on Fifth Avenue (see above). These houses were, typically, essays in a particular style; often they were based on one specific monument from the past. Scholarship was valued, especially in the handling of detail, but composition, though rooted in Classical principles, was quite free. The second category of artistic houses included those that were usually more modest in size—typically single- or double-width townhouses, most frequently built one at a time but sometimes in groups of two or three by owners who might live in one and settle their children in the others or just lease them out, or by developers who saw the marketing advantages of individual expression and found ways to achieve facade diversity while building fundamentally repetitious units. Though the designers of these houses relied on the grammar and vocabulary of traditional architecture, frequently their intention was to create distinctly modern designs by combining wide-ranging stylistic eclecticism with an even looser handling of Classical composition than in the Vanderbilt mansions. Their ambition was not merely to make each house design individual but to push architecture toward some reformulation that, by means of a process of continual synthesis and resynthesis, might lead to the creation of a "modern" style. Better still, given the period's nationalism, it was hoped that this process would lead to the formulation of a distinctly American style.

The search for a distinctly modern style grew out of the theorizing of the first half of the nineteenth century, especially in the Neo-Classicism of French and German practice and the Gothicism of the English and the French, so it was not surprising that the first architect to advocate the individuality of the urban house was Richard Morris Hunt. Hunt's studies at the Ecole des Beaux-Arts had made him intimately aware of the European debates about

Rossiter–Parmly house, 11 West Thirty-eighth Street.
Richard Morris Hunt, 1855–57. View to the northeast.
The Octagon, AAF.

Rossiter–Parmly house, 11 West Thirty-eighth Street.
Richard Morris Hunt, 1855–57. Watercolor presentation drawing.
The Octagon, AAF.

what constituted modern style, and his brilliant training gave him the design skills to handle the styles that brought the debates to life.

The break with brownstone uniformity can best be traced back to 1855, when Hunt arrived in New York from Paris and immediately undertook the design of a townhouse, Hunt's first. It was commissioned by Dr. Eleazer Parmly, a dentist, who intended it for the use of his daughter and son-in-law, the painter Thomas P. Rossiter, a friend of Hunt's.[357] The Rossiter-Parmly house (1855–57), at 11 West Thirty-eighth Street, set the agenda for the stylistically and compositionally liberated artistic townhouse. As dramatic an artistic break with rowhouse uniformity as had yet been seen in New York, the house was a star-crossed project. Based on ideas of Rossiter's, Hunt had prepared early sketches in Paris and continued work on the project in New York. Parmly, an extensive landholder, was, as the saying goes, "very close with a dollar," and tension between the architect and his client existed from the first time they met, in September 1855. Believing that Hunt's design would be too expensive to build, Parmly instructed the fledgling architect to reduce its size, narrowing its width from fifty feet to thirty-seven and a half feet. The situation went from bad to worse when Rossiter's wife died in Paris and Parmly decided to add an

additional floor to what had been a three-story design so that he could live in it with his son-in-law, an arrangement that did not work out because Rossiter remarried within a year of his first wife's death. The house was placed on the market in 1860.

During the course of construction, Hunt, who had accepted a temporary job to help Thomas U. Walter with work on the United States Capitol, turned the supervision of the project over to Joseph C. Wells, an experienced architect, resuming his responsibilities on his return to New York, in May 1856. But when the house was nearly complete in November 1857, Parmly refused to honor Hunt's bills, which were for five percent of the cost of construction and included designs for interior decoration. Hunt, who had not entered into a contract with Parmly specifying his authorship of the design and his responsibilities during construction, took Parmly to court, where a number of leading architects testified on his behalf. Parmly denied that he had retained Hunt "to make a line of architecture for me in my life, in any way, shape or manner."[358] The problem between the two could be traced to Parmly's decision to act as his own contractor, employing a carpenter-builder and others to carry out the work. Although Hunt often visited the site, providing the builder with details, Parmly refused to acknowledge the value of his service.

While the decision was for Hunt, he only received a two and a half percent fee—the minimum commission charged by architects at the time—and not the five percent to which he felt entitled. The case was nonetheless an important one for the profession, helping to establish the prestige of the architect as a representative of the client and not as a mechanic in the building field.

The Rossiter-Parmly house was notable not only for its introduction of the Neo-Grec style to New York but also for its status as a highly ambitious, self-conscious—indeed, self-proclamatory—work. Its rigorous symmetry, complex layering of facade elements including an arched pediment, and scholarly use of such obscure sources as the French Order, designed by the sixteenth-century architect Philibert de l'Orme, evidenced a young architect out to show his stuff. In the trial against Parmly, Hunt testified to the uniqueness of his work:

This house was peculiar in construction; there was a marked difference from any house I have seen in this city, both in its general plan and its elevation; the object to be attained was to have with one entrance door two entrances in fact—one to the public and the other to the private part, that is to say, after entering the vestibule there were two doors, one leading to the house and the other to a public exhibition-room, portrait studio and also to a large atelier, where Mr. Rossiter was to have his scholars; the whole house was distributed in such a way that in every story a person having a certain pass-key could get in to the private house, but strangers could only go into the exhibition room, portrait studio and up to the top, without being able to see the private part of the house at all; it was a thing that necessitated a good deal of study and trouble; there is also another feature in the house which is peculiar, the center room is two stories high with a gallery around it on the second story; the front of the house is also different from any in the city, in its way.[359]

In 1895 Montgomery Schuyler reflected on the already demolished house:

The first town-house designed by Mr. Hunt must have been a surprise to New York of that time. . . . It is not only an unmistakable product of the Beaux Arts, but it is specifically inspired by Lefuel's work on the Louvre, as witness the banded shafts and the carved pediment that crowns the centre. The absolute symmetry decreed at Paris is maintained, it will be observed, even to the construction at the flank opposite the entrance of an architectural counterpart of the entrance and to the blind arches that flank the opening of the upper story. For the rest it is an evidently educated performance and as such was calculated to exert a beneficial effect in the prevailing chaos.[360]

Hunt did not build another house in New York until 1868, when the sculptor John Quincy Adams Ward, with whom Hunt was collaborating on the Seventh Regiment Memorial in Central Park, commissioned a double house with a connected studio on a twenty-five-foot-wide lot at 7–9 West Forty-ninth Street.[361] Hunt's design, with its paired stoops and limited fenestration, suggested a single house of generous size rather than the two twelve-and-a-half-foot-wide units that were in fact the case. The house was very tall—sixty-nine feet—and its flat facade, crowned by a boldly modeled cornice and a steep mansard above, was notable for the use of incised decoration similar to that of the Neo-Grec that had been favored in Paris when Hunt was a student. At the rear, Ward's studio stretched across the entire lot. While the Rossiter-Parmly house was New York's first example of the Neo-Grec and inaugurated the idea of the individual "artistic" house, it was built at a time when New York was not quite ready for it. Moreover, the Civil War subsequently halted construction of private townhouses. But the timing of the Ward house, finished in 1869, was in at least one way just right: it set the trend for the decoration of rowhouse facades in the 1870s, when flat walls and incised decoration were well within the technical and budgetary reach of new specula-

John Quincy Adams Ward house, 7–9 West Forty-ninth Street. Richard Morris Hunt, 1868–69. View to the north. The Octagon, AAF.

tive construction. In 1882 Ward abandoned 7–9 West Forty-ninth Street for 119 West Fifty-second Street, where Hunt designed a house-studio large enough for the sculptor to work on his monumental public designs—such as his statue of George Washington, which, on November 26, 1883, was unveiled at its location on the steps of the United States Subtreasury, at the northeast corner of Wall and Nassau Streets—and to entertain friends, clients, and influential public officials in an elaborately decorated, Pompeii-inspired reception room.[362]

Hunt followed the Forty-ninth Street Ward house with twin houses for William H. Osborne and Jonathan Sturgis, at 32 and 34 Park Avenue (1869–70), between Thirty-fifth and Thirty-sixth Streets.[363] The boldly detailed, vigorously modeled, three-and-a-half-story, mansarded, unequally wide pair of stone-trimmed brick houses were treated as a unit. Identical scrolled pedimented dormers crowned a tier of bay windows that, in the case of the larger house to the south, belonging to Osborne, rose from the basement, and in the smaller house, belonging to Sturgis, projected forward only at the second floor. Next door, Charles D. Gambrill and H. H. Richardson's less individualistic pair of mansarded houses (1869–70) for Jonathan Sturges and his son Frederick, at 38 Park Avenue and 40 East Thirty-sixth Street, attempted to suggest the grander scale of an urban palazzo. Though they revealed none of the bravura of Richardson's later house pair (1884–86) for John Hay and Henry Adams in Washington, D.C., Montgomery Schuyler deemed them "two sober and respectable houses."[364]

Hunt, ever the professional, was even willing to undertake the design of a row of speculative houses. His four-house group (1873–74) at 219–225 East Sixty-second Street, between Second and Third Avenues, was commissioned by Thomas and John D. Crimmins, building contractors.[365] The modest, seventeen-foot-wide Second Empire–style brownstone houses, intended for middle-class tenants, were only wide enough for two windows per floor. The group was built on land that constituted the twenty-four-acre farm of Adam Treadwell, a merchant, until the late 1860s. The new owners of the tract voluntarily entered into a protective covenant that assured certain standards for the size and quality of the houses to be built, which may explain why Hunt was retained by the Crimminses. The commission led to further work on the former Treadwell property, including a three-story, one-family house (1873–74) for the Crimminses' own use, at 203 East Sixty-first Street, and a seven-unit row of five-story, four-family houses (1872–74), at 1031–1043 Third Avenue, between Sixty-first and Sixty-second Streets, each with street-level shops and built by the same developers.[366]

In 1878 Richard Morris Hunt again returned to the paired townhouse type that had become something of a specialty for him. Frederic Bronson and Egerton Winthrop commissioned a design to be built at the northwest corner of Madison Avenue and Thirty-third Street, with forty-nine feet on Madison Avenue and seventy-six feet on Thirty-third Street.[367] Though the idea of a coor-

William H. Osborne and Jonathan Sturgis houses, 32 and 34 Park Avenue, between East Thirty-fifth and East Thirty-sixth Streets. Richard Morris Hunt, 1869–70. View to the west. The Octagon, AAF.

dinated pair of dwellings was hardly new, the project, completed in 1879, created quite a stir. As the New York correspondent of the *American Architect and Building News* reported: "A spirit of exclusiveness and a desire for privacy have prevented in great measure the carrying out of anything like combination in the design of private dwellings."[368] The editors of the *Real Estate Record and Builders' Guide* deemed it a "quaint specimen of the Old English dwelling," though in fact the houses were just as much French in inspiration, with high mansards. They went on to praise Hunt's design as "a real combination . . . in plan as well as in outward design. . . . Instead of cutting [the lot] into a pair of equal parallelograms, a give-and-take policy has been followed" so that "the two houses are in no wise flats, since there is a distinct party wall between them, though this wall is not built in one plane."[369] The principal facade facing Madison Avenue consisted of a triple and a double bay, giving an individual identity to each house. The detailing was simple to the point of severe, in Philadelphia brick trimmed with Belleville stone. Compared with the Rossiter-Parmly and Osborne-Sturgis houses, these designs were very restrained, so much so that the *American Architect and Building News* was moved to comment on Hunt's "reappearance upon the

Frederic Bronson and Egerton Winthrop houses, northwest corner of Madison Avenue and East Thirty-third Street. Richard Morris Hunt, 1878–79. View to the southwest. The Octagon, AAF.

field, with work we should hardly know as his . . . ; it is so much more quiet and sober than that to which he has accustomed us to in the past."[370]

Winthrop's house was well known for its scheme of interior decoration, especially that of the drawing room, which introduced New York to pure Louis XVI design. Winthrop was a stickler for accurate historical detail in an era that typically valued modern interpretation. As George W. Sheldon noted: "Few apartments in this city have been treated with such persistent determination to reproduce in all respects the forms, color, and feeling of a particular era."[371] A lawyer and a connoisseur of paintings, furniture, and literature, Winthrop was descended from both Governor Peter Stuyvesant of New York and Governor John Winthrop of Massachusetts. He shared his interests with the much younger Edith Wharton and introduced her to contemporary French naturalism and to the writings of Charles Darwin, Herbert Spencer, and Thomas Henry Huxley. Wharton later immortalized Winthrop as Sillerton Jackson, the society gossip who figures prominently in her novel *The Age of Innocence* (1920) and in "The Old Maid" and "New Year's Day," two of the four novellas published as *Old New York* (1924). Recalling Winthrop's drawing room forty years after she had first known it, Wharton wrote that it exemplified an "educated taste" that "replaced stuffy upholstery and rubbishy 'ornaments' with objects of real beauty in a simply designed setting."[372]

Less ambitious in size and less integrative in conception than McKim, Mead & White's six-house Villard Houses (see above) and that firm's three-house Tiffany mansion (see below) was Richard Morris Hunt's three-house group

Egerton Winthrop house, 23 East Thirty-third Street. Richard Morris Hunt, 1878–79. Drawing room. AH. CU.

Henry G. Marquand three-house group, northwest corner of Madison Avenue and East Sixty-eighth Street. Richard Morris Hunt, 1881–84. View to the northwest. Bogart. MCNY.

(1881–84) for Henry G. Marquand, a banker, real estate investor, and patron of the Metropolitan Museum of Art.[373] At 11 East Sixty-eighth Street, on the northwest corner of Madison Avenue, the design was nonetheless an important example of Hunt's traditional approach to the problem of the grouped townhouse. Marquand had been a long-standing patron of Hunt's, commissioning Linden Gate in Newport, Rhode Island, the Marquand Chapel at Princeton University, and the Guernsey Building at 160–164 Broadway (see chapter 3). Though he admired both, Montgomery Schuyler preferred the Marquand house to Hunt's William K. Vanderbilt mansion, seeing in it "the work of an architectural artist." Schuyler deemed the principal residence of the Marquand group the more Classical and favored it over the two narrower houses, which rose with the site's climb up Madison Avenue to form a "brilliantly successful . . . wall, and not a sash frame, a very wally wall . . . covered with emphatic and varied roofs. It is admirable how a flat front has been made to yield so much architectural interest, and how very piquant the composition is without being restless." He concluded his assessment with the observation that though "Hunt was rightly congratulated when his Vanderbilt house was finished, upon having designed the best dwelling house in New York it is at least questionable whether [the Marquand house] is not, merely as a piece of architectural design, even better. Certainly it is more valuable for the suggestions it gives for the treatment of the ordinary New York street front, which most architects find so intractable, and which they are so apt to make either tame or wild, either hopelessly stupid or outrageously vulgar."[374]

The four-story height of the brick and sandstone principal portion of the composition dominated its brownstone neighborhood. It shared a heavy, rusticated basement with the two twenty-five-foot-wide houses facing Madison Avenue, but these were each treated somewhat individually; the roofline and cornice of the northernmost house was higher, a feature Schuyler particularly admired. Though at first glance the composition seemed distinctly symmetrical, in fact there was a remarkable syncopation in the handling of such large elements as the towers and windows, and a wealth of delightful detail kept the eye continually engaged. Marquand's own house stretched 125 feet along Sixty-eighth Street and was entered at the center. Near Madison Avenue the house stepped back to shelter a conservatory, a weakness of mass at the most public corner of the group, producing an utterly surprising transparency that flew in the face of traditional composition,

Henry G. Marquand house, northwest corner of Madison Avenue and East Sixty-eighth Street. Richard Morris Hunt, 1881–84. Hall. SHA. CU.

Henry G. Marquand house, northwest corner of Madison Avenue and East Sixty-eighth Street. Richard Morris Hunt, 1881–84. Japanese room. AR. CU.

which treated corners with maximum emphasis. Inside there was the typical range of rooms, each handled in a distinct stylistic manner. Most notable were the drawing room, where the ceiling was the work of Sir Frederic Leighton and the piano case, chairs, and other furnishings that of Sir Lawrence Alma-Tadema; the requisite Moorish den; a Spanish dining room; and a Japanese living room, designed by Manly N. Cutter, who took three years to craft what was probably the most elaborate Japanese detailing in the city, with exquisitely intricate lacquered woodwork, shelves, and cupboards to display Marquand's important collection of Oriental porcelains.

Another direction in the design of artistic houses was influenced by the writing of Charles Eastlake, whose widely read *Hints on Household Taste* (1868) lamented the lack of picturesque street architecture, and the innovative work of such English architects as Richard Norman Shaw. Shaw's London houses, especially his Lowther Lodge (1872) and his townhouses at Chelsea Embankment, Cadogan Square, and Queen's Gate (1875–79), and, to a lesser extent, his New Zealand Chambers (1871), a small office building, came to the attention of New York architects, who immediately began to make their own versions in houses and commercial buildings.[375] By the late 1870s, Shavian work, known in America as the Queen Anne style, was well known and was being widely disseminated by such influential architects as

Henry G. Marquand house, northwest corner of Madison Avenue and East Sixty-eighth Street. Richard Morris Hunt, 1881–84. Moorish room. SHA. CU.

Edward N. Dickerson house, 64 East Thirty-fourth Street. McKim, Mead & Bigelow, 1877–79. View to the south. Levy. AIC.

Edward N. Dickerson house, 64 East Thirty-fourth Street. McKim, Mead & Bigelow, 1877–79. Drawing room. AH. CU.

Henry Hudson Holly, best known for his book *Holly's Country Seats* (1863). In his subsequent book, *Modern Dwellings in Town and Country* (1878), Holly recommended the Queen Anne approach as the most appropriate to modern conditions.[376]

McKim, Mead & Bigelow was credited by Montgomery Schuyler with introducing the "out-and-out Queen Anne" taste to New York with the firm's Edward N. Dickerson house (1877–79), at 64 East Thirty-fourth Street, between Madison and Fourth Avenues.[377] Dickerson was a patent lawyer and inventor, so the house was also remarkable for its many technical innovations: it was served by a water-powered Otis elevator featuring a safety lock, patented by Dickerson, that prevented the doors from being opened except when the elevator arrived at a given landing. The house featured a system of forced-air ventilation and a network of electric bells throughout. Telephones, introduced only two years before the building was completed, allowed communication in every room.

The Dickerson house, five stories and a basement, virtually filled its twenty-five-by-one-hundred-foot midblock site. The interior decoration by the firm was also interesting, impressing Mrs. M.E.W. Sherwood, who praised the house to the readers of *Harper's New Monthly Magazine*: "We can not look through the tasteful and artistic interiors of New York without a pleasurable sense of having lived through a very dark night, to be rewarded with an exceedingly fresh and brilliant morning."[378] Sherwood

found proof of her claim in the stained-glass windows and subtle tonal harmonies of the drawing room, especially its woodwork and furniture of satinwood, the light blue satin damask on the wall panels, and the ceiling's gold pattern on a pale gray ground. The drawing room was notably eclectic: a collection of Japanese pottery was combined with a painting of an Eastern European peasant girl and a Louis XV mantel centerpiece of silverwork on blue porcelain. For Sherwood, the mixture of different styles and periods was acceptable so long as the objects had inherent virtues and colors and scale were harmoniously balanced. But it was the house's facade that announced a new point of view, with the charming, Japanese-inspired delicacy of some of the details. Attributing the design to Charles F. McKim, Schuyler dismissed it as looking "less like a work of architectural art than a magnified piece of furniture 'with the Chippendale feeling.'"[379] He compared it to "furniture, and in its treatment of architectural members is not unlike a monumental sideboard . . . a tall and narrow gabled front of red brick over a basement of the fine-grained and soft-colored Wyoming blue-stone, which is also used in the wrought work above. . . . The lack of emphasis in the divisions of the front gives it an appearance of weakness which is enhanced by the irrelevancy of the decoration to the structure, and the triviality of the decoration by itself." For Schuyler it betrayed the belief "that refinement consists in the absence of vigor."[380]

George B. Post's asymmetrically composed house

Henry M. Braem house, 15 East Thirty-seventh Street. George B. Post, 1877. View to the north. Levy. AIC.

Frederick F. Thompson house, 283 Madison Avenue, between East Fortieth and East Forty-first Streets. McKim, Mead & White, 1879–81. View to the east showing part of the James Morris house (George E. Harney, 1878) on the left. MCNY.

Frederick F. Thompson house, 283 Madison Avenue, between East Fortieth and East Forty-first Streets. McKim, Mead & White, 1879–81. Dining room and conservatory. AH. CU.

(1877) for Henry M. Braem, at 15 East Thirty-seventh Street, though less formally inventive, was, as probably the "first strictly architectural terra cotta building" in the city, just as innovative.[381] Nonetheless, technological innovation was not enough for the New York correspondent of the *American Architect and Building News*, who, after noting Post's combination of terra cotta with brick and bluestone, went on to state that with "all respect to Mr. Post, the terra cotta panels would be more in scale were they placed on top of the Western Union Telegraph Building. He has so much really good work standing in New York that we do not fear to call attention to this fact."[382]

McKim, Mead & Bigelow, which was reorganized in 1879 as McKim, Mead & White, followed its Dickerson house with a forty-two-foot-wide house (1879–81) for the banker and amateur printer and photographer Frederick F. Thompson, at 283 Madison Avenue, between Fortieth and Forty-first Streets.[383] One of the most deliberately convenient, and even comfortable, houses of the period, it provided for the convenience of arriving guests a concealed stair leading from the inner vestibule to a second-floor toilet, while in the outer vestibule an exposed steam coil warmed the feet of telegraph messengers awaiting replies. The house also had an elevator. The exterior, while not betraying a specific source in the past, and at first glance certainly an example of the Queen Anne, used motifs from French rather than English Renaissance precedent, not only revealing the architects' commanding eclecticism but also suggesting the kind of serious scholarship Richard Morris Hunt was contemporaneously carrying forward in his William K. Vanderbilt house. The house's asymmetrical composition, with a wide, two-story-high bay, was nonetheless relaxed in an almost suburban way that mirrored the spacious plan, comparable to that of Shingle Style country houses, of loosely interconnected rooms wrapped around a central hall. The interior detailing was inventive to the point of exuberance, with the rooms appointed in a notably functional manner, particularly the three-thousand-book, thirty-foot-square, Moorish-inspired library with its mix of upholstered furniture, a slat-back Windsor armchair, and cane-seat bentwood chairs. The rooms were notably well lit, with the dining

J. Coleman Drayton house, 374–380 Fifth Avenue, between West Thirty-fifth and West Thirty-sixth Streets. McKim, Mead & White, 1882–83. View to the west. AR. CU.

Charles T. Barney house, 8–10 East Fifty-fifth Street. McKim, Mead & White, 1881–83. View to the south. Levy. AIC.

room bathed in light from a conservatory that virtually filled one end of the room as well as a skylight that filled the flat ceiling at the center of the high cove. While the living room was Japanese in style, on the second story, facing the avenue, were the Colonial Room and the Governor's Room. The former was one of the first in a fashionable house to be furnished with hundred-year-old American antiques, while the latter, so-named because it was often occupied by Mrs. Thompson's father, a former governor of New York State, was also furnished with old American pieces.

J. Coleman Drayton's house (1882–83), at 374–380 Fifth Avenue, between Thirty-fifth and Thirty-sixth Streets, was the next of McKim, Mead & White's artistic townhouse designs.[384] Even more than the Thompson house, it was a departure from the spiky rooflines and panelized facade treatment of the Dickerson house, exhibiting instead not a little of the characteristics of Hunt and especially of Richardson, so much so that in 1895 Russell Sturgis confessed to having long "thought it a piece of H. H. Richardson's work, and . . . assumed that his early Paris teaching and his later Romanesque strivings were pleasantly at odds in its design."[385] Until their divorce in 1896, Drayton was married to Charlotte Astor, daughter of William B. and Caroline Astor, who paid for the house. The design, attributed to Stanford White, was notable for the broad expanse of unbroken wall achieved because there were only two large windows per floor, and for the visible hipped roof sitting on a cornicelike stone-trellis frieze, a favorite detail of Charles F. McKim's. Although it incorporated French Renaissance details, the brick facade, trimmed in Potsdam sandstone, was its own thing, relatively severe except for a three-sided bay window lighting the third-floor library and a small, festooned oculus between the windows on the fourth floor. The arched entrance, above a broad, shallow flight of stairs, was emphasized with massive carved impost blocks that reminded Sturgis of the Mycenaean Tomb at Orchomenus. Montgomery Schuyler was pleased with its "simply and quietly treated streetfront in brick and sandstone," which he felt could "certainly not be called Queen Anne, in spite of the three rows of egg and dart moulding . . . which crown its rock-face basement."[386] Despite its rusticated base and the bold color contrasts between the light-colored stone and the red pressed brick, for Sturgis the "real charm" of the Drayton house was "that it is a modern New York house," raising hope "for one step more out of the fetters of the past. With one such step or maybe two of them the designer would reach unencumbered ground."[387]

Similar to the Drayton house in some of its details but more restless in its composition, McKim, Mead & White's double house (1881–83) for McKim's close friend the financier Charles T. Barney, at 8–10 East Fifty-fifth Street, was so free of a specific style that Russell Sturgis, reviewing the firm's work in 1895, insisted that it "be judged on its merits." Sturgis was thereby able to concentrate on the building's composition and detailing, especially "the almost inevitable crowding of the parts together in the front of the narrower house." Despite the design's faults, Sturgis deemed the pair of unidentically sized houses "an agreeable front, a relief to the eye, something to come upon with real pleasure in our monotonous streets."[388] Fourteen years earlier, Montgomery Schuyler had not been nearly so kind. "To the unanointed eye," he wrote, the Barney house is "simply a piece of insanity," recalling the "wildest freaks of Mr. [Edward William] Godwin and the other mad wags in the 'artistic quarter' of Chelsea."[389] The composition of the facade was undoubtedly restless—Schuyler deemed it an "aberration," his first use of the opprobrious term he would virtually make his own in the 1890s. Schuyler was particularly vexed with the detailing of the subtly panelized red brick wall that sat above the rock-faced pink granite base, which he characterized as a "very flat, very thin brick wall . . . covered with a trellis of brick weather-strips, so to speak, of which the angles are not moulded nor chamfered, but channelled." This effect combined with the chevron pattern of the brick to yield "an instability given to the wall by its design," improbably capped by what

> appears a heavy granite cornice, and over this again a solid granite parapet, behind which the pediments of two tin dormers of great, but unequal size, assert themselves. . . . One feels at once that this is not a work of reason, but of inspiration, and therefore must not be analyzed from a rational point of view. But then the theory of plenary inspiration in architecture, as in theology, gives rise to difficulties. It is hard to adopt the old theological distinction, to be sure what is above reason, and what is only contrary to reason. One would say without hesitation that the erection of this thin and liny brick screen over this rocky wall, and the crowning of the screen with a granite fortification, was irrational, but he cannot be sure that it is not supra-rational.[390]

While the Barney house exterior seemed to pose an unresolvable debate between rationalism and the Queen Anne, the interior appears to have been an unqualified success, at least for a writer in the *New York Sun* who, though he had doubts about the outside, found within "the best interior in New York, from an artistic point of view. As is everywhere the case, there is a considerable mixing up of styles. One room is in the Renaissance manner, another is arabesque, and a third is said to be 'Colonial;' but with some slips and hitches, they have been so well combined as to be very peacefully disposed toward one another." Most interesting of all to the *Sun*'s writer was the library, "quite probably, the most interesting [interior] in the city," designed by George Fletcher Babb, one of the McKim firm's bright young stars, who would soon go out on his own as partner in the firm Babb, Cook & Willard. The library was small, so much so that it seemed more like "the full size model of a room, in building which the architect's motive must have been to show what a beautiful room he could build if he should ever get the means." Almost devoid of ornament, the nearly square space

Charles L. Tiffany house, northwest corner of Madison Avenue and East Seventy-second Street. McKim, Mead & White, 1882–85. View to the northwest. BHS.

Charles L. Tiffany house, northwest corner of Madison Avenue and East Seventy-second Street. Sketch by Louis Comfort Tiffany, c. 1882. LCT. CU.

capped by a flattened groin was said to possess "a beauty of its own—the rarest kind of beauty in this era of building— architectural beauty."[391]

McKim, Mead & White's Charles L. Tiffany house (1882–85), at the northwest corner of Madison Avenue and Seventy-second Street, was the most palatial example of the artistic house.[392] Built by the head of the famous jewelry company, it was intended to be home to the owner's daughter Louise and to his recently widowed son, the artist Louis Comfort Tiffany, who since 1878 had been living with his three small children in a remarkably decorated suite at the Bella (see above). The project seems to have been conceived in part with a therapeutic purpose in mind, since Charles Tiffany left to his still-grieving son the day-to-day responsibility for working with Stanford White on the design. In fact, a drawing by Louis Comfort

Tiffany seems to have been the basis for the design. Early drawings for the project reveal only outlines for the upper portion of the house, where Louis Comfort Tiffany's studio was to be located, suggesting that he may very well have designed this part of the house himself—certainly he was responsible for its remarkable, proto–Art Nouveau interior. Louis Comfort Tiffany also guided the spirit of the other interiors, which he directed White to do in what he called the "Old Dutch style." In White's hands, this entailed a mix of simplified Queen Anne and freestyle that formed an important step along the route of progressive design, which began with the work of Richard Norman Shaw and climaxed in the spare, white-painted interiors of the British architect Charles F. A. Voysey.[393]

Tiffany's sketch outlined the basic components of the remarkable design, a heavily rusticated base carrying a tri-partite composition facing Seventy-second Street, with pronounced pedimented gables and a projecting oriel at the corner. Under White's direction the house emerged much taller, bolder, and simpler, with a colossal steel-framed gable running east-west, sheltering Tiffany's studio and tying the composition together. While the example of Richardson as well as precedents for overall massing in various northern European countries can be cited, and for certain details the revived Classicism of Palladio, the design of the Tiffany house—from its use of multihued soft buff to deep golden brown speckle-glazed thin Roman

brick, developed by White in association with the Perth Amboy Brick Company, to its dark tile roof, like that of only a handful of work in its period, including McKim, Mead & White's Phoenix house (see below)—can be described as virtually *sui generis*, a point made by Mariana Van Rensselaer: "It is a style of its own—one which must be judged by intrinsic standards and not by reference to bygone fashions and antiquarian dogmas."[394]

From the first, the house was appreciated for its size and for the boldness of its composition, especially given that its nearest neighbor was the simple, white-painted Lenox farmhouse, the only building on the block, immediately to the south. In May 1884, as the house was nearing completion, the editors of the *Real Estate Record and Builders' Guide* deemed it to be "already the most conspicuous dwelling house in the city. The gable on the Madison Avenue front must be very nearly seventy-five feet wide at the base, and the pitch is steep, so that the roof is a towering object. The house is also conspicuous for its magnitude and material."[395] Two months later the editors judged it almost, "if not quite, the largest private dwelling in New York." Dimensions alone, they continued, "would suffice to make the house very conspicuous" as well as its unusual materials. However, they found that it was "only the novelty of the material" that made the house conspicuous because the yellow brick yielded an overall effect that was quite the opposite: "It is quiet in color and its mottled surface offers a very effective

View to the northwest from Madison Avenue and East Seventy-first Street, 1885, showing Lenox farm buildings and the American Museum of Natural History (Calvert Vaux and Jacob Wrey Mould, 1874–77) in the distance across Central Park. MCNY.

Louis Comfort Tiffany apartment, northwest corner of Madison Avenue and East Seventy-second Street. McKim, Mead & White and Louis Comfort Tiffany, 1882–85. Entrance to studio. AR. CU.

contrast to the blue stone of the basement. It has the great advantage of making a brand new building look as if it might be old, without invoking any trickery to the purpose."[396] But the calm composition of almost plain surfaces and elemental shapes did not find quite so much favor with the *Record and Guide*'s critic, probably Montgomery Schuyler, who found it "tending to monotony," even though "as our buildings go" such was "a fault on the right side." All in all, especially when viewed in perspective, "the composition . . . [was] very spirited and picturesque, in spite of the blankness of the great gable. The fault one finds at last with the building is that it is scarcely a building, as a work of architecture must primarily be. That is to say, it seems like an attempt not so much to make a picture out of a building as to make a building out of a picture," referring to the picturesque handling of chimneys and balconies and other "structural solecisms" that gave "an unreal and fictitious character to a building which in general composition, in choice and arrangement of material and many points even of detail is thoroughly admirable."[397]

White's design was far more vertical and imposing if somehow less strictly tectonic than Tiffany's original sketch, as Schuyler suggested. This was so in part because of the extensive use of balconies and loggias, which made the house more distinctly residential and picturesque, so much so that it can be argued that the Tiffany block was an urban version of the kind of suburban and resort work

Louis Comfort Tiffany apartment, northwest corner of Madison Avenue and East Seventy-second Street. McKim, Mead & White and Louis Comfort Tiffany, 1882–85. Studio. AR. CU.

Louis Comfort Tiffany apartment, northwest corner of Madison Avenue and East Seventy-second Street. McKim, Mead & White and Louis Comfort Tiffany, 1882–85. Library. AR. CU.

Louis Comfort Tiffany apartment, northwest corner of Madison Avenue and East Seventy-second Street. McKim, Mead & White and Louis Comfort Tiffany, 1882–85. Dining room. AR. CU.

of which White and his partners were then the masters. There was an irony to this mix of huge size and cozy domesticity, since some contemporary observers insisted on describing the triple mansion as an apartment house. Mariana Van Rensselaer addressed her criticism to the dilemma of scale and character posed by the design:

> To me this is a beautiful house as well as a very good one. But I know there are many eyes which, while acknowledging its excellence as a piece of construction and an architectural design (as to this there can hardly be serious question), find it too uncompromisingly massive, too grave and somber, too forbidding, almost, to fit in with the idea of what is beautiful in domestic building. I can but reiterate that I myself do not feel this about it, and then explain why, whether it be very beautiful or not, it seems to me the most interesting and most promising house we have yet constructed—more interesting even and more promising than

Mr. Hunt's indisputably beautiful French chateau [the William K. Vanderbilt house]. This is because when we come into its presence we do not for a moment think of asking what "style" it follows, or care a whit whether it follows none or draws inspirations from a dozen. Style it has—that style which means harmony of proportions, accord of features, unity of effect; which means that the artist has had a definite, homogeneous conception to express, and has expressed it clearly, coherently, and in each and every proportion, form and detail. . . . For this reason I believe it must have a good influence upon our art; not as inciting to direct imitation,—that would perhaps be a dangerous essay,—but as showing that it is possible to be "original" without being fantastic or unscholarly (no work is unscholarly which is perfectly coherent and harmonious), and to build admirably without a particle of ornamentation. Nothing could be more instructive than to compare

Louis Comfort Tiffany apartment, northwest corner of Madison Avenue and East Seventy-second Street. McKim, Mead & White and Louis Comfort Tiffany, 1882–85. Studio. AR. CU.

(or, rather, to *contrast*) the two finest houses New York has yet to show—this house and Mr. Hunt's. They prove how wide are the limits that bound architectural excellence even in the one branch of city domestic work; how foolish it is to try and fetter effort with narrow artistic creeds, with rigid dogmas as to style and treatment and amount of decoration. Each is an admirable house in its own way—I am almost afraid to say how admirable in my eyes when judged by the standard of current performance even in its better phases, and even in Europe as well as here. Yet no two houses could well be more unlike in idea, in material, in treatment, or in degree of ornamentation.[398]

Entered through a wrought-iron portcullis set in a version of a typical Richardsonian arch, the six-story, fifty-seven-room house presented separate doors that led via stairs and an elevator to Charles Tiffany's apartment on the two lower floors, Louise Tiffany's on the third, and Louis Comfort Tiffany's on the fourth and in the attic. Charles Tiffany, however, never occupied his apartment, which was subse-

quently rented out. Louis Comfort Tiffany's apartment, one of the great interiors of the nineteenth century, included a large studio, the iron framing for which was left exposed and vividly contrasted with exposed concrete and plaster. In order to create as large a room as possible, all the flues serving the furnace and numerous fireplaces housed below were bundled together in the center of the studio, "modeled" to form what Charles de Kay described in 1914 as "a shaft as easy of line as the bole of a great tree . . . hollowed out" on four sides "so that the wide and lofty studio—almost as wide as the area of the building, high as the peak of the roof permitted—is lighted up at night in every direction by smouldering log fires." Presiding over the studio was an organ loft, though the keyboard was set on the studio floor. The studio incorporated bits and pieces from an unidentified two-thousand-year-old Indian palace and was filled with treasures gathered from around the world, including, to decorate the corners of a bay window, a collection of Japanese sword guards, Pompeian glass, and especially the Favrile glass that became

Louis Comfort Tiffany apartment, northwest corner of Madison Avenue and East Seventy-second Street. McKim, Mead & White and Louis Comfort Tiffany, 1882–85. Breakfast room. AR. CU.

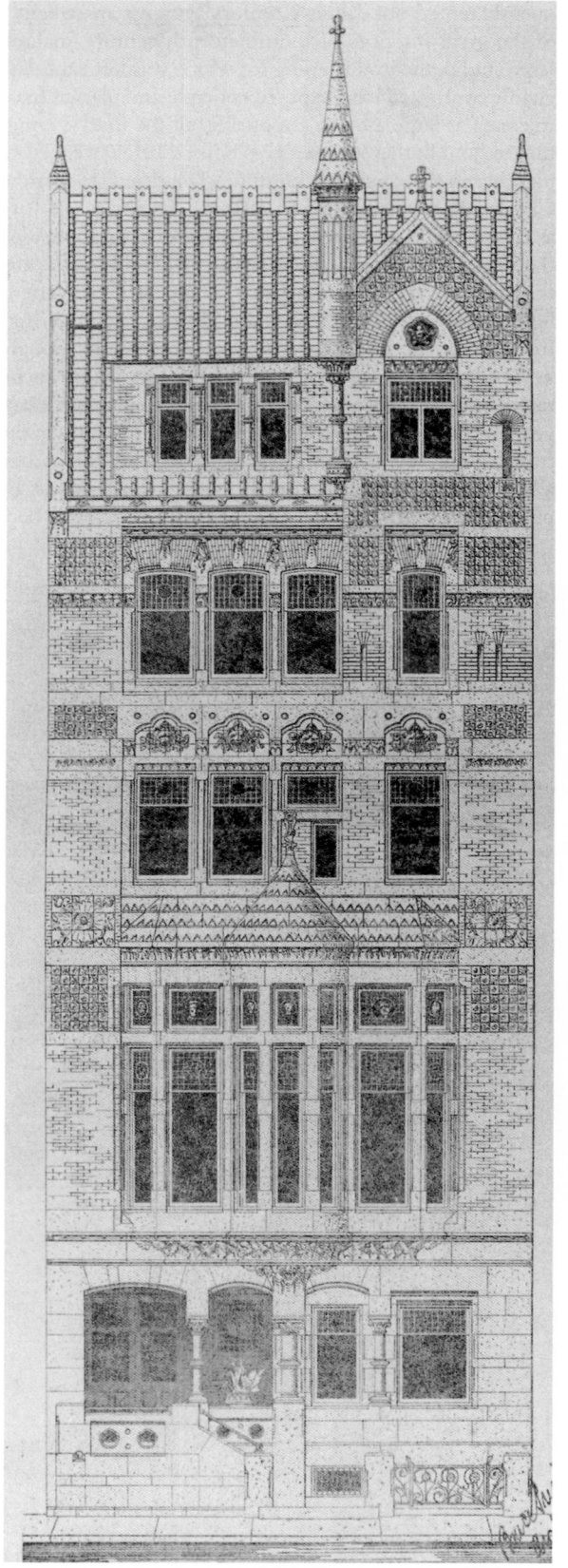

Proposed rowhouse designs. Bruce Price, 1879. Elevations. AABN. CU.

Tiffany's most famous art form. The natural light that streamed in from near the top of the twenty-foot-high, partially skylit studio, which opened to a rooftop terrace, was supplemented by suspended lamps, the colored shades of which created pools of red, rose, cream, and yellow. According to de Kay, "At night the glow from the hearths round the central stack lights up the brightest of the vases and bowls and plaques, gleams with dull rich notes on copper and bronze and throws broad spaces of the irregular apartment into deep shadow. The suspended lamps of many shades of red, rose, yellow and creamy white are foiled against the blackness of the high roof-ceiling. If at that moment a skilled hand touches the keys of the organ the great studio merges into fairy-land."[399] Tiffany's apartment also included an east-facing breakfast room, a west-facing dining room, and a ballroomlike drawing room with a fireplace flanked by wall cases displaying rare Oriental porcelain and Favrile glass.

The Tiffany house marked the apogee of McKim, Mead & White's Queen Anne work and also its virtual conclusion. As construction progressed, the firm began to design the strictly Classical Villard Houses (see above), a project as diagrammatically precise in plan, section, and elevation as the Tiffany house was intuitive and picturesquely complex. The Tiffany house was more than the culmination of a stylistic trend—it really was a special moment in the young firm's work. It was, as the English critic Edmund Gosse, visiting New York in November 1884, put it, "the realization of an architect's dream; and . . . the most beautiful modern domestic building I have almost ever seen. . . . The Tiffany house gave me the same impression as some of the grand Seventeenth Century châlets in Switzerland give; a sort of vastness, as if it had grown like a mountain."[400]

After McKim, Mead & White, Bruce Price was perhaps the city's leading designer of artistic houses. Price first made his mark in 1878 with a Queen Anne–style houselike apartment building on East Twenty-first Street (see above). He followed that success with two designs for a twenty-five-foot-wide rowhouse. Never built, the drawings were published in 1879 and revealed brilliantly controlled facades that formed nothing short of an elaborate mosaic of motifs and materials.[401] The two schemes shared a remarkably open plan featuring a large, centrally located stair. Price's five-story brick and Belleville stone house (1881) at 36 West Fifty-sixth Street, built by the developer David H. King Jr. and occupied by Dr. William J. Morton, recalled in a much-chastened way the composition of the unrealized house designs.[402] Montgomery Schuyler found it touched by "spirit and picturesqueness,"[403] and Russell Sturgis found nothing to criticize "unless it be in the mere choice of some of the sculptured details, and the general effect of the picturesque and spirited front to enliven the dull street is most delightful."[404] In comparison with its unrealized prototypes, the Morton house was notably singular, even severe, in its design, in effect an arch supporting a bracketed pediment atop a rusticated stone base. Only a shallow bay forming a third-floor balcony relieved the composition, which was notable for its bold scale.

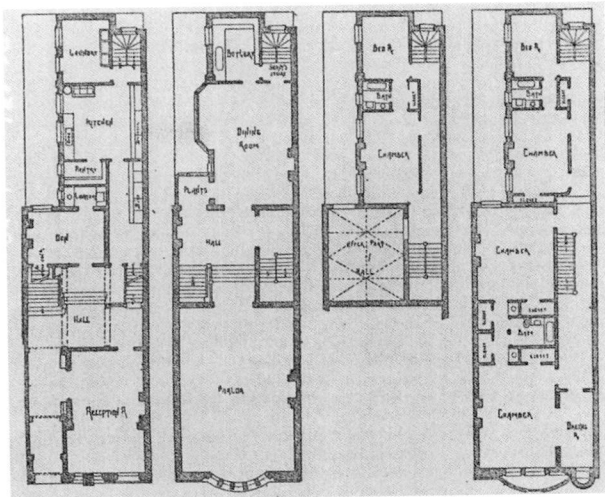

Proposed rowhouse designs. Bruce Price, 1879. Plans. AABN. CU.

Dr. William J. Morton house, 36 West Fifty-sixth Street. Bruce Price, 1881. View to the south. Levy. AIC.

Price's bold, pedimented, twenty-foot-wide house (1884) for Dr. Theodore G. Thomas, at 600 Madison Avenue, between Fifty-seventh and Fifty-eighth Streets, offered, according to Sturgis, a "pleasant suggestion of Dutch post and lintel architecture."[405] In effect the design was much more a recollection of French Medieval design and, according to Vincent Scully, a close adaptation of the sixteenth-century House of Diane de Poitiers at Rouen, demonstrat-

Dr. Theodore G. Thomas house, 600 Madison Avenue, between East Fifty-seventh and East Fifty-eighth Streets. Bruce Price, 1884. View to the west. AABN. MMA.

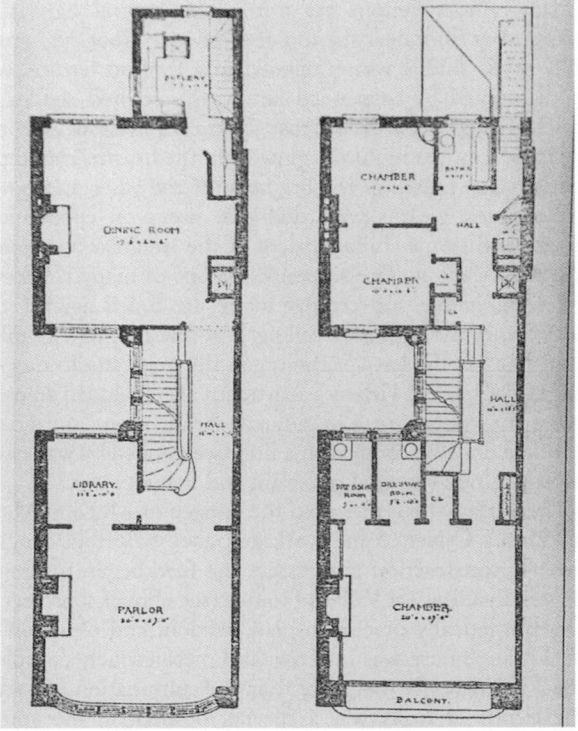

Dr. Theodore G. Thomas house, 600 Madison Avenue, between East Fifty-seventh and East Fifty-eighth Streets. Bruce Price, 1884. First- and second-floor plans. AABN. MMA.

ing the importance in the 1880s of the influence of the so-called Francis I style, "combining, as this did, medieval skeleton construction with Renaissance detail and the beginnings of Renaissance control."[406] The house immediately attracted attention because of its extensive horizontal bands of glazing, its shallow-swell bay at the second floor, and its exuberant decorative detail, with most of the facade at the second and third stories clad in copper ornamented with heraldic designs. The editors of *Building* magazine

described Price's influential design in detail: "The third story is recessed, giving a narrow balcony on the street, and the copper work is continued up to the fourth story, which presents a pointed gable of brick and tiles. The use of copper for the front instead of iron has the advantage of allowing much more delicate ornamentation, and it need not be painted, the dull surface of the copper harmonizing effectively with the brick and brown-stone work of the rest of the house." But they were not impressed with the internal arrangements of the house, finding "no peculiar features" in the plan, with a "cramped" staircase hall in the center and stairs too small to allow room for an adequately sized light well.[407] Dr. Thomas's consulting rooms were on the first floor, his living and dining rooms on the second (the latter connecting via a pantry to a kitchen in the cellar), and bedrooms above. One unusual feature was a small hospital located on the roof, put there, according to the *American Architect and Building News*, to carry "out a hobby of the doctor's for quarantining any member of his own family stricken with any infectious disease."[408]

Price's four-story brick and stone house (1888–89) for John E. Griswold, at 1 East Thirty-fourth Street, was one of the last important houses to be built on what only twenty years earlier had been the upper end of fashionable Fifth Avenue but was soon to become home to high-class commerce. The *Real Estate Record and Builders' Guide* commented: "Anyone walking up the avenue cannot help noticing the beautiful new

4–8 West Fifty-seventh Street. Russell Sturgis, 1872–73. View to the south. AR. CU.

house. . . . Price has designed one of the most striking houses in the city. The style is of a composite order, leaning to the Romanesque, with an immense bay window on the first floor. The house is 25 x 100 and contains about twenty-five rooms. Another feature is the large open air and light shaft on the side wall. The front is uncut brown stone."[409]

According to a less-than-enthralled Montgomery Schuyler, however, the new individualistic houses were mostly to be seen even farther uptown: on Fifty-seventh Street between Fifth and Sixth Avenues, and along Fifth Avenue and its immediate side streets between Fifty-ninth and Eightieth Streets. Together these were "the chief scenes of the new movement in which . . . it is somewhat difficult to distinguish inspiration from simple dementia." For Schuyler the south side of Fifty-seventh Street was the battleground of "a particularly active and acrimonious architectural competition" among George E. Harney, Russell Sturgis, Lamb & Wheeler, J. C. Cady, Edward E. Raht, and W. Wheeler Smith.[410] Russell Sturgis's 4, 6, and 8 West Fifty-seventh Street (1872–73), combining aspects of Neo-Grec, Italianate, and Gothic manners, were the first important houses to be built on the block.[411] According to Schuyler, who was not impressed, Sturgis's group consisted of "three flat-roofed houses which [were] treated in Gothic, [are] not pretentious, and have no appearance of having been designed in competition."[412] Of the group, number 6 was occupied by Theodore Roosevelt Sr. and

Theodore Roosevelt Sr. house, 6 West Fifty-seventh Street. Russell Sturgis, 1872–73. View of dining room designed by Frank Furness, c. 1880. TRC.

View to the south showing, from left to right, part of the William H. De Forest house (Lamb & Wheeler, 1879–82), 12 West Fifty-seventh Street, the E. A. Wickes house (J. C. Cady, 1879), 14 West Fifty-seventh Street, and the A. D. Juilliard house (Edward E. Raht, 1879), 16 West Fifty-seventh Street. MCNY.

William H. De Forest house, 12 West Fifty-seventh Street. Lamb & Wheeler, 1879–82. Hall. AH. CU.

number 4 by his brother James Alfred, while number 8 was the home of J. S. Kennedy. Roosevelt, the father of the future president, had inherited a great deal of money and also ran a successful glass-importing business. He was one of the city's leading philanthropists and a founding member of both the Metropolitan Museum of Art and the American Museum of Natural History. For the interiors, Roosevelt made a surprising choice, hiring the Philadelphia architect Frank Furness. Furness was then at the beginning of the most productive phase of his career, and he was put in charge of the library, dining room, and hall and was responsible for furnishings for one or more bedrooms. Roosevelt was very proud of the house and took an active role in its construction and decoration, specifying a top-floor gymnasium for the children. After his first night in the house he wrote to his wife: "It seems like another landmark reached on my life's journey. We have now probably one abiding-place for the rest of our days."[413]

Lamb & Wheeler's fifty-foot-wide, four-story, gable-fronted gray limestone and red brick house (1879–82) for William H. De Forest, at 12 West Fifty-seventh Street, was, according to Schuyler, "treated now with Gothic and now with classic detail, and of an uneasy and notoriety-hunting appearance."[414] George W. Sheldon, who admired Queen Anne eclecticism as much as Schuyler did not, reveled in the house's interior decorating, especially that of the Early English–style hall with its Japanese-inspired ceiling, where Hugh Lamb "allowed himself much freedom of expression, and introduced into his very eclectic and interesting scheme the salient and most enticing qualities of various schools and epochs, thus avoiding what otherwise might have been some loudly-resounding clashing."[415] Schuyler was dismissive of Edward E. Raht's four-story brownstone house (1879) for A. D. Juilliard, at 16 West Fifty-seventh Street, which, "except for some study of detail here and there, would not deserve to be distinguished from the ordinary brownstone front."[416] W. Wheeler Smith's E. W. Chapin house (1880), at 34 West Fifty-seventh Street, was the last in the group of Queen Anne houses detested by Schuyler, who found it full of "more 'things'" than any of the others, "or perhaps any two, of the others, and as many, it seems, as could conveniently be put into a twenty-five foot front. It is equally elaborate in form and in color, which seems a clear error"—all in all a "fretful building."[417]

Two houses in the block met with Schuyler's approval: J. C. Cady's E. A. Wickes house (1879), at 14 West Fifty-seventh Street, and George E. Harney's Frederick W. Stevens house (1875–76), at 2 West Fifty-seventh Street, on the southwest corner of Fifth Avenue. Cady's "not very noticeable" four-story Wickes house combined brick and brownstone in a design that seemed to Schuyler the product of a search for "domestic peace. The color is deep and quiet, and much of the detail is refined, as it could scarcely

Frederick W. Stevens house, southwest corner of Fifth Avenue and West Fifty-seventh Street. George E. Harney, 1875–76.
View to the southwest showing part of 4–8 West Fifty-seventh Street (Russell Sturgis, 1872–73) on the far right. Levy. AIC.

Frederick W. Stevens house, southwest corner of Fifth Avenue and West Fifty-seventh Street. George E. Harney, 1875–76. Ballroom. AH. CU.

fail to be . . . thoroughly classic and . . . [overall] a mixture of 'Old New York' with more orthodox Renaissance."[418] Harney's Stevens house was the first freestanding house to be built on a corner of what would soon become a key area of mansions—Robert Mook's seven-unit row for Mary Mason Jones already occupied the northeast corner (see above).[419] The Stevens house, which enjoyed only twenty-five feet of avenue frontage, was surprisingly underscaled considering the Stevenses' wealth and lavish social program. The Stevenses' entertaining would be curtailed by their divorce, in 1886, after which Mrs. Stevens became the Duchess de Talleyrand. The interior decor was elaborate but unexceptional, save for the century-old Flemish ballroom, purchased in Ghent, Belgium, with its flat, light-colored, planelike walls, parquet floor, and furniture upholstered in Beauvais tapestries. Harney's design also impressed Alfred J. Bloor, who found its "ample dimensions, . . . several towers and particularly its round tower, and some of its other features" reminiscent "of a French chateau; but it is full of modern feeling, gracefully rendered. The interior, with its spacious, lofty living-rooms, its mosaic hall floor, its gallery, its lace and leather hangings, and its general appointments, is luxuriously worked out."[420] Writing in 1881, Schuyler felt that the Stevens house gained in respectability as its neighbors were built.[421]

A few important artistic houses were built outside midtown's cordon of fashion. Van Campen Taylor's house for Lockwood de Forest (1887), at 7 East Tenth Street, was the city's most unusual artistic house, made special by the extensive use of Indian-inspired teakwood details designed by de Forest, who was descended from a socially prominent family that had made its money in South American and Caribbean shipping.[422] After studying with the landscapist Frederic Church, de Forest went on to a modestly successful career as a painter, but his interests in architecture and decoration led him to join Louis Comfort Tiffany and others in founding Associated Artists, a short-lived,

Lockwood de Forest house, 7 East Tenth Street. Van Campen Taylor and Lockwood de Forest, 1887. View to the north. BLDG. CU.

Fourth Avenue and Irving Place.[423] The house was in fact an extensive renovation of a house (1844–45) that had already been altered in 1863 by Griffith Thomas soon after its purchase by Tilden, a prominent lawyer and politician who would narrowly lose the 1876 presidential race. In 1874 Tilden, just elected governor of New York, purchased the house west of his and hired Vaux & Radford to combine the two, creating a new facade that represented to Schuyler a viable architectural direction "stopped short by the new [Queen Anne] 'movement.'" Schuyler found the Tilden house an "interesting piece of Gothic work, though . . . distinctly Victorian Gothic." He took particular pleasure

> in the detail of form and color [rather] than in general composition, since the building is architecturally only a street front, and since the slightness of the projections and the lack of visible and emphasized depth in the wall itself give it the appearance rather of a screen than of one face of a building, and the small gables which surmount it too evidently exist for the sole purpose of animating the sky-line. But the color treatment of this front is admirable [and] . . . an unusually large variety of colors, and those of the most positive tints that natural stones supply, has here been employed and harmonized; and what is even rarer, they have all been used with architectural propriety to accentuate the construction and to heighten its effect. An ingenious and novel use of dark granite, which when polished is almost black, and which is employed in narrow bands precisely where it is wanted, deserves particular remark. The decorative carving attracts attention chiefly by its profusion, and by the exquisite crispness and delicacy of its execution.[424]

Although some of Thomas's work on the inside of the house was not altered, Vaux & Radford designed a large library on the ground floor of number 14, lit by a stained-glass dome made in Boston by Donald MacDonald, as well as new drawing and dining rooms on the ground floor of number 15. George W. Sheldon was impressed by the dining room, where "the architect has produced, with complex material, an effect of great richness and perfect unity." He was particularly taken with the treatment of its ceiling:

> The ceiling, thirty-one feet square—and this squareness of dimension adds its own note of fitness to the general effect—is divided transversely, by satin-wood beams, into four parts, each end of the beams terminating in an octagonal panel of the same wood, and each division of the ceiling covered with blue tiles eight inches square, every tile being framed in ribs of satin-wood, and caught by four projections from the center of each rib, and fastened in the back to an iron plate above it. The glaze of these encaustic, turquoise-hued Low tiles gives the ceiling almost a mirror effect, and produces the great charm of changing, shifting tones.[425]

Though the followers of the Queen Anne, as Schuyler pointed out, were intent on escaping the wild, untutored work of the post–Civil War era, they took up a way of designing that was itself frequently as eclectic and undis-

high-minded decorating company that was influenced by Asian and Eastern Mediterranean art and specialized in intricate handwork and in the rich use of color. De Forest continued to work with Tiffany after the Associated Artists group broke up, in 1883. De Forest also pursued his own ventures; he had been introduced to Indian art on his wedding trip, and he established a cabinet shop in Ahmadabad to produce Indian-style furniture for Americans. In 1887 de Forest bought two lots on East Tenth Street, selling one, number 9, for development as a small apartment house (see above) and commissioning Van Campen Taylor to design a house for de Forest's own use on the other. Taylor's design was simple to the point of anonymity. Probably the first house in New York not to have a stoop, it served merely as a background for de Forest's decorative embellishments, principally intricately carved teak woodwork from India as well as the house's most memorable exterior feature, on the second floor, a filigreed teak-framed oriel carried on heavy brackets and overlayed with spectacular naturalistic carving. The interiors included red sandstone from Asia, blue tiles from Damascus, a patterned brass ceiling in the parlor, and Indian-style furniture.

Another individualistic house of note south of midtown was Calvert Vaux and George K. Radford's Samuel J. Tilden house (1881–84), at 14–15 Gramercy Park South, between ciplined as that which they sought to avoid. But some young American architects, such as Charles F. McKim, began to see in American late-Colonial and post-Colonial work a way to combine the discipline of Classicism with forms that were characteristically, if not uniquely, American. McKim, Mead & White's H.A.C. Taylor house (1894), at 3 East Seventy-first Street, is frequently cited as the first Georgian Revival building in New York, although the firm had already produced a number of country houses along the same line, starting with the Newport, Rhode Island, house they designed for the same client in 1882.[426] As early as 1878, however, George E. Harney had anticipated this antiquarian bent in the design of his four-story, Connecticut brownstone house for James Morris, at 289 Madison Avenue, between Fortieth and Forty-first Streets, next door to McKim, Mead & White's Frederick S. Thompson house (see above). Perhaps the earliest example of the Colonial Revival, the Morris house fascinated and annoyed Schuyler, who at first criticized Harney's choice of stylistic model and then went on to see the scholarly approach that lay behind the design as a failure of nerve. "Swell fronts were never so characteristic of New York as they were and are of Boston, but still a goodly number of them used to be built," Schuyler wrote in 1881. "Mr. Harney's work is, in except some few and unimportant details, an exact reproduction of the type he has chosen. . . . The effect of the copy like that of the original is at best simply void of offence. If it be a success from an educated architect in the year 1881 to equal, by copying it, the work of a mechanic of 1840 when educated architects were unknown to New York, Mr. Harney is to be congratulated upon attaining that

Samuel J. Tilden house, 14–15 Gramercy Park South. Vaux & Radford, 1881–84. View to the southwest. AABN. CU.

Samuel J. Tilden house, 14–15 Gramercy Park South. Vaux & Radford, 1881–84. Dining room. AH. CU.

Phillips and Lloyd Phoenix house, 21 East Thirty-third Street. McKim, Mead & White, 1882–84. View to the north. AABN. CU.

Gibson Fahnestock house, 30 East Fifty-first Street. McKim, Mead & White, 1886–89. View to the south. BLDG. CU.

success."[427] Schuyler did not see Harney's house as the reaction to the excesses of the Queen Anne that it clearly was. Rather, he saw it as emblematic of the shift from the progressive Gothicism of the 1860s and early 1870s to the reactive Queen Anne: "We might ask Mr. Harney, for example, who has been one of the noteworthy contributors to the works of both periods, whether in falling to 'grace' he has not fallen from something more important." While Schuyler believed Harney had much to be proud of

in his Stevens house, "it seems to have been morbid sensitiveness to the defects of his work which led [him] to abandon altogether and in despair the practice of architectural design . . . and when he had another city house to do, to dispute the design of it to some unknown carpenter who died before he was born," by reproducing "accurately in Madison Avenue a Vandam or Charlton Street house built out of due time, with a familiar 'old New York' doorway, in the jambs of which quoins intercept sheaves of mouldings. This confession that a carpenter of 1825 was a better-trained designer than an educated architect of 1880 is very possibly credited to the personal modesty of the latter; but Mr. Harney's own earlier works sufficiently testify that it does not do him justice."[428]

Far more promising to Schuyler as a direction for architecture was McKim, Mead & White's Phillips and Lloyd Phoenix house (1882–84), at 21 East Thirty-third Street, which sat next door to Richard Morris Hunt's Egerton Winthrop house (see above).[429] Built for two bachelor brothers, the small house was highly individual and thoroughly "artistic" but had nothing "picturesque" about it. In one respect this house can be seen as the Queen Anne pushed to its logical conclusion: in its search for a modern way of design, it achieved what many adherents of the Queen Anne had all along been searching for, a virtually modern language born out of so complex a synthesis of things from the past that the final result defied stylistic categorization. But in another way it had almost nothing to do with the Queen Anne and everything to do with the new taste for Classicism. In the Phoenix house, McKim, Mead & White took the Renaissance and essentialized it, creating a Classicism comparable in its purity to that which flourished in late-eighteenth-century France. As Vincent Scully, deriving his point from an observation of Henry-Russell Hitchcock's, has written, the Phoenix house was a "highly original" interpretation of the Renaissance, "where the principle of order and clarity was seen in essential rather than representational terms."[430] This was just the direction in which Schuyler, who believed the Queen Anne to be a waste of effort, a skittering-about on the surface of things, had hoped the restless search for modern expression would lead. What would happen, Schuyler asked in 1883, if architects turned to the essentials of the great styles, "if they faithfully scrutinize their precedents, and faithfully discard such as are inapplicable, in arriving at free architecture will arrive, so far as style is concerned, at much the same result. If this process were to be carried on for a generation, it would be as difficult, and as purely a matter of speculative curiosity, to trace the sources of English and American architecture as the sources of the composite and living English language, which is adequate to every expression."[431]

The Phoenix house plan was not remarkable except that each brother had an identical front-facing master bedroom. But the facade was noteworthy in its flatness. The pure astylar elevation was carefully controlled, with ornament concentrated in panels that visually tied the windows together to form a strong figure. Above a buff sandstone base that expressed the public rooms behind it, light yellow brick and slightly darker terra cotta were combined in a structurally expressive manner—the brick side walls suggesting support, the terra cotta a light skin or cladding. Russell Sturgis deemed it "a very sagacious partial answer to the question what our small house-fronts ought to be. . . . It is . . . the large manner of framing-in the second and third stories of windows that especially

attracts, together with the separation of the upper wall, which was to be so different in its openings, by a marked difference in material from the basement."[432]

The purity of the Phoenix house was difficult to sustain. McKim, Mead & White's four-story Gibson Fahnestock house (1886–89), at 30 East Fifty-first Street, also built of Roman brick set on a sandstone base, was a wider version, "more refined in detail," as Sturgis put it, "but the great width of the undivided windows tends to confuse the scale of the whole."[433] Like the Phoenix house, except for a heavy modillioned cornice, the facade was virtually free of specific Classical details, although the arched hood over the entrance was carried on console brackets. In contrast with the smooth finish of the base at the Phoenix house, the Fahnestock design was rusticated.

Upper Fifth Avenue

While fashion favored Fifth Avenue in the Fifties and the side streets immediately to the east and west of it, the obvious advantages of a location on the avenue where it bordered Central Park slowly began to be appreciated, and by the end of the 1880s top society was relocating to Fifth Avenue's park blocks. Jacob Wrey Mould's Ruskin-Gothic residence (1865–69) for Runyon W. Martin Jr., at 816 Fifth Avenue, just south of Sixty-third Street, was the first house to be built facing Central Park.[434] The narrow facade of the four-and-a-half-story house was busily broken up with a projecting pedimented porch, a second-floor bay window, and a fourth-floor projecting balcony. Besides the park itself, upper Fifth Avenue's most significant attraction was Richard Morris Hunt's Lenox Library (1870–77), at Seventieth Street (see chapter 2). James Lenox's farm surrounded the library and slowly he began to sell off parcels for speculatively built rowhouses catering to the well-to-do. Most of the new houses were developed by builders, many of whom resorted to the typical brownstone type. In 1881 Montgomery Schuyler gave a decidedly downbeat assessment of the new construction, finding, for example, D. & J. Jardine's French Renaissance–inspired house and adjoining stable (1877–78) for the Standard Oil mogul Jabez A. Bostwick, at 800 Fifth Avenue, on the northeast corner of Sixty-first Street, "pure Peorian," making up "in restless vulgarity what it loses in monotony."[435] Schuyler delivered an insidious backhanded compliment to Charles W. Clinton for his H. R. Bishop house (1880), at 881 Fifth Avenue, between Sixty-ninth and Seventieth Streets. The wide, fifty-four-by-ninety-foot, four-story, midblock brownstone front struck the critic as "a well-behaved, correct, and rather rich piece of formal Renaissance," going so far as to proclaim it as "one of the most elegant specimens in New York of Renaissance in domestic work . . . distinctly better than its architect's work in . . . the Seventh Regiment Armory."[436] He was a little fonder of Herter Brothers's four-story, 50-by-104-foot David Dows house (1879), at the northeast corner of Fifth Avenue and Sixty-ninth Street, which he found "a great relief" compared to the majority of the work in the neighborhood. This brick and brownstone house, with ample frontage on both streets, was "very simple in composition, and rather affectedly prim and precise in treatment."[437] In a subsequent assessment, written two years later, he praised it again by listing its deficiencies:

> . . . the absence of any emphatic cornice, the general primness and precision of the detail, and the irrelevancy of what little architecture there is to the building to which the architecture is applied. The architecture consists mainly of an ineffectual porch . . . and a row of irrelevant brownstone pilasters along an upper story. . . . There is nothing offensive or extravagant about the house. It does not call out to you in boisterous and profane language to come and look at it. It is only thin and flat and spiritless and tame, and comes as near to be unnoticeable as a big house can.[438]

While development was slow to come to upper Fifth Avenue, the Lenox Hill side streets, between Sixty-third and Seventy-first Streets and extending as far east as Fourth Avenue, were rapidly filling up, typically with three- to five-house groups developed on speculation. Sometimes the developers employed architects, frequently with good results, as in the case of the three-house, brick and sandstone group of four-story, sixteen-foot-wide houses (1879) for James Sinclair, at 2–6 East Sixty-third

Street, by Cyrus L. W. Eidlitz.[439] Schuyler found that despite a "not promising" high-stoop basement scheme cramming three houses onto two lots "so that a look of stilting was almost inevitable," the houses were "a pleasure to come upon." He praised the group as "rational, clear and vigorous," with a strong sense of the exterior wall as a work of construction and not merely "sash frames," resulting in an overall "design [that] is eminently sane and manly."[440] Also notable was a bay-windowed, Queen Anne–style group (1878–80) at 6–10 East Sixty-seventh Street, designed by James E. Ware for the developer Ira E. Doying,[441] and Lamb & Wheeler's house (1881–82) for John Wolfe, the prominent art collector, at 8 East Sixty-eighth Street.[442] Detlef Lienau was hired for the interiors of the Wolfe house, where his notably architectonic dining room, in the Italian Renaissance style and paneled in black walnut, was the only view of the house included in George W. Sheldon's *Artistic Houses*.

After 1880 upper Fifth Avenue and its environs really began to take off as a fashionable neighborhood. While most of the construction was concentrated below Seventy-ninth Street, at least one significant house was built far uptown: a mansion (1881–83) for the beer baron Jacob H. Ruppert, whose brewery stood on the east side of Third Avenue and Ninety-first Street, commissioned from

Runyon W. Martin Jr. house, 816 Fifth Avenue, between East Sixty-second and East Sixty-third Streets. Jacob Wrey Mould, 1865–69. View to the east, c. 1870. NYHS.

Jabez A. Bostwick house, northeast corner of Fifth Avenue and East Sixty-first Street. D. & J. Jardine, 1877–78. View to the northeast, c. 1880. MCNY.

William Schickel.[443] The house, of brick and Belleville stone, stood on a fifty-by-one-hundred-foot lot at 1115 Fifth Avenue, on the southeast corner at Ninety-third Street. The restlessly massed, turreted, and gabled house was ridiculed by the *Real Estate Record and Builders' Guide*: "Coarse and ignorant, it is evident the house cost a great deal of money."[444] But the mansion and its owner were taken seriously enough to be included in Sheldon's *Artistic Houses*, in which, with the exception of the light-toned drawing room, photographs revealed dark, heavy interiors designed by Herter Brothers. In the basement were a bil-

liards room and a barrel-vaulted *Trinkstube*, modeled on similar rooms in old German taverns but with dark oak wainscoting embellished with a wide frieze of grapes highlighted by colored-glass jewel inserts.

In the mid-1880s the *Record and Guide* observed: "Fifth Avenue, above Fifty-ninth Street, is now in an active state of transition. Rookeries still standing, cheek-by-jowl, with fine houses, serve to show through what phases a great city must pass; but they are fast giving way before the march of handsome residences, which will soon make a stately border to this side of the park and the most notable part of

John Wolfe house, 8 East Sixty-eighth Street. Lamb & Wheeler, 1881–82. Dining room designed by Detlef Lienau. AH. CU.

Jacob H. Ruppert house, southeast corner of Fifth Avenue and East Ninety-third Street. William Schickel, 1881–83. Drawing room. AH. CU.

Jacob H. Ruppert house, southeast corner of Fifth Avenue and East Ninety-third Street. William Schickel, 1881–83.
View to the southeast, c. 1925. NYPL.

At first slowly, and then with a rush toward the end of the 1880s, the avenue began to fill up. R. H. Robertson's inventively composed, thirty-foot-wide, pressed brick and Belleville stone Joseph B. Kennedy house (1881–83), at 846 Fifth Avenue, between Sixty-fifth and Sixty-sixth Streets, was an early example of the trend toward relatively compact, individually designed rowhouses, a type that would fill up most of the park blocks between Sixtieth and Seventy-ninth Streets by 1890.[447] Originally designed for a somewhat wider site, with an elaborately asymmetrical French Renaissance–inspired composition culminating in a gable pierced by a Serlian window, the executed design, with its second-floor bay supported on a swelling central bracket, was praised by Schuyler in 1896 for its "conformity and decorum. . . . If one can add a touch of picturesqueness without disturbing the air of peacefulness and good neighborhood which is the first essential of a town house, all the better."[448]

Schuyler was not very fond of a lot of the new work. One of his least favorite designs was Lamb & Rich's four-house, four-story, brick and brown sandstone, Queen Anne–style row of houses (1881–83), the principal one of which was occupied by H. O. Armour, at the southeast corner of Sixty-seventh Street.[449] Schuyler abhorred these houses:

> There is no composition whatever, and the effect is so scattering, and the whole is so fortuitous an aggregation of unrelated parts, that it is impossible to describe the houses or to remember them when one's back is turned. Their fragments only recur to memory as the blurred images of a hideous dream. So one recalls the Batavian grace of the bulbous gables, the oriel-windows so set as to seem in imminent danger of toppling out, the egg and dart moulding niggled up and down jambs of brickwork connected by flat key-stones, the whip-lashes cut in sandstone blocks, the decorative details fished from the slums of the Rococo. These are not subjects for architectural criticism; they call for the intervention of an architectural police. They are cases of disorderly conduct done in brick and brown stone. Hazardous as the superlative degree generally is, it is not much of a hazard to say that they are the most thoroughly discreditable buildings ever erected in New York, and it is to be noted that they are thoroughly characteristic of the period. Such a nightmare might perhaps have entered the brain of some speculative builder during the wildest vulgarity of the brown-stone period, but he would not have had the effrontery to build it, being deterred by the consideration that nobody would face public ridicule by consenting to live in it. Some speculator is, however, convinced there is now a market for a house upon the street corner and screeches for people to come and look at it when there is nothing in it worth looking at; and we must take shame to ourselves from the reflection that the speculator may be right in counting upon this extreme vulgarization of the public taste, and that, at any rate, there is no police to prevent the emission of the screech upon the public highway.[450]

Joseph B. Kennedy house, 846 Fifth Avenue, between East Sixty-fifth and East Sixty-sixth Streets. R. H. Robertson, 1881–83. View to the east. AR. CU.

town. The architecture here is more varied, and here are to be found some of the handsomest interiors."[445] Though the new houses were luxurious, they were not the lavish palaces seen farther downtown. Some even were built on speculation. These were quickly gobbled up, as Montgomery Schuyler, reviewing the current building boom, noted:

> While the sign "Flat to Let" meets the eye of the stroller, especially in the upper part of the City, quite frequently the sign "house to rent" is rarely met with, except now and then in some newly settled section. This state of things is in part explained by the very generally accepted theory that New York is more and more tending to become the home of the rich, who are crowding here from all parts of the country, and also by the fact that there has been no adequate provision made for this influx. One reason for this is that many people are in a quandary as to the trend of the future. Upper Fifth Avenue is experiencing a slow development, and its exact position is not yet clearly defined.[446]

Sheldon, who usually concentrated on the interiors of his patrons' houses, described the Armour facade at some length:

> Its round, mullioned bay-windows run up to the third story; beneath them, on the Sixty-seventh Street side, are carved panels, in the style of the Italian Renaissance; above them, pretty balustrades of wrought-iron work, and, higher still, Queen Anne gables. The projecting porch on Fifth Avenue shows caryatides supporting a richly-carved pediment; and the steps have three broad landings, with two turns, the balustrade a massive panel of bronze. The basement walls and the circular bay-windows are both of stone. Simplicity of effect, especially in the picturesque sky-lines, seems to have been the leading aim of the architects . . . and they have accomplished it without falling into barrenness.[451]

In 1886 Mariana Van Rensselaer also took a look at the houses, agreeing more with Schuyler than with Sheldon and marveling that four houses "built at the same time and by the same hands" could be "as different as possible from its neighbors, and each . . . as distressingly fantastic as a house could be."[452]

At the same time that the Armour group was going up, Lamb & Rich was at work on a much larger group of coordinated Queen Anne houses (1881–82), although they were built far to the east in Yorkville and intended for a much more modest clientele.[453] Developed as rental units by the wealthy fur importer and maker of fur hats John C. Henderson, these thirty-two, three-story, mostly seventeen- and eighteen-foot-wide red brick houses occupied the full west blockfront of Avenue B (renamed East End Avenue in 1890) from Eighty-sixth to Eighty-seventh Street. The half-acre development also included 100-foot portions on the two side streets as well as a new cul-de-sac, Henderson Place, located on Eighty-sixth Street 100 feet west of the avenue and running back 140 feet through the block. Henderson had purchased the land, originally part of the eighteenth-century farm of William Waldron, from John Jacob Astor II, over three years, from 1855 to 1857. The *Real Estate Record and Builders' Guide* was impressed with the effort although leery of some of the details, remarking that the houses

> are noteworthy in the general scheme, in the details of management, and in the architecture. The most striking peculiarity of the arrangement is the introduction of a court or private street, faced by houses. . . . The street is not properly a street, as it should be open from end to end, but only extends half way through the block and is there stopped by a brick wall. This interrupting not only interferes with the free circulation of air which is desirable, but has sentimental consequences even more important in giving the inhabitants of the court the disagreeable feeling of living in what the French call a bag's end.

Although the journal found the architecture "bright, varied and animated," as at the Armour group, but to a much lesser degree, the design suffered from

H. O. Armour house, southeast corner of Fifth Avenue and East Sixty-seventh Street. Lamb & Rich, 1881–83. View to the southeast. BSFA. CU.

too much pretentiousness and too much strain after variety. Each front is treated quite by itself, and each has an unusual number of features. . . . The long front on Avenue B is a symmetrical composition with a pagoda roof at each end, and four little roofs of the same kind, which are entirely meaningless, as the central feature. . . . With all the variety and attempt at individualization, it is not always possible to make out from the outside where one house ends and another begins or to which house a given door belongs, and this is an annoying fault. If the designer had selected, say the best third of the motives he has employed, and chastened them more finely, he would have done better than he has done by building whatever occurred to him in the form in which it occurred to him.

But for all its concerns, the *Record and Guide* concluded on a positive note: "Nevertheless these cottages are welcome innovations upon the conventional street fronts. Their exaggeration and violence are by no means so excessive that we would exchange them as we would sometimes exchange those qualities even for conventional stupidity."[454] Another, more modest development of Queen Anne houses (1886–87) worthy of note was built by William Rhinelander at 146–156 East Eighty-ninth Street, between Lexington and Third Avenues.[455] The ten four-story houses, brick with stone and terra cotta trim, were designed by Hubert, Pirsson & Co., far better known for their pioneering apartment-house work (see above). All of the houses in the row were twelve and a half feet wide, except for number 146, which measured slightly over twenty feet.

The *Real Estate Record and Builders' Guide*'s critic, probably Montgomery Schuyler, reviewed the Fifth Avenue scene in 1883 and found fault with a number of examples, including the Robert Leighton Stuart house (William Schickel, 1881), at 871 Fifth Avenue, on the northeast corner of Sixty-eighth Street.[456] The Connecticut brownstone residence for Stuart, a sugar refiner, was designed in a stolid version of the French Second Empire, with projecting bay windows, corner quoins, a rusticated stone base, and polished Aberdeen granite columns supporting the entrance porch. The house fronted 55 feet on the avenue, making it wider than many, and 136 feet along Sixty-eighth Street. The critic deemed the Stuart house "overloaded," a "very 'thingy' edifice," the "most pretentious feature . . . and about the most ungainly" being the "sort of tower" placed atop a classic porch, "an original idea, we believed [but] one not likely to be repeated."[457] The *Record and Guide*'s writer characterized the William H. Fogg house (Edward D. Lindsey, 1882–85), then under construction on the northeast corner of Fifth Avenue and Sixty-seventh Street, as "disappointing. . . . It stands opposite the wild, wild work of the 'Armour houses,' and it is almost as tame as they are wild. It does give evidence, however, of having interested its designer. It is . . . a composition of two elevations with a round tower in the corner. . . . The style of the house is rather Tudor than anything else."[458] The *Record and Guide*'s critic did praise James E. Ware's brick and light sandstone pair of four-story houses (1882–85) belonging to Andrew J. White, at the southeast corner of Fifth Avenue and Sixty-sixth Street, noting that they showed "a more practiced hand," although he found them "not great things, to be sure."[459] *Art Age* was more positive, praising the interior decoration of White's houses, which was executed by George A. Schastery, as "noteworthy not only for its beauty, but for its mechanical perfection. The smaller house has a Japanese drawing room. . . . The bay in the end of the room has transoms of Tiffany glass with Japanese forms."[460]

Along with Jacob H. Ruppert, Henry H. Cook was one of the first to commission a really big house on upper Fifth Avenue.[461] Cook, a banker and railroad developer, owned the entire block bounded by Fifth and Madison Avenues and Seventy-eighth and Seventy-ninth Streets, and he

John C. Henderson houses, west side of Avenue B between East Eighty-sixth and East Eighty-seventh Streets. Lamb & Rich, 1881–82. View to the southwest, 1892. MCNY.

Andrew J. White houses, southeast corner of Fifth Avenue and East Sixty-sixth Street. James E. Ware, 1882–85. View to the southeast. Parshley. BLDG. CU.

Henry H. Cook house, northeast corner of Fifth Avenue and East Seventy-eighth Street. W. Wheeler Smith, 1883–84. View to the northeast showing, from right to left, the Cook house, the Isaac D. Fletcher house (C.P.H. Gilbert, 1899), and the Isaac Vail Brokaw house (Rose & Stone, 1887–88). MCNY.

chose to build his home at the northeast corner of Fifth Avenue and Seventy-eighth Street, one block south of what would remain for some time the northern boundary of fashion. To design his house (1883–84) Cook turned to W. Wheeler Smith, whose Renaissance Revival design occupied one half of the Fifth Avenue blockfront. The *Real Estate Record and Builders' Guide* claimed that the Cook house was "one of the most conspicuous, perhaps the most conspicuous, of the new mansions going up opposite the park." The freestanding house was separated from the street by a dry moat set behind a balustrade, "which give the impression that even a millionaire cannot afford to have his domestic affairs transacted above ground, but must resort to one or two subterranean stories." As the granite Cook house was being completed, and its steeply pitched, pyramidal slate roof was taking shape, the massiveness deemed by the *Record and Guide* to be "its main general merit" became quite clear.[462] Seven years later,

reviewing Fifth Avenue's architectural development, the *Record and Guide* was even more blunt: "[It is] one of the largest residences on the avenue. The building is more remarkable for its solidity and massive appearance than for its architectural beauty. It is a fine house and a costly one—that is the principal word it has for the passer-by."[463] The *Record and Guide*'s editors were even less kind about William Cauvet's four-story, twenty-four-by-eighty-five-foot house (1882–86) for William Van Antwerp, at 930 Fifth Avenue, on the northeast corner of Seventy-fourth Street, which they found to be "extremely and even comically bad. The architect would probably describe it as neo-Gothic, and it is one of the numerous buildings which explain a dislike of that style. It is of brick and dark brownstone, with numerous features, and is singularly cheap and shabby for this part of Fifth Avenue, with its cornices and dormers in sheet metal."[464]

In the late 1880s, once the mid-decade economic slump

Ogden Mills house, southeast corner of Fifth Avenue and East Sixty-ninth Street. Richard Morris Hunt, 1885–87. View to the southeast. The Octagon, AAF.

was over, the park-facing blocks along Fifth Avenue below Seventy-ninth Street rapidly filled up with the homes of the very rich, who patronized some of the city's top architects. The new houses, as the *Record and Guide* noted, tended to be more stylistically conservative: "As times and tastes change, intelligent and watchful architects change with them, and each successive month shows increasing conformity to the prevailing desire for antique and ornamental styles in building . . . ; but these styles are more restrained, and are never carried to such extremes there as they sometimes are in other parts of the city."[465] Ogden Mills, whose father, Darius, had made a fortune in the California Gold Rush, chose Richard Morris Hunt for his three-and-a-half-story, fifty-foot-wide, eighty-foot-deep brick and stone house (1885–87), at the southeast corner

of Sixty-ninth Street.[466] Hunt's quietly restrained, somewhat Venetian Gothic, somewhat Romanesque-inspired design had nothing of the Richardsonian about it. Nor did it fit in with Hunt's scholarly, even academic designs, such as the William K. Vanderbilt house, which he had just completed when Mills hired him. Instead the design looked back to the synthesis of Neo-Grec and medievalism that had been the architect's stock-in-trade in the 1870s. The *Record and Guide* found the design "chaste, elegant and almost severe . . . yet . . . very gracefully relieved by small columns with richly carved capitals and other ornamental features."[467] Inside, there was a grand white marble staircase that served as the focal point for the Millses' entertaining. Next door, at 6 East Sixty-ninth Street, Hunt designed a five-story brownstone-faced house (1887) for Mills's father-in-law, Maturin Livingston.[468]

A burst of construction at the end of the 1880s filled in much of the south side of Seventy-eighth Street between Fifth and Madison Avenues with three contiguous houses (1887) by Alfred Zucker.[469] The houses were built for Edward Lauterbach, at 2 East Seventy-eighth Street; Arnold Falk, at 4 East Seventy-eighth Street; and Louis M. Hornthal, at 6 East Seventy-eighth Street. Zucker's houses were notable for featuring entrances decorated with elaborately carved mythological animals. One block north stood Rose & Stone's châteauesque house (1887–88) for Isaac Vail Brokaw, at the northeast corner of Seventy-ninth Street and Fifth Avenue.[470] The mansion for Brokaw, a prominent clothier and realtor, raised concerns similar to those raised by critics of Hunt's William K. Vanderbilt house. "Is not a city chateau an incongruity?" asked the *Real Estate Record and Builders' Guide*.[471] The house was large—fifty feet wide on the avenue and seventy-five feet

Edward Lauterbach house, 2 East Seventy-eighth Street. Alfred Zucker, 1887. View to the south. AZ. CU.

Isaac Vail Brokaw house, northeast corner of Fifth Avenue and East Seventy-ninth Street. Rose & Stone, 1887–88. View to the northeast. AR. CU.

Isaac Vail Brokaw house, northeast corner of Fifth Avenue and East Seventy-ninth Street. Rose & Stone, 1887–88. Dining room. AR. CU.

long on Seventy-ninth Street—though at three stories it was also comparatively low, "a rather unusual liberality for a New York house."[472] A tower with a high pyramidal roof rose above the otherwise low mass at the northwest corner, and various oriels and a swelling bay helped to relieve the austere granite box. The *Record and Guide* found it "almost as large and decidedly more architectural in character" than W. Wheeler Smith's Cook house. But it was still somehow bland, at least by comparison with Hunt's Vanderbilt house, perhaps because Rose & Stone was intent on "simplifying [its] design to accord with the situation on a city street." The generosity of this contextual response notwithstanding, the design had a "prim, stiff appearance far from satisfactory."[473] The interiors were far more intricate and lavish, however, than the severe exteriors might have implied.

Two more essays in the French Renaissance closed Fifth Avenue's Gilded Age: fittingly, one was a design of Richard Morris Hunt, the other of C. C. Haight. Hunt collaborated with his son Richard Howland Hunt on William V. Lawrence's house (1890–91), at 969 Fifth Avenue, on the southeast corner of Seventy-eighth Street.[474] The stone-trimmed brick design very narrowly

faced Fifth Avenue with a four-and-a-half-story round tower, stretching a three-and-a-half-story mass along the side street. The design, with its carefully molded window frames, its gabled, buttressed dormer, and its superbly melded roof planes, showed no diminution in the senior Hunt's powers. It was in fact a subtle evocation, in a lower key, of his William K. Vanderbilt house, perhaps intended as a reply to Rose & Stone's clumsy effort.

The second of the two last great statements, C. C. Haight's house (1889–90) for Henry Osborne Havemeyer, at 1 East Sixty-sixth Street, on the northeast corner of Fifth Avenue, was New York's largest and most prominently sited Richardsonian Romanesque townhouse.[475] Haight was not particularly well known for houses, but he may have been selected at the suggestion of Louis Comfort Tiffany, who, with the assistance of the artist Samuel Colman, would design the interiors. Haight and Tiffany had recently collaborated on the renovation of Leonard P. Jerome's former mansion, now serving as the Manhattan Club, and were at work on Christ Episcopal Church on the West Side. Though rooted in H. H. Richardson's taste, Haight's design occupied its own independent ground, resembling nothing more closely than his own design for

Isaac Vail Brokaw house, northeast corner of Fifth Avenue and East Seventy-ninth Street. Rose & Stone, 1887–88. Hall. AR. CU.

William V. Lawrence house, southeast corner of Fifth Avenue and East Seventy-eighth Street. Richard Morris Hunt, 1890–91. View to the southeast. Parshley. The Octagon, AAF.

View to the southeast along Fifth Avenue from Seventy-eighth Street, 1901, showing, from left to right, part of the Henry H. Cook house (W. Wheeler Smith, 1883–84), the William V. Lawrence house (Richard Morris Hunt, 1890–91), the Jacob Schiff house (Charles C. Thain, 1901), and two houses built for the developer William A. Mathesius (R. Napier Anderson, 1893). The construction site on the far right is for the William A. Clark house (Hewlett & Hull and Henri Deglane, 1899–1907). Byron. MCNY.

Henry Osborne Havemeyer house, northeast corner of Fifth Avenue and East Sixty-sixth Street. C. C. Haight, 1889–90. View to the northeast showing Haight's 1891–92 addition on the left. NYHS.

Henry Osborne Havemeyer house, northeast corner of Fifth Avenue and East Sixty-sixth Street. C. C. Haight, 1889–90. Interiors by Louis Comfort Tiffany. Picture gallery. AR. CU.

Henry Osborne Havemeyer house, northeast corner of Fifth Avenue and East Sixty-sixth Street. C. C. Haight, 1889–90. Interiors by Louis Comfort Tiffany. Drawing room. AR. CU.

Henry Osborne Havemeyer house, northeast corner of Fifth Avenue and East Sixty-sixth Street. C. C. Haight, 1889–90. Interiors by Louis Comfort Tiffany. Entrance hall. AR. CU.

the Cancer Hospital (1884–90) (see chapter 6). Montgomery Schuyler praised it as "a rudimentary and still highly classic Romanesque in the two upper of its three stories," finding "the only specific Romanesque . . . in the round-arched openings of the ground floor, and yet the massiveness and severity of the whole treatment undoubtedly recall the style."[476] Surely the most notable features of the composition were the tile-roofed conical corner towers that framed the Sixty-sixth Street facade.

Although Havemeyer and his wife, Louisine Waldron Elder, were no doubt good clients to Haight, they chose to concentrate their energies on the house's interiors. Influenced by a visit to the 1876 Centennial Exhibition, in Philadelphia, accompanied by Samuel Colman, Havemeyer began a collection of Japanese crafts. After his marriage to Louisine, in 1883—he had previously been married to her aunt—Havemeyer turned his collecting passions to paintings, a field in which he took his cues from his wife and her friend the artist Mary Cassatt. To create a proper setting for their rapidly growing collections, the Havemeyers eschewed conventional decorating firms and, probably at the direction of Colman, who had been a teacher of Louis

Comfort Tiffany's, turned to the Tiffany Studios. While Tiffany often contributed a room to fashionable houses, this was to be a complete set of interiors, comparable to but far larger than the artist's apartment at the Bella and his own recently completed suite in the triple mansion built by his father on Madison Avenue (see above). The Havemeyer interiors, constituting one of the great monuments of the Artistic movement, were all the more surprising in a prominent Fifth Avenue house owned by one of the nation's principal business barons. From an architectural point of view, the high point of Tiffany's scheme was the second-floor gallery, a double-height volume ringed by a narrow balcony reached by a spectacular iron, latticelike double staircase that was suspended from the third floor. The staircase, a tour de force in structural and spatial gymnastics, was no mere piece of structural exhibitionism, but a weblike frame highlighted with gold filigree and small crystal balls that caught the light, especially when the Havemeyers hosted concerts there on alternate Sundays. After the concerts, when tea was served, the stair was alive with movement made musical by the tinkle of the fringes of the crystal pendants that edged the landing.

Henry Osborne Havemeyer house, northeast corner of Fifth Avenue and East Sixty-sixth Street. C. C. Haight, 1889–90. Interiors by Louis Comfort Tiffany. Watercolor gallery. AR. CU.

Metropolitan Opera, Broadway to Seventh Avenue, West Thirty-ninth to West Fortieth Street. J. C. Cady, 1882. View to the northwest. MOA.

CHAPTER 5

&ઉ Amusements &ઉ

That the floating population of New York steadily increases is shown by the great number of places of amusement in every part of the city.
—*Real Estate Record and Builders' Guide*, 1883 [1]

Theaters

In 1893 Moses King summed up the importance of the theater world to New York:

> Among all the cities of America New York stands first in the strength and scope of its interest in the drama. There is good reason, too, for claiming first position in the world, for, aside from its purely local enterprises, New York is distinctly a metropolis in the dramatic field. It is the great clearing-house and outfitting depot for the theatrical enterprises of the entire continent. In this respect it is a city of greater importance than London, Paris, Berlin or Vienna. As many new plays are produced in New York in a season as are brought forward in London or Paris. . . . Then, too, New York is the only city in the world in which the music drama, or grand opera, is maintained as a permanent institution without assistance from a public or royal treasury. [2]

New York's fascination with theatrical entertainment and the city's central role in the nation's entertainment business as a whole were already established by the early 1870s; though New York City had only half the population of Paris, residents and visitors spent almost three-quarters as much money as was spent on entertainment in the French capital. [3] Commercial travelers as well as comparatively affluent single people living in boardinghouses patronized and fueled the entertainment industry, which followed in the northward march of the city's principal middle- and upper-class residential neighborhoods, from Union Square to Murray Hill. Over the course of twenty-five years, from 1865 to 1890, the theater district, which before the Civil War was located below Union Square, regrouped mostly along Broadway from Union Square to Forty-first Street. [4]

The idea of a theater district was in itself a concept that was distinctly New York's, as Samuel Osgood, an English writer, noted in 1866: "Unlike the system that exists in London of scattering the theatres, the plan adopted in New York has been to bring them as nearly as possible together, so that the overflow of one house finds another theatre ready at hand. Hence the New York houses are nearly all situated in the Broadway, and have therefore a continual stream of life passing backward and forward before their doors." The implications of this clustering, Osgood wrote, created a uniquely New York theater typology: "With some few exceptions the . . . theatres are not distinguishable from the surrounding houses until a close proximity reveals the name, lights, and other outside paraphernalia of a place of amusement: for on either side [of] the spacious entrance are usually to be found shops or cafes, and above the windows of an hotel or retail store." [5]

The Broadway Athenaeum (1865), located at 728–730 Broadway, opposite Waverly Place, was probably the city's first postwar playhouse and certainly one of its most unusual. [6] In 1865 the department store entrepreneur Alexander T. Stewart, working with the architect J. H. Hackett, converted the former Unitarian Church of the

Broadway Athenaeum, 720–730 Broadway. J. H. Hackett, 1865. Alteration of the Church of the Messiah (1838). View to the southeast. NYHS.

Theatre Français, 105–109 West Fourteenth Street. Alexander Saeltzer, 1866. View to the northeast. NYHS.

Messiah (1838) into a theater to showcase his favorite talent, Lucy Rushton (after whom the theater was later to be named). Tradition had it that a young student, A. Oakey Hall, later mayor during the heyday of Boss Tweed, had recited a prophetic couplet when the building was still a church: "Even in some future age / This pulpit may be a stage."[7] The tower of the church was removed in 1869,

when the unsuccessful Athenaeum was relaunched as the New York Theater, at which time, presumably, a steep mansard and crocketed roof and a street-level arcade were added, virtually obscuring the theater's ecclesiastical origins. Operated under many managers, it was known as one of the unluckiest of New York theaters, going through a number of name changes until 1881, when it was again renovated as the Theatre Comique, only to burn to the ground on December 23, 1884.

The Theatre Français (1866), designed by Alexander Saeltzer, who was also the architect of the Academy of Music (1854), was the first new purpose-built theater to open after the Civil War, and one of the city's most consequential playhouses.[8] Built on the site of the famous pleasure garden Cremorne Garden, the Theatre Français was, according to John W. Kennion, a "notable step in the right direction, and though not at all remarkable as a piece of architecture" it was at least one with "a facade of its own, relieving it from the penurious effect of a store front, behind which the other theatres hide themselves as it were in their poverty."[9] Kennion's opinion notwithstanding, the Theatre Français, located at 105–109 West Fourteenth Street, between Sixth and Seventh Avenues, confronted the street with a bold, double-story pedimented Corinthian portico that sheltered both orchestra and gallery audiences from the weather while making a gesture to the street that implied high culture and civic responsibility. If anything, the design was overambitious. A shallow lobby led to the 1,600-seat auditorium, which the *New York World* deemed "very high, too high in fact." The editors also complained that "in the arrangement of the thirty-eight private boxes . . . insufficient regard has been had for the necessities of feminine fashions. The small door-ways may prove a source of inconvenience to ladies on entering or retiring. But this remains to be demonstrated."[10] To the *New York Daily Tribune*, the theater seemed like the Academy of Music done "in little."[11]

The Union Square Theater, at 58 East Fourteenth Street, opened on September 11, 1871.[12] It was not a new building but an alteration within the shell of what had been the Union Place Hotel, facing Union Square between Broadway and Fourth Avenue. Typical of most New York theaters, it was a largely hidden asset, concealed behind the dour facade of the old hotel. The theater was, however, distinguished by what the *New York Daily Tribune* described as "a cheerful and commodious entrance. . . . The name of the new theater appears, in letters of fire, above the portal." Inside, the *Tribune* noted, "The vestibule stretches from beneath spacious porticos, and is brilliantly frescoed, in green and red, and brilliantly lighted."[13] In order to pack 1,200 seats into a comparatively small area, the auditorium was built very high, so that, as the *New York Herald* put it, "the appearance of the family circle, which rises tier above tier, is exceedingly stiff-backed. But in spite of this, the house has a compact comfortable look about it that impresses one rather favorably. In point of arrangement and decoration there is nothing to complain of."[14] In keeping with local tradition, access to the cheap seats at the top of the theater was kept separate from the rest—in this case, on Fourth Avenue. At a time when bathing, not to mention personal deodorants, were largely unknown except to the very rich, the separation probably had some practical benefits. So great was the theater's interior height that the *Herald*'s correspondent complained that from the parquet "the decoration of the dome and even those over the proscenium are scarcely visible." This, however, may not have been a great loss. As the *Herald* noted, "Art, too, has been called in to aid in making the Union Theatre a fit temple for the muses. We cannot say that the art is of a very high quality, but in view of the very low state of decorative painting in America, it is not, perhaps, fair to be over-fastidious."[15] A fire in February 1888 destroyed the roof and parts of the auditorium, and the theater reopened in 1889, rebuilt to designs reputedly by Leopold Eidlitz and John E. Terhune, although some thought the design was by Charles P. Palmer, the manager of the property. The interior of the rebuilt theater was painted in gold and ivory and the proscenium arches contained a large medallion incorporating a painting of Shakespeare.

Renwick & Sands's exuberant New Hampshire granite, French Second Empire–style Booth Theater (1867–69) was the city's most important, opulent, and technically innovative playhouse constructed during the post–Civil War Bonanza economy, and perhaps during the century as

Union Square Theater (1871), 58 East Fourteenth Street. Alteration of Union Place Hotel. View to the south, c. 1875. LH.

a whole.[16] The theater was commissioned by the immensely popular actor-manager Edwin Booth, brother of the presidential assassin John Wilkes Booth. Edwin Booth, who had broken all New York precedents by playing Hamlet for one hundred consecutive appearances in the 1864–65 season, dedicated the playhouse to Shakespeare and to the Greek muse of tragedy, Melpomene. The theater pioneered the neighborhood above Union Square as a theatrical center, occupying the southeast corner of Sixth Avenue and Twenty-third Street. Built at a cost of over one million dollars, it was among the most expensive theater complexes of its time, consisting of two components: a thirty-four-foot deep, five-story building facing Sixth Avenue with ground-floor shops, two floors of double-height acting studios, and an intermediate floor of offices, as well as an occupied low mansard; and behind this, facing Twenty-third Street, the 150-foot-wide, 100-foot-deep theater itself. The theater was principally entered on Twenty-third Street, although a second entrance opened to Sixth Avenue. The design of the commercial building was relatively restrained, but Renwick & Sands pulled out all the stops in the pavilioned, mansarded, crocketed, 120-foot-high theater. In response to requirements imposed by the recently enacted building code of 1867, the 1,750-seat auditorium was placed lengthwise in the building so that its emergency doors led directly to Twenty-third Street. For this reason the tripar-

Booth Theater, southeast corner of Sixth Avenue and West Twenty-third Street. Renwick & Sands, 1867–69. View to the southeast. MCNY.

Booth Theater, southeast corner of Sixth Avenue and West Twenty-third Street. Renwick & Sands, 1867–69. Rendering of auditorium by Charles Witham. MCNY.

tite organization of the facade was somewhat misleading: the doors at the west end were for public entrance to the theater, those on the east led backstage, and those in the center were only for use as fire exits. The *New York World*'s architecture critic, Montgomery Schuyler, dismissed the complicated composition as an "incoherent jumble of openings of all sizes and shapes, thrown together as if by accident, and in themselves of the most uncouth and ungainly forms." But, the critic added, "the theatre itself [was] unquestionably one of the handsomest—and if we consider the difficulties of the case—one of the most skillful and ingenious ever erected in this city."[17] Visiting the theater ten days after its opening, the prolific diarist George Templeton Strong described it as a "very handsome building, within and without." He also noted that for a performance of *Romeo and Juliet*, the building was "well filled. I'm glad of this and hope it may last, for if this theatre goes on as it has begun, it will be a humanizing and educating influence."[18]

The Booth was not only the city's most imposing theater, it was also the best equipped, with excellent backstage facilities as well as a ventilation system that employed a huge fan to modulate the auditorium's temperature year-round. The theater nonetheless fell victim to mismanagement and the boom-and-bust economy of the early 1870s. It had been built with funds mortgaged against Booth's future earnings, and after Booth's bankruptcy in 1874, the

Park Theater, southeast corner of Broadway and Twenty-third Street. Frederic Diaper, 1873–74. View to the southeast of the theater on fire, October 30, 1882. MCNY.

theater was renovated to provide additional orchestra-level seating and then reopened, passing under the direction of a number of noteworthy theater managers during the next few years, including Junius Brutus Booth, Dion Boucicault, Jarret & Palmer, Augustin Daly, John Stetson, and Henry E. Abbey. In 1883 it was converted to accommodate the department store of James T. McCreery, which was relocating from Broadway and Eleventh Street; many of the theater's interior fittings were at that time reinstalled in the New Park Theater (1883), on the corner of Broadway and Thirty-fifth Street.[19]

Well planned though it was in so many ways, Booth's theater was not without deficiencies. As the *New York Times* noted, "though its exterior grandeur . . . [was] equaled by the beauty and brightness of the interior decorations it was lacking in the spacious freedom of the Grand Opera House, and [was] particularly deficient in lobby room."[20] Perhaps more significantly, Montgomery Schuyler argued with Renwick & Sands's use of a historical vocabulary, contending that

> aesthetic scholarship is good, excellence of execution is good, but they are only helps to a real artist to express what is within himself. If he have no idea of his own to realize, it does not help him nor us to galvanize the corpses of a bygone world. . . . We conclude then that though the new theatre is a splendid triumph of upholstery and mechanical contrivance, it is not, in any degree,

a work of art. . . . It is no worse . . . to be sure, than any other theatre, or almost any pretentious public building. It is, with the exception of the Brooklyn Academy, the finest place of public amusement we possess. As far as comfort and commodiousness go, it is perfect; but it is by no means the ideal theatre.[21]

Writing twelve years later, however, in a reflection of his evolving perspective and of the ever-changing winds of architectural fashion, Schuyler would uncategorically state that the theater constituted "one of the most carefully studied and effective pieces of Renaissance [architecture] in New York."[22] *Appletons' Journal* stated that the theater was "in the opinion of many, the finest design in the city." Noting that the building's principal facade formed "an almost perfect whole," the journal found the theater to constitute "one of the architectural jewels of the city."[23]

The Park Theater (1873–74), at the southeast corner of Twenty-second Street and Broadway, was designed by Frederic Diaper, a former partner of Alexander Saeltzer and a fine interpreter of Classical, Renaissance, and Second Empire styles.[24] The Park Theater pioneered a real estate–driven strategy that would become standard for the era's theaters: entrances confined to narrow street frontages on busy avenues such as Broadway, with space-consuming, windowless auditoria set behind on cheaper side-street sites. The Park was developed for Dion Boucicault, the actor, manager, and playwright, but he lost

Eagle Theater (1876), 1287 Broadway. View to the west. MCNY.

Wallack Theater, 844 Broadway. Thomas R. Jackson, 1861. View to the east. NYHS.

control of the enterprise before the new playhouse opened on April 13, 1874. The site had 110 feet facing Broadway and a near equal amount on Twenty-second Street. To maximize real estate values, however, the decision was made to develop the Broadway frontage with a white marble–faced building to house a corner restaurant, situating the theater entrance at the least valuable, midblock location. The theater entrance led to a sixty-foot-square, nine-hundred-seat auditorium that featured what was perhaps New York's first fully sunken orchestra pit, virtually invisible from the parquet. In contrast to the marble lavished on the Broadway facade, the Twenty-second Street elevation of the auditorium was clad in Philadelphia red brick and trimmed with Nova Scotia sandstone, a design the *New York Times* found "plain and substantial rather than ornamental." That austerity carried through to the auditorium, where, as the *Times* remarked, "There is an absence of bright colors, of gorgeous upholstery, and elaborate fresco such as we are little accustomed to in our City theaters. Nothing could be more simple and, at the same time, so chaste as the design of the auditorium. The softest pink and white and gray prevail throughout."[25]

The fame of the Park Theater peaked when, on December 18, 1875, it presented the debut of A. Oakey Hall, the former mayor, acting in a play he had also written, *The Crucible*.[26] Notoriety marked the theater's demise: the theater burned down late in the afternoon of October 30, 1882, the day on which Lily Langtry, the English superstar, was to have made her American debut on its stage. Langtry, a guest at the nearby Albemarle Hotel (Renwick & Auchmuty, 1860), watched the fire from a window in her suite. The Park was not rebuilt, and the site became home to C. C. Haight's Brooks Brothers Building (see below).

Josh Hart's Eagle Theater, completed in 1876 at 1287 Broadway, between Thirty-second and Thirty-third Streets, had a short but complicated history.[27] Hart, a prominent vaudeville manager, opened the theater on October 18, 1875, only to find that the seats were too small and too compactly arranged. Correcting these defects, he then learned that the pitch of the balconies was too slight to provide a good view of the stage, requiring a second overhaul. While nothing is known of the decoration of the theater's interior, which was destroyed by fire in 1883, the principal facade was a busy but engaging French Second Empire design, consisting of two stories and a mansard, surmounted by a soaring eagle. After the fire, the eagle was mounted on the new, six-story-high building, which housed a 1,200-seat auditorium that was, according to Moses King, "decorated in conventional style, with little attempt at artistic effect."[28]

Lester Wallack's first theater, at 485 Broadway, just south of Broome Street, opened in 1858. In 1861 he commissioned from Thomas R. Jackson a second theater, at 844 Broadway, at Thirteenth Street, and for twenty years this would be the most famous theater in the United States. By 1880, however, the theater was losing out to new uptown competitors such as the Booth (see above), so Wallack redecorated the interior. Sensing that something more drastic was required, Wallack closed the theater in 1881 and hired George A. Freeman Jr. to design a new playhouse, to be built at 1220 Broadway, at the northeast corner of Thirtieth Street, next door to Henry Engelbert's Grand Hotel (see chapter 4).[29] The old Wallack Theater was renamed the Star and continued under other management.[30] The new Wallack Theater set an unprecedented standard for safety: it had a center aisle that tapered from six feet four inches at the entry vestibule to four feet six inches at the stage, brick fire-walls separating the auditorium from the back stage, and a glass skylight over one third of the stage that could be opened in the event of fire. Freeman carried the skylit flytower much higher than the auditorium ceiling and located the actors' dressing rooms in a separate building. The theater's lower two stories were made of rock-faced stone, while the upper stories were of imported Carlisle stone and Philadelphia brick. The auditorium contained an arcade of papier-mâché and bronze as well as sixteen mural-sized paintings illustrating the history of drama, and was surmounted by a cast-iron, gold-leafed dome. From the dome, a suspended chandelier had as its principal feature a blue porcelain ball supporting four eight-foot-high gold dragons carrying three thousand lights. The chandelier also concealed vents that allowed hot air to escape and fresh air to enter, the latter pushed

Wallack Theater, 1220 Broadway. George A. Freeman Jr., 1881. View to the east showing the Grand Hotel (Henry Engelbert, 1868) on the left. MCNY.

Wallack Theater, 1220 Broadway. George A. Freeman Jr., 1881. View across parquet of mezzanine and boxes. MCNY.

Hoyt's Madison Square Theater, south side of West Twenty-fourth Street between Fifth and Sixth Avenues. Francis H. Kimball and Thomas Wisedell, 1879–80. Alteration of the Fifth Avenue Hall. View to the south showing a corner of the Fifth Avenue Hotel (William Washburn, 1859) on the left. MCNY.

into the room by a fan located on the roof. The *New York Daily Graphic* praised the theater before its completion for both its location and its architecture: "It was a considerable jump from Broome to Thirteenth street, and it is not so great a jump as from Thirteenth to Thirtieth streets, considering how much of the city now lies above that point. The theatres seem to begin to concentrate around one particular locality, however, and it is probable that the new Wallack's will be in the right spot for centuries to come. Its interior is already one of the sights of the metropolis, and the exterior when completed, will be one of the ornaments of upper Broadway."[31]

According to a comprehensive discussion of American theaters published in 1891 by the English architect Horace Townsend, Francis H. Kimball and Thomas Wisedell, working closely with the "somewhat erratic actor and dramatic manager" Steele MacKaye, "introduced what may fairly be called a new era of American

theatrical architecture" in their transformation of the Fifth Avenue Hall into the Madison Square Theater (1879–80), located on the south side of Twenty-fourth Street west of Fifth Avenue, next door to the Fifth Avenue Hotel (William Washburn, 1859).[32] (After 1891, the theater was known as Hoyt's Madison Square Theater.) They replaced the then-standard horseshoe balcony with a new arrangement employing a deep, irregularly sloped central balcony that put most patrons in much better relationship to the proscenium by virtually eliminating all the visually challenged side seats. A second, shallower balcony was also included in the design. In addition, to accelerate scene changes, two stages were placed one on top of the other so that the upper could be lifted up into the fly by elevators and the lower could be dropped by a similar means into a deep basement that had been excavated out of rock at considerable cost. Further technical innovations included advanced fire-fighting sys-

Casino Theater, southeast corner of Broadway and West Thirty-ninth Street. Francis H. Kimball and Thomas Wisedell, 1882. View to the southeast showing the Hotel Normandie (William H. Hume, 1887) on the right. NYHS.

tems; summer cooling, which enabled the Madison Square to remain open year-round, that worked by passing cool air over enormous blocks of ice; and, in the mid-1880s, electric footlights installed by Thomas A. Edison. As the *New York Times* noted, "Mr. MacKaye has succeeded in establishing a play-house remarkable for the originality of its stage mechanisms."[33] MacKaye, who had been in Conway's Theater in Brooklyn on the night of its widely publicized fire, in 1876, was particularly concerned about the safety of his patrons and had installed in the basement a pump that supplied water to several hydrants on stage and in the auditorium. These were soon put to use when, on the night of February 26, 1880, the curtain caught fire as an inexperienced stagehand was lighting the gaslights. Within three minutes, six stagehands put out the fire with water from one of the hydrants. Sadly the curtain, designed by Louis Comfort Tiffany and the decorative artist Candace Wheeler, was irreparably damaged.

The curtain had been noted as especially handsome, in keeping with MacKaye's desire to provide "a warm, rich and cheerful auditorium without distracting from the stage-opening as the optic focus of the house and without fatiguing the eyes."[34] The fire did not diminish the rest of what apparently was a memorable interior that, according to the *New York Times*, included proscenium boxes made of "imitation ebony and bronze, fashioned somewhat after the Moorish style of decoration."[35]

The Madison Square Theater occupied what had formerly been home to Christy's Minstrel Hall (1865). Originally developed as an evening stock exchange in 1862 by Amos R. Eno, in 1869, under the ownership of Jim Fisk, the building was renovated to be Brougham's Theater. The *New York Times* noted: "Seldom has space been so economized . . . to the outside gazer, [the theater] looks painfully narrow, but the happy idea of a genius in having the side walls of the interior plated with mirrors

Casino Theater, southeast corner of Broadway and West Thirty-ninth Street. Francis H. Kimball and Thomas Wisedell, 1882. View to the southeast. MCNY.

Casino Theater, southeast corner of Broadway and West Thirty-ninth Street. Francis H. Kimball and Thomas Wisedell, 1882. Main entrance. AR. CU.

affords a most agreeable illusion of immensity to the seated audience."[36] Rechristened the Fifth Avenue Theater in 1870, it burned three years later, on January 1, 1873, and was rebuilt (1876–77) to the designs of D. & J. Jardine, which reused the old marble front.[37]

It was not until Kimball and Wisedell's reconstruction, however, that the old house, rechristened yet again, achieved, along with its technical innovations, genuine architectural distinction. The *New York Times*, reporting on the Madison Square Theater's opening night, informed its readers that the "orchestra occupied their little gallery above the stage, and were as carefully secluded as Oriental houris, and the double stage performed its necromantic movements advertised by the management. . . . The result is an exquisite little theater, which in appearance and mechanical contrivances is unique in New York."[38] In his monograph on Kimball, published in 1898, Montgomery Schuyler wrote that "the reconstruction . . . produced one of the most attractive and artistic interiors of its kind, in the 'bijou' class."[39]

Kimball and Wisedell followed their triumphant Madison Square renovation with a totally new theater, the nearly six-story-tall, 1,300-seat Casino (1882), at the southeast corner of Broadway and Thirty-ninth Street, by far the most architecturally inventive of New York's post–Civil War playhouses.[40] In 1881 it had been announced that George B. Post would be the architect for a 60-foot-tall, 1,400-seat facility on the 100-by-200-foot

Casino Theater, southeast corner of Broadway and West Thirty-ninth Street. Francis H. Kimball and Thomas Wisedell, 1882. View across parquet of mezzanine and boxes. MCNY.

Casino Theater, southeast corner of Broadway and West Thirty-ninth Street. Francis H. Kimball and Thomas Wisedell, 1882. Box. MCNY.

Casino Theater, southeast corner of Broadway and West Thirty-ninth Street. Francis H. Kimball and Thomas Wisedell, 1882. Roof garden. MCNY.

Proctor's Theater, 141 West Twenty-third Street. H. Edwards Ficken, 1888. Alteration of the Temple Theater (1882–83). View to the northwest. MCNY.

site, a project developed by twenty investors led by Rudolph Aronson. According to the *Real Estate Record and Builders' Guide*, the proposed theater was to include a roof garden, probably the city's first, a "novel feature" of which was to be "the winding walks and the fine fountain that will occupy the center."[41] But it was Kimball and Wisedell who designed the Moorish-inspired theater that opened, somewhat prematurely, on October 21, 1882. No sooner had the curtain risen than a rainstorm blew over the city, revealing poor workmanship on the roof garden, forcing the owners to close down for two months of repairs. The *New York Daily Tribune* contended that more than the roof was unfinished: "Saturday night found it in a very incomplete state. Great stretches of unbleached muslin, draperies of the National tri-color and frowzy hangings concealed gaps in the walls and did service for partitions, but marred sadly the picturesque effect presented by the ceiling and proscenium and the general design of the house. Beside these offenses . . . and the masses of rubbish which littered the place, the comfort of a large audience was destroyed by cold blasts of air that came from thousands of crannies."[42]

Despite the new theater's shortcomings, the editors of the *Real Estate Record and Builders' Guide* greeted the Casino with enthusiasm, finding it "one of the most effective and picturesque buildings, which relieve its monotony without adding monstrosities." The Casino, they continued, joined Temple Emanu-El, the Central Synagogue

(see chapter 2), and "an iron shopfront on Broadway, which does not call for much ornament"—presumably Richard Morris Hunt's 474–476 Broadway (see chapter 3)—as the only Moorish-inspired works in the city. The editors felt that the use of this exotic style was appropriate:

Moorish architecture is distinctly "indicated," as the doctors say, by the requirements of the Casino. It was to have a fantastic and festal appearance, to be the expression of an irregular plan on an irregular site, and to make free use of such ornamentation as could be well executed from moldings in baked clay. No historical style contains so many precedents applicable to this problem as the Moresque, and as for the people who clamor for a "new style" and demand that the architect of a building like this should invent not only the details of decoration, but a decorative system, without any reference to any historical architecture, it is safe to dismiss them with the simple remark that they do not know what they are talking about. Architectural styles grow, they are not invented. You might as well quarrel with a man for not inventing a language, and criticize a poem because words of it are all to be found in that some old unabridged dictionary.[43]

The *Record and Guide* took pleasure in the direct handling of the pictorial elements, praising the "sweep of the auditorium here on the north side, visible externally . . . carrying its bracketed wooden balcony, and the manner in which it is set onto the angular base, the contrast, piquant without being discordant, between this and the straight side on Broadway and, finally, the solid and vigorous tower at the angle, which resolves into a harmony the contrast between the sides, and ties the parts into an architectural whole—these are among the happiest and most effective features of the design." Though the interiors were incomplete, the *Record and Guide* felt confident in concluding: "In view of this beautiful and artistic work, our wonder is renewed that when these treasures are open to them, that so many young architects should have turned to the meager and starved detail of the so-called Queen Anne style, which is not a style, and which has never produced a monument."[44]

In the survey of American architecture that he published in 1889, Karl Hinckeldeyn, the former technical attaché to the German legation at Washington, D.C., also admired Kimball and Wisedell's pleasure palace:

The interior of the Casino [is] . . . doubtless . . . of high artistic order . . . [with] original and varied forms and magnificence of colors [that] unite in impressing the visitor, carrying his mind into the sphere of imagination. But it seems a somewhat strange whim on the part of the architects . . . to select for the front of a New York theater the forms of Moresque architecture, the massive wall-spaces and small openings of which are adapted alike for defensive purposes and for affording shelter against the rays of the sun in a hot climate.[45]

Horace Townsend greeted the Casino with total enthusiasm, calling it "one of the most beautiful theatres in the world."[46] Inside, according to Moses King, the two-thousand-seat auditorium, with its forty-foot-wide, thirty-two-foot-deep stage, was a "low horse-shoe arch, the semi-spherical dome, the low colonnade, and the lattice work . . . characteristic of Moorish architecture. . . . The [roof] garden, tower, and overhanging balcony are brilliantly lighted with electricity at night."[47] All in all, Montgomery Schuyler wrote in 1898, "in the recognition of the capabilities of terra cotta . . . [it] surpasses every other building in New York."[48]

Proctor's Theater, at 141 West Twenty-third Street, designed by H. Edwards Ficken, was in its way as picturesque as the Casino.[49] The building had originally been home to the Seventy-ninth Regiment Armory and was converted into the Temple Theater (1882–83) by the eccentric playwright Salmi Morse, who intended to use it for a passion play of his own styling. Public opposition forced Morse to abandon his plan, and as the Twenty-third Street Theater the playhouse offered more conventional fare under other managers. Then, in a stroke of irony, it was renamed the Twenty-third Street Tabernacle and used for religious purposes. When H. Edwards Ficken renovated the building in 1888 to accommodate F. F. Proctor's "refined vaudeville," he transformed the seventy-five-foot-wide, thirty-seven-and-a-half-foot-deep former armory and church into a Dutch- or Flemish-inspired theater with an ornamental brick facade, crowstepped central and end gables, and a tile-covered enclosed porch extending across the entire frontage.[50]

The Lyceum (1884–85), adjoining the National Academy of Design (see chapter 2) on Fourth Avenue between Twenty-third and Twenty-fourth Streets, was initially intended to serve as workshop space for Steel MacKaye's Lyceum School of Acting.[51] As designed by Philip G. Hubert, the severe fifty-foot-wide, three-story-high, red brick facility was less interesting than the interior decoration, by Louis Comfort Tiffany, who received the commission over John La Farge because he waived his fee in favor of a percentage of the theater's profits. Conveniently, since 1881 Tiffany's decorating concern had occupied a four-story building located a block away on the southeast corner of Fourth Avenue and Twenty-fifth Street as well as the adjacent five-story building to the south. The corner building, designed by J. C. Markham in 1875, incorporated Gothic-inspired detail and a central atrium. The Lyceum was said to be the first theater entirely lighted by electricity, and its 75-by-48-foot, 727-seat auditorium included a musicians box as wide as the stage. The orchestra could be lifted up into the fly when not needed, so the box could form the top part of the proscenium frame, an innovation that, like many others by MacKaye, soon proved impractical. The *New York Times* praised the Lyceum as "a comfortable and attractive little playhouse, a trifle strange in its appointments and in the conglomerate character of its decorations, but on the whole one that pleased the visitor, after he has become used to it."[52]

By the late 1880s Broadway's "theater row" stretched almost to Forty-second Street. J. B. McElfatrick's Broadway Theater (1887–88), built on a block-long site on

Lyceum Theater, 312–316 Fourth Avenue. Philip G. Hubert, 1884–85. View to the southwest showing a corner of the National Academy of Design (Peter B. Wight, 1863–65) on the left. MCNY.

Lyceum Theater, 312–316 Fourth Avenue. Philip G. Hubert, 1884–85. Interior decoration, Louis Comfort Tiffany, 1885. Watercolor rendering by Louis Comfort Tiffany of view toward proscenium. MMA.

Broadway Theater, south side of West Forty-first Street between Seventh Avenue and Broadway. J. B. McElfatrick, 1887–88. View to the southeast. MCNY.

the south side of Forty-first Street between Seventh Avenue and Broadway, marked the northernmost point of a district that was coming to be called the Rialto.[53] On the former site of the Metropolitan Concert Hall (see below), the five-story, Romanesque-inspired Broadway consisted of arcaded brownstone and Anderson red pressed brick. The design pleased the *New York Times* even though it was "not of an ornate style of architecture."[54] The "Persian style" auditorium accommodated about 1,800 theatergoers, who were able to move about across broad aisles. But, as the *Real Estate Record and Builders' Guide* rather bluntly put it, the "theatre has commended itself to the playgoer's point of view, however, without making any addition of value to our street architecture. The list of pretty auditoriums is much longer than that of theaters the outside of which strains the mark of an artistic designer. In the latter class one is inclined to begin and end with the Casino." The article concluded quite decisively: "the new theatre is not externally an ornament to Broadway."[55] A reporter for the *New York Daily Graphic* was more kindly disposed toward the theater's interior, though at a loss in categorizing its architectural vocabulary: "I don't know, and I doubt if anybody but the architect knows, the style of the interior decorations, or could give the style a name without inventing one. The effect of the innovations made in the decorations remains to be seen. . . . It is only possible to say just now that the best talent has been employed and the newest inventions have been utilized to make the Broadway of tonight as nearly a perfect theatre as possible."[56]

Opera Houses

Throughout the Gilded Age, opera was a mainstay of New York's musical life and, equally significantly, its social life.[57] Italian opera had made its first appearance in New York in 1825. Eight years later, the Italian Opera House was built; it burned in 1839.[58] In 1843, the Palmo Opera House opened on Chambers Street, and for four years it

was home to Italian opera.[59] But the Palmo was too far downtown, and in 1847 the Astor Place Opera House was opened, a building that two years later became notorious as the site of a demonstration between the supporters of two rival Shakespearean actors, the American Edwin Forrest and the Englishman William Charles Macready, which gave it the nickname "Massacre Place Opera House."[60]

Beginning on October 2, 1854, opera could be heard on a regular basis at the Academy of Music, a theater built with money raised by public subscription.[61] Designed by Alexander Saeltzer, it occupied a 117-by-204-foot site on the northeast corner of Fourteenth Street and Irving Place, and was most like a grand opera house of any such space in the city. The Academy burned on May 21, 1866, reopening in 1868 after a renovation by Thomas R. Jackson, which added Corinthian pilasters and elaborate moldings as well as replaced a wrought-iron balcony with one of stone, all on a building that was a relatively diagrammatic essay in the Rundbogenstil. The renovated 70-foot-wide, 102-foot-deep, white-and-gold auditorium arranged piled tiers of balconies around the orchestra, a design that was praised by *Ballou's Pictorial Drawing-Room Companion*:

> Let the reader look upon the engraving, and imagine every line in the picture to be a gold stripe, with the brilliant effect of a thousand gas lights shining thereupon, the private and stage boxes upholstered in the richest manner—and he may perhaps form some faint conception of the magnificent ensemble of this interior. Spacious and commodious, it is admirably adapted for seeing and hearing. The seats are all single, and constructed in the plan of those in the Boston and European theaters, the seat being so hinged that when the sitter rises it folds up against the back, allowing "ample room and verge enough" to move about and make one's exit without inconvenience.[62]

For almost thirty years, the Academy of Music was the center of New York's social scene. *The Age of Innocence*, Edith Wharton's novel of upper-class New York life in the 1870s, begins at an Academy performance featuring Christine Nilsson in Charles-François Gounod's *Faust*:

Academy of Music, northeast corner of Irving Place and East Fourteenth Street. Alexander Saeltzer, 1854; renovation, Thomas R. Jackson, 1868. View of renovated auditorium from stage. NYHS.

Academy of Music, northeast corner of Irving Place and East Fourteenth Street. Alexander Saeltzer, 1854. View to the northeast. NYHS.

Academy of Music, northeast corner of Irving Place and East Fourteenth Street. Alexander Saeltzer, 1854; renovation, Thomas R. Jackson, 1868. View to the northeast. Byron. MCNY.

Pike's Opera House, northwest corner of Eighth Avenue and West Twenty-third Street. Griffith Thomas, 1868. View to the northwest. NYHS.

Pike's Opera House, northwest corner of Eighth Avenue and West Twenty-third Street. Griffith Thomas, 1868. View of auditorium from stage. Byron. MCNY.

Though there was already talk of the erection in the remote metropolitan distances "above the Forties," of a new Opera House which would compete in costliness and splendor with those of the great European capitals, the world of fashion was still content to reassemble every winter in the shabby red and gold boxes of the sociable old Academy. Conservatives cherished it for being small and inconvenient, and thus keeping out the "new people" whom New York was beginning to dread and yet be drawn to; and the sentimental clung to it for its historic associations, and the musical for its excellent acoustics, always so problematic a quality in halls built for the hearing of music.[63]

In 1868, the Academy of Music was challenged by a new enterprise farther uptown, Samuel N. Pike's 1,883-seat opera house, at the northwest corner of Twenty-third Street and Eighth Avenue, which proved almost out of fashion's bounds by being so far west.[64] Designed by Griffith Thomas, the four-story, marble-faced palazzo, with its hefty balustrades partially obscuring a mansarded roof, contained an elaborately decorated auditorium beneath a seventy-foot-high dome. The proscenium was defined by superimposed columns three orders high. The stage, said to be one of the biggest in the United States, was eighty feet wide and seventy feet deep. But the most memorable feature of the interior was the grand foyer, the largest of any theater in the city.

The only successful evening Pike's Opera House enjoyed was opening night, January 6, 1868. After that triumphant debut, the serious opera audience returned to the Academy, leaving Pike, a hapless distiller and distributor of alcoholic beverages from Cincinnati, Ohio, on the brink of financial collapse. His enterprise was rescued from ruin by Jim Fisk and Jay Gould, who bought the building, renamed it the Grand Opera House, and turned its office floors into headquarters for the Erie Railroad. It was here that Fisk's body lay in state following his murder in 1872 in a dispute over the affections of his mistress. The opera house subsequently became the only theater in the city to pass inspection after the 1876 fire in Conway's Theater, in Brooklyn.

While Pike had clearly built his opera house too far west, by the 1870s Twenty-third Street between Fifth and Sixth Avenues was deemed acceptable and actually threatened to rival Union Square and Fourteenth Street as the center of the city's theatrical life. The Booth Theater (see above), on the southeast corner of Sixth Avenue and Twenty-third Street, set the tone, quickly followed by Stephen D. Hatch's four-story, one-thousand-seat, mansarded, Italianate Bryant's Opera House (1870), on the north side of Twenty-third Street just west of Sixth Avenue. Montgomery Schuyler praised Bryant's as "one of the best things of its kind yet erected in New York. There is no pretense about it."[65]

In 1876, it was proposed that a new opera house, to be designed by Arthur Gilman and managed by Maurice Strakosch, be built on a full-block site bounded by Forty-third and Forty-fourth Streets and Madison and Vanderbilt Avenues. The site belonged to William H. Vanderbilt, who was reported to be interested in the pro-

Bryant's Opera House, north side of West Twenty-third Street between Sixth and Seventh Avenues. Stephen D. Hatch, 1870. View to the north. NYHS.

ject. Other sites were also considered, including a lot on the corner of Fifth Avenue and Twenty-fourth Street, but by the end of 1877 it was reported that the Madison Avenue site had been purchased and that Gilman had developed a design calling for an Italian Renaissance–style building, identical in size to La Scala in Milan. No sooner had the new opera house been publicly announced, however, than negotiations with Vanderbilt collapsed, terminating plans for the project.

Clearly the impulse to build a new opera house was not simply musical. The social set that dominated the opera scene at the Academy of Music included the Belmonts, the Lorillards, the Cuttings, the Schuylers, and the Astors, but by the late 1870s a new-money crowd was emerging. The desire among these parvenus for boxes of their own could not be accommodated in the old house. An 1880 scheme, also engineered by Strakosch, to establish a second opera company, the Metropolitan Opera Association, was no doubt intended to address this situation, as it was initially underwritten by the newly monied Goulds, Whitneys, Morgans, and Vanderbilts.[66] Recognizing the threat, the Academy's management tried to add more boxes, but the proposed number fell short of the demand.

Among the sites considered for a new opera house were the same square block bounded by Forty-third and Forty-fourth Streets and Madison and Vanderbilt Avenues that Strakosch had tried to secure earlier, as well as a site at Fourth Avenue and Thirty-ninth Street. Both were controlled by William H. Vanderbilt, who, citing a deed restriction forbidding their use for places of amusement, forced the new opera company to look elsewhere. After considering a site in Reservoir Square, the company chose one farther west, filling the irregularly shaped block between Broadway and Seventh Avenue and Thirty-ninth and Fortieth Streets.[67] Before the Madison Avenue site had been ruled out, however, a competition for the new opera house was held. The entrants were George B. Post, George E. Harney, Potter & Robertson,[68] and J. C. Cady. Cady, who was ultimately chosen as the architect for the building, to be erected on the Broadway site, was in many ways an unlikely choice. He had never designed a theater and he had never been to Europe, so he had not visited the world's greatest opera houses; indeed, he had never attended an opera. Cady's scheme, submitted as "Lyre"—a name that perhaps referred to the shape of the boxes, which incorporated a gentle curve as they neared the stage—was widely believed to have been chosen because of its comparatively low construction cost and its emphasis on fireproofing. Cady was apparently heavily assisted in the design by one of his employees, Louis De Coppet Bergh, who had studied architecture and civil engineering in Germany and came from a musical family: his father had been the organist for the Episcopal Church of the Transfiguration, and his sister, a singer, had sent him pictures of opera houses while touring Europe. After winning the design competition, Cady went to London to examine Covent Garden (Sir Robert Smirke, 1808–10). Bergh, who later changed the spelling of his surname to Berg, became a partner of Cady's in the early 1880s when, together with Milton See, they practiced as Cady, Berg & See.

The Cady-designed Metropolitan Opera opened in 1882. The auditorium, said to be the largest of its type in the world, accommodated 3,045 people in all, well in excess of the 2,156 accommodated at the Paris Opera (Jean-Louis-Charles Garnier, 1860–75), which, though it occupied a much larger site, used more of its real estate for grand salons and elaborate backstage facilities, both of which the Metropolitan lacked in abundance. Nonetheless, in keeping with the American obsession with size, the Metropolitan boasted the largest stage in the United States, 101 feet wide and 90 feet deep, with a 50-foot rise from stage to roof and a 48-by-50-foot curtain opening. An immense proscenium arch was flanked by two monumentally scaled paintings by Francis Maynard titled *The Chorus* and *The Ballet*. The Renaissance-inspired interior, which maintained a gold and burgundy color scheme, was done by the Boston-based decorator E. P. Treadwell.

From the point of view of function, the new opera house—which at a total cost of $1,732,978.21 more than twice exceeded the original budget—was a relative success. The acoustics seemed to meet most listeners' expectations. But "Colonel" James H. Mapleson, the director of the rival

Metropolitan Opera, Broadway to Seventh Avenue, West Thirty-ninth to West Fortieth Street. J. C. Cady, 1882. View to the northwest. MOA.

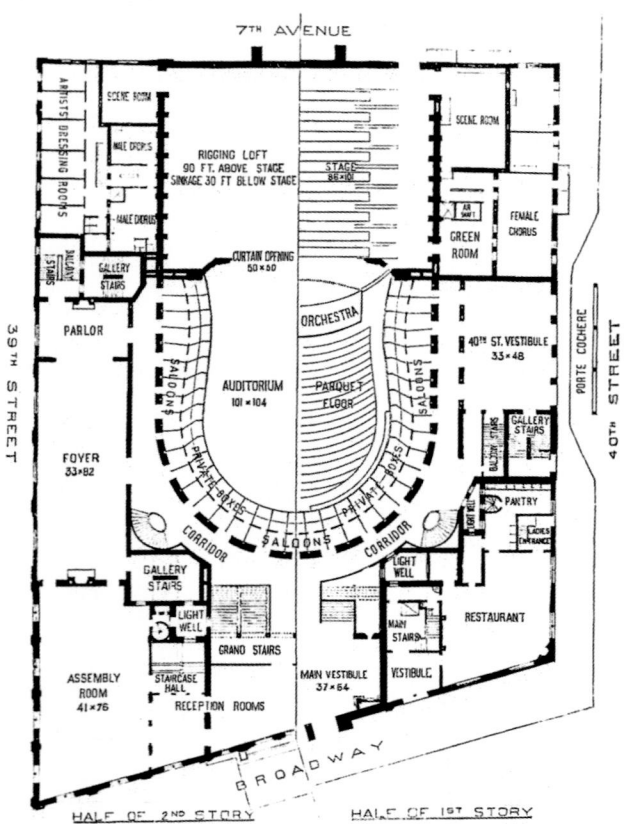

Metropolitan Opera, Broadway to Seventh Avenue, West Thirty-ninth to West Fortieth Street. J. C. Cady, 1882. Half plans of first floor (right) and second floor (left). HNM. CU.

Academy of Music, who had at one time sung opera under the stage name Enrico Mariana, could not resist making a crack about the decision to locate a portion of the orchestra under the stage apron. Mapleson told a reporter:

> That new-fangled arrangement for [the] orchestra under that vast wilderness of stage is my salvation. They spent $120,000 blasting out rocks to get a stage with a cellar depth of thirty feet, and put the orchestra in the cellar. The result, in addition to breaking them up financially, is that all the sound is swallowed by the cellar—singers, band, and everything. I am magnanimous to save [Henry E.] Abbey [the Metropolitan Opera's managing director], who is a pretty good sort of fellow. It is a well-known fact in acoustics that if you put glass saltcellars under the legs of a piano it increases the sonority of the instrument. The same thing is true of singers. If Abbey will shoe his tenors and prima donnas with saltcellars their voices can be heard. This improvement can be made readily—he can get the saltcellars anywhere—and the public will be mystified and gratified by the great change. Science is a wonderful thing. Abbey needs its aid to enable him to give opera up town in that Broadway pitfall.[69]

If less prejudiced voices such as Montgomery Schuyler's can be trusted, the auditorium and its acoustics were a suc-cess, but the decor of the room itself was a bit dull. Although the corridors, particularly those serving the highly prized boxes, were distinctly undersized, this was unlikely to prove dangerous, as Schuyler pointed out, because there were only 222 box seats on each tier and because the opera house, unlike most theaters, occupied an entire block, making possible multiple fire exits and eliminating the need for a grand street-level lobby. To meet the needs of the box-holders and other affluent operagoers, however, the second level contained a grand suite of foyers and assembly rooms. All in all, Schuyler reported, the acoustics and sight lines were "so satisfactory that it is safe to say there is no theatre in which there are fewer bad seats in proportion to its size, nor any opera-house in which the difference between the best and the worst boxes is so small."[70]

Every effort was made to ensure the building's fire-resistance, with wood only sparingly used in the interior decoration and for the stage. Iron stairways were housed in brick wells. Partitions were brick, fireproof arches were used between iron beams, and the floors of all corridors were tiled. Most importantly, the stage house was treated as an independent entity that would function as a flue in case of fire, with a large, specially weighted skylight that would fall open if the temperature rose above normal. An innovative sprinkler system was located above the stage, served by a rooftop water tank.

The opera house's light yellow brick exterior, trimmed with terra cotta of a similar hue, was severe in its unornamented directness, leading some to compare it with a brewery. The massing was somewhat compromised by the introduction at each of the two Broadway corners of a seven-story, seventy-foot-square tower intended to be rented out to offset the inevitable financial losses of the opera company. The ground floor of the south tower was occupied by the Bank of New Amsterdam, and that of the north tower by a restaurant. The second floor of the Thirty-ninth Street side held the opera house's suite of assembly rooms, while the upper floors of both towers were given over to residential apartments.

The critical reception for the new opera house was mixed at best. Some of it was scathing, none more so than that of the *New York World*, which proclaimed in an editorial that a "more amazing example of wealth working without taste or conviction or public spirit was never seen":

> Enough money has been spent on this structure to make it a monument and a valuable architectural addition to our city. It is in reality one of the most conspicuously ugly of the many ugly buildings that disgrace our good taste. There appears to have been no sense of decorative obligation to the community whatever. The Opera-house is ill-designed, antiquated and altogether inharmonious in its plan and proportions, and not only poverty-stricken but absolutely painful in its embellishment. . . . The general impression . . . is that the capitalists instructed their architect to build a house as big as possible and not bother about its appearance or convenience. The interior is modeled after the corridors of a state prison, and its

Metropolitan Opera, Broadway to Seventh Avenue, West Thirty-ninth to West Fortieth Street. J. C. Cady, 1882. Renderings of interiors, including architectural features and details. NYDG. CU.

Metropolitan Opera, Broadway to Seventh Avenue, West Thirty-ninth to West Fortieth Street. J. C. Cady, 1882. View to the northeast of Seventh Avenue facade. AR. CU.

gloomy crypts and stone aisles have a Catacomb massiveness combined with all the painful gorgeousness of color one finds in a packing box. It is in vain that one looks for a grand entrance, a grand staircase, a central foyer or any objective point where the eye can rest on the gay multitude assembled. The attempts at decoration over the curtain are pallid conventional allegories that would not be tolerated in a modern variety show. The ceiling is the traditional fresco-work of the beer saloon, and the garish effect of the yellow over the whole auditorium is exactly that of a coat of priming. The vestibules are cheerless stone courts, and the number of them separates the audience and destroys all idea of sociability. Looked at from the street the building appears like an enormous malthouse. Inside it has the appearance of a Mississippi steamboat. If the stockholders wished to beautify New York, while at the same time they made a corner in music, they went about it the wrong way. But no one, we suspect, will accuse them of any such design.[71]

So disappointed was Cady in the critical response to his building that he wrote a letter to the *New York Daily Tribune*, defensively stating that "probably no other building in the country has received so much care and thought."[72]

As the building failed to please, neither did the location pass muster. Montgomery Schuyler would have preferred the Madison Avenue plot, although he admitted that it was tight compared with the one on Thirty-ninth Street, where the irregularly shaped block allowed for sixty feet of additional length. Schuyler found the building's exterior pleasing because it was

considerably less like the stereotyped treatment of an opera-house than the interior. Costly as the building is, it is so very large as to limit the expenditure upon its external architecture. And this limitation seems to have determined the architect, together with other considerations, to seek for the effect of the great building through simplicity and the expressiveness of general composition. . . . The style, in deference, possibly, to the purpose of the building is Italian, and in the Broadway entrance, which is more capriciously decorated than any other part, is a correct and academic Italian Renaissance. This style has more elegance than vigor. The portico on Broadway is noteworthy not only for the refinement of the detail which never fails Mr. Cady in whatever style he is working, but for the breadth of the composition.[73]

Compared to most, Mariana Van Rensselaer was quite supportive, characterizing Cady's design as "reserved and unpretentious." Van Rensselaer found the light yellow brick to be of "beautiful quality, though perhaps a trifle paler in tone than might have been desirable—a trifle paler, I think than the new *Post* building downtown [see chapter 3], which shows the most successful use of the material which New York as yet can boast." She thought that the rear elevation was exemplary, "the part which has been least considered with regard to architectural effect, but which by its simply-told expression of its purpose and its immense size is very impressive and very admirable. Here the proportions of the front are reversed, the side wings which contain the dressing-rooms, etc., very comparatively low, and the center is a height of over one hundred and fifty feet, supported by two strongly projecting buttresses." Van Rensselaer went on to find "the dignity and even beauty which it attains by such simple means . . . quite remarkable. No factor in architecture is so potent toward producing an effect of grandeur and dignity as mere brute size. . . . The immense wall is not like a brewery-wall, even apart from the strength secured by the rarity of its openings, for it is *designed*, and not simply built. . . . It does not pretend to be anything but what it is, the *back* of an opera house." For Van Rensselaer the opera house lacked the grandeur of European theaters, in part because it lacked a monumental setting; she argued that "it is a utilitarian rather than a monumental work. . . . If we expect the magnificent *foyers*, stairways and corridors of Paris, Dresden or Vienna, magnificent in size and in material, we shall be grievously disappointed. Space had to be economized as well as money."[74]

Returning to the subject as part of her impressive survey of American architecture published in *Century Magazine* in 1884, Van Rensselaer further recognized the limitations placed on Cady by his client:

> We can only congratulate ourselves that we have got as much as we have—an honest, unaffected, scholarly, dignified pile, as well designed in mass as was possible under the circumstances, expressive, at all events, of its structural fashioning, and happy in the imposition of its voids and solids. So simple and scholarly and unaggressive is it, indeed, that I fear "the public" does not half realize the debt of gratitude it owes the architect. . . . Is it not a vast improvement on such a hideous nullity as our old Academy of Music? And, on the other hand, should we not be happier if the Casino Theatre had been less fantastic, and if the Eden Museum [see chapter 2] on Twenty-third Street had relied on structural beauty and appropriate, subordinated decoration for its effect . . . ?

For Van Rensselaer, the Seventh Avenue facade showed Cady at his best, where he

> could work in a more untrammeled way than upon his principal fronts. . . . I believe there are even persons who claim that it is not different in any way from the breweries which deform our suburbs. But believe me, it is very different. Mere massing may be, of course, an immense element in architectural power, and the mass of this wall counts for much in its impressiveness . . . because it has

been intelligently handled. . . . The ponderous bulk of Mr. Cady's wall is *designed*, not merely built, and designed so as to prove its strength most clearly, it has parts and features which are organic, and, though simple, are potent and expressive. . . . I am of so optimistic a frame of mind while contemplating the fact that one of our architects has done so well when daring to do so honestly and simply, that I can even look forward to a day when a malt-house itself may do us credit, not dishonor.[75]

Van Rensselaer may have been supportive, but Schuyler, though he appreciated the essential dignity of Cady's design, properly insisted that it was victimized by an inadequate site and budget. In his 1897 assessment of Cady's work, Schuyler regretted the lack of grand interior spaces and the compromising role of the flanking towers, concluding that on the whole the building was "a good story marred in the telling, a design deprived in its due effect in part by the conditions of the problem, and in part by the architect's fear of loudness and exaggeration."[76]

Though the new house was designed to suit its medium, it was not built so much for the acoustic and aesthetic sake of opera as to satisfy the demands of a new monied class for social recognition. As Schuyler put it: "The interest in opera is at least three parts social to one part musical."[77] This point was echoed by Henry T. Finck, writing in the *New York Evening Post*: "From an artistic and musical point of view, the large number of boxes in the Metropolitan is a decided mistake. But as the house was avowedly built for social purposes rather than artistic, it is useless to complain about this, or the fact that the opportunity was not taken to make of the building itself an architectural monument of which the city might be proud."[78]

For a time after the Metropolitan's opening, members of the old guard clung to their Fourteenth Street bastion, where the high quality of music remained undiminished under the direction of Mapleson. For his part, Mapleson, who also ran Covent Garden in London, did not rest on his laurels, seeing the new opera house as a real challenge. An all-out war between the Academy of Music and the Metropolitan was staged to capture the public's attention, as well as to satisfy the egos of two leading singers: Adelina Patti at the Academy of Music and Christine Nilsson, formerly a star at the Academy, who opened at the Metropolitan as Marguerite in Gounod's *Faust*. Fashionable New York greeted the 1883–84 season, the inaugural one for the Metropolitan, with a battle between opera houses tantamount to what the *New York Times* described as "a social war of extermination."[79] Opening night at the Academy on October 22, 1883, was an unalloyed artistic and social triumph, despite competition from the opening of the National Horse Show, Tony Pastor's variety house, and the new Metropolitan Opera. The Metropolitan's opening the night before had been an event in which the bejeweled new rich created a scene that the *New York Evening Telegram* described as "almost ravishing."[80] Despite an unimpressive presentation of *Faust*, the

Steinway Hall (1866), 71–73 East Fourteenth Street. Renovation by Heinrich Beck, 1868. View to the northeast. MCNY.

Metropolitan Opera had the advantage of a new home, no matter how controversial some of its features, and the support of a monied group, albeit one that seemed to many exceptionally vulgar—so vulgar, in fact, that the phenomenon drew tremendous attention in the press and attracted audiences solely to view the scene. The *New York Dramatic Mirror*'s critic was direct: "There was a big crowd Monday night at the new Metropolitan Opera House. All the *nouveau riches* were on hand. The Goulds and Vanderbilts and people of that ilk perfumed the air with the odor of crisp greenbacks. The tiers looked like cages in a menagerie of monopolists. When somebody remarked that the house looked *as bright as a new dollar*, the appropriate character of the assemblage became apparent. To a refined eye, the decorations of the edifice seemed in extremely bad taste."[81]

Social glitter did not immediately prove to be enough, and the Metropolitan's first season was not successful. Henry E. Abbey's management was terminated in the spring of 1884, and for the following season the Metropolitan inaugurated a German opera series under the management of Edward C. Stanton and the musical direction of Leopold Damrosch. This proved a great success and remained the Metropolitan's policy for six seasons. Mapleson held on at Fourteenth Street, but Stanton's strategy of introducing hitherto unfamiliar German opera

to a public that to a considerable degree understood German and not Italian, combined with the inviolable authority of the investment the Goulds and especially the Vanderbilts were willing to make in the new Metropolitan enterprise, ultimately presented competition too fierce. As Mapleson so aptly put it, "I simply could not fight a battle with all Wall Street."[82] And on November 28, 1885, the Academy of Music staged its last opera performance, before taking on new life as a playhouse. Whatever its architectural shortcomings, the Metropolitan Opera House was a potent symbol of the city's changed social order: the new money had arrived.

Concert Halls

Until the 1891 completion of the Music Hall on Fifty-seventh Street (see below), the performance of serious music largely fell under the purview of the leading piano manufacturers, Steinway and Chickering, each of which built combined showrooms and recital halls. From the first concert in its 1,800-seat auditorium, on October 31, 1866, with Theodore Thomas conducting, the mansionesque, somewhat Italianate Steinway Hall, at 71–73 East Fourteenth Street, was known as the "cradle of classical music in this country."[83] In 1868 Steinway Hall was thoroughly overhauled and redecorated by Heinrich Beck, a

Chickering Hall, northwest corner of Fifth Avenue and West Eighteenth Street. George B. Post, 1875. View to the northwest. NYHS.

Music Hall, southeast corner of Seventh Avenue and West Fifty-seventh Street. William B. Tuthill, 1889–91. View to the southwest showing main entrance, on West Fifty-seventh Street. CHA.

Viennese architect hired on the strength of his work on theaters and pleasure gardens in Austria. According to the *New York Times*, Beck's services were desperately needed: "Steinway Hall, as last seen, was plain in all its appointments, almost to poverty—austere as a country church." The renovated theater, adopting what the *Times* described as "the elaborate yet chaste style of ornamentation known as that of Louis Quatorze," served in the winter of 1868 as the location of a series of highly popular lectures by Charles Dickens.[84]

George B. Post's Chickering Hall (1875), at the northwest corner of Fifth Avenue and Eighteenth Street, was larger and far more imposing than Steinway Hall, to which it was a would-be rival.[85] A robust building of red brick trimmed in brownstone and gray marble, occupying a site that measured 75 feet on Fifth Avenue and 135 feet along Eighteenth Street, Chickering Hall was four stories tall, although the two middle floors were expressed as one. The ground floor was used for showrooms, with stairs leading from the building's principal entrance, on Fifth Avenue, up to the 103-foot-deep, 73-foot-wide, and 49-foot-high auditorium, which was capable of seating 1,450 concertgoers. The 56-foot-wide, 28-foot-deep stage easily accommodated as many as 250 orchestral and choral performers. The venue became particularly popular beginning in 1875, when the pianist Hans von Bülow gave a recital series there. The northward migration of fashion proved too much for the concert hall, however, and by 1893 the entire building had been transformed to accommodate retail space.

The Music Hall (1889–91), a gift of the steel baron Andrew Carnegie, was without question New York's most important concert hall, unique in that it was free of commercial sponsorship and exclusively devoted to musical performance.[86] It was also far larger than its predecessors. The idea of a hall that could serve New York's diverse musical groups had originated with Leopold Damrosch, who, in addition to conducting the Metropolitan Opera's orchestra, had founded the Oratorio Society and the New York Symphony. Damrosch died in 1885. Two years later, his twenty-five-year-old son, Walter, sailing to Germany to continue his musical training, was introduced to fellow passenger Andrew Carnegie, then on his honeymoon. Carnegie had served on the board of the Oratorio Society. At first Carnegie did not seem interested in the music hall project, but further conversations between the two at last won him over and in 1889 he pledged two million dollars to secure the nucleus of what would become the Music Hall's site. At the southeast corner of Seventh Avenue and Fifty-seventh Street, the location was considered quite far west of fashion until the construction of the luxurious Osborne apartment house (James E. Ware, 1883) (see chapter 4) on the diagonally opposite corner. In July 1889 the site was expanded so that it extended 175 feet along Seventh Avenue and 150 feet along Fifty-seventh Street, with a 25-foot-wide strip of land connecting to Fifty-sixth Street at the lot's southeast corner. By the time construction began, the site had been further enlarged, with 235

feet on Fifty-seventh Street and more frontage on Fifty-sixth Street.

The architect hired to design the Music Hall, which was renamed Carnegie Hall in 1898 after its donor, was William B. Tuthill, a comparatively unknown thirty-four-year-old who may have been chosen as much for his skills as a cellist and singer as for his architectural prowess. Tuthill was not without some experience in the design of concert facilities, however, having in 1882 created a music pavilion for the Seventh Regiment Armory.[87] No doubt because of his comparative youth and inexperience, Tuthill was asked to consult with Richard Morris Hunt and with the Chicago-based engineer Dankmar Adler, whose work in partnership with Louis Sullivan on the Auditorium Building (1887–89), in Chicago, was widely admired, not only for its handling of a much more complex mix of uses than was being considered for the New York project but also for the superb acoustical properties of its ingeniously engineered performance space.

Tuthill's concert hall was a rather stiff, six-story, orange gold Roman brick, Italian Renaissance–inspired block surmounted by a mansard roof. The principal facades were articulated with numerous arches, belt courses, and delicate terra cotta decorative work. Inside, the approximately 3,000-seat red, white, and gold auditorium, at once magnificent in scale and intimate in feeling, featured curved boxes and an elliptical ceiling. The hall opened on May 5, 1891, to a packed house. Early in the performance Tuthill looked up at the crowded top tiers and began to worry about the weight capacity of the slender iron posts that carried them. He left the hall and went home to double-check the calculations that had determined the posts' manufacturing design, only to find that they were fine. The hall's inaugural event commenced with the hymn "Old Hundred," followed by a long speech from the Reverend Henry C. Potter, then bishop of New York's Episcopal diocese, and a massed singing of "America the Beautiful." Walter Damrosch then conducted the New York Symphony Orchestra in a performance of Beethoven's *Leonore Overture no. 3*. Damrosch was followed by Peter Ilich Tchaikovsky, who conducted a solemn march of his own composition, whereupon Damrosch returned to the podium to conclude the program with Hector Berlioz's *Te Deum*, which Tchaikovsky regarded as "dullish."[88] That Tchaikovsky had been invited to participate in the opening concert signaled the management's high ambitions for the hall. Leopold Damrosch had been an early champion in America of the composer's work, and Walter Damrosch continued that tradition. On what was the first trip to the United States of the world's most famous living composer, Tchaikovsky found the new building "magnificent," and the hall itself "unusually impressive and grand" when "illuminated and filled with an audience."[89] From the first notes, the acoustical properties of the Music Hall were deemed "perfect," as the *New York Herald* exclaimed, noting that "there was no echo, no undue reverberation. Each note was heard."[90]

Music Hall, southeast corner of Seventh Avenue and West Fifty-seventh Street. William B. Tuthill, 1889–91. View to the southeast. CHA.

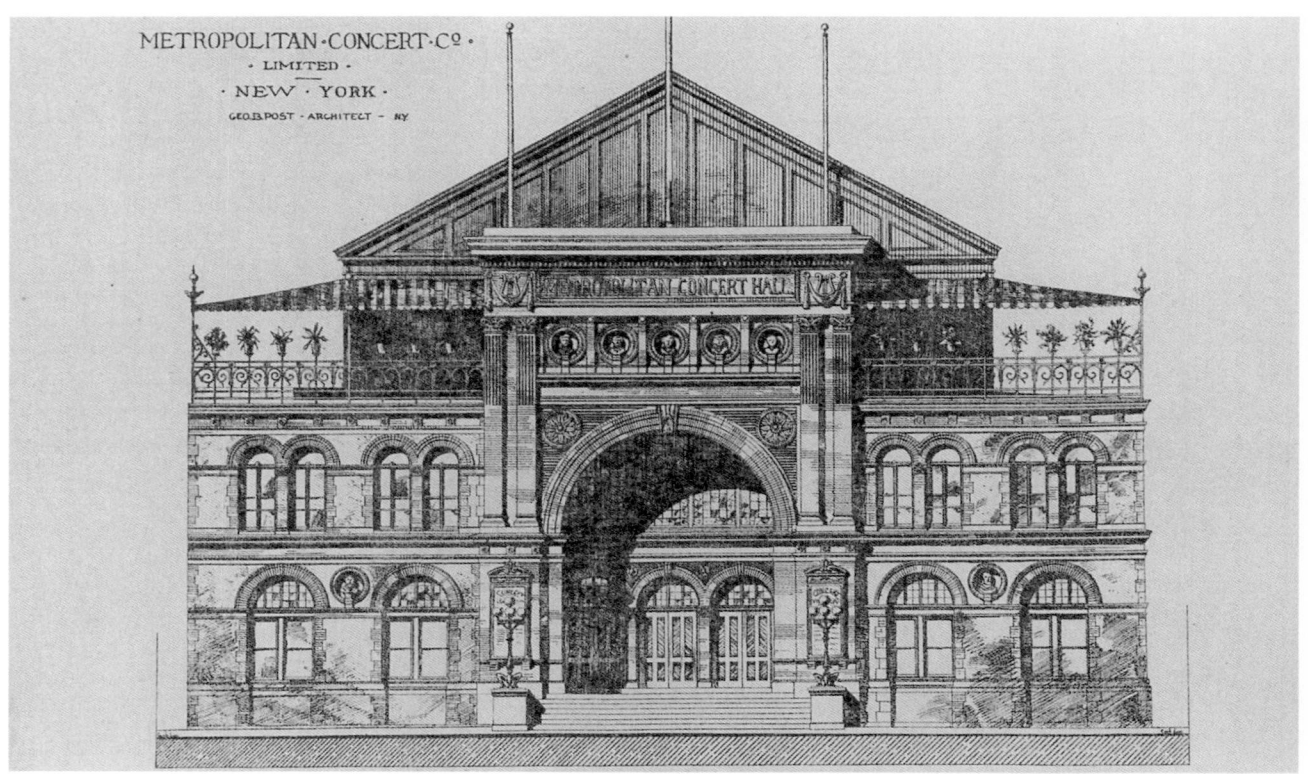

Metropolitan Concert Hall, southwest corner of Broadway and West Forty-first Street. George B. Post, 1880. Broadway elevation. AABN. CU.

Metropolitan Concert Hall, southwest corner of Broadway and West Forty-first Street. George B. Post, 1880. Section and plan. AABN. CU.

Central Park Garden (1875), west side of Seventh Avenue, West Fifty-eighth to West Fifty-ninth Street. View to the southwest. MCNY.

Pleasure Gardens

In addition to theaters, opera houses, and concert halls, the city abounded in another building type designed to contain public entertainments—the pleasure garden. Pleasure gardens tended to have interiors that were more spatially flexible than those of other kinds of theaters and halls and they were aimed at less highbrow attractions and events. The type flourished in lower Manhattan in the early part of the nineteenth century. Despite its name, the Metropolitan Concert Hall (1880), at the southwest corner of Broadway and Forty-first Street, was a pleasure garden.[91] As designed by George B. Post, the brick and stucco building faced Broadway and contained an elaborately detailed iron shed that filled most of the block to Seventh Avenue. A forty-by-ninety-foot portion of the building's roof was capable of being retracted in two and a half minutes to create an open-air theater for summer concerts. Conceived of by the conductor Rudolph Aronson, the Metropolitan Concert Hall was to be a place, as the *American Architect and Building News* reported, "where the people of New York, with their families, may enjoy recreation of a lighter order than Italian opera or symphony concerts, at a reasonable price."[92] Farther uptown, on the west side of Seventh Avenue between Fifty-eighth and Fifty-ninth Streets, the Central Park Garden (1875) was another pleasure garden, initially used for summer concerts conducted by Theodore Thomas.[93]

Webster Hall (Charles Rentz, 1887), at 119 East Eleventh Street, between Third and Fourth Avenues, contained one of the city's largest places of assembly and was most often utilized as a dance hall.[94] Social dancing rapidly gained popularity during the 1880s and 1890s, particularly in working-class and immigrant neighborhoods. By 1895 it was estimated that the city contained 130 dance halls, most located on the Lower East Side.

In their 1896 history of New York, Martha J. Lamb and Mrs. Burton Harrison wrote that in "size, situation, architectural beauty, and lavish provision for the multitudes it is intended to harbor, McKim, Mead and White's Madison Square Garden [1887–90] completes, with the Metropolitan Opera House and the Carnegie Music Hall, the list of the most important places of amusement in New York."[95] Because of the sensational event of 1906 when Stanford White was killed on its rooftop, and its introduction to New York of a glittering Classicism such as the city had never before seen, the story of Madison Square Garden belongs in part to the period covered in *New York 1900*. The early history of the project leading to its opening on June 16, 1890, however, is surely as much a story of the 1870s and 1880s.

The site of Madison Square Garden was exceptionally prominent and had a long and complex history. Situated at the northeast corner of Madison Square Park, bounded by Madison and Fourth Avenues and Twenty-sixth and Twenty-seventh Streets, the site had been a train yard

Madison Square Garden (1874), Fourth to Madison Avenue, East Twenty-sixth to East Twenty-seventh Street. View to the northeast, c. 1879. NYHS.

since 1837, serving from 1853 until 1871 as the Union Depot of the New York and Harlem Railroad and its successors. In the 1850s the railroad's operations also included the reception of milk trains and the delivery of milk and produce at night. In 1873 the combined carbarn and passenger depot, made redundant by the new Grand Central Depot, was leased to P. T. Barnum. By the spring of 1874, Barnum had completed a large but rather temporary and structurally crude building known as the Great Hippodrome, which he used for spectacular shows, including the "Congress of Monarchs," a colossal equestrian entertainment.[96] Barnum's hall was also the setting for large religious revival meetings, including those led by Campbell N. Moody and Ira David Sankey. Barnum additionally used the Great Hippodrome for performances of his circus. In summers beginning in 1875, under the management of Patrick Gilmore, it functioned as a concert ground, which on May 11, 1876, was the setting for the American debut of the French composer and conductor Jacques Offenbach. After Gilmore's financial failure in 1879, the complex was for a time run by William H. Vanderbilt under the name Madison Square Garden. In 1880 Barnum proposed building a new mixed-use facility, a veritable coliseum that would transcend the constraints of conventional building types, including pleasure gardens, containing within a single structure large and small con-

Madison Square Garden (1874), Fourth to Madison Avenue, East Twenty-sixth to East Twenty-seventh Street. View to the northwest, c. 1879. NYHS.

cert rooms, an opera house to be "the most spacious in America," an arena for horse shows, a winter garden, an aquarium, a skating rink, stores, offices, and a 250-foot-tall observatory.[97] Barnum's scheme failed to go forward, and Philip G. Hubert and James W. Pirsson subsequently proposed that the block be developed as a complex of Home Club apartments, another idea that failed to materialize (see chapter 4).

When Barnum could not move his vision into reality, Madison Square Garden became home to various sporting events, including boxing, which had recently been legalized. The idea of a vast entertainment center continued to fascinate investors and the public alike, however, and early in 1887 Vanderbilt sold the property to the Madison Square Amusement Company, a syndicate set up by officers of the National Horse Show Association. The newly formed group retained William R. Ware, a professor at Columbia, as its architectural advisor. The idea for the new Madison Square Garden had started with Hiram Hitchcock, one of the founders of the Garfield Bank and an original proprietor of the Fifth Avenue Hotel. Hitchcock convinced others to invest, including J. Pierpont Morgan, James Stillman, Herman Oelrichs, James T. Hyde, Adrian Iselin, Edward S. Stokes, and Stanford White. White not only served as the project's architect but also was the impresario responsible for pro-

ducing the shows, pageants, and events that were to fill the complex's halls. Andrew Carnegie was to have been an investor, but he withdrew his support in favor of the concert hall planned for Fifty-seventh Street (see above).

Francis H. Kimball, the architect, with Thomas Wisedell, of the highly regarded Casino Theater (see above), was rumored to be a likely choice for the job of designing the entertainment complex. As reported by the *Real Estate Record and Builders' Guide*, Kimball had a few years before prepared "a complete set of plans for an immense amphitheater, grand dining hall, exhibition room and theater, and submitted them to Commodore Vanderbilt," presumably at Barnum's behest.[98] By July 1887, word was out that the old Madison Square Garden building would be torn down and replaced by "one of the largest places of amusement in the country," and that six architects had been retained to prepare designs for the new building.[99] Despite these speculations, the job went to McKim, Mead & White.

In September 1887, White, assisted by Joseph Morrill Wells, proceeded to work on the design. By early the following spring, it was heavily rumored that the ambitious project would not be able to generate enough income to provide the investors with a satisfactory return. In March, a *New York Times* reporter cornered White after a meeting with a client. Acknowledging problems with the project,

Madison Square Garden (1874), Fourth to Madison Avenue, East Twenty-sixth to East Twenty-seventh Street. View of interior, 1883, showing a choral society on stage. NYHS.

the architect said that there had been "some objection to the proposed tower," which, based on the Giralda Tower in Seville, was to be one of the great glories of his design.[100] Taking this as a serious blow to civic pride, the *New York Times* editorialized: "While accounts of the wonderful tower of Eiffel were coming across the ocean from Paris, the modern Babylon, the city of New York was hugging herself with the belief that she was to have a tower too, but one in which quality not quantity was to be shown." The dream might be "shattered," the *Times* went on, if the desires of many of the project's stockholders prevailed. That would be a loss for what the editors labeled a new "palace of pleasure . . . which was to supply what New York grievously lacks, a beautiful piece of architecture not badly and oppressively designed for money making, but beautiful first and then profitable in a minor and 'genteel' way." The *Times*, anticipating the mood of enlightened civicism that was to be so important in the nineteenth century's last decade, argued that the point of the tower was not its sheer height, as was the case with Gustave Eiffel's tower, but its role as a "crown" that would finish the "prospect of a town view already somewhat pleasing." The structure would also confirm that

> we had for that purpose not only the architects capable of designing a beautiful tower, but citizens of wealth who had the courage and civic spirit to undertake its erection. . . . The steeple as an adjunct of a church has become a superfluity in cities. Still, one steeple holds its own as an external badge of the church, because it permits the architect to leave the dusty road of fact and soar a little into the poetry of his profession. . . . The abandonment of the tower as a means of obtaining a bird's eye view of the city . . . and as the one thing which dignified and made important the main building, is a fact somewhat crushing. . . . If New York is proud of the new Madison Square Garden as a work of art, everything connected with it will succeed.[101]

White persisted in lobbying for his tower, making such a fuss that in order to "shut him up somehow" David H. King Jr., the builder, petitioned a key member of the committee, offering to pay for half the tower's cost if the other half could be raised by the investors.[102]

The fate of the new building hung in the balance until early 1889, when the decision was made to complete the plans in accordance with White's proposed vision. Only half the funds needed for the project had been raised, however, and as late as June construction had not yet been authorized. On August 7, 1889, the work of tearing down what had been the old Madison Square Garden began. After bemoaning that "New York has no building devoted to amusement which is at the same time a work of art," singling out the recently completed Metropolitan Opera House as "substantial" but possessing "no beauty" and the Metropolitan Museum as "a triumph of ugliness," the *New York Times* almost gleefully editorialized that the city was "about to have . . . something in the way of a Palace of Amusements. . . . The problem is exceedingly complex. The roof is to have Summer and Winter gardens. The

View to the northeast along Twenty-sixth Street showing Madison Square Garden (McKim, Mead & White, 1887–90), with the tower, in the center, the Leonard P. Jerome house (Thomas R. Jackson, 1859) across Twenty-sixth Street to the right, and Madison Square Park on the lower right. NYHS.

north side is to have studios. The body of the structure is to contain halls and lecture rooms. A theater, a hippodrome, a restaurant, and baths are said to be other requirements. . . . But as a further complication there is the task of making this Palais de Gaietés a handsome object to the eye."[103] To the editors of the *Times* the project was of civic importance—no matter that it was to be privately funded—and they asked that the various architectural drawings be put on public view.

By November 1889 "the huge building" was "commencing to show itself," and on June 16, 1890, Madison Square Garden, including the tower, was ready for service.[104] Twelve thousand people attended a gala opening event that heralded a new era in entertainment and, perhaps more importantly, exemplified a powerful sense of civic idealism. Oddly, despite the complex's vast size, there was a shortage of public space, a problem that vexed the opening-night audience members, who had come to hear Eduard Strauss, Johann's brother, conduct a forty-piece Viennese orchestra, and to see two short ballets deemed "inartistic and almost indecent" by an unidentified blue-stockinged reporter for the *New York World*.[105] Whatever its reaction to the performance, and despite the crowded conditions of the corridors, the audience could not help but be impressed by the building and its interiors. White had seen to every detail of the project; he even designed the ushers' flashy orange cutaway swallow tailcoats, orange trousers, and cardinal red waistcoats ornamented with outsize silver buttons.

From the first, the public loved the building's Spanish- and Venetian-inspired exterior. The main mass of White's building rose sixty feet, filling the block with walls of buff-colored Roman brick trimmed with white terra cotta. The principal rooms were illuminated by tall, arched windows surmounted by oeils-de-boeuf. At the parapet a colonnade and eight belvederes screened a roof garden while providing a transition to the culminating thrust of the great tower, which soared 341 feet above the sidewalk, 66 feet higher than its Spanish prototype. A year after the building's completion, to help accommodate the crush of arriving and departing crowds, arcades were built over the Madison Avenue sidewalk and along one hundred feet of each side street. The arcades had been part of the original design, but permission for their construction had been delayed by municipal authorities, forcing Madison Square Garden's board to seek special enabling legislation for their construction.

The principal room of the complex could function either as a vast amphitheater or an exhibit hall, capable of seating eight thousand to ten thousand people, depending on the event, with many more able to promenade on an upper level from which they could gaze at the crowd below. The roof was a considerable piece of engineering, with exposed steel trusses spanning 277 feet carried on twenty-eight columns. By day the room was illuminated by an enormous skylight that moved so quietly it could be rolled aside during summer performances to help with ventila-

Madison Square Garden, Fourth to Madison Avenue, East Twenty-sixth to East Twenty-seventh Street. McKim, Mead & White, 1887–90. View to the northwest showing the Fourth Avenue facade on the right. NYHS.

View to the northeast from Madison Square Park showing Madison Square Garden (McKim, Mead & White, 1887–90) in the center and the Leonard P. Jerome house (Thomas R. Jackson, 1859) on the right. NYHS.

Madison Square Garden, Fourth to Madison Avenue, East Twenty-sixth to East Twenty-seventh Street. McKim, Mead & White, 1887–90. View to the northeast showing the Madison Avenue facade on the left. NYHS.

tion. In the evening the room sparkled with light from incandescent bulbs lining the trusses. Echoing Roman precedent, the floor could be flooded for water spectacles and, as at the Colosseum, animals employed in the various spectacles were housed in basement stalls. When the amphitheater opened on June 16, 1890, the *New York Daily Tribune* found its "vast dimensions" to be "tremendously imposing." There was "something exceedingly agreeable in the excellence of its proportions and the impression of combined strength and gracefulness in its constructive details."[106] Mariana Van Rensselaer was particularly taken with the room, praising its "appreciable proportions." But she found the exposed steel columns and trusses "thin and bare" unless decorated for a special event, which was frequently done.[107] Some other observers were not impressed. The editors of *Town Topics* gloated that "the big, bare, cheerless Madison Square Garden is to become a beer hall, after all. Well, that's about all it's fit for."[108] It was even rumored that John D. Wanamaker, the Philadelphia merchant, wanted to convert it into a New York branch of his department store.

The 1,200-seat-capacity Madison Square Garden Theater, located at the building's northwest corner, opened on September 27, 1890. It was an intimate, luxuriously appointed white, gold, and light brown playhouse, with red seats and carpet. Mariana Van Rensselaer found it "prettier and more truly architectural for its charm than any other in New York," combining an "unusual air of joyousness . . . with refinement."[109] A 1,500-seat, Louis XVI–style, gold and white concert hall was located at the building's southwest corner above a restaurant space. The room never prospered as a place for serious music but found its niche as a home for light musical fare.[110] Van Rensselaer quipped, "It is an old joke in New York to speak of [the firm] as Messrs. McKim, White-and-gold; but it is a very friendly joke, for we know that they have done us good service in popularizing the types of decoration which it indicates."[111] The restaurant space was never used. Although it was offered free of charge to Delmonico's and Sherry's, both restaurants declined to establish branches there, claiming that the variety of events attracted very different crowds, which would require constantly varied menus that would not be in keeping with their standards. The room was infrequently used as an exhibition hall. The roof garden, the last part of the Madison Square Garden complex to open, on May 30, 1892, occupied about two hundred by eighty feet at the Madison Avenue end of the building. Nearly three hundred tables were arranged to supply food and drinks to customers enjoying nighttime entertainment amid

Madison Square Garden, Fourth to Madison Avenue, East Twenty-sixth to East Twenty-seventh Street. McKim, Mead & White, 1887–90. Night view of the amphitheater. NYHS.

Madison Square Garden, Fourth to Madison Avenue, East Twenty-sixth to East Twenty-seventh Street. McKim, Mead & White, 1887–90. View toward the amphitheater proscenium. MMWA. CU.

varicolored electric lights, Chinese lanterns, fountains, flowers, and shrubs.

While Madison Square Garden's dizzying array of facilities, all of which could function simultaneously, was undeniably spectacular, it was the 38-foot-square, 341-foot-tall tower that particularly captured the public's imagination. It perfectly embodied the synthesis between hedonism and civicism that was the building's most distinguishing characteristic. Unlike its Spanish prototype, the tower was devoted to sensual pleasure, not religious devotion. An elevator wrapped by a stair led to the roof garden. Above that level, in the tower proper, seven stories of apartments were crowned by a loggia intended to serve as a summer café. A winding stair connected the loggia with a toplit chamber from which a ladder climbed to a small, usually guarded balcony, where intrepid visitors could command some of the best aerial views of the city.

To crown it all, in homage to Seville and with a showman's flair, White commissioned from his friend the sculptor Augustus Saint-Gaudens a revolving statue. So important did the two men deem this feature that they agreed to pay for it with their own money. Saint-Gaudens's eighteen-foot-high figure of Diana was made of beaten sheet copper fastened to a wrought-iron pipe frame. The spectacular statue depicted the huntress poised for action with her left foot set on a large rotating ball, her right leg extended back, a bow in her left hand, and the shaft of an arrow in her right. Set upon a crescent moon of plate glass that rose about twelve feet from tip to tip, and lit from within by sixty-six incandescent lamps, White and Saint-Gaudens's *Diana*, in its blatant hedonism bordering on vulgarity, was surely like no other civic sculpture, anytime, anywhere. The statue was placed directly atop the still unfinished tower in October 1891. White rejoiced in the sight of it but he had some doubts: "My heart reacts at times, however, at the thought that it is going to be too big."[112]

When the tower opened to the public on November 2, 1891, Van Rensselaer King, the son of the building's contractor, was the first to ascend. Later in the evening, after an hour of fireworks, White staged a spectacle of electric light, which was still a comparative novelty. White's show featured 6,600 incandescent bulbs decorating the base building, 1,400 bulbs outlining the tower, and 100 lights picking out particular features of the design. In one of the early displays of the kind of theatrical hoopla that would soon become typical on Broadway, two powerful searchlights shone upward, illuminating *Diana* against the darkening night sky.

The building's positive effect on the public and the press was overwhelming. The French writer Paul Bourget, arriving for his first visit to New York, in August 1893, held it in high regard as "the first evidence of beauty that I have seen since I set foot outside of the ship."[113] The *New York Sun* summed up the feeling of many when it pronounced the tower and its sculpture "the greatest artistic achievement of the nineteenth century . . . unrivaled by any creation of art in how many centuries."[114] Less hyperbolically, Mariana Van Rensselaer stated: "The finest of all [the building's] features is the tower. One cannot but think first and chiefly of this whenever the Madison Square Garden is named."[115]

Triumph aside, White and Saint-Gaudens felt in retrospect that the statue of Diana was indeed too large; White claimed that he had not anticipated that it "would become such a noticeable and prominent feature."[116] One Saturday afternoon, as White was examining various solutions to the problem with his assistant Francis Hoppin, Charles F. McKim came out of his private office to gently mock the miscalculation: "Stan, that was a very beautiful pedestal you made for Saint-Gaudens's statue, but I thought he was going to make a finial for your Tower."[117] In October 1892, eleven months after being set in place, *Diana* was taken down. Cholly Knickerbocker reported in the *New York Recorder* that "our pretty Diana, the highest kicker of them all" had been sent to Chicago for display at the World's Columbian Exposition of 1893.[118] It was ostensibly to be prepared for display in the Women's Building, set to open in the spring of 1893, but that building had no suitable pinnacle. Moreover, a wave of protest against the display of the virtually nude statue at the fair had begun to rise, led by the Women's Christian Temperance Union. The *Chicago Herald* protested that the "Windy City" not "be made a dumping-ground, an asylum for all the cast-off statues, the errors in judgment of New York."[119] *Diana* did find a home at the fair, atop McKim, Mead & White's Agriculture Building, and after the event she served as a weathervane for Montgomery Ward & Company. The statue was later exhibited at the Art Institute of Chicago, and eventually it was returned to New York, where it was placed in a storage warehouse. A second version of the statue, five feet shorter as well as slimmer, simpler, and with a somewhat different pose, was put in place on top of Madison Square Garden's tower in November 1893. This time the glass crescent moon was eliminated.

Writing in 1894, Mariana Van Rensselaer summarized the aesthetic and civic significance of White's achievement:

> If I should try to name the most beautiful building in New York, plausible contradictions would immediately follow; for there is no critical balance in which architectural works of widely different sorts may rightly be weighed against one another. But it is neither rash nor invidious to name the building which most conspicuously increases the beauty of New York. Size, type, station, environment now limit the field for comparisons; and when intrinsic beauty is appraised within this narrowed field, Madison Square Garden asserts itself without a rival. Nothing else in all New York has done so much to dignify, adorn, and enliven its neighborhood; nothing else would be so sorely missed by all New Yorkers were ruin to overtake their dearest architectural possessions.[120]

Stores

> What cannot be found here [in New York], is not to be found in any shopping district anywhere.
> —Moses King, 1893[121]

The post–Civil War boom economy, though felt throughout the nation, was particularly strong in New York, catapulting the city into its role as the nation's leading marketplace. New York's status as the country's de facto capital of consumerism had a civic dimension as well: it compelled the construction of imposing shopping palaces, department stores, and elaborate retail venues on a scale which the nation—and the world—had never before seen.

New York's retail establishments captured the popular imagination. Not only was shopping in New York efficient, it was fun, particularly for upper-middle-class women, who formed the largest and most important group of consumers. Savvy retailers capitalized on extra leisure time recently afforded to affluent women by labor-saving housekeeping devices and cheap domestic help, the twin results of widespread industrialization and massive immigration. While politicians and lawyers performed in the architecturally impressive settings of courthouses and other civic buildings, and businessmen and bankers pursued their tasks in equally grand surroundings, women were celebrated and catered to in department stores—palaces dedicated to consumerism. Within the perfectly controlled confines of a department store—which combined the variety and vitality of the traditional shopping street with the high level of organization that could be provided by centralized management—women could not only shop, they could meet with each other and enjoy themselves. In the post–Civil War era, department stores thus transformed the hitherto mundane act of shopping for "dry goods" into an amusement.

Moses King vividly described the realities and the near-mythic aspect of New York's stores:

> Ill fares the rural or provincial purse whose owner ventures before these attractive windows, extending for miles on miles, ever diversified and varied; a perfect kaleidoscope of silks and velvets, laces and jewels, rich books and music, paintings and statuary, rifles and racquets, confections and amber-like bottles, *cloisonnée* and cut-glass, everything imaginable for use or luxury, massed in perfect affluence, and displayed in the most attractive way possible.[122]

A. T. Stewart & Co. was America's first great department store. Stewart, a Scotch-Irish immigrant, had founded his business in 1823 at 283 Broadway, basing it on a selling system that he is credited with pioneering: rather than negotiating prices for individual sales, Stewart advertised set prices, employing small markups and mandating cash-only purchases, ideas now taken for granted that turned shopping into a cornerstone of democratic capitalism. Set prices became a key factor in the transformation of shopping from a somewhat unpleasant and potentially embarrassing private necessity to a very public entertainment by freeing customers from the uncertainties of bar-

A. T. Stewart & Co., Fourth Avenue to Broadway, Ninth to Tenth Street. John Kellum, 1862–70. View to the southeast. MCNY.

gaining and the possibility of selecting items beyond their means. Additionally, the introduction of the "free entrance," which made it possible for shoppers to browse independently rather than be accompanied by a store employee, also served to render shopping a pleasurable pastime. Stewart prospered rapidly by virtue of his business acumen and understanding of human psychology, raising the status of shopkeepers to that of merchants; in the process, he became the first merchant prince. In 1846, after moving his business several times to ever larger quarters in the neighborhood, he built the so-called Marble Palace, at 280 Broadway, on the northeast corner of Chambers Street.[123] The white Tuckahoe marble–clad Anglo-Italianate building was designed by Trench & Snook, drawing inspiration from Sir Charles Barry's Travelers' Club (1829–31), in London, as well as from Frances Trollope's Bazaar (Seneca Palmer, 1828–29), in Cincinnati, Ohio. Trench & Snook's design incorporated two elements that would become standard features of the department-store type: expansive display windows and an imposing dome. Located between the impressive Corinthian columns that punctuated the building's

facades, unprecedentedly large plate-glass windows easily lured customers away from exclusive shops nearby. Inside, a ninety-foot-high main hall rose to a dome, dignifying the commercial emporium by nodding to the traditional architectural vocabulary of public buildings, including City Hall (Joseph François Mangin and John McComb Jr., 1803–11), located just across Broadway.

Following fashion's northward migration, in 1862 Stewart abandoned the Marble Palace for a new site, at the southeast corner of Broadway and Tenth Street, where over an eight-year period he built a vast cast-iron building that occupied the entire 200-by-328-foot block between Broadway and Fourth Avenue and Ninth and Tenth Streets.[124] Designed by John Kellum, the building consisted of five stories plus an attic and was soon known as the Palace of Trade, incorporating eight acres of selling space in an extensively glazed and arcaded design, the metalwork of which had been manufactured by the Cornell Iron Works. Stewart's, like many cast-iron buildings, was painted white, a fact that pleased its owner. As *Architectural Record* put it, "In its dress of white paint Mr. Stewart used often to liken his iron front to puffs of

View to the north along Broadway showing A. T. Stewart & Co. (John Kellum, 1862–70) in the foreground and Grace Church (James Renwick Jr., 1845) in the background. NYHS.

white clouds, arch upon arch, rising eighty-five feet above the sidewalk."[125] Straightforward to a point of repetitiousness that reflected the mass-produced efficiencies of cast-iron construction, Stewart's new store found little favor with the individualistic taste of post–Civil War observers such as James D. McCabe Jr., who in 1869 remonstrated the merchant and his architect for failing to make an "attempt at outward display" and relying instead for "fine effect" on "vast size and . . . symmetry."[126] Montgomery Schuyler, writing in 1871, was also highly critical of Kellum's building, castigating it as a "huge wilderness of cast-iron elliptic arches"[127] and lambasting it as a "conspicuous example" of the

> overpowering effect of mere size upon the eye. . . . This building has been over and over again trumpeted to the world as a specimen of architectural magnificence, as if the costliness and splendor of the wares inside were any offset to the painful poverty of invention traced upon its exterior, from top to bottom. It is impossible to conceive anything more glaringly monotonous, more utterly devoid of inventive skill than such a building. . . . A block of dead walls covering the same space, although not quite so useful for the purpose of commerce, would be quite as pleasing to look at, and do quite as much towards the cultivation of architecture as a fine art.[128]

The building was, however, not without its admirers. Writing in the *Architectural Review and American Builders' Journal* in 1869, William J. Fryer stated: "Let an observer stand on any of the four corners of Stewart's immense dry goods store, and take in with his eye the frontage on two streets. Those plain round columns and moulded arches and projecting corners could not be mistaken for stone. There is too much lightness and grace for anything but iron; and both the expansive elevations are beautiful, too, in being iron."[129]

Inside, Stewart's was served by broad staircases on the Ninth and Tenth Street sides as well as five steam elevators, two of which were reserved for freight. At the center of the building, an eighty-by-forty-eight-foot open rotunda rose to an oval dome of tessellated glass. The *New York Daily Tribune* stated:

> For one not versed in architecture, a description of this dome is impossible. It is supported on the lower floor by sixteen immense iron columns . . . the capitals of which are highly ornamented. . . . The sides of these pillars are elaborately embossed, having on two of their faces, just below the capital, two Cupids, and below them beautiful designs of leaves and flowers; on the other sides, in addition to these ornaments, each pillar contains the coat of arms of the Stewart family, bearing the monogram, "A. T. S.". . . . Standing beneath the dome and gazing up through story after story til one eye reaches the top, one is made dizzy and bewildered by the sight.[130]

Summing up Stewart's achievements as an architectural patron, however, Peter B. Wight, the Ruskin-inspired Gothicist architect, had nary a kind word for Stewart or for Kellum's design, which he deemed

absolutely beneath criticism . . . [with] nothing about it to attract the attention of the ordinary observer, except its great size. Built of cast-iron, it has no more interest than the commonest iron railing, with its oft-repeated balusters. It bears all over it an evidence of cheapness, especially when we observe that it is of iron,—a cheapness which comes from the desire to save pattern-making. In all probability, not more than six patterns were required to cast the several thousand tons which are put in this great iron wall. There is nothing inside of this store except iron columns, all cast from one pattern; and no end of plaster-corniced girders, save the great cast-iron well-hole over the glove-counter, with its bull's eye skylight above. This is a perfect mine of wasted iron, which, if properly used, would construct several respectable buildings. It is safe to say that this building has done more to retard architectural progress in New York than any other dozen buildings of the worst possible design. It overawes the thoughtless by its size, and seizes the sympathy of the sentimental by the purity of the white paint— when it is fresh. It was while building his retail store, that Mr. Stewart made the acquaintance of the late John Kellum; and, from that time forward, all his building enterprises were put into that gentleman's hands, including the finishing of the retail store. Thereafter all his architectural work was characterized by wastefulness and extravagance, and the almost total absence of artistic design.[131]

As if to soften the blow of his negative assessment, Wight praised Stewart's old headquarters, the so-called Marble Palace, which was still serving the company as a wholesale store:

> Even the Westchester marble was a novelty. Soon it began to be copied, but only in an indifferent way. Cast-iron had just been introduced in the first store fronts as a substitution for granite; and immediately Stewart's marble Corinthian columns were copied in that material; and to this day they are considered by the average New York architect to be the proper thing for first-class wholesale stores. Since the Devil had not yet invented galvanized-iron cornices, Stewart's cornice was copied generally in wood, and sometimes in stone or marble, while his Italian windows were imitated everywhere; but invariably the details were made coarse and clumsy. For, though the architects were for years trying to copy this building, they never produced anything half so good, and the old building stands to this day as the best example of classic or Italian store architecture.[132]

While architectural critics on the whole dismissed Kellum's design, other observers were much kinder; at least one journalist, from Cincinnati, found it "like some fairy palace of ancient story," with "white parapets extended against the evening sky and its innumerable windows full of lights. . . . With the picturesque marble Gothic Grace Church across the way, the most practical quarter of Broadway, New York, is thus transformed into a beautiful fable, a dream."[133]

Stewart's stores were important not only architecturally but in terms of their role in the domestic liberation of

James McCreery & Co., northwest corner of Broadway and East Eleventh Street. John Kellum, 1868. Rendering of view to the northwest. King, 1893. CU.

middle-class women. Ready-to-wear clothing was an innovative feature at a time when most women shopped for fabrics to take home or to their dressmakers for crafting into various articles of clothing. In 1869, after visiting Stewart's, where she saw the workshops that produced ready-to-wear as well as custom-made garments, Jane Croly, a fashion editor and feminist, wrote: "There is no reason why manufacturing houses should not supply every article worn at the cost of material and labor, labor being gauged, not by old methods, but by the application of the sewing machine and other labor-saving machines.... The days of family sewing are numbered."[134]

After Alexander T. Stewart's death, in 1876, the great store foundered; it was closed in 1882. The role it had played in New York's history and the significance of its loss were assessed by the editors of *The Nation*, who viewed the city's commercialism with an ambivalence bordering on contempt:

> Finally, much as we must all mourn the disappearance of Stewart's from the surface of New York life, as moralists our regret cannot but be tempered by a feeling that its importance as an "institution," like all things that came down to the great New York of today from the little provincial New York of the period before the war, was somewhat exaggerated. It was undoubtedly a great store in its day, but that one of the chief capitals of the world should regard a dry goods store as one of its most unassailable titles to respect and consideration—that when asked what it had to show among the other cities of the modern world, it should, in the place of monuments of

art and science, buildings or galleries, have triumphantly pointed to a dry goods store, and proudly told the stranger who wanted to see what New York really was to go to Stewart's—was after all a little melancholy. Twenty years ago the disappearance of Stewart's would have been regarded as an irreparable public calamity. In the great city which New York has grown to be, the wreck makes one less among the old provincial landmarks, and the moralist may awake with cheerful surprise to the fact that after all it was not Stewart's that made New York, but New York that made, and unmade, Stewart's.[135]

At the time of its completion, Stewart's uptown store was at the northern end of Broadway's retail district, then concentrated around Canal Street. The retailer James T. McCreery followed Stewart uptown in 1868, opening a substantial store, James McCreery & Co., at the northwest corner of Eleventh Street and Broadway.[136] McCreery also commissioned a design from John Kellum, who obliged with elegant four-story, arcaded, cast-iron facades crowned by an imposing occupied mansard. The building had a midblock extension toward Twelfth Street, featuring a continuous north-facing skylight that flooded the back wall of the ground-floor silk department with the even light needed to see true colors. Kellum introduced a new kind of show window, lining the store's Broadway facade with glassy bays protected by a galvanized wire fender, a feature that Samuel Sloan, the Philadelphia architect and publisher, writing in 1869, predicted would replace "obsolete straight fronts with long outside shutters." So extensive was the glazing, according to Sloan, that the building appeared to have "no apparent structure from the ground," creating a sense of "apparent weakness . . . such as to produce a feeling of discomfort, arising from a doubt of safety," an issue that troubled many as higher and higher buildings were built that had glassy storefronts at the base.[137]

Stewart had not in fact moved far enough uptown: by the late 1860s, the city's unprecedented commercial

James McCreery & Co., northwest corner of Broadway and East Eleventh Street. John Kellum, 1868. Rendering of silk department. King, 1893. CU.

Proposed Tiffany & Co., 11–15 Union Square West.
George B. Post, c. 1868. Competition-entry perspective. NYHS.

growth pushed out the top-class residential quarter that ringed Union Square, leaving Stewart's and McCreery's slightly below the new fashionable retailing district that would eventually come to be called Ladies' Mile.[138] In the 1870s and 1880s, stores and shops extended along Broadway from Fourteenth to Twenty-third Street. Tiffany & Co., founded in 1837, was the first important retailer to occupy a purpose-built commercial building in the hitherto residential area, moving in 1869 from 550 Broadway (R. G. Hatfield, 1853–54), at Spring Street, to 11–15 Union Square West, on the southwest corner of Fifteenth Street.[139] Its five-story cast-iron building, designed by John Kellum, replaced what Montgomery Schuyler described as "the ugly old Puritan church," James Renwick Jr.'s Church of the Puritans (1846).[140] Prior to hiring Kellum to design its new building, Tiffany's had conducted a competition. George B. Post prepared a submission, but the identities of the other participants are not known. Post's entry called for a dramatically massed composition in the French Second Empire style, with a corner tower rising high above the curved-profile mansard that crowned the five-story design.

To meet the explosive increase in demand for luxury goods that characterized post–Civil War trade, Tiffany's building incorporated salesrooms as well as manufacturing

Tiffany & Co., 11–15 Union Square West. John Kellum, 1869. View to the northwest, c. 1870, showing the Spingler House, formerly the Springler Institute (1847), on the left and Tiffany & Co. on the right. FLC.

Tiffany & Co., 11–15 Union Square West. John Kellum, 1869. View to the southwest, c. 1885, showing Tiffany & Co. in the center and the Spingler Building (Benjamin Warner, 1878) to the left. NYHS.

space housing two hundred workers. Kellum molded his 78-by-141-foot cast-iron palazzo along traditional lines, with the first story consisting of widely spaced columns framing large sheets of plate glass. Above these was a conventional, not very inspiring pattern of elliptical and segmental arched windows. The *Real Estate Record and Builders' Guide*'s critic, most likely Montgomery Schuyler, disliked the "squatty little detached Corinthian columns relieved here and there by massive rusticated shafts running up the entire height of the building, and crowned by that greatest of all architectural novelties—a balustrade." In the end, the critic noted: "Monotony and insipidity are stamped upon every square inch of the surface. . . . It is, like A. T. Stewart's upper store, just one huge mass of architectural nothingness."[141] Writing in the *New York World*, Schuyler regarded the prominent jeweler's move uptown as a descent in architectural quality: "Tiffany's old marble building, with its Atlas carrying a huge clock, [con-

stitutes] a structure which, old fashioned as it is, exhibits more design than the present iron thing of Mr. Tiffany's on Union Square." Most of all, true to his moralistic view of architecture, Schuyler objected to the handling of the cast iron:

Were this edifice really erected of Ohio stone—as by the color of its pigment it evidently pretends to be—we should still condemn it as a very ordinary and unartistic production: but when we look at its solid masses, all made out of cast iron and painted to look like stone, the impression is still more unsatisfactory. We think it was a sorry day for the fine arts when we commenced to build our fronts as we build our kitchen stoves; but if we will have iron fronts, let us at least build them of iron shapes and boldly proclaim them iron—as Sir Joseph Paxton did in his crystal palace—[and] not attempt to imitate the massive forms of granite and marble out of thin iron plates, smeared with paint. Considering its conspicuous loca-

Decker's Piano Store, 33 Union Square West. Leopold Eidlitz, 1870. View to the west. AR. CU.

tion, and the grand opportunity that was here offered for architectural display, we look upon this building as one of the most painful failures in the city.[142]

As was often the case, the general press had rather a different view; when Tiffany's opened, the *New York Times* proclaimed it "a jewel palace," and stated that the "new and magnificent store . . . was opened for inspection and the sale of goods and the number of ladies who visited the establishment and made purchases was quite large. The building is the largest of its kind devoted to this business of any in the world, and the collection of bronzes is the largest and most magnificent to be found in any city in Europe or America." The *Times* also took note of many of the building's interior features, including "a dummy engine" that "hoists goods and persons from one floor to another on a sliding platform" and the provision of "a retiring-room for ladies and children," a feature motivated by the fact that "very many ladies residing in the country, or in towns adjacent to New York, come here to purchase

their holiday goods, and almost invariably . . . bring their children with them," making "such toilet-rooms . . . an absolute necessity."[143] Two years after the building's opening, the *Times* noted that it had taken on a nearly civic dimension, serving not only as a place to shop but as a destination in its own right. In an editorial extolling the city's virtues, the *Times* singled out Tiffany's as "'the South Kensington Museum' of New York. Hours may be spent there with the greatest interest and profit; and indeed there is no public exhibition in the City which can offer attractions anything like so great or so varied."[144] The frequently acerbic diarist George Templeton Strong welcomed Tiffany's as a replacement for the demolished Church of the Puritans, asserting that "real jewels will be sold there instead of bogus ones. [Reverend] Cheever's few holders paid high prices for their bogus acquisitions. Tiffany's customers will pay still higher sums, but they will secure a genuine article."[145] Architecturally, however, the new store proved no better to Strong than the old church: "Tiffany is moving into his hideous new iron store that occupies the site of Cheever's hideous meetinghouse."[146]

In contrast to his harsh dismissal of Tiffany's Classicized box, Montgomery Schuyler nearly swooned with praise for the Venetian Gothic–inspired Decker's Piano Store (1870), at 33 Union Square West, designed by his friend and mentor Leopold Eidlitz, which, though "only a comparatively small edifice, with no advantage of a corner location," was deemed by the critic to be a model piece of urban architecture: "Look at the cunning and tasteful arrangement of the entrance steps; the variety and beauty of detail scattered over the whole front; the ingenious way in which ornamentation is blended with construction . . . to form part of it and not a mere adjunct; the exquisite care and judgment with which the various materials have been contrasted; the elegant and meaning proportions of all the openings, whether large or small."[147] A week later Schuyler had more to say about the building, finding it "a charming little Gothic edifice of brick relieved by Ohio-stone trimmings . . . which, contrasted with Tiffany's, goes to show the difference between well and ill-directed taste. Everything about the little Gothic building is truthful, well studied, meaning; in the other all is sham and vulgarity, showing no more invention than there is in a lead bullet shot out of a mould."[148] Despite what might have been a conflict of interest given the relationship between the architect and the critic, Schuyler appears to have been within his bounds, in fact echoing the praise of the editors of the *Real Estate Record and Builders' Guide*—although circumstantial evidence suggests he may well have been that journal's architectural critic as well. Nine months before the *New York World*'s review, the *Record and Guide* reported:

Everything about this little front:—the bold arrangement of the stoop at the entrance,—the pleasing sunk paved space leading to the store below, and occupied by Brentano's literary emporium,—the variety of ingenious forms adopted for windows in the several stories,—the distribution and meaning of the ornamentation,—the tasteful combination and contrasts of different stories and brick work,—all exhibit traces of artistic thought and skill. The windows are large and wide enough for all the purposes for which they were intended, and although the architect has freely availed himself of the pointed arch, the moulding and other ornamental forms of Gothic architecture, there is certainly nothing either gloomy or monastic about the building.[149]

Renwick & Sands's building for the offices and salesrooms of Wheeler & Wilson, a manufacturer of sewing machines and supplies, was completed at 44 West Fourteenth Street in 1874, as the effects of the Panic of 1873 were being felt. The building's imposing principal facade was described by the *New York Daily Graphic* as both "rich and chaste," with "pale clay-tinted Indiana stone, producing a very soft and pleasing effect."[150] Clusters of composite pilasters and columns supported a massive architrave. The company's monograms and elaborately carved stone rosettes provided decoration, while the building was surmounted by a balustrade and arched frieze emblazoned with the company's name. Inside, offices as well as sales and instruction rooms were elegantly appointed in a Classical manner. In reference to the Wheeler & Wilson building, the *Daily Graphic* somewhat grandly stated:

The Aristocracy of Idleness in the Old World monopolizes the splendors of art. In the New World the artist and artisan clasp hands, and the Aristocracy of Industry claims the tributes of genius and wealth. . . . But why such an expenditure of money on decoration? Why not give it to the poor when want presses so sorely? Answer: Charity is best dispensed as wages earned; far better than given as alms. Now that business is so depressed, the wealthy might set the wheels of industry and commerce in motion if they would pursue the improvements needed in all directions. The money which Wheeler & Wilson have thus expended is largely a gift to the public. The whole city is enriched by improvements that all enjoy. . . . The business facilities of Paris cannot be compared to those of New York, and yet the former city is the cynosure of the world.[151]

Commercial development not only lined Union Square but also pushed itself northward along Broadway. In 1868, the dry-goods retailer Arnold Constable found itself marooned in its store, known as Marble House, designed by Griffith Thomas, at 307–311 Canal Street, on the northeast corner of Mercer Street, completed only eleven years earlier, in 1857. Moving in 1869 to 881–887 Broadway, on the southwest corner of Nineteenth Street, Arnold Constable became the first large-scale retailer to

Arnold Constable, 881–887 Broadway. Griffith Thomas, 1869. View to the west along Nineteenth Street. King, 1893. CU.

relocate above the square.[152] Its new five-story, brick and cast-iron emporium was also designed by Thomas and was second in size only to Stewart's Palace of Trade. The business had developed from a dry-goods store founded in 1825 by Aaron Arnold, an immigrant from the Isle of Wight. As the business, first located on Front Street, prospered, Arnold took in his nephews, George and James Hearn, who in 1842 set out on their own as James A. Hearn & Son Dry Goods Company (see below). At the same time, Arnold's daughter Henrietta married James Constable, who was also taken into the business, which became Arnold Constable in 1853. In 1857, the store had moved from Front Street to Marble House.

Thomas's new building, at Broadway and Nineteenth Street, was a spirited design very much influenced by the architecture of the late years of France's Second Empire. With a modeled facade distinguished by boldly projecting columns and deeply recessed windows, as well as an elaborate skyline that articulated the mansard into towerlike pavilions, Arnold Constable was far more complex in composition than its New York department-store predecessors, proudly attention grabbing and stylistically up-to-date. The store was built in conjunction with the Hoyt Building, an identical design by Thomas, which stretched the complex through to Eighteenth Street. For Montgomery Schuyler, the combined block-long development, "although not of any great architectural pretension, is, from its size and general arrangement and detail, very effective, and gives quite a dignity to that part of the city."[153] But Schuyler, who did not find the exterior "graceful or imposing," objected to the inadequacy of the glassy base in visually supporting the ponderous mass above, itself "a mixture of Corinthian, Ionic and something else not easily definable, upon which one gazes with puzzled but neither soothed nor fascinated eyes."[154]

Inside, Arnold Constable was, as Schuyler put it, "just what it was intended to be—a spacious, convenient place for the sale of all varieties of dry goods." The ground floor, where the counting house was located, was devoted to "foreign dress goods" and gentlemen's furnishings, with the second floor for cloaks, mantillas, and other similar items for women and children.[155] The third floor was left vacant for future expansion—soon enough the store carried carpets and upholstery—while the fourth and fifth floors were occupied by male and female garment workers employed in making women's clothing. In the basement, space was provided for a staff lunchroom and for a supplementary salesroom.

The building's lot spanned only 83 feet along Broadway and 171 feet along Nineteenth Street, so in 1872 the building was renovated and expanded, with a two-story mansard built on top and a wing, incorporating a new entrance, extending 50 feet west along Nineteenth Street. In 1876 the store was extended again, reaching 150 feet farther west to Fifth Avenue—the first department store to do so. As Broadway was still the city's principal shopping street, however, the new wing did not accommodate retail space, instead housing the wholesale department, which previously had been left behind on Canal Street. The extension replaced Leopold Eidlitz's Fifth Avenue Presbyterian Church (1853). While the 1876 work resembled the 1872 renovation that had reconfigured the rooftop of the original building, this time Thomas eschewed marble for cast iron. With the additions, the *Real Estate Record and Builders' Guide* claimed that the expanded store was "one of the largest business establishments in the world."[156] The *New York Daily Graphic* praised the facility as "a new palace of trade, a prominent and ornamental addition to the street architecture of New York."[157] The building was enlarged once again, in 1883, when William Schickel extended it, midblock, south to Eighteenth Street.

Lord & Taylor, one of the city's leading dry-goods stores, had been founded in 1826 by Samuel Lord and George W. Taylor. When it was decided that the store would follow fashion north, from Broadway and Grand Street, land was leased from the real estate developers Ogden and Robert Goelet and an adjoining landholder to build an enormous cast-iron-fronted store (James H. Giles, 1869–70), at 901 Broadway, on the southwest corner of Twentieth Street.[158] With this addition to the neighborhood, the status of this stretch of Broadway was cemented as the city's leading shopping venue. According to the *New York Times*, the new Lord & Taylor building also made the construction of "one's own business palace" a "test of commercial business standing." Moreover, the *Times* observed, the trend toward large-scale mercantile palaces "has worked wonderful transformations on Broadway . . . and promises to be the leading agent in correcting that tendency to build on single lots, which, generally operative until 1860, has converted Broadway into a thoroughfare of slices of buildings, of variable height, set one against another, without regard to harmony proper, or even to harmonious contrast."[159]

Lord & Taylor had over the years simultaneously maintained stores at several locations in New York City as well as in Newtown, the East River village on Long Island where Samuel Lord lived. The company had kept its store at Grand and Chrystie Streets in order to continue catering to middle-class shoppers, while moving its "carriage trade" store from 461–467 Broadway (Griffith Thomas, 1858–59), at Grand Street, to the new location.[160] To design the uptown commercial palace, Lord & Taylor and the landowners from whom the property was leased mutually decided on James H. Giles, an architect specializing in cast-iron work. Giles's bold design, four stories plus a mansard, dominated Broadway with its expressively detailed iron. At the corner a diagonal tower rose to a truncated pyramid, a full story higher than the building, but the main entrance was located farther down Broadway, where a double-height entrance broke the scale of the four-story facade and the roofline was interrupted by a wide dormer carrying a low truncated pyramidal mansard. At street level the building was lined with broad

Lord & Taylor, 901 Broadway. James H. Giles, 1869–70. View to the southwest. MCNY.

show windows containing beautiful displays that came to be considered "among the sights of Broadway."[161] According to the critic of the *Real Estate Record and Builders' Guide*, probably Montgomery Schuyler, a large "semi-circular glazed space" corresponding "in form to that of their old store at the corner of Grand Street and Broadway . . . [had] the advantage at least of singularity, if not of beauty or meaning."[162]

Beneath the semicircular window, an eighteen-foot-high, twenty-five-foot-long, twelve-foot-deep porch, paved with variegated marble, sheltered the entrance to the eighteen-foot-high selling space on the main floor, which was finished in ash and black walnut. At the rear of the main floor was a "dark room," a new type of display space where fabrics and fashions could be viewed under gaslight. The store contained two steam elevators, one for freight and the other for passengers; the passenger elevator was the first in a department store and was said to have been ridden by ten thousand people during its initial three days of operation. The store also incorporated a reception room, complete with a piano, where female shoppers could meet and socialize, leading the *New York Daily Graphic* to note, "In this new feature in shopping, New York is ahead of any city in the world."[163]

In designing Lord & Taylor, Giles disregarded the rationalist, panelized repetitiousness of early cast-iron architecture, also eschewing the copybook Classicism that was a common feature of cast-iron designs. Instead he cre-

Paran Stevens Building, 1160 Broadway. Richard Morris Hunt, 1871. View to the northeast. The Octagon, AAF.

ated a highly elaborate program of decoration that rendered the building anything but standardized, going perhaps as far toward craft-based customization as any cast-iron building ever would. The use of cast-iron cladding for warehouses and other relatively minor commercial buildings had troubled some observers, who deemed the stamped-out Classicism of many examples an uninventive failure. There was also a belief that cast iron not only lacked the permanence but also the dignity of other materials, particularly stone. Giles's Lord & Taylor store demonstrated that the new material and building technology were capable of inspiring aesthetic expression unique to their own properties. Montgomery Schuyler seized upon the issue of materiality as the paramount consideration in assessing the design, finding Lord & Taylor

> by far the most beautiful, sensible, and perfect iron building yet erected in New York. We do not mean to say that it does not, in some cases, run into the fault of imitating stone forms, but in this case the details are so cut up into a multiplicity of forms, and richness is so florid, that the eye at once recognizes the fact that so much extravagance of ornamentation could only result from the mould, and could not be from the laborious work of the chisel. In other words, it challenges criticism on its very face as an iron building, and nothing else. Allowing this, we must say that the details are exceedingly pleasing and appropriate . . . [but] we wonder that Messrs. Lord and Taylor should have fallen into the common error of painting the building one color, when such a temptation was offered for the use of polychromy. All those little detailed columns and projections, moulded caps, elaborate balconies of curved shapes, and light iron ornamentations, would look gorgeous if judiciously picked out in varied colors and tastefully enriched by gilding. Well treated in this manner, it might be made the most magnificent exterior in the whole city.[164]

In 1871, a small, five-story building containing both retail and loft space, designed by Richard Morris Hunt and located at 1160 Broadway, was completed for the entrepreneur Paran Stevens, owner of the imposing Stevens House, also by Hunt (see chapter 4), and widely known as the "Napoleon of Hotel Keepers."[165] Both the Stevens House and the commercial building became the subjects of a legal dispute, with Hunt suing Stevens for payment due. Hunt eventually won the case, in the process validating the fee guidelines and schedules of the American Institute of Architects, thus fortifying evolving standards of professional architectural practice in the United States. The building's importance, however, was also architectural. The design incorporated a boldly expressed, bonelike cast-iron structure as well as a mansard punctuated by a dormer and pyramidal tower. The building was stylistically significant as an early example of Hunt's interest in medieval French architecture, exhibited in this case in a somewhat less than resolved combination of forms than would be seen in the architect's subsequent work.

The Panic of 1873 halted the development of the

View to the north from Union Square Park showing the Parish Building (Detlef Lienau, 1883–84) in the center, the Century Company Building (William Schickel, 1880–81) on the right, and part of Everett House (1854) on the far right. MCNY.

uptown shopping district, and for three or four years the stretch of Broadway between Union and Madison Squares remained an odd jumble of imposing retail buildings towering over the remaining houses of the gentry, including one belonging to the Goelets, on the northeast corner of Nineteenth Street.[166] Deemed a palace when completed in 1850, with its own garden stocked with animals including peacocks, by the 1870s the house looked almost puny, and certainly incongruous. By 1878, the *New York Daily Graphic* could state, "No better evidence of the tendency of trade to seek the central part of the metropolis is wanting than the marvelous transformations that are being made year by year in the appearance of many of the aristocratic thoroughfares between Union Square and Thirtieth Street, on the west side . . . [where] palatial business structures loom up over the spot where once stood the elegant mansions of the rich, and almost weekly old and familiar landmarks disappear only to give place to the ever increasing demands of business."[167]

When business picked up in the 1880s, the Parish family's namesake building (1883–84), at 860 Broadway, on the northeast corner of Seventeenth Street, was one of the more interesting new designs, a late work of Detlef Lienau.[168] The Parish Building was developed by descendants of Henry Parish, the dry-goods merchant, whose Italianate brownstone mansion (R. G. Hatfield, 1847–48) previously occupied the site and was home to the Union

Parish Building, 860 Broadway. Detlef Lienau, 1883–84. Perspective view to the northeast. Lienau Collection. CU.

W. & J. Sloane, 884 Broadway. W. Wheeler Smith, 1881. View to the southwest along East Nineteenth Street toward Broadway. AABN. CU.

League Club from its founding in 1863 until the completion of its new clubhouse, on Fifth Avenue, in 1881 (see chapter 2). The design was characteristic of Lienau, whose studies in Paris in the 1840s under Henri Labrouste were evident in the way he adapted the stripped Classicism of the 1840s so that it anticipated the Classical revival of the late 1880s, with severe, carefully proportioned brick facades trimmed in stone and terra cotta ornamented along the lines of the Neo-Grec. The building quickly became home to jewelers, silversmiths, and home-furnishings merchants, including Thonet Brothers. But the design seemed so old-fashioned that the critic of the *Real Estate Record and Builders' Guide*, possibly Montgomery Schuyler, found it wanting: "The general division" of the facade "is not effective, giving the building the look of two buildings set one on top of the other" with "nothing . . . made of the corner." The critic went on to state that "the commonplace of the design . . . [is] not redeemed by any grace of detail. Indeed, the work would be scarcely worth talking about at all, except for its conspicuousness."[169]

In 1881, the rug and carpet emporium W. & J. Sloane became the first important retail establishment to relocate uptown after the Panic of 1873, moving from 649–655 Broadway, near Bleecker Street, to a six-story building at 884 Broadway, on the southeast corner of Nineteenth Street.[170] Designed by W. Wheeler Smith, the building broke with the hitherto self-aggrandizing architecture of most department stores, a structurally straightforward essay in brick and cast iron that could as easily suit a factory or warehouse. Smith's design was consequently condemned, with the *Real Estate Record and Builders' Guide* dismissing it as one "that looks very well lighted, and is not otherwise noticeable except for a treatment of a frieze over the basement, which suggests that the real construction is invisible."[171] But the design made up in rigor what it lacked in ornamental excess: it had a strong A-A-B-A-A rhythm of bays along Broadway and coupled the second and third floors, as well as the fourth and fifth floors, to create a near-Classical composition of base, double-story middle, and attic, with piers treated as plain Corinthian pilasters and punctuated at their midpoints by Neo-Grec medallions. The effect was one of extraordinary structural directness, which was pointed out early on by Karl Hinckeldeyn, who found in its "treatment of the pillars, in the arrangement of the large light-openings, in the placement of the intermediate columns of iron . . . in the composition of the whole, as well as of the details, a fine artistic spirit, confident of success."[172]

Sloane's was followed by the music publisher Oliver Ditson & Co., which constructed a five-story, Romanesque-inspired, brownstone-trimmed, red brick building (1882–83) combining a retail store and offices at 867–869 Broadway, on the southwest corner of Eighteenth Street, designed by George W. Pope, a Boston architect.[173] Henry Fernbach's six-story Hess Building (1883–84), at 876–878 Broadway, between Eighteenth and Nineteenth Streets, housed the prominent decorating company of David S. Hess, who used

Gorham Building, 889–891 Broadway. Edward H. Kendall, 1883–84. Rendering of view to the northwest showing Lord & Taylor (James H. Giles, 1869-70) on the right. King, 1893. CU.

it as a warehouse and showroom.[174] The building's Renaissance-inspired design was more distinguished in its details than in its overall conception: a glassy ground floor was framed by stylized Ionic pilasters detailed to convey the Hess Company's specialties, which included drafting equipment, builders' tools, and architectural elements.

Edward H. Kendall's Queen Anne–style Gorham Building (1883–84), at 889–891 Broadway, on the northwest corner of Nineteenth Street, placed six stories of bachelor apartments atop two stories of retail space leased by the silver manufacturer whose name identified the building.[175] Kendall may have turned to the Queen Anne in order to convey an appropriate domesticity in the upper-floor apartments, but the location soon proved unsuitable for residences and in 1893 he was asked to renovate the upper floors for Gorham's, which thereafter occupied the entire building, bringing its retail sales and manufacturing facilities together under one roof. Kendall's pink brick building, trimmed with terra cotta and gray Belleville sandstone, rose to a high, steeply pitched slate roof. A rounded corner emerged above the roof as a slender, domed minaret, easing the transition between the

View to the north along Broadway from East Nineteenth Street, c. 1885, showing the Gorham Building (Edward H. Kendall, 1883–84) on the far left and Lord & Taylor (James H. Giles, 1869–70) two buildings to the north. NYHS.

facades to fit the awkward geometry of the trapezoidal site. The design was notable for its ornament, characteristic of the Queen Anne style, which included panels featuring sunflower and other floral motifs as well as bay windows flanked by scroll motifs rendered in brick. Scrolled and stepped gable dormers broke free of the roof, creating a vigorously modeled silhouette. A boldly scaled, steeply raked pediment announcing the store's entrance managed to complement the much taller and deeper arched entry porch of Lord & Taylor (see above), with which Gorham's shared the Broadway blockfront.

By the time the Gorham Building was finished, the taste for the Queen Anne was waning, as could be seen in Mariana Van Rensselaer's reluctance to "really approve" of the design, "with its trivial 'Queen Anne' detail appropriate only to a structure one-tenth its size." She admitted that at least it was not "loud or vulgar" and was "in happy contrast with such a neighbor as Lord & Taylor's iron shop," a building that only recently had been deemed virtually the best in New York by Van Rensselaer's mentor, the then-youthful Montgomery Schuyler, but which was now thought of as the epitome of vulgarity.[176] Van Rensselaer was in some ways echoing the review in the *Real Estate Record and Builders' Guide*, probably written by Schuyler, who observed that "the purpose of the designer was evidently to make [the building] noticed, and he has succeeded. Nobody will find it feasible to overlook his work." The critic deemed the main entrance of the Gorham Building particularly disagreeable, with "a steep ugly pediment of the advanced Queen Anne kind we know so well." But the critic reserved his principal displeasure for

> the chief feature of the building . . . a turret which surmounts the truncated angle, and after clearing the walls is roofed with an open cupola of copper. The idea of the feature is not at all bad, but the treatment is unfortunate. It is not at all clear what the object is for, and the treatment of the rest of the building does not suggest that it is merely monumental architecture. Moreover it has not been studied in relation to the roofs of the building, being either too important or not important enough, and upon the whole does not look at home in its place. In itself it is much the best thing in the building, and if the building "lived up to it," the building would be much more effective and show a much less painful effort to be effective than it is and does.[177]

Van Rensselaer regarded C. C. Haight's Brooks Brothers Building (1883–84), at 932–938 Broadway, on the southeast corner of Twenty-second Street, "a much better work" than the Gorham Building; though "weak in composition," the critic found it to be "quiet, straightforward, unpretentious, and agreeable. With others of its class it proves, if nothing more, that rampant ostentation is going out of fashion."[178] Brooks Brothers, the gentlemen's clothiers, had been comparatively late in moving uptown; operating two stores, its northerly branch was from 1857 to 1870 at Broadway and Grand Street. It was then moved

to Fourteenth Street opposite Union Square, where it remained only four years, at which time the downtown store, at Catherine and Cherry Streets, was abandoned after fifty-six years of business. All activity was then concentrated in a new building (George E. Harney, 1873–74), at 670–674 Broadway, on the northeast corner of Bond Street, extending back to Jones Alley, replacing the once-imposing house of Samuel Ward, the noted epicure. Montgomery Schuyler, in his history of the Romanesque Revival in New York, noted that "though it cannot be called an example of Romanesque," Harney's design constituted "a tolerably distinct reminiscence of the Norman variety of the style." Praising it as "very respectable . . . in spite of the drawbacks of detail," Schuyler posited it as "an oasis in . . . the dreary architectural desert of middle Broadway."[179] But Brooks Brothers's decision to settle below Fourteenth Street was a mistake. Once in the heart of the retail shopping district, the location was quickly becoming outmoded, and in ten years the store moved still farther uptown, to Twenty-second Street. C. C. Haight's new store replaced the Park Theater (see above), which had burned in 1882, with a tectonically straightforward building of five stories and a mansard, graced by such Queen Anne details as pedimented dormers and a bay window on a chamfered corner. Bruce Price, working with George A. Freeman Jr., had also prepared a design for the store building.[180] This proposal was bolder than Haight's and very much influenced by Richard Norman Shaw's New Zealand Chambers (1871), in London, in its handling of the extensively paned windows. Price and Freeman's design, like Haight's, featured a chamfered corner, but one that rose five floors to a turret supporting a

Proposed Brooks Brothers Building, 932–938 Broadway. Bruce Price, 1883. Perspective. AABN. CU.

Charles R. Yandell & Co., 140 Fifth Avenue. McKim, Mead &
White, 1886–87. Perspective. NYHS.

steep cantilevered roof that was broken up by numerous
gables and many chimneys—a veritable paradigm of the
kind of Queen Anne exuberance that Haight was far too
reticent a designer to exhibit. Like Haight's, Price's design
was distinctly residential in feeling. According to the *Real
Estate Record and Builders' Guide*, whose writer may have
been Schuyler, Haight's building was "Elizabethan, or
more properly Jacobean in type, and might be criticized as
more appropriate to a dwelling than to a commercial
building. But we do not get a piece of architecture so skillful and circumspect as this among the new work often
enough to quarrel with the pleasure it gives us, both for
what we receive and what we have escaped."[181]

In the 1870s and 1880s, while Broadway was emerging
as the city's primary shopping street, Fifth Avenue between
Fourteenth and Twenty-third Streets, even more than
Broadway once a high-profile stretch of grand houses, was
being rebuilt with clubs, office buildings, and stores. In
1879, on the northeast corner of Fifth Avenue and
Fourteenth Street, called "the old Delmonico corner" after
the famous restaurant that had been located there between
1861 and 1876 (see below), Edward H. Kendall designed
the Blatchford Building, five stories with a mansard,
expressly to be occupied by a retail store.[182] At 140 Fifth
Avenue, on the southwest corner of Nineteenth Street,
McKim, Mead & White renovated Charles R. Yandell &
Co.'s furniture store (1886–87), glamorizing a 27-by-143-
foot, one-story building of the type later called a "taxpayer."
The additions included glassy bays to serve as show windows, a Moorish arch over a carriageway, and a "Florentine
doorway and steps with wrought iron railing" that the *Real
Estate Record and Builders' Guide* said "greatly improved" the
premises.[183] In 1886, at 123 Fifth Avenue, between
Nineteenth and Twentieth Streets, Henry J. Hardenbergh
renovated the lower two floors of a five-story dwelling dating from 1850.[184] He incorporated a generously scaled cast-
iron arch with open spandrels—a Beaux-Arts–inspired
motif that Richard Morris Hunt had introduced to New
York in his Roosevelt Building (1873–74) (see chapter 3)—

Brooks Brothers Building, 932–938 Broadway. C. C. Haight, 1883–84. View to the southeast across Broadway. NYHS.

Western Union Building, southwest corner of Fifth Avenue and West Twenty-third Street. Henry J. Hardenbergh, 1882–83. View to the southwest. HRE. CU.

View to the northwest, c. 1890, showing the Sixth Avenue elevated railroad in the foreground, B. Altman & Co. (D. & J. Jardine, 1876–77) on the left, and O'Neill & Co. (Mortimer C. Merritt, 1887), with corner turrets, on the right. NYHS.

united by decorative themes including grotesque masks and griffins similar to those employed in the ironwork of Hardenbergh's recently completed Dakota apartments (see chapter 4).

Farther uptown, Hardenbergh's seven-story, red brick and terra cotta Western Union Building (1882–83), at the southwest corner of Fifth Avenue and Twenty-third Street, was an attempt to bridge the gap between the area's commercial and residential scales.[185] The Fifth Avenue facade was slender and incorporated a metal-framed oriel, rising to a pedimented gable roof; around the corner, the Twenty-third Street front was boldly scaled with its six-bay, double-height, extensively glazed, arcaded treatment and a skyline enlivened with six gables. Hardenbergh's building was a principal branch office of the company—there were over 130 similar but smaller offices throughout the city—and provided communication services that connected businesses and shoppers as well as neighborhood residents via pneumatic tube to the headquarters, at Broadway and Dey Street. The *Real Estate Record and Builders' Guide*'s correspondent, probably Montgomery Schuyler, found much to admire in Hardenbergh's design: "The arrangement and the modeling of the openings emphasize the weight of the wall. The general aspect of the building is sober and quiet, with that sense of straightforwardness and naturalness which can only come by following out and giving expression to the actual facts of the building."[186] In his mono-graph on Hardenbergh, published thirteen years after the completion of Western Union's uptown branch, Schuyler praised it as "in its kind, one of the most successful commercial buildings we have, and its quaint picturesqueness is the more valuable for seeming to have come unsought from the most straightforward treatment of the problem. . . . The treatment of the lower stage is especially ingenious," and the oriel facing Fifth Avenue "one of the happiest bits of our street architecture."[187]

Throughout the early and mid-1870s, as Ladies' Mile flourished along Broadway and to a lesser extent along Fifth Avenue, Fourteenth Street west of Union Square and the stretch of Sixth Avenue between Fourteenth and Twenty-third Streets remained comparative backwaters.[188] The construction of the elevated railroad along Sixth Avenue in 1878, however, transformed that thoroughfare and the adjacent blocks of Twenty-third Street into major retail locations, permitting dedicated shoppers to make a continuous loop that included these streets as well as Broadway, with only a slight detour needed to go farther down along Broadway to visit Stewart's and McCreery's. No city in the world had so long and varied a continuous shopping route. While the great stores along Broadway were squarely aimed at the so-called carriage trade, the Fourteenth Street and Sixth Avenue emporiums were more democratic and ultimately larger, achieving vast physical size by the end of the 1880s.

The impact of the elevated railroad on Sixth Avenue was tremendous. According to an 1878 report from the New York correspondent of the *Philadelphia Ledger*, those people who predicted that the avenue would be "ruined" by steam transit "are beginning to revise their opinions. The immense travel which has been turned into that street is doing wonders for the retail trade," and forcing some shopkeepers to relocate from Broadway.[189] Within a year of the elevated railroad's opening, the stretch of Sixth Avenue between Fourteenth and Twenty-third Streets became the city's leading retail location in terms of volume, even attracting such higher-status operations as James A. Hearn & Son Dry Goods Company, operated by the two nephews of Aaron Arnold, which in 1879 moved from 733 Broadway, between Waverly Place and Eighth Street, where it had been located for twenty-three years, to the Dry Goods Palace, as their new four-story store at 30 West Fourteenth Street was called.[190] As designed by John B. Snook, Hearn's new store was only twenty-five feet wide but stretched through the block to Thirteenth Street. In order to help bring natural light into the building's heart, the store was divided into a four-story front and a two-story extension at the rear, which permitted the installation of what the *New York Times* extolled as "an ingenious system of sloping sky-lights" as well as "three large oval wells in each floor," permitting "floods of light [to] penetrate even the remotest corners of the store," including the basement, which was reserved for the sale of white goods and calicoes and was "as carefully lighted as any of the upper floors." Wisely, James Hearn saw that the uptown trend might leave his store's location behind, but he told the *Times* that he was "convinced that for the next 10 or 15 years Fourteenth Street, between Broadway and Sixth-avenue, is to be the great center of the retail dry goods trade of the City."[191]

J. & J. Dobson's carpet store was housed in a five-story building (W. Wheeler Smith, 1879) at 40–42 West Fourteenth Street, between Fifth and Sixth Avenues, that also ran through to Thirteenth Street.[192] Dobson's was twice as wide as Hearn's. Entering through an imposing thirty-foot-long, eighteen-foot-wide vestibule, shoppers were greeted by an interior illuminated by a dome measuring twenty by forty feet and surrounded by galleries, all carried on cast-iron columns. In 1879 Ludwig Brothers, a dry-goods store, occupied 28 West Fourteenth Street, again running through to Thirteenth Street and designed by W. Wheeler Smith.[193] The severely uniform iron and glass facade of Ludwig Brothers functioned as a kind of warm-up for the stripped-down realism of Smith's W. & J. Sloane store, to be constructed two years later (see above). D. & J. Jardine's cast-iron-fronted Bauman's (1880), a carpet store, at 22–26 East Fourteenth Street, between University Place and Fifth Avenue, offered passersby a rich Classical filigree of composite columns, garlands, festoons, and floral bas-relief playing off an extensively glazed window wall.[194]

Rowland H. Macy was the retailer who to a greater extent than any other established the importance of Sixth Avenue as a retail destination for New Yorkers and tourists alike.[195] Established in 1858 at 204–206 Sixth Avenue, between Thirteenth and Fourteenth Streets, by 1876 Macy's had become, according to the *New York Times*, "one of the show places of . . . New York."[196] The store occupied a series of cast-iron buildings that held only passing architectural interest but were technologically innovative: Macy's was illuminated by arc lights in 1879, automatic cash-carrying tubes were installed in 1880, and telephones were hooked up in 1881.

B. Altman & Co. was the second important retailer to locate on Sixth Avenue.[197] An outgrowth of the modest retail establishment of Benjamin Altman's parents, the company began in 1865 at 39 Third Avenue, between Ninth and Tenth Streets; the business did well and moved to larger quarters, at 43 Third Avenue. In 1868, a branch was opened at 331 Sixth Avenue, between Twenty-first and Twenty-second Streets, and in 1870 the Third Avenue store was closed. The Altman family enterprises survived the Panic of 1873 and prospered enough to build a grand Neo-Grec cast-iron-fronted store (D. & J. Jardine, 1876–77), six stories tall and 65 feet wide by 125 feet deep, at 625–629 Sixth Avenue, on the southwest corner of Nineteenth Street, with a 25-foot-wide extension leading to Eighteenth Street, where a carriage entrance was located. After Alexander T. Stewart's death in 1876 and the subsequent collapse of his enterprise through mismanagement, Benjamin Altman became the city's leading retailer, proclaiming his store a "Palace of Trade" and augmenting it with a cavalry-like fleet of delivery vans drawn by matched "high-steppers."[198] In 1880 Altman's was expanded along Nineteenth Street in brick face by the Jardines. In 1887 the store grew again, along both Sixth Avenue and Eighteenth Street, but this time the expansion was designed by the architect William H. Hume in cast iron to closely resemble the original Jardine design; taken together, the building and its extensions formed a block-

Simpson, Crawford & Simpson, 307 Sixth Avenue. Thomas Stent, 1879. Rendering of view to the northwest. NYHS.

Ehrich Brothers, 695–709 Sixth Avenue. Alfred Zucker, 1886–87; William Schickel, 1889. View to the northwest, c. 1912, showing the Sixth Avenue elevated railroad in the foreground. NYHS.

long superstore. New York's first store building to have central heating, Altman's also incorporated an interior court illuminated through a delicately filigreed shallow dome of glass and iron that was carried on boldly scaled, lavishly decorated iron beams.

Simpson, Crawford & Simpson was another important retailer located on Sixth Avenue.[199] Begun in the 1860s as Ronaldson & Meares, the store was first located in a converted brick rowhouse at 307 Sixth Avenue, on the northwest corner of Nineteenth Street. In 1874, after Ronaldson's death, the firm became Meares & Co., and in 1878 William Crawford became a partner. Meares retired the next year, and Thomas and James Simpson joined the enterprise, which became Simpson, Crawford & Simpson and was housed in a four-story, Renaissance-style building (Thomas Stent, 1879) on the same site as the first Ronaldson & Meares store. The new building included an almost complete reconstruction of the original shop's interior. As designed by Stent, the new building, faced in cast

iron painted black with decoration highlighted in wine, olive, and gold, was a palatial facility, in keeping with the company's status as a carriage-trade retailer. The store tried to appear more like an art gallery or clubhouse than a dry-goods enterprise: items never carried price tags, and liveried attendants helped customers with their packages.

While Altman's and Simpson, Crawford & Simpson catered to a well-heeled clientele, O'Neill & Co. was a middle-class department store.[200] Hugh O'Neill, the store's founder, was an Irish immigrant who had come to New York in 1857 as a thirteen-year-old, and, after some education and military service, opened a millinery and notions shop on Hudson Street near Broome Street with his brother. In 1867 the store moved to Broadway near Twentieth Street, and three years later to Sixth Avenue, where it operated in two houses and then expanded into an adjacent building. By 1879, when O'Neill's brother retired, the firm had acquired the entire west blockfront between Twentieth and Twenty-first Streets. Part of the site had

Rendering of view to the southwest along West Twenty-third Street between Fifth and Sixth Avenues, 1879, showing, from left to right, Stern Brothers (Henry Fernbach, 1878), the Calvary Baptist Church (John R. Thomas, 1854), and the Booth Theater (Renwick & Sands, 1867–69). NYHS.

been purchased from the Shearith Israel congregation, which had used it as a cemetery until 1851, when the city prohibited burials south of Eighty-sixth Street. It was not until 1886, however, when all the tenant leases had expired, that the firm set out to build a new store building, hiring Mortimer C. Merritt to design what in 1887 was the city's grandest department store and among the largest cast-iron-fronted buildings ever realized. O'Neill's move was widely applauded. The *New York Daily Tribune* reported: "Anyone who has shopped in the yellow-faced brick buildings" of the previous O'Neill store "will remember the low ceilings and sloping floors of the old, made-over houses, the dense crowding and pressure everywhere of a retail trade squeezed into half its rightful compass." The six-month-long construction of the new four-story building was a feat of planning ingenuity, taking place with the store in continuous operation. The neutral, Neo-Grec facades, with their rhythmic grouping of windows, were painted a "dazzling white" and rendered exceptional by a central pediment emblazoned with the store's name and by two five-story corner turrets.[201] The turrets were articulated with composite columns, illuminated by curved-glass windows, and crowned with bulbous domes, suggesting a very stylish and faintly exotic bazaar.

The Ehrich Brothers department store (Alfred Zucker, 1886–87; William Schickel, 1889), at 695–709 Sixth Avenue, between Twenty-second and Twenty-third Streets, was New York's last grand cast-iron store.[202] The popular mart was opened in 1868 at 279 Eighth Avenue, but in the late 1870s the Ehrichs began to plan a move to Sixth Avenue. They acquired the site just abandoned by Stern Brothers, which was moving to Twenty-third Street (see below). At first the Ehrichs maintained a stagecoach service to take their customers from the Twenty-third Street elevated station to their store, but when they carried nine thousand people on the day

View to the east along Twenty-third Street, c. 1902, from near Sixth Avenue, showing Stern Brothers (Henry Fernbach, 1878–80; Hugo Kafka, 1886; William Schickel, 1892) in the center and the Fuller Building (D. H. Burnham & Co., 1902) in the background. A sign identifying the Eden Musée can be seen on the far left. NYHS.

before Christmas, 1885, the die was cast. In 1886, they had Alfred Zucker file plans for a five-story building in the middle of the block, with a T-shaped plan that connected to the side streets. The building soon expanded, ultimately occupying the entire Sixth Avenue blockfront except for the Twenty-third Street corner, where the jeweler William Mori refused to give up the five-story cast-iron-faced building he had commissioned in 1871.[203] Difficulty in acquiring key leases delayed the expansion's completion until 1889, by which time William Schickel had taken over from Zucker.

While Zucker's cast-iron facades were legal when designed and filed with the New York City Building Department in 1886, technically they did not meet the more stringent safety requirements enacted in 1887. But because Schickel's plan was, from the point of view of the Building Department, an amendment to Zucker's plan, he was permitted to continue with it, thus making Ehrich Brothers the city's last cast-iron building of consequence. The use of a giant order to group the building's stories and the arithmetical progression of the windows suggested that despite the building's use of an "old-fashioned" material, the architect was anxious to distance himself from the past and embrace the new popular taste for Classical architecture. Inside, Ehrich Brothers was paneled in quartered oak, with mahogany used for the counters.

In 1878 Stern Brothers became the first retailer to abandon Sixth Avenue, where the company had been conducting business since 1867.[204] The store moved from 337 Sixth Avenue, at Twenty-second Street, to 32–36 West Twenty-third Street, occupying a six-story, sixty-five-foot-wide, cast-iron building designed by Henry Fernbach, who chose a dramatically scaled three-story arch as the dominant feature of the building's principal facade. Shoppers entered through imposing twelve-foot-high walnut doors; inside, the vestibule floor was covered in multicolored Minton tiles, and mahogany and cherry elevator cabs supplemented an elaborate staircase that rose through a central rotunda famed for the massive, sparkling chandelier that almost filled its upper reaches. The *Real Estate Record and Builders' Guide* described the building as a "magnificent bazaar" and "an ornament" to its setting.[205] The company prospered in its new location, taking advantage of its proximity to both the mass markets of Sixth Avenue and the more exclusive venues along Broadway and Fifth Avenue below Madison Square. The store was expanded in 1879 with an addition at the rear, facing Twenty-second Street, designed by Fernbach, who also designed a second rear addition in 1880. In 1886, three years after Fernbach's death, Hugo Kafka realized a one-hundred-foot-wide extension following the late architect's design, and in 1892, another addition, designed by William Schickel, adapted Fernbach's arch entrance for use in a new pavilion developed in the center of the now vastly enlarged complex. Schickel also added a sixth floor to Fernbach's buildings, but in most respects stayed close to his predecessor's work.

Restaurants

> Nowhere else in this country do men live so largely at restaurants as in New York.
> —Junius Henri Browne, 1869 [206]

In 1869, the author Junius Henri Browne reported that there were between five thousand and six thousand restaurants in the city and analyzed the phenomenon:

> One wonders how even this great City can support so many eating-houses. It could not but for the great distance between business and residence quarters, and the consequent necessity of the commercial classes dining or lunching downtown. Nearly three quarters of the restaurants below Canal Street owe their support to that fact; for as soon as the mercantile tide sets northward, their trade is over for the day. . . . Nowhere else are lodging and eating so completely and strictly divided. Probably 150,000 of our population rent rooms up town, and get their meals down town. They adopt that mode of existence because they are not able to live at hotels, and they are unwilling to put up with what is termed, by an ingenious figure of speech, boarding-house accommodations.[207]

Thirteen years later, the *Real Estate Record and Builders' Guide* would observe that the situation remained largely unchanged: "A distinctive feature of New York is its vast and varied system of restaurants. Paris doubtless has a greater number of places where choice meals can be served up . . . ; but while in the metropolis of France eating at the cafe is a social custom, using a restaurant in New York is a business necessity."[208] This aspect of daily life affected not only the number of restaurants, but the tone of business. According to Browne, "Eating is done in the Metropolis with the haste of Americans intensified. From 12 o'clock to 3 in the afternoon, the down-town eating houses are in one continuous roar. The clatter of plates and knives, the slamming of doors, the talking and giving of orders by customers, the bellowing of waiters, are mingled in a wild chaos. The sole wonder is how any one gets anything. . . . Everybody talks at once; everybody orders at once; everybody eats at once; and everybody seems anxious to pay at once."[209]

Not surprisingly, these midday meal factories were universally banal in their architecture and design. During the post–Civil War period, however, a different type of restaurant began to emerge, operating later in the day and catering to a pleasure-seeking clientele. As Browne stated:

> When evening comes and the business of the day is ended, the down-town restaurants are closed, and those up-town have their active season. Then [these restaurants] thrive, particularly toward midnight, after the theatres and the concerts and the operas are over. The up-town restaurants furnish quite a contrast to those in the lower quarter of the City. They have no confusion, no bustling, no jostling, no door-slamming. Ladies elegantly and elaborately dressed go with their escorts to upper Broadway and Fourteenth Street.[210]

Of the city's many restaurants, however, only two

Delmonico's (1861), northeast corner of Fifth Avenue and East Fourteenth Street. Alteration of the Moses H. Grinnell house. View to the northeast. NYHS.

achieved any degree of architectural distinction—Delmonico's and Sherry's. Delmonico's was the city's premier restaurant in terms of both its cuisine and its reputation as a social magnet, a place in which to see and be seen, playing a pivotal role in teaching New Yorkers—and the still young and puritanical nation as a whole—how to enjoy itself in public.[211] Indeed, as the journalist and restaurant critic John Mariani recently put it, "The restaurant as Americans know it began . . . when the Swiss brothers John and Peter Delmonico opened a small establishment. . . . Taverns, coffee houses, and eating houses existed in American cities at the time, but restaurants that offered fine dining did not. Based on the Parisian model, Delmonico's established the pattern for all restaurants in the United States."[212]

The restaurant was founded in 1827 and occupied a building at 23 William Street, expanding and upgrading its operations to 25 William Street four years later. In 1834, Delmonico's opened another restaurant, at 76 Broad Street. The great fire of 1835 destroyed the William Street

restaurant, and John and Peter Delmonico moved their establishment to a purpose-built building erected nearby at the geometrically spectacular intersection of South William and Beaver Streets. A local newspaper described the building as possessing "a scale of splendour, comfort and convenience far surpassing anything of the kind in this country."[213] John Delmonico died suddenly in 1842 while on a Long Island hunting expedition, and Peter Delmonico took his nephew Lorenzo into partnership; three years later, the restaurant opened a branch at 233–235 Broadway, on the southwest corner of Morris Street. In 1855, with Lorenzo serving as sole proprietor, the branch restaurant moved, this time to a building at the northwest corner of Broadway and Chambers Street.

Still maintaining its facility at South William and Beaver Streets, in 1861 Delmonico's opened a restaurant in the former Moses H. Grinnell mansion, on the northeast corner of Fifth Avenue and Fourteenth Street.[214] Operating from this luxurious if understated four-story, red brick residence, Delmonico's first gained a national

Delmonico's, south side of West Twenty-sixth Street, Fifth Avenue to Broadway. Griffith Thomas, 1876. Alteration of the Dolworth Building. View to the northwest of Fifth Avenue facade, with sidewalk café. NYHS.

reputation; it was here that Charles Ranhofer, one of Delmonico's chefs, reputedly originated Lobster Newburg and Baked Alaska, each mainstays of American cuisine in the Gilded Age. According to Henry Collins Brown's history of Delmonico's, the restaurant's "beautiful ballrooms and dining rooms at once eclipsed the glories of all its former establishments and inaugurated a new and brilliant gastronomic era."[215] The *New York Times* noted that the former mansion

> has been fitted up with faultless taste, and is without any exception, the handsomest place of the kind in the City. We doubt, indeed, if Europe can boast its equal in quiet elegance and real comfort of decoration. The large restaurant on the ground floor is an extremely cheerful apartment, commanding from its windows a view of the always animated promenades of Fifth-avenue and Fourteenth-street. On the same level, but quite detached from it, is a cafe in the true Parisian style, being fitted up with small marble-top tables, and destitute of a bar. This is a new experiment, which we trust will succeed. Upstairs there are innumerable private apartments, large and small, intended for dinner and supper parties, and all fitted up with lavish luxuriousness, but without the slightest excess that can be called garish or vulgar. The establishment is, in fact, as unique as it is beautiful.[216]

Shortly after the restaurant opened in its new location, it served as the venue for a dinner honoring Samuel F. B. Morse, at which the professor and inventor sent and received, from his table, the world's first cablegram. Ward McAllister, the lawyer and high-society tastemaker who helped to create the social circle known as the Four Hundred, writing in his book of 1890, *Society As I Have Found It*, depicted the restaurant as an apt setting for gatherings of the city's elite:

> The Assemblies were always given at Delmonico's in Fourteenth Street, the best people in the city chosen as a committee of management, and under the patronage of ladies of established position. They were large balls, and embraced all who were in what may be termed General Society. They were very enjoyable. A distinguished banker, the head of one of our old families, then gave the first *private* ball at Delmonico's to introduce his daughter to society. It was superb. The Delmonico rooms were admirably adapted to such an entertainment. . . . Being a success, it then became the fashion to give private balls at Delmonico's, and certainly one could not have found better rooms for such a purpose. One of the grandest and handsomest fancy balls ever given [in New York] was given in these rooms a little after.

McAllister went on to describe another particularly memorable event at Delmonico's that became known as the Swan Ball:

> A man of wealth, who had accumulated a fortune here, resolved to give New Yorkers a sensation; to give them a banquet which should exceed in luxury and expense anything before seen in this country. . . . The banquet was given at Delmonico's, in Fourteenth Street. There were

seventy-two guests in the large ballroom, looking on Fifth Avenue. The table covered the whole length and breadth of the room, leaving a passageway for the waiters to pass around it. It was a long extended oval table, and every inch of it was covered with flowers, excepting a space in the centre, left for a lake, and a border around the table for the plates. This lake was indeed a work of art . . . four superb swans, brought from Prospect Park, swam in it, surrounded by high banks of flowers of every species and variety, which prevented them from splashing the water on the table. There were hills and dales; modest little violet carpeting the valleys, and other bolder sorts climbing up and covering the tops of those miniature mountains. . . . It seemed like the abode of fairies; and when surrounding this fairyland with lovely young American womanhood, you had indeed an unequaled scene of enchantment.[217]

In 1876 Delmonico's moved yet farther uptown, this time to a location in the heart of the city's most fashionable residential neighborhood, on the south side of Twenty-sixth Street between Fifth Avenue and Broadway.[218] For its new restaurant, which was an alteration of the former Dolworth Building, Delmonico's hired Griffith Thomas, whose design incorporated a sixty-six-by-seventy-foot café and a thirty-three-by-sixty-foot restaurant on the ground floor, with a twenty-five-by-fifty-seven-foot grand dining room and smaller private dining rooms on the floors above. To help dissipate the heat and smells, the kitchen was located on the fifth floor. The alterations resulted in an elegant brick and brownstone palazzo. A segmental pediment, emblazoned with the restaurant's crest set between two white scrolls, confronted Fifth Avenue, where elaborate wrought-iron balustrades enclosed second-floor balconies and a street-level sidewalk café. While on his second trip to the United States, in 1879, sixteen years after his first visit, the English writer George Augustus Sala noted, "When I was here last the fashionable or 'uptown' Delmonico occupied a large building at the corner of East Fourteenth-street, and Fifth-avenue. But East Fourteenth-street is now 'down town' and the existing Palazzo Delmonico fronts Broadway, Fifth-avenue, and Twenty-sixth-street. The furniture and hangings are splendid, but very quiet and refined."[219]

As Delmonico's business prospered uptown the restaurateurs expanded and beautified the downtown facilities. In 1886, James Brown Lord was retained to renovate two floors and the basement at 341 Broadway, between Worth and Leonard Streets, to provide a café, restaurant, and private dining rooms.[220] Three years later, Delmonico's hired Lord to design an eight-story, iron-spot Roman brick, brownstone, and salmon terra cotta building on the triangular lot at the corner of Beaver and South William Streets, where the restaurant had been located for more than fifty years.[221] Completed in 1891, the arcaded building, combining aspects of the Richardsonian Romanesque with high Renaissance Classicism, effectively filled its wedge-shaped site while complementing George B. Post's

Delmonico's (c.1835), South William and Beaver Streets. View to the west, c. 1884. NYHS.

Cotton Exchange (1883–85) (see chapter 3) across the street. A sweeping curve facing the intersection incorporated two double-height colonnades as well as the building's principal entrance, which was enframed by a cornice and marble columns taken from the original Delmonico's building; the columns were reportedly Pompeian artifacts imported by John Delmonico. The arcades of Lord's elegant design spanned the third through sixth floors and were outlined in terra cotta banding decorated in a checkerboard pattern. Inside, dining rooms, which served men only, were located on the first and second floors and connected to an eighth-floor kitchen by means of hydraulic elevators and pneumatic tubes. The building's remaining space was rented out for offices. The *New York Times* praised the building as "admirable in its simplicity and elegance."[222]

Delmonico's only rival was Sherry's, which catered to the faster, new-money crowd. Louis Sherry was a native of St. Alban's, Vermont, who came to prominence after working in the dining room of the Brunswick Hotel in

New York and as maître d' in a fashionable summer hotel in Elberon, New Jersey. There he met Henry Clews, Frederic Coudert, and William Dinsmore, who in 1881 backed Sherry in a confectionary and restaurant venture that occupied a nondescript building at 662 Sixth Avenue.[223] Sherry really hit his mark as the caterer of high-society parties, but in 1889 he embarked on creating a full-fledged grand restaurant, hiring Stanford White to renovate a four-story house owned by the Goelet estate, at the southwest corner of Thirty-seventh Street and Fifth Avenue.[224] White added a floor to the house and gutted the interior. Two lots, one at 402 Fifth Avenue and another on Thirty-seventh Street, were added to the project and provided space for a ballroom. But it was not until nine years later, in 1898, when a new era defined by unprecedented wealth and metropolitan grandeur had taken hold of New York, that White completed his most significant work for Sherry's, a twelve-story building on the southwest corner of Fifth Avenue and Forty-fourth Street that epitomized the new era's lavish standards.[225]

Delmonico's, South William and Beaver Streets. James Brown Lord, 1891. View to the west. OMH.

Charles Ward Apthorpe house (Elmwood) (1774), near Columbus Avenue and West Ninety-first Street. View c. 1890. NYHS.

Dr. Valentine Mott house (1835), the Boulevard and West Ninety-fourth Street. View c. 1853. Prevost. NYHS.

CHAPTER 6

❧ New Neighborhoods ❧

The new quarter, amounting to a new and strange city, . . . has been built up within the past few years upon the "West Side." So strange and exotic of aspect is this new quarter that a New Yorker of 1880 even, who might be suddenly dropped into it, would never recognize it as part of the downtown brown stone city that he knew.

—Montgomery Schuyler, 1891[1]

WEST SIDE

During the post–Civil War era, the area bounded by Fifty-ninth and 110th Streets and Eighth Avenue and the Hudson River was transformed from a sparsely developed, almost rural landscape into a thriving urban district, known alternately as the West Side or the West End, with its own distinctive character. In the seventeenth century, Dutch settlers had called the area Bloemendal, meaning "vale of flowers," also the name of a place in the Netherlands near Haarlem.[2] For most of the city's early history the area was home to scattered estates as well as a number of small residential settlements at Harsen's Lane (Seventy-first Street), Strycker's Bay (Ninety-sixth Street), which had been settled as early as 1764 by Gerrit Strycker, and, farther north, Bloomingdale Village. Bloomingdale Road, the area's principal route, was also the primary means of surface travel between New York and Albany. Travel across the island to the Boston Post Road on the East Side went via Harsen's Lane and via Apthorpe Lane at Ninety-third Street. Along the cliffs looking west toward the Hudson, leading landholders built fine houses, some of which were occupied in the summer by downtown families such as the Apthorpes, the de Lanceys, and the Livingstons. The de Lancey house, built in the 1750s, stood at Eighty-sixth Street and Riverside Drive, and the Charles Ward Apthorpe house, Elmwood, was built around 1774 farther inland, at Columbus Avenue and Ninety-first Street.[3] In 1835 the celebrated surgeon Dr. Valentine Mott built his house at Ninety-fourth Street so far back from the river that in 1868 it had to be moved to make way for the construction of the Boulevard.[4] Another grand house, built in the mid-1830s by William P. Furniss, commanded the river at Ninety-ninth Street.

The development of suburban-style villas continued well into the nineteenth century. As late as 1851, the architect Leopold Eidlitz built a chalet-like residence at the terminus of Eighty-sixth Street.[5] In 1866 Cyrus Clark, who would become a leading investor in and champion of the West Side, purchased the Brockholst Livingston house and its extensive property; the house was a craggy stone pile that sat on what would become Ninetieth Street and Riverside Drive.[6] While retaining some of the property, in 1889 Clark sold the house to John H. Matthews, the "Soda Water King," whose bottling plant occupied two full blocks in the East Twenties. Matthews tore the house down and replaced it with a rambling, Richardsonian Shingle Style cottage (1892) by Lamb & Rich, at the northeast corner of Ninetieth Street.[7]

The decision to create Central Park focused attention on the West Side's real estate potential for the first time, although the area remained isolated from the city until after the Civil War. So undeveloped—and, more to the point, so unlikely to attract development—was the area that only one streetcar line ran above Fifty-ninth Street, and even that one line, along Eighth Avenue, consisted of

Leopold Eidlitz house, near the Hudson River and West Eighty-sixth Street. Leopold Eidlitz, 1851. View to the northeast. NYHS.

a single pair of tracks on which a single car plied its route back and forth between Fifty-ninth and Eighty-fourth Streets. When the elevated was extended along Ninth Avenue to Eighty-first Street, in June 1879, quick connections to the central city were finally available. Since the extension carried trains from both the Sixth and Ninth Avenue lines, in typical New York fashion the track on the west side of the street was built by the New York Elevated Railway Company while that on the east was the project of the Metropolitan Railway Company.[8]

The extension of the El was the decisive event in the development of the West Side. Nonetheless, as West Side property owners pointed out in a meeting held in 1878 at the new American Museum of Natural History (see chapter 2), there were still serious impediments to growth: "Scarcely a single street or avenue north of Fifty-ninth Street is completely ready for building: the water supply is deficient; Manhattan Square repels instead of attracts; the smaller parks are incomplete, and Ninth Avenue, which should be the first finished, is impassable."[9] Furthermore, the area's appeal was not enhanced by the Fifty-ninth Street yards of the New York Central Railroad, home to the Union Stock Yards, the malodorous scent of which wafted from the west across the entire surrounding area.[10] It would be some time before the problem went away: it was not until 1898 that slaughtering in Manhattan was restricted to Abattoir Place, near the Hudson River at

View to the northeast, c. 1892, of Riverside Drive and West Ninetieth Street, showing the John H. Matthews house (Lamb & Rich, 1892) on the left and the Cyrus Clark house (Henry F. Kilburn, 1889) on the right. MCNY.

View to the west, 1868, of the New York Central Railroad's Fifty-ninth Street Yards, showing the Union Stock Yards in the foreground and the Hudson River in the background. WS. CU.

Thirty-ninth Street, and Abattoir Center, near the East River in the East Forties.

Beginning in the 1860s, when the construction of Central Park robbed them of their rookeries, the West Side was also home to squatters, thousands upon thousands of them, especially after the Panic of 1873.[11] Some squatters were quite entrepreneurial, leasing land from its legal owners and setting up as landlords themselves, building rows of shacks to rent. By around 1880 it was estimated that there were ten thousand squatters. Most were from Ireland and Germany, although there was also a colony of Dutch immigrants settled on an ash dump at Eighty-first Street. Until

the squatters were driven away in the early 1880s, West Seventieth Street from Central Park West to Columbus Avenue was the "main street" for one shanty village, which included shops as well as a saloon occupying an old frame house perched on a rocky outcropping that was reached from the street by a flight of wooden steps. Although they were inherently makeshift, some of the shanties looked like permanent houses. By no means were all the residents unemployed. According to *Harper's Weekly*, the most prestigious houses might have belonged to reasonably well-compensated workers: "There would be more tin on the roof, the windows would look as though they might be

View to the south, 1887, from the roof of the Dakota (Henry J. Hardenbergh, 1882–84), at Eighth Avenue and West Seventy-second Street. NYHS.

View to the northwest, c. 1872, of the Boulevard from West Seventy-second Street. NYHS.

mates, an extra chimney or two would impart an air of wealth and comfort to the ambitious structure."[12]

One last and most intransigent obstacle to the West Side's development was its daunting topography of deep glaciated furrows running north to south between sharply tilted ledges of tough schist. Frequent rock outcroppings thirty feet or more in height had to be blasted to make way for streets and buildings. Many were so formidable that developers were unwilling in even the most prosperous times to undertake the cost of blasting them away. In addition, underground streams as well as various ponds and rivulets not only plagued road builders but also scared off property developers. Some of the water features were charming, if occasionally pestilential: inclement weather turned Arch Brook, at Eighty-seventh Street and Tenth Avenue, into a half-mile-wide swamp that proved a perfect breeding ground for cholera, malaria, and, on occasion, yellow fever.[13] Fortunately, the engineer and surveyor Egbert L. Viele, who had been a key lobbyist for the Metropolitan Health Law of 1866, had lived in the area since 1872, occupying a red brick villa overlooking the Hudson at Eighty-eighth Street.[14] Viele pushed for the construction of storm and sanitary sewers along with the new streets; by 1876, when hardly more than a handful of new buildings had been erected in the area, the makings of a sophisticated sewer system were in place.

Despite the implemented and proposed improvements, the West Side's real estate future remained glum. In 1868 the newly founded *Real Estate Record and Builders' Guide* reported that "notwithstanding the greatest inducements offered to builders on the West side of the city, and the impetus given to move in the direction of the new Boulevard, the great majority of buildings contemplated, will be erected on the East side, the Nineteenth Ward seeming to be the chosen locality."[15] Moreover, when at last the attention of the real estate community focused on the West Side at the frenzied peak of the Bonanza economy, the price of land became artificially inflated, typically rising

some two hundred percent and occasionally much higher, thereby further retarding development.[16] As the *Record and Guide* noted: "This may be readily accounted for in the theory that people do not care to pay two or three or ten times as much for a plot of ground as for the house they erect upon it. The demand for small, one-family, moderate-priced houses is almost universal, and such cannot be erected on the West side of the city and insure anything like a respectable return on an investment. Hence it is that while few very costly houses are built on the East side of the city, still fewer moderate priced houses are built on the West side."[17] Just as swiftly as the boom came, after the Panic of 1873 so too came collapse. Quickly the West Side, which had attracted many German Jews as investors, became known as the "Hebrew Graveyard."[18]

When mortgage rates declined in 1876 and 1877, interest in West Side real estate resumed, with many large properties purchased at auction. But the new investors were cautious, pricing their properties high and holding out for top-quality development. This had the effect of turning the table on the farther reaches of the East Side, which bore the brunt of low-level speculative development in the 1880s boom, quickly filling up block after block with working-class tenements and closing the open-space gap between what had been uptown and the suburb of Harlem. The West Side building boom, which began after about 1885 and continued with hardly a break until around 1910, was largely aimed at providing housing for the middle class and the rich but not the super-rich. By and large, the needs of the working poor, so amply satisfied east of Third Avenue, were not addressed on the West Side.[19] Two of the major West Side developers were also not individual entrepreneurs such as those who typically built rowhouses and tenements on the East Side but socially prominent individuals with access to large private fortunes: Edward Clark, president of the Singer Sewing Machine Company, and W.E.D. Stokes, heir to a fortune derived from banking.

View to the southwest, c. 1872, of the Boulevard, with West Seventy-second Street in the foreground. NYHS.

The Boulevard

Although the Commissioners' Plan of 1811 provided for the expansion of the city to 155th Street, the construction of Central Park, with its dramatic interruption of the grid, encouraged a second look at the city's physical layout, particularly in the as-yet-undeveloped West Side. This was undertaken by the Board of Commissioners of Central Park under the state legislature's act of April 24, 1867. The area was considered to be of great importance to the growing city because, despite the fact that it was virtually undeveloped, it was owned by individuals who collectively paid more taxes than did the population of the entire island above Astor Place in 1811, when the Commissioners' Plan was adopted. Under the leadership of Andrew Haswell Green, comptroller of the park, a West Side plan was prepared. Released in November 1867, the proposal showed new streets, avenues, and public squares, as well as various waterfront features, especially new piers and bulkhead lines.[20] The plan put an end to the wandering route of the old Bloomingdale Road, creating in its place an extension of Broadway in the form of a 160-foot-wide thoroughfare, until 1899 called the Boulevard, the principal features of which were the twin rows of elm trees planted in beds on each fifteen-foot-wide sidewalk and the series of thirty-foot-wide landscaped islands separating the north- and southbound carriageways. Part of the motivation in creating the Boulevard was to raise real estate values, but its construction was also intended to produce jobs for those laid off as the result of Central Park's completion.

Land acquisition for the Boulevard was approved in July 1868 by the New York Supreme Court, which had jurisdiction over the commissioners; certain pieces of land at the key intersections of Ninth, Tenth, and Eleventh Avenues, however, were excluded. The new street's path had in fact been graded in 1867 with the expectation that the roadway would be open for travel in January 1871.[21] Yet another manifestation of the city's enchantment with

Second Empire Paris, the Boulevard was imagined as a kind of Champs Elysées lined with imposing mansions and villas. Sadly, the very admirably conceived road came to be a symbol of Boss Tweedism at its worst; as the *Real Estate Record and Builders' Guide* noted, it was a "magnificent monument of the era of fraud . . . , a standing menace and rebuke to corrupt officials and daring speculators."[22] Though opened more or less on schedule, the Boulevard failed to become a prestigious address. Part of the problem lay in its associations with the Tweed Ring's excesses, part in the city's decision to pave it in gravel, a situation exacerbated by shoddy construction, which resulted in numerous craterlike ditches that frequently filled with water. It was not until 1890, when the Boulevard was surfaced in asphalt, that it became home to leading hotels and apartment houses.

Although the plan for the new Boulevard, or Grand Boulevard, as it was sometimes called, was approved, debate swirled about the proposal to widen the already opened stretch of Broadway between West Fifty-ninth and Seventieth Streets, with the *New York Times* supporting the strong objections of abutting landlords to public usurpation of their land.[23] But the plans for the widening were approved in 1869, as were plans for the creation of a traffic circle, to be called the Grand Circle, at the southwest corner of Central Park. Andrew Green's plan also called for a broken chain of parks extending from the northwest corner of Central Park, incorporating the escarpments known as Morningside and St. Nicholas Heights, as well as a new park facing the Hudson River to be known as Riverside Park.[24]

Riverside Park

The idea of turning the Hudson River's shore into Riverside Park was probably initiated by William R. Martin, an early president of the neighborhood advocacy group the West Side Association, who boldly claimed: "The westward tendency on this island has the force of law, as

View to the northwest, c. 1895, of a squatter's shack on the east side of Riverside Drive between West Eightieth and West Eighty-first Streets. NYHS.

powerful and as unobserved as the law of gravitation."[25] Martin's pamphlet of 1865, *The Growth of New York*, outlined in some detail the vision to which the idealistic Frederick Law Olmsted, with the assistance of Leopold Eidlitz in one small portion of the work, would later give specific form. Martin imagined a time when

> [West Side] residents . . . could come out of a summer afternoon upon the Riverside Park, and, through its drives and walks, among its flowers, under the cool shade of its old trees, in its casinos and refreshment houses, could have in the city all the enjoyments of the millionaire in his one-hundred-thousand-dollar villa at Irvington. Assuredly this region will be the site of the future magnificence of this metropolis. During the coming five or ten years the Fifth avenue will no doubt be soonest built up and built up grandly, but the city will not stop on that account; it will be succeeded by an age of imperial magnificence. That will be the day for the now neglected west side of the island. The poetical prophecy—"Westward the star of empire takes its way," and which is fast becoming historical truth, will receive another illustration.[26]

Plans for the creation of Riverside Park and the new road to run along its edge, dubbed Riverside Avenue by Frederick Law Olmsted (in 1908 the name was officially changed to Riverside Drive), as well as for the construction of Morningside Park, were not only delayed by the 1873 crash but also by "reason of the [Tweed] Ring frauds and the empty treasury they left behind them" and by litigation.[27] By 1875 taxpayers were being assessed for improvements despite the fact that Riverside Drive was not opened to the public until March 1, 1880, with some portions remaining incomplete until 1902.[28] The new park and adjacent avenue, the latter in fact a reworked Twelfth Avenue, were seen as a spur to development, showing to the public "how matchless and unique this location is."[29] While many hoped that the combination of the park and the distant views of the Hudson River and New Jersey Palisades from the new avenue would lure some of the upper-class market away from Fifth Avenue, the *Real Estate Record and Builders' Guide* rather pragmatically pointed out that this would not take place soon: "There [is] wealth in New York, but as yet not enough to fill the whole West Side with ornamental residences."[30]

The design for the park and the avenue was prepared by Olmsted between 1872 and 1873, although a final plan was not issued until January 18, 1875.[31] An earlier proposal was prepared in 1865 by William R. Martin.[32] The legislation authorizing the project along with other West Side improvements was passed in Albany in 1867, and land acquisition by condemnation, which cost the city dearly at some six million dollars, was begun in 1872.

In keeping with comparisons between the West Side and London's West End, Riverside Drive was from the first contrasted with Hyde Park's Rotten Row, which boosters claimed it would surpass. In creating Riverside Drive Olmsted abandoned the irregularly inclined and winding road as first proposed in 1868 in favor of a much more gradually graded avenue that would command river views at important points and that would also provide a pedestrian promenade along the park's edge. Where topography required, the new road was separated from residential cross streets, thereby creating picturesque enclaves such as were almost unknown in New York, as well as separating through and local traffic. In these ways Riverside Drive took the parkway idea, which Olmsted was also proposing for Brooklyn, one step further toward his ultimate goal of creating a limited-access highway, as he had first proposed in 1869 for Riverside, Illinois, but not realized. The drive terminated above the Harlem Valley, where it completed a loop around the Claremont, an existing house from the early 1800s that had for some time been used as an inn. Olmsted's plan showed no specific development for the sloping parkland. In accordance with general practice, the land west of the shore-level railroad tracks would be developed with commercial docks. As Olmsted pointed out to the Department of Public Parks, the plan eliminated "the imaginary line by which the site for the avenue was divided from the site for the park" in favor of a plan that utilized "in the greatest degree practicable, the advantages offered by the territory, *as a whole* for the several purposes—first, of a means of access to the property on its east side; second, of a pleasure drive, commanding a fine view over the river, airy and shaded; third, of a foot promenade, commanding the same view, and also airy and shaded."[33] The land selected for the park was, in Olmsted's view, remarkably suitable, because "the river bank had been for a century occupied as the lawns and ornamental gardens in front of the country seats along its banks. Its foliage was fine, and its views magnificent."[34]

In 1876 construction began on the three-mile-long terraced drive, said to be the largest single municipal road-building project undertaken to date in New York.[35] By the fall of 1879 the graded country road was complete between Seventy-second and Eighty-fifth Streets, while most of the work up to 113th Street was quite far along. But disputes with the city led the contractors to post guards and block off the cross streets with derricks, tim-

bers, and heaps of stone, preventing the area's few residents from gaining access to their houses. Egbert L. Viele complained that he was forced to grope his way home at night "at the imminent risk of being bitten by the vicious dogs the shanty-dwellers kept to harass the bailiffs."[36] When a property owner, Christopher R. Robert, was actually harassed by the guards in the spring of 1880, he got a court order relieving them of their posts. Around midnight on May 6, 1880, about 150 men "liberated" the new road at Seventy-second Street, hurling the derricks over Olmsted's parapet, leading the *New York Times* to report that the "sun rose upon Riverside-avenue yesterday open, for the first time, from one end to another. The citizens along the avenue were jubilant and all of them conveniently ignorant as to the man under whose orders the barriers had been destroyed."[37]

In its first years, the lack of transportation and the cold winter winds proved to be obstacles to progress, and only a few houses were built along Olmsted's new drive.[38] By 1887 *Phillip's Elite Directory of Private Families and Ladies Visiting and Shopping Guide for New York City*, which had first covered Riverside Avenue five years earlier, listed only eighteen worthy families on that thoroughfare.[39] Among these were George Noakes and his family, who lived in a turreted, hip-roofed, French-inspired, rock-faced stone mansion (1884) between 113th and 114th Streets, designed by Arthur B. Jennings on a full block of terraced lawn.[40] Soon in residence was the family of Samuel Gamble Bayne, who had started out his career peddling oil equipment and had risen to be head of the Seaboard Bank. The Bayne house (1888–91), on the southeast corner of 108th Street, was described by the *Real Estate Record and Builders' Guide* as "the best house thus far erected on the Drive. It is pretty and artistic in itself, and is eminently appropriate to its site and its surroundings." The magazine found the Bayne house, designed by Frank Freeman,

> conspicuous by the choice and combination of material.
> A basement and principal story in light gray sandstone, framed and enriched with brown sandstone in two tints,

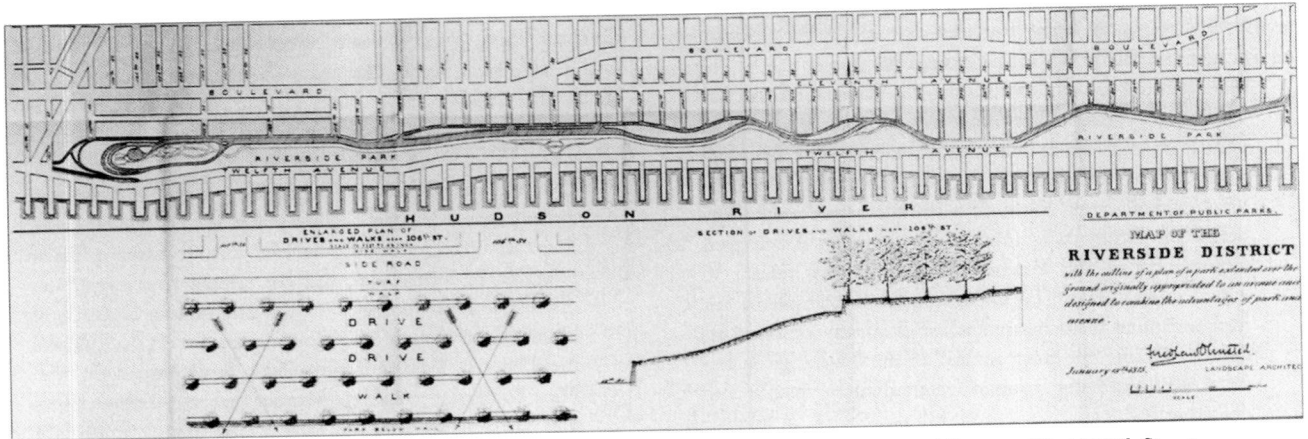

Map of the Riverside District, west side of Tenth Avenue to the Hudson River, West Seventy-second Street to West 129th Street. Frederick Law Olmsted, 1875. FLONHS.

George Noakes house, east side of Riverside Drive between West 113th and West 114th Streets. Arthur B. Jennings, 1884. Rendering of view to the northeast. NYHS.

carries a second story in brown brick, repeating the tint of the darker brown stone and rising into a tower and gables that form half of a third story, and are relieved against a pyramidal roof of flat tiles with hip rolls of the same material. . . . The building, in its treatment of form and its combination of color, strongly recalls Mr. Richardson's work, and is one that he need not have been ashamed to own.[41]

Freeman soon designed another villa, on the northeast corner of 108th Street, for Henry F. S. Davis, a yellow brick mass trimmed in rich red sandstone with a roof of varnished black tile.[42] According to Montgomery Schuyler, the general composition of the Davis mansion, of "which the motive is the pyramidization of the whole mass to the apex of the crowning roof with the tall arcade of the larger tower," was "admirably conceived and admirably executed."[43] On the southeast corner of Ninetieth Street, Cyrus Clark commissioned a turreted Romanesque granite house (1889) from Henry F. Kilburn.[44] The *Real Estate Record and Builders' Guide* found the design not particularly distinguished but contended that it at least had "the advantage of being unmistakably a villa and not a city house, and in this respect [set] a good example for succeeding builders."[45] In 1891, Schuyler characterized the area's architectural progress:

> The building thus far done along the Riverside Drive has sufficed to commit that boulevard to a suburban rather than a strictly urban character. It is especially fortunate since among the villas already erected, which are for the most part decorous and dull, with one or two exceptions which are highly undecorous and even duller, it has given opportunity to Mr. Freeman to put up two villas . . . which are not only by far the most artistic examples of the Richardsonian Romanesque in our domestic architecture, but are among the most artistic of our dwellings in any style. Without being grouped, each enhances the effect of the other.[46]

Other men of great wealth and position, such as Benjamin Altman and Jacob Schiff, bought land on the drive but did not follow through with their intentions of building villas or mansions. Presumably they preferred the social safety of the East Side.

Riverside Avenue's development was held in check, in part, by the commercial nature of the waterfront. In addition to their continued steam-powered freight service on shore-hugging railroad tracks, the New York Central and Hudson River Railroads had the right to develop the shorefront itself, filling in the Hudson River to the west of the tracks between Seventy-second and Seventy-sixth Streets to create a dock and freight depot. Immediately to the north, the Department of Docks constructed a bulkhead, assigning the area to the Street Cleaning Department for the creation of landfill from the excess debris created from the leveling of the West Side area. The Department of Docks also gave landings at Seventy-ninth and Ninety-sixth Streets to the West End Association to use for off-loading building materials. Not all the waterfront was commercial, however. At the foot of Eighty-sixth Street, the Columbia Yacht Club, founded in 1867, built a boathouse designed by William B. Tuthill.[47] The more modest Hudson River Yacht Club was located at Ninety-second Street, and in the 1890s other clubs could be found at Seventy-fifth, Seventy-seventh, and 102nd Streets.

The West Side Boom

In order to stimulate the West Side's development, an effort was made early on to promote the area as a distinct, visually identifiable enclave within the city, with many promoters preferring to call it the West End and advocating special names for the area's important streets.[48] Edward Clark suggested that the names be taken from those of the new states: Eighth Avenue would be known as Montana Place, Ninth as Wyoming Place, Tenth as Arizona Place, and Eleventh as Idaho Place. He also believed that "the very poor and common name, 'Central Park,'" be changed to Irving Park, presumably after Washington Irving.[49] Eleventh Avenue above Seventy-second Street was the first to be renamed, becoming West End Avenue on February 10, 1880. Eighth Avenue became Central Park West, Ninth became Columbus Avenue, and Tenth became Amsterdam Avenue on the same day, April 22, 1890.[50] The *Real Estate Record and Builders' Guide* doubted that a name change would bring Eighth Avenue to life:

> This title, which is more megalophonous than 8th avenue, is also much more accurately descriptive. . . . Even an ordinance of the Aldermen, however, cannot make a street populous or fashionable, and the comparative stagnation of Central Park West is a curious and striking illustration of the uncertainty of operations in real estate. . . . [While the Dakota pioneered high-class development on the West Side], for years this pioneer had no follower. Even now there is scarcely any very interesting or important evidence of building activity between the Dakota at 72d street and the Cancer Hospital at 106th Street.[51]

With the opening of the elevated railroad and the concurrent rebirth of the city's economy, the West Side once again attracted attention. The New York correspondent of the Boston-based *American Architect and Building News* speculated on its future: "What will be done in that peculiar district lying north of Fifty-ninth Street and west of the Park it will be difficult to say. With the finest views, the healthiest location, the most desirable surroundings, the best appointed roads, this region is yet a desert, so far as humanity is concerned. Now that rapid transit is pushing up into it a move may be made, but it is not the side where activity and push is looked for."[52]

The group that took the greatest interest in the area's development was the West Side Association, founded in 1866 and largely made up of local residents and landholders, including Dwight H. Olmstead, a lawyer who advocated reform for New York State real estate laws. At a meeting of the association in December 1879, the area's future was debated, with the various participants arguing about whether the neighborhood should be dominated by tenements, modest rowhouses, mansions, or apartment houses. But Egbert L. Viele, who published a map of the West Side plateau in 1879, had a clearer vision, claiming that as "westward the empire runs," the trend of fashionable growth in great cities such as London, Paris, Berlin, and Naples was also westward and that New York would inevitably experience the same movement, especially given the West Side's sunset views and pollution-free summer breezes.[53] Viele believed that the West Side would replace Murray Hill as a "synonyme of fashion . . . [combining] in its general aspect all that is magnificent in the leading capitals of Europe. In our Central Park, we have the fine Prater of Vienna, in our grand Boulevard the rival of the finest avenues of the gay capital of France, in our Riverside Avenue the equivalent of the Chiara of Naples and the Corso of Rome, while the beautiful 'Unter den Linden' of Berlin and the finest portions of the West End of London are reproduced again and again."[54]

But no matter the new parks or the evocative street names, the bright future would not materialize until the shanties and their residents were removed. Early in 1880 the members of the West Side Association, many of whom were landlords to shanty dwellers, vowed to oust these residents by May. The massive forced relocation could not take place without incurring the danger of civil unrest, the threat of which began to build as the self-imposed deadline approached. The *New York Times* reported on May 20:

> Two weeks ago, a Deputy Marshal, wandering about Eighty-first street serving papers, was seized, and a milk-can, half filled, was turned over his head like a hat. Two other deputies were beset by dogs kept for the purpose of harassing bailiffs. . . . Seventy-ninth Street is said to be the most dangerous locality, and any well-dressed strangers found prowling about there are roughly handled. One old man refuses to leave his shanty at all, fearing that in his absence his house will be pulled down. Not all of these people are poor. Two Germans boast a bank

account of $30,000. These people will not converse with strangers, and a reporter for the *Times* who visited the district in pursuit of the facts herein narrated, found it safer and pleasanter to continue his investigations in other quarters.[55]

The May deadline passed and the squatters remained. Nearly a year later, in April 1881, the *Times* reported:

> [The] locality from Sixty-fifth to Seventy-second street, between Ninth and Eighth avenues, is the paradise of squatters and goats, whose shanties disfigure the landscape. This is really one of the most valuable sections of the West Side, and is destined in the natural course of events to be rapidly built up as soon as the squatter element is banished. The squatter colony—which for so long made the region bounded by Seventy-ninth and Eighty-third streets and Ninth and Tenth avenues, unsightly— has been mostly cleared away, and the owners of the property between Eighth and Ninth avenues have promised the West Side Association that the squatters shall vacate the premises before the first of May.[56]

By the mid-1880s, the largest shanty villages were a thing of the past.

These changes had been fueled by something of a boom in the entire city during the early 1880s; by the middle of the decade it was in full swing, and had an impact on the West Side as well.[57] According to the *Real Estate Record and Builders' Guide*, in 1885 the character of the West Side seemed "to have determined itself. Between Fifty-ninth and Sixty-seventh streets will be largely given over to flats. Glancing north we find that from Sixty-seventh street to Seventieth street, between Eighth and Ninth avenues, the ground scarcely appears to have been touched. This is no doubt principally owing to the immense quantities of rock which hang as a millstone over the sale of this realty. . . . West of Ninth Avenue, however, quite a number of improvements are underway."[58] Another deterrent to growth in the area were covenants, imposed by the original landholders of what had been Jacob Harsen's farm, which restricted development to single-family houses. But the *New York Times* was boosterish:

> The West Side of the city presents just now a scene of building activity such as was never before witnessed in that section, and which gives promise of the speedy disappearance of all the shanties in the neighborhood and the rapid population of this long neglected part of New York. The huge masses of rock which formerly met the eye, usually crowned by a rickety shanty and a browsing goat, are being blasted out of existence. Streets are being graded, and thousands of carpenters and masons are engaged in rearing substantial buildings where a year ago nothing was seen but market gardens or barren rocky fields.[59]

After 1885 the West Side's fortunes changed, almost overnight. By 1887 not only the amount but the variety, individuality, and quality of the buildings that comprised the new district were obvious to observers. Here truly was, as described by the *Real Estate Record and Builders' Guide* with only a little exaggeration, a new city, to all intents and purposes, and not an extension of the old. The New Yorker of 1867 might perambulate almost the whole region between Central Park and Riverside Park without learning or being reminded that he was in his own city at all. Once in five blocks or so he might come upon a familiar-looking row of brown stone fronts, looking more sombre and monotonous than ever, and also, it must in truth be owned, looking sometimes more respectable than ever by reason of the strange company with which they are surrounded. But for the most part there is not a trace of middle New York in upper New York, not an architectural feature that recalls the era that immediately preceded this eruption of what the designers and builders who have broken out with it call art, and what the old-fashioned and sober-sided citizen would, in his unenlightened way, describe as gingerbread. Whether stately uniformity or picturesque unity and irregularity are the more desirable note for the street architecture of a city is an open question among architects. New York at all events affords ample material for making the comparison. . . . One who is endeavoring to estimate the architectural value of the new work on the west side finds his task very difficult, by reason of the bewildering complexity of the subject, and he is continually diverted from it by considerations not architectural. What a great work it is that has been undertaken and is now accomplishing between the Park and the Hudson. It is an attempt made, not at all upon philanthropic and benevolent grounds, but as a mere matter of commercial supply and demand, to do a work by the greatest possible philanthropy and benevolence. Twenty years ago one needed to be a rich man to occupy the whole of a house in New York. The result was that people who were not rich took houses intended for single families, and in the endeavor to keep them up made themselves really miserable. Here was the burden of the advertisement: "A private family, having more room than they require." Twenty years ago there were a hundred advertisements beginning in that wearisome and pathetic strain where now there is one. . . . All that is past and gone now, thanks to French flats and apartment houses, the elevated roads and the great tract of land they have made for the first time accessible and habitable.[60]

In many ways the West Side was New York's equivalent to Boston's Back Bay, a neighborhood of rowhouses.[61] While not every house or group of rowhouses was designed by an architect, many were. Although the quality of a lot of the work was pretty run of the mill—the work of "contract architects," as Montgomery Schuyler put it—in many cases the West Side provided opportunities for young, up-and-coming talents, who, indulging their taste for individuality in architectural expression, with the Queen Anne and Richardsonian Romanesque as the dominant styles, frequently produced such exuberant facades that Schuyler derided them as "artchitects." Many would become known for much larger, public work later in their careers. But in the second half of the 1880s, the West Side

was their playground for architectural invention. In their anxiety not to be conventional, these architects frequently produced designs that some found risible, leading the *Real Estate Record and Builders' Guide* to observe "that an artistic architect can make a very decided improvement on the brownstone front, but that in the absence of such a functionary it is safer to stick even to that dreary old pattern than to strike out for novelty."[62]

More than in any other section of the city, when presented with a row of five or more houses architects working on the West Side approached these projects not as a series of repeated individual houses but as a unit, balanced between the desire to express the individuality of each dwelling and the desire to create an overall composition. The architects and builders seemed bound by a sense that this new area represented a great chance to right the wrongs of the lower city, to make special architecture for what was widely perceived as a special enclave of manageable size and definite extent, bounded by parks and a riverfront. The sense about the neighborhood was that it would be planned in relationship to its particular assets and not just as real estate. This was not truly the case, as Sarah Bradford Landau has pointed out: "In actuality there was no master plan, just the belated but still viable image of New York as a city of private houses."[63]

Another reason the West Side gave the impression of having been planned as a community was that developers assembled larger numbers of adjacent lots than was customary on the East Side; especially along West End Avenue, whole blockfronts were designed as single groups. This sense of a physically planned community also had an impact on daily life, as the *New York Daily Tribune*, with some amazement, observed in 1889:

> There is actually a local public spirit on the West Side, something apparently unknown in any other quarter of this great heterogeneous town, which is made up of a jumble of every people under the sun. There are associations for the improvement of the streets, for furthering legislation at Albany in the interest of the section, and for fighting jobs that are regarded as inimical. . . . There are well-authenticated cases of people living on the West Side who know who their Representative in Congress is and who is their Assemblyman in Albany. This is a unique development in the history of this city.[64]

The most fashionable areas were the so-called park blocks, between Eighth and Ninth Avenues and Sixty-eighth and Eighty-first Streets, and west of the Boulevard between Seventy-second and Eighty-sixth Streets. The area above Eighty-sixth Street, considered somewhat remote even though the Ninth Avenue elevated had stations above that point beginning in mid-1879, would not be extensively developed until the 1890s.[65] Rowhouses were typically built on the east-west streets, with the most impressive efforts located on West Seventy-second Street, which in a largely treeless city was intended to be a kind of parkway connection between Riverside and Central Parks, and along West End Avenue, which also had wide, tree-

Houses, north side of West Seventy-third Street, Eighth to Ninth Avenue. Henry J. Hardenbergh, 1879–80. View to the northwest, 1884. NYHS.

shaded sidewalks. In contrast to Fifth Avenue, only a few houses and one great apartment house, the Dakota (1882–84) (see chapter 4), were built on Eighth Avenue. The avenue did not come into its own until after 1890, when it became home to large apartment houses and hotels as well as to clubs and houses of worship. Initially, real estate interests projected that West End Avenue would be the area's principal shopping street, serving the big houses lining Riverside Drive and the Boulevard. But the Boulevard failed to catch on, and West End Avenue became the heart of an area frequently called the West End, which from the late 1880s into the new century would be a preferred address of the prosperous merchant and professional class.

In 1878 Edward Clark began what would be not only the first important development on the West Side but also one of its most distinguished when he committed to build the Dakota, an apartment house at Seventy-second Street and Eighth Avenue, as well as two long rows of houses on the north side of Seventy-third Street, one stretching from two hundred feet west of Eighth Avenue to within thirty feet of Ninth (where he concluded the row with a complementary five-story tenement), and the other stretching from thirty-one feet west of Ninth Avenue to within three hundred feet of Tenth.[66] Taken together, Clark's group set a standard for the West Side that was unmatched in the city as a whole. Henry J. Hardenbergh was the architect for both rows of houses as well as for the Dakota, setting in place the image of a coherent community, an image that would happily prevail as the area developed, whether under the direction of a banal architecture firm, such as Thom & Wilson, or an inspired one, such as Lamb & Rich.

The twenty-five houses designed by Hardenbergh for Clark built to the west of Ninth Avenue (1879–80) were somewhat timid.[67] Inspired by the Renaissance, with Neo-Grec elements in the detailing, the nine four-story and sixteen three-story buildings seemed to look back to the work of the early 1870s. There were also eight four-story, Connecticut brownstone rowhouses (1880–81), at 156–170 West Seventy-third Street, between Ninth and Tenth Avenues, designed in a similar manner by Hardenbergh for Daniel Herbert.[68] Clark and Hardenbergh concentrated most of their energy on the row nearest the park, where four-story houses with traditional high stoops featured olive sandstone at the basement and first floor, and buff-colored or red brick above. The sandstone and sometimes salmon-colored, sometimes buff-colored brick echoed the palette of the Dakota while the red brick introduced more color and added spice to a composition that, given its length, might otherwise have been bland. In contrast to typical practice, Hardenbergh's row was not made up of a repeated single facade. Nor did it conclude with a decisive cornice and a flat roof. Instead, there were a number of distinctly different designs arranged according to a

syncopated rhythm, so that corbeled oriels, two-story bays, projecting windows, and the intermittent use of shallow arches, as well as a variety of highly visible roofs, most with gabled pediments, combined to create the impression of a neighborhood of individual houses. The various roofs also helped orchestrate the composition of the 20- or 22-foot-wide houses in the 550-foot-long row, which the *Real Estate Record and Builders' Guide* was quick to praise as "a significantly interesting experiment in street architecture":

> The effect of unity is obtained by a high basement of Dorchester stone running through the whole series [but individuality is achieved through the use] sometimes of red pressed brick and sometimes of the salmon colored Perth Amboy brick. Sixteen of the houses are in red brick, and the remaining eleven of yellow brick, the latter material being used in two groups of three houses each, and elsewhere in single dwellings interpolated in the red brick. The yellow brick walls, whenever they occur, are projected a few inches beyond the normal plane of the front, the angles being quoined in stone up to the cornice lines, and each house is divided from the next by a row of quoins marking the line of the party wall. There are many diversities of detail. In fact there are only two adjoining houses in the whole row which are identical in design, although the design has been repeated in the single houses in yellow brick. These diversities are slight, being

Houses, north side of West Seventy-third Street, Eighth to Ninth Avenue. Henry J. Hardenbergh, 1879–80. View to the northeast, c. 1897. AR. CU.

Houses, west side of Eighth Avenue, West Eighty-fourth to West Eighty-fifth Street. Edward L. Angell, 1887–88. View to the northwest, c. 1900. AAR. CU.

such differences of roof treatment as the change of a pair of dormers for a single dormer, of this for a gable. . . . Slight as these differences are they fully answer their purpose of individualizing every house, and of assuring the spectator that he has not seen all where he has seen one. . . . As with the Dakota, the treatment of these houses has more affinity with French Renaissance than with any other historical style of architecture. It is, however, everywhere free and modern in handling. The features are such as are actually appropriate to a city house in the nineteenth century and might have been devised for it whether they actually were or not.[69]

Montgomery Schuyler, in an 1897 assessment of Hardenbergh's work, essentially echoed the *Record and Guide*, adding the critical observation that the Clark row was "a work of 1884, when there were no precedents for such an attempt at unity in variety, and when the choice was between rows depressingly tame and rows outrageously wild. This work set a precedent."[70]

Aside from the Dakota, only one other large-scale development facing Eighth Avenue was undertaken in the 1880s. Taking up a full blockfront, like many similar rows that would be built on West End Avenue, were Edward L. Angell's nine houses (1887–88) between Eighty-fourth

and Eighty-fifth Streets for William Noble.[71] This development came closer than the Dakota to the real estate community's original vision for the street as a rival to mansion-lined Fifth Avenue, though Angell's design, with its bold scale, strong modeling, and robust character, did not completely please the *Record and Guide*:

> In size and in apparent costliness these houses give a very gratifying earnest [*sic*] of the character of the improvements in this quarter. They are distinctly "first-class residences." There are only nine of them in the block front, making an average width of something over 22 feet; they are of four stories, including a roof story and a basement, and they are built of choice brick with a very profuse use of carved stone, of which the basements and first stories are mainly composed. In design, these houses are typical specimens of west side architecture. . . . It is in the skyline that the strain of the designer's effort after variety is most apparent. The line broken at the ends by turrets, and intermittently by four gables, obviously shows since the ridge of the roof does not run back more than 3 or 4 feet. The effect of the whole is confusing.[72]

Edward Clark died in 1882, leaving the as-yet-unfinished Dakota and his other, surrounding properties to his twelve-year-old grandson, Edward Severin Clark. In 1883

Proposed stable for the Dakota, south side of West Seventy-fifth Street, Tenth Avenue to the Boulevard. Charles W. Romeyn, 1883. Rendering of view to the southwest. AABN. CU.

48–54 West Eightieth Street. Detlef Lienau, 1886–87. North elevation. Lienau Collection. CU.

plans were announced for an addition to the Dakota complex, a livery stable designed by Charles W. Romeyn for a site on Tenth Avenue at the southwest corner of Seventy-fifth Street.[73] The site extended to the Boulevard, surely a blow to that street's potential prestige as a high-class residential avenue, and it placed Tenth Avenue even lower than the El-shadowed Ninth Avenue in the hierarchy of West Side avenues. Romeyn's grandly conceived brick and terra cotta design, which was to have contained stalls for forty-five horses, was not built, but in 1891 and 1894 another stable was constructed in two sections on the site, designed by Bradford Lee Gilbert on a commission from Edmund Coffin, a banker and real estate investor.[74] Gilbert's five-story, Romanesque-inspired palazzo was more massive but far less picturesque than Romeyn's unbuilt design. By the early 1890s the surrounding area was home to a number of other stables, including the five-story brick building of the New York City Cab Company (1888–89), at 201 West Seventy-fifth Street, designed by a lesser-known architect, C. Abbott French.[75]

In 1885 and 1886 the Clark estate, having expanded its West Side holdings, undertook the construction of fourteen rowhouses at 53–75 West Eighty-fifth Street, between Eighth and Ninth Avenues, designed by the comparatively unknown George Griebel, whose brick and yellow stone Queen Anne design, echoing the example set by Hardenbergh, employed a complex alternating rhythm of pediments, bay windows, and boldly scaled arches.[76]

The Clark family's exemplary developments set a high standard for the West Side, and their scale would seldom be matched. Small, stylish projects were more typically the order of the day, such as the one built by the architect George W. DaCunha for his own account, a three-house, Queen Anne–style group (1884–85) at 55–57 West Eighty-third Street, between Eighth and Ninth Avenues.[77] Another interesting group was a four-house row at 48–54 West Eighty-second Street (1886–87), designed by Hardenbergh's mentor, Detlef Lienau, for the architect's own use and for Mary M. Wilhaus, who also commissioned two rows of six sixteen-foot-wide houses from the same architect, at 37–47 West Eighty-second Street (1883–84) and 46–56 West Eighty-third Street (1883–84).[78] Lienau occupied 48 West Eighty-second Street. Behind the quiet street elevations, notable for their Dutch-inspired pedimented dormers, Lienau experimented with a relatively unusual plan that modified the typical brownstone type, which placed the stair to one side of a narrow hallway, with an arrangement that located the stairs deeper inside the house in a hall that ran its full width, creating a memorable room at the expense of strictly usable space.

John D. Crimmins, the New York City Park Commissioner, having sought agreement with fellow landholders on the block of Sixty-eighth Street between Eighth and Ninth Avenues to impose deed restrictions limiting development to private houses, hired D. & J. Jardine to design a row of houses (1884–85) on the north side of the street; the group seems not to have been built.[79] Crimmins subsequently hired Charles W. Romeyn to design an eight-house, four-story, Romanesque-inspired row (1887–88) on the south side of the block at 50–64 West Sixty-eighth Street.[80] Romeyn adopted an interesting A-B-C-B-A composition pattern, and would carry these ideas to further simplicity with his Grolier Club (1890), at 29 East Thirty-second Street (see chapter 2).

Hubert, Pirsson & Co., the firm better known for its Home Club apartment houses, designed for Sarah J. Doying a three-unit Queen Anne–style row (1886–89) at 61–65 West Sixty-ninth Street,[81] and three more of the same on Seventieth Street,[82] as well as a five-unit group on the north side of Seventy-ninth Street east of Tenth Avenue.[83] There was no effort to create a unified whole out of Doying's Queen Anne groups; the architects instead sought to syncopate the placement of elements so that the facade of each essentially identical house had an individual character. Farther west on Sixty-ninth Street, Arthur M. Thom and James W. Wilson, who some would argue qualified, in a time before professional certification was required, more as inspired builders than as architects, were responsible for thirty-one different houses. They designed many more on the West Side, making them the most prolific but by no means the most interesting architects working in the area.[84] Their earliest group, at 123–127 West Sixty-ninth Street (1882), between Columbus Avenue and Broadway, a Neo-

Grec, brownstone-clad, three-house row, enjoyed the park-like setting of William H. Day's Gothic Chapel of the Transfiguration (1880), the modesty of which was enhanced in 1887 by Sidney V. Stratton, who added to the west side of the building's north facade a porch surmounted by a tower.[85] At about the same time, George Martin Huss designed a rather dour townhouse (1884–85) at 120 West Sixty-ninth Street for Edward C. Houghton.[86] Addraetta Goodwin asked Charles W. Clinton to design a five-house Romanesque Revival row (1888–89) at 30–38 West Seventieth Street, setting the tone for the even grander houses that would follow on that block, between Eighth and Ninth Avenues, in the early 1890s.[87]

By the end of the decade, with the West Side boom in full flower, the park blocks were beginning to fill up. Lamb & Rich's 24–30 West Seventy-first Street consisted of four houses (1887–90) designed with great originality in the Queen Anne style.[88] Three of the houses, numbers 26–30 (1887–88), constituted a group developed by Hugh Lamb and J. H. Andrew, with number 30 reserved for the Andrew family. The cozily domestic three-house group consisted of a classicizing center house graced by a fourth-floor

26–30 West Seventy-first Street. Lamb & Rich, 1887–88. Rendering of view to the south. AABN. CU.

24 West Seventy-first Street. Lamb & Rich, 1890. View to the south, c. 1911. NYPL.

balconied loggia and a high, corniced attic, bracketed by two very similar houses that had as their principal differences the roofs, one hipped and finished in clay tile, the other a steeply profiled gable pediment. Directly to the east, number 24, commissioned by Elizabeth Milbank, was not only taller but clearly more self-important than numbers 26–30. The Romanesque design, which incorporated Renaissance-inspired decorative elements, was distinguished by particularly prominent window enframements.[89] Farther down the block to the west, John H. Duncan's 32–40 West Seventy-first Street (1887), commissioned by Cornelius Luyster, an important investor in the area, confronted the street with identical facades that both incorporated elements from the Romanesque, especially the round-arched windows that made for a cloister-like attic story, and also revealed a severity and stiffness that spoke to Duncan's more characteristic Classicism.[90]

West Seventy-second Street

West Seventy-second Street, sometimes referred to as West Seventy-second Street Parkway because of its wide sidewalks and generously sized planting beds, was a premier residential address. What should have been its grandest block, however, between Eighth and Ninth Avenues, was compromised by the decision of the Edward Clark estate to keep the lots west of the Dakota off the market and to deliberately hold back the development of properties adjacent to the Dakota.[91] Another hindrance to the full realization of Seventy-second Street's potential was the fact that the Ninth Avenue elevated station not only made it more crowded than other streets but also blocked the vista that would otherwise have visually linked the two parks. Only in 1894, when Alfred Zucker's eleven-story Hotel Majestic, at the southwest corner of Central Park West, opened, did the park block of Seventy-second Street come into its own.[92] Designed in 1889 for Jacob Rothschild, the Majestic was the second important tall building on Central Park West and, indeed, on the entire West Side. With the Dakota, the Majestic formed a symbolic gateway to the neighborhood, especially when viewed from the Central Park drive leading to it. In 1887 the *Real Estate Record and Builders' Guide*, whose anonymous reporter was almost certainly Montgomery Schuyler, had expressed a belief in West Seventy-second Street's potential as "the principal approach to the new city [of the West Side]." Though "already a very important street," continued Schuyler, "it is destined to be far more important as the main driveway between Central Park and Riverside Park." The report was confined to the development of the block between Ninth and Tenth Avenues, "the scene at present of the greatest building activity in the street," but an "opportunity [that] has been worse than wasted. The houses are by no means as unpretentious as those that make up the bulk of the west side buildings. They are four stories in height, and of at least twenty feet in frontage. By a perverse fate it happens that not one of these has fallen into the hands of an architect. One or two of them have

View to the west, 1898, of West Seventy-second Street from near Ninth Avenue, showing numbers 137 and 139 (Thom & Wilson, 1885–86), with conical roofs, on the right, and the Hotel St. Andrew (Andrew Craig, 1893) in the background. MCNY.

points of interest, but, in all but one or two the artchitect [*sic*] has had his wicked will, and they seemed to have been designed by contract. It is too bad."[93]

Half a year before the *Record and Guide* had admired the four-story, twenty-two-foot-wide, five-house row (1885–86) that Thom & Wilson designed for Robert Irwin at 135–143 West Seventy-second Street, praising "certain elements taken from different architectural styles, united in such a way as to produce a novel and striking effect."[94] Schuyler was not so sure. He singled out numbers 137 and 139, praising the treatment of the bays of the two identical houses as towers rising to slated conical roofs, but he regretted the "crude, unskillful way" the work was detailed. Nonetheless, "it would be unfair . . . to class this with the architecture done by contract. One can imagine the designer really being interested in what he was doing, and enjoying it, and so it is possible to regard his work with sympathy, even though it falls far short of being completely successful." As much as he had nice things to say about Thom & Wilson's turreted pair, Schuyler found only negative words for number 141, which he deemed "another atrocity." Objecting to the "central oriel rising through the second and third stories," which "sustains what was perhaps meant to simulate a balcony" but which was not really a balcony because it could not be reached from inside the house, he found the device "a most queer and absurd object."[95]

Schuyler was unhappy with Gilbert A. Schellenger's Renaissance-inspired, three-house row (1883–84) at 145–149 West Seventy-second Street, which was certainly quiet to the point of banality, as well as Schellenger's five-house brownstone row (1883–84) at 130-138 West Seventy-second Street, which rose to a metal cornice; he also disliked D. & J. Jardine's ten-house brownstone row (1883–84) at 151–169 West Seventy-second Street, which also had the type of tin cornice he deplored.[96] But it was Thom & Wilson's five-house group (1885–87) at 140–148 West Seventy-second Street that really riled Schuyler. Calling it a "triumph of contract architecture," he found the combination of Renaissance and Moorish devices far too individualistic: "But a long brown stone row does not 'collar' the eye, no matter how wild the design may be. One has to look at these houses in order to perceive in what monstrosities of form they abound." After regaling the reader with a litany of the houses' detailing horrors, Schuyler went on to say that "these things are as ugly in themselves as they are natural in their application. They not only show a complete absence of skill in design, but an equally complete absence of intention. It is impossible that they could have given pleasure to any human being, even to the designer while he was doing them. They are not meant to give pleasure, but only to show that they have cost money. Of course this is a vulgar purpose, and it effectually vulgarizes these 'elegant brown stone mansions.'"[97]

All in all Schuyler used the new houses of West Seventy-second Street as an opportunity to lament that "while the architect and the public had reason to be grateful for the increased freedom given him by the public tolerance of novelty, and demand for it, the demand had done nothing but mischief when the 'architect' undertook to respond to it, and that he might better confine himself to repeating the stupid and stereotyped brown stone front of which what is now middle New York has some miles to show."[98]

In 1889 Schuyler returned to the subject of West Seventy-second Street. Expanding the scope of his view beyond the street's middle block to its entire length, he was able to find some good individual work. For example, he deemed the design of Thom & Wilson's 48–50 West Seventy-second Street (1888), on the Central Park block, "good, the red stone in the substructure [harmonizing] with the tint of red brick used. There is no straining after effect which in so many cases on this thoroughfare has given rise to distortions in decoration such as the brown stone bust pinioned like a trophy against the transom of the window on the block."[99] Numbers 48–50 were part of a five-house row built for J. T. Farley, who filled out the rest of the south side of the street to Ninth Avenue with two more buildings designed by Thom & Wilson, both constructed in 1888, a four-story, twenty-foot-wide house and a six-story flat at the corner.[100] On his revisit Schuyler failed to soften his attack on the houses on the north side of the street between Ninth and Tenth Avenues, where "it seems that our friend, the contract 'architect,' or his cousin had much to do in making of that block. The designs are poor, and the enrichments are not only overdone, but poorly done, and in some cases are fearfully and wonderfully made, notably in certain pretentious dwellings in the centre of the block." His overall impression was mixed, at best: "The first appearance of 72d street viewed in its length is decidedly 'taking.' The street is wide, is planted in part with trees; there are grass plots on the sidewalks, and the architectural effect of more than one half a mile of costly residences is very fine. Few streets in the city look better. Inspection of the architecture in detail, however, does not yield so satisfactory results. Indeed, the architecture of the street is, on the whole, not perfect. . . . The work is pretentious, but in many cases inartistic, and sometimes positively vulgar."[101]

Above Seventy-second Street

With the north side of West Seventy-third Street's park block lined with Henry J. Hardenbergh's row for Edward Clark and the south side of Seventy-fourth Street largely held by the Clark family as an investment for future development, expansion skipped to the north side of Seventy-fourth Street, which quickly filled up with three- and five-house rows. Most were of no particular significance, although numbers 3–19, designed by Daniel Burgess in 1890, constituted a lively essay in the Queen Anne.[102] West of Ninth Avenue, Seventy-fourth Street was home to a variety of rowhouses, far and away the most interesting of which were Lamb & Rich's nine-house row (1886) at 161–169 West Seventy-fourth Street and 303–309 Amsterdam Avenue,[103] and James Brown Lord's seven-

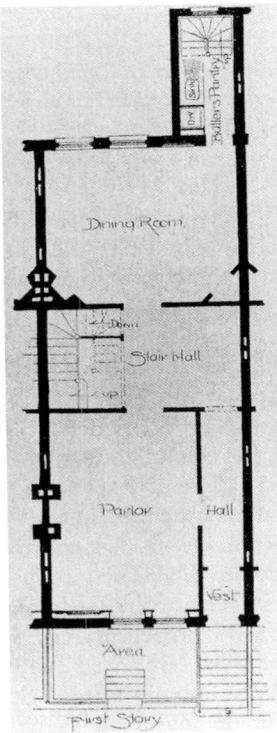

147–159 West Seventy-fourth Street. James Brown Lord, 1886–87. Rendering of view to the north. BLDG. CU.

house development (1886–87) for Charles T. Barney at 147–159 West Seventy-fourth Street.[104] Also noteworthy was Lord's seven-house row (1887–88), which Barney built one block north at 156–168 West Seventy-fifth Street.[105] Lamb & Rich's combined rowhouse and tenement development was in every respect worthy of Hardenbergh's prototype, with a varied roofline of hipped and gabled dormers and, at the corner, a sophisticated lifting of the scale with a strong gable parallel to the avenue. Lord's Seventy-fourth Street row was admirably restrained, with a continuous gable punctuated by alternating pedimented and hipped dormers in an A-B-B-A-B-B-A pattern. The low flight of steps reflected a new direction in rowhouse planning that would culminate in the 1890s in the so-called American basement plan, wherein the traditional stoop was eliminated in favor of a ground-level entrance leading to an entry hall, central stair, and, behind it, a dining room, thereby freeing the entire street frontage of the upper floors for occupiable rooms.[106] Edward L. Angell's five-house row (1888–89) at 140–148 West Seventy-fourth Street was interesting for its framed, pedimented bay that suggested half-timbering in brick.[107] Less successful was the same architect's attempt to introduce themes from the nascent Classicism that would flower in the 1890s in a five-house row completed a year or so later (1889–90), next door at 150–158 West Seventy-fourth Street.[108]

147–159 West Seventy-fourth Street. James Brown Lord, 1886–87. Typical first-floor plan. BLDG. CU.

305–307 West Seventy-eighth Street. Rafael Guastavino, 1885–86. View to the north, 1912. NYPL.

Manhattan Square

Manhattan Square, bounded by Eighth and Ninth Avenues and Seventy-seventh and Eighty-first Streets, was one of four small parks proposed in the Commissioners' Plan of 1811. With the construction of Central Park, Manhattan Square, which was the only open space to abut it, was given over to the newly founded American Museum of National History (see chapter 2). The blocks around Manhattan Square, with the convenience of an elevated station at Eighty-first Street and Ninth Avenue and the prestige of the museum, were among the first on the West Side to be sufficiently developed to constitute a neighborhood.

Bernard S. Levy, an established property developer, commissioned Rafael Guastavino to design two facing rows of houses (1885–86) on Seventy-eighth Street, filling most of the block between Ninth and Tenth Avenues,[109] a five-house row on West Seventy-seventh Street facing the square,[110] and a pair of houses on West Eighty-second Street.[111] Trained as a musician, the Spanish-born Guastavino had worked for a time in Barcelona, where he may

have come into contact with Antonio Gaudí. Guastavino developed a system of vaulted construction based on thin-shell Catalan masonry techniques. He called the system "cohesive construction," and it produced exceptionally fire-proof results because of its combination of laminated tiles, plaster of Paris, and Portland cement. Guastavino applied his system to factories in Spain before bringing it in 1881 to the United States, where he settled in New York and soon after began listing himself as an architect. He worked on the Progress Club (1883–84) with Henry Fernbach (see chapter 2) and on B'nai Jeshurun Synagogue (1884–85) with Schwarzmann & Buchman (see chapter 2), two projects that may have brought him to Levy's attention. The first phase, on the north side of Seventy-eighth Street, did not employ the cohesive-construction system, suggesting that Levy retained the architect because of his familiarity with Moorish forms, which the developer may have wanted as part of a plan to market the houses to Jews (Levy chose number 121 West Seventy-eighth Street as his own). In any case, the *Real Estate Record and Builders' Guide* was impressed with Guastavino's work on Seventy-eighth Street:

> The six new houses . . . are good examples of the novel and tasteful dwellings with which the region west of Central Park is building up. . . . The houses are three and four stories high, 16 and 18 x 70 x 102. The basements are fronted with rock-faced brown stone and the upper stories are brick and terra cotta, with heavy courses of Nova Scotia stone. The windows are encased in this stone, including the handsome bay windows of the second stories. The architectural style is Spanish Renaissance, and the fronts attract much attention by their novelty and beauty. . . . A pretty minor feature is the inlaid work in light blue, brown and white tiles, which ornaments the floors of the vestibules.[112]

In the second group of houses, on the south side of the street, Levy introduced Guastavino's system of construction, which used "low arches of fire-proof tiling" to support the floors, "taking up no more space than ordinary beams and leaving the cellar entirely unobstructed."[113] For the even choicer location on West Seventy-seventh Street, facing the square, Guastavino's designs catered to a more affluent market. According to the *Record and Guide*:

> The designs for these mansions were made by a Spanish gentleman who has displayed in his work the graceful artistic spirit for which his countrymen are noted. We miss in these houses the lugubrious heaviness of many west side dwellings. The design of each of the five residences is different. With the exception of the central one, which is Gothic with many Spanish details, they represent different phases of the Renaissance—Italian, French and German—successfully treated to form a harmonious whole, and tendency to monotony in material is broken by the alternation of the soft red of Scotch Carlisle sandstone and the white of Ohio limestone. The buildings are five and six stories high, measuring 25 x 92 x 104.[114]

Other architects contributed to the architectural rich-

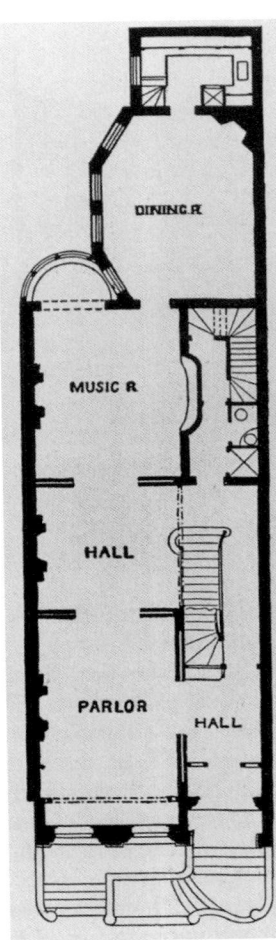

27 West Eighty-first Street. Berg & Clark, 1889. First-floor plan. HCC. CU.

ness of the Manhattan Square neighborhood. Russell Sturgis took particular note of the plan of the house at 27 West Eighty-first Street (Berg & Clark, 1889), which occupied "nearly the whole of its hundred-foot lot" but in such a way that "the four rooms en suite are made all accessible and convenient, whether used separately or together."[115] West Eighty-first Street between Ninth and Tenth Avenues soon filled up with a number of exceptionally vivacious Queen Anne rows commissioned from important architects. At 153–165 West Eighty-first Street, Henry J. Hardenbergh's seven-house row (1884–85) of three-story brownstone buildings for Daniel Herbert was severely detailed, with a central bay on the second floor and a steeply raked pedimented dormer at the top.[116] Other architects represented on the block, all doing Queen Anne work, were the gifted and inventive H. Edwards Ficken, with a house at 135 West Eighty-first Street (1886–88) consisting of four stories and a basement,[117] and Rossiter & Wright, with a four-house, four-story row (1886–87) at 137–143 West Eighty-first Street.[118]

French Flats

The success of the Dakota inspired at least two developers besides Edward Clark to consider Eighth Avenue as a likely setting for an apartment house. In 1883 Carl Pfeiffer was reported to be at work designing an apartment building intended for the northwest corner of Eighth Avenue and Sixty-second Street, but the project was not carried out.[119] In 1889, the six-story Beresford, an apartment hotel designed by Theodore E. Thompson on the northwest corner of Eighth Avenue and Eighty-first Street, was completed.[120] Built for Alva Walker, the Beresford was somewhat distinguished, although more as a precursor of large-scale apartment buildings to come than on its own terms. Apartment houses far less grand than the Dakota were built on Tenth and especially Ninth Avenues, beginning with the Bedford (1881), at the northeast corner of Tenth Avenue and Eighty-second Street.[121] Though largely unmemorable in appearance, O. P. and R. G. Hatfield's building was important from a social point of view: intended for genteel families of moderate means—according to the *New York Times*, bookkeepers, confidential clerks, and secretaries and their families—the Bedford provided at a reduced scale many of the amenities found in luxurious apartment houses, such as state-of-the-art heating and plumbing, setting the tone for many more such buildings that would be built on the West Side.

Thom & Wilson was responsible for many of Ninth Avenue's flats, supplying the market with skillfully composed but inherently banal versions of the Neo-Grec.[122] The firm's Graystone (1886–87), at 286–294 Ninth Avenue, on the southwest corner of Seventy-fourth Street, was perhaps the grandest of the group.[123] Charles Buek, another builder-architect, also was responsible for a number of plain buildings along Ninth Avenue. But to the *Real Estate Record and Builders' Guide*, his two flat buildings (1888–89) that filled the east side of the avenue between Seventy-second and Seventy-third Streets were "elegant."[124] While their design was not particularly notable, their greater-than-usual height—seven stories—and the provision of both passenger and service elevators were out of the ordinary. Gilbert A. Schellenger was another important contributor to the Ninth Avenue flat-building spree, producing at its end, in 1890 and 1891, Romanesque-inspired designs in buff brick.[125] Perhaps Schellenger's most felicitous building was the Greylock (1890–91), at 301–303 Ninth Avenue, on the northeast corner of Seventy-fourth Street, a seven-story block.[126] Cleverdon & Putzel's 302 Ninth Avenue (1889–90), between Seventy-fourth and Seventy-fifth Streets, with its elaborate metalwork pediment, was commissioned by the J. M. Horton Ice Cream Co., which no doubt used the street-level shop to dispense its popular product.[127] Edward L. Angell's six-story, vaguely Renaissance-style Sylvia (1889–90), at 341–349 Ninth Avenue, on the northeast corner of Seventy-sixth Street, was hardly up to the designer's capabilities.[128] But with his seven-story,

Hotel Endicott, 440–444 and 446–456 Ninth Avenue.
Edward L. Angell, 1889–91. Rendering of view to the northwest.
RERG. CU.

Brockholst, west side of Ninth Avenue between West Eighty-fifth
and West Eighty-sixth Streets. John G. Prague, 1889–90. View to
the southwest. RERG. CU.

Romanesque-inspired Hotel Endicott (1889–91), at 440–444 and 446–456 Ninth Avenue, along the west blockfront from Eighty-first to Eighty-second Street, of red brick and stone with terra cotta trim, Angell utilized a generous site and robustly handled the mass to establish a strong architectural presence by grouping two independent apartment buildings around a central light court.[129] Facing the avenue, the building contained commercial space on its ground floor. According to the *Real Estate Record and Builders' Guide*, the Endicott, intended to cater to a higher class of tenants than Angell's previous efforts had, was planned by its developer, Charles Fuller, as a rival to the Dakota.

John G. Prague's six-story Brockholst (1889–90), on the west side of Ninth Avenue between Eighty-fifth and Eighty-sixth Streets, shared its stylistic inspiration and marketing ambitions with the Hotel Endicott.[130] But its effort

Apartment building, northwest corner of Ninth Avenue and
West 100th Street. Rafael Guastavino, 1887. Rendering of view
to the northwest. RERG. CU.

to be more engagingly residential than the Endicott was not well served by a dark exterior finished in rock-faced brownstone and brick. Across Eighty-sixth Street, Prague's Queen Anne–style Amy (1886–87), which filled the block to Eighty-seventh Street, was a suitable companion.[131]

Farther uptown, in 1887, at the northwest corners of Ninety-ninth and 100th Streets and Ninth Avenue, Raphael Guastavino designed for his own account and for Fernando Miranda two five-story-high brick "moderate-priced flats . . . which must, in time," as the *Real Estate Record and Builders' Guide* put it, "overturn present methods." The magazine was not only impressed with Guastavino's innovative tile-vault construction system but also with

> another merit which these new flats possess which should not be forgotten, and that is an architectural one. The public is learning that the "complex" fronts, so much affected by the ordinary west side architect, are offenses against good taste. To be handsome a building need not be constructed of a score of different materials with ornamentation stuck in every possible position. The buildings . . . are thoroughly good architectural work. The material used is a fine quality red brick, which so treated as to form its own ornamentation. There is no striving for effect, and yet the structures are among the most striking and satisfactory, on the west side.[132]

While most of the West Side's apartments were on Ninth Avenue, a few buildings were located on side streets. One of particular sophistication, 167–173 West Eighty-third Street (1885), was designed by McKim, Mead & White for the socially well-connected developer and builder David H. King Jr.[133] The five-story, four-unit row contained floor-through apartments and was aimed at middle-class tenants. The McKim firm's Romanesque-inspired facade, with its triple-floored pilaster arcade and sensitive window patterns, immediately distinguished the building from the ordinary working-class tenement. Inside, the appointments were also fine, including vestibules paved with an interlocking pattern of pink, white, and gray marbles and, in the apartments, raised ceiling decorations, stained wood wainscoting, and paneled doors. King presumably imagined that his building would sit amid the neighborhood's typical side-street rowhouses, but for whatever reasons the block quickly took on the aspect of a service street, especially in 1889, when the completion of the four-story, twenty-five-foot-wide Engine Company Number 56, at 120 West Eighty-third Street, designed by Napoleon Le Brun & Sons, itself a modest enough facade culminating in a quirkily proportioned Serlian window in a steeply raked gable, brought with it the clatter and clang of the fire department.[134] Soon enough the rest of the block filled up with less inventively designed flats, such as Gilbert A. Schellenger's five-story 100–102 West Eighty-third Street (1889).[135]

West End Avenue

> West End Avenue, alone of all city avenues, has a chance of remaining a site of private residences exclusively and permanently.
>
> —West End Association, 1888 [136]

More so than any other street in the district, perhaps even in the city, Eleventh Avenue, which above Fifty-ninth Street became West End Avenue in 1880, was to become a premier rowhouse location.[137] Because it was built up in a short period of time by developers with a shared vision, West End Avenue exuded an aura of overall aesthetic intentionality that was unrivaled in Gilded Age New York. The unification had not only to do with building type but also with a shared sense of the area's image of urban domesticity, comparable to that of London's West End. In 1889 Montgomery Schuyler took the readers of a special supplement of the *Real Estate Record and Builders' Guide* on a walking tour of West End Avenue and its immediately adjacent side streets. Because he chose to go north from Seventy-second Street, Schuyler skipped Edward L. Angell's row of six three-story Queen Anne–style houses (1885–86) at 220–230 West End Avenue, designed for the developer Charles Fuller, extending from the northeast corner of Seventieth Street, which was praised by the *Record and Guide* as "of a kind that will naturally be selected by those who have been used to elegant surroundings, but whose fortunes are not yet made."[138] Directly north of this row, at number 232 (1886–87), Angell designed a three-story, twenty-by-forty-eight-foot brick residence for Forrest Lowther.[139] Schuyler also missed the nine-house row (c. 1887) designed by W. Holman Smith on the north side of Seventy-first Street near West End Avenue, which the *Record and Guide* had recently described as "not of imposing character, but ... [of] attractive ... appearance," with each three-story house "a different design, and each front . . . a study in itself."[140] He additionally passed over six houses consisting of three stories and a basement that J. C. Cady designed for the south side of Seventy-first Street east of

Bicycle Club, east side of West End Avenue between West Seventy-first and West Seventy-second Streets. Renwick, Aspinwall & Russell, 1888–89. View to the southeast. RERG. CU.

West End Avenue,[141] and Renwick, Aspinwall & Russell's townhouselike, boldly modeled Bicycle Club (1888–89), on the east side of West End Avenue between Seventy-first and Seventy-second Streets.[142]

Beginning his tour at Seventy-second Street and West End Avenue, Schuyler found interesting work on two of the four corners. On the southwest corner there was Lamb & Rich's five-house "small block of dwellings," a group (1889–90) that would "surely attract attention" when finished. "It is of the Romanesqued style," he wrote, reflecting a disdain for what he described as the stylistic "fad of the hour" whereby an "architect 'Romanesques' his work by putting into it 'features' from the style desired. It might be said that this is 'archaeology, not architecture,' but archaeology is much too dignified a term to apply to a merely superficial copyism." Nonetheless Schuyler found in some of the "features" employed by Lamb & Rich a "design [that] is effective and meritorious, but the choice of material—light stone with red stone trimming—is so strongly suggestive of the little confectionery edifices turned out by caterers that it is doubtful whether the color scheme will not be found more than the design can successfully carry."[143] Schuyler returned to these houses in his article on

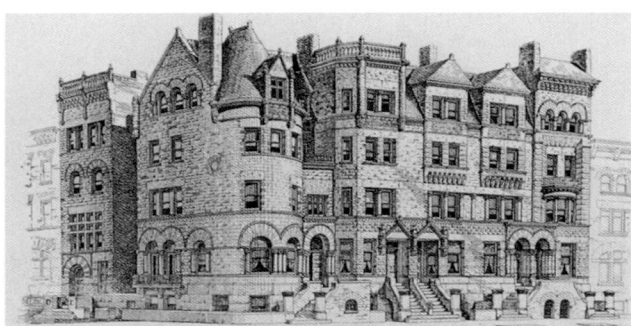

Houses, southwest corner of West End Avenue and West Seventy-second Street. Lamb & Rich, 1889–90. Rendering of view to the southwest. RERG. CU.

Houses, southwest corner of West End Avenue and West Seventy-second Street. Lamb & Rich, 1889–90. Rendering of typical stair hall. RERG. CU.

Houses, southwest corner of West End Avenue and West Seventy-second Street. Lamb & Rich, 1889–90. Rendering of typical dining room. RERG. CU.

301–319 West End Avenue. William J. Merritt, 1889. View to the northwest. RERG. CU.

the Romanesque Revival in New York, praising "the color treatment . . . [as] the most striking and the most successful element of the design, an olive sandstone being employed in effective combination with a reddish sandstone that much enhances its value. . . . The general composition is highly effective, individualizing the houses without destroying the unity of the group, and the massiveness of the style does not often degenerate into the clumsiness which is its besetting tendency."[144]

Schuyler was less taken with William J. Merritt's six-house group (1889) at 301–319 West End Avenue, on the northwest corner of Seventy-second Street, developed for W.E.D. Stokes. He deemed them

> merely negations. The design consists practically of a flat wall with a gable above, repeated as many times as there are houses. It is difficult to make much out of so limited a scheme, and criticism is compelled to deal more with what there is not than what there is. The designer evidently can do better. At any rate there is a suggestion to this effect in the bay carried on two columns which is an excellent feature in one of the central houses of the group. A little more work of this kind would have made the row noticeably good. As it is, it cannot be said that it is bad, but then it is not noticeable. The restraint does not suggest anything more artistic than economy.[145]

Farther east on Seventy-second Street, between the Boulevard and West End Avenue, Schuyler found houses more to his liking than the ones he had encountered two years earlier, when he toured the block between Ninth and Tenth Avenues. Nonetheless, he felt that if C.P.H. Gilbert's red brick and brownstone rowhouse group (1886–87) at 216–224 West Seventy-second Street "does not display any striking excellencies [it] is in nothing offensive, while the ornamentation is restrained and the carving good and appropriate."[146] Even less to his taste was "the weak Gothicism stereotyped in each of the houses" in George B. Pelham's five-unit, four-story row "of lightstone dwellings" (1887) at 248–256 West Seventy-second Street, which "may best be passed in silence."[147] In 1887, for a site on the south side of Seventieth Street between West End Avenue and the river, Lamb & Rich had prepared designs for three eighteen-foot-wide, three-story, brick and brownstone houses, as well as for seven two- and three-story brick stables, but the development went unrealized.

In February 1885, the *Real Estate Record and Builders' Guide* announced plans for the first important houses to be built on the avenue above Seventy-second Street: "Lamb & Rich, architects, propose to commence within a few weeks the erection of twelve brick buildings, with brown stone and terra cotta trimmings, six on the southeast corner of Seventy-fifth Street and a similar number on the southeast corner of that avenue and Seventy-fourth Street. They will be of different dimensions, the frontages being from 18 to 20 feet, with varying depths from 36 to 50 feet."[148] By August 1885 the project was reported to be in construction, but increased to nine brick, stone, and terra

Proposed houses, east side of West End Avenue between West Seventy-fourth and West Seventy-fifth Streets. Lamb & Rich, 1885. Rendering of view to the east. BLDG. CU.

Houses, southeast corner of West End Avenue and West Seventy-fifth Street. Lamb & Rich, 1886. Rendering of view to the southeast. BLDG. CU.

cotta "ornate dwellings" of three stories and a basement on each corner.[149] That increase of units, resulting in smaller houses, reflected the growing certainty that West End Avenue would be a middle-class stronghold. In 1886, after the nine-house rows were completed, *Art Age* singled out the Seventy-fourth Street group for praise, noting that the architects had made the corner "notable with a block of Old Colonial houses."[150] Schuyler also admired Lamb & Rich's intricately planned split row, deeming the houses "good work" that "shine by comparison with what is opposite them," William J. Merritt's development (1886) for W.E.D. Stokes, which filled the entire west blockfront between Seventy-fourth and Seventy-fifth Streets.[151] Schuyler was not impressed by Merritt's effort, although it exhibited a significant degree of skill in the design of individual houses and a considerable capacity to create a coherent row out of them. Schuyler sarcastically regretted that "the architects (for it is hard to think that one man is answerable for so much)" of this row "could not be made to study for a time [the] piece of composition" that was Charles T. Mott's six-house group (1887) at the northeast

Houses, northwest corner of West End Avenue and West Seventy-fourth Street. William J. Merritt, 1886. Rendering of view to the northwest. BLDG. CU.

Houses, northeast corner of West End Avenue and West Seventy-fifth Street. Charles T. Mott, 1887. View to the northeast. RERG. CU.

Houses, northeast corner of West End Avenue and West Seventy-fifth Street. Charles T. Mott, 1887. View to the north of entrance, facing West Seventy-fifth Street. RERG. CU.

corner of Seventy-fifth Street and West End Avenue.[152] Mott had, ironically, been commissioned to design that group by William J. Merritt himself, acting as developer. Schuyler believed that Mott's robustly turreted row was "by far the best group of houses in this part of the west side. . . . The architect has succeeded in obtaining diversity with unity of design without the use of forced expedients. The material used throughout is red stone and vitrified brick. Very little ornamentation is used, and that only in panels, the architect trusting for effect mainly to the disposition of masses. The treatment of the roof both as to form and material is good, and is the most picturesque piece of work on the west side."[153]

In an essay on the small city house as a type, Schuyler deemed the blockfront designed by Merritt as the worst possible example of small-house construction in the city. Schuyler berated developers, anxious to meet the market's demand for individuality, for using untrained architects to design houses in the area. "While the public wanted variety in their brown-stone facades," Schuyler wrote in 1899, by which time taste had shifted to a preference for a uniform Classicism, "the speculative builders didn't know how to provide this tastefully and instead produced the 'wildest of the wild works'":

> Our street architecture nowhere presents a worse aspect than in these productions of an incompetent designer working under the purpose of a real or imagined demand for novelty and variety. Perhaps in no other is it so bad. Such a block-front . . . is an atrocity compared to which a

row of merely dull and dismal brown-stone fronts takes on repose and dignity. Not that the features of this bad architecture are necessarily bad in themselves. Some of them, such as the archway spanning the whole front, and the loggia, were crude suggestions of good things. But in the hands of the speculative builder's draughtsman, they remained hopelessly crude and unstudied.[154]

Not everyone shared Schuyler's opinion. In 1886 the *Real Estate Record and Builders' Guide* commented favorably on Merritt's ten-house row:

> The old English features are strongly marked, and the design handsomely illustrates the architectural style now most in favor on the west side, especially on this avenue and in its neighborhood. The style is closely related to that revival of the antique of which Queen Anne has been chosen as the patron saint, but unites all modern elements of luxury and convenience with the quaint old gables, the small squares of glass, and all the ancient graces that time has mellowed and endeared to the hearts of the home-seekers of our day. The fronts are tastefully varied in design, so that the owner can never be charged, by those who rebel against the old uniform fashion in brown stone, with offering houses by the yard, like cloth cut from the same piece. The . . . southern corner house . . . is noteworthy for handsome exterior effects and for its interior arrangement, the airy and sunny situation having been well improved by the designer.[155]

Merritt also designed two rows (1886–87) of side street Queen Anne houses at 254–256 West Seventy-fifth Street and 231–247 West Seventy-sixth Street, between the Boulevard and West End Avenue.[156]

Between Seventy-fifth and Seventy-sixth Streets on the west side of the avenue, where three lots were still open, with the one at the southwest corner of Seventy-sixth Street having been recently bought by Theodore Low De Vinne, was Berg & Clark's eight-house group (1886–88), running north from Seventy-fifth Street. This group was admired by Russell Sturgis, who included the row's plans in his important discussion of the evolution of the city house.[157] Sturgis was impressed by the handling of the stair and its hall, which separated the narrow front parlor from the dining room. The dining room occupied the full width of the house at the rear. Around the corner at 302 West Seventy-sixth Street, Lamb & Rich's five-story, twenty-five-by-sixty-foot brick house (1888–89) for Percival Knauth was one of the West End's most interesting designs.[158] A fine expression of the aesthetic taste of the 1880s and a worthy competitor in its way to the best inventive work to be seen in London or by Wilson Eyre in Philadelphia, the house's round-arched windows, carved wood and glass entry doors, bottle-glass transoms on the second-floor windows, and many other decorative features were said to be Spanish Renaissance in inspiration. The Knauth house, bigger than was typical on the avenue, was an early example of the 1890s trend of building large mansions on the sloping river blocks. Schuyler was quick to praise the Knauth house as

> a five-story dwelling which is a thoroughly good piece of architecture. It is constructed of brown stone, red brick and terra cotta and is an example of how effective a simple design may be. The width of the building is not sufficient for the height, but presumably this cannot be charged to the architect. It was his misfortune, not his fault. In the stone substructure are two plain, square windows and a deep but rather low doorway. Above are three round, arched openings of terra cotta springing from terra cotta columns. The next two stories are marked with only two square openings each. These, with the floor beneath them, form the middle division of the design carried out in red brick. Above this are four arched openings topped with a far projecting cornice. The building is obviously the work of a well-trained architect. There is too little of such work on the west side.[159]

Schuyler ventured over to Riverside Drive, where he saw nearing completion Lamb & Rich's four-house, granite and Indiana limestone group (1888–89) at 35–38 Riverside Drive, between Seventy-fifth and Seventy-sixth Streets, for George and Charles Lowther.[160] He reported them to be "heavy-looking buildings of a design of no great merit. There is, however, nothing meretricious in the work, though the windows in the roof, which suggest a Mother Hubbard hat and the helmet of a cuirassier, are absurd. The entrances, consisting of an inverted oyster shell supported on corbels could be—at any rate with effort—improved upon. The build-

Percival Knauth house, 302 West Seventy-sixth Street. Lamb & Rich, 1888–89. Rendering of view to the northeast. RERG. CU.

George and Charles Lowther houses, 35–38 Riverside Drive. Lamb & Rich, 1888–89. View to the east. AABN. CU.

ings seem to be well constructed, but the design is ineffectual."[161] Amazingly, Schuyler seemed to overlook Theodore Low De Vinne's house (1888–89), at the southwest corner of West End Avenue and Seventy-sixth Street.[162] De Vinne turned to the same architects who had in 1885–86 designed his monumental business headquarters (see chapter 3), Babb, Cook & Willard. The firm's severely disciplined design took excellent advantage of the corner with a severe, fresh interpretation of the Georgian-style house of red brick and light stone trim that was characteristic of early republican New York. Facing Seventy-sixth Street, a short flight of

steps parallel to the house led to a small hall with a stair behind it. A reception room led to the dining room at the west, where a bay window provided partial views of Riverside Park. A shallow bow window comprised most of the West End Avenue facade. Schuyler also overlooked Edward L. Angell's four-story brick, brownstone, and granite, Romanesque-inspired row of five houses (1889–90) at 340–346 West End Avenue, on the northeast corner of Seventy-sixth Street, which was stiff and comparatively flat except for boldly swelling two-story bays.[163] In 1889–91 Lamb & Rich built fourteen three-and-a-half-story, French- and Spanish-inspired

Theodore Low De Vinne house, southwest corner of West End Avenue and West Seventy-sixth Street. Babb, Cook &
Willard, 1888–89. View to the southwest showing the main entrance, facing West Seventy-sixth Street. AABN. CU.

Houses, northwest corner of West End Avenue and West Seventy-eighth Street. Frederick B. White, 1885–86. View to the northwest. BLDG. CU.

houses at 341–357 West End Avenue, 301–305 West Seventy-sixth Street, and 302–306 West Seventy-seventh Street, forming what was probably West End Avenue's largest single group of houses. These are discussed in *New York 1900*.[164]

"At Seventy-sixth Street," Schuyler reported, "the building on West End avenue terminates with the old dilapidated frame dwelling, used for business purposes, on which is displayed the suggestive name of Poignant. For the space of several blocks north of this there is nothing on the avenue with the exception of the few houses under construction on the northeast corner of Seventy-sixth Street."[165] At the northwest corner of Seventy-eighth Street, eight houses (1885–86) designed by Frederick B. White formed what was probably the most unusual and complexly planned group on the avenue, although the Queen Anne–style paired houses of Philadelphia and molded red brick trimmed with terra cotta and granite failed to capture Schuyler's fancy.[166] Bridling at the pairing of entrances under one arch, a device that enhanced the scale of the group, Schuyler pronounced it a "method [that] is never really successful. It can scarcely be called a sham, yet it seems an attempt to indicate what is not."[167] The *Real Estate Record and Builders' Guide* perhaps better understood what the young, recently deceased, Princeton-trained architect had been attempting to achieve: a group of houses that was "neat, substantial and chaste in design, moderate in cost, and yet decidedly elegant and in keeping with the prevailing taste of the day. . . . The impression that they convey at the first glance is one that is very well expressed by the word 'conscientiousness'—freedom from all meretricious tricks of ornament, and thorough honesty in the whole plan and style of construction. They are built for comfortable and luxurious though not ostentatious homes."[168]

Schuyler reported that there was little building on the side streets in the vicinity of Seventy-ninth Street, and "what there is is poor." But above Eighty-first Street, "buildings

again become thick, both on the avenue and on some of the side streets."[169] At the northwest corner of Eighty-second Street, Lamb & Rich had just finished a row of seven houses (1887) in which an A-B-A rhythm was adopted, with two-and-a-half-story units treated as hyphens between bolder, wider houses that rose a full three stories.[170] The same firm was also responsible for another row of five three- and four-story houses (1887–88), at the northwest corner of Eighty-first Street, which Schuyler deemed "passably good, but the avenue front of the row is spoiled by the ogeed metal imitation gables on the roof. No amount of paint can make them like stone or connect them with architecture. They are simply attempts at imposition."[171] Farther up the avenue, past the Old Church, a picturesque carpenter-Gothic structure that remained from the time when the area was still deep country, Schuyler came upon McKim, Mead & White's five-house brownstone and mottled-brick group (1885) at the northwest corner of Eighty-third Street, which he considered "good" although he quarreled with the use of "imitation gables [that] are here no better though there is less of them" than at number 341 West End Avenue, about which Schuyler was also lukewarm.[172] Schuyler nonetheless had much to praise, seeing the group as a timely evocation of the kind of Dutch Colonial houses that were rapidly falling to the wrecker's ball in the lower city. Expressing a wish that the group had occupied an entire blockfront, Schuyler still took pleasure in the "general composition and the detail," which he found "almost equally successful. It was a happy thought that alternated the gables of the longer front with the houses that exhibit the roof to the ridge line, converting the upper story into an open loggia of which the roof is carried upon two unmistakably wooden posts."[173]

North of Eighty-sixth Street, Schuyler reported, was the domain of the contract architect. The brown stone monstrosities on Eighty-sixth Street, west of the avenue, strike the beholder with gloom. As to the houses going up

Houses, northwest corner of West End Avenue and West Eighty-second Street. Lamb & Rich, 1887. Rendering of view to the northwest. BLDG. CU.

by the dozen on the northwest corner of the street and the avenue [designed by Joseph H. Taft for W.E.D. Stokes], ornamented from end to end with large rings and festoons in painful regularity with decanter-like gables on the roof, it is perhaps not right to speak as they are not yet completed. Still it may be best to consider them in their present state and not later on when the design is revealed in its entirety. North of Eighty-sixth Street the seeker after architectural beauty feels that he is in a land of his enemies, and when he reaches the symphony of ochre, light yellow, green, scarlet and blue, between Eighty-ninth and Ninetieth streets, he is delighted to find that beyond stretch rural felicities, and kitchen gardens, for there there is peace.[174]

Among the colorful rows Schuyler was likely to have had in mind were the five four-story brick and stone houses (1889) designed by Joseph H. Taft and developed by W.E.D. Stokes on the northeast corner of Eighty-seventh Street and West End Avenue,[175] and the same architect's ten-house group of four-story townhouses (1887–89), also for Stokes, at 308–310 West Eighty-ninth Street, wrapping around to 591–599 West End Avenue.[176] The latter group was notable for its boldly curved three-story-high bays, slate tile roofs, and deeply carved pediment ornament that pushed Flemish decoration toward the Art Nouveau. Schuyler also may have been thinking about Thom & Wilson's ten-house, four-story group (1888) at 601–619 West End Avenue, occupying the entire west blockfront between Eighty-ninth and Ninetieth Streets.[177]

Eighty-sixth Street, like Seventy-second Street, was treated as a parkway, with broad sidewalks punctuated with planting beds. While it is not difficult to imagine Schuyler's reaction to some of the Eighty-sixth Street work, it is interesting to contemplate what he might have said about the pair of houses (1890) on that street designed by Cyrus L. W. Eidlitz, numbers 341–343. In 1896 Schuyler would illus-

Houses, southwest corner of West End Avenue and West Eighty-ninth Street. Joseph H. Taft, 1887–89. View to the southwest, 1919. NYPL.

trate the houses in his review of the work of the architect, son of Schuyler's mentor, Leopold Eidlitz, but chose not to describe or comment on them, especially on their restless and spikily composed dormers that seemed part Gothic, part Romanesque in their sources.[178]

In contrast to his typically banal brownstone rows, John G. Prague's five-house group (1887–90) at 111–119 West Eighty-sixth Street, between Ninth and Tenth Avenues,

601–609 West End Avenue, West Eighty-ninth to West Ninetieth Street. Thom & Wilson, 1888. View to the west. RERG. CU.

341–343 West Eighty-sixth Street. Cyrus L. W. Eidlitz, 1890. View to the north. AR. CU.

111–119 West Eighty-sixth Street. John G. Prague, 1887–90. View to the north. AABN. CU.

was a sophisticated composition executed with such admirable restraint that the *American Architect and Building News*, which did not frequently publish Prague's work, included a full-page photograph of the group in its international edition.[179] Prague also designed a comparable group of buildings on the south side of Eighty-seventh Street.

Houses of Worship

The residential development of the West Side naturally enough necessitated new institutional buildings, particularly churches. One significant new church predating the opening of the West Side to real estate development, the 125-foot-wide, 285-foot-long Church of St. Paul the Apostle (1876–85), occupied what the *American Architect and Building News* called a "rather forlorn, out-of-the-way corner of the city" at the southwest corner of Sixtieth Street and Ninth Avenue.[180] It was far and away the grandest Catholic church undertaken in New York, or indeed in all the United States, except for James Renwick Jr.'s St. Patrick's Cathedral (1850–79, 1888) (see chapter 2). Designed by Jeremiah O'Rourke, a Newark-based architect who died before the plans were complete, it was finished under the direction of Paulist Father George Deshon, Ulysses S. Grant's roommate at West Point. The Paulist Fathers were founded in 1858 by Isaac Hecker, who sixteen years earlier had left his family's thriving flour and baking business and converted to Catholicism. Hecker, who may have provided some funding for the new church, had a strong hand in its design, proposing the thirteenth-century Cathedral of Santa Croce in Florence as a model. At the building's dedication, on January 25, 1885, the *New York Daily Tribune* described the hulking Tarrytown granite mass with its never-completed twin towers as "vast, plain, fortress-like in its solidity—almost repelling in the ascetic cast without and within; yet it is the most August, unwordly [*sic*] interior on this continent."[181] The critic Mariana Van Rensselaer was also impressed, especially by its sixty-five-foot-wide nave flanked by huge alternating round and octagonal blue limestone columns, with clerestory windows that flooded the room with light and made mysterious the dark blue ceiling. Later, stained glass by John La Farge added to the drama, as did a large, high baldachino carried on columns of colored porphyry inlaid with onyx, alabaster, and gold marble mosaic, built from 1887 to 1890 according to Stanford White's design.

As the West Side grew, most of the new churches were built for Protestant denominations, suggesting that even the modest apartment houses along Ninth and Tenth Avenues were out of the reach of the city's working class, a great many of whom were Irish and Italian and therefore mostly Roman Catholic. Those Roman Catholics who lived in the area presumably worshiped at the Church of St. Paul the Apostle until 1887, when plans were announced for the construction of a "more or less temporary" red brick seventy-five-by-one-hundred-foot building, designed by Napoleon Le Brun & Sons, to house the Roman Catholic Church of the Blessed Sacrament, at 148 West Seventy-first Street, east of the Boulevard.[182] Poor Jews were trapped along with other immigrant groups on the Lower East Side, while prosperous Jews preferred the Upper East Side, so no synagogues were built in the early days of the West Side's development.

For the most part, the new West Side was an upper-middle-class Protestant stronghold. In 1854, the Park Presbyterian Church, founded several years earlier, moved into a frame building at the northeast corner of Eighty-fourth Street and West End Avenue.[183] The congregation was small until 1879, when Anson Phelps Atterbury, who was one of the Phelps-Dodge mining family, became pastor. In 1883, sensing that the new elevated railway would foster growth, Atterbury secured a large site at the northeast corner of Eighty-sixth Street and Amsterdam Avenue, commissioning Leopold Eidlitz, whose nearby riverfront villa overlooked the Hudson River at Eighty-sixth Street, to design a large brownstone chapel midblock on Eighty-sixth Street. Eidlitz left the corner site free for a compatibly designed principal sanctuary (1889–90) by Henry F. Kilburn, whose somewhat stiff and vertical Romanesque-inspired church of rock-faced Long Meadow brownstone trimmed in Lake Superior red stone culminated in a bell tower crowned by a steep, ribbed, bell-shaped dome.

Another early church was Samuel B. Reed's Bloomingdale Reformed Church (1885), which occupied a generously sized lot at the northeast corner of the Boulevard and Sixty-eighth Street.[184] The site was part of a cemetery formerly attached to the old Bloomingdale Church, which had been taken down when Broadway was widened to form the Boulevard. Reed's Gothic-style, Kentucky limestone church, incorporating a parsonage and Sunday school, seated one thousand worshipers in a square, column-free sanctuary. With its eighty-foot-tall tower carrying an eighty-foot-tall spire, the building was a prominent monument.

Many of the leading Protestant churches were built as branches of downtown congregations or had strong ties to established ministries. William H. Day's Protestant Episcopal Chapel of the Transfiguration (1880), at 120 West Sixty-ninth Street, between Ninth Avenue and Broadway, was presided over by Edward C. Houghton, whose father was minister of the "Little Church Around the Corner," at 1 East Twenty-ninth Street.[185] R. H. Robertson's Rutgers Riverside Presbyterian Church (1887–89), at the southwest corner of Seventy-third Street and the Boulevard, was the new home of a congregation that was moving uptown from Madison Avenue and Twenty-ninth Street, where it had been located since 1873.[186] While awaiting the completion of the new church, the congregation worshiped in a temporary chapel west of the church site on Seventy-third Street, also designed by Robertson. The Romanesque-inspired design of the permanent church employed three types of sandstone: reddish Potsdam sandstone for the walls, purplish New Jersey stone for most of

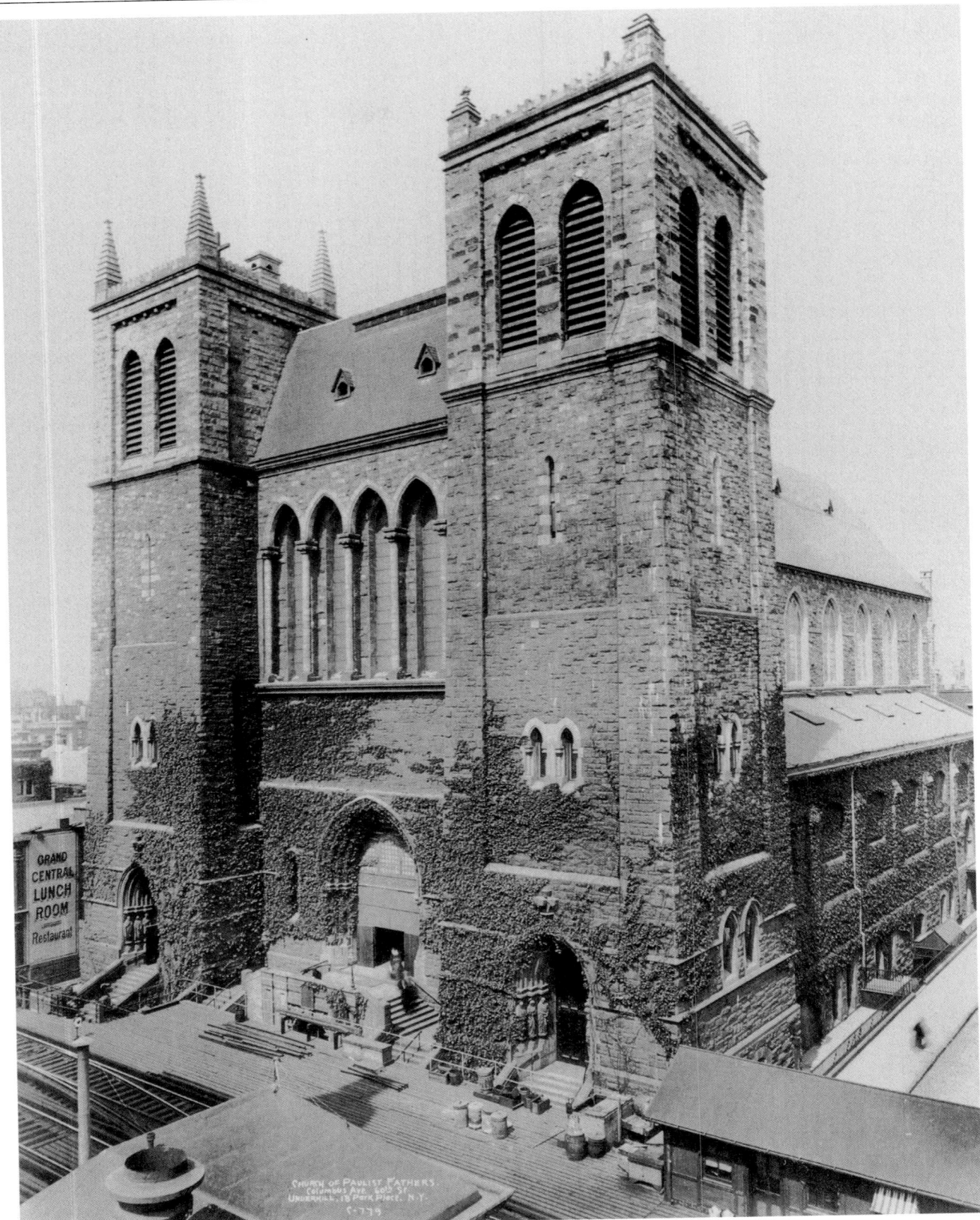

Church of St. Paul the Apostle, southwest corner of Ninth Avenue and West Sixtieth Street. Jeremiah O'Rourke, 1876–85.
View to the southwest, c. 1895. Underhill. NYHS.

Park Presbyterian Church, northeast corner of Amsterdam Avenue and West Eighty-sixth Street. Henry F. Kilburn, 1889–90. View to the northeast showing the chapel (Leopold Eidlitz, 1884) on the right. NYHS.

the trim, and darker Long Meadow stone for the voussoirs of the arches. Montgomery Schuyler praised the design, finding it "as free" as Robertson's St. James Protestant Episcopal Church (1883–84) (see chapter 2) on Madison Avenue,

> and showing no more care for the praise of "correctness." . . . The plan turns to architectural account the peculiarities of the site and . . . converts apparently unpromising requirements into sources of effectiveness and individuality. The street corner upon which the church stands is an obtuse angle, and the church is nevertheless set upon it rectangularly, the front being perpendicular to the line of the street. This leaves a considerable space between the avenue (the Broadway Boulevard) and the inner angle of the church, and this space is utilized by the erection here of the tower, thus well protected from the church, to its considerable advantage. The detachment is nearly complete, for the space behind the tower, as far as the transept, is also reserved so as to secure the ample lighting of the interior, no matter what disposition may be made in the adjoining lot.[187]

This tower, like that of Robertson's St. James Protestant Episcopal Church, was not completed.

C. C. Haight's Christ Protestant Episcopal Church (1889–90) was built for another congregation that was moving uptown.[188] The congregation was relocating from the southeast corner of Fifth Avenue and Thirty-fifth Street, where it had since 1858 occupied a building (1854–56) originally designed for a Baptist congregation.[189] Located at the northwest corner of Seventy-first Street and the Boulevard, two blocks from the Rutgers Riverside Presbyterian Church, its design was also inspired by the Romanesque but in this case that of Normandy in France. As built, the church was only a shadow of the far more ambitious scheme initially proposed. The salmon-colored brick building, relieved with dark red terra cotta and roofed in glazed and corrugated black tile, was comparatively small, seating eight hundred people in a building only 57 by 117 feet. Its character was austere and so different from what originally had been designed that Schuyler felt it "quite possible that the architect would object to being judged by the existing building, since the changes are all reductions and seem to have been made in the interest of economy." In the original design, a massive tower sat at the corner. Never built, it was, as Schuyler put it, "architecturally necessary . . . [to] relieve the building of the look of hardness and squareness which is its principal defect."[190]

Farther uptown, J. C. Cady's St. Andrew's Methodist Episcopal Church (1889), at 120 West Seventy-sixth Street, between Ninth and Tenth Avenues, incorporated a rectory and a low bell tower in a Romanesque-inspired limestone building that provided space for one thousand worshipers in its domed sanctuary.[191] On the north side of 104th Street between Tenth Avenue and the Boulevard, Cady's Grace Methodist Episcopal Church (1888) occupied a 150-foot-deep, 82-foot-wide, irregularly shaped midblock site that

Park Presbyterian Church, northeast corner of Amsterdam Avenue and West Eighty-sixth Street. Henry F. Kilburn, 1889–90. View to the east of main entrance, facing Amsterdam Avenue. MCNY.

Bloomingdale Reformed Church, northeast corner of the Boulevard and West Sixty-eighth Street. Samuel B. Reed, 1885.
View to the northeast, c. 1895, showing the Dakota (Henry J. Hardenbergh, 1882–84) in the background. NYHS.

permitted the construction of a small chapel with a class-room above at the rear of the eight-hundred-seat, Lombardic-Romanesque–inspired main church.[192]

All Angels' Protestant Episcopal Church (1888–90), at the southeast corner of Eighty-first Street and West End Avenue, replaced a smaller wood-frame church on the same site.[193] As designed by Samuel B. Snook of the firm of J. B. Snook & Sons, the English Gothic–inspired, Indiana limestone building exemplified the return to the stricter handling of stylistic detail that would characterize the work of the 1890s. Handsome enough, the church was particularly important for its plan, which brought worshipers into the building at the corner under a diagonally oriented tower, leading them into the fundamentally square sanctuary, which remarkably accommodated a 140-foot-long nave along the diagonal within the confines of a 100-by-100-foot lot. The effect of the building's cathedral-like scale was further enhanced by the use of columns and piers that described a cruciform plan, though the "aisles" were in effect vestigial triangles taking up the difference between the two geometries.

Rutgers Riverside Presbyterian Church, southwest corner of the Boulevard and West Seventy-third Street. R. H. Robertson, 1887–89. View to the southwest. King, 1893. CU.

St. Andrew's Methodist Episcopal Church, 120 West Sixty-ninth Street. J. C. Cady, 1889. View to the southwest. NYHS.

All Angels' Protestant Episcopal Church, southeast corner of West End Avenue and West Eighty-first Street. Samuel B. Snook, 1888–90. View to the southeast. AAC.

The decision of Trinity Church Parish to build a chapel and a school on the West Side signified as much as any other factor that the new district had at last arrived.[194] One of a series of "chapels-of-ease," St. Agnes represented Trinity's northernmost outpost. In July 1888, Trinity announced a competition for a 1,500-seat church building with a clergy house and school, to be erected on a 225-foot-wide midblock site extending from Ninety-first to Ninety-second Street between Ninth and Tenth Avenues. Rumor had it that Trinity proposed the new facility as a replacement for St. Luke's Church in Greenwich Village, but this proved false. Six firms were each paid one thousand dollars to compete: C. C. Haight, Henry M. Congdon, Frederick Clarke Withers, Richard Morris Hunt, W. Halsey Wood, and McKim, Mead & White. Additionally, William A. Potter, who was the half-brother of Bishop Henry Codman Potter, the head of the diocese, asked to be able to compete at his own expense. Bishop Potter was very sensitive about nepotism, and the issue would soon surface again in reference to the commission for the Cathedral of St. John the Divine (see chapter 2). Amid the grumblings of the others, William A. Potter was permitted to compete. And when Potter was chosen, Richard Morris Hunt, one of the competitors and arguably the most respected American architect at the time, wrote a letter of congratulation, thereby validating the selection procedure and its outcome.

All Angels' Protestant Episcopal Church, southeast corner of West End Avenue and West Eighty-first Street. Samuel B. Snook, 1888–90. View to the southwest from near West Eighty-second Street between the Boulevard and West End Avenue. Bracklow. NYHS.

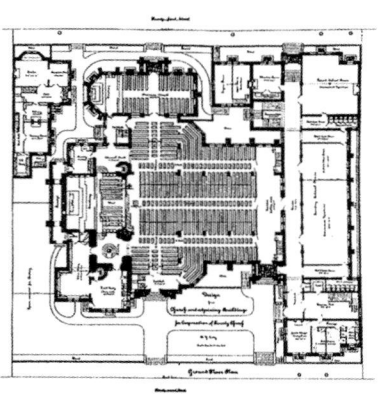

Proposed church, clergy house, and school of Trinity Church Parish, between Ninth and Tenth Avenues, West Ninety-first to West Ninety-second Street. Henry M. Congdon, 1888. Competition-entry elevation of south facade and ground-floor plan. AABN. CU.

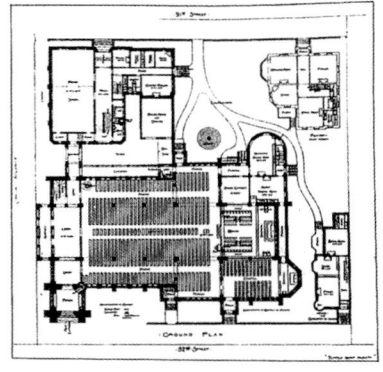

Proposed church, clergy house, and school of Trinity Church Parish, between Ninth and Tenth Avenues, West Ninety-first to West Ninety-second Street. Frederick Clarke Withers, 1888. Competition-entry perspective rendering showing view to the north-east from West Ninety-first Street and ground-floor plan. AABN. CU.

Proposed church, clergy house, and school of Trinity Church Parish, between Ninth and Tenth Avenues, West Ninety-first to West Ninety-second Street. Richard Morris Hunt, 1888. Competition-entry perspective rendering showing view to the southwest from West Ninety-second Street. AABN. CU.

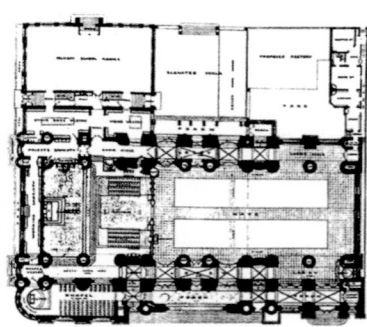

Proposed church, clergy house, and school of Trinity Church Parish, between Ninth and Tenth Avenues, West Ninety-first to West Ninety-second Street. W. Halsey Wood, 1888. Competition-entry perspective rendering showing view to the southwest from West Ninety-second Street and plan. AABN. CU.

St. Agnes Chapel, between Ninth and Tenth Avenues, West Ninety-first to West Ninety-second Street. William A. Potter, 1889. View to the southwest from West Ninety-second Street. NYHS.

Though the site was inconspicuously located in the middle of a long block, a fifty-foot-wide strip of land that was part of the Croton Aqueduct system bounded it on the east, guaranteeing light as well as some prominence when approached from Ninth Avenue or viewed from the elevated railway. The competition brief asked that the church be entered from the north, in part because Ninety-second Street was closer to the elevated station at Ninety-third Street. Two of the competitors, Wood and Congdon, proposed a liturgically correct east-west orientation. Hunt surprised with a Romanesque-inspired design, clearly influenced by H. H. Richardson.

Montgomery Schuyler felt that the combination of functional elements and materials initiated by Potter in his Holy Trinity Church in Harlem (see below) was "better managed" in his light granite and brownstone St. Agnes Chapel, which was completed in 1889. The presence of the school at the rear and the decision not to build completely to the flanking property lines rendered St. Agnes unusual as a freestanding church on a midblock site. Reminiscent of Richardson's Trinity Church in Boston, St. Agnes fea-

tured a central lanternlike tower, or *cimborio*, placed over the crossing as well as a tall, campanile-like bell tower rising from the west transept, an arrangement that made confusing the composition of the building as a whole. Although in 1891 Schuyler praised the triple-arched entrance front as "truly and nobly Romanesque,"[195] in 1909 he reconsidered the building and found fault with the composition: "There is no dominating feature. The two features of which either might dominate in the absence of the other are not cooperative, but competitive. One is the big and rather bad 'cimborio' which covers the crossing . . . ; the other the tall unbuttressed campanile which had its inspiration in the tower of Richardson's Albany City Hall. But these faults do not, and worse faults would not, prevent St. Agnes' from attaining architectural success." Schuyler found the interior "a very straightforward, expressive and impressive example of the Romanesque which, even in its architectural detail, and still more in its interesting furniture and fittings, harks back from the western Romanesque to the eastern, to the Byzantine."[196] Upon the chapel's completion, the *New York Times*

St. Agnes Chapel, between Ninth and Tenth Avenues, West Ninety-first to West Ninety-second Street. William A. Potter, 1889. View to the northeast from West Ninety-first Street showing the church's school in the foreground. NYHS.

praised St. Agnes extravagantly: "Magnificent in dimension and excellently planned—Trinity Parish's best building [and] not only the finest church structure under the jurisdiction of Trinity Parish, but the finest church structure, barring the cathedral [St. Patrick's], in New York City. It is perhaps the most perfectly equipped structure for religious work of all sorts in the United States."[197]

Caring Institutions

The construction of the elevated railroad made the West Side particularly attractive as a site for caring institutions, which needed large, affordable sites but could settle for outlying locations provided they were accessible. In 1881 Richard Morris Hunt, probably on the strength of his work for the Presbyterian Hospital (1868–72) (see chapter 2), was hired to design an old-age home, the Association Residence for Respectable and Indigent Females, on the east block of Tenth Avenue between 103rd and 104th Streets.[198] One of the city's oldest charitable organizations, the association had been formed in 1813 by socially prominent women to aid war widows. Originally support was in the form of money, food, and clothing, given "to relieve and to comfort those aged females, who once

Proposed Association Residence for Respectable and Indigent Females, Fourth Avenue between East Seventy-eighth and East Seventy-ninth Streets. Richard Morris Hunt, 1868. Elevation of the entrance facade. The Octagon, AAF.

Association Residence for Respectable and Indigent Females, east side of Tenth Avenue between West 103rd and West 104th Streets. Richard Morris Hunt, 1883. View to the southeast. King, 1893. CU.

enjoyed a good degree of affluence, but now reduced to poverty by the vicissitudes of Providence." In 1833 a subscription was begun to construct a building, completed in 1838, at 226 East Twentieth Street on three lots donated by Peter G. Stuyvesant, for an asylum, which was intended as an alternative to "the common almshouse, filled as it usually is with the dregs of society; [which] is not a place of comfort to persons of refined sensibilities."[199] The association continued to grow, acquiring a site on Fourth Avenue between Seventy-eighth and Seventy-ninth Streets and, in 1868, commissioning Hunt to prepare plans for a new, French-inspired building. But concerns about the rapid growth of the neighborhood and the site's proximity to the steam-belching railroad encouraged the association to delay until 1881, when it began in earnest to look for "some location farther uptown, where a site easy of access and suitable for the purpose might be obtained at a cost much less than one in the heart of the city."[200] For the new Manhattan Valley site, Hunt was once again retained. After providing several variations, a design was selected for the building as well as for two adjoining houses. In December 1883, amid some ceremony, the building was opened to any respectable, non–Roman Catholic (Protestants only) gentlewoman over sixty years of age, on payment of $150 and surrender of any property she possessed. Like Hunt's earlier design for the association, and like his work for the Presbyterian Hospital and other of his work of the 1870s and early 1880s, the new building was French Second Empire in its character though Gothic in its details, moving Montgomery Schuyler to observe that "it would not be unfair to describe [it] . . . as a persistent but unsuccessful attempt to avoid Gothic architecture. It was quite feasible to avoid medieval detail, but the spirit and idea, the composition and grouping distinctly recalled Gothic work in buildings in which not a single Gothic form was suffered to appear."[201] The C-shaped, load-bearing, three-story building, of dark red brick, contained eighty-five rooms. A strong mansard sheltered dormered rooms and the composition was broken up into pavilions articulated by three implied towers, with the one at the 104th Street corner rising some distance above the mass. A bold, rock-faced granite porch marked the entrance off Tenth Avenue. In 1887, the Association Residence was joined by a neighbor across the street on the southwest corner of 104th Street: the Home for the Relief of the Destitute Blind, founded in 1869 to help both men and women.[202] Designed by F. Carles Merry, the complexly pavilionated, three-story building was far more eclectic, notable for an ogee dome that dominated the Tenth Avenue blockfront. The firm of D. & J. Jardine designed two other charitable institutions in the area: the vaguely Romanesque Methodist Episcopal Church Home (1885), occupying the east blockfront of Tenth Avenue from Ninety-second to Ninety-third Street, and the mansarded Home for the Aged of the Little Sisters of the Poor (1884-87), on the north side of 106th Street between Ninth and Tenth Avenues.[203]

*Home for the Relief of the Destitute Blind, southwest corner of Tenth Avenue and West 104th Street. F. Carles Merry, 1887.
View to the southwest. Bracklow. NYHS.*

*Roosevelt Hospital, Ninth to Tenth Avenue, West Fifty-eighth to West Fifty-ninth Street. Carl Pfeiffer, 1871.
View to the northeast from West Fifty-eighth Street. NYHS.*

Roosevelt Hospital Syms Operating Theater (W. Wheeler Smith, 1892), southwest corner of Ninth Avenue and West Fifty-ninth Street, on the left, and the Roosevelt Hospital Surgical Pavilion (Carl Pfeiffer, 1871), on the right. View to the southeast. OMH.

Another important institution to locate on the West Side was Roosevelt Hospital, founded in 1864 with a bequest from James H. Roosevelt, an uncle of Theodore Roosevelt.[204] Opened in November 1871 as a family-supported charity that would twenty years later be described as "to all intents and purposes, a free public hospital," it stretched from Fifty-eighth to Fifty-ninth Street between Ninth and Tenth Avenues.[205] As a private hospital that received no public support but provided free health care to those patients who could not afford fees, Roosevelt's organization was similar to that of New York Hospital. The new Roosevelt complex consisted of a four-story administration building flanked by two pavilions for patients, linked by open arcades, reflecting the latest thinking in hospital design. The vertical Gothic massing of the red brick and light-colored Ohio stone central building rising to a central flèche-like steeple set at forty-five degrees to the ridge, designed by Carl Pfeiffer, was also stylistically up-to-date. In 1887, W. Wheeler Smith's four-story brick Sloane Maternity Hospital, at the northeast corner of Fifty-ninth Street and Tenth Avenue, was added to the complex, a gift of Mrs. Sloane, a Vanderbilt. Sloane's Broadway furniture emporium (1881) had also been designed by Smith (see chapter 5).

In 1892, as a result of the generosity of a retired gun merchant, William J. Syms, an operating theater bearing his name was added in a separate wing, also designed by Smith. Said to be "the finest structure in the world for surgical operations," the granite-trimmed deep red brick building rose to a semi-conical skylight. Nonetheless, the *New York Times* noted in 1891 that the surgical pavilion was outdated before it was finished. Connected to the main building by means of a corridor, it was "only one story high, the belief being at the time it was constructed that surgical spaces were safe only in a structure of this character. But since the introduction of antiseptic treatment and the improved methods of ventilation, a surgical building can run up to any reasonable heights with safety to the patients that can be gathered under its roof."[206] *Harper's Weekly* felt that in conceiving the mildly Romanesque building Smith had sacrificed "beauty of exterior . . . to utility of interior," but in reality the building was quite handsome, employing subtly decorated brick walls and curved corners and the particularly memorable semi-conical roof, which sheltered the operating theater that Smith designed in close collaboration with Dr. Charles McBurney, who achieved international recognition for his identification of the point on the abdomen from which appendicitis can be diagnosed.[207] Inside, in an effort to combat infection, walls and ceilings were sheathed in marble and all corners were curved so that they could be easily cleaned and disinfected. Even the laundry chute was lined with marble so that it could be easily disinfected. The operating room could seat 134 students from the Columbia College of Physicians and Surgeons, which trained its students at the hospital, although the two institutions were not otherwise affiliated with each other.

C. C. Haight's New York Cancer Hospital (1884–90), on Eighth Avenue between 105th and 106th Streets, was the nation's first facility of its kind and one of the city's most important experiments in health care.[208] Additionally, it was, along with the Dakota (1882–84) (see chapter 4),

New York Cancer Hospital, west side of Eighth Avenue between West 105th and West 106th Streets. C. C. Haight, 1884–90. View to the northwest. AR. CU.

the second building of consequential size to be constructed facing Central Park on the West Side since the American Museum of Natural History (1874–77) (see chapter 2) and one of the city's grandest public buildings. From the first, the marriage of Haight's individualistic, French Renaissance–inspired imagery to an inventive plan of forty-foot-diameter circular towers was widely discussed. In 1885, the *Real Estate Record and Builders' Guide*'s reporter, possibly Montgomery Schuyler, observed that "the group of round towers, that give the building its resemblance to a sixteenth century French chateau, is an outgrowth of the plan, since in the diseases to the treatment of which this hospital is devoted it is especially desirable to avoid corners which prevent the cleansing of rooms. The architect has carried out the motive thus furnished him so as to produce a work marked by repose and dignity and much simple elegance of detail."[209]

The idea to build an independent cancer hospital had been formulated after a bequest made by John Jacob Astor II to the Woman's Hospital in 1882 to fund a pavilion for the treatment of cancer patients was rejected. Working with John E. Parsons and Elizabeth Hamilton Cullum, a cousin of Astor's wife, the New York Cancer Hospital realized the aspirations to establish the institution, which was built in three stages. The Astor money paid for the first third of the new facility. The Astor pavilion was to treat women only, but by the time it opened plans were under way for a companion facility for the treatment of men, also funded by Astor. At the same time a chapel was added near the 105th Street corner, dedicated to the memory of the recently deceased Elizabeth Cullum.

UPPER MANHATTAN

Harlem

Perhaps no other part of New York more dramatically reflected the city's almost overnight transformation in the post–Civil War era from open land and independent villages to densely developed streetscapes of rowhouses and apartment buildings than did Harlem.[1] The area known as Harlem had traditionally included both the broad, relatively flat plain of land known as the Harlem Plain, or the "Flats," an expanse extending north from about 110th Street to about 155th Street and east from Morningside and Washington Heights (known since the 1920s as Hamilton Heights) to the East and Harlem Rivers; and the high land, generally known as the Harlem Heights, an area on a steep bluff north of 125th Street, sloping west to the Hudson River. The Harlem Valley, connecting the Plain with the Hudson River, lay along the present-day 125th Street, at the foot of Morningside and Harlem Heights. But Harlem was also the name of a historic village, independent of New York and almost as old as the city itself, established by Peter Stuyvesant as Nieuw Haarlem in 1658 and located at what later became 125th Street and First Avenue. In 1664, when the British defeated the Dutch, the name of the village was changed to Lancaster. At the same time, Nieuw Amsterdam became New York. In 1668 the two communities were connected by a road built by black slaves of the Dutch West India Company. As early as the 1680s, municipal records indicated that at least for judicial purposes Harlem was considered part of New York. By the early nineteenth century the old Dutch name, Harlem, was once again used. The legal relationship between Harlem and New York during the post–Civil War period is now surprisingly unclear; what is known, however, is that at the beginning of the period Harlem was, in terms of its character, separate and unique, and that by the period's close it had become an integral part of New York.

In the early nineteenth century, and for a while to come, with only about ninety families in the Harlem area, most of the land east of Fifth Avenue between 110th and 125th Streets belonged to James Roosevelt, who had it farmed until he sold it in 1825 as the once-lush soil began to deteriorate. With farming in decline, properties were abandoned only to be taken over by Irish squatters. Soon the

squatters began to give way to well-to-do suburbanites, who after 1837 were able to travel back and forth to the city on the New York and Harlem Railroad. Far-sighted observers looked forward to the time when Harlem, nearby Yorkville, and the established city to the south would merge into a single conurbation.[2] In 1836, anticipating the transformation of Harlem into a densely developed neighborhood, the city of New York purchased a square of land, to be used as a public park, interrupting Fifth Avenue between 120th and 124th Streets and running from Madison Avenue on the east to a point four hundred feet west of Fifth Avenue, where a new north-south street, eventually called Mount Morris Park West, was established between Fifth and Sixth Avenues.[3] At the same time, the city fathers, bottom-line-oriented as ever,

View to the southeast, 1883, showing West 121st Street in the foreground, the intersection with Sixth Avenue in the middle ground, and Mount Morris Park in the background. NYHS.

Fire watchtower, Mount Morris Park, Fifth Avenue to Mount Morris Park West, West 120th to West 124th Street. Julius Kroehl, 1856. Bracklow. NYHS.

saw to it that the loss of taxable property due to the creation of Mount Morris Park was compensated for by the elimination of Harlem Square, which the Commissioners' Plan of 1811 had called for, between Sixth and Seventh Avenues and 117th and 121st Streets.[4] Not much more than a massive rock outcrop, the land for Mount Morris Park was ignored until the mid-1850s. Unusual in the otherwise relatively flat area, and certainly a hindrance to development, the very intractability of the rock and the consequent unsalability of the land was probably why the city decided to hold on to it. In 1856 a fire watchtower, one of many in the city, was built at the park's highest point. As designed by an engineer, Julius Kroehl, its construction resembled the system James Bogardus had developed for post-and-lintel structural framing in cast iron.[5] Five years later, the first efforts were made to transform the outcrop into a park and to grade the surrounding streets.[6] By the late 1870s, the *Real Estate Record and Builders' Guide* was extolling Mount Morris Park as "the most charming, delightful and picturesque park in the city. . . . Its dense foliage, its velvety green sward, its bed of flowers, its bushes of roses, together with its elevated promontory from which a widely extended view may be comfortably had, are features in which it has no rival. Yet with all its conceded attractions it has failed to exert any active influence upon property immediately surrounding it."[7]

Though the new park did not immediately stimulate adjacent development, suburbanization did come to nearby areas in the form of scattered, small, villalike houses built by working class or artisanal families—such as the two-and-a-half-story wood-frame house (c. 1863) on a seventy-five-foot-wide lot on the south side of 129th Street between Fifth and Sixth Avenues that was shared by the families of two carpenters, William Paul and Thomas Wilson.[8] The same block also included two Greek Revival houses from the 1840s. The arrival of workers and artisans meant that the Dutch- and English-descended residents who had previously dominated the area were forced to give way to Irish immigrants, as well as Germans, a considerable number of whom were Jews.

House, east of Broadway near 140th Street. J. C. Cady, c. 1877. AR. CU.

The area's first postwar religious building, however, was St. Johannes Kirche (1873), at 217 East 119th Street, between Second and Third Avenues, which catered to German Lutherans.[9]

Quickly the remote village of Harlem was becoming a haven for commuters, although many were forced to live in shantytowns that, according to a health inspector in 1866, were more densely packed than a Third Avenue horsecar, with "men, women and children, dogs, cows, pigs, goats, geese, ducks, and chickens . . . almost promiscuously mixed together." The shantytowns rendered the streets "rank with filth and stench" to such an extent "that mortality holds high command there."[10] Soon enough, with the construction of the elevated railroads along Third and Second Avenues, East Harlem became a socially complex working-class tenement district that included, along the East River, the same kind of manufacturing that characterized the East Side farther downtown.

The completion of Grand Central Depot, in 1871, brought with it improvements to the tracks along Fourth Avenue between Forty-second Street and Harlem.[11] Tunnels, trestles, and an open cut were constructed to provide an uninterrupted, more or less level right-of-way, and by 1875 four tracks were in use, two of which were exclusively devoted to local service, utilizing a station at 125th Street. Like the growth pattern of the West Side, however, until the economy picked up and brought about the building boom of the 1880s these improvements had comparatively little immediate effect on Harlem's development. The 1880s boom included the construction of the Second, Third, and Ninth Avenue elevated railways, which plunged the Harlem Flats headlong into an urbanism so dense that by 1883 a writer in the *Real Estate Record and Builders' Guide*, almost certainly Montgomery Schuyler, could lament that "Harlem, speaking architecturally, and speaking generally, is one of the most depressing quarters of New York. There is in its streets the thoughtless and conventional repetition of forms intrinsically bad which makes up the bulk of the architecture of this island. But in Harlem, owing to the suburban character of the place, this character is mixed with the character of a frontier town, with something particularly raw and Peorian."[12] A year later Schuyler restated his case for a larger audience, the readers of *Lippincott's Magazine*: "Harlem, to be sure, is populous, and the tide of progress has spread out over its expanse of alluvium and 'filling,' to results no doubt commodious, but as far as possible from being picturesque. In truth, there is very little that is suburban in the character of Harlem, which simply repeats the monotony of the lower island in its most monotonous parts."[13]

The Harlem Plain was the last easily developable area of land on Manhattan Island, but it was not without its problems. Parts of the area were plagued by environmental abuses that were at their worst in lower Harlem, where in some areas inadequate sewage and the runoff from nearby breweries created serious health hazards.[14] These problems notwithstanding, the Flats boomed in the 1880s, moving the boosterish editors of the *New York Daily Tribune* to report that "the Harlem of the goats and rocks has disappeared to be succeeded by a great and beautiful city, almost independent and entirely local in its peculiar characteristics. The wealthy home-owner no longer contemplates the picturesque hideousness of the hovel of the laborer perched on the rocks across the street. The 'shanty' has disappeared, the rocks have been blasted away and on the spots where they stood other houses have arisen."[15]

All in all, Harlem's evolution virtually mirrored that of the neighborhoods growing up east of Central Park, with the significant exception that it lacked the high-profile luxury district that filled the blocks between Fourth, Madison, and Fifth Avenues. In the 1880s the architecture of the Harlem Flats consisted almost entirely of two residential building types: apartment houses, which appeared in relatively small numbers, and rowhouses, which filled block upon block. An exception to this was one of J. C. Cady's earliest works, a one-and-a-half-story villa built east of Broadway near 140th Street in the 1870s for David Maitland Armstrong. The red and yellow brick mansarded cottage (c. 1877) was, with its iron roof cresting and scrollwork, as charming an example of post–Civil War cottage building as any in the city. Reviewing Cady's career in 1897, Montgomery Schuyler looked back on this house as a work of youth: "That was the day of small things, evidently, with the architect as well as with the client. But the evidence that this unpretentious dwelling afforded that intelligent and artistic pains had been ungrudgingly bestowed upon every detail of the design made it a particularly welcome object, especially in what was then and still elsewhere is the distressing ugliness of suburban New York."[16]

The middle-class apartment houses of the Harlem Flats were principally built along Eighth, Manhattan, and Morningside Avenues as well as on nearby side streets, but one of the earliest such apartment houses, Hubert, Pirsson

& Co.'s Mount Morris (1883), was located farther east at 10–12 East 130th Street, between Fifth and Madison Avenues.[17] Built as a Home Club cooperative for the Mount Morris Apartment Association, the fifty-foot-wide, eight-story apartment house contained two units per floor, included an elevator and a goods lift, and was notable for its logical plan. While the designers of many similar apartments placed the kitchen at the rear, far from

Mount Morris, 10–12 East 130th Street. Hubert, Pirsson & Co., 1883. View to the south. BLDG. CU.

Washington Apartments, 2034–2040 Seventh Avenue. Mortimer C. Merritt, 1883–84. View to the northeast, 1888. NYHS.

the dining room, in order to isolate heat and cooking odors, Hubert, Pirsson & Co. located the Mount Morris kitchens at the narrow portion of the "dumbbell" to serve the dining rooms toward the front, and grouped the bedrooms together in the back.

Harlem's grandest apartment house, and its first intended for middle-class tenants who would commute downtown via the elevated train from the nearby station, at Eighth Avenue and 125th Street, was Mortimer C. Merritt's eight-story Washington Apartments (1883–84), at 2034–2040 Seventh Avenue, on the northeast corner of West 122nd Street, constructed for the speculative developer Edward H. M. Just.[18] Merritt's Queen Anne design of brick trimmed in terra cotta, stone, and iron, with its

Apartment house, east side of St. Nicholas Avenue between West 118th and West 119th Streets. Richard R. Davis, 1890. Rendering of view to the southeast. RERG. CU.

projecting balconies, overscaled frontispiece, and decorative panels, was lively but in no way as stylish as its contemporary, Henry J. Hardenbergh's Dakota (see chapter 4), on Eighth Avenue and Seventy-second Street, which of course catered to a much more affluent clientele. The two buildings nonetheless had aspects in common. Like the Dakota, the Washington rose up amid a ragtag landscape. But in place of the Dakota's view of Central Park juxtaposed against a shantytown, the Washington overlooked isolated wood-frame houses of some substance as well as single-family rowhouses. In each case the construction of the Ninth Avenue elevated train, with nearby stations, made the project viable. The thirty-unit Washington occupied a far smaller site than the Dakota, with only 101 feet on Seventh Avenue. It was also far less handsome. The building's artistic deficiencies did not go unnoticed. The *Real Estate Record and Builders' Guide* reported in 1885 that though the Washington "is more or less bragged about in Harlem . . . the brag must be founded on the fact that it is big. It is undeniably big . . . [but] in general design the big building is nothing but a big box. The only architectural interest that attaches to any part of it is the mechanical execution of the carving in the basement. This is very good, but the design even of this detail is of no account, and it is merely absurd to ascribe any importance to this edifice from the architectural point of view, however important it may be from a real estate point of view."[19]

The Washington's deficiencies notwithstanding, it was far superior to the much larger development, completed in 1890, that filled the east side of Ninth Avenue between

119th and 120th Streets (by 1898 that portion of Ninth Avenue was renamed Morningside Park East, to be subsequently identified as Morningside Avenue). Designed for John H. Wellwood by the Harlem-based architect Richard R. Davis, the project consisted of nine individual five-story walk-up buildings grouped together. Attempts to give the complex a unified impression included rounded corners that continued as conical towers above the roofline. While the *Real Estate Record and Builders' Guide* noted that the buildings had "no particular architectural pretensions," they deemed them "superior in design to many of the flats built nowadays," calling out for notice the use of Philadelphia brick and brownstone as well as many of the interior appointments.[20] Davis also designed four red brick apartment buildings (1887–88) at 2300–2306 Seventh Avenue, on the northwest corner of West 135th Street.[21] The buildings were distinguished by their brickwork, terra cotta decoration, and iron cornices. As designed by Edward L. Angell, the Lotta apartments (c. 1889) consisted of three stylistically coordinated, five-story, brick and stone-trimmed buildings on the northeast corner of Seventh Avenue and 118th Street.[22] Adopting a Romanesque-inspired architectural vocabulary, the Lotta's facades incorporated lively compositions with arched windows, recessed bays, and a silhouette punctuated by gables and finials. On the ground level, facing the street intersection, a heavily glazed storefront was framed by stone archways and contained an entrance placed on the diagonal and recessed beyond a corner column.

Rowhouses, not apartments, formed the principal building blocks of the district, beginning in the 1860s with Italianate brownstone rows similar in design to those elsewhere on Manhattan Island and in the city of Brooklyn. Given the area's flat and relatively featureless character, fashionable development was concentrated in the few places where topographical irregularities tended to foster a sense of place: around Mount Morris Park, at the edge of Morningside Park, and on Washington Heights, particularly just west of the Convent of the Sacred Heart (see below). The east side of Mount Morris Park, formed by Madison Avenue, was but a short block away from the railroad, so the most important residential development took place where the houses could be buffered by the park from the railroad's noise and dirt, along Fifth and Sixth (renamed Lenox in 1887) Avenues and on the side streets that lay in between.[23] Lenox Avenue was an exceptionally grand, 150-foot-wide street, with sidewalks interspersed with grassy, tree-planted plots. In 1891, in a letter to the *New York Times*, one Simon Stern, citing Lenox Avenue's success, suggested that Seventh Avenue also be renamed, recommending the name Knickerbocker Avenue, but the change was not adopted.[24] Madison Avenue, along the east side of Mount Morris Park, marked the eastern border of fashionable Harlem. The first construction facing the park was a row of ten brownstone-faced houses (1883) between 122nd and 123rd Streets.[25] The five houses at the northern end were designed by Charles W. Romeyn, who built

Lotta, northeast corner of Seventh Avenue and West 118th Street. Edward L. Angell, c. 1889. Rendering of view to the northeast. BLDG. CU.

extensively on the East Side as well as in Harlem, and the other five houses were the work of Charles Baxter, although there was little to distinguish the two groups. Each Italianate house consisted of three stories and a basement and had a full-height, three-sided bay window, a high stoop, and a boldly bracketed cornice.

Fashionable houses were typically to be found on Harlem's east-west streets no farther south than 119th Street and no farther north than 129th Street, although this was less true of the district's avenues. It was an unrealized dream of many realtors that Fifth Avenue's fashionable stretch would expand continuously northward from the park blocks to the Harlem River. While most of the houses built around Mount Morris Park, like those in Harlem's other fashionable neighborhoods, were rowhouses, there were occasional freestanding townhouses,

E. Augustus Neresheimer house, southeast corner of Sixth Avenue and West 119th Street. Arthur B. Jennings, 1886. Rendering of view to the southeast. AABN. CU.

John Dwight house, 31 Mount Morris Park West. Frank H. Smith, 1889–90. Rendering of main entrance. AABN. CU.

131 West 122nd Street. Julius Franke, 1890. View to north, c. 1940. NYPL.

8–12 West 122nd Street. William B. Tuthill, 1888–89. View to the south, c. 1940. NYPL.

such as the one Arthur B. Jennings designed for E. Augustus Neresheimer (1886) at the southeast corner of Sixth Avenue and 119th Street, a two-and-a-half-story stone mansion featuring porches on each floor and a rising roofline that included Dutch-inspired crowstepped gables.[26] In 1889–90, an individual house was built for John Dwight, whose fortune derived from Arm and Hammer baking soda, at 31 Mount Morris Park West, on the northwest corner of West 123rd Street.[27] As designed by Frank H. Smith, the mansion, which introduced Italian Renaissance–inspired facade design to Harlem, was distinguished by an impressive main entrance flanked by columns and surmounted by an elegantly articulated arched canopy. In 1890, the architect Julius Franke completed an individual house at 131 West 122nd Street; with a front of rough-hewn limestone, the house adopted a Romanesque vocabulary that included round-arched windows and a similarly articulated entrance.[28]

More typical than individual houses were three- or five-house rows. The row at 26–30 Mount Morris Park West (A. B. Van Dusen, 1880–81) adopted a Neo-Grec vocabulary and incorporated prominent porticos framing the main entrances.[29] As designed by Charles Baxter, the brownstone row at 4–26 West 123rd Street (1880–82) also adopted a Neo-Grec style.[30] More lighthearted was an

Houses, northeast corner of Lenox Avenue and West 121st Street. F. Carles Merry, 1889. View to the northeast. RERG. CU.

adjacent pair of houses at 28–30 West 123rd Street; as designed by John E. Terhune, the Queen Anne houses, each only thirteen feet wide, had facades of brick and variously colored and textured stone as well as decorative carvings depicting floral forms.[31] A Tudor Gothic–inspired red brick and unglazed terra cotta five-house row (c. 1885) at 17–25 West 129th Street, between Fifth and Sixth Avenues, moved Montgomery Schuyler to write that "there was no shame about the front of this house," but that "an undue solicitude for variety, which spoils so many buildings, makes its appearance fretful, uneasy and disagreeable."[32] The English-trained architect Francis H. Kimball packed in a wealth of bravura Queen Anne flourishes in a six-house row (1885–87) designed for C. W. Gould at 133–143 West 122nd Street, between Sixth and Seventh Avenues.[33] The row, certainly among the most accomplished Queen Anne–style house groupings in the city, incorporated an early use of terra cotta decoration. In 1888, deMeuron & Smith completed a distinguished row at 200–218 Lenox Avenue, on the west side of the avenue between 120th and 121st Streets, which incorporated a mansard roof and iron cresting.[34] Thom & Wilson's five-house group (1887–88) at 103–111 West 122nd Street contained a rich array of decorative carving.[35] William B. Tuthill, the architect of Carnegie Hall (see chapter 5),

designed a brownstone-fronted row at 4–16 West 122nd Street (1888–89) that was enlivened by stained-glass transoms and massive stoops incorporating grandly scaled newel posts.[36] Another row, designed by F. Carles Merry at the northeast corner of Lenox Avenue and 121st Street, adjoining Holy Trinity Church, was completed in 1889.[37] The brick and stone row contained a variety of imaginatively conceived units of varying widths, featuring generously scaled box stoops and two-story bay windows, with a boldly projecting, four-story, turretlike bay marking the corner. Brick facades surmounted both smooth and rough stone bases. Decorative features drew from both Renaissance and Romanesque sources. Inside, apartments were richly finished, incorporating complexly patterned parquet floors, mahogany and oak woodwork, distinctive built-in furniture and mantlepieces, and stained-glass windows. In 1885 McKim, Mead & White designed a modest rowhouse nearby at 47 West 119th Street for the personal use of the contractor-developer James C. Miller, for whom the firm would complete the Wanaque (1886–87), an understated French flat at 359 West Forty-seventh Street (see chapter 4).[38]

The block of 121st Street between Lenox and Seventh Avenues formed one of Harlem's most notable rowhouse streets. While most of the block's houses were faced in

128–134 West 121st Street. Cleverdon & Putzel, 1891.
View to the southeast. RERG. CU.

View to the northwest showing 1 West 121st Street on the left
and 11–14 Mount Morris Park West on the right. James E. Ware,
1887–89. RERG. CU.

brownstone, the stretch displayed neither the stylistic uniformity typical of the 1860s and 1870s nor the extreme individuality of the Queen Anne style. Rather, as typified in the seven-house group (1891) designed by Cleverdon & Putzel and developed by S. O. Wright at 128–134 West 121st Street, a subtle variety of window groupings and cornice details counterbalanced the repetitious stoops and round bay windows to form an overall composition that could not be considered distinguished architecture but was certainly good urbanism.[39] Farther east at 1 West 121st Street and 11–14 Mount Morris Park West, the developers Dr. James V. S. Wooley and G. Grant Brinckerhoff Jr. built a group of five French Gothic–inspired brick and brownstone houses (1887–89) consisting of four stories and a basement, four facing the park and the fifth facing 121st Street.[40] Among the most remarkable in the city, they were designed by James E. Ware, who let each house rise to a distinct, steeply pitched pedimented dormer. An additional dormer punctuated the roof facing 121st Street, and at the corner an oriel rising to a conical roof provided one further note of distinction.

North of 125th Street, urbanization mostly followed the same pattern as around Mount Morris Park, although the rowhouses were frequently more modest in size and less aesthetically ambitious. The slow pace of development in the 1860s and 1870s created an odd ghostlike urbanism of widely spaced rowhouse groups, including those along 133rd Street as well as the Italianate, brownstone-faced house group (1869) on the south side of 127th Street between Fifth and Sixth Avenues designed by Alexander Wilson.[41] Between Fifth and Sixth Avenues 126th Street remained undeveloped until 1871, when Calvert Vaux and Frederick Clarke Withers completed a three-story house at number 28 for Edward Gleason, the superintendent of the Union League Club.[42] Beneath a mansard roof punctuated by a dormer, the house's principal facade consisted of dark red Philadelphia brick trimmed with light-colored Ohio stone and decorated with carvings that presaged those of Vaux & Withers's Jefferson Market Courthouse, completed six years later (see chapter 2). Development picked up around 1883, when Henry J. Hardenbergh was at work on plans for six eighteen-foot-wide, four-story brick houses, erected on the southwest corner of Sixth Avenue and 128th Street, as well as six more, twelve-and-a-half feet wide, on 128th Street west of Sixth Avenue.[43] The narrow size of the houses clearly reflected the market's sense that this neighborhood would cater to a barely middle-class clientele. At the same time Charles W. Romeyn was at work on a house for Charles J. Fisk, a three-story mansarded brick and stone design constructed at 2069 Fifth Avenue, between 127th and 128th Streets.[44] Completed around 1889, James Brown Lord's five-house group for E. S. Higgins, at the northeast corner of 130th Street and Seventh Avenue, was one of the city's most interesting townhouse developments.[45] Designed to look like a single mansion, the solid block turned a long, steeply sloped gable parallel to the avenue while a series of elaborately ornamented pedimented

View to the northeast, c. 1877, of West 133rd Street between Fifth and Sixth Avenues. NYHS.

dormers and clustered chimneys broke up the skyline. Only the projection of flights of stooplike steps suggested that the space within consisted of individual houses.

Just before the development of Harlem was in full swing, William B. Astor II erected twenty-eight houses (1880–83) at 8–62 West 130th Street, between Fifth and Sixth Avenues.[46] Astor's grandfather John Jacob Astor had acquired the land in 1844 but had left it in its rural state. Nearby, west of Fifth Avenue between 131st and 132nd Streets, stood what was known as the Hall Mansion, a three-story farmhouse raised on a high basement and wrapped by porches on all but the top floor; the house was sufficiently picturesque to inspire the architect Charles W. Stoughton to

sketch it.[47] When John Jacob Astor died in 1848, the property was inherited by his son William B. Astor; upon the younger Astor's death, in 1875, the property was divided in two, with the northern portion of the property, facing 130th Street, inherited by William B. Astor II, and the southern half, facing 129th Street, inherited by his brother, John Jacob Astor III. William B. Astor II hired Charles Buek, a prolific rowhouse architect, to design numbers 8–22 (1880–81). The rest of the development was completed in two campaigns: 24–38 West 130th Street (1882–83) and 40–62 West 130th Street (1883). Both of these were built without Buek's assistance even though the houses were similar to his designs, but with a notable exception: Buek's group consisted of

E. S. Higgins houses, northeast corner of Seventh Avenue and West 130th Street. James Brown Lord, c. 1889. Rendering of view to the northeast. BLDG. CU.

Hall Mansion, Fifth to Sixth Avenue, West 131st to West 132nd Street. Rendering by Charles W. Stoughton, c. 1886. AABN. CU.

12 West 130th Street. Charles Buek, 1880–81. View to the south, 1932. NYPL.

that a drawing of one of the houses by itself would convey the idea of a rural dwelling. . . . The architecture of the houses . . . enhance the suburban look given to them by their semi-detachment. Each is quite different from the others, even in color, the visible materials being painted brick, stone, tile, slate and wood." But as usual, Schuyler was not completely pleased:

> There are, even in each taken singly, too many features, and the result is that the houses look somewhat miscellaneous and "thingy." There is too much cheap ornament in wood—not badly done however—which in a few years will look very shabby. Most of the detail is Queen Anne, and it is rather queer and silly Queen Anne. The houses are two-story with mansard roofs and the roofs are enlivened with fantastic double gables and odd dormers that are beyond reasonable license, even for suburban cottages. Nevertheless, the aspect of the whole, though it lacks sobriety, has brightness, poignancy and picturesqueness, and one would like to see the hint supplied by these buildings extensively taken in suburban districts.[48]

In 1883 H. M. Blasdell, inspired by William B. Astor II's development on 130th Street, commissioned twenty three-story double houses from Lamb & Rich for the west blockfront of Sixth Avenue between 130th and 131st Streets. Eight houses, ranging in width from approximately twenty-three to twenty-six feet, were built on the avenue in "a style similar to those of the Astors' . . . though," according to the *Real Estate Record and Builders' Guide*, "somewhat more artistic in appearance."[49] Twelve more houses, planned for the adjacent side streets, were never realized.

Harlem was to become home to one more exemplary group of houses, perhaps the most distinguished undertaking of its kind in all of the United States: David H. King Jr.'s Model Houses (1891), a comprehensive development filling both sides of 138th and 139th Streets between Seventh and Eighth Avenues as well as the avenue frontages.[50] Designed and planned with the assistance of Stanford White, James Brown Lord, and Bruce Price, King's Model Houses represented the furthest

freestanding pairs of houses set back from the street behind small yards, while the two subsequent groups, also set back, formed a continuous row, although a deep recess between each pair maintained the rhythm of the original design. Buek's notably simple three-story houses with their wide front porches sheltering brick facades looked back to Harlem's earlier development as a rural suburbia. Nearby, at 57–65 East 129th Street, on the land John Jacob Astor III owned, a group of five similar rowhouses was built in 1889.

The *Real Estate Record and Builders' Guide*'s anonymous critic, unmistakably Montgomery Schuyler, was impressed with Buek's design: "In the design of these it is assumed that the building of houses in Harlem ought to be of a suburban rather than a strictly urban character, insomuch

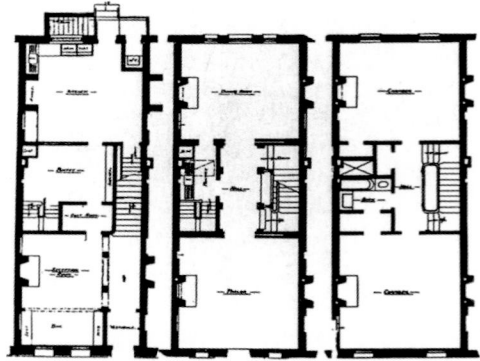

David H. King Jr.'s Model Houses, Seventh to Eighth Avenue, West 138th to West 139th Street. McKim, Mead & White, James Brown Lord, and Bruce Price, 1891. Site plan. KMH. CU.

David H. King Jr.'s Model Houses, Seventh to Eighth Avenue, West 138th to West 139th Street. McKim, Mead & White, James Brown Lord, and Bruce Price, 1891. Floor plans of typical house on West 139th Street. McKim, Mead & White, 1891. KMH. CU.

David H. King Jr.'s Model Houses, Seventh to Eighth Avenue, West 138th to West 139th Street. McKim, Mead & White, James Brown Lord, and Bruce Price, 1891. View to the north showing gated entrance to midblock lane, north side of West 139th Street (McKim, Mead & White, 1891). NYHS.

advance to date in the sporadic efforts made by architects and developers to establish architecturally and urbanistically coherent enclaves within the limitations of the city's gridiron of streets and avenues. This type of effort had been pioneered by Samuel B. Ruggles, whose most important project was the creation of Gramercy Park (1831) and its surrounding development.[51] The idea for the overall plan, which provided for spacious, fountain-punctuated midblock lanes wide enough for two carriages to pass, apparently belonged to Stanford White. The lanes were accessible to the street from two midblock wrought-iron-gated lanes that broke the otherwise relentless wall of the typical New York block. In an undated promotional brochure published around 1891, the layout was described as "ample enough to 'Create a Neighborhood,' independent of surrounding influences. It is the largest enterprise of its kind ever undertaken by any one builder on Manhattan Island."[52] King's plan for 160 individual units mostly provided rows of townhouses that were just slightly wider than those typically on the market. It also included modest four-story apartment houses designed by McKim, Mead & White, each accommodating six families, which were built along Eighth Avenue facing the elevated railway. These, as well as the rowhouses facing Seventh Avenue, enjoyed exceptionally wide, thirty-foot setbacks from the street (the side-street houses were set back twelve feet).

Although the overall plan was proposed by White, his firm designed only the apartment houses and the row of houses on the north side of 139th Street, which were the biggest units in the development. Because all the houses conformed to the new taste for Classical design, however, there was a remarkable sense of commonality. James Brown Lord's red brick rows lined the south side of West 138th Street and faced Seventh Avenue. Bruce Price, who worked with Clarence Luce, designed the houses on the north side of 138th Street and the south side of 139th Street, as well as those facing Seventh Avenue on that block, using buff-colored brick with white stone trim, a lighter palette than White's, whose houses combined brownstone at the base with glazed speckled Roman brick

David H. King Jr.'s Model Houses, Seventh to Eighth Avenue, West 138th to West 139th Street. McKim, Mead & White, James Brown Lord, and Bruce Price, 1891. Rendering of midblock lanes. KMH. CU.

David H. King Jr.'s Model Houses, Seventh to Eighth Avenue, West 138th to West 139th Street. McKim, Mead & White, James Brown Lord, and Bruce Price, 1891. View showing houses (McKim, Mead & White, 1891) on the north side of West 139th Street. NYHS.

David H. King Jr.'s Model Houses, Seventh to Eighth Avenue, West 138th to West 139th Street. McKim, Mead & White, James Brown Lord, and Bruce Price, 1891. Rendering of view to the north showing houses (James Brown Lord, 1891) on West 138th Street between Seventh and Eighth Avenues. KMH. CU.

David H. King Jr.'s Model Houses, Seventh to Eighth Avenue, West 138th to West 139th Street. McKim, Mead & White, James Brown Lord, and Bruce Price, 1891. Rendering of main hall in typical house by James Brown Lord. KMH. CU.

David H. King Jr.'s Model Houses, Seventh to Eighth Avenue, West 138th to West 139th Street. McKim, Mead & White, James Brown Lord, and Bruce Price, 1891. Rendering of parlor in typical house by James Brown Lord. KMH. CU.

trimmed in matching terra cotta. While Lord and Price cozied their Classicism with Georgian-inspired details, White took the high road with a severe, almost unornamented Renaissance-inspired vocabulary that suppressed the individuality of the units for the grand gesture of a palatial row.

Montgomery Schuyler was lavish in his praise of King's development, finding the experiment "so successful that one would like to have it again and again repeated, not merely for the sake of having something entertaining to look at . . . but because the idea of taking a block front and giving it to one designer who is asked to create one design would retain the only redeeming feature of the brownstone period, the uniformity of a single blockfront," and bring into play "the additional advantage gained of detail that was interesting as well as an ensemble that was impressive. . . . These are 'second-rate, genteel houses' in which nobody will be ashamed in dwelling. Mere decorum is a considerable achievement, as our street architecture goes." According to Schuyler, King "was a public benefactor, and if he had seen his way to covering the whole flat from Morningside to the Harlem River with like houses, he would have been a public benefactor of the very first order."[53]

Harlem's growing population brought with it a pressing need not only for housing but also for many different types of public facilities. Some of these were housed in architecturally interesting buildings. Small schools had been built in Harlem since the 1840s, but when the elevated railways filled the streets of East Harlem with tenements and rowhouses, the New York City Board of Education commissioned one of the city's largest schools, a superscaled, factorylike, 1,800-student facility, Public School 72 (1879–82), on the west side of Lexington Avenue between 105th and 106th Streets.[54] Designed by David I. Stagg, the symmetrically composed Neo-Grec building was com-

Public School 72, west side of Lexington Avenue between East 105th and East 106th Streets. David I. Stagg, 1879–82. View to the northwest. TC.

Harlem Police Court and District Court, 170 East 121st Street. Thom & Wilson, 1891–93. View to the southeast. King, 1893. CU.

pleted in two phases, beginning with the south wing in 1881 and the north wing a year later. Stagg had begun his career in 1834 as a carpenter with the Board of Education, rising to the position of superintendent of school buildings in part because of his singular honesty. His vaguely Lombardic design, consisting of thirty-six classrooms on four floors plus a janitor's apartment in the penthouse, was served by fire-resistant slate and iron stairways. Student toilets were only to be found on the ground floor. Classrooms on the second and fourth floors of the south wing were fitted out with sliding walls, allowing rooms to be combined to create large areas that functioned as indoor playrooms as well as auditoriums. In each classroom, exterior windows were supplemented by clerestories facing the interior corridor, allowing for through ventilation.

Big-city life brought big-city problems, so to help mete out justice, a substantial, Gothic Revival and Romanesque-inspired building (1891–93) to house the police court and the district court was constructed at 170 East 121st Street, on the southeast corner of Sylvan Terrace.[55] An uncharacteristically inventive design by the frequently heavy-handed Thom & Wilson, the red brick building, incorporating bluestone and terra cotta trim, culminated in a five-story, gable-ended pavilion that served as the principal entrance and a round tower surmounted by an octagonal gabled belfry rising to a six-sided spire that anchored the corner.

As Harlem matured, its long-term residents, resisting the notion that their village was being swallowed up by the

city, continued to think of their neighborhood as a quasi-independent suburb. Not surprisingly, they developed their own cultural and social institutions. Just as Harlem was being annexed to New York in 1873, the Harlem Library, founded in 1825, built a new, thirty-foot-wide, brownstone-fronted, extensively glazed building designed by B. Walther, at 2238 Third Avenue, between 121st and 122nd Streets.[56] Reading rooms were open to one and all, though a yearly membership fee was required of patrons who wished to borrow books. By 1891 the location was no longer central to the community—or at least to its upper strata—and a new building was commissioned for a lot located at 32 West 123rd Street, near Lenox Avenue, purchased from the Harlem Club (see below), which was located next door.[57] Edgar K. Bourne, a library trustee, was selected as architect. His design for the thirty-four-foot-wide, four-story building was remarkably sympathetic to Lamb & Rich's Harlem Club and incorporated above its two library floors two floors of bachelor apartments, which were leased to the club. Just as the new building was opened, a distributing station of the New York Free Circulating Library was established near the corner of Lexington Avenue and 125th Street. The free library made inroads on the fee-based readership of the Harlem Library, leading to the eventual merger of the two.

Lamb & Rich had followed the success of the firm's Mount Morris Bank (see below), one of Harlem's most architecturally distinguished buildings, with the design of the Harlem Club (1888–89), at the southeast corner of Lenox Avenue and 123rd Street.[58] The nearly eight-

Harlem Library, 32 West 123rd Street. Edgar K. Bourne, 1891. View to the south, 1920. HNYPL. CU.

Harlem Club, southeast corner of Lenox Avenue and West 123rd Street. Lamb & Rich, 1888–89. View to the southeast. AABN. CU.

St. James Methodist Episcopal Church, northeast corner of Madison Avenue and East 126th Street. Rembrandt Lockwood, 1869–71. View to the northeast. MCNY.

cotta, capped by a tall, clay tile–covered hipped roof interrupted by pedimented and turreted dormers and boldly massed chimneys. Montgomery Schuyler thought that the design would not have been possible without the example of the Romanesque Revival, "but it can scarcely be said to be in the academic sense an example of Romanesque architecture . . . in spite of the round-headed arcade, of the pairs of round arches under relieving arches in the second story, of the stout colonnade in the gable and of the carved ornament, which is consistently Byzantine and particularly good."[59]

In 1873 the *New York Times* reported that Harlem's citizens "are not neglectful of their spiritual welfare, as witness the many new and handsome churches which have been recently built or are now in course of erection."[60] Among these was Rembrandt Lockwood's Norman Gothic–style St. James Methodist Episcopal Church (1869–71), at the northeast corner of Madison Avenue and 126th Street.[61] The church, founded in 1830 as the First Methodist Episcopal Church of Harlem, had moved from its wooden building (1833) on East 125th Street between Fourth and Madison Avenues. The new, rough brownstone building was visually dominated by a corner tower which in turn supported a 188-foot steeple. Inside, a forty-six-foot-high sanctuary was enclosed by a column-free parabolic-arch ceiling.

One of Harlem's oldest congregations was St. Andrew's Protestant Episcopal, founded in 1829, which built its first home in 1830 but did not begin to take on the proportions

hundred-member club was organized in 1879 and incorporated in 1886. Until completing its new building, it had been located at 2056 Fifth Avenue. The project had been awarded through competition, with Lamb & Rich beating Francis H. Kimball, Henry F. Kilburn, Arthur B. Jennings, and Henry J. Hardenbergh, among others. Lamb & Rich's spectacular design called for a three-and-a-half-story, forty-by-ninety-foot, mansionlike clubhouse finished in reddish brown sandstone, red brick, and matching terra

St. Andrew's Protestant Episcopal Church, northeast corner of Fifth Avenue and East 127th Street. Henry M. Congdon, 1889–90. View to the northeast. NYHS.

St. Andrew's Protestant Episcopal Church, between Lexington and Fourth Avenues, East 127th to East 128th Street. Henry M. Congdon, 1873. View to the northeast. NYSB. CU.

Church of the Puritans, 15 West 130th Street. Attributed to Hubert, Pirsson & Co., 1873–78. View to the northwest. King, 1893. CU.

West Harlem Methodist Episcopal Church, northwest corner of Seventh Avenue and West 129th Street. John R. Thomas, 1887. View to the northwest. King, 1893. CU.

of a substantial congregation until much later. In 1873, after a fire destroyed its home on a midblock site running from 127th to 128th Street between Fourth and Lexington Avenues, St. Andrew's moved into a new church designed for the same site by the twenty-nine-year-old architect Henry M. Congdon. In 1876 the *New-York Sketch-Book of Architecture* reported that Congdon's new, rose-colored Niantic granite St. Andrew's, with a 125-foot-long nave leading to a chancel, 80-foot-wide transepts, and seats for about 960 people, was "picturesquely situated, for a city church, in its own graveyard."[62] A slender tower rising to a steep near-pyramidal roof anchored the graceful composition. By the late 1880s the congregation had so expanded that Congdon was asked to dismantle the building and supervise its reconstruction and expansion (1889–90) on a new and much more prominent, 100-by-160-foot site on the northeast corner of Fifth Avenue and 127th Street.[63] The new church, housing one thousand worshipers, was so situated that its slender, soaring clock tower and spire were located at the eastern end of the nave, hard up against the south transept, leaving to the corner the welcoming gesture of the main entrance.

The Church of the Puritans (1873–78), attributed to Hubert, Pirsson & Co., at 15 West 130th Street, was a new congregation.[64] Organized as the Second Presbyterian Church of Harlem, it changed its name as a stipulation of its benefactor, the Reverend Dr. George B. Cheever. Cheever had given the congregation the money to build the new church, proceeds from the 1869 sale to the jeweler Tiffany & Co. of the old Church of the Puritans (James Renwick Jr., 1846), located on the southwest corner of Fifteenth Street and Broadway, facing Union Square.[65] The new rock-faced granite Gothic-style church was sited with a low tower to the west, a north-south nave, and, at the rear of the site, a transept and vestry that formed an ell to create a small landscaped forecourt.

The prosperity of the mid-1880s and Harlem's great growth stimulated a wave of church building. Many of the new houses of worship, serving Methodists and Baptists, were more auditorium-like than those of the high-church Protestant denominations. John R. Thomas was a prolific architect reputed to have completed more buildings in New York than any other architect of his generation.[66] His Calvary Baptist Church (1883), on West Fifty-seventh Street (see chapter 2), was an important example of the auditorium approach. Thomas designed for the four-year-old West Harlem Methodist Episcopal congregation a brick and stone church as well as a chapel and parsonage (1887) occupying a 99-by-125-foot site on the northwest corner of Seventh Avenue and 129th Street.[67] The *Real Estate Record and Builders' Guide* found it to be

> another attempt at the chronic problem of a Protestant church, that is to say of giving an ecclesiastical character to the most convenient form of a lecture room. . . . The church is not successful as an architectural expression of the "auditorium," which, indeed, only appears in the dis-

position of the roof, though it may be inferred from the equal length of the two faces, which constitute one of the difficult points of the problem. So many good architects have failed, however, to give this problem a satisfactory solution that the designer of the West Harlem Methodist Church need not be abashed by his lack of complete success. His dispositions are sensible and result naturally from his conditions. His detail, though never exquisite, is never weak or silly, his . . . windows are effective features and the shaft of his tower is excellent.[68]

Whatever the shortcomings of Thomas's design, the congregation grew dramatically, and after only three years, the architect was asked to expand the building to double its size. At the time of its completion in 1890, the expanded building contained the largest Protestant church auditorium in the city.

At about the same time that he was working for the Methodists, Thomas designed the rock-faced Reformed Low Dutch Church of Harlem (1885–87), at 267 Lenox Avenue, on the northwest corner of 123rd Street, notable for a tall slender corner spire.[69] Thomas also designed the original portion of the limestone New York Presbyterian Church (1884–85), at 151 West 128th Street, between Sixth and Seventh Avenues, providing for a small lecture room that served double duty as a chapel, built with the intention of creating a proper sanctuary later on, which was realized in 1889–90.[70] In 1885 the *Real Estate Record and Builders' Guide* described the incomplete church at length:

> . . . a promising fragment . . . built of a light stone, used rough faced, over a base of reddish stone, and with polished shafts of red granite in the jambs of the doorways. The fragment is an apsidal chapel, covered with a steep roof, and showing a small gable on the street front over a rose window. In its present detached condition the fragment necessarily has an awkward look, although it may very possibly have more force and impressiveness than it will have when it comes to take its place as part of a complete composition. The detail is scholarly and good. The tracery of the rose window is especially well designed.

After finding fault with other details, the *Record and Guide* concluded that "what is already built gives promise of being an effective piece of architecture, more so than any other church in Harlem, except the granite Episcopal Church of St. Andrew."[71] But Thomas was not hired for the later work, which went instead to Richard R. Davis, whose gabled and towered design complemented the original but was bolder, with a wide, fan-shaped sanctuary that could open to the original lecture room when needed. By comparison with the prolific Thomas, Davis was an obscure figure who broadcast the entire design as his own, although in fact even the portion that was his responsibility seemed very similar to that of the western section of Thomas's Reformed Low Dutch Church of Harlem, just a few blocks away. In any case, though Davis's corner tower was never realized, the mix of Gothic and Romanesque Revival features made for a powerful design, heavy in its massing, with an extraordinarily prominent conical roof.

New York Presbyterian Church, 151 West 128th Street. John R. Thomas, 1884–85; Richard R. Davis, 1889–90. View to the northwest. NYHS.

Proposed New York Presbyterian Church, 151 West 128th Street. Richard R. Davis, 1889. Perspective rendering showing proposed corner tower. RERG. CU.

Mount Morris Baptist Church, 2050 Fifth Avenue. Henry F. Kilburn, 1888. Rendering of view to the west. NYDG. CU.

Henry F. Kilburn's severe Mount Morris Baptist Church (1888), at 2050 Fifth Avenue, between 126th and 127th Streets, was the second home on the site of the parish, organized in 1843.[72] The Romanesque-inspired design of brick and Longmeadow stone turned its gable end to the street and could seat eight hundred people. Kilburn's First German Baptist Church of Harlem (c. 1889), with its entrance enclosed by a distinctive half-round arch, stood at 220 East 118th Street, between Second and Third Avenues.[73]

William A. Potter's Holy Trinity Church (1887–89), at the southeast corner of Lenox Avenue and 122nd Street, ranked in importance and status with the most prominent in the city and was certainly one of Harlem's most archi-

Holy Trinity Church, southeast corner of Lenox Avenue and West 122nd Street. William A. Potter, 1887–89. View to the southeast. HTC.

tecturally interesting houses of worship.[74] Potter came to the Richardsonian version of the Romanesque rather belatedly—in fact, at just about the same time that its progenitor died of Bright's disease. On a 100-by-150-foot site, Holy Trinity, the first church in a series by Potter in the style, was, as Montgomery Schuyler put it, "not only a church but a complete parochial 'plant' so to speak, includ-

ing a rectory and an extensive parish building." In order to house all these functions on the site, the axis of the nave was located parallel to the church front along 122nd Street, with the transept occupying the street-facing gable, resulting in what Schuyler praised as "a picturesque and effective grouping." A massive square tower, located above the entrance, rising from an elongated belfry to a steep

All Saints' Church Rectory, north side of East 125th Street between Fifth and Madison Avenues. Variously attributed to Renwick, Aspinwall & Russell and Renwick, Aspinwall & Owen, 1889. View to the northeast. BLDG. CU.

Lenox Avenue Unitarian Church, northwest corner of Lenox Avenue and West 121st Street. Charles B. Atwood, 1889–91. View to the northwest. NYHS.

pyramidal roof, was very effective, punctuating what Schuyler described as "a real architectural composition and a very successful one, as it is also unmistakably and emphatically a structure of masonry. There are few churches in New York so dignified and solemn and 'churchly' in expression, or that so strongly recommend Romanesque as suitable for church building."[75] The composition was unusual and ingenious, with the seventeen-foot-wide parish house located between the west end of the church and Lenox Avenue. Like the church itself, the parish house was a vigorously detailed structure of rock-faced sandstone trimmed with darker, smooth-faced stone, punctuated by two steep gables at either end and a small spire set between. Here, as in the tower, the handling of the arched windows was inventive. The "simple and massive" bell tower was the outstanding feature of the design, deemed by the editors of the *Real Estate Record and Builders' Guide* to be "one of the most dignified and impressive objects in the architecture of New York [with] . . . clustered shafts and heavily-moulded arches and deep reveals."[76] Impressive also was the vaulted interior with transept galleries carried on iron columns. The editors were so taken by this room, capable of seating one thousand, that they compared it favorably with

Leopold Eidlitz's Assembly Chamber (1877–83) in the New York State Capitol in Albany.

The Gothic-inspired All Saints' Church, variously attributed to Renwick, Aspinwall & Russell and Renwick, Aspinwall & Owen, also ranked among the area's most accomplished houses of worship. Located on the northeast corner of Madison Avenue and 129th Street, it was built in two stages, beginning with the Venetian Gothic, limestone-trimmed, elaborately ornamented brick rectory, completed in 1889,[77] and continuing five years later with the completion of the church.[78] The complex was designed by James Renwick Jr. in 1875 and was ultimately built from more refined drawings produced by his nephew William W. Renwick; it constituted James Renwick Jr.'s last church design and was among his finest. Drawing on both French and Italian precedents, the church was, like the rectory, notably detailed, with Gothic tracery and terra cotta ornament played against buff, honey-colored, and brown brick walls. Inside, the church was distinguished by a polygonal transept and a dramatic use of polychromy, including columns painted dark green. One other Gothic church of note, the Lenox Avenue Unitarian Church (1889–91), at 225 Lenox Avenue, on the northwest corner of 121st Street, was the third Unitarian church in New York. It was

*St. Cecilia's, East 106th Street between Lexington and
Fourth Avenues. Napoleon Le Brun & Sons, 1883–87.
View to the southwest. King, 1893. CU.*

designed by the spectacularly talented Charles B. Atwood,
who had been so important in the design of the Vanderbilt
houses (see chapter 4) and who would shortly relocate to
Chicago, where he would make important contributions to
the design of the World's Columbian Exposition of 1893.[79]

As on the West Side, most Harlem churches were built
for Protestant congregations, although there were exceptions. The St. Cecilia Roman Catholic Church (1883–87),
designed by Napoleon Le Brun & Sons, occupied a 75-
foot-wide, 118-foot-deep midblock site at 120 East 106th
Street, between Fourth and Lexington Avenues, and
served a working-class congregation.[80] St. Cecilia's
Romanesque-inspired facade, of Collsburg and Philadelphia molded red brick elaborately ornamented with glazed
terra cotta, was a powerful and much-welcome break
amid the rowhouse- and tenement-dominated townscape.
Tuckett & Thompson's limestone and brick Gothic-style
St. Charles Borromeo (1888), at 211 West 141st Street,
between Seventh and Eighth Avenues, was another
notable Roman Catholic church.[81]

While there was a Jewish community in Harlem, it was
neither large enough nor established enough to undertake
synagogue-building projects. Consequently, existing facilities, including abandoned churches, were renovated as synagogues. One example of this trend was the 1890 adaptation
of the old Carmel Baptist Church, at 357 East 121st Street,
for use by the ten-year-old Congregation Ateres Zwie.[82]

The opening of the 125th Street station of the New
York and Harlem Railroad in 1837 guaranteed that street
a key role in Harlem's development. But it was not until a
half-century later that 125th Street between Third and
Seventh Avenues began to take on the character of an
impressive commercial center, exemplified by the construction of the Mount Morris Bank Building (1883–84;
1889–90), at the northwest corner of Fourth Avenue,

View to the southeast, c. 1895, of East 125th Street from near Lexington Avenue. Byron. MCNY.

View to the east, 1905, of West 125th Street from near Eighth Avenue, showing the Hamilton Bank (J. B. McElfatrick & Sons, 1890) and, immediately to the right, the Harlem Opera House (J. B. McElfatrick & Sons, 1889), both on the north side of the street. NYHS.

Mount Morris Bank Building, northwest corner of Fourth Avenue and East 125th Street. Lamb & Rich, 1883–84; 1889–90.
View to the northwest. NYHS.

which provided sure evidence that Harlem had arrived as an important urban neighborhood of New York City.[83] In January 1883, Lamb & Rich had been awarded the commission through competition. Other entrants included Silliman & Farnsworth, McKim, Mead & White, and

J. C. Cady. Lamb & Rich's boldly massed, intricately and vigorously detailed design of Philadelphia red brick and sandstone trimmed in terra cotta was realized in two sections, the first in 1883–84, the second in 1889–90. Combining headquarters for the recently organized Mount

Morris Bank on the ground floor and the Mount Morris Safe Deposit Company in the basement, above which were six French flats constituting an apartment house called the Morris, the building employed features of the Queen Anne and the Romanesque in a design that brought together a rich mix of materials and details, including broad oriels and Classical ornament. A boldly scaled porch projected into the street at the corner, leading visitors to the bank. A more delicately detailed, smaller porch at the building's west end served the residents of the Morris. The extension of the building resulted in the addition of four tiers of narrow iron balconies facing Fourth Avenue. Montgomery Schuyler greeted Lamb & Rich's building with enthusiasm, particularly given his view of Harlem as an architectural wasteland:

> It gives us especial pleasure to say that this work in Harlem, like the Commercial building at Broome Street and Broadway [486 Broadway; see chapter 3], and in a less degree the Henderson cottages at Eighty-sixth Street and Avenue B [see chapter 4], is an exception to the thoughtless routine, showing, as it does, some purpose, apart from the purpose of making an exception. To be sure, that is not of itself very high praise. A low degree of skill calls for an exaggerated expression of gratitude, such as the dismal character of our routine building. But this building offers interesting points of composition and interesting points of detail.[84]

The Bank of Harlem, later the Hamilton Bank, soon followed the Mount Morris Bank to 125th Street, occupying a far less picturesque building (1890) at 213–217 West 125th Street, designed by J. B. McElfatrick & Sons. Located next door to the same firm's Harlem Opera House (see below), the loosely Classical, five-story-high building greeted the street with an intricately gridded facade described by the *Real Estate Record and Builders' Guide* as being "in the Renaissance style of architecture, neither distinctly Italian nor French Renaissance, but partaking of the character of both."[85]

By the late 1880s, 125th Street was Harlem's principal shopping street, replacing the upper reaches of Third Avenue, which had hitherto enjoyed that distinction. It included the Harlem-based architect Julius Munckwitz's three-story (with provisions for three more stories), extensively glazed emporium for the E. D. Farrell Furniture Company (1891), on the south side of 125th Street east of Seventh Avenue.[86] The windows in Farrell's storefronts were said to be the largest in the city. At 132–140 West 125th Street, William H. Hume's Koch Emporium (1891) was built for H.C.F. Koch & Co., an established dry-goods business that followed its patrons from the lower city up to the new suburb.[87] Founded in 1860 at Carmine and Bleecker Streets, from 1875 until 1891 Koch's was located on Sixth Avenue and Twenty-ninth Street. Other notable retailers were D. M. Williams, which was located in a string of renovated and purpose-built buildings on the northwest corner of Third Avenue and 125th Street, and Corn, Kaliske & Co., which occupied a glassy, iron-

Bank of Harlem, 213–217 West 125th Street. J. B. McElfatrick & Sons, 1890. Rendering of view to the north. RERG. CU.

E. D. Farrell Furniture Company, south side of West 125th Street between Lenox and Seventh Avenues. Julius Munckwitz, 1891. North elevation. RERG. CU.

Koch Emporium, 132–140 West 125th Street. William H. Hume, 1891. Rendering of view to the southwest. RERG. CU.

Corn, Kaliske & Co. (1889), 144–146 West 125th Street. Rendering of view to the south. RERG. CU.

D. M. Williams (c. 1890), building row on the north side of East 125th Street west of Third Avenue. Rendering of view to the north, with the corner of East 125th Street and Third Avenue on the far right. RERG. CU.

fronted, four-story building (1889) at 144–146 West 125th Street, running through to 124th Street.[88] Both establishments were pioneering New York examples of the so-called arcade shopfront, wherein the store entrance was deeply recessed from the sidewalk, resulting in increased show-window area.

The importance of the 125th Street business district was further cemented on September 30, 1889, with the opening of Oscar Hammerstein's Harlem Opera House, at 207

Harlem Opera House, 207 West 125th Street. J. B. McElfatrick & Sons, 1889. View of the auditorium from the stage. Byron. MCNY.

Harlem Opera House, 207 West 125th Street. J. B. McElfatrick & Sons, 1889. View to the northeast showing part of the Hamilton Bank (J. B. McElfatrick & Sons, 1890) on the left. Byron. MCNY.

West 125th Street, just west of Seventh Avenue.[89] As designed by J. B. McElfatrick & Sons, which specialized in theaters, the Harlem Opera House occupied seventy-five feet of frontage on 125th Street but extended through to 126th Street, where the lot was twenty-five feet wider. The 125th Street portion housed the entrance and lobby as well as a 100-by-75-foot music or concert hall. A frescoed and tiled arcade led to the opera house itself, which was located along 126th Street, seated 1,800 people on three levels, and had a 70-by-40-foot stage, one of the largest in the city. The *New York Times* found the bright blue opera

house decorations "pleasing in spite of their excessive gorgeousness."[90] Hammerstein also owned and managed the Columbus Theater, at 114 East 125th Street running through to 124th Street, a two-hundred-by-one-hundred-foot building designed by J. B. McElfatrick & Sons which opened a year later, on October 1, 1890.[91]

Bradford Lee Gilbert's five-story, fifty-foot-wide building for the Young Men's Christian Association (1887), at 5 West 125th Street, was a second home for the Harlem branch, which was established in 1868.[92] Despite the incorporation of ground-level shops flanking the entrance,

*Young Men's Christian Association, Harlem branch, 5 West 125th
Street. Bradford Lee Gilbert, 1887. View to the north. YMCA.*

the building's Dutch-inspired, brick and iron facade,
including two three-sided oriels roofed in tile and a crowstepped roof parapet buttressing a steep gable, established
a clublike expression for a facility that incorporated a gymnasium and a five-hundred-seat auditorium as well as a
parlor and library.

Despite its small size, Napoleon Le Brun & Sons's four-
story, twenty-five-foot wide Fire Hook & Ladder Company No. 14 (1889), at 120 East 125th Street, between
Park and Lexington Avenues, exerted a strong civic presence on the street.[93] Adopting a Romanesque vocabulary,
the building's principal facade incorporated a rusticated
brownstone base above which a red brick wall was punctuated by two tripartite windows. The building culminated
in a gable containing an arched window.

Manhattanville

The hamlet of Manhattanville was located approximately one mile west of the village of Harlem, between
Morningside and Washington Heights.[94] Established
around 1806, Manhattanville had been surveyed and laid
out by Adolphus Loss in the area formerly known as
Harlem Cove. In 1808 a ferry line connected Manhattanville to New Jersey. The area first attracted attention at
the beginning of the nineteenth century because it was

View to the northeast, c. 1876, of Manhattanville, showing Manhattan Street between Morningside and Tenth Avenues in the center and part of the main building (1847) of Manhattanville College of the Sacred Heart in the distance. SC.

View to the northwest, c. 1876, from near West 123rd Street, showing Manhattanville in the distance. SC.

Manhattan College, northeast corner of the Boulevard and West 131st Street. View to the northeast from the Boulevard, c. 1883, showing expanded main buildings on the left and the Church of the Annunciation (Edson & Englebert, 1854) on the right. SC.

thought that its elevated riverfront site and its distance from New York rendered it a healthy environment. The *Public Advertiser* noted: "There can be no doubt of a rise in value of these lots [in Manhattanville], even should the city remain free from the epidemic, but in case it should again be visited by that dreadful scourge, a great advance in the value of these situations is certain."[95] According to the *New York Gazette and General Advertiser*, initial land sales were made "principally to tradesmen."[96]

Manhattan Street, the village's principal thoroughfare, ran from Morningside Avenue in Harlem to the Hudson River, and after 1811 interrupted the mapped street grid.[97] By 1853 the area was served by Third Avenue Railroad streetcars, with lines running along Manhattan Street and north along Tenth Avenue to 186th Street. Located on or in the nearby vicinity of Manhattan Street were not only houses but several important institutions. The Manhattan Presbyterian Church (1851), at the southwest corner of Ninth Avenue and West 126th Street (in 1890, this section of Ninth Avenue was renamed Columbus Avenue, and later Morningside Avenue), was built in the Greek Revival style, an architectural vocabulary arguably more appropriate to the building's use, after 1875, as a courthouse.[98] Located on the same block, at the northwest cor-

ner of Ninth Avenue and Manhattan Street, St. Joseph's Roman Catholic Church (1860–63) adopted an austere, vaguely Lombardic style.[99] A somewhat more robustly articulated Sabbath School (Herter Brothers, 1889) was added directly to the north of the church.[100]

The two most prominent institutions in Manhattanville were Catholic places of higher learning. Manhattan College was founded by the Christian Brothers in 1853 and was an outgrowth of the Academy of the Holy Infancy, itself an outgrowth of the first parish school of the Brothers of the Christian Schools, established in 1848 at 16 Canal Street.[101] Manhattan College was housed in a formidable collection of buildings dating from the 1850s and early 1860s that crowned a prominent hill leading up to Washington Heights; the college campus would ultimately be bounded by 131st and 133rd Streets, Bloomingdale Road (Old Broadway), and what after 1871 would become the Boulevard. At the time of the college's establishment the cross streets were not yet cut through. Indeed, though the hamlet of Manhattanville was thriving, the area was still quite rural, encouraging the founders to boast that their campus could provide a true refuge from the nearby city, and thus an appropriate environment for serious study: "The situation of the college is not surpassed in landscape beauty, or salubrity,

Manhattan College, northeast corner of the Boulevard and West 131st Street. View to the northeast, c. 1867, prior to the northward continuation of the Boulevard, showing main buildings on the left and the Church of the Annunciation (Edson & Englebert, 1854) on the right. SC.

Manhattanville College of the Sacred Heart, site bounded by Convent, Cliff, and Hamlin Avenues and West 130th and West 137th Streets. View to the north of the main building (1847). SC.

by that of any similar institution in the country. . . . The hum and the bustle of the busy world are excluded by sloping hills and shady groves, the *tout ensemble* of which, as seen from the recitation-rooms and dormitories, is well calculated to give the youthful mind a studious and thoughtful turn."[102] The college founders had been attracted to the site in large part because of its proximity to another important Catholic institution, the Convent of the Sacred Heart. One founding member of the faculty wrote to another upon surveying the proposed Manhattanville site, "You see, Brother, the height crowned with a cross. To the left you see another, though lower eminence. Now, we gentlemen have been thinking how gratifying it would be to the Catholics of New York to see another cross crowning the summit opposite the Convent."[103]

On the site when the college took over were two wood-frame buildings with attached barns. These were divided and converted into classrooms, dormitories, a refectory, and a chapel. By 1863 a four-story main building, incorporating a mansard roof and a tower surmounted by a cross, had been completed. In 1867 excavation work began for the northward continuation of the Boulevard, slicing so close to the school's main building that the extensive rock outcropping on which it stood was blasted out and the building reconstructed, yielding two additional "basement" stories. A wing fronting the newly created Boulevard was added and a new principal entrance facing the thoroughfare established, taking away from the campus's sense of seclusion and lending the college more of a civic presence in an increasingly urban part of the city. The main building was expanded again in 1883. By the early 1890s construction in the surrounding area had been so extensive that the college no longer commanded views of the Hudson River.

Just northeast of Manhattan College stood the Manhattanville College of the Sacred Heart, founded in 1841 as a convent and academy for women.[104] The college occupied the former Lorillard estate high above the heart of Manhattanville on a parklike site ultimately bounded by 130th and 137th Streets and Convent, Cliff, and Hamlin Avenues.

View to the northwest, c. 1896, from West 110th Street west of Morningside Drive, showing, from left to right, the Leake and Watts Orphan Asylum (Ithiel Town, 1843), the Cathedral of St. John the Divine (Heins & La Farge, 1889–1911), seen under construction, and St. Luke's Hospital (Ernest Flagg, 1892–96). MCNY.

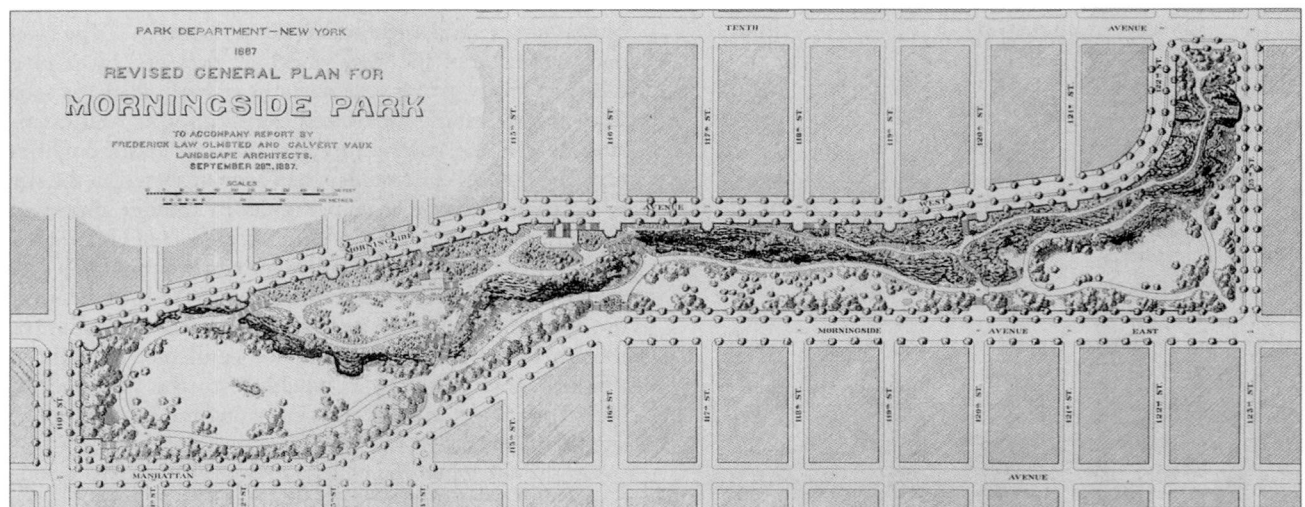

Morningside Park, Morningside Avenue to Morningside Drive, West 110th to West 123rd Street. Frederick Law Olmsted and Calvert Vaux with Jacob Wrey Mould, 1887. Revised plan. FLONHS.

In 1847 Manhattanville College erected a three-and-a-half story, battlemented, Romanesque main building. When fire destroyed the building in 1888, the college built expanded facilities designed by William Schickel.[105] The new buildings were vaguely medieval in their appearance, incorporating pointed-arch windows and towers with conical roofs.

Morningside Heights

The elevated ground immediately to the south of Manhattanville was in the seventeenth century largely covered by farms and known as Vanderwater's Heights, bearing the name of a local landowner. In the eighteenth century the area was known as Harlem Heights, a name made famous by the Revolutionary War's Battle of Harlem Heights, which took place in 1776 west of Broadway between 107th and 130th Streets.[106] By the 1870s the area was known as Morningside Heights.[107] In contrast to Washington Heights to the north, which by that time was dominated by suburban villas, Morningside

Heights was largely undeveloped except for the presence of two charitable institutions: the Bloomingdale Insane Asylum, which beginning in 1818 enjoyed a campuslike setting bounded by Broadway and Amsterdam Avenue and 116th and 120th Streets (the site was later expanded to extend from 113th to 122nd Street), and the Leake and Watts Orphan Asylum, which beginning in 1843 occupied a site bounded by Amsterdam Avenue and the escarpment to the east and 110th and 112th Streets. Even after 1880, the area languished in relative isolation because the Ninth Avenue elevated swerved eastward at 110th Street to avoid the steep climb up Morningside Heights. Since 1872, Morningside Heights had been permanently isolated from the plain below by Morningside Park, designed by Frederick Law Olmsted and Calvert Vaux, with Jacob Wrey Mould. The men had been charged with the task of turning a truly formidable geographic obstacle into a landscape amenity.[108] Morningside Park, stretching from 110th to 123rd Street and

Morningside Park, Morningside Avenue to Morningside Drive, West 110th to West 123rd Street. Frederick Law Olmsted and Calvert Vaux with Jacob Wrey Mould, 1887. View to the north. Johnston. NYHS.

Morningside Park, Morningside Avenue to Morningside Drive, West 110th to West 123rd Street. Frederick Law Olmsted and Calvert Vaux with Jacob Wrey Mould, 1887. View to the northeast from Morningside Drive between West 115th and West 116th Streets. NYHS.

from Morningside Avenue to Morningside Drive, though small by comparison with Central Park or Riverside Park, was deemed critical to the future growth of northern Manhattan. According to an 1872 article in the *New York Times*, the thirty-two-acre park was probably given its name by Olmsted, who was said to have chosen it because of the "fact that it possesses a sunny exposure in the early morning hours. From it a clear and unobstructed view of the [Long Island] Sound and its mooring craft can be obtained at all times."[109]

The decision in 1867 to revise the street grid and create a park, as well as to create what would become Morningside Avenue and Morningside Drive, was hardly idealistic, as Olmsted and Vaux pointed out in 1887: "Had it been determined to carry streets through the property . . . at the usual intervals . . . [there] would have been . . . a difference of millions of dollars in the cost of preparing them in the usual manner for close permanent building. The simplest way to avoid this was for the city to take possession of the ground, and the easiest legal way to take possession of the ground was to ordain, as a matter of form, that it should be called a park."[110] Olmsted and Vaux were in fact reluctant to take the project on, believing that the city did not need another pastoral park, which the real estate community, seeking to repeat the successes that followed the construction of Central Park, vigorously advocated. Instead, the park designers pointed to other types of open space that New York lacked:

> The city is still deficient in many provisons which unquestionably will soon be urged upon it by advancing civilization: such as already exist in the principal towns of Europe, and for which considerable spaces of open ground are necessary. New York, for example, has no ground for the athletic exercises of young men, the open spaces of the Central Park not being suitable for this purpose, and being already devoted to the athletic education of the children of the city, for whose use they will eventually prove much too small—no grand promenade, the Central Park roads and walks being designed for rural and not for urban recreation. It has no proper market places, no fair grounds nor places adapted to the display of fireworks or other exhibitions. Within four miles of Morningside Park there is no ground suitable to exercises in arms, civic receptions, or any great public ceremonies. There is no ground in the city or its suburbs adapted to special education in general botanical science, arboriculture, horticulture, pharmacy or zoology, nor have any of the thirty-five reservations, large and small, termed parks, in New York and Brooklyn, been selected for or devoted to any of these purposes. Unfortunately Morningside Park but adds another public ground chosen without the slightest reference to any of these special requirements of the city, and happens to be singularly incapable of being adapted to them.[111]

Despite their belief that the site might be put to better use, Olmsted and Vaux began to plan Morningside Park in 1873, three years after the land had been acquired by the city. Work did not proceed until 1881, when construction of Morningside Drive was begun according to detailed plans prepared by Jacob Wrey Mould, who had a thirty-year association with the New York City Department of Public Parks, serving as its architect in chief from 1870 to 1871. Naively ignoring the likelihood of future development on the Harlem Plain, Olmsted and Vaux had envisioned Morningside Drive as an urban promenade that would take advantage of a spectacular view eastward "far out across a wide range of beautiful country, and over waters and islands of the river and sound, the eastern seagate of the metropolis" while forming a link between Central Park and Riverside Park so that pleasure seekers in carriages or on horseback could complete a circuit through a chain of parks that would have the West Seventy-second Street Parkway as its final link. At the southeast corner of Morningside Park, adjoining the 110th Street connection to Central Park, Olmsted and Vaux proposed an aquatic garden of subtropical plants. The middle portion of the park was to be developed in "an urban and gardenesque style," while the northern end would be home to a lawn as well as an alpine rock garden.[112] The city had stipulated that the park contain a large exhibition building; Olmsted and Vaux proposed placing the structure between 113th and 114th Streets, a site that would have required considerable leveling.

In August 1887, after Mould's design for Morningside Drive had been largely executed, Olmsted and Vaux were called back to the job and asked to "revise and complete their plan" for the park proper, which would be finished by the end of the year.[113] In October the designers made their report. Though they found Mould's handling of Morningside Drive a bit more monumental than they would have liked, they were primarily concerned with the impact of the now rapidly urbanizing Harlem Plain on the park. Especially important to them was the construction of an elevated railroad along 110th Street between Eighth and Ninth Avenues and an elevated station at 116th Street and Eighth Avenue. Much to Olmsted and Vaux's credit, the new urban realities were recognized and the park, once envisioned as a preserve for carriage-parading swells, was redesigned as a destination for urban straphangers. Where Central Park and Morningside Park were to have connected, the construction of the elevated railroad formed a distinct barrier between the two. Acknowledging this in their new design, Olmsted and Vaux relocated the main entrance from 110th Street to 116th Street and Morningside Avenue. Inside the park, pathways were accordingly reconfigured. Additionally, the exhibition hall was eliminated from the plan and the park's increased accessibility, according to the designers, "makes necessary a more careful avoidance of nooks and passages which, with crowds entering them, are likely to be glutted, and requires that precautions should be observed against dangers that increase with the pressure of throngs."[114]

View to the west of Carmansville, Tenth Avenue to the Hudson River, West 142nd to West 158th Street, showing the Hudson River and New Jersey in the distance. MCNY.

View to the south of Carmansville, Tenth Avenue to the Hudson River, West 142nd to West 158th Street, showing the Hudson River on the right. MCNY.

Carmansville

At the beginning of the post–Civil War period most of Harlem's choice sites, on the comparatively isolated high ground, remained in a more or less natural state. The land of Richard F. Carman was the first high-ground site to be developed with housing, becoming Carmansville, a suburban village stretching from 142nd to 158th Street and from the Hudson River to Tenth Avenue.[115] Carman had been poor as a child and rose to wealth as a building and land speculator in New York after the fire of 1835. When Carman's neighboring landowner, John James Audubon, died in 1851, Audubon's widow stimulated the area's suburban development by subdividing some of her twenty-four acre estate, Minnie's Land—the name of which had been taken from the Scottish term of endearment for Lucy Audubon's first name—into Audubon Park. Writing in

John James Audubon house (c. 1841), west of Riverside Drive between West 155th and West 156th Streets. View to the northeast, c. 1865. MCNY.

Trinity Cemetery suspension bridge, spanning the Boulevard at West 155th Street. Vaux & Withers, 1872. View to the northeast. NYHS.

Harper's New Monthly Magazine, the journalist T. Addison Richards described Audubon Park as a development of "charming country seats, all sharing in common the rural pleasures of a broad woodland stretch along a river marge."[116] Earlier, Lucy Audubon had sold other holdings to Trinity Church, which in 1842 had established the new Trinity Cemetery, between Amsterdam Avenue and Riverside Drive and 153rd and 155th Streets.[117] The creation of the Boulevard, which necessitated the exhumation of bodies, created a significant spatial interruption in the ruralesque cemetery. In 1872 Vaux & Withers linked the cemetery's two halves across the Boulevard with a spectacular suspension bridge, probably engineered by George K. Radford. At each end, brownstone towers with portcullis-like entries anchored the span and enhanced the landscape setting. In 1876 the cemetery was walled in, and five years later it was landscaped by Vaux & Co. In 1883, Calvert Vaux, with George K. Radford and Samuel Parsons Jr., designed a gatehouse and gatekeeper's lodge.

Commuters could reach New York from Carmansville via the Hudson River Railroad, which had its Carmansville station at the foot of 152nd Street. A village grew up in the 1860s, with a hotel and several churches soon followed by a police station (1871–72), the 32nd Precinct, located at 1854 Tenth Avenue, on the southwest corner of 152nd Street.[118] The French Second Empire–style building replaced an earlier precinct house (1864) on the site and was designed by the police department's official architect, Nathaniel D. Bush, who had been appointed to the job in the early 1860s as part of a citywide effort to modernize facilities. Bush's design was built from brick painted white and trimmed in brownstone and consisted of three stories plus a slate-shingled, iron-crested mansard. The

Trinity Cemetery suspension bridge, spanning the Boulevard at West 155th Street. Vaux & Withers, 1872. View to the north. MCNY.

32nd Precinct Police Station, 1854 Tenth Avenue. Nathaniel D. Bush, 1871–72. View to the southwest. King, 1893. CU.

complex included a stable building as well as an annex incorporating a jail and lodging space for vagrants.

In addition to suburban-style villas, churches, and civic buildings, the area was home to an ironworks and to Joseph Loth & Co.'s formidably scaled "Fair and Square" ribbon factory (1886), at 1828 Tenth Avenue, between 150th and 151st Streets.[119] Also in Carmansville were a number of New York–based institutions for healing and child care. The Colored Orphan Asylum and Association, founded in 1838, was the first to relocate to the Carmansville vicinity, moving from its property facing Fifth Avenue between Forty-third and Forty-fifth Streets after a savage attack on the orphanage during the Draft Riots of 1863, when the building was set on fire with 233 children inside.[120] Although the children were rescued, the building was destroyed. The trustees of the institute immediately moved the children into temporary housing at the Hickson Fields mansion, at 151st Street, until a new building, constructed on a campuslike site between 143rd and 144th Streets and Tenth and Eleventh Avenues, was completed in 1867. As designed by Carl Pfeiffer, the three-story-high, mansard-roofed, brick building, with its bold skyline, married the Rhenish Romanesque of the architect's native Germany to the era's prevailing taste for French

Joseph Loth & Co.'s "Fair and Square" ribbon factory (1886), 1828 Tenth Avenue. View to the northwest. RERG. CU.

Second Empire architecture. In addition, the orphan asylum's campus contained various outbuildings, including dormitories, a chapel, and an observatory.

In 1877, with the Colored Orphan Asylum and Association established on its own campus, the Fields mansion became home to the Hebrew Sheltering Guardian Society until the completion of a purpose-built facility (1881–84) for one thousand children, between 136th and 138th Streets and the Boulevard and Tenth Avenue.[121] Established in 1860 by the Hebrew Benevolent Society, the asylum, which previously had been housed in a much smaller facility at Third Avenue and Seventy-sixth Street, catered to orphans as well as to children from abusive or broken homes. As designed by William H. Hume, who was awarded the job through a competition, the sprawling, pressed-brick, sandstone-trimmed, mansarded building had a central 60-by-150-foot, four-story pavilion flanked by two three-story wings, each 50 by 145 feet. The building's opening was attended by the political leader and journalist Carl Schurz and by Mayor Franklin Edson.

Close by, another Jewish charity, the Montefiore Home for Chronic Invalids, established in 1884 to serve 140 incurables of both sexes, was housed in an elegantly detailed, four-story, pavilionated hospital (1889) occupy-

Colored Orphan Asylum and Association, Tenth to Eleventh Avenue, West 143rd to West 144th Street. Carl Pfeiffer, 1867. Rendering of view to the northwest. MCNY.

Hebrew Sheltering Guardian Society, Tenth Avenue to Bloomingdale Road, West 136th to West 138th Street. William H. Hume, 1881–84. View to the northwest of the Tenth Avenue facade. NYHS.

Montefiore Home for Chronic Invalids, east side of Broadway between West 138th and West 139th Streets. Brunner & Tryon, with Buchman & Deisler, 1889. View to the east. NYHS.

Sheltering Arms, south side of West 129th Street between Tenth Avenue and Old Broadway. View to the southeast showing, from right to left, Furness Cottage (Ralph Townsend, 1881), May Cottage (Ralph Townsend, 1879), and Sheltering Arms's main building (C. C. Haight, 1869). SC.

Sheltering Arms, south side of West 129th Street between Tenth Avenue and Old Broadway. C. C. Haight, 1869. View to the southwest. SC.

ing a site on the east side of the Boulevard between 138th and 139th Streets. The plan of the new hospital, designed by Brunner & Tryon in association with Buchman & Deisler, was, according to *Building* magazine—"now accepted as a model for this class of building—that is, of a central or 'administrative' building and two wings—one for male and one for female patients."[122] A far cry from the mansarded irregularities of Hume's building for the Hebrew Sheltering Guardian Society, the freely adapted elements of the French Renaissance style were admirably suited to a plan inspired by the most advanced hospital design then to be found, that of the pavilionated hospitals of Paris.

Another notable charitable institution located near Carmansville was Sheltering Arms, devoted to homeless children.[123] Founded in 1864 by the rector of St. Michael's Church, in 1869 Sheltering Arms moved from 101st Street and Broadway to its first purpose-built home, on the southwest corner of Amsterdam Avenue and 129th Street, where it occupied a red brick Gothic Revival building consisting of two stories and a mansard, designed by C. C. Haight to house two hundred children.[124] Two red brick buildings known as the May and Furness Cottages were completed in 1879 and 1881 respectively; designed by Ralph Townsend, they occupied the western end of Sheltering Arms's blocklong site on the south side of 129th Street between Old Broadway and Amsterdam Avenue.[125] Just to the south, facing the north side of Lawrence Street, Napoleon Le Brun completed the red brick and stone-trimmed Engine House Number 37 in 1882.[126]

Engine House Number 37, north side of Lawrence Street between Tenth Avenue and Old Broadway. Napoleon Le Brun, 1882. View to the northeast. SC.

Washington Heights

Beyond Carmansville, roughly between 135th and 145th Streets, was Washington Heights.[127] (Beginning in the 1920s the name Washington Heights referred exclusively to the area in upper Manhattan bounded by the Harlem and Hudson Rivers and 155th and Dyckman Streets.) Like other areas above the Harlem Flats, Washington Heights was an oasis of suburban-style villas until the 1880s, when the elevated along Eighth Avenue made it relatively easy to travel back and forth on a daily basis between downtown and home, at least for those willing to negotiate the hill. One important survivor of the area's rural past was Alexander Hamilton's grand country house, the Grange, designed by John McComb Jr., which had been built in 1801 near what would become the intersection of Convent Avenue and 145th Street. In 1886, when what had been Hamilton's twenty-three-acre estate became the property of William H. De Forest, the future of the Grange was at risk just as the artistic importance of the long-neglected house was coming to be appreciated, a situation not lost on the *Real Estate Record and Builders' Guide*: "[The] Hamilton mansion . . . is one of the finest remaining specimens of the Colonial Classic style of architecture—a style which has a great deal of intrinsic merit, together with its interesting associations, and is often reproduced by leading architects at this day."[128] In 1889 the house was rescued for posterity when it was moved two blocks south from its historic site to 143rd Street and Convent Avenue, where it was put to service as the rectory for R. H. Robertson's St. Luke's Church.

Washington Heights was still a desirable place in which to build a villa during the late 1870s, when Eugene Kelly began building an elaborate spread that stood nearby at 136th Street; it was later extended north from just above 135th Street to 137th Street on the west side of the Boulevard by the prominent publisher Oswald Ottendorfer.[129] The compound included a rather fanciful Moorish pavilion (1879) designed by William Schickel, as well as a two-and-a-half-story Swiss cottage for the groundskeeper and a stable, also designed by Schickel. In 1887 the architectural firm of Brunner & Tryon published plans for a development of six stone villas to be built on Tenth Avenue north of 140th Street.[130] But perhaps because the future of Washington Heights as a more intensely developed city neighborhood was becoming clear to developers, the building group was never realized.

When the sale of the Hamilton estate resulted in the development of the historic landholding in the mid-1880s, real estate pressures had rendered the construction of freestanding houses largely a thing of the past. Nonetheless, in 1886 Theodore Minot Clark, a Boston architect who had assisted H. H. Richardson, designed three houses on adjacent sites, one of which was not built and one of which was realized for Nathan Hobart on the northwest corner of 146th Street and St. Nicholas Avenue.[131] The forty-by-sixty-foot, picturesquely massed villa, consisting of three

Grange (John McComb Jr., 1801), originally near the intersection of Convent Avenue and West 145th Street. View to the northeast, c. 1892, after the house's relocation in 1889 to the east side of Convent Avenue opposite West 143rd Street. MCNY.

Oswald Ottendorfer estate, west side of the Boulevard between West 135th and West 137th Streets. View to the west showing the pavilion (William Schickel, 1879). SC.

Nathan Hobart house, northwest corner of St. Nicholas Avenue and West 146th Street. Theodore Minot Clark, 1886. View to the north-west and ground-floor plan. BLDG. CU.

Nathan Hobart house, northwest corner of St. Nicholas Avenue and West 146th Street. Theodore Minot Clark, 1886. View to the southwest and second-floor plan. BLDG. CU.

stories and a basement, was notable for its boldly projecting domed corner tower and elaborately dormered and chimneyed roofline. More in keeping with development trends in the area, Clark also completed three houses (1885–86) of a four-house row he designed for the west side of St. Nicholas Avenue between 146th and 147th Streets.[132] The houses, like several others in the area, were faced with Manhattan schist, and also featured brick, yellow terra cotta, and wood shingles, and culminated in conical turrets. William Mowbray was the architect of a row of eight houses (1886–90) at 453–467 West 144th Street, between Convent and Amsterdam Avenues, developed and built by Mowbray's father, Anthony, working together with William H. De Forest Jr.[133] One of the most ambitious undertakings in the area, Mowbray's row was carefully adjusted to the sloping street. With generous setbacks, it provided raised terraces separating the front yards from the sidewalk. A varied mix of motifs suggesting inspiration from the Romanesque, Gothic, and Tudor styles gave each house in the row a distinct individuality.

Houses, southwest corner of St. Nicholas Avenue and West 147th Street. Theodore Minot Clark, 1885–86. View to the northwest. MCNY.

Mowbray also designed eight similar houses on the south side of the street at 452–466 West 144th Street, built by De Forest, who had inherited the property from his father and who constructed buildings on most of the remaining open land of the former Hamilton estate.[134] Other fine rows of houses were built, including Adolph Hoak's picturesque fifteen-house row (1887–90) at 311–339 Convent Avenue,[135] and a five-house Romanesque-inspired group (1887–90) by T. Hurtell Dunn, built for Jacob D. Butler at the northeast corner of West 144th Street and Convent Avenue.[136] H. L. Page and William W. Kent proposed a five-house row on West 144th Street near Tenth Avenue, but the project was never realized.[137] Dunn's elaborate six-house group (1889) at 413–423 West 144th Street, on the northeast corner of Convent Avenue, erected for A. H. Powell, formed a carefully composed row that assured the individuality of each house.[138] Perhaps the area's most imposing row was at 718–730 St. Nicholas Avenue (1889), between 146th and 147th Streets, a limestone-faced group of seven houses designed for George

453–459 West 144th Street. William Mowbray, 1886–90. View to the north. SA. CU.

Houses, northeast corner of Convent Avenue and West 144th Street. T. Hurtell Dunn, 1887-90. View to the northeast. BLDG. CU.

718–730 St. Nicholas Avenue. Arthur B. Jennings, 1889. View to the northeast. OMH.

St. Luke's Church, north side of West 141st Street between Hamilton Terrace and Convent Avenue. R. H. Robertson, 1892. Rendering showing unrealized tower at the northeast corner of Convent Avenue and West 141st Street. AR. CU.

Daiker by Arthur B. Jennings, who bookended the row with strongly modeled turrets rising to conical roofs.[139]

Commanding a spectacular site on Washington Heights, R. H. Robertson's St. Luke's Church (1892), on the north side of 141st Street between Hamilton Terrace and Convent Avenue, was among the city's most impressive churches.[140] The church was built in recognition of the northward migration of the downtown St. Luke's parishioners; the original church, located on Hudson Street in Greenwich Village, was sold to Trinity Church Parish for use as a mission parish in what had become a densely populated working-class neighborhood. The new church was believed by Montgomery Schuyler to be "the most successful" of Robertson's Romanesque-inspired churches. Like Robertson's St. James Protestant Episcopal Church (1883–84) (see chapter 2) and his Rutgers Riverside Presbyterian Church (1887–89) (see above), St. Luke's remained incomplete, with the critical tower element missing. Robertson took advantage of the dramatically sloping site, which was a full story lower at the east beneath the apse, where he created a raised terrace, upon which he set his boldly scaled, elaborately worked, clearly articulated stone church. Despite the fact that the church was never finished, Schuyler found much to like, praising the "notably severe" treatment of the composition for "its effect on the disposition and proportion of its masses alone. This has been so successfully studied that the result is one of our most noteworthy churches."[141]

Reverend Dr. Maunsell Van Rensselaer house, 22 St. Nicholas Place. Carl Pfeiffer, 1884. Rendering of view to the northeast. BLDG. CU.

F. W. Seagrist house, St. Nicholas Place at West 153rd Street. C.P.H. Gilbert, 1887. Rendering. BLDG. CU.

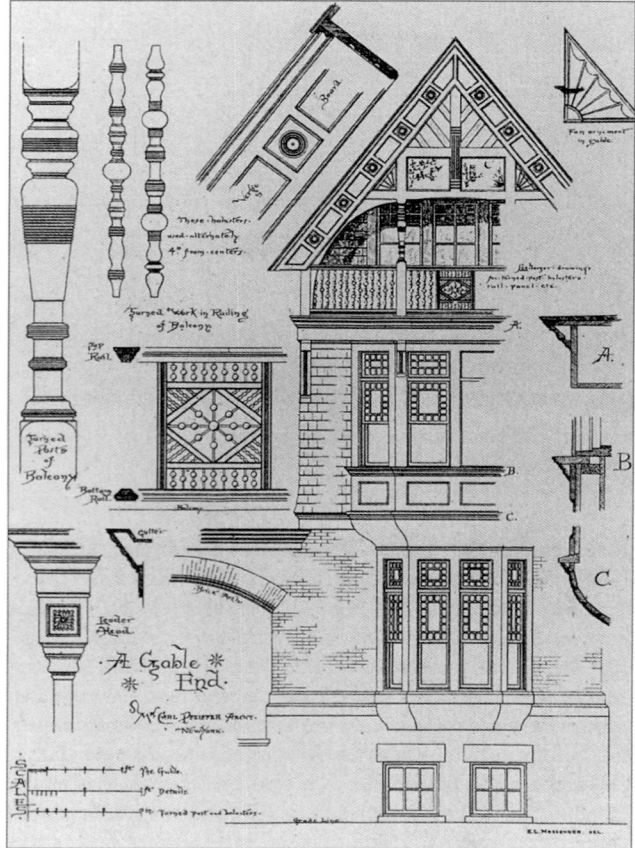

Reverend Dr. Maunsell Van Rensselaer house, 22 St. Nicholas Place. Carl Pfeiffer, 1884. Gable details. BLDG. CU.

The Island's Northern Tip

North of Washington Heights, Manhattan Island remained rural, with a few notable houses such as the imposing turreted and half-timbered double house (1884) of the Reverend Dr. Maunsell Van Rensselaer, designed by Carl Pfeiffer, at 22 St. Nicholas Place.[142] In 1887, C.P.H. Gilbert published drawings of a three-story, stone-faced, Queen Anne–inspired house for F. W. Seagrist; despite a narrow site, the house, on St. Nicholas Place at 153rd Street, managed to incorporate a gravel drive along the side leading back to a three-stall stable.[143] In 1888, construction concluded on Samuel B. Reed's sprawling, turreted, stone-faced, gabled house (1886–88) at 10 St. Nicholas Place, on the northeast corner of 150th Street, for James Anthony Bailey, partner in the famous Barnum & Bailey Circus, which had been founded in 1881.[144] The Bailey house, an appropriately flamboyant design for a great showman, incorporated the exterior use of Belcher mosaic glass. Inside it contained rooms designed by Joseph Burr Tiffany, a cousin of Louis Comfort Tiffany. Occupying the southwest corner of Convent Avenue and West 150th Street was a remarkable row of two-and-a-half-story Shingle Style townhouses, completed in 1887, that incorporated a varied building silhouette punctuated by dormers, chimneys, and a turreted corner tower.[145] The row brilliantly demonstrated the adaptability of the style to an urban context. The row has been attributed to John H. Duncan, but that architect's work was usually in the Classical mode.

Farther north still, the house that had belonged to Madame Eliza Jumel, the widow of Alexander Hamilton's

James Anthony Bailey house, 10 St. Nicholas Place. Samuel B. Reed, 1886–88. View to the northeast. MCNY.

View to the north, c. 1890, of St. Nicholas Place, showing St. Nicholas Avenue on the left and the James Anthony Bailey house (Samuel B. Reed, 1886–88), with turreted tower, on the right. MCNY.

Houses, southwest corner of Convent Avenue and West 150th Street. John H. Duncan, 1887. View to the southwest, 1932. NYPL.

nemesis, Aaron Burr, enjoyed a happier fate than that of the Grange, escaping both the wrecker's ball and adaptive reuse.[146] Located near what would become the intersection of Edgecombe Avenue and 160th Street, the mansion had been built in 1764 by its first occupants, Colonel Roger Morris, a member of the British Executive Council of the Province of New York, and his wife, Mary Philips Morris, who reputedly had a romantic liaison with George Wash-

ington before her marriage. Sometimes attributed to the architect John Edward Pryor, the house, with a double-story portico and octagonal wing, was an excellent essay in Palladian aesthetics, and clearly reflected the tastes of Morris, whose father was a well-established Palladian architect in England. In 1783, with the cessation of the Revolutionary War, the house was confiscated, and after serving as a popular inn was purchased in 1810 by Stephen

Madame Eliza Jumel house, near the intersection of Edgecombe Avenue and West 160th Street. Attributed to John Edward Pryor, 1764. View to the north, 1902, showing the Harlem River in the distance. Bracklow. NYHS.

Madame Eliza Jumel house, near the intersection of Edgecombe Avenue and West 160th Street. Attributed to John Edward Pryor, 1764. View to the north, 1890. Bracklow. NYHS.

View to the west, c. 1900, of Sylvan Terrace, showing rows of houses (George Robinson Jr., 1882) with St. Nicholas Avenue in the background. LPC.

Isabella Heimath residence, west side of Tenth Avenue north of West 190th Street. William Schickel & Co., 1889. View to the northwest. King, 1893. CU.

and Eliza Jumel. After Stephen Jumel died in 1832, Eliza Jumel married Aaron Burr; following Burr's death four years later, Jumel became a recluse, remaining in the house until her death in 1861. The property was in litigation for the next sixteen years. When the house was returned to use in 1887 as a result of Seth Milliken's purchase of the property, public awareness of its significance had grown to such an extent that the *Real Estate Record and Builders' Guide* called for its preservation by the New-York Historical Society "or some association."[147] Though the house was preserved, some of its land was sold off. To its west, in 1882, on land formerly part of the estate, George Robinson Jr. designed two rows of ten small wooden houses, each lining a side of a new street, Sylvan Terrace, that ran east from St. Nicholas Avenue to Jumel Terrace, where its vista was closed by the mansion itself.[148] Robinson's scheme, with its narrow street, tall wooden stoops running parallel to the houses, and simple clapboard facades, re-created the spirit of the old New York that was rapidly being destroyed downtown.

One important charitable institution chose the open country of northern Manhattan for its facility: in 1889, the Isabella Heimath, a home for old indigent German women, was opened at Fort George on Tenth Avenue just north of 190th Street.[149] First established in 1875 in Astoria, the institution had been founded as the result of a gift from Oswald Ottendorfer and his family, who had a villa nearby (see above), in honor of his late daughter, Isabella. As designed by William Schickel & Co., the new building consisted of a principal basement-and-three-story main portion with gabled dormers and a central cupola, as well as projecting wings forming a central court. The design was somewhat surprising, given Ottendorfer's heritage and his position as publisher of the *New Yorker Staats-Zeitung*, the city's leading German-language newspaper, owing far more to the English architecture of the Georgians than to anything German or Austrian.

Long Island Historical Society, southwest corner of Pierrepont and Clinton Streets. George B. Post, 1878–81. View to the south, c. 1881. BHS.

CHAPTER 7

❧ Brooklyn ❧

We have not, in a modern city like Brooklyn, such marked specimens of magnificent architecture as the ancient or mediaeval cities presented, and many of whose ruins yet remain. For *our* architectural greatness consists in the hundreds and thousands of suburban private dwellings, for the comfort and luxury of the great body of middle class people—a kind of architecture unknown until comparatively late times, and nowhere known to such an extent as in Brooklyn.

—Walt Whitman, 1862[1]

Brooklyn is no longer a village, but supports several business centres; and, as it spreads farther towards what is now its outskirts, other centres will spring up without interfering with the old ones.

—*Brooklyn Daily Eagle*, 1869[2]

The Historic Village

The land that became the village of Brooklyn was purchased from the Native Americans in 1636 by William A. Bennet and Jacques Bentyu. When it was declared a city by the state legislature, effective April 8, 1834, it consisted of five inhabited wards as well as four outlying ones devoted to agriculture. The new city's population of twenty-four thousand lived within a radius of about three-quarters of a mile from the area known as Fulton Ferry, beyond which there were no streets of consequence. The geographic area of the new city was bounded by the East River on the north and west, by Fulton Street on the east, and by Atlantic Avenue on the south. Twenty years earlier Robert Fulton had opened his steam-propelled ferry connecting New York and Brooklyn, choosing as his landing place the site where the village had begun, just below what would come to be known as Brooklyn Heights. Fulton's ferry not only opened the village to development as a bedroom suburb of New York but also fostered the development of a busy commercial and industrial hub. Ferry service between the two cities had been in operation since 1642 but steam power made it faster and more reliable than anything before, transforming Brooklyn so rapidly that it became an important center, leading to its incorporation as a village in 1816 and as a city eighteen years later. To honor Fulton's innovation, Ferry Road, which connected Brooklyn to Jamaica and the eastern end of Long Island, was rechristened Fulton Street.[3]

By the Civil War, ferries connected other points in Brooklyn to New York's downtown, but the Fulton Ferry, now part of the Union Ferry Company's system, remained the principal carrier. In 1865, just as plans were being formulated for the East River bridge that would eighteen years later render waterborne commutation between the two cities an anachronism, the Union Ferry Company built a new, picturesquely massed, elaborately wood-framed ferry house featuring a tower surmounted by a truncated, pyramidal, French Second Empire–style roof.[4] A statue of Robert Fulton was placed in a niche on the Fulton Street facade. The new Fulton Ferry Terminal may have been designed by Leopold Eidlitz, the architect of the company's Hamilton Ferry House (c. 1858).[5]

The commercial character of the area around Fulton Ferry was largely established by the 1830s, but important new buildings were added between the Civil War and the Panic of 1873. When the economy began to recover in the late 1870s, the inevitability of the bridge, rendering the ferry superfluous, doomed the neighborhood to backwater status. Front Street, Brooklyn's equivalent to Wall Street, was home to banks and insurance companies, the grandest of which were the office buildings that housed the recently founded Long Island Safe Deposit Company and the *Brooklyn-Union* newspaper. The Long Island Safe Deposit Building (William A. Mundell, 1868–69), at 1 Front Street, on the northwest corner of Old Fulton Street, was a two-story-high, boldly scaled, Venetian-inspired design

Fulton Ferry Terminal (1865), foot of Fulton Street. View to the northwest, c. 1870. BHS.

that presented its corner site with two finely detailed cast-iron facades.[6] A diagonal corner entrance led to the banking room, which was framed and ornamented in cast iron. Across the street, also with a diagonal corner entrance, was Leopold Eidlitz's severe, five-story, Ruskin-inspired Brooklyn-Union Building (1868).[7] Built by a short-lived newspaper founded during the Civil War to express Republican sentiment, the brick, sandstone-trimmed structure rose past a corbeled cornice to a mansard interrupted by elaborately treated pedimented dormers.

Among the Fulton Ferry area's memorable postwar buildings were two warehouses and a manufacturing plant. The first to be built, Nesmith & Sons' Empire Stores, was a powerfully massed, simple brick design notable for long rows of round-arched windows and doors, occupying almost the entire waterfront block between Main and Dock Streets, Water Street, and the East River.[8] Though in final appearance suggesting a single building, this commodities warehouse was in fact built in two stages, beginning in 1870 with Nesmith & Sons' four-story unit at the western end and concluding with

Brooklyn-Union Building, 2 Front Street. Leopold Eidlitz, 1868. View to the east, c. 1870, showing Old Fulton Street on the right. BHS.

Empire Stores, 53–83 Water Street, between Dock and Main Streets. Nesmith & Sons, 1870. View from the East River, c. 1880. BHS.

Thomas Stone's five-story portion (1884–85). The Gair Building (William Higginson, 1887–88), at 1 Main Street, was the first of a series of pioneering reinforced-concrete loft buildings built by Robert Gair, an early entrepreneur in the corrugated-box business.[9]

Last built among the Fulton Ferry area's great commercial buildings, Frank Freeman's Eagle Warehouse and Storage Company (1893), at 28 Old Fulton Street, on the southeast corner of Elizabeth Street, was one of a series of the architect's significant early designs based on H. H. Richardson's version of the Romanesque.[10] Arguably Brooklyn's leading architect, the Canadian-born Freeman immigrated to the United States in 1885, quickly settling in Brooklyn but maintaining an office in Manhattan. The facade of the six-story brick building was dominated by a monumental, low-sprung, vaulted archway displaying the inscription "Eagle Warehouse Storage Company" and by a severe, monumentally scaled parapet resting on a row of small corbeled arches. The high parapet incorporated a clock flanked by the company's name. Above the base, which was pierced by a slightly random pattern of iron-gated windows, a brick wall punctuated by five vertical tiers of flat-arched, boldly keystoned windows extended up through four stories.

Eagle Warehouse and Storage Company, 28 Old Fulton Street, southeast corner of Elizabeth Street. Frank Freeman, 1893. View to the south showing 1906 addition by Freeman on the left. PHB. CU.

Kings County Courthouse, southwest corner of Joralemon and Fulton Streets. Gamaliel King and Herman Teckritz, 1861–65. View to the southeast, c. 1870. BHS.

Farther up Fulton Street lay Brooklyn's Greek Revival City Hall (Gamaliel King, 1846–51), which, in an act of political foresight, had its front entrance on the north side, facing New York.[11] With the consolidation in 1855 of Brooklyn, Williamsburg, and Bushwick, new local and federal government buildings began to cluster around City Hall, including the Tuckahoe marble–clad, colonnaded, enthusiastically Classical Kings County Courthouse (Gamaliel King and Herman Teckritz, 1861–65), at the southwest corner of Joralemon and Fulton Streets and extending to Livingston Street.[12] King and Teckritz won the commission in competition, beating out the fledgling architect Peter B. Wight, whose oddly conceived, round-arched palazzo with a high mansard tower was influenced by the work of Eidlitz and by the ideas of Ruskin.[13] The architect of the Municipal Building (1876–78), just west of the County Courthouse, facing Joralemon Street, was also picked through competition.[14] Cornwall & Maynicke submitted a French Second Empire–style design, but Ditmars & Mumford won with its scheme for a five-story, 100-by-150-foot, marble-fronted, brick building, a severe version of the French Renaissance rising to a florid skyline of steep mansarded pavilions and a small dome. On the other side of the County Courthouse, on the southwest corner of Fulton Street and Boerum Place, stood William A. Mundell's 102-by-192-foot, white limestone and brick Hall of Records (1885–87), consisting of two stories and an attic.[15] The *New York Daily Tribune* observed that the "architecture is of the classic Renaissance period" and that "a handsome portico covers the main entrance."[16] Nearby,

the imposing, granite, castellated, four-story Kings County Jail (1879), on Raymond Street between Willoughby Street and DeKalb Avenue, also designed by Mundell, was, like New York's Tombs, a formidable symbol of public morality.[17]

Mifflin E. Bell's General Post Office (1885–91), on Johnson Street between Washington and Adams Streets, was the most grandly scaled building in Brooklyn's government center.[18] The somewhat academic design combined the Richardsonian Romanesque with more stiffly handled Classical elements from the Renaissance, an awkward mixture which can no doubt be attributed to the fact that the original architect was replaced in the course of construction by William A. Freret, Bell's successor as supervising architect of the Treasury Department, who was surely influenced by the period's emerging Classicism. But the deeply carved, boldly modeled, rock-faced and polished granite turrets and the steep, slate-covered roof overcame the ambiguities of style and the defects of the essentially blocky mass to make the building the area's most imposing monument.

Though not the biggest of the new civic structures, Frank Freeman's Fire Headquarters (1891–92), at 365–367 Jay Street, between Willoughby Street and Myrtle Avenue, was by far the most distinguished.[19] One of the most inventive essays in the Richardsonian Romanesque, Freeman's midblock building was broken into two unequal bays, the narrower of which was taller, rising two additional floors to form a campanile-like watchtower. The composition was highly articulated, from the bold,

Proposed Kings County Courthouse, southwest corner of Joralemon and Fulton Streets. Peter B. Wight, 1861. Elevation. AIC.

Municipal Building, south side of Joralemon Street between Fulton and Court Streets. Ditmars & Mumford, 1876–78. View to the southeast, 1910, showing the Kings County Courthouse (Gamaliel King and Herman Teckritz, 1861–65) on the left. BHS.

View to the southeast along the Fulton Avenue elevated, 1888, showing, from left to right, the Hall of Records (William A. Mundell, 1885–87), Kings County Courthouse (Gamaliel King and Herman Teckritz, 1861–65), and part of City Hall (Gamaliel King, 1846–51). Visible above City Hall is the top of the Municipal Building (Ditmars & Mumford, 1876–78). BHS.

Kings County Jail, east side of Raymond Street between Willoughby Street and DeKalb Avenue. William A. Mundell, 1879. View to the northeast, 1905. BHS.

low-sprung arch serving as a portal to the equipment shed to the tourelle-like corner piers and clustered intervening piers, suggesting that behind the picture of the facade lay a rigorous discipline based on the structural frame. Freeman was also responsible for two fine clubhouses in the area. For the Kings County Democrats he designed the three-bay-wide, seven-story, stone, terra cotta, and molded brick, Richardson-inspired Thomas Jefferson Association Building (1889–90), located on Boerum Place opposite the Hall of Records, featuring tourelle-like piers, two arched entryways, and a large bust of Jefferson set in a niche where the center bay concluded with a hipped roof.[20] Also in 1889–90 Freeman designed the four-story, sixty-by-one-hundred-foot Germania Club, at 120 Schermerhorn Street, between Smith Street and Boerum Place, in the Richardsonian Romanesque but far more volumetric than the Jefferson Club.[21] Home to the four-hundred-member German-American society, which was founded in 1860 and had been previously located in a building on Atlantic Avenue, the red Gatelawbridge stone, brick, and terra cotta building broke with the quiet streetwall of brick and brownstone rowhouses, pushing a bay window and a tower forward to the building line. Boldly paired party-wall chimneys gave the impression that the building's

manifest destiny was as a freestanding building on a much larger lot.

Commerce, in the form of shops and small office buildings, inevitably sprung up near the government buildings. Just past City Hall, where Fulton Street assumed an east-west orientation, lay Brooklyn's shopping district, one element of but by no means the greatest contributor to the area's visual clutter, which so troubled Montgomery Schuyler.[22] Here could be found the usual assortment of midcentury brownstone-faced commercial buildings and some residential buildings converted to commercial uses, such as 372–374 Fulton Street (1875), into which the restaurateurs Charles M. Gage and Eugene Tollner relocated their well-established eatery in 1892.[23] They remodeled the ground floor of the Italianate-style facade to provide a painted Neo-Grec storefront leading under a portico supported on paired modified Doric columns to a twenty-five-by-ninety-foot room furnished with a paneled bar and mahogany tables brought from their previous place of business. Nearby were such notable commercial enterprises as Ovington's (R. B. Eastman, 1883), at 250 Fulton Street, retailers of glass and ceramics. The store, according to *Building* magazine, was an essay in the Neo-Grec, making "free use . . . of

General Post Office, north side of Johnson Street between Washington and Adams Streets. Mifflin E. Bell and William A. Freret, 1885–91. View to the northwest, c. 1896. BHS.

Fire Headquarters, 365–367 Jay Street, between Willoughby Street and Myrtle Avenue. Frank Freeman, 1891–92. View to the east, 1910. Underhill. BPL.

terra-cotta in combination with brick, the peculiar construction compelling the use of the latter material in large blocks."[24] Parfitt Brothers, one of Brooklyn's most prolific architectural firms, designed two neighboring store buildings on Fulton Street between Gallatin Place and Hoyt Street in 1885: 418–420, a six-story, Euclid, Ohio, stone and terra cotta store and showroom, and 414–416, a six-story, twenty-six-by-ninety-foot stone building for the J. M. Horton Ice Cream Co.[25] Liebman Brothers occupied a four-story, stone, brick, and terra cotta building at 446 Fulton Street, on the southwest corner of Hoyt Street, designed by W. H. Beers in 1888.[26] George L. Morse's five-story building (1884–85) for Wechsler & Abraham, a department store, at 422–432 Fulton Street with an extension running to Gallatin Place, was a fairly dignified study in the Romanesque using Roman brick, brownstone, and granite.[27] Six years later, P. J. Lauritzen designed a seven-story building for the Wechsler store, now named S. Wechsler & Brother, at 203–215 Fulton Street.[28] Lauritzen also designed an eight-story, Nova Scotia stone, yellow brick, and terra cotta building (1889–90) for the clothiers Smith, Gray & Co.[29] Lauritzen took advantage of the prominent site at the junction of Fulton Street, Flatbush Avenue, and Nevins

Thomas Jefferson Association Building, east side of Boerum Place between Livingston and Fulton Streets. Frank Freeman, 1889–90. View to the east, c. 1900. BHS.

Germania Club, 120 Schermerhorn Street, between Smith Street and Boerum Place. Frank Freeman, 1889–90.
View to the southeast, c. 1896. BHS.

View to the north, 1890, toward the intersection of Fulton, Court, and Washington Streets from City Hall Park, showing the Fulton Street elevated railway (1887). BHS.

Street with a design reminiscent of H. H. Richardson's R. and F. Cheney Building (1875–76) in Hartford, Connecticut, featuring a series of Romanesque arcades at the base and a pyramidally roofed clock tower. Less than two years after its opening, the building was destroyed in a massive fire, on February 28, 1892.

The impact of ragtag commercial building on the dignity of the civic center was comparatively benign compared with that of the elevated railway (1887), which ran above Fulton Street from the Brooklyn Bridge south and east to Clinton and Bedford. Downtown merchants such as Ovington's and Wechsler & Abraham had advocated the construction of elevated railroads along Fulton Street and Myrtle Avenue as early as 1879, arguing that they were needed, as the *New York Times* put it, "to keep business in the city."[30] So startling was the impact of the elevated that Montgomery Schuyler, writing anonymously in the first volume of *Architectural Record*, remarked:

> Brooklynites seem to have devoted themselves of late to disfiguring [their civic center] with great energy and with a success which cannot be questioned. Unfortunately for them this region around about the City Hall, is the most conspicuous, the most thoroughly "in evidence" of the whole city, and it is also the most outrageous of aspect. The elevated road is the chief factor in this disfigurement, and perhaps remonstrance about that would be foolish as well as futile. "Business" is the Juggernaut before which we meekly prostrate, not only ourselves, but all our civic adornments and properties. . . . Anything like the con-

geries of ten-story office buildings and two-story sheds and litter and confusion that now characterizes it [the civic center] can scarcely be seen anywhere else this side of the Rocky Mountains. It looks, indeed, like a mining camp and a "boom" in active operation. It does not look like a Western city. It is much too "Western" and too crude. . . . Yet it is suffused without remonstrance by the inhabitants of the fourth city of the Union with a history going back two-hundred years.[31]

Montague Street, running west from Fulton Street to Furman Street, was Brooklyn's principal stretch of cultural institutions, beginning in 1861 with the construction of Leopold Eidlitz's Brooklyn Academy of Music, a turning point in Brooklyn's reputation as a city.[32] As the *New York Times* rather indelicately put it in 1865: "Five years ago Brooklyn was the worst appointed city in the North. Its public buildings were with one or two exceptions, devoted to religious worship, and for all purposes of amusement and entertainment there were but two respectable and popular places—the Brooklyn Institute and the Atheneum." But the Brooklyn Academy of Music changed all that, serving "as a lever with which the tone of the entire city has been changed."[33] Walt Whitman expressed the city's pride, extolling the building as a symbol that Brooklyn was no longer to be considered a provincial backwater. Said Whitman, the Brooklyn Academy of Music is "magnificent . . . so beautiful outside and in, and on a scale commensurate with similar buildings, even in some of the largest and most polished capitals of

View to the southeast along Montague Street, c. 1895, showing the Brooklyn Art Association (J. C. Cady, 1869–72) on the right and the Brooklyn Academy of Music (Leopold Eidlitz, 1861) in the center. BHS.

Europe."[34] The severe, pavilionated, German Romanesque–inspired design was Eidlitz's first important secular building. Montgomery Schuyler, in one of his earliest works of architectural criticism, praised Eidlitz's design extravagantly: "If anyone wishes to see how exquisitely the most varied material can be contrasted in the same frontage let him go and study attentively the facade of the Academy of Music. . . . See here how little the dark red surface of the walls is allowed to interfere with the form and outline of the beautifully enriched openings; how distinctly each door and window tells its own story; whether seen near or from a distance; and while the eye pleasantly takes in the whole mass, there is no funny fretting of details to mar the harmony."[35] Schuyler, who would remain a lifelong admirer of Eidlitz's work as well as a friend of the architect's, was not entirely blind to the design's peculiarities. In his 1883 review of J. C. Cady's recently completed—and in its way, equally severe—Metropolitan Opera House (see chapter 5), Schuyler recalled that the Brooklyn Academy had been described "by a satirist as an edifice which the subscribers intended to look as much like a church, in which 'they could hold a religious revival if they wanted to, and a Shakespearean revival if they had to.'"[36] In his memorial tribute to the architect published in 1908, five years after the Brooklyn Academy's destruction by fire, Schuyler gave the building its full due:

> Confined to a single street front, parallel with the axis of the interior, it was an attempt, then novel on this side of the ocean and not common on the other, to express a theatre in its exterior. There cannot be any question of the success. . . . The popular success was immediate and deci-

Proposed Mercantile Library, 195–199 Montague Street, between Clinton and Court Streets. Richard Morris Hunt, 1865. Elevation. The Octagon, AAF.

sive and the people of Brooklyn became and remained very proud of the place which for a generation was the centre and focus of their civic life, a function for which the very successful acoustics of the interior especially fitted it. The unusual expanse of the street front is relieved of monotony by the expression of each of its component parts, the green-room, the stage, the auditorium, the foyer, and it is full of character. That it is not an expression of the special character of a theatre was an early criticism. There is, indeed, something severe and almost monastic about the long front, with such sparing decoration as could be afforded under the conditions, at the ends and especially at the entrance . . . where the ornament, admirable in its kind and unfailingly placed and "scaled" was wisely concentrated. But blank wall, after all, is that of which the exterior of an auditorium must largely and the exterior of a stage almost exclusively consist, and blank wall, with even a minimum of architectural "treatment" is sure of making its impression. . . . The interior, in which the timber construction was exhibited throughout, in spite of the very pretty and rather festal and rather elaborate design and decoration of the proscenium, with its open gallery above, lighted from the ends, was also found by many observers architecturally too "strenuous" for a theatre, if not for an "Academy of Music." . . . But it would be hard to point to one of the successors of the Brooklyn Academy in either city or in any line, and quite hopeless to designate any successor in its own line which shows greater architectural individuality, or as great a power of robust, vigorous and masculine architectural expression.[37]

Proposed Mercantile Library, 195–199 Montague Street, between Clinton and Court Streets. Peter B. Wight, c. 1865. Preliminary design. AIC.

Though the writer for the *New York Times* seemed to share Schuyler's concerns about the exterior, he was lavish in his praise of the auditorium:

> The *tout ensemble* of the auditorium will strike everyone at first with astonishment, then with pleasure. The whole room, in its pillars, arches, panelings, and general decorations is, in form, technically Gothic; but all these are finished with most brilliant colorings, after the Moorish style, so that the whole effect is Moorish; and if closer inspection did not convince us that those decorative forms strictly belonged within the pale of the Gothic school we should not have had any other ideas than that they were drawn from Saracenic models. The colors are mostly brilliant reds and yellows, tempered by neighboring more delicate tints. The pigments are not in any way blended with each other, but put on pure and simple. This style of coloring is a remnant of a barbaric age, and gives also a certain barbaric splendor to the hall. The manner of decoration is by sawing out patterns of Gothic device in wood, fixing them upon the surface which they are to adorn, then laying in these rich Moorish colors, which by contrast and concord form a certain wild harmony, both unique and pleasing.[38]

With the opening of the Brooklyn Academy of Music, Montague Street almost overnight became the heart of Brooklyn's cultural life, attracting the Mercantile Library and the Brooklyn Art Association, which were built facing each other, the latter next door to Eidlitz's music hall. The commission for the Mercantile Library (1865–68), to be located on the north side of Montague Street, was awarded to Peter B. Wight through competition.[39] Wight won over Eidlitz, Jacob Wrey Mould, John Kellum, Charles Alexander, George Hathorne (who submitted an unsolicited plan), and Richard Morris Hunt, who proposed a symmetrically disposed, three-story, Ruskin-inspired Venetian design of exceptional refinement. The library had only been founded in 1857, so this building was to be its first permanent home. Wight's competition entry called for a red brick, Gothic-inspired building, Ruskinian in spirit but in no way Venetian, echoing the work of the English architect G. G. Scott. A charming oriel window counterpointing the crocketed Gothic arch over the entrance was eliminated in the final scheme, which was decidedly more severe, featuring a simplified porch framing the central entrance. Inside, a general reading room on the first floor was adequately illuminated by windows on the building's front and back, supplemented by a skylight. The library itself was on the second floor, where two levels of alcoves surrounded a central open space lit by a narrow clerestory. Despite the extensive use of cast iron for decorative features, Wight, who would in a few years become a leading proponent of fireproof construction, framed the building in wood, perhaps, as Sarah Bradford Landau has suggested, because he was already losing faith in cast iron as a fire-resistant material; Wight later was to claim that weak wood posts were better in a fire than strong iron ones. The library's interiors were brilliantly stenciled and furnished with pieces specially designed by Wight, reflecting the architect's particular antipathy to the mass-produced products in the market.

The library was soon joined by the Brooklyn Art Association (1869–72), J. C. Cady's first important commission.[40] To complete the job Cady joined forces with Henry M. Congdon in what can be assumed to have been a professional marriage of convenience—Congdon's father, Charles, was a member of the Brooklyn Art Association's council. The four-story building was boldly scaled and intensely Gothic, with motives said to have been derived from thirteenth-century French work but sifted through mid-nineteenth-century English taste, especially the work of William Burges, whose competition entry for the Law Courts (1866), in London, was one of the defining projects of the era. The design was influenced by a sense that Montague Street could become Brooklyn's equivalent to the promenading streets of government and culture taking form at the time in Europe, in particular, as Kathleen A. Curran has suggested, Munich's Ludwigstrasse. This point was not lost on A. A. Low, a prominent developer and one of the founders of the association, who at the building's dedication compared Cady's design to that of Friedrich von Gärtner's Staatsbibliothek (1831–40).[41] Cady's severe and planar scheme became fussily ornamented when executed—what had been Ruskinian became spikily Gothic. The impression of big scale came not only from the bold use of various gray, brown, and pink stones on the facade and from the polished serpentine colonnettes on the third-

Mercantile Library, 195–199 Montague Street, between Clinton and Court Streets. Peter B. Wight, 1865–68.
View to the northeast, 1876. BHS.

floor porch but also from the fact that the building rose sheer from the street and had its very foreshortened main entrance across a moat spanned by a half-flight of steps. A bold roofline, combining a dormer set in a steeply sloped slated roof with an exaggeratedly vertical tower gable, rendered the building an urban aggressor. Built on a vacant, fifty-foot-wide, one-hundred-foot-deep lot adjoining the Brooklyn Academy of Music, from which it was separated by about fifteen feet, Cady's Ohio stone building, trimmed in bluestone, Nova Scotia granite, and white and colored marbles, managed to hold its own. The asymmetrical composition of the facade with a corner entrance and a steeply pitched towerlike gable gave the impression that the building belonged to a venerable institution which had, before the city's recent burst of growth, enjoyed greater space. Inside, the building housed an art school as well as exhibition galleries, with one very long gallery connecting to the adjoining Academy of Music via a small covered bridge so that on important occasions it could be made available for assemblies and promenades.

Looking back on Cady's building twenty-five years after its completion, Montgomery Schuyler labeled it "a distinctly Gothic work. . . . It is not an imitation . . . in any sense that at all diminishes the credit of the . . . author."[42] Schuyler had been less kind in 1871, when he visited the Art Association during construction:

It is an elaborate Gothic front, unfortunately too much circumscribed in space, and thus, apparently, strung to make up in richness of detail what it could not obtain in space and perspective effects. Indeed there is no other alternative left to any building so situated. In this respect, therefore, the Academy of Art can be considered a success. The enrichments are very fine; evidently designed with much care and as carefully executed. The various stories that enter into the composition are well contrasted; the light Ohio stone against the darker cream color, producing a rich effect, and the slender Gothic shafts of variegated polished marbles are grand in appearance.

"From what can be seen in its unfinished" state, Schuyler continued, "the grand staircase at the entry appears to be a malformation." He particularly objected to the fact that the stair from the first to the second floor ran from back to front:

. . . as well might a gentleman be expected to present his back instead of his face to you on a first formal introduction. As for anyone on entering a public building be saluted by the soffit of the staircase! And the thing in the entrance hall bids fair to be a failure, and that is lining the walls internally with white bricks checkered with red. The effect is at best but very poor, and more fitted to a stable than anything else. But apart from this, the so-called white bricks have already become time-stained in all sorts of colors, from gamboge to brown sepia, producing a most motley appearance. Why such an innovation when we know our walls can be so beautifully decorated by the fresco-painter?[43]

One block away, at 128 Pierrepont Street, on the southwest corner of Clinton Street, would soon rise George B. Post's very red, Romanesque-inspired Long Island Historical Society (1878–81), the final component of Brooklyn's cultural center.[44] The society, founded in 1863, was part of the burst toward maturity that marked Civil War Brooklyn—the New-York Historical Society had been founded almost sixty years before, in 1804. After a short time in rented space the Long Island Historical Society secured a site, and in 1870 the building committee commissioned Leopold Eidlitz to prepare a design. The project was put aside when the society fell into debt, in part as a result of costs incurred repairing its collections after a fire in its rented quarters. In 1877, with the revival of the economy and the society's finances, a number of architects, including Eidlitz, were invited to participate in a competition. The caliber of architects who agreed to participate reflected the national importance of the project, and the sheer number underscored the fact that the depression had left architects with little work. The list included J. Pickering Putnam, from Boston; Herman J. Schwarzmann, a Philadelphia architect who would soon move to New York and join up with Albert Buchman; Solon Spencer Beman, of Chicago; from New York, Julius W. Adams, Alexander Jackson Davis, Hugh Lamb, Emlen T. Littel, George L. Morse, J. C. Cady, Alfred Thorp, Richard M. Upjohn, George B. Post, and Henry Hudson Holly; and three architects from Brooklyn, including Parfitt Brothers. Post's design was chosen over Cady's by a narrow margin. Of the other proposals, Putnam's Gothic scheme complemented Cady's Brooklyn Art Association, perhaps too much; Parfitt Brothers's design, despite its bays, dormers, corner turrets, and various other more or less Gothic features, was in fact very clear in its internal planning; and Henry Hudson Holly's proposal, with its large, Serlian-inspired windows, broad piers, and overall symmetry, was an accomplished and stylistically advanced reflection of the prevailing English Queen Anne taste.

Post's building was vivid without being garish, featuring tiles, vibrant red brick laid in black oil putty instead of black mortar, and brownstone and terra cotta—it was said to be the first building to use American-made terra cotta. One of the most distinguished public buildings of the 1870s, the boldly hipped roof design, with piled arcades and a banded attic story, was in some ways a warm-up for the architect's New York Produce Exchange (1881–84) (see chapter 3). To one side, facing Pierrepont Street, an asymmetrically placed tower with a pedimented dormer interrupting a pyramidal hipped roof marked the entrance, which was further decorated with a projecting porch. Portrait heads in the arcades by Olin Levi Warner and terra cotta ornament by Truman Hiram Bartlett lent a note of vivacious exuberance to the design, reflecting Post's sure sense of Classical form and detail.

The challenge presented to the architect by the society's trustees had less to do with aesthetics than with function: to produce a fireproof building that was well ventilated,

Proposed Long Island Historical Society, southwest corner of Pierrepont and Clinton Streets. J. Pickering Putnam, c. 1878. Perspective of view to the southwest. AABN. CU.

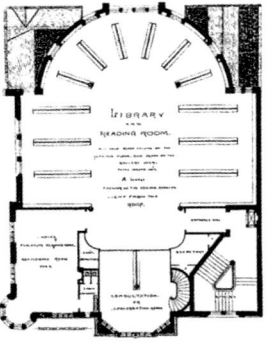

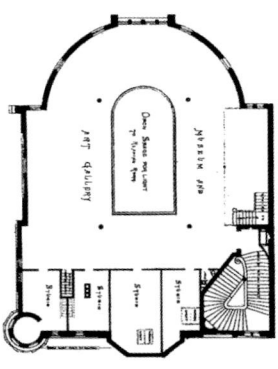

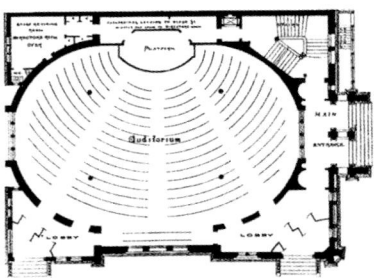

Proposed Long Island Historical Society, southwest corner of Pierrepont and Clinton Streets. Parfitt Brothers, c. 1878. Pierrepont Street elevation and plans. AABN. CU.

Long Island Historical Society, southwest corner of Pierrepont and Clinton Streets. George B. Post, 1878–81. View to the southwest, c. 1881, showing the Church of the Holy Trinity (Minard Lafever, 1844–47) on the left. BHS.

Long Island Historical Society, southwest corner of Pierrepont and Clinton Streets. George B. Post, 1878–81. Library, c. 1881. BHS.

Long Island Historical Society, southwest corner of Pierrepont and Clinton Streets. George B. Post, 1878–81. Auditorium, c. 1881. BHS.

and to incorporate both a library, which Post located on the second floor, and an auditorium, which he placed at street level. A remarkable space, the eighty-by-fifty-foot galleried library rose to twenty-four feet and was lit on three sides to bathe books, brick piers, black ash woodwork, and readers in an even light. Montgomery Schuyler found the building "simple in plan and outline," though he was quick to point out that the design was similar to Post's Chickering Hall (1875) (see chapter 5), in New York. Schuyler did not like the addition of a tower to the Brooklyn version, although he deemed Post's Brooklyn cornice "much less aggressive" than the one on the New York hall.[45] Russell Sturgis, looking back on Post's career in 1898, saw the Long Island Historical Society building as an early step in the revival of Classicism. He admired in particular the entrance porch, "adorned by, perhaps, the initial attempt to put the work of first-rate sculptors to use for architectural enrichment."[46]

The cultured ambience of Montague Street soon proved irresistible to commerce. The Brooklyn Real Estate Exchange (1890), at 189–191 Montague Street running through to Pierrepont Street, directly opposite the Brooklyn Academy of Music, was the first prominent commercial building on the street. Montgomery Schuyler, assessing the New York–based architect George H. Edbrooke's design as the third in his series of "architectural aberrations," viewed the building's great height—nine stories—as an almost unforgivable intrusion: "In truth [Edbrooke] could not have prevented himself from spoiling the street, whatever he did, and even if he had produced something that was in itself worth looking at. He could not have subordinated his commercial building to the public buildings." Nevertheless, Schuyler suggested, the architect turned bad to worse by designing "a building so reckless, in the face of quiet buildings a building so noisy, and in the face of harmonious buildings a building so discordant as to prove that he went about what to an artist would have been an ungrateful task in gaiety of heart; and he has produced a monument of what may be called aggressive and militant insensibility to architecture."[47]

Brooklyn Real Estate Exchange, 189–191 Montague Street, between Clinton and Court Streets. George H. Edbrooke, 1890. View to the northwest showing the Mercantile Library (Peter B. Wight, 1865–68) on the right. BHS.

Hotel Margaret, northeast corner of Columbia Heights and Orange Street. Frank Freeman, 1889. View to the northeast. PHB. CU.

Farther west along Montague Street was one of Brooklyn's earliest, most luxurious, and most architecturally distinguished apartment houses, Parfitt Brothers's Montague (1885–86), at 103–105 Montague Street, between Henry and Hicks Streets.[48] With a 51-foot frontage, the building was only twice as wide as a typical rowhouse, but its great depth of 90 feet and height of 150 feet made for an imposing mass, further enhanced by the strongly modeled, large-sized, Queen Anne–style pedimented gable that crowned the granite, brick, and terra cotta facade. Beyond the tiled vestibule was a hall serving the elevator accessing the building's seven floors, which contained fourteen apartments, fourteen servant bedrooms, a laundry and drying room, and a thirty-three-by-sixteen-foot attic party room for tenants. Other luxurious apartment houses were built nearby, including Parfitt Brothers's twin, seven-story, Queen Anne–style Berkeley and Grosvenor Apartments (1885–86), at 111–113 and 115–117 Montague Street.[49] Also of note was Montrose W. Morris's ten-story, fifty-by-ninety-two-foot, stone, brick, and terra cotta Arlington Apartments (1887), at 62–64 Montague Street, between Montague Terrace and Hicks Street, which contained twenty large apartments and ten bachelor apartments.[50]

Frank Freeman's Hotel Margaret (1889), at 97 Columbia Heights, on the northeast corner of Orange Street, a ten-story luxury apartment house built on a seventy-five-by-one-hundred-foot site, was a slightly less exuberant example of its designer's often Richardsonian work.[51] Housing thirty-nine families in what was the highest building in Brooklyn Heights and, after the Brooklyn Bridge, the area's most prominent landmark, the Margaret was executed in copper, buff brick, red pressed brick, terra cotta, and brownstone. It was notable for its fine detailing, ranging from Classical-inspired floral friezes to medieval strapwork to a technological representationalism manifest in a proliferation of projecting bolt-heads. Balconies and complexly banded corner towers rising to elaborately framed, hip-roofed belvederes further enhanced its distinction. A Roman entrance hall led to a lobby set under an immense glass dome.

A few blocks away, on the block bounded by Hicks, Henry, Oak, and Pineapple Streets, stood the Hotel St. George.[52] Designed by Augustus Hatfield in 1885 as eight stories and an attic, the building received numerous additions, beginning with Montrose W. Morris's work in 1890. An architecturally ambitious apartment house was built for a site nearby, at 105 Clark Street (1888–90).[53] As designed by C.P.H. Gilbert and rendered by the twenty-one-year-old architect and illustrator Bertram Grosvenor Goodhue, the five-story-high, townhouselike, forty-nine-by-eighty-foot brick and stone building, with an asymmetrical, steeply raked, pedimented gable and corner oriel rising to a faceted tile roof, skillfully merged a Richardsonian sense of tectonic simplicity with a Queen Anne domesticity. There was nothing about the design pointing to the scholarly essays in French Renaissance design that would be Gilbert's stock-in-trade in the coming decades.

105 Clark Street. C.P.H. Gilbert, 1888–90. Rendering by Bertram Grosvenor Goodhue. AABN. CU.

In 1890, on a site near the docks bounded by 2–34 Columbia Place, 315–345 Furman Street, and 20–26 Joralemon Street, Alfred T. White, a civil engineer who had graduated from Rensselaer Polytechnic Institute and inherited considerable wealth from a family-owned mercantile fur business, commissioned William Field & Son to create a version of the highly successful worker housing, the Tower and Home Buildings, that White had sponsored and Field had designed thirteen years before in South Brooklyn (see below).[54] Field's fortresslike, red brick and terra cotta Riverside dwellings, his and White's largest undertaking in the field of affordable housing, accommodated 280 families in nine buildings that wrapped a 255-by-115-foot landscaped courtyard and covered only 49 percent of the lot. The court featured a children's play area and a rustic, open-roofed, circular bandshell where White sponsored Saturday concerts. Though the rooms in the Riverside complex were small, the shallow plan ensured that they were bright and well ventilated. In a three-room apartment, two of the rooms were designated bedrooms while the third was reserved for living, dining, and, in a separate extension, cooking. Each apartment had its own toilet at the end of the kitchen but bathing facilities were communal and in the basement. There were a variety of unit sizes, ranging from two to four rooms. Rents were

Riverside, 2–34 Columbia Place, 315–345 Furman Street, and 20–26 Joralemon Street. William Field & Son, 1890.
View to the south of the Joralemon Street building, c. 1892. Riis. MCNY.

Riverside, 2–34 Columbia Place, 315–345 Furman Street, and 20–26 Joralemon Street. William Field & Son, 1890. View to the north of the courtyard, c. 1892. Riis. MCNY.

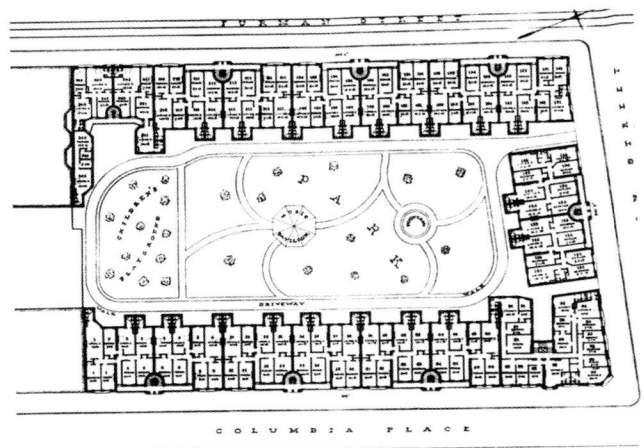

Riverside, 2–34 Columbia Place, 315–345 Furman Street, and 20–26 Joralemon Street. William Field & Son, 1890. Plan. MCNY.

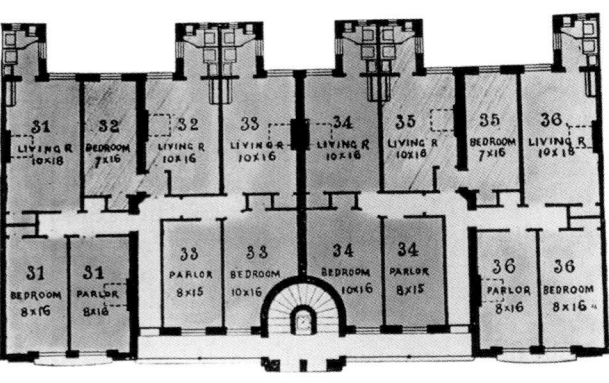

Riverside, 2–34 Columbia Place, 315–345 Furman Street, and 20–26 Joralemon Street. William Field & Son, 1890. Plan. MCNY.

Charles S. Kimball house, Columbia Heights near Fulton Street. Frederick Clarke Withers, 1865. Presentation drawing. M. and M. Karolik Collection. MFA.

Daniel Chauncey house, 129 Joralemon Street, between Henry and Clinton Streets. C.P.H. Gilbert, 1890. View to the north, c. 1893. BHS.

skewed, based on floor, location, and size of rooms. In his influential book *How the Other Half Lives* (1890), the reform-oriented journalist Jacob Riis applauded the Riverside apartments as "the *beau ideal* of the model tenement."[55]

Rowhouses were the most common type of residential construction undertaken in Brooklyn Heights in the mid-1880s. The three-house group at 108–112 Willow Street (1883), between Clark and Pierrepont Streets, was designed for the banker Spencer Trask by W. Halsey Wood, the Newark-based architect better known for his ecclesiastical work.[56] Terra cotta reliefs enlivened already lively facades filled with richly detailed doorways, bay windows, a turret, and profuse dormers, a particularly successful adaptation of the Queen Anne to a relatively dense urban setting. Each house retained its individuality yet somehow managed to contribute to an overall sense of the group. William B. Tubby's six-house row (1887–88) for Mrs. Packer, at 262–272 Hicks Street, on the southwest corner of Joralemon Street, was just about as delightful, with corbeled brickwork, shingles, and strong shapes conveying a sense of individuality to each house in the row.[57]

Many of the important single-family houses in Brooklyn Heights were built before the Civil War, especially in the 1850s when there was a surge in mansion building. One notable exception was put up after the war, Frederick Clarke Withers's Charles S. Kimball house (1865), on

Columbia Heights near Clark Street.[58] The three-bay, three-story, highly articulate, banded stone-faced essay in Ruskinian Gothic was notable for the rich polychromy of its facade and for its dramatic silhouette, a striking departure from its flat-roofed, comparatively sedate, prewar Italianate neighbors.

Little in the way of important townhouse construction seems to have taken place in Brooklyn Heights in the 1870s and 1880s. In 1890 a new scale came to the area with a series of massive houses by C.P.H. Gilbert, Parfitt Brothers, and Frank Freeman. Gilbert's Daniel Chauncey house, at 129 Joralemon Street, between Henry and Clinton Streets, was a grandly scaled, forty-foot-wide design consisting of three stories and an attic, featuring an exterior of thin Roman brick.[59] Parfitt Brothers's Hattie L. James residence (1890), at 6 Pierrepont Street, a Romanesque-inspired design with fine carving at the entrance stairs, was locked into its site by a broad bay window overlooking the harbor.[60] Farther inland, Frank Freeman's Herman Behr residence (1888–90), at 82 Pierrepont Street, on the southwest corner of Henry Street, was a vigorous Romanesque-inspired design with rock-faced walls, bay windows, and, at the top, a steeply pitched clay-tile roof.[61] Unlike Freeman's Germania Club (see above), the Behr house had a corner site that justified the three-dimensional modeling of the composition.

Not surprisingly given Brooklyn's reputation as a city of

Hattie L. James house, 6 Pierrepont Street, between Pierrepont Place and Willow Street. Parfitt Brothers, 1890. View to the south, 1922. BHS.

Herman Behr house, southwest corner of Pierrepont and Henry Streets. Frank Freeman, 1888–90. View to the southwest, c. 1891. AB. CU.

churches, there were some notable religious buildings in Brooklyn Heights, most dating from before the Civil War, including Richard Upjohn's Church of the Pilgrims (1844–46), at the northeast corner of Remsen and Henry Streets, and his Grace Church (1847–49), at the southwest corner of Hicks Street and Grace Court.[62] Minard Lafever's Church of the Savior (1842–44) stood at the northeast corner of Pierrepont Street and Monroe Place, and his Church of the Holy Trinity (1844–47) at the northwest corner of Clinton and Montague Streets.[63] Right after the war, Patrick C. Keely, the prolific architect specializing in Roman Catholic churches, designed the St. Charles Borromeo Church (1868), at 21 Sidney Place, reportedly his 325th church design.[64] The modest Gothic Revival house of worship catered to Roman Catholics living at the fringes of the hitherto almost exclusively upper-class Protestant neighborhood. Keely also designed St. Ann's Roman Catholic Church (1860), at the northwest corner of Gold and Front Streets.[65]

The still dominant Protestants were the great church builders, beginning with Renwick & Sands's elaborate St. Ann's Episcopal Church (1867–69), at the northeast corner of Clinton and Livingston Streets, a brownstone and terra cotta design combining Gothic Revival correctness with Ruskinian passion.[66] Lawrence B. Valk's two-story, brick and sandstone First Baptist Church (1877–78), at the northeast corner of Pierrepont and Clinton Streets,

St. Charles Borromeo Church, northeast corner of Sidney Place and Livingston Street. Patrick C. Keely, 1868. View to the northeast, c. 1870. BHS.

St. Ann's Episcopal Church, northeast corner of Clinton and Livingston Streets. Renwick & Sands, 1867–69. View to the northeast, c. 1910. BHS.

built on the site of an 1843 Baptist church, was notable for the ingenious plan of its worship room, a forty-foot-high, elliptically shaped, amphitheater-style auditorium, ringed on all sides by a gallery, oriented diagonally on the nearly square corner site, with the pulpit placed at the inside corner.[67] This arrangement would be adopted by Samuel B. Snook for his All Angels' Protestant Episcopal Church (1888–90), in New York at the southeast corner of West End Avenue and Eighty-first Street (see chapter 6). On the downslope of the Heights toward Atlantic Avenue was J. C. Cady's one-thousand-seat, fifty-four-by-one-hundred-

foot, Romanesque Revival German Reformed Church (1888), at 63 Schermerhorn Street, between Boerum Place and Court Street.[68] In 1889–91 the church architect John Welch designed a Belleville stone, bluestone, and brick, 75-by-107-foot home for the Sands Street Methodist Episcopal Church, at the southwest corner of Clark and Henry Streets, which had been forced out of its previous location by the encroachments of the Brooklyn Bridge.[69] The Romanesque Revival design featured a large square tower and a monumental round-arched corner entrance, forming a highly inventive, intensely site-specific composition.

First Baptist Church, northeast corner of Pierrepont and Clinton Streets. Lawrence B. Valk, 1877–78. View to the northeast, 1891. BHS.

Sands Street Methodist Episcopal Church, southwest corner of Clark and Henry Streets. John Welch, 1889–91. View to the southwest, 1891, showing the First Presbyterian Church (W. B. Olmsted, 1846) on the left. BHS.

South Brooklyn

Below Atlantic Avenue—that is to say, south of Brooklyn Heights—lay South Brooklyn, an area of farms and orchards which began to be developed as a residential quarter in the mid-1830s, when a dock was opened at the end of Atlantic Avenue and a ferry to New York was established.[70] While in some ways an extension of the Heights, principally because it enjoyed the same street grid, South Brooklyn was more a working-class neighborhood than a home to gentry because it was not elevated above the harbor and its western edge was lined with docks.

Atlantic Avenue, the boundary between South Brooklyn and the Heights, served each neighborhood as a business street, lined with a number of important banking structures. The Tuckahoe marble South Brooklyn Savings Bank (E. L. Roberts, 1871), at the southeast corner of Clinton Street, was a Neo-Grec design featuring elaborately finished interiors and an ingeniously constructed vault.[71] Across the street Journeay & Burnham established the area's largest retail dry-goods store, expanding over time.[72] The company, one of Brooklyn's largest, completed its holdings with a three-and-a-half-story iron, stone, and brick building at 121–125 Pacific Street (1879–81) designed in the Neo-Grec style by John A. Raymond.

Unquestionably, South Brooklyn's most significant post–Civil War development was the group of model row

South Brooklyn Savings Bank, southeast corner of Atlantic Avenue and Clinton Street. E. L. Roberts, 1871. View to the southeast, c. 1910. BHS.

Tower Buildings, 417–435 Hicks Street, 129–135 Baltic Street, and 136–142 Warren Street. William Field & Son, 1878–79. View to the southeast, 1891. BHS.

and apartment houses built for working-class families in 1876–79 by Alfred T. White.[73] White had visited model tenements developed by Alderman Sidney Waterlow's Industrial Dwelling Company in London and modeled his own project after their example. Waterlow's experiments had been reported to Brooklyn newspaper readers by Walt Whitman, who, in an article published in the *Brooklyn Times* on May 1, 1857, begged for builders to "mingle a little philanthropy with their money-making and to construct tenement houses with a view to comfort of the inmates as well as the maximum of rent."[74] White was also inspired by the 1865 report of the Council of Hygiene and Public Health, a subcommittee of the Citizens' Associa-

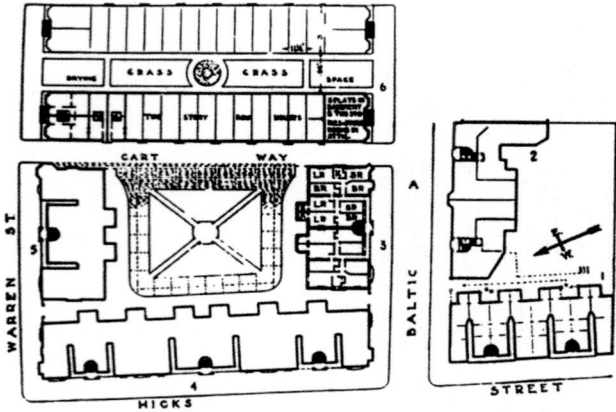

Tower and Home Buildings and Warren Place mews, east side of Hicks Street between Baltic and Warren Streets, 129–147 Baltic Street, 136–154 Warren Street, and Warren Place between Warren and Baltic Streets. William Field & Son, 1876–79. Plan. HHNYC. CU.

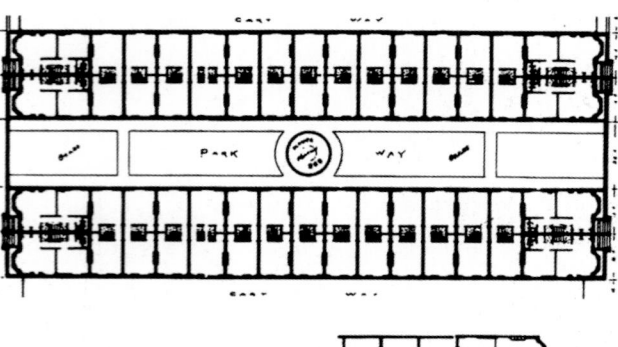

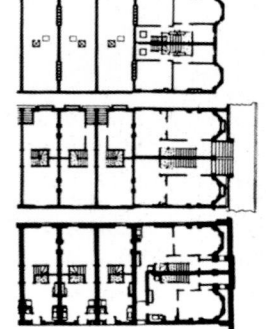

Warren Place mews, 139–147 Baltic Street, 146–154 Warren Street, and Warren Place between Warren and Baltic Streets. William Field & Son, 1878. Plan. BHW. CU.

tion of New York, which led to the passage in New York of the Tenement House Law of 1867.

White's development strategy was captured in the phrase "philanthropy plus seven percent." In his *Improved Dwellings for the Laboring Classes*, first published in 1877, White outlined his housing philosophy:

> Legislation is not the only thing needed; *private endeavor* must show the possibility of improving existing dwellings, or erecting improved dwellings which shall yield *a fair return on the capital invested*. It is not worth while to consider the Old World experiments in providing homes for the poor furnished in whole or in part *as a charity*, for this is neither necessary nor to be commended. The laboring classes now pay rents in New York which would yield a large interest on the cost of well-constructed and well-aired houses; but beyond this, the reception of a home as a species of charity is quite as harmful to the poor, quite as discouraging to the industrious, as the direct receiving of alms without adequate return in labor.[75]

White justified housing philanthropy as a way to help provide a transitional step for those on their way up the ladder to the middle class, though he offered no idea about other economic and social strategies to foster that transition.

White capped his house-building career in 1890 with the Riverside dwellings, on the downslope of Brooklyn Heights (see above), but his first efforts, in South Brooklyn, document his evolving ideas, beginning with two apartment houses (1876–77) on the southeast corner of Hicks and Baltic Streets, called the Home Buildings, designed by William Field & Son. In 1878–79 White added three more structures, called the Tower Buildings, on a site bounded by Baltic, Hicks, and Warren Streets. The U-shaped group created a courtyard that provided the individual dwelling units with through ventilation and abundant light. The buildings were simple to the point of starkness, but the use of open balconies on the street side leading to units from a central open stair tower serving each pair of buildings provided visual interest, broke down the scale of the overall complex, and eliminated the nearly airless corridors and stairwells typical of most tenements. More or less simultaneously, White completed two rows of two-story mews houses running north-south between Baltic and Warren Streets, providing the fourth wall to the courtyard. All in all, 218 units were built, representing the first significant investment of private capital in large-scale working-class housing in the United States.

The Home Buildings were built in two stages, with some improvements made in the second half. The press was quick to see the virtues of White's idea and William Field & Son's plans. In 1877 a correspondent to the *American Architect and Building News* reported: "Two parts have already been erected, and have given such satisfaction that additional land was bought, and new work begun. These designs are worthy of special notice, as fulfilling the requirements of economy, privacy, excellent sanitary appli-

Warren Place mews, 139–147 Baltic Street, 146–154 Warren Street, and Warren Place between Warren and Baltic Streets. William Field & Son, 1878. Elevation. BHS.

Tower Buildings, 417–435 Hicks Street, 129–135 Baltic Street, and 136–142 Warren Street. William Field & Son, 1878–79. Courtyard. THP. CU.

North Gate, Green-Wood Cemetery, Fifth Avenue and Twenty-fifth Street. Richard Upjohn & Son, 1860–65. View to the east, 1899. Byron. MCNY.

East Gate, Green-Wood Cemetery, Fort Hamilton Parkway west of Gravesend Avenue. Richard M. Upjohn, 1876. View to the north. King, 1904. CU.

ances, strength, fire-proof qualities and cheapness, at one and the same time."[76] The *New York Times* published an enthusiastic editorial, only quibbling with the fact that the units were too deep, leaving the middle rooms dark. The paper had nothing but praise for White, however, and urged other rich businessmen to follow his example: "When one considers the amount of wealth earned during the last twenty-five years in this City by individuals, many of whom were anxious to found some permanent benefaction for their native City, and the well-known miseries and evils from our present tenement-house system, it seems almost incredible that nothing has thus far been done in the direction of 'model tenements.' . . . The City waits for its special benefactor."[77] When the second building of the Home group was completed, in October 1877, the *Times* found it an "improvement," with every room "light and airy."[78] By the late 1880s the Home Buildings were recognized as "the pioneer of all the good tenement houses in New York . . . and so admirably planned that the New York buildings [of the Improved Dwellings Association] modeled from it have found little opportunity for improvement."[79]

The scheme of William Field & Son's subsequent Tower Buildings consisted of six-story apartment buildings (1878–79) at 417–435 Hicks Street, 129–135 Baltic Street, and 136–142 Warren Street, grouped around three sides of a large landscaped courtyard reserved exclusively for the use of tenants. The brick Tower Buildings were not only more boldly detailed than their predecessors but the planning was a bit more complex as well, with the Hicks Street buildings, which included street-facing shops, served by three stair towers leading via open balconies to four apartments at every floor. The houses on the side streets were each served by a single common stair tower. Within the group there was a sense of hierarchy, with the

most elaborate brickwork reserved for the buildings facing Hicks Street, where the stair towers were handled sculpturally and carried above the roof.

Warren Place, the jewel of the complex, was planned in 1878 as a private, landscaped mews closed to vehicles of any kind and defined by twenty-six eleven-and-a-half-foot-wide, thirty-two-foot-deep, charmingly detailed, two-story brick rowhouses. Also designed by William Field & Son, the houses were grouped in pairs under a continuous cornice, with arched doorways paired under a common segmental arch crowned by a steep Gothic gable. Behind the houses, narrow service alleys ran through the block, while at the ends of each row, pairs of three-story, sixteen-foot-wide gateway houses, larger and more imposing than those fronting the mews, faced outward onto either Warren or Baltic Street.

In 1878, in search of more space, the venerable Church of the Pilgrims decided to expand from Brooklyn Heights and build a chapel in South Brooklyn on a nearly one-hundred-foot-square plot at the southwest corner of Henry and Degraw Streets.[80] As designed by J. C. Cady, the Philadelphia pressed brick, terra cotta, and Belleville stone, Italian Gothic–style church featured a 1,200-seat chapel and a 100-foot-high campanile. The *New York Times* was impressed: "The walls and ceilings are handsomely decorated, and the windows are filled with rolled cathedral glass of beautiful designs. The building is handsome, both within and without, and is an ornament to the locality, as well as a benefit."[81] But the area's most magnificent structure, and one of the most remarkable structures in all the United States, was not a church but part of a sacred place, Green-Wood Cemetery. Located at Fifth Avenue and Twenty-fifth Street, Richard Upjohn & Son's flamboyantly Gothic gateway to Green-Wood, with its striking, multicolored, slate-roofed, flanking pavilions, was commissioned by the cemetery's trustees in 1860 but was not completed until 1865.[82] Envisioned by Henry E. Pierrepont, who was inspired by Mount Auburn Cemetery (1831) in Cambridge, Massachusetts, as a parklike necropolis, the 478-acre cemetery, laid out by Major David B. Douglass in 1838–40, crowned what was then known as Gowanus Heights. Douglass's plan provided for curving roads leading past burial sites on which would soon be built elaborate mausoleums in a panoply of styles. It quickly became popular as both a tourist attraction and as a park. By the 1890s, as a writer observed, "All that wealth can command, everything that taste can suggest, all that local pride can bestow, has been lavished in the efforts to beautify this silent city."[83] The gate, built of New Jersey brownstone from the Belleville quarries, was set well back from Fifth Avenue to form an impressive entrance plaza. Two arches guarded by portcullises, leading to the burial park within, flanked a central pier carrying a 106-foot-tall steeple containing a double-dialed clock and a belfry that was tolled for each funeral procession. In 1868, in a long article describing the entire cemetery, which the Upjohn firm had been associated with since the 1840s, the *New York Times* singled out the Fifth Avenue gate, probably the work of Richard M. Upjohn, for special praise: "The architectural design of the northern entrance cannot escape the admiration of the visitor. . . . In the panels over the gateways we observe sculptured groups of allegorical figures which at once commend themselves to patient study. There is no other object in the cemetery upon which the lover of art is willing to gaze so long or so constantly as these groups."[84] In 1876 Richard M. Upjohn designed another gate, for the east entrance to the cemetery at Fort Hamilton Parkway.[85] While the 1865 gateway included a superintendent's house, a stone cottage for the porter, a tool house, and a stable, the east entrance was more modest. Flanking the gate were two fussily detailed, unidentical Belleville stone buildings crowned by steeply pitched, iron-crested slate roofs, to be used as a porter's lodge and a visitors' cottage.

Fort Greene

As Brooklyn Heights and South Brooklyn began to fill up in the 1850s, major residential development, mostly targeted at the upper classes, moved eastward from Brooklyn's historic core into the Fort Greene area, named for the military structure that was its principal landmark between 1814 and 1850. Fort Greene began to blossom as a middle-class neighborhood after 1867, when Frederick Law Olmsted and Calvert Vaux were hired to redesign Washington Park on the site of the nineteenth-century fort, bounded by Cumberland and Canton Streets and DeKalb and Myrtle Avenues.[86] The thirty-three-acre park, Brooklyn's first public outdoor recreational area, had been initiated in 1848 largely through the efforts of Walt Whitman, then editor of the *Brooklyn Daily Eagle*. Opened in 1850, it was laid out along the naturalistic lines advocated by Andrew

Washington Park, Cumberland to Canton Street, DeKalb to Myrtle Avenue. Frederick Law Olmsted and Calvert Vaux, 1867. Plan. BHS.

Jackson Downing. By 1858 the park was so intensely used that Edwin Spomer, a prominent park promoter, began to argue for an even larger facility, leading seven years later to the creation of Prospect Park (see below). In 1867, with considerable progress already achieved at Prospect Park, a proposal was put forward by the park commissioners to demap Washington Park, which most people continued to call Fort Greene, and sell it off as building lots. By then the park had begun to show the ill effects of extreme popularity, with injured trees and bare lawns. Poor policing made it unsafe for women and children. Rather than eliminate the park, however, Olmsted and Vaux were hired to revive its fortunes. A key part of their redesign was the construction of a vault to house the bones of the thousands of American soldiers who had perished on the British prison ships that had been anchored for six years in nearby Wallabout Bay during the War of 1812. Classifying the park as an enlarged town square and taking advantage of the superb view afforded by its central elevated height, Olmsted and Vaux called for a closely planted rolling landscape traversed by shady walks. Work began in 1868 and the major part of the reconstruction was completed in the following year. The Panic of 1873 curtailed plans for such features as an observatory and rostrum (in effect a covered reviewing stand), and only the vault and foundation for the Gothic-inspired Martyrs Memorial were finished. But the renewed park was nonetheless a roaring success, so much so that on July 4, 1876, it was the focus of Brooklyn's Centennial Parade, when thousands came to celebrate and to honor the dead soldiers.

Stimulated by the revitalization of Washington Park, construction boomed. The area was quickly filled with brownstone rowhouses built in French Second Empire, Neo-Grec, or Italianate styles, mostly designed by such builder-architects as T. B. Jackson or Robert Dixon, who in 1879 designed a row of four three-story brownstone,

Washington Park, Cumberland to Canton Street, DeKalb to Myrtle Avenue. Frederick Law Olmsted and Calvert Vaux, 1867. Unbuilt Martyrs Memorial scheme. BHS.

Washington Park, Cumberland to Canton Street, DeKalb to Myrtle Avenue. Frederick Law Olmsted and Calvert Vaux, 1867. View to the east, c. 1904. BHS.

Neo-Grec houses at 297–303 Clermont Avenue[87] and two years later designed three more in the same style at 11–15 South Elliott Place.[88] Dixon began his career apprenticed to his father, a carpenter, and later studied in the office of Marshall J. Morrill, a prolific Brooklyn architect. In 1879 Dixon set up his own office, working extensively in the Fort Greene and Clinton Hill areas as well as in Park Slope. Dixon's mentor, Morrill, was represented by four Italianate townhouses (1873) at 265–269 Carlton Avenue and 197 DeKalb Avenue, and five narrow Neo-Grec four-story brownstone houses at 2–4 South Oxford Street and 153–155 DeKalb Avenue (1875).[89] A number of single-family houses were also built in the Fort Greene neighborhood. Compared to his mostly conventional rowhouse

Lafayette Avenue Presbyterian Church, southeast corner of Lafayette Avenue and South Oxford Street. Grimshaw & Morrill, 1860–62. View to the southeast. BHS.

designs, Morrill's three-story house (1881) for Chester B. Lawrence, at 192 Washington Park, mixed Neo-Grec details with an asymmetrical composition closer to the domestic Queen Anne.[90] But Morrill and Dixon, though active, were not particularly gifted, nor was the early work of the also prolific Parfitt Brothers, a firm that would become important in the 1880s. Parfitt Brothers consisted of three English-born siblings: Henry, who arrived in the United States in 1863; Walter, who immigrated in 1872; and Albert, who came about eight years later. Two of the brothers were represented in the Fort Greene neighborhood by three three-story Neo-Grec brick buildings (1876) at the southeast corner of DeKalb and Clermont Avenues, which had commercial ground floors.[91] Also in the Neo-Grec taste but far more elegant were Charles Werner's three-story brownstone designs at 25–27 South Elliott Place (1881)[92] and two others at 61–61A South Elliott Place (1885), which featured beautifully detailed high stories leading to richly elaborated arched doorways.[93]

Frank Freeman's Romanesque-inspired, four-floor, four-family tenement (1890) at 33 South Elliott Place, the only example of that building type known to have been designed by the Canadian-born architect, was a minor work though one not without interest for its ornamental use of pale yellow pressed brick, galvanized-iron cornice replete with dwarf columns and corbeled shapes echoing the brick corbels below, and a fine terra cotta plate memorializing the building's date of construction.[94] While the construction of a tenement such as Freeman's reflected Brooklyn's rapidly increasing population, it was a relative anomaly in Fort Greene given the availability of land in outlying areas and the comparative stability within the neighborhood. Nonetheless, it was not alone: the five-story San Carlos (1890), at 69–71 South Oxford Street, was designed by Montrose W. Morris, a prolific and gifted architect whose offices were in Manhattan but who mostly worked in Brooklyn.[95] The San Carlos was a dramatically massed apartment house with Romanesque Revival details, its high, rock-faced basement pierced by three arched openings and the gentle swelling of its two bays on the second and third floors enhancing the building's scale and presence on the street.

Most of Fort Greene's church buildings were constructed around the time of the Civil War. The Lafayette Avenue Presbyterian Church (Grimshaw & Morrill, 1860–62), at 102–108 Lafayette Avenue, an early and particularly fine example of the round-arched churches that Brooklyn abounded in, was home to a liberal congregation that had broken with the more conservative Synod in New York.[96] Under the leadership of the charismatic preacher Theodore L. Cuyler, the new independent congregation blossomed. After a short time in a brick chapel on Carlton Street that had belonged to another church, ground was broken in November 1860 for a new home. Faced in Belleville freestone, a form of brownstone, Grimshaw & Morrill's design was austere and straightforward in a style highly popular with dissenting sects anxious to distance themselves from high church ritual and focus on preaching. The simple massing, with unequally high square towers flanking a gabled central section, led inside to a room planned along the lines of Joseph C. Wells's Puritan Congregational Church (1849), at 56–64 Orange Street, between Henry and Hicks Streets. The taller tower was topped by a corbeled gable that in turn supported an ornate, essentially Gothic, wooden spire.

The story of one of Brooklyn's more important church structures, that of the Reformed Episcopal Church of the Messiah, is unusually convoluted.[97] Founded in 1848 or 1849, the congregation was the third Episcopal church in the area but the first to follow progressive, low-church principles. The new congregation first built a small wooden chapel (1852) on Adelphi Street but it was soon deemed inadequate and a new brick church (1859) was constructed next door. In 1863 the growing congregation found the brick church to be too small and purchased the building of the Greene Avenue Presbyterian Church, at the southeast corner of Clermont Avenue, which was unfinished, lacking a roof. After completing the Greene Avenue church in 1865, the congregation sold its wooden chapel and brick church on Adelphi Street to St. Mark's Protestant Episcopal Church (see below). The Greene Avenue Church (1865), attributed to James H. Giles, was, like the Lafayette Avenue Presbyterian Church, a round-arched brick structure with towers of unequal height flanking the principal facade. Some twenty-five years later, the prominent architect R. H. Robertson was called in to alter the church, adding a beehive spire on the taller tower as well as an ornate porch. Robertson also designed a new chapel for the church and a Byzantine-inspired chancel with decorations by J. N. Stent, whose direct inspiration was St. Mark's in Venice. Montgomery Schuyler was pleased with Robertson's renovations: "There is no patent incongruity between the new work and the old. . . . The designer has contrived to impart a positive and grateful architectural character to that which before was absolutely characterless and commonplace."[98]

The congregation of St. Mark's Protestant Episcopal Church, which had been founded in 1849 as a chapel of Holy Trinity Protestant Episcopal Church in Brooklyn Heights, in 1885 elected to demolish the wooden chapel (1852) on Adelphi Street that had been purchased in 1865 from the Church of the Messiah and replace it with a new chapel.[99] Designed by Lawrence B. Valk, the building featured a principal facade of red sandstone laid in random ashlar trimmed with terra cotta and pierced by a pointed-arch window with tracery and a small bay. According to *The Churchman*, the "beautiful new chapel . . . possessed many good points of ecclesiastical architecture and made the old church look even worse than it really was."[100] In 1888 the congregation hired Marshall & Walter, successors to Pugin & Walter, architects of the Memorial Presbyterian Church in Park Slope (see below), to design a new house of worship next to Valk's chapel, replacing the

Reformed Episcopal Church of the Messiah, southeast corner of Greene and Clermont Avenues. James H. Giles, 1865; R. H. Robertson, 1888–93. View to the southeast, 1894, showing the Episcopal Residence (Patrick C. Keely, 1883–87) on the left. BHS.

Church of the Messiah's old brick church (1859).[101] Marshall & Walter's Gothic design, executed in Carlisle stone laid in random ashlar trimmed with sandstone, was conventional in plan, with a single tower rising one hundred feet above the south entrance. Only one aspect of the design failed to please the congregation: Marshall & Walter's decision to place a rooster, instead of the typical cross, atop the "candle extinguisher" steeple. The *New York Times* covered the controversy in March 1889, about six weeks before the church was officially dedicated:

A rooster whose habits are as changing as the winds, who does not welcome the morning with his clarion, and whose resplendent tail feathers are never plucked by any envious rival, sits serene upon the apex of St. Mark's Protestant Episcopal Church . . . and defies the congregation. . . . The fowl, whose humble duty it is to face the wind, which is tempered according to the needs of Kings County lambs, has, among things that are not appreciated by the parishioners, given the edifice the title of the Church of the Holy Rooster among the unchosen, and when the Warden and Vestrymen stray forth they are asked solicitously by the children of the vicinity concerning the condition of the chickens. As a result of all this the ladies of the parish have arisen and protested that a barnyard was the place for a rooster and not a sacred building. . . . The architects protested against the change, declaring that the rooster was frequently used in Europe on both Episcopalian and Roman Catholic churches, but that made no difference. . . . Next Sunday a cross will gleam where yesterday the festive rooster twirled on the weather vane.[102]

Far and away the most ambitious church project undertaken in Brooklyn was the Roman Catholic Cathedral of the Immaculate Conception, intended for the block bounded by Clermont, Greene, Vanderbilt, and Lafayette Avenues.[103] A Pugin-inspired version of the cathedral at Rouen, as designed by Patrick C. Keely it was to have been the second largest cathedral in the country, exceeded only by New York's St. Patrick's (see chapter 2), then under construction. A symbolic representation of the fact that the number of followers of the Roman Catholic faith in the United States was increasing significantly, as well as a bid for social position in what was still a nearly exclusively Protestant society, the cathedral was conceived at a monumental scale as "an enterprise of magnificent proportions, such as only a prosperous and growing city could sustain."[104] As described in 1871, the approach taken by Keely abounded in "clustered shafts, moulded bases, decorated caps, richly-traceried windows, varied statuary, pinnacled and gabled canopies."[105] The cathedral was to have been built of blue granite. Two 98-foot-wide, 350-foot-high corner

Proposed Roman Catholic Cathedral of the Immaculate Conception, Vanderbilt to Clermont Avenue, Greene to Lafayette Avenue. Patrick C. Keely, 1868. Elevation. PCK. CU.

towers were to have marked the 160-foot-wide entrance facade facing Lafayette Avenue, beyond which was to sit the 354-foot-long church with its 98-foot-high, white granite nave soaring to a roof framed in oak. The project was extremely ambitious given that the Diocese of Brooklyn had only been in existence for eight years when the site was acquired in 1860, but Bishop John Loughlin was deeply committed to the idea of the cathedral as a beacon for Catholicism in Protestant Brooklyn, as were many laypeople, forty thousand of whom showed up for the laying of the cornerstone on June 21, 1868. Nonetheless, the walls of the cathedral only reached between ten and twenty feet high before money ran out and construction was halted. Only the Chapel of Saint John (1878) was finished. In 1883 Keely designed an Episcopal residence at the northeast corner of Clermont and Greene Avenues, an austere composition of dark gray dressed Connecticut granite blocks and a mansard roof, completed in 1887 to serve as the residence for the bishop and clergy attached to the cathedral.[106] In 1898–99, at the invitation of Charles Edward McDonnell, Bishop of Brooklyn, John Francis Bentley, the architect of London's Roman Catholic Cathedral of Westminster (1894–1903), visited Brooklyn and prepared new designs for the cathedral.[107] But shortly before Bishop McDonnell could visit Bentley in London and see the drawings, the architect died.

Clinton Hill

While the Fort Greene neighborhood was clearly an eastward expansion of the historic city of Brooklyn, beginning in the 1850s Clinton Hill, a few blocks beyond in the area roughly bounded by Fulton Street, Vanderbilt, Myrtle, and Classon Avenues, had been developed at a distinctly suburban scale.[108] In the 1870s, however, as development of the Fort Greene neighborhood was maturing, urban pressures came to Clinton Hill. Spacious properties were subdivided and undeveloped areas were rapidly filled in so that by 1880, except for Clinton Avenue, the neighborhood was a grander version of Fort Greene. Beginning in the late 1870s and continuing into the 1890s, the seven blocks of Clinton Avenue between Myrtle and Atlantic Avenues took on a new identity that was unique in both Brooklyn and New York, becoming a landscaped, mansion-lined thoroughfare comparable to Euclid Avenue in Cleveland or Delaware Avenue in Buffalo or South Prairie Avenue in Chicago.[109]

Originally laid out as a tree-lined boulevard in 1832 by George Washington Pine, a merchant and auctioneer, by 1860 Clinton Avenue was home to mostly freestanding wood-frame villas set back from the street on deep lots that extended to Vanderbilt and Waverly Avenues, where stables, carriage houses, and other outbuildings were constructed. The transformation of Clinton Avenue, and Clinton Hill as a whole, began in 1874 when Charles Pratt decided to build a mansion at 232 Clinton Avenue, between DeKalb and Willoughby Avenues.[110] Pratt was a partner in the paint and oil firm of Reynolds, Devoe &

Charles Pratt house, 232 Clinton Avenue, between DeKalb and Willoughby Avenues. E. L. Roberts, 1874. View to the northwest. King, 1904. CU.

Pratt, and after 1867 head of Charles Pratt & Co., oil refiners and manufacturers of "Pratt Astral Oil," a less flammable lighting fuel. The product attracted the attention of John D. Rockefeller, who in 1874 acquired Pratt's company for his Standard Oil conglomerate, making Pratt a leading player in the nation's boldest corporate enterprise and Brooklyn's richest citizen. To design his house Pratt retained the Brooklyn-based architect E. L. Roberts, who ten years later would design Standard Oil's Manhattan headquarters (see chapter 3). The somewhat blocky, three-story house consisted of brick with sandstone trim and derived from Italianate and Neo-Grec inspiration, with low-pitched pedimented gables, bay windows, and porches as the principal grace notes. In 1874, just as Pratt's house was being built, his business associate James H. Lounsbery bought a site a block away, between Lafayette and DeKalb Avenues, also commissioning Roberts to design a house, which he did not live long enough to occupy.[111] At 321 Clinton Avenue, the four-story, cubelike brownstone villa (1875) was similar to Pratt's in its Italianate and Neo-Grec detailing.

The Panic of 1873 curtailed building activity, but in 1882 the economy's revitalization was marked by the completion of Parfitt Brothers's residence for Dr. Cornelius N. Hoagland, at 410 Clinton Avenue, between Gates and Greene Avenues.[112] While Parfitt Brothers's early practice was little different from that of builder-architects, the opportunity to work for Dr. Hoagland, originator of the formula for baking powder marketed under the name Royal Baking Powder, marked a distinct advance in the firm's prestige. Parfitt Brothers made the most of the opportunity, designing a three-story, Queen Anne–style, red brick mansion, subtle in its asymmetrical composition and charming in its details, with variously shaped oriel windows, molded brickwork, corbeled brick chimneys, and roof cresting that hinted of Japan.

While the Hoagland house was under way, Abraham Gould Jennings, a leading lace manufacturer, commissioned a three-and-a-half-story Neo-Grec house (1882) at 313 Clinton Avenue, between DeKalb and Lafayette Avenues, from George L. Morse, a somewhat less prominent Brooklyn architect whose mansarded brick design,

*Abraham Gould Jennings house (George L. Morse, 1882), 313
Clinton Avenue, on the left, and John Arbuckle house (Montrose
W. Morris, 1887–88), 315 Clinton Avenue, on the right.
View to the east, c. 1941. BHS.*

*Alfred Pouch house, 345 Clinton Avenue, between Greene
and Lafayette Avenues. William A. Mundell, 1887, 1890.
View to the northeast, c. 1900. BHS.*

*Alfred Pouch house, 345 Clinton Avenue, between Greene and
Lafayette Avenues. William A. Mundell, 1887, 1890. View of
the main hall, c. 1900. BHS.*

trimmed with stone and terra cotta, looked back to the architecture of the 1860s and 1870s.[113] Also of interest was William A. Mundell's brownstone house and adjoining stables for the wallpaper manufacturer Robert Graves, at 345 Clinton Avenue (1887), between Greene and Lafayette Avenues.[114] Graves died before moving in, so the house was known for its second owner, the oil executive Alfred Pouch, who bought it in 1890 and added a wooden extension to house his art collection.

John Arbuckle's mansion (1887–88) at 315 Clinton Avenue, between Lafayette and DeKalb Avenues, designed by Montrose W. Morris, was the avenue's next important landmark.[115] Arbuckle, prominent in the coffee business as an importer and packager, staged a competition, which Morris won with his design for a thirty-by-ninety-foot, symmetrically massed, brick and rock-faced brownstone house; though somewhat stiff, the scheme was a powerful representation of the Romanesque Revival style. Also included was a forty-by-fifty-foot, two-story brick stable built at the rear, at 306–308 Waverly Avenue. In 1889 another Brooklyn-based architect, William B. Tubby, who had worked as a draftsman in E. L. Roberts's office, provided an extraordinary house for Charles Adolph Schieren, a German-born inventor, banker, and manufacturer of leather goods.[116] Set on a rock-faced stone base, Schieren's thirty-two-by-seventy-foot house, at 405 Clinton Avenue, between Gates and Greene Avenues, was a deep red Roman brick, sandstone-trimmed superstructure capped by a roof of imbricated shingles. The house was entered up a stoop through a heavy stone porch with segmented arches. Above, a curving Flemish gable pierced by a Palladian window punctuated the exceptionally tall hipped roof to provide a particularly strong silhouette. Tubby's success with the Schieren house, and the fact that he took over Roberts's practice after that architect's death in 1890, brought him to the attention of Charles Pratt. For Pratt's oldest son, Charles Millard Pratt, also an active participant in the affairs of Standard Oil, Tubby designed 241 Clinton Avenue (1890–93), between DeKalb and Willoughby Avenues, and a twelve-horse stable facing Vanderbilt Avenue.[117] The house represented the climax of the impact of the Richardsonian Romanesque on urban villa building, and was the avenue's grandest dwelling of the period. The house was a wedding gift from the elder Pratt, who would eventually commission a Clinton Avenue house for each of his other two sons.[118] The two-and-a-half-story, orange Roman brick house, trimmed with matching sandstone and capped by a steeply pitched, green Spanish tile roof with rakishly flared eaves, was articulated into three parts, with an enormous, low, arched porte cochere subsumed into the building mass and balanced by a projecting rock-faced tower-bay crowned by its own tiled conical roof. Despite its masonry, Tubby's design had about it some of the taut skinlike closure typically associated with wood villas in what would come to be called the Shingle Style. Byzantine-inspired detail on moldings and decorative ironwork softened the composition, while details such as an eyelid dormer and a triple-window shed dormer further contributed to its sense of puckish lightness, so rarely found in a house of this scale and pretension.

Clinton Avenue was also the setting for some fine rowhouses, most notably John Mumford's three three-story Neo-Grec brownstone residences (1878), at 469–473 Clinton Avenue, on the southeast corner of Gates Avenue; the three atypically shared a common front porch.[119] Also fine was a row of four houses designed by R. H. Robertson and A. J. Manning at 215–221 Clinton Avenue (1891), on the southeast corner of Willoughby Avenue.[120] Illuminating the transition from the synthesizing stylistic eclecticism of the Richardsonian Romanesque, of which Robertson had been an inspired interpreter during the late 1880s, to the more strict and constraining Renaissance-based Classicism he would embrace in the 1890s, the tan-colored brick mass was set on a rock-faced stone base. Numerous decorative details firmly placed the design of the three-and-a-half-story row in the Romanesque, though the paired windows separated by Corinthian colonettes and the dentil courses used to visually separate the parlor floor from those above, as well as various details in the attic gables, revealed new sympathy for the strictly Classical. Langston & Dahlander's five-story apartment house (c. 1892) at 487 Clinton Avenue, between Gates Avenue and Fulton Street, the first of its type on the

Charles Adolph Schieren house, 405 Clinton Avenue, between Gates and Greene Avenues. William B. Tubby, 1889. View to the northeast. King, 1904. CU.

Charles Millard Pratt house, 241 Clinton Avenue, between DeKalb and Willoughby Avenues. William B. Tubby, 1890–93. View to the east showing part of the George D. Pratt house (Babb, Cook & Willard, 1901) on the right. King, 1904. CU.

avenue, suggested a Loire Valley château built in the Romanesque style.[121] Using Roman brick above a base of rough stone laid in random ashlar, the design was dominated by a massive archway leading to the entry and a full-height brick tower projecting from the mass and capped by a corbeled cornice with a diaper-work frieze, French-style dormer windows, a tall chimney, and a snub-nosed roof.

Clinton Avenue was the most impressive street in Clinton Hill, but Washington Avenue, which was also wider than normal, came a close second, although the building blocks of its urbanism were groups of rowhouses rather than individual mansions. Notable among these were W. H. Gaylor's Neo-Grec five-house row (1879) at 235–243 Washington Avenue, on the southeast corner of Willoughby Avenue, a three-story block with a high basement set behind deep gardens;[122] Parfitt Brothers's three three-story Neo-Grec brownstone rowhouses (1878) at 331–335 Washington Avenue, between DeKalb and Lafayette Avenues;[123] Amzi Hill's pair of three-and-a-half-story Neo-Grec brownstone houses (1879) at 388–390 Washington Avenue, between Lafayette and Greene Avenues;[124] Hill's imposing three-and-a-half-story Neo-Grec brownstones (1885–86) at 323–325 Washington Avenue, between DeKalb and Lafayette Avenues;[125] John Mumford's three-house group (1880) in the Queen Anne style at 301–305 Washington Avenue, on the northeast corner of DeKalb Avenue, consisting of two-and-a-half-story mansarded designs built of Philadelphia brick, with stone, wood, and terra cotta trim, and composed as a unit with the end houses projecting forward;[126] Marshall J. Morrill's pair of four-story, mirror-image Queen Anne–style houses (1887) at 280–282 Washington Avenue, between Willoughby and DeKalb Avenues;[127] Adam E. Fischer's inventive pair of four-story Queen Anne townhouses (1887) set behind low stone garden walls, at 396–398 Washington Avenue, between Lafayette

229–231 Washington Avenue, northeast corner of Willoughby Avenue. J. G. Glover, 1892. View to the northeast, 1942. Sperr. NYPL.

and Greene Avenues;[128] and Mercein Thomas's three highly picturesque, Queen Anne–style rowhouses (1885) at 400–404 Washington Avenue, on the northwest corner of Greene Avenue, which combined overall symmetry with individuality in the design of each house.[129] J. G. Glover's pair of Romanesque Revival houses (1892) at 229–231 Washington Avenue, on the northeast corner of Willoughby Avenue, was designed as a single unit for two brothers, John and Henry von Glahn, wholesale grocers.[130] Mercein Thomas's 407–409 Washington Avenue (1889), between Greene and Gates Avenues, pushed the scale of accommodation, disguising as one unit what in effect was a small, four-story apartment house.[131] Henry Olmsted & Son was franker in its handling of the same building type with its five-story, twenty-five-by-seventy-two-foot, brick, and Nova Scotia stone, Romanesque Revival apartment house (1890) at 478 Washington Avenue, between Greene and Gates Avenues.[132]

While Waverly and Vanderbilt Avenues were mostly lined with the carriage houses and other back buildings of the Clinton Avenue mansions, St. James Place, lying east of Washington Avenue and its rowhouses, was home to two-and-a-half- and three-story houses of a more moderate stripe, ranging from builder brownstone rows from the late 1860s to a handful of highly individual designs in the block between Gates Avenue and Fulton Street. This block was the last to be developed not only along St. James Place but also in the Clinton Hill area as a whole, taking form in 1890 such that some of its best houses exactly mirrored the contemporaneous shift of style from the Richardsonian Romanesque to the Classical Renaissance. The story of St. James Place can be said to have begun with Napoleon Le Brun & Sons's two-story Romanesque Revival office building and shop for the Nassau Gas-Light Company (1877), at number 191, between Gates Avenue and Fulton Street, with its high rock-faced stone base and upper story of brick trimmed with terra cotta.[133] Two years later George L. Morse produced two brownstone designs in the Neo-Grec taste, including three French flats at 211–215 St. James Place and a pair of townhouses at

301–305 Washington Avenue, northeast corner of DeKalb Avenue. John Mumford, 1880. View to the northeast, 1942. NYPL.

217–219 St. James Place.[134] In the late 1880s a renewed burst of activity began with Mercein Thomas's mirror-image pair of eleven-and-a-half-foot-wide, red brick, Romanesque Revival–style houses (1888), at 177–177A St. James Place,[135] and continued with Thomas's Romanesque Revival mirror houses at 202–204 St. James Place (1889), which, despite arched entries and dormer porches, used Corinthian columns and a Renaissance cornice to reveal the designer's shifting taste.[136] The comparatively unknown Benjamin Wright's three three-story, brick-faced, Romanesque Revival houses (1890), at 206–210 St. James Place, constructed for Charles Pratt's Morris Building Company, took fewer risks and seemed content with the Romanesque.[137] William B. Tubby's two houses (1892) for the same owner, however, at 179–183 St. James Place, revealed the architect's superior grasp of the issues, seemingly summarizing the stylistic preoccupations of the late 1880s with a self-assured synthesis between Romanesque Revival and Queen Anne motifs.[138] The three virtually identical houses were raised a half-level from the street, as was Mercein Thomas's group next door, and had a strong second-floor bay window centered in each unit and a four-window arched arcade on the third floor holding the street wall against the sloping imbricated

shingle roof. The center arcade carried a flamboyantly scaled Flemish gable, which was echoed in a quiet way in the stepped profile of the party walls.

Other exceptional rowhouses in Clinton Hill included Montrose W. Morris's 285–289 DeKalb Avenue (1889), on the northwest corner of Waverly Avenue, a three-house group powerfully massed as a single house as grand as any in the Richardsonian taste,[139] and a five-house group by the same architect across the street, at 282–290 DeKalb Avenue (1890),[140] on the southwest corner of Waverly Avenue. All were built for Joseph Fahys, a watchcase maker who moved into number 285. Morris was selected for the first group in a three-firm competition. His design, though more flamboyant than H. H. Richardson's influential two-house group for John Hay and Henry Adams in Washington, D.C. (1884–86),[141] nonetheless understood and mastered the problem just as well. Morris separated the two pavilionated end units, with the one at the corner expressed as a turret with an independent conical roof, and enhanced the prestige of the center with a concatenation of elements piling a bay window upon a pedimented frontispiece. The second, larger group was quieter in its composition, unified with a pediment over the central unit and symmetrical turrets at each end. This group was by com-

Adelphi Academy, east side of St. James Place between Clifton Place and Lafayette Avenue. View to the northeast, c. 1896, showing C. C. Haight's building (1888) on the right and Mundell & Teckritz's building (1867, 1873, 1880) on the left. BHS.

position, if not by style, more Classical, suggesting a shift of interest on the designer's part. At 69–77 Downing Street, between Gates and Putnam Avenues, Augustus Walbridge, a jeweler, commissioned from the Brooklyn-based architect George P. Chappell an equally fine but far less bombastic five-house row (1890) in the Queen Anne style.[142] Set atop a high base of rock-faced Belleville stone, each unit was entered via a high stoop, and the group took on the look of an outbuilding on a suburban, Shingle Style estate, with the slightly projecting second floor clad in wood shingles. An off-center bay window set beneath a pediment broke the design's remarkable horizontality.

Clinton Hill was home to one of Brooklyn's finest schools, the coeducational Adelphi Academy, established in 1863 on Adelphi Street and relocated four years later to a new, four-story Romanesque Revival–style building at the southeast corner of Lafayette Avenue and St. James Place.[143] Designed by Mundell & Teckritz, the school would be expanded with wings added in 1873 and 1880 according to the architects' original plans. In 1888 Charles Pratt, who had paid for part of the academy's new east wing, agreed to fund an entirely new building to house the school's collegiate division.[144] C. C. Haight, who had extensive experience with educational clients, including Columbia College and the General Theological Seminary (see chapter 2), was retained as architect. Fronting on Clifton Place, Haight's four-and-a-half-story building was connected to the older building by a one-thousand-seat chapel. Although the use of round arches to frame the entrances as well as the windows on the main floor and in the pediments and dormers suggested a connection with the Romanesque, Haight's red brick mass, with its regular rhythm of exceptionally large windows, was remarkably straightforward.

At the same time that Pratt was helping the Adelphi Academy to expand, he was founding an institute, which would bear his name, for the purpose "of enabling the youth of the country to obtain a thorough technical education, coupled with a practical manual training."[145] According to Pratt, "the idea was not to teach . . . any trade, but to educate [the students] to work patiently and systematically in the use of hand, eye, and brain."[146] Pratt hired Lamb & Rich, the firm with which he was working on the Astral Apartments in Greenpoint (see below), to design what would soon be called the Main Building (1885–87) of his Pratt Institute.[147] A six-story, Romanesque, turreted block entered up a double staircase leading through a projecting portico with paired brownstone arches resting on colonettes, the Main Building included a free reading room and circulating library on the first floor, open to Brooklyn residents over the age of fourteen. The Pratt Institute grew rapidly, and in 1889–91 Charles Pratt commissioned an addition from his current favorite architect, William B. Tubby, who designed a three-story red brick building that was even more severe than the vaguely militaristic Main Building.[148]

Pratt Institute, east side of Ryerson Street between DeKalb and Willoughby Avenues. View to the east, 1910, showing the Main Building (Lamb & Rich, 1885–87) on the left and William B. Tubby's addition (1889–91) on the right. Underhill. BPL.

Lincoln Club, 65 Putnam Avenue, between Irving Place and Classon Avenue. Rudolph L. Daus, 1889. View to the north. King, 1904. CU.

Clinton Hill was also home to the Lincoln Club, a Republican organization founded in 1878.[149] Rudolph L. Daus's four-story clubhouse (1889), at 65 Putnam Avenue, between Irving Place and Classon Avenue, located on the site of the club's previous headquarters, was an exuberant essay mixing elements from the Romanesque with those more specifically associated with the Queen Anne. The asymmetrical arrangement of the facade pivoted about a slender, conical, roof-capped tourelle that rose as the highest element, suggesting what Ludwig II's castle at Neuschwanstein might have looked like had John Ruskin or William Burges been awarded the commission. The building abounded in extraordinary details, most notably the recessed keystones over the fourth-floor windows and the elaborate way the club's initials and the building's date were worked into the upper half of the gable's end.

With a distinguished school, an institute for higher education, and a fine clubhouse, only churches were necessary to render Clinton Hill complete as a desirable suburban neighborhood. While the religious needs of most of the area's residents were met in nearby Fort Greene or in the established, fashionable churches of Brooklyn Heights, a few new churches were built. Richard T. Auchmuty's ruralesque, English-inspired St. Mary's Episcopal Church (1858–59), at 230 Classon Avenue, perfectly echoed Clinton Hill's

Emmanuel Baptist Church, northwest corner of Lafayette Avenue and St. James Place. Francis H. Kimball, 1887. View to the northwest, 1910. BHS.

Emmanuel Baptist Church, northwest corner of Lafayette Avenue and St. James Place. Francis H. Kimball, 1887. Interior. AR. CU.

St. Luke's Episcopal Church, 520 Clinton Avenue, between Fulton Street and Atlantic Avenue. John Welch, 1888–91.
View to the northwest, 1894. BHS.

early history as a suburb,[150] while Francis H. Kimball's French Gothic Emmanuel Baptist Church (1887), at 279 Lafayette Avenue, reflected Clinton Hill's new status as Brooklyn's most fashionable neighborhood.[151] When Emmanuel Baptist was undertaken the congregation had only recently been formed, by 194 members who had broken with the Washington Avenue Baptist Church. From the architect of that church, E. L. Roberts, the new congregation commissioned a small, Gothic-style, two-story interim chapel on St. James Place (1882–83).[152] In 1884 fund-raising for a new church began in earnest, with Charles Pratt bearing most of the burden, and the cornerstone was laid for Kimball's new church two years later. Construction advanced quickly, and on April 17, 1887, what can be regarded as one of its designer's most spectacular efforts was dedicated, an extraordinary synthesis of the cathedral type and the Baptist preaching church. Montgomery Schuyler admired Emmanuel Baptist, deeming it "a very rich scholarly and well considered design, in which the triple porch, with its stilted arches, and the treatment of the towers especially recall Mr. Burges's work, and in which the mullioned windows both in the aisle wall and in the centre of the front are very admirably designed and detailed, and of which the deep reveals are so modeled as to get the utmost advantage of their depth." But what really impressed Schuyler was Kimball's interior. Unlike many Baptist churches in which the font was hidden under the platform, Kimball made "the font with its pool . . . the central and most conspicuous object in the church, walled in by an enclosure of sumptuous marble and flanked by open arcades which enable the converts to make their exits and entrances with decorum."[153] The distinctions of the interior included not only the handling of the Baptist ritual but also the stenciled walls, boldly scaled and profiled wooden cove ceiling, lamps and other furnishings, and, most surprisingly, the arclike arrangement of pews, positioned to meet the needs of a preaching church.

John Welch was awarded the commission to design St. Luke's Episcopal Church (1888–91) in a competition that included Richard M. Upjohn, Rudolph L. Daus, and J. W. Walter.[154] At 520 Clinton Avenue, between Fulton Street and Atlantic Avenue, Welch's building replaced a much-expanded (Wills & Dudley, 1853) Greek Revival structure built for a different congregation in 1835. Welch, a leading Brooklyn-based church architect, married elements from the North Italian Romanesque with a Ruskinian taste for polychromy, exhibited in the use of three shades of brownstone. The complex composition kept the church plant, one of the largest in Brooklyn, from overwhelming its context by separating the church proper—with its projecting round-arched entrance porch, large wheel window, corbeled cornice, and small octagonal towers—from the chapel and its magnificent tower, based on Romanesque campaniles. The church interior was beautifully detailed. St. Luke's was also one of the first buildings in Brooklyn to be lit by electricity.

Bedford

Southeast of Clinton Hill lay what remained of the colonial village of Bedford, which, though platted for streets in 1835, remained largely farmland until the Civil War.[155] While precise borders for Bedford are difficult to draw, a strong southern edge was created with the construction of the Eastern Parkway (1870–74), while the historic village of Williamsburg, lying north and east of Wallabout Bay, provided a northern boundary. To the west lay Prospect Heights, Fort Greene, and Clinton Hill, and to the east what had until 1855 been the independent village of Bushwick. Bushwick, Williamsburg, and Greenpoint were together typically referred to as the Eastern District. At the core of the new neighborhood was Grant Square, formed by the angular intersection of Bedford Avenue with Rogers Avenue and Dean and Bergen Streets.

At first Bedford was developed as a suburban retreat. Dean Sage's villa at 839 St. Mark's Avenue (1869), on the northeast corner of Brooklyn Avenue, was a powerful essay in the Romanesque designed by the eminent Ruskinian architect Russell Sturgis.[156] Nearby, at 96 Brooklyn Avenue, on the northwest corner of Dean Street, another imposing house, this one containing fifty rooms, was designed by Parfitt Brothers for John and Elizabeth Truslow.[157] Completed in 1888, the house was substantially set back from both streets. Built of red brick and trimmed with brownstone, the house, which incorporated some Romanesque-inspired details, was principally distinguished by two gabled wings articulated with towers, chimneys, and finials, imbuing the overall composition with a lively silhouette. Despite the architectural interest of these freestanding houses, a denser form of urbanism would dominate the area, with the rowhouse becoming the principal development unit, typically built in groups as small as three houses but sometimes extending for whole block lengths. Among the area's first rowhouse developments were two long rows of three-story-tall Italianate-style houses developed by Curtis L. North, an insurance agent, at 111–127 MacDonough Street (1872), between

Dean Sage house, northeast corner of St. Mark's and Brooklyn Avenues. Russell Sturgis, 1869. View to the northeast, 1929. Sperr. NYPL.

Montrose W. Morris house, 236 Hancock Street, between Marcy and Tompkins Avenues. Montrose W. Morris, 1885. Reception hall. AR. CU.

Tompkins and Throop Avenues, and 221–247 MacDonough Street (1872), between Sumner and Lewis Avenues.[158] Small gardens ringed with iron railings and gates separated the houses from the sidewalk—an arrangement that would prevail in the area for a long time, making for a suburban type of rowhouse urbanism wholly distinct from equivalent contemporary developments in New York. In 1876, for the developer John Robus, Charles Ringle designed a row of five two-story brownstone houses with rusticated basements at 295–303 MacDonough Street, between Lewis and Stuyvesant Avenues, blending an essentially Italianate design with French Neo-Grec details, a style combination that would become the neighborhood standard for the next ten years or so.[159]

During the 1880s, paralleling the emergence of the Queen Anne style for suburban resort houses and H. H. Richardson's version of the Romanesque, designers began to place a greater emphasis on the individuality of each unit within the row. No architect working in Brooklyn understood the need to establish individuality within the context of the whole better than Montrose W. Morris, a prolific practitioner of real distinction whose early work included houses, rowhouses, and apartment houses.[160] Born in the Long Island village of Hempstead, Morris grew up in Brooklyn but, beginning in 1883, conducted his architectural practice from New York, presumably in order to be close to where his clients worked. His timing

was exact: the completion of the Brooklyn Bridge stimulated a vast building boom in the suburban city where the young, entrepreneurial Morris, impatient for clients, bought land, in the Stuyvesant Heights section of Bedford, on Hancock Street at Marcy Avenue. Intending to build model homes, he began with one for his own use at 236 Hancock Street (1885), east of Marcy Avenue, and opened it for public inspection.[161] A vigorously detailed, three-story, terra cotta and brick, Queen Anne–style, twenty-by-thirty-two-foot, party-wall townhouse with a sixteen-by-sixteen-foot extension, it caught the eye with bay windows that projected from an elaborately articulated pedimented central motif, all set against a steeply sloping pyramidal roof. The *Brooklyn Daily Eagle* enthused over Morris's paneled English-, French-, and Japanese-inspired interiors, especially the double-height oak-paneled reception hall with its second-floor balcony and stained-glass dome and the bamboo-paneled billiards room, also lit by a stained-glass dome, somewhat hyperbolically deeming them "unprecedented in the annals of architecture."[162] Morris's investment paid off wisely and his career boomed. Three years later he designed two more houses next to his own, at 232–234 Hancock Street (1888), on the southeast corner of Marcy Avenue, slate-roofed brick and stone houses that turned the corner with a second-floor turret and confronted Marcy Avenue with a bold pedimented cross-gable.[163] In 1889 Morris continued in building speculative houses on the Hancock Street block between Marcy and Tompkins Avenues, including four limestone and terra cotta buildings consisting of three stories and a basement at 246–252 Hancock Street (1889)[164] and, across the street, at 255–259 Hancock Street (1889).[165] Three simple tin-roofed, sandstone and terra cotta houses, also of three stories and a basement, these latter designs were brought to life with round stone arches at the base, identical bay windows at the second floor, and inventive handling of the third floors in an A-B-A pattern with the end openings hinting at inspiration from Japan. Morris's success resulted in his capturing the commission to design two rowhouse developments for Joseph Fahys, on DeKalb Avenue in Clinton Hill (see above), as well as the Henry Carlton Hulbert mansion in Park Slope (see below). In 1892, for Charles C. Lloyd, Morris designed a pair of large, three-story houses in the Romanesque Revival style at 855–857 St. Mark's Avenue, between Brooklyn and Kingston Avenues.[166] Using brick and limestone, Morris stamped the structure as his own with a corner tower crowned by a bell-shaped roof.

Though Morris was far and away the most prolific of the gifted designers working in Bedford in the late 1880s, the prevailing taste for individualistic design inspired remarkably interesting work from others. E.G.W. Dietrich's single-family house, consisting of two stories and an attic, at 673 St. Mark's Avenue (1888), between Rogers and Nostrand Avenues, provided a welcome note of Queen Anne eccentricity to a somewhat self-important street.[167] George P. Chappell's three-story, thirty-by-forty-

Alhambra, west side of Nostrand Avenue between Halsey and Macon Streets. Montrose W. Morris, 1889–90. View to the northwest, c. 1910, showing the Renaissance Apartments (Montrose W. Morris, 1892) on the far right. BHS.

nine-foot, brick and Belleville stone house (1888) for Thomas Prosser Jr. at 387–389 Stuyvesant Avenue, on the northeast corner of Bainbridge Street, combined Romanesque Revival and Queen Anne elements in a confidently asymmetrical composition that included a picturesque tower and decorated metal gable.[168] Prosser was a member of the firm Thomas Prosser & Son, American agents of Krupp, the German industrial powerhouse. Even the usually conventional architectural firm Amzi Hill & Son, which typically specialized in Neo-Grec rowhouses in Bedford, Fort Greene, and Clinton Hill, was moved to vary its formula when designing 300–332 MacDonough Street (1888–90), between Lewis and Stuyvesant Avenues, a row of sixteen three-story townhouses which incorporated alternating Neo-Grec, Romanesque Revival, and Queen Anne units.[169] Amzi Hill & Son was also the designer of ten three-story brick Romanesque Revival houses (1891–93) at 154–174 MacDonough Street, between Throop and Sumner Avenues, exhibiting a touch of the Queen Anne in asymmetrical facades, dormer windows, steep, decoratively slated roofs, and sunbursts.[170] But it was the thirty-three-unit 73–139 Bainbridge Street (Magnus Dahlander, 1892) that came closest to a tour de force, juxtaposing Romanesque Revival, Queen Anne, and Renaissance Revival elements in a series of individually designed three-story brownstone houses that flowed together to form a coherent group.[171] Francis Stryker's ten-

house row at 281–299 Decatur Street (1890), between Lewis and Stuyvesant Avenues, was more static in composition and consistent in its Romanesque Revival style, but atypical in its inclusion of a four-story apartment house, at 301 Decatur Street, serving as the row's terminal unit.[172] The building featured a polygonal bay rising full height on the short Decatur Street front, a base of stone, and upper floors of orange Roman brick with stone trim to tie in but render more monumental the vocabulary of the row itself. While most of the work of the late 1880s tended toward the large-scale, heftily detailed, near-monumental Romanesque, George P. Chappell's 1164–1182 Dean Street (1889–90), between Bedford and Nostrand Avenues, consisted of ten seventeen- and eighteen-foot-wide Queen Anne–style rowhouses of two stories and a basement, with brick, limestone, terra cotta, wooden shingles, and Spanish tile fleshing out an eclectic mixture of stepped and peaked gables.[173]

Luxury apartment houses began to be built in Bedford in the late 1880s, in many respects as ambitious, if not as large, as some of the grand buildings then being realized in New York on the south and west sides of Central Park. In 1889 the *Real Estate Record and Builders' Guide* reported that Montrose W. Morris had "prepared plans and placed the contracts for what will be one of the largest and finest apartment houses in Brooklyn," the Alhambra (1889–90), at 500–518 Nostrand Avenue and 29–33 Macon Street.[174] The two-hundred-by-seventy-foot, five-story, electrically lit building occupied the entire block of Nostrand Avenue between Halsey and Macon Streets and was set back fifteen feet from the street on a terrace, with broad steps leading up to an arched entrance. Between the two wings on Nostrand Avenue, an open court big enough for a tennis court lay behind an arcade of columns and arches. The Romanesque-inspired design was faced in stone on the first story and light Roman brick with terra cotta above. Inside there were six suites of eight or nine rooms each on every floor, with sliding doors that allowed the parlor, library, reception, and dining rooms to be united into one large room for receptions. The Alhambra was developed by Louis Seitz, who had admired Morris's model house on Hancock Street. Despite its name, the apartment building had no Moorish details. A superb example of Morris's ability to synthesize elements from the Romanesque Revival and the Queen Anne in a fashion at once monumental and picturesque, it abounded in contrasting textures and terra cotta details that complemented its highly articulated mass, which incorporated six towers, steep dormered roofs, loggias, and arcades.

On the next block to the north, Morris followed up with the Renaissance Apartments (1892), at 488 Nostrand Avenue, on the southwest corner of Hancock Street, a smaller but in some ways more imposing design that reflected a stronger basis in geometrical composition than did the Alhambra.[175] The châteauesque, five-story, terra cotta–trimmed, buff Roman brick mass, with conical capped towers at each corner, rose to a high, pitched slate mansard roof, connecting the design strongly to the tradition of the French Renaissance. Between the towers, monumental Palladian windows framed the second, third, and fourth floors, a sure sign of Morris's increasing interest in Classicism. Morris capped his career as an apartment-house architect with another châteauesque design, the yellow brick and white terra cotta Imperial Apartments (1892), at 1198 Pacific Street, on the southeast corner of Bedford Avenue.[176] Also stylistically transitional, the Imperial faced both Pacific Street and Bedford Avenue with a basement story atop which a three-story arcade, consisting of two-story-high, colossal paired Corinthian terra cotta columns carrying terra cotta arches, rose to a pitched roof broken by a long shed dormer framed by smaller dormers to provide light to the fifth-floor units. On the second and third floors, bronze-clad bay windows were set between the paired columns. At the Renaissance, three six-story towers simply marked the building's corners. But at the Imperial, the middle tower, sitting at the corner of Bedford Avenue and Pacific Street, commanded a strategic vista of Grant Square and formed a visible marker for travelers on Bedford Avenue, an important thoroughfare. The six-story towers rose to conical roofs, which together with the steep mansards even more specifically connected the Imperial with the château architecture of the French Renaissance. Both the Imperial and the Renaissance were also developed by Louis Seitz.

Compared to Morris's three splendid apartment houses, most others in Bedford were more modest in layout, size, and architectural ambition. Francis Stryker's four-story 375 Stuyvesant Avenue (1890), at the northwest corner of Decatur Street, placed a yellow Roman brick superstructure over a brownstone base.[177] Magnus Dahlander's 376–380 Lewis Avenue (1892), between Macon and MacDonough Streets, a pair of four-story orange brick and brownstone apartment buildings, showed, like Montrose W. Morris's grander designs, an interest in combining features of the Romanesque Revival with those of the French Renaissance.[178] Like Morris, Dahlander used a stone wall to continue the base of the two buildings and thereby suggest that they function as a unit.

A break in the residential landscape came in the form of a modest park, Frederick Law Olmsted and Calvert Vaux's Tompkins Park (1870–71), a small oasis bounded by Greene, Lafayette, Marcy, and Tompkins Avenues.[179] The plan was simple, with a straight, bench-lined perimeter walk and diagonal paths leading from the corners to a central mall, where a fountain and a flagstaff occupied symmetrical places of honor. A dense thicket of trees at the edge lent a sense of privacy and, near the center, widely spaced trees provided room for sunny lawns.

In addition to residential development, Bedford was also the home of the Union League Club of Brooklyn, a Republican stronghold which appropriately enough had its clubhouse (1889–90) facing Grant Square on Bedford Avenue, on the southeast corner of Dean Street.[180] P. J. Lauritzen won the commission through a seven-firm competition in which he beat, among others, Henry F. Kilburn; Kilburn had produced a palazzo-like design, a version of which he would eventually see built, in 1894, in New York for the recently founded Colonial Club, at the southwest corner of Broadway and Seventy-second street.[181] Lauritzen had recently relocated to New York from Philadelphia after winning the competition for the Manhattan Athletic Club, on Madison Avenue (see chapter 2). He was also the architect of the building for Smith,

Imperial Apartments, southeast corner of Pacific Street and Bedford Avenue. Montrose W. Morris, 1892. View to the southeast, c. 1910. BHS.

Union League Club, southeast corner of Bedford Avenue and Dean Street. P. J. Lauritzen, 1889–90. View to the southeast, c. 1896. BHS.

Gray & Co., at Flatbush Avenue and Fulton and Nevins Streets (see above). The Union League Club was Brooklyn's most magnificent clubhouse. Four stories tall, with a base consisting of three arches forming a deep arcade at the entrance, it was elsewhere relieved by courses of rock-faced brownstone set against a granite, brick, and Belleville stone composition. A three-sided bay window at the corner was an implied tower, rising above the roofline to resolve itself as an octagonal loggia capped by a steeply pitched tiled conical roof. Balancing the mock tower was a broad mass rising to a hipped roof—all in all an ambitious melange held in check by the banded base and the band courses tying together and indicating the various floors. The interior consisted of bowling alleys and a shooting gallery in the basement, dining and reception rooms on the first floor, a library and a billiards room on the second, private dining rooms and bachelor apartments on the third, a

Proposed Union League Club, southeast corner of Bedford Avenue and Dean Street. Henry F. Kilburn, 1889. Competition-entry perspective. BLDG. CU.

fourth-floor gymnasium, and a rooftop pavilion for summer refreshments.

Two blocks north of the Union League Club was the site of Fowler & Hough's Twenty-third Regiment Armory (1891–94), at 1322 Bedford Avenue, between Atlantic Avenue and Pacific Street, which consisted of a midblock, 62,965-square-foot drill hall and, facing Grant Square, a cross-gabled administration building in part influenced by H. H. Richardson's Allegheny County Courthouse and Jail (1883–88), in Pittsburgh.[182] Seven seventy-foot-tall crenellated circular towers were located at the corners and flanking the two-story-high, round-arched entrance, which was ornamented with terra cotta friezes. At the corner of Bedford Avenue and Pacific Street an eighth tower, 136 feet tall, pierced the skyline,

enjoying an urbanistically witty dialogue with the towers of Montrose W. Morris's Imperial Apartments, across the street. In 1897, while describing the armory, the *New York Daily Tribune* paid particular attention to the interior of the main reception room:

> This has an unusually lofty ceiling, and the whole interior is trimmed with massive carved oak in the old English style. As the chairs and tables are also of heavy carved oak, the effect is that of a mediaeval knightly banquet hall. The old armor and weapons that decorate the walls complete the effect. Certainly nothing in any other American armory approaches it, and visitors from abroad say they have never seen anything like it. Something of its generous proportions may be judged from the fact that the fireplace and mantel reach up twenty-four feet.[183]

Twenty-third Regiment Armory, 1322 Bedford Avenue, between Atlantic Avenue and Pacific Street. Fowler & Hough, 1891–94. View to the northwest, 1900. Underhill. BPL.

Girls' High School, 475 Nostrand Avenue, between Halsey and Macon Streets. James W. Naughton, 1885–86. View to the northeast, c. 1896. BHS.

Bedford was home to some of the more interesting post–Civil War school buildings constructed in both New York and Brooklyn. Between 1879 and 1898 James W. Naughton, an Irish-born architect trained at the University of Wisconsin and the Cooper Union, was superintendent of buildings for the Board of Education of the City of Brooklyn. Designed by Naughton, Brooklyn's schools tended to be more sprawling and with fewer floors than their site-constricted New York counterparts. Naughton had a fine eye for detail, and under his direction the schools shed their factory-like aura and became more institutional in character. Naughton's Central Grammar School (1885–86), at 475 Nostrand Avenue, between Halsey and Macon Streets, was in effect the first purpose-built high school to be constructed in either New York or Brooklyn.[184] A striking design consisting of three red brick stories atop a stone basement, the building combined Gothic and French Second Empire features and included a pavilion at each corner and a projecting central tower rising to a cupola capped by a high pyramid. Despite its size, the demand for space was such that a decision was made to restrict it to 2,300 girls and to build a separate high school for boys. Hence, almost from opening day, the building was known as Girls' High School. Public School 73 (1888), at 241 MacDougal Street, on

the northeast corner of Rockaway Avenue, in the farthest reaches of Bedford, was a remarkably handsome Romanesque Revival design that demonstrated Naughton's willingness to take pains with even the most remotely located facility.[185] Closer to Bedford's heart, Naughton's Public School 79 (1889), at 322–328 Kosciusko Street, between Throop and Sumner Avenues, was similar and not any grander, revealing the school board's evenhanded approach.[186] Boys' High School (1891), at 832 Marcy Avenue, between Putnam Avenue and Madison Street, was Naughton's most ambitious design and Brooklyn's most impressive public school facility.[187] With four floors of classrooms set on a high rusticated base, the school, which occupied one end of a city block, marked an important milestone in the evolution of a new building type, lifting it into the realm of serious architecture. While not completely in control of his Richardsonian Romanesque–derived design, Naughton did achieve one brilliant feature which would serve the school in good stead—a four-sided tower at the corner of Marcy Avenue and Madison Street, a version of the tower H. H. Richardson used to crown his Allegheny County Courthouse. Essentially blank, the tower was pierced only by narrow, vertical air slits, relieved by an exceptionally high pilaster arcade and anchored at the corner by slender

Public School 79, 322–328 Kosciusko Street, between Throop and Sumner Avenues. James W. Naughton, 1889. View to the southwest, c. 1900. BHS.

tourelles. It rose to an open arcade supporting a cornice and a steep pyramidal roof.

New churches were required for the new neighborhood. Richard M. Upjohn's brownstone St. George Episcopal Church (1886–87), occupying an 80-by-112-foot site at the southwest corner of Gates and Marcy Avenues, looked back to an earlier stage of ecclesiastical practice with a low-massed Ruskinian Gothic design in red brick trimmed with stone and roofed in slate.[188] Entered from Marcy Avenue, the nave, covered by a steep-pitched slate roof, was flanked by aisles sheltered under roofs of a shallower pitch. A polygonal tower next to the entrance porch served as a chimney. Enriched with slender stone colonettes and tiny supporting gables, and rendered in a checkerboard of brick and stone, it formed a uniquely memorable feature. In 1889 Upjohn added an extension to St. George to accommodate the Sunday school and other parish activities. George P. Chappell's brick and granite Tompkins Avenue Congregational Church (1888–89), on the southwest corner of Tompkins Avenue and MacDonough Street, featured an immense, 140-foot-tall campanile reminiscent of St. Mark's in Venice.[189] Built by what was said to be the nation's largest Congregational congregation, it was frequently called Dr. Meredith's Church in

Boys' High School, 832 Marcy Avenue, between Putnam Avenue and Madison Street. James W. Naughton, 1891.
View to the northwest, c. 1900. BHS.

Tompkins Avenue Congregational Church, southwest corner of Tompkins Avenue and MacDonough Street. George P. Chappell, 1888–89. View to the southwest, c. 1910. BHS.

Throop Avenue Presbyterian Church, southwest corner of Throop and Willoughby Avenues. Fowler & Hough, 1889–90. View to the southwest, c. 1900. BHS.

honor of its pastor. The interior featured a semicircular auditorium seating 2,100 people in a forty-seven-foot-high, column-free room, the flat roof above carried by a Howe bridge truss. The church replaced an earlier structure across the street that was both too small and plagued by bad acoustics; that building was retained for use as a Sunday school.[190] Chappell's St. Bartholomew's Episcopal Church (1890), at 1227 Pacific Street, between Bedford and Nostrand Avenues, near Grant Square, was a charming, countrified antiphony to Upjohn's St. George.[191] The congregation began as an offshoot of St. Luke's Church in Clinton Hill, meeting in the former Bedford Congregational Church, which was torn down to make way for the new building. The highly picturesque composition was dominated by a high, wide, and unusually detailed tower of battered red brick, with rough-stone corners that grew out of the stone base to tie the entire complex together. An open-sided covered porch led under the bell tower to the nave.

Fowler & Hough's 900-seat, Romanesque-inspired Throop Avenue Presbyterian Church (1889–90), at the southwest corner of Throop and Willoughby Avenues, a terra cotta–trimmed brick structure resting on a base of Lake Superior stone, had at its corner a 110-foot-high belfry with no bell.[192] In 1889 the cornerstone was laid for three new buildings for the New York Avenue Methodist Church, a 101-by-103-foot church, a 62-by-90-foot Sunday school, and a 31-by-50-foot parsonage, all designed by J. C. Cady for the east side of New York Avenue between Bergen and Dean Streets.[193] The Romanesque church, of Colobaugh brick with Lake Superior sandstone trim, was completed in 1891 and featured a 100-foot-tall tower in the center of the New York Avenue facade and a 1,100-seat auditorium shaped in the form of a Greek cross and covered by a dome carried on four massive columns. The church organ, the largest in Brooklyn and said to be one of the five largest in the country, had 3,917 pipes.

Parfitt Brothers's one-thousand-seat Temple Israel (1890–92), at 1005 Bedford Avenue, on the northeast corner of Lafayette Avenue, was a superb, restrained design in light-colored brick, with a clear geometry of crossed gables supporting a gilded dome.[194] Said to be modeled on the Church of St. Sophia in Constantinople, it was Brooklyn's largest synagogue, replacing an earlier facility on Greene Avenue near Carlton Avenue. Entered through a low-sprung arch set in a pedimented facade flanked by two square towers crowned by pyramidal roofs, Temple Israel was a notable, remarkably abstract piece of elemental composition. Covering the dedication services, the *New York Times* described the building as "one of the most magnificent of the new church edifices in Brooklyn."[195] Parfitt Brothers's chapel for the Embury Methodist Episcopal Church (1894), at 230 Decatur Street, between Lewis and Stuyvesant Avenues, was a boldly asymmetrical Romanesque Revival design combining orange Roman brick, brownstone, copper, and red tile.[196]

New York Avenue Methodist Church, east side of New York Avenue between Bergen and Dean Streets. J. C. Cady, 1889–91. View to the southeast, c. 1910. BHS.

Temple Israel, northeast corner of Bedford and Lafayette Avenues. Parfitt Brothers, 1890–92. View to the northeast, c. 1910. BHS.

Prospect Park

Prospect Park (1866–73) was Frederick Law Olmsted and Calvert Vaux's second major commission and, some would have it, their best.[197] Though graced with natural advantages of landscape and topography that Central Park lacked, Prospect Park was not simply an adaptation of a site to park purposes but a complete reconsideration of its assets leading to a superb work of public art. According to Olmsted and Vaux, the park "would be a work of art, and the combination of the art thus defined, with the art of architecture in the production of landscape compositions, is what we denominate landscape architecture."[198]

On April 18, 1859, Brooklyn citizens, impressed by New York's Central Park, succeeded in lobbying the New York State Legislature to establish a commission to study the feasibility of creating a park system for their city. The cornerstone of the park system was to be Mount Prospect, located on the Brooklyn-Flatbush boundary line. The site was the highest point in the city still to be virtually uninhabited. Other sites considered were at Ridgewood, Bay Ridge, and New Lots; sites for small local parks were also mentioned, one a block in Brooklyn Heights bounded by Montague Terrace and Remsen, Furman, and Montague Streets, intended to preserve the harbor view for all. Though the Mount Prospect site was at the edge of the mostly built-up city of Brooklyn, it was in fact central to the larger urban district that inevitably would wrap it but which now consisted of the open farmland of Flatbush and New Lots to the south and west and, on the east, the still-rural areas of the slope extending down to the harbor. The Mount Prospect site also enjoyed the value of historical association—it had been the site of the Battle of Long Island on August 27, 1776, the first major battle between the Continental Army under George Washington and the British Army after the signing of the Declaration of Independence.

An act of the legislature on April 17, 1860, established the Board of Park Commissioners and allocated funds to

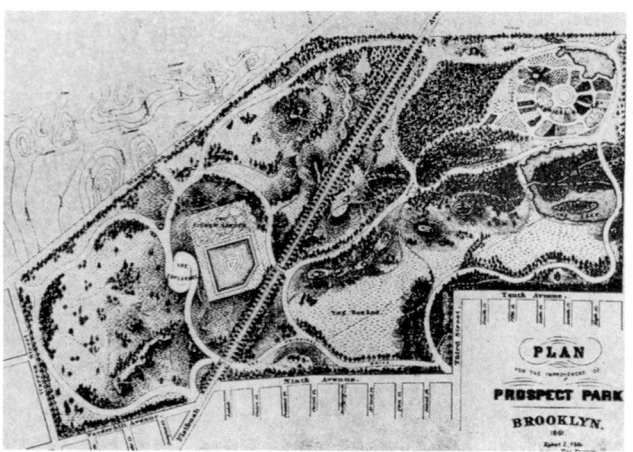

Plan for the Improvement of Prospect Park. Egbert L. Viele, 1861. BHS.

lay out the proposed park, which was to encompass 350 acres. Egbert L. Viele, the engineer who had initially been in charge of Central Park, was appointed chief engineer. Viele, in keeping with the ideas of Andrew Jackson Downing and Olmsted, saw the park as a "rural resort, where people of all classes, escaping from the turmoil of the city, might find relief for the mind, and physical recreation."[199] But Viele was not a great designer, and his "Plan for the Improvement of the Park" was rather banal and gardenesque. Stalled by the Civil War, the park began to take shape after 1865, when successive acts of the legislature provided funds for land acquisition, leading to the addition of more than 200 acres to the original tract, so that 562 acres were soon dedicated to the project. And on May 29, 1866, the state legislature replaced Viele with Frederick Law Olmsted and Calvert Vaux, who were appointed landscape architects of Prospect Park. Their design, prepared at the behest of the Board of Park Commissioners in 1866, even before they were hired by the legislature, differed from Viele's not only in size but in concept. Viele had proposed to extend the park north and east of Flatbush Avenue, then the city's principal link to the outer village of Flatbush and to the ocean some five or six miles beyond, thus creating what would be a split park, a condition he proposed to rectify with overpasses. The site east of Flatbush Avenue was important because it would shelter the reservoir from urban development, thereby protecting the city's drinking water. But the reservoir, combined with the 198-foot-high Mount Prospect itself, presented considerable obstacles to park development. Moreover, much of the land east of Mount Prospect was little more than an ash dump, which would require fifteen feet of fill. Viele also intended the park to extend only as far as Ninth Street. In 1861, Viele stated that the park "requires but little aid from art to fit it for all the purposes of health and recreation."[200] Though his plan favored existing topographical features, it nonetheless also called for an awkward arrangement of familiar park elements, including a parade ground and a flower garden.

James S. T. Stranahan, president of the Board of Park Commissioners, was particularly displeased with Viele's ideas. Even before Olmsted and Vaux's appointment, Stranahan hired Vaux to join him in a survey of the grounds, leading to the decision to sell the land east of Flatbush Avenue and to extend the park to the west between Ninth and Tenth Avenues and to the south, where the flat land was suitable for a lake. It was ironic that this solution resulted in the exclusion from the park of Mount Prospect, which had given the park its name. Though the park was expanded beyond Ninth Street, the eastern piece of land was not sold and Olmsted and Vaux recommended that the land instead be used for a museum and other educational institutions, which it was.[201]

When Vaux was asked to survey the park in January 1865, he described the project in a letter to Olmsted, who was in California, enclosing a sketched plan and asking

Olmsted to return to New York to resume their partnership and work on Prospect Park with him.[202] Olmsted, concerned about his health and still smarting over the political feuding that surrounded the design and construction of Central Park, was slow to reply to Vaux's offer. He nonetheless joined the project in November after Vaux catered to his vanity and craving for public recognition: "If I go on and do Brooklyn alone, well or ill," Vaux wrote to his colleague, "you suffer because the public will naturally say, if Olmsted really was the prime mover in the C.P. [*sic*] why is he not ready to go forward in the path he started in. . . . I shall not advise but, if . . . in the Fall you should happen to be here again disengaged and willing to devote a decade to Landscape art, why, there is the half of Brooklyn to begin on. . . . My position is that I have defended you from yourself and that 'Olmsted & Vaux' is an institution that ought not to be a mere bubble to be blown away heedlessly."[203] Flattery combined with the failure of his Mariposa, California, mine project brought Olmsted back to New York.

In 1868 Olmsted and Vaux issued their report for Prospect Park.[204] Their plan not only laid out a superb sylvan retreat but also proposed a comprehensive parkway system that would frame and foster the development of Brooklyn for a generation or more. The parkways, in effect broad boulevards providing for local and through traffic and flanked by carefully controlled development lots, were

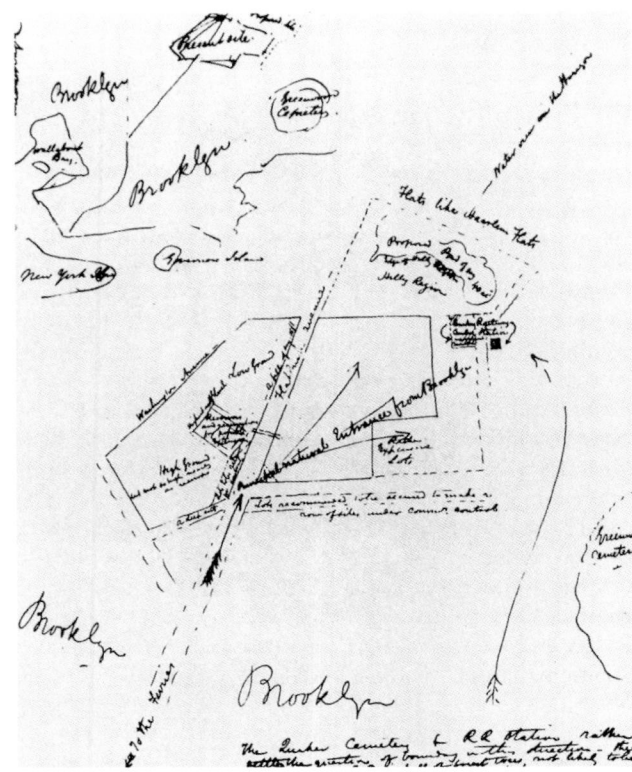

Sketch plan for Prospect Park. Calvert Vaux, 1865. FLONHS.

View of Prospect Park site, 1865. The two men holding the drawing sheet in the center of the photograph are thought to be Calvert Vaux (left) and Frederick Law Olmsted (right). BHS.

to connect the park with the sea at Coney Island and the farther reaches of Long Island to the east.

Two years before they issued their report, Olmsted and Vaux had presented a preliminary plan accompanied by a long essay that clearly described the designers' intentions. In a report to the Brooklyn Common Council, the Board of Park Commissioners summarized Olmsted and Vaux's proposal: "The ground features of the plan are simple and easily comprehended; but the Commissioners wish to direct attention to three regions of distinct character embodied in it, in each of which, it will be observed, the suggestions of the natural condition of the land are proposed to be developed. They are, first, a region of open meadow, with large trees singly and in groups; second, a hilly district, with groves and shrubbery; and third, a lake district, containing a fine sheet of water, with picturesque shores and islands." The plan also allowed for playgrounds, zoological gardens, "and other special purposes," all "connected with each other . . . by a carefully adjusted system of rides, drives and rambles."[205] The designers actually thought the natural scenery of the site was in some ways a distraction from the park's attraction: "The largest provision is required for the human presence. Men must come together, and must be seen coming together, in carriages, on horseback and on foot, and the concourse of animated life which will thus be formed, must in itself be made, if possible, an attractive and diverting spectacle."[206]

An elaborate, Gothic-inspired stone lookout tower, designed by Vaux, was included in the initial plan, as was a sheltered dining area overlooking the lake; neither were built. From the time when Vaux made a rough sketch while undertaking his first survey, Prospect Park's main entrance was to be at its northwest corner, where a large elliptical plaza was to become a hub for a sophisticated road system. Smaller plazas were to define each of the other important park entrances. In 1867, as a result of a public subscription, a large statue of Abraham Lincoln was erected at the northern end of the elliptical plaza at the main entrance. A fountain was placed in the plaza's center in 1871.

In 1871 the diarist George Templeton Strong was one of 250,000 visitors to the new park. In his diary entry for July 18 of that year, Strong recorded the impressions of his first visit:

> Crossed at Fulton Ferry. Inspected the Brooklyn pier of the future bridge. It is about thirty feet high, and the great mass of granite masonry looks like business. Then a long horse railroad car ride up Fulton Street and Flatbush Avenue, and reached the "Plaza," a large open place with a most lovely fountain and a tolerable statue of Lincoln. Reservoir on the left, with a kind of observatory. The outlook thence is panoramic and most striking. It takes in New York, Brooklyn with its numerous suburbs, the Jersey hills, the Bay, Staten Island, the Navesink Highlands, an expanse of ocean, Canarsie or Jamaica Bay, and the great belt of level ground that extends eastward from the Narrows to a latitude south of Jamaica. Then explored the

Proposed lookout tower, Prospect Park. Calvert Vaux, 1870. BHS.

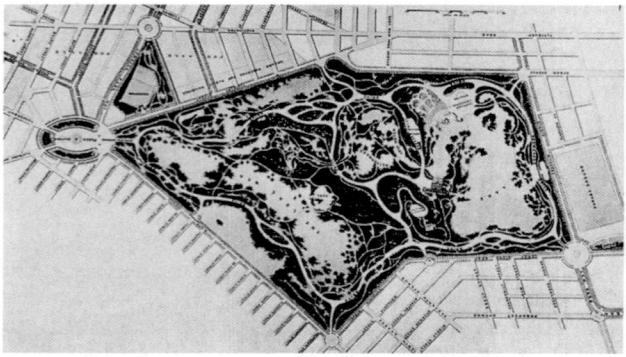

Prospect Park, bounded by Flatbush Avenue, Ocean Avenue, Franklin Avenue, Coney Island Road, Fifteenth Street, Ninth Avenue, and Plaza Street. Frederick Law Olmsted and Calvert Vaux, 1866–73. Plan, 1871. BHS.

View to the south of the Long Meadow, c. 1870, Prospect Park. Frederick Law Olmsted and Calvert Vaux, 1866–73. Visible on the far right is part of the Picnic House (Calvert Vaux, 1869). BHS.

View of typical rustic shelter, c. 1890, Prospect Park. Frederick Law Olmsted and Calvert Vaux, 1866–73. BHS.

Park, even to "Lookout Hill," from which one gets a fine view to the south and west. We almost saw the crest of the surf breaking on Coney Island beach. . . . This Park beats Central Park ten to one in trees. Its wealth of forest is most enviable. I think we cannot match its softly undulating lawns. But we beat it in rock and . . . in water and bridges. . . . But it beats us in views and is a most lovely pleasance.

On his way back Strong reflected on the discomforts of commuting: "The ferry boats coming in as we left our car were a phenomenon. Each . . . carried just as many men as could stand on her deck. If I wanted to buy a house in Brooklyn (and I envy residents on the Heights overlooking the Bay), the necessity of using such an overcrowded conveyance morning and evening would reduce the value of any piece of Brooklyn real estate . . . at least thirty per cent. The bridge, if ever completed, will remove this drawback."[207]

Strong was not the only one to see the natural advantages of Prospect Park over Central Park. In 1868 John W. Kennion wrote:

> Instead of a long and narrow parallelogram, restricted by the encroachments of municipal and private boundary lines, and obstructed by an obstinate entanglement of rock ledges, barrens and morasses, the Prospect Park . . . opens at once,

from the main entrance, right and left, into a breadth and variety of ground which has enabled the designers to arrange the plan with reference to the most desirable class of effects for a genuine city park. The advantages of this are such that, although actually less in area than the Central Park, the interior scenery of the "Prospect" will be larger in character, the landscapes broader and more truly rural, and the space will seem to be actually greater.[208]

In contrast with the slow pace required to complete Central Park, Prospect Park was pushed to completion in a comparatively short time. Three hundred men worked on the park in the summer of 1866; 1,825 worked on it during the following summer; 1,100 in 1868; close to 1,000 in 1869; 750 in 1870; and 1,100 in 1871. In the depression year of 1873 only about 500 were employed. Despite the natural beauties of the site, extensive grading was required to create the seventy-five-acre Long Meadow, which suggested infinite distance as it extended nearly a mile into the heart of the park from the plaza entrance. Of all the park's features, the Long Meadow was perhaps the most remarkable, not only for its size and subtly curving plan but for its part in the principal entrance sequence to the park. Pedestrians progressed from the formal oval plaza through a shady vestibule that was big enough to close off the noise and dust of the city, then under the park drive by means of the Endale Arch, "a thing of beauty" in the opinion of the *New York Times*, whereupon the vastness of the Long Meadow opened up in its full glory.[209]

A fifteen-acre lake was dug, supplied by a well said to be one of the largest ever. An arbor shaded a portion of the children's playground, where the park's first carousel was opened in 1874. Various rustic shelters dotted the park, but the most unusual one, an extraordinary umbrella-like circular shelter for horses and carriages designed by Vaux in 1869, was not realized. The earliest permanent structures were the arches that allowed pedestrians to avoid the traffic carried above on the main drive. The first was the Eastwood Arch (1867–68), near the Willink Entrance, and the second was the Endale Arch (1867–69), originally called the Enterdale Arch, near the plaza; both were built of yellow Berea sandstone from Ohio and reddish brownstone from New Jersey. Even more spectacular was the Meadowport Arch (1868–70), balancing the Endale Arch on the west side of the Long Meadow, with its Mogul-inspired cornices. The passages through all three arches were lined with wood, with the Endale featuring alternating bands of black walnut and yellow pine. Grander still was the triple-span, four-bay-deep Nethermead Arch (1868–70), carrying the central drive near the heart of the park, with inner vaults faced in hard brick laid in patterns. The final underpass, Cleft Ridge Span (1871–72), was built of molded concrete blocks, known as *béton coignet*, alternately colored red, ocher, and pale gray. With only three different molds, complex patterns were achieved on the arch's interior surface.

The Concert Grove House (1872) was a chalet designed by Vaux to provide toilet facilities and light refreshments. It resembled the park's Dairy (1869), also designed by Vaux. More unusual was Vaux's Concert Grove Pavilion (1874), in which eight cast-iron posts modeled after early Hindu columns carried a complexly curved, forty-by-eighty-foot hipped roof. In good weather, tables and chairs were placed under this shelter for the use of parkgoers, who, if their timing was right, could take in concerts from orchestras and bands set on an island, an idea that proved acoustically ill-advised. A temporary music pavilion was set up in the Lullwood in 1871, and in 1888 the Music Pagoda was added near the Lily Pond.

Olmsted and Vaux's plans also called for improvements to nearby streets. Vanderbilt and Ninth Avenues were widened to one hundred feet and Fifteenth Street, Coney Island Road, and Franklin Avenue were also widened. The designers believed that dark parks invited crime, so sidewalks along the outside of the park were gaslit for public strolling after the gates to the park were closed in the evening. Southeast of the park, on a separate tract provided by the state in 1868, lay the Parade Ground, a forty-acre marching field adjoining Park Circle. In 1869 a wood structure with steep, picturesque roofs was built to provide officers' quarters in the central, two-story pavilion and open shelters at either side for observing the proceedings.

In 1873 Olmsted and Vaux disbanded their partnership so that Vaux could concentrate on his architectural commissions. Olmsted was then retained as a consultant to the Board of Park Commissioners, remaining in this capacity until 1878. After that, during the 1880s, he had little connection with the park and the increasing mishandling of its maintenance, a problem that also plagued him at Central Park. In each case the commissioners were ignorant of his ideas and frequently just as ignorant of sound gardening principles. Olmsted was particularly disappointed in the

Proposed shelter for horses and carriages, Prospect Park. Calvert Vaux, 1869. BHS.

View to the south of Endale Arch, c. 1894, Prospect Park. Calvert Vaux, 1867–69. BHS.

View to the west of Meadowport Arch, c. 1894, Prospect Park. Calvert Vaux, 1868–70. BHS.

View to the west of Nethermead Arch, c. 1894, Prospect Park. Calvert Vaux, 1868–70. BHS.

View to the east through Cleft Ridge Span, c. 1874, Prospect Park. Calvert Vaux, 1871–72. BHS.

View to the west of Cleft Ridge Span, c. 1880, Prospect Park. Calvert Vaux, 1871–72. BHS.

View to the southeast, c. 1880, of Concert Grove House (1872) on the left and Concert Grove Pavilion (1874) on the right, Prospect Park. Calvert Vaux. BHS.

View to the north, c. 1895, of the Plaza (Frederick Law Olmsted and Calvert Vaux, 1870), with the Montauk Club (Francis H. Kimball, 1889–91) on the left. BHS.

decision to scrap Music Island, which he felt was the victim of a trumped-up attack, especially since the entire shorefront landscape around it, as well as the pedestrian and carriage concourses, were all designed to focus on the offshore concerts. When the commissioners planned to convert the great entrance oval outside the park into a kind of public garden, the newly founded, highly influential magazine *Garden and Forest* blasted them in an editorial of July 4, 1888:

> The noble plaza outside the principal entrance of the park is described by the Commissioners in their report [27th annual report, 1888] as a "great failure, suggestive of Siberia in winter and Sahara in summer," and it is suggested to convert it into a garden after the fashion of the Public Garden in Boston. It is evident that the Commissioners do not understand the motives which led to the creation of the plaza, which is really one of the great features of the park, and which provides, among other things, a proper place in which great public meetings can be held outside the park itself. To those who have seen the effects of public meetings upon the London parks, the establishment of this broad paved plaza will seem a wise provision indeed. It greatly facilitates, too, the entrance of carriages into the park as the currents of street traffic approach here upon lines coming from six different directions, which without the plaza would create hopeless confusion.[210]

James S. T. Stranahan was also no longer part of the picture. In 1882, the recently elected mayor of Brooklyn, Seth Low, had removed "the father of Prospect Park" from his position as president of the Board of Park Commissioners, which Stranahan had held for twenty-two years, because of a ten-thousand-dollar discrepancy found in the commission's books—which Stranahan had promptly recompensed with his own money. Behind Stranahan's dismissal was Low's belief that Brooklyn was now big enough to run its own departments and that state-appointed commissions like the one Stranahan headed needed to be replaced by municipal departments. About Stranahan's forced retirement the *Brooklyn Daily Eagle* somewhat hyperbolically wrote:

> Prospect Park is pre-eminently his work. But for his foresight and perseverance we should not now be in possession of that noble resort; . . . The truth is, that Mr. Stranahan is one of the very few men who have creative genius. In the not remote future, the question will be asked by intelligent writers, who were the real architects of Brooklyn? who were the men who lifted her out of the cowpaths of village advance and put her on the road track of Metropolitan importance? When that question is answered, the name named with greatest honor will be that of James S. T. Stranahan.[211]

Eastern and Ocean Parkways

Frederick Law Olmsted and Calvert Vaux saw Prospect Park as a key feature in a comprehensive plan for the development of Brooklyn and for its integration with New York. In this they were nothing short of visionary, proposing that Prospect Park be connected to Central Park by a "shaded pleasure drive" that would skirt the developed portions of Brooklyn and run "through the rich country lying back" of it, "until it can be turned, without striking through any densely occupied ground, so as to approach the East River, and finally reach the shore at or near Ravenswood," where either "ferry or high bridges" would carry it over "the two narrow straits into which the East River is divided in this neighborhood" and connect with "one of the broad streets leading directly into Central Park, and thus with the system of somewhat similar sylvan roads leading northward, now being planned by the Commissioners of Central Park. Such an arrangement," Olmsted and Vaux continued in their preliminary report of 1866, "would enable a carriage to be driven on the half of a summer's day, through the most interesting parts both of the cities of Brooklyn and New York, through their most attractive and characteristic suburbs, and through both their great parks. . . . The whole might be taken in a circuit without twice crossing the same ground, and would form a grand municipal promenade, hardly surpassed in the world either for extent or continuity of interest."[212] In addition to this roadway, a much-reduced version of which would be realized as Eastern Parkway (1870–74),[213] Olm-

Plan for Eastern Parkway. Frederick Law Olmsted and Calvert Vaux, 1868. BHS.

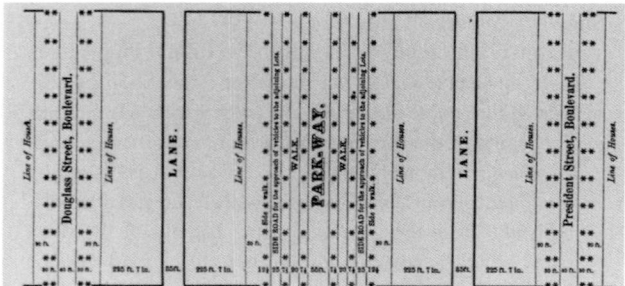

Plan for Eastern Parkway. Frederick Law Olmsted and Calvert Vaux, 1873. BHS.

sted and Vaux also proposed a second thoroughfare, to extend from the southern entrance of Prospect Park to the sea, which in time was completed as Ocean Parkway (1874–76).[214]

In their report of 1868 Olmsted and Vaux returned to the idea of a system of arterial roads. Now they argued that broad boulevards with various carriageways devoted to local and through traffic would attract suburban villa development. But they did not propound a picturesque, curving, topographically varied network of roads, favoring instead a type of street that had its origins in French boulevard planning, in particular the 429-foot-wide Avenue of the Empress (now Avenue Foch) in Paris and the Unter den Linden in Berlin. Olmsted and Vaux spelled out their ideas in detail, noting that cities could now spread out because workers and employers alike were no longer confined to living quarters located within walking distance from workplaces; these roads could thus serve as the backbone of a pattern of suburban development, which Olmsted and Vaux very much favored. Olmsted's experiences as executive secretary of the United States Sanitary Commission during the Civil War had convinced him that crowded living conditions fostered disease. He saw urban salvation in the suburbs and especially the detached villa, which he believed should be built on lots that were at least one hundred feet wide.

Eastern and Ocean Parkways, with their central drives surrounded by island paths suitable for promenading or horseback riding, and their flanking exterior roads, all extensively planted with trees, would not only serve modern traffic conditions and act as a fire barrier but would also help to establish distinct neighborhoods in the otherwise essentially flat and featureless Brooklyn landscape that stretched south and east of Prospect Park. Olmsted's plan for Eastern Parkway, which was to lie in the path of Sackett Street, also called for service lanes to replace Union Street to the south and DeGraw Street to the north. In addition, Douglass and President Streets were to be realigned so that they could be widened to incorporate double rows of trees on each sidewalk. All in all, the parkways, had they been executed according to Olmsted and Vaux's plans, would not only have been traffic arteries but also linear suburbs.

Neither Eastern nor Ocean Parkway was built to the elaborate specifications originally proposed. Ocean Parkway did fulfill Olmsted and Vaux's vision of a road to the sea, but Eastern Parkway, which abruptly terminated at Ralph Avenue, about two and a half miles east of the plaza, was not the link to New York and outer Long Island that Olmsted had hoped for. When the five-and-a-half-mile-long, 210-foot-wide Ocean Parkway opened late in 1876, the *New York Daily Tribune* pronounced it "the finest public drive in America."[215] The central, seventy-foot-wide road was flanked by two twenty-five-foot-wide bridle paths separated from the driving tracks by twenty-foot-wide grassy plots planted with young trees. The road was virtually flat for its entire length. The Board of Park

Ocean Parkway. Frederick Law Olmsted and Calvert Vaux, 1874–76. View c. 1890. BHS.

Eastern Parkway. Frederick Law Olmsted and Calvert Vaux, 1870–74. View to the east from Washington Avenue, 1900. BPL.

Commissioners was responsible for maintaining the new road, its jurisdiction extending thirty feet to either side of the parkway, a protected area in which "no buildings or other erections, except porches, piazzas, fences, fountains and statuary shall remain or be at any time placed; which space on each side of the avenue and in addition thereto, shall be used for courtyards only, and may be planted with trees, shrubbery, and otherwise ornamented, at the discretion of the respective owners or occupants thereof; but such an ornamentation shall be under the direction of the said Park Commissioners."[216] The *New York Times* was also impressed with the new parkway. Six months after its opening, the *Times* reported: "New York is almost entirely ignorant, and even Brooklyn but partially aware of the fact, that between these two great cities and the ocean there has been constructed a connecting link, a grand avenue, which for colossal proportions has scarce an equal in the world. Other cities may have their Champs Elysée, their Prater, their Cachina, but Ocean Parkway . . . as a work of suburban embellishment is without a rival."[217]

Park Slope

Park Slope, on the hill running to the harbor from Prospect Park, was the last of Brooklyn's three great upper-middle-class neighborhoods to develop in the Gilded Age.[218] Although it was laid out in the early 1850s and some construction took place in the 1870s, Park Slope, like Bedford, did not come into its own until the mid-1880s, when renewed prosperity combined with the opening of the Brooklyn Bridge and the establishment of elevated-train service to New York made the neighborhood's development possible. Not even the completion of its incomparable focus, Prospect Park, ten years before had such an impact.

Better than any other neighborhood in Brooklyn, perhaps even in all the New York area, Park Slope distilled and reified the sociology of the traditional American town. With a dramatic topography to reinforce the era's penchant for precise social stratification, Park Slope was in some ways a miniature version of a typical New England port town, rising up from shorefront commerce to a privileged world of big houses at the top of the hill and open countryside beyond, here in the form of Prospect Park. As the slope climbed from the industrial area around the Gowanus Canal to the park, so too rose the social profile. The bottomland was at Fourth Avenue, an arterial street leading to what would become Sunset Park and Bay Ridge. Fifth Avenue was not much higher. Here an elevated railroad was put in service in 1885, creating a tangible border for the zone of respectability beyond. Sixth Avenue was the first of the area's avenues to become a grand residential address, bounded by row upon row of houses occasionally interspersed with churches. On Seventh Avenue, as on Fifth, there was some local commerce as well as a number of churches. Above Seventh Avenue was an area, once the family farm of Johannus Theodorus Polhemus, that began to be subdivided by his descendant

Theodore Polhemus in 1866. Polhemus sold lots mostly to investors and developers, attaching to the deeds of sale covenants that restricted the land to the construction of high-class residences. Above Seventh Avenue, where most of the development of the 1880s and 1890s took place, relatively uniform rowhouses were joined by single and paired houses that were individual in character.

Prospect Heights was the name sometimes used to describe the area above Seventh Avenue, where top businesspeople and other professionals settled, many from established families who lived elsewhere in Brooklyn.[219] Some, as in the equivalent fashionable areas in New York, came from "nowhere," being newly rich. Development of the choicest land, from just west of Eighth Avenue to Ninth Avenue (not named Prospect Park West until 1895), came at the end of the 1880s. Here the handiwork of talented architects was almost everywhere to be seen, in high-class speculatively developed and individually commissioned townhouses as well as in spectacular freestanding mansions comparable to those on Clinton Avenue. As a result, Park Slope was one of the most interesting new residential quarters in America, containing by 1890 an extraordinary number of superb buildings, mostly houses, in either the Queen Anne or Romanesque Revival style. By far the majority were Romanesque, creating a remarkable streetscape that managed at once to be homogeneous by virtue of color, scale, and proximate mass, and extraordinarily varied by virtue of individual composition and detail.

Though typical of their type and similar to those in Fort Greene or Clinton Hill, the rowhouses of lower Park Slope, between Fifth and Seventh Avenues, were notable for their sheer number. Given that the land was open pasture until the Civil War, there were no impediments to development save those of the marketplace. As a result, long, unbroken rows tended to be built at one time. Probably the earliest row was 8–16 Seventh Avenue (1860), just south of Flatbush Avenue, the main point of access to the neighborhood from the built-up portion of Brooklyn.[220] Constructed without an architect, as were many of the early rowhouse groups, these were three-story brick dwellings set on a high rusticated-stone basement. The war and the Panic of 1873 virtually halted any further development in the area, but in 1876 a row of Neo-Grec houses consisting of three stories and a basement was built at 128–146 Sixth Avenue, featuring stoops balustraded in cast iron.[221] The row was notable in that it filled the complete blockfront between Sterling and St. John's Places, and because it was designed by a prominent Brooklyn architect, Marshall J. Morrill. As in other growing districts of New York and Brooklyn, the Neo-Grec was the preferred style, especially for details, which were precisely incised into the stone fronts; moldings and cornices, however, were often as not in the Italianate taste. Such was the aesthetic case of the work of another Brooklyn architect, Robert Dixon, whose six-house row (1877) at 188–194 Sixth Avenue stretched down the block from the corner of

Stewart L. Woodford house, 825 President Street, between Seventh and Eighth Avenues. Henry Ogden Avery, 1885. View to the north. Henry Ogden Avery Collection. CU.

north-south streets inserted into the grid between Carroll Street and Garfield Place to break up the long avenue blocks and create intimate residential settings) Parfitt Brothers's noticeably restrained group (1889–90) for J. F. Ranson, displaying Romanesque and Italian Renaissance tendencies, consisted of two distinctly different houses that, because the basements and parapets aligned, formed a unit.[226]

Henry Ogden Avery's house for Stewart L. Woodford (1885), at 825 President Street, between Seventh and Eighth Avenues, was the first significant single-family house in Park Slope.[227] Woodford, once ambassador to Spain, moved to Park Slope from 67 Cambridge Place in Clinton Hill. After attending the Cooper Union and apprenticing with Russell Sturgis, Avery had studied architecture at the Ecole des Beaux-Arts in Paris. He returned to New York and worked as a draftsman in Richard Morris Hunt's office, where he assisted with designs for the base of the Statue of Liberty (see chapter 2). In 1883 he established an independent practice in New York, perhaps making the decision to do so on the strength of the Woodford commission. Avery's design for the thirty-six-foot-wide house was a remarkable break with prevailing practice. With no raised basement or stoop, it was entered almost at street level. Its elevation, simple to the point of severity, was symmetrical, with the entrance at the center. Broad, simple brick wall surfaces were enlivened by an alternating pattern of square-edged and chamfered bricks forming door and window frames. The facade's design was quirky, with an almost syncopated rhythm of openings. Three round-arched openings at the ground floor were surmounted by two two-sided oriel windows on the second floor, leaving the center blank except for the tiniest square opening high above the central entrance arch; on the third floor were three square openings, each holding a pair of windows. A structurally expressive roof was carried on projecting wood struts in a manner reminiscent of Eugène-Emmanuel Viollet-le-Duc.

Rudolph L. Daus's pair of houses for Drs. William M. Thallon and Edward Brinker (1887–88), at 176–178 St. John's Place, between Sixth and Seventh Avenues, was also quirky, but in that jumpy sort of way generally described as Queen Anne.[228] A caduceus, symbol of the medical profession, appeared in the elaborately ornamented gable of number 178, the wider of the two red brick and brownstone houses. Despite the houses' comparatively narrow dimensions, a variety of gables and dormer windows fit onto a shared slate roof, the skyline of which was broken by a conical-roofed tower.

Montrose W. Morris was represented in Park Slope with Henry Carlton Hulbert's house (1889), which, if not Morris's best Romanesque work, certainly constituted his grandest.[229] A double dwelling commissioned by Hulbert, a financier and industrialist in the paper-supply business, it housed the patron in one half with the other half leased to his daughter and son-in-law, Joseph H. Sutphin, who was also a partner in H. C. Hulbert & Co. When completed, Hulbert's house was quite isolated, facing Prospect

Berkeley Place.[222] Farther up Park Slope at 36–44 Seventh Avenue (1881), between Sterling and St. John's Places, Dixon designed a group consisting of five twenty-two-foot-wide, four-story, Neo-Grec brownstone houses, each with full-height, two-sided, oriel-type bay windows.[223] Close by, Thomas F. Houghton's four-house brownstone row (1882) at 13–19 Seventh Avenue, between Park and Sterling Places, was grander though only three stories high.[224] The row had full-height, two-sided bays and high stoops leading to segmental arched doorways, bringing a new sense of artistic vitality to Park Slope that would find its fulfillment in the larger houses built closer to Prospect Park in the late 1880s.

While the most interesting work of the mid- and late 1880s was designed for the high-end market, rowhouses aimed at those who were less well-to-do continued to be built. Not surprisingly, these reflected the prevailing taste of those at the top of the hill: the desire for individuality of expression that went with the rich and permissive vocabularies and compositional strategies of the Queen Anne and the Romanesque. At 21–27 Seventh Avenue (1887), between Sterling and St. John's Places, Lawrence B. Valk designed an elaborately detailed four-unit row of Romanesque houses.[225] At 18–20 Fiske Place (one of two

Henry Carlton Hulbert house, southwest corner of Ninth Avenue and First Street. Montrose W. Morris, 1889. View to the southwest, c. 1893. BHS.

Henry Carlton Hulbert house, southwest corner of Ninth Avenue and First Street. Montrose W. Morris, 1889. Main hall, c. 1893. BHS.

Park on the southwest corner of Ninth Avenue and First Street, a location still largely undeveloped. A subtly asymmetrical structure, clad not in the usual brownstone but in lighter-colored rough-cut limestone, with a gray slate roof that closely matched the stone, it featured balanced but differently shaped corner towers facing Ninth Avenue, lending the house a châteauesque character. The Hulbert house, with its equally elaborate interiors, ushered in an era of mansion building in Park Slope, and the sheer ambition of the undertaking rivaled anything to be found in Clinton Hill. According to a somewhat promotion-minded article in the *Brooklyn Daily Eagle*, the house was "the most startling private residence, from an architectural point of view, which has been erected in Brooklyn for some time."[230]

Lansing C. Holden's forty-foot-wide house for Mrs. M. V. Phillips (1887), at 70–72 Eighth Avenue, on the northwest corner of Union Street, was almost as imposing as Morris's Hulbert house.[231] The freestanding, picturesquely massed and imaginatively detailed three-story brick and brownstone Romanesque design featured Queen Anne details, including a Jacobean gable facing Union Street. Mrs. Phillips's house complemented F. Carles Merry's house for the New York jeweler Henry E. Beguelin (1886), at 52 Eighth Avenue, on the southwest corner of Berkeley Place, a Romanesque design that was distinguished by a spectacular curved stoop leading to the front door.[232] Entirely formed of cut stone, each story was defined by a different texture or design: at the basement, rough-faced random ashlar; above the parlor-floor windows, a checkerboard pattern; and above the next floor, a wide brick band of diagonal studding. A principal element was the corner bay topped by a truncated, cone-shaped tile roof. Facing Berkeley Place, the side elevation was dramatic with its molded brick chimney stack and curved bay. The next year, in 1887, Merry designed a similar house nearby for James Foster, at 240 Berkeley Place, between Seventh and Eighth Avenues, this one a three-story, twenty-by-fifty-foot, brick, Euclid stone, and terra cotta design.[233]

Lamb & Rich designed two memorable houses in Park Slope: one for F. L. Babbott (1886–87), at 153 Lincoln Place, between Sixth and Seventh Avenues,[234] and the other for George P. Tangeman (1890–91), at 276 Berkeley Place, between Plaza Street and Eighth Avenue.[235] The Babbott house, though situated in the middle of the block, could be seen in three-quarter view thanks to a wide side yard. Its main facade, facing Lincoln Place, combined a sweeping roofline and a complex intersection of elements, including a corner bay and a high chimney, for maximum picturesque effect. The Tangeman house, though distinctly Romanesque, with picturesque symmetry and a shingled pediment, also revealed strong hints of a turn toward Classicism. This could be seen especially in the details, which included an egg-and-dart frieze, an anthemion frieze above the front door, swagged garlands, and shells used for decorative relief. Yet the real interest stemmed from the decision to turn the ridge of the tiled gambrel roof parallel to the

George P. Tangeman house, 276 Berkeley Place, between Eighth Avenue and Plaza Street. Lamb & Rich, 1890–91. View to the south, c. 1892. AABN. CU.

street, framed with stepped end gables and giant chimneys and punctuated in the center by a three-windowed dormer crowned with a flared, slightly hipped roof.

Frank Freeman's house (1889) at the southwest corner of Plaza Street and Lincoln Place, for Guido Pleissner, a New York dry-goods merchant, was perhaps Brooklyn's finest Romanesque residence.[236] A squarish mass of stone, off of which turretlike bays seemed to pinwheel, it was organized into distinct, asymmetrical facades facing the two streets. Entered from Lincoln Place through a double-arched porch not unlike the one at Morris's Hulbert house, the basically unornamented design climaxed on the Plaza Street side in an elaborately decorated, high-peaked, gabled dormer with a triple window of Chicago School proportions.

Among architects based in New York, C.P.H. Gilbert made the greatest contribution to the architectural distinction of Park Slope. Between 1887 and 1892, Gilbert designed virtually all of Montgomery Place.[237] He was put in charge of the work by Harvey Murdock, a developer who commissioned from Gilbert twenty of the forty-six houses on the block, including Murdock's own, thereby creating one of the period's great urban ensembles.

Guido Pleissner house, southwest corner of Plaza Street and Lincoln Place. Frank Freeman, 1889. View to the southwest, c. 1895. BHS.

Gilbert's work on Montgomery Place began with two three-house groups facing each other across the street: 14, 16, and 18 for William A. Holliday, Frederick W. Starr, and George A. Price respectively; and 11, 17, and 19 for Murdock, William F. Brown, and Thomas L. Gill.[238] Though each house had its own identity, the groups were visually unified through the use of the same materials—rough-faced, random ashlar brownstone for the first floor, with amber-colored speckled brick above arched entrances. Numbers 14, 16, and 18 featured second-story oriels and steep roof gables. A little more variety was found across the street, where the Murdock house was understandably the showpiece, sporting a Dutch stepped gable above a very wide, bow-shaped, two-story bay with stone frames around stained-glass transoms.

Gilbert's work was not confined to the Montgomery Place development. At the far edge of Park Slope, on the south side of Ninth Street between Fifth and Sixth Avenues, he designed four seventeen-foot-wide brownstone houses (1887) consisting of three stories and a basement.[239] Closer to the fashionable quarter, a double residence of four stories and an attic at 115–119 Eighth

Avenue (1888), on the northeast corner of Carroll Street, was commissioned by Thomas Adams Jr., the chewing-gum mogul whose Chiclets brand was internationally famous and who had also invented the coin-operated machines that dispensed the gum.[240] Half of the house served John Dunbar Adams, a family member. Gilbert's Romanesque Revival design, in its ambitions the equal of Frank Freeman's Pleissner house, was vastly larger than his Montgomery Street houses. Picturesquely massed with a bold profile featuring a corner tower and a central projecting gable-roofed entrance bay, it was nonetheless somewhat stiff in its overall composition and sharp-edged detailing.

Soon to move in across the street from Adams, the chewing-gum king, in what was surely an amusing juxtaposition, was John H. Hanan, the shoe king.[241] Gilbert also designed this four-story, thirty-five-by-sixty-foot house (1890), at the northwest corner of Carroll Street and Eighth Avenue. Hanan's Romanesque-inspired house, with its swelling corner turret, was imposing if somewhat conventional. Inside, its arcaded main hall, anticipating the Renaissance Classicism of the 1890s, was spatially

14–18 Montgomery Place, between Eighth and Ninth Avenues. C.P.H. Gilbert, 1887–88. View to the southwest, c. 1893. BHS.

Harvey Murdock house, 11 Montgomery Place, between Eighth and Ninth Avenues. C.P.H. Gilbert, 1887. View to the north, c. 1893. BHS.

William F. Brown house, 17 Montgomery Place, between Eighth and Ninth Avenues. C.P.H. Gilbert, 1887–88. View to the north, c. 1893. BHS.

Thomas L. Gill house, 19 Montgomery Place, between Eighth and Ninth Avenues. C.P.H. Gilbert, 1887–88. View to the north, c. 1893. BHS.

Thomas Adams Jr. house, northeast corner of Eighth Avenue and Carroll Street. C.P.H. Gilbert, 1888. View to the north, c. 1893. BHS.

John H. Hanan house, northwest corner of Eighth Avenue and Carroll Street. C.P.H. Gilbert, 1890. View to the northwest, c. 1893. BHS.

John H. Hanan house, northwest corner of Eighth Avenue and Carroll Street. C.P.H. Gilbert, 1890. Main hall, c. 1893. BHS.

expansive and complex. Around the corner on Carroll Street, Gilbert designed three houses in a row in 1887, each thirty-two feet wide: 846 Carroll Street, a stone and Perth Amboy brick house of three stories and a basement for Charles Robinson Smith;[242] 842 Carroll Street, a buff-colored Roman brick and brownstone-trimmed house of four stories and a basement for George W. Kenyon;[243] and 838 Carroll Street, a stone and brick house of four stories and a basement for the lawyer James H. Remington.[244] On Garfield Place, Gilbert designed a house (1889) for Louis B. Jones at number 313, between Eighth and Ninth Avenues, a twenty-six-foot-wide, four-story brick house with a Spanish-tile mansard roof.[245] Another house (1889) on Garfield Place, and one of Gilbert's best, was built for Rodney Allen Ward, at number 319.[246] Beneath a Classical cornice, Gilbert superimposed smooth walls of orange-colored brick on a base of rough-faced random stonework rising through the basement and parlor-floor levels.

George P. Chappell, who might have been counted on to counterpoint Park Slope's urbanism with a more rural-esque approach, instead went along with the neighborhood's trend. His 283–289 Garfield Place (1889), between Seventh and Eighth Avenues, was a row of four three-story, seventeen-by-fifty-foot, variegated brick, brown-stone, and tile Romanesque houses unified by an overall symmetry, with the emphasis placed on the end gables and

Charles Robinson Smith house, 846 Carroll Street, between Eighth and Ninth Avenues. C.P.H. Gilbert, 1887. View to the southwest, c. 1893. BHS.

George W. Kenyon house, 842 Carroll Street, between Eighth and Ninth Avenues. C.P.H. Gilbert, 1887. View to the south, c. 1893. BHS.

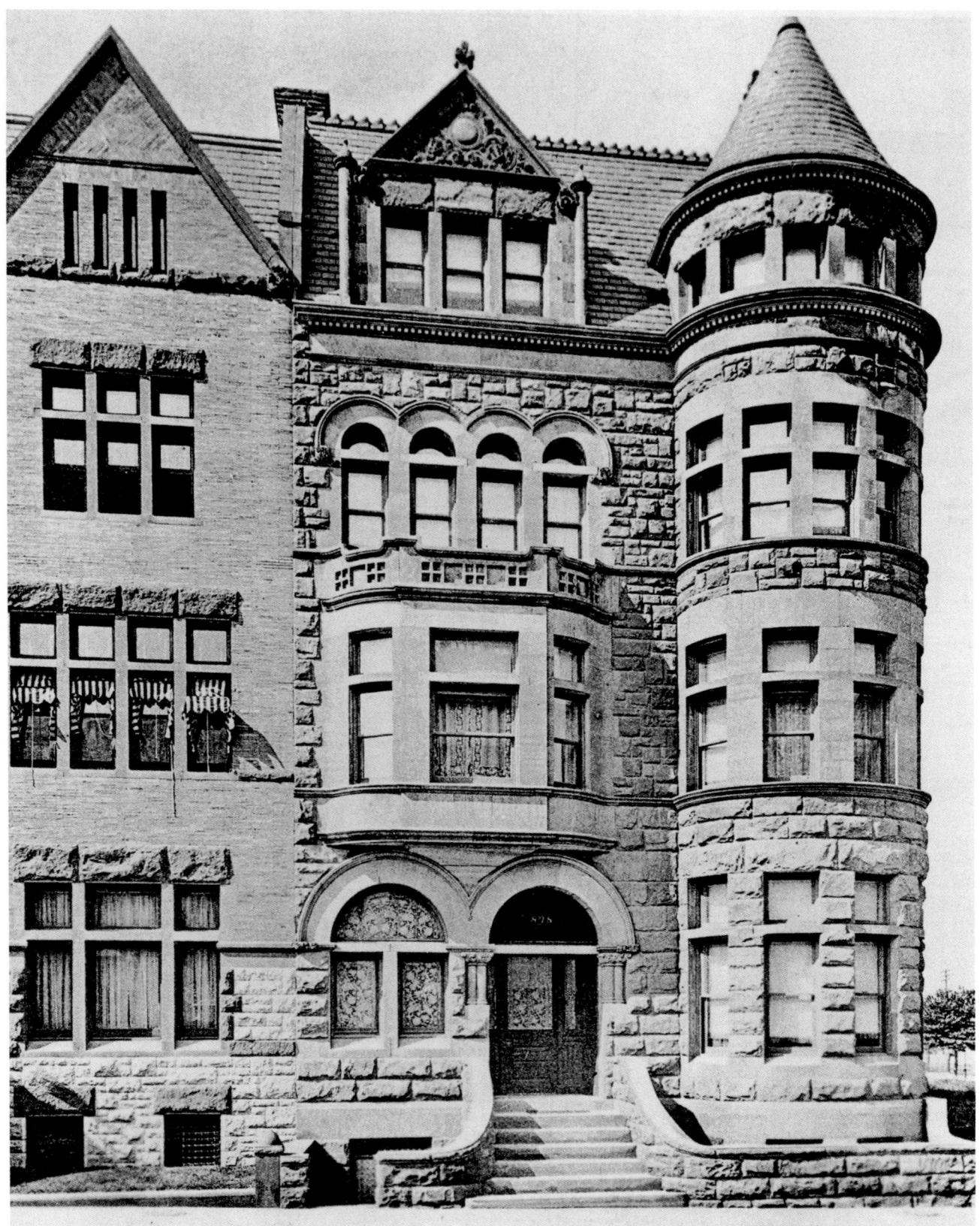

James H. Remington house, 838 Carroll Street, between Eighth and Ninth Avenues. C.P.H. Gilbert, 1887. View to the south, c. 1893. BHS.

Rodney Allen Ward house, 319 Garfield Place, between Eighth and Ninth Avenues. C.P.H. Gilbert, 1889. View to the north, c. 1893. BHS.

Episcopal Church of the Redeemer, northwest corner of Fourth Avenue and Pacific Street. Patrick C. Keely, 1870. View to the northwest, c. 1910. BHS.

on chimneys rising above the roofline, while the middle houses, slightly set back, featured gabled dormers set into the steep tiled roof.[247] Chappell's houses echoed the stiff formality of much of Gilbert's work. By contrast, William B. Tubby designed a fine, almost suburban, three-story, brick, stone, and tile, five-house Queen Anne row (1887) at 864–872 Carroll Street, between Eighth and Ninth Avenues.[248] Two years later, however, Tubby also turned to the Romanesque with his three-story, twenty-five-by-fifty-five-foot, brick and sandstone house for S. E. Buchanan, at 234 Lincoln Place, between Seventh and Eighth Avenues.[249] Napoleon Le Brun & Sons, which rarely designed houses, made an exception for the engineer William R. Webster.[250] Located at 863 Carroll Street, between Eighth and Ninth Avenues, the house (1890) combined brownstone and reddish Roman brick in a manner that seemingly straddled the dramatic chasm between the loose eclecticism of the 1880s and the strict formalism that was to come.

As with other Brooklyn neighborhoods, churches were important civic-scaled features of the Park Slope townscape. The area's first churches catered to the working-class residents who were its first settlers. Patrick C. Keely's low-slung, Gothic-inspired, rock-faced ashlar Episcopal Church of the Redeemer (1870), at the northwest corner of Fourth Avenue and Pacific Street, was the area's first house of worship, located in the bottomland at some distance from the middle-class development above Fifth Avenue.[251] In 1880 Lawrence B. Valk's Sixth Avenue Baptist Church (1880), on the northeast corner of Lincoln Place, was built to serve the growing middle-class population now living midslope.[252] Valk's eighty-seven-by-one-hundred-foot Gothic-style church was charmingly picturesque yet suited to its urban setting with a certain toughness most clearly manifested in the sandstone bands set perfectly flush with the flat brick walls. Two years later, Parfitt Brothers's six-hundred-seat, brownstone and terra cotta–trimmed Grace United Methodist Episcopal Church, at 31–35 Seventh Avenue, anchored the northeast corner of St. John's Place with a more boldly patterned but equally picturesque Gothic design that also exhibited some exotic touches, including references to Romanesque and even Moorish sources.[253] A corner tower culminating in a tall octagonal cone helped establish the church as an important local landmark. St. John's Episcopal Church (1869–70; 1885), at 139 St. John's Place, between Sixth and Seventh Avenues, was built for a congregation moving from its original home, at Washington and Johnson Streets, where it had been founded in 1826.[254] On June 15, 1869, the cornerstone was laid for a chapel that was completed a year later, and the street's name was changed from Douglass to St. John's Place in honor of the church. Edward T. Potter designed the charmingly modest, Gothic-inspired chapel of rough-faced Belleville brownstone trimmed with light Ohio

Grace United Methodist Episcopal Church, northeast corner of St. John's Place and Seventh Avenue. Parfitt Brothers, 1882. View to the northeast, c. 1910. BHS.

stone. A simple, steeply gabled rectangle crowned by a stone bell gable that rose above the roof ridge, St. John's had at its west end a bold stone wall pierced by tall lancet windows. The chapel was intended as a part of a larger church, and in 1885 John R. Thomas incorporated it as the transepts of his expanded facility. Next to the church, Potter also designed a large Gothic rectory (1869–70). The Memorial Presbyterian Church (1881–82), at 42–48 Seventh Avenue, on the southwest corner of St. John's Place, was designed by Pugin & Walter.[255] Built entirely of random ashlar Belleville stone, it presented a far less restless appearance than the typically polychromed Gothic churches of the period, although the rust-colored terra cotta cresting at the roof stood out. In 1888 the successor firm of Marshall & Walter added a chapel that mostly followed the lines of the church.

By the mid-1870s the new neighborhood was populous enough to require schools. Public School 39 (1876–77), at 417 Sixth Avenue, on the northeast corner of Eighth Street, was designed by Samuel B. Leonard, superintendent of buildings for the Board of Education of the City of Brooklyn.[256] The high-shouldered, vertically proportioned, three-story brick facility married a mansard roof and the overall proportions of the French Second Empire style with Italianate detailing. The narrow, pavilionated facade, with projecting ends and an upthrusting central tower containing the stooped entrance, was altogether memorable. Public School 107 (1894), at 1301–1323 Eighth Avenue, on the northeast corner of Thirteenth Street, was designed by Leonard's successor, James W.

St. John's Episcopal Church, 139 St. John's Place, between Sixth and Seventh Avenues. Edward T. Potter, 1869–70. View to the northwest showing the rectory (Edward T. Potter, 1869–70) on the left. EWP. CU.

View to the north along Seventh Avenue, 1891, showing the Memorial Presbyterian Church (Pugin & Walter, 1881–82) on the left and Grace United Methodist Episcopal Church (Parfitt Brothers, 1882) on the right. BHS.

Public School 39, northeast corner of Sixth Avenue and Eighth Street. Samuel B. Leonard, 1876–77. View to the northeast, 1941. BHS.

Montauk Club, northeast corner of Eighth Avenue and Lincoln Place. Francis H. Kimball, 1889–91. View to the northeast, with Eighth Avenue facade on the left, 1894. BHS.

Naughton, who took over the design of Brooklyn's public schools in 1879.[257] Naughton's four-story, brick and Lake Superior stone, Romanesque Revival design was bigger in size and far more expansive in scale than Leonard's school, consisting of five bays stretching along Eighth Avenue with a central projecting bay containing the arched entrance and crowned by a high brick gable.

While churches and schools were scattered through the new neighborhood so as to be accessible to virtually all classes of people living in Park Slope, pride of place, facing the Plaza, was given to the newly founded Montauk Club (1889–91), the social focus for the richest families living on or near what was coming to be called the Gold Coast.[258] Park Slope's architectural high point, and a fair rival to the great New York clubs, the Montauk Club, occupying a 100-by-117-foot site on the northeast corner of Eighth Avenue and Lincoln Place, was designed by Francis H. Kimball. Kimball was awarded the commission over a number of other architects, including C.P.H. Gilbert, who, it was reported, had expected to get the job.

The club was incorporated on March 15, 1889, and the cornerstone was laid for the palatial clubhouse on December 14 of the same year, four months later than had first been announced in the *Real Estate Record and Builders' Guide*. After seeing the drawings, the editors of the *Record and Guide* were moved to observe that they "promise a striking example of the Venetian style, a decided contrast to the Romanesque which will surround the clubhouse."[259] The building was dedicated at a gala reception on May 23, 1891. Kimball's design, an essay in the Venetian Gothic, was specifically an interpretation of the Ca d'Oro (1427–36), on the Grand Canal. Although Montgomery Schuyler had reservations about specific aspects of the design, he admired Kimball's approach: "It is a style especially appropriate to a club-house, first by reason of its undeniably festal aspect which it wears more strikingly, perhaps, than any other mode of mediaeval architecture, and also, more specifically, because the Venetian palazzo resembled a modern club-house in the simplicity of its division into few and large apartments, a division naturally

Montauk Club, northeast corner of Eighth Avenue and Lincoln Place. Francis H. Kimball, 1889–91. View to the northwest, with Plaza Street facade on the right, c. 1907. BHS.

expressed by its exterior architecture."[260] Kimball's palette of brownstone, tawny-colored brick, and reddish-brown brick, with brownish-orange terra cotta reserved for the ornament, yielded a warm golden hue that set the building off from its mostly darker context. The use of terra cotta was a Kimball trademark. The material had only begun to come into its own after 1877, when, in response to architects' demands for more than the then-standard gray, it became available in a variety of colors. Particularly remarkable was the frieze over the second-floor quatrefoil arcade on the south side, illustrating the inscription, "1659 Wyandanch Sachame of Pamanack, his wife and his son Wiankabone giving a deed to Lion Gardiner of Saybrook, Easthampton, Long Island, July 14, 1659." The history of the Montauk Indians was presented in a continuous narrative frieze above the third floor. This frieze, like all the other ornamental features of the building, only spanned three sides. The fourth, north side of the building was kept very simple in anticipation of the need for expansion. The main entrance, by means of a

steep stoop, was on the club's narrow end, facing Eighth Avenue. To the right, a bay window provided for a second-floor balcony carried on lion-head brackets, a smaller companion to the grand balcony. To the left of the main entrance, a second door, smaller in scale but with its own stoop, served as an entrance for ladies. Though the club was one of the first to open its doors to women, the separate entrance permitted unescorted females to reach the second-floor dining hall without crossing the main lobby, where presumably the behavior of the gentlemen might be too raffish. Above the main entrance was a carved stone band of American Indian heads. At the second floor the spandrels between the round-arched windows depicted Classically inspired trophies fused with American Indian motifs, while above a small frieze depicted the founders and builders laying the cornerstone. The compositional and allegorical complexities met on the Plaza Street side, where a two-story bay window swelled to take in the park views and provide a balcony for the third-floor dining room.

Flatbush

South of Prospect Park lay the village of Flatbush, first settled in 1630 as Midwout; though it was renamed by the British in 1664 it remained until the 1880s very Dutch in character.[261] Flatbush was the seat of Kings County until 1832, when Brooklyn began to gain commercial power. Beyond the village lay the open spaces of Flatlands along the Atlantic Ocean, where there were summer resorts at Coney Island and Brighton and Manhattan Beaches. Flatbush Avenue, between Fulton Street and the Brooklyn border, was opened in 1858. Two years later, horsecar service was established between Flatbush and Brooklyn, leading Edmund D. Fisher, a local historian, to claim: "The doom of Flatbush as a country place was forever sealed when in July, 1860, the first car of the Brooklyn City R.R. Co. was driven into the town."[262] The 1878 opening of the Brooklyn, Flatbush, and Coney Island Railroad, which linked Brighton Beach with Prospect Park, where travelers changed to horsecars for the rest of the trip to the Brooklyn ferries, made suburbanization possible. Nonetheless, given the length of the trip and the inconveniences of multiple transfers—from railroad to horsecar to ferry—suburbanization came slowly, such that, as Montgomery Schuyler observed in 1884, even though "Flatbush . . . has not been protected from change by eminence," Flatbush Avenue, "through which the horse-cars run, has a quaint and ancient aspect, and you have only to drive half a mile away on either side to forget that you are in a world where a horse-car exists. There are long and leafy lanes which look very much as they must have looked when the British riflemen marched through them a hundred and eight years ago this August, past farmhouses which even then were old, and of which many are still standing."[263] When horsecar service was replaced by continuous train service in 1889, Flatbush's growth began in earnest.

In 1873 the citizens of Flatbush and other surrounding towns defeated an annexation proposal similar to the one that successfully joined New York with parts of lower Westchester. The proposal would have bound the towns politically with Brooklyn, a merger that did not take place until 1894. With independence seemingly assured, local residents and newspapers called for the construction of a town hall, authorized in 1874 by the Flatbush Board of Improvement. The new Town Hall (1874–75), on the north side of Grant Street between Flatbush Avenue and Locust Street, was designed by John Y. Culyer, one of the engineers of Prospect Park.[264] Set atop a high, random-stone basement, the red-brick-fronted, two-story, Gothic building, trimmed in horizontal bands of buff stone, sat in splendid near-isolation close to the site of the August 1776 Battle of Long Island. A tower culminating in a steep pyramidal roof ensured the building's visual prominence in a townscape of widely spaced, low-lying houses.

In 1869 the state legislature passed a bill establishing a street grid for all of Kings County, a sure early warning of the urbanization to come. In 1886, three years after the opening of the Brooklyn Bridge, and surely in anticipation of continuous train service to New York, the developer Richard Ficken began to construct Tennis Court, a quintessential suburban development named after the recently popular lawn game favored by the upper classes.[265] Ficken's development, consisting of frame houses built along lushly planted streets marked by entrance gateposts, included portions of Ocean Avenue, East Eighteenth and East Nineteenth Streets, and the grounds of the Knickerbocker Field Club, established in 1889. First housed in a small facility that quickly proved inadequate, the Knickerbocker Field Club commissioned from Parfitt Brothers an elegant, gambrel-roofed, clapboard and shingle clubhouse (1892), at 114 East Eighteenth Street.[266] In 1893 the *Brooklyn Daily Eagle* described the club as "an old-time family mansion, cozy but substantial," going on to praise the contrast between the yellow and white color scheme and the surrounding greenery.[267] The club was surrounded by comfortable wooden houses such as the one designed by E.G.W. Dietrich and A. M. Stuckert for W. A. Porter (1887), a tightly massed version of the Shingle Style.[268]

View to the southeast of Flatbush Avenue near Vernon Avenue, 1877, showing the Van Beuren house (c. 1711) on the left, Flatbush. BHS.

Town Hall, north side of Grant Street between Flatbush Avenue and Locust Street, Flatbush. John Y. Culyer, 1874–75. View to the northeast, c. 1877. Brainard. BPL.

Knickerbocker Field Club, 114 East Eighteenth Street, between Albemarle Road and Church Avenue, Flatbush. Parfitt Brothers, 1892. View to the southwest, c. 1905. BHS.

Coney Island

South of Flatbush lay Coney Island, a resort accessible from Brooklyn by train or via the newly completed Ocean Parkway, and from New York by steamship.[269] By the Centennial, Coney Island, once a denizen of hoodlums, had been transformed into a popular seaside pleasure ground, "the true republic of watering-places," with wooden hotels served by six railway lines built between 1869 and 1877, when Coney Island's development was aided by the construction of the 250-foot-wide, 3,000-foot-long Coney Island Concourse, an asphalt road running parallel to the surf.[270] The *New York Times* was impressed with the new road:

> Excellent arrangements have been made for the safety of pedestrians, the driving road on the Concourse being separated from the footpath. Overlooking the water, as a protection for visitors, two large shelters have been erected, each house capable of holding 4,500 people, where, safe from the glaring sun or passing squalls, in ease and comfort, during the Summer heats, the cool, pure air of the ocean can be imbibed. In completing this, the Brooklyn Park Commissioners have certainly accomplished a colossal work.[271]

Two years later, in 1879, Coney Island was made even more convenient with the completion of a new pier, the double-decked, one-thousand-foot-long Iron Steamboat Pier, at West Brighton, which not only incorporated toilet facilities but also numerous saloons to serve day-trippers.[272] By 1882 Coney Island was host to five million visitors annually. Surprisingly, Coney Island met the exacting standards of Frederick Law Olmsted, who found it "the only notable instance in this country in which capital has been used with . . . boldness in advance of demand."[273]

Austin Corbin's New York and Manhattan Beach Railway Company was linked to the Long Island Railroad, and thereby offered the most convenient route to Coney Island from Greenpoint, which was reached from New York by ferry. The railroad had its terminus at the site of a new hotel, the Manhattan Beach Hotel, constructed by the company in 1877 on extensive grounds.[274] The wood-framed, shingle-clad hotel was designed by J. Pickering Putnam, a Boston architect. Said to be the largest of its kind when built, the 600-foot-long, 225-foot-deep, 150-bedroom summer palace sat on a foundation of hard pine piles eight and twelve inches in diameter, its heavy frame strapped to the piles with iron and, in the architect's own words, "well braced and trussed to withstand the severest winter gales."[275] Behind the hotel lay the train shed, connected to it by a covered passageway. Inside, the hotel contained a dining hall as well as a restaurant and lunchroom, each sixty-eight by one hundred feet, as well as open-air

Iron Steamboat Pier (1879), west of West Fifth Street, West Brighton. View to the southeast, c. 1890. BHS.

dining facilities of nearly the same capacity, "they being of the same character as those which proved so popular at the Centennial Exhibition at Philadelphia."[276] Towers containing colossal water tanks, a fire-prevention necessity, provided an additional impression of grandeur. Corbin catered to a top-notch crowd. His ban on lower- and middle-class "Hebrews" had the effect of instituting a boycott of all Jews, which may have been his original goal. Despite its management's prejudices, the hotel prospered, and in 1879 Corbin more than doubled it in size, employing the architect Maurice Fornachon, who had his offices in New York.[277]

In 1878 the New York architect John G. Prague, who specialized in speculatively built middle-class rowhouses and tenements, designed the Hotel Brighton, similar in style to the Manhattan Beach Hotel and likewise a large, wood-framed structure; the Brighton also catered to a monied crowd.[278] The *New York Daily Tribune* described the Brighton as a piece of "Gothic architecture, a long, low, rambling building, having a frontage of 325 feet. . . . It is painted a cream color, relieved by red window sashes, and fretwork in the cornices of the same color." Inside, the paper was most impressed with the main parlor, "a sumptuous apartment, 80 feet by 40, covered with a heavy Wilton carpet, of dark-red color, and furnished with Eastlake sets, in dark-green raw-silk, with lambrequins to match."[279] Bruce Price's St. George's Inn (1880), a much

smaller hotel intended for Coney Island, was a charming, three-and-a-half-story design that appears not to have been realized.[280]

By the mid-1880s, Brooklyn's oceanfront resorts were very popular, far outstripping the appeal of those at Williamsburg which had flourished in the middle of the century. The resorts consisted not only of hotels but also included "attractions," the most famous of which was J. Mason Kirby's "Elephantine Colossus" (1884–85), located at West Brighton, a 122-foot-high elephant topped by a howdah that afforded superb views of the ocean and surrounding countryside.[281] Deemed the eighth wonder of the world by its manager, C. A. Bradenburgh, the elephant could accommodate five thousand people and, in addition to the observatory, included the 60-by-35-foot "Stomach Room" and a 298-foot-long gallery.

Coney Island's buildings took a lot of punishment from the sea. In 1883 it was reported that one hotel, Paul Bauer's West Brighton Hotel, "the largest on the west end of the island," was to be lifted one floor above the sand.[282] In the winter of 1887–88, the same winter that brought a famously crippling blizzard to New York, the seas were raised so high at Coney Island that the Hotel Brighton was standing in water and seriously undermined. On April 3, 1888, after a coffer dam of sheet piling was built to hold the water back, and twenty-four lines of railroad track

Manhattan Beach Hotel, west of Ocean Avenue, Manhattan Beach. J. Pickering Putnam, 1877; Maurice Fornachon, 1879. View to the northeast, c. 1890. BHS.

Hotel Brighton, west of Coney Island Avenue, Brighton Beach. John G. Prague, 1878. View to the northwest, c. 1900. BHS.

Proposed St. George's Inn, Coney Island. Bruce Price, 1880. Perspective rendering. AABN. CU.

Moving the Hotel Brighton (John G. Prague, 1878), west of Coney Island Avenue, Brighton Beach. View to the east, April 3, 1888. BHS.

were laid up to the hotel, the building was jacked up and moved 600 feet back on timbers spread across twenty-four trains comprising 112 flatcars.[283] Six engines attached to ropes with sheaves, which multiplied the force of each by about eight times, did the work. It was an amazing feat— probably the largest building ever moved in one piece. So gentle was the operation that the plaster did not crack nor the window glass break, and the furniture as well as the crockery kept their places without damage.

Despite Coney Island's prosperity, the resort's halcyon days were numbered. There were reports of water pollution caused by garbage being dumped too close to land and the railroads aggressively promoted the crowds of day-trippers who came as much for horse-racing, which was introduced in the late 1870s, as for the sea.[284] At the resort's peak, perhaps the most spectacular building was Gilmore's Pavilion (1887–88), at Manhattan Beach, built to the designs of Francis H. Kimball. Designed to replace a canvas tent, Montgomery Schuyler described it as a "permanent tent, reared upon a base hung with parti-colored wood shingles, open to the air above that, and covered with a roof that is merely a velarium. If one looks closely he may detect Gothicism in the decorative detail in wood with which as a festal place it is properly provided. But upon the whole it is a piece of free architecture in which the picturesqueness of the result is not only appropriate and unforced, but proceeds from the special conditions of the problem."[285]

Moving the Hotel Brighton (John G. Prague, 1878), west of Coney Island Avenue, Brighton Beach. View to the southeast, April 3, 1888. BHS.

Gilmore's Pavilion, west of Ocean Avenue, Manhattan Beach. Francis H. Kimball, 1887–88. View to the northwest, 1898, showing the Manhattan Beach Hotel (J. Pickering Putnam, 1877; Maurice Fornachon, 1879) on the right. BHS.

View to the northwest of West Brighton between West Eighth and West Twelfth Streets, c. 1889, showing the "Elephantine Colossus" (J. Mason Kirby, 1884–85). BHS.

Grand View Hotel (c. 1875), foot of Fifth Avenue, Fort Hamilton. View from Gravesend Bay, c. 1890. BHS.

Bensonhurst-by-the-Sea

While Coney Island attracted a fast crowd, Bensonhurst-by-the-Sea and its adjoining communities, Bath Beach, Blythebourne, and Bay Ridge—until 1894 all parts of the town of New Utrecht, originally settled in 1662 and known for its potato and cabbage farms—were developed largely as suburban areas appealing to middle-class families.[286] As a Bensonhurst-by-the-Sea promotional brochure of 1890 succinctly stated, "There is no intention of setting up a fashionable resort. It is to be a quiet all-the-year living place."[287] There was at least one large hotel in the area, however, the Grand View, a magnificent, porch-wrapped, seven-story, wood-framed, elaborately carpentered palace built in the 1870s by the Brooklyn City Railroad Company on a spectacular cliffside perch where Fifth Avenue joined the sea.[288] Since the middle of the nineteenth century, elaborate villas such as the clapboarded, Gothic-style Dellwood House had been built along Bay Ridge, which until 1853 had been called Yellow Hook after the yellow clay deposits found there; following a yellow-fever epidemic, the name took on a negative connotation and was changed.[289] Some houses built in Bay Ridge belonged to vacationing New Yorkers, while others, like the board-and-batten, Gothic-style Andrew G. Cropsey cottage, at Eighty-fourth

and Bay Sixteenth Streets, belonged to families long established in the area.[290] Development picked up in Bay Ridge after 1890. One single-family house of note was the Shingle Style dwelling (1892) built by Samuel and Phoebe How on an eighty-foot-wide lot at 217 Eighty-second Street, between Second and Third Avenues.[291] Possibly designed by Parfitt Brothers, the house's entrance was on the side, at the base of an octagonal tower. The kitchen was located in the basement and the first floor was devoted to one large entertaining space, with French doors leading to the long porch facing the front, which was graced by Ionic columns.

Bensonhurst-by-the-Sea, connected to New York by a line of the Brooklyn, Bath Beach, and West End Railroad, was a planned suburb built beginning in 1887 on the two-hundred-year-old farmland of the Benson family. The family's farmhouse, called Bensonhurst, a simple, dormered cottage built in the early 1800s, served as the still rather rural retreat where in the 1890s Martha J. Lamb coauthored much of her widely read history of New York City.[292] Developed by James D. Lynch, who incrementally acquired the Benson farm and adjoining properties until he controlled one square mile, Bensonhurst-by-the-Sea incorporated a plan worked on by a team that included the surveyor Samuel H. McElroy, the landscape architects B. S. and G. S. Olmstead, the

217 Eighty-second Street (1892), between Second and Third Avenues, Bay Ridge. View to the northeast, 1892. Thomas. BRHS.

Dellwood House (c. 1860), Bay Ridge. View c. 1870. BHS.

Bensonhurst-by-the-Sea. Developed by James D. Lynch, beginning in 1887; plan by Samuel H. McElroy, B. S. and G. S. Olmstead, Colonel George E. Waring Jr., and Parfitt Brothers. Rendering of the Bensonhurst Marine and Field Club. BBS. CU.

Daniel W. Tallmadge house, Bensonhurst-by-the-Sea. Stanley S. Covert, 1889. Rendering. BLDG. CU.

sanitary engineer Colonel George E. Waring Jr., and the architectural firm Parfitt Brothers. Located approximately six miles from lower Manhattan and more easily reached by means of rapid transit than many parts of Harlem and upper Manhattan, Bensonhurst-by-the-Sea was hyped as

a suburban quarter near New York, with a southerly exposure on the ocean [developed] to the highest attainable state of perfection, by the aid of the most approved modern appliances. . . . Plans were devised to cover these acres with comfortable and tasteful homes suited to persons of moderate incomes. To the hamlet thus laid out was given the good Saxon name of those who had dwelt there so long. . . . Thus what was a quaint, quiet, retired rural region redolent with suggestions of Peter Stuyvesant and our Dutch ancestors has within a few years been endowed with all of the best and none of the worst features of the Metropolis.[293]

Unlike many real estate developers, Lynch decided to build the infrastructure of his town before selling lots. In addition, he laid out the beachfront between Bay Twenty-seventh and Bay Twenty-ninth Streets as a park to be shared by all the residents. While the community's promoters stated that deed restrictions "exclude no desirable inhabitants, but invite and make room for thrifty people of refined taste, and protect all classes," they nonetheless boasted, with more than a hint of xenophobia, that "the Park will be for Bensonhurst what the Battery was to New York in the early part of this century, before that lovely breathing place was invaded by the elevated railroads and became the camping ground of immigrants."[294] Tennis courts and a clubhouse for the Bensonhurst Marine and Field Club were also provided. The community contained an architecturally noteworthy train station, perhaps designed by Parfitt Brothers, incorporating a hipped, dormered roof punctuated by a conical-roofed tower, a feature that gave the building an easily identifiable silhouette. To enhance connections with Brooklyn, Lynch built Twenty-first Avenue as a one-hundred-foot-wide boulevard leading from Ocean Parkway at Parkville to his new suburban town. The house lots were uniformly twenty by one hundred feet. The first house was built in July 1888, and by August 1890 about one hundred houses were built or in construction, with the architect Walter E. Parfitt in residence as well as prominent doctors, engineers, and politicians. Daniel W. Tallmadge, an influential state assemblyman and the secretary of the Brooklyn Board of Education, occupied a shingle-clad, Classically detailed house designed in 1889 by little-known New York architect Stanley S. Covert.[295]

Although Twenty-first Avenue connected back to Ocean Parkway, according to the *Real Estate Record and Builders' Guide*, by 1890, when ten miles of streets were opened and in use, the "handsomest" was Twenty-second Avenue, by which "Brooklynites who take their daily drive through Prospect Park and the Ocean Driveway [*sic*] generally take a short cut to the sea . . . ; Twenty-first Avenue also runs from the Bay to the Parkway, but it is not so wide a thoroughfare."[296] Eighty-sixth Street, another one-hundred-foot-wide street, was the only place in Bensonhurst-by-the-Sea other than beachfront property where nonresidential development was permitted.

Vaux & Radford's Children's Aid Society Health Home or Sanitarium (1882) occupied a four-acre seaside lot at 1750–1818 Cropsey Avenue, facing Bath Beach on Gravesend Bay, that had been donated by A. B. Stone.[297] The resortlike, ninety-by-forty-foot, porch-wrapped, slate-colored building, with a sixty-five-foot-long service wing at the rear, was paid for by D. Willis James. With long porches facing the sea and casually massed dormers and stairs, the expansive facility permitted mothers to stay with their sick children while they were being treated. The charitable organization also built other structures on the campuslike property, including two Shingle Style buildings that served as refuges from inner-city neighborhoods for poor children seeking to escape the heat.[298] One of the buildings, named the Haxtun Cottage, incorporated deep

Children's Aid Society Health Home or Sanitarium, 1750–1818 Cropsey Avenue, between Bay Seventeenth and Bay Nineteenth Streets, Bath Beach. Vaux & Radford, 1882. Rendering. CAS.

Green Corridor Cottage (c. 1885), Children's Aid Society, Cropsey Avenue between Bay Seventeenth and Bay Nineteenth Streets, Bath Beach. View c. 1936. Abbott. MCNY.

porches, while the other, the Green Corridor Cottage, was distinguished by a five-story-high cylindrical tower capped by a conical roof. Occupying the adjacent block to the north was an elegantly detailed, three-story wooden house, built around 1850 for John V. Voorhees, whose family had lived in the vicinity for a century; the structure was converted into a hotel in 1893, with one story added, and was opened for business during the summer season.[299]

The Eastern District:
Williamsburg, Greenpoint, and Bushwick

Founded in 1802, and an independent city for only fifteen years before it was consolidated into the city of Brooklyn in 1855, Williamsburg began as a resort for New Yorkers, who arrived by ferry.[300] Williamsburg's main street was Broadway, an important conduit leading southeast from the ferry through Bushwick to Jamaica, along which Bushwick farmers carried produce to New York markets. Immediately after the Civil War, Williamsburg prospered, absorbing some overflow of residential population and manufacturing from New York's Lower East Side. According to the *New York Times* in 1867, the "limited accommodations furnished by the City of New York for business and residences has given a grand impetus to building in the City of Brooklyn, and particularly in the Eastern District, more familiarly known as Williams-

burg. . . notwithstanding many discouragements, such as antiquated ferry facilities, a 'one horse' Post-office, and other such-like farcical institutions."[301] A sign of prosperity was the decision to widen Broadway, which also required property owners along the street to renovate the facades of their buildings.

One substantial new building was King & Wilcox's Dorchester stone Kings County Bank Building (1868), three stories and a mansard, at 135 Broadway, on the northeast corner of Bedford Avenue, located at a strategic intersection of two important arterial roads.[302] Despite its Italianate detailing, the richly modeled, deeply carved, three-bay facade was a highly sophisticated representation of the new taste for the architecture of Second Empire France. On the second and third floors, slender Ionic and Corinthian columns alternated to emphasize the already emphatically banded columns carrying a pediment ornamented with a plaited Indian hut. Far grander was George B. Post's Williamsburgh Savings Bank (1869–75), at 175 Broadway, on the northwest corner of Driggs Avenue, a stylistic pioneer mixing Roman and Renaissance Classicism in ways that would not become typical in American architecture for another twenty years.[303] (The bank retained the original spelling of *Williamsburgh*, ending in the *h* the community had eliminated when it became part of Brooklyn, in 1855.) Post

Proposed Williamsburgh Savings Bank, northwest corner of Broadway and Driggs Avenue. Original scheme by George B. Post, 1869. NYHS.

was awarded the job in a competition, beating Peter B. Wight, whose brother-in-law, Samuel Mundy Meeker, was a charter member of the bank's board of trustees. Before the decision had been made, Post proposed that if he won the commission, Wight could decorate the bank's interior for five thousand dollars. Wight's design called for a three-and-a-half-story, French Second Empire-inspired building with a bold mansard and a central tower rising above the Serlian entrance porch. Inside, the central banking room was to be topped by a shallow cupola. Post's design, with its broad, low dome and monumental pedimented entrance, was certainly more unusual and impressive than Wight's. In presenting the revised design, the *New-York Sketch-Book of Architecture* took pains not only to justify the bank's monumental scale and character, but to explain why there was now a high dome and cupola:

> The bank is one of the wealthiest and most popular in the State of New York, and the present banking-hall is frequently crowded by so great a number of depositors, that the proper ventilation is almost impossible. In view of this difficulty the present banking-room, at the suggestion of the trustees, has been given a great height and provided with a continuous row of windows at the base of the dome. It is 60 feet square, and 100 feet high. The side walls are lined with freestone. The pilasters carrying the main interior cornice are of granite, with Corinthian

Proposed Williamsburgh Savings Bank, northwest corner of Broadway and Driggs Avenue. Competition entry by Peter B. Wight, 1869. Elevation. AIC.

Williamsburgh Savings Bank, northwest corner of Broadway and Driggs Avenue. George B. Post, 1869–75. View to the northwest. NYHS.

caps, and bases of marble. The dome is of iron, supported at the angles on pendentive bracketting of freestone. The shafts of the pilasters, the panels of the wainscoting, and the friezes of the cornices are of polished granite, as are also the counters, with the exception of the panels which are in colored marbles. The mouldings and rail of the counter are being made of bronze. The bank occupies the entire building, which is fireproof throughout.[304]

True to their agreement, Wight undertook the ceiling decoration of Post's building, producing a refined floral pattern. The architect Alfred J. Bloor in 1876 described Post's design succinctly, if critically: "Outside of governmental and ecclesiastical structures, there is probably no more monumental—and no more misplaced—building in the country than the Williamsburgh Savings Bank recently finished by Post, the interior polychromatic work being, however, from the designs of Wight. Both the exterior and the interior effect of the dome are very imposing; and the rest of the work, in a Renaissance tinged with Neo-Grec feeling though motived by Roman examples, is not unworthy of it."[305] Another bank of note was Theobald Engelhardt's North Side Bank (1889), at 33–35 Grand Street, between Kent and Wythe Avenues, a bold Romanesque building of brick and Lake Superior stone located closer to the ferry landing.[306]

In 1876, William B. Ditmars's Temple Beth Elohim, at 274 Keap Street, was built to serve Williamsburg's growing Jewish population.[307] It was commissioned by the first Jewish congregation in Brooklyn, a group of Orthodox German Jews who in 1850 organized themselves as Kahal Kodesh Beth Elohim, but who adopted the Reform ritual by the time they built their new house of prayer. The midblock, brick and stone, Gothic-style synagogue was decidedly churchlike. At one side, interrupting the prominent steep facade gable, a belfrylike tower rose to a steep pyramidal roof. In 1884 J. C. Cady designed St. Paul's German Evangelical Lutheran Church, on the southeast corner of South Fifth and Ninth Streets, which was dedicated the following year.[308] The Philadelphia brick and Belleville stone church, with a 100-foot tower at the corner, sat 1,100 worshipers in the main sanctuary. A smaller chapel was also provided.

Colored School No. 3, located at 270 Union Avenue, was a rather architecturally imposing building serving the needs of the area's black children before public education had been integrated in New York City.[309] As designed by Samuel B. Leonard and built in 1879–81, the brick, brownstone-trimmed building adopted a Romanesque vocabulary, complete with a principal facade dominated by a centrally located entrance tower flanked by pairs of ninefoot-high, round-arched windows.

North of Williamsburg lay Greenpoint, an independent village developed by two prominent New Yorkers, Ambrose C. Kingsland and Samuel J. Tilden.[310] In 1855 Greenpoint became part of Brooklyn. A working-class residential area serving the shorefront industry, including shipbuilding and the so-called black arts of printing, pot-

Temple Beth Elohim, 274 Keap Street, between Division and Marcy Avenues. William B. Ditmars, 1876. View to the south, c. 1910. BHS.

tery, glass, and iron, it had some houses not built as parts of rows. In 1889 Theobald Engelhardt, whose diverse practice kept him busy in Williamsburg and Bushwick as well as in other areas of Brooklyn, designed a two-and-a-half-story Queen Anne–style brick house for Dr. S. M. Lyons, at 143 Kent Street, west of Manhattan Avenue.[311] Most off Greenpoint's streets, however, were lined with rowhouses built for a less well-to-do clientele, comparable to the dwellings found in the lower reaches of Park Slope. Like other Brooklyn neighborhoods, Greenpoint was served by schools designed by Samuel B. Leonard and James W. Naughton. Public School 34, at 131 Norman Avenue, occupying the entire blockfront between Eckford Street and McGuiness Boulevard, was begun by Leonard in 1867 and expanded by Naughton in 1887–88.[312] The original portion of the building, based on the German Romanesque style of the 1840s, consisted of a two-and-a-half-story temple form entered at the gable end. Naughton's two-story flanking pavilions were respectful.

Greenpoint's churches included the hefty, early Romanesque Revival–style Reformed Dutch Church of Greenpoint (William B. Ditmars, 1870), at 149 Kent Street, between Manhattan Avenue and Franklin Street, and its rather more charming Florentine, baptistry-like octagonal Sunday School (W. Wheeler Smith, 1879).[313]

Reformed Dutch Church of Greenpoint, 149 Kent Street, between Manhattan Avenue and Franklin Street. William B. Ditmars, 1870. View to the northwest, c. 1880, showing the Sunday School (W. Wheeler Smith, 1879) on the right. BHS.

Henry Dudley's English-inspired, symmetrically massed, stone Church of the Ascension (1865–66) was a short distance away at 129 Kent Street.[314] The most prominent of Greenpoint's churches was the Roman Catholic St. Anthony of Padua (1874), at 862 Manhattan Avenue, at the end of Milton Street.[315] It was designed by the prolific church architect Patrick C. Keely, whose scheme of Philadelphia pressed red brick trimmed with Belleville and Nova Scotia freestone, with its 240-foot spire, was a landmark for all of Greenpoint.

Theobald Engelhardt's Greenpoint Home for the Aged (1887), at 137 Oak Street, at the head of Guernsey Street, was an imposing, if somewhat stylistically old-fashioned, two-story brick facility with Italianate massing and Romanesque arches.[316] Greenpoint's most unusual building was the Astral Apartments (Lamb & Rich and E. L. Roberts, 1885–86), at 184 Franklin Street, between Java and India Streets, a palatial, six-story, red brick and terra cotta apartment house underwritten by the oil merchant Charles Pratt, who named it after his leading product, Astral Oil, which was produced in a nearby refinery.[317] Built to provide adequate housing for Pratt's workers, the Astral was designed by the same firm (joined by Roberts) to which Pratt had entrusted the design of the first building of his new institute, in Clinton Hill (see above). The multi-entried Astral reflected ideas developed in England at the Peabody Flats and by Henry Roberts for the Society for Improving the Condition of the Laboring Classes. The Astral's architects were surely also aware of the work of William Field & Son on the Tower and Home Build-

Greenpoint Home for the Aged, 137 Oak Street, at the head of Guernsey Street. Theobald Engelhardt, 1887. View to the north, c. 1890. BHS.

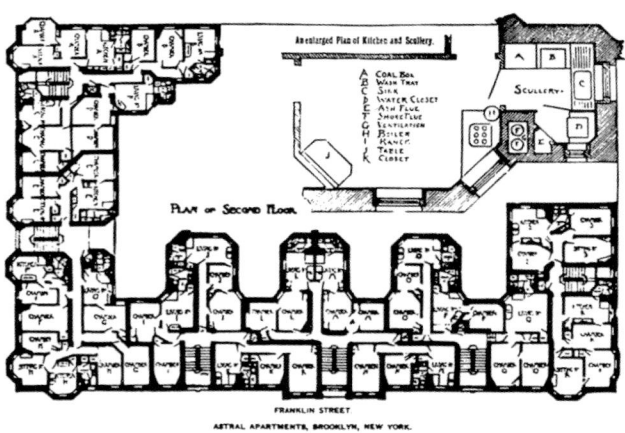

Astral Apartments, 184 Franklin Street, between Java and India Streets. Lamb & Rich and E. L. Roberts, 1885–86. View to the northeast. Erich. PILA.

ings, in South Brooklyn (see above). Though the Astral's exterior architecture was a bit fussy—especially the somewhat stagy Dutch-inspired stepped gable that marked the center of the Franklin Street facade—the bold use of Palladian-inspired motifs to tie the third, fourth, and fifth floors together, the vigorously modeled arches at the entry, and the skillful incorporation of shops at each corner suggested a grasp of the possibilities of multifamily architecture that to date only Henry J. Hardenbergh had realized, in his Dakota apartments (1882–84) (see chapter 4). The generously sized rear courtyard guaranteed light and air to back apartments. Inside, each apartment was outfitted with a kitchen with a scullery alcove off of which opened a separate room containing a toilet. Large tubs were included in each apartment, as well as hot and cold water, steam heat, and marble floors, wainscoting, and polished ash woodwork. Dumbwaiters located in the halls at each

Astral Apartments, 184 Franklin Street, between Java and India Streets. Lamb & Rich and E. L. Roberts, 1885–86. Plan. HWP. CU.

floor facilitated the daily routines of package handling and trash removal. A large lecture room was located in the basement, and the retail shops at the Java and India Street corners were organized on a cooperative basis. All in all, the Astral was a true people's palace.

Bushwick, lying to the southeast, was the third of the so-called Eastern District communities to join Brooklyn in 1855.[318] Largely a working-class area, it was home to workers in the breweries that opened midcentury, after the political uprisings of 1848 fostered a mass migration of Germans to the United States. Broadway was Bushwick's main thoroughfare, leading from Williamsburg to the farmland farther east on Long Island. Paralleling that street one block to the east was Bushwick Avenue, which was lined with large, deliberately imposing, freestanding houses typically commissioned by the brewery owners. Theobald Engelhardt's Italianate house (1886) for a brewer's widow, Catherine Lipsius, at 680 Bushwick Avenue, on the southwest corner of Willoughby Avenue, was stylistically surprising—such a house would have been more likely to have been designed twenty or more years earlier.[319] More up to date was the house of the

William Ulmer house (c. 1885), northwest corner of Bushwick and Willoughby Avenues. Rendering of view to the northwest. BHS.

brewer William Ulmer, across the street at 670 Bushwick Avenue (c. 1885), on the northwest corner of Willoughby Avenue, an imposing Romanesque Revival mass with a three-story corner tower rising free of the mansard to a conical copper roof.[320] Even more interesting was the brewer Gustav Doerschuck's residence (1890), at 999 Bushwick Avenue, on the northeast corner of Grove Street, a Romanesque Revival design by Engelhardt in brick and Lake Superior stone that split its principal facade between a two-and-a-half-story gable and a three-story square tower rising to a pyramidal roof.[321] Across the street at 1001 Bushwick Avenue (I. D. Reynolds, 1888), on the southeast corner of Grove Street, another brewer, Charles Lindemann, lived in a Shingle Style villa with turrets and porches.[322] And across from Lindemann's home was the house (1887) Engelhardt designed for the millwork manufacturer and future hotel owner Louis Bossert, at 1002 Bushwick Avenue, on the southwest corner of Grove Street.[323] Bossert's was a red brick box with a slate-covered mansard roof pierced by Gothic bracketed dormers on the street side. A bit farther down the avenue at 1020 Bushwick Avenue, on the northwest corner of Linden Street, and 37–53 Linden Street (E. F. Gaylor, 1885), was a fine row of Queen Anne townhouses executed in red brick and terra cotta with the most intricate treatment reserved for the corner unit, the elaborately plaited facades of which rose to a cast-iron-crested mansard.[324]

Parfitt Brothers's Bushwick Avenue Congregational Church (1894–96), at 1160 Bushwick Avenue, on the northwest corner of Cornelia Street, was a remarkably inventive, late-Romanesque design, with a square, hip-roofed meeting hall lit by a clerestory of round arches and rising behind brick gables pierced by enormous, vaguely Gothic windows, trimmed and mullioned in smooth-faced sandstone.[325] An octagonal, slender brick campanile topped by an open-work belfry rose at the corner, a third again as high as the church.

In contrast to Republican Bedford, Bushwick was a Democratic stronghold. The Bushwick Democratic Club (Frank Freeman, 1892) did not match the rival Union League Club in size but exceeded it in artistic significance.[326] Located at 719 Bushwick Avenue, on the northwest corner of Hart Street, the clubhouse maintained a domestic character in keeping with its location on Bushwick's finest residential street. A masterwork of Freeman's Romanesque period, "looking like a big Queen Anne cottage," according to the *New York Times*, its curved, semi-turreted corner, with deep stone mullions, was embellished with spectacularly intricate foliate ornament continued in the frieze.[327] The ornament was but one feature of a complex scheme offering two distinct impressions, one of bold, near-institutional scale fronting on Bushwick Avenue, and a lower-key and slightly more playful facade on Hart Street, where below the pedimented gable, with its projecting balconette, the design displayed a compositional duality of round arches and negative bay windows creating deep shadows. The

Bushwick Avenue Congregational Church, northwest corner of Bushwick Avenue and Cornelia Street. Parfitt Brothers, 1894–96. View to the northwest, c. 1905. BHS.

Times, which covered both the laying of the club's cornerstone and its opening as front-page events, was impressed with the building, describing it as "one of the finest political clubhouses in America . . . that may almost be described as palatial. . . . The building . . . is a most imposing structure. . . . The exterior style is modeled on easy, graceful lines, and might serve as the design for a millionaire's mansion."[328]

The area was served by a particularly well-designed police station, William B. Tubby's 20th Precinct Station House and Stable (1894–95), on the northeast corner of Hamburg and DeKalb Avenues, a castellated red brick fortress trimmed with yellow and ocher Roman brick.[329] With two-story-high Romanesque Revival–inspired arches and a strong corner tower rising one floor above the three-story building, the design appropriately expressed power and strength. Above the entrance, a frieze contained the seal of the City of Brooklyn with the Dutch motto "Eendraght Maakt Magt" (unity makes might), which was perhaps a subtle plea for the unification of Brooklyn and New York, then under discussion, to be implemented in 1898.

Bushwick Democratic Club, northwest corner of Bushwick Avenue and Hart Street. Frank Freeman, 1892. View to the northwest, c. 1900. BHS.

New York Central and Hudson River Railroad station at Mott Haven, north side of East 138th Street between Mott and Park Avenues, Annexed District. R. H. Robertson and A. J. Manning, 1885–87. View to the north. DD. CU.

CHAPTER 8

❧ The Suburban Ideal ❧

> The suburbs of an island city are apt to be sharply distinguished in character from those of a city on the mainland. The long ridge of rock that constitutes Manhattan cannot merge by imperceptible transitions into the surrounding expanse, like London or Philadelphia, nor does the topography allow of a periphery of dependencies like those which are known to the facile humorists as the "sub-hubs" of Boston.
>
> —Montgomery Schuyler, 1884[1]

Suburban development, which began in New York in 1814 when Robert Fulton inaugurated steam-ferry service between the city and Brooklyn, was by the 1850s intense, largely spurred on by newly constructed railroads on Long Island and in New Jersey which connected with ferries to lower Manhattan. The railroad opened up vast areas of the hinterland to those willing to commute two to four hours each day.[2] By 1869 many breadwinners were making an eighty-minute trip each way between their homes in still-suburban Harlem (see chapter 6) and their jobs downtown.[3]

The suburban trend was not universally admired. "From a domestic point of view," James Richardson observed in 1874, "New York . . . is a city of paradoxes. It is full of palatial dwellings and homeless people [boarders] . . . paying for unsocial subsistence a price that, under a wiser system, might give them every domestic comfort the heart could wish. Thousands who would live in the city could they find suitable homes here, and who would be worth millions to the city, are driven to the surrounding country to build up Jersey and all the regions round about; while no small proportion of those who must remain" find themselves "herded" into hotels and boardinghouses, "a manner of living which violates the very first requirements of the life we most affect, namely, individual privacy and family seclusion."[4]

According to the *New York Times*, suburban living rapidly increased in popularity as a direct consequence of the "financial reaction and commercial depression" that

began in September 1873: "The dullness of trade and scarcity of money . . . drove thousands and tens of thousands into the adjacent country—Westchester County, Long Island, Staten Island, and New Jersey, where comparatively low rents prevailed." By 1878, the *Times* reported, about 300,000 people commuted on a daily basis between New York and the suburbs, "so that the continuous region from twenty to thirty miles around is little else than a vast dormitory of New York."[5] As a result of preferable economic conditions in the suburbs many city houses went unrented as did rooms in hotels and boardinghouses, even though city rents did decline in the 1870s. While the rich could move to new houses farther uptown, or to elaborate apartments in the new French flats, by 1878 it was pretty much agreed, as the journalist Raymond Westbrook wrote in the *Atlantic Monthly*, that "the middle class are hardly expected to stay on the island at all." Already they were "spread out into the country by rail, [forming] vast settlements of ornamental cottages, while New York itself is given up to the rich and poor."[6]

Though the suburbs offered an affordable and comfortable alternative to living in Manhattan, they seemed to many a badge of failure, a kind of retreat from the city's sophistication to a smaller-scaled, vastly more provincial urbanism that existed elsewhere in the country's interior. Social stigma aside, however, there was little choice for many middle-class people other than the grinding daily commute between the outer reaches of Brooklyn, the

Annexed District, Queens, and Staten Island, or towns in New Jersey and Westchester County, and New York's business district.[7] Other middle-class families chose to remain in New York even though their living conditions were poorer than they might be in the suburbs. *Harper's New Monthly* pointed out in 1882: "Myriads of inmates of the squalid, distressing tenement-houses, in which morality was as impossible as happiness, would not give them up, despite their horrors, for clean, orderly, wholesome habitations in the suburbs, could they be transported there and back free of charge. They are in some unaccountable way terribly in love with their own wretchedness."[8] But to many, the suburbs did offer better middle-class living conditions. Westbrook argued that "in everything except proximity to their business,—and there is not so much difference even here, . . . the suburban people, in their spacious houses, designed often by the best professional skill, and affording in their interiors light for works of art and room for the varied activities of a refined life, have the best of it."[9]

The Annexed District

In 1874, the towns of Morrisania, West Farms, and Kingsbridge, all located in southwestern Westchester County, west of the Bronx River and south of Yonkers, established two years earlier as an independent city, were annexed to New York City.[10] With this act of annexation the city, for the first time opened up to the mainland, began to embrace a more complex urbanism, with the establishment of new suburban neighborhoods that would potentially allow the middle class a fair shot at living decently in New York. At the time of annexation, New York consisted of 14,000 acres of land, 1,000 of which were given over to parkland. With the addition of the former towns, New York's size swelled to about 22,000 acres.

The creation of the so-called Annexed District had its origins in the arrival of the railroad in lower Westchester County in the early 1840s, leading to the formation in 1846 of the town of West Farms.[11] By 1855 West Farms grew so populous that a new town, Morrisania, was created, with its northern boundary drawn from 164th Street and Summit Avenue east to the Bronx River. In 1863, the Mott Haven section of Morrisania was laid out in a grid-iron pattern of streets that followed the numbering pattern of New York. Clearly annexation was anticipated, in large part because the population of West Farms and especially of Morrisania had outstripped the capacity of the town governments to function efficiently. In 1869 the Board of Commissioners of Central Park was authorized by the legislature to formulate a street system to replace the approximately twelve different village plans within Morrisania. This domain was extended east to the Hutchinson River in 1871. The vote for annexation was overwhelmingly favorable, and on December 31, 1873, the Westchester County Board of Supervisors wound up the affairs of the lower county. Ten years later, the city began to press vigorously for the annexation of the land east of the Bronx River. The likelihood of this was so great that the Depart-

ment of Public Parks proposed new parks within the area in January 1884, angering landholders. The acquisition of the eastern half of Bronx Park and all 1,756 acres of Pelham Bay Park was authorized on June 14, 1884, even though this land did not yet fall within city limits. After lawsuits, title was taken in 1888.

By the advent of the Civil War, the chronic shortage of housing had become a hallmark of New York life. The physical growth of the city would not significantly alleviate this situation unless, as the *New York Times* pointed out in an 1873 editorial, "improved facilities for intercommunication" between Manhattan Island and the mainland were put in place.[12] Following annexation, five new bridges were constructed over the Harlem River: the Northern Railroad Bridge, above Seventh Avenue (1877); the Madison Avenue Bridge (1884); a bridge at Second Avenue for elevated trains (1885); the Washington Bridge (1886–89); and the Broadway Bridge (1894). In addition, in 1896 a new bridge replaced the outmoded crossing (1813) at Macombs Dam. Elevated train service, which came to Manhattan in the 1870s, would not reach the Annexed District until 1886, when a new station was opened at 133rd Street and Willis Avenue.[13]

In 1885, just as the first elevated railway connection was being forged, the New York Central and Hudson River Railroad announced plans for a large station (1885–87) at Mott Haven.[14] There was something mildly preposterous about the project, though R. H. Robertson and A. J. Manning's Richardsonian Romanesque design was very fine. When the building was completed, the *Real Estate Record and Builders' Guide* stated:

> At first sight it seems odd that so large and important a station . . . should be erected for the use of Mott Haven, at present one of the least important as well as one of the most depressing and disreputable in aspect of the suburbs of New York. Mott Haven has that temporary and tentative appearance which denotes, what is in fact, that the line of its development has not yet been determined and that its property-owners are waiting to ascertain this before they commit themselves to any improvements of a permanent or a costly kind. It does not yet appear what it shall be, but it does appear that the march of improvement, when it begins, will find little or nothing in the present building of Mott Haven to obstruct it, or that cannot be removed without trouble, expense or regret. It is not for Mott Haven alone, however . . . that the new station is built. It is rather a transfer than a local station. Passengers from the East, bound up the Hudson River, are now carried to Forty-second Street. By awaiting the up-river trains at One Hundred and Thirty-eighth Street they save some ten miles of distance and two journeys through the tunnel. . . . These considerations justify the Hudson River Company . . . in providing a new and important building which, to the lover of architecture, needs no justification, but is its own excuse for being. The new station is, in extreme dimensions, not far from 200 x 50. The northern half of it, which is 100 feet by 30, is given to one large

View to the northwest, c. 1897, of Bedford Park Boulevard from Southern Boulevard, Annexed District. BCHS.

waiting-room, or possibly refreshment-room, opening along its whole length upon a sheltered platform some 15 feet wide. . . . Over the center of the building is a clock tower some 15 feet square, and at the southern end is an open loggia with a porch. To the baggage yard on the west access is gained through a large archway some 20 feet in span, in a wall which continues the southern front.

The plan is extremely simple and straightforward, and the architectural problem in such a case is how to get out of such a building which can properly be but one story, or counting its subordinate rooms a story and a-half in height, anything but a long, low, monotonous shed, without features, and without variety or contrast. These elements are gained here by widening the building at the southern end, by the arrangement of roofs . . . by the introduction of the clock tower and by the treatment of the southern front. . . . The material throughout is baked clay, common brick for the walls, pressed brick for the jambs and arches, red tile for the roofs, red terra cotta for the ornament. The bases of the round piers in the loggia are quarry-faced sandstone. . . . Candor compels us to say that the interior, though very good as such interiors go, is not equal to the exterior architecture, and that the structural use of wood in the main room is by no means as straightforward or so effective as the use of masonry. The exterior . . . seems to us the most uniformly successful work he [Robertson] has yet done. It shows a strong liking for the Romanesque work of Provence, and especially for the work of the late Mr. Richardson. But there is nothing in it which does not show independent thought and study, and indeed it manifests a very different artistic temperament from the vigorous impetuosity that can be inferred from Mr. Richardson's work. . . . We have to thank

Mr. Robertson for a very artistic building, which it seems a pity to waste upon Mott Haven, but we may hope that Mott Haven will grow up to it.[15]

Montgomery Schuyler, who deemed the station "one of the most admirable works that the Romanesque revival has produced in New York,"[16] placed it in the first rank of its architect's works:

In this there are not only elaborated single features which we rarely fail to find even in those of his works in which we fail to find a composition to the total effect of which all the parts contribute. We find also unity, unity in variety, and the features are parts of physiognomy. The buildings and its dependencies are nearly a monochrome in red—nearly, but not quite . . . and the slight variations of tint that result add life and charm to the design. There is scarcely any building more featureless than a railway station reduced to its simplest expression. It is a low shed with a sheltered platform. But then it may without incongruity have a porch, a clock-tower is especially appropriate to it, and the baggage yard may be allowed its own gate. With no other sources of variety than these an artistic architect may make a charming building, as we see here. . . . Perhaps the most successful point in the general composition is the skill with which the whole low substructure, by means of the separate treatment of its separate roofs, is grouped about the central tower and made to converge to it. . . . Upon the whole this seems to me the most uniformly and consistently excellent, of the work the designer has yet done.[17]

While as a result of annexation lower Westchester became part of the nation's largest city, it was to remain for many years a collection of separate villages and neighbor-

Jockey Club, site of the former James Bathgate estate, near Paul Avenue and West 195th Street, Annexed District. BCHS.

hoods. During the post–Civil War era, the principal building activity remained the construction of rather typical suburban-style villas, especially in Fordham Heights, Mount Hope, and the area just south of St. Mary's Park, as well as in Morris Heights, where, in the words of the architect Albert E. Davis, chairman of the boosterish North Side Board of Trade, Sedgwick Avenue was "bordered with handsome residences [belonging to] some of New York's wealthiest and most prominent citizens."[18]

In contrast to the neighborhoods consisting of isolated villas, there was a particularly interesting planned community, Bedford Park, in the northwest section of the Annexed District.[19] A twenty-five-acre development, it was established in 1882 by two real estate entrepreneurs, Daniel R. Kendall and Horace B. Chalfin, the latter a well-known New York "merchant prince," on land bounded by Berriam Avenue, Brook Street, Williamsbridge Road, and Bainbridge and Southern Boulevards. Bedford Park, modeled after the widely publicized and admired development of the same name established by Jonathan Thomas Carr in 1876 on the western outskirts of London,[20] was intended to provide, as the *New York Times* put it in February 1884, "New Yorkers of moderate means a chance to become owners of comfortable homes on easy terms." The article went on to praise the newly completed "pretty cottages" as "healthful, cleanly and cheerful."[21] Two months later, the *New York Daily Graphic* noted:

The planting of elm and maple trees . . . commenced some years ago; more recently . . . Queen Anne cottages have

been erected. . . . These residences at present number about a dozen, of which three or four have been sold. They are reached . . . by a stone-paved pathway that curves around the end of the meadow, which it divides from the wooded slopes on the other side, forming a pleasant rural walk. . . . The view from all points of this upland is fine, extending on the countryside over wooded hills to a great distance. A picturesque part of the Bronx is reached by a walk of fifteen minutes. . . . Some of the new cottages contain seven rooms and others eight, with prices ranging for them from \$3,750 to \$7,000, but the first built and now occupied are of a different type—more like that of mansions. . . . A building for stores has been erected by the association controlling the property, but from being only one story in height and on lower ground apart from the residences, the villa effect is not marred. The shops are intended to provide only immediate domestic necessities, including those from butcher and druggist.[22]

While most development in the Annexed District was residential, a few architecturally distinguished buildings of other types were also completed. In 1866, in an effort to rescue horse racing from the disreputable state into which it had fallen, Leonard P. Jerome persuaded the American Jockey Club to buy the 230-acre James Bathgate estate, on which the Jerome Park Villa Site Company would build a racetrack that would attract New York's fashionable set.[23] Designed by Thomas R. Jackson, the Jockey Club (1868) wrapped around part of the racetrack and contained a ballroom and dining rooms as well as guest bedrooms. To connect his racetrack with New York, Jerome persuaded the Township of West Farms to issue bonds covering the cost of a broad street, later called Jerome Avenue, running north from 153rd Street and the Harlem River, where it was possible to cross on the Macombs Dam Bridge. The racetrack was an immediate success, but in 1887, as the Annexed District began to fill up with houses, the city announced its intention to condemn the track and build a reservoir on the site, which took place in 1894.

Located to the east of the Annexed District, the village of West Chester was one of the first settlements in what would become the county of the same name; as urbanization spread northward throughout the post–Civil War era, the character of the village changed, and in 1896 it became part of New York City. By the end of the Civil War the village had at its center a green, named Westchester Square, onto which faced St. Peter's Church, designed by Leopold Eidlitz and completed in 1855 (restored in 1879 in collaboration with Eidlitz's son Cyrus), and, after 1868, an adjacent Sunday school, also designed by Leopold Eidlitz.[24] Both buildings adopted a Gothic vocabulary, with the more visually dramatic church distinguished by a steeply pitched roof and a slender spire. Also fronting the public square was Frederick Clarke Withers's Van Schaick Reading Room (1882–83), at 9 Westchester Square, the posthumous gift of Peter C. Van Schaick, a local philanthropist, to the village of West Chester.[25] A modest design, partly in the spirit of the early Gothic Revival of the 1840s but also reflecting the increasingly flamboyant work of the 1880s Queen Anne, the red brick building, with a tower set over an arched entrance, contained a reading room and a chess room. The building proved more than the citizens

St. Peter's Church, 2500 Westchester Avenue, West Chester. Leopold Eidlitz, 1855. View to the southeast. BCHS.

Van Schaick Reading Room, 9 Westchester Square, West Chester. Frederick Clarke Withers, 1882–83. Rendering of view to the southwest. BCHS.

Riverdale Presbyterian Chapel, 2550 Independence Avenue, Riverdale, Annexed District. Francis H. Kimball, 1889. View to the northeast. BCHS.

Christ Church, 5030 Riverdale Avenue, Riverdale, Annexed District. Richard Upjohn & Son, 1865–66. View to the southwest, c. 1897. BCHS.

were prepared for; claiming that it would cost too much to maintain, they refused to open the facility until 1890, when the railroad tycoon Collis P. Huntington, who had recently bought the summer mansion of Henry Osborne Havemeyer in nearby Throgs Neck, purchased the reading room and, after sympathetically expanding it with the assistance of William Anderson, endowed it and renamed it after himself. Huntington, whose charities were few, had the dates changed in the terra cotta rondels of the original building and replaced the central plaque so that his name and not Van Schaick's was on the building.

In 1852 five wealthy businessmen—William Woodworth of Yonkers and Charles W. Foster, Henry L. Atherton, William D. Cromwell, and Samuel D. Babcock of New York City—purchased one hundred acres overlooking the Hudson River for the purpose of developing a summer residential suburb they called Riverdale.[26] Located in the most remote part of the Annexed District, Riverdale was of all the area's settlements the one most able to retain an independent and cohesive identity over time, ultimately becoming, as the city grew up around it, a powerful exemplar of *rus in urbe*. The plan was to have five large estates with villas and outbuildings. The villas, at least one of which was designed by Thomas S. Wall, faced Independence Avenue. A station of the Hudson River Railroad was established to serve the community.

The Panic of 1857 and the Civil War hampered development, but by the 1860s there were enough families in the area to support two churches, James Renwick Jr.'s Riverdale Presbyterian Church (1863), at Riverdale Avenue and 249th Street,[27] and, two blocks north on the same avenue, Richard Upjohn & Son's Christ Church (1865–66), built

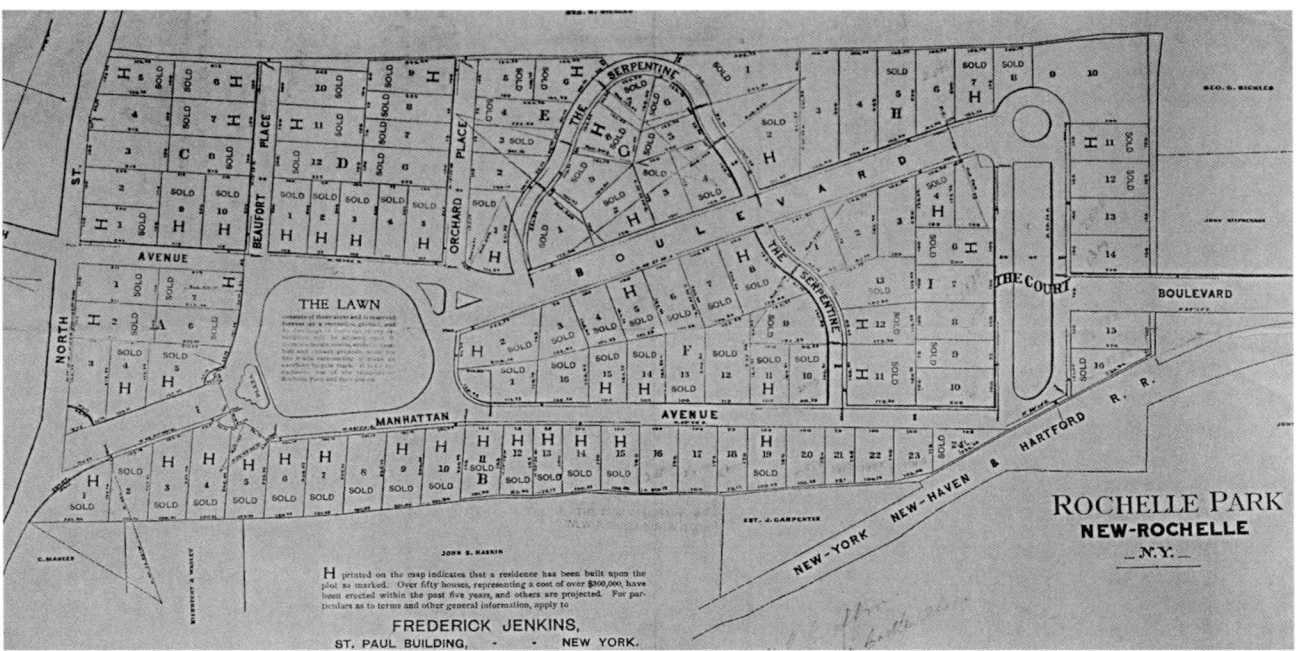

Rochelle Park, New Rochelle. Nathan F. Barrett, c. 1885. Site plan. NRPL.

for an Episcopal congregation.[28] Renwick's modest design resembled an English parish church, with fieldstone walls and a steeply sloped slate roof. Upjohn's church, built with funds donated by parishioners, was stylistically more complex and grander in every way. Locally quarried stone was combined with brick to create a patterned facade that was echoed in the striped slate roof. At the west end of the nave a belfry crowned the ridge, while a small porch to the side served as the principal entrance.

At the time the churches were being built, William Earl Dodge Jr., a merchant and member of the family whose fortune grew from copper mining, commissioned a grand villa from James Renwick Jr., which he called Greyston (1863–64), probably taking the name from the random ashlar, gray granite walls of the house.[29] The picturesque Gothic-inspired cottage-villa, with numerous gables, was wrapped by wooden porches commanding the river views.

In 1874, when New York took over the West Bronx, Riverdale and its hillside villas were threatened by a proposal to plat the forested area in conformance with the city's typical gridiron plan. But in 1876, Frederick Law Olmsted and the municipal civil engineer J. James R. Croes submitted a report calling for the area's future development as an in-city suburbia, with a recommendation that the prevailing street pattern, which closely followed the site's natural topography, be maintained.[30] By this time Olmsted had formulated his definition of suburbia: "detached dwellings with sylvan surroundings yet supplied with a considerable share of urban convenience."[31] Acceptance of the report was particularly sweet to Olmsted, who, together with a group of reformers, had in 1866 lost a battle to prevent the extension of the gridiron plan to the as-yet-undeveloped upper por-

tion of Manhattan. At that time Olmsted argued that areas of varied topography needed to be preserved in a more or less natural state for an emerging middle class "struggling to maintain an honorable independence."[32]

In their report, Olmsted and Croes wrote: "So far as the plan of New York remains to be formed, it would be inexcusable that it should not be the plan of a Metropolis: adapted to serve and serve well, every legitimate interest of the wide world; not of ordinary commerce only, but of humanity, religion, art, science and scholarship. If a house to be used for many different purposes must have many rooms and passages of various dimensions and variously lighted and furnished, not less must such a metropolis be specially adapted at different points to different ends."[33] Olmsted's plan for Riverdale's streets was adopted by the Department of Public Parks in 1877.[34]

Riverdale saw little in the way of new construction toward the end of the Gilded Age, but in 1889 its Presbyterian congregation commissioned a charming Shingle Style chapel, known as the Riverdale Presbyterian Chapel, designed by Francis H. Kimball, at 2550 Independence Avenue, to serve the workers of the Johnson Iron Foundry at nearby Spuyten Duyvil, a small factory village.[35] The design was inventive yet modest, with a high stone base carrying a superstructure of shingles and half-timbered gables. Oddly, Isaac G. Johnson, who owned the foundry and started the project, was a Baptist. A partner's wife, Mary E. Cox, donated the land.

One notable Westchester County village that did not get annexed bears discussion here. Rochelle Park (c. 1885) was perhaps the nation's first suburban enclave set within an existing suburban town.[36] Samuel Swift, the author of a pioneering series on American suburbs that appeared in

Main entrance to Rochelle Park, New Rochelle. View to the west, 1889, from within the enclave. NRPL.

Main entrance to Rochelle Park, New Rochelle. View to the northeast, 1889, from North Street. NRPL.

early issues of *House and Garden*, observed in 1904 that "if Llewellyn Park [see below] be an expression of idealistic aims of a wise dreamer, then Rochelle Park may be declared an embodiment of commercial expediency. . . . The case of Rochelle Park might be matched within the land tributary to any one of a dozen American cities; while Llewellyn Park and our exclusive and fashionable communities are the products of exceptional conditions."[37] With its clearly defined boundaries and self-contained internal circulation system that made only two connections to the city's street system, Rochelle Park was intended to foster a sense of separateness from New Rochelle, a small city in Westchester County that was "just forty-five minutes from Broadway," as George M. Cohan was to put it in a popular song of the pre–World War I era.

The site of Rochelle Park, seventy-five acres of former farmland that had been purchased under foreclosure by the

Manhattan Life Insurance Company, was bounded on one side by the tracks of the New York, New Haven, and Hartford Railroad. The site's varied and largely inhospitable topography, including swampland and craggy rock outcroppings, was a challenge for the community's planner, the landscape architect Nathan F. Barrett, who, according to Swift, had as his "watchword . . . the commercial value of sentiment," and for his associate Horace Crosby.[38] Nearly one-third of the site was devoted to roads and open spaces: six acres for parkland, including an open meadow called the Lawn, and fifteen or more acres for the streets, sidewalks, and planting borders, leaving some 115 building plots averaging a scant half-acre each. The location of the New Rochelle train station, a ten-minute walk to the southwest, dictated the diagonal orientation of the principal street, the Boulevard, the formality of which was counterbalanced by the Serpentine, an avenue that looped its way through the

View to the southwest, 1889, of houses on Manhattan Avenue, Rochelle Park, New Rochelle. NRPL.

community. Together, these streets embodied a dialogue between the organic and the geometric, between naturalistic form and Classicizing form, a highly unusual integration in a time that tended to favor one or the other mode of composition and expression but not the combination of the two. Although no gates were provided, stone walls with terminal posts designed by Edward A. Sargent, an English-born architect whose practice at the time was based on Staten Island, defined Rochelle Park's borders, "giving more the idea of a large private estate than a public park," according to the *New York Daily Graphic*.[39] Within, the Rochelle Park Community Association maintained a tennis court on the Lawn and lawn bowls on the long rectilinear space at the end of the Boulevard known as the Court.

Rochelle Park was intended for persons of moderate means. The lots were comparatively small, one hundred by two hundred feet, with houses expected to cost from $3,500 to $5,000. While there was no formal program of architectural review, designs for moderate-size villas were prepared by Sargent. An article published in the *Real Estate Record and Builders' Guide* in 1887, signed by "Wanderer"— probably Montgomery Schuyler, who lived nearby— praised Rochelle Park as "attractive."[40] Rochelle Park was effectively promoted for its views over Long Island Sound and its convenience to New York. "There is no comparison in the advantages of this situation over New Jersey towns," the *Daily Graphic* reported in 1887, "with the inconveniences and delays experienced in crossing" the Hudson River.[41] So attractive to home buyers was Rochelle Park that it stimulated a building boom. Between 1885 and 1887 New Rochelle saw the completion of more houses than had been built there in the previous fifteen years, and in the process the once rather sleepy village became a bustling suburban satellite.

Queens

Lying on the western end of Long Island, Queens County, extending east to Suffolk County, was almost as large as New York City, the Annexed District, and Staten Island combined. Forcing out the local Native American population, early Dutch settlers began farming in the area during the first half of the seventeenth century and established a Dutch form of government. The English took over in 1664, and the rural character of the scattered villages and towns prevailed until long after the Revolution. In 1839, a new pattern was begun with the incorporation of Astoria, founded by fur trader Stephen Halsey, the first new village in the county since the seventeenth century. Over the next thirty years, along with several other partners, Halsey set out to promote and develop Astoria as a suburb. At about the same time, Charles and Peter Roach acquired a long stretch of shoreline opposite Blackwell's Island, developing it as Ravenswood, Long Island's first neighborhood of riverfront mansions. New villages were also founded at sites relatively remote from New York ferries. Woodhaven began as a real estate promotion in 1835, followed two years later by Queens Village. Maspeth came along in 1852 and Winfield, Corona, and College Point in 1854. All of these were to slumber for a generation; only after the Civil War did Queens begin to take off. In keeping with its rural character, Queens also became home to many of the region's cemeteries, a result of the state legislature's enactment in 1847 of the Rural Cemetery Act, which banned new graveyards in New York City and initiated large-scale burial areas in nearby counties, organized by corporations authorized to sell plots to individuals. In less than ten years large cemeteries were established for Catholics near Newtown Creek, for Lutherans in present-day Middle Village, and for Jews in Cypress Hills.

In July 1870 the thirty-four-year-old William Steinway, head of his family's piano manufacturing company, purchased some eighty acres facing Bowery Bay with the intention of establishing a works to supplement the principal plant (1859–60), which was located in New York on the full block bounded by Fourth and Lexington Avenues and Fifty-second and Fifty-third Streets.[42] Henry Steinweg (the family name was changed in 1866), William's father, had been a piano maker in Germany since the 1830s, immigrating to the United States in 1850 with three of his sons. William first worked as an apprentice to the soon-to-be bankrupt William Nunns & Co. before joining his father and brothers in creating Steinway & Sons. The family business quickly prospered, in no small part due to a combination of dedication to detail and craftsmanship and the ready embrace of new technologies, inclinations that would characterize William for the remainder of his life in a variety of different ventures. By the time of the Queens land purchase, Steinway & Sons was not only the leading piano maker in the United States but its innovative methods were the standard in Europe as well.

Two different impulses lay behind William Steinway's

Steinway & Sons factory (1859–60), Lexington to Fourth Avenue, East Fifty-second to East Fifty-third Street. View to the northeast. LWA.

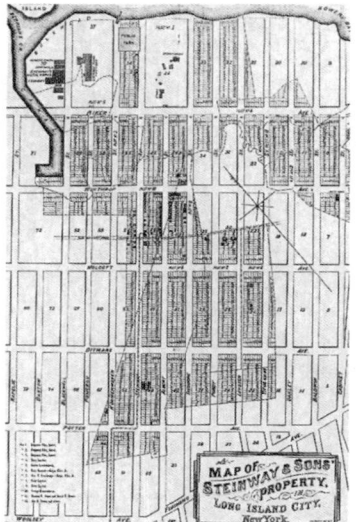

Steinway Village, Queens. Site plan, c. 1880. LWA.

decision to expand in such a dramatic manner. One grew out of a series of protracted strikes that plagued the company in 1869, leading Steinway to believe that business could be more agreeably conducted outside the city. As he observed in the 1890s: "We wished to escape the machinations of the Anarchists and Socialists, who . . . were continually breeding discontent among our workmen and inciting them to strike. . . . We felt that if we could withdraw our workmen from contact with these people and the other temptations of city life in the tenement districts they would be more content and their lot would be a happier one." The other reason for the move was the nature of the piano manufacturing business. The New York plant, besides its now-inadequate size, was landlocked: "We needed . . . shipping facilities near the water and a basin in which logs could be stored in water to keep them moist and prevent them from cracking."[43]

The land that Steinway purchased in 1870 had belonged to the German Cabinetmakers' Association of New York,

William Steinway house (c. 1850), between Steinway Avenue and Theodore Street, Riker Avenue and the East River, Steinway Village, Queens. View to the north, c. 1881. LWA.

Workers' houses (c. 1875), Steinway Village, Queens. LWA.

Steinway & Sons piano factory and offices (1877), Steinway Village, Queens. View to the northeast from Riker Avenue. LWA.

which had hoped to establish a cooperative community. Within a year of the original purchase, Steinway increased his holdings to some four hundred acres. "At that time it was a beautiful garden spot, surrounded by waste lands and vacant lots . . . [and] was partly wooded," Steinway would later recall.[44] Most significant, the location enjoyed more than half a mile of East River waterfront and possessed a navigable canal. Technically located in Long Island City, which the state legislature had incorporated in 1871, combining the villages of Hunter's Point, Ravenswood, and Astoria, the site was opposite the stretch of land between 100th and 120th Streets in New York. Also included in the original purchase, and now located basically in the center of the Steinway holdings, was what Steinway considered to be a "splendid chateau . . . with over 14 acres of waterfront," a rather ponderous granite mansion built in the 1850s by Benjamin Pike, a prominent New York optician.[45] The house was used as a summer residence for the extended Steinway family.

Steinway quickly began clearing land and laying roads (originally named after family members), establishing in 1872 the first factory buildings, at the water's edge, including a massive steam sawmill, iron and brass foundries, boiler and engine houses, and a structure for the drilling, finishing, and japanning of iron frames and other metal pieces used in the construction of pianos. A 384-foot dock and bulkhead was also installed, enclosing a 100-by-300-foot basin that contained millions of square feet of logs. At this time Steinway also began commissioning plans for housing for workers and others who might be interested in living in the new community. He formed the Astoria Homestead Company and began selling lots as early as 1873, achieving some success the following year, with thirty-five lots sold at substantial profit. Also in 1873 Steinway built six frame houses and opened up Steinway Avenue, running through the center of his property.

Although Steinway was clearly farsighted in his business

Steinway Reformed Church (1891), northeast corner of Albert Street and Ditmars Boulevard, Steinway Village, Queens. View to the northeast. QBPL.

affairs and well informed regarding social issues, he was not a visionary planner and his town grew over time according to no particular pattern. In addition to the workers' houses, which ranged from four-bedroom single cottages to three-bedroom rowhouses, all set about a third of a mile back from the shore, Steinway also built houses for more affluent families on higher ground farther east. Vernacular cottages exhibiting features from a mixture of styles, the houses were dignified by flush stone lintels and recessed entrances.

From 1874 to 1876 Steinway built twenty-nine company rowhouses intended for skilled workmen along Forty-first, Forty-second, and Steinway Streets between Twentieth Road and Twentieth Avenue. These two-story, brick, vaguely Italianate houses, each on a twenty-by-one-hundred-foot lot, featured recessed doorways and boldly scaled stone lintels incised with Neo-Grec details. Unlike later houses built by Steinway, these were rental units remaining under company control. In fact, the decision to sell rather than rent the majority of housing to both workers and others set Steinway Village apart from a traditional company town, although Steinway's control over most aspects of village life was still significant.

In 1877, in keeping with his desire to move as much of his manufacturing operations out of New York and into Queens as possible, Steinway completed facilities for keyboard making and wood carving. Two years later, a four-story, 248-by-60-foot case factory was built. Four-story-high, 40-by-100-foot brick buildings contained drying kilns and drying rooms that held over 500,000 square feet of lumber. Between the dock basin and the factories, over 5,000,000 square feet of lumber was stored in open-air yards; the wood needed to remain in that state for at least two years. Clearly, an operation of this type and size could not have been accommodated in the Fourth Avenue fac-

tory, which now concentrated on varnishing and polishing operations and the installation of soundboards.

By the late 1870s a majority of Steinway workers were employed in the Astoria works, although only a small percentage actually lived in the village. Even though the number of residences was small—as late as 1881 there were merely 130 houses—Steinway was committed to creating a complete, functioning town. His first significant public work was an eight-hundred-student-capacity school, completed in 1877, which was operated under the supervision of Long Island City's Board of Education, although a special teacher was hired to instruct children in German and music. Two years later Steinway funded the construction of the five-hundred-seat Protestant Union Church, located in the center of the village at Shore Road and Albert Street. The church would serve the community for the next decade before being replaced by the 1,000-seat Steinway Reformed Church (1891), located on a 100-by-125-foot site on the corner of Albert Street and Ditmars Boulevard. The wood-framed, shingle-clad country chapel had as its principal feature a boldly articulated bell tower rising to a steep pyramidal roof. It also contained the cathedral organ that had been previously housed in Steinway Hall, on Fourteenth Street in Manhattan (see chapter 5). The old church building was not abandoned and served to house the village's kindergarten, in the basement, as well as the Steinway Free Circulating Library. In 1881 the federal government recognized Steinway Village with its first post office. That same year Steinway constructed a one-hundred-by-fifty-foot public bath on the East River shore. The free facility featured over fifty dressing rooms and was soon graced by an adjoining 250-by-200-foot public park. In keeping with Steinway's beliefs, and in contrast with the typical company town, the various stores that served the community were privately run.

In 1881, with the recession of the 1870s over as well as the strikes of 1878 and 1880 concluded (work stoppages did not affect operations in the new, suburban location), Steinway expanded his operations again, beginning with the construction of twelve rental cottages designed by Horace Greely Knapp.[46] Nearby, Knapp was building "a commodious residence" for William H. Williams, who operated a veneer-cutting business begun with Steinway's financial support.[47] Also in 1881 Knapp built a fifty-eight-by-eighty-five-foot stable for Steinway & Sons.[48] In 1884 the *Real Estate Record and Builders' Guide* reported that Andrew Spence was designing fifty three-story "double apartment houses 30 x 60 each," to be "interspersed with stores." These were "principally intended for the accommodation of the numerous employees of the company," and were built in "installments."[49] In addition, some single-family houses were built by prosperous individuals. One of these, designed by the second-tier house architect Nicholas Gillesheimer, had its own stable behind, a sure sign of the client's prosperity.[50]

Even though Steinway boasted that his town was located in "the geographical centre of Greater New York" and "nearer to the city than Harlem," as well as only five miles from City Hall and four miles from the Fourth Avenue factory, he well understood that its success depended on transportation, both water connections from New York and land connections to other parts of Queens.[51] Indeed, Steinway would apply almost as much energy on this subject as any other, culminating in his 1890 appointment to the Rapid Transit Commission, one of the few government positions he was willing to accept. Although he was ultimately not particularly successful as a transportation entrepreneur, Steinway managed accurately to predict the technological advances that would render Queens truly convenient, and in the process nearly became the father of the American automobile as well.

Access from New York was primarily by way of the Astoria Ferry, which had a dock at East Ninety-second Street. Steinway purchased approximately ten thousand dollars worth of Island Shore Railroad's stock and influenced the company to extend its route to the village, thereby making travel between the Fourth Avenue factory and Steinway Village relatively convenient. In eight years' time Steinway controlled the line, which was renamed the Steinway and Hunter's Point Railroad. In 1884 a new line, the Broadway and Bowery Bay Railroad, also controlled by Steinway, was opened to serve the village. In less than a decade all the horsecar lines in Long Island City provided transportation to the town. But Steinway, ever mindful of technological advances, quickly saw the limitations of horsecar travel. An equine distemper epidemic in the 1870s had seriously interrupted operations, and the expense of upkeep on the horses, whose usefulness generally lasted only five years, was significant. In 1886 Steinway cultivated the friendship of Gottlieb Daimler, of Canstatt, Germany, who was pioneering work on the internal combustion engine, producing a remarkably light model fueled by liquid petroleum. Two years later Steinway acquired the North American rights to all of Daimler's existing and future patents. In 1890 the first engines were built in the United States, in a Hartford machine shop, and Steinway began preparing for their man-

ufacture in Queens. He spent a great deal of money and oversaw the production of what was a technologically successful product that achieved mixed business results. Steinway simply did not live long enough to see, much less profit from, the impact the engine would have on all forms of transportation.

As early as 1875, Steinway sought to increase access to the town with the construction of an East River bridge intended to align with Seventy-seventh Street. Although over the course of five years he raised more than $350,000 with the help of other Long Island City businessmen, the bridge project proved too expensive. Another attempt to traverse the river was made in 1891, when Steinway became the largest stockholder in the New York and Long Island Railway Company, which intended to build a freight and passenger tunnel to connect Queens and New York roughly at Forty-second Street in Manhattan. But tragedy struck early in the process, with a December 1892 explosion killing some five people, including two women who were dining in a restaurant at 25 Jackson Avenue in Queens; the accident was grimly headlined in the *New York World* as "Death in Dynamite."[52] Lawsuits stopped future progress, and the tunnel, named after Steinway, was not completed until 1907, long after his death in 1896.[53]

Besides problems of transportation, another hindrance to the success of Steinway Village was the deteriorating condition of the surrounding area, especially to the south along the waterfront. The once bucolic Astoria had, since its 1871 incorporation into Long Island City, evolved into something of a dump, becoming a major depository for New York's manure and slaughterhouse refuse. It also became home to the fat and bone boilers that had been banned across the river. In 1879, in a rare show of force from the notoriously corrupt Long Island City government, the Newtown Creek Ammonia Works was finally disciplined and its polluting deemed "a public nuisance."[54]

To provide for the leisure-time pleasure of village residents as well as to create a major destination point for citizens of greater New York, Steinway joined forces in 1886

Grand Pier (1887), Bowery Bay, Queens. View to the northeast. Geipel. QHS.

Fort Totten Battery, Willets Point, Queens. William Petit Trowbridge, 1862–64. View to the south showing Long Island Sound in the foreground. QBPL.

with George A. Ehret, owner of the Hell Gate Brewery, in Yorkville, to form the Bowery Bay Improvement Company. The company would develop a version of Coney Island's seaside amusement park, but with a difference: this resort was to cater to "respectable" people, a point emphasized from the very beginning, with an opening-day advertisement in the *New York Sun* declaring it the "Safest place, with ample police protection."[55] In fact, one year after the resort's opening, Long Island City resident William Powers filed a ten-thousand-dollar suit against the company for too *much* police protection, claiming that two overzealous officers from the Steinway private police force "unmercifully clubbed him about the head and body" without provocation and kept him locked up for seventeen hours without water.[56] The beachfront along Bowery Bay had been functioning as a summer resort for quite some time, crowded with city dwellers. Local residents complained of the "indecent way in which bathing is permitted," making it "impossible for ladies during the hot weather to pass along the road abutting the bay in the afternoons and evenings" because "full grown men bathe there without the slightest regard to decency, wearing no bathing suits or drawers, and naked men and boys may be seen running about or drying themselves after this bath without any appearance of shame and utterly regardless of the fact that they are within sight of a public thoroughfare."[57] Steinway and Ehret quickly banned nude bathing and set about creating a major attraction, building a substantial seawall, grading the streets, transforming estate houses into hotels, and constructing bathhouses. A quaint peasant's cottage was built to give the development a German character. The *New York Times* effusively greeted the resort's opening: "From its natural beauty, splendid facilities for recreation, and close proximity to the metropolis [Bowery Bay] bids fair to become a formidable rival to Coney Island. . . . The grounds abound in well-shaded walks, lawns, rambles, croquet grounds, artificial lakes . . . and furnish views of the most picturesque character." The *Times* also made the significant observation that "no sewage whatever flows into the bay."[58]

The attraction was immediately successful, and the following year Steinway and Ehret constructed the $50,000, 110-foot-wide Grand Pier, which extended 500 feet into the water and was big enough to accommodate the 2,000-passenger ferryboats of the New York and College Point Ferry Company, in which Steinway bought a half-interest in 1890. By the following year he owned the entire company, which had a dock on East Ninety-ninth Street. The resort was also serviced by the so-called summer cars of the Steinway and Hunter's Point Railroad, which picked up passengers from the Astoria and Hunter's Point ferries. Steinway additionally created another horse railroad line to reach Bowery Bay, the Rikers Avenue and Sanford's Point Railway. And in a direct assault on Coney Island, the tracks of the Brooklyn Heights Railway Company were extended to link up with the new recreation complex.

But success had its price. For one thing, the privacy of the Steinway family mansion, located between the village and the beach, was forever compromised. Furthermore, as the development prospered it became less bucolic and more an urban resort, in many ways like Coney Island despite Steinway's desire to dissociate from that great destination. In 1891 the name of the resort was changed to North Beach, eschewing Bowery Bay because of its associations with the time-honored bawdy street in New York and with its namesake in Coney Island. But the name change was not enough to stem the tide of urbanism, and North Beach quickly became a Coney Island in all but name.

Steinway Village was William Steinway's pet project, and he poured enormous energy and vast amounts of the family fortune into its development. In 1883, after more than a dozen years of steady expenditures that neither realized a significant return nor guaranteed a happy labor force, Steinway remained idealistic. He explained his motivations for building the town in testimony before the United States Senate:

> I consider one of the greatest evils under which workingmen live, especially in the city of New York, is the horrors of the tenement houses—the terrible rents they have to pay. . . . The horrors of the tenement houses are having a

Poppenhusen Institute, 114–04 Fourteenth Road, College Point, Queens. Mundell & Teckritz, 1868. View to the northwest. QBPL.

Flushing Town Hall (1862), 137–35 Northern Boulevard, Flushing, Queens. View to the northwest. QBPL.

very baneful effect upon the morals and character of the coming generation; in fact, I may say a terrible effect. But I do not see what legislation can do. Capitalists consider tenement houses a poor investment, paying poor returns. The only thing I can imagine is to do as *we* have done, remove the very large factories requiring much room and many men from out of the city of New York into the suburbs. . . . I think every effort ought to be directed to having the large establishments go out to the suburbs of the city, in order to give the workingmen a chance to live as human beings ought to live.[59]

By 1896, the year of Steinway's death, the population of the village had grown to seven thousand. That same year the *New York Times*, which had only sporadically covered the project, published three pages of almost unqualified praise: "A striking object lesson of the efficacy of wealth, when coupled with energy, enterprise and philanthropy, as an adjunct to excellent business methods, is found in that thriving town of Steinway."[60] Four years earlier, Moses King, in his boosterish guide, had proclaimed Steinway Village an "Arcadia."[61] Although hardly the unqualified success portrayed in the press, William Steinway's vision, not to mention his relative restraint given such enormous power over so many people, was admirable. The workers' housing was solidly built and included indoor bathrooms at a time when backyard privies were still commonplace. Although he controlled almost all aspects of town life in much the same way that Steinway & Sons oversaw all elements of piano making—the firm even designed and built the large brass keys used for locking the keyboards— William Steinway allowed workers their *lagerbier* at market prices, not to mention the opportunity to own their own homes.

While no other contemporary development within Queens County rivaled Steinway Village in terms of architectural, urbanistic, and sociological significance, there were nonetheless scattered throughout the sprawling area of villages and residential neighborhoods a handful of noteworthy buildings. The Fort Totten Battery on Willets Point was built between 1862 and 1864 as part of a network of seacoast fortifications masterminded by Joseph C. Totten, the United States Army's chief engineer, whose so-called Totten System incorporated vaulted chambers with embrasures through which guns could be fired. At the brick and stone Fort Totten Battery, built under the supervision of the engineer William Petit Trowbridge, two ramparts formed a shallow V-shape; a polygonal bastion marked the vortex.[62]

The Poppenhusen Institute, at 114–04 Fourteenth Road, in the village of College Point in Flushing, was completed in 1868, just twelve years after several large farms had been broken up and College Point as well as the villages of nearby Strattonport and Flammersburg were established.[63] As designed by the firm of Mundell & Teckritz, the three-story brick building combined Italianate-inspired detail with a French Second Empire mansard roof. Founded by Conrad Poppenhusen, a German immigrant who had become a prosperous rubber manufacturer, with a factory in

Queens County Court House, 25–10 Court House Square, Long Island City, Queens. George Hathorne, 1874. View to the east. QBPL.

College Point, the institute incorporated what was reputedly the country's first tuition-free kindergarten and served also as a civic center; in time the building housed a meeting hall, a free library, a jail, and the College Point Savings Bank. The dignified building exerted a commanding civic presence in the developing working-class area.

As designed by Vaux & Radford, a one-room brick chapel (1885) located on the grounds of the Tifereth Israel Cemetery, the Long Island burial ground of the Spanish Portuguese Synagogue of New York City, incorporated both decorative brickwork and stone accents.[64] The building, at once imposing and understated, featured an arcaded entrance porch. The firm also designed the cemetery's entrance gate.

Two civic buildings, built twelve years apart, dramatically reflected the growth of individual towns. The Flushing Town Hall (1862), at 137–35 Northern Boulevard, was a modestly sized, nine-thousand-square-foot, two-story, Romanesque-inspired, brick building.[65] Tall, narrow buttresses rose past the roofline, delicately scaled round-arched corbels supported a simply articulated cornice, and a triple-arched entrance portico adorned the front. It was distinctly different from the almost bombastic Queens County Court House (1874), at 25–10 Court House Square, at Jackson and Thompson Avenues in Long Island City, designed by George Hathorne.[66] A monumental, five-story brick building trimmed with three types of granite, its arcades of double-height arched windows were surmounted by boldly scaled mansard roofs that in turn supported decorative cresting. A mansarded tower contained the principal entrance.

Garden City

The department-store magnate Alexander T. Stewart's Garden City, located in a part of Queens County that would later split off to join a new county, Nassau, was initially called Hygiea. The original name reflected the motivation for the community's founding: to provide a more healthful place to live than the city. The same impetus had inspired Llewellyn Haskell to create Llewellyn Park, in West Orange, New Jersey, in 1853 (see below). In 1879, a reporter identified only as "M.," but perhaps Montgomery Schuyler, writing in the Boston-based journal the *American Architect and Building News*, explained that from the first the development had "pretensions to be something more than a sanitarium. It is a suburb, a sanitarium, and a cathedral town, all made at once and all made to order," promising "an economic and an architectural interest, in addition to its sanitary interest."[67] In contrast to Llewellyn Park, Garden City occupied a basically uncongenial site. Whereas the New Jersey community had been set on hilly, hard to develop, but picturesque land, Garden City, nineteen miles east of the East River, occupied a portion of the basically treeless, seven-thousand-acre Hempstead Plains, common lands of the Town of Hempstead, that Stewart had acquired in 1869. Stewart's favorite architect, John Kellum, came from the nearby village of Hempstead, and he no doubt encouraged the purchase, which eventually consisted of about 10,000 acres of land assembled at a total cost of $450,000. As planned by Stewart and Kellum, the village was to comprise five hundred acres located between Mineola and Hempstead, along the Long Island Railroad branch serving those two villages. In 1870, before construction began, Stewart had a small public cemetery moved and initiated the construction of a new rail line, completed in 1873, connecting directly to Long Island

Map, 1888, drawn by Chester Woolverton, of Garden City, Long Island. Alexander T. Stewart and John Kellum, 1869. GCA.

View to the north of Garden City, Long Island, 1878, showing two "Apostles" houses (John Kellum, 1872), left and center, and the Cathedral of the Incarnation (Henry G. Harrison, 1885), under construction, on the right. GCA.

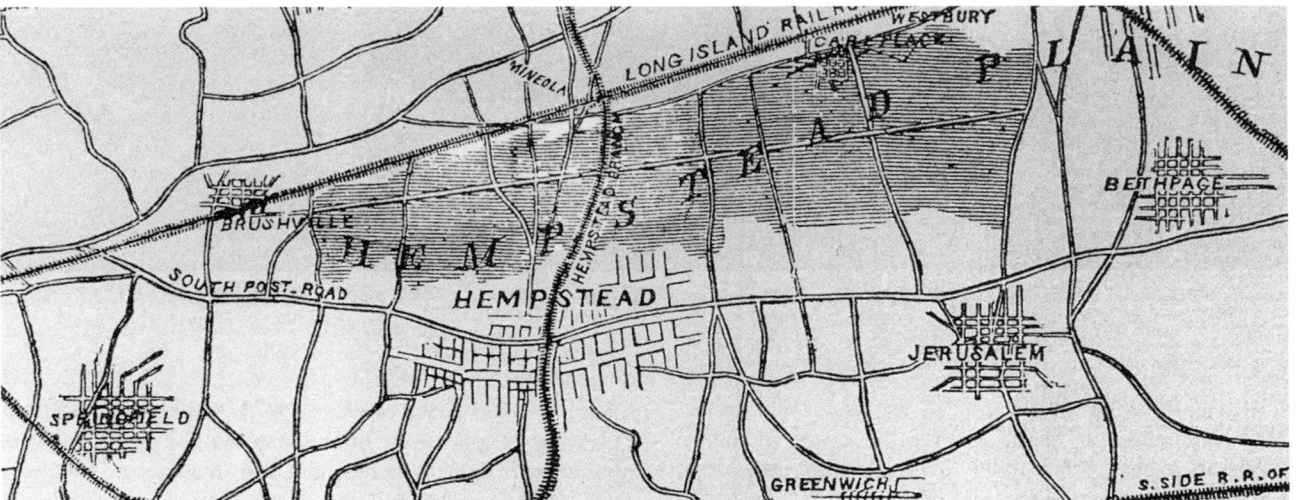

Map, c. 1869, showing, in the darkened area, the site purchased by Alexander T. Stewart on the Hempstead Plains for Garden City, Long Island. GCA.

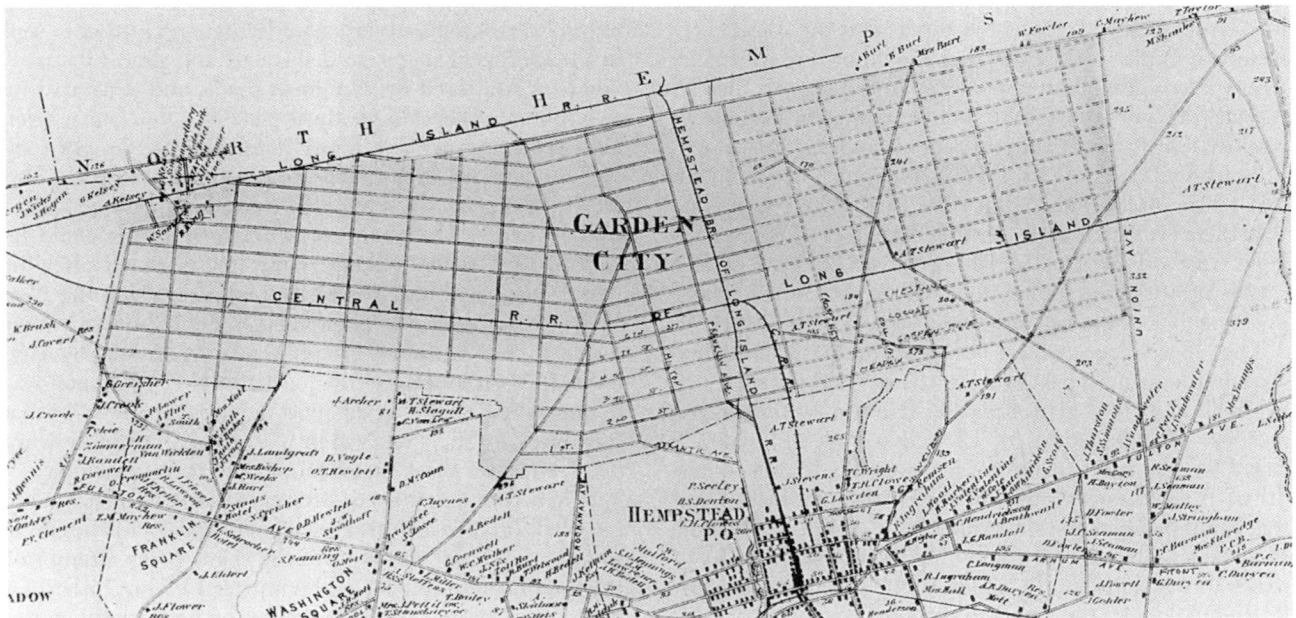

Map, 1873, showing the master plan of Garden City, Long Island. Alexander T. Stewart and John Kellum, 1869. GCA.

Garden City Hotel, in the park bounded by Hilton, Cathedral, and Cherry Valley Avenues, Sixth and Eighth Streets, Garden City, Long Island. John Kellum, 1874. View to the north. GCA.

City via Flushing. According to the *New York Herald*, Stewart intended to "build a city to be rented by men of moderate means, who prefer to hire houses rather than invest in real estate the capital they need in their business."[68] Stewart had in mind a town of ten thousand houses "for clerks and . . . businessmen, and it is known that he intended that not one single house should be sold in Garden City. It is conjectured that he desired to bequeath to the world a city that should own itself—a city whose every inhabitant should pay house-rent to the city treasury direct—a city that should ultimately become so wealthy that it might support schools and encourage art." Stewart died on April 10, 1876, before much development had taken place, leading the *New York Herald* to predict that there "is little doubt that the executors of [Stewart's] great trust will eventually sell homes in Garden City as a means of attracting a class that will be welcomed there," presumably a polite way of saying "people with money."[69]

The new village, which occupied about five hundred acres in the western part of the tract, was laid out on a grid by Kellum, at first glance placing it in opposition to the arcadian planning ideals of Llewellyn Park or Frederick Law Olmsted and Calvert Vaux's Riverside, Illinois, established in 1869, a new town nine miles west of Chicago that was being planned and developed more or less at the same time. But Kellum's grid, containing twenty-seven miles of roadway, was quite subtly manipulated, respecting the gentle undulations of the site with diagonal avenues that conformed to natural drainage patterns. A series of large

neighborhood parks combined with a fifty-thousand-tree planting program were little appreciated by early observers but came in time to be regarded as distinct assets. No street was less than eighty feet wide. Individual blocks were large: 500 feet wide, they extended between 1,000 and 1,500 feet in the east-west direction. Houses were required to be set back seventy-five feet from the street. At the town's center, a simple brick railroad station and a manager's office as well as a brick row of shops faced a "square and almost flat treeless park, traversed by rectilinear roads, and decorated by two fountains kept diligently at play."[70] A four-story, brick and stone, twenty-five-room hotel (1874), designed by Kellum and set in its own twenty-three-acre park, also faced the square. Stewart undertook the hotel's construction so that, as he put it, prospective residents could be well-housed "while looking at the houses that I offer for rent."[71] Stewart himself lived in the hotel, which the *New York Herald* labeled a "phenomenal country-house"; after his death, his "sumptuous room" was "sacredly kept by Mrs. Stewart."[72] According to the journalist "M.," the hotel was designed by Kellum "in the most nefarious manner," with a "raw brick front . . . relieved by a veranda, shiny with white paint, and by a sheet-metal cornice of great projections."[73]

When first announced, Stewart's plans were favorably received. In 1869 *Harper's Weekly* rejoiced: "This design is so gigantic that it throws into the shade every attempt of the kind hitherto made. . . . Hempstead Plains, hitherto a desert, will be made to blossom as the rose; it will be the most beautiful suburb in the vicinity of New York. God speed the undertaking!"[74] But the following year the *New York World* was not so sure: Stewart's "purchase of Hempstead Plains, simply because it was the cheapest large property near New York, is certainly against the judgment of real estate operators. He is attempting a daring experiment, nothing less than a community which should have churches, schools, water, gas and all the appliances of municipal life, without a single other person having interest in a foot of the whole domain. He proposes to be landlord, mayor, alderman, in fact the whole municipality."[75]

At least at first, Garden City was a failure as a town, constituting merely a bedroom community for New Yorkers. While Llewellyn Park was a small enclave, Garden City was to be a large town, but not much thought seemed to be given to providing any commercial activity. Only a few shops were built to serve the residents, so that, as a shopkeeper put it, "the gentlemen, they go into New York every morning, and the ladies,—well, the ladies go in too."[76]

As designed by Kellum and completed in 1872, ten large houses set the tone for the new development's architecture. Quickly dubbed "the Apostles," the houses were soon followed by smaller brick and frame houses sometimes called "the Disciples." By 1879 the development consisted of about sixty houses, some brick, some wood, but all, according to "M.," "suburban villas of the deepest dye, and apparently designed out of *The Practical Builder's Assistant*."[77] Some of

the houses were by Kellum, but his death in 1871 had left the town artistically rudderless. Eighteen cottages were built on Franklin Avenue in 1872 to house families of the skilled workmen, many of them recent immigrants from Poland. A central waterworks (1876) was constructed, featuring a great well fifty feet in diameter and forty feet deep. The four-story, mansarded Cathedral School of St. Paul, designed by E. H. Harris, was completed in 1883.

Upon Stewart's death, his widow, Cornelia Clinch Stewart, set out to build a cathedral church and Episcopal center in Garden City as a memorial. She hired Henry G. Harrison, who had helped in laying out the community, to design the building. It would take Cornelia Stewart nearly a decade to realize her project; the Cathedral of the Incarnation was dedicated on June 2, 1885, four months before her death. The circumstances surrounding the cathedral's construction were nothing short of melodramatic. On November 7, 1878, it was reported that Stewart's corpse had been stolen from the churchyard of St. Mark's-in-the-Bouwerie, in New York, where it had been temporarily deposited pending final burial in the new cathedral. Two years later, Stewart's executor, Judge Henry Hilton, paid a ransom, and Stewart's body was finally interred. The cathedral, made from Belleville, New Jersey, brownstone, was 175 feet long and 96 feet wide, with steep, slate-covered roofs and an 80-foot-tall bell tower atop which a tapering spire rose 130 feet. Harrison's design for the

"Apostles" house, Garden City, Long Island. John Kellum, 1872. View to the northwest, 1877, showing the Cathedral of the Incarnation (Henry G. Harrison, 1885) under construction in the background. GCA.

Workers' cottages (1872), east side of Franklin Avenue between Fifth Street and the Long Island Railroad crossing, Garden City, Long Island. View to the southeast. GCA.

Cathedral of the Incarnation, Cathedral Avenue to Rockaway and Cherry Valley Avenues, Fourth Street to the Long Island Railroad crossing, Garden City, Long Island. Henry G. Harrison, 1885. View to the northwest. GCA.

church was not especially admired. "M." was more impressed with its height than any other aspect: "There are no powerful masses of structure felt through [its] . . . meshes of ornament, no leading lines to accentuate with all these moulded subdivisions. The whole is not large enough, in mere physical magnitude or in idea, to dominate this multiplicity of petty parts, and the cathedral becomes a toy, and recalls the attenuated confectionary of 'Greenwood Gothic,'" the last a reference to Richard Upjohn & Son's highly decorated gateway (1860–65) to Brooklyn's Green-Wood Cemetery (see chapter 7). In short, the reporter concluded, "the memorial cathedral of Long Island, as an architectural work, must be added to the long list of lost opportunities."[78]

With the national economy's recovery in the 1880s, Garden City began to prosper. But even as late as 1885, it was still known as "Stewart's Folly," with only 550 residents. Montgomery Schuyler, in his 1884 survey of New York's suburbs, was almost completely negative in his assessment of Garden City:

> When the late A. T. Stewart "went out of his business," his excursions were apt to be as unsuccessful as his exertions in his own line were uniformly successful. Garden City was one of the boldest of these excursions and one is not surprised to hear that as an investment it has not been profitable. The site has nothing to recommend it except salubrity, nor indeed anything to explain its selection. The village simply occurs on the great Long Island plain in the same fortuitous way in which villages crop out on the Western prairies, with nothing to indicate why it should be here rather than elsewhere. And Mr. Stewart was by no means so fortunate in his architects as the proprietor of Short Hills [see below]. . . . Neither the hotel nor any of the houses has the slightest interest as a visual object. . . . Though the cathedral be the architectural lion not only of Garden City but of all Long Island, it does not remove one's wonder at the patient suburban people who can endure to live in a place where there is nothing else to look at.[79]

Cathedral of the Incarnation, Cathedral Avenue to Rockaway and Cherry Valley Avenues, Fourth Street to the Long Island Railroad crossing, Garden City, Long Island. Henry G. Harrison, 1885. View of the nave toward the chancel. GCA.

New York Yacht Club, former Henry and Anne McFarlane house (mid-1840s), 30 Hylan Boulevard, Clifton, Staten Island. Rendering, 1872, showing view to the southwest. NYYC.

Staten Island

Two-and-a-half times the size of Manhattan Island, Staten Island had very little to do with New York until the early years of the nineteenth century, when sixteen-year-old Cornelius Vanderbilt invested one hundred dollars and established a passenger and produce ferry service run by Daniel D. Tompkins. By the 1830s the northern part of the island began to flourish as a summer resort, catering to prosperous if not necessarily prominent families from New York and the South who settled New Brighton (1834–36), a planned community modeled on English resorts such as Brighton and the Isle of Wight.[80] According to its developer, George A. Ward, New Brighton promised "men in active business . . . the means . . . of withdrawing from the labors and anxiety of commerce to the quiet of their own families."[81] In 1836 Ward, working with a group of New York businessmen, took over land that a wealthy Manhattan developer, Thomas E. Davis, had begun to amass adjoining the property of Sailors' Snug Harbor, a seamen's retreat that was in the process of establishing itself on the island. The Panic of 1837 stalled the town's promising architectural development. Among other buildings, John Haviland, the English-born, Philadelphia-based architect who was then in New York working on the Tombs, a prison, had proposed Washington Crescent, a Classical

terrace.[82] Plans for this development, as well as for eclectically designed houses that would potentially have been major American versions of contemporary English work, went unrealized. Other developments were built, including nearby Clifton, established by the Staten Island Association in 1837, and Elliottville, founded by the eminent eye specialist Dr. Samuel McKenzie Elliott in 1839, where patients including such important writers as Henry Wadsworth Longfellow and Francis Parkman stayed to recuperate from surgery.[83] Frederick Law Olmsted was also attracted to Staten Island, establishing an experimental wheat farm on Raritan Bay near the mouth of the Great Kills, which he worked from 1848 to 1850.[84] Hamilton Park, in the New Brighton area, a suburban enclave built on an elevated site bounded by Third Street and Franklin, Prospect, and York Avenues, was created by the real estate developer Charles Kennedy Hamilton.[85] It opened in 1853 and was at first largely unconnected to the surrounding street grid. The development included brick Italianate houses that were initially rented rather than offered for purchase. In 1863 Carl Pfeiffer added twelve houses of stucco-covered brick incorporating towers, corner oriel windows, and porches in a highly picturesque manner.

During the Civil War, Staten Island, which had been host to many Southern summertime guests, was an assem-

Staten Island Athletic Club boathouse, near Richmond Terrace, Livingston, Staten Island. Edward A. Sargent, 1877. View to the east showing the Kill Van Kull on the left and the tracks of the Staten Island Rapid Transit Railroad on the right. Almstaedt. SIHS.

bly point for organizing Union regiments, with fields and orchards turned into camps and training grounds. But postwar growth was so sluggish that in 1871 the legislature appointed a committee to investigate the causes. Its report, written by Olmsted, pointed to such problems as malaria caused by mosquitos in the marshes and poor ferry service plagued by serious safety issues.[86]

One segment of Staten Island's economy did continue to prosper: leisure-time activities. In 1870 members of the New York Yacht Club watched the first defense of the America's Cup from the latticed veranda of the rambling, two-and-a-half-story clapboard Henry and Anne McFarlane house (mid-1840s), at 30 Hylan Boulevard, which James Gordon Bennett Jr. had bought for the club's use two years earlier, when he was its vice commodore.[87] In 1877 the Staten Island Athletic Club built a picturesquely massed but severely geometric Queen Anne–style boathouse designed by Edward A. Sargent, perhaps the island's most prominent architect.[88] Nine years later a passing barge destroyed the building. It was replaced in the following year by another structure designed by Sargent, who this time wrapped the building in an envelope of shingles. Built on pilings and consisting of water-level boat storage and a veranda-surrounded clubhouse crowned by an openwork domed cupola, the building was described by the *New York Daily Graphic* as "probably the largest boat

house" in the country, and "one of the handsomest."[89] Mary E. Outerbridge, a Staten Island resident who had seen lawn tennis played while on a trip to Bermuda, introduced the game to the United States in 1874 at the Staten Island Cricket and Baseball Club, near St. George Ferry.[90] On September 1, 1880, the club, which maintained a houselike facility incorporating a broad veranda, hosted the first National Lawn Tennis Tournament.

The late 1880s and early 1890s witnessed the zenith of Staten Island's heyday as a resort, culminating in the construction of C.P.H. Gilbert's Hotel Castleton (1891), in New Brighton. Gilbert's four-hundred-room, wood-frame hotel, approximately the size of Wentworth-by-the-Sea (Charles E. Campbell and David Chase, 1874; Frank Jones, 1880–81), in New Castle, New Hampshire, or Mason & Rice's Grand Hotel (1887), on Mackinac Island, Michigan, was deemed a "revelation to Staten Islanders and others" who remembered its predecessor, the Peteler (later St. Mark) Hotel, which the new design subsumed.[91]

In the post–Civil War era, Staten Island also served as a suburban haven for New Yorkers. In 1865 the *Richmond County Gazette* reported that the "demand for dwelling houses has never before been equaled. There is a daily rush from the city of ladies and gentlemen . . . in search of residences at moderate rents. The deluge of people, we suppose, is mainly to be attributed to the fact that rents in the

*Staten Island Athletic Club boathouse, near Richmond Terrace, Livingston, Staten Island. Edward A. Sargent, 1877. View to the south-
west showing the Kill Van Kull in the foreground and the tracks of the Staten Island Rapid Transit Railroad in the background. SIIAS.*

Staten Island Athletic Club boathouse, near the intersection of Richmond Terrace and Bement Avenue, Livingston, Staten Island. Edward A. Sargent, 1887. View to the northeast, c. 1900, across the tracks of the Staten Island Rapid Transit Railroad. Benedict. SIHS.

Staten Island Athletic Club boathouse, near the intersection of Richmond Terrace and Bement Avenue, Livingston, Staten Island. Edward A. Sargent, 1887. View to the northeast, c. 1890, across the tracks of the Staten Island Rapid Transit Railroad. SIHS.

Hotel Castleton, St. Mark's Place, New Brighton, Staten Island. C.P.H. Gilbert, 1891. View to the southwest. SIHS.

Prohibition Park, Westerleigh, Staten Island. View to the southwest of houses (1887) on the Boulevard, showing part of the development's auditorium building on the far right. SIIAS.

H. H. Richardson house, 45 McClean Avenue, Arrochar, Staten Island. H. H. Richardson, 1868–69. View to the northwest. SIHS.

cities of New York and Brooklyn have been raised to an enormous figure, and quite impossible for anyone to hire a respectable tenement and pay for it and yet have money enough to buy bread for his family."[92] One of the more interesting suburban enclaves was Prohibition Park, in Westerleigh, south of Port Richmond, which was established in 1887 with a very specific ideological mission: Dr. Isaac Funk, a co-founder of the publishing house Funk and Wagnalls, Dr. William Boole, a Methodist minister, and other prohibitionists planned the enclave as a temperance-supporting community.[93] The development included a four-thousand-seat auditorium and a hotel, where lectures and events were held regularly, as well as commodious Queen Anne–style houses. Another important development, St. George, occupied the island's north shore in the vicinity of the ferry landing. It appears to have been so named in 1885 by the promoter Erastus Wiman in honor of financier George Law, who had made the site available. Law also helped forge an integrated system linking the ferry to the recently consolidated Staten Island Rapid Transit Railroad Company, which connected the populated north end of the island with the remote village of Tottenville in the south.[94]

Most of the suburban houses of the late 1860s and early 1870s conformed to the prevailing French Second Empire taste. Twelve ten- to twelve-room "cottages" designed by Carl Pfeiffer for the developer Charles Kennedy Hamilton were built on the east side of Harvard Avenue between Park Place and East Buchanan Street.[95] The enclave, begun in 1853 and known as Hamilton Park, was in many ways similar to the gated community of Llewellyn Park, New Jersey (see below), which opened the same year. The most significant dwelling of the Bonanza economy was a boldly massed two-and-a-half-story house (1868–69) with a steeply sloped, slated, and crocketed mansard, which the fledgling architect H. H. Richardson designed for his own use at 45 McClean Avenue in Arrochar.[96] Sheathed in clapboard, the walls were articulated by flat boards suggesting a structural frame. While Richardson was working on this house, he also prepared a design for George and Elizabeth Redmond, Staten Island friends of his, about which nothing is known.[97]

With the revival of the economy in the late 1870s, a number of interesting new houses were completed. Particularly distinguished and stylistically innovative were two houses by the English-trained architect Bassett Jones, who had begun practicing in New York in 1873, establishing the partnership of Oakey & Jones. The young architect Bruce Price, who made his mark in the 1880s with modest Queen Anne–inspired cottages, was the first to call attention to the character of Jones's work on Staten Island. According to Price, Jones, "fresh from the studio and influence of Norman Shaw," built "lovely cottages on Staten Island . . . inspired by the Queen Anne revival then starting up in England, but so modified and adapted under his skillful treatment as to distinctly be his own."[98] Jones's cottage (1877) for Alexander J. Hamilton was especially notable, perched about fifty feet

Alexander J. Hamilton cottage, Shore Road, between New Brighton and the Quarantine, Staten Island. Bassett Jones, 1877. Rendering. AABN. CU.

William Krebs gardener's cottage, Staten Island. Bassett Jones, 1877. Rendering. AABN. CU.

above the water on Shore Road, halfway between New Brighton and the Quarantine.[99] One of the first of the new, vernacular-inspired, Queen Anne–style houses to be realized anywhere, the Hamilton cottage was comparable in character to Charles F. McKim's Fairchild stable, in Newport, Rhode Island, which had been completed in the previous year. Jones's gardener's cottage and stable for William Krebs (1877) came even closer to McKim's design.[100] In publishing the Krebs cottage, the *American Architect and Building News*, then in its second year of publication, stated that the "style both of the cottage and stable is a somewhat free adaptation of Queen Anne forms," the first time that stylistic designation was used in what had quickly become the nation's most influential architectural magazine.[101] By the mid-1880s, when the economy was roaring and parts of Staten Island were in the midst of a boom, "a taste for the Queen Anne," as the *Real Estate Record and Builders' Guide* put it,

Mary and Dr. Theodore Walser double house, northeast corner of St. Mark's Place and Westervelt Avenue, New Brighton, Staten Island. Edward A. Sargent, 1891. View to the northeast showing St. Mark's Place on the right. SIHS.

pervaded Staten Island like an exhalation from the soil. An intricate landscape combination of ridges and ravines, with sloping hill-sides, valleys and wooded peaks, the island offers every opportunity for a picturesque display; and whatever opinions may be held on this style of construction, when illustrated on graded streets and among carefully aligned buildings, its adaptability for rural or suburban cottages, where the surrounding scenery is favorable, is beyond question. . . . Some of the finest specimens of the [Queen Anne] style are to be seen in the town of Castleton. They stand singly and in large groups, and nestling among foliage, or relieved against a background of trees or precipitous hills, there are few instances where the treatment is not effective. . . . The largest and finest of these groups is probably to be found on the block bounded by Lafayette and Clinton avenues and Second and Fourth streets, at the foot of the bluff, in the village of New Brighton. There are ten dwellings in

this group, seven of which were built last spring by Mr. John C. Henderson, after designs by Messrs. Lamb & Rich. . . . These new buildings are in the English style, pure and simple, with large exterior chimneys, rendered picturesque in the treatment, projecting porches, gables and heavy sloping roofs. The coloring . . . may be pronounced highly successful, made by a tasteful mingling of russet, green, orange and brown.[102]

Between 1885 and 1892 New Brighton, the center of the residential construction boom, was transformed into a charming Shingle Style suburbia.[103] In 1887 Mary and Dr. Theodore Walser commissioned a double house (1891) at 1–5 St. Mark's Place, on the northeast corner of Westervelt Avenue, from Edward A. Sargent, taking advantage of property purchased in the late 1860s that had become valuable as a result of the 1886 opening of the Staten Island Railroad's New Brighton station.[104] The Walsers had been active developers in the 1870s, but

View to the north, c. 1894, of St. Mark's Place, New Brighton, Staten Island. SIHS.

this project was far more architecturally distinguished than anything they had previously undertaken. Located on a corner, the two-and-a-half-story house had an angled corner tower that broke away from the main mass, rising to a steep, dramatically flared roof. The mixture of clapboard and decorative shingles banded together with horizontally grouped windows to create a remarkably rich effect. At about the same time (c. 1890) Sargent was hired to design what may have been his most interesting house, for Frederick L. Rodewald, at 103 St. Mark's Place, with an astonishingly original central pediment incorporating a large, Queen Anne–inspired window, deep porches, and a gable pierced with small square openings that was no doubt intended for birds.[105] Rounded corners enhanced the slipcover effect of the shingles, while a profusion of details provided almost unending visual interest. Sargent's Stephen H. Brown house (c. 1890), at 115 St. Mark's Place, was only slightly

less remarkable.[106] A rounded corner tower, half timbering on multiple gables, staggered shingles, and bargeboards all contributed to the design. Sargent's 119 St. Mark's Place (1889–91), built for Vernon H. Brown, who was the developer of the Stephen H. Brown house, combined elements of the Rodewald and Stephen H. Brown houses to a calmer effect that was more appropriate to its midblock location.[107] In 1892 Sargent undertook for Henry H. Cammann, a manufacturer of petroleum jelly, a house at 125 St. Mark's Place.[108] That design exhibited more compositional rigor, with a shingled, conical, French Norman tower forming its principal feature in clear evocation of McKim, Mead & White's Francis L. Skinner house, in Newport, Rhode Island, completed ten years earlier.

Inspired by the Walsers, in 1890 Anson Phelps Stokes, whose own sprawling, mansarded Bay Villa commanded a hilltop site between Hamilton Avenue and St. Mark's

Anson Phelps Stokes house (Bay Villa) (c. 1870), between Hamilton Avenue and St. Mark's Place, New Brighton, Staten Island. View to the northwest. SIHS.

Place, undertook an eleven-house development on two new cul-de-sac streets, one on the southwest and the other on the southeast corner of his estate.[109] Stokes hired Douglas Smyth to design eight double and three single houses, to be sold or rented out. Although the two- and three-story efforts were uneven in character, the overall effect was a remarkable demonstration of an approach conceived for sprawling villas instead used for compactly massed, almost urban townhouses.

While the developments at New Brighton catered to the upper middle class, Kreischerville was a small village run as a quasi–company town by a local industrialist, Balthasar Kreischer.[110] Begun as a hamlet called Androvetteville, near the junction of Arthur Kill and Sharrotts Roads, part of Westfield on the southeastern side of the island, Kreischerville grew up after the mid-1850s, when refractory fireclays were discovered in the vicinity, leading Kreischer to develop a firebrick manu-

facturing works, one of the first in the United States. Kreischer also had a plant in New York but closed it in 1876. Two years later, fire swept the Staten Island works, which were immediately rebuilt, at which time Kreischer retired and turned the business over to his children, concentrating on the development of his town, which by then included two large tenements built to house workers. Soon after he followed with a group of semidetached houses, which became the village's dominant building type. Because the town was isolated, it needed to be self-sufficient. Kreischer built stores for lease and in 1883 he erected a small building for St. Peter's German Evangelical Reformed Church, a modest, wood-framed vernacular structure.[111] Kreischer's attitude toward the town was paternalistic but not overbearing. Nonetheless, he had it fenced and closed its gates early in the evening. Kreischer himself lived there, in a villa probably built in the 1860s, and his sons, Charles and Edward, constructed a pair of

View, c. 1910, of Kreischerville, Staten Island, showing clay bank in the foreground. Grimshaw. SIHS.

View to the northwest of Kreischerville, Staten Island, showing Kreischer Road in the foreground and Balthasar Kreischer's firebrick manufacturing works in the distance. Guether. SIHS.

Episcopal Church of the Holy Comforter, Southfields, Staten Island. Richard M. Upjohn, 1865; moved and enlarged, 1869–72. View to the south of the enlarged church, Amboy Road east of Richmond Avenue, Southfields (Eltingville), Staten Island. SIHS.

St. John's Church, 1331 Bay Street, Clifton, Staten Island. Arthur D. Gilman, 1871. View to the northeast showing the church on the left, the chapel (Arthur D. Gilman, 1882) in the center, and the rectory (Arthur D. Gilman, 1886) on the right. Almstaedt. SIHS.

St. Paul's Memorial Church, 225 St. Paul's Avenue, Edgewater Village, Staten Island. Edward T. Potter, 1866–70. View to the northeast, c. 1900. Burdick. SIHS.

similar, imposing Stick Style villas (c. 1886) attributed to Palliser & Palliser; the Charles Kreischer residence was located at 4500 Arthur Kill Road.[112]

A number of churches were built to meet the requirements of the island's growing population. Richard M. Upjohn's Episcopal Church of the Holy Comforter (1865) served the village of Southfields (now Eltingville), at the island's southern tip.[113] A charmingly modest Gothic Revival board-and-batten country chapel designed in the manner of the 1830s or 1840s, it quickly proved inadequate and, in 1869–72, was moved to a new site six hundred feet away and enlarged with transepts and a bell tower, with Upjohn probably again serving as architect. The Brighton Heights Reformed Church (1866), at 320 St. Mark's Place, on the southwest corner of Fort Place, designed by the architect John Correja, known primarily for the design

of warehouses in New York (see chapter 3), was a delicate, white-painted, wood-frame building.[114]

Arthur D. Gilman's St. John's Church (1871), at 1331 Bay Street, on the southeast corner of New Lane, was the island's first imposing religious structure.[115] Gilman continued to work for the congregation, completing a building that housed a chapel, Sunday school, and facilities for a parish house in 1882, and a rectory in 1886. Three years later he designed a separate parish house. In 1871, fresh from the success of his Equitable Building (see chapter 3), in New York, he replaced an earlier church (1844) with one inspired by an English parish, possibly Holy Trinity in Stratford-upon-Avon. The new, somewhat stiff, rose-colored granite church was crowned by a banded, gabled high spire above a square tower at the crossing, which became an instant and enduring landmark for ships coming

Church of St. Andrew, southeast corner of Arthur Kill and Old Mill Roads, Richmondtown, Staten Island. William H. Mersereau, 1872. View to the northeast. SIHS.

through the Narrows. Edward T. Potter's Episcopal St. Paul's Memorial Church (1866–70), at 225 St. Paul's Avenue, in the heart of Edgewater Village, about a quarter of a mile from the Tompkinsville landing, commanded a grand vista of the harbor from Sandy Hook past the Narrows to Fort Hamilton in Brooklyn.[116] Intended to be crowned with a 140-foot-tall tower, the ultimately towerless church and its adjoining rectory nonetheless made for a memorable presence, with subtly crafted, Connecticut brownstone–trimmed, dark gray traprock walls and polished granite dwarf columns capped by naturalistically carved foliated capitals. William H. Mersereau's English Norman

Church of St. Andrew (1872), at Old Mill and Arthur Kill Roads, in Richmondtown, was in fact the final reconstruction of a building that began in the eighteenth century as a small stone church (1709–12).[117] Mersereau, a Staten Island native who lived on the south shore and studied architecture at Columbia College under William R. Ware, reused the original stone walls for his simple design, which to one side had a square tower and belfry surmounted by a plain octagonal spire presiding over a country graveyard.

The Mission of the Immaculate Virgin, also known as Mount Loretto, was founded in 1883 by Father Drumgoole as a refuge for homeless and orphaned children.[118]

Mission of the Immaculate Virgin (c. 1883), Sharrott to Richard Avenue, Raritan Bay to Amboy Road, Richmond Valley, Staten Island. View to the northeast, c. 1915, showing the Church of Saint Joachim and Saint Anne (Benjamin E. Lowe, 1891) in the center. Grimshaw. SIHS.

Mission of the Immaculate Virgin (c. 1883), Sharrott to Richard Avenue, Raritan Bay to Amboy Road, Richmond Valley, Staten Island. View to the northwest of the main buildings. SIHS.

The institution occupied a campuslike site in Richmond Valley, with commanding views of Raritan Bay and the entire Lower New York Bay, and was housed in a variety of buildings. Visually dominating the building group was an imposing Gothic church (1891), dedicated to Saint Joachim and Saint Anne, designed by Benjamin E. Lowe.

One other religious structure bears notice, not a house of worship but a burial place: Richard Morris Hunt and Frederick Law Olmsted's Vanderbilt Mausoleum (1884–89), near the Moravian Cemetery at New Dorp.[119] In 1884 William H. Vanderbilt, recognizing that his son's Fifth Avenue house, designed by Hunt, was more impressive than his own, hired the Paris-trained architect to design the family tomb on a twenty-two-acre site behind the Moravian Cemetery, where his father, the Commodore, was buried. William had previously tried to buy a plot in the cemetery but had given up the idea because the owners asked exorbitant prices. Hunt, working with Olmsted for the first time since their clash over the Albany Capitol ten years earlier, set the mausoleum on a high

knoll commanding superb views of Staten Island and the harbor. Vanderbilt, mindful of the shocking fate of Alexander T. Stewart's remains (see above), wanted a secure burial place. Hunt's first proposal seemed too showy, and Vanderbilt died on December 8, 1885, before construction on the revised design, which he had apparently approved, had been completed. The design was derived from the twelfth-century Romanesque Church of St. Gilles, near Arles, France. Only the mausoleum's principal facade, dominated by an elaborately framed, Quincy granite, triple-entry portal, as well as two cupolas that decorated the roof, could be seen; the rest of the structure was set into the hillside.

Staten Island had comparatively few public works of distinction. Of these, Alfred B. Mullett's French Second Empire–style office building for the Third District United States Lighthouse Depot (1868–71), at 1 Bay Street, a bold, three-story, granite and red brick structure that could easily be mistaken for a grand villa, was far and away the most impressive.[120] Edward A. Sargent's Queen

Vanderbilt Mausoleum, near the Moravian Cemetery, New Dorp, Staten Island. Richard Morris Hunt and Frederick Law Olmsted, 1884–89. View to the northeast. The Octagon, AAF.

Samuel R. Smith Infirmary, Castleton Avenue opposite Cebra Avenue, New Brighton, Staten Island. Alfred E. Barlow, 1887–89. View to the northeast. Steinrock. SIHS.

Anne–style Public School 15 (c. 1888), at the southeast corner of Grant and St. Paul's Avenues, in Richmond, was also noteworthy.[121] Staten Island's two village halls were somewhat architecturally distinguished. As designed by James Whitford and completed in 1871, the brick New Brighton Village Hall adopted a French Second Empire style.[122] The Edgewater Village Hall (1889), designed by Paul Kühne, was more eclectic in its style, combining a dormered entrance tower with Romanesque-inspired round-headed windows.[123] Both Whitford and Kühne were Staten Island–based architects. After occupying a succession of buildings near the ferry terminal, the Samuel R. Smith Infirmary moved into a red brick, castlelike building (Alfred E. Barlow, 1887–89) on Castleton Avenue, in New Brighton.[124] With four corner towers rising to conical roofs, perhaps reflecting the influence of C. C. Haight's New York Cancer Hospital (see chapter 6), then under construction, Barlow's building was an imposing addition to the first private hospital on Staten Island, founded by the Richmond County Medical Society in 1861 and named after a local doctor who had devoted himself to the poor. The sophisticated design was a clear signal that Staten Island had shaken off its rural past.

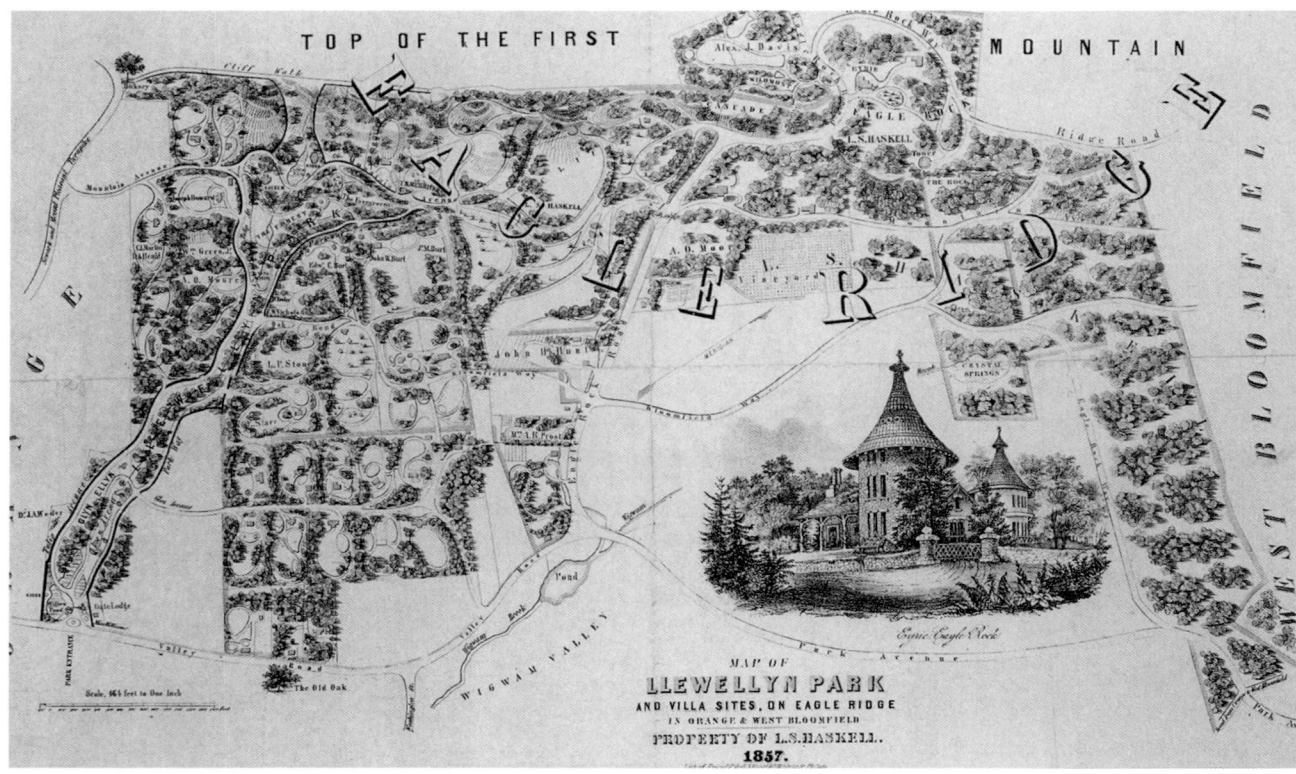

Llewellyn Park, New Jersey. Llewellyn Haskell and Alexander Jackson Davis, 1853. Plan. MMA.

New Jersey Suburbs

The towns of New Jersey were fertile ground for suburban homesteading. But two planned developments, Llewellyn Park, founded in 1853, and Short Hills, founded in 1877, gave New Jersey distinction not only as a suburban haven but also as a home to important experiments in town planning. Llewellyn Park, a gated community in West Orange, New Jersey, was established by a New York– and Philadelphia-based pharmaceutical dealer, Llewellyn Haskell.[125] Haskell, an ardent supporter of the proposal to create Central Park, enjoyed a wide group of spiritually minded intellectuals as friends, including Washington Irving, William Cullen Bryant, and the architect Alexander Jackson Davis.

Haskell abandoned his country estate in Belleville on the nearby Passaic River after concluding that its swampy site was at least partly to blame for the deaths of four of his five sons as well as his own bouts with rheumatism. The estate had contained a villa designed by Davis, featuring a salon, dining room, and parlor respectively labeled "Mind," "Body," and "Soul." Haskell found better air at higher ground on Orange Mountain, twelve miles west of the Hudson, where, on February 20, 1853, he bought and renovated a twenty-one-and-a-half-acre farm and commissioned Davis to transform the existing house into a charming villa. The area was near a mineral springs and had been a popular resort destination in the 1820s. By the 1840s Orange was already on its way to becoming a haven for rich commuters, a neighborhood of estates made more villagelike as a result of the decision of Matthias Ogden Halsted to occupy only a portion of a hundred-acre farm there, parceling off the remaining land to his city friends. At his own expense Halsted built a depot on the newly opened Morris and Essex Railroad, which in turn agreed to have one inbound train in the morning and one outbound train in the evening stop there, making possible an hour-long commute to and from New York via rail and ferry, approximately the same amount of time it took a rush-hour trolley to go from lower Manhattan to Central Park.

But Haskell had more in mind than establishing his own house, and with other investors soon assembled about seven hundred acres of land on which he conceived, probably on the advice of Davis, a unique, gated residential enclave filled with "country homes for city people."[126] Haskell was surely involved in devising the suburban development's plan, and two landscape gardeners, Eugene A. Baumann and Howard Daniels, likely also contributed significantly to the community's layout. Baumann, recently arrived from France, had a reputation as a designer of small suburban sites, and Daniels's submission to the 1858 competition for Central Park (see chapter 1) had received third-runner-up prize.

Set behind a barrier of evergreen plantings and fencing, the enclave seemed as "if its residents had thrown up an abatis against an insurrection of visitors from the town."[127]

View, c. 1870, of Llewellyn Park, New Jersey. Llewellyn Haskell and Alexander Jackson Davis, 1853. NJIC.

The core of the development encompassed 350 acres, including a 50-acre linear strip of common parkland known as the Ramble (but called Llewellyn Park until about 1860), which served as the community's spine. A picturesque, fifty-acre ravine crisscrossed by paths and bridges, it contained a miniature waterfall and ornamental ponds. One of the principal roadways along the Ramble was called the Park Way, the first use of the term that Frederick Law Olmsted would later adopt to describe a new kind of highway. Ten miles of curving streets encircled the Ramble and branched out to the house sites, which were laid out in a largely unmanicured landscape that flew in the face of conventional practice. Covenants not only protected the park area but also stipulated that no house be built on less than one acre in order to help preserve the area's pastoral character. Many sites were much larger. By common consent, hedges rather than fences were used to demarcate property lines.

Davis's unique involvement with Llewellyn Park during its early days was in large part responsible for the enclave's architectural consistency; he is said to have built twelve houses in Llewellyn Park, as well as the ornamental shelters and the entrance lodge. It was as though Davis and Haskell imagined the property as an English estate, with houses for the yeomanry and a few castles for the lords of the manor. In addition to the close relationship between architect and developer, Llewellyn Park's architectural unity resulted from the fact that the houses tended to be subsumed by the

View from Eagle Rock, Llewellyn Park, New Jersey. NJIC.

View to the northwest of the entrance to Llewellyn Park, New Jersey, showing the Porter's Lodge (Alexander Jackson Davis, 1857) on the right. NJIC.

Llewellyn Haskell cottage (the Eyrie), Llewellyn Park, New Jersey. Alexander Jackson Davis, 1853–54. NJIC.

View to the northeast of Willow Pond, Llewellyn Park, New Jersey, showing the Porter's Lodge (Alexander Jackson Davis, 1857) on the right. NJIC.

Arcade Cottage, Llewellyn Park, New Jersey. Alexander Jackson Davis, 1857. View to the southeast. ANT. CU.

landscape. Llewellyn Park was a triumph of associationism, in which a dramatic landscape of rocky summits, springs, and forests was intended to match Gothic villas and romantic, independent-minded residents. Davis renovated Haskell's farmhouse, transforming it into a picturesque cottage called the Eyrie (1853–54). Planned as a temporary residence that was to become the gatehouse of a much larger estate that was never realized, it featured two asymmetrical towers, one of wood and the other of local traprock. Next door Davis built his own house, Wildmont, on twenty-five acres, where he lived on weekends and during the summer until 1870 and from which he was able to exercise substantial influence on the planning of the community as well as on the design of villas built there.

Davis's turreted stone Porter's Lodge (1857), flanking Willow Pond, guarded Llewellyn Park's fenced-in preserve; along with a nearby rustic, lakeside kiosk, it set the architectural tone for the community so that even the more elaborate houses, such as the Gothic-inspired Castlewood, designed by Davis in 1859 for the prominent local businessman Joseph C. Howard, seemed almost

Joseph C. Howard house (Castlewood), Llewellyn Park, New Jersey. Alexander Jackson Davis, 1859. Southeast elevation. Alexander Jackson Davis Collection. CU.

modest. Complete with two massive towers constructed of rough-hewn stone from the town's quarries, and a long "cloister" connecting the main house to its stone stables, Castlewood was a wonderful evocation of an imaginary past, an American dream of the English Middle Ages as it had never been.

By no means were all the houses grand. Arcadia (1857), or Arcade Cottage, as it was first known, was designed by Davis and built by Haskell in a simple Italianate style. Another modest cottage (1858–59) by Davis, for Edward W. Nichols, a landscape artist, became home to the abolitionist James Miller McKim in 1866. Shortly after moving in, McKim's Quaker wife, Sarah Allibone McKim, wrote to her son Charles F. McKim, who was in his freshman year at Harvard, and claimed that the house was too "fanciful" for her, with "a funny pitched roof and clustered chimneys and bull's-eye windows, and niches for statuettes, and all sorts of artistic arrangements, that don't quite suit my plain taste." Nonetheless she found the "Park . . . beautiful and the views from our house . . . lovely. . . . The roads are so fine that it makes driving pleasant."[128] Of the two, Castlewood was more premonitory than the McKim cottage: by the 1880s, the suburb began to throw off its cloak of modesty and emerge as an enclave whose exclusivity was defined principally by material wealth rather than romantic ideals.

In April 1865, by which time about twenty-five houses had been built, the *New York Times* repeated an account from the *Independent* on Theodore Tilton's visit to Llewellyn Park. The well-known editor and Swedenborgian compared it to the "project of the ancient architects to carve Mount Athos into a statue of a king, holding a city in his right hand, and a basin of rivers in his left," transforming what had been "a rough, shaggy mountain side . . . into an enchanted ground, or fairy land."[129]

Haskell's interests in health and the spiritual life attracted like-minded residents. The abolitionists Wendell Phillips Garrison, son of William Lloyd Garrison, and the previously mentioned James Miller McKim, both journalists connected with the founding of *The Nation* magazine, occupied relatively modest homes. Other early co-investors, such as Edwin C. Burt and Levi P. Stone, built more substantial houses. In 1858 George Fletcher Babb designed Lakewood for D. C. Otis on property that became part of Llewellyn Park in 1860. Soon the place became known as a haven for freethinkers, "famous," as an original resident, Edward D. Page, wrote, "for its long-haired men and short-haired women."[130] But most of all Llewellyn Park was a retreat from the city, as Davis himself made clear in a letter describing the view from his own home: "From these windows and frequently, under the chromatic (blue) of the heavens we behold the Atlantic sea, even its agitated billows, gleaming in the horizon, its ships riding high above the monuments of mortal life: the great city, its Greenwood, its cypress hills, its many parks for healthy pleasure, starry pointing spires, its lofty bridges and its busy crows of men. . . . What an association of ideas

Thomas Alva Edison house (Glenmont), Llewellyn Park, New Jersey. Henry Hudson Holly, 1881. View to the northwest. NJIC.

Thomas Alva Edison house (Glenmont), Llewellyn Park, New Jersey. Henry Hudson Holly, 1881. Hall. NJIC.

View to the north, 1878, of Hobart Avenue, Short Hills, New Jersey. MSHHS.

of the great future of hopes, rise to the mind, while look-ing over the scene."[131]

By 1860, despite reverses suffered in the Panic of 1857, Haskell owned five hundred acres of land. The Civil War interrupted development, but by 1870 Haskell had added another 250 acres, intended to provide sites for one hun-dred families, of which thirty were already in residence elsewhere in the community. But the tastes of the Bonanza economy era had evolved away from simple cottage styles to the mansarded grandeur of the French Second Empire, and even Davis succumbed to the shifting winds—the Mrs. Elwood Byerly house (1868) was one of his best efforts in the new manner. The depression of the 1870s slowed things to a near halt, but with the return of pros-perity in the 1880s large new houses began to go up. In 1886 Thomas Alva Edison, filled with the first flush of success, settled in Llewellyn Park, from which he com-muted to the factory he built just outside the community's gates, in West Orange. Edison's house, Glenmont, had been completed in 1881 for Henry C. Peddler, who was later convicted of building the house with funds he had embezzled from his employer, Aaron Arnold, the co-owner of the New York department store Arnold Consta-ble. In order to retrieve some of his losses, Arnold took over the house and sold it, fully furnished, to Edison. Glenmont was a vast, turreted palace of wood painted red, designed by Henry Hudson Holly, who had published many books on suburban-house design in which he advo-cated rational planning and grandiloquent architectural expression. The popularity of Holly's books was to make him one of the most influential house architects of his generation. Haskell did not live to see this phase in

Llewellyn Park's development, which in many ways con-tradicted his original vision; he was seriously injured in a railroad accident in 1865. An early casualty of the eco-nomic turmoil of the 1870s, he had already been forced to surrender much of his control by the time he died, in 1872.

Nearby, at Short Hills, a different strategy for achieving the suburban ideal was pursued.[132] In contrast to the rural escapism of Llewellyn Park and the spacious rectilinearity of Garden City, Short Hills was a pleasant village that gracefully spilled out into the countryside. More like Llewellyn Park and in distinct contrast to Garden City, Short Hills incorporated a great variety of architectural styles—Shingle Style, Colonial, and Queen Anne, among others—to give a sense of a stable, long-settled, preindus-trial settlement. Short Hills was founded by Stewart Hartshorn in 1877, six years after he had prospered suffi-ciently in the window-shade business to move to the New Jersey countryside. He first settled in Springfield, where he began to plan his model community. Three years later he moved with his family to Short Hills, a part of Millburn, a commuter village that had been founded in 1857. He began his town there by purchasing thirteen acres of land not too far from the Erie and Lackawanna Railroad sta-tion, continuing to acquire land until he eventually owned almost 1,600 acres.

Hartshorn laid out the village himself, calling it Short Hills Park. The development was the product of Hartshorn's boyhood dream of founding an ideal town. The streets were graded and curved to complement the natural, undulating hillside. The irregularly shaped build-ing lots were large, varying from one to five acres. Hartshorn, who in about equal proportion built houses to

View to the east, 1878, along Hobart Avenue, Short Hills, New Jersey. MSHHS.

rent and sold properties to buyers who would construct their own, picked his fellow Short Hills citizens carefully. He wanted nature-loving people to live in his community, as he believed such people had taste and initiative. But to assure that their taste jibed with his own, he reserved the right to review all plans even after the land was sold. Hartshorn's requirements included the stipulation that no two houses be alike. Perhaps not surprisingly, given Hartshorn's need for control, the suburb grew slowly, reaching thirty-three houses in 1885. By the time of Hartshorn's death in 1937, at the age of ninety-seven, Short Hills had only 150 houses.

Hartshorn started his development in July 1879 with a small, clapboard-sheathed railroad station on the Erie and Lackawanna line, giving his new suburb an identity independent from Millburn's. He commissioned the fledgling firm McKim, Mead & White to design the community's social center (1879–80), first called the Casino but soon known as the Music Hall, a generously sized facility located near the railroad station that featured a large gabled hall and a rounded tower with a square-planned, pedimented, gabled crown, sheathed in shingles and decorated with Japanese-inspired latticework and shell motifs. The Music Hall also served as home to the first Short Hills School, and for several years as the weekly meeting place of an Episcopalian congregation. For much longer it also functioned as a town hall. Sufficiently admired to be included in George W. Sheldon's *Artistic Country-Seats*, this boldly composed, imaginatively detailed design, with its daringly juxtaposed geometries and delicately detailed windows and gable end, was essentially a glorified barn. Montgomery Schuyler was not

completely impressed, finding fault with its "starveling and stringy classicized detail" and being troubled by what he deemed Stanford White's formalistic bombast: "But when one moves the previous question why a round tower should be crowned with a square roof, the building does not yield an answer, and the roof begins to look very irrelevant to the tower which it crowns, and the tower to the building of which it relieves the monotony." Though he deemed the Music Hall "the most important building of Short Hills thus far," he asserted that the "balloon-framed monument seems to involve a contradiction in terms. . . . It is an example of that kind of design in which the 'effect' precedes the cause, and which must continually be compromising itself, no matter how cleverly it is done, when it comes to be adjusted to the actual requirements of a building instead of being developed out of these requirements, so that the impression it ultimately leaves is not so much architectural as scenic."[133]

In mid-1879, several months before work began on the Music Hall in November, Hartshorn hired McKim, Mead & White to design a five-thousand-dollar model house located close to the new passenger depot. Visible from passing trains, like the Music Hall it functioned as an advertisement for the community. The many-gabled house, with bargeboards and half-timbering, seemed quaintly out-of-date, a late recollection of cottages designed a generation earlier by Andrew Jackson Downing, and in no way as stylistically sophisticated as the Music Hall. Most of Short Hills's houses were sited for less pragmatic purposes than McKim, Mead & White's model. Hartshorn approved of houses picturesquely set on knolls, and forbade any outbuildings or fences that

Music Hall, 162 Hobart Avenue, Short Hills, New Jersey. McKim, Mead & White, 1879–80. View to the south. NYHS.

Music Hall, 162 Hobart Avenue, Short Hills, New Jersey. McKim, Mead & White, 1879–80. View to the southwest. NYHS.

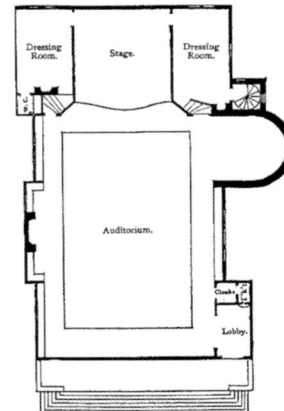

Music Hall, 162 Hobart Avenue, Short Hills, New Jersey. McKim, Mead & White, 1879–80. Ground-floor plan. ACS. CU.

Music Hall, 162 Hobart Avenue, Short Hills, New Jersey. McKim, Mead & White, 1879–80. View to the east. MSHHS.

Music Hall, 162 Hobart Avenue, Short Hills, New Jersey. McKim, Mead & White, 1879–80. View to the west. MSHHS.

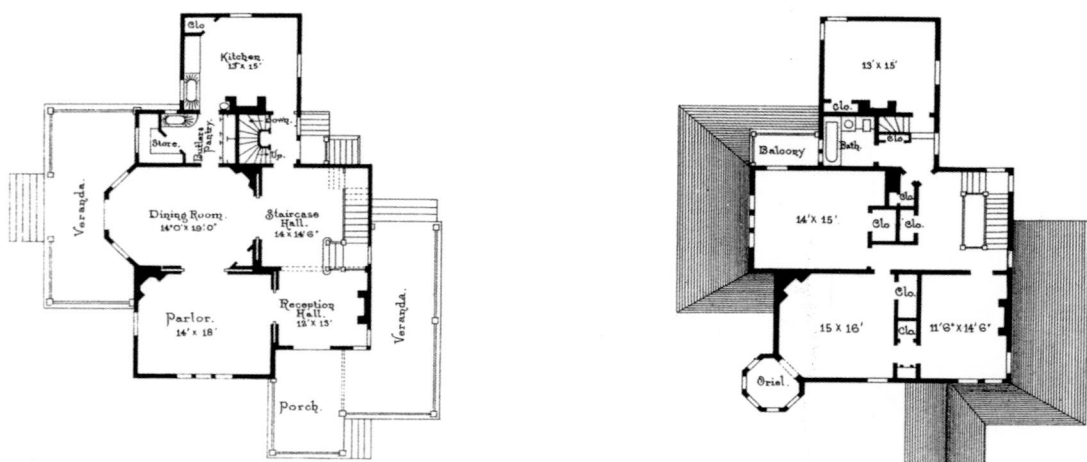

40 Knollwood Road (the Anchorage), Short Hills, New Jersey. Lamb & Wheeler, c. 1880. Rendering of view to the northeast, first-floor plan (left), and second-floor plan (right). WTC. CU.

Reverend Alonzo Rich house (Sunset Cottage), 12 The Crescent, Short Hills, New Jersey. Charles Rich, 1881–82. View to the southwest. ACS. CU.

would mar the view. In order to preclude the need for outbuildings, he provided a community stable as well as a sewage and water system.

Firms such as Lamb & Wheeler and its successor, Lamb & Rich, designed houses that gave Short Hills its reputation for innovative and individualistic domestic architecture. Lamb & Wheeler built extensively, including the Anchorage (c. 1880), at 40 Knollwood Road, a cross-gabled house with a distinctive corner oriel-like turret, a fine example of the complexly massed, eclectically detailed Queen Anne cottage. The twenty-six-year-old Charles Rich designed Sunset Cottage (1881–82) for his father, the Reverend Alonzo Rich, with whom the architect still lived; the plan included a studio and photography darkroom for the son. According to Sheldon, Sunset Cottage was one of the first houses in the United States to have its "weatherboards or shingles . . . stained in gradations so as to give the appearance of age."[134] The color varied from yellow gray at the top to dark India red below. The freely massed house, with towers, chimneys, and dormers that seemed to burst from the sloping roof, incorporated rough stone, brick, shingles, and a rough plaster panel proclaiming "Sunset Cottage" in seashells. In 1878 Lamb & Rich made extensive renovations for Franklin H. Tinker, the new owner of the William Russell house,

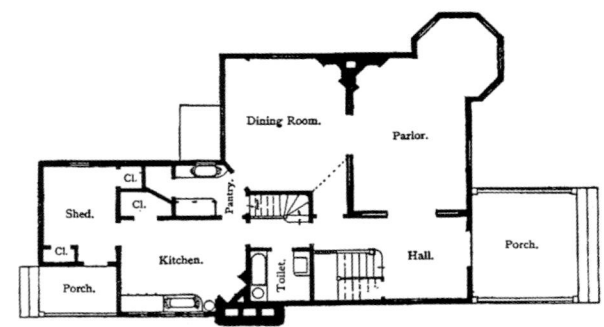

Reverend Alonzo Rich house (Sunset Cottage), 12 The Crescent, Short Hills, New Jersey. Charles Rich, 1881–82. Ground-floor plan. ACS. CU.

Sunnyside. The Russells later moved to Redstone (1882), also designed by Lamb & Rich. Redstone was distinguished by soaring ribbed chimneys and innumerable gables rising from a Richardson-inspired stone base. The *American Architect and Building News* was impressed with the house, especially the splendid interiors, most particularly the hall: "If you do not believe in open fireplaces, and large ones, too, just step in here and sit down for a minute before the hall fireplace. . . . The hall itself runs two stories high, with an open-beam

Franklin H. Tinker house (Sunnyside), 39 Knollwood Road, Short Hills, New Jersey. Renovated by Lamb & Rich, 1878. Library. AH. CU.

William Russell house (Redstone), southeast corner of Knollwood Road and Wells Lane, Short Hills, New Jersey. Lamb & Rich, 1882. View to the south of the entrance facade. MSHHS.

William Russell house (Redstone), southeast corner of Knollwood Road and Wells Lane, Short Hills, New Jersey. Lamb & Rich, 1882. Hall. MSHHS.

John Farr house, 54 Western Drive, Short Hills, New Jersey. James Brown Lord, 1883. Perspective rendering of view to the southwest. AABN. CU.

ceiling; the walls are colored in Indian red, and on one side of the second-story runs a regular Romeo and Juliet balcony. . . . Whole logs disappear within this cavern . . . and give out not only heat, but a sense of hospitable cheer and comfort."[135]

James Brown Lord's 54 Western Drive (1883), a house commissioned by Hartshorn on behalf of John Farr, combined a gray stone base with windows and doors framed in Philadelphia pressed brick and a shingled superstructure that incorporated half-timbering in its gables. W. Halsey Wood, better known for his ecclesiastical designs, designed Greystone Cottage (c. 1880), at 177 Hobart Avenue, a largely stone house notable for its conical turret. Arthur B. Jennings was the architect of Knollwood (c. 1880) and the Lodge (c. 1880), two more romantically conceived cottages. The Lodge was quite small, in fact the "smallest house in the park," according to the *American Architect and Building News*, and "so minute and pretty that many an eye has looked upon it with envy." Knollwood was much larger, a brick house with spacious piazzas and balconies, commanding views of the Narrows, the heights of Staten Island, Navesink, and Newark Bay, and "scattering here and there in the middle distance . . . villages looking like so many little paper boxes."[136]

Charles Rich designed the village's only church, Christ Church (1883–84), a superbly crafted, slate-roofed chapel built of traprock from the Hartshorn quarry in Springfield. The *American Architect and Building News* characterized it as a "veritable little mountain church, with stone bell-turret, from which ere long will issue the sound of a chime of bells. . . . Step under the low massive arch into the chancel, and look back; the afternoon sun streams through a large and magnificent memorial window, and floods the nave with subdued light, bringing out the tints of the wall, and the warm wood-work of the benches and little wineglass pulpit."[137]

By 1884, when a history of Essex County was published, Short Hills was an established success:

[It] has been brought into existence as the solution of a long baffling problem of how to make beautiful and healthy suburban homes. Mr. Hartshorn has made such homes, with all the happiness and comfort which they imply . . . and his enterprise in this direction . . . is perhaps the most practically successful one which has been undertaken in this country and it may be added that its result is at least as fair to the aesthetic eye as to the examination of the utilitarian. Mr. Hartshorn entered on his work with a love for it. . . . His conception of what a town should be was thoroughly formed. . . . There was never a rude clearing of the land. The noblest trees were left about the sites of future homes, and thus the place was given the appearance of a great park, by which term, indeed, Short Hills is better described than by any other.[138]

Hartshorn controlled the only store in the village, and there were no saloons or factories. This was a residential enclave, pure and simple, one which, as the *American Architect and Building News* reported, was "the original and only garden wherein Mother Eve and Father Adam built their home and commenced housekeeping."[139] In his survey of New York's suburbs, Montgomery Schuyler, himself a resident of New Rochelle, in Westchester County, was particularly taken with Short Hills:

A very pleasant place Short Hills must have been even before it occurred to an enterprising merchant of New York to buy it and convert it into an artistic and unique suburb,—an undulating piece of ground on the farther slope of the Orange Mountains, where they decline into the "Short Hills," with a wide southwestward outlook and fine old trees scattered about it. The distinction of Short Hills is that its colonization was coincident with the emancipation of American architecture, and the proprietor has invited a number of the bright young freedmen to design him each a house. . . . It is characteristic of the northern spirit in which Short Hills has been conceived that a music hall was one of its earliest buildings, having at present attained the relative venerableness of five or six years, while a church is only now under construction. . . . That is more or less the general impression of Short Hills. It is scene-painters' architecture in an opera village, as it were, where the houses have no further function than to look pretty and to possess "practical" doors out of which you momentarily expect a chorus of happy villagers to emerge with a view to dancing on the sward. We see at Short Hills what the satirist meant when he declared that American humor never found full expression except in architecture.

In conclusion, Schuyler wrote: "You certainly derive a distinct impression that all these places must be inhabited by very nice people, which is not a bad impression for a collection of country houses to make. And you must be of an unthankful spirit if when you leave Short Hills you do not invoke blessings upon its proprietor for having afforded you so much entertainment by building you this unique and delightful suburb."[140]

Christ Church, northeast corner of Highland and Forest Avenues, Short Hills, New Jersey. Charles Rich, 1883–84. View to the northwest. MSHHS.

Court of Honor, World's Columbian Exposition of 1893, Chicago, Illinois. View to the west showing, from left to right, the Agriculture Building (McKim, Mead & White), the Machinery Building (Peabody & Stearns), the Administration Building (Richard Morris Hunt), the Electricity Building (Van Brunt & Howe), and the Manufactures and Liberal Arts Building (George B. Post), with the sculpture Republic *(Daniel Chester French) in the foreground. Arnold. CHS.*

General Grant National Memorial, Riverside Drive at West 122nd Street. John H. Duncan, 1890–97. View to the northwest. Hall. NYHS.

Afterword

New York's Gilded Age came to an end in 1890 with a lost opportunity. When the United States House of Representatives selected Chicago over New York to host the World's Columbian Exposition of 1893, New Yorkers were powerfully alerted to the fact that economic hegemony alone would not render their city truly world-class. In the twenty-five years following the Civil War, New York had transformed itself into the nation's richest and most important city, surpassing its former rivals, Boston and Philadelphia. Now, with the federal government's refusal to grant New York the world's fair, the city was presented with a direct challenge: could New York remake itself again, this time focusing on goals loftier than material prosperity? Could the reigning capital of capitalism adopt an idealistic attitude toward the public realm and the built environment that would render it a model for American urbanism and a worthy counterpart to the mature capitals of Europe?

Post–Civil War New York had been defined by simultaneous expansion and consolidation. The city had become rich, its coffers filled in large part by profits reaped from its year-round port and its state-of-the-art railroad connections. With the 1874 annexation of part of Westchester County it had grown physically, and its sense of its own geography had been transformed in 1883 by the completion of the Brooklyn Bridge, an event as important for the independent cities of New York and Brooklyn as the completion of the first transcontinental railroad, in 1869, had been for the nation as a whole. As the city grew, it had likewise consolidated with the introduction of telephone service, electric lights, and steam-powered elevated trains, as well as with the completion of the Croton Aqueduct System, making New York a highly efficient, modern metropolis. The post–Civil War period had also witnessed the growth of New York as a cultural center, with its wealthiest citizens, often newly rich industrialists, financing the establishment and expansion of great colleges and seminaries, libraries and museums, and concert halls and opera houses. Yet despite this cultural flowering, the Gilded Age building programs of New York's institutions were compromised at best—they tended to provide cramped accommodations in buildings sorely lacking in formal monumentality and civic grandeur.

More than any other event or influence, the World's Columbian Exposition catapulted New York into its next phase of development. Despite the Chicago locale, the fair's design team was dominated by architects, planners, and artists from New York, already the "front office" of the architectural profession in the United States. Richard Morris Hunt, McKim, Mead & White, Frederick Law Olmsted, and Augustus Saint-Gaudens seized the opportunity to help create a daringly monumental ensemble of Classical buildings, thereby announcing that America, which would soon emerge as an imperialist world power with the acquisition of protectorates in the Caribbean and the Pacific, was the rightful heir to the Classical world.

The fair's buildings, formal courts, sculpture, and landscaping inspired Americans to reconsider their cities, catalyzing a movement that would come to be known as the American Renaissance. Returning from Chicago in triumph, the fair's New York–based architects set out to rebuild their own city, erecting nobly proportioned and rigorously articulated buildings, monuments, and public spaces. Seeking to overthrow the previously dominant conception of urbanism—a brutal utilitarianism rooted in the belief of the nation's founding fathers that cities were at best a necessary evil—a new political and architectural power elite embraced an enlightened civicism that celebrated the city as a cultural artifact. New York's physical evolution would no longer be seen predominantly in terms of programmatic necessity and economic expediency but also as an exercise in civic art and grand place-making.

The new approach would encompass a dramatic and profound stylistic break from the romantic eclecticism that had characterized the architecture of the Gilded Age. That era's frequently astylar buildings had bypassed a didactic agenda in favor of highly individualistic, inventive statements. In fin de siècle New York, architectural exoticism would give way to a call for a uniform Classicism. This Classical revival in part derived from new money, new building materials, and new building technologies. It also reflected both a nostalgia for the country's early republican past and a bold confidence in the nation's destiny as the last, best hope for Western civilization. Believing that their fiercely bottom-line-oriented hometown could become a City Beautiful, New Yorkers developed a heightened sensitivity to the ways in which architecture and planning could improve the daily lives of self-proclaimed American aristocrats and newly arrived immigrants alike. And that, in large measure, is the story of *New York 1900*.

❧ Photographic Sources ❧

PHOTOGRAPHERS

Abbott: Berenice Abbott
Almstaedt: I. Almstaedt
Anthony: Edward and Henry T. Anthony
Arnold: C. D. Arnold
Beal: Joshua H. Beal
Beer: S. Beer
Benedict: Colman Benedict
Bill: Charles K. Bill
Bogart: Leonard Hassam Bogart
Bracklow: Robert L. Bracklow
Brainard: George Brainard
Burdick: Burdick Photographic
Byron: Joseph and Percy Byron
Cox: George Cox
Day: J. P. Day
Erich: Frederick William Erich Jr.
Geipel: Paul Geipel
Grimshaw: W. J. Grimshaw
Gubelman: Gubelman Photographers
Guether: William Guether
Gurney: Jeremiah Gurney
Hall: George P. Hall & Son
Hepp: August Hepp
Holmes: S. A. Holmes
Ingalls: Frank M. Ingalls
Instantaneous Photo Company:
    Instantaneous Photo Company
Jenkins: J. Cameron Jenkins
Johnston: John S. Johnston
Levy: Albert Levy
Mora: José Maria Mora
O'Neil: H. O'Neil
Pach: Pach Brothers
Parshley: F. E. Parshley
Pelletreau: W. S. Pelletreau
Powelson: Gustavus A. Powelson
Powers: C.V.V. Powers
Prevost: Victor Prevost
Riis: Jacob A. Riis
Rockwood: George G. Rockwood
Schulz: George Schulz
Seehuysen: E. Seehuysen
Sperr: P. L. Sperr
Stadtfeld: Maurice Stadtfeld
Steinrock: C. Steinrock
Stoddard: S. R. Stoddard
Thomas: Samuel Winter Thomas
Underhill: Irving Underhill
Waks: Albert Waks
Wurts: Wurts Brothers

COLLECTIONS

AAC: All Angels' Church, New York, New York
AIC: Art Institute of Chicago, Chicago, Illinois. All photographs ©1999, The Art Institute of Chicago, All Rights Reserved. Albert Levy, Photographic Series of Modern American Architecture: First Series, Nos. 134, 143, 217; Thirty-first Series, No. 707; Thirty-third Series, Nos. 756, 758. Peter Bonnett Wight, American, 1838–1925: Williamsburgh Savings Bank, PBW147; Brooklyn Mercantile Library, PBW156; Kings County Courthouse, PBW161; Mutual Life Insurance Company, PBW163; National Park Bank, PBW168.
AMNH: Courtesy Department of Library Services, American Museum of Natural History, New York, New York. Nos. 313491, 324747, 325486, 338001.
Archive Photos: Archive Photos, New York, New York
BCHS: Courtesy of The Bronx County Historical Society Collection, The Bronx, New York
BCN: Bibliothèque du Conservatoire National des Arts et Métiers, Paris, France
BF: Bibliothèque Forney, Paris, France
BHS: The Brooklyn Historical Society, Brooklyn, New York
BNY: Bank of New York, New York, New York

BPL: Brooklyn Public Library - Brooklyn Collection, Brooklyn, New York
BRHS: Bay Ridge Historical Society, Brooklyn, New York
CA: Century Association Archives Foundation, New York, New York
CAS: Children's Aid Society, New York, New York
CHA: Carnegie Hall Archives, New York, New York
CHS: Chicago Historical Society, Chicago, Illinois
CS: Archives of Central Synagogue, New York, New York
CU: Columbia University, New York, New York (Rare Book and Manuscript Library; the University Archives and Columbiana Library; and the Collection of the Avery Architectural and Fine Arts Library, including the Drawings Collection)
CUHSD: Archives & Special Collections, Columbia University Health Sciences Division, New York, New York
DC: Collection of Dartmouth College Library, Hanover, New Hampshire
DO: Dumbarton Oaks, Trustees for Harvard University
ELAS: The Equitable Life Assurance Society of the United States, New York, New York
FLC: Frederick Lightfoot Collection
FLONHS: Courtesy of the National Park Service, Frederick Law Olmsted National Historic Site, Brookline, Massachusetts
GCA: Garden City Archives, Garden City, New York
GTS: St. Mark's Library, General Theological Seminary, New York, New York
HLHU: Houghton Library, Harvard University, Cambridge, Massachusetts
HM: Courtesy of Herbert Mitchell, New York, New York
HTC: Collection of the Holy Trinity Church, New York, New York

LH: Courtesy of Luther Harris, New York, New York

LHL: Linda Hall Library, Kansas City, Missouri

LPC: Landmarks Preservation Commission of the City of New York, New York

LWA: The La Guardia and Wagner Archives, La Guardia Community College/The City University of New York, Long Island City, New York

MA: Municipal Archives, New York, New York

MB: Musée Bartholdi, Colmar, France, reprod. C. Kempf

MCNY: Museum of the City of New York, New York. Including the Leonard Hassam Bogart Collection; Byron Collection; Changing New York Collection, photographed by Berenice Abbott; J. Clarence Davies Collection; McKim, Mead & White Collection; Jacob A. Riis Collection; William Seymour Collection; Underhill Collection; and the Wurts Collection. All photography by Arthur Vitols, Helga Photo Studio.

MFA: Courtesy Museum of Fine Arts, Boston, Massachusetts

MIT: Courtesy of the Rotch Library Visual Collections, M.I.T., Cambridge, Massachusetts

MMA: Metropolitan Museum of Art, New York, New York

MOA: Metropolitan Opera Archives, New York, New York

MONY: Mutual of New York, New York, New York

MSHHS: From the collection and through the courtesy of the Millburn–Short Hills Historical Society, Short Hills, New Jersey

MSMC: The Archives of Mount Sinai Medical Center, New York, New York

NJIC: New Jersey Information Center, Newark Public Library, Newark, New Jersey

NRPL: New Rochelle Public Library, New Rochelle, New York

NYCPP: New York City Parks Photo Archive, New York, New York

NYHC: New York Hospital–Cornell Medical Center, New York, New York

NYHS: New-York Historical Society, New York, New York

NYPL: New York Public Library, New York, New York (including the Local History and Genealogy Division, Map Division, and Rare Book Division, New York Public Library, Astor, Lenox and Tilden Foundations)

NYSEA: New York Stock Exchange Archives, New York, New York

NYUA: New York University Archives, New York, New York

NYYC: New York Yacht Club, New York, New York

The Octagon, AAF: The Prints & Drawings Collection, an architectural records collection, is owned by The Octagon, the Museum of The American Architectural Foundation, Washington, D.C. Its holdings include architectural drawings, historic photographs, sketchbooks, scrapbooks, manuscript material, slides, and architectural models. Architects represented in the collection date from the 18th century to the present. Material from the Hunt Collection was photographed by Lee Stasworth, Chief Photographer at The Hirshhorn Museum and Sculpture Garden, Smithsonian Institution, Washington, D.C., where he has worked for twenty-five years.

OECHA: The Otis Elevator Company Historic Archives, Farmington, Connecticut

OMH: Office for Metropolitan History, New York, New York

PES: Archives of Park East Synagogue, New York, New York

PILA: Pratt Institute Library, Archives, Brooklyn, New York

PTC: The Parish of Trinity Church in the City of New York, New York

QBPL: Long Island Division, The Queens Borough Public Library, Jamaica, New York

QHS: Queens Historical Society, Flushing, New York

SC: Schomburg Center for Research in Black Culture, New York Public Library, New York, New York

SIHS: Courtesy of the Staten Island Historical Society, Staten Island, New York

SIIAS: From the Collection of the Staten Island Institute of Arts and Sciences, Staten Island, New York

SMB: Collection of the Societé Miège et Buhler, Paris, France

STM: Archives of St. Thomas More Church, New York, New York

TC: Special Collections, Milbank Memorial Library, Teachers College, Columbia University, New York, New York

TRC: Theodore Roosevelt Collection, Harvard College Library, Cambridge, Massachusetts

UT-AAA: The Alfred Zucker Collection, 1880–1904. Alexander Architectural Archive, Architecture and Planning Library, The General Libraries, The University of Texas at Austin

UTS: Burke Library of the Union Theological Seminary in the City of New York, New York

WF: William Frost, New York, New York

YMCA: Kautz Family YMCA Archives, YMCA of Greater New York Collection, Chicago, Illinois

BOOKS AND PERIODICALS

AABN: *American Architect and Building News*

AAR: *American Architectural Review*

AB: *Architecture and Building*

ACS: G. W. Sheldon, *Artistic Country-Seats*, 2 vols. (New York: D. Appleton, 1886)

AH: G. W. Sheldon, *Artistic Houses: Being a Series of Interior Views of a Number of the Most Beautiful and Celebrated Homes in the United States, with a Description of the Art Treasures Contained Therein*, 2 vols. (New York: D. Appleton, 1883–84)

AJB: Amos J. Bicknell, *Wooden and Brick Buildings with Details* (New York: A. J. Bicknell, 1875)

ANT: *Antiques*

AR: *Architectural Record*

ARCH: *Architecture*

AZ: *Photographed from Designs for Buildings and from Buildings Erected by Alfred Zucker, Architect* (New York: National Chemigraph Co., 1894)

BBS: *Bensonhurst-by-the-Sea* (New York: New York Engraving and Printing, 1890)

BHW: Alfred Tredway White, *Better Homes for Workingmen* (New York: Putnam, 1885)

BLDG: *Building*

BPUR: *Illustrated Description of the Broadway Pneumatic Underground Railway* (New York, 1870)

BSFA: *Collins' Both Sides of Fifth Avenue* (New York: J.F.L. Collins, 1910)

CAB: *Canadian Architect and Builder*

CD: *Competitive Designs for the Cathedral of St. John the Divine in New York City* (Boston: Heliotype Printing Co., c. 1891)

CM: *Century Magazine*

CO: *The Cosmopolitan*

CPA: *The Central Park Apartments* (New York: American Banknote, 1881)

DD: Edwin P. Alexander, *Down at the Depot: American Railroad Stations from 1831 to 1920* (New York: Clarkson N. Potter, 1970)

DDB: Daniel D. Badger, *Illustrations of Cast Iron Architecture Made by the Architectural Iron Works of the City of New York* (New York: Baker & Godwin, 1865)

DGCP: Richard Morris Hunt, *Designs for the Gateways of the Southern Entrances to the Central Park* (New York, 1866)

EWP: Sarah Bradford Landau, *Edward T. and William A. Potter: American Victorian Architects* (New York: Garland, 1979)

HCC: Russell Sturgis et al., *Homes in City and Country* (New York: Charles Scribner's Sons, 1893)

HHNYC: Richard Plunz, *A History of Housing in New York City* (New York: Columbia University Press, 1990)

HHR: Henry-Russell Hitchcock, *The Architecture of H. H. Richardson and His Times* (New York: Museum of Modern Art, 1936)

HLT: Theodore W. Scull, *Hoboken's Lackawanna Terminal* (New York: Quadrant Press, 1987)

HMMA: Winifred E. Howe, *A History of the Metropolitan Museum of Art* (New York: Metropolitan Museum of Art, 1913)

HNM: *Harper's New Monthly Magazine*

HNYC: John Benson Lossing, *History of New York City* (New York: Perine, 1884)

HNYPL: Harry Miller Lydenberg, *History of the New York Public Library* (New York: New York Public Library, 1923)

HOHL: Jacob A. Riis, *How the Other Half Lives* (New York: Charles Scribner's Sons, 1890)

HRE: *A History of Real Estate, Building and Architecture in New York City During the Last Quarter of a Century* (New York: Real Estate Record Association, 1898)

HW: *Harper's Weekly*

HWP: Elgin R. L. Gould, *The Housing of the Working People: Eighth Special Report of the Commissioner of Labor* (Washington, D.C.: GPO, 1895)

IBB: *Insurance Blue Book, 1876–1877* (New York: C. C. Hine, 1877)

INPS: I. N. Phelps Stokes, *The Iconography of Manhattan Island*, 6 vols. (New York: Robert H. Dodd, 1915–28)

JBW: James Blaine Walker, *Fifty Years of Rapid Transit, 1864–1917* (New York: Law Printing Co., 1918)

King, 1893: Moses King, *King's Handbook of New York* (Boston: Moses King, 1893)

King, 1895: Moses King, *King's Photographic Views of New York* (Boston: Moses King, 1895)

King, 1904: Moses King, *King's Views of Brooklyn* (Boston: Moses King, 1904)

KMH: *The King Model Houses* (New York: D. H. King, c. 1891)

LAA: *L'Architecture américaine* (Paris: André, Daly fils et Cie, 1886), republished as Arnold Lewis and Keith Morgan, *American Victorian Architecture* (New York: Dover, 1975)

LAD: *L'Architecture et la décoration aux Palais du Louvre et des Tuileries* (Paris, 1905–07)

LCT: Charles de Kay, *The Art Work of Louis C. Tiffany* (privately published, 1914)

MAH: *Magazine of American History*

MMW: *A Monograph of the Works of McKim, Mead & White, 1879–1915* (New York: Architectural Book Publishing Co., 1915)

MMWA: Leland M. Roth, *McKim, Mead & White, Architects* (New York: Harper & Row, 1983)

MUS: Leo Lerman, *The Museum: One Hundred Years and the Metropolitan Museum of Art* (New York: Viking, 1969)

MVHC: Edward Strahan [Earl Shinn], *Mr. Vanderbilt's House and Collection* (Boston: G. Barrie, 1883–84)

NAD: *The National Academy of Design. Ceremonies on the Occasion of Laying the Corner-Stone, October 21, 1863, and the Inauguration of the Building, April 27, 1865* (New York: Miller and Mathews, 1865)

NM: E. Idell Zeisloft, ed., *The New Metropolis* (New York: D. Appleton & Co., 1899)

NYDG: *New York Daily Graphic*

NYDT: *New York Daily Tribune*

NYF: Andrew Alpern, *New York's Fabulous Luxury Apartments* (New York: McGraw-Hill, 1975; New York: Dover, 1987)

NYJA: *38th Annual Report of the New York Juvenile Asylum* (New York, 1890)

NYSB: *New-York Sketch-Book of Architecture*

NYTN: Edward B. Watson, *New York Then and Now* (New York: Dover, 1976)

PCK: Francis W. Kervick, *Patrick Charles Keely, Architect: A Record of His Life and Work* (South Bend, Ind., 1953)

PHB: Brooklyn Daily Eagle, *The Pictorial History of Brooklyn* (Brooklyn: Brooklyn Daily Eagle, 1916)

PSE: *Plumber and Sanitary Engineer*

RCR: Robert C. Reed, *The New York Elevated* (South Brunswick, N.J., and New York: A. S. Barnes, 1978)

RERG: *Real Estate Record and Builders' Guide*

RK: Robert Koch, *Louis C. Tiffany: Rebel in Glass* (New York: Crown, 1964)

RMH: Paul R. Baker, *Richard Morris Hunt* (Cambridge, Mass.: MIT Press, 1980)

RNS: Andrew Saint, *Richard Norman Shaw* (New Haven, Conn., and London: Yale University Press, 1976)

SA: *Scientific American*, including the Architects and Builders Edition

SAH: James Ford, *Slums and Housing, with Special References to New York City: History, Conditions, Policy* (Cambridge, Mass.: Harvard University Press, 1936)

SHA: Harry W. Desmond and Herbert Croly, *Stately Homes in America* (New York: D. Appleton, 1903)

SM: *Scribner's Monthly*

SSNY: Matthew Hale Smith, *Sunshine and Shadow in New York* (Hartford, Conn.: J. B. Burr, 1868)

ST: Simon Cohen, *Shaaray Tefila: A History of Its Hundred Years* (New York: Greenberg, 1945)

THP: Robert W. De Forest and Lawrence Veiller, eds., *The Tenement House Problem* (New York: Macmillan, 1903)

TSSB: Annette Blaugrund, *The Tenth Street Studio Building*, exhibition catalogue (Southampton, N.Y.: Parish Art Museum, 1997)

WKV: John Vredenburgh Van Pelt, *A Monograph of the William K. Vanderbilt House, Richard Morris Hunt, Architect* (New York, 1925)

WS: *The Westsider*

WTC: William T. Comstock, *Modern Architectural Designs and Details* (New York: William T. Comstock, 1881)

Notes

Preface

1. Robert A. M. Stern, Gregory Gilmartin, and John Montague Massengale, *New York 1900: Metropolitan Architecture and Urbanism 1890–1915* (New York: Rizzoli International Publications, 1983), 7–8; Karin May Elizabeth Alexis, "Russell Sturgis: Critic and Architect" (Ph.D. diss., University of Virginia, 1986).

2. Cynthia Doering Kinnard, "The Life and Works of Mariana Griswold Van Rensselaer, American Art Critic" (Ph.D. diss., Johns Hopkins University, 1977); Lois Dinnerstein, "Opulence and Ocular Delight, Splendor and Squalor: Critical Writings in Art and Architecture by Mariana Griswold Van Rensselaer" (Ph.D. diss., City University of New York, 1979); Stern, Gilmartin, and Massengale, *New York 1900*, 8; David Gebhard, "Introduction," in Mariana Griswold Van Rensselaer, *Accents as Well as Broad Effects: Writings on Architecture, Landscape, and the Environment, 1876–1925* (Berkeley: University of California Press, 1996), 1–28.

3. William H. Jordy and Ralph Coe, "Editors' Introduction," in Montgomery Schuyler, *American Architecture and Other Writings*, 2 vols. (Cambridge, Mass.: Harvard University Press, Belknap Press, 1961); William John Thorn, "Montgomery Schuyler: The Newspaper Architectural Articles of a Protomodern Critic (1868–1907)" (Ph.D. diss., University of Minnesota, 1976); Stern, Gilmartin, and Massengale, *New York 1900*, 7.

4. Mark Twain and Charles Dudley Warner, *The Gilded Age: A Tale of To-Day* (Hartford, Conn.: American Publishing Co., 1873).

5. For the Panic of 1873, see Eric Foner, *Reconstruction: America's Unfinished Revolution, 1863–1877* (New York: Harper & Row, 1988), 512–63.

6. Editorial, *American Architect and Building News* 1 (April 8, 1876): 118.

7. "The Crisis in Real Estate," *Real Estate Record and Builders' Guide* 16 (November 27, 1875): 761–62; "The Crisis in Real Estate, Part II," *Real Estate Record and Builders' Guide* 16 (December 4, 1875): 775–76; "The Crisis in Real Estate, Part III," *Real Estate Record and Builders' Guide* 16 (December 11, 1875): 789–90; "Mr. S. E. Church's Letter," *Real Estate Record and Builders' Guide* 16 (December 18, 1875): 805–6; "The Crisis in Real Estate, Part IV," *Real Estate Record and Builders' Guide* 16 (December 25, 1875): 825–26; "The Crisis in Real Estate, Part V," *Real Estate Record and Builders' Guide* 17 (January 1, 1876): 1–2; "The Crisis in Real Estate, Part VI," *Real Estate Record and Builders' Guide* 17 (January 8, 1876): 19–20; "The Crisis in Real Estate, Part VII," *Real Estate Record and Builders' Guide* 17 (January 15, 1876): 35–36; "The Crisis in Real Estate, Part VIII," *Real Estate Record and Builders' Guide* 17 (January 22, 1876): 53–54; "Are New Buildings Needed?" *Real Estate Record and Builders' Guide* 18 (July 8, 1876): 525.

8. Maunsell Van Rensselaer to James W. Beekman, November 27, 1876, James W. Beekman Papers, New-York Historical Society, quoted in Albert Fein, "Centennial New York, 1876," in Milton M. Klein, ed., *New York: The Centennial Years 1676–1976* (Port Washington, N.Y.: Kennikat Press, 1976), 73–120.

CHAPTER 1
Introduction

1. James D. McCabe Jr., *The Secrets of the Great City* (Philadelphia: Jones Brothers & Co., 1868), 15.

2. Junius Henri Browne, *The Great Metropolis; a Mirror of New York* (Hartford, Conn.: American Publishing Co., 1869), 697, 699–700.

3. "Mr. Stewart's New Residence," *Harper's Weekly* 13 (August 14, 1869): 521, 525–26.

4. *Miller's New York as It Is; or, Stranger's Guide-book to the Cities of New York, Brooklyn and Adjacent Places* (New York: J. Miller, 1866; New York: Schocken Books, 1975), 20.

5. George Templeton Strong, diary entries dated August 6, 1866, and October 22, 1867, in *The Diary of George Templeton Strong*, eds. Allan Nevins and Milton Halsey Thomas, 4 vols. (New York: Macmillan, 1952), vol. 4: 96–97, 155–56.

6. William R. Martin, *The Growth of New York* (New York: George W. Wood, 1865), 15–16.

7. John A. Roebling, "Report of John A. Roebling, C.E., to the President and Directors of the New York Bridge Company, On the Proposed East River Bridge" (New York, 1867), quoted in Alan Trachtenberg, *Brooklyn Bridge: Fact and Symbol* (Chicago and London: University of Chicago Press, 1965), 75–76.

8. Albert Fein, "Centennial New York, 1876," in Milton M. Klein, ed., *New York: The Centennial Years 1676–1976* (Port Washington, N.Y.: Kennikat Press, 1976), 73–120.

9. Stern, Gilmartin, and Massengale, *New York 1900*, 11–25.

10. Martin, *The Growth of New York*, 17.

11. *Miller's New York as It Is*, 22.

12. Henry James to George Du Maurier, April 17, 1883, in *Letters/Henry James*, ed. Leon Edel, 4 vols. (Cambridge, Mass.: Harvard University Press, Belknap Press, 1974–84), vol. 2: 409.

13. "Back Buildings," *Real Estate Record and Builders' Guide* 23 (May 17, 1879): 397–98. Also see John F. Sprague, *New York the Metropolis* (New York: New York Recorder, 1893), 36; Stern, Gilmartin, and Massengale, *New York 1900*, 13.

14. Talbot Hamlin, "The Rise of Eclecticism in New York," *Journal of the Society of Architectural Historians* 11 (May 1952): 3–8; Ellen W. Kramer, "Detlef Lienau, an Architect of the Brown Decades," *Journal of*

the Society of Architectural Historians 14 (March 1955): 18–25; Ellen W. Kramer, "The Domestic Architecture of Detlef Lienau: A Conservative Victorian" (Ph.D. diss., New York University, 1957): 92–113.

15. "The Mansard Mania," editorial, *New York Times* (November 12, 1872): 4.

16. Montgomery Schuyler, "A Great American Architect: Leopold Eidlitz. Parts 1–3," *Architectural Record* 24 (September 1908): 164–79, (October 1908): 277–92, (November 1908): 365–78, excerpted in Montgomery Schuyler, *American Architecture and Other Writings*, eds. William H. Jordy and Ralph Coe, 2 vols. (Cambridge, Mass.: Harvard University Press, Belknap Press, 1961), vol. 1: 136–87; Stephen S. Garmey, "Leopold Eidlitz," in *Macmillan Encyclopedia of Architects*, 4 vols. (New York: Free Press; London: Collier Macmillan, 1982), vol. 2: 13–16.

17. Leopold Eidlitz, quoted in Schuyler, "A Great American Architect: Leopold Eidlitz. Part 1": 169.

18. *A History of Real Estate, Building and Architecture in New York City During the Last Quarter of a Century* (New York: Real Estate Record Association, 1898), 595.

19. Paul R. Baker, *Richard Morris Hunt* (Cambridge, Mass.: MIT Press, 1980), esp. chapter 5; Paul R. Baker, "Richard Morris Hunt," in *Macmillan Encyclopedia of Architects*, vol. 2: 436–44; Paul R. Baker, "Richard Morris Hunt: An Introduction," in Susan Stein, ed., *The Architecture of Richard Morris Hunt* (Chicago: University of Chicago Press, 1986), 3–10; Sarah Bradford Landau, "Richard Morris Hunt: Architectural Innovator and Father of a 'Distinctive' American School," in Stein, ed., *The Architecture of Richard Morris Hunt*, 46–77.

20. "Rebuilding New York," *Real Estate Record and Builders' Guide* 28 (October 1, 1881): 921.

21. Russell Sturgis, "The Works of George B. Post," *Architectural Record* 4 (June 1898): 1–102; Winston Weisman, "The Commercial Architecture of George B. Post," *Journal of the Society of Architectural Historians* 31 (December 1972): 176–203; Winston Weisman, "George Browne Post," in *Macmillan Encyclopedia of Architects*, vol. 3: 460–63; Diana Balmori, "George B. Post: The Process of Design and the New American Architectural Office (1868–1913)," *Journal of the Society of Architectural Historians* 46 (December 1987): 342–55; Sarah Bradford Landau, *George B. Post, Architect: Picturesque Designer and Determined Realist*, Sources of American Architecture, ed. Robert A. M. Stern (New York: Monacelli Press, 1998), 53–77, 84.

22. Montgomery Schuyler, "The New Stock Exchange," *Architectural Record* 12 (September 1902): 413–20.

23. Baker, *Richard Morris Hunt*, 82–87, 210, 212–13; Leland M. Roth, ed., *America Builds: Source Documents in American Architecture and Planning* (New York: Harper & Row, 1983), 216–31.

24. Baker, *Richard Morris Hunt*, 98–107.

25. Balmori, "George B. Post": 342–55.

26. Turpin C. Bannister, "Bogardus Revisited, Part I," *Journal of the Society of Architectural Historians* 15 (December 1956): 12–22. Also see Margot Gayle and Edmund V. Gillon Jr., *Cast-Iron Architecture in New York* (New York: Dover, 1974), viii–xiii; Sarah Bradford Landau and Carl W. Condit, *Rise of the New York Skyscraper, 1865–1913* (New Haven, Conn., and London: Yale University Press, 1996), 48; Margot Gayle and Carol Gayle, *Cast-Iron Architecture in America: The Significance of James Bogardus* (New York: W. W. Norton, 1998), esp. chapter 3.

27. Christopher Gray, "Streetscapes/James Bogardus," *New York Times* (August 20, 1995), IX: 7.

28. Bannister, "Bogardus Revisited, Part I": 12–22; Nathan Silver, *Lost New York* (Boston: Houghton Mifflin, 1967), 167; Gayle and Gillon, *Cast-Iron Architecture in New York*, xiii; Landau and Condit, *Rise of the New York Skyscraper, 1865–1913*, 47–48.

29. Landmarks Preservation Commission of the City of New York, LP-0017 (November 23, 1965); Gayle and Gillon, *Cast-Iron Architecture in New York*, 142–43; Paul Goldberger, *The City Observed: New York* (New York: Random House, 1979), 60–61; John Tauranac, *Essential New York* (New York: Holt, Rinehart and Winston, 1979), 38–39; Norval White and Elliot Willensky, *AIA Guide to New York City*, 3rd ed. (New York: Macmillan, 1988), 4; David W. Dunlap, *On Broadway: A Journey Uptown Over Time* (New York: Rizzoli International Publications, 1990), 74–77; Barbaralee Diamonstein, *The Landmarks of New York II* (New

York: Harry N. Abrams, 1993), 122–23; Christopher Gray, "Restoring a Richly Sculpted Venetian Palace," *New York Times* (January 1, 1995), IX: 5.

30. William Fogarty, "The Conditions and Prospects of Architecture in the United States," *Van Nostrand's Engineering Magazine* 14 (January 1876): 70, quoted in Carl W. Condit, *American Building Art: The Nineteenth Century* (New York: Oxford University Press, 1960), 38–39.

31. "A Great Dry Goods Fire," *New York Times* (January 18, 1879): 1; "Over Three Millions Lost," *New York Times* (January 19, 1879): 2; "The Recent Large Fires," *New York Times* (February 8, 1879): 3; "The Late Fire in Worth Street, N.Y.," *American Architect and Building News* 5 (February 15, 1879): 49.

32. Silver, *Lost New York*, 164; Christopher Gray, "Links to the Cast-Iron Era Awaiting Reconstruction," *New York Times* (June 10, 1990), VIII: 8.

33. New York Legislature, *Laws of the State of New York Passed at the One Hundred and Eighth Session of the Legislature* (Albany, N.Y., 1885), 772–73; "Some New Laws Proposed," *New York Times* (January 28, 1885): 2; Cervin Robinson, "Late Cast Iron in New York," *Journal of the Society of Architectural Historians* 30 (May 1971): 164–69.

34. "Buildings Projected," *Real Estate Record and Builders' Guide* 43 (April 20, 1889): 570; "Some Examples in Good Building," *Real Estate Record and Builders' Guide* 45 (May 10, 1890): 688–89; Landmarks Preservation Commission of the City of New York, *Soho—Cast-Iron Historic District Designation Report* (New York, 1973), 137; Gayle and Gillon, *Cast-Iron Architecture in New York*, 62–63; White and Willensky, *AIA Guide* (1988), 99.

35. "Some Commercial Buildings," *Real Estate Record and Builders' Guide* 33 (March 1, 1884): 202.

36. Montgomery Schuyler, "Architecture of New York," *New York World* (December 17, 1871): 3.

37. Montgomery Schuyler, "Polychromy in Street Architecture," *New York World* (March 31, 1872): 4.

38. "Metropolitan Improvements," *New York Evening Post* (March 10, 1871): 1; Schuyler, "Polychromy in Street Architecture": 4; *A History of Real Estate, Building and Architecture in New York City During the Last Quarter of a Century*, 622.

39. "A New Broadway Store," *Real Estate Record and Builders' Guide* 31 (March 3, 1883): 81–82.

40. Henry-Russell Hitchcock, *The Architecture of H. H. Richardson and His Times*, rev. ed. (New York: Museum of Modern Art, 1936; Hamden, Conn.: Archon Books, 1961), 150–51; Vincent J. Scully Jr., *The Shingle Style and the Stick Style: Architectural Theory and Design from Richardson to the Origins of Wright*, rev. ed. (New Haven, Conn., and London: Yale University Press, 1955, 1971), 25–33; Richard Guy Wilson, "Charles F. McKim and the Development of the American Renaissance: A Study of Architecture and Culture" (Ph.D. diss., University of Michigan, 1972), vol. 1: 103–17, 131–36, 141–42; Leland M. Roth, *McKim, Mead & White, Architects* (New York: Harper & Row, 1983), 36, 38.

41. "Old House at Newport, R.I.," *New-York Sketch-Book of Architecture* 1 (December 1874): 1–2, plate 45; Scully, *The Shingle Style and the Stick Style*, 26; Roth, ed., *America Builds*, 232–34.

42. Scully, *The Shingle Style and the Stick Style*, 8.

43. A. J. Bloor, "Annual Address," *Proceedings of the Tenth Annual Convention of the American Institute of Architects, 1876* (Boston, 1877): 15–34.

44. Montgomery Schuyler, "Recent Building in New York," *Harper's New Monthly Magazine* 67 (September 1883): 557–78.

45. Schuyler, "Recent Building in New York": 557.

46. Schuyler, "Recent Building in New York": 558–60.

47. Mariana Griswold Van Rensselaer, *Henry Hobson Richardson and His Works* (Boston: Houghton Mifflin, 1888; New York: Dover, 1969), 79–80, 132–38; Hitchcock, *The Architecture of H. H. Richardson and His Times*, rev. ed., 56–57.

48. See Richard Chafee, "Richardson's Record at the Ecole des Beaux-Arts," *Journal of the Society of Architectural Historians* 36 (October 1977): 175–88.

49. "Stores for Messrs. R. and F. Cheney, Hartford, Conn.," *New-York Sketch-Book of Architecture* 2 (September 1875): plate 35; Van Rensselaer, *Henry Hobson Richardson and His Works*, 67; Henry-Russell Hitchcock, *Architecture: Nineteenth and Twentieth Centuries* (Baltimore: Penguin

Books, 1958), 238–39, fig. 116a; Jeffrey Karl Ochsner, *H.H. Richardson: Complete Architectural Works* (Cambridge, Mass., and London: MIT Press, 1982), 153–55.

50. Montgomery Schuyler, "The Romanesque Revival in New York," *Architectural Record* 1 (July–September 1891): 7–38.

51. Schuyler, "The Romanesque Revival in New York": 15, 38.

52. Strong, diary entry dated April 26, 1866, in *The Diary of George Templeton Strong*, vol. 4: 80.

53. James Richardson, "The New Homes of New York: A Study of Flats," *Scribner's Monthly* 8 (May 1874): 63–76.

54. W., "New Work," *American Architect and Building News* 5 (March 1, 1879): 69–70. Also see "Architecture and Building," *Real Estate Record and Builders' Guide* 1 (March 21, 1868): 2.

55. Quoted in "Notes and Clippings," *American Architect and Building News* 1 (September 2, 1876): 288.

56. "Old Dutch House, New York, N.Y. Sketched by Mr. Max Schroff, Architect," *American Architect and Building News* 8 (November 6, 1880): 223, plate; Mary Black, *Old New York in Early Photographs* (New York: Dover, 1973), 56.

57. "A New-York Fashion," editorial, *New York Times* (November 2, 1879): 6.

58. "Rebuilding New York," (October 1, 1881): 921.

59. Richard Grant White, "Old New York and Its Houses," *Century Magazine* 26 (October 1883): 845–59.

60. Browne, *The Great Metropolis*, 338.

61. "Stores on Fifth-Avenue," editorial, *New York Times* (March 17, 1878): 6. Also see "Trade Invading Fifth-Avenue," editorial, *New York Times* (May 14, 1877): 4.

62. Raymond Westbrook, "Open Letters from New York," *Atlantic Monthly* 41 (January 1878): 91–99.

63. Strong, diary entry dated July 22, 1871, in *The Diary of George Templeton Strong*, vol. 4: 374–75.

64. Strong, diary entry dated September 2, 1869, in *The Diary of George Templeton Strong*, vol. 4: 253.

65. For the St. Cloud, see "A New Up-Town Hotel," *New York Times* (May 4, 1868): 1; Montgomery Schuyler, "Buildings on Broadway," *New York World* (September 24, 1871): 3; Montgomery Schuyler, "Improvements in New York Architecture," *New York World* (November 26, 1871): 3; Black, *Old New York in Early Photographs*, 176; Dunlap, *On Broadway*, 165. For the Rossmore, see "The Rossmore Hotel," *Frank Leslie's Illustrated Newspaper* (February 26, 1876): 129; Black, *Old New York in Early Photographs*, 176; Mary Ann Clegg Smith, "The Commercial Architecture of John Butler Snook" (Ph.D. diss., Pennsylvania State University, 1974): 145–47, 218; Dunlap, *On Broadway*, 165.

66. Christopher Gray, "Streetscapes/50th Street from Broadway to Seventh Avenue," *New York Times* (September 13, 1998), XI: 7.

67. Schuyler, "Buildings on Broadway": 3.

68. Schuyler, "Buildings on Broadway": 3. Also see "Buildings Projected," *Real Estate Record and Builders' Guide* 6 (November 19, 1870): 7; "Buildings Projected," *Real Estate Record and Builders' Guide* 6 (November 26, 1870): 8.

69. George Augustus Sala, *America Revisited: From the Bay of New York to the Gulf of Mexico, and from Lake Michigan to the Pacific*, 2 vols. (London: Vizetelly & Co., 1882), vol. 1: 35, 53–54.

70. Edith Wharton, *The Age of Innocence* (New York: D. Appleton, 1920; New York: Collier Books, 1992), 70–71.

71. O. B. Bunce, "The City of the Future," *Appletons' Journal* 7 (February 10, 1872): 156–58.

72. Frederick Law Olmsted, "Public Parks and the Enlargement of Towns," paper read before the American Social Science Association, February 25, 1870, quoted in Albert Fein, "Introduction," in Albert Fein, ed., *Landscape into Cityscape: Frederick Law Olmsted's Plans for New York City* (Ithaca, N.Y.: Cornell University Press, 1967), 38.

73. Frederick Law Olmsted, *Preliminary Report upon the Proposed Suburban Village at Riverside, near Chicago* (New York, 1868), 5, quoted in Fein, "Introduction," in Fein, ed., *Landscape into Cityscape*, 40.

74. Bunce, "The City of the Future": 156–58.

75. Editorial, *Real Estate Record and Builders' Guide* 28 (October 15, 1881): 963.

76. "Grouping in Architecture," *Real Estate Record and Builders' Guide* 32 (November 17, 1883): 899–900.

77. Landau and Condit, *Rise of the New York Skyscraper, 1865–1913*, 35–37, 66–67, 169–70.

78. "Buildings Projected," *Real Estate Record and Builders' Guide* 43 (June 8, 1889): 824; Landau and Condit, *Rise of the New York Skyscraper, 1865–1913*, 169.

79. "A Welcome Return," editorial, *New York Times* (January 18, 1880): 6.

80. George Townsend Fox, *American Journals* (June 1868), quoted in Fein, "New York Centennial, 1876," in Klein, ed., *New York: The Centennial Years 1676–1976*, 75.

81. Browne, *The Great Metropolis*, 23.

82. "The City of Luxury," editorial, *New York Times* (May 21, 1877): 4.

83. Ira Rosenwaike, *Population History of New York City* (Syracuse, N.Y.: Syracuse University Press, 1972), 42, 67.

84. Martin, *The Growth of New York*, 24.

85. "New York's Influx," *Real Estate Record and Builders' Guide* 26 (November 6, 1880): 961.

86. Lewis Mumford, "The City," in Harold E. Stearns, ed., *Civilization in the United States* (New York: Harcourt, Brace & Co., 1922), 17.

87. "The Past and Future of New York," *Real Estate Record and Builders' Guide* 38 (August 7, 1886): 994–96.

88. Browne, *The Great Metropolis*, 35.

89. James D. McCabe Jr., *Lights and Shadows of New York Life; or, The Sights and Sensations of the Great City* (Philadelphia: National Publishing, 1872; New York: Farrar, Straus & Giroux, 1970), 123.

90. "A Welcome Return," editorial, *New York Times* (January 18, 1880): 6.

91. I. N. Phelps Stokes, *The Iconography of Manhattan Island*, 6 vols. (New York: Robert H. Dodd, 1915–28; New York: Arno Press, 1967), vol. 5: 1899; Nelson Manfred Blake, *Water for the Cities: A History of the Urban Water Policy Problem in the United States* (Syracuse, N.Y.: Syracuse University Press, 1956), 144–71; Landmarks Preservation Commission of the City of New York, LP-0319 (July 12, 1967); Goldberger, *The City Observed*, 321; White and Willensky, *AIA Guide* (1988), 463; Christopher Gray, "The High Bridge Water Tower," *New York Times* (October 9, 1988), X: 12, reprinted in Christopher Gray, *Changing New York: The Architectural Scene* (New York: Dover, 1992), 66; Andrew S. Dolkart, *Guide to New York City Landmarks* (Washington, D.C.: Preservation Press, 1992), 140–41; Diamonstein, *The Landmarks of New York II*, 161; Christopher Gray, "Streetscapes/The Old Croton Aqueduct," *New York Times* (May 11, 1997), IX: 5.

92. Peter Shaver, *New York State Office of Parks, Recreation and Historic Preservation Survey Report* (August 25, 1992); "Gatehouse Sale, with Conditions," *New York Times* (February 7, 1993), X: 1.

93. "The Croton Question," editorial, *New York Times* (December 8, 1867): 4; "An Increased Water Supply," *New York Daily Tribune* (January 20, 1876): 8; "The Croton Water Works," *New York Daily Graphic* (March 21, 1881): 168–69; Editorial, *Real Estate Record and Builders' Guide* 30 (December 23–30, 1882): 139; "The People and the Aqueduct Scheme," editorial, *New York Times* (June 3, 1883): 6; "City Note-Book," *Building* 2 (June 1884): 104; "Croton Versus Well Water," *Building* 2 (August 1884): 127; "Gate-house for the New Croton Aqueduct," *Building* 5 (November 1886): 247–49; "The Progress of the New Aqueduct," *New York Daily Graphic* (October 17, 1887): 861; Charles Barnard, "The New Croton Aqueduct," *Century Magazine* 39 (December 1889): 205–24; "Almost Ready for Use," *New York Times* (June 12, 1890): 8; "The New Aqueduct Opened," *New York Times* (July 16, 1890): 5; "A Leak in the New Aqueduct," *New York Times* (July 17, 1890): 8; "New and Old Aqueducts," *New York Times* (May 31, 1892): 9; Moses King, *King's Handbook of New York* (Boston: Moses King, 1893), 196–201; Rebecca Read Shanor, *The City That Never Was* (New York: Viking Penguin, 1988), 193–96; Christopher Gray, "Streetscapes/The Croton Gatehouse," *New York Times* (July 28, 1991), X: 6; Dolkart, *Guide to New York City Landmarks*, 141.

94. "The Removal of the Reservoir," *New York Times* (June 23, 1882): 3; "The Fifth Avenue Reservoir," *New York Times* (June 29, 1882): 3; "The Fifth Avenue Reservoir," *New York Times* (June 30, 1882): 3; "The Fifth Avenue Reservoir," *New York Times* (September 20, 1882): 8.

95. Stern, Gilmartin, and Massengale, *New York 1900*, 91, 94–95; Shanor, *The City That Never Was*, 52–53.

96. "The Sewerage System Law," *New York Times* (September 12, 1865): 2.

97. "Sanitary Suggestions for Architects," *American Architect and Building News* 1 (January 15, 1876): 19–20.

98. Editorial, *American Architect and Building News* 1 (February 5, 1876): 41.

99. King, *King's Handbook of New York* (1893), 204; Sandra Opdycke, "Sewers," in Kenneth T. Jackson, ed., *The Encyclopedia of New York City* (New Haven, Conn., and London: Yale University Press; New York: New-York Historical Society, 1995), 1062.

100. "The Piers of New York," editorial, *New York Times* (August 31, 1865): 4.

101. *Report of the Joint Committee of the Senate and General Assembly of the State of New Jersey on the Encroachments upon the Bay and Harbor of New York, with the Report of Egbert L. Viele, State Topographical Engineer* (Trenton, 1855), 6, quoted by Fein, "New York Centennial, 1876," in Klein, ed., *New York: The Centennial Years 1676–1976*, 81.

102. "Our Wharves and Piers," editorial, *New York Times* (February 16, 1869): 2; Ann L. Buttenwieser, *Manhattan Water-Bound: Planning and Developing Manhattan's Waterfront from the Seventeenth Century to the Present* (New York and London: New York University Press, 1987), 61–62.

103. Buttenwieser, *Manhattan Water-Bound*, 62–64; Mary Beth Betts, "Masterplanning: Municipal Support of Maritime Transport and Commerce 1870–1930s," in Kevin Bone, ed., *The New York Waterfront: Evolution and Building Culture of the Port and Harbor* (New York: Monacelli Press, 1997), 36–81.

104. For a biography of McClellan's life, see Stephen W. Sears, *George B. McClellan: The Young Napoleon* (New York: Ticknor & Fields, 1988).

105. "The Docks and Wharves," editorial, *New York Times* (April 12, 1870): 4. Also see "The City Water Front," editorial, *New York Times* (January 26, 1870): 4; "Our Wharves and Piers," editorial, *New York Times* (February 11, 1870): 4; "River Front Improvements," *New York Times* (March 31, 1870): 3; "New System of Docks Needed," *Real Estate Record and Builders' Guide* 5 (April 16, 1870): 3; "Our Wharves and Piers," *New York Times* (April 22, 1870): 2; "Our City Wharves," *New York Times* (June 2, 1870): 2.

106. *Public Meetings of the Department of Docks to Hear Persons Interested in Improving the Waterfront, June and July 1870* (New York: New York Printing Company, 1870); Buttenwieser, *Manhattan Water-Bound*, 64–73; Betts, "Masterplanning," in Bone, ed., *The New York Waterfront*, 46–56.

107. "Our Dangerous Docks," editorial, *New York Times* (April 20, 1871): 4; "Don't Stop Improvement," *Real Estate Record and Builders' Guide* 8 (December 2, 1871): 233; Buttenwieser, *Manhattan Water-Bound*, 73–76; Betts, "Masterplanning," in Bone, ed., *The New York Waterfront*, 56–60, 65–67; Kevin Bone, "Horizontal City: Architecture and Construction in the Port of New York," in Bone, ed., *The New York Waterfront*, 84–151.

108. "Hell Gate Excavation," *New York Daily Tribune* (July 1, 1876): 3; "The Great Mine Fired," *New York Daily Tribune* (September 25, 1876): 1, 5; Fein, "New York Centennial, 1876," in Klein, ed., *New York: The Centennial Years 1676–1976*, 81; Gina Pollara, "Transforming the Edge: Overview of Selected Plans and Projects," in Bone, ed., *The New York Waterfront*, 151–89.

109. "The Great Mine Fired": 1.

110. Stern, Gilmartin, and Massengale, *New York 1900*, 49–50.

111. Landmarks Preservation Commission of the City of New York, LP-0918 (July 12, 1977); Carl Condit, "The Development of the Dock, Rail, and Bridge System of New York City, 1870–1920," in Josef Paul Kleihues and Christina Rathgeber, eds., *Berlin–New York: Like and Unlike* (New York: Rizzoli International Publications, 1993), 32–45; Diamonstein, *The Landmarks of New York II*, 187; Betts, "Masterplanning," in Bone, ed., *The New York Waterfront*, 65; Bone, "Horizontal City," in Bone, ed., *The New York Waterfront*, 122, 124–25; Bonnie Yochelson, *Berenice Abbott: Changing New York* (New York: New Press and the Museum of the City of New York, 1997), 340, plate 3.

112. "The City's Water Front," editorial, *New York Daily Tribune* (November 29, 1886): 4.

113. King, *King's Handbook of New York* (1893), 70.

114. Stokes, *The Iconography of Manhattan Island*, vol. 5: 1963, 1966–68, 1971, 1982; Bern Dibner, "Communication," in Melvin Kranzberg and Carroll W. Pursell Jr., eds., *Technology in Western Civilization*, 2 vols. (New York: Oxford University Press, 1967), vol. 1: 452–68; Thomas W. Smith, "Late Nineteenth-Century Communication: Techniques and Machinery," in Kranzberg and Pursell, eds., *Technology in Western Civilization*, vol. 1: 636–48; George David Smith, "Telephony," in Jackson, ed., *The Encyclopedia of New York City*, 1158–59.

115. Landau and Condit, *Rise of the New York Skyscraper, 1865–1913*, 38.

116. "Broadway Illuminated by Electricity Last Monday Night," *New York Daily Graphic* (December 22, 1880): 382, 384; Stokes, *The Iconography of Manhattan Island*, vol. 5: 1975.

117. Editorial, *Real Estate Record and Builders' Guide* 28 (September 24, 1881): 902.

118. "Miscellaneous City News: Edison's Electric Light," *New York Times* (March 1, 1881): 2; "Edison's Electric Light for Houses," *New York Times* (April 16, 1881): 8; "Edison's Latest Achievement," *New York Times* (October 5, 1881): 3; "The Edison Electric Light," *New York Times* (December 2, 1881): 8; "The Edison Dark Lanterns," *New York Times* (March 9, 1882): 8; "Miscellaneous City News: Edison's Electric Light," *New York Times* (September 5, 1882): 8; "After Two Years of Preparation," *American Architect and Building News* 12 (September 9, 1882): 117; King, *King's Handbook of New York* (1893), 202–4; Stokes, *The Iconography of Manhattan Island*, vol. 5: 1976, 1979; Harold I. Sharlin, "Applications of Electricity," in Kranzberg and Pursell, eds., *Technology in Western Civilization*, vol. 1: 563–78; *Where They Lit Up New York* (New York: Con Edison, 1987), 4–5; Martin V. Melosi, *Thomas A. Edison and the Modernization of America* (Glenview, Ill.: Scott, Foresman, 1990), 58–76; William J. Hausman, "Light and Power," in Jackson, ed., *The Encyclopedia of New York City*, 673–75.

119. Editorial, (September 24, 1881): 902.

120. "Miscellaneous City News: Edison's Electric Light," (September 5, 1882): 8.

121. "The Telegraph Pole Nuisance," *Real Estate Record and Builders' Guide* 4 (February 19, 1870): 1. Also see "Kite Tails vs. Telegraph Poles," *Real Estate Record and Builders' Guide* 4 (March 12, 1870): 1.

122. "The United States Underground Telegraph Company," *New York Daily Graphic* (March 23, 1882): 160.

123. "Telegraph Poles and Wires," *Real Estate Record and Builders' Guide* 32 (August 25, 1883): 624–25.

124. "A Determined Attempt," *American Architect and Building News* 13 (January 6, 1883): 2; "A Serious Attempt," *American Architect and Building News* 14 (December 6, 1883): 265.

125. Editorial, *American Architect and Building News* 15 (January 12, 1884): 14; Editorial, *American Architect and Building News* 15 (April 19, 1884): 181.

126. "In West Fifty-seventh Street," *Real Estate Record and Builders' Guide* 36 (September 12, 1885): 992–93.

127. "The Underground Wires," *New York Times* (January 17, 1886): 1; "Combining the Merits," *New York Times* (January 18, 1886): 2; "The Combination Plan," *New York Times* (January 19, 1886): 1; "Only Biding Their Time," *New York Times* (February 1, 1886): 1; "Experienced in Laying Wires," *New York Times* (May 26, 1886): 1; "The Electrical Subway Schemers Uncertain of Their Ground," *New York Times* (June 7, 1886): 8; "The Subways Report," editorial, *New York Times* (July 2, 1886): 4; "In and About the City: Getting Into the Subway," *New York Times* (August 13, 1886): 8; "The Place for the Wires," *New York Times* (September 14, 1886): 1; "His Subway Work Done," *New York Times* (November 7, 1886): 3; "Mr. Flower's Succession," *New York Times* (November 10, 1886): 8; "The Subway Commission," *New York Times* (November 12, 1886): 8; "Work in the Subways," *New York Times* (February 5, 1887): 8; "The Underground Wires," *New York Times* (February 9, 1887): 8; "In and About the City: Building the Conduits," *New York Times* (September 7, 1887): 8; "The Poles to Come Down," *New York Times* (November 28, 1887): 8; "Subways Ready for Use," *New York Times*

(November 4, 1888): 8; Stokes, *The Iconography of Manhattan Island*, vol. 5: 1985.

128. "In a Blizzard's Grasp," *New York Times* (March 13, 1888): 1; Stokes, *The Iconography of Manhattan Island*, vol. 5: 1995; Richard F. Shephard, "Calling the Blizzard of 1888," *New York Times* (January 14, 1988), C: 23; "The Icy Nightmare of '88," editorial, *New York Times* (March 11, 1988): 34; "The Blizzard that Spanned 100 Years of Memories," *New York Times* (March 12, 1988): 33. Also see José Martí, "New York Under the Snow," *La Nación* (1888), reprinted in Phillip Lopate, ed., *Writing New York: A Literary Anthology* (New York: Library of America, 1998), 271–77.

129. "Subways Must Be Used," *New York Times* (February 19, 1889): 8.

130. "In and About the City: Raid on the Wires," *New York Times* (April 16, 1889): 8; "No Trifling Permitted," *New York Times* (April 26, 1889): 8.

131. "Local Intelligence: The Broadway Bridge," *New York Times* (April 16, 1867): 8; Stokes, *The Iconography of Manhattan Island*, vol. 3: 926, vol. 5: 1927, 1932; John A. Kouwenhoven, *The Columbia Historical Portrait of New York* (Garden City, N.Y.: Doubleday, 1953), 314–15; Frederick S. Lightfoot, ed., *Nineteenth-Century New York in Rare Photographic Views* (New York: Dover, 1981), fig. 17.

132. "Metropolitan Conveyances—The Omnibus Nuisance," editorial, *New York Herald* (October 2, 1864): 4.

133. "Our City's Need," editorial, *New York Daily Tribune* (February 2, 1866): 4.

134. *Laws of N.Y. (1869), chap. 919*, quoted in Stokes, *The Iconography of Manhattan Island*, vol. 5: 1935. Also see "An Architectural Ramble," *Real Estate Record and Builders' Guide* 6 (September 17, 1870): 3–4; "The New Union Depot," *Real Estate Record and Builders' Guide* 6 (November 5, 1870): 3–4; "The New Railway Depot," *Real Estate Record and Builders' Guide* 7 (June 24, 1871): 311; "The New Railroad Depot at Forty-second Street and Fourth Avenue," *Scientific American* 25 (July 15, 1871): 40; "A Death Trap," *New York Times* (November 16, 1871): 1; "Railroad Abuses," *New York Times* (November 17, 1871): 5; "Vanderbilt's Latest Claims to Fame," *New York Times* (November 17, 1871): 4; Fair Play, F.F.M. Jr., Charles F. Boessoher, and Sufferer, "A Shameful Abuse," letters to the editor, *New York Times* (November 17, 1871): 5; "The Grand Central Depot," editorial, *New York Times* (November 18, 1871): 4; "The Railroad Trap," *New York Times* (November 18, 1871): 1; "Real Estate Injured," *New York Times* (November 18, 1871): 1; Nineteenth Ward Tax-Payer, J.M., J.L.R. Jr., and H.B., "The Grand Central Depot," letters to the editor, *New York Times* (November 18, 1871): 1; "Grand Central Depot," *Harper's Weekly* 16 (February 3, 1872): 104–5, 108–9; "The Grand Central Depot, New York City," *Scientific American* 32 (June 25, 1875): 399; "Grand Central Depot Signal System," *Scientific American* 33 (December 25, 1875): 399, 402; "Pictures of the Day," *New York Daily Graphic* (January 15, 1877): 511, 516; Walter G. Berg, *Buildings and Structures of American Railroads* (New York: John Wiley & Sons, 1893), 431–32; King, *King's Handbook of New York* (1893), 111–12, 115, 123; Stokes, *The Iconography of Manhattan Island*, vol. 3: 975, vol. 5: 1935, 1946; Wheaton J. Lane, *Commodore Vanderbilt: An Epic of the Steam Age* (New York: Alfred A. Knopf, 1942), 281–89; Lloyd Morris, *Incredible New York* (New York: Bonanza Books, 1951), 107–8; Carroll L. V. Meeks, *The Railroad Station: An Architectural History* (New Haven, Conn., and London: Yale University Press, 1956; New York: Dover, 1995), 49, 51–52, 73, 86–87, 100–101, figs. 98, 119–21; Ada Louise Huxtable, "Grand Central Depot—1869–71," *Progressive Architecture* 37 (October 1956): 135–38; Silver, *Lost New York*, 156; Edwin P. Alexander, *Down at the Depot: American Railroad Stations from 1831 to 1920* (New York: Clarkson N. Potter, 1970), 255–59; Black, *Old New York in Early Photographs*, plate 139; Smith, "The Commercial Architecture of John Butler Snook": 126, 134–40, 153–54, 195–96, 216, 331–33; John Grafton, *New York in the Nineteenth Century* (New York: Dover, 1977), 256; Carl W. Condit, *The Port of New York: A History of the Rail and Terminal System from the Beginnings to Pennsylvania Station* (Chicago and London: University of Chicago Press, 1980), 83–105; Elaine Abelson, "The Vanderbilt Collection," in Deborah Nevins, ed., *Grand Central Terminal: City Within the City* (New York: Municipal Art Society, 1982), 110–14;

Deborah Nevins, "Grand Central: Architecture as a Celebration of Daily Life," in Nevins, ed., *Grand Central Terminal*, 20, 61–63; Elliot Willensky, "Grand Central: Shaper of a City," in Nevins, ed., *Grand Central Terminal*, 87–99; M. Christine Boyer, *Manhattan Manners: Architecture and Style, 1850–1900* (New York: Rizzoli International Publications, 1985), 54, 61, 135–38.

135. "Vanderbilt's Latest Claims to Fame": 4.

136. "An Architectural Ramble": 3.

137. "The New Union Depot": 3.

138. "The New Railway Depot": 311.

139. "The New Railroad Depot at Forty-second Street and Fourth Avenue": 40.

140. "A Death Trap": 1.

141. Lane, *Commodore Vanderbilt*, 285.

142. "Railway Reform," *New York Times* (December 11, 1871): 2; "'Sink the Track,'" *New York Times* (December 20, 1871): 8; Christopher Gray, "Streetscapes/Historical Panorama," *New York Times* (October 19, 1997), X: 5.

143. Browne, *The Great Metropolis*, 466.

144. "Our City's Need": 4.

145. Stokes, *The Iconography of Manhattan Island*, vol. 5: 1709; Robert C. Reed, *The New York Elevated* (South Brunswick, N.J., and New York: A. S. Barnes, 1978), 23–25; Condit, *The Port of New York*, 79.

146. "Randall's [sic] Elevated Railway," *Scientific American* 3 (November 6, 1847): 52; "Elevated Railroads," *Scientific American* 18 (February 8, 1868): 86; "An Old Broadway Elevated Railroad," *New York Daily Graphic* (July 6, 1885): 35–36; Stokes, *The Iconography of Manhattan Island*, vol. 3: 699–700, plate 133a, vol. 5: 1796–97, 1805–6; Condit, *The Port of New York*, 79–80; Michael W. Brooks, *Subway City: Riding the Trains, Reading New York* (New Brunswick, N.J., and London: Rutgers University Press, 1997), 13–17.

147. "Randall's [sic] Elevated Railway": 52.

148. "Elevated Railway for New York City," *Scientific American* 15 (August 18, 1866): 119; "An Elevated Railroad Authorized," *New York Times* (May 25, 1867): 8; "Relief of the City—Elevated Railroads," *Scientific American* 16 (May 25, 1867): 332; John W. Kennion, *Architects' and Builders' Guide* (New York: Fitzpatrick & Hunter, 1868), part 2: 79–81; "The Elevated Railway," *New York Times* (January 12, 1868): 4; Editorial, *Real Estate Record and Builders' Guide* 1 (May 23, 1868): 1; "The Elevated Railway," *New York Times* (July 4, 1868): 2; "The West Side Elevated Railway," *Scientific American* 19 (July 15, 1868): 42; "The Elevated Railway," *Harper's Weekly* 12 (July 25, 1868): 476–77; "The Elevated Railway," *New York Times* (September 7, 1869): 4; "The Greenwich-Street Elevated Railway," *New York Times* (November 6, 1869): 2; "The Elevated Railway," *Real Estate Record and Builders' Guide* 5 (August 27, 1870): 1; "Rapid Transit in New York," *Appletons' Journal* 4 (May 1878): 393–408; James Blaine Walker, *Fifty Years of Rapid Transit, 1864–1917* (New York: Law Printing Co., 1918; New York: Arno Press, 1970), 60, 72–79; Stokes, *The Iconography of Manhattan Island*, vol. 3: 884, plate 27Bb, vol. 5: 1923–24, 1926–28, 1932; William Fullerton Reeves, *The First Elevated Railroads in Manhattan and the Bronx of the City of New York* (New York: New-York Historical Society, 1936), 5–14; John Anderson Miller, *Fares, Please! From Horse-Cars to Streamliners* (New York and London: D. Appleton-Century Co., 1941), 71–75; Black, *Old New York in Early Photographs*, plate 55; Stan Fischler, *Uptown, Downtown: A Trip Through Time on New York's Subways* (New York: Hawthorn Books, 1976), 11–13; Reed, *The New York Elevated*, 31–43; Condit, *The Port of New York*, 80; Benson Bobrick, *Labyrinths of Iron: Subways in History, Myth, Art, Technology, and War* (New York: William Morrow, 1981), 198–201; Brian J. Cudahy, *Under the Sidewalks of New York*, rev. ed. (Lexington, Mass.: Stephen Greene Press, 1988), xii–xiii; Shanor, *The City That Never Was*, 90–91; Joseph Cunningham and Leonard O. DeHart, *A History of the New York City Subway System*, rev. ed. (New York: Cunningham and DeHart, 1993), part 1: 5; Clifton Hood, *722 Miles: The Building of the Subways and How They Transformed New York* (New York: Simon & Schuster, 1993), 48–50; Brooks, *Subway City*, 31.

149. "The Elevated Railway," *Harper's Weekly*: 477.

150. "An Underground Railroad," *New York Illustrated News* (April 6,

1864): 386; *Proposed (Underground) Metropolitan Railway* (New York: Clayton and Medole, 1865); "The Proposed Tunneling of Broadway," *New York Times* (January 29, 1866): 2; Walker, *Fifty Years of Rapid Transit, 1864–1917*, 10–39; Stokes, *The Iconography of Manhattan Island*, vol. 5: 1912, 1916, 1918; Fischler, *Uptown, Downtown*, 10; Brooks, *Subway City*, 17–20.

151. A. P. Robinson, quoted in *Proposed (Underground) Metropolitan Railway*, quoted in Walker, *Fifty Years of Rapid Transit, 1864–1917*, 28–29.

152. *Arcade Underground Railroad: Evidence Before Senate R. R. Committee* (New York, 1868); "The Arcade Railroad," *Real Estate Record and Builders' Guide* 1 (April 11, 1868): 1; "City Transit Again," editorial, *New York Times* (May 4, 1868): 4; "Defeat of the Arcade," *Real Estate Record and Builders' Guide* 1 (May 9, 1868): 1; "The Underground Arcade," editorial, *New York Times* (March 15, 1869): 4; "Railroad Projects," editorial, *New York Times* (April 16, 1869): 4; "The Arcade Railroad," *New York Times* (March 21, 1870): 2; "The Future of New York," *Galaxy* 9 (April 1870): 548–53; "Arcade Railroad—A Gigantic Scheme of Plunder," editorial, *New York Times* (April 21, 1870): 4; "The Arcade Railroad in the Legislature," editorial, *New York Times* (April 23, 1870): 4; "The Arcade Railroad," *New York Times* (April 26, 1870): 2; "The Arcade Railroad Again," editorial, *New York Times* (April 26, 1870): 4; "The Arcade Railway," *New York Times* (April 29, 1870): 8; McCabe, *Lights and Shadows of New York Life*, 222–24; "Rapid Transit in New York," *Appletons' Journal*: 393–95; Stokes, *The Iconography of Manhattan Island*, vol. 3: 700–701, plate 133b, vol. 5: 1939; Morris, *Incredible New York*, 105–6; Shanor, *The City That Never Was*, 86–90; Brooks, *Subway City*, 27–30.

153. "The Arcade Railroad," *Real Estate Record and Builders' Guide*: 1.

154. "Rapid Transit in New York," *Appletons' Journal*: 394–95.

155. "City Transit Again": 4.

156. Leopold Eidlitz and John W. Serrell, *A Viaduct Railway for the City of New York* (New York, 1870); "The New City Railroad," *New York Daily Tribune* (June 7, 1871): 1; Septuagenarian, "The Viaduct Railroad," letter to the editor, *New York Times* (June 13, 1871): 2; "The Viaduct Railroad," *Real Estate Record and Builders' Guide* 7 (June 24, 1871): 1; "The Viaduct Railway," *New York Daily Tribune* (July 8, 1871): 1; "The Viaduct Railroad," *Real Estate Record and Builders' Guide* 8 (July 8, 1871): 1; Reeves, *The First Elevated Railroads in Manhattan and the Bronx of the City of New York*, 9; Brooks, *Subway City*, 24–26. Also see William Jordy and Ralph Coe's note in Schuyler, *American Architecture and Other Writings*, vol 1: 172–73 (n. 86).

157. "Plans for the Proposed Underground Railway, New York City," *New York Daily Graphic* (September 7, 1880): 502, 504; "A Ride Under Broadway," *New York Times* (June 26, 1882): 8; "Broadway Underground Railway," *New York Daily Graphic* (April 13, 1883): 308–10, 313; "Proposed Arcade Railway," *Harper's Weekly* 28 (March 19, 1884): 209; "The Underground Railroad," *New York Times* (August 17, 1884): 9; "The Arcade Scheme Dead," *New York Times* (March 13, 1885): 2; "Arcade Railway," *New York Daily Graphic* (April 3, 1886): 313; Stokes, *The Iconography of Manhattan Island*, vol. 5: 1977, 1989–90; Brooks, *Subway City*, 30–31.

158. "The 'Central Underground Railroad,'" *Real Estate Record and Builders' Guide* 1 (April 25, 1868): 1–2; "The Central Underground Railroad of this City—Reported Progress of the Scheme," *New York Times* (November 29, 1869): 2; Walker, *Fifty Years of Rapid Transit, 1864–1917*, 94–104; Stokes, *The Iconography of Manhattan Island*, vol. 5: 1931, 1937, 1965, 1967.

159. "The Pneumatic Dispatch," *Scientific American* 16 (January 5, 1867): 1–2; "Official Report of Patents and Claims," *Scientific American* 17 (November 23, 1867): 331; *Illustrated Description of the Broadway Pneumatic Underground Railway* (New York, 1870); "The Broadway Pneumatic Tunnel," *Frank Leslie's Illustrated Newspaper* (February 19, 1870): 381; "The Pneumatic Tunnel under Broadway, New York," *Scientific American* 22 (February 19, 1870): 127; "Under Broadway," *New York Herald* (February 27, 1870): 7; "The Pneumatic Railway," *New York Daily Tribune* (February 28, 1870): 5; "The Pneumatic Tunnel under Broadway, N.Y.," *Scientific American* 22 (March 5, 1870): 154–56; "The Pneumatic Railway," *Scientific American* 22 (April 30, 1870): 290; "The Broadway Underground Railway," *Real Estate Record and Builders' Guide* 6 (Decem-

ber 31, 1870): 1; McCabe, *Lights and Shadows of New York Life*, 224; "Underground Railroads," *Scientific American* 27 (November 2, 1872): 279–80; "The Broadway Underground Railway," *Scientific American* 28 (May 3, 1873): 272; "Broadway Underground Railway," *New York Daily Graphic* (May 22, 1873): 2, 5; Walker, *Fifty Years of Rapid Transit, 1864–1917*, 87–94; Stokes, *The Iconography of Manhattan Island*, vol. 5: 1931, 1934, 1937, 1943, 1948, 1953; Morris, *Incredible New York*, 104–5; Fischler, *Uptown, Downtown*, 19–27; Cunningham and DeHart, *A History of the New York City Subway System*, part 1: 1–4; Hood, *722 Miles*, 42–48; Brooks, *Subway City*, 20–27.

160. "Under Broadway," *New York Herald*: 7.

161. "The Pneumatic Tunnel under Broadway, New York," *Scientific American*: 127.

162. "The Broadway Underground Railway," *Real Estate Record and Builders' Guide*: 1.

163. "Rapid Transit in New York," *Appletons' Journal*: 395–97; Shanor, *The City That Never Was*, 95–99; Brooks, *Subway City*, 12–13.

164. "Rapid Transit in New York," *Appletons' Journal*: 396.

165. "The Rapid-Transit Routes," *New York Daily Graphic* (September 13, 1875): 557, 560–61; "Rapid Transit in New York," *Appletons' Journal*: 400; Walker, *Fifty Years of Rapid Transit, 1864–1917*, 105–7; Stokes, *The Iconography of Manhattan Island*, vol. 5: 1949; Reeves, *The First Elevated Railroads in Manhattan and the Bronx of the City of New York*, 16–22; Reed, *The New York Elevated*, 23, 29–30, 53–57; Bobrick, *Labyrinths of Iron*, 201–4; Shanor, *The City That Never Was*, 92–95; Hood, *722 Miles*, 50–51; Brooks, *Subway City*, 13, 15. Other notable elevated schemes included William Hemstreet's of 1866, Richard P. Morgan's of 1869, and Franz Sigel's of 1872. See Reeves, *The First Elevated Railroads in Manhattan and the Bronx of the City of New York*, 59–60; Brooks, *Subway City*, 13–14, 16.

166. "The Dying Horses," editorial, *New York Times* (October 26, 1872): 6; "Quietus to Quadrupeds," *New York World* (October 27, 1872): 5.

167. Stokes, *The Iconography of Manhattan Island*, vol. 5: 1939, 1945–46, 1948, 1958; Reed, *The New York Elevated*, 49–51; Fischler, *Uptown, Downtown*, 13–14; Brooks, *Subway City*, 31.

168. "Steam in Sixth Avenue," *New York Daily Tribune* (May 1, 1878): 2. Also see "The Gilbert Elevated Railway," *New York Daily Tribune* (August 17, 1876): 2; "The Gilbert Road's Future," *New York Daily Tribune* (March 3, 1877): 3; "The Gilbert Elevated Railway," *New York Daily Graphic* (December 27, 1877): 369; "The Depots of the Gilbert Elevated Railroad—The Station at Forty-second Street and Sixth Avenue," *New York Daily Graphic* (April 1, 1878): 216; "The Gilbert Elevated Road," *New York Times* (April 30, 1878): 10; "The Opening of the Gilbert Elevated Railroad," *New York Daily Graphic* (June 6, 1878): 681.

169. "Rapid Transit's Progress," *New York Daily Tribune* (December 16, 1878): 2.

170. "Rapid Transit in Earnest," *Frank Leslie's Illustrated Newspaper* (April 27, 1878): 132–34, quoted in Stephen Garmey, *Gramercy Park: An Illustrated History of a New York Neighborhood* (New York: Balsam Press, 1984), 162.

171. "City Steam Transit," *New York Daily Graphic* (May 1, 1876): 492, 494; "Rapid Transit on the West Side," *New York Daily Tribune* (November 17, 1876): 2; "Rapid Transit Work," *New York Daily Tribune* (March 27, 1877): 2; "Opposed to Elevated Railways," *New York Daily Tribune* (June 22, 1877): 2; "Advocating Rapid Transit," *New York Times* (June 30, 1877): 8; "The Progress of Rapid Transit," *New York Daily Graphic* (November 21, 1877): 137; "Correspondence," *American Architect and Building News* 3 (January 26, 1878): 32–33; "Rapid Transit in New York," *Appletons' Journal*: 403–8; "Rapid Transit in New York," *New York Daily Graphic* (May 8, 1878): 469; "How Will Elevated Railways Effect City Streets?" *American Architect and Building News* (June 28, 1878): 223–24; W., "What the Elevated Railway Actually Does for Street Architecture," *American Architect and Building News* 4 (July 13, 1878): 15–16; "Rapid Transit," *Harper's Weekly* 22 (July 20, 1878): 578; Editorial, *American Architect and Building News* 4 (September 28, 1878): 106; Editorial, *American Architect and Building News* 4 (October 12, 1878): 121; "Travelling Up in the Air," *New York Times* (October 13, 1878): 5; "Rapid Transit Problems," *New York Daily Tribune* (January 11, 1879): 5;

Charles Barnard, "The Railroad in the Air," *St. Nicholas Magazine* 6 (October 1879): 801–8; Editorial, *American Architect and Building News* 7 (January 10, 1880): 9; "A Ride on the Elevated," *New York Times* (August 1, 1880): 5; "Fast Time Up in the Air," *New York Times* (September 20, 1880): 2; "Life on the Elevated Road," *New York Daily Tribune* (July 4, 1882): 3; Walker, *Fifty Years of Rapid Transit, 1864–1917*, 108–22; Stokes, *The Iconography of Manhattan Island*, vol. 5: 1966–68, 1970–71; Reeves, *The First Elevated Railroads in Manhattan and the Bronx of the City of New York*, 22–33; Fischler, *Uptown, Downtown*, 251–54; Reed, *The New York Elevated*, 58–61; Bobrick, *Labyrinths of Iron*, 204–12; David C. Hammack, *Power and Society: Greater New York at the Turn of the Century* (New York: Columbia University Press, 1987), 231–33; Cunningham and DeHart, *A History of the New York City Subway System*, part 1: 6–9; Brooks, *Subway City*, 34–39.

172. "Suburban Rapid Transit," *New York Daily Graphic* (January 22, 1884): 68–69; Reeves, *The First Elevated Railroads in Manhattan and the Bronx of the City of New York*, 34–38, 125–26; Fischler, *Uptown, Downtown*, 253–55; Reed, *The New York Elevated*, 144–45.

173. Frederick Law Olmsted, "The Future of New York," *New York Daily Tribune* (December 28, 1879): 5.

174. Editorial, *Real Estate Record and Builders' Guide* 36 (August 22, 1885): 927; "Electricity on the Elevated Roads," *New York Daily Graphic* (August 25, 1885): 378, 380; "Run by Electricity," *New York Times* (November 27, 1888): 8; Stokes, *The Iconography of Manhattan Island*, vol. 5: 1986, 1996.

175. "Rapid Transit in New York," *Appletons' Journal*: 408. Also see William S. Talbot, *Jasper F. Cropsey, 1823–1900* (New York and London: Garland, 1977), 218–19; Barbara Finney, "Jasper F. Cropsey: Architect," in Mishoe Brennecke, *Jasper F. Cropsey: Artist and Architect* (New York: New-York Historical Society, 1987), 134–50.

176. Reeves, *The First Elevated Railroads in Manhattan and the Bronx of the City of New York*, 14–16. The section of the Third Avenue elevated along the Bowery was not rebuilt until 1915.

177. "New York's Grand West End," *Real Estate Record and Builders' Guide* 24 (November 11, 1879): 871–72.

178. William Dean Howells, *A Hazard of New Fortunes* (New York: Harper & Brothers, 1890; New York: New American Library, 1965), 66–67. Also see Brooks, *Subway City*, 39–46.

179. Henry James, *The Bostonians* (London: Macmillan & Co., 1886; New York: Viking Penguin, 1984), 436.

180. King, *King's Handbook of New York* (1893), 138.

181. Browne, *The Great Metropolis*, 100.

182. Brian J. Cudahy, *Over and Back: The History of Ferryboats in New York Harbor* (New York: Fordham University Press, 1990), 112.

183. "Ferry-Houses, Hoboken, N.J. Mr. H. Edwards Ficken, Architect, New York, N.Y.," *American Architect and Building News* 13 (February 3, 1883): 56, plates. Also see Harry J. Smith Jr., *Romance of the Hoboken Ferry* (New York: Prentice-Hall, 1931), 81–82.

184. Cudahy, *Over and Back*, 122.

185. Among the most useful overviews of Central Park are Clarence C. Cook, *A Description of the New York Central Park* (1869; New York: Benjamin Blom, 1972); "Central Park," *Scribner's Monthly* 6 (September 1873): 523–39; "Central Park: II," *Scribner's Monthly* 6 (October 1873): 673–91; Edward Hagaman Hall, "Central Park in the City of New York," *Annual Report of the American Scenic and Historic Preservation Society* 16 (1911): 379–489; Stokes, *The Iconography of Manhattan Island*, vol. 3: 730–65, plates 149, 151, 164b; Frederick Law Olmsted Jr. and Theodora Kimball, eds., *Forty Years of Landscape Architecture: Central Park* (New York: G. P. Putnam's Sons, 1928); Eugene Kinkead and Russell Maloney, "Central Park, Part I: Grass on Manhattan," *New Yorker* 17 (September 13, 1941): 24–28, 30, 32, 34, 36–37; Eugene Kinkead and Russell Maloney, "Central Park, Part II: A Nasty Place," *New Yorker* 17 (September 20, 1941): 34–38, 40, 42, 44–45; Eugene Kinkead and Russell Maloney, "Central Park: Part III: What a *Nice* Municipal Park!" *New Yorker* 17 (September 27, 1941): 23–26, 28, 31–33; Clay Lancaster, "Central Park, 1851–1951," *Magazine of Art* 44 (April 1951): 123–28; Fein, ed., *Landscape into Cityscape*, 45–88, 391–440; Henry Hope Reed and Sophia Duckworth, *Central Park: A History and a Guide* (New York: Clarkson N. Potter, 1967); Elizabeth Barlow, *Frederick Law Olmsted's New York* (New York: Praeger, 1972); Ian R. Stewart, "Central Park, 1851–71: Urbanization and Environmental Planning in New York City" (Ph.D. diss., Cornell University, 1973); Landmarks Preservation Commission of the City of New York, LP-0851 (April 16, 1974); Elizabeth Barlow, *The Central Park Book* (New York: Central Park Task Force, 1977); Henry Hope Reed, *Central Park: A Photographic Guide* (New York: Dover, 1979); Bruce Kelly, "Art of the Olmsted Landscape," in Bruce Kelly, Gail Travis Guillet, and Mary Ellen M. Hern, eds., *Art of the Olmsted Landscape* (New York: New York City Landmarks Preservation Commission and The Arts Publisher, 1981), 4–71; Henry Hope Reed, "Central Park: The Genius of the Place," in Kelly, Guillet, and Hern, eds., *Art of the Olmsted Landscape*, 124–32; Ian R. Stewart, "The Fight for Central Park," in Kelly, Guillet, and Hern, eds., *Art of the Olmsted Landscape*, 86–97; M. M. Graff, *The Men Who Made Central Park* (New York: Greensward Foundation, 1982); Charles E. Beveridge and David Schuyler, eds., *The Papers of Frederick Law Olmsted, Vol. 3: Creating Central Park, 1857–1861* (Baltimore: Johns Hopkins University Press, 1983); M. M. Graff, *Central Park, Prospect Park: A New Perspective* (New York: Greensward Foundation, 1985); Roy Rosenzweig and Elizabeth Blackmar, *The Park and the People: A History of Central Park* (Ithaca, N.Y.: Cornell University Press, 1992); Jordan Mejias, "Central Park," in Kleihues and Rathgeber, eds., *Berlin–New York: Like and Unlike*, 71–80; Diamonstein, *The Landmarks of New York II*, 126–27; Phyllis Lambert, ed., *Viewing Olmsted: Photographs by Robert Burley, Lee Friedlander, and Geoffrey James* (Montreal: Canadian Center for Architecture; Cambridge, Mass.: MIT Press, 1997); Malcolm Jones Jr., "Scenic Overlooks," *Newsweek* 192 (February 24, 1997): 70; Adam Gopnik, "A Critic at Large: Olmsted's Trip," *New Yorker* 73 (March 31, 1997): 95, 97–98, 100–102, 104; Frances Morrone, "The Way Olmsted Saw," *New Criterion* 15 (April 1997): 41–45; Francis R. Kowsky, *Country, Park and City: The Architecture and Life of Calvert Vaux* (New York: Oxford University Press, 1998), 96–135, 163–66, 189–94. For useful discussions of specific aspects of the park and its development, also see "The Fruits of Legislative Action in the City," editorial, *New York Times* (July 1, 1864): 4; "Local Intelligence: Central Park," *New York Times* (July 16, 1864): 3; "Central Park and the Means of Getting There," editorial, *New York Times* (July 16, 1865): 8; "Central Park," *New York Times* (April 22, 1866): 5; "Local Intelligence: The Central Park," *New York Times* (June 10, 1866): 8; "Central and Prospect Parks," editorial, *New York Times* (April 21, 1867): 4; "Summer Evenings in Town—Concerts in the Central Park," editorial, *New York Times* (August 4, 1867): 4; "Fish in the Park," *New York Times* (September 10, 1870): 1; "The Central Park," editorial, *New York Times* (October 31, 1870): 4; "The Central Park Meadows," *New York Times* (December 22, 1870): 4; "The Aldermen Request Light in the Central Park," *New York Times* (June 28, 1872): 2; "Central Park: Progress of the Work of Improvement Now Being Prosecuted," *New York Times* (November 28, 1872): 3; "City Improvements," *New York Times* (December 6, 1873): 4; "Improvements at Central Park," *New York Times* (April 9, 1874): 8; "Sunday in Central Park," *New York Times* (June 29, 1875): 8; "Saturday in Central Park," *New York Times* (July 4, 1875): 2; "Miniature Yachting in Central Park," *New York Times* (July 8, 1875): 5; "Draining the Park Ponds," *New York Daily Tribune* (March 16, 1876): 8; "A Crowd Scattered by Rain," *New York Times* (June 5, 1876): 10; "Central Park Menagerie," *New York Daily Tribune* (September 8, 1876): 8; "The Central Park Menagerie," *New York Times* (September 8, 1876): 8; "Central Park Improvements," *New York Daily Tribune* (November 6, 1876): 8; Editorial, *New York Daily Tribune* (March 5, 1877): 4; C. Vaux, "The Central Park Plan," letter to the editor, *New York Daily Tribune* (February 19, 1878): 5; C. Vaux, "The Central Park Plan," letter to the editor, *New York Daily Tribune* (February 22, 1878): 5; "The Proposed Zoological Garden," editorial, *New York Times* (March 3, 1878): 6; "A City Zoological Garden," *New York Times* (March 3, 1878): 10; "The Proposed Botanical Garden," *New York Times* (April 18, 1878): 8; Calvert Vaux, "A Plea for the Artistic Unity of Central Park," *New York Times* (August 27, 1879): 5; "The Mismanagement of the Park," *New York Times* (September 8, 1879): 8; Editorial, *New York Times* (September 8, 1879): 4; "An Amateur Menagerie," editorial, *New York Times* (April 22, 1881): 4; "Where New York Is Poor," editorial, *New York Times* (June 5, 1881): 6; "Improving Manhattan Square: The Beauties of Central Park Revealed by the Two New Driveways," *New York*

Times (October 1, 1882): 4; "Music in Central Park," *New York Times* (June 3, 1883): 9.

186. Andrew Jackson Downing, "Public Cemeteries and Public Gardens," *Horticulturalist* (July 1849), reprinted in Andrew Jackson Downing, *Rural Essays* (New York: G. P. Putnam, 1853), 154–55.

187. William Cullen Bryant, "A New Public Park," editorial, *New York Evening Post* (July 3, 1844): 2.

188. William Cullen Bryant, quoted in Norval White, *New York: A Physical History* (New York: Atheneum, 1987), 92–93.

189. Ambrose Kingsland, quoted in Stewart, "The Fight for Central Park," in Kelly, Guillet, and Hern, eds., *Art of the Olmsted Landscape*, 92.

190. "The Middle Park," editorial, *New York Times* (June 23, 1853): 4.

191. George W. Curtis, "Editor's Easy Chair," editorial, *Harper's New Monthly Magazine* 11 (June 1855): 125.

192. Quoted in "A Hundred Acre Public Park," *New York Herald-Tribune* (June 8, 1847): 1.

193. Andrew Jackson Downing, "The New-York Park," *Horticulturalist* (August 1851): 347.

194. *Report of the Croton Aqueduct Department Made to the Common Council, December 31, 1851* (1852), 18–20, quoted in Rosenzweig and Blackmar, *The Park and the People*, 40.

195. "Central Park: II," *Scribner's Monthly*: 677.

196. Frederick Law Olmsted, "The Beginning of Central Park: A Fragment of Autobiography" (1877), in Fein, ed., *Landscape into Cityscape*, 61.

197. William Cullen Bryant, quoted in Olmsted and Kimball, eds., *Forty Years of Landscape Architecture: Central Park*, 28.

198. "The Central Park," *Harper's Weekly* 1 (November 28, 1857): 757.

199. Calvert Vaux, memorandum, November 1894, Calvert Vaux Papers, Rare Books and Manuscripts Division, New York Public Library, Astor, Lenox and Tilden Foundations, quoted in Shanor, *The City That Never Was*, 169.

200. For the life and work of Frederick Law Olmsted, see Mariana G. Van Rensselaer, "Frederick Law Olmsted," *Century Magazine* 46 (October 1893): 860–67; Lewis Mumford, *The Brown Decades: A Study of the Arts in America, 1865–1895* (New York: Harcourt, Brace, 1931), 79–96; S. B. Sutton, ed., *Civilizing American Cities: A Selection of Frederick Law Olmsted's Writing on City Landscapes* (Cambridge, Mass.: MIT Press, 1971); Albert Fein, *Frederick Law Olmsted and the American Environmental Tradition* (New York: George Braziller, 1972); Laura Wood Roper, *FLO: A Biography of Frederick Law Olmsted* (Baltimore: Johns Hopkins University Press, 1973); Elizabeth Stevenson, *Park Maker: A Life of Frederick Law Olmsted* (New York: Macmillan, 1977); Dana F. White and Victor A. Kramer, *Olmsted's South: Old South Critic, New South Planner* (Westport, Conn.: Greenwood, 1979); Graff, *The Men Who Made Central Park*; Roger Starr, "The Motive Behind Olmsted's Park," *The Public Interest* (winter 1984): 66–76, reprinted in Nathan Glazer and Mark Lilla, eds., *The Public Face of Architecture: Civic Culture and Public Spaces* (New York: Macmillan, 1987), 264–75; Dana F. White, "Frederick Law Olmsted, the Placemaker," in Daniel Schaffer, ed., *Two Centuries of American Public Planning* (Baltimore: Johns Hopkins University Press, 1988), 87–112; Melvin Kalfus, *Frederick Law Olmsted* (New York: New York University Press, 1990); Charles E. Beveridge and Paul Rocheleau, *Frederick Law Olmsted: Designing the American Landscape* (New York: Rizzoli International Publications, 1995); Lee Hall, *Olmsted's America: An "Unpractical" Man and His Vision of Civilization* (Boston: Little, Brown, 1995).

201. Gopnik, "A Critic at Large: Olmsted's Trip": 101.

202. Frederick Law Olmsted, *A Journey in the Seaboard Slave States in the Years 1853–54* (1856; New York: G. P. Putnam's Sons, 1904).

203. Frederick Law Olmsted, *Walks and Talks of an American Farmer in England* (New York: Dix, Edwards, 1853).

204. For an extensive discussion of Calvert Vaux's life and work, see William Alex, *Calvert Vaux: Architect and Planner* (New York: Ink, 1994).

205. Morrone, "The Way Olmsted Saw": 42.

206. *Description of Designs for the Improvement of Central Park* (1858), 13, quoted in Shanor, *The City That Never Was*, 173.

207. *Description of Designs for the Improvement of Central Park* (1858), 35, quoted in Shanor, *The City That Never Was*, 172.

208. Frederick Law Olmsted and Calvert Vaux, quoted in Olmsted and Kimball, eds., *Forty Years of Landscape Architecture: Central Park*, 46.

209. J. B. Jackson, "The American Space," *The Public Interest* (winter 1984): 52–65, reprinted in Glazer and Lilla, eds., *The Public Face of Architecture: Civic Culture and Public Spaces*, 276–91.

210. Van Rensselaer, "Frederick Law Olmsted": 864–65.

211. Frederick Law Olmsted, quoted in Michael Pye, *Maximum City: The Biography of New York* (London: Sinclair-Stevenson, 1991), 270.

212. Rosenzweig and Blackmar, *The Park and the People*, 64–73; Douglas Martin, "Before Park, Black Village," *New York Times* (April 7, 1995), B: 1–2; Paul Schwartzman, "Central Park's Vanished Black Settlement," *New York Daily News* (January 19, 1997): 29; Douglas Martin, "A Village Dies, a Park Is Born," *New York Times* (January 31, 1997), C: 1, 4; Clyde Haberman, "The History Central Park Almost Buried," *New York Times* (February 28, 1997), B: 1; Eric K. Washington, "Unearth Truth in Central Park," *New York Daily News* (May 20, 1997): 31.

213. *Description of Designs for the Improvement of Central Park* (1858), 45, quoted in Christopher Gray, "Central Park Transverses: Neglected and Abused Crosstown Roads," *New York Times* (November 5, 1989), X: 10, reprinted in Gray, *Changing New York*, 104.

214. See Christopher Gray, "The Challenge of Restoring Long-Neglected Trails," *New York Times* (January 2, 1994), X: 5.

215. Christopher Gray, "Neighborhood: Frozen in Time," *Avenue* (February 1987): 148–53; Janet Allon, "The Skating Boom," *New York Times* (December 24, 1995), XIII: 1, 10; Gopnik, "A Critic at Large: Olmsted's Trip": 102.

216. "Central Park: II," *Scribner's Monthly*: 679.

217. Frederick Law Olmsted to H. G. Stebbins, memorandum, "Examination of the Design of the Park and of Recent Changes Therein," February 1872, quoted in Kelly, "Art of the Olmsted Landscape," in Kelly, Guillet, and Hern, eds., *Art of the Olmsted Landscape*, 28.

218. Frederick Law Olmsted, *Annual Report to Central Park Commissioners* (1868), quoted in Kelly, "Art of the Olmsted Landscape," in Kelly, Guillet, and Hern, eds., *Art of the Olmsted Landscape*, 28.

219. Alex, *Calvert Vaux*, 114–15. Also see Francis R. Kowsky, "Jacob Wrey Mould: Master of Color," *Preservation League of New York State Newsletter* 11 (March–April 1985): 4–5.

220. "Pictures of the Day," *New York Daily Graphic* (June 4, 1873): 1–2. Also see "The Talk of the Town: Angel," *New Yorker* 31 (July 2, 1955): 13–14.

221. "Central Park: II," *Scribner's Monthly*: 683.

222. Frederick Law Olmsted, *Report to the Commissioners of Central Park* (1871), quoted in Kelly, "Art of the Olmsted Landscape," in Kelly, Guillet, and Hern, eds., *Art of the Olmsted Landscape*, 45.

223. Calvert Vaux, fragment, Olmsted Papers, quoted in Kelly, "Art of the Olmsted Landscape," in Kelly, Guillet, and Hern, eds., *Art of the Olmsted Landscape*, 45.

224. Alex, *Calvert Vaux*, 119.

225. Alex, *Calvert Vaux*, 129.

226. "New Boat-House Now Being Erected on the Lake in Central Park," *New York Daily Graphic* (April 28, 1876): 474.

227. Alex, *Calvert Vaux*, 120–21.

228. For a discussion of Central Park's bridges, see Henry Hope Reed, Robert M. McGee, and Esther Mipaas, *Bridges of Central Park* (New York: Greensward Foundation, 1990). Also see Alex, *Calvert Vaux*, 122–28.

229. See Gopnik, "A Critic at Large: Olmsted's Trip": 101.

230. Vaux, fragment, Olmsted Papers, quoted in Kelly, "Art of the Olmsted Landscape," in Kelly, Guillet, and Hern, eds., *Art of the Olmsted Landscape*, 53.

231. Clarence Cook, "Mr. Hunt's Designs for the Gates of Central Park," *New York Daily Tribune* (August 2, 1865): 8; "The Proposed Designs for the Central Park Gates," *The Nation* 1 (August 10, 1865): 186–88; C.P., "The Designs for the Central Park Gates," letter to the editor, *The Nation* 1 (September 28, 1865): 410–12; Richard Morris Hunt, *Designs for the Gateways of the Southern Entrances to the Central Park* (New York, 1866); Montgomery Schuyler, "The Works of the Late Richard M. Hunt," *Architectural Record* 5 (October–December 1895): 97–180; Baker, *Richard Morris Hunt*, 146–56; Francis R. Kowsky, "The Central Park

Gateways: Harbingers of French Urbanism Confront the American Landscape Tradition," in Stein, ed., *The Architecture of Richard Morris Hunt*, 78–89; Gregory F. Gilmartin, *Shaping the City: New York and the Municipal Art Society* (New York: Clarkson Potter, 1995), 240.

232. Calvert Vaux to Clarence Cook, June 6, 1865, Frederick Law Olmsted Papers, Manuscript Division, Library of Congress, quoted in Kowsky, "The Central Park Gateways," in Stein, ed., *The Architecture of Richard Morris Hunt*, 78–79.

233. Cook, "Mr. Hunt's Designs for the Gates of Central Park": 8.

234. "The Proposed Designs for the Central Park Gates": 188.

235. Vaux to Cook, June 6, 1865, quoted in Kowsky, "The Central Park Gateways," in Stein, ed., *The Architecture of Richard Morris Hunt*, 84.

236. Schuyler, "The Works of the Late Richard M. Hunt": 104.

237. Kowsky, "The Central Park Gateways," in Stein, ed., *The Architecture of Richard Morris Hunt*, 86–87.

238. Margot Gayle and Michele Cohen, *The Art Commission and the Municipal Art Society Guide to Manhattan's Outdoor Sculpture* (New York: Prentice Hall, 1988), 214.

239. Gayle and Cohen *The Art Commission and the Municipal Art Society Guide to Manhattan's Outdoor Sculpture*, 205.

240. "Joseph Mazzini," *New York Daily Graphic* (May 29, 1878): 625; Gayle and Cohen, *The Art Commission and the Municipal Art Society Guide to Manhattan's Outdoor Sculpture*, 240.

241. Gayle and Cohen, *The Art Commission and the Municipal Art Society Guide to Manhattan's Outdoor Sculpture*, 194.

242. Gayle and Cohen, *The Art Commission and the Municipal Art Society Guide to Manhattan's Outdoor Sculpture*, 206.

243. Report of Committee on Statues in the Park, April 25, 1873, reprinted in Olmsted and Kimball, eds., *Forty Years of Landscape Architecture: Central Park*, 491.

244. Report of Committee on Statues in the Park, April 25, 1873, reprinted in Olmsted and Kimball, eds., *Forty Years of Landscape Architecture: Central Park*, 489.

245. Olmsted and Vaux to S. H. Wales, March 4, 1874, in Olmsted and Kimball, eds., *Forty Years of Landscape Architecture: Central Park*, 496.

246. "Statue of Daniel Webster to Be Unveiled in Central Park Today," *New York Daily Graphic* (November 25, 1876): 174.

247. Gayle and Cohen, *The Art Commission and the Municipal Art Society Guide to Manhattan's Outdoor Sculpture*, 207–8.

248. Gayle and Cohen, *The Art Commission and the Municipal Art Society Guide to Manhattan's Outdoor Sculpture*, 203.

249. Baker, *Richard Morris Hunt*, 145, 301, 539; Gayle and Cohen, *The Art Commission and the Municipal Art Society Guide to Manhattan's Outdoor Sculpture*, 241.

250. Gayle and Cohen, *The Art Commission and the Municipal Art Society Guide to Manhattan's Outdoor Sculpture*, 220.

251. "Cleopatra's Needle Exhumed," *New York Daily Tribune* (June 18, 1877): 1; "Pictures of the Day," *New York Daily Graphic* (September 27, 1877): 607, 609; "Egypt in New York," editorial, *New York Daily Tribune* (October 8, 1877): 4; Chas. Storrs, "Cleopatra's Needles," letter to the editor, *New York Times* (October 8, 1877): 5; Edward W. Serrell Jr., "Cleopatra's Needle," letter to the editor, *New York Times* (October 9, 1877): 5; "The Obelisk Secured," *New York Daily Tribune* (October 15, 1877): 1; "The Obelisk and Its Place," editorial, *New York Daily Tribune* (October 16, 1877): 4; Edward W. Serrell Jr., "The Obelisk," *New York Daily Tribune* (October 18, 1877): 8; "The Rise of the Obelisk," editorial, *New York Daily Tribune* (October 20, 1877): 4; Editorial, *American Architect and Building News* 2 (October 27, 1877): 342; Editorial, *American Architect and Building News* 5 (June 28, 1879): 201; Editorial, *American Architect and Building News* 6 (August 16, 1879): 49; "Cleopatra's Needle: The Machinery for Transporting It," *American Architect and Building News* 6 (October 25, 1879): 135; Edward T. Potter, letter to the editor, *American Architect and Building News* 6 (November 15, 1879): 160; "Pictures of the Day," *New York Daily Graphic* (July 22, 1880): 152, 154; Editorial, *New York Times* (July 27, 1880): 8; "Pictures of the Day," *New York Daily Graphic* (July 28, 1880): 195–96; Editorial, *American Architect and Building News* 31 (July 31, 1880): 49–50; "The Obelisk as It Will Appear When Erected on the Selected Site in Central Park," *New York Daily Graphic* (July 31, 1880): 225; "Removing the Pedestal of the

Obelisk," *New York Daily Graphic* (August 6, 1880): 264, 267; Editorial, *American Architect and Building News* 8 (August 7, 1880): 61; "Laying the Corner-stone for the Foundation of the Obelisk in Central Park Last Saturday Afternoon," *New York Daily Graphic* (October 12, 1880): 776; Editorial, *American Architect and Building News* 8 (October 16, 1880): 181; "Pictures of the Day," *New York Daily Graphic* (October 20, 1880): 838, 840; Editorial, *American Architect and Building News* 8 (November 20, 1880): 242; "Pictures of the Day," *New York Daily Graphic* (December 2, 1880): 234, 236; "Constructing the Incline and Supports for the Placing of the Obelisk on the Pedestal in Central Park," *New York Daily Graphic* (December 21, 1880): 374, 376; "The Obelisk Partly Uncased," *New York World* (December 24, 1880): 4; "Pictures of the Day," *New York Daily Graphic* (January 22, 1881): 608, 615–17; "The Journey Ended," *New York Daily Graphic* (January 27, 1881): 646; Genera diCesnola, "Obelisks," *American Architect and Building News* 9 (May 28, 1881): 258–60, "Designs for a Proposed Railing Around the Obelisk in Central Park," *New York Daily Graphic* (March 20, 1882): 132; Elbert E. Farman, "The Negotiations for the Obelisk," *Century Magazine* 24 (May–October 1882): 879–89; "Pictures of the Day," *New York Daily Graphic* (November 11, 1885): 65–66; "An Address Delivered before the New York Academy of Sciences, November 23, 1885, by R. M. Caffall on His Process for Waterproofing and Preserving Buildings as Recently Applied to the Obelisk in Central Park," pamphlet (New York, 1886); Adolf Cluss, "New Reasons Advanced for the Delay of the New York Obelisk," *Building* 8 (March 17, 1888): 90–91; New York City Department of Parks, "Copy of Report on the Condition of the Obelisk in the Central Park, New York by a Committee of Experts Appointed by the Department of Public Parks," pamphlet (New York, 1890); Charles E. Moldenke, *The New York Obelisk: Cleopatra's Needle* (New York: A.D.F. Randolph, 1891); Geoffrey T. Hellman, "That Was New York: A Needle for Central Park," *New Yorker* 14 (September 3, 1938): 24–32; "The Obelisk," scrapbook consisting of articles taken from American and English newspapers and periodicals and other memorabilia, 1879–1941, Thomas J. Watson Library, Metropolitan Museum of Art, New York; Ruth McKenney and Eileen Bransten, "Ordeal by Obelisk," *Holiday* 43 (June 1968): 68, 76–78; Seymour Z. Lewin, George E. Wheeler, and A. E. Charola, "Stone Conservation and Cleopatra's Needle: A Case History and an Object Lesson," 1983, Department of Objects Conservation, Metropolitan Museum of Art, New York; Erhard M. Winkler, "Historical Implications in the Complexity of Destructive Salt Weathering: Cleopatra's Needle, New York," *Association for Preservation Technology Bulletin* 12 (1980): 94–102; E. A. Wallis Budge, *Cleopatra's Needles and Other Egyptian Obelisks* (London: Religious Tract Society; New York: Dover, 1990), 172–73; Martina D'Alton, "The New York Obelisk: Or How Cleopatra's Needle Came to New York and What Happened When It Got Here," *Metropolitan Museum of Art Bulletin* 50 (spring 1993): 1–74.

252. "Pictures of the Day," (December 2, 1880): 234, 236.

253. "The Obelisk and Its Place": 4.

254. Editorial, (June 28, 1879): 201.

255. "What May Be Learned at the Central Park," editorial, *Architects' and Mechanics' Journal* 2 (August 18, 1860): 191.

256. Martin, *The Growth of New York*, 34.

257. "The Central Park," *New York Times* (March 25, 1865): 5.

258. Frederick Law Olmsted, quoted in Olmsted and Kimball, eds., *Forty Years of Landscape Architecture: Central Park*, 58–59.

259. Central Park ordinances, 1859, quoted in Olmsted and Kimball, eds., *Forty Years of Landscape Architecture: Central Park*, 410.

260. "The Central Park," *New York Times* (July 25, 1861): 5.

261. Browne, *The Great Metropolis*, 122.

262. See "Farewell to Central Park," editorial, *New York Times* (October 2, 1870): 4.

263. "The Central Park," editorial, *New York Times* (December 21, 1870): 2–3. Also see "Is the Central Park in Danger?" editorial, *New York Times* (October 20, 1870): 4; "The Central Park," editorial, *New York Times* (March 22, 1871): 4; "The Central Park, and How It Fell into the Hands of the Ring," editorial, *New York Times* (August 17, 1871): 4.

264. "A 'Picture on the Ground,'" editorial, *New York Times* (March 25, 1872): 2–3. Also see Editorial, *New York Times* (November 5, 1875): 4;

"A Bankrupt Pleasure-Ground," editorial, *New York Times* (November 22, 1876): 4; "Tammany Rule and Central Park," *New York Times* (January 9, 1878): 5; Editorial, *New York Times* (September 30, 1879): 4.

265. "A 'Picture on the Ground'": 2.

266. Frederick Law Olmsted, *The Spoils of the Park, with a Few Leaves from the Deep-Laden Note-Books of a 'Wholly Unpractical Man'* (1882), reprinted in Olmsted and Kimball, eds., *Forty Years of Landscape Architecture: Central Park*, 117–55.

267. "Central Park Lots," *Real Estate Record and Builders' Guide* 18 (November 18, 1876): 851–52. Also see M., "More Parks for New York," letter to the editor, *New York Times* (January 9, 1882): 3.

268. "The Fifth Avenue," *Real Estate Record and Builders' Guide* 21 (June 15, 1878): 515–16; "The Limits of Central Park," *Real Estate Record and Builders' Guide* 21 (June 29, 1878): 555–56. Also see Boyer, *Manhattan Manners*, 18.

269. Henry James, *The Bostonians* (1886; New York: Viking Penguin, 1984), 319.

270. W. D. Howells, *Impressions and Experiences* (New York: Harper & Brothers, 1896), 227.

271. Van Rensselaer, "Frederick Law Olmsted": 856–66.

272. Significant discussions of the Brooklyn Bridge and the Roeblings include Hamilton Schuyler, *The Roeblings: A Century of Engineers, Bridge-builders and Industrialists* (Princeton, N.J.: Princeton University Press, 1931); D. B. Steinman, *The Builders of the Bridge: The Story of John Roebling and His Son* (New York: Harcourt, Brace, 1945); David B. Steinman and Sara Ruth Watson, *Bridges and Their Builders*, rev. ed. (New York: Dover, 1957), 205–47; Trachtenberg, *Brooklyn Bridge: Fact and Symbol*; David McCullough, *The Great Bridge* (New York: Simon and Schuster, 1972); Sharon Reier, *The Bridges of New York* (New York: Quadrant Press, 1977), 10–27; David McCullough, "The Treasure from the Carpentry Shop: The Extraordinary Original Drawings of the Brooklyn Bridge," *American Heritage* 31 (December 1979): 19–29; David P. Billington, *The Tower and the Bridge: The New Art of Structural Engineering* (New York: Basic Books, 1983), 72–87; Deborah Nevins et al., *The Great East River Bridge, 1883–1983* (Brooklyn: Brooklyn Museum, 1983); Ellen M. Snyder-Grenier, *Brooklyn! An Illustrated History* (Philadelphia: Temple University Press, 1996), 67–81.

273. *Report of John A. Roebling, C.E., to the President and Directors of the New York Bridge Company, On the Proposed East River Bridge* (New York, 1867), quoted in Reier, *The Bridges of New York*, 11.

274. Thomas Pope, *A Treatise on Bridge Architecture, in Which the Superior Advantages of the Flying Pendant Are Fully Proved* (New York: Alexander Niven, 1811). Also see Reier, *The Bridges of New York*, 11; Nevins et al., *The Great East River Bridge, 1883–1983*, 123.

275. David Jacobs and Anthony E. Neville, *Bridges, Canals and Tunnels* (New York: American Heritage, 1968), 73–75.

276. John Roebling, "Correspondence," *Architects' and Mechanics' Journal* 2 (June 14, 1860): 13–14. Also see "Bridging the East River," *Architects' and Mechanics' Journal* 1 (March 31, 1860): 209.

277. "Shall the East River Be Bridged?" editorial, *New York Times* (January 21, 1867): 4; "The East River Bridge," *New York Times* (September 11, 1867): 5; "The Bridge Across East River," editorial, *New York Times* (March 21, 1868): 4; "The East River Bridge," editorial, *New York Times* (April 16, 1868): 4; "The East River Bridge," editorial, *New York Times* (December 23, 1868): 4; "A Bridge to Brooklyn," editorial, *New York Times* (December 28, 1868): 4; "The Brooklyn Bridge," *Real Estate Record and Builders' Guide* 2 (January 2, 1869): 1; "The East River Suspension Bridge Project," *New York Times* (February 5, 1869): 2; "The Brooklyn Bridge," editorial, *New York Times* (February 8, 1869): 4; George W. Dow, "East River Bridge and Docks," letter to the editor, *New York Times* (February 15, 1869): 2; W. S. Livingston, "A Tubular Bridge Across the East River," letter to the editor, *New York Times* (March 14, 1869): 5; "The East River Bridge," *New York Times* (March 14, 1869): 6; D., "The East River Suspension Bridge vs. the Dock System," letter to the editor, *New York Times* (March 17, 1869): 2; "Bridging the East River," editorial, *New York Times* (March 21, 1869): 4; "Bridging East River," editorial, *New York Times* (July 8, 1869): 4; "The East River Bridge," *New York Times* (December 3, 1869): 3; Shanor, *The City That Never Was*, 127–28.

278. Kennion, *Architects' and Builders' Guide*, part 2: 49–50.

279. "The Brooklyn Bridge Project," editorial, *New York Times* (April 3, 1868): 4.

280. "East River Bridge," *New York Times* (March 20, 1870): 8; "The East River Bridge," *New York Times* (June 19, 1870): 8; "The East River Bridge," *New York Times* (August 30, 1870): 3; "Completion of the Caisson of the East River Bridge," *New York Times* (December 23, 1870): 6; "The East River Bridge," *New York Times* (March 27, 1872): 5; "The Brooklyn Bridge," *New York Times* (June 24, 1872): 5; "The East River Bridge," *New York Times* (July 2, 1872): 4; "The Brooklyn Bridge," *Real Estate Record and Builders' Guide* 11 (June 7, 1873): 263.

281. "The Brooklyn Bridge," *New York Daily Tribune* (November 11, 1875): 2; Editorial, *American Architect and Building News* 1 (August 5, 1876): 249; "The Brooklyn Bridge Upheld," *New York Daily Tribune* (August 5, 1876): 9; "The East River Bridge," *New York Times* (August 15, 1876): 8; "Stretching the First Wires Across the East River Bridge Last Monday," *New York Daily Graphic* (August 16, 1876): 311; "The Brooklyn Bridge Ropes," *New York Daily Tribune* (August 17, 1876): 2; "Local Miscellany: The East River Bridge," *New York Times* (August 20, 1876): 2; "A Ride Over East River," *New York Times* (August 26, 1876): 8; "The East River Bridge," *New York Times* (August 27, 1876): 12; "Local Miscellany: Work on the East River Bridge," *New York Times* (August 30, 1876): 8; Editorial, *American Architect and Building News* 1 (September 2, 1876): 289; "Contracts for the Brooklyn Bridge," *New York Daily Tribune* (September 8, 1876): 8; "The Work on the East River Bridge," *New York Times* (September 15, 1876): 8; "The East River Bridge," *New York Daily Tribune* (September 30, 1876): 6; "Another Rope Across the River," *New York Daily Tribune* (October 17, 1876): 2; "The Work of the Great Bridge," *New York Times* (October 17, 1876): 2; "The Work on the Bridge," *New York Times* (October 18, 1876): 5; "The Work on the East River Bridge," *New York Times* (November 4, 1876): 2; "Local Miscellany: The East River Bridge," *New York Times* (November 12, 1876): 12; "The Building of the Bridge," *New York Times* (November 25, 1876): 2; "New York's Great Bridge," *New York Times* (January 28, 1877): 12; A Sufferer, "A Growl Over the Brooklyn Bridge," letter to the editor, *New York Times* (January 30, 1877): 5; "Local Miscellany: A Down-Town Boulevard," *New York Daily Tribune* (February 21, 1877): 2; "Opposing the Down-Town Boulevard," *New York Daily Tribune* (March 3, 1877): 2; "The Down-Town Boulevard Opposed," *New York Daily Tribune* (March 9, 1877): 2; "The Great East River Bridge," *New York Times* (June 6, 1877): 8; "The New York and Brooklyn Bridge, as It Will Appear When Completed," *New York Daily Graphic* (June 20, 1877): 774–75; "The East River Bridge," *New York Times* (July 7, 1877): 8; "The Brooklyn Bridge," *New York Times* (July 13, 1877): 2; "Correspondence," *American Architect and Building News* 2 (July 28, 1877): 241–42; "The Suspension Bridge: Progress of the Great Work," *New York Times* (September 11, 1877): 5; "Local Miscellany: Passing Beneath the Cables," *New York Times* (September 17, 1877): 8; "The Demolition of Buildings to Make Room for the New York Approach of the East River Bridge," *New York Daily Graphic* (October 17, 1877): 745; "Is the Bridge a Nuisance," *New York Times* (October 31, 1877): 8; "Taking Lands for the Bridge," *New York Times* (December 18, 1877): 3; "Up Among the Spiders; or, How the Great Bridge Is Built," *Appletons' Journal* 4 (January 1878): 1–11; "Progress of the Great Bridge," *New York Daily Tribune* (February 5, 1878): 8; "Rapid Transit Over the Bridge," *New York Daily Tribune* (May 25, 1878): 10; "Opposition to the Bridge," *New York Daily Tribune* (August 21, 1878): 8; "East River Bridge Approaches," *New York Times* (August 28, 1878): 8; "Condition of the Brooklyn Bridge," *New York Daily Tribune* (October 5, 1878): 2; "Work on the Bridge," *New York Daily Tribune* (December 6, 1878): 5.

282. "Pictures of the Day," *New York Daily Graphic* (December 10, 1879): 286, 289.

283. "A Bit of Bridge History: The Opponents of the Structure Testifying," *New York Times* (March 21, 1879): 3; "Work on the Great Bridge," *New York Daily Tribune* (October 27, 1879): 2; Editorial, *New York Times* (November 18, 1879): 4; "The Great Engineer in New York: Count De Lesseps Inspecting the East River Bridge," *New York Daily Graphic* (February 28, 1880): 859–60; "The Brooklyn Bridge," *New York*

Times (April 1, 1880): 3; Editorial, *New York Times* (June 6, 1880): 4; "Work on the Great Bridge," *New York Times* (February 19, 1881): 8; "The Approach to the Bridge," *New York Times* (June 17, 1881): 8; "The Approach to the Bridge," *New York Times* (June 28, 1881): 8; "The East River Bridge," *New York Daily Graphic* (February 7, 1882): 674, 676–77; "Brooklyn Bridge Affairs," *New York Times* (September 7, 1882): 2; "Work on the Brooklyn Bridge," *New York Times* (September 21, 1882): 8; "More Room for Traffic," *New York Times* (November 23, 1882): 8; "Section of the East River Bridge, Showing Tramway, Wagon Road and Passenger Way," *New York Daily Graphic* (February 19, 1883): 765, 767.

284. *The New York and Brooklyn Bridge* (Brooklyn: Frederick Loeser & Co., 1883); *Opening Ceremonies of the New York and Brooklyn Bridge* (Brooklyn, 1883); "The Bridge Informally Opened," *New York Times* (April 2, 1883): 8; "The East River Bridge," *Building* 1 (May 1883): 106; "The East River Bridge Opening," *New York Evening Post* (May 17, 1883): 1; Editorial, *New York Times* (May 20, 1883): 6; "Traffic Over the Bridge," editorial, *New York Times* (May 23, 1883): 4; "The Great Event," *New York Daily Graphic* (May 24, 1883): 590–92; "The Building of the Bridge," *New York Times* (May 24, 1883): 2; "The Opening of the Bridge Yesterday," *New York Daily Graphic* (May 25, 1883): 595, 599–600; "Two Great Cities United," *New York Times* (May 25, 1883): 1–2; "The Opening of the Brooklyn Bridge Last Thursday," *New York Daily Graphic* (May 26, 1883): 603–4; "The People and the Bridge," editorial, *New York Times* (May 26, 1883): 4; "Traffic on the Bridge," *New York Times* (May 27, 1883): 1; "New York and Brooklyn," editorial, *New York Times* (May 29, 1883): 6; "The Grips Attached to the Bottom of Cars on the Brooklyn Bridge," *New York Daily Graphic* (August 14, 1883): 295; "The Bridge Railroad," *New York Times* (August 14, 1883): 8; "The Cars of the Brooklyn Bridge," *New York Daily Graphic* (August 27, 1883): 387; Stephen M. Ostrander, *A History of the City of Brooklyn and Kings County* (Brooklyn, 1894), 178–90.

285. "Two Great Cities United": 1.

286. Abram Hewitt, opening remarks, May 24, 1883, reprinted in *Opening Ceremonies of the New York and Brooklyn Bridge*, n.p.

287. "The Bridge Horror," *New York Daily Graphic* (May 31, 1883): 629–30; "Dead on the New Bridge," *New York Times* (May 31, 1883): 1–2; "The Disaster on the Brooklyn Bridge," *Building* 1 (June 1883): 120; "The Rush on the Bridge," *New York Daily Graphic* (June 1, 1883): 643–44; "Victims of the Crush," *New York Times* (June 1, 1883): 1–2.

288. "Our Impending Ruin," editorial, *New York Times* (October 15, 1883): 4.

289. Montgomery Schuyler, "The Bridge as a Monument," *Harper's Weekly* 27 (May 26, 1883): 326, reprinted in Schuyler, *American Architecture and Other Writings*, vol. 2: 331–44.

290. Schuyler, "A Great American Architect: Leopold Eidlitz. Part 1": 178.

291. Seth Low, opening remarks, May 24, 1883, quoted in McCullough, *The Great Bridge*, 536.

292. Gustav Lindenthal, "A Discussion of Long Span Bridges," *Engineering News* 19 (March 3, 1888): 155; "The Proposed Hudson River Suspension Bridge," *Scientific American* 64 (May 23, 1891): 319, 323; Condit, *The Port of New York*, 253, 256–58; Shanor, *The City That Never Was*, 134–41.

293. Editorial, *Building* 3 (August 5, 1885): 122; "The New Harlem Bridge," *New York Times* (July 17, 1886): 3; "Erection of the Harlem River Bridge at 181st Street," *Scientific American* 58 (February 18, 1888): 101; "The New Manhattan Bridge," *New York Times* (July 3, 1888): 8; William R. Hutton, *The Washington Bridge Over the Harlem River* (New York: Leo von Rosenberg, 1889); "Washington Bridge," editorial, *New York Times* (May 1, 1889): 4; King, *King's Handbook of New York* (1893), 176, 189–90; Kouwenhoven, *The Columbia Historical Portrait of New York*, 416; Reier, *The Bridges of New York*, 78–81; Landmarks Preservation Commission of the City of New York, LP-1222 (September 14, 1982); Dolkart, *Guide to New York City Landmarks*, 151; Diamonstein, *The Landmarks of New York II*, 195.

294. Montgomery Schuyler, "Art in Modern Bridges," *Century Magazine* 38 (May 1900): 12–25, reprinted in Schuyler, *American Architecture and Other Writings*, vol 2: 351–71.

CHAPTER 2
Representative Places

Government Buildings

1. Henry James to Sarah Butler Wister, January 23, 1875, in *Letters/Henry James*, ed. Leon Edel, 4 vols. (Cambridge, Mass.: Harvard University Press, Belknap Press, 1974–84), vol. 1: 470. Henry James to Isabella Stewart Gardner, December 7, 1881, in *Letters/Henry James*, vol. 2: 364.

2. "The New City Hall," *New York Times* (April 10, 1855): 1. Also see "A New City Hall," *New York Times* (March 20, 1857): 8; "The New City Hall Bill," *New York Times* (April 24, 1857): 8; I. N. Phelps Stokes, *The Iconography of Manhattan Island*, 6 vols. (New York: Robert H. Dodd, 1915–28; New York: Arno Press, 1967), vol. 6: 973; Deborah S. Gardner, "The Architecture of Commercial Capitalism: John Kellum and the Development of New York, 1840–1875" (Ph.D. diss., Columbia University, 1979): 162–74.

3. "The New City Hall," (April 10, 1855): 1.

4. "Beekman Street Expansion," *Architects' and Mechanics' Journal* 1 (November 1859): 30.

5. "Accepted Designs for New Municipal Buildings in the City of New York, Charles B. Atwood, Architect," *Building* 9 (December 29, 1888): plates; "Tower, New City Hall, N.Y., Charles B. Atwood, Arch't.," *American Architect and Building News* 27 (February 1, 1890): plate; Stern, Gilmartin, and Massengale, *New York 1900*, 61.

6. "The New Court House," *New York Times* (December 27, 1861): 3; "The County Court House," *New York Times* (July 15, 1862): 5; "The New Court House," *New York Times* (June 10, 1863): 8; "The County Court House," *New York Times* (July 15, 1865): 5; "The New County Court House," *New York Times* (December 26, 1865): 8; "The New County Court House and Charges of Corruption," editorial, *New York Times* (February 28, 1866): 4; "Board of Supervisors," *New York Times* (February 28, 1866): 8; "Letter from a Taxpayer," letter to the editor, *New York Times* (March 3, 1866): 4; "The New County Court House," *New York Times* (March 3, 1866): 8; "The New Court House Job," editorial, *New York Times* (March 11, 1866): 4; "Board of Supervisors," *New York Times* (June 27, 1866): 2; "What It Costs to Investigate Fraud," editorial, *New York Times* (November 17, 1866): 4; "The Marble in the New Court-House—A Very Rich Quarry," editorial, *New York Times* (December 26, 1866): 4; "The Court of Appeals and the New County Court-House," *New York Times* (March 12, 1867): 6; "The County Court-House Job," *New York Times* (May 6, 1867): 8; "The County Court-House: Extravagance and Plunder," editorial, *New York Times* (October 11, 1867): 4; John W. Kennion, *Architects' and Builders' Guide* (New York: Fitzpatrick & Hunter, 1868), part 3: 96; "The New County Court-House," *New York Times* (April 22, 1868): 8; "County Court-House," *Real Estate Record and Builders' Guide* 1 (September 12, 1868): 8; "Our Architecture Reviewed," *Architectural Review and American Builders' Journal* 1 (December 1868): 354; "The New County Court-House," *New York Times* (December 15, 1868): 8; "A Gulf for the Public Money," editorial, *New York Times* (December 2, 1870): 4; "Completing the New Court-House," *New York Times* (December 6, 1870): 5; "The New Court-House," *New York Times* (December 21, 1870): 8; "The New Court-House," *Real Estate Record and Builders' Guide* 4 (December 31, 1870): 3; "The New Court-House—What Has Been Done and What Remains to Be Accomplished," *New York Times* (April 4, 1871): 2; "Supplement," *New York Times* (July 2, 1871): n.p.; "Who Is Responsible," editorial, *New York Times* (July 3, 1871): 4; "Our Proofs of Fraud Against the City Government," editorial, *New York Times* (July 23, 1871): 4; "Repairs of New Buildings—Decay of Public Architecture," editorial, *New York Times* (July 28, 1871): 4–5; "Court-House Expenditures," *New York Times* (August 2, 1871): 3; "The Great Carpet Trick: The Real Cost of the Court-House Carpets—An Estimate by an Eminent Firm as to the Actual Quantity Required," *New York Times* (August 30, 1871): 1; "Notes and Clippings," *American Architect and Building News* 1 (April 22, 1876): 136; Montgomery Schuyler, "Architectural Malpractice," *New York World* (May 28, 1876): 4; Editorial, *American Architect and Building News* 1 (June 3, 1876): 1; "John Kellum," *American Architect and Building News* 1 (June 24, 1876): 204; "Correspondence," *American Architect and*

Building News 1 (June 24, 1876): 206–7; "New Court-House Extension," *New York Daily Tribune* (October 24, 1876): 8; "Notes and Clippings," *American Architect and Building News* 1 (November 4, 1876): 360; "The New Barn," editorial, *New York Times* (December 10, 1876): 6; William H. Morrell, "The Renewed 'New Court-House Impositions,'" *New York Times* (April 13, 1877): 2; "The Court-House Swindle," *New York Times* (April 29, 1877): 7; "Municipal Extravagance," *New York Times* (May 8, 1877): 2; "Court House Summary," *American Architect and Building News* 2 (November 17, 1877): 366; Warrington, "Correspondence," *American Architect and Building News* 3 (March 16, 1878): 94; Moses King, *King's Handbook of New York* (Boston: Moses King, 1893), 838–39; Montgomery Schuyler, "A Great American Architect: Leopold Eidlitz. Part 1," *Architectural Record* 24 (September 1908): 163–79; Alexander B. Callow Jr., *The Tweed Ring* (New York: Oxford University Press, 1966), 197–206; Gardner, "The Architecture of Commercial Capitalism: John Kellum and the Development of New York, 1840–1875": 161–210; Paul Goldberger, *The City Observed: New York* (New York: Random House, 1979), 29–30; White and Willensky, *AIA Guide* (1988), 62; Barbaralee Diamonstein, *The Landmarks of New York II* (New York: Harry N. Abrams, 1993), 138–39; Gregory F. Gilmartin, *Shaping the City: New York and the Municipal Art Society* (New York: Clarkson Potter, 1995), 47–48; Mary Elizabeth Brown, "Tweed Courthouse," in Kenneth T. Jackson, ed., *The Encyclopedia of New York City* (New Haven, Conn., and London: Yale University Press; New York: New-York Historical Society, 1995), 1206.

7. "The New County Court House," (December 26, 1865): 8.

8. For William Tweed and the so-called Tweed Ring, see Gustavus Meyers, *The History of Tammany Hall*, 2d rev. ed. (1917; New York: Dover, 1965); Dennis Lynch, *Boss Tweed: The Story of a Grim Generation* (New York: Bone and Liveright, 1927); M. R. Werner, *Tammany Hall* (Garden City, N.Y.: Doubleday, 1928); Seymour J. Mandelbaum, *Boss Tweed's New York* (New York: John Wiley & Sons, 1965); Callow, *The Tweed Ring*; Leo Hershkowitz, *Tweed's New York: Another Look* (Garden City, N.Y.: Doubleday, 1977); Oliver E. Allen, *The Tiger: The Rise and the Fall of Tammany Hall* (Reading, Mass.: Addison-Wesley, 1993).

9. Kennion, *Architects' and Builders' Guide*, part 3: 96.

10. For a discussion of the impact of the *New York Times*'s series of articles on the Tweed Ring, see Frank Luther Mott, *American Journalism 1690–1940* (New York: Macmillan, 1941), 382–84.

11. "Supplement," *New York Times*: n.p.

12. For a discussion of Thomas Nast's series of cartoons, see Albert Bigelow Paine, *Thomas Nast* (New York: Macmillan, 1904), 152–86.

13. "John Kellum," *American Architect and Building News*: 204.

14. Quoted in Callow, *The Tweed Ring*, 198.

15. "Jefferson Market and the New Courthouse," *New York Times* (February 3, 1874): 2; "Study for City Prison and Courts of New York, by C. Vaux and F. C. Withers, Architects," *New York Daily Graphic* (March 9, 1874): 57; Calvert Vaux and R. G. Hatfield, "The New City Prison," letter to Hon. William F. Havemeyer, Chairman of New City Prison Commission, January 23, 1874, reprinted in *New York Daily Graphic* (March 9, 1874): 60; Calvert Vaux, letter to William F. Havemeyer, February 10, 1874, reprinted in *New York Daily Graphic* (March 9, 1874): 60; "Study for City Prison and Courts, New York. Messrs. C. Vaux and F. C. Withers, Architects," *New-York Sketch-Book of Architecture* 1 (April 1874): 1–2, plate; "Design for Court House, Third Judicial District, New York. Messrs. Frederick C. Withers and C. Vaux, Architects," *New-York Sketch-Book of Architecture* 1 (July 1874): plate; "The New Jefferson Market Court-House," *New York Daily Graphic* (October 22, 1874): 815; "Pictures of the Day," *New York Daily Graphic* (May 31, 1875): 614, 617; "Court House, Bell Tower and Prison, Third Judicial District, New York," *New-York Sketch-Book of Architecture* 2 (June 1875): 1, plate; "Notes and Clippings," *American Architect and Building News* 1 (March 18, 1876): 96; "A Ninth Ward Resident and Taxpayer," letter to the editor, *New York Times* (July 9, 1876): 2; Editorial, *American Architect and Building News* 2 (February 10, 1877): 41; "Correspondence: The Third District Court-House Investigations," *American Architect and Building News* 2 (February 10, 1877): 45; "The Jefferson Market Court-House," *New York Daily Tribune* (February 10, 1877): 1–2; "A County Court-House," *New York Daily Tribune* (May 8, 1877): 5; "Municipal Extravagance": 2; "The Jefferson Market Monument," *New York Times* (May 9,

1877): 4; Editorial, *New York Daily Tribune* (June 19, 1877): 4; "The Jefferson Market Prison Opened," *New York Daily Tribune* (April 4, 1878): 1–2; "The Third District Court-House, Bell Tower, and Prison, New York. Messrs. F. C. Withers and C. Vaux, Architects," *American Architect and Building News* 3 (June 15, 1878): 209, plate; "Correspondence," *American Architect and Building News* 5 (February 1, 1879): 37–38; "Rebuilding Jefferson Market," *New York Times* (June 22, 1882): 8; "The Jefferson Market (Third District) Court-House, New York, N.Y. Mr. F. C. Withers, Architect, N.Y.," *American Architect and Building News* 18 (July 25, 1885): 42, plate; C. Hinckeldeyn, "A Foreigner's View of American Architecture," *American Architect and Building News* 25 (May 25, 1889): 243–44; King, *King's Handbook of New York* (1893), 262, 839; Stokes, *The Iconography of Manhattan Island*, vol. 5: 1984; John A. Kouwenhoven, *The Columbia Historical Portrait of New York* (Garden City, N.Y.: Doubleday, 1953), 480; Alan Burnham, ed., *New York Landmarks* (Middletown, Conn.: Wesleyan University Press, 1963), 138–39; Nathan Silver, *Lost New York* (Boston: Houghton Mifflin, 1967), 104–5; Landmarks Preservation Commission of the City of New York, *Greenwich Village Historic District Designation Report* (New York, 1969), 183, 185; *New York City Architecture: Selections from the Historic American Buildings Survey*, no. 7 (Washington, D.C.: U.S. Department of the Interior, Historic American Buildings Survey, 1969); Edward B. Watson, *New York Then and Now* (New York: Dover, 1976), 96–97; Francis R. Kowsky, "The Architecture of Frederick C. Withers (1828–1901)," *Journal of the Society of Architectural Historians* 35 (May 1976): 83, 105; Goldberger, *The City Observed*, 80–81; Francis R. Kowsky, *The Architecture of Frederick Clarke Withers* (Middletown, Conn.: Wesleyan University Press, 1980), 109–18; White and Willensky, *AIA Guide* (1988), 119–20; William Alex, *Calvert Vaux: Architect and Planner* (New York: Ink, 1994), 194–95; Christopher Gray, "A Stopped Clock Sired the Preservation Movement," *New York Times* (April 3, 1994), X: 5; Margot Gayle, "Jefferson Market Courthouse," in Jackson, ed., *The Encyclopedia of New York City*, 616–17; Robert A. M. Stern, Thomas Mellins, and David Fishman, *New York 1960: Architecture and Urbanism Between the Second World War and the Bicentennial* (New York: Monacelli Press, 1995), 1131–32, 1146.

16. Kowsky, *The Architecture of Frederick Clarke Withers*, 109.

17. "The Jefferson Market Monument": 4.

18. "Municipal Extravagance": 2.

19. "The Jefferson Market Monument": 4.

20. "Study for City Prison and Courts, New York. Messrs. C. Vaux and F. C. Withers, Architects": plate.

21. "The Jefferson Market Court-House," *New York Daily Tribune*: 1.

22. "Jefferson Market," *Real Estate Record and Builders' Guide* 32 (September 15, 1883): 633–34. Also see "Brick Architecture in New York," *Building* 1 (May 1883): 105–6; "Municipal Architecture," *Real Estate Record and Builders' Guide* 33 (March 15, 1884): 260–61; "New York Markets," *Building* 2 (May 1884): 94.

23. "Municipal Architecture," (March 15, 1884): 260–61.

24. "The New Post-Office," *New York Times* (May 22, 1866): 2; "Civilization in New York," *Harper's Weekly* 11 (January 5, 1867): 2; "The Architects and the Post-Office Commissioners," *New York Daily Tribune* (February 19, 1867): 4; "The New Post-Office," *New York Times* (June 7, 1867): 2; "The New York Post Office," *New York Times* (June 16, 1867): 3; "The New Post-Office," *New York Times* (December 29, 1867): 8; Kennion, *Architects' and Builders' Guide*, part 1: 67–70; "Architectural Cheese-Parings," editorial, *New York Daily Tribune* (February 28, 1868): 4; "The New Post-Office," *New York Times* (February 29, 1868): 8; "The New Post-Office in the Park," editorial, *New York Times* (March 1, 1868): 4; "Report on the New Post-Office," *Real Estate Record and Builders' Guide* 1 (April 11, 1868): 1–2; "Report on the New Post-Office," *Real Estate Record and Builders' Guide* 1 (April 18, 1868): 1–2; "A Suggestion," *Real Estate Record and Builders' Guide* 1 (July 18, 1868): 1; "The New Post Office," *New York Times* (August 10, 1869): 1; George Templeton Strong, diary entries dated August 10, 1869, February 24, 1874, and May 7, 1874, in *The Diary of George Templeton Strong*, eds. Allan Nevins and Milton Halsey Thomas, 4 vols. (New York: Macmillan, 1952), vol. 4: 251, 515, 520; "The Post-Office Building, New York," *Harper's Weekly* 13 (October 23, 1869): 676, 679; "The New City Post-Office," *Harper's Weekly* 14 (November 12, 1870): 725, 727; "The New York Post-Office,"

editorial, *New York Times* (December 6, 1870): 4; "Public Improvements," *Real Estate Record and Builders' Guide* 6 (December 10, 1870): 1; "The New Post-Office," editorial, *New York Times* (December 25, 1870): 4; "The New York Post-Office," *New York Times* (April 26, 1871): 4; "The New Post-Office," *New York Times* (November 1, 1871): 2; "The New York City Post-Office," *Builder* [London] 29 (November 25, 1871): 924, 927; James D. McCabe Jr., *Lights and Shadows of New York Life; or, The Sights and Sensations of the Great City* (Philadelphia: National Publishing, 1872; New York: Farrar, Straus & Giroux, 1970), 449–60; "New Post-Office," *Real Estate Record and Builders' Guide* 10 (September 28, 1872): 1; Montgomery Schuyler, "Mullett and Logan," *New York World* (June 28, 1874): 4; Montgomery Schuyler, "Mullett's Monkeyshines," *New York World* (July 5, 1874): 4; "The New York Post-Office," *New York Daily Graphic* (December 24, 1874): 399, 401; Montgomery Schuyler, "The New Post-Office," *New York World* (January 24, 1875): 5; Montgomery Schuyler, "The New Tribune Building," *New York World* (May 2, 1875): 4–5; "The New Post Office," *New York Times* (July 22, 1875): 8; "The New Post-Office," *New York Daily Tribune* (July 30, 1875): 2; "The New United States Court-Rooms," *New York Times* (July 30, 1875): 3; "Law Reports," *New York Times* (August 4, 1875): 3; "The New York Post Office," *New York Times* (August 24, 1875): 2; "The New Post-Office," *New York Daily Tribune* (August 25, 1875): 8; "Plans of the New Post Office," *New York Daily Graphic* (August 27, 1875): 434; "The New York Post Office," *New York Times* (August 27, 1875): 2; "The New Post-Office," *New York Daily Graphic* (August 28, 1875): 437, 439; "In the New Post Office," *New York Times* (August 28, 1875): 2; Editorial, *New York Times* (August 29, 1875): 6; "The New Post Office," *New York Times* (August 30, 1875): 1; "Pictures of the Day," *New York Daily Graphic* (August 31, 1875): 456, 458; "The New Post Office," *New York Times* (August 31, 1875): 8; "The New Post Office—Interior View of the Main Room," *New York Daily Graphic* (September 4, 1875): 492; "The New Post-Office," *New York Daily Graphic* (September 7, 1875): 516; "Interior Views in the New Post-Office," *New York Daily Graphic* (September 9, 1875): 533; Editorial, *New York Times* (November 11, 1875): 4; "A Wonderful Workshop," *New York Times* (January 1, 1876): 2; A.F.O., "A Chapter on Architecture," letter to the editor, *Real Estate Record and Builders' Guide* 17 (May 20, 1876): 388–89; "Training Post Office Clerks," editorial, *New York Times* (July 23, 1876): 6; "Architectural New York," editorial, *New York Times* (March 25, 1883): 8; Editorial, *New York Times* (September 21, 1883): 4; "A New Post Office Station," *New York Times* (May 14, 1890): 8; "An Up-Town Post Office," *New York Times* (October 13, 1890): 2; "The Need for a New Post Office," editorial, *New York Times* (October 15, 1890): 4; "How Is This for a Dicker?" *New York Times* (October 26, 1890): 16; Editorial, *New York Times* (November 16, 1890): 4; "Its Facilities Outgrown," *New York Times* (May 23, 1891): 8; "It Is Very Much Needed," *New York Times* (May 25, 1891): 3; King, *King's Handbook of New York* (1893), 265–66; Stokes, *The Iconography of Manhattan Island*, vol. 3: 845–46, 935, 974, plate 163, vol. 5: 1923, 1927–29, 1931, 1934–35, 1947, 1955, 1958; "Topics of The Times: An Ohio Builder," *New York Times* (August 17, 1938): 18; Rosalie Thorne McKenna, "James Renwick, Jr., and the Second Empire Style in the United States," *Magazine of Art* 44 (March 1951): 97–101; Silver, *Lost New York*, 106; Lawrence Wodehouse, "Alfred B. Mullett and His French Style Government Buildings," *Journal of the Society of Architectural Historians* 31 (March 1972): 27–37; Mary Black, *Old New York in Early Photographs* (New York: Dover, 1973), plates 39–40, 42; John Grafton, *New York in the Nineteenth Century* (New York: Dover, 1977), 177–78; Sarah Bradford Landau, *Edward T. and William A. Potter: American Victorian Architects* (New York: Garland, 1979), 291; Paul R. Baker, *Richard Morris Hunt* (Cambridge, Mass.: MIT Press, 1980), 171–72, 540; Donald J. Lehman, "Alfred B. Mullett," in *Macmillan Encyclopedia of Architects*, 4 vols. (New York: Free Press; London: Collier Macmillan, 1982), vol. 3: 249–51; Stern, Gilmartin, and Massengale, *New York 1900*, 61, 165; Robert A. M. Stern, Gregory Gilmartin, and Thomas Mellins, assisted by David Fishman and Raymond W. Gastil, *New York 1930: Architecture and Urbanism Between the Two World Wars* (New York: Rizzoli International Publications, 1987), 94, 96, 713; Mary E. Bellor, "Biographies of the Architects," in *Architectural Drawings of the Old Executive Office Building, 1871–1888: Creating an American Masterpiece*, exhibition catalogue (Washington, D.C.: AIA Press, 1988), 68; David W. Dunlap, *On Broadway: A Journey Uptown Over Time* (New York: Rizzoli International Publications, 1990), 45; Lawrence Wodehouse, "Designs by Mullett as Supervising Architect of the Treasury Department, 1865–74," in D. Mullett Smith, *A. B. Mullett: His Relevance in American Architecture and Historic Preservation* (Washington, D.C.: Mullett-Smith, 1990), 29–37; Stern, Mellins, and Fishman, *New York 1960*, 1091.

25. "Report on the New Post-Office," (April 11, 1868): 1–2.

26. "A Suggestion": 1.

27. "Civilization in New York": 2.

28. "The New Post-Office," (June 7, 1867): 2.

29. Roger Hale Newton, *Town & Davis, Architects* (New York: Columbia University Press, 1942), 306–8, fig. 31; Talbot Hamlin, "The Rise of Eclecticism in New York," *Journal of the Society of Architectural Historians* 11 (May 1952): 3–8; Francis R. Kowsky, "Simplicity and Dignity: The Public and Institutional Buildings of Alexander Jackson Davis," in Amelia Peck, ed., *Alexander Jackson Davis: American Architect 1803–1892*, with an introduction by Jane B. Davies (New York: Metropolitan Museum of Art and Rizzoli International Publications, 1992), 40–57. Also see untitled manuscripts in the A. J. Davis Collection in the New-York Historical Society.

30. Alexander Jackson Davis, note in the A. J. Davis Collection, New-York Historical Society.

31. "Architectural Cheese-Parings": 4.

32. Strong, diary entry dated August 10, 1869, in *The Diary of George Templeton Strong*, vol. 4: 251.

33. "New Post-Office," (September 28, 1872): 1.

34. *Annual Report, Supervising Architect, United States Treasury Department* (1873), 4–5, quoted in Stokes, *The Iconography of Manhattan Island*, vol. 5: 1955.

35. Strong, diary entry dated February 24, 1874, in *The Diary of George Templeton Strong*, vol. 4: 515.

36. Strong, diary entry dated May 7, 1874, in *The Diary of George Templeton Strong*, vol. 4: 520.

37. Schuyler, "Mullett's Monkeyshines": 4.

38. Schuyler, "The New Post-Office": 5.

39. For useful general discussions of the evolution of the New York City Police Department, see McCabe, *Lights and Shadows of New York Life*, 171–85; Augustine Costello, *Our Police Protectors* (New York: A. E. Costello, 1885; Montclair, N.J.: Patterson Smith, 1972); King, *King's Handbook of New York* (1893), 522–26; Stokes, *The Iconography of Manhattan Island*, vol. 3: 675; James F. Richardson, *The New York Police: Colonial Times to 1901* (New York: Oxford University Press, 1970); Joseph P. Viteritti, "Police," in Jackson, ed., *The Encyclopedia of New York City*, 910–13.

40. "Police Headquarters," *New York Times* (July 14, 1869): 8; McCabe, *Lights and Shadows of New York Life*, 182–85; King, *King's Handbook of New York* (1893), 525.

41. "Police Headquarters": 8.

42. White and Willensky, *AIA Guide* (1988), 79.

43. "Municipal Architecture," (March 15, 1884): 260–61.

44. "Two Model Structures," *New York Times* (September 26, 1885): 8; "The Costly and Substantial Buildings of 1886," *Real Estate Record and Builders' Guide* 39 (January 1, 1887): 6; White and Willensky, *AIA Guide* (1988), 359.

45. For discussions of the development of firefighting in New York, see McCabe, *Lights and Shadows of New York Life*, 430–32; Augustine Costello, *Our Fireman: A History of the New York Fire Department* (New York: A. E. Costello, 1887); Stokes, *The Iconography of Manhattan Island*, vol. 3: 586, 713, vol. 5: 1915–16; Lowell M. Limpus, *History of the New York Fire Department* (New York: E. P. Dutton, 1940); Donald J. Cannon, "Firefighting," in Jackson, ed., *The Encyclopedia of New York City*, 408–12.

46. Landmarks Preservation Commission of the City of New York, *SoHo—Cast-Iron Historic District Designation Report* (New York, 1973), 168; Rebecca Zurier, *The American Firehouse* (New York: Abbeville, 1982), 82–83; White and Willensky, *AIA Guide* (1988), 100.

47. "A New Engine House," *Real Estate Record and Builders' Guide* 36 (October 10, 1885): 1096; Montgomery Schuyler, "The Work of N. Le Brun & Sons," *Architectural Record* 27 (May 1910): 364–81; Stern, Gilmartin, and Massengale, *New York 1900*, 69.

48. "A New Engine House": 1096.

49. Schuyler, "The Work of N. Le Brun & Sons": 373–74.

50. Landmarks Preservation Commission of the City of New York, *Tribeca West Historic District Designation Report* (New York, 1991), 293–94.

51. Landmarks Preservation Commission of the City of New York, LP-1962 (June 17, 1997).

52. "Out Among the Builders," *Real Estate Record and Builders' Guide* 33 (June 28, 1884): 698; "Two Model Structures": 8; "The New Fire Headquarters," *New York Daily Graphic* (May 14, 1887): 618, 621; "Fire Department Headquarters," *Real Estate Record and Builders' Guide* 39 (June 18, 1887): 830; Schuyler, "The Work of N. Le Brun & Sons": 372, 374; Zurier, *The American Firehouse*, 96–97; Stern, Gilmartin, and Massengale, *New York 1900*, 69; White and Willensky, *AIA Guide* (1988), 359.

53. "Fire Department Headquarters": 830.

54. Schuyler, "The Work of N. Le Brun & Sons": 374.

Places of Learning

1. For useful histories of Columbia College, which became Columbia University in the City of New York in 1912, from its founding as King's College through the post-Civil War period, see James D. McCabe Jr., *Lights and Shadows of New York Life; or, The Sights and Sensations of the Great City* (Philadelphia: National Publishing, 1872; New York: Farrar, Straus & Giroux, 1970), 672–73; "Columbia College," *Harper's New Monthly Magazine* 69 (November 1884): 813–31; Moses King, *King's Handbook of New York* (Boston: Moses King, 1893), 270, 272–74; *A History of Columbia University, 1754–1904* (New York: Columbia University Press, 1904); Frederick Paul Keppel, *Columbia* (New York: Oxford University Press, 1914); Robert Arrowsmith, *Columbia of Yesterday* (New York: Columbia University, 1926); John William Robson, *A Guide to Columbia University* (New York: Columbia University Press, 1937); William F. Russel, ed., *The Rise of a University* (New York: Columbia University Press, 1937); John A. Kouwenhoven, *The Columbia Historical Portrait of New York* (Garden City, N.Y.: Doubleday, 1953), 7, 67, 126, 199, 252, 256–57; David C. Humphrey, *From King's College to Columbia, 1746–1800* (New York: Columbia University Press, 1976); Thomas Bender, *New York Intellect: A History of Intellectual Life in New York City from 1750 to the Beginnings of Our Own Time* (New York: Alfred A. Knopf, 1987), 19–25, 92; Harold Wechsler, "Columbia," in Kenneth T. Jackson, ed., *The Encyclopedia of New York City* (New Haven, Conn., and London: Yale University Press; New York: New-York Historical Society, 1995), 259–61; Barry Bergdoll, "The Genesis and Legacy of McKim, Mead & White's Master Plan for Columbia University," in Barry Bergdoll, Hollee Haswell, and Janet Parks, *Mastering McKim's Plan: Columbia's First Century on Morningside Heights* (New York: Columbia University, 1997), 22–34.

2. Reverend Andrew Burnaby, quoted in Milton Halsey Thomas, "The King's College Building," *New-York Historical Society Quarterly* 39 (January 1955): 23–61.

3. Adolf Placzek, "Design for Columbia College 1813," *Journal of the Society of Architectural Historians* 11 (May 1952): 22–23; Paul Venable Turner, *Campus: An American Planning Tradition* (New York: Architectural History Foundation; Cambridge, Mass.: MIT Press, 1984), 110–11; Bergdoll, "The Genesis and Legacy of McKim, Mead & White's Master Plan for Columbia University," in Bergdoll, Haswell, and Parks, *Mastering McKim's Plan: Columbia's First Century on Morningside Heights*, 23. Plans and renderings of Renwick's proposed building are housed in the Drawings and Archives Collection of Avery Library, Columbia University.

4. C. C. Haight, quoted in "Columbia College," *Harper's New Monthly Magazine*: 820.

5. Montgomery Schuyler, "Architecture of American Colleges, IV—New York City Colleges," *Architectural Record* 27 (June 1910): 442–69. Also see Charles Lockwood, *Manhattan Moves Uptown* (Boston: Houghton Mifflin, 1976), 104.

6. Robson, *A Guide to Columbia University*, 14.

7. "Columbia College Removal," *New York Times* (April 1, 1857): 1; "Columbia College Excelsior," *New York Times* (May 12, 1857): 3; *A History of Columbia University, 1754–1904*, 130–34; I. N. Phelps Stokes, *The Iconography of Manhattan Island*, 6 vols. (New York: Robert H. Dodd,

1916–28; New York: Arno Press, 1967), vol. 3: 940, vol. 5: 1869; Kouwenhoven, *The Columbia Historical Portrait of New York*, 199.

8. Christopher Gray, "Neighborhood: A History of Park Avenue, Part II," *Avenue* (November 1982): 68–75.

9. "Columbia College," *Harper's New Monthly Magazine*: 824.

10. "The Demolition of Columbia College," *New York Times* (April 15, 1857): 3; "The Last Prayers at Old Columbia," *New York Times* (May 9, 1857): 3; Stokes, *The Iconography of Manhattan Island*, vol. 3: 712, vol. 5: 1868.

11. "Columbia College," *New York Evening Post* (May 11, 1857): 3. Also see Stokes, *The Iconography of Manhattan Island*, vol. 3: 171, plate 142b, vol. 5: 1869.

12. "Departmental News," *School of Mines Quarterly* 11 (1889–90): 94.

13. "School of Mines, Columbia College, New York City. Mr. C.C. Haight, Architect," *New-York Sketch-Book of Architecture* 3 (January 1876): 1, plate; Montgomery Schuyler, "The Works of Charles Coolidge Haight," *Architectural Record* 6 (July 1899): 1–102; Stokes, *The Iconography of Manhattan Island*, vol. 5: 1920.

14. Steven M. Bedford, "History I: The Founding of the School," in Richard Oliver, ed., *The Making of an Architect, 1881–1981* (New York: Rizzoli International Publications, 1981), 5–12; Steven M. Bedford and Susan M. Strauss, "History II: 1881–1912," in Oliver, ed., *The Making of an Architect, 1881–1981*, 23–48; David G. DeLong, "William R. Ware and the Pursuit of Suitability: 1881–1903," in Oliver, ed., *The Making of an Architect, 1881–1981*, 13–22.

15. Schuyler, "The Works of Charles Coolidge Haight": 4–5.

16. "School of Mines, Columbia College, New York City. Mr. C.C. Haight, Architect": 1.

17. "Columbia College Improvements," *New York Daily Tribune* (May 28, 1878): 8; "New York's Chief College," editorial, *New York Daily Tribune* (May 28, 1878): 4; W., "Correspondence," *American Architect and Building News* 3 (June 8, 1878): 201–2; Editorial, *Columbia Spectator* (January 13, 1879): 86; Montgomery Schuyler, "Recent Building in New York—I," *American Architect and Building News* 9 (April 9, 1881): 176–77; "The Ten Best Buildings in the U.S.," *American Architect and Building News* 17 (June 13, 1885): 282; "Meeting of the American Association for the Advancement of Science, New York, 1887," *Scientific American* 57 (August 13, 1887): 95, 100; Schuyler, "The Works of Charles Coolidge Haight": 5–8, 11; *A History of Columbia University, 1754–1904*, 144–45; Nathan Silver, *Lost New York* (Boston: Houghton Mifflin, 1967), 99; Arnold Lewis and Keith Morgan, *American Victorian Architecture* (New York: Dover, 1978), 28, 143; Bergdoll, "The Genesis and Legacy of McKim, Mead & White's Master Plan for Columbia University," in Bergdoll, Haswell, and Parks, *Mastering McKim's Plan: Columbia's First Century on Morningside Heights*, 26–27.

18. Schuyler, "Recent Building in New York—I": 176–77.

19. Schuyler, "Recent Building in New York—I": 176–77.

20. "Columbia College," *Harper's New Monthly Magazine*: 824–25.

21. "The Ten Best Buildings in the U.S.": 282.

22. Schuyler, "The Works of Charles Coolidge Haight": 8.

23. "Out Among the Builders," *Real Estate Record and Builders' Guide* 27 (April 23, 1881): 391; "Out Among the Builders," *Real Estate Record and Builders' Guide* 29 (March 25, 1882): 271; "The New Building," *Columbia Spectator* (January 11, 1883): 91–92; Russell Sturgis, "New Building for Columbia College," *Building* 1 (May 1883): 104; M. G. Van Rensselaer, "Recent Architecture in America—I," *Century Magazine* 28 (May 1884): 48–67; "Columbia College," *Harper's New Monthly Magazine*: 826; Russell Sturgis, "Good Things in Modern Architecture," *Architectural Record* 8 (July–September 1898): 92–110; Schuyler, "The Works of Charles Coolidge Haight": 8–10; Bergdoll, "The Genesis and Legacy of McKim, Mead & White's Master Plan for Columbia University," in Bergdoll, Haswell, and Parks, *Mastering McKim's Plan: Columbia's First Century on Morningside Heights*, 26, 29.

24. Sturgis, "New Building for Columbia College": 104.

25. "Columbia College," *Harper's New Monthly Magazine*: 826.

26. Van Rensselaer, "Recent Architecture in America—I": 64–65.

27. Schuyler, "The Works of Charles Coolidge Haight": 8–9.

28. "Columbia College," *Real Estate Record and Builders' Guide* 31 (April 21, 1883): 165–66.

29. Van Rensselaer, "Recent Architecture in America—I": 64–65. For an extensive discussion of American quadrangular campus planning, see Turner, *Campus*, 215–47.

30. Arrowsmith, *Columbia of Yesterday*, 31.

31. "Money for a Gymnasium," *New York Times* (April 12, 1887): 9; "A Columbia Clubhouse," *New York Times* (March 28, 1890): 3.

32. "Out Among the Builders," *Real Estate Record and Builders' Guide* 42 (May 12, 1888): 604–5. Plans for Haight's proposed building are housed in the Drawings and Archives Collection of Avery Library, Columbia University.

33. "Columbia College Improvements," *Building* 11 (September 28, 1889): 108.

34. "Columbia College," *Harper's New Monthly Magazine*: 828, 831.

35. "Barnard College," *Columbia Spectator* (April 25, 1889): 50–51; "Barnard College," *New York Times* (October 8, 1889): 2; King, *King's Handbook of New York* (1893), 274; Stokes, *The Iconography of Manhattan Island*, vol. 5: 2000; Annie Nathan Meyer, *Barnard Beginnings* (Boston: Houghton Mifflin, 1935), 147–53; Robson, *A Guide to Columbia University*, 9; Jane Allen, "Barnard College," in Jackson, ed., *The Encyclopedia of New York City*, 77.

36. Frederic S. Lee, "The School of Medicine," in *A History of Columbia University, 1754–1904*, 307–34.

37. "Out Among the Builders," *Real Estate Record and Builders' Guide* 34 (November 15, 1884): 1150; "City News," *Building* 14 (February 20, 1886): 96.

38. "To Go to White Plains," *New York Times* (May 19, 1888): 5.

39. "The Removal of Columbia," editorial, *New York Times* (February 28, 1892): 4. Also see "The Prospects of Removal to Bloomingdale," *Columbia Spectator* (January 7, 1892): 99; "The Bloomingdale Grounds," *Columbia Spectator* (February 4, 1892): 127; Stern, Gilmartin, and Massengale, *New York 1900*, 404–11.

40. "The Bloomingdale Grounds": 127.

41. McCabe, *Lights and Shadows of New York Life*, 669; King, *King's Handbook of New York* (1893), 269, 271; Samuel W. Patterson, *Hunter College: Eighty-Five Years of Service* (New York: Lantern, 1955), 13–76; Selma Berrol, "Hunter College," in Jackson, ed., *The Encyclopedia of New York City*, 575–76.

42. "The General Theological Seminary," *Real Estate Record and Builders' Guide* 31 (May 26, 1883): 216; "The General Theological Seminary," *The Churchman* (February 2, 1884): 119–20; "Sherred Hall," *Real Estate Record and Builders' Guide* 33 (March 29, 1884): 313–14; W. S. Perry, *The History of the American Episcopal Church*, 2 vols. (Boston, 1885), vol 2: 512; "The Chapel of the Good Shepherd of the General Theological Seminary, N.Y.," *The Churchman* (October 27, 1888): plate; "Chapel of the General Theological Seminary," *Architectural Record* 1 (September 1891): 60, plate; King, *King's Handbook of New York* (1893), 281–83; Schuyler, "The Works of Charles Coolidge Haight": 19–33; Theodore M. Riley, *A Memorial Biography of the Very Reverend Eugene Augustus Hoffman* (Jamaica, N.Y.: Marion, 1904), 622–26; Samuel Macauley Jackson, *The New Schaff-Herzog Encyclopedia of Religious Knowledge* (New York: Funk and Wagnalls, 1911), 384–85; Stokes, *The Iconography of Manhattan Island*, vol. 5: 1604, 1981, 1987; William Wilson Manross, *A History of the American Episcopal Church* (New York: Morehouse-Gorham, 1950), 239–45; Powel Mills Dawley, *The Story of the General Theological Seminary* (New York: Oxford University Press, 1969); Landmarks Preservation Commission of the City of New York, *Chelsea Historic District Designation Report* (New York, 1970), 21–25; Sarah Bradford Landau, *Edward T. and William A. Potter: American Victorian Architects* (New York: Garland, 1979), 332; Bernice L. Thomas, *Dean Hoffman's "Grand Design": The General Theological Seminary 1879–1902* (New York: General Theological Seminary, 1988); White and Willensky, *AIA Guide* (1988), 174; Christopher Gray, "Restoration Drive Begun for Chelsea Landmark," *New York Times* (May 1, 1988), X: 14, reprinted in Christopher Gray, *Changing New York: The Architectural Scene* (New York: Dover, 1992), 48; Sally Siddiqi, "Restoring a Nineteenth Century Seminary," *Metropolis* 8 (April 1989): 21; Barbaralee Diamonstein, *The Landmarks of New York II* (New York: Harry N. Abrams, 1993), 446; J. Robert Wright, "General Theological Seminary," in Jackson, ed., *The Encyclopedia of New York City*, 457–58.

43. Schuyler, "The Works of Charles Coolidge Haight": 21–22.

44. Eugene Augustus Hoffman, quoted in Thomas, *Dean Hoffman's "Grand Design": The General Theological Seminary 1879–1902*, 5.

45. Schuyler, "The Works of Charles Coolidge Haight": 27. For Cobb's plan, see Charles E. Jenkins, "The University of Chicago," *Architectural Record* 4 (October–December 1894): 229–46.

46. "The General Theological Seminary," *The Churchman*: 120.

47. "The General Theological Seminary," *Real Estate Record and Builders' Guide*: 216.

48. "Sherred Hall": 313.

49. Schuyler, "The Works of Charles Coolidge Haight": 28.

50. Schuyler, "The Works of Charles Coolidge Haight": 32–33.

51. *Union Theological Seminary, New-York, 1872*, n.p., Registrar's Archives, Union Theological Seminary, New York; "Union Theological Seminary, New York, N.Y., Messrs. W.A. Porter [*sic*] and J. Brown [*sic*], Architects, New York, N.Y.," *American Architect and Building News* 11 (April 15, 1882): 174, plate; "The Union Theological Seminary," *Real Estate Record and Builders' Guide* 32 (September 22, 1883): 706; "Union Theological Seminary, Park Avenue," *Harper's Weekly* 28 (February 9, 1884): 96; "The New Building of the Union Theological Seminary," *New York Daily Graphic* (April 4, 1884): 257; *Services in Adams Chapel at the Dedication of the New Buildings of the Union Theological Seminary* (New York, December 9, 1884); "New Theological Buildings: The Many Handsome Gifts to the Union Seminary," *New York Times* (December 10, 1884): 3; "The Union Theological Seminary, Park Avenue and 69th Street, New York City," *Building* 4 (March 27, 1886): 150, plate; George Lewis Prentiss, *The Union Theological Seminary in the City of New York* (New York: Anson D. F. Randolph, 1889); King, *King's Handbook of New York* (1893), 282, 284; Montgomery Schuyler, "The Work of William A. Potter," *Architectural Record* 26 (September 1909): 176–96; Stokes, *The Iconography of Manhattan Island*, vol. 5: 1738, 1750, 1755, 1987; Charles Ripley Gillet, "Detailed History of the Union Theological Seminary," 1937, unpublished typescript in the collection of the Union Theological Seminary; Landau, *Edward T. and William A. Potter: American Victorian Architects*, 329–32, 477, figs. 219–22; Robert T. Handy, *A History of the Union Theological Seminary in New York* (New York: Columbia University Press, 1987); Randall Balmer, "Union Theological Seminary," in Jackson, ed., *The Encyclopedia of New York City*, 1211–12.

52. Paul R. Baker, *Richard Morris Hunt* (Cambridge, Mass.: MIT Press, 1980), 539.

53. Roswell Dwight Hitchcock, quoted in Handy, *A History of the Union Theological Seminary in New York*, 57.

54. King, *King's Handbook of New York* (1893), 282.

55. "The Union Theological Seminary," *Real Estate Record and Builders' Guide*: 706.

56. Schuyler, "The Work of William A. Potter": 190–91.

57. "Improvements and Additions to Trinity Church Schools. Mr. Richard M. Upjohn, Architect," *New-York Sketch-Book of Architecture* 1 (June 1874): 1, plate 21; "Trinity Parish School, New York, N.Y., R. M. Upjohn, Architect," *American Architect and Building News* 3 (April 6, 1876): 121, plate.

58. George Templeton Strong, diary entry dated April 21, 1871, in *The Diary of George Templeton Strong*, eds. Allan Nevins and Milton Halsey Thomas, 4 vols. (New York: MacMillan, 1952), vol. 4: 351.

59. "Trinity Parish School, New York, N.Y., R. M. Upjohn, Architect": 121.

60. Montgomery Schuyler, "The Works of Cady, Berg & See," *Architectural Record* 6 (April–June 1897): 517–53.

61. For discussions of public education in New York, see "The Public Schools of New York," *Tribune Monthly* (March 1896): 1–126; Diane Ravitch, *The Great School Wars—New York City, 1805–1973: A History of the Public Schools as Battlefield of Social Change* (New York: Basic Books, 1974); Diane Ravitch and Ronald K. Goodenow, eds., *Educating an Urban People: The New York City Experience* (New York: Teachers College Press, 1981); David Ment, "Public Schools," in Jackson, ed., *The Encyclopedia of New York City*, 955–61.

62. "Municipal Architecture," *Real Estate Record and Builders' Guide* 33 (March 15, 1884): 260–61.

63. White and Willensky, *AIA Guide* (1988), 162; Landmarks Preservation Commission of the City of New York, LP-1836 (June 25, 1996).

64. White and Willensky, *AIA Guide* (1988), 135; Landmarks Preservation Commission of the City of New York, LP-1836 (June 25, 1996), 7.

65. New York City Board of Education, *Annual Financial and Statistical Report* (New York, 1906–08), 39.

66. White and Willensky, *AIA Guide* (1988), 161; Landmarks Preservation Commission of the City of New York, LP-1836 (June 25, 1996), 7.

67. "The Costly and Substantial Buildings of 1886," *Real Estate Record and Builders' Guide* 39 (January 11, 1887): 6–8; "The Public Schools of New York," *Tribune Monthly*: 7–8.

68. "The Costly and Substantial Buildings of 1886": 6–8; "The Public Schools of New York," *Tribune Monthly*: 13–14; New York City Board of Education, *Annual Financial and Statistical Report*, 6.

69. For schools designed by C.B.J. Synder and under his jurisdiction, see Stern, Gilmartin, and Massengale, *New York 1900*, 79–86.

Museums

1. "New-York Historical Society," *New York Times* (October 18, 1855): 2; Moses King, *King's Handbook of New York* (Boston: Moses King, 1893), 330–31; Robert H. Kelby, *The New-York Historical Society, 1804–1904* (New York: New-York Historical Society, 1905); I. N. Phelps Stokes, *The Iconography of Manhattan Island*, 6 vols. (New York: Robert H. Dodd, 1915–28; New York: Arno Press, 1967), vol. 3: 957, vol. 5: 1862, 1870; Robert Vail, *Knickerbocker Birthday: A Sesqui-Centennial History of the New-York Historical Society, 1804–1954* (New York: New-York Historical Society, 1954); Rebecca Read Shanor, *The City That Never Was* (New York: Viking Penguin, 1988), 38–39.

2. Kelby, *The New-York Historical Society, 1804–1904*, 53.

3. "The New-York Historical Society," *New York Times* (November 22, 1865): 8; "A Public Museum in the Central Park," *New York Times* (May 21, 1866): 2; Stokes, *The Iconography of Manhattan Island*, vol. 5: 1931; Jay E. Cantor, "The Museum in the Park," *Metropolitan Museum of Art Bulletin* 26 (April 1968): 333–40; Paul R. Baker, *Richard Morris Hunt* (Cambridge, Mass.: MIT Press, 1980), 154–55; Sarah Bradford Landau, "Richard Morris Hunt: Architectural Innovator and Father of a 'Distinctive' American School," in Susan R. Stein, ed., *The Architecture of Richard Morris Hunt* (Chicago: University of Chicago Press, 1986), 50–51; Lewis I. Sharp, "Richard Morris Hunt and His Influence on American Beaux-Arts Sculpture," in Stein, ed., *The Architecture of Richard Morris Hunt*, 122–23; Shanor, *The City That Never Was*, 38–42, 44, 46, 50.

4. New York City Board of Commissioners of the Central Park, *Documents*, no. 1 (February 26, 1866): 2.

5. "A Public Museum in the Central Park": 2.

6. Thomas S. Cummings, *Historic Annals of the National Academy of Design, New-York Drawing Association, Etc., with Occasional Dottings by the Way-Side, from 1825 to the Present Time* (Philadelphia: George W. Childs, 1865); Eliot Clark, *History of the National Academy of Design: 1825–1953* (New York: Columbia University Press, 1954). For the Pennsylvania Academy of the Fine Arts, see Helen W. Henderson, *The Pennsylvania Academy of the Fine Arts* (Boston: L. C. Page, 1911).

7. Mary Ann Clegg Smith, "The Commercial Architecture of John Butler Snook" (Ph.D. diss., Pennsylvania State University, 1974): 103; David W. Dunlap, *On Broadway: A Journey Uptown Over Time* (New York: Rizzoli International Publications, 1990), 93.

8. "Designs in Competition," *Architects' and Mechanics' Journal* 1 (January 19, 1861): 154; "National Academy of Design," *Architects' and Mechanics' Journal* 1 (March 23, 1861): 245; "The National Academy of Design," *New York Evening Post* (October 22, 1863): 1; "New National Academy of Design," *New York Times* (October 22, 1863): 2; "National Academy of Design," *New York Daily Tribune* (October 23, 1863): 3; Russell Sturgis, "An Important Gothic Building," *The New Path* 2 (June 1864): 17–32; Cummings, *Historic Annals of the National Academy of Design*, 280–87, 292–301, 313–15, 322–28, 332–53; *The National Academy of Design. Ceremonies on the Occasion of Laying the Corner-Stone, October 21, 1863, and the Inauguration of the Building, April 27, 1865* (New York: Miller and Mathews, 1865); "National Academy of Design," *New York Evening Post* (April 28, 1865): 1; "Opening of the Academy of Design," *New York World* (April 28, 1865): 5; "The National Academy of Design—The Corridor," *New York Times* (May 12, 1865): 4; Russell

Sturgis, "National Academy of Design—Fortieth Annual Exhibition. Introduction—Interior of the New Building," *The New Path* 2 (June 1865): 81–85; *National Academy of Design. Photographs of the New Building, with an Introductory Essay and Description by P. B. Wight, Architect* (New York: S. P. Avery, 1866); "Academy of Design, Corner of Fourth Avenue and Twenty-third Street, New York City," *New-York Sketch-Book of Architecture* 3 (November 1876): plate 32; King, *King's Handbook of New York* (1893), 287, 308–9; "The Academy of Design, New York, N.Y. Mr. P. B. Wight, Architect, Chicago, Ill.," *American Architect and Building News* 46 (November 24, 1894): 83, plate; "Academy of Design's Future," *New York Times* (April 21, 1899): 3; "Academy of Design Sold," *New York Times* (June 2, 1899): 5; Peter B. Wight, "Reminiscences of the Building of the Academy of Design," *New York Times* (April 22, 1900): 25; Stokes, *The Iconography of Manhattan Island*, vol. 3: 518, 957, vol. 5: 1655, 1816, 1827, 1910, 1917; Clark, *History of the National Academy of Design: 1825–1953*, 76, 79–83; John Grafton, *New York in the Nineteenth Century* (New York: Dover, 1977), 142–43; Francis R. Kowsky, *The Architecture of Frederick Clarke Withers and the Progress of the Gothic Revival in America After 1850* (Middletown, Conn.: Wesleyan University Press, 1980), 15; Sarah Bradford Landau, *Peter B. Wight: Architect, Contractor, and Critic, 1838–1925* (Chicago: Art Institute of Chicago, 1981), 16–21, 101, 104–6; Frederick S. Lightfoot, ed., *Nineteenth-Century New York in Rare Photographic Views* (New York: Dover, 1981), plate 103; "Academy Moves Uptown and Downtown," *The Academy Bulletin* 8 (spring 1989): 2; Christopher Gray, "Venetian Blind," *Avenue* (October 1991): 56–60.

9. *The National Academy of Design. Ceremonies on the Occasion of Laying the Corner-Stone, October 21, 1863, and the Inauguration of the Building, April 27, 1865*, 68.

10. Smith, "The Commercial Architecture of John Butler Snook": 103.

11. Baker, *Richard Morris Hunt*, 119–20, 539; Landau, *Peter B. Wight: Architect, Contractor, and Critic, 1838–1925*, 17; Landau, "Richard Morris Hunt: Architectural Innovator and Father of a 'Distinctive' American School," in Stein, ed., *The Architecture of Richard Morris Hunt*, 50; Sharp, "Richard Morris Hunt and His Influence on American Beaux-Arts Sculpture," in Stein, ed., *The Architecture of Richard Morris Hunt*, 122, 124.

12. Sturgis, "An Important Gothic Building": 29.

13. "The National Academy of Design—The Corridor": 4.

14. George P. Putnam, quoted in Morrison H. Heckscher, "The Metropolitan Museum of Art: An Architectural History," *Bulletin of the Metropolitan Museum of Art* 53 (summer 1995): 5. Also see "A Great Art Enterprise," *New York Times* (November 24, 1869): 1; "A Museum for New York," editorial, *New York Times* (November 25, 1869): 3; Winifred E. Howe, *A History of the Metropolitan Museum of Art* (New York: Metropolitan Museum of Art, 1913; New York: Arno Press, 1974), 99–121; Stokes, *The Iconography of Manhattan Island*, vol. 5: 1936; Calvin Tomkins, *Merchants and Masterpieces: The Story of the Metropolitan Museum of Art* (New York: E. P. Dutton, 1970), 25–31.

15. Richard Morris Hunt, quoted in W. C. Bryant et al., *A Metropolitan Art-Museum in the City of New York: Proceedings of a Meeting* (New York, 1869), 17–18, also quoted in Morrison H. Heckscher, "Hunt and the Metropolitan Museum of Art," in Stein, ed., *The Architecture of Richard Morris Hunt*, 172–87. Also see Baker, *Richard Morris Hunt*, 172–74.

16. Montgomery Schuyler, "The Metropolitan Art Museum," editorial, *New York World* (November 25, 1869): 5.

17. Quoted in "The Metropolitan Museum of Art," *New York Times* (January 19, 1870): 2–3. Also see Howe, *A History of the Metropolitan Museum of Art*, 121–25; Stokes, *The Iconography of Manhattan Island*, vol. 5: 1938–39; Tomkins, *Merchants and Masterpieces*, 31–32; Elizabeth McFadden, *The Glitter and the Gold* (New York: Dial, 1971), 114.

18. Howe, *A History of the Metropolitan Museum of Art*, 153–55; Tomkins, *Merchants and Masterpieces*, 22, 33–37.

19. A.K.D., "The Metropolitan Museum," letter to the editor, *New York Times* (January 15, 1874): 2; Howe, *A History of the Metropolitan Museum of Art*, 164; Stokes, *The Iconography of Manhattan Island*, vol. 5: 1968; Tomkins, *Merchants and Masterpieces*, 61.

20. J.R.G. Hassard, "An American Museum of Art," *Scribner's Monthly* 2 (August 1871): 409–15; Cantor, "The Museum in the Park": 333–40; Alison Sky and Michelle Stone, *Unbuilt America* (New York: McGraw-Hill, 1976), 36–37; Shanor, *The City That Never Was*, 42–45.

21. *Thirteenth Annual Report of the Board of Commissioners of the Central Park for the Year Ending December 31, 1869* (New York, 1870), 24. Also see Heckscher, "Hunt and the Metropolitan Museum of Art," in Stein, ed., *The Architecture of Richard Morris Hunt*, 174–75.

22. Quoted in Heckscher, "The Metropolitan Museum of Art: An Architectural History": 10. Also see Howe, *A History of the Metropolitan Museum of Art*, 150; Stokes, *The Iconography of Manhattan Island*, vol. 5: 1943–44.

23. Howe, *A History of the Metropolitan Museum of Art*, 151–52.

24. Howe, *A History of the Metropolitan Museum of Art*, 152–53. Also see "City Improvements," *New York Times* (December 6, 1873): 4.

25. Howe, *A History of the Metropolitan Museum of Art*, 143; Stokes, *The Iconography of Manhattan Island*, vol. 5: 1947; Tomkins, *Merchants and Masterpieces*, 41–43.

26. Quoted in Howe, *A History of the Metropolitan Museum of Art*, 143.

27. Howe, *A History of the Metropolitan Museum of Art*, 160–65; Stokes, *The Iconography of Manhattan Island*, vol. 5: 1952; Tomkins, *Merchants and Masterpieces*, 44–45; Heckscher, "The Metropolitan Museum of Art: An Architectural History": 7–8.

28. George Templeton Strong, quoted in Heckscher, "The Metropolitan Museum of Art: An Architectural History": 16.

29. Howe, *A History of the Metropolitan Museum of Art*, 153.

30. Howe, *A History of the Metropolitan Museum of Art*, 178.

31. "The Metropolitan Museum of Art," *New York Daily Graphic* (February 19, 1879): 745; "Fine Arts: Metropolitan Art Museum," *New York Daily Tribune* (March 28, 1880): 7; "The Metropolitan Museum," editorial, *New York Evening Post* (March 30, 1880): 2; "A Metropolitan Museum," *New York Times* (March 30, 1880): 10; "The New Museum," *New York World* (March 30, 1880): 1; "The Opening of the Metropolitan Museum," editorial, *New York World* (March 30, 1880): 4; "The City's Art Museum," *New York Daily Tribune* (March 31, 1880): 1–2; "The Metropolitan Art Museum," editorial, *New York Sun* (March 31, 1880): 2; "The New Museum Opened," *New York Times* (March 31, 1880): 8; "A Start in Art Development," editorial, *New York Times* (April 4, 1880): 6; "The Fine Art Museum," *New York Times* (April 30, 1880): 2; "The Metropolitan Museum of Art," *Harper's New Monthly Magazine* 60 (May 1880): 863–78; Jacob Wrey Mould, "Mr. Mould and the Museum of Art," letter to the editor, *New York Times* (May 1, 1880): 5; Howe, *A History of the Metropolitan Museum of Art*, 174–84, 189–99; Stokes, *The Iconography of Manhattan Island*, vol. 5: 1950; John David Sigle, "Calvert Vaux: An American Architect" (master's thesis, University of Virginia, 1967): 49–51; Cantor, "The Museum in the Park": 340; Leo Lerman, *The Museum: One Hundred Years and the Metropolitan Museum of Art* (New York: Viking, 1969), 21, 40, 44–45, 63–66; Tomkins, *Merchants and Masterpieces*, 15–24, 60–61; McFadden, *The Glitter and the Gold*, 183–90; Baker, *Richard Morris Hunt*, 174–76; Heckscher, "Hunt and the Metropolitan Museum of Art," in Stein, ed., *The Architecture of Richard Morris Hunt*, 175; Shanor, *The City That Never Was*, 46–50; Barbaralee Diamonstein, *The Landmarks of New York II* (New York: Harry N. Abrams, 1993), 166; William Alex, *Calvert Vaux: Architect & Planner* (New York: Ink, 1994), 23–24, 206–9; Heckscher, "The Metropolitan Museum of Art: An Architectural History": 10–20.

32. Frederick Law Olmsted and Calvert Vaux, quoted in Heckscher, "The Metropolitan Museum of Art: An Architectural History": 10.

33. Quoted in Heckscher, "The Metropolitan Museum of Art: An Architectural History": 15. Also see Howe, *A History of the Metropolitan Museum of Art*, 178.

34. Mould, "Mr. Mould and the Museum of Art": 5.

35. Heckscher, "The Metropolitan Museum of Art: An Architectural History": 16.

36. "The Fine Art Museum": 2.

37. "Fine Arts: Metropolitan Art Museum": 7.

38. James Jackson Jarves, quoted in Heckscher, "The Metropolitan Museum of Art: An Architectural History": 18.

39. Quoted in Heckscher, "The Metropolitan Museum of Art: An Architectural History": 18.

40. "The Metropolitan Museum of Art," *Harper's New Monthly Magazine*: 872–73, 875.

41. "Fine Arts: Metropolitan Art Museum": 7.

42. Heckscher, "The Metropolitan Museum of Art: An Architectural History": 21.

43. Louis Palma di Cesnola, quoted in Heckscher, "The Metropolitan Museum of Art: An Architectural History": 21.

44. "Out Among the Builders," *Real Estate Record and Builders' Guide* 34 (July 5, 1884): 722; "Out Among the Builders," *Real Estate Record and Builders' Guide* 34 (July 19, 1884): 769; "The Metropolitan Museum Addition," *Art Age* 3 (January 1886): 100; "City News," *Building* 4 (February 20, 1886): 96; "The New Addition to the Metropolitan Museum of Art," *New York Daily Graphic* (November 5, 1887): 45; "Enlargement of the Metropolitan Museum of Art, Central Park, New York," *Building* 8 (February 25, 1888): 65, plate; "The New Addition to the Metropolitan Museum of Art," *New York Daily Graphic* (February 27, 1888): 858; "The Metropolitan Museum," *New York Times* (December 18, 1888): 5; "A Treasure-House of Art," *New York Daily Tribune* (December 19, 1888): 7; "Art, Eloquence, Music and Beauty: Opening of the New Wing of the Metropolitan Museum of Art," *New York Herald* (December 19, 1888): 5; "Art Museum's New Wing," *New York Times* (December 19, 1888): 8; Editorial, *New York Times* (December 19, 1888): 4; "The Reopening of the Metropolitan Museum," *Harper's Weekly* 32 (December 29, 1888): 1004–6; "The Well-Named Metropolitan Museum of Art," *American Architect and Building News* 7 (April 10, 1889): 189; King, *King's Handbook of New York* (1893), 303–6; Howe, *A History of the Metropolitan Museum of Art*, 216–17, 231–37; Stokes, *The Iconography of Manhattan Island*, vol. 5: 1997; Tomkins, *Merchants and Masterpieces*, 75; Baker, *Richard Morris Hunt*, 441–42; Heckscher, "Hunt and the Metropolitan Museum of Art," in Stein, ed., *The Architecture of Richard Morris Hunt*, 175–77; Christopher Gray, "A Diminished Garden Courtyard for an Old Facade," *New York Times* (March 19, 1989), X: 12, reprinted in Christopher Gray, *Changing New York: The Architectural Scene* (New York: Dover, 1992), 82; Diamonstein, *The Landmarks of New York II*, 166; Heckscher, "The Metropolitan Museum of Art: An Architectural History": 21–29.

45. "Out Among the Builders," (July 5, 1884): 722.

46. Richard Morris Hunt to John T. Johnston, July 10, 1884, quoted in Heckscher, "Hunt and the Metropolitan Museum of Art," in Stein, ed., *The Architecture of Richard Morris Hunt*, 176.

47. John T. Johnston to Louis Palma di Cesnola, July 11, 1884, quoted in Heckscher, "Hunt and the Metropolitan Museum of Art," in Stein, ed., *The Architecture of Richard Morris Hunt*, 177.

48. Theodore Weston to Louis Palma di Cesnola, July 19, 1884, quoted in Heckscher, "Hunt and the Metropolitan Museum of Art," in Stein, ed., *The Architecture of Richard Morris Hunt*, 177.

49. "The Metropolitan Museum Addition": 100.

50. "The Reopening of the Metropolitan Museum": 1006.

51. "Museum of Natural History," *New York Times* (May 30, 1874): 2; "Natural History Museum," *New York Times* (June 3, 1874): 3; "Laying the Corner-Stone of the American Museum of Natural History in Central Park on Tuesday," *New York Daily Graphic* (June 4, 1874): 725; "The American Museum of Natural History, New York. Messrs. Vaux and Mould, Architects," *American Architect and Building News* 1 (August 12, 1876): 261, plates; "Visitors to the Central Park Museum," *New York Daily Tribune* (October 9, 1876): 12; "A Great School of Science," *New York Times* (April 15, 1877): 10; "Natural History Museum," *New York Times* (December 20, 1877): 2; "The New Building of the American Museum of Natural History Opened at Central Park To-day," *New York Daily Graphic* (December 22, 1877): 348; "New York's New Museum," *New York Daily Tribune* (December 22, 1877): 2–3; Editorial, *New York Times* (December 22, 1877): 4; "An Imposing Ceremony," *New York Herald* (December 23, 1877): 5; "Ex-Gov. Hayes' Movements: Yesterday's Show at the Opening of the American Museum," *New York Sun* (December 23, 1877): 1; "New York's New Museum," *New York Times* (December 23, 1877): 1; "Notes and Clippings," *American Architect and Building News* 2 (December 29, 1877): 420; *Ninth Annual Report of the American Museum of Natural History: 1877* (New York, 1878), 57; King, *King's Handbook of New York* (1893), 306–8; Martha J. Lamb and Mrs. Burton Harrison, *History of the City of New York* (New York: A. S. Barnes & Co., 1896), 781–82; Stokes, *The Iconography of Manhattan Island*, vol. 3: 956, vol. 5: 1934, 1936, 1943–44, 1956, 1958, 1967; "Theodore Roosevelt Park: 1807–1958," *Curator* 3, no. 2 (1960): 161–82; Sigle, "Calvert Vaux:

An American Architect": 47–49, plates 36–37; John Michael Kennedy, "Philanthropy and Science in New York City: The American Museum of Natural History, 1868–1968" (Ph.D. diss., Yale University, 1968): 12–15, 37–46, 55–64, 68–70; Stern, Gilmartin, and Massengale, *New York 1900*, 370; M. Christine Boyer, *Manhattan Manners: Architecture and Style, 1850–1900* (New York: Rizzoli International Publications, 1985), 11, 199–200; Douglas J. Preston, *Dinosaurs in the Attic: An Excursion into the American Museum of Natural History* (New York: St. Martin's Press, 1986), 13–20; White and Willensky, *AIA Guide* (1988), 325–26; Diamonstein, *The Landmarks of New York II*, 164; Alex, *Calvert Vaux*, 202–5; Christopher Gray, "A Vaux Masterpiece Eroded and, Now, Ignored," *New York Times* (June 19, 1994), X: 7.

52. "The Central Park," *New York Times* (August 8, 1868): 2; "Meeting of the Lyceum of Natural History—Prof. Waterhouse Hawkins' Report on the Paleozoic Museum at Central Park," *New York Times* (March 7, 1871): 5; Edwin H. Colbert and Katharine Beneker, "The Paleozoic Museum in Central Park, or the Museum that Never Was," *Curator* 2, no. 2 (1959): 137–50; Adrian J. Desmond, "Central Park's Fragile Dinosaurs," *Natural History* 83 (October 1974): 64–71; Preston, *Dinosaurs in the Attic*, 8–12.

53. Quoted in Preston, *Dinosaurs in the Attic*, 11.

54. Preston, *Dinosaurs in the Attic*, 11.

55. "The Central Park Captives," *New York Times* (April 28, 1871): 8; Stokes, *The Iconography of Manhattan Island*, vol. 5: 1950; Kennedy, "Philanthropy and Science in New York City: The American Museum of Natural History, 1868–1968": 51–53.

56. Albert Smith Bickmore, "An Autobiography" (unpublished manuscript), quoted in "Theodore Roosevelt Park: 1807–1958": 162.

57. "The American Museum of Natural History, New York. Messrs. Vaux and Mould, Architects": 261.

58. "Squatter Life in New York," *Harper's New Monthly Magazine* 61 (September 1880): 562–69.

59. "Competitive Design for the American Museum of Natural History, New York, N.Y., Mr. R. H. Robertson, Architect, New York, N.Y.," *American Architect and Building News* 26 (July 27, 1889): 37, plate.

60. "The Museum of Natural History," editorial, *New York Daily Tribune* (February 24, 1888): 4; "Plans Seriously Criticized," *New York Times* (March 8, 1888): 8; "The New Museum Building," *New York Times* (March 29, 1888): 8; "Enlarging the Museum," *New York Times* (September 5, 1888): 8; "The Museum of Natural History," editorial, *New York Daily Tribune* (January 17, 1889): 6; "For the Natural History Museum," *New York Daily Tribune* (February 8, 1889): 2; "Monster Girders," *New York Times* (May 17, 1889): 8; "Museum of Natural History," *Architectural Record* 1 (April–June 1890): 481; "A Museum Worth Seeing," *New York Times* (February 14, 1892): 10; "More Money for the Museum," *New York Times* (April 12, 1892): 8; "In and About the City: Museum of Natural History," *New York Times* (November 3, 1892): 3; Montgomery Schuyler, "The Works of Cady, Berg & See," *Architectural Record* 6 (April–June 1897): 517–53; "Theodore Roosevelt Park: 1807–1958": 170–71; Alan Burnham, ed., *New York Landmarks* (Middletown, Conn.: Wesleyan University Press, 1963), 162–63; Kennedy, "Philanthropy and Science in New York City: The American Museum of Natural History, 1868–1968": 88–89; Stern, Gilmartin, and Massengale, *New York 1900*, 370–71; Kathleen A. Curran, *A Forgotten Architect of the Gilded Age: Josiah Cleaveland Cady's Legacy* (Hartford, Conn.: Trinity College, 1993), 20–25.

61. "Monster Girders": 8.

62. "A Museum Worth Seeing": 10.

63. "The Forty-second Street Reservoir Unnecessary," *New York Daily Tribune* (May 11, 1877): 2; "A Proposed Polytechnic Institute," *New York Times* (July 1, 1877): 7; "Plans of the Proposed Metropolitan Museum of Scientific Industry, in Reservoir Square," *New York Daily Graphic* (July 2, 1877): 4; "A Museum in Place of the Reservoir," *New York Daily Tribune* (July 2, 1877): 2; "Correspondence," *American Architect and Building News* 2 (July 7, 1877): 218; "Proposed Metropolitan Museum of Scientific Industry," *American Architect and Building News* 2 (August 11, 1877): 85, plate; "The Reservoir Park," *New York Times* (October 24, 1877): 8.

64. For the Crystal Palace, see John A. Kouwenhoven, *The Columbia Historical Portrait of New York* (Garden City, N.Y.: Doubleday, 1953), 242–43.

65. "Buildings Projected," *Real Estate Record and Builders' Guide* 31 (March 24, 1883): 197; "Obituaries," *Building* 2 (December 1883): 36; "A Moral Wax-Work Show," *New York Times* (January 1, 1884): 3; "The Eden Musée," *New York Daily Tribune* (March 29, 1884): 5; "Opening the Eden Musée," *New York Evening Post* (March 29, 1884): 1; "Scenes and Figures in Wax," *New York Times* (March 29, 1884): 4; "The Eden Musée, New York, N.Y., Mr. Henry Fernbach and Mr. Theodore DeLemos, Architects, New York, N.Y.," *American Architect and Building News* 15 (May 24, 1884): 247, plate; M. G. Van Rensselaer, "Recent Architecture in America—II," *Century Magazine* 28 (July 1884): 323–34; "Crushed by a Heavy Stone," *New York Daily Tribune* (September 25, 1884): 1; King, *King's Handbook of New York* (1893), 605; *A History of Real Estate, Building and Architecture in New York City During the Last Quarter of a Century* (New York: Real Estate Record Association, 1898), 640; Stokes, *The Iconography of Manhattan Island*, vol. 3: 983, vol. 5: 1984; Lloyd Morris, *Incredible New York* (New York: Bonanza Books, 1951), 190; Arnold Lewis and Keith Morgan, *American Victorian Architecture* (New York: Dover, 1975), 25, 142.

66. Van Rensselaer, "Recent Architecture in America—II": 327.

Libraries

1. "Architecture," *Crayon* 2 (July 1856): 214–15; Moses King, *King's Handbook of New York* (Boston: Moses King, 1893), 328–29; Austin Baxter Keep, *History of the New York Society Library* (New York: DeVinne, 1908); Marion King, *Books and People: Five Decades of New York's Oldest Library* (New York: Macmillan, 1954); Cynthia A. Kierner, "New York Society Library," in Kenneth T. Jackson, ed., *The Encyclopedia of New York City* (New Haven, Conn., and London: Yale University Press; New York: New-York Historical Society, 1995), 843–44.

2. Philip Hone, diary entry dated April 6, 1842, in *The Diary of Philip Hone*, ed. Allan Nevins, 2 vols. (New York: Dodd, Mead & Co., 1936), vol. 2: 595; "The Astor Library," *Gleason's Pictorial* 3 (September 25, 1852): 200; "The Astor Library," *Putnam's* 2 (1853): 13; "The Modern Architecture of New York," *New York Quarterly* 4 (April 1855): 105–23; "The Astor Library," *New York Times* (January 10, 1854): 8; Frank H. Norton, "Ten Years in a Public Library," *Galaxy* 8 (October 1869): 528–37; James D. McCabe Jr., *Lights and Shadows of New York Life; or, The Sights and Sensations of the Great City* (Philadelphia: National Publishing, 1872; New York: Arno Press, 1970), 514–15; "The Astor Library," supplement, *Harper's Weekly* 19 (October 2, 1875): 81; "The Astor and Lenox Libraries," *The Nation* 36 (May 31, 1883): 462–63; John Benson Lossing, *History of New York City* (New York: Perine, 1884), vol. 2: 701–4; Martha J. Lamb, "A Neglected Corner of the Metropolis," *Magazine of American History* 16 (July 1886): 1–29; Frederick K. Saunders, "The Astor Library," *New England* 2 (April 1890): 148–59; King, *King's Handbook of New York* (1893), 325–26; Charles H. Haswell, *Reminiscences of New York by an Octogenarian* (New York: Harper & Brothers, 1896), 122, 440, 456, 485; Martha J. Lamb and Mrs. Burton Harrison, *History of the City of New York* (New York: A. S. Barnes & Co., 1896), 753–55, 860–61; Harry Miller Lydenberg, *History of the New York Public Library* (New York: New York Public Library, 1923), 1–94; George Watson Cole, "Early Library Development in New York State (1800–1900)," *Bulletin of the New York Public Library* 30 (November 1926): 849–57, (December 1926): 917–25; I. N. Phelps Stokes, *The Iconography of Manhattan Island*, 6 vols. (New York: Robert H. Dodd, 1915–28; New York: Arno Press, 1967), vol. 5: 1816, 1818, 1827, 1847, 1857, 1881; Frank L. Tolman, "Libraries and Lyceums," in Alexander C. Flick, ed., *History of the State of New York: Mind and Spirit* (New York: Columbia University Press, 1937), vol. 9: 47–91; Alan Burnham, ed., *New York Landmarks* (Middletown, Conn.: Wesleyan University Press, 1963), 118–19; Landmarks Preservation Commission of the City of New York, LP-0016 (October 26, 1965); Ellen W. Kramer, "Contemporary Descriptions of New York City and Its Public Architecture c. 1850," *Journal of the Society of Architectural Historians* 27 (December 1968): 264–80; Paul Goldberger, *The City Observed: New York* (New York: Random House, 1979), 68–69; Thomas Bender, *New York Intellect: A History of Intellectual Life in New York City from 1750 to the Beginnings of Our Own Time* (New York: Alfred A. Knopf, 1987), 112–14, 216; Barbara lee Diamonstein, *The Landmarks of New York II* (New York: Harry N. Abrams, 1993), 107; Phyllis Dain, "Libraries," in Jackson, ed., *The Encyclopedia of New York City*, 667–70.

3. Lamb, "A Neglected Corner of the Metropolis": 17.

4. Stokes, *The Iconography of Manhattan Island*, vol. 5: 1818.

5. "The Modern Architecture of New York": 115.

6. Cole, "Early Library Development in New York State (1800–1900)": 919.

7. "Pictures of the Day," *New York Daily Graphic* (February 13, 1880): 752, 754; "The Astor Library, N.Y.," *American Architect and Building News* 7 (May 22, 1880): 224, plate; "No. 27 Lafayette Place," *Real Estate Record and Builders' Guide* 40 (September 3, 1887): 1124.

8. "No. 27 Lafayette Place": 1124.

9. "The Lenox Library, New York," *Architectural Review and American Builders' Journal* 2 (February 1870): 483; Montgomery Schuyler, "Improvements in New York Architecture," *New York World* (November 26, 1871): 3; McCabe, *Lights and Shadows of New York Life*, 518; "New York Architecture," *New York Times* (July 5, 1873): 2; "The Lenox Library," *New-York Sketch-Book of Architecture* 3 (April 1876): 1–2, plate 13; A. J. Bloor, "Annual Address," *Proceedings of the Tenth Annual Convention of the American Institute of Architects, 1876* (Boston, 1877): 15–34; "Lenox Library, New York, Mr. R. M. Hunt, Architect," *American Architect and Building News* 2 (September 1, 1877): 280–81, plates; "Opening of the Lenox Library," *New York Daily Tribune* (December 12, 1877): 5; "Mr. James Lenox," *New York Daily Graphic* (February 21, 1880): 815; "The Astor and Lenox Libraries," *The Nation*: 463; M. G. Van Rensselaer, "Recent Architecture in America—I," *Century Magazine* 28 (May 1884): 48–67; "Notes About Town," *Real Estate Record and Builders' Guide* 36 (October 24, 1885): 1160; "The Lenox Library, New York, N.Y. Mr. R. M. Hunt, Architect, New York, N.Y.," *American Architect and Building News* 20 (August 28, 1886): 98, plate; King, *King's Handbook of New York* (1893), 326; Montgomery Schuyler, "The Works of the Late Richard M. Hunt," *Architectural Record* 5 (October–December 1895): 97–180; *A History of Real Estate, Building and Architecture in New York City During the Last Quarter of a Century* (New York: Real Estate Record Association, 1898), 600–601, 622; Lydenberg, *History of the New York Public Library*, 95–128; Talbot Hamlin, *The American Spirit in Architecture* (New Haven, Conn.: Yale University Press, 1926), 174; Stokes, *The Iconography of Manhattan Island*, vol. 3: 763, vol. 5: 1937; Franklin F. Hopper, *Three Men—Their Intellectual Contribution to America* (Princeton, N.J.: Princeton University Press, 1944), 12–14; Henry Stevens, *Recollections of James Lenox and the Formation of His Library* (New York: New York Public Library, 1951); Burnham, ed., *New York Landmarks*, 43; Paul R. Baker, *Richard Morris Hunt* (Cambridge, Mass.: MIT Press, 1980), 181–86; Sarah Bradford Landau, "Richard Morris Hunt: Architectural Innovator and Father of a 'Distinctive' American School," in Susan R. Stein, ed, *The Architecture of Richard Morris Hunt* (Chicago: University of Chicago Press, 1986), 46–77; David Van Zanten, "The Lenox Library: What Hunt Did and Did Not Learn in France," in Stein, ed., *The Architecture of Richard Morris Hunt*, 90–117.

10. King, *King's Handbook of New York* (1893), 326.

11. "The Astor and Lenox Libraries," *The Nation*: 463.

12. "New York Architecture": 2.

13. "Opening of the Lenox Library": 5.

14. Van Zanten, "The Lenox Library: What Hunt Did and Did Not Learn in France," in Stein, ed., *The Architecture of Richard Morris Hunt*, 91.

15. Bloor, "Annual Address": 27.

16. *A History of Real Estate, Building and Architecture in New York City During the Last Quarter of a Century*, 600–601.

17. Schuyler, "The Works of the Late Richard M. Hunt": 112.

18. John Rose Greene Hassard, "The New York Mercantile Library," *Scribner's Monthly* 1 (February 1871): 353–67. Also see *Addresses of John Romeyn Broadhead, Esq. and His Excellency, Gov. Horatio Seymour, Delivered before the Clinton Hall Association and Mercantile Library Association* (New York: George F. Nesbitt, 1854); *Fiftieth Anniversary Celebration of the Mercantile Library Association* (New York: George F. Nesbitt, 1871); McCabe, *Lights and Shadows of New York Life*, 515; Lamb, "A Neglected Corner of the Metropolis": 27–28; Haswell, *Reminiscences of New York by an Octogenarian*, 119, 476, 493; Stokes, *The Iconography of Manhattan*

Island, vol. 5: 1612, 1614, 1626, 1675, 1858, 1923; Richard D. Lyons, "Redevelopment Aids Cultural Institutions," *New York Times* (March 21, 1990), D: 23; Elaine Weber Pascu, "Mercantile Library Association," in Jackson, ed., *The Encyclopedia of New York City*, 750–51.

19. Hassard, "The New York Mercantile Library": 358.

20. "Building Prospects for 1889," *Building* 10 (January 5, 1889): 1; "In and About the City," *New York Times* (July 17, 1890): 8; "The Mercantile Library," *New York Times* (November 10, 1891): 9.

21. Haswell, *Reminiscences of New York by an Octogenarian*, 476.

22. D., "A Few Words About Reading Rooms," letter to the editor, *New York Times* (October 14, 1869): 2.

23. "The Free Circulating Library," *New York Times* (May 4, 1880): 8; "The New York Free Circulating Library," *Harper's Weekly* 26 (January 21, 1882): 34; "Free Reading for Everybody," *Harper's Weekly* 26 (February 4, 1882): 66–67; Viola Roseboro, "New York Free Public Libraries," *The Cosmopolitan* 3 (May 1887): 169–73; "The Free Libraries of New York," *New York Daily Graphic* (May 9, 1888): 527–29; Lamb and Harrison, *History of the City of New York*, 861; Stokes, *The Iconography of Manhattan Island*, vol. 5: 1973, 1984; Landmarks Preservation Commission of the City of New York, LP-0969 (September 20, 1977).

24. "The Free Libraries of New York," *New York Daily Graphic*: 527–29.

25. Editorial, *New York Times* (December 4, 1884): 4. Also see "Shall We Have a Public Library," editorial, *New York Times* (February 26, 1871): 4; "Lack of Library Facilities," editorial, *New York Times* (November 16, 1879): 6–7.

26. *Second Annual Report of the New York Free Circulating Library* (1880–81), quoted in Landmarks Preservation Commission of the City of New York, LP-0969 (September 20, 1977), 2.

27. Landmarks Preservation Commission of the City of New York, LP-0969 (September 20, 1977); White and Willensky, *AIA Guide* (1988), 166; Diamonstein, *The Landmarks of New York II*, 184.

28. Editorial, (December 4, 1884): 4.

29. "In West Forty-second Street," *Real Estate Record and Builders' Guide* 41 (January 14, 1888): 34. Also see King, *King's Handbook of New York* (1893), 331–32.

30. "A Munificent Gift from George W. Vanderbilt," *New York Daily Graphic* (July 9, 1888): 50, 53; King, *King's Handbook of New York* (1893), 331–32; Wayne Andrews, *The Vanderbilt Legend* (New York: Harcourt, Brace, 1941), 331; Landmarks Preservation Commission of the City of New York, *Greenwich Village Historic District Designation Report* (New York, 1969), 199; Paul R. Baker, "Richard Morris Hunt: An Introduction," in Stein, ed., *The Architecture of Richard Morris Hunt*, 7; White and Willensky, *AIA Guide* (1988), 122.

Clubs

1. An Old New Yorker, "Clubs—Club Life—Some New York Clubs," *Galaxy* 22 (August 1876): 227–38. For an English perspective on American clubs, including those in New York, see "Like Railway Stations," *New York Times* (April 18, 1886): 5.

2. Paul R. Baker, *Richard Morris Hunt* (Cambridge, Mass.: MIT Press, 1980), 115–16, 142–43, 539; Lewis I. Sharp, "Richard Morris Hunt and His Influence on American Beaux-Arts Sculpture," in Susan R. Stein, ed., *The Architecture of Richard Morris Hunt* (Chicago: University of Chicago Press, 1986), 122; Susan R. Stein, "Role and Reputation: The Architectural Practice of Richard Morris Hunt," in Stein, ed., *The Architecture of Richard Morris Hunt*, 116; David Van Zanten, "The Lenox Library: What Hunt Did and Did Not Learn in France," in Stein, ed., *The Architecture of Richard Morris Hunt*, 95–97.

3. John W. Kennion, *Architects' and Builders' Guide* (New York: Fitzpatrick & Hunter, 1868), part 2: 102; "Clubs in New York," editorial, *New York Times* (November 28, 1870): 4; James D. McCabe Jr., *Lights and Shadows of New York Life; or, The Sights and Sensations of the Great City* (Philadelphia: National Publishing, 1872; New York: Farrar, Straus & Giroux, 1970), 394, 396; "The Fire at the Union League Club House Last Sunday Morning," *New York Daily Graphic* (April 27, 1875): 428; An Old New Yorker, "Clubs—Club Life—Some New York Clubs": 235–36; I. N. Phelps Stokes, *The Iconography of Manhattan Island*, 6 vols.

(New York: Robert H. Dodd, 1915–28; New York: Arno Press, 1967), vol. 3: 939, vol. 5: 1906, 1915, 1920, 1931, 1958; Frederick S. Lightfoot, ed., *Nineteenth-Century New York in Rare Photographic Views* (New York: Dover, 1981), fig. 104.

4. W., "New Work," *American Architect and Building News* 5 (March 1, 1879): 69–70; W., "Correspondence," *American Architect and Building News* 5 (April 26, 1879): 133–34; W., "The Union League Clubhouse," *American Architect and Building News* 5 (May 3, 1879): 141; "Competitive Design for the Union League Club-House, New York, N.Y. Messrs. Potter & Robertson, Architects, New York," *American Architect and Building News* 5 (May 31, 1879): 173, plate; "Competitive Design for the Union League Club-House, New York, N.Y. Messrs. McKim, Mead & Bigelow, Architects, New York," *American Architect and Building News* 5 (June 7, 1879): 180, plates; "Competitive Design for the Union League Club-House, New York, N.Y. Mr. E. E. Ralet [*sic*], Architect, New York," *American Architect and Building News* 5 (June 14, 1879): 189, plates; "Competitive Design for the Union League Club-House, New York, N.Y. Messrs. Gambrill & Ficken, Architects, New York," *American Architect and Building News* 5 (June 21, 1879): 197, plate; "Competitive Design for the Union League Club-House, New York, N.Y. Mr. G. E. Harney, Architect, New York," *American Architect and Building News* 5 (June 28, 1879): 204, plates; "Competitive Design for the Union League Club-House, New York, N.Y. Mr. R. M. Hunt, Architect, New York," *American Architect and Building News* 6 (July 5, 1879): 4, plates; "Competitive Design for the Union League Club-House, New York, N.Y. Mr. S. D. Hatch, Architect, New York," *American Architect and Building News* 6 (July 12, 1879): 12, plates; "Competitive Design for the Union League Club-House, New York, N.Y. Messrs. Thorp & Price, Architects, New York," *American Architect and Building News* 6 (August 23, 1879): 60, plates; "The Accepted Design for the Union League Club-House, New York, N.Y. Messrs. Peabody & Stearns, Architects, Boston, Mass.," *American Architect and Building News* 6 (September 20, 1879): 92, plates; "Competitive Design for the Union League Club-House, New York, N.Y. Mr. James Renwick, Architect, New York," *American Architect and Building News* 6 (October 11, 1879): 117, plates; "Competitive Design for the Union League Club-House, New York, N.Y. Messrs. West & Anderson, Architects, New York," *American Architect and Building News* 6 (October 18, 1879): 124, plates; "The Union League Club House," *Real Estate Record and Builders' Guide* 26 (October 9, 1880): 872; "Rich Painting and Glass: Decorations in the New Union League Club-House," *New York Daily Tribune* (February 16, 1881): 5; "Union League's New Home," *New York Daily Tribune* (February 16, 1881): 2; "A New Palace for a Club," *New York Times* (March 4, 1881): 8; S. H. Wales, "The New Club-House," letter to the editor, *New York Times* (March 5, 1881): 5; Montgomery Schuyler, "The Union League Club-House," *New York World* (March 5, 1881): 4; "Local Miscellany: The First Day in Its New Quarters," *New York Daily Tribune* (March 6, 1881): 12; "The Union League's New Home," *New York Times* (March 6, 1881): 7; "The Union League Club Building," *Real Estate Record and Builders' Guide* 27 (March 19, 1881): 246–47; Montgomery Schuyler, "Recent Building in New York—I," *American Architect and Building News* 9 (April 9, 1881): 176–77; M. G. Van Rensselaer, "Recent Architecture in America—V," *Century Magazine* 31 (February 1886): 548–58; Moses King, *King's Handbook of New York* (Boston: Moses King, 1893), 544–45; Martha J. Lamb and Mrs. Burton Harrison, *History of the City of New York* (New York: A. S. Barnes & Co., 1896), 778–79; Russell Sturgis, "Boston Architects. Part II—Peabody & Stearns," *Architectural Record* 3 (July 1896): 53–94; Montgomery Schuyler, "A Great American Architect: Leopold Eidlitz. Part I," *Architectural Record* 24 (September 1908): 163–79; Stokes, *The Iconography of Manhattan Island*, vol. 5: 1976; Wheaton Arnold Holden, "Robert Swain Peabody of Peabody and Stearns in Boston: The Early Years (1870–1886)" (Ph.D. diss., Boston University, 1969): 111–14, figs. 132, 134; Richard Guy Wilson, "Charles F. McKim and the Development of the American Renaissance: A Study in Architecture and Culture" (Ph.D. diss., University of Michigan, 1972): 231–32; Sarah Bradford Landau, *Edward T. and William A. Potter: American Victorian Architects* (New York: Garland, 1979), 314–20, figs. 206–7; Baker, *Richard Morris Hunt*, 203, 539, 544, fig. 35; Leland M. Roth, *McKim, Mead & White, Architects* (New York: Harper & Row, 1983),

50–51; Stern, Gilmartin, and Massengale, *New York 1900*, 227–29. For Dickel's Riding Academy (1879), located on the south side of Fifty-sixth Street between Fifth and Sixth Avenues, see "A Model Riding School," *New York Daily Graphic* (October 2, 1879): 660.

5. "A New Palace for a Club": 8.

6. W., "Correspondence," (April 26, 1879): 133–34.

7. W., "Correspondence," (April 26, 1879): 134.

8. W., "Correspondence," (April 26, 1879): 134.

9. Schuyler, "Recent Building in New York—I": 176–77.

10. "A New Palace for a Club": 8.

11. Schuyler, "A Great American Architect: Leopold Eidlitz. Part I": 171.

12. Schuyler, "The Union League Club-House," *New York World*: 4.

13. "A New Palace for a Club": 8. Also see the letter to the editor of the *New York Times* from Salem H. Wales, a member of the Union League Club's building committee, pointing out that there was no theater in the club: Wales, "The New Club-House": 5.

14. Van Rensselaer, "Recent Architecture in America—V": 553.

15. An Old New Yorker, "Clubs—Club Life—Some New York Clubs": 229; "Events in the Metropolis," *New York Times* (April 2, 1881): 5; "Out Among the Builders," *Real Estate Record and Builders' Guide* 28 (December 3, 1881): 1120; King, *King's Handbook of New York* (1893), 546; Stokes, *The Iconography of Manhattan Island*, vol. 3: 938, vol. 5: 1942, 1979.

16. An Old New Yorker, "Clubs—Club Life—Some New York Clubs": 229; "Notes of Current Interest," *Building* 5 (January 22, 1887): 4; "Out Among the Builders," *Real Estate Record and Builders' Guide* 39 (April 9, 1887): 479–80; "New Homes for Two Clubs," *New York Daily Tribune* (May 6, 1888): 9; "The New Home of the New York Club," *New York Daily Graphic* (May 12, 1888): 557, 559; "Furniture for the Club-House of the New York Club, New York, N.Y. Mr. R. H. Robertson, Architect, New York, N.Y.," *American Architect and Building News* 24 (October 27, 1888): 194, plate; "A Club's House-Warming," *New York Daily Tribune* (November 11, 1888): 4; "Showing Their New House," *New York Times* (November 11, 1888): 3; "Alterations to Building of the New York Club. Mr. R. H. Robertson and Mr. A. J. Manning, Associated Architects, New York, N.Y.," *American Architect and Building News* 25 (June 1, 1889): 258, plate; James Grant Wilson, *The Memorial History of the City of New York*, 4 vols. (New York: New York History, 1892–93), vol. 1: 236–37; King, *King's Handbook of New York* (1893), 545–46; Stokes, *The Iconography of Manhattan Island*, vol. 5: 1795, 2006.

17. "Out Among the Builders": 479–80.

18. "New Homes for Two Clubs": 9.

19. "The New Home of the New York Club": 559.

20. Quoted in An Old New Yorker, "Clubs—Club Life—Some New York Clubs": 233–34. Also see McCabe, *Lights and Shadows of New York Life*, 394–95; Stokes, *The Iconography of Manhattan Island*, vol. 3: 937; Christopher Gray, "The Century Association Clubhouse," *New York Times* (December 11, 1988), X: 10, reprinted in Christopher Gray, *Changing New York: The Architectural Scene* (New York: Dover, 1992), 72.

21. "Out Among the Builders," *Real Estate Record and Builders' Guide* 43 (February 28, 1889): 245–46; "New Home of the Century Club in New York," *Harper's Weekly* 33 (November 2, 1889): 876; "Some Fine New Buildings," *New York Times* (December 15, 1889): 11; "Art Notes," *New York Times* (October 16, 1890): 4; "The Century Club in Its New Home," *New York Daily Tribune* (January 11, 1891): 2; "In and About the City," *New York Times* (January 11, 1891): 3; A. R. Macdonough, "The Century Club," *Century Magazine* 41 (March 1891): 673–89; Wilson, *The Memorial History of the City of New York*, vol 1: 244; King, *King's Handbook of New York* (1893), 548; Russell Sturgis, "The Works of McKim, Mead & White," *Architectural Record* 4 (May 1895): 1–111; *A History of Real Estate, Building and Architecture in New York City During the Last Quarter of a Century* (New York: Real Estate Record Association, 1898), 598; Stokes, *The Iconography of Manhattan Island*, vol. 3: 937, vol. 5: 2000; Charles C. Baldwin, *Stanford White* (New York: Dodd, Mead & Co., 1931), 229–31; Alan Burnham, ed., *New York Landmarks* (Middletown, Conn.: Wesleyan University Press, 1963), 164–65; Leland Roth, "McKim, Mead & White Reappraised," in *A Monograph of the Works of McKim, Mead & White, 1879–1915* (New York: Architectural Book Publishing Co., 1915; New York: Benjamin Blom, 1973), 38; Leland M. Roth, "The Urban Architecture of McKim, Mead and White,

1870–1910" (Ph.D. diss., Yale University, 1973): 292–94; Leland Roth, *The Architecture of McKim, Mead & White, 1870–1920: A Building List* (New York and London: Garland, 1978), 40; Roth, *McKim, Mead & White, Architects*, 143–45; Stern, Gilmartin, and Massengale, *New York 1900*, 231–32; Christopher Gray, "Clubhouse Row," *Avenue* (September 1987): 84–87; White and Willensky, *AIA Guide* (1988), 241–42; Lawrence Wodehouse, *White of McKim, Mead and White* (New York and London: Garland, 1988), 165; David Garrard Lowe, *Stanford White's New York* (New York: Doubleday, 1992), 153–57.

22. Sturgis, "The Works of McKim, Mead & White": 3, 10.

23. "To Build a New Clubhouse," *New York Times* (May 2, 1885): 5; "Out Among the Builders," *Real Estate Record and Builders' Guide* 35 (May 16, 1885): 564; "The Costly and Substantial Buildings of 1886," *Real Estate Record and Builders' Guide* 39 (January 1, 1887): 6–8; "The Down-Town Club," *Real Estate Record and Builders' Guide* 40 (July 2, 1887): 890–91; Montgomery Schuyler, "The Romanesque Revival in New York," *Architectural Record* 1 (July–September 1891): 7–38; King, *King's Handbook of New York* (1893), 558; Montgomery Schuyler, "The Works of Charles Coolidge Haight," *Architectural Record* 6 (July 1899): 1–102; Stokes, *The Iconography of Manhattan Island*, vol. 3: 937–38, vol. 5: 1882; Andrew S. Dolkart, *Lower Manhattan Architectural Survey Report* (New York: Lower Manhattan Cultural Council, fall 1987), no. 72; White and Willensky, *AIA Guide* (1988), 36.

24. "The Down-Town Club," *Real Estate Record and Builders' Guide*: 890–91.

25. Schuyler, "The Romanesque Revival in New York": 26.

26. An Old New Yorker, "Clubs—Club Life—Some New York Clubs": 236–37; McCabe, *Lights and Shadows of New York Life*, 394; Wilson, *The Memorial History of the City of New York*, vol. 1: 259; King, *King's Handbook of New York* (1893), 567; Ellen Kramer, "The Domestic Architecture of Detlef Lienau: A Conservative Victorian" (Ph.D. diss., New York University, 1957): 216–18, fig. 88. Also see drawings in the Lienau Collection, Drawings Collection, Avery Library, Columbia University.

27. "Local Miscellany: A Racket Club House," *New York Times* (June 4, 1876): 2; "The Racquet Club House," *New York Sun* (June 21, 1876): 1; A. J. Bloor, "Annual Address," *Proceedings of the Tenth Annual Convention of the American Institute of Architects* (Boston, 1877): 15–34; Montgomery Schuyler, "Two Commercial Palaces," *New York World* (March 31, 1878): 6; W., "Correspondence," *American Architect and Building News* 4 (July 13, 1878): 15–16; Augustus Stonehouse, "Club Buildings in New York," *The Art Review* 1 (March 1887): 11; Wilson, *The Memorial History of the City of New York*, vol. 1: 257; Montgomery Schuyler, "The Work of William A. Potter," *Architectural Record* 26 (September 1909): 176–96; Stokes, *The Iconography of Manhattan Island*, vol. 3: 938, vol. 5: 1958; Sarah Bradford Landau, "The Tall Office Building Artistically Reconsidered: Arcaded Buildings of the New York School, 1870–1890," in Helen Searing, ed., *In Search of Modern Architecture: A Tribute to Henry-Russell Hitchcock* (New York: Architectural History Foundation; Cambridge, Mass.: MIT Press, 1982), 143–45; Sarah Bradford Landau, "The Old Racquet Club," *Village Views* 3 (summer 1986): 24–32; White and Willensky, *AIA Guide* (1988), 178; Landmarks Preservation Commission of the City of New York, LP-1709 (October 3, 1989); Christopher Gray, "Streetscapes: Readers' Questions: The Coogan Building," *New York Times* (June 2, 1991), IX: 6.

28. Stonehouse, "Club Buildings in New York": 11.

29. "Local Miscellany: A Racket Club House": 2.

30. Schuyler, "Two Commercial Palaces": 6.

31. Schuyler, "The Work of William A. Potter": 176.

32. "A New Home for the Racquet Club," *New York Times* (February 11, 1890): 5; "The Racquet Club's New House," *New York Times* (June 13, 1890): 8; Schuyler, "The Romanesque Revival in New York": 26; King, *King's Handbook of New York* (1893), 566; Montgomery Schuyler, "Cyrus L. W. Eidlitz," *Architectural Record* 5 (April–June 1896): 411–35; Stokes, *The Iconography of Manhattan Island*, vol. 5: 2001.

33. Schuyler, "The Romanesque Revival in New York": 26.

34. Duncan Edwards, "Life at the Athletic Clubs," *Scribner's* 18 (July 1895): 4–23.

35. "Out Among the Builders," *Real Estate Record and Builders' Guide* 31 (May 19, 1883): 205; "Out Among the Builders," *Real Estate Record and Builders' Guide* 32 (November 17, 1883): 905; "Near the Athletic Building," *Real Estate Record and Builders' Guide* 36 (September 5, 1885): 968; Editorial, *American Architect and Building News* 19 (January 16, 1886): 25–26; H. Edwards Ficken, "The Case of H. Edwards Ficken, Architect, Against the New York Athletic Club," *American Architect and Building News* 19 (February 6, 1886): 69–70; "Trouble Among Athletes," *New York Daily Tribune* (March 1, 1886): 2; "New York Athletic Club, H. Edwards Ficken, Arch't," *American Architect and Building News* 19 (April 10, 1886): 175, plate; King, *King's Handbook of New York* (1893), 565; Stokes, *The Iconography of Manhattan Island*, 3: 938; Stern, Gilmartin, and Massengale, *New York 1900*, 228, 231.

36. Editorial, (January 16, 1886): 25.

37. "Near the Athletic Building": 968.

38. "The New Manhattan Athletic Club," *Real Estate Record and Builders' Guide* 36 (November 14, 1885): 1250; "Manhattan Athletic Club," *New York Daily Graphic* (December 8, 1887): 265, 267.

39. "Out Among the Builders," *Real Estate Record and Builders' Guide* 41 (June 23, 1888): 807; "Out Among the Builders," *Real Estate Record and Builders' Guide* 41 (June 30, 1888): 836–37; "The Manhattan Athletic Club's New Building," *Real Estate Record and Builders' Guide* 42 (July 14, 1888): 888; "To Build a New House," *New York Times* (July 15, 1888): 9; "Out Among the Builders," *Real Estate Record and Builders' Guide* 42 (July 28, 1888): 948–49; "The Manhattan Athletic Club," *Real Estate Record and Builders' Guide* 42 (September 11, 1888): 1065; "Competitive Design for the Manhattan Athletic Club," *Building* 10 (June 1, 1889): 177, plate; "Cherry Diamond Athletes," *New York Daily Tribune* (December 15, 1889): 19; "Some Fine New Buildings": 11; "The Growth of Clubs in New York City," supplement, *Real Estate Record and Builders' Guide* 45 (March 8, 1890): 1–13; "The Manhattan Athletic Club," *Real Estate Record and Builders' Guide* 46 (August 30, 1890): 270–71; "A Palace for Athletes," *New York Daily Tribune* (November 30, 1890): 19; King, *King's Handbook of New York* (1893), 564–65; Stokes, *The Iconography of Manhattan Island*, vol. 5: 1967, 2000; Stern, Gilmartin, and Massengale, *New York 1900*, 228; Matthew Postal, "Members Only," *Avenue* (April 1995): 16.

40. "The Manhattan Athletic Club," (August 30, 1890): 270–71.

41. King, *King's Handbook of New York* (1893), 565.

42. "City News," *Building* 4 (May 15, 1886): 240; "Sketch of the Riding Club," *Building* 5 (September 25, 1886): 151, plate; King, *King's Handbook of New York* (1893), 572–73.

43. "The Costly and Substantial Buildings of 1886": 6–8; "New Houses East of Central Park," *Real Estate Record and Builders' Guide* 39 (January 29, 1887): 130–31; "A New Club House," *Real Estate Record and Builders' Guide* 41 (June 9, 1888): 731; Wilson, *The Memorial History of the City of New York*, vol. 1: 257; King, *King's Handbook of New York* (1893), 551; Sturgis, "The Works of McKim, Mead & White": 66, 71; Baldwin, *Stanford White*, 317; Wilson, "Charles F. McKim and the Development of the American Renaissance: A Study in Architecture and Culture": 305, 388; Roth, "The Urban Architecture of McKim, Mead and White, 1870–1910": 209–10; Roth, *The Architecture of McKim, Mead & White, 1870–1920: A Building List*, 61; Roth, *McKim, Mead & White, Architects*, 100–101; Stern, Gilmartin, and Massengale, *New York 1900*, 231.

44. "A New Club House": 731.

45. Sturgis, "The Works of McKim, Mead & White": 66, 71.

46. "Out Among the Builders," *Real Estate Record and Builders' Guide* 39 (February 19, 1887): 233–34; "A New Turnhalle," *New York Times* (April 24, 1887): 9; "Laying a Foundation Stone," *New York Times* (September 6, 1887): 2; "Architectural Notes," *Real Estate Record and Builders' Guide* 40 (September 10, 1887): 1152; "Important Buildings Under Way. III. Between Fifty-ninth and Eighty-sixth Streets," *Real Estate Record and Builders' Guide* 43 (June 8, 1889): 798; "The Central Turnverein," *Real Estate Record and Builders' Guide* 44 (September 14, 1889): 1233–34; "The Growth of Clubs in New York City": 4–6; Wilson, *The Memorial History of the City of New York*, vol. 1: 257; King, *King's Handbook of New York* (1893), 566; White and Willensky, *AIA Guide* (1988), 395.

47. "The Growth of Clubs in New York City": 4.

48. "Another Club in Trouble," *New York Times* (January 15, 1893): 8; "Turned Over to Mr. Ruppert," *New York Times* (February 7, 1893): 2.

49. "Out Among the Builders," *Real Estate Record and Builders' Guide* 41 (March 24, 1888): 363; King, *King's Handbook of New York* (1893), 569; White and Willensky, *AIA Guide* (1988), 165.

50. "Out Among the Builders," *Real Estate Record and Builders' Guide* 43 (March 23, 1889): 392–94; "Laying a Cornerstone: The New House of the Oldest German Club," *New York Times* (December 5, 1889): 2; "Some Fine New Buildings": 11; "The Growth of Clubs in New York City": 3–4; "Club News and Gossip," *New York Times* (July 26, 1891): 14; King, *King's Handbook of New York* (1893), 551; "Deutscher Verein Club, 59th Street, Near 6th Avenue, New York. McKim, Mead & White, Architects," *Architecture and Building* 19 (August 19, 1893): 90, plate; Sturgis, "The Works of McKim, Mead & White": 18–19; Roth, "The Urban Architecture of McKim, Mead and White, 1870–1910": 211, 239; Roth, *The Architecture of McKim, Mead & White, 1870–1920: A Building List*, 54; Roth, *McKim, Mead & White, Architects*, 100; Stern, Gilmartin, and Massengale, *New York 1900*, 231.

51. "Out Among the Builders," *Real Estate Record and Builders' Guide* 31 (January 20, 1883): 28; "Out Among the Builders," *Real Estate Record and Builders' Guide* 33 (February 16, 1884): 160–61; "Front Elevation of the New Building for the Progress Club in Fifty-ninth Street," *New York Daily Graphic* (April 19, 1884): 373; "The Progress Club Progresses," *New York Times* (October 20, 1884): 8; "The Progress Club. Sixty-third Street and Fifth Avenue, New York, N.Y.," *American Architect and Building News* 30 (December 6, 1890): plate; George R. Collins, "The Transfer of Thin Masonry Vaulting from Spain to America," *Journal of the Society of Architectural Historians* 27 (October 1968): 178–201; Stern, Gilmartin, and Massengale, *New York 1900*, 464 (n. 74).

52. "Out Among the Builders," (February 16, 1884): 160–61.

53. "Out Among the Builders," *Real Estate Record and Builders' Guide* 40 (July 30, 1887): 1012–13; "Architectural Notes," *Real Estate Record and Builders' Guide* 40 (November 19, 1887): 1441; "Out Among the Builders," *Real Estate Record and Builders' Guide* 41 (March 24, 1888): 363; "A Handsome Clubhouse," *New York Times* (March 28, 1888): 5; "Important Buildings Projected and Under Way," *Real Estate Record and Builders' Guide* 41 (April 28, 1888): 529; "A Club of Progress," *New York Daily Tribune* (November 29, 1888): 10; "In and About the City: To Cost Half a Million," *New York Times* (November 29, 1888): 8; "The Progress Club," *Real Estate Record and Builders' Guide* 43 (January 12, 1889): 33; "Important Buildings Under Way. III. Between Fifty-ninth and Eighty-sixth Streets": 798; "Out Among the Builders," *Real Estate Record and Builders' Guide* 44 (August 17, 1889): 1134; "A Florentine Palace," *New York Daily Tribune* (February 23, 1890): 19; "The Progress Club Has a House-Warming," *New York Daily Tribune* (March 2, 1890): 2; "A $600,000 Clubhouse," *New York Times* (March 8, 1890): 2; "The Growth of Clubs in New York": 6–11; "A Reception by the Progress Club," *New York Daily Tribune* (March 9, 1890): 4; "Progress Club at Home," *New York Times* (March 9, 1890): 2; "The East Side—Its Streets and Buildings," supplement, *Real Estate Record and Builders' Guide* 45 (May 3, 1890): 1–11; "The Progress Club, Fifth Avenue and Sixty-third Street, New York," *Architecture and Building* 12 (May 31, 1890): 259, plates; "The Progress Club-House, Sixty-third Street and Fifth Avenue, New York, N.Y. Messrs. Alfred Zucker & Co., Architects, New York," *American Architect and Building News* 30 (December 6, 1890): 154, plate; King, *King's Handbook of New York* (1893), 551; Stokes, *The Iconography of Manhattan Island*, vol. 3: 938, vol. 5: 1911; Mary Kathryn Stroh, "The Commercial Architecture of Alfred Zucker in Manhattan" (master's thesis, Pennsylvania State University, 1973): 8; Stern, Gilmartin, and Massengale, *New York 1900*, 231.

54. "The Growth of Clubs in New York": 6.

55. "The Growth of Clubs in New York": 9–10.

56. "The Catholic Club's New House," *New York Times* (March 14, 1891): 8; King, *King's Handbook of New York* (1893), 556, 574; "The Catholic Club-House, West 59th St., New York, N.Y. Messrs. Wm. Schickel & Co., Architects, New York, N.Y.," *American Architect and Building News* 48 (June 15, 1895): 111–12, plates; Stokes, *The Iconography of Manhattan Island*, vol. 3: 937, vol. 5: 1942, 2010; Stern, Gilmartin, and Massengale, *New York 1900*, 231; Christopher Gray, "Central Park South," *Avenue* (June–August 1983): 50–59.

57. "Good News for Masons," *New York Times* (December 1, 1869): 2; "The New Masonic Temple," *Real Estate Record and Builders' Guide* 8 (July 22, 1871): 1; "Out Among the Builders," *Real Estate Record and Builders' Guide* 33 (May 24, 1884): 566; King, *King's Handbook of New York* (1893), 570–71; Edward B. Watson, *New York Then and Now* (New York: Dover, 1976), 156.

58. For discussions of the Young Men's Christian Association's founding and growth, see Verranus Morse, *An Analytical Sketch of the Young Men's Christian Association in North America* (New York: International Committee of Young Men's Associations, 1901); C. Howard Hopkins, *History of the Y.M.C.A. in North America* (New York: Association, 1951).

59. Kennion, *Architects' and Builders' Guide*, part 3: 18–24; "The New Building for the Young Men's Christian Association," *New York Times* (March 16, 1868): 8; "A Christian Club," *New York Times* (July 18, 1869): 5; "The New Building of the Young Men's Christian Association," *New York Times* (August 10, 1869): 3; "Young Men's Christian Association of this City—Details of Their New Building," *New York Times* (October 22, 1869): 5; "Y.M.C.A.," *New York Times* (December 1, 1869): 5; "Young Men's Christian Association," *Frank Leslie's Illustrated Newspaper* (December 18, 1869): 219; Lyman Abbott, "The Y.M.C.A.," *Harper's New Monthly Magazine* 41 (October 1870): 641–54; McCabe, *Lights and Shadows of New York Life*, 811–15; "City Gymnasiums," *New York Times* (July 26, 1875): 8; "The Y.M.C.A. Convention," *New York Daily Graphic* (February 20, 1888): 809–10; King, *King's Handbook of New York* (1893), 414–15; *Young Men's Christian Association Buildings* (Chicago: Young Men's Era, 1895), 6–7; Lamb and Harrison, *History of the City of New York*, 783; Stokes, *The Iconography of Manhattan Island*, vol. 5: 1932, 1936; Rosalie Thorne McKenna, "James Renwick, Jr., and the Second Empire Style in the United States," *Magazine of Art* 44 (March 1951): 97–101; Robert Koch, *Louis C. Tiffany: Rebel in Glass*, 3rd rev. ed. (New York: Crown, 1982), 7; Stephen Garmey, *Gramercy Park: An Illustrated History of a New York Neighborhood* (New York: Balsam Press, 1984), 67–68; M. Christine Boyer, *Manhattan Manners: Architecture and Style, 1850–1900* (New York: Rizzoli International Publications, 1985), 83–84.

60. "The Young Men's Institute, 222 and 224 Bowery, Bowery Branch for the Young Men's Christian Association, of New York City," *Building* 4 (January 16, 1886): 30, plates; "The Y.M.C.A. Convention": 809–10; King, *King's Handbook of New York* (1893), 414, 416; *Young Men's Christian Association Buildings*, 6; White and Willensky, *AIA Guide* (1988), 80.

61. "The German Branch Growing: Its Tenth Anniversary Is About to Be Celebrated," *New York Times* (January 18, 1891): 8; King, *King's Handbook of New York* (1893), 416.

62. "For French Residents," *New York Times* (March 19, 1889): 8; King, *King's Handbook of New York* (1893), 416.

63. "The Costly and Substantial Buildings of 1886": 6–8; "The Hudson River Branch Y.M.C.A.," *Real Estate Record and Builders' Guide* 40 (August 20, 1887): 1079–80; "Cheers for Vanderbilt: Opening the New Railroad Men's Building," *New York Times* (October 4, 1887): 5; "Cornelius Vanderbilt's Gift," *New York Daily Graphic* (October 5, 1887): 765; Editorial, *Real Estate Record and Builders' Guide* 40 (October 8, 1887): 1252; "The Y.M.C.A. Convention": 809–10; "Railroad Employees Club House, New York," *Building* 8 (February 25, 1888): 65, plate; King, *King's Handbook of New York* (1893), 415, 417; Montgomery Schuyler, "The Works of R. H. Robertson," *Architectural Record* 6 (October–December 1896): 184–219; Stokes, *The Iconography of Manhattan Island*, vol. 5: 1993.

64. "The Hudson River Branch Y.M.C.A.": 1079–80.

65. Schuyler, "The Works of R. H. Robertson": 197.

66. "Woman's Work for Her Sex," *New York Daily Tribune* (March 31, 1876): 8; "Out Among the Builders," *Real Estate Record and Builders' Guide* 35 (May 16, 1883): 564; "Young Women's Christian Association Building, Mr. R. H. Robertson, Architect, New York, N.Y.," *American Architect and Building News* 17 (June 13, 1885): 283, plate; "The New Building for the Young Women's Christian Association," *New York Daily Graphic* (November 18, 1885): 114, 116; "Aid for Young Women," *New York Times* (December 2, 1885): 8; "An Aid to Workingwomen," *New York Times* (January 19, 1887): 8; King, *King's Handbook of New York* (1893), 416–17; Schuyler, "The Works of R. H. Robertson": 194–95, 197; Stokes, *The Iconography of Manhattan Island*, vol. 3: 956, vol. 5: 1965–66, 1989, 1992; "The Side Streets of 'The Ladies Mile': R. H. Robertson and the Early

Days of the Young Women's Christian Association," *Village Views* 2 (fall 1985): 2–12; White and Willensky, *AIA Guide* (1988), 186–87.

67. "An Aid to Workingwomen": 8.

68. Schuyler, "The Works of R. H. Robertson": 194.

69. "A Home for Women," *New York Times* (December 3, 1889): 2; "The Margaret Louisa Home for Women Dedicated," *New York Times* (January 20, 1891): 3; "A Woman's Gift to Women," *New York Times* (June 14, 1891): 10; King, *King's Handbook of New York* (1893), 417–18; Schuyler, "The Works of R. H. Robertson": 196; "The Side Streets of 'The Ladies' Mile': R. H. Robertson and the Early Days of the Young Women's Christian Association": 2–12; White and Willensky, *AIA Guide* (1988), 186–87; Landmarks Preservation Commission of the City of New York, *Ladies' Mile Historic District Designation Report* (New York, 1989), 430–33.

70. Quoted in *Ladies' Mile Historic District*, 430.

71. Schuyler, "The Works of R. H. Robertson": 196.

72. Schuyler, "The Works of R. H. Robertson": 196.

73. "Out Among the Builders," *Real Estate Record and Builders' Guide* 33 (January 26, 1884): 87; "The Hebrew Institute," *New York Times* (November 8, 1891): 11; "For Work Among Hebrews," *New York Times* (November 9, 1891): 8; King, *King's Handbook of New York* (1893), 418; White and Willensky, *AIA Guide* (1988), 84.

74. Wilson, *The Memorial History of the City of New York*, vol. 1: 257; King, *King's Handbook of New York* (1893), 318–19.

75. "A New Building for the Arion," *New York Times* (December 31, 1885): 2; "Club House for the Arion Society of New York," *Building* 4 (April 24, 1886): 198, plate; "The Costly and Substantial Buildings of 1886": 6–8; "The Arion Society Building," *Real Estate Record and Builders' Guide* 39 (June 11, 1887): 796; Wilson, *The Memorial History of the City of New York*, vol. 1: 257; King, *King's Handbook of New York* (1893), 319, 574; Stokes, *The Iconography of Manhattan Island*, vol. 3: 937; Collins, "The Transfer of Thin Masonry Vaulting from Spain to America": 192; White and Willensky, *AIA Guide* (1988), 876.

76. "Out Among the Builders," *Real Estate Record and Builders' Guide* 33 (June 21, 1884): 674; "Near the Athletic Building": 968; King, *King's Handbook of New York* (1893), 318; Schuyler, "The Works of R. H. Robertson": 197–98, 201.

77. "Near the Athletic Building": 968.

78. "At the Clubs," *New York Times* (May 10, 1891): 19; "For Music and Musicians," *New York Times* (April 17, 1892): 20; "Mendelssohn Glee Club," *New York Times* (December 7, 1892): 4; "Mendelssohn Glee Club, 113 to 119 West Fortieth Street, New York. R. H. Robertson, Architect," *Architecture and Building* 19 (November 18, 1893): 247, plate.

79. "Celebration of the Fourth," *New York Times* (July 5, 1867): 1; Kennion, *Architects' and Builders' Guide*, part 1: 102; "Tammany Hall," *Harper's Weekly* 12 (July 11, 1868): 433, 438–39; King's *King's Handbook of New York* (1893), 561–62; Stokes, *The Iconography of Manhattan Island*, vol. 5: 1927–28; Watson, *New York Then and Now*, 152.

80. "The Growth of Clubs in New York": 1, 11; Wilson, *The Memorial History of the City of New York*, vol. 1: 247; King, *King's Handbook of New York* (1893), 553; "The Grolier Club-House, 29 East 32nd St., New York, N.Y. Messrs. Romeyn & Stever, Architects, New York, N.Y.," *American Architect and Building News* 48 (June 1, 1895): 91, plates; Stokes, *The Iconography of Manhattan Island*, vol. 3: 938, vol. 5: 1983; Landmarks Preservation Commission of the City of New York, LP-0597 (August 18, 1970); Stern, Gilmartin, and Massengale, *New York 1900*, 231; White and Willensky, *AIA Guide* (1988), 216; Barbaralee Diamonstein, *The Landmarks of New York II* (New York: Harry N. Abrams, 1993), 205.

81. "A New College Fraternity," *New York Daily Tribune* (September 8, 1879): 8; "Delta Psi Chapter House, New York City. J. Renwick, Archt.," *American Architect and Building News* 7 (June 19, 1880): 272, plate; "The Twenty-five Foot House," *Real Estate Record and Builders' Guide* 34 (August 9, 1884): 829–30.

82. "The Twenty-five Foot House": 830.

83. "Presented by Edwin Booth," *New York Times* (April 29, 1888): 16; King, *King's Handbook of New York* (1893), 553–54; Stokes, *The Iconography of Manhattan Island*, vol. 3: 938, vol. 5: 1997; Baldwin, *Stanford White*, 253, 318; Burnham, ed., *New York Landmarks*, 170–71; Landmarks Preservation Commission of the City of New York, LP-0222

(March 15, 1966); Roth, *The Architecture of McKim, Mead & White, 1870–1920: A Building List*, 121; Roth, *McKim, Mead & White, Architects*, 138, 143; Garmey, *Gramercy Park*, 135–37, 139; White and Willensky, *AIA Guide* (1988), 197; Lowe, *Stanford White's New York*, 148–53; Diamonstein, *The Landmarks of New York II*, 96.

Armories

1. For useful overviews of New York's armories, see Robert Koch, "The Medieval Castle Revival: New York Armories," *Journal of the Society of Architectural Historians* 14 (October 1955): 23–29; Pamela Whitney Hawkes, "An American Phenomenon," *Metropolis* 7 (November 1987): 74–75, 77, 81; Pamela W. Hawkes, "Armories," in Kenneth T. Jackson, ed., *The Encyclopedia of New York City* (New Haven, Conn., and London: Yale University Press; New York: New-York Historical Society, 1995), 53–55.

2. Robert M. Fogelson, *America's Armories: Architecture, Society and Public Order* (Cambridge, Mass., and London: Harvard University Press, 1989), 4–5.

3. Koch, "The Medieval Castle Revival: New York Armories": 23; Landmarks Preservation Commission of the City of New York, LP-0312 (October 12, 1967); Barbaralee Diamonstein, *The Landmarks of New York II* (New York: Harry N. Abrams, 1993), 101.

4. "The New Market," *New York Times* (September 17, 1857): 4; "The Tompkins Market," *New York Times* (April 12, 1860): 8; "Opening of the New Tompkins Market," *New York Times* (August 9, 1860): 8; "The New Seventh Regiment Armory," *New York Times* (October 2, 1860): 8; "The National Guard Armory," *New York Times* (January 10, 1861): 8; I. N. Phelps Stokes, *The Iconography of Manhattan Island*, 6 vols. (New York: Robert H. Dodd, 1915–28; New York: Arno Press, 1967), vol. 5: 1865, 1870, 1887–88; Nathan Silver, *Lost New York* (Boston: Houghton Mifflin, 1967), 95; Judith Saltzman, "The Armories of Manhattan" (research paper, Columbia University, April 1980): 2, 13; Frederick S. Lightfoot, ed., *Nineteenth-Century New York in Rare Photographic Views* (New York: Dover, 1981), fig. 98.

5. "The Tompkins Market": 8.

6. "The National Guard Armory": 8.

7. "The Sanitary Fair in New York," *Frank Leslie's Illustrated Newspaper* (March 12, 1864): 396; "The Metropolitan Sanitary Fair," *Frank Leslie's Illustrated Newspaper* (April 16, 1864): 49–50, 56–57, 60–61; George W. Wingate, *History of the Twenty-second Regiment of the National Guard of the State of New York from Its Organization to 1895* (New York: Edwin W. Dayton, 1896), 139–41; Stokes, *The Iconography of Manhattan Island*, vol. 3: 924.

8. "The Seventh Regiment Armory: A New One to Be Erected at the Expense of the Regiment," *New York Times* (January 18, 1876): 8; "The Seventh Regiment: Its Proposed New Armory," *New York Times* (January 23, 1876): 2; "Perspective View and Plans of a Design for Armory for Seventh Regiment, N.G. N.Y.S. Mr. Henry D. Casey, Architect," *New-York Sketch-Book of Architecture* 3 (July 1876): 1, plates 27–28; "Laying a Corner-Stone," *New York Times* (October 14, 1877): 12; "Laying the Corner-Stone of the New Seventh Regiment Armory Last Saturday Afternoon," *New York Daily Graphic* (October 16, 1877): 733–34; "The Long List of Subscribers," editorial, *New York Daily Tribune* (January 8, 1878): 4; "Seventh Regiment Fair—Exterior of the Armory Building," *New York Daily Graphic* (November 17, 1879): 122, 124; "The Opening of the Seventh Regiment Armory Fair Yesterday," *New York Daily Graphic* (November 18, 1879): 129–30, 132; "Opening the Great Fair," *New York Times* (November 18, 1879): 8; "Second Week of the Fair," *New York Times* (November 25, 1879): 2; "After the Fair," *New York Times* (December 8, 1879): 8; "The Seventh's New Home," *New York Times* (April 10, 1880): 8; "The Seventh's 'Good-Bye,'" *New York Daily Tribune* (April 25, 1880): 1; "Taking Possession of the New Armory," *New York Daily Tribune* (April 27, 1880): 8; Clarence C. Buel, "The New York Seventh," *Scribner's Monthly* 20 (May 1880): 63–80; "New York City—Views of the Interior of the Seventh Regiment's New Armory," *New York Daily Graphic* (May 13, 1880): 637; "The Seventh's New Home," *New York Daily Tribune* (September 26, 1880): 12; "National Guard Gossip," *New York Times* (September 26, 1880): 9; "Veterans Housed Sumptuously," *New York Times* (April 23, 1881): 2; William C. Brownell, "Decoration in the Seventh Regiment Armory," *Scribner's Monthly* 22 (July 1881): 370–80; George Augustus Sala, *America Revisited: From the Bay of New York to the Gulf of Mexico, and from Lake Michigan to the Pacific*, 2 vols. (London: Vizetelly & Co., 1882), vol. 1: 59–60, 65–66, 69–71; *Seventh Regiment Armory Illustrated*, pamphlet (New York: Decorator and Furnisher, 1885); Colonel Emmons Clark, *History of the Seventh Regiment of New York, 1806–1889*, 2 vols. (New York: Seventh Regiment, 1890); Moses King, *King's Handbook of New York* (Boston: Moses King, 1893), 532–33; Stokes, *The Iconography of Manhattan Island*, vol. 3: 923, vol. 5: 1956, 1967, 1971, 1973; Koch, "The Medieval Castle Revival: New York Armories": 23–29; Alan Burnham, ed., *New York Landmarks* (Middletown, Conn.: Wesleyan University Press, 1963), 142–43; Silver, *Lost New York*, 218–19; Landmarks Preservation Commission of the City of New York, LP-0417 (June 9, 1967); Elton Robinson, "Rediscovery: A Tiffany Room," *Art in America* 57 (July–August 1969): 72-77; Saltzman, "The Armories of Manhattan": 3–5, 14–16; Robert Koch, *Louis C. Tiffany: Rebel in Glass*, 3rd rev. ed. (New York: Crown, 1982), 14–37; Sophia Duckworth Schachter, "The Seventh Regiment Armory of New York City: A History of Its Construction and Decoration" (master's thesis, Columbia University, 1985); White and Willensky, *AIA Guide* (1988), 356–57; Diane Petzke, "A Call to Arms," *On the Avenue* (June 4, 1988): 10, 12; Fogelson, *America's Armories*, 1–3, 12, 18–55, 102–5, 127–30, 150–51, 156–67, 168; David Garrard Lowe, *Stanford White's New York* (New York: Doubleday, 1992), 82–85; Diamonstein, *The Landmarks of New York II*, 173; Katherine S. Howe et al., *Herter Brothers: Furniture and Interiors for a Gilded Age* (New York: Harry N. Abrams, 1994), 75–77, 93–96; Landmarks Preservation Commission of the City of New York, LP-1884 (July 19, 1994).

9. "View of Reservoir Square, with Armory for Seventh Regiment N.G. S.N.Y.," *New York Daily Graphic* (April 21, 1873): 2, 8.

10. "The Superfluous Reservoir," *New York Daily Tribune* (February 5, 1878): 8; "An Armory on Washington Square," *New York Daily Tribune* (February 19, 1878): 8; Fogelson, *America's Armories*, 94–100, 103–5.

11. Clark, *History of the Seventh Regiment of New York, 1806–1889*, vol. 2: 291–99, quoted in Fogelson, *America's Armories*, 3.

12. James F. O'Gorman, *The Architecture of Frank Furness* (Philadelphia: Philadelphia Museum of Art, 1973), 41, 94–95.

13. Colonel Emmons Clark, quoted in "The Seventh's New Home," *New York Daily Tribune*: 12.

14. "The Armory as a Club House," *Seventh Regiment Gazette* (February 1890): 43, quoted in Landmarks Preservation Commission of the City of New York, LP-1884 (July 19, 1994), 7.

15. *Seventh Regiment Armory Illustrated*, quoted in Schachter, "The Seventh Regiment Armory of New York City: A History of Its Construction and Decoration": 74.

16. *The Veterans' Room, Seventh Regiment N.G. S.N.Y. Armory* (New York, 1881), quoted in Koch, *Louis C. Tiffany*, 15.

17. Brownell, "Decoration in the Seventh Regiment Armory": 380.

18. *The Armory Board, 1884–1911* (New York, 1912), 5–7, cited in Koch, "The Medieval Castle Revival: New York Armories": 25.

19. "Out Among the Builders," *Real Estate Record and Builders' Guide* 34 (October 4, 1884): 1001; "Out Among the Builders," *Real Estate Record and Builders' Guide* 34 (October 18, 1884): 1053; "The Great Building Movement on the West Side," *Real Estate Record and Builders' Guide* 36 (August 29, 1885): 951–52; "Pictures of the Day," *New York Daily Graphic* (September 28, 1885): 610, 612; "Armory for the Twelfth Regiment," *Building* 4 (May 8, 1886): 222; Mitchell, "The New City on the West Side," *Real Estate Record and Builders' Guide* 38 (August 7, 1886): 999–1000; "The Twelfth Regiment Armory," *Real Estate Record and Builders' Guide* 39 (March 26, 1887): 396; "On the March Again," *New York Times* (April 12, 1887): 9; "Bayonets Used on Guests," *New York Daily Tribune* (April 22, 1887): 1; "Sorry but Helpless," *New York Times* (April 23, 1887): 3; King, *King's Handbook of New York* (1893), 535–36; Stokes, *The Iconography of Manhattan Island*, vol. 3: 924; Koch, "The Medieval Castle Revival: New York Armories": 25–26; Fogelson, *America's Armories*, 81–82, 130–33.

20. "The Twelfth Regiment Armory": 396.

21. King, *King's Handbook of New York* (1893), 535.

22. "The Twenty-second's New Armory," *New York Daily Graphic* (June 4, 1887): 771–72; "Out Among the Builders," *Real Estate Record and Builders' Guide* 40 (December 10, 1887): 1549; "Out Among the Builders," *Real Estate Record and Builders' Guide* 41 (May 26, 1888): 672–73; "Out Among the Builders," *Real Estate Record and Builders' Guide* 41 (June 16, 1888): 772–73; "Armory Plans Selected," *New York Times* (July 24, 1888): 5; "Twenty-second Regiment Armory," *New York Times* (September 9, 1888): 16; "Its New Armory," *New York Times* (September 27, 1888): 8; "Laying the Cornerstone," *New York Times* (May 12, 1889): 9; "The Twenty-second's Home," *New York Daily Tribune* (May 31, 1889): 7; "Cornerstone Laid," *New York Times* (May 31, 1889): 5; "Important Buildings Under Way—VI. Between Fifty-ninth and One Hundred and Twenty-fifth Streets, West of Eighth Avenue," *Real Estate Record and Builders' Guide* 43 (June 29, 1889): 912; "National Guard Gossip," *New York Times* (November 10, 1889): 20; "Very Few Defects to Be Found," *New York Times* (February 4, 1890): 8; "Trouble About an Armory," *New York Times* (May 28, 1890): 9; "Their New Armory Opened," *New York Times* (February 1, 1891): 3; "Officers in a Police Court," *New York Times* (February 4, 1891): 2; "Mr. Leo Out in the Cold," *New York Daily Tribune* (July 28, 1891): 4; King, *King's Handbook of New York* (1893), 536; Wingate, *History of the Twenty-second Regiment of the National Guard of the State of New York from Its Organization to 1895*, 482–97; Fogelson, *America's Armories*, 62, 106, 118, 135.

23. "Armory Plans Selected": 5.

24. King, *King's Handbook of New York* (1893), 536.

25. "Out Among the Builders," *Real Estate Record and Builders' Guide* 34 (November 8, 1884): 1129; "Out Among the Builders," *Real Estate Record and Builders' Guide* 34 (December 6, 1884): 1226; "Out Among the Builders," *Real Estate Record and Builders' Guide* 39 (April 16, 1887): 518–19; "Eighth Regiment's Armory," *New York Times* (June 18, 1887): 8; "Out Among the Builders," *Real Estate Record and Builders' Guide* 40 (December 10, 1887): 1549; "Important Buildings Projected and Under Way," *Real Estate Record and Builders' Guide* 41 (April 28, 1888): 529; "For Its New Armory," *New York Times* (September 29, 1888): 5; "Reviewing the Militia," *New York Daily Tribune* (October 20, 1888): 7; "The Cornerstone Laid," *New York Times* (October 20, 1888): 8; "Razed in a Few Seconds," *New York Times* (November 12, 1888): 1; "Work on New Armories," *New York Times* (December 8, 1888): 2; "Important Buildings Under Way—IV. Between Eighty-sixth and One Hundred and Twenty-fifth Streets, East of Fifth Avenue," *Real Estate Record and Builders' Guide* 43 (June 15, 1889): 838–39; "The Eighth Regiment Armory," *Real Estate Record and Builders' Guide* 44 (November 9, 1889): 1501–3; "A Model Military Home," *New York Times* (December 2, 1889): 9; "A Handsome New Armory," *New York Daily Tribune* (December 22, 1889): 19; "The East Side—Its Streets and Buildings," supplement, *Real Estate Record and Builders' Guide* 45 (May 3, 1890): 1–11; "Armory for the Eighth Regiment, N.Y. N.G., Fourth Ave., New York, N.Y. Mr. J. R. Thomas, Architect, New York, N.Y.," *American Architect and Building News* 32 (April 11, 1891): 29–30; King, *King's Handbook of New York* (1893), 534; Stokes, *The Iconography of Manhattan Island*, vol. 3: 923, vol. 5: 1943, 1967, 2001; Koch, "The Medieval Castle Revival: New York Armories": 26; Mary C. Black, *Old New York in Early Photographs* (New York: Dover, 1973), plate 170; Fogelson, *America's Armories*, 55, 105–6, 133–35.

26. "Out Among the Builders," (December 6, 1884): 1226.

27. Stokes, *The Iconography of Manhattan Island*, vol. 5: 1967.

28. "The Eighth Regiment Armory," *Real Estate Record and Builders' Guide*: 1501–2.

29. "A Model Military Home": 9.

Hospitals and Charities

1. For a brief general discussion of the history of hospitals in New York, see Sandra Opdycke and David Rosner, "Hospitals," in Kenneth T. Jackson, ed., *The Encyclopedia of New York City* (New Haven, Conn., and London: Yale University Press; New York: New-York Historical Society, 1995), 561–63. Also see David Rosner, *A Once Charitable Enterprise: Hospitals and Health Care in Brooklyn and New York, 1885–1915* (New York: Cambridge University Press, 1982).

2. *New York As It Is* (New York: J. Miller, 1866; New York: Schocken, 1975), 41; "The New York Hospital," *New York Times* (April 9, 1866): 2; James D. McCabe Jr., *Lights and Shadows of New York Life; or, The Sights and Sensations of the Great City* (Philadelphia: National Publishing, 1872; New York: Farrar, Straus & Giroux, 1970), 648; Society of the New York Hospital, *New York Hospital. Report of the Building Committee, Together with an Address Delivered on the Occasion of the Inauguration of the Building, on the 16th March, 1877, by William H. Van Buren* (New York: L. W. Lawrence, 1877); Eric Larrabee, *The Benevolent and Necessary Institution: The New York Hospital, 1771–1971* (Garden City, N.Y.: Doubleday, 1971); Adele A. Lerner, "New York Hospital," in Jackson, ed., *The Encyclopedia of New York City*, 833.

3. Pliny Earle, *History, Description and Statistics of the Bloomingdale Asylum for the Insane* (New York: Egbert, Hovey & King, 1848); McCabe, *Lights and Shadows of New York Life*, 648. For an extensive discussion of the New York Hospital's presence on Morningside Heights, see Rosner, *A Once Charitable Enterprise*, 164–86.

4. "New York Illustrated—No. 2," *Appletons' Journal* 1 (June 12, 1869): 1–8; "Competitive Design for New York Hospital. Mr. J. Cleaveland Cady, Architect," *New-York Sketch-Book of Architecture* 3 (May 1876): plate 19; "Competitive Design for New York Hospital. R. H. Robertson, Architect," *American Architect and Building News* 1 (August 19, 1876): 269, plate; A. J. Bloor, "Annual Address," *Proceedings of the Tenth Annual Convention of the American Institute of Architects, 1876* (Boston, 1877): 15–34; "New York Hospital. G. B. Post Architect," *American Architect and Building News* 2 (March 17, 1877): 85, plate; "Opening of the New York Hospital, West 16th Street, Yesterday," *New York Daily Graphic* (March 17, 1877): 116; "Opening of the New York Hospital," *New York Times* (March 17, 1877): 8; "The New York Hospital," *Harper's Weekly* 21 (April 7, 1877): 267, 272; Moses King, *King's Handbook of New York* (Boston: Moses King, 1893), 463–64; Russell Sturgis, "The Works of George B. Post," *Architectural Record* 4 (June 1898): 1–96; I. N. Phelps Stokes, *The Iconography of Manhattan Island*, 6 vols. (New York: Robert H. Dodd, 1915–28; New York: Arno Press, 1967), vol. 3: 884, vol. 6: 1106, plate 27C; Winston Weissman, "The Commercial Architecture of George B. Post," *Journal of the Society of Architectural Historians* 31 (October 1972): 176–203; Christopher Gray, "Neighborhood: Ward Healers," *Avenue* (January 1992): 16–20; Sarah Bradford Landau, *George B. Post, Architect: Picturesque Designer and Determined Realist*, Sources of American Architecture, ed. Robert A. M. Stern (New York: Monacelli Press, 1998), 33–34, 36, plate 9.

5. King, *King's Handbook of New York* (1893), 464.

6. Sturgis, "The Works of George B. Post": 45–46.

7. Bloor, "Annual Address": 23.

8. McCabe, *Lights and Shadows of New York Life*, 648–49; Robert J. Carlisle, M.D., ed., *An Account of Bellevue Hospital with a Catalogue of the Medical and Surgical Staff from 1736 to 1894* (New York: Society of the Alumni of Bellevue Hospital, 1893), 1–93; *Bellevue: A Short History of Bellevue Hospital and of the Training Schools* (New York: Alumnae Association of Bellevue, Pension Fund Committee, 1915), n.p.; Stokes, *The Iconography of Manhattan Island*, vol. 3: 1822; Page Cooper, *The Bellevue Story* (New York: Thomas Y. Crowell, 1948); John Star, *Hospital City* (New York: Crown, 1957), 1–129; Don Gold, *Bellevue: A Documentary of a Large Metropolitan Hospital* (New York: Harper & Row, 1975), xi–xii; Jane E. Mottus, "Bellevue Hospital," in Jackson, ed., *The Encyclopedia of New York City*, 98–99.

9. Rosner, *A Once Charitable Enterprise*, 74.

10. "Metropolitan Improvements," *New York Evening Post* (March 10, 1871): 1; "The Busy Builders," *New York Times* (September 3, 1871): 6; Montgomery Schuyler, "Improvements in New York Architecture," *New York World* (November 26, 1871): 3; McCabe, *Lights and Shadows of New York Life*, 650; "Presbyterian Hospital, New York City. Mr. R. H. Hunt, Architect," *New-York Sketch-Book of Architecture* 3 (September 1876): 1, plate 34; Bloor, "Annual Address": 23; "Mr. James Lenox," *New York Daily Graphic* (February 21, 1880): 815; "Some New East Side Buildings," *Real Estate Record and Builders' Guide* 39 (January 1, 1887): 5–6; "Gelatine Print—Dispensary of the Presbyterian Hospital, Madison Avenue and Seventieth Street, New York City," *Building* 9 (November 24, 1888): 189, plate; "Ventilating Tower for the Presbyterian Hospital,

Madison Ave., New York, N.Y. Messrs. J. C. Cady & Co., Architects, New York, N.Y.," *American Architect and Building News* 25 (March 9, 1889): 114, plate; King, *King's Handbook of New York* (1893), 468–69; Montgomery Schuyler, "The Works of the Late Richard M. Hunt," *Architectural Record* 5 (October–December 1895): 97–180; Martha J. Lamb and Mrs. Burton Harrison, *History of the City of New York* (New York: A. S. Barnes & Co., 1896), 415; Montgomery Schuyler, "The Works of Cady, Berg & See," *Architectural Record* 6 (April–June 1897): 517–53; *A History of Real Estate, Building and Architecture in New York City During the Last Quarter of a Century* (New York: Real Estate Record Association, 1898), 600; David Bryson Delavan, *Early Days of the Presbyterian Hospital in the City of New York* (privately published, 1926), 49–53; Albert Richard Lamb, *The Presbyterian Hospital and the Columbia-Presbyterian Medical Center, 1868–1943: A History of a Great Medical Adventure* (New York: Columbia University Press, 1955), 3–38; Paul R. Baker, *Richard Morris Hunt* (Cambridge, Mass.: MIT Press, 1980), 177–81; Frederick S. Lightfoot, ed., *Nineteenth-Century New York in Rare Photographic Views* (New York: Dover, 1981), fig. 119; Sarah Bradford Landau, "Richard Morris Hunt: Architectural Innovator and Father of a 'Distinctive' American School," in Susan R. Stein, ed., *The Architecture of Richard Morris Hunt* (Chicago: University of Chicago Press, 1986), 46–77; Gray, "Neighborhood: Ward Healers": 18; Kathleen A. Curran, *A Forgotten Architect of the Gilded Age: Josiah Cleaveland Cady's Legacy* (Hartford, Conn.: Trinity College, 1993), 41–44, fig. 38; Jane E. Mottus, "Presbyterian Hospital," in Jackson, ed., *The Encyclopedia of New York City*, 936–37; Landau, *George B. Post, Architect*, 15, plate 2.

11. Bloor, "Annual Address": 23.

12. Schuyler, "Improvements in New York Architecture": 3.

13. Schuyler, "The Works of the Late Richard M. Hunt": 104–5.

14. Schuyler, "The Works of Cady, Berg & See": 531, 534.

15. King, *King's Handbook of New York* (1893), 474–75; George R. Stuart, *A History of St. Vincent's Hospital in New York City* (New York: Alumnae Association of St. Vincent's Hospital School of Nursing, 1938), 11–12.

16. *New York As It Is*, 41–42; Barbara J. Niss, "Mount Sinai Hospital," in Jackson, ed., *The Encyclopedia of New York City*, 777.

17. "New Buildings," *New York Times* (May 15, 1870): 6; "Mount Sinai Hospital," *New York Times* (May 26, 1870): 2; "Metropolitan Improvements": 1; McCabe, *Lights and Shadows of New York Life*, 651; "Correspondence. New Work.—Mr. Potter's Retirement," *American Architect and Building News* 1 (August 12, 1876): 262–63; King, *King's Handbook of New York* (1893), 469–70; Lamb and Harrison, *The History of the City of New York*, 416; Stokes, *The Iconography of Manhattan Island*, vol. 3: 1840, 1853–54; "Mount Sinai Hospital," *West-Sider* (July–October 1938): 34; Jane Benedict, comp., *The Story of the First Fifty Years of Mount Sinai Hospital, 1852–1902* (New York: Mount Sinai Hospital, 1944), 1–82; Joseph Hirsh and Beka Doherty, *The First Hundred Years of the Mount Sinai Hospital of New York 1852–1952* (New York: Random House, 1952), 3–64; Tina Levitan, *Islands of Compassion: A History of the Jewish Hospitals of New York* (New York: Twayne, 1964), 22–31; White and Willensky, *AIA Guide* (1988), 359; Gray, "Neighborhood: Ward Healers": 19; Barbara J. Niss, "Mount Sinai Hospital," in Jackson, ed., *The Encyclopedia of New York City*, 777.

18. "Important Buildings Under Way. III. Between Fifty-ninth and Eighty-sixth Streets," *Real Estate Record and Builders' Guide* 43 (June 8, 1889): 798; "The East Side—Its Streets and Buildings," supplement, *Real Estate Record and Builders' Guide* 45 (May 3, 1890): 1–11; Landmark Preservation Commission of the City of New York, LP-1053 (January 29, 1980); Barbaralee Diamonstein, *The Landmarks of New York II* (New York: Harry N. Abrams, 1993), 203.

19. John W. Kennion, *Architects' and Builders' Guide* (New York: Fitzpatrick & Hunter, 1868), part 2: 33–35; "New German Hospital," *New York Times* (September 14, 1869): 2; McCabe, *Lights and Shadows of New York Life*, 650; King, *King's Handbook of New York* (1893), 476.

20. "Out Among the Builders," *Real Estate Record and Builders' Guide* 41 (January 21, 1888): 80.

21. King, *King's Handbook of New York* (1893), 476, 488; Landmarks Preservation Commission of the City of New York, LP-0924 (November 9, 1976); White and Willensky, *AIA Guide* (1988), 166; Diamonstein, *The Landmarks of New York II*, 185.

22. "N.Y. State Woman's Hospital," *New York Times* (October 11, 1867): 2; Kennion, *Architects' and Builders' Guide*, part 2: 105–11; McCabe, *Lights and Shadows of New York Life*, 651; King, *King's Handbook of New York* (1893), 479; Stokes, *The Iconography of Manhattan Island*, vol. 3: 1875; *Woman's Hospital in the State of New York 1855–1930*, pamphlet (New York, 1930), 2–8.

23. McCabe, *Lights and Shadows of New York Life*, 651; King, *King's Handbook of New York* (1893), 480; Centennial Committee of New York Nursery and Child's Hospital, *A Century of Service to Mothers and Children, 1823–1923* (New York, 1923).

24. King, *King's Handbook of New York* (1893), 479–80.

25. "An Architectural Ramble," *Real Estate Record and Builders' Guide* 6 (September 17, 1870): 1–2; Montgomery Schuyler, "Our City Architecture," *New York World* (October 1, 1871): 6–7; King, *King's Handbook of New York* (1893), 486; Lamb and Harrison, *History of the City of New York*, 415; Frank Beekman, *Hospital for the Ruptured and Crippled* (New York: New York Society for the Relief of the Ruptured and Crippled, 1939).

26. Quoted in Beekman, *Hospital for the Ruptured and Crippled*, 21.

27. Dr. James Knight, quoted in Beekman, *Hospital for the Ruptured and Crippled*, 21.

28. Schuyler, "Our City Architecture": 7.

29. "An Architectural Ramble": 1.

30. King, *King's Handbook of New York* (1893), 484.

31. "Eye and Ear Hospitals," *New York Times* (August 5, 1869): 2; "Out Among the Builders," *Real Estate Record and Builders' Guide* 27 (April 23, 1881): 391; "Manhattan Eye and Ear Hospital of New York," *Building* 3 (February 1885): 53; King, *King's Handbook of New York* (1893), 483.

32. "Correspondence," *American Architect and Building News* 1 (October 21, 1876): 343; "The New Hahneman [*sic*] Hospital," *New York Daily Tribune* (October 26, 1876): 8; "The Hahnemann Hospital Opened," *New York Daily Tribune* (November 11, 1878): 2; King, *King's Handbook of New York* (1893), 475; Stokes, *The Iconography of Manhattan Island*, vol. 3: 1939.

33. "Correspondence": 343.

34. "The New Homeopathic Hospital," *New York Daily Graphic* (February 7, 1888): 715; "Out Among the Builders," *Real Estate Record and Builders' Guide* 42 (July 21, 1888): 920–21; "Important Buildings Under Way. III. Between Fifty-ninth and Eighty-sixth Streets": 798.

35. "The New Homeopathic Hospital": 715.

36. "Out Among the Builders," *Real Estate Record and Builders' Guide* 43 (March 9, 1889): 315–17; "An Unexpected Local Improvement," *Real Estate Record and Builders' Guide* 43 (May 25, 1889): 729; "New York Academy of Medicine, New York, N.Y. Mr. R. H. Robertson, Architect, New York, N.Y.," *American Architect and Building News* 26 (August 31, 1889): 98, plate; "Laying the Cornerstone," *New York Times* (October 3, 1889): 9; "Proud and Happy Doctors," *New York Times* (November 21, 1890): 1; Montgomery Schuyler, "The Works of R. H. Robertson," *Architectural Record* 6 (October–December 1896): 184–219; *A History of Real Estate, Building and Architecture in New York City During the Last Quarter of a Century*, 587.

37. Schuyler, "The Works of R. H. Robertson": 201–2.

38. Landmarks Preservation Commission of the City of New York, LP-0908 (March 23, 1976); Diamonstein, *The Landmarks of New York II*, 52–53.

39. King, *King's Handbook of New York* (1893), 500.

40. Landmarks Preservation Commission of the City of New York, LP-0910 (March 23, 1976); Diamonstein, *The Landmarks of New York II*, 52–53.

41. Charles Dickens, *American Notes* (London: Chapman & Hall, 1842; London: Oxford University Press, 1959), 94.

42. King, *King's Handbook of New York* (1893), 462.

43. Nellie Bly, "Behind Asylum Bars: The Mystery of the Unknown Insane Girl," *New York World* (October 9, 1887): 25. Also see Nellie Bly, *Ten Days in a Madhouse, or Nellie Bly's Experience on Blackwell's Island* (New York: N. L. Monroe, 1887); "Light on a Dark Subject," editorial, *New York World* (October 9, 1887): 4.

44. Junius Henri Browne, *The Great Metropolis; a Mirror of New York* (Hartford, Conn.: American Publishing Co., 1869), 77, 79; King, *King's Handbook of New York* (1893), 461; Rosalie Thorne McKenna, "James Renwick, Jr., and the Second Empire Style in the United States," *Magazine of Art* 44 (March 1951): 97–101; Christopher Gray, "Piles of Rubble Where Grim Gray Walls Once Stood," *New York Times* (October 16, 1994), XIII: 7.

45. Quoted in McKenna, "James Renwick, Jr., and the Second Empire Style in the United States": 100.

46. Landmarks Preservation Commission of the City of New York, LP-0909 (March 23, 1976); Diamonstein, *The Landmarks of New York II*, 52–53.

47. Kennion, *Architects' and Builders' Guide*, part 3: 11–17; King, *King's Handbook of New York* (1893), 501.

48. "The New Building for the Department of Charities and Corrections," *New York Times* (March 9, 1869): 7; Christopher Gray, "A 'Costly Looking Barn' for the Charities Agency," *New York Times* (September 17, 1989), X: 12.

49. "The New Building for the Department of Charities and Corrections": 7.

50. *The Children's Aid Society of New York: Its History, Plan and Results* (New York: Children's Aid Society, 1893); *The Crusade for Children: A Review of Child Life in New York During 75 Years, 1853–1928* (New York: Children's Aid Society, 1928).

51. M. G. Van Rensselaer, "Frederick Law Olmsted," *Century Magazine* 46 (October 10, 1893): 860–67.

52. *The Children's Aid Society of New York: Its History, Plan and Results*, 38; Christopher Gray, "Pioneer Home for the Homeless," *New York Times* (March 31, 1991), X: 7; William Alex, *Calvert Vaux: Architect & Planner* (New York: Ink, 1994), 214–23.

53. "The New East Side Boys' Lodging House and Industrial School," *New York Daily Graphic* (May 29, 1880): 763; Alex, *Calvert Vaux*, 216, 218–19.

54. "The New East Side Boys' Lodging House and Industrial School": 763.

55. "Newsboys' Lodging-House, New York, N.Y. Messrs. Vaux & Radford, Architects, New York, N.Y.," *American Architect and Building News* 6 (September 13, 1879): 85, plate; "Out Among the Builders," *Real Estate Record and Builders' Guide* 31 (June 21, 1883): 324; "The Opening of the West Side Lodging House for Homeless Boys Last Thursday Night," *New York Daily Graphic* (May 24, 1884): 633; "Newsboys' Lodging-House, New York, N.Y. Messrs. Vaux & Radford, Architects, New York, N.Y.," *American Architect and Building News* 16 (November 29, 1884): 25, plate; "Design for a Newsboys' Lodging-House. Mr. R. H. Robertson, Architect, New York, N.Y.," *American Architect and Building News* 18 (August 15, 1885): 78, plates; *The Children's Aid Society of New York: Its History, Plan and Results*, 12–18; Alex, *Calvert Vaux*, 220–21.

56. White and Willensky, *AIA Guide* (1988), 163–64; Gray, "Pioneer Home for the Homeless": 7; Alex, *Calvert Vaux*, 222–23.

57. *The Children's Aid Society of New York: Its History, Plan and Results*, 22; White and Willensky, *AIA Guide* (1988), 164; Alex, *Calvert Vaux*, 224.

58. White and Willensky, *AIA Guide* (1988), 410; Christopher Gray, "A $1.9 Million Effort to Rectify the Alteration of an 1891 Relic," *New York Times* (January 15, 1989), IX: 11, reprinted in Christopher Gray, *Changing New York: The Architectural Scene* (New York: Dover, 1992), 76; Alex, *Calvert Vaux*, 225.

59. Alex, *Calvert Vaux*, 226.

60. "Out Among the Builders," *Real Estate Record and Builders' Guide* 43 (May 18, 1889): 694–95; Alex, *Calvert Vaux*, 216.

61. Landmarks Preservation Commission of the City of New York, LP-0960 (July 12, 1977); White and Willensky, *AIA Guide* (1988), 80; Diamonstein, *The Landmarks of New York II*, 200; Alex, *Calvert Vaux*, 225.

62. "An Industrial School," *Real Estate Record and Builders' Guide* 42 (December 29, 1888): 1538. Also see *The Children's Aid Society of New York: Its History, Plan and Results*, 30.

63. *37th Annual Report of the New York Juvenile Asylum* (New York, 1889); Alex, *Calvert Vaux*, 228.

64. Alex, *Calvert Vaux*, 216.

65. White and Willensky, *AIA Guide* (1988), 116; Alex, *Calvert Vaux*, 216.

66. Christopher Gray, "Where the Poor Learned 'Plain and Fine Sewing,'" *New York Times* (September 6, 1987), VIII: 9, reprinted in Gray,

Changing New York, 22; White and Willensky, *AIA Guide* (1988), 181; Landmarks Preservation Commission of the City of New York, LP-1632 (October 2, 1990); Diamonstein, *The Landmarks of New York II*, 388.

67. White and Willensky, *AIA Guide* (1988), 196.

68. Montgomery Schuyler, "Recent Building in New York—I," *American Architect and Building News* 9 (April 9, 1881): 176–77.

69. "New Buildings—The Catholic Male Orphan and Inebriate Asylums," *New York Times* (August 12, 1867): 8; Kennion, *Architects' and Builders' Guide*, part 2: 29–31; "An Architectural Ramble": 1–2; Schuyler, "Our City Architecture": 6–7.

70. "An Architectural Ramble": 1–2.

71. Schuyler, "Our City Architecture": 6–7.

Places of Worship

1. James D. McCabe Jr., *Lights and Shadows of New York Life; or, The Sights and Sensations of the Great City* (Philadelphia: National Publishing, 1872; New York: Farrar, Straus & Giroux, 1970), 491, 497–98. For a brief general discussion of churches in New York, see Susanna A. Jones, "Churches," in Kenneth T. Jackson, ed., *The Encyclopedia of New York City* (New Haven, Conn., and London: Yale University Press; New York: New-York Historical Society, 1995), 221–22.

2. Montgomery Schuyler, "The Churches of New York," *New York World* (October 22, 1871): 2.

3. Schuyler, "The Churches of New York": 2.

4. "New York Illustrated—No. 2," *Appletons' Journal* 1 (June 12, 1869): 1–8; "An Architectural Ramble," *Real Estate Record and Builders' Guide* 6 (September 17, 1870): 1–2; Montgomery Schuyler, "Our City Architecture," *New York World* (October 1, 1871): 6–7; Effingham P. Humphrey, "The Churches of James Renwick, Jr." (master's thesis, New York University, 1942): 61–62.

5. "New York Illustrated—No. 2": 1–8.

6. "An Architectural Ramble": 2.

7. Alan Burnham, ed., *New York Landmarks* (Middletown, Conn.: Wesleyan University Press, 1963), 132–33; Landmarks Preservation Commission of the City of New York, LP-1046 (September 11, 1979); White and Willensky, *AIA Guide* (1988), 217; "Restoration: Desooting a Church's Facade," *New York Times* (November 10, 1991), X: 1; Barbaralee Diamonstein, *The Landmarks of New York II* (New York: Harry N. Abrams, 1993), 144.

8. John W. Kennion, *Architects' and Builders' Guide* (New York: Fitzpatrick & Hunter, 1868), part 2: 100; I. N. Phelps Stokes, *The Iconography of Manhattan Island*, 6 vols. (New York: Robert H. Dodd, 1915–28; New York: Arno Press, 1967), vol. 5: 1918.

9. Kennion, *Architects' and Builders' Guide*, part 2: 112–15.

10. Schuyler, "Our City Architecture": 6. Also see "Laying of the Corner-Stone of the Church of the Messiah," *New York Times* (October 4, 1866): 8; "An Architectural Ramble": 1; Schuyler, "The Churches of New York": 2; Stokes, *The Iconography of Manhattan Island*, vol. 3: 902, vol. 5: 1924.

11. Kennion, *Architects' and Builders' Guide*, part 2: 11.

12. Schuyler, "Our City Architecture": 7; Schuyler, "The Churches of New York": 2; Moses King, *King's Handbook of New York* (Boston: Moses King, 1893), 352; Arthur Bartlett Maurice, *Fifth Avenue* (New York: Dodd, Mead, 1918), 277, 279; Stokes, *The Iconography of Manhattan Island*, vol. 5: 929; Sarah Bradford Landau, *Edward T. and William A. Potter: American Victorian Architects* (New York: Garland, 1979), 152–53, figs. 52–54.

13. Schuyler, "The Churches of New York": 2.

14. Quoted in Maurice, *Fifth Avenue*, 277.

15. Schuyler, "Our City Architecture": 7.

16. Schuyler, "The Churches of New York": 2.

17. Montgomery Schuyler, untitled editorial, *New York World* (January 3, 1875): 5.

18. White and Willensky, *AIA Guide* (1988), 236.

19. White and Willensky, *AIA Guide* (1988), 222.

20. "The Busy Builders," *New York Times* (September 3, 1871): 6; Newbury Frost Read, *The Story of St. Mary's* (New York: privately printed, 1931); J. Robert Wright, "Church of St. Mary the Virgin," in Jackson, ed., *The Encyclopedia of New York City*, 223.

21. White and Willensky, *AIA Guide* (1988), 254; Kathleen A. Curran, *A Forgotten Architect of the Gilded Age: Josiah Cleaveland Cady's Legacy* (Hartford, Conn.: Trinity College, 1993), 29.

22. "Dr. Tyng's Church," *New York Times* (January 29, 1866): 6; Montgomery Schuyler, "Modern Churches," editorial, *New York World* (October 19, 1873): 4; Montgomery Schuyler, "The Church of the Holy Trinity," *New York World* (October 19, 1873): 1; "Pictures of the Day," *New York Daily Graphic* (April 28, 1874): 436, 439; "Church of the Holy Trinity, Forty-Second Street and Madison Avenue, New York. Mr. Leopold Eidlitz, Architect," *New-York Sketch-Book of Architecture* 3 (December 1876): plate 45; George Wolfe Shinn, *King's Handbook of Notable Episcopal Churches in the United States* (Boston: Moses King, 1889), 106–7; *A History of Real Estate, Building and Architecture in New York City During the Last Quarter of a Century* (New York: Real Estate Record Association, 1898), 624; Montgomery Schuyler, "A Great American Architect: Leopold Eidlitz. Part 1," *Architectural Record* 24 (September 1908): 163–79; Nathan Silver, *Lost New York* (Boston: Houghton Mifflin, 1967), 149; White and Willensky, *AIA Guide* (1988), 196. For further discussion of Dr. Stephen Tyng Sr., see Charles Rockland Tyng, *Record of the Life and Work of the Rev. Stephen Higginson Tyng, D.D. and History of St. George's Church, New York to the Close of His Rectorship* (New York: E. P. Dutton, 1890).

23. Schuyler, "The Church of the Holy Trinity": 1.

24. Schuyler, "A Great American Architect: Leopold Eidlitz. Part 1": 175.

25. "Pictures of the Day": 436.

26. Schuyler, "A Great American Architect: Leopold Eidlitz. Part 1": 175.

27. Kennion, *Architects' and Builders' Guide*, part 2: 9–10; George Templeton Strong, diary entry dated May 31, 1871, in *The Diary of George Templeton Strong*, eds. Allan Nevins and Milton Halsey Thomas, 4 vols. (New York: MacMillan, 1952), vol. 4: 361; Schuyler, "The Churches of New York": 2; "St. Thomas's Church, Fifth Avenue, New York City. Mr. Richard M. Upjohn, Architect," *New-York Sketch-Book of Architecture* 3 (May 1876): 1, plate 17; "St. Thomas's Chancel," *American Architect and Building News* 2 (November 3, 1877): 354–55; "Art Work in the Chancel," *New York Times* (May 6, 1878): 5; Shinn, *King's Handbook of Notable Episcopal Churches in the United States*, 129–32; Schuyler, "A Great American Architect: Leopold Eidlitz. Part 1": 175; Maurice, *Fifth Avenue*, frontispiece, 281–82; Everard M. Upjohn, *Richard Upjohn: Architect and Churchman* (New York: Columbia University Press, 1939), 178–80; George E. DeMille, *Saint Thomas Church in the City and County of New York 1823–1954* (Austin, Texas: Church Historical Society, 1958); Helene Barbara Weinberg, "La Farge's Eclectic Idealism in Three New York City Churches," *Winterthur Portfolio* 10 (1975): 199–228.

28. "Out Among the Builders," *Real Estate Record and Builders' Guide* 27 (April 23, 1881): 391; Montgomery Schuyler, "The Works of Charles Coolidge Haight," *Architectural Record* 6 (July 1899): 1–102.

29. Strong, diary entry dated May 31, 1871, in *The Diary of George Templeton Strong*, vol. 4: 361.

30. Schuyler, "The Churches of New York": 2.

31. Schuyler, "A Great American Architect: Leopold Eidlitz. Part 1": 175.

32. "The Old Dutch Church," *New York World* (May 26, 1869): 5; Schuyler, "Our City Architecture": 6–7; Schuyler, "The Churches of New York": 2; *Historical Sketch of the Origin and Organization of the Reformed Church in America and of the Collegiate Church of the City of New York* (New York: Reformed Protestant Dutch Church, 1899), 36–38; Maurice, *Fifth Avenue*, 277, 279–80; Stokes, *The Iconography of Manhattan Island*, vol. 5: 1935; Stern, Mellins, and Fishman, *New York 1960*, 1106.

33. Schuyler, "Our City Architecture": 7.

34. Schuyler, "The Churches of New York": 2.

35. "The Building Outlook," *New York Daily Tribune* (June 17, 1873): 5; Montgomery Schuyler, "Architectural Notes," *New York World* (January 24, 1875): 5; "An Old Church," *New York Daily Tribune* (April 12, 1875): 3; "Dr. Hall's New Church," *New York World* (May 6, 1875): 8; "The New Fifth Avenue Presbyterian Church. Mr. Carl Pfeiffer, Architect," *New York Daily Graphic* (May 8, 1875): 520; "Dr. Hall's New Church," *New York Times* (May 10, 1875): 2; "Notes and Clippings," *American Architect and Building News* 1 (October 7, 1876): 328; "The Fifth Avenue Presbyterian Church, New York, N.Y.," *American Architect and Building News* 13 (March 24, 1883): 139–40, plate; M. G. Van Rensselaer, "Recent Architecture in America—IV," *Century Magazine* 29 (January 1885): 323–38; Henry W. Jessup, *History of the Fifth Avenue Presbyterian Church of New York City, New York, from 1808 to 1908* (New York: Fifth Avenue Presbyterian Church, 1909); Stokes, *The Iconography of Manhattan Island*, vol. 5: 1846; Deacon George T. Peck, "Historical Account of Fifth Avenue Presbyterian Church," in *A Noble Landmark* (New York: Fifth Avenue Presbyterian Church, 1960), 46–51; David Meerse, "Fifth Avenue Presbyterian Church," in Jackson, ed., *The Encyclopedia of New York City*, 402–3.

36. "Dr. Hall's New Church": 8.

37. Van Rensselaer, "Recent Architecture in America—IV": 334.

38. "St. Bartholomew's Church," *Real Estate Record and Builders' Guide* 10 (October 19, 1872): 1; "Consecrating a Church," *New York Times* (February 22, 1878): 8; "A Noble Charity Founded," *New York Times* (July 5, 1890): 5; Montgomery Schuyler, "The Romanesque Revival in New York," *Architectural Record* 1 (July–September 1891): 7–38; King, *King's Handbook of New York* (1893), 151, 358; "Death of James Renwick, Architect," *American Architect and Building News* 48 (June 29, 1895): 125; *A History of Real Estate, Building and Architecture in New York City During the Last Quarter of a Century*, 64; Montgomery Schuyler, "Recent Church Building in New York," *Architectural Record* 13 (June 1903): 408–34; Edward Clowes Churley, *The Centennial History of Saint Bartholomew's Church* (New York: Saint Bartholomew's Church, 1935); Humphrey, "The Churches of James Renwick, Jr.": 63–65; M. Christine Boyer, *Manhattan Manners: Architecture and Style, 1850–1900* (New York: Rizzoli International Publications, 1985), 34.

39. "St. Bartholomew's Church": 1.

40. King, *King's Handbook of New York* (1893), 358–59.

41. "Consecrating a Church": 8.

42. "Out Among the Builders," *Real Estate Record and Builders' Guide* 30 (August 19, 1882): 305; "A New Methodist Church," *New York Times* (November 12, 1882): 7; "Park Avenue Methodist Episcopal Church," *New York Evening Post* (November 14, 1882): 3; "Opening a New Chapel," *New York Times* (June 4, 1883): 5; "Various Notes," *New York Evening Post* (March 24, 1884): 3; "Methodists in a New Home," *New York Times* (March 24, 1884): 8; Van Rensselaer, "Recent Architecture in America—IV": 334; "Park Avenue M. E. Church, Corner Park Avenue and 86th Street, New York, N.Y. Messrs. J. C. Cady & Co., Architects, New York, N.Y.," *American Architect and Building News* 36 (April 16, 1892): 46, plate; King, *King's Handbook of New York* (1893), 377; Montgomery Schuyler, "The Works of Cady, Berg & See," *Architectural Record* 6 (April–June 1897): 517–53; *A History of Real Estate, Building and Architecture in New York City During the Last Quarter of a Century*, 635.

43. "Methodists in a New Home": 8.

44. Van Rensselaer, "Recent Architecture in America—IV": 334.

45. "The New Calvary Baptist Church," *New York Daily Tribune* (January 13, 1881): 2; "The Calvary Baptist Church," *New York Times* (August 9, 1882): 3; "The Calvary Baptist Church," *Real Estate Record and Builders' Guide* 31 (May 5, 1883): 178; "Calvary Baptist Church," *Building* 2 (October 1883): 6, plate; "The Madison Avenue Methodist Church," *Real Estate Record and Builders' Guide* 32 (November 10, 1883): 876–77; "The Calvary Baptist Church," *New York Times* (December 24, 1883): 8; "Calvary Baptist Church," *New York Evening Post* (February 4, 1884): 10; "The Calvary Baptist Church," *New York Daily Graphic* (October 11, 1884): 755, 761; Van Rensselaer, "Recent Architecture in America—IV": 334–35; "In West Fifty-Seventh Street," *Real Estate Record and Builders' Guide* 36 (September 19, 1885): 992–93; King, *King's Handbook of New York* (1893), 380–81; Stokes, *The Iconography of Manhattan Island*, vol. 5: 1983.

46. "The Calvary Baptist Church," *Real Estate Record and Builders' Guide*: 178.

47. Van Rensselaer, "Recent Architecture in America—IV": 334–35.

48. "The Madison Avenue Methodist Church": 876.

49. "In West Fifty-seventh Street": 992–93.

50. Humphrey, "The Churches of James Renwick, Jr.": 65; Landmarks Preservation Commission of the City of New York, *Upper East Side Historic District Designation Report* (New York, 1981), 741; White and Willensky, *AIA Guide* (1988), 372–73.

51. "St. James Lutheran Church and Rectory, New York," *American Architect and Building News* 31 (July 4, 1891): plates; "St. James Lutheran Church," *Scientific American Architects' and Builders' Edition* 12 (November 1892): 71; Landau, *Edward T. and William A. Potter: American Victorian Architects*, 220–21, figs. 125–26.

52. "Phillips Presbyterian Church. Mr. R. H. Robertson, Architect," *New-York Sketch-Book of Architecture* 1 (April 1874): 2, plate; "Phillips Presbyterian Church," *New York Times* (October 19, 1874): 8; "Pictures of the Day," *New York Daily Graphic* (October 20, 1874): 796, 802; "Phillips Presbyterian Church, Madison Avenue, New York City, Mr. R. H. Robertson, Architect," *New-York Sketch-Book of Architecture* 3 (August 1876): 1, plate; King, *King's Handbook of New York* (1893), 370; Montgomery Schuyler, "The Works of R. H. Robertson," *Architectural Record* 6 (October–December 1896): 184–219; *A History of Real Estate, Building and Architecture in New York City During the Last Quarter of a Century*, 624, 691.

53. Schuyler, "The Works of R. H. Robertson": 184–85.

54. "Church to Be Built on Madison Avenue, New York City," *American Architect and Building News* 9 (April 30, 1881): 210, plate; "Out Among the Builders," *Real Estate Record and Builders' Guide* (May 14, 1881): 492; "Church of the Holy Spirit," *New York Daily Graphic* (October 4, 1884): 703, 709; "A Church Tower, Madison Avenue, Corner Sixty-sixth Street, New York City," *Building* 7 (August 13, 1887): 53, plate.

55. "Church to Be Built on Madison Avenue, New York City": 210.

56. "Church of the Holy Spirit": 703.

57. "Out Among the Builders," (May 14, 1881): 492.

58. "Out Among the Builders," *Real Estate Record and Builders' Guide* 28 (September 24, 1881): 903; "Out Among the Builders," *Real Estate Record and Builders' Guide* 28 (December 3, 1881): 1120; "A New Methodist Church," *New York Times* (April 22, 1882): 8; "Laying a Corner-Stone," *New York Times* (August 1, 1882): 3; "Opening a New Church," *New York Times* (November 12, 1883): 2; "The New Methodist Church," *New York Times* (November 19, 1883): 8; "Methodists in a New Home," *New York Times* (March 24, 1884): 8; "Madison Avenue M. E. Church," *Building* 5 (August 28, 1886): 103, plates; James Fergusson, *A History of Architecture in All Countries, from the Earliest Times to the Present Day*, 3rd rev. ed. by Robert Kerr (London: J. Murray, 1891), 364–66; Schuyler, "The Works of R. H. Robertson": 187–88; William Wallace Martin, *Manual of Ecclesiastical Architecture* (Cincinnati: Curtis & Jennings; New York: Eaton & Mains, 1897), 403–4; *A History of Real Estate, Building and Architecture in New York City During the Last Quarter of a Century*, 635, 691.

59. Schuyler, "The Works of R. H. Robertson": 187–88.

60. "A New Methodist Church," (April 22, 1882): 8.

61. Fergusson, *A History of Architecture in All Countries, from the Earliest Times to the Present Day*, 366.

62. Schuyler, "The Works of R. H. Robertson": 187–88.

63. Schuyler, "The Works of R. H. Robertson": 189. Also see "Out Among the Builders," *Real Estate Record and Builders' Guide* 31 (May 19, 1883): 205; "Various Notes," *New York Evening Post* (April 15, 1884): 3; "Upper Madison Avenue," *Real Estate Record and Builders' Guide* 33 (May 24, 1884): 560; "The New St. James's Church," *New York Times* (June 25, 1884): 8; "St. James' Church," *Real Estate Record and Builders' Guide* 34 (November 22, 1884): 1172; "The New St. James's Church," *New York Evening Post* (January 21, 1885): 1; "The Newest St. James's Church," *New York Times* (January 22, 1885): 3; "St. James Church, Corner Seventy-first Street and Madison Avenue, New York, N.Y., Mr. R. H. Robertson, Architect, New York, N.Y.," *American Architects and Building News* 17 (April 25, 1885): 199, plate; Fergusson, *A History of Architecture in All Countries, from the Earliest Times to the Present Day*, 363; Stokes, *The Iconography of Manhattan Island*, vol. 5: 1984; Christopher Gray, *History of a New York Parish: St. James' Church 1810–1985* (New York: St. James' Church, 1985).

64. Humphrey, "The Churches of James Renwick, Jr.": 62–63.

65. "Upper Madison Avenue": 560.

66. "St. James' Church," (November 22, 1884): 1172.

67. Schuyler, "The Works of R. H. Robertson": 189.

68. "A New Presbyterian Church," *New York Times* (April 1, 1875): 5.

69. "Laying a Cornerstone," *New York Times* (December 12, 1887): 8; Curran, *A Forgotten Architect of the Gilded Age: Josiah Cleaveland Cady's Legacy*, 29.

70. "The New Forsyth-Street Church," *New York Times* (March 15, 1890): 3; Paul Goldberger, *The City Observed: New York* (New York: Random House, 1979), 54; Curran, *A Forgotten Architect of the Gilded Age: Josiah Cleaveland Cady's Legacy*, 29–30, fig. 27.

71. "The New Forsyth-Street Church": 3.

72. King, *King's Handbook of New York* (1893), 388–90. Also see "The Catholic Apostolic Church," *Real Estate Record and Builders' Guide* 41 (January 7, 1888): 2; John S. Davenport, "The Catholic Apostolic Church," letter to the editor, *Real Estate Record and Builders' Guide* 41 (January 14, 1888): 36; James Taylor, "The History of Terra Cotta in New York City," *Architectural Record* 2 (October–December 1892): 136–48; Montgomery Schuyler, "The Work of Francis H. Kimball and Kimball & Thompson," *Architectural Record* 7 (April–June 1898): 479–518; White and Willensky, *AIA Guide* (1988), 225; Christopher Gray, "On West 57th Street, a Striking Victorian Sanctuary," *New York Times* (July 7, 1996), VIII: 5.

73. White and Willensky, *AIA Guide* (1988), 181.

74. "The Catholic Apostolic Church": 2.

75. Schuyler, "The Works of Francis H. Kimball and Kimball & Thompson": 494.

76. "City Intelligence: Chapel for Grace Church," *New York Times* (March 23, 1860): 8; "Building Operations in New York," *Architects' and Mechanics' Journal* 2 (September 1, 1866): 218; "Burning of Barnum's; Destruction of the Circus Building, Grace Chapel and the Adjoining Edifices in Fourteenth Street," *New York Herald* (December 25, 1872): 3; "New York Fires," *New York Times* (December 25, 1872): 8; "The Hippodrome Burned," *Harper's Weekly* 17 (January 11, 1873): 29–30; Stokes, *The Iconography of Manhattan Island*, vol. 5: 1886, 1951.

77. "Grace Chapel. Messrs. W. A. Potter and R. H. Robertson, Architects," *New-York Sketch-Book of Architecture* 2 (June 1875): 2, plate 22; "The New Grace Chapel, Fourteenth Street, Opposite the Academy of Music," *New York Daily Graphic* (January 28, 1876): 692; "A Mission for the Italians," *New York Times* (March 5, 1883): 8; Shinn, *King's Handbook of Notable Episcopal Churches in the United States*, 63; King, *King's Handbook of New York* (1893), 348–50; William Rhinelander Stewart, *Grace Church and Old New York* (New York: E. P. Dutton, 1924); Carl Carmer, *The Years of Grace* (New York: Grace Church, 1958); Landau, *Edward T. and William A. Potter: American Victorian Architects*, 185–86, fig. 85.

78. "The New Memorial Chapel of St. Mark's Parish at Tenth Street and Avenue A," *New York Daily Graphic* (June 14, 1884): 774, 777; Humphrey, "The Churches of James Renwick, Jr.": 70; White and Willensky, *AIA Guide* (1988), 163.

79. "Out Among the Builders," *Real Estate Record and Builders' Guide* 41 (May 26, 1888): 673; "Chapel of the Good Shepherd, Blackwell's Island, New York, N.Y., Mr. Frederick C. Withers, Architect, New York, N.Y.," *American Architect and Building News* 26 (July 20, 1889): 27, plate; Francis R. Kowsky, *The Architecture of Frederick Clarke Withers and the Progress of the Gothic Revival in America After 1850* (Middletown, Conn.: Wesleyan University Press, 1980), 143–45; White and Willensky, *AIA Guide* (1988), 473.

80. Christopher Gray, "St. Thomas Moore Roman Catholic Church," *New York Times* (April 2, 1989), VIII: 12, reprinted in Christopher Gray, *Changing New York: The Architectural Scene* (New York: Dover, 1992), 84.

81. "Opening a New Church," *New York Times* (May 25, 1885): 8; "The Broome Street Tabernacle, New York City," *Building* 4 (June 26, 1886): 306, plate; King, *King's Handbook of New York* (1893), 387; Curran, *A Forgotten Architect of the Gilded Age: Josiah Cleaveland Cady's Legacy*, 29, figs. 23–24.

82. "Old Trinity Renovated," *New York Times* (June 17, 1877): 2; "An Impressive Ceremonial," *New York Times* (June 30, 1877): 2; "New York—The Altar and Reredos in Trinity Church," *The Churchman* 35 (June 30, 1877): 726–27; "Correspondence," *American Architect and Building News* 2 (July 7, 1877): 218; *The Year Book and Register of Trinity Church in the City of New York, 1878* (New York: Trinity Church, 1878), 52–55; "Alterations at Trinity Church," *American Architect and Building News* 3 (February 2, 1878): plate; Clifford P. Morehouse, *Trinity: Mother of Churches* (New York: Seabury, 1973), 171–74; Kowsky, *The Architecture of Frederick Clarke Withers*, 122–27.

83. "Correspondence": 218.

84. Schuyler, "The Works of Charles Coolidge Haight": 14.

85. "Laying of the Corner-Stone of the Free Chapel of St. Chrysostum," *New York Times* (October 29, 1868): 2; Montgomery Schuyler, "Trinity's Architecture," *Architectural Record* 25 (June 1909): 411–25; E. Clowes Chorley, ed., *Quarter of a Millennium: Trinity Church of the City of New York, 1697–1947* (Philadelphia: Church Historical Society, 1947), 73–74; Morehouse, *Trinity: Mother of Churches*, 157.

86. Schuyler, "Trinity's Architecture": 423.

87. "A New Church for Trinity Parish," *New York Times* (January 16, 1876): 12; "New Trinity Chapel of St. Augustine, Now Building at the Corner of The Bowery and Houston Street, New York City," *New York Daily Graphic* (March 22, 1876): 174; "St. Augustine Chapel and Schools, Trinity Parish, New York, Messrs. Potter and Robertson, Architects," *American Architect and Building News* (July 8, 1876): 220, plate; "Church Corner-Stone Laid," *New York Times* (September 3, 1876): 12; "Trinity's New Chapel," *New York Daily Graphic* (September 6, 1876): 458; "Chapel of St. Augustine," *New York Times* (December 1, 1877): 8; Shinn, *King's Handbook of Notable Episcopal Churches in the United States*, 179–82; King, *King's Handbook of New York* (1893), 346–47; *A History of Real Estate, Building and Architecture in New York City During the Last Quarter of a Century*, 628; Schuyler, "Trinity's Architecture": 424; Chorley, ed., *Quarter of a Millennium*, 74–77; Morehouse, *Trinity: Mother of Churches*, 157–59; Landau; *Edward T. and William A. Potter: American Victorian Architects*, 186–88, figs. 86–88.

88. "Trinity's New Chapel": 458.

89. Schuyler, "Trinity's Architecture": 424.

90. For useful discussions of the Roman Catholic Church in New York, see John Talbot Smith, *The Catholic Church in New York* (New York: Hall and Locke, 1905); Florence D. Cohalan, *A Popular History of the Archdiocese of New York* (Yonkers, N.Y.: United States Catholic Historical Society, 1983); T. J. Shelley, "Catholics," in Jackson, ed., *The Encyclopedia of New York City*, 190–93.

91. "New York City: Laying the Cornerstone of the New St. Patrick's Cathedral," *New York Times* (August 11, 1858): 8; "Dedication of St. Patrick's Cathedral," *New York Times* (March 18, 1868): 8; "Our Architectural Progress," *New York Times* (April 5, 1868): 3; "New York Illustrated—No. 2": 7; "St. Patrick's Cathedral in New York," *Harper's Weekly* 13 (October 18, 1869): 808–12; "An Architectural Ramble": 2; Schuyler, "The Churches of New York": 2; "A Protestant Cathedral," editorial, *New York World* (November 9, 1873): 4; "The Altar for the New York Cathedral," *New York Times* (May 7, 1875): 9; "The Catholic Cathedral," *New York Times* (August 24, 1875): 2; "The Marble Altar and Throne for St. Patrick's Cathedral, Fifth Avenue," *New York Daily Graphic* (January 8, 1876): 537; "New York Roman Catholic Cathedral, Fifth Avenue, New York City," *New-York Sketch-Book of Architecture* 3 (November 1876): 1, plate 41; "Notes and Clippings," *American Architect and Building News* 1 (November 18, 1876): 376; "The New Catholic Cathedral," *New York Daily Tribune* (November 18, 1876): 2; "Opening the New Cathedral," *New York Daily Tribune* (November 30, 1877): 3; "St. Patrick's Roman Catholic Cathedral, New York," *American Architect and Building News* 3 (January 19, 1878): 20, plate; "The New St. Patrick's," editorial, *New York Daily Tribune* (October 23, 1878): 5; Clarence Cook, "The New Catholic Cathedral in New York," *Atlantic Monthly* 42 (February 1879): 173–77; "The Catholic Cathedral," *New York Times* (May 18, 1879): 10; "The New Cathedral," *New York Daily Graphic* (May 26, 1879): 607–9; Editorial, *New York Times* (May 27, 1879): 4; "Spires for the Cathedral," *New York Times* (September 25, 1885): 8; "St. Patrick's Cathedral, New York, N.Y., Messrs. Renwick & Sands, Architects, New York, N.Y.," *American Architect and Building News* 19 (March 27, 1886): 150, plate; "St. Patrick's Cathedral," *Building* 5 (August 14, 1886): 79, plates; "St. Patrick's Cathedral, New York City," *Building* 5 (September 4, 1886): 115, plates; "Two Dwellings," *Real Estate Record and Builders' Guide* 42 (July 28, 1888): 944–45; "The Spires Completed," *New York Times* (October 7, 1888): 13; "Costly New York Buildings," *New York Times* (October 5, 1890): 11; King, *King's Handbook of New York* (1893), 391–94; Cardinal John Murphy Farley, *History of St. Patrick's Cathedral* (New York: Archdiocese of New York, 1908); Maurice, *Fifth Avenue*, 280–81; Stokes, *The Iconography of Manhattan Island*, vol. 5: 1877, 1967–68; Humphrey, "The

Churches of James Renwick, Jr.": 25–60; Rosalie Thorne McKenna, "James Renwick, Jr., and the Second Empire Style in the United States," *Magazine of Art* 44 (March 1951): 97–101; Robert C. Broderick, *Historic Churches of the United States* (New York: Wilfred Funk, 1958), 152, 154–55, 157; Burnham, ed., *New York Landmarks*, 140–41; Landmarks Preservation Commission of the City of New York, LP-0267 (October 19, 1966); Leland A. Cook, *St. Patrick's Cathedral* (New York: Quick Fox, 1979); Roger Kennedy, *American Churches* (New York: Stewart, Tabori & Chang, 1982), 90–93; White and Willensky *AIA Guide* (1988), 266; Edward Norman, *The House of God* (London: Thames and Hudson, 1990), 277, 279; Diamonstein, *The Landmarks of New York II*, 128–29; Margaret M. McGuinness, "St. Patrick's Cathedral," in Jackson, ed., *The Encyclopedia of New York City*, 1037.

92. John Gilmary Shea, ed., *The Catholic Churches of New York City* (New York: Lawrence G. Goulding, 1878), 81–106; White and Willensky, *AIA Guide* (1988), 79.

93. "An Architectural Ramble": 1.

94. Schuyler, "The Churches of New York": 2.

95. "A Protestant Cathedral": 4.

96. "The New St. Patrick's," (October 23, 1878): 5.

97. Landmarks Preservation Commission of the City of New York, LP-0267 (October 19, 1966); White and Willensky, *AIA Guide* (1988), 79.

98. "Out Among the Builders," *Real Estate Record and Builders' Guide* 28 (December 3, 1881): 1120; "Some Up-Town Buildings," *Real Estate Record and Builders' Guide* 33 (January 5, 1884): 2–3; White and Willensky, *AIA Guide* (1988), 266.

99. "Some Up-Town Buildings": 2.

100. "Two Dwellings": 944.

101. Shea, ed., *The Catholic Churches of New York City*, 718–22; White and Willensky, *AIA Guide* (1988), 354; Diamonstein, *The Landmarks of New York II*, 179.

102. Landmarks Preservation Commission of the City of New York, LP-1052 (May 19, 1981); White and Willensky, *AIA Guide* (1988), 354–55; Diamonstein, *The Landmarks of New York II*, 179.

103. Shea, ed., *The Catholic Churches of New York City*, 338–45; White and Willensky, *AIA Guide* (1988), 208.

104. White and Willensky, *AIA Guide* (1988), 182.

105. Kennion, *Architects' and Builders' Guide*, part 2: 5–6; "Catholic Church Notes: Church of the Holy Cross Nearly Ready for Consecration," *New York Times* (December 27, 1885): 4; King, *King's Handbook of New York* (1893), 398; White and Willensky, *AIA Guide* (1988), 227.

106. "Correspondence," *American Architect and Building News* 1 (June 24, 1876): 206; Shea, ed., *The Catholic Churches of New York City*, 107–24; "St. Agnes's to Have a New Altar," *New York Times* (September 11, 1892): 16; Robert D. McFadden, "Fire Guts St. Agnes, a Historic Manhattan Church," *New York Times* (December 11, 1992), B: 1; Nick Ravo, "St. Agnes Gets a New Face As It Is Rebuilt," *New York Times* (October 22, 1995), IX: 41.

107. "In and About the City: An Architectural Gem," *New York Times* (November 25, 1887): 8. Also see "Building a New Church," *New York Times* (November 11, 1880): 8; "Architectural Notes," *Art Age* 3 (July 1886): 213–14.

108. Shea, ed., *The Catholic Churches of New York City*, 178–88; "The New Church of St. Anthony of Padua, New York City," *Building* 4 (June 5, 1886): 270, plate; "Blessing a Cornerstone," *New York Times* (June 15, 1886): 8; "St. Anthony's of Padua," *New York Times* (June 11, 1888): 2.

109. Kennion, *Architects' and Builders' Guide*, part 2: 506; Shea, ed., *The Catholic Churches of New York City*, 274–83; King, *King's Handbook of New York* (1893), 398; Montgomery Schuyler, "The Work of N. Le Brun & Sons," *Architectural Record* 27 (May 1920): 364–81; White and Willensky, *AIA Guide* (1988), 212.

110. Shea, ed., *The Catholic Churches of New York City*, 413–24; Schuyler, "The Work of N. Le Brun & Sons": 372–73; White and Willensky, *AIA Guide* (1988), 212.

111. "Out Among the Builders," *Real Estate Record and Builders' Guide* 33 (February 9, 1884): 134–35; "Out Among the Builders," *Real Estate Record and Builders' Guide* 33 (April 5, 1884): 343–44.

112. "A New Catholic Church," *New York Times* (April 17, 1884): 8; "Beginnings of New Churches," *New York Times* (July 14, 1884): 8; White and Willensky, *AIA Guide* (1988), 224.

113. For informative discussions of the history of Jews in New York, see Hyman B. Grinstein, *The Rise of the Jewish Community of New York, 1654–1860* (Philadelphia: Jewish Publication Society of America, 1945); Moses Rischin, *The Promised City: New York's Jews, 1870–1914* (Cambridge, Mass.: Harvard University Press, 1962); Marc D. Angel and Jeffrey S. Garock, "Jews," in Jackson, ed., *The Encyclopedia of New York City*, 620–23.

114. "Local Intelligence: The Temple Emanu El," *New York Times* (November 1, 1866): 2; Kennion, *Architects' and Builders' Guide*, part 2: 73–74; "Local Intelligence: The New Temple Emanuel," *New York Times* (September 11, 1868): 2; Montgomery Schuyler, "Temple Emanu-el," *New York World* (September 12, 1868): 7; "Architects Criticized," *Real Estate Record and Builder's Guide* 2 (September 26, 1868): 1; Strong, diary entry dated November 3, 1869, in *The Diary of George Templeton Strong*, vol. 4: 261–62; "An Architectural Ramble": 1–2; McCabe, *Lights and Shadows of New York Life*, 494; "Jewish Synagogue, 5th Avenue, New York City," *New-York Sketch-Book of Architecture* 3 (February 1876): 1, plate 6; "The Alcazar Casino," *Real Estate Record and Builder's Guide* 30 (November 18–25, 1882): 74–75; "Temple Emanuel, New York, N.Y.," *American Architect and Building News* 18 (October 31, 1885): 210, plate; King, *King's Handbook of New York* (1893), 402; Meyer Stern, *The Rise and Progress of Reform Judaism Embracing a History Made from the Official Records of Temple Emanu-el of New York* (New York: Meyer Stern, 1895); Schuyler, "A Great American Architect: Leopold Eidlitz. Part 1": 176–77, 179; Montgomery Schuyler, "A Great American Architect: Leopold Eidlitz. Part 2," *Architectural Record* 24 (October 1908): 277–92; Maurice, *Fifth Avenue*, 269; Rachel Wischnitzer, *Synagogue Architecture in the United States* (Philadelphia: Jewish Publication Society of America, 1955), 72, 74–76; Silver, *Lost New York*, 150; Brian de Breffny, *The Synagogue* (New York: Macmillan, 1975), 168; Frederick S. Lightfoot, ed., *Nineteenth-Century New York in Rare Photographic Views* (New York: Dover, 1981), fig. 112; Dorothy B. Dubin, "Extant Manhattan Synagogues Organized Before the Civil War" (master's thesis, Columbia University, 1983): 46–49; Stern, Gilmartin, and Massengale, *New York 1900*, 109; Joy Kestenbaum, "Synagogue Architecture in New York," *Village Views* 5 (1989): 56–79; Jenna Weisman Joselit, "Temple Emanu-El," in Jackson, ed., *The Encyclopedia of New York City*, 1161; David Gonzalez, "A Walk Down 150 Years of Faith and Tradition," *New York Times* (April 3, 1995), B: 3.

115. Schuyler, "Temple Emanu-el": 7.

116. For further discussion of the development of Reform Judaism, see David Philipson, *The Reform Movement in Judaism* (Cincinnati: Ktav, 1967).

117. "Proposed Parsonage for Temple Emanuel, New York. Mr. Henry Fernbach, Architect," *American Architect and Building News* 2 (April 2, 1877): 124, plate.

118. Carol Herselle Krinsky, *Synagogues of Europe: Architecture, History, Meaning* (New York: Architectural History Foundation; Cambridge, Mass.: MIT Press, 1985), 265–70.

119. Wischnitzer, *Synagogue Architecture in the United States*, 72.

120. Arnold Brunner, quoted in Abram S. Isaacs, "Recent American Synagogue Architecture," *American Architect and Building News* 94 (September 2, 1908): 73–76, also quoted in Christopher Gray, "A $500,000 Restoration of an 1872 Masterwork," *New York Times* (April 2, 1995), IX: 7.

121. Schuyler, "Temple Emanu-el": 7.

122. Schuyler, "A Great American Architect: Leopold Eidlitz. Part 2": 277.

123. Schuyler, "Temple Emanu-el": 7.

124. Schuyler, "The Churches of New York": 2.

125. Strong, diary entry dated November 3, 1869, in *The Diary of George Templeton Strong*, vol. 4: 261–62.

126. King, *King's Handbook of New York* (1893), 404; Simon Cohen, *Shaaray Tefila: A History of Its Hundred Years* (New York: Greenberg, 1945), 25–38; Wischnitzer, *Synagogue Architecture in the United States*, 84–85; Dubin, "Extant Manhattan Synagogues Organized Before the Civil War": 49–51.

127. Quoted in Wischnitzer, *Synagogue Architecture in the United States*, 84.

128. King, *King's Handbook of New York* (1893), 404.

129. "The New Synagogue," *Harper's Weekly* 16 (July 6, 1872): 532; "The Alcazar Casino": 74–75; Wischnitzer, *Synagogue Architecture in the United States*, 77–78, 80–81; Landmarks Preservation Commission of the City of New York, LP-0276 (June 7, 1966); Dubin, "Extant Manhattan Synagogues Organized Before the Civil War": 51–54; White and Willensky, *AIA Guide* (1988), 249–50; Kestenbaum, "Synagogue Architecture in New York": 68–69; Oscar Israelowitz, *Synagogues of the United States* (New York: Israelowitz, 1992), 45, 104; Diamonstein, *The Landmarks of New York II*, 158–59; H. A. Meek, *The Synagogue* (London: Phaedon, 1995), 194; Gray, "A $500,000 Restoration of an 1872 Masterwork": 7.

130. Henry Fernbach, quoted in Wischnitzer, *Synagogue Architecture in the United States*, 77–78.

131. Quoted in Gray, "A $500,000 Restoration of an 1872 Masterwork": 7.

132. Krinsky, *Synagogues of Europe*, 157–59.

133. "Dedication of a New Synagogue," *New York Times* (July 3, 1872): 2; "Anshi Chesed," *New York Times* (March 8, 1874): 5; King, *King's Handbook of New York* (1893), 403–4; Wischnitzer, *Synagogue Architecture in the United States*, 78; Dubin, "Extant Manhattan Synagogues Organized Before the Civil War": 55, 135.

134. King, *King's Handbook of New York* (1893), 404.

135. "Buildings Projected," *Real Estate Record and Builders' Guide* 33 (March 22, 1884): 309; "Dedicating a Synagogue," *New York Times* (March 26, 1885): 8; King, *King's Handbook of New York* (1893), 400–402; Israel Goldstein, *A Century of Judaism in New York: B'nai Jeshurun* (New York: Congregation B'nai Jeshurun, 1930); Wischnitzer, *Synagogue Architecture in the United States*, 78; Dubin, "Extant Manhattan Synagogues Organized Before the Civil War": 58–59, 128, 136; Kestenbaum, "Synagogue Architecture in New York": 70–71; Jenna Weissman Joselit, "B'nai Jeshurun," in Jackson, ed., *The Encyclopedia of New York City*, 121; Christopher Gray, "Future Uncertain, 1919 Synagogue Begins Repairs," *New York Times* (February 11, 1996), IX: 6.

136. King, *King's Handbook of New York* (1893), 404–5. Also see "The New Ephraim Memorial," *New York Times* (November 29, 1889): 8; "The East Side—Its Streets and Buildings," supplement, *Real Estate Record and Builders' Guide* 45 (May 3, 1890): 1–11; "Two Synagogues Dedicated," *New York Times* (September 8, 1890): 8; Landmarks Preservation Commission of the City of New York, LP-1056 (January 29, 1980); White and Willensky, *AIA Guide* (1988), 359–60; Kestenbaum, "Synagogue Architecture in New York": 68, 70; Diamonstein, *The Landmarks of New York II*, 204; Meek, *The Synagogue*, 194.

137. "The East Side—Its Streets and Buildings": 9.

138. Wischnitzer, *Synagogue Architecture in the United States*, 83–84; Gerard R. Wolfe, *The Synagogues of New York's Lower East Side* (New York: New York University Press, 1978), 42–50; Landmarks Preservation Commission of the City of New York, LP-1107 (July 8, 1980); Roberta Brandes Gratz, "Eldridge Street Synagogue Symbolizes Lower East Side Heritage," *Preservation League of New York State Newsletter* 13 (spring 1987): 1–2; White and Willensky, *AIA Guide* (1988), 82; "The Talk of the Town: Restoration," *New Yorker* 54 (September 26, 1988): 33–35; Roberta Brandes Gratz, *The Living City* (New York: Simon and Schuster, 1989), 388–90; Kestenbaum, "Synagogue Architecture in New York": 68–70; Israelowitz, *Synagogues of the United States*, 57; Diamonstein, *The Landmarks of New York II*, 193.

139. "A New Synagogue," *New York Times* (May 17, 1890): 2; "Three New Buildings," *New York Times* (October 18, 1890): 5; King, *King's Handbook of New York* (1893), 403; Wischnitzer, *Synagogue Architecture in the United States*, 86–89; *Upper East Side Historic District*, 928; Dubin, "Extant Manhattan Synagogues Organized Before the Civil War": 60–62; Kestenbaum, "Synagogue Architecture in New York": 70; Israelowitz, *Synagogues of the United States*, 75.

140. Henry Codman Potter, "Letter to the Citizens of New York," quoted in "A Great Cathedral Plan," *New York Daily Tribune* (June 2, 1887): 1, "New Cathedral Planned," *New York Times* (June 2, 1887): 5, "An Episcopal Cathedral," *New York World* (June 2, 1887): 2. Also see "A Cathedral for New York," editorial, *New York Daily Tribune* (June 3, 1887): 4; "The Great Cathedral," *New York Times* (June 3, 1887): 8; "Plans for the Cathedral," *New York World* (June 3, 1887): 10; "Making Cordial Response," *New York Times* (June 6, 1887): 5; "For the Cathe-

dral," *New York Times* (June 10, 1887): 8; Editorial, *Real Estate Record and Builders' Guide* 39 (June 11, 1887): 795; "What Architects Say About the Proposed Cathedral," *Real Estate Record and Builders' Guide* 39 (June 11, 1887): 798–99; "A Pastoral Letter by Bishop Potter," *New York Daily Tribune* (June 13, 1887): 2.

141. Potter, "Letter to the Citizens of New York," quoted in "A Great Cathedral Plan": 1.

142. For a thorough discussion of the competition and its aftermath, see Janet Adams Strong, "The Cathedral of Saint John the Divine in New York: Design Competitions in the Shadow of H. H. Richardson, 1889–1891" (Ph.D. diss., Brown University, 1990). Also see Stern, Gilmartin, and Massengale, *New York 1900*, 396–402.

143. "The Proposed Episcopalian Cathedral," *New York Times* (September 23, 1873): 2; Stokes, *The Iconography of Manhattan Island*, vol. 5: 1953.

144. Strong, "The Cathedral of Saint John the Divine in New York," vol. 1: 61–62.

145. See "Henry Codman Potter," in *Cyclopaedia of American Biography* (New York: Press Association Compilers, 1918), vol. 8: 309–10.

146. "A Site for the Cathedral," *New York Daily Tribune* (October 9, 1887): 9; "The Cathedral's Site," *New York Times* (October 10, 1887): 8; "The New Cathedral Site," *Real Estate Record and Builders' Guide* 40 (October 15, 1887): 1236–37; "To Rival Old World Piles," *New York Times* (November 6, 1887): 9; "In and About the City," *New York Times* (November 9, 1887): 8; Editorial, *New York Times* (November 16, 1887): 4; "Plans for the Cathedral," *New York Times* (November 26, 1887): 3.

147. King, *King's Handbook of New York* (1893), 430; Stokes, *The Iconography of Manhattan Island*, vol. 5: 1752, 1782.

148. "A Site for the Cathedral," *New York Daily Tribune*: 9.

149. Stokes, *The Iconography of Manhattan Island*, vol. 5: 2004.

150. Quoted in "Plans for the Cathedral," *New York Times*: 3.

151. Editorial, (June 11, 1887): 795.

152. "Out Among the Builders," *Real Estate Record and Builders' Guide* 40 (September 24, 1887): 1203.

153. D., "The New Cathedral," letter to the editor, *Real Estate Record and Builders' Guide* 40 (November 12, 1887): 1412. Also see Agnostic, "The Proposed Cathedral," letter to the editor, *Real Estate Record and Builders' Guide* 40 (December 10, 1887): 1506; Architect, "Is the Cathedral Possible?" letter to the editor, *Real Estate Record and Builders' Guide* 40 (December 31, 1887): 1644; H.M.T., "An Objection to the Proposed Cathedral," *Real Estate Record and Builders' Guide* 40 (December 31, 1887): 1642–43.

154. "The Bishop's Seat," editorial, *New York Times* (January 8, 1888): 4. Also see Francis Schell, "The New Cathedral," letter to the editor, *Real Estate Record and Builders' Guide* 41 (January 7, 1888): 7; L., "Some Difficulties Attending the Designing of the Proposed Episcopal Cathedral," *American Architect and Building News* 23 (February 18, 1888): 77–78; John Beverly Robinson, "How to Approach the Designing of the New York Cathedral," letter to the editor, *American Architect and Building News* 23 (March 10, 1888): 119.

155. For J. C. Cady & Co.'s entry, see Strong, "The Cathedral of Saint John the Divine in New York," vol. 2: 114–18. For Haight's entry, see Strong, "The Cathedral of Saint John the Divine in New York," vol. 3: 226–27. For Withers's entry, see "Competitive Design for the Cathedral of St. John the Divine, New York, N.Y. Mr. Frederick C. Withers, Architect, New York, N.Y.," *American Architect and Building News* 26 (November 2, 1889): 231, plates; *Competitive Designs for the Cathedral of St. John the Divine in New York City* (Boston: Heliotype Printing Co., c. 1891; New York: Da Capo Press, 1982), 109–13; Kowsky, *The Architecture of Frederick Clarke Withers*, 147–48; Strong, "The Cathedral of Saint John the Divine in New York," vol. 3: 327–31. For Gibson's entry, see "Competitive Design for the Cathedral of St. John the Divine, New York, N.Y. Mr. R. W. Gibson, Architect, New York, N.Y.," *American Architect and Building News* 26 (October 19, 1889): 182–83, plates; *Competitive Designs for the Cathedral of St. John the Divine in New York City*, 67–71; Strong, "The Cathedral of Saint John the Divine in New York," vol. 3: 196–210. For Congdon's entry, see *Competitive Designs for the Cathedral of St. John the Divine in New York City*, 43–47; Strong, "The Cathedral of Saint John the Divine in New York," vol. 2: 146–55. For Hunt's entry, see Paul R. Baker, *Richard Morris Hunt* (Cambridge, Mass.: MIT Press,

1980), 547; Strong, "The Cathedral of Saint John the Divine in New York," vol. 3: 239–48. For Renwick, Aspinwall & Russell's entry, see *Competitive Designs for the Cathedral of St. John the Divine in New York City*, 97–101; Strong, "The Cathedral of Saint John the Divine in New York," vol. 3: 270–77. For McKim, Mead & White's entry, see Strong, "The Cathedral of Saint John the Divine in New York," vol. 3: 256. For Potter & Robertson's entry, see "The Cathedral of St. John the Divine: The Second Competition," *American Architect and Building News* 32 (May 9, 1891): 81–92, plates; *Competitive Designs for the Cathedral of St. John the Divine in New York City*, 23–31; Landau, *Edward T. and William A. Potter: American Victorian Architects*, 210–19; Strong, "The Cathedral of Saint John the Divine in New York," vol. 2: 43–59. For Van Brunt & Howe's entry, see "Competitive Design for the Cathedral of St. John the Divine, New York, N.Y. Messrs. Van Brunt & Howe, Architects, Kansas City, Mo.," *American Architect and Building News* 26 (November 2, 1889): 206, plates; *Competitive Designs for the Cathedral of St. John the Divine in New York City*, 103–7; Strong, "The Cathedral of Saint John the Divine in New York," vol. 3: 311–17. For Wood's entry, see "The Cathedral of St. John the Divine: The Second Competition": 81–85, plates; *Competitive Designs for the Cathedral of St. John the Divine in New York City*, 5–15; Strong, "The Cathedral of Saint John the Divine in New York," vol. 2: 60–80. Vaughan dropped out of the contest and Furness's entry was submitted by Baker & Dallett, the partners of which had been junior partners in Furness's firm. See Strong, "The Cathedral of Saint John the Divine in New York," vol. 2: 105–6.

156. "Competitive Design for the Cathedral of St. John the Divine, New York, N.Y. Messrs. Carrère & Hastings, Architects, New York, N.Y.," *American Architect and Building News* 26 (October 5, 1889): 158–59, plates; *Competitive Designs for the Cathedral of St. John the Divine in New York City*, 79–83; Strong, "The Cathedral of Saint John the Divine in New York," vol. 2: 122–33.

157. For Herter Brothers's scheme, see "Design for the Proposed Protestant Cathedral of St. John the Divine," *Real Estate Record and Builders' Guide* 44 (October 12, 1889): 1366; Strong, "The Cathedral of Saint John the Divine in New York," vol. 3: 236–38. For Huss & Buck's scheme, see "The Cathedral of St. John the Divine: The Second Competition": 87–89, plates; *Competitive Designs for the Cathedral of St. John the Divine in New York City*, 1–3; Strong, "The Cathedral of Saint John the Divine in New York," vol. 2: 29–42. For Roth's scheme, see "Competitive Design for the Cathedral of St. John the Divine, New York," *Building* 11 (November 16, 1889): 165, plate; Strong, "The Cathedral of Saint John the Divine in New York," vol. 3: 285–88. For Casey's scheme, see *Competitive Designs for the Cathedral of St. John the Divine in New York City*, 51–53; Strong, "The Cathedral of Saint John the Divine in New York," vol. 2: 136–39. For Jennings's scheme, see Strong, "The Cathedral of Saint John the Divine in New York," vol. 3: 249–50. For Mellen, Westel & Kirby's scheme, see Strong, "The Cathedral of Saint John the Divine in New York," vol. 3: 253–55, 257. For Upjohn's scheme, see Strong, "The Cathedral of Saint John the Divine in New York," vol. 3: 304–9. For Winterburn's scheme, see "Cathedral of St. John the Divine. Competitive Design Submitted by F. W. Winterburn, Architect, New York," *Building* 11 (December 28, 1889): 231, plate; Strong, "The Cathedral of Saint John the Divine in New York," vol. 3: 323–26. For Goodhue's scheme, see *Competitive Designs for the Cathedral of St. John the Divine in New York City*, 73–75; Richard Oliver, *Bertram Grosvenor Goodhue* (New York: Architectural History Foundation; Cambridge, Mass.: MIT Press, 1983), 8–10; Strong, "The Cathedral of Saint John the Divine in New York," vol. 3: 211–14. For Parfitt Brothers's scheme, see "Competitive Design for the Cathedral of St. John the Divine, New York, N.Y. Messrs. Parfitt Bros., Architects, Brooklyn, N.Y.," *American Architect and Building News* 26 (November 23, 1889): 243, plates; *Competitive Designs for the Cathedral of St. John the Divine in New York City*, 85–89; Strong, "The Cathedral of Saint John the Divine in New York," vol. 3: 258–63. For Cusack's scheme, see Strong, "The Cathedral of Saint John the Divine in New York," vol. 2: 173.

158. For Peabody & Stearns's scheme, see *Competitive Designs for the Cathedral of St. John the Divine in New York City*, 91–95; Strong, "The Cathedral of Saint John the Divine in New York," vol. 3: 264–69. For Faxon's scheme, see *Competitive Designs for the Cathedral of St. John the*

Divine in New York City, 53–55; Strong, "The Cathedral of Saint John the Divine in New York," vol. 2: 187–91. For Rotch & Tilden's scheme, see Strong, "The Cathedral of Saint John the Divine in New York," vol. 3: 284. For Sturgis & Cabot's scheme, see Strong, "The Cathedral of Saint John the Divine in New York," vol. 3: 301–3. For Warren's scheme, see "Competitive Design for the Cathedral of St. John the Divine, New York, N.Y. Mr. H. L. Warren, Architect, Boston, Mass.," *American Architect and Building News* 26 (December 14, 1889): 279, plates; Strong, "The Cathedral of Saint John the Divine in New York," vol. 3: 319–22. For Hay's scheme, see "Competitive Design for the Cathedral of St. John the Divine, New York, N.Y. Mr. Alexander Hay, Architect, Lowell, Mass.," *American Architect and Building News* 26 (December 21, 1889): 290, plates; Strong, "The Cathedral of Saint John the Divine in New York," vol. 3: 228–34. For Earle's scheme, see *Competitive Designs for the Cathedral of St. John the Divine in New York City*, 49–51; Strong, "The Cathedral of Saint John the Divine in New York," vol. 2: 180–84. For Chandler's scheme, see *Competitive Designs for the Cathedral of St. John the Divine in New York City*, 61–65; Strong, "The Cathedral of Saint John the Divine in New York," vol. 2: 140–44. For Cope & Stewardson's scheme, see *Competitive Designs for the Cathedral of St. John the Divine in New York City*, 39–41; Strong, "The Cathedral of Saint John the Divine in New York," vol. 2: 156–60. For Deery's scheme, see Strong, "The Cathedral of Saint John the Divine in New York," vol. 2: 174–77.

159. For Buffington's scheme, see "Competitive Design for the Cathedral of St. John the Divine, New York City," *Building* 11 (July 13, 1889): 13–14; "Competitive Design for the Cathedral of St. John the Divine, New York, N.Y. Mr. L. S. Buffington, Architect, Minneapolis, Minnesota," *American Architect and Building News* 26 (November 23, 1889): 242, plates; *Competitive Designs for the Cathedral of St. John the Divine in New York City*, 33–37; Francis Swales, "Master Draftsman III: Harvey Ellis (1852–1907)," *Pencil Points* 5 (July 1924): 49–54; Strong, "The Cathedral of Saint John the Divine in New York," vol. 2: 81–86. For Brown's scheme, see "Competitive Design for the Cathedral of St. John the Divine, New York, N.Y. Mr. Glenn Brown, Architect, Washington, D.C.," *American Architect and Building News* 27 (January 4, 1890): 12–13, plates; Strong, "The Cathedral of Saint John the Divine in New York," vol. 2: 110–13. For Fraser's scheme, see "Competitive Design for the Cathedral of St. John the Divine, New York, N.Y. Mr. W. S. Fraser, Architect, Pittsburgh, Pa.," *American Architect and Building News* 26 (October 5, 1889): 157, plates; *Competitive Designs for the Cathedral of St. John the Divine in New York City*, 57–61; Strong, "The Cathedral of Saint John the Divine in New York," vol. 2: 192–95. For Gorsuch's scheme, see Strong, "The Cathedral of Saint John the Divine in New York," vol. 3: 215. For Keller's scheme, see Strong, "The Cathedral of Saint John the Divine in New York," vol. 3: 251.

160. For Carpenter & Ingelow's scheme, see Strong, "The Cathedral of Saint John the Divine in New York," vol. 2: 120–21. For Dudley's scheme, see Strong, "The Cathedral of Saint John the Divine in New York," vol. 2: 178–79. For Emerson's scheme, see Strong, "The Cathedral of Saint John the Divine in New York," vol. 2: 185–86. For Stark's scheme, see "Design for the Proposed Cathedral, New York," *The Architect* (London) 42 (September 13, 1889): 149, plates; Strong, "The Cathedral of Saint John the Divine in New York," vol. 3: 297–300. For Boesch's scheme, see Strong, "The Cathedral of Saint John the Divine in New York," vol. 2: 107. For Bossan's scheme, see Strong, "The Cathedral of Saint John the Divine in New York," vol. 2: 108–9. For Gosset's scheme, see "A Competitive Design for the Cathedral of St. John the Divine, New York. M. Alphonse Gosset, Architect," *American Architect and Building News* 84 (June 18, 1904): 99, plates; Strong, "The Cathedral of Saint John the Divine in New York," vol. 3: 216–25. For Kin's scheme, see Strong, "The Cathedral of Saint John the Divine in New York," vol. 3: 252. For Rhind's scheme, see "Competitive Design for the Cathedral of St. John the Divine, New York. James R. Rhind, Architect, Montreal, Que.," *Canadian Architect and Builder* 3 (February 1890): 16, plate; Strong, "The Cathedral of Saint John the Divine in New York," vol. 3: 279–83.

161. *Competitive Designs for the Cathedral of St. John the Divine in New York City*, 75–77; Strong, "The Cathedral of Saint John the Divine in New York," vol. 2: 161–72; Douglass Shand-Tucci, *Boston Bohemia, 1881–1900, Volume One of Ralph Adams Cram: Life and Archi-*

tecture (Amherst, Mass.: University of Massachusetts Press, 1995), 108–10, 131–33.

162. "The Cathedral of St. John the Divine: The Second Competition": 89–91, plates; *Competitive Designs for the Cathedral of St. John the Divine in New York City*, 15–23; Strong, "The Cathedral of Saint John the Divine in New York," vol. 2: 1–28. In April 1891, before the ultimate winner was picked, Kent sued Heins and La Farge because they did not include his name on their revised submission. Eventually Heins and La Farge settled the case by paying Kent ten thousand dollars and Kent gave up any claim to the design. See "Architect Kent's Complaint," *New York Times* (April 25, 1891): 8.

163. Strong, "The Cathedral of Saint John the Divine in New York," vol. 3: 289–96.

164. "Plans for the Cathedral," *New York Times* (January 16, 1889): 4; "Plans for the Cathedral," *New York Times* (January 26, 1889): 8; "Fair Play," *Building* 10 (February 9, 1889): 41; "The New Cathedral," *Real Estate Record and Builders' Guide* 43 (February 23, 1889): 242; "The New York Cathedral Competition," *American Architect and Building News* 25 (March 16, 1889): 121; "The New Cathedral," *New York Times* (March 16, 1889): 8; "Plans for the Cathedral," *New York Times* (April 11, 1889): 8; "The New York Cathedral Competition," *American Architect and Building News* 25 (April 20, 1889): 181; "Cathedral Plans," *New York Times* (May 9, 1889): 8; "Plans for the New Cathedral," *New York Times* (May 10, 1889): 8; "New Cathedral Plans," *New York Times* (May 17, 1889): 8; "The Cathedral Designs," *New York Times* (May 18, 1889): 8; "The New York Cathedral Competition," *American Architect and Building News* 25 (May 25, 1889): 241; "The Cathedral Competition," editorial, *New York Times* (May 26, 1889): 4; Editorial, *New York Times* (May 31, 1889): 4; S., "The New Cathedral," letter to the editor, *New York Times* (May 31, 1889): 5; "A Charge of Suppressing Information," *American Architect and Building News* 25 (June 1, 1889): 253; A Non-Competitor, "The New York Cathedral Competition," letter to the editor, *American Architect and Building News* 25 (June 8, 1889): 275; "Exhibition of the New York Cathedral Plans Impossible," *American Architect and Building News* 25 (June 8, 1889): 275; "The Cathedral Competition," *Building* 10 (June 8, 1889): 181–82; "The Architects Objected," *New York Times* (June 8, 1889): 5; "The Late Competition for the Proposed Cathedral of St. John the Divine," *American Architect and Building News* 25 (June 22, 1889): 296–99; "The Cathedral of St. John the Divine," *Building* 11 (July 27, 1889): 34; "Out Among the Builders," *Real Estate Record and Builders' Guide* 44 (July 27, 1889): 1049–50.

165. "The Cathedral Competition," (May 26, 1889): 4.

166. "The Designs for the Cathedral of St. John the Divine," *American Architect and Building News* 26 (September 28, 1889): 141; Alexander Graham, "Cathedral for New York," *Journal of the Royal Institute of British Architects* 6 (November 7, 1889): 46–47, reprinted in *American Architect and Building News* 26 (December 7, 1889): 267; "The Architectural League," *New York Daily Tribune* (December 28, 1889): 6–7; A Layman, "The Architectural League Exhibition, Part I," *American Architect and Building News* 27 (January 18, 1890): 40–41; A Layman, "The Architectural League Exhibition, Part II," *American Architect and Building News* 27 (January 25, 1890): 57–58.

167. "More Time Allowed," *New York Times* (January 23, 1890): 9; "The Episcopal Cathedral," *New York Times* (October 21, 1890): 8; "Plans for the Cathedral," *New York Times* (March 5, 1891): 5; "The Cathedral Plans," *New York Times* (March 19, 1891): 3; "The Protestant Cathedral," *New York Times* (March 22, 1891): 4; "Shall the Cathedral Be Romanesque?" editorial, *New York Times* (April 26, 1891): 4; "The Cathedral of St. John the Divine: The Second Competition": 81–92, plates.

168. Mariana Griswold Van Rensselaer, *Henry Hobson Richardson and His Works* (Boston: Houghton Mifflin, 1888; New York: Dover, 1969), 22–23, 86–89, 145–47; Strong, "The Cathedral of Saint John the Divine in New York," vol. 2: 87–98.

169. Strong, "The Cathedral of Saint John the Divine in New York," vol. 2: 81–86.

170. W. A. Potter and R. H. Robertson, "The Potter and Robertson Design," *American Architect and Building News* 32 (May 9, 1891): 85.

171. "A Cathedral with Four Spires," editorial, *New York Times* (April 20, 1891): 4.

172. Montgomery Schuyler, "The Work of William A. Potter," *Architectural Record* 26 (September 1909): 176–96.

173. "Some Questions of Art: Cathedral Designs at the Academy: First Notice," *New York Sun* (April 26, 1891): 14.

174. "Mr. Wood's Cathedral," editorial, *New York Times* (April 12, 1891): 4.

175. "The Cathedral of St. John the Divine: No. 1," *Real Estate Record and Builders' Guide* 47 (April 11, 1891): 552–53. Also see "The Cathedral of St. John the Divine: II," *Real Estate Record and Builders' Guide* 47 (April 18, 1891): 603–4.

176. See George L. Collins, "The Transfer of Thin Masonry Vaulting from Spain to America," *Journal of the Society of Architectural Historians* 27 (October 1968): 176–201.

177. "Some Questions of Art: Cathedral Designs at the Academy: Second Notice," *New York Sun* (May 3, 1891): 14.

178. "The Cathedral of St. John the Divine: No. 1," *Real Estate Record and Builders' Guide*: 553.

179. "The Protestant Cathedral," *New York Times* (March 22, 1891): 4.

180. "The Architects Chosen," *New York Times* (July 26, 1891): 9.

181. "A Church for the People," *New York Times* (December 27, 1892): 1–2; "Great Work Well Begun," *New York Times* (December 28, 1892): 1; Stokes, *The Iconography of Manhattan Island*, vol. 5: 2011.

182. Stern, Gilmartin, and Massengale, *New York 1900*, 15–17, 396–402; Stern, Gilmartin, and Mellins, *New York 1930*, 147, 151, 155–57; Stern, Mellins, and Fishman, *New York 1960*, 754–56.

Memorials and Monuments

1. Paul R. Baker, *Richard Morris Hunt* (Cambridge, Mass.: MIT Press, 1980), 144–45. Also see vestry minutes and letters in the Trinity Church Archives, New York.

2. "An American Sculptor," *Harper's New Monthly Magazine* 57 (June 1878): 66; Adeline Adams, *John Quincy Adams Ward: An Appreciation* (New York: Gillis, 1912), 22–29; Lewis I. Sharp, "John Quincy Adams Ward: Historical and Contemporary Influences," *American Art Journal* 4 (November 1972): 71–79; Baker, *Richard Morris Hunt*, 145; Lewis I. Sharp, *John Quincy Adams Ward: Dean of American Sculpture* (Newark, N.J.: University of Delaware Press; London: Associated University Presses, 1985), 51–54, 172–77; Margot Gayle and Michele Cohen, *The Art Commission and the Municipal Art Society Guide to Manhattan's Outdoor Sculpture* (New York: Prentice Hall, 1988), 241.

3. "The Farragut Statue," editorial, *New York Times* (May 25, 1881): 4; "History of a Day," *New York Daily Graphic* (May 26, 1881): 638, 641; "Unveiling the Statue," *New York Times* (May 26, 1881): 8; "History of a Day," *New York Daily Graphic* (May 27, 1881): 646, 648; Richard Watson Gilder, "The Farragut Monument," *Scribner's Magazine* 22 (June 1881): 161–67; "The Statue of Farragut," *Harper's Weekly* 25 (June 11, 1881): 375; Editorial, *American Architect and Building News* 9 (June 25, 1881): 301; M. G. Van Rensselaer, "Mr. St. Gaudens's Statue of Admiral Farragut in New York," *American Architect and Building News* 10 (September 10, 1881): 119–20; Richard H. Titherington, "Picturesque Points on Fifth Avenue," *Munsey's Magazine* 6 (November 1891): 122–33; Moses King, *King's Handbook of New York* (Boston: Moses King, 1893), 175; Homer Saint-Gaudens, ed., *The Reminiscences of Augustus Saint-Gaudens* (New York: Century, 1913), 162; I. N. Phelps Stokes, *The Iconography of Manhattan Island*, 6 vols. (New York: Robert H. Dodd, 1916–28; New York: Arno Press, 1967), vol. 3: 796, vol. 5: 1976, 2006; Alan Burnham, ed., *New York Landmarks* (Middletown, Conn.: Wesleyan University Press, 1963), 144–45; Louise Hall Tharp, *Saint-Gaudens and the Gilded Era* (Boston: Little, Brown, 1969), 102–3, 106; Lois Goldreich Marcus, "Studies in Nineteenth Century Sculpture: Augustus Saint-Gaudens (1848–1907)" (Ph.D. diss., City University of New York, 1979): 35–75; Burke Wilkinson, *Uncommon Clay: The Life and Work of Augustus Saint-Gaudens* (New York: Harcourt Brace Jovanovich, 1981); Stern, Gilmartin, and Massengale, *New York 1900*, 118, 122; Kathryn Greenthal, *Augustus Saint-Gaudens: Master Sculptor* (New York: Metropolitan Museum of Art, 1985), 91; Gayle and Cohen, *The Art Commission and the Municipal Art Society Guide to Manhattan's Outdoor Sculpture*, 105–6; White and Willensky, *AIA Guide* (1988), 190; Michele H. Bogart, *Public Sculpture* and the Civic Ideal in New York City, 1890–1930 (Chicago: University of Chicago Press, 1989), 27–33; Michele H. Bogart, "Augustus Saint-Gaudens," in Kenneth T. Jackson, ed., The Encyclopedia of New York City (New Haven, Conn., and London: Yale University Press; New York: New-York Historical Society, 1995), 1033–34; Donald Martin Reynolds, Monuments and Masterpieces: Histories and Views of Public Sculpture in New York City (New York: Thames and Hudson, 1997), 70–72; Claire Nicholas White, ed., Stanford White: Letters to His Family (New York: Rizzoli International Publications, 1997), 82, 90–105.

4. Stanford White to Augustus Saint-Gaudens, December 17, 1879, in White, ed., Stanford White: Letters to His Family, 98.

5. Gilder, "The Farragut Monument": 161.

6. Van Rensselaer, "Mr. St. Gaudens's Statue of Admiral Farragut in New York": 119.

7. Editorial, (June 25, 1881): 301.

8. Stanford White to Augustus Saint-Gaudens, September 16 or 17, 1879, in White, ed., Stanford White: Letters to His Family, 90.

9. Stanford White to Augustus Saint-Gaudens, February 24, 1880, in White, ed., Stanford White: Letters to His Family, 101.

10. "The Farragut Statue," New York Times: 4.

11. Significant discussions of the Statue of Liberty include Benjamin Levine and Isabelle F. Story, Statue of Liberty, National Park Service Historical Handbook Series No. 11 (Washington, D.C., 1952); Andre Gschaedler, True Light on the Statue of Liberty and Its Creator (Narberth, Penn.: Livingston Publishing Co., 1966); Oscar Handlin, Statue of Liberty (New York: Newsweek, 1971); Marvin Trachtenberg, The Statue of Liberty (New York: Viking Press, 1976); Landmarks Preservation Commission of the City of New York, LP-0931 (September 14, 1976); James B. Bell and Richard I. Abrams, In Search of Liberty: The Story of the Statue of Liberty and Ellis Island (Garden City, N.Y.: Doubleday & Co., 1984); Leslie Allen, Liberty: The Statue and the American Dream (New York: The Statue of Liberty-Ellis Island Foundation, 1985); Christian Blanchet and Bertrand Dard, Statue of Liberty, trans. by Bernard A. Weisberger (New York: American Heritage, 1985); Sue Burchard, The Statue of Liberty: Birth to Rebirth (San Diego: Harcourt Brace Jovanovich, 1985); Charles Mercer, Statue of Liberty (New York: G. P. Putnam's Sons, 1985); William E. Shapiro, The Statue of Liberty (New York: Franklin Watts, 1985); Michael Grumet, Images of Liberty (New York: Arbor House, 1986); Frank Spiering, Bearer of a Million Dreams: The Biography of the Statue of Liberty (Ottowa, Ill.: Jameson Books, 1986); The New York Public Library and the Comité officiel franco-americain pour la célébration du centenaire de la Statue de la Liberté, with Pierre Provoyeur and June Hargrove, Liberty: The French-American Statue in Art and History (New York: Harper & Row, 1986); Wilton S. Dillon and Neil G. Kotler, eds., The Statue of Liberty Revisited (Washington, D.C., and London: Smithsonian Institution Press, 1994). Also see Stern, Gilmartin, and Massengale, New York 1900, 118, 121; White and Willensky, AIA Guide (1988), 7–8; Bogart, Public Sculpture and the Civic Ideal in New York City, 1890–1930, 23–25; Barbaralee Diamonstein, The Landmarks of New York II (New York: Harry N. Abrams, 1993), 171.

12. Janet Headley, "Voyage of Discovery: Bartholdi's First American Visit (1871)," in Liberty: The French American Statue in Art and History, 100–105.

13. Jeffrey Karl Ochsner, H. H. Richardson: Complete Architectural Works (Cambridge, Mass.: MIT Press, 1982), 73–77.

14. Frédéric-Auguste Bartholdi, The Statue of Liberty Enlightening the World (New York: North American Review, 1885; New York: New York Bound, 1984), 18–19.

15. "The Lafayette Statue," New York Daily Graphic (September 5, 1876): 452; "Bronze Statue of General Lafayette Unveiled at Union Square Yesterday," New York Daily Graphic (September 7, 1876): 463; Gayle and Cohen, The Art Commission and the Municipal Art Society Guide to Manhattan's Outdoor Sculpture, 97.

16. "Liberty Enlightening the World," Scientific American 52 (June 13, 1885): 367, 375–76; Pierre Provoyeur, "Technical and Industrial Challenges," in Liberty: The French-American Statue in Art and History, 106–19.

17. "The Arm of Bartholdi's Colossal Statue of Liberty," New York Daily Graphic (March 20, 1877): 133; Mary Black, Old New York in Early Photographs (New York: Dover, 1973), plate 119.

18. Charles de Kay, "France to America," Scribner's Monthly 14 (June 1877): 129–36. Also see Editorial, American Architect and Building News 2 (February 17, 1877): 50; "Notes and Clippings: The Statue of Liberty," American Architect and Building News 2 (March 3, 1877): 72.

19. June Hargrove, "The American Committee," in Liberty: The French-American Statue in Art and History, 148–55.

20. "Progress of Work on the Foundation for the Statue of Liberty on Bedloe's Island," New York Daily Graphic (August 7, 1883): 244, 246; "Pedestal of the Statue of Liberty," Building 2 (November 1883): 23; "Progress of Work on the Pedestal for the Bartholdi Statue of Liberty on Bedloe's Island," New York Daily Graphic (May 31, 1884): 672; "The Bartholdi Statue Pedestal," Building 2 (June 1884): 108; "The Statue of Liberty," editorial, New York Times (August 5, 1884): 4; "Liberty's Place of Rest," New York Times (August 6, 1884): 8; Baker, Richard Morris Hunt, 314–22; Lewis I. Sharp, "Richard Morris Hunt and His Influence on American Beaux-Arts Sculpture," in Susan R. Stein, ed., The Architecture of Richard Morris Hunt (Chicago: University of Chicago Press, 1986), 120–49; Susan R. Stein, "Richard Morris Hunt and the Pedestal," in Liberty: The French-American Statue in Art and History, 176–85.

21. Montgomery Schuyler, "The Works of the Late Richard M. Hunt," Architectural Record 5 (October–December 1895): 97–180.

22. Editorial, Building 2 (February 1884): 51; June Hargrove, "The American Fund-Raising Campaign," in Liberty: The French-American Statue in Art and History, 156–65.

23. See Heinrich E. Jacob, The World of Emma Lazarus (New York: Schocken Books, 1949).

24. Editorial, New York Times (December 4, 1884): 4; "San Francisco Will Take the Statue," New York Times (December 13, 1884): 6.

25. Editorial, American Architect and Building News 16 (July 12, 1884): 13; "Bartholdi's Statue Presented," New York Times (July 14, 1884): 1.

26. "A Glorious Achievement," editorial, New York World (August 11, 1885): 4. Also see "One Hundred Thousand Dollars!" New York World (August 11, 1885): 1.

27. "Bartholdi's Statue on the Way," New York Times (May 22, 1885): 1; "The Great Statue Here," New York Times (June 18, 1885): 1; "The Reception of the Statue," editorial, New York Times (June 20, 1885): 4; "Welcoming the Statue," New York Times (June 20, 1885): 2.

28. "The Great Statue," New York Daily Graphic (May 22, 1886): 687, 697; "The Great Statue—Progress of the Work on Liberty Island," New York Daily Graphic (June 26, 1886): 962, 964; June Hargrove, "Reassembly on Bedloe's Island," in Liberty: The French-American Statue in Art and History, 186–97.

29. "The Day that Was Celebrated," editorial, New York Daily Tribune (October 29, 1886): 4; "World-Lighting Liberty," New York Daily Tribune (October 29, 1886): 1–2; "France's Gift Accepted," New York Times (October 29, 1886): 1–3; "The Unveiling of the Statue," editorial, New York Times (October 29, 1886): 4; "The Lesson of the Statue," editorial, New York World (October 29, 1886): 4; "To Liberty!" New York World (October 29, 1886): 1; June Hargrove, "Unveiling the Colossus," in Liberty: The French-American Statue in Art and History, 198–203.

30. "The Lesson of the Statue": 4.

World's Fair

1. For a discussion of late-nineteenth- and early-twentieth-century American world's fairs, see Robert W. Rydell, All the World's a Fair: Visions of Empire at American International Expositions, 1876–1916 (Chicago and London: University of Chicago Press, 1984). Also see John Allwood, The Great Exhibitions (London: Studio Vista, 1977), 179–85.

2. For the Philadelphia Centennial Exhibition, see Rydell, All the World's a Fair, 9–37. For the New York Crystal Palace Exhibition, see Charles Hirschfeld, "America on Exhibition: The New York Crystal Palace," American Quarterly 9 (summer 1957): 101–16.

3. "Arrangements for a World's Fair," New York Daily Tribune (February 19, 1879): 8.

4. A.V.W., "A Proposed Site for Next Exhibition," letter to the editor, New York Times (February 20, 1879): 2.

5. "Talking About a World's Fair," New York Times (May 8, 1879): 8; "The World's Fair," Real Estate Record and Builders' Guide 24 (October 11, 1879): 302.

6. Vaux & Radford, "A Site for the Exhibition," *New York Daily Tribune* (April 18, 1879): 5. Also see "A Site for the World's Fair," *New York Daily Tribune* (May 1, 1879): 1; "The Coming Exhibition," *New York Daily Tribune* (May 15, 1879): 2.

7. "The Proposed World's Fair: Action of the Executive Committee—Central Park Believed to Be the Most Desirable Site," *New York Times* (March 28, 1879): 8; E., "No Encroachment on the Park," letter to the editor, *New York Times* (April 4, 1879): 2; "A Site for the Exhibition," editorial, *New York Daily Tribune* (April 10, 1879): 4; Richard C. McCormick, "A World's Fair in New York," letter to the editor, *New York Daily Tribune* (April 10, 1879): 5; One of the People, "Site for the Next Exhibition," letter to the editor, *New York Times* (April 14, 1879): 2; "Exhibition Sites," editorial, *New York Daily Tribune* (April 19, 1879): 4.

8. "Map of the World's Fair in New York in 1883," *Demorest's Monthly Magazine* 14 (November 1879): 600–602.

9. "In 1883," *Real Estate Record and Builders' Guide* 24 (October 18, 1879): 823. Also see "The Coming World's Fair," *New York Times* (May 18, 1879): 2.

10. "Sketch for the New York International Exhibition Building, 1883. Mr. William G. Preston, Architect, Boston," *American Architect and Building News* 7 (March 13, 1880): 106, plates; Alison Sky and Michelle Stone, *Unbuilt America* (New York: McGraw-Hill, 1976), 202. For William G. Preston, see Henry F. Withey and Elise Rathburn Withey, *Biographical Dictionary of American Architects (Deceased)* (Los Angeles: New Age, 1956), 486–87. For the Paris fair, see Allwood, *The Great Exhibitions*, 42–48.

11. "The Proposed World's Fair," *New York Times* (April 26, 1879): 3; Editorial, *New York Times* (May 17, 1879): 4; "The World's Fair," *New York Times* (May 22, 1879): 8; "Organizing for the World's Fair," *New York Times* (June 17, 1879): 8; "A World's Fair Convention," *New York Daily Tribune* (June 19, 1879): 8; "Considering the World's Fair," *New York Times* (June 19, 1879): 5; "Considering a World's Fair," *New York Times* (June 20, 1879): 3; "The World's Fair Again," *New York Times* (June 24, 1879): 8; "The Proposed World's Fair," *New York Times* (July 19, 1879): 8; "The Organization of a World's Fair," *New York Daily Tribune* (July 21, 1879): 8; "The World's Fair Committee," *New York Times* (September 9, 1879): 2; "The World's Fair Committee," *New York Times* (October 7, 1879): 3; "The World's Next Fair," *New York Times* (November 14, 1879): 8.

12. "A Site for the World's Fair," *New York Times* (April 20, 1879): 7; "A Site for the World's Fair," *New York Times* (October 2, 1879): 8.

13. "The Proposed World's Fair," *New York Times* (May 2, 1879): 2. Also see Lespinasse & Friedman, "A Site for the Exhibition of 1883," letter to the editor, *New York Times* (May 4, 1879): 10.

14. "Appeals for a World's Fair," *New York Daily Tribune* (January 15, 1880): 5; "The International Fair," *New York Times* (January 15, 1880): 5.

15. "The World's Fair Project," editorial, *New York Daily Tribune* (January 21, 1880): 4.

16. "The World's Fair Bill," *New York Daily Tribune* (April 1, 1880): 1; Editorial, *American Architect and Building News* 7 (April 10, 1880): 149; "New York to Have the Exhibition," *New York Daily Tribune* (April 20, 1880): 1; "The World's Fair of 1883," *New York Times* (April 21, 1880): 3; "The World's Fair," *New York Times* (May 2, 1880): 7; "The New York World's Fair and the Manager's Responsibilities," *Real Estate Record and Builders' Guide* 25 (May 22, 1880): 483; "New York World's Fair," *New York Daily Tribune* (May 23, 1880): 5; F., "The World's Fair of 1883," letter to the editor, *New York Times* (June 20, 1880): 5; "Notes from the Capital," *New York Times* (June 27, 1880): 1; "The Exhibition of 1883," editorial, *New York Daily Tribune* (July 13, 1880): 4.

17. Editorial, *Real Estate Record and Builders' Guide* 26 (July 24, 1880): 667; "The New York Exposition," editorial, *New York Daily Tribune* (August 5, 1880): 4; "The Site of the Fair," editorial, *New York Daily Tribune* (August 15, 1880): 6; "The Great World's Fair," editorial, *New York Times* (August 23, 1880): 4; "The Coming Exhibition," *New York Times* (August 27, 1880): 4; "World's Fair Sites Considered," *New York Times* (October 30, 1880): 3.

18. Editorial, *New York Times* (November 6, 1880): 4. Also see "A Blundering Committee," editorial, *New York Times* (November 19, 1880): 4; "The World's Fair," editorial, *New York Times* (November 20, 1880): 4.

19. "The Site of the Fair," editorial, *New York Daily Tribune* (November 17, 1880): 4. Also see "The Park and the Fair," editorial, *New York Daily Tribune* (November 19, 1880): 4; "Get Out," editorial, *New York Daily Tribune* (November 24, 1880): 4; "A Site Beyond Criticism," editorial, *New York Daily Tribune* (November 28, 1880): 6; "Site of the World's Fair," *New York Daily Tribune* (November 30, 1880): 2; "A Sluggish Committee," editorial, *New York Daily Tribune* (December 2, 1880): 4; "Pleading for the Park," *New York Daily Tribune* (December 2, 1880): 2; Port Morris, "The Advantages of Port Morris," letter to the editor, *New York Times* (December 20, 1880): 3; "The Park and the Fair," editorial, *New York Daily Tribune* (December 23, 1880): 4. The Boston-based journal *American Architect and Building News* also opposed the Central Park site. See Editorial, *American Architect and Building News* 8 (November 20, 1880): 241.

20. "Hints to the Promoters of the World's Fair," *Real Estate Record and Builders' Guide* 26 (September 18, 1880): 807.

21. Editorial, *American Architect and Building News* 8 (November 6, 1880): 217.

22. D. G. Croly, "A Grand Hygiearium Proposed," *Real Estate Record and Builders' Guide* 26 (October 9, 1880): 873.

23. "Giving Up the Park Site," *New York Times* (December 2, 1880): 1.

24. "The Fair Site," editorial, *New York Daily Tribune* (December 10, 1880): 4; "Inwood as the Fair Site," *New York Times* (December 10, 1880): 8; "The Inwood Site," *Real Estate Record and Builders' Guide* 26 (December 11, 1880): 1083; "A Look at the Inwood Site," *New York Daily Tribune* (December 13, 1880): 5; "The Inwood Site," editorial, *New York Daily Tribune* (December 13, 1880): 4; "The World's Fair: Merits of the Inwood Site," *New York Daily Tribune* (December 18, 1880): 7; J.J.R. Croes, "International Exhibition Site," letter to the editor, *New York Times* (December 20, 1880): 3; Egbert L. Viele, "The Site Selected for the World's Fair," letter to the editor, *New York Times* (December 25, 1880): 3; "Plans for a World's Fair: Inwood Designated as the Site," *New York Daily Tribune* (January 11, 1881): 2.

25. "The World's Fair," editorial, *New York Daily Tribune* (December 26, 1880): 6. Also see "Can the Big Fair Be Held," *New York Times* (November 21, 1880): 1; Editorial, *New York Times* (November 22, 1880): 4.

26. "General Grant for President of the World's Fair," *Real Estate Record and Builders' Guide* 26 (September 4, 1880): 771. Also see Benjamin Perley Poore and Rev. O. H. Tiffany, *Life of U. S. Grant* (New York: Union Publishing House, 1892), 480–87; William B. Hesseltine, *Ulysses S. Grant, Politician* (New York: Frederick Ungar, 1957), 444.

27. "The World's Fair Commission: Gen. Grant Accepts the Presidency," *New York Daily Tribune* (January 15, 1881): 8; "Miscellaneous City News: World's Fair Commission," *New York Times* (January 15, 1881): 8.

28. "World's Fair Commission: Gen. Grant Tenders His Resignation as President," *New York Times* (March 24, 1881): 5. Also see "The International Fair," *New York Daily Tribune* (February 17, 1881): 2; "Obstacles to the Fair," *New York Daily Tribune* (February 24, 1881): 2; "New York City and the World's Fair," *Real Estate Record and Builders' Guide* 27 (February 26, 1881): 175; "Will There Be a World's Fair," *New York Times* (March 13, 1881): 10; "The World's Fair," *Real Estate Record and Builders' Guide* 27 (March 26, 1881): 273; "The World's Fair," *Real Estate Record and Builders' Guide* 27 (April 2, 1881): 300–301.

29. "The World's Fair," editorial, *New York Times* (April 22, 1881): 4.

30. "A Moribund Project," editorial, *New York Daily Tribune* (May 9, 1881): 4.

31. "Events in the Metropolis: The World's Fair Project," *New York Times* (August 21, 1881): 12; "Shall We Have a World's Fair?" editorial, *New York Daily Tribune* (August 28, 1881): 6; "Miscellaneous City News: The World's Fair Project Dead," *New York Times* (September 7, 1881): 8; "Reviving the World's Fair," *New York Times* (October 21, 1881): 8.

32. "The Abortive World's Fair," editorial, *New York Times* (May 6, 1881): 4.

33. "World's Fair," editorial, *Building* 6 (May 28, 1887): 193.

34. "A World's Fair in 1892," editorial, *New York Times* (June 25, 1889): 4.

35. "Sites for a World's Fair," *New York Times* (July 9, 1889): 2; "Exposition of 1892," *Building* 11 (July 13, 1889): 9; "Pelham Bay Park Urged,"

New York Times (July 20, 1889): 8; "Another Good Fair Site," *New York Times* (July 21, 1889): 6.

36. "A New World's Fair Site," *New York Times* (July 13, 1889): 8.

37. "The First Steps Taken," *New York Daily Tribune* (July 26, 1889): 1–2; "For the Big World's Fair," *New York Daily Tribune* (July 31, 1889): 10; "Grant's Difficult Task," *New York Times* (August 7, 1889): 8; "To Manage the Fair," *New York Daily Tribune* (August 11, 1889): 9; "Planning for the Fair," *New York Times* (August 14, 1889): 8; "All About the Great Fair," *New York Times* (August 16, 1889): 8; Editorial, *New York Daily Tribune* (August 21, 1889): 6; "The Crank Correspondence Bureau," editorial, *New York Daily Tribune* (August 23, 1889): 6.

38. "National Board of Trade," *New York Times* (January 21, 1887): 3. Also see Editorial, *American Architect and Building News* 26 (July 20, 1889): 22; "Congress and the World's Fair," editorial, *New York Daily Tribune* (August 6, 1889): 6.

39. "Foolish Rivalry," editorial, *New York Times* (August 14, 1889): 4. Also see Honesty, "Rough on Chicago," letter to the editor, *New York Times* (September 25, 1889): 5; Francis L. Lederer II, "Competition for the World's Columbian Exposition: The Chicago Campaign," *Journal of the Illinois State Historical Society* 45 (1972): 365–81; Robert D. Parmet, "Competition for the World's Columbian Exposition: The New York Campaign," *Journal of the Illinois State Historical Society* 45 (1972): 382–94; Rydell, *All the World's a Fair*, 41–42.

40. "Chicago and the World's Fair," editorial, *New York Daily Tribune* (July 31, 1889): 6. Also see "Chicago Goes into Retirement," editorial, *New York Daily Tribune* (August 3, 1889): 6.

41. Stanley Appelbaum, *The Chicago World's Fair of 1893: A Photographic Record* (New York: Dover, 1980), 1.

42. "What Site Shall Be Selected?" *Real Estate Record and Builders' Guide* 44 (August 10, 1889): 1102; "Erastus Wiman on the World's Fair," *Real Estate Record and Builders' Guide* 44 (August 17, 1889): 1130; J. B. James Jr., "The Site for the Exposition," letter to the editor, *Real Estate Record and Builders' Guide* 44 (August 17, 1889): 1131; "The Topic of the Hour—The Exposition," *Real Estate Record and Builders' Guide* 44 (August 24, 1889): 1155; "Many Sites Suggested," *New York Times* (August 27, 1889): 5; "People Are Interested: Scores of Letters about the World's Fair," *New York Times* (August 28, 1889): 8; "Lessons of the Fair," *New York Times* (August 29, 1889): 8; "The Site for the Exposition of 1892," *Building* 11 (August 31, 1889): 67; "Ideas of Various People," *New York Times* (August 31, 1889): 8; "World's Fair Schemes," *New York Times* (September 4, 1889): 8; "More Sites for the Fair," *New York Times* (September 5, 1889): 8; "More Places for the Fair," *New York Times* (September 7, 1889): 8; "Suggestions for the Fair," *New York Times* (September 8, 1889): 9; "More Plans for the Fair," *New York Times* (September 10, 1889): 8; Frederick J. Stone, "Is the Committee Packed?" letter to the editor, *Real Estate Record and Builders' Guide* 44 (September 14, 1889): 1236; "Liberty's Great Temple," *New York Times* (September 16, 1889): 5.

43. Quoted in "The Territory Proposed to Be Taken for the Great World's Fair," *New York Times* (September 21, 1889): 1. Also see "The Site Decided Upon," *New York Times* (September 19, 1889): 1–2; "Diagram Showing the World's Fair Site and How It Can Be Used," *New York Times* (September 29, 1889): 16.

44. William Waldorf Astor, quoted in "The Site Selected," *Real Estate Record and Builders' Guide* 44 (September 21, 1889): 1264–65. Also see Newland Maynard, "The Park's Advantages," letter to the editor, *New York Times* (September 21, 1889): 3; "The Use of Central Park Bad Policy," *Building* 11 (September 28, 1889): 99; "Editorial Notes and Comments," *Building* 11 (October 5, 1889): 109.

45. Frederick Law Olmsted, "Mr. Olmsted on the Site," letter to the editor, *New York Times* (September 26, 1889): 8.

46. "The Rev. Morgan Dix Speaks," *New York Times* (September 23, 1889): 5; "Not All Smooth Sailing: Site Problems Not Easily Settled," *New York Times* (September 24, 1889): 5; "Prospects Are Brighter: Solutions of the Site Problem Suggested," *New York Times* (September 25, 1889): 8; "Opposed to the Site," *New York Times* (September 26, 1889): 8; "Site Problems in View," *New York Times* (September 26, 1889): 8; "To Rally Site Owners," *New York Times* (September 28, 1889): 5; Diplomaticus, "The Site Question," letter to the editor, *New York Times* (October 1, 1889): 8; Editorial, *Real Estate Record and Builders' Guide* 44 (October 5, 1889): 1323–24; "World's Fair Legislation," *New York Times* (December 29, 1889): 16; "The World's Fair Bill," editorial, *New York Daily Tribune* (January 31, 1890): 6; "A Few Plain Words," editorial, *New York Daily Tribune* (February 17, 1890): 6; "The Fair Assured," editorial, *New York Daily Tribune* (February 18, 1890): 6; "All Agreed for a World's Fair," editorial, *New York Times* (February 18, 1890): 4; "The City and the Fair," editorial, *New York Daily Tribune* (February 19, 1890): 6; Rydell, *All the World's a Fair*, 42.

47. "An Appeal to Citizens," *New York Times* (October 24, 1889): 5; "Subscribing for the Fair," *New York Times* (October 27, 1889): 12; "Pushing the Fair Project," *New York Times* (October 31, 1889): 8; "Booming the Fair Fund," *New York Times* (December 27, 1889): 5.

48. A Layman, "The Architectural League Exhibit," *Real Estate Record and Builders' Guide* 45 (January 11, 1890): 35–36.

49. Editorial, *Real Estate Record and Builders' Guide* 45 (February 22, 1890): 253. Also see "New York's Argument," editorial, *New York Daily Tribune* (January 10, 1890): 6; "New York City Is the Place," *New York Daily Tribune* (January 12, 1890): 22; "Our Title to the Fair," editorial, *New York Daily Tribune* (January 12, 1890): 6; "World's Fair Claimants: The Other Cities Losing Hope of Defeating New York," *New York Times* (January 23, 1890): 2.

50. "Chicago Wins the Fight," *New York Daily Tribune* (February 25, 1890): 1–2; "Enthusiasm in Chicago," *New York Daily Tribune* (February 25, 1890): 2; "New York Was Amazed," *New York Daily Tribune* (February 25, 1890): 2; "The Triumph of Chicago," editorial, *New York Daily Tribune* (February 25, 1890): 6.

51. Editorial, *Real Estate Record and Builders' Guide* 45 (March 1, 1890): 291. Also see William O. McDowell, "Why New York Lost the Fair," letter to the editor, *New York Daily Tribune* (March 3, 1890): 5; Editorial, *Real Estate Record and Builders' Guide* 45 (March 15, 1890): 363.

CHAPTER 3
Workplaces

The Rise of the Office Building

1. Walt Whitman, "Wicked Architecture," *Life Illustrated* (July 19, 1856), reprinted in Emory Holloway, ed., *Complete Poetry and Selected Prose and Letters* (London: Nonesuch Press, 1938), 607.

2. "A Telegraph Palace," *New York Daily Graphic* (June 3, 1873): 1.

3. Notable recent attempts to arrive at an inclusive definition of the skyscraper type include J. Carson Webster, "The Skyscraper: Logical and Historical Considerations," *Journal of the Society of Architectural Historians* 18 (December 1959): 126–39; Winston Weisman, "A New View of Skyscraper History," in Edgar Kaufmann Jr., ed., *The Rise of an American Architecture* (New York: Praeger, 1970), 115–60; Rosemarie Haag Bletter, "The Invention of the Skyscraper: Notes on Its Diverse Histories," *Assemblage* 2 (February 1987): 110–17; Thomas A. P. van Leeuwen, *The Skyward Trend of Thought: The Metaphysics of the American Skyscraper* (Cambridge, Mass.: MIT Press, 1988); Sarah Bradford Landau and Carl W. Condit, *Rise of the New York Skyscraper, 1865–1913* (New Haven, Conn., and London: Yale University Press, 1996), esp. preface and chapters 1–4.

4. For discussions of pre–Civil War office buildings in New York, see Winston Weisman, "Commercial Palaces of New York: 1845–1875," *Art Bulletin* 36 (December 1954): 285–302; Lee Edward Gray, "The Office Building in New York City: 1850–1880" (Ph.D. diss., Cornell University, 1993): esp. chapters 1–2.

5. Russell Sturgis, "The Works of George B. Post," *Architectural Record* 4 (June 1898): 1–102.

6. Henry-Russell Hitchcock, *Architecture: Nineteenth and Twentieth Centuries*, 4th ed. (Baltimore: Penguin, 1971), 327. For a discussion of the relationship between architecture and the emerging insurance industry in New York, see Kenneth Turney Gibbs, "Business Architectural Imagery in America, 1870–1930" (Ph.D. diss., Cornell University, 1976): 21–66. Also see Gray, "The Office Building in New York City: 1850–1880": 88–96.

7. M. F. Sweetser, *New York: The American Cosmopolis* (Boston: Moses King, 1894), 30.

8. "The Manhattan Life Insurance Company's Building," *New York Times* (March 17, 1865): 7; *Insurance Blue Book, 1876–1877* (New York: C. C. Hine, 1877), 120–24; Mary Ann Clegg Smith, "The Commercial Architecture of John Butler Snook" (Ph.D. diss., Pennsylvania State University, 1974): 108–10, 212; Gibbs, "Business Architectural Imagery in America, 1870–1930": 21–22; Gray, "The Office Building in New York City: 1850–1880": 90–92.

9. "Mutual Life Insurance Company Building," advertisement, *Banker's Magazine* 19 (June 1865): 94; *Insurance Blue Book, 1876–1877*, 96–100; Winston Weisman, "New York and the Problem of the First Skyscraper," *Journal of the Society of Architectural Historians* 12 (March 1953): 13–21; Weisman, "A New View of Skyscraper History," in Kaufmann, ed., *The Rise of an American Architecture*, 124–25; Deborah S. Gardner, "The Architecture of Commercial Capitalism: John Kellum and the Development of New York, 1840–1875" (Ph.D. diss., Columbia University, 1979): 103–25; Gray, "The Office Building in New York City: 1850–1880": 92–96; Landau and Condit, *Rise of the New York Skyscraper, 1865–1913*, 76.

10. Sarah Bradford Landau, *Peter B. Wight: Architect, Contractor, and Critic, 1838–1925* (Chicago: Art Institute of Chicago, 1981), fig. 11, plate 163.

11. John W. Kennion, *Architects' and Builders' Guide* (New York: Fitzpatrick & Hunter, 1868), part 1: 57–60; "New York Life Insurance Co.'s New Building," *Real Estate Record and Builders' Guide* 1 (March 28, 1868): 4; "New Buildings," *New York Daily Tribune* (April 24, 1869): 1–2; "New-York Illustrated—No. 2," art supplement, *Appletons' Journal* 1 (June 12, 1869): 1–8; "Mercantile Palaces," *New York Herald* (October 18, 1869): 5; "The New York Life Assurance Company's Offices, Broadway, New York—Mr. Griffith Thomas, Architect," *Builder* 29 (September 16, 1871): 727, 729; Montgomery Schuyler, "Buildings on Broadway," *New York World* (September 24, 1871): 3; *Insurance Blue Book, 1876–1877*, 104–8; *A History of Real Estate, Building and Architecture in New York City During the Last Quarter of a Century* (New York: Real Estate Record Association, 1898), 555; I. N. Phelps Stokes, *The Iconography of Manhattan Island*, 6 vols. (New York: Robert H. Dodd, 1915–28; New York: Arno Press, 1967), vol. 5: 1930; Weisman, "New York and the Problem of the First Skyscraper": 13–21; Weisman, "A New View of Skyscraper History," in Kaufmann, ed., *The Rise of an American Architecture*, 124–25; Gibbs, "Business Architectural Imagery in America, 1870–1930": 28; Gardner, "The Architecture of Commercial Capitalism: John Kellum and the Development of New York, 1840–1875": 122–24; David W. Dunlap, *On Broadway: A Journey Uptown Over Time* (New York: Rizzoli International Publications, 1990), 55; Gray, "The Office Building in New York City: 1850–1880": 120–29; Landau and Condit, *Rise of the New York Skyscraper, 1865–1913*, 76–78.

12. Stokes, *The Iconography of Manhattan Island*, vol. 5: 1861, 1926, vol. 6: 466.

13. J. F. Richmond, *New York and Its Institutions, 1609–1872* (New York: E. B. Treat, 1872), 125, quoted in Dunlap, *On Broadway*, 55.

14. Schuyler, "Buildings on Broadway": 3.

15. "Improvement on Broadway," *New York Evening Post* (March 5, 1868): 1; "Another Broadway Palace," *New York Daily Tribune* (May 11, 1868): 2; "Demolition of Seven Buildings on Broadway—One Imposing Structure to Take Their Place," *New York Times* (May 24, 1868): 6; "New Buildings," *New York Daily Tribune* (April 24, 1869): 1–2; "The Equitable Life Insurance Building," *Real Estate Record and Builders' Guide* 4 (October 16, 1869): 2; "Mercantile Palaces": 5; "A Grand Commercial Edifice," *New York Sun* (November 4, 1869): 4; "Hints to Building Proprietors," *Real Estate Record and Builders' Guide* 4 (November 20, 1869): 3; Montgomery Schuyler, "Our City Architecture," *New York World* (September 7, 1871): 3; Arthur Gilman, "Cheap Fire-Proof Building," letter to the editor, *New York Times* (January 16, 1873): 5; *History of Architecture and the Building Trades of Greater New York* (New York, 1899), 55, 57; Montgomery Schuyler, "The 'Sky-Scraper' Up to Date," *Architectural Record* 8 (January–March 1899): 231–57; James W. Alexander, James H. Hyde, and William Alexander, *Henry Baldwin Hyde: A Biographical Sketch* (New York: Equitable Life Assurance Society of America, 1901), 119–20, 125; Stokes, *The Iconography of Manhattan Island*, vol. 3: 779, vol. 5: 1880, 1940; Weisman, "New York and the Problem of the First Sky-

scraper": 13–21; Weisman, "Commercial Palaces of New York: 1845–1875": 285–302; Carl W. Condit, *American Building Art: The Nineteenth Century* (New York: Oxford University Press, 1960), 43–44; Henry-Russell Hitchcock, *The Architecture of H. H. Richardson and His Times*, rev. ed. (Cambridge, Mass.: MIT Press, 1966), 76–77, 131, 153, 275, 309, fig. 8; Carl W. Condit, *American Building: Materials and Techniques from the First Colonial Settlements to the Present* (Chicago and London: University of Chicago Press, 1968), 115–16; Weisman, "A New View of Skyscraper History," in Kaufmann, ed., *The Rise of an American Architecture*, 119, 125; Winston Weisman, "The Commercial Architecture of George B. Post," *Journal of the Society of Architectural Historians* 31 (December 1972): 176–203; Arnold Lehman, "The New York Skyscraper: A History of Its Development, 1870–1939" (Ph.D. diss., Yale University, 1974): 33–36; Edward B. Watson, *New York Then and Now* (New York: Dover, 1976), 4; Gardner, "The Architecture of Commercial Capitalism: John Kellum and the Development of New York, 1840–1875": 122–24; Paul R. Baker, *Richard Morris Hunt* (Cambridge, Mass.: MIT Press, 1980), 501, 503, 539–40; Jeffrey Karl Ochsner, *H. H. Richardson: Complete Architectural Works* (Cambridge, Mass.: MIT Press, 1982), 38–40; Sarah Bradford Landau, "The Tall Office Building Artistically Reconsidered: Arcaded Buildings of the New York School, 1870–1890," in Helen Searing, ed., *In Search of Modern Architecture: A Tribute to Henry-Russell Hitchcock* (New York: Architectural History Foundation; Cambridge, Mass.: MIT Press, 1982), 136–64; M. Christine Boyer, *Manhattan Manners: Architecture and Style, 1850–1900* (New York: Rizzoli International Publications, 1985), 121; Sarah Bradford Landau, "Richard Morris Hunt: Architectural Innovator and Father of a 'Distinctive' American School," in Susan Stein, ed., *The Architecture of Richard Morris Hunt* (Chicago: University of Chicago Press, 1986), 54; Susan Stein, "Role and Reputation: The Architectural Practice of Richard Morris Hunt," in Stein, ed., *The Architecture of Richard Morris Hunt*, 115; David Van Zanten, "The Lenox Library: What Hunt Did and Did Not Learn in France," in Stein, ed., *The Architecture of Richard Morris Hunt*, 100, 106; Diana Balmori, "George B. Post: The Process of Design and the New American Architectural Office (1868–1913)," *Journal of the Society of Architectural Historians* 46 (December 1987): 342–55; Dunlap, *On Broadway*, 26; Gray, "The Office Building in New York City: 1850–1880": 130–91; Landau and Condit, *Rise of the New York Skyscraper, 1865–1913*, 62–71; Sarah Bradford Landau, *George B. Post, Architect: Picturesque Designer and Determined Realist*, Sources of American Architecture, ed. Robert A. M. Stern (New York: Monacelli Press, 1998), 13–15, plate 1.

16. Baker, *Richard Morris Hunt*, 539–40; Landau, "Richard Morris Hunt: Architectural Innovator and Father of a 'Distinctive' American School," in Stein, ed., *The Architecture of Richard Morris Hunt*, 54; Stein, "Role and Reputation: The Architectural Practice of Richard Morris Hunt," in Stein, ed., *The Architecture of Richard Morris Hunt*, 115; Zanten, "The Lenox Library: What Hunt Did and Did Not Learn in France," in Stein, ed., *The Architecture of Richard Morris Hunt*, 100; Gray, "The Office Building in New York City: 1850–1880": 143–48.

17. Hitchcock, *The Architecture of H. H. Richardson and His Times*, 77, 131, 275, fig. 8; Ochsner, *H. H. Richardson: Complete Architectural Works*, 38–40; Landau, "The Tall Office Building Artistically Reconsidered: Arcaded Buildings of the New York School, 1870–1890," in Searing, ed., *In Search of Modern Architecture: A Tribute to Henry-Russell Hitchcock*, 141–42; Gray, "The Office Building in New York City: 1850–1880": 147–52.

18. "Mercantile Palaces": 5, quoted in Gray, "The Office Building in New York City: 1850–1880": 156.

19. Henry Baldwin Hyde, quoted in *The Condition of Life Insurance Companies of the State of New York: Testimony Taken Before the New York Assembly Committee on Insurance* (Albany, N.Y.: W. S. Manning, 1877), 45, also quoted in Gray, "The Office Building in New York City: 1850–1880": 158.

20. Montgomery Schuyler, "The Evolution of the Skyscraper," *Scribner's Magazine* 46 (September 1909): 257–71.

21. "Mercantile Palaces": 5, quoted in Gray, "The Office Building in New York City: 1850–1880": 190.

22. "The Equitable Life Insurance Building," *Real Estate Record and Builders' Guide*: 2.

23. "A Grand Commercial Edifice": 4, quoted in Gray, "The Office Building in New York City: 1850–1880": 191.

24. *Insurance Blue Book, 1876–1877*, 148–52; Stokes, *The Iconography of Manhattan Island*, vol. 6: 313; Gibbs, "Business Architectural Imagery in America, 1870–1930": 28; Gardner, "The Architecture of Commercial Capitalism: John Kellum and the Development of New York, 1840–1875": 120–25.

25. Moses King, *King's Handbook of New York* (Boston: Moses King, 1893), 673–74; Gibbs, "Business Architectural Imagery in America, 1870–1930": 28.

26. *History of Architecture and the Building Trades of Greater New York*, 55, 57.

27. Henry Baldwin Hyde, quoted in Gibbs, "Business Architectural Imagery in America, 1870–1930": 26. Also see Alexander, Hyde, and Alexander, *Henry Baldwin Hyde: A Biographical Sketch*, 119.

28. Henry Hyde to George B. Post, June 1, 1893, quoted in Gibbs, "Business Architectural Imagery in America, 1870–1930": 40.

29. "A New Business Center," *New York Times* (March 8, 1872): 8; "The Highest Business Block," *New York Daily Tribune* (April 25, 1873): 8; "A Telegraph Palace": 1; "Western Union Telegraph Building," *The Aldine* 7 (January 1, 1875): 258, reprinted in *The Operator* (January 1, 1875): 2; "An Immense Telegraphing Establishment," *Scientific American* 32 (March 6, 1875): 144–45; A. J. Bloor, "Annual Address," *Proceedings of the Tenth Annual Convention of the American Institute of Architects, 1876* (Boston, 1877): 15–34; "Sky Building in New York," *Building News* 45 (September 7, 1883): 363–64; Schuyler, "The 'Sky-Scraper' Up to Date": 232–33; Montgomery Schuyler, "The Skyscraper Problem," *Scribner's Magazine* 34 (September 1903): 253–56; Stokes, *The Iconography of Manhattan Island*, vol. 3: 777, plate 155a, vol. 5: 1948, 1952; John Kouwenhoven, *The Columbia Historical Portrait of New York* (Garden City, N.Y.: Doubleday, 1953), 357; Weisman, "New York and the Problem of the First Skyscraper": 13–21; Hitchcock, *Architecture: Nineteenth and Twentieth Centuries*, 239–40, 244, fig. 115a; Weisman, "A New View of Skyscraper History," in Kaufmann, ed., *The Rise of an American Architecture*, 127; Weisman, "The Commercial Architecture of George B. Post": 181–82; Lehman, "The New York Skyscraper: A History of Its Development, 1870–1939": 36–41; Gibbs, "Business Architectural Imagery in America, 1870–1930": 71, 73; Landau, "The Tall Office Building Artistically Reconsidered: Arcaded Buildings of the New York School, 1870–1890," in Searing, ed., *In Search of Modern Architecture: A Tribute to Henry-Russell Hitchcock*, 142; Balmori, "George B. Post: The Process of Design and the New American Architectural Office (1868–1913)": 342–55; Dunlap, *On Broadway*, 25; Gray, "The Office Building in New York City: 1850–1880": 194–214; Landau and Condit, *Rise of the New York Skyscraper, 1865–1913*, 78–83; Landau, *George B. Post, Architect*, 25, 30–36.

30. George B. Post to William Orion, August 5, 1872, quoted in Balmori, "George B. Post: The Process of Design and the New American Architectural Office (1868–1913)": 347.

31. Quoted in Gray, "The Office Building in New York City: 1850–1880": 200.

32. "Western Union Telegraph Building," *The Aldine*: 258.

33. "The Highest Business Block": 8.

34. Bloor, "Annual Address": 25.

35. Schuyler, "The Skyscraper Problem": 253–56.

36. See Gray, "The Office Building in New York City: 1850–1880": 68–87.

37. "Press Palaces," *American Builder* (September 1873): 200, quoted in van Leeuwen, *The Skyward Trend of Thought*, 93.

38. "The New Herald Building," *New York Herald* (April 21, 1867): 3; "New Buildings," *New York Herald* (July 7, 1867): 5; Schuyler, "Our City Architecture": 3; Kennion, *Architects' and Builders' Guide*, part 3: 49–54; Bloor, "Annual Address": 24; Weisman, "New York and the Problem of the First Skyscraper": 13–21; Gardner, "The Architecture of Commercial Capitalism: John Kellum and the Development of New York, 1840–1875": 147–60; Gray, "The Office Building in New York City: 1850–1880": 105–9.

39. George Templeton Strong, diary entry dated July 13, 1865, in *The Diary of George Templeton Strong*, eds. Allan Nevins and Milton Halsey Thomas, 4 vols. (New York: Macmillan, 1952), vol. 4: 17.

40. Kennion, *Architects' and Builders' Guide*, part 3: 51.

41. Schuyler, "Our City Architecture": 3.

42. "Office of the New Yorker Staats-Zeitung," *Real Estate Record and Builders' Guide* 10 (November 9, 1872): 173; Bloor, "Annual Address": 24; King, *King's Handbook of New York* (1893), 56–57, 613; Stokes, *The Iconography of Manhattan Island*, vol. 3: 777, plate 155a.

43. "Office of the New Yorker Staats-Zeitung": 173.

44. "The Evening Post Building," supplement, *New York Evening Post* (July 1, 1875): n.p.; "New York City News: Hathorne Vs. the 'Evening Post'—The Case Summed Up," *New York World* (October 9, 1875): 2; Bloor, "Annual Address": 24; "The Post Building," *Real Estate Record and Builders' Guide* 30 (November 11–18, 1882): 72–73; "Sky Building in New York": 364; "Very Tall Building," *The Architect* 30 (September 15, 1883): 155–56; King, *King's Handbook of New York* (1893), 610–12; Weisman, "A New View of Skyscraper History," in Kaufmann, ed., *The Rise of an American Architecture*, 127; Gibbs, "Business Architectural Imagery in America, 1870–1930": 72–73; Dunlap, *On Broadway*, 34; Landau and Condit, *Rise of the New York Skyscraper, 1865–1913*, 94–96.

45. "The Post Building": 72–73.

46. "The Evening Post Building": n.p.

47. "The Bennett Building," *New York Herald* (December 11, 1872): 5; "Fire-Proof Buildings," advertisement, *New York Daily Tribune* (December 17, 1872): 8; King, *King's Handbook of New York* (1893), 835; *A History of Real Estate, Building and Architecture in New York City During the Last Quarter of a Century*, 624; Weisman, "New York and the Problem of the First Skyscraper": 13–21; Mary Black, *Old New York in Early Photographs* (New York: Dover, 1973), plate 33; Andrew S. Dolkart, *Lower Manhattan Architectural Survey Report* (New York: Lower Manhattan Cultural Council, fall 1987), no. 99; White and Willensky, *AIA Guide* (1988), 41; Gray, "The Office Building in New York City: 1850–1880": 214–25, 329–35; Landau and Condit, *Rise of the New York Skyscraper, 1865–1913*, 98–99; Christopher Gray, "Streetscapes/The Bennett Building," *New York Times* (January 7, 1996), IX: 7.

48. "Fire-Proof Buildings": 8.

49. "Local Improvements—Tearing Down the Tribune Building," *New York Daily Graphic* (May 29, 1873): 2, 4; "The New Tribune Building, in Course of Erection, from the Plans of Mr. Hunt, Architect," *New York Daily Graphic* (August 4, 1873): 234, 236; "The New Tribune Building," *New-York Sketch-Book of Architecture* 1 (January 1874): 1–2, plate 1; "Competitive Design for the New Tribune Building. Mr. J. Cleaveland Cady, Architect," *New-York Sketch-Book of Architecture* 1 (July 1874): 1, plate 25; "The New Tribune," *New York Daily Tribune* (April 10, 1875): 9–10; "The Best Lawyers' Offices in the City," *New York Daily Tribune* (April 17, 1875): 7; "The Tribune's New Building," *New York Daily Tribune* (May 1, 1875): 2; Montgomery Schuyler, "The New Tribune Building," *New York World* (May 2, 1875): 4–5; "The Tribune Building, New York," *New-York Sketch-Book of Architecture* 3 (July 1876): 1, plate 26; "Notes and Clippings," *American Architect and Building News* 1 (December 23, 1876): 416; Bloor, "Annual Address": 24; "The Post Building": 72–73; "Sky Building in New York": 364; "Very Tall Building": 155–56; Montgomery Schuyler, "The Works of the Late Richard M. Hunt," *Architectural Record* 5 (October–December 1895): 97–180; Martha J. Lamb and Mrs. Burton Harrison, *History of the City of New York* (New York: A. S. Barnes & Co., 1896), 441, 791; *A History of Real Estate, Building and Architecture in New York City During the Last Quarter of a Century*, 556; Schuyler, "The 'Sky-Scraper' Up to Date": 233–34; Schuyler, "The Skyscraper Problem": 253–56; Weisman, "New York and the Problem of the First Skyscraper": 13–21; Weisman, "Commercial Palaces of New York: 1845–1875": 285–302; Hitchcock, *Architecture: Nineteenth and Twentieth Centuries*, 169, 239–40; Vincent Scully, *American Architecture and Urbanism* (New York: Frederick A. Praeger, 1969), 174; Weisman, "A New View of Skyscraper History," in Kaufmann, ed., *The Rise of an American Architecture*, 120–22, 125; Black, *Old New York in Early Photographs*, plate 44; Lehman, "The New York Skyscraper: A History of Its Development, 1870–1939": 36–41; Baker, *Richard Morris Hunt*, 219–23; Landau, "The Tall Office Building Artistically Reconsidered: Arcaded Buildings of the New York School, 1870–1890," in Searing, ed., *In Search of Modern Architecture: A Tribute to Henry-Russell Hitchcock*, 142–43; Gibbs, "Business Architectural Imagery in America, 1870–1930": 69–70, 73;

van Leeuwen, *The Skyward Trend of Thought*, 94–99; Gray, "The Office Building in New York City: 1850–1880": 251–323, 366–477; Kathleen A. Curran, *A Forgotten Architect of the Gilded Age: Josiah Cleaveland Cady's Legacy*, exhibition catalogue (Hartford, Conn.: Trinity College, 1993), 45–48; Landau and Condit, *Rise of the New York Skyscraper, 1865–1913*, 83–90.

50. Frederic Hudson, *Journalism in the United States from 1690 to 1872* (New York: Harper & Bros., 1873), 573, quoted in Gray, "The Office Building in New York City: 1850–1880": 252.

51. Landau and Condit, *Rise of the New York Skyscraper, 1865–1913*, 84. For the Metropolitan Life Tower, see Stern, Gilmartin, and Massengale, *New York 1900*, 171–73, 176.

52. Bayard Taylor to Whitelaw Reid, May 3, 1873, quoted in Gray, "The Office Building in New York City: 1850–1880": 276.

53. "A Telegraph Palace": 1.

54. Schuyler, "The New Tribune Building": 4–5.

55. Schuyler, "The Works of the Late Richard M. Hunt": 105.

56. Schuyler, "The Skyscraper Problem": 253–56.

57. Weisman, "Commercial Palaces of New York: 1845–1875": 298.

58. Leonard Huxley, *Life and Letters of Thomas Henry Huxley*, 2 vols. (New York: D. Appleton & Co., 1900), vol. 1: 494, quoted by William H. Jordy and Ralph Coe in Montgomery Schuyler, *American Architecture and Other Writings*, eds. William H. Jordy and Ralph Coe, 2 vols. (Cambridge, Mass.: Harvard University Press, Belknap Press, 1961), vol. 2: 425 (n. 76).

59. "Correspondence: New York—Mr. Potter's Retirement," *American Architect and Building News* 1 (August 12, 1876): 262–63; Montgomery Schuyler, "Recent Building in New York—II," *American Architect and Building News* 9 (April 16, 1881): 183–84; Montgomery Schuyler, "The Works of Henry Janeway Hardenbergh," *Architectural Record* 6 (January–March 1897): 335–75; *A History of Real Estate, Building and Architecture in New York City During the Last Quarter of a Century*, 628.

60. "Buildings Projected," *Real Estate Record and Builders' Guide* 27 (April 16, 1881): 383; "Out Among the Builders," *Real Estate Record and Builders' Guide* 27 (May 14, 1881): 492; *A History of Real Estate, Building and Architecture in New York City During the Last Quarter of a Century*, 634.

61. King, *King's Handbook of New York* (1893), 155, 750–51; Moses King, *King's Views of New York, 1896* (Boston: Moses King, 1896; New York: Benjamin Blom, 1974), 9; *A History of Real Estate, Building and Architecture in New York City During the Last Quarter of a Century*, 624; Stokes, *The Iconography of Manhattan Island*, vol. 3: 842, plate 159b, vol. 6: 312; Weisman, "New York and the Problem of the First Skyscraper": 13–21.

62. "The Building Outlook: New Business Structures," *New York Daily Tribune* (June 17, 1873): 5; "The Delaware and Hudson Canal Company's New Building," *New York Times* (March 14, 1874): 3; Delaware and Hudson Canal Company, *Description of the Coal and Iron Exchange Building* (New York: Baker & Godwin, Printers, 1876); "The Coal and Iron Exchange," *New York Daily Tribune* (January 28, 1876): 3; "The Post Building": 72–73; M. G. Van Rensselaer, "Recent Architecture in America—III," *Century Magazine* 28 (August 1884): 511–23; King, *King's Handbook of New York* (1893), 130–31; Schuyler, "The Works of the Late Richard M. Hunt": 109; *A History of Real Estate, Building and Architecture in New York City During the Last Quarter of a Century*, 624; Stokes, *The Iconography of Manhattan Island*, vol. 5: 1952; Weisman, "New York and the Problem of the First Skyscraper": 13–21; Baker, *Richard Morris Hunt*, 163, 217–19, 502, 543; Landau, "Richard Morris Hunt: Architectural Innovator and Father of a 'Distinctive' American School," in Stein, ed., *The Architecture of Richard Morris Hunt*, 55; Gray, "The Office Building in New York City: 1850–1880": 225–50; Landau and Condit, *Rise of the New York Skyscraper, 1865–1913*, 90–93.

63. Van Rensselaer, "Recent Architecture in America—III": 518.

64. Schuyler, "The Works of the Late Richard M. Hunt": 109.

65. "Buildings Projected," *Real Estate Record and Builders' Guide* 27 (April 30, 1881): 446; "The Post Building": 72–73; King, *King's Handbook of New York* (1893), 690; Schuyler, "The Works of the Late Richard M. Hunt": 107; *A History of Real Estate, Building and Architecture in New York City During the Last Quarter of a Century*, 561; Gibbs, "Business Archi-

tectural Imagery in America, 1870–1930": 67–69, 73; Baker, *Richard Morris Hunt*, 223–25, 293, 504, 544; Landau, "Richard Morris Hunt: Architectural Innovator and Father of a 'Distinctive' American School," in Stein, ed., *The Architecture of Richard Morris Hunt*, 72.

66. Schuyler, "The Works of the Late Richard M. Hunt": 107.

67. W., "Correspondence," *American Architect and Building News* 3 (April 20, 1878): 138; B.W., "Correspondence," *American Architect and Building News* 5 (January 11, 1879): 12–13; "The Boreel Building," *Real Estate Record and Builders' Guide* 23 (February 22, 1879): 146; Montgomery Schuyler, "Two Office Buildings," *New York World* (May 25, 1879): 4; W., "Correspondence: Iron Fronts—New Office Buildings," *American Architect and Building News* 6 (July 5, 1879): 6–7; Montgomery Schuyler, "Recent Building in New York—II," *American Architect and Building News* 9 (April 16, 1881): 183–84; "The Post Building": 72–73; *A History of Real Estate, Building and Architecture in New York City During the Last Quarter of a Century*, 557, 629; Weisman, "A New View of Skyscraper History," in Kaufmann, ed., *The Rise of an American Architecture*, 126–27, 132–33; Gibbs, "Business Architectural Imagery in America, 1870–1930": 74; Dunlap, *On Broadway*, 26.

68. "The Boreel Building": 146.

69. B.W., "Correspondence," (January 11, 1879): 13.

70. W., "Correspondence: Iron Fronts—New Office Buildings": 7.

71. Schuyler, "Recent Building in New York—II": 183–84; "A Mammoth Insurance Company," *New York Daily Graphic* (June 2, 1881): 695–96; "Sky Building in New York": 364; King, *King's Handbook of New York* (1893), 662; *A History of Real Estate, Building and Architecture in New York City During the Last Quarter of a Century*, 629; Stokes, *The Iconography of Manhattan Island*, vol. 6: 312.

72. Schuyler, "Recent Building in New York—II": 183–84.

73. "The Morse Building," *Real Estate Record and Builders' Guide* 23 (January 18, 1879): 44–45. Also see Schuyler, "Two Office Buildings": 4; "Artistic Brickwork," *Carpentry and Building* 1 (June 1879): 101–3, (July 1879): 121–22; W., "Correspondence: Iron Fronts—New Office Buildings": 6–7; B.W., "Correspondence," *American Architect and Building News* 6 (November 11, 1879): 12–13; "Sky Building in New York": 364; "Very Tall Building": 155; Van Rensselaer, "Recent Architecture in America—III": 517; King, *King's Handbook of New York* (1893), 830–31; *A History of Real Estate, Building and Architecture in New York City During the Last Quarter of a Century*, 515–16, 560; Montgomery Schuyler, "Architectural Aberrations—No. 18: The Nassau-Beekman," *Architectural Record* 12 (May 1902): 93–98; Weisman, "A New View of Skyscraper History," in Kaufmann, ed., *The Rise of an American Architecture*, 126–27, 133; Dolkart, *Lower Manhattan Architectural Survey Report*, no. 109; White and Willensky, *AIA Guide* (1988), 41; Landau and Condit, *Rise of the New York Skyscraper, 1865–1913*, 102, 104–5.

74. "The Morse Building": 44–45.

75. Schuyler, "Two Office Buildings": 4.

76. Schuyler, "Two Office Buildings": 4.

77. W., "Correspondence: Iron Fronts—New Office Buildings": 6.

78. Schuyler, "Recent Building in New York—II": 183–84.

79. Schuyler, "Architectural Aberrations—No. 18: The Nassau-Beekman": 96.

80. "Sky Building in New York": 364; "Very Tall Building": 155; "Out Among the Builders," *Real Estate Record and Builders' Guide* 43 (February 23, 1889): 245; King, *King's Handbook of New York* (1893), 831, 833; *A History of Real Estate, Building and Architecture in New York City During the Last Quarter of a Century*, 634; Weisman, "The Commercial Architecture of George B. Post": 188; Dolkart, *Lower Manhattan Architectural Survey Report*, no. 110; White and Willensky, *AIA Guide* (1988), 41; Landau and Condit, *Rise of the New York Skyscraper, 1865–1913*, 116–17; David W. Dunlap, "Around City Hall, the Past Is New," *New York Times* (April 19, 1998), XI: 1, 6.

81. "New Office Buildings," *Real Estate Record and Builders' Guide* 30 (December 30, 1882): 144. Also see "The Welles Building, Broadway and Beaver Streets, New York, N.Y. Messrs. G. R. and R. G. Shaw, Architects, Boston, Mass.," *American Architect and Building News* 11 (June 10, 1882): 270, plate; "The Standard Oil Company's Building, New York, N.Y. Mr. E. L. Roberts, Architect, New York, N.Y.; and the Welles Building, Messrs. G. R. & R. G. Shaw, Architects, Boston, Mass.," *Amer-*

ican Architect and Building News 19 (February 27, 1886): 102, plate; Dunlap, *On Broadway*, 18; Landau and Condit, *Rise of the New York Skyscraper, 1865–1913*, 133–34.

82. "Out Among the Builders," *Real Estate Record and Builders' Guide* 33 (January 26, 1884): 87; "Out Among the Builders," *Real Estate Record and Builders' Guide* 33 (March 21, 1884): 319; "Two Business Buildings," *Real Estate Record and Builders' Guide* 34 (November 29, 1884): 1196; "A Model Business Structure," *New York Daily Graphic* (July 27, 1885): 179, 181; "Lower Broadway," *Real Estate Record and Builders' Guide* 36 (August 15, 1885): 905; "The Standard Oil Company's Building, New York, N.Y. Mr. E. L. Roberts, Architect, New York, N.Y.; and the Welles Building, Messrs. G. R. & R. G. Shaw, Architects, Boston, Mass.": 102, plate; *A History of Real Estate, Building and Architecture in New York City During the Last Quarter of a Century*, 640; Dunlap, *On Broadway*, 18; Landau and Condit, *Rise of the New York Skyscraper, 1865–1913*, 133–34.

83. "Two Business Buildings": 1196.

84. "New Office Buildings," (December 30, 1882): 144. Also see *A History of Real Estate, Building and Architecture in New York City During the Last Quarter of a Century*, 635.

85. *A History of Real Estate, Building and Architecture in New York City During the Last Quarter of a Century*, 624; Baker, *Richard Morris Hunt*, 504, 542; Landau, "Richard Morris Hunt: Architectural Innovator and Father of a 'Distinctive' American School," in Stein, ed., *The Architecture of Richard Morris Hunt*, 54–55; Landau and Condit, *Rise of the New York Skyscraper, 1865–1913*, 93–94.

86. For Sullivan's buildings, see Hugh Morrison, *Louis Sullivan: Prophet of Modern Architecture* (New York: Museum of Modern Art and W. W. Norton & Co., 1935), 60–62, 295, 297, plate 4.

87. "Correspondence," *American Architect and Building News* 2 (July 7, 1877): 218; "The Queen's Insurance Company's Building, New York, N.Y. Messrs. Clinton and Pirsson, Architects," *American Architect and Building News* 2 (September 29, 1877): 313, plate; "The Orient Building in Wall Street," *Real Estate Record and Builders' Guide* 21 (March 9, 1878): 200; "A New Building in Wall Street," *American Architect and Building News* 5 (May 3, 1879): 141; "The Orient Mutual Insurance Company's Building, Wall St., N.Y.," *American Architect and Building News* 3 (March 2, 1878): 76, plate; Montgomery Schuyler, "Two Commercial Palaces," *New York World* (March 31, 1878): 3; "The Orient Building, Wall Street," *New York Daily Graphic* (April 6, 1878): 260; *A History of Real Estate, Building and Architecture in New York City During the Last Quarter of a Century*, 628; Stokes, *The Iconography of Manhattan Island*, vol. 5: 1822; Arnold Lewis and Keith Morgan, *American Victorian Architecture* (New York: Dover, 1975), 38; Landau and Condit, *Rise of the New York Skyscraper, 1865–1913*, 101–3.

88. "The Queen's Insurance Company's Building, New York, N.Y. Messrs. Clinton and Pirsson, Architects": 313, plate; Schuyler, "Two Commercial Palaces": 6; *A History of Real Estate, Building and Architecture in New York City During the Last Quarter of a Century*, 628; Lewis and Morgan, *American Victorian Architecture*, 35, 38, 144; Landau and Condit, *Rise of the New York Skyscraper, 1865–1913*, 101–3.

89. "Correspondence," (July 7, 1877): 218.

90. "The Queen's Insurance Company's Building, New York, N.Y. Messrs. Clinton and Pirsson, Architects": 313.

91. Schuyler, "Two Commercial Palaces": 3.

92. Schuyler, "Recent Building in New York—II": 183–84; Van Rensselaer, "Recent Architecture in America—III": 518, 520; *A History of Real Estate, Building and Architecture in New York City During the Last Quarter of a Century*, 629, 673; Dunlap, *On Broadway*, 20.

93. Van Rensselaer, "Recent Architecture in America—III": 518, 520.

94. "New Down-Town Buildings," *Real Estate Record and Builders' Guide* 32 (September 29, 1883): 729–30; "The Commercial Union Insurance Co. Building," *Real Estate Record and Builders' Guide* 32 (December 15, 1883): 996; "Commercial Union Assurance Co. Building, New York, by Geo. E. Harney, Architect, 149 Broadway, New York," *Building* 3 (December 1884): 29, plate; *A History of Real Estate, Building and Architecture in New York City During the Last Quarter of a Century*, 640.

95. "The Commercial Union Insurance Co. Building," *Real Estate Record and Builders' Guide*: 996.

96. "The Corbin Building, Northeast Corner of John Street and Broadway, New York City. Mr. Francis H. Kimball, Architect, 40 Broadway, New York City," *Building* 11 (September 28, 1889): 105; James Taylor, "A Review of Architectural Terra-Cotta," in *A History of Real Estate, Building and Architecture in New York City During the Last Quarter of a Century*, 520, 522–24, 646; Montgomery Schuyler, "The Works of Francis H. Kimball and Kimball & Thompson," *Architectural Record* 7 (April–June 1898): 479–518; Landau and Condit, *Rise of the New York Skyscraper, 1865–1913*, 155–56, 158.

97. Schuyler, "The Works of Francis H. Kimball and Kimball & Thompson": 502.

98. "Out Among the Builders," *Real Estate Record and Builders' Guide* 31 (April 21, 1883): 163; "Out Among the Builders," *Real Estate Record and Builders' Guide* 32 (July 14, 1883): 501; "A New Building in Park-Row," *New York Times* (July 20, 1883): 8; "The Potter Building," *Real Estate Record and Builders' Guide* 35 (June 20, 1885): 701–2; "The Potter Building," *New York Daily Graphic* (February 27, 1886): 829; King, *King's Handbook of New York* (1893), 824–25; *A History of Real Estate, Building and Architecture in New York City During the Last Quarter of a Century*, 640; Stokes, *The Iconography of Manhattan Island*, vol. 5: 1982; Dolkart, *Lower Manhattan Architectural Survey Report*, no. 106; White and Willensky, *AIA Guide* (1988), 41; Andrew Alpern, *Luxury Apartment Houses of Manhattan: An Illustrated History* (New York: Dover, 1992), 174–76; Landau and Condit, *Rise of the New York Skyscraper, 1865–1913*, 137–42.

99. "The Potter Building," *Real Estate Record and Builders' Guide*: 701–2.

100. Margot Gayle and Edmund V. Gillon Jr., *Cast-Iron Architecture in New York* (New York: Dover, 1974), 159; White and Willensky, *AIA Guide* (1988), 155; Dunlap, *On Broadway*, 102–3; Landau and Condit, *Rise of the New York Skyscraper, 1865–1913*, 137.

101. "Buildings Projected," *Real Estate Record and Builders' Guide* 31 (June 23, 1883): 453; "Out Among the Builders," *Real Estate Record and Builders' Guide* 31 (June 23, 1883): 248; "In West Twenty-third Street," *Real Estate Record and Builders' Guide* 33 (June 28, 1884): 693–94; Schuyler, "The Works of Henry Janeway Hardenbergh": 342–46; *A History of Real Estate, Building and Architecture in New York City During the Last Quarter of a Century*, 567, 681.

102. Schuyler, "The Works of Henry Janeway Hardenbergh": 342–46.

103. "In and Around New York," *New York World* (August 30, 1881): 5; "Mr. Field's New Building," *New York Times* (November 17, 1881): 8; "The Old Washington Hotel at Bowling Green, Now Being Demolished," *New York Daily Graphic* (January 6, 1882): 454, 457; "Cyrus W. Field's Purchases," *New York Times* (January 6, 1882): 8; "Important Real Estate Transfers," *New York Times* (June 2, 1882): 8; "Out Among the Builders," *Real Estate Record and Builders' Guide* 29 (June 3, 1882): 553; "The Field Building," *Real Estate Record and Builders' Guide* 31 (March 24, 1883): 114; Edward H. Kendall, letter to the editor, *Real Estate Record and Builders' Guide* 31 (April 7, 1883): 135; "Competitive Design for an Office-Building on Battery Place, New York, Facing the Park and Bay, for Cyrus Field, Esq., Mr. Charles B. Atwood, Architect, New York, N.Y.," *American Architect and Building News* 13 (April 21, 1883): 186–87, plates; "Twelve Hundred Feet Deep," *New York Times* (August 25, 1883): 2; "Sky Building in New York": 364; "The Washington Building," *New York Daily Graphic* (August 4, 1884): 247–48; Van Rensselaer, "Recent Architecture in America—III": 518; "Walls Rising in Broadway," *New York Daily Tribune* (September 19, 1886): 13; "The Washington Building," *Real Estate Record and Builders' Guide* 43 (April 27, 1889): 583; Horace Townsend, "English and American Architecture—A Companion and a Prophecy," *Art Journal* 54 (October 1892): 294–300; King, *King's Handbook of New York* (1893), 820–21; *A History of Real Estate, Building and Architecture in New York City During the Last Quarter of a Century*, 635; Stokes, *The Iconography of Manhattan Island*, vol. 2: 216, vol. 5: 1977–78, vol. 6: 436, 513, 619; Weisman, "The Commercial Architecture of George B. Post": 188; Christopher Gray, "A 1922 Facade that Hides Another from the 1880's," *New York Times* (March 26, 1995), IX: 7; Landau and Condit, *Rise of the New York Skyscraper, 1865–1913*, 125–29.

104. "The Field Building," (March 24, 1883): 114.

105. Van Rensselaer, "Recent Architecture in America—III": 518.

106. For a discussion of arcaded buildings before Richardson, see Landau, "The Tall Office Building Artistically Reconsidered: Arcaded Buildings of the New York School, 1870–1890," in Searing, ed., *In Search of Modern Architecture: A Tribute to Henry-Russell Hitchcock*, 136–45.

107. "The United Bank Building," *New York Daily Graphic* (April 4, 1881): 257; "United Bank Building, N.Y. Messrs. Peabody & Stearns, Architects, Boston, Mass.," *American Architect and Building News* 9 (April 23, 1881): 199, plate; Schuyler, "Recent Building in New York—II": 183–84; "The United Bank Building," *New York Daily Graphic* (June 27, 1881): 881–82; "The United Bank Building," *Real Estate Record and Builders' Guide* 30 (November 4–11, 1882): 59–60; "Sky Building in New York": 364; "Very Tall Building": 155; King, *King's Handbook of New York* (1893), 724–25; *A History of Real Estate, Building and Architecture in New York City During the Last Quarter of a Century*, 629; Wheaton Arnold Holden, "Robert Swain Peabody of Peabody and Stearns in Boston: The Early Years (1870–1886)" (Ph.D. diss., Boston University, 1969): 122–24, fig. 153; Wheaton A. Holden, "The Peabody Touch: Peabody and Stearns of Boston, 1870–1917," *Journal of the Society of Architectural Historians* 32 (May 1973): 114–31; Landau, "The Tall Office Building Artistically Reconsidered: Arcaded Buildings of the New York School, 1870–1890," in Searing, ed., *In Search of Modern Architecture: A Tribute to Henry-Russell Hitchcock*, 148–49; Manfred Bock, *Anfänge einer neuen Architektur* ('s-Gravenhage: Staatsuitgeverij; Wiesbaden: Franz Steiner Verlag, 1983); 295; Dunlap, *On Broadway*, 25; Landau and Condit, *Rise of the New York Skyscraper, 1865–1913*, 110, 220.

108. For Richardson's Cheney Building, see Hitchcock, *Architecture: Nineteenth and Twentieth Centuries*, 238–39, fig. 116A; Ochsner, *H. H. Richardson: Complete Architectural Works*, 153–55; James F. O'Gorman, *Living Architecture: A Biography of H. H. Richardson* (New York: Simon & Schuster, 1997), 125.

109. Schuyler, "Recent Building in New York—II": 183–84.

110. "The United Bank Building," *Real Estate Record and Builders' Guide*: 59–60.

111. "Buildings Projected," *Real Estate Record and Builders' Guide* 37 (April 10, 1886): 480; "Walls Rising in Broadway": 13; "Aldrich Court," *Real Estate Record and Builders' Guide* 39 (March 5, 1887): 288; King, *King's Handbook of New York* (1893), 826; *A History of Real Estate, Building and Architecture in New York City During the Last Quarter of a Century*, 641; Landau, "The Tall Office Building Artistically Reconsidered: Arcaded Buildings of the New York School, 1870–1890," in Searing, ed., *In Search of Modern Architecture: A Tribute to Henry-Russell Hitchcock*, 154–55; White and Willensky, *AIA Guide* (1988), 862; Dunlap, *On Broadway*, 19; Landau and Condit, *Rise of the New York Skyscraper, 1865–1913*, 149–50.

112. "Aldrich Court": 288.

113. "Out Among the Builders," *Real Estate Record and Builders' Guide* 41 (January 21, 1888): 80; "Out Among the Builders," *Real Estate Record and Builders' Guide* 41 (January 28, 1888): 115; "Out Among the Builders," *Real Estate Record and Builders' Guide* 41 (February 11, 1888): 181; "Buildings Projected," *Real Estate Record and Builders' Guide* 41 (March 3, 1888): 287; "Out Among the Builders," *Real Estate Record and Builders' Guide* 41 (March 10, 1888): 302–3; "Competitive Design for Office Building of the United States Trust Building [*sic*], Messrs. Babb, Cook & Willard, Architects, New York, N.Y.," *American Architect and Building News* 23 (March 17, 1888): 127, plate; "Important Buildings Projected and Under Way," *Real Estate Record and Builders' Guide* 41 (April 28, 1888): 529; "New Premises for the United States Trust Company, Wall St., New York. Mr. R. W. Gibson, Architect, New York, N.Y.," *American Architect and Building News* 23 (June 16, 1888): 282, plate; "Laying the Cornerstone," *New York Times* (June 28, 1888): 8; "Important Buildings Under Way: Part II," *Real Estate Record and Builders' Guide* 42 (September 15, 1888): 1110; "The United States Trust Company," *Real Estate Record and Builders' Guide* 42 (December 22, 1888): 1509; "United States Trust Company's Building, Wall Street, New York, N.Y.," *American Architect and Building News* 27, international edition (January 18, 1890): plate; Montgomery Schuyler, "The Romanesque Revival in New York," *Architectural Record* 1 (July–September 1891): 7–38; Townsend, "English and American Architecture—A Companion and a Prophecy": 297; King, *King's Handbook of New York* (1893), 758–59;

A History of Real Estate, Building and Architecture in New York City During the Last Quarter of a Century, 646, 679; Landau and Condit, *Rise of the New York Skyscraper, 1865–1913*, 103, 155.

114. Schuyler, "The Romanesque Revival in New York": 28–29.

115. "The United States Trust Company," (December 22, 1888): 1509.

116. "Out Among the Builders," *Real Estate Record and Builders' Guide* 41 (March 31, 1888): 396–97; "Important Buildings Projected and Under Way," (April 28, 1888): 529; "Important Buildings Under Way," *Real Estate Record and Builders' Guide* 42 (September 1, 1888): 1065; "The Market and Fulton National Bank," *Real Estate Record and Builders' Guide* 43 (March 16, 1889): 347–48; Schuyler, "The Romanesque Revival in New York": 27, 29–31; King, *King's Handbook of New York* (1893), 727–28; *A History of Real Estate, Building and Architecture in New York City During the Last Quarter of a Century*, 579, 646; Moses King, *King's Views of New York, 1908–1909* (Boston: Moses King, 1908; New York: Benjamin Blom, 1974), 43; Bock, *Anfänge einer neuen Architektur*, 295; van Leeuwen, *The Skyward Trend of Thought*, 89–90.

117. "The Market and Fulton National Bank," (March 16, 1889): 347–48.

118. Schuyler, "The Romanesque Revival in New York": 29, 31.

119. "Out Among the Builders," *Real Estate Record and Builders' Guide* 30 (November 25–December 2, 1882): 96; "Out Among the Builders," *Real Estate Record and Builders' Guide* 30 (December 16–23, 1882): 131; "New Down-Town Buildings," *Real Estate Record and Builders' Guide* 32 (September 29, 1883): 729–30; "The Mutual Building," *Real Estate Record and Builders' Guide* 33 (January 12, 1884): 25–26; "The Mutual Life Building," *Real Estate Record and Builders' Guide* 33 (January 19, 1884): 57; Engineer, "The Mutual Life Building," letter to the editor, *Real Estate Record and Builders' Guide* 33 (January 26, 1884): 83; Civil Engineer, "Engineer Answered," letter to the editor, *Real Estate Record and Builders' Guide* 33 (February 2, 1884): 111; "Our Trade Palaces," *Building* 2 (May 1884): 100; "The New Building of the Mutual Life Ins. Co.," *New York Times* (June 26, 1884): 5; "Artistic Wood-Finishing," *New York Times* (July 13, 1884): 7; "Marble for Interiors," *New York Times* (July 20, 1884): 7; Van Rensselaer, "Recent Architecture in America—III": 518; "Remarkable Building Work," *New York Times* (October 3, 1884): 5; "A Deluge of Water," *New York Times* (October 12, 1884): 9; "Offices of the Mutual Life Insurance Company of New York. Mr. C. W. Clinton, Architect, New York," *American Architect and Building News* 21 (January 22, 1887): 42, plates; King, *King's Handbook of New York* (1893), 664–66; *A History of Real Estate, Building and Architecture in New York City During the Last Quarter of a Century*, 569, 640; Landau and Condit, *Rise of the New York Skyscraper, 1865–1913*, 131–33.

120. Van Rensselaer, "Recent Architecture in America—III": 518.

121. "New Down-Town Buildings": 729–30.

122. "The Mutual Building": 25–26.

123. "Our Trade Palaces": 100.

124. Sturgis, "The Works of George B. Post": 4.

125. "Cortlandt Street Improvements," *Real Estate Record and Builders' Guide* 24 (October 25, 1879): 848; Schuyler, "Recent Building in New York—II": 183–84; "The Mills Building," *Real Estate Record and Builders' Guide* 30 (October 28–November 4, 1882): 46–47; *A History of Real Estate, Building and Architecture in New York City During the Last Quarter of a Century*, 114, 690; Weisman, "The Commercial Architecture of George B. Post": 185.

126. Schuyler, "Recent Building in New York—II": 183–84.

127. Weisman, "The Commercial Architecture of George B. Post": 185.

128. "A New Office Building," *New York World* (December 25, 1880): 8; Schuyler, "Recent Building in New York—II": 183–84; "The Post Building": 72–73; "Brick Architecture in New York," *Building* 1 (May 1883): 105–6; Van Rensselaer, "Recent Architecture in America—III": 511–23; *A History of Real Estate, Building and Architecture in New York City During the Last Quarter of a Century*, 562, 629, 690; Sturgis, "The Works of George B. Post": 34–36; Weisman, "The Commercial Architecture of George B. Post": 185–86; Landau and Condit, *Rise of the New York Skyscraper, 1865–1913*, 113–14; Landau, *George B. Post, Architect*, 52–53.

129. Schuyler, "Recent Building in New York—II": 183–84.

130. "The Post Building": 72–73.

131. "Out Among the Builders," *Real Estate Record and Builders' Guide* 27 (May 14, 1881): 492; "Immense New Structures," *New York Times* (June 2, 1881): 8; Editorial, *Real Estate Record and Builders' Guide* 28 (September 10, 1881): 869; "Safety of the Mills Building," *New York Daily Tribune* (January 24, 1882): 8; "Safety of the Mills Building," *New York Daily Tribune* (February 3, 1882): 8; "The Mills Building," *New York Times* (February 3, 1882): 8; "The Mills Building," *Real Estate Record and Builders' Guide*: 46–47; "Wrought-Iron Grille of the Mills Building, New York, N.Y., Mr. George B. Post, Architect, New York, N.Y.," *American Architect and Building News* 12 (October 14, 1882): 182, plate; "The Mills Building," *New York Daily Graphic* (November 28, 1882): 199, 201, 203; "Brick Architecture in New York": 105–6; "Sky Building in New York": 364; "Very Tall Building": 155; Van Rensselaer, "Recent Architecture in America—III": 517; "Gelatine Print—The Mills Building, Broad Street, New York City," *Building* 9 (November 10, 1888): 171, plate; Townsend, "English and American Architecture—A Companion and a Prophecy": 297; King, *King's Handbook of New York* (1893), 822–23; L. Gmelin, "Architektonisches ans Nord Amerika," *Deutsche Bauzeitung* 28 (October 27, 1894): 532; *A History of Real Estate, Building and Architecture in New York City During the Last Quarter of a Century*, 566, 690; Sturgis, "The Works of George B. Post": 38–40, 42; Weisman, "A New View of Sky-scraper History," in Kaufmann, ed., *The Rise of an American Architecture*, 132–33; Weisman, "The Commercial Architecture of George B. Post": 186–87; Lewis and Morgan, *American Victorian Architecture*, 41, 145; Landau and Condit, *Rise of the New York Skyscraper, 1865–1913*, 113–16; Landau, *George B. Post, Architect*, 53–57, 60.

132. Weisman, "The Commercial Architecture of George B. Post": 186.

133. "The Mills Building," *Real Estate Record and Builders' Guide*: 46–47.

134. Van Rensselaer, "Recent Architecture in America—III": 517.

135. Sturgis, "The Works of George B. Post": 38, 42.

136. "Out Among the Builders," *Real Estate Record and Builders' Guide* 33 (February 16, 1884): 160–61; "Out Among the Builders," *Real Estate Record and Builders' Guide* 33 (April 12, 1884): 378–79; "Out Among the Builders," *Real Estate Record and Builders' Guide* 33 (May 17, 1884): 536; "The Mortimer Building," *Real Estate Record and Builders' Guide* 34 (December 13, 1884): 1247–48; "The Mortimer Building," *New York Times* (February 15, 1885): 7; "The Mortimer Building, New York, N.Y. Mr. George B. Post, Architect, New York, N.Y.," *American Architect and Building News* 19 (May 22, 1886): 246, plate; King, *King's Handbook of New York* (1893), 842; Sturgis, "The Works of George B. Post": 38; *A History of Real Estate, Building and Architecture in New York City During the Last Quarter of a Century*, 690; Weisman, "The Commercial Architecture of George B. Post": 190–91; Landau, *George B. Post, Architect*, 64, 66.

137. "The Mortimer Building," *Real Estate Record and Builders' Guide*: 1247–48.

138. "Walls Rising in Broadway": 13; William Alexander, *Description of the New Equitable Building* (New York: J. K. Lees, 1887); "A Huge Office Building," *New York Daily Tribune* (January 10, 1887): 5; "A Great Insurance Building," *New York Times* (January 10, 1887): 5; "The New Equitable Building," *Real Estate Record and Builders' Guide* 39 (January 15, 1887): 65; *A History of Real Estate, Building and Architecture in New York City During the Last Quarter of a Century*, 690; King, *King's Views of New York, 1908–1909*, 30; Weisman, "The Commercial Architecture of George B. Post": 197–98; Gibbs, "Business Architectural Imagery in America, 1870–1930": 112; Dunlap, *On Broadway*, 26; Landau and Condit, *Rise of the New York Skyscraper, 1865–1913*, 71–75; Landau, *George B. Post, Architect*, 67, 70–73.

139. "The New Equitable Building": 65.

140. "A Great Insurance Building": 5.

141. William Allen Butler, *History of The Lawyers Club* (New York: The Lawyers Club, 1921), 11–20.

142. "Out Among the Builders," *Real Estate Record and Builders' Guide* 40 (November 12, 1887): 1417; "Important Buildings Projected and Under Way," (April 28, 1888): 529; "Another Landmark Goes," *New York Times* (May 13, 1888): 5; "A View Showing the Manner of Reconstruct-

ing 'The Times' Building," *New York Times* (May 20, 1888): 1; "The New 'Times' Building," *New York Times* (May 23, 1888): 4; "The 'Times's' New Building," *New York Times* (June 8, 1888): 8; "A Night View of 'The Times's' Building, Showing the Progress of the Work," *New York Times* (June 10, 1888): 1; "The New Times Building," *New York Herald* (June 12, 1888): 5; "The New 'Times' Building," *New York Times* (June 13, 1888): 4; "The New 'Times' Building," *Scientific American* 59 (August 25, 1888): 117; "Men and Things," *Real Estate Record and Builders' Guide* 42 (September 1, 1888): 1064; "The New 'Times' Building," *Building* 9 (October 6, 1888): 110–11, plate; "The New Building of the New York 'Times'—George B. Post, Architect," *Harper's Weekly* 32 (October 27, 1888): 817–18; "The 'Times' Building," *Real Estate Record and Builders' Guide* 43 (January 12, 1889): 32; "A Lesson in Architecture," *New York Times* (January 31, 1889): 4; "A Newspaper at Home," *New York Times* (April 8, 1889): 5; "A Great Problem Solved," *New York Times* (April 29, 1889): 9–11; "The New York Times Building," *New York Times* (April 29, 1889): 9; "'The Times' and Its New Home," *New York Times* (May 5, 1889): 4; "New York Architects," *New York Times* (June 4, 1889): 2; "The Times's New Home," *New York Times* (June 21, 1889): 4; Schuyler, "The Romanesque Revival in New York": 31–33; Townsend, "English and American Architecture—A Companion and a Prophecy": 297, 300; King, *King's Handbook of New York* (1893), 618–19; *A History of Real Estate, Building and Architecture in New York City During the Last Quarter of a Century*, 580, 690; Sturgis, "The Works of George B. Post": 10–12, 15–17; Weisman, "The Commercial Architecture of George B. Post": 192–93; Landau, "The Tall Office Building Artistically Reconsidered: Arcaded Buildings of the New York School, 1870–1890," in Searing, ed., *In Search of Modern Architecture: A Tribute to Henry-Russell Hitchcock*, 156; Dolkart, *Lower Manhattan Architectural Survey Report*, no. 107; White and Willensky, *AIA Guide* (1988), 61; Landau and Condit, *Rise of the New York Skyscraper, 1865–1913*, 149, 151–55; Landau, *George B. Post, Architect*, 67, 71, 75.

143. "The Times Building," *New York Times* (May 26, 1858): 1, quoted in Gray, "The Office Building in New York City: 1850–1880": 85. Also see "The New York Times," *New York Times* (May 13, 1857): 4; Black, *Old New York in Early Photographs*, plate 43; Landau, "The Tall Office Building Artistically Reconsidered: Arcaded Buildings of the New York School, 1870–1890," in Searing, ed., *In Search of Modern Architecture: A Tribute to Henry-Russell Hitchcock*, 139, 141; Landau and Condit, *Rise of the New York Skyscraper, 1865–1913*, 50–51.

144. Augustus Maverick, *Henry J. Raymond and the New York Press* (Hartford, Conn.: Hale & Co., 1870), 157–58, quoted in Gray, "The Office Building in New York City: 1850–1880": 85.

145. "The New 'Times' Building," *Building*: 110–11.

146. "The New Times Building," *New York Herald*: 5, quoted in Landau, *George B. Post, Architect*, 67, 71.

147. "The 'Times' Building," *Real Estate Record and Builders' Guide*: 32.

148. Schuyler, "The Romanesque Revival in New York": 31–32.

149. Sturgis, "The Works of George B. Post": 15, 17.

150. "Building Prospects for 1889," *Building* 10 (January 5, 1889): 1; "Out Among the Builders," *Real Estate Record and Builders' Guide* 43 (March 23, 1889): 392–94; "Important Buildings Under Way: South of 14th Street," *Real Estate Record and Builders' Guide* 43 (May 25, 1889): 728–29; Observer, "The Union Trust Company's New Building," *Real Estate Record and Builders' Guide* 44 (November 16, 1889): 1534; "The Union Trust Company," *Real Estate Record and Builders' Guide* 45 (February 1, 1890): 149; "Union Trust Company's Building, Broadway Near Wall Street," *Architecture and Building* 12 (February 1, 1890): 55, plate; "A Fine New Building," *New York Times* (October 22, 1890): 8; Schuyler, "The Romanesque Revival in New York": 33–35; "Union Trust Company's Building, 80 Broadway, New York, N.Y., George B. Post, Architect," *American Architect and Building News* 42 (October 21, 1893): plate; *A History of Real Estate, Building and Architecture in New York City During the Last Quarter of a Century*, 592–93, 647, 690; Sturgis, "The Works of George B. Post": 17–20; Schuyler, "The 'Sky-Scraper' Up to Date": 233–34; Weisman, "A New View of Skyscraper History," in Kaufmann, ed., *The Rise of an American Architecture*, 115, 136; Weisman, "The Commercial Architecture of George B. Post": 195; Landau, "The Tall Office

Building Artistically Reconsidered: Arcaded Buildings of the New York School, 1870–1890," in Searing, ed., *In Search of Modern Architecture: A Tribute to Henry-Russell Hitchcock*, 157; Stern, Gilmartin, and Massengale, *New York 1900*, 148–49; Dunlap, *On Broadway*, 21; Landau and Condit, *Rise of the New York Skyscraper, 1865–1913*, 194–97; Landau, *George B. Post, Architect*, 74, 76.

151. Schuyler, "The 'Sky-Scraper' Up to Date": 233.

152. "The Union Trust Company," *Real Estate Record and Builders' Guide*: 149.

153. Schuyler, "The Romanesque Revival in New York": 33–35.

154. Schuyler, "The 'Sky-Scraper' Up to Date": 233.

155. "Buildings Projected," *Real Estate Record and Builders' Guide* 45 (April 19, 1890): 589; *A History of Real Estate, Building and Architecture in New York City During the Last Quarter of a Century*, 652; Sturgis, "The Works of George B. Post": 27–29; Dunlap, *On Broadway*, 98; Herbert Muschamp, "Beyond Organic Architecture: The Office as Oasis," *New York Times* (July 26, 1992), II: 26; Landau, *George B. Post, Architect*, 94, plate 19.

156. Sturgis, "The Works of George B. Post": 29.

157. "Men and Things," (September 1, 1888): 1064; "Competitive Design for the World Building, New York, N.Y. Mr. R. H. Robertson, Architect, New York, N.Y.," *American Architect and Building News* 25 (February 9, 1889): 66, plate; "Out Among the Builders," *Real Estate Record and Builders' Guide* 43 (March 23, 1889): 392–94; "Not as High as 'The Times' Building," *New York Times* (June 1, 1889): 8; "A New Newspaper Building," *New York Times* (October 11, 1889): 2; "The Laying of the Corner-Stone," *New York World* (October 11, 1889): 1–2; *The World: Its History and Its New Home, the Pulitzer Building* (New York, 1890); "The New World Building," *Real Estate Record and Builders' Guide* 45 (June 14, 1890): 879; "The New York World Building," *Engineering and Building Record* 22 (November 1, 1890): 342–43; "The New York World Building," *Engineering and Building Record* 22 (November 8, 1890): 358–60; "The Pulitzer Building," souvenir supplement, *New York World* (December 10, 1890): n.p.; "At Home! The Pulitzer Building Formally Opened," *New York World* (December 11, 1890): 1–3; King, *King's Handbook of New York* (1893), 620–21; *A History of Real Estate, Building and Architecture in New York City During the Last Quarter of a Century*, 647, 686, 691; Sturgis, "The Works of George B. Post": 11, 14–16; Barr Ferree, "The Art of the High Building," *Architectural Record* 15 (May 1904): 445–66; Stokes, *The Iconography of Manhattan Island*, vol. 5: 1409, 1819–20; Weisman, "The Commercial Architecture of George B. Post": 191–92, 197–98; Lehman, "The New York Skyscraper: History of Its Development, 1870–1939": 51–53; Gibbs, "Business Architectural Imagery in America, 1870–1930": 98; Landau, "The Tall Office Building Artistically Reconsidered: Arcaded Buildings of the New York School, 1870–1890," in Searing, ed., *In Search of Modern Architecture: A Tribute to Henry-Russell Hitchcock*, 156; Stern, Gilmartin, and Massengale, *New York 1900*, 145–48; van Leeuwen, *The Skyward Trend of Thought*, 102–5; Landau and Condit, *Rise of the New York Skyscraper, 1865–1913*, 197–201; Landau, *George B. Post, Architect*, 74, 77, 84.

158. "Buildings Projected," *Real Estate Record and Builders' Guide* 27 (March 12, 1881): 237; "The 'World' and Its New Home," *New York Daily Graphic* (April 10, 1882): 281, 283.

159. "The Post Building": 72–73. Also see "Flames in a Death-Trap," *New York Times* (February 1, 1882): 1; "A Disastrous Fire," *New York World* (February 1, 1882): 1; "That Fire," *Real Estate Record and Builders' Guide* 29 (February 4, 1882): 95–96.

160. Don C. Seitz, *Joseph Pulitzer: His Life and Letters* (New York: Simon & Schuster, 1924), 48–49, 168–83; George Juergens, *Joseph Pulitzer and the New York World* (Princeton, N.J.: Princeton University Press, 1966), 6–7; W. A. Swanberg, *Pulitzer* (New York: Charles Scribner's Sons, 1967), 162–64.

161. "The New World Building," *Real Estate Record and Builders' Guide*: 879.

162. *The World: Its History and Its New Home, the Pulitzer Building*, 86, quoted in van Leeuwen, *The Skyward Trend of Thought*, 105.

163. "The New World Building," *Real Estate Record and Builders' Guide*: 879.

164. "Important Buildings Projected and Under Way," (April 28, 1888): 529; "Important Buildings Under Way," (September 1, 1888): 1065; "The Tower Building," *Real Estate Record and Builders' Guide* 43 (February 16, 1889): 207; "The Tower Building, No. 50 Broadway, New York," *Architecture and Building* 12 (March 1, 1890): 103, plate; Louis De Coppet Berg, "Iron Construction in New York City," *Architectural Record* 1 (April–June 1892): 448–68; William J. Fryer, "A Review of the Development of Structural Iron," in *A History of Real Estate, Building and Architecture in New York City During the Last Quarter of a Century*, 467–71; "The First 'Skeleton' Building," *Real Estate Record and Builders' Guide* 64 (August 12, 1899): 239; Schuyler, "The Evolution of the Sky-scraper": 257–71; "New York's First Skyscraper and Its Architect," *Real Estate Record and Builders' Guide* 88 (October 21, 1911): 589; Weisman, "New York and the Problem of the First Skyscraper": 13–21; Condit, *American Building Art: The Nineteenth Century*, 46–48; Condit, *American Building: Materials and Techniques from the First Colonial Settlements to the Present*, 118; Weisman, "A New View of Skyscraper History," in Kaufmann, ed., *The Rise of an American Architecture*, 142–43; Lehman, "The New York Skyscraper: A History of Its Development, 1870–1939": 53–57; Landau, "The Tall Office Building Artistically Reconsidered: Arcaded Buildings of the New York School, 1870–1890," in Searing, ed., *In Search of Modern Architecture: A Tribute to Henry-Russell Hitchcock*, 155, 157; Stern, Gilmartin, and Massengale, *New York 1900*, 146, 148; Landau and Condit, *Rise of the New York Skyscraper, 1865–1913*, 161–66.

165. Berg, "Iron Construction in New York City": 449–51, 463–64; Fryer, "A Review of the Development of Structural Iron," in *A History of Real Estate, Building and Architecture in New York City During the Last Quarter of a Century*, 471, 581, 647; "The First 'Skeleton' Building": 239; Roger Hale Newton, "New Evidence on the Evolution of the Sky-scraper," *Art Quarterly* 4 (winter 1941): 56–70; Curran, *A Forgotten Architect of the Gilded Age: Josiah Cleaveland Cady's Legacy*, 45; Landau and Condit, *Rise of the New York Skyscraper, 1865–1913*, 203.

166. Berg, "Iron Construction in New York City": 450.

167. Stern, Gilmartin, and Massengale, *New York 1900*, 158; Landau and Condit, *Rise of the New York Skyscraper, 1865–1913*, 201–3.

168. "Limit to High Buildings," *New York Daily Tribune* (December 30, 1894): 5.

169. Thomas Hastings, quoted in "Limit to High Buildings": 5.

170. For discussions of Wall Street's early history, see James D. McCabe Jr., *Lights and Shadows of New York Life; or, The Sights and Sensations of the Great City* (Philadelphia: National Publishing, 1872; New York: Farrar, Straus & Giroux, 1970), 258–63; Thomas A. Janvier, *In Old New York* (New York: Harper & Brothers, 1894; New York: Garrett Press, 1969), 6–15; Mrs. Schuyler Van Rensselaer, *History of the City of New York in the Seventeenth Century*, 2 vols. (New York: Macmillan, 1909), vol. 2: 253–55, 331–37; Stokes, *The Iconography of Manhattan Island*, vol. 2: 214–15, vol. 6: 601; Lois Severini, *The Architecture of Finance: Early Wall Street* (Ann Arbor, Mich.: UMI Research Press, 1983), esp. chapters 1–2.

171. Schuyler, "Recent Building in New York—II": 183–84. Also see W., "A New Building in Wall Street," *American Architect and Building News* 5 (May 3, 1879): 141; "New Office Building on Wall St., New York. G. E. Harney, Architect, N.Y.," *American Architect and Building News* 7 (May 1, 1880): 192, plate.

172. Stokes, *The Iconography of Manhattan Island*, vol. 6: 343.

173. W., "A New Building in Wall Street": 141.

174. W., "A New Building in Wall Street": 141.

175. "New Office Building on Wall St., New York. G. E. Harney, Architect, N.Y.": 192.

176. Schuyler, "Recent Building in New York—II": 183–84.

177. "Out Among the Builders," *Real Estate Record and Builders' Guide* 33 (April 26, 1884): 436–37; "Building for the Eagle Fire Company, New York City," *Building* 4 (April 3, 1886): 162, plate; *A History of Real Estate, Building and Architecture in New York City During the Last Quarter of a Century*, 640.

178. "Out Among the Builders," *Real Estate Record and Builders' Guide* 31 (April 28, 1883): 174; "New Work in Wall Street," *Real Estate Record and Builders' Guide* 33 (February 9, 1884): 127–28; "The Best Ten Buildings in the United States," *American Architect and Building News* 17

(April 11, 1885): 178; King, *King's Handbook of New York* (1893), 705–6, 708; King, *King's Views of New York, 1896*, 15; *A History of Real Estate, Building and Architecture in New York City During the Last Quarter of a Century*, 691; Landau and Condit, *Rise of the New York Skyscraper, 1865–1913*, 31, 131–32.

179. "New Work in Wall Street": 127–28.

180. Schuyler, "The Works of Henry Janeway Hardenbergh": 342–43. Also see "Buildings Projected," *Real Estate Record and Builders' Guide* 35 (April 25, 1885): 483; "Astor Building, Wall Street, New York City," *Building* 5 (December 25, 1886): 307; "Astor Building, Wall Street, New York City," *Building* 7 (November 9, 1887): 169; James Taylor, "The History of Terra Cotta in New York City," *Architectural Record* 2 (October–December 1892): 136–48; *A History of Real Estate, Building and Architecture in New York City During the Last Quarter of a Century*, 641, 681.

181. "Buildings Projected," *Real Estate Record and Builders' Guide* 37 (January 30, 1886): 148–49; "The Gallatin Bank's New Building," *New York Daily Tribune* (January 31, 1886): 2; "The Costly and Substantial Buildings of 1886," *Real Estate Record and Builders' Guide* 39 (January 1, 1887): 6–8; "Recent Building in Wall Street," *Real Estate Record and Builders' Guide* 40 (July 16, 1887): 950; "Gelatine Print—The Gallatin Bank Building, Wall Street, New York City. Messrs. J. C. Cady & Co., Architects," *Building* 9 (August 11, 1888): 45, plate; Berg, "Iron Construction in New York City": 462–63; King, *King's Handbook of New York* (1893), 716–17; Montgomery Schuyler, "The Works of Cady, Berg & See," *Architectural Record* 6 (April–June 1897): 517–53; *A History of Real Estate, Building and Architecture in New York City During the Last Quarter of a Century*, 575, 641; Curran, *A Forgotten Architect of the Gilded Age: Josiah Cleaveland Cady's Legacy*, 44–45; Landau and Condit, *Rise of the New York Skyscraper, 1865–1913*, 132, 148–49. For the Thompson Building, see "Buildings Projected," *Real Estate Record and Builders' Guide* 37 (March 6, 1886): 306.

182. "Recent Building in Wall Street": 950.

183. "Important Buildings Under Way," (September 1, 1888): 1065; "The Bank of America," *Real Estate Record and Builders' Guide* 43 (May 4, 1889): 615–16; King, *King's Handbook of New York* (1893), 708, 710–11; *A History of Real Estate, Building and Architecture in New York City During the Last Quarter of a Century*, 586, 646; Landau and Condit, *Rise of the New York Skyscraper, 1865–1913*, 169.

184. "The Bank of America": 616.

185. "Buildings Projected," *Real Estate Record and Builders' Guide* 42 (November 3, 1888): 1326; "Out Among the Builders," *Real Estate Record and Builders' Guide* 43 (January 19, 1889): 76–77; "Important Buildings Under Way: South of 14th Street": 728–29; King, *King's Handbook of New York* (1893), 708–9; *A History of Real Estate, Building and Architecture in New York City During the Last Quarter of a Century*, 646.

186. "Buildings Projected," *Real Estate Record and Builders' Guide* 37 (April 24, 1886): 557; "The Costly and Substantial Buildings of 1886": 6–8; King, *King's Handbook of New York* (1893), 762–64; *A History of Real Estate, Building and Architecture in New York City During the Last Quarter of a Century*, 641.

187. "Buildings Projected," *Real Estate Record and Builders' Guide* 43 (March 9, 1889): 337; King, *King's Handbook of New York* (1893), 155; King, *King's Views of New York, 1896*, 12; *A History of Real Estate, Building and Architecture in New York City During the Last Quarter of a Century*, 647.

188. "Domestic Sewing Machine Company," *New York Daily Graphic* (June 23, 1873): 8; "Opening of the Domestic Sewing-Machine Company's New Building," *New York Times* (June 25, 1873): 8; Robert Macoy, *How to See New York and Its Environs* (New York: Robert Macoy, 1876), 62; *A History of Real Estate, Building and Architecture in New York City During the Last Quarter of a Century*, 624; Weisman, "New York and the Problem of the First Skyscraper": 13–21; Dunlap, *On Broadway*, 102–3, 108.

189. "The Death of J. Morgan Slade, Architect of New York," *American Architect and Building News* 12 (December 9, 1882): 273; Lewis and Morgan, *American Victorian Architecture*, 58, 146.

190. "The Century Co.'s New Home," advertising section, *Century Magazine* 25 (November 1882): 25; "Middle Broadway," *Real Estate Record and Builders' Guide* 33 (February 2, 1884): 106; Landmarks Preservation Commission of the City of New York, LP-1539 (October 7, 1986); White and Willensky, *AIA Guide* (1988), 186; Barbaralee Diamonstein, *The Landmarks of New York II* (New York: Harry N. Abrams, 1993), 175.

191. "Middle Broadway": 106.

192. Taylor, "The History of Terra Cotta in New York City": 143, 148; J. C., "The Havemeyer Building—A Type," *Real Estate Record and Builders' Guide* 51 (April 29, 1893): 654–58; Montgomery Schuyler, "The Works of R. H. Robertson," *Architectural Record* 6 (October–December 1896): 184–219; *A History of Real Estate, Building and Architecture in New York City During the Last Quarter of a Century*, 574, 691; Boyer, *Manhattan Manners*, 125; White and Willensky, *AIA Guide* (1988), 186; Landmarks Preservation Commission of the City of New York, LP-1536 (July 12, 1988); Diamonstein, *The Landmarks of New York II*, 391; Landau and Condit, *Rise of the New York Skyscraper, 1865–1913*, 193–95.

193. J. C., "The Havemeyer Building—A Type": 657.

194. King, *King's Handbook of New York* (1893), 748–49; Schuyler, "The Works of R. H. Robertson": 216–17, 219; *A History of Real Estate, Building and Architecture in New York City During the Last Quarter of a Century*, 652; Boyer, *Manhattan Manners*, 124, 126; William Conklin, "Ladies' Mile: The Architecture of Commerce," *Village Views* (summer 1986): 8–9; White and Willensky, *AIA Guide* (1988), 187; Landmarks Preservation Commission of the City of New York, *Ladies' Mile Historic District Designation Report* (New York, 1989), 66–70; Dunlap, *On Broadway*, 116, 124–25.

195. Schuyler, "The Works of R. H. Robertson": 216.

196. "Out Among the Builders," *Real Estate Record and Builders' Guide* 39 (May 28, 1887): 736–37; "Recent Attempts at Gothic," *Real Estate Record and Builders' Guide* 40 (December 8, 1887): 1505; Taylor, "The History of Terra Cotta in New York City": 140; White and Willensky, *AIA Guide* (1988), 157; Dunlap, *On Broadway*, 106.

197. "Recent Attempts at Gothic": 1505.

198. "Out Among the Builders," *Real Estate Record and Builders' Guide* 40 (November 5, 1887): 1385; "Out Among the Builders," *Real Estate Record and Builders' Guide* 40 (November 12, 1887): 1417; "Out Among the Builders," *Real Estate Record and Builders' Guide* 40 (December 17, 1887): 1584; "Out Among the Builders," *Real Estate Record and Builders' Guide* 41 (February 11, 1888): 181; "Important Buildings Projected and Under Way," (April 28, 1888): 529; "Laying the Cornerstone," *New York Times* (May 24, 1888): 8; "The Methodist Book Concern," *Real Estate Record and Builders' Guide* 43 (May 11, 1889): 646–47; "The Methodist Book Concern," *New York Daily Tribune* (December 1, 1889): 3; "A Century of Honor," *New York Daily Tribune* (December 7, 1889): 4; "Rejoicing in Methodism," *New York Daily Tribune* (February 12, 1890): 4; "A Methodist Jubilee," *New York Times* (February 14, 1890): 8; "The Methodist Book Concern, New York, N.Y. Mr. Edward H. Kendall, Architect, New York, N.Y.," *American Architect and Building News* 30 (November 8, 1890): 90, plate; King, *King's Handbook of New York* (1893), 630–31; Henry Collins Brown, *Fifth Avenue: Old and New, 1824–1924* (New York: The Fifth Avenue Association, 1924), 47–48; Boyer, *Manhattan Manners*, 125; White and Willensky, *AIA Guide* (1988), 188; *Ladies' Mile Historic District*, 252–55.

199. "The Methodist Book Concern," *Real Estate Record and Builders' Guide*: 646–47.

200. "Out Among the Builders," *Real Estate Record and Builders' Guide* 41 (May 5, 1888): 564–65; "Out Among the Builders," *Real Estate Record and Builders' Guide* 41 (May 12, 1888): 604–5; "Out Among the Builders," *Real Estate Record and Builders' Guide* 41 (June 2, 1888): 705–6; "Important Buildings Under Way: Part II," (September 15, 1888): 1110; "The 'Judge' Building," *Real Estate Record and Builders' Guide* 44 (October 26, 1889): 1436; "Supplement—The Judge Building, Corner Fifth Avenue and Sixteenth Street, New York City," *Architecture and Building* 12 (March 1, 1890): 103, plate; King, *King's Handbook of New York* (1893), 635; Russell Sturgis, "The Works of McKim, Mead & White," *Architectural Record* 4 (May 1895): 1–111; *A History of Real Estate, Building and Architecture in New York City During the Last Quarter of a Century*, 646; Russell Sturgis, "The Warehouse and the Factory in Architecture," *Architectural Record* 15 (January 1904): 1–18; Henry W.

Desmond and Herbert Croly, "The Work of Messrs. McKim, Mead & White," *Architectural Record* 20 (September 1906): 153–268; Leland M. Roth, "The Urban Architecture of McKim, Mead and White: 1870–1910" (Ph.D. diss., Yale University, 1973): 311–12; Leland M. Roth, *The Architecture of McKim, Mead & White, 1870–1920: A Building List* (New York and London: Garland, 1978), 65; Landau, "The Tall Office Building Artistically Reconsidered: Arcaded Buildings of the New York School, 1870–1890," in Searing, ed., *In Search of Modern Architecture: A Tribute to Henry-Russell Hitchcock*, 155–57; Leland M. Roth, *McKim, Mead & White, Architects* (New York: Harper & Row, 1983), 169–70; White and Willensky, *AIA Guide* (1988), 187; Lawrence Wodehouse, *White of McKim, Mead and White* (New York and London: Garland, 1988), 157–59; Paul R. Baker, *Stanny: The Gilded Life of Stanford White* (New York: Macmillan, 1989), 112; *Ladies' Mile Historic District*, 198–201; Brooks Peters, "The Goelets," *Quest* (March 1989): 40–45.

201. "The 'Judge' Building," *Real Estate Record and Builders' Guide*: 1436.

202. Sturgis, "The Works of McKim, Mead & White": 63.

203. Sturgis, "The Warehouse and the Factory in Architecture": 8, 10.

204. "Walls Rising in Broadway": 13; "New Commercial Buildings," *Real Estate Record and Builders' Guide* 38 (December 11, 1886): 1524; "The Costly and Substantial Buildings of 1886": 6–8; "Out Among the Builders," *Real Estate Record and Builders' Guide* 41 (May 5, 1888): 564–65; "Gelatine Print—The Goelet Building, Twentieth Street and Broadway, New York City," *Building* 8 (May 26, 1888): 169, plate; Sturgis, "The Works of McKim, Mead & White": 65–66; *A History of Real Estate, Building and Architecture in New York City During the Last Quarter of a Century*, 641; Desmond and Croly, "The Work of Messrs. McKim, Mead & White": 165; Lewis Mumford, *The Brown Decades: A Study of the Arts in America, 1865–1895* (New York: Harcourt, Brace & Co., 1931), 128–29; Richard Guy Wilson, "Charles F. McKim and the Development of the American Renaissance: A Study in Architecture and Culture" (Ph.D. diss., University of Michigan, 1972): 303, fig. 222; Leland Roth, "McKim, Mead & White Reappraised," in *A Monograph of the Works of McKim, Mead & White, 1879–1915* (New York: Architectural Book Publishing Co., 1915; New York: Benjamin Blom, 1973), 33, 36–37; Roth, "The Urban Architecture of McKim, Mead and White, 1870–1910": 222–23; Roth, *The Architecture of McKim, Mead & White, 1870–1920: A Building List*, 64; Landau, "The Tall Office Building Artistically Reconsidered: Arcaded Buildings of the New York School, 1870–1890," in Searing, ed., *In Search of Modern Architecture: A Tribute to Henry-Russell Hitchcock*, 154–55; Roth, *McKim, Mead & White, Architects*, 199, fig. 120; Boyer, *Manhattan Manners*, 124–25; White and Willensky, *AIA Guide* (1988), 188; Wodehouse, *White of McKim, Mead and White*, 156–57; Baker, *Stanny: The Gilded Life of Stanford White*, 112; *Ladies' Mile Historic District*, 93–97; Peters, "The Goelets": 40–45; Dunlap, *On Broadway*, 119–22; David Garrard Lowe, *Stanford White's New York* (New York: Doubleday, 1992), 103–5; Christopher Gray, "The Invisible Clan," *Avenue* (February 1992): 26–30; Landau and Condit, *Rise of the New York Skyscraper, 1865–1913*, 145, 147.

205. "Walls Rising in Broadway": 13.

206. "Walls Rising in Broadway": 13.

207. Sturgis, "The Works of McKim, Mead & White": 66.

208. "Bits of Street Architecture," *Real Estate Record and Builders' Guide* 40 (July 9, 1887): 920; Sturgis, "The Works of McKim, Mead & White": 83; Roth, "The Urban Architecture of McKim, Mead and White, 1870–1910": 222, 239; Baker, *Stanny: The Gilded Life of Stanford White*, 112–13; Gray, "The Invisible Clan": 28.

209. "Bits of Street Architecture": 920.

Banks and Exchanges

1. For an overview of the emerging combination bank and office building during the 1850s, see Lee Edward Gray, "The Office Building in New York City: 1850–1880" (Ph.D. diss., Cornell University, 1993): 38–61.

2. "The New Banking House of the Bank of New York," *New York Times* (March 26, 1858): 4, quoted in Gray, "The Office Building in New York City: 1850–1880": 38.

3. "The New Banking House of the Bank of New York": 4; I. N. Phelps Stokes, *The Iconography of Manhattan Island*, 6 vols. (New York: Robert H. Dodd, 1915–28; New York: Arno Press, 1967), vol. 5: 1809; Lois Severini, *The Architecture of Finance: Early Wall Street* (Ann Arbor, Mich.: UMI Research Press, 1983), 58–59, fig. 77; Gray, "The Office Building in New York City: 1850–1880": 39–43.

4. Joan C. Weakley, "Frederic Diaper," in *Macmillan Encyclopedia of Architects*, 4 vols. (New York: Free Press; London: Collier Macmillan, 1982), vol. 1: 570; Severini, *The Architecture of Finance: Early Wall Street*, 59, fig. 77.

5. Sarah Bradford Landau, "The Tall Office Building Artistically Reconsidered: Arcaded Buildings of the New York School, 1870–1890," in Helen Searing, ed., *In Search of Modern Architecture: A Tribute to Henry-Russell Hitchcock* (New York: Architectural History Foundation; Cambridge, Mass.: MIT Press, 1982), 136–64; Severini, *The Architecture of Finance: Early Wall Street*, 59–60, fig. 85; Sarah Bradford Landau and Carl W. Condit, *Rise of the New York Skyscraper, 1865–1913* (New Haven, Conn., and London: Yale University Press, 1996), 45–47.

6. "Bank Architecture in New York," *Bankers' Magazine* 9 (February 1855): 588–90; Stokes, *The Iconography of Manhattan Island*, vol. 5: 1858; Mary Black, *Old New York in Early Photographs* (New York: Dover, 1973), plate 50; Gray, "The Office Building in New York City: 1850–1880": 48–49, 51.

7. "Recent Bank Architecture," *Bankers' Magazine* 10 (February 1856): 9; Moses King, *King's Handbook of New York* (Boston: Moses King, 1893), 708–9; Severini, *The Architecture of Finance: Early Wall Street*, 66–68; Gray, "The Office Building in New York City: 1850–1880": 42, 44–47.

8. "Bank of New York," *Builder* (February 1858): 126–27; "The Bank of New York," *Architects' and Mechanics' Journal* 2 (May 5, 1860): 44, 47; King, *King's Handbook of New York* (1893), 703–4; Stokes, *The Iconography of Manhattan Island*, vol. 5: 1865; Arthur Channing Downs Jr., letter to the editor, *Journal of the Society of Architectural Historians* 36 (March 1977): 61; Severini, *The Architecture of Finance: Early Wall Street*, 73–76; Gray, "The Office Building in New York City: 1850–1880": 53–61; William Alex, *Calvert Vaux: Architect and Planner* (New York: Ink, 1994), 9–10, 19, 184; Francis R. Kowsky, *Country, Park and City: The Architecture and Life of Calvert Vaux* (New York: Oxford University Press, 1998), 82–85.

9. King, *King's Handbook of New York* (1893), 752; Sarah Bradford Landau, *Edward T. and William A. Potter: American Victorian Architects* (New York: Garland, 1979), 239–42, 453, fig. 145; Landau and Condit, *Rise of the New York Skyscraper, 1865–1913*, 55–56.

10. "The Park Bank Building," *New York Herald* (January 5, 1867): 7; John W. Kennion, *Architects' and Builders' Guide* (New York: Fitzpatrick & Hunter, 1868), part 3: 8, 62–67; "Down Town Building Improvements," editorial, *New York Herald* (January 5, 1868): 4; "Architecture in New York," *New York World* (January 25, 1868): 4; "The New Park Bank," *New York World* (February 18, 1868): 11–12; "The New Park Bank," *Real Estate Record and Builders' Guide* 1 (April 4, 1868): 2; "Building in New York," *New York Times* (May 4, 1868): 4–5; "The Park Bank Building," *New York Daily Tribune* (December 16, 1868): 5; "The New Park Bank," *New York Sun* (December 16, 1868): 3; "Hints to Building Proprietors," *Real Estate Record and Builders' Guide* 4 (November 20, 1869): 1; James D. McCabe Jr., *Lights and Shadows of New York Life; or, The Sights and Sensations of the Great City* (Philadelphia: National Publishing, 1872; New York: Farrar, Straus & Giroux, 1970), 278; A. J. Bloor, "Annual Address," *Proceedings of the Tenth Annual Convention of the American Institute of Architects, 1876* (Boston, 1877): 15–34; King, *King's Handbook of New York* (1893), 732–33; *A History of Real Estate, Building and Architecture in New York City During the Last Quarter of a Century* (New York: Real Estate Record Association, 1898), 615; Stokes, *The Iconography of Manhattan Island*, vol. 5: 1926; Winston Weisman, "Commercial Palaces of New York: 1845–1875," *Art Bulletin* 36 (December 1954): 285–302; Winston Weisman, "A New View of Skyscraper History," in Edgar Kaufmann Jr., ed., *The Rise of an American Architecture* (New York: Praeger, 1970), 115–60; Black, *Old New York in Early Photographs*, plate 37; Sarah Bradford Landau, *P. B. Wight: Architect, Contractor, and Critic, 1838–1925* (Chicago: Art Institute of Chicago, 1981), 26, 103; David W. Dunlap, *On Broadway: A Journey Uptown Over Time* (New

York: Rizzoli International Publications, 1990), 38; Gray, "The Office Building in New York City: 1850–1880": 110–19; Landau and Condit, *Rise of the New York Skyscraper, 1865–1913*, 57–58, 239.

11. Landau and Condit, *Rise of the New York Skyscraper, 1865–1913*, 57.

12. *D. Appleton's New York Illustrated* (New York: D. Appleton, 1871), 11.

13. "The Park Bank Building," *New York Daily Tribune*: 5.

14. "The New Park Bank," *Real Estate Record and Builders' Guide*: 2.

15. Bloor, "Annual Address": 25.

16. "The Farmer's Loan and Trust Company's Building," *Real Estate Record and Builders' Guide* 31 (March 31, 1883): 125–26; "The Farmer's Loan and Trust Company," *Real Estate Record and Builders' Guide* 45 (March 8, 1890): 323–24.

17. "The Metropolitan Savings Bank," *New York Times* (May 22, 1867): 5; Kennion, *Architects' and Builders' Guide*, part 2: 15–16; Landmarks Preservation Commission of the City of New York, LP-0183 (November 19, 1969); White and Willensky, *AIA Guide* (1988), 165; Barbaralee Diamonstein, *The Landmarks of New York II* (New York: Harry N. Abrams, 1993), 151.

18. "The Bond Street Savings Bank," *New York Daily Graphic* (June 26, 1874): 886, 892; Landmarks Preservation Commission of the City of New York, LP-0192 (January 11, 1967); White and Willensky, *AIA Guide* (1988), 160–61; Diamonstein, *The Landmarks of New York II*, 161.

19. Montgomery Schuyler, "Our City Architecture," *New York World* (October 1, 1871): 6–7; Stokes, *The Iconography of Manhattan Island*, vol. 5: 1946; Nathan Silver, *Lost New York* (Boston: Houghton Mifflin, 1967), 165.

20. "New Building of the Union Dime Savings Bank," *New York Daily Graphic* (January 4, 1877): 441; King, *King's Handbook of New York* (1893), 781; *A History of Real Estate, Building and Architecture in New York City During the Last Quarter of a Century*, 601, 628; Moses King, *King's Views of New York, 1908–1909* (Boston: Moses King, 1908; New York: Benjamin Blom, 1974), 68; Dunlap, *On Broadway*, 142.

21. "Dry Dock Savings Bank, Corner of Bowery and Third Street, New York City," *New-York Sketch-Book of Architecture* 2 (October 1875): 1, plate 38; "Dry Dock Savings Bank, Corner of Bowery and Third Street, New York," *New-York Sketch-Book of Architecture* 3 (August 1876): 1, plate 24; King, *King's Handbook of New York* (1893), 777; Montgomery Schuyler, "A Great American Architect: Leopold Eidlitz. Part 2," *Architectural Record* 24 (October 1908): 277–92; H. Allen Brooks Jr., "Leopold Eidlitz (1823–1908)" (master's thesis, Yale University, 1955): 16–17; Winston Weisman, "The Commercial Architecture of George B. Post," *Journal of the Society of Architectural Historians* 31 (October 1972): 176–203; Black, *Old New York in Early Photographs*, plate 83; Sarah Bradford Landau, *George B. Post, Architect: Picturesque Designer and Determined Realist*, Sources of American Architecture, ed. Robert A. M. Stern (New York: Monacelli Press, 1998), 20, plate 5.

22. Weisman, "The Commercial Architecture of George B. Post": 179, 181; Landau, "The Tall Office Building Artistically Reconsidered: Arcaded Buildings of the New York School, 1870–1890," in Searing, ed., *In Search of Modern Architecture: A Tribute to Henry-Russell Hitchcock*, 142, 144; Landau and Condit, *Rise of the New York Skyscraper, 1865–1913*, 83, 100.

23. Schuyler, "A Great American Architect: Leopold Eidlitz. Part 2": 289.

24. Bloor, "Annual Address": 25.

25. M. G. Van Rensselaer, "Recent Architecture in America—III," *Century Magazine* 28 (August 1884): 511–23; "Building of the American Safe Deposit Company, New York, N.Y., Messrs. McKim, Mead & White, Architects, N.Y.," *American Architect and Building News* 19 (January 30, 1886): 55, plate; Charles C. Baldwin, *Stanford White* (New York: Dodd, Mead & Co., 1931; New York: Da Capo Press, 1971), 123; Richard Guy Wilson, "Charles F. McKim and the Development of the American Renaissance: A Study in Architecture and Culture" (Ph.D. diss., University of Michigan, 1972): 301–2; Leland M. Roth, "The Urban Architecture of McKim, Mead and White: 1870–1910" (Ph.D. diss., Yale University, 1973): 220–21; Leland M. Roth, *The Architecture of McKim, Mead & White, 1870–1920: A Building List* (New York and London: Garland, 1978), 21; Landau, "The Tall Office Building Artistically Reconsidered: Arcaded Buildings of the New York School, 1870–1890," in Searing, ed., *In Search of Modern Architecture: A Tribute to Henry-Russell*

Hitchcock, 152; Leland M. Roth, *McKim, Mead & White, Architects* (New York: Harper & Row, 1983), 108–9; Lawrence Wodehouse, *White of McKim, Mead and White* (New York and London: Garland, 1988), 143–44.

26. Baldwin, *Stanford White*, 123.

27. "The Stock Exchange," *New York Times* (August 21, 1865): 1; "The New Stock Exchange," *New York Times* (December 10, 1865): 8; "The Board of Brokers—Great Opening of the New Building," *Frank Leslie's Illustrated Newspaper* (December 30, 1865): 227; McCabe, *Lights and Shadows of New York Life*, 264–66; Stokes, *The Iconography of Manhattan Island*, vol. 5: 1919; Deborah S. Gardner, "The Architecture of Commercial Capitalism: John Kellum and the Development of New York, 1840–1875" (Ph.D. diss., Columbia University, 1979): 125–46; Frederick S. Lightfoot, ed., *Nineteenth-Century New York in Rare Photographic Views* (New York: Dover, 1981), fig. 14; Landau and Condit, *Rise of the New York Skyscraper, 1865–1913*, 55. Also see Robert Sobel, *The Big Board: A History of the New York Stock Market* (New York: Free Press, 1965), 1–80.

28. "The Board of Brokers—Great Opening of the New Building": 227.

29. Gardner, "The Architecture of Commercial Capitalism: John Kellum and the Development of New York, 1840–1875": 91–93.

30. "The New Stock Exchange," *New York Times*: 8.

31. "The Stock Exchange's New Building," *New York Times* (April 23, 1880): 3; "The New Stock Exchange Building, Broad Street, Near Wall," *New York Daily Graphic* (January 28, 1881): 654; Montgomery Schuyler, "Recent Building in New York—I," *American Architect and Building News* 9 (April 9, 1881): 176–77; "The Stock Exchange Improvement," *Real Estate Record and Builders' Guide* 27 (May 14, 1881): 491; "A New Stock Exchange," *New York Daily Tribune* (November 23, 1881): 1; King, *King's Handbook of New York* (1893), 788–92; Moses King, *King's Views of New York, 1896* (Boston: Moses King, 1896; New York: Benjamin Blom, 1974), 12; Stokes, *The Iconography of Manhattan Island*, vol. 5: 1978.

32. Schuyler, "Recent Building in New York—I": 176–77.

33. "A New Commercial Year: Annual Meeting of the Produce Exchange," *New York Times* (May 28, 1879): 8; "A Building Committee Chosen," *New York Times* (July 30, 1879): 8; "Miscellaneous City News: The New Produce Exchange," *New York Times* (December 3, 1879): 2; "The New Produce Exchange," *New York Times* (August 6, 1880): 3; "Local Miscellany: The New Produce Exchange," *New York Daily Tribune* (November 15, 1880): 8; "Produce Exchange's New Building," *New York Times* (January 19, 1881): 8; Whitehall, "The Produce Exchange Designs," letter to the editor, *New York Times* (February 22, 1881): 5; Montgomery Schuyler, "The New Produce Exchange," *New York World* (March 1, 1881): 4; "A New Building," *New York Daily Tribune* (March 2, 1881): 5; "The Produce Exchange," *New York Times* (March 3, 1881): 8; "The New Produce Exchange," *New York Times* (March 4, 1881): 8; "The New Produce Exchange Building," *New York Times* (March 6, 1881): 7; Montgomery Schuyler, "The New York Produce Exchange Competition," *American Architect and Building News* 9 (March 12, 1881): 123–24; Schuyler, "Recent Building in New York—I": 176–77; "Competitive Design for the New York Produce Exchange, New York, N.Y. Mr. F. C. Withers, Architect, New York, N.Y.," *American Architect and Building News* 9 (April 9, 1881): 174, plates; "Immense New Structures," *New York Times* (June 2, 1881): 8; "Competitive Design for the New York Produce Exchange, New York, N.Y. Mr. C. B. Atwood, Architect, New York, N.Y.," *American Architect and Building News* 9 (June 11, 1881): 285, plates; "The Produce Exchange," *Real Estate Record and Builders' Guide* 27 (June 14, 1881): 572; "Laying a Corner-Stone," *New York Daily Tribune* (June 7, 1882): 8; "Produce Men Jubilant," *New York Times* (June 7, 1882): 8; "Laying the Corner Stone of the New Produce Exchange, Corner of Broadway and Beaver Street, Last Tuesday," *New York Daily Graphic* (June 9, 1882): 708, 710; "Iron Architecture," *New York Times* (July 9, 1882): 6; Clarence Cook, "Architecture in America," *North American Review* 135 (September 1882): 243–52; "The New Produce Exchange," *Real Estate Record and Builders' Guide* 30 (October 7–14, 1882): 9; "The New Produce Exchange," *Real Estate Record and Builders' Guide* 31 (January 13, 1883): 12–13; "Brick Architecture in New York," *Building* 1 (May 1883): 105; "Competitive Design for the New York Produce Exchange, New York, N.Y., Mr. R. M. Upjohn, Architect, New

York, N.Y.," *American Architect and Building News* 14 (September 8, 1883): 115, plate; "The Union Theological Seminary," *Real Estate Record and Builders' Guide* 32 (September 22, 1883): 706; "Grouping in Architecture," *Real Estate Record and Builders' Guide* 32 (November 17, 1883): 899–900; "Statistics of a Large Building," *New York Daily Tribune* (November 18, 1883): 4; New York Produce Exchange, *Ceremonies on Leaving the Old and Opening the New Produce Exchange, May 5th and 6th, 1884* (New York: Art Interchange Press, 1884); New York Produce Exchange, *Origin, Growth, and Usefulness of the New York Produce Exchange* (New York: Historical Publishing, 1884); "Our Trade Palaces," *Building* 2 (May 1884): 100; "The New Produce Exchange," *Harper's Weekly* 28 (May 3, 1884): 285, 287; "Going Into a New Home," *New York Times* (May 4, 1884): 3; "The Produce Exchange," *New York Daily Tribune* (May 7, 1884): 2; "Merchants in a New Home," *New York Times* (May 7, 1884): 8; "The New Produce Exchange," *New York Daily Graphic* (May 9, 1884): 515, 517; "Around the Produce Exchange," *Real Estate Record and Builders' Guide* 33 (May 10, 1884): 496; Montgomery Schuyler, "The New Produce Exchange," *The Manhattan* 4 (August 1884): 208–14; Van Rensselaer, "Recent Architecture in America—III": 520; M. G. Van Rensselaer, "Berlin and New York—II," *American Architect and Building News* 18 (July 25, 1885): 40–42; "The Produce Exchange, New York, N.Y. Mr. George B. Post, Architect, New York, N.Y.," *American Architect and Building News* 19 (June 26, 1886): 305–6, plate; Richard Wheatly, "The New York Produce Exchange," *Harper's New Monthly Magazine* 73 (July 1886): 189–218; C. Hinckeldeyn, "A Foreigner's View of American Architecture," *American Architect and Building News* 25 (May 25, 1889): 243–44; Montgomery Schuyler, "The Romanesque Revival in New York," *Architectural Record* 1 (July–September 1891): 7–38; King, *King's Handbook of New York* (1893), 794–98; *A History of Real Estate, Building and Architecture in New York City During the Last Quarter of a Century*, 563, 634, 690; Russell Sturgis, "The Works of George B. Post," *Architectural Record* 4 (June 1898): 1–96; Stokes, *The Iconography of Manhattan Island*, vol. 5: 1979, 1985; John A. Kouwenhoven, *The Columbia Historical Portrait of New York* (Garden City, N.Y.: Doubleday, 1953), 335; Carl W. Condit, *American Building Art: The Nineteenth Century* (New York: Oxford University Press, 1960), 44–45; Silver, *Lost New York*, 102–3; Carl W. Condit, *American Building: Materials and Techniques from the First Colonial Settlements to the Present* (Chicago and London: University of Chicago Press, 1968), 116–17; Arnold Lehman, "The New York Skyscraper: History of Its Development, 1870–1939" (Ph.D. diss., Yale University, 1974): 41–42; Weisman, "A New View of Skyscraper History," in Kaufmann, ed., *The Rise of an American Architecture*, 133–35; Weisman, "The Commercial Architecture of George B. Post": 188–90; John Grafton, *New York in the Nineteenth Century* (New York: Dover, 1977), 225; Francis R. Kowsky, *The Architecture of Frederick Clarke Withers and the Progress of the Gothic Revival in America After 1850* (Middletown, Conn.: Wesleyan University Press, 1980), 135–37; Landau, "The Tall Office Building Artistically Reconsidered: Arcaded Buildings of the New York School, 1870–1890," in Searing, ed., *In Search of Modern Architecture: A Tribute to Henry-Russell Hitchcock*, 149–50; Dunlap, *On Broadway*, 15; Landau and Condit, *Rise of the New York Skyscraper, 1865–1913*, 116–25; Landau, *George B. Post, Architect*, 58–64, plate 11.

34. Schuyler, "The Romanesque Revival in New York": 12. Also see "The New Produce Exchange," *Architects' and Mechanics' Journal* 2 (December 8, 1860): 92; Schuyler, "A Great American Architect: Leopold Eidlitz. Part 2": 282, 284; Brooks, "Leopold Eidlitz (1823–1908)": 15; Severini, *The Architecture of Finance: Early Wall Street*, 78–79.

35. Schuyler, "The Romanesque Revival in New York": 12.

36. Schuyler, "A Great American Architect: Leopold Eidlitz. Part 2": 284.

37. Schuyler, "The New Produce Exchange," *New York World*: 4.

38. "The New Produce Exchange," (March 4, 1881): 8.

39. George B. Post, quoted in New York Produce Exchange, *Origin, Growth, and Usefulness of the New York Produce Exchange*, 57, also quoted in Landau and Condit, *Rise of the New York Skyscraper, 1865–1913*, 123–24.

40. Schuyler, "The New Produce Exchange," *The Manhattan*: 209.

41. New York Produce Exchange, *Origin, Growth, and Usefulness of the New York Produce Exchange*, 60, quoted in Landau and Condit, *Rise of the New York Skyscraper, 1865–1913*, 119.

42. Post's claim was made in a speech delivered on June 5, 1895, to the New York Architectural League. See "Steel-Frame Building Construction," *Engineering Record* 32 (June 15, 1895): 44; Landau and Condit, *Rise of the New York Skyscraper, 1865–1913*, 413 (n. 26).

43. Condit, *American Building: Materials and Techniques from the First Colonial Settlements to the Present*, 116.

44. Weisman, "The Commercial Architecture of George B. Post": 188–90.

45. Cook, "Architecture in America": 252.

46. Schuyler, "Recent Building in New York—I": 176–77.

47. Schuyler, "The New Produce Exchange," *New York World*: 4.

48. "Around the Produce Exchange," (May 10, 1884): 496.

49. Van Rensselaer, "Recent Architecture in America—III": 520.

50. Hinckeldeyn, "A Foreigner's View of American Architecture": 244.

51. "The Union Theological Seminary": 706.

52. For the Marshall Field Warehouse, see Jeffrey Karl Ochsner, *H. H. Richardson: Complete Architectural Works* (Cambridge, Mass.: MIT Press, 1982), 380–84. For the Auditorium Building, see Carl W. Condit, *The Chicago School of Architecture: A History of Commercial and Public Building in the Chicago Area, 1875–1925* (Chicago and London: University of Chicago Press, 1964), 69–78, figs. 31–39.

53. Sturgis, "The Works of George B. Post": 32.

54. "House the Children Well," *New York Times* (October 17, 1887): 4; "The Army Building," *Real Estate Record and Builders' Guide* 40 (October 29, 1887): 1348; "The New Army Building," *New York Times* (July 24, 1888): 8; "Laying the Armory Cornerstone," *New York Times* (October 26, 1888): 5; Schuyler, "The Romanesque Revival in New York": 12; King, *King's Handbook of New York* (1893), 541–42; White and Willensky, *AIA Guide* (1988), 862; Christopher Gray, "The Old U.S. Army Building on Whitehall Street," *New York Times* (March 5, 1995), IX: 7; Landau and Condit, *Rise of the New York Skyscraper, 1865–1913*, 55, 149, 151.

55. "The Army Building," *Real Estate Record and Builders' Guide*: 1348.

56. "Out Among the Builders," *Real Estate Record and Builders' Guide* 31 (April 28, 1883): 1–4; "The New Cotton Exchange," *New York Daily Graphic* (March 14, 1884): 100; "Prominent Buildings Under Way," *Real Estate Record and Builders' Guide* 33 (April 5, 1884): 341; "The Cotton Exchange," *Real Estate Record and Builders' Guide* 34 (November 1, 1884): 1100; "In Their New Building: Cotton Brokers Change Their Place of Business," *New York Times* (May 1, 1885): 8; "The Plumbing and Water Supply of the New York Cotton Exchange," *Carpentry and Building* 7 (December 1885): 228–30; James Taylor, "The History of Terra Cotta in New York City," *Architectural Record* 2 (October–December 1892): 136–48; King, *King's Handbook of New York* (1893), 799–801; *A History of Real Estate, Building and Architecture in New York City During the Last Quarter of a Century*, 573, 640, 690; Sturgis, "The Works of George B. Post": 36–38; Stokes, *The Iconography of Manhattan Island*, vol. 6: 313; Silver, *Lost New York*, 101; Weisman, "The Commercial Architecture of George B. Post": 190–91; Landau and Condit, *Rise of the New York Skyscraper, 1865–1913*, 127–28, 130–31; Landau, *George B. Post, Architect*, 64–65.

57. "Out Among the Builders," *Real Estate Record and Builders' Guide* 33 (March 1, 1884): 210–11; "Out Among the Builders," *Real Estate Record and Builders' Guide* 33 (April 5, 1884): 343–44; "Out Among the Builders," *Real Estate Record and Builders' Guide* 33 (June 14, 1884): 649; "Out Among the Builders," *Real Estate Record and Builders' Guide* 33 (June 28, 1884): 698; "The Mercantile Exchange," *Real Estate Record and Builders' Guide* 34 (July 5, 1884): 718–19; "The New Mercantile Exchange," letter to the editor, *Real Estate Record and Builders' Guide* 34 (July 5, 1884): 720; "Home for New York Merchants," *New York Times* (December 4, 1884): 2; "Entertaining Its Friends: The Members' Reception in the New Mercantile Exchange," *New York Times* (April 7, 1886): 2; "The Formal Opening: Yesterday's Proceedings at the New Mercantile Exchange," *New York Times* (April 8, 1886): 8; King, *King's Handbook of New York* (1893), 803–4; *A History of Real Estate, Building and Architecture in New York City During the Last Quarter of a Century*, 640; White

and Willensky, *AIA Guide* (1988), 55; Landmarks Preservation Commission of the City of New York, *Tribeca West Historic District Designation Report* (New York, 1991), 230–31.

58. "The Mercantile Exchange": 718–19.

59. "The New Mercantile Exchange": 720.

60. "The Consolidated Stock and Petroleum Exchange's New Building," *Real Estate Record and Builders' Guide* 39 (June 1, 1887): 5; "Laying the Corner Stone of the New Consolidated Exchange," *New York Daily Graphic* (September 10, 1887): 562, 573; "Consolidated Stock and Petroleum Exchange, New York City. George Dinkelberg and Fred. Harding, Architects, New York City," *Building* 7 (November 12, 1887): 161; "Architectural Notes," *Real Estate Record and Builders' Guide* 41 (April 7, 1888): 425; "The New Consolidated Stock Exchange," *Real Estate Record and Builders' Guide* 41 (April 14, 1888): 455–56; "The New Consolidated Stock and Petroleum Exchange, Broadway and Exchange Place," *New York Daily Graphic* (April 16, 1888): 352–53; John Arbuckle, "The New York Consolidated Exchange," *The Cosmopolitan* 5 (May 1888): 233–42; King, *King's Handbook of New York* (1893), 792–94; *A History of Real Estate, Building and Architecture in New York City During the Last Quarter of a Century*, 646; Dunlap, *On Broadway*, 23–24.

61. "The New Consolidated Stock Exchange," (April 14, 1888): 455–56.

Warehouses

1. See Mary Black, *Old New York in Early Photographs* (New York: Dover, 1973), plate 10.

2. Landmarks Preservation Commission of the City of New York, *Soho—Cast-Iron Historic District Designation Report* (New York, 1973), 183–84; Margot Gayle and Edmund V. Gillon Jr., *Cast-Iron Architecture in New York* (New York: Dover, 1974), ix–x. For Thomas's five-story building at 80–82 Greene Street (1872–73), built for C. Henry Gardiner, see "Projected Buildings," *Real Estate Record and Builders' Guide* 9 (June 29, 1872): 305; *Soho—Cast-Iron Historic District*, 101; White and Willensky, *AIA Guide* (1988), 97. Thomas also built two five-story buildings (1869–72) for the prominent financier Samuel D. Babcock at 116–118 Franklin Street and 121–123 Franklin Street. See "Projected Buildings," *Real Estate Record and Builders' Guide* 3 (June 19, 1869): 10; Landmarks Preservation Commission of the City of New York, *Tribeca East Historic District Designation Report* (New York, 1992), 152–53.

3. *Soho—Cast-Iron Historic District*, 99–100, 178; Gayle and Gillon, *Cast-Iron Architecture in New York*, 72–74; Paul Goldberger, *The City Observed: New York* (New York: Random House, 1979), 58; White and Willensky, *AIA Guide* (1988), 97.

4. *Tribeca East Historic District*, 253–54; Landmarks Preservation Commission of the City of New York, *Tribeca South Historic District Designation Report* (New York, 1992), 84, 86, 108.

5. *A History of Real Estate, Building and Architecture in New York City During the Last Quarter of a Century* (New York: Real Estate Record Association, 1898), 685; Gayle and Gillon, *Cast-Iron Architecture in New York*, 128–29; Landmarks Preservation Commission of the City of New York, LP-1650 (August 19, 1989); Barbaralee Diamonstein, *The Landmarks of New York II* (New York: Harry N. Abrams, 1993), 387.

6. *Soho—Cast-Iron Historic District*, 181–83; Gayle and Gillon, *Cast-Iron Architecture in New York*, 136; Mary Ann Clegg Smith, "The Commercial Architecture of John Butler Snook" (Ph.D. diss., Pennsylvania State University, 1974): 148–49; David W. Dunlap, *On Broadway: A Journey Uptown Over Time* (New York: Rizzoli International Publications, 1990), 71.

7. *Soho—Cast-Iron Historic District*, 181–83; Gayle and Gillon, *Cast-Iron Architecture in New York*, 144; Smith, "The Commercial Architecture of John Butler Snook": 149–50; Dunlap, *On Broadway*, 73.

8. Gayle and Gillon, *Cast-Iron Architecture in New York*, 14–15; Deborah S. Gardner, "The Architecture of Commercial Capitalism: John Kellum and the Development of New York, 1840–1875" (Ph.D. diss., Columbia University, 1979): 37–41; White and Willensky, *AIA Guide* (1988), 71.

9. Gardner, "The Architecture of Commercial Capitalism: John Kellum and the Development of New York, 1840–1875": 413–14; White and Willensky, *AIA Guide* (1988), 94; Dunlap, *On Broadway*, 76–77.

10. Gayle and Gillon, *Cast-Iron Architecture in New York*, v, 28–29; Gardner, "The Architecture of Commercial Capitalism: John Kellum and the Development of New York, 1840–1875": 413–14; White and Willensky, *AIA Guide* (1988), 68; Landmarks Preservation Commission of the City of New York, LP-1651 (March 22, 1988); Diamonstein, *The Landmarks of New York II*, 386.

11. White and Willensky, *AIA Guide* (1988), 69; Christopher Gray, "Remnant of a Major 19th-Century Architectural Fad," *New York Times* (June 18, 1995), IX: 7.

12. "Metropolitan Improvements," *New York Evening Post* (March 10, 1871): 1; Amos J. Bicknell, *Wooden and Brick Buildings with Details* (New York: A. J. Bicknell, 1875), vol. 2: plate 87; *Soho—Cast-Iron Historic District*, 56; Gayle and Gillon, *Cast-Iron Architecture in New York*, 46; Francis R. Kowsky, *The Architecture of Frederick Clarke Withers and the Progress of the Gothic Revival in America After 1850* (Middletown, Conn.: Wesleyan University Press, 1980), 97–98; White and Willensky, *AIA Guide* (1988), 101.

13. Montgomery Schuyler, "Frederick C. Withers," *Real Estate Record and Builders' Guide* 67 (January 12, 1901): 42, quoted in Kowsky, *The Architecture of Frederick Clarke Withers*, 97.

14. "The Building Outlook," *New York Daily Tribune* (June 17, 1873): 5; "An Iron Store-Front on Broadway, New York, R. M. Hunt Architect," *American Architect and Building News* 1 (June 10, 1876): 188, plate; A. J. Bloor, "Annual Address," *Proceedings of the Tenth Annual Convention of the American Institute of Architects, 1876* (Boston, 1877): 15–34; Montgomery Schuyler, "Recent Building in New York—II," *American Architect and Building News* 9 (April 16, 1881): 183–84; "The Post Building," *Real Estate Record and Builders' Guide* 30 (November 11–18, 1882): 72–73; Montgomery Schuyler, "The Works of the Late Richard M. Hunt," *Architectural Record* 5 (October–December 1895): 97–180; *A History of Real Estate, Building and Architecture in New York City During the Last Quarter of a Century*, 624; Winston Weisman, "Commercial Palaces of New York: 1845–1875," *Art Bulletin* 36 (December 1954): 285–302; Winston Weisman, "The Chicago School of Architecture: A Symposium—Part I," *Prairie School Review* 9 (first quarter, 1972): 6–30; *Soho—Cast-Iron Historic District*, 37–38; Gayle and Gillon, *Cast-Iron Architecture in New York*, 140–41; Goldberger, *The City Observed*, 60–61; Paul R. Baker, *Richard Morris Hunt* (Cambridge, Mass.: MIT Press, 1980), 215–17, 543; Sarah Bradford Landau, "Richard Morris Hunt: Architectural Innovator and Father of a 'Distinctive' American School," in Susan Stein, ed., *The Architecture of Richard Morris Hunt* (Chicago: University of Chicago Press, 1986), 46–77; White and Willensky, *AIA Guide* (1988), 95–96; Dunlap, *On Broadway*, 72.

15. "An Iron Store-Front on Broadway, New York, R. M. Hunt Architect," *American Architect and Building News* 1 (July 15, 1876): 228, plates; Bloor, "Annual Address": 27; Schuyler, "Recent Building in New York—II": 183–84; "The Post Building": 72–73; Schuyler, "The Works of the Late Richard M. Hunt": 110; *A History of Real Estate, Building and Architecture in New York City During the Last Quarter of a Century*, 622; Gayle and Gillon, *Cast-Iron Architecture in New York*, xiv–xv; Baker, *Richard Morris Hunt*, 214–16; 542; Landau, "Richard Morris Hunt: Architectural Innovator and Father of a 'Distinctive' American School," in Stein, ed., *The Architecture of Richard Morris Hunt*, 60.

16. Quoted in Baker, *Richard Morris Hunt*, 214.

17. Bloor, "Annual Address": 27.

18. Schuyler, "Recent Building in New York—II": 183–84.

19. Schuyler, "The Works of the Late Richard M. Hunt": 110. Also see James Fergusson, *A History of Architecture in All Countries, from the Earliest Times to the Present Day*, vol. 5: *A History of the Modern Styles of Architecture*, 3rd ed., rev. and ed. by Robert Kerr (London: J. Murray, 1891), 353–55; Baker, *Richard Morris Hunt*, 217.

20. Richard Morris Hunt, quoted in "Cast Iron in Decorative Architecture," *Crayon* 6 (1859): 24.

21. "Buildings Projected," *Real Estate Record and Builders' Guide* 11 (April 19, 1873): 183; Baker, *Richard Morris Hunt*, 504, 543; White and Willensky, *AIA Guide* (1988), 35.

22. W., "Correspondence: Iron Fronts—New Office Buildings," *American Architect and Building News* 6 (July 5, 1879): 6–7. Also see Weisman, "The Chicago School of Architecture: A Symposium—Part I":

18–19; Karin May Elizabeth Alexis, "Russell Sturgis: Critic and Architect" (Ph.D. diss., University of Virginia, 1986): 107–8, plate 33.

23. Gayle and Gillon, *Cast-Iron Architecture in New York*, 96–97.

24. "Buildings Projected," *Real Estate Record and Builders' Guide* 11 (May 17, 1873): 234; Gayle and Gillon, *Cast-Iron Architecture in New York*, 67.

25. "Buildings Projected," *Real Estate Record and Builders' Guide* 13 (April 11, 1874): 198; Gayle and Gillon, *Cast-Iron Architecture in New York*, 43.

26. "Buildings Projected," *Real Estate Record and Builders' Guide* 17 (April 1, 1876): 251; "Store No. 31 Green [*sic*] Street, New York. Designed by C. W. Romeyn, Architect," *American Architect and Building News* 2 (February 24, 1877): 60, plate; *Soho—Cast-Iron Historic District*, 91–92; White and Willensky, *AIA Guide* (1988), 96.

27. "Buildings Projected," *Real Estate Record and Builders' Guide* 35 (April 25, 1885): 484; "Out Among the Builders," *Real Estate Record and Builders' Guide* 35 (May 2, 1885): 495; *Soho—Cast-Iron Historic District*, 85, 91.

28. "Buildings Projected," *Real Estate Record and Builders' Guide* 24 (September 13, 1879): 732; "New York's Model Warehouse," *Real Estate Record and Builders' Guide* 26 (July 31, 1880): 684; *Soho—Cast-Iron Historic District*, 37–38; Gayle and Gillon, *Cast-Iron Architecture in New York*, 138–39; White and Willensky, *AIA Guide* (1988), 96; Dunlap, *On Broadway*, 72.

29. "New York's Model Warehouse": 684.

30. "Buildings Projected," *Real Estate Record and Builders' Guide* 23 (May 10, 1879): 390; Gayle and Gillon, *Cast-Iron Architecture in New York*, 88–89; Landmarks Preservation Commission of the City of New York, LP-1038 (May 22, 1979); White and Willensky, *AIA Guide* (1988), 151–52; Diamonstein, *The Landmarks of New York II*, 174.

31. "Buildings Projected," *Real Estate Record and Builders' Guide* 6 (December 17, 1870): 9; "The Work of the Flames," *New York Times* (March 8, 1877): 5; "Local Miscellany: The Bond Street Fire," *New York Times* (March 9, 1877): 2; "Firemen as Building Inspectors," letter to the editor, *New York Times* (March 12, 1877): 4.

32. "Buildings Projected," *Real Estate Record and Builders' Guide* 2 (September 19, 1868): 9; *Tribeca East Historic District*, 189–91.

33. "Buildings Projected," *Real Estate Record and Builders' Guide* 3 (July 24, 1869): 10; Gayle and Gillon, *Cast-Iron Architecture in New York*, 26; *Tribeca East Historic District*, 184–85.

34. "Buildings Projected," *Real Estate Record and Builders' Guide* 9 (June 22, 1872): 295; *Soho—Cast-Iron Historic District*, 99–100; White and Willensky, *AIA Guide* (1988), 97. For Fernbach's five-story 58–60 Greene Street (1871), see "Buildings Projected," *Real Estate Record and Builders' Guide* 7 (June 10, 1871): 293; *Soho—Cast-Iron Historic District*, 100; White and Willensky, *AIA Guide* (1988), 97. For his five-story 19–21 Greene Street (1871-72), see "Buildings Projected," *Real Estate Record and Builders' Guide* 8 (October 28, 1871): 184; *Soho—Cast-Iron Historic District*, 92; Gayle and Gillon, *Cast-Iron Architecture in New York*, 81; White and Willensky, *AIA Guide* (1988), 96. For the series of buildings numbering 67–81 Greene Street (1872–78), see "Buildings Projected," *Real Estate Record and Builders' Guide* 10 (July 13, 1872): 16; "Buildings Projected," *Real Estate Record and Builders' Guide* 17 (May 13, 1876): 383; "Buildings Projected," *Real Estate Record and Builders' Guide* 17 (June 17, 1876): 485; "Buildings Projected," *Real Estate Record and Builders' Guide* 19 (May 12, 1877): 389; "Buildings Projected," *Real Estate Record and Builders' Guide* 21 (June 1, 1878): 489; *Soho—Cast-Iron Historic District*, 98–99; White and Willensky, *AIA Guide* (1988), 97. For his three five-story buildings at 92, 94, and 96 Greene Street (1879), see "Buildings Projected," *Real Estate Record and Builders' Guide* 23 (April 26, 1879): 342; *Soho—Cast-Iron Historic District*, 103; White and Willensky, *AIA Guide* (1988), 98. For his two five-story buildings at 101 and 103–105 Greene Street (1879), see "Buildings Projected," *Real Estate Record and Builders' Guide* 23 (April 26, 1879): 341; *Soho—Cast-Iron Historic District*, 102; White and Willensky, *AIA Guide* (1988), 98. For his three six-story buildings at 93–99 Greene Street (1881), see "Buildings Projected," *Real Estate Record and Builders' Guide* 27 (April 2, 1881): 321; *Soho—Cast-Iron Historic District*, 101-2; White and Willensky, *AIA Guide* (1988), 98. For his two six-story buildings at 133 and 135–137

Greene Street (1882–83), see "Buildings Projected," *Real Estate Record and Builders' Guide* 29 (April 8, 1882): 348; *Soho—Cast-Iron Historic District*, 106; White and Willensky, *AIA Guide* (1988), 100. For his five-story 113 Greene Street (1882–83), see "Buildings Projected," *Real Estate Record and Builders' Guide* 30 (September 2, 1882): 813; *Soho—Cast-Iron Historic District*, 103; Gayle and Gillon, *Cast-Iron Architecture in New York*, 71; White and Willensky, *AIA Guide* (1988), 98. For his two six-story buildings at 108 and 110–112 Greene Street (1883-84), see "Buildings Projected," *Real Estate Record and Builders' Guide* 31 (May 12, 1883): 348; *Soho—Cast-Iron Historic District*, 104; White and Willensky, *AIA Guide* (1988), 98.

35. "Out Among the Builders," *Real Estate Record and Builders' Guide* 27 (May 7, 1881): 455; "Buildings Projected," *Real Estate Record and Builders' Guide* 27 (June 4, 1881): 592; *Soho—Cast-Iron Historic District*, 103–4.

36. "Buildings Projected," *Real Estate Record and Builders' Guide* 29 (April 8, 1882): 348; White and Willensky, *AIA Guide* (1988), 100; *Soho—Cast-Iron Historic District*, 105–6.

37. "Out Among the Builders," *Real Estate Record and Builders' Guide* 32 (December 22, 1883): 1030; "Buildings Projected," *Real Estate Record and Builders' Guide* 33 (February 2, 1884): 124; *A History of Real Estate, Building and Architecture in New York City During the Last Quarter of a Century*, 691; *Soho—Cast-Iron Historic District*, 108; Mary Kathryn Stroh, "The Commercial Architecture of Alfred Zucker in Manhattan" (master's thesis, Pennsylvania State University, 1973): 13–16, 94. In 1890, Zucker designed the six-story Scholle Building, at 716 Broadway, between Fourth Street and Astor Place, which featured whimsical ornamental details and a predominantly cast-iron facade, although it was also built of stone and terra cotta. See "Buildings Projected," *Real Estate Record and Builders' Guide* 45 (March 22, 1890): 426; "The New Mercantile District," supplement, *Real Estate Record and Builders' Guide* 46 (October 25, 1890): 1–48; *A History of Real Estate, Building and Architecture in New York City During the Last Quarter of a Century*, 692; Stroh, "The Commercial Architecture of Alfred Zucker in Manhattan": 36–41, 87, 104; Dunlap, *On Broadway*, 99.

38. "Sale of St. John's Park," *New York Times* (October 20, 1866): 8; "St. John's Park," *New York Times* (March 9, 1867): 1; "St. John's Park," editorial, *New York Times* (March 9, 1867): 4; "Local Intelligence: St. John's Park," *New York Times* (November 15, 1867): 8; John W. Kennion, *Architects' and Builders' Guide* (New York: Fitzpatrick & Hunter, 1868), part 1: 60–63; Albert Degroot, "A Monument to Commodore Vanderbilt," letter to the editor, *New York Times* (February 17, 1868): 5; "The Statue to Vanderbilt," *New York Times* (March 17, 1868): 4–5; "Commodore Vanderbilt," *New York Times* (September 2, 1869): 4; "The Vanderbilt Monument," *Harper's Weekly* 13 (September 25, 1869): 620; "The Vanderbilt Bronzes," *New York Daily Tribune* (November 11, 1869): 2; "Vanderbilt: Unvailing the Memorial Bronze Yesterday," *New York Times* (November 11, 1869): 2; "Dangerous Buildings," *New York Times* (July 8, 1871): 5; Bloor, "Annual Address": 25; Moses King, *King's Handbook of New York* (Boston: Moses King, 1893), 814; I. N. Phelps Stokes, *The Iconography of Manhattan Island*, 6 vols. (New York: Robert H. Dodd, 1915–28; New York: Arno Press, 1967), vol. 5: 1924, 1929; "Razing Freight Depot," *New York Times* (July 22, 1936): 37; Frank W. Crane, "Lower West Side Landmark Passing," *New York Times* (July 26, 1936), XI: 1–2; Smith, "The Commercial Architecture of John Butler Snook": 116–21, 214; Frederick S. Lightfoot, ed., *Nineteenth-Century New York in Rare Photographic Views* (New York: Dover, 1981), figs. 120–21; Ann L. Buttenwieser, *Manhattan Water-Bound: Planning and Developing Manhattan's Waterfront from the Seventeenth Century to the Present* (New York and London: New York University Press, 1987), 75, fig. 14; Landmarks Preservation Commission of the City of New York, *Tribeca North Historic District Designation Report* (New York, 1992), 22–24; Gregory F. Gilmartin, *Shaping the City: New York and the Municipal Art Society* (New York: Clarkson Potter, 1995), 335.

39. See Carl W. Condit, *The Port of New York: A History of the Rail and Terminal System from the Beginnings to Pennsylvania Station* (Chicago and London: University of Chicago Press, 1980), 32–40.

40. "St. John's Park," editorial, *New York Times*: 4.

41. *Tribeca North Historic District*, 114–15.

42. "Buildings Projected," *Real Estate Record and Builders' Guide* 5 (June 11, 1870): 10; "Buildings Projected," *Real Estate Record and Builders' Guide* 10 (October 12, 1872): 135; *Tribeca North Historic District*, 50–51, 96–97, 113–14.

43. "Buildings Projected," *Real Estate Record and Builders' Guide* 30 (December 16, 1882): 1081; *Tribeca North Historic District*, 112–13.

44. "Out Among the Builders," *Real Estate Record and Builders' Guide* 33 (May 17, 1884): 536; "Buildings Projected," *Real Estate Record and Builders' Guide* 33 (June 21, 1884): 688; *Tribeca North Historic District*, 62–63.

45. "Buildings Projected," *Real Estate Record and Builders' Guide* 23 (April 19, 1879): 321; "A New Grocery House," *New York Daily Graphic* (April 18, 1881): 362; Landmarks Preservation Commission of the City of New York, *Tribeca West Historic District Designation Report* (New York, 1992), 274.

46. "Out Among the Builders," *Real Estate Record and Builders' Guide* 28 (October 29, 1881): 1009; "Out Among the Builders," *Real Estate Record and Builders' Guide* 29 (March 4, 1882): 187; "Buildings Projected," *Real Estate Record and Builders' Guide* 29 (April 1, 1882): 316; *Tribeca West Historic District*, 280–81.

47. "Buildings Projected," *Real Estate Record and Builders' Guide* 27 (March 5, 1881): 212; *Tribeca West Historic District*, 272–73.

48. "White Street and Vicinity," *Real Estate Record and Builders' Guide* 26 (July 17, 1880): 650. Also see "Buildings Projected," *Real Estate Record and Builders' Guide* 25 (January 10, 1880): 44.

49. "Buildings Projected," *Real Estate Record and Builders' Guide* 17 (April 15, 1876): 295; "Correspondence," *American Architect and Building News* 1 (May 6, 1876): 150–51; King, *King's Handbook of New York* (1893), 878; Winston Weisman, "The Commercial Architecture of George B. Post," *Journal of the Society of Architectural Historians* 31 (October 1972): 176–203; *Soho—Cast-Iron Historic District*, 98.

50. "Correspondence": 150.

51. "Out Among the Builders," *Real Estate Record and Builders' Guide* 27 (April 30, 1881): 422; "Buildings Projected," *Real Estate Record and Builders' Guide* 27 (May 7, 1881): 481; *Tribeca West Historic District*, 97–98.

52. "Buildings Projected," *Real Estate Record and Builders' Guide* 33 (April 19, 1884): 425; *Tribeca West Historic District*, 260–61.

53. "Buildings Projected," *Real Estate Record and Builders' Guide* 45 (March 22, 1890): 426; *Tribeca West Historic District*, 87–88.

54. "Buildings Projected," *Real Estate Record and Builders' Guide* 5 (April 16, 1870): 9; *Soho—Cast-Iron Historic District*, 31–32; Gayle and Gillon, *Cast-Iron Architecture in New York*, 135; Dunlap, *On Broadway*, 69.

55. "Buildings Projected," *Real Estate Record and Builders' Guide* 7 (March 11, 1871): 123; *Tribeca East Historic District*, 135–36.

56. "Buildings Projected," *Real Estate Record and Builders' Guide* 30 (September 30, 1882): 897; *Tribeca North Historic District*, 76–77.

57. "Out Among the Builders," *Real Estate Record and Builders' Guide* 32 (August 4, 1883): 567; "Buildings Projected," *Real Estate Record and Builders' Guide* 32 (August 25, 1883): 639; *Tribeca North Historic District*, 54–55.

58. "Buildings Projected," *Real Estate Record and Builders' Guide* 32 (September 29, 1883): 750; *Tribeca North Historic District*, 53–54.

59. "Buildings Projected," *Real Estate Record and Builders' Guide* 36 (October 31, 1885): 1210; *Tribeca North Historic District*, 75.

60. "Buildings Projected," *Real Estate Record and Builders' Guide* 37 (February 27, 1886): 273; *Tribeca North Historic District*, 99–100.

61. "Buildings Projected," *Real Estate Record and Builders' Guide* 35 (April 18, 1885): 448; "Buildings Projected," *Real Estate Record and Builders' Guide* 43 (June 22, 1889): 897; *Tribeca West Historic District*, 232–34.

62. "Buildings Projected," *Real Estate Record and Builders' Guide* 41 (June 2, 1888): 722; "Important Buildings Under Way," *Real Estate Record and Builders' Guide* 42 (September 1, 1888): 1065; *Tribeca West Historic District*, 111–12.

63. "A New Broadway Store," *Real Estate Record and Builders' Guide* 31 (March 3, 1883): 80–81. Also see "Out Among the Builders," *Real Estate Record and Builders' Guide* 29 (March 25, 1882): 271; "Buildings Projected," *Real Estate Record and Builders' Guide* 29 (April 22, 1882): 406;

M. G. Van Rensselaer, "Recent Architecture in America—III," *Century Magazine* 28 (August 1884): 511–23; *A History of Real Estate, Building and Architecture in New York City During the Last Quarter of a Century*, 689; Soho—*Cast-Iron Historic District*, 53–54; White and Willensky, *AIA Guide* (1988), 94–95; Dunlap, *On Broadway*, 73.

64. "A New Broadway Store": 80–81.

65. Van Rensselaer, "Recent Architecture in America—III": 519.

66. "Buildings Projected," *Real Estate Record and Builders' Guide* 27 (March 12, 1881): 237; "Buildings Projected," *Real Estate Record and Builders' Guide* 27 (April 23, 1881): 412; "Out Among the Builders," *Real Estate Record and Builders' Guide* 27 (April 23, 1881): 391; *Tribeca East Historic District*, 160–61.

67. *A History of Real Estate, Building and Architecture in New York City During the Last Quarter of a Century*, 635, 681; *Tribeca North Historic District*, 108–9.

68. "Out Among the Builders," *Real Estate Record and Builders' Guide* 23 (May 26, 1883): 215; "Buildings Projected," *Real Estate Record and Builders' Guide* 31 (June 16, 1883): 437; *A History of Real Estate, Building and Architecture in New York City During the Last Quarter of a Century*, 681; *Tribeca North Historic District*, 55–56.

69. "Out Among the Builders," *Real Estate Record and Builders' Guide* 33 (March 1, 1884): 210–11; "Buildings Projected," *Real Estate Record and Builders' Guide* 33 (May 10, 1884): 524.

70. Montgomery Schuyler, "The Works of Charles Coolidge Haight," *Architectural Record* 6 (July 1899): 1–102. Also see "Out Among the Builders," *Real Estate Record and Builders' Guide* 41 (March 24, 1888): 363; "Buildings Projected," *Real Estate Record and Builders' Guide* 41 (May 19, 1888): 661; "Important Buildings Under Way," (September 1, 1888): 1065; "The New Mercantile District": 43; *Tribeca West Historic District*, 277–78.

71. Schuyler, "The Works of Charles Coolidge Haight": 43–44.

72. "Buildings Projected," *Real Estate Record and Builders' Guide* 45 (April 5, 1890): 502; *A History of Real Estate, Building and Architecture in New York City During the Last Quarter of a Century*, 681; Schuyler, "The Works of Charles Coolidge Haight": 85; *Tribeca West Historic District*, 321–22.

73. Russell Sturgis, "The Warehouse and the Factory in Architecture," *Architectural Record* 15 (January 1904): 1–18.

74. Schuyler, "Recent Building in New York—II": 183–84; Van Rensselaer, "Recent Architecture in America—III": 512; *A History of Real Estate, Building and Architecture in New York City During the Last Quarter of a Century*, 629, 673; Sturgis, "The Warehouse and the Factory in Architecture": 2, 4; Sarah Bradford Landau, "The Tall Office Building Artistically Reconsidered: Arcaded Buildings of the New York School, 1870–1890," in Helen Searing, ed., *In Search of Modern Architecture: A Tribute to Henry-Russell Hitchcock* (New York: Architectural History Foundation; Cambridge, Mass.: MIT Press, 1982), 136–64; Alexis, "Russell Sturgis: Critic and Architect": 258–59; White and Willensky, *AIA Guide* (1988), 57–58; *Tribeca West Historic District*, 192; Sarah Bradford Landau and Carl W. Condit, *Rise of the New York Skyscraper, 1865–1913* (New Haven, Conn., and London: Yale University Press, 1996), 415 (n. 51).

75. Van Rensselaer, "Recent Architecture in America—III": 512.

76. Sturgis, "The Warehouse and the Factory in Architecture": 4.

77. "Out Among the Builders," *Real Estate Record and Builders' Guide* 34 (October 18, 1884): 1049; Editorial, *Real Estate Record and Builders' Guide* 34 (October 25, 1884): 1074; *A History of Real Estate, Building and Architecture in New York City During the Last Quarter of a Century*, 673; Sturgis, "The Warehouse and the Factory in Architecture": 6, 8–9; Landau, "The Tall Office Building Artistically Reconsidered: Arcaded Buildings of the New York School, 1870–1890," in Searing, ed., *In Search of Modern Architecture: A Tribute to Henry-Russell Hitchcock*, 150–52; Alexis, "Russell Sturgis: Critic and Architect": 262–63.

78. Sturgis, "The Warehouse and the Factory in Architecture": 6, 8.

79. Editorial, *Real Estate Record and Builders' Guide*: 1074.

80. Homer Saint-Gaudens, ed., *The Reminiscences of Augustus Saint-Gaudens* (New York: Century Co., 1913), 283. Also see "The De Vinne Press Building, New York," *Sanitary Engineer* 13 (May 13, 1886): 561, plate; "Example of a Modern Factory Building," *Art Age* 3 (June 1886): 19; "A Printing House," *Art Age* 3 (June 1886): 197; "No. 27 Lafayette

Place," *Real Estate Record and Builders' Guide* 40 (September 3, 1887): 1124; Theodore L. De Vinne, "The Printing of 'The Century,'" *Century Magazine* 41 (November 1890): 87–99; James Taylor, "The History of Terra Cotta in New York City," *Architectural Record* 2 (October–December 1892): 136–48; *A History of Real Estate, Building and Architecture in New York City During the Last Quarter of a Century*, 641, 673; Sturgis, "The Warehouse and the Factory in Architecture": 2–7; Henry-Russell Hitchcock, *The Architecture of H. H. Richardson and His Times*, rev. ed. (New York: Museum of Modern Art, 1936; Hamden, Conn.: Archon Books, 1961), 296; Henry-Russell Hitchcock, *Architecture: Nineteenth and Twentieth Centuries* (Baltimore: Penguin Books, 1958), 242–43; Landmarks Preservation Commission of the City of New York, LP-0201 (October 19, 1966); Goldberger, *The City Observed*, 67; John Tauranac, *Essential New York* (New York: Holt, Rinehart and Winston, 1979), 61–63; Landau, "The Tall Office Building Artistically Reconsidered: Arcaded Buildings of the New York School, 1870–1890," in Searing, ed., *In Search of Modern Architecture: A Tribute to Henry-Russell Hitchcock*, 152–53; Irene Tichenor, "Theodore Low De Vinne (1828–1914): Dean of American Printers" (Ph.D. diss., Columbia University, 1983): 49–55, 61; Alexis, "Russell Sturgis: Critic and Architect": 258–62; White and Willensky, *AIA Guide* (1988), 154; Diamonstein, *The Landmarks of New York II*, 185; Landau and Condit, *Rise of the New York Skyscraper, 1865–1913*, 9, 143–46.

81. Sturgis, "The Warehouse and the Factory in Architecture": 6.

82. "No. 27 Lafayette Place": 1124.

83. "Out Among the Builders," *Real Estate Record and Builders' Guide* 35 (April 25, 1885): 466; "Buildings Projected," *Real Estate Record and Builders' Guide* 35 (June 20, 1885): 772; Landau, "The Tall Office Building Artistically Reconsidered: Arcaded Buildings of the New York School, 1870–1890," in Searing, ed., *In Search of Modern Architecture: A Tribute to Henry-Russell Hitchcock*, 154, 163 (n. 43); White and Willensky, *AIA Guide* (1988), 103. Teale, a onetime president of the American Society of Magicians, was the author of *Higher Magic: Magic for the Artist* (New York: Adams Press, 1920). See Brander Matthews, "Modern Magic and Conjurer's Tricks," book review, *New York Times* (September 19, 1920), III: 6.

84. "Buildings Projected," *Real Estate Record and Builders' Guide* 35 (April 11, 1885): 413; *Tribeca West Historic District*, 339–40.

85. "Buildings Projected," *Real Estate Record and Builders' Guide* 50 (December 3, 1892): 747; King, *King's Handbook of New York* (1893), 912; "Explosion: Section of Two Blocks Wrecked," *New York Evening Post* (October 29, 1900): 1; "Death and Havoc Follow Explosion," *New York Times* (October 30, 1900): 1; Sturgis, "The Warehouse and the Factory in Architecture": 10, 12–13; Stokes, *The Iconography of Manhattan Island*, vol. 5: 2042.

86. "Buildings Projected," *Real Estate Record and Builders' Guide* 29 (May 27, 1882): 544; Sarah Bradford Landau, *Edward T. and William A. Potter: American Victorian Architects* (New York: Garland, 1979), 321–22, 477; Landau, "The Tall Office Building Artistically Reconsidered: Arcaded Buildings of the New York School, 1870–1890," in Searing, ed., *In Search of Modern Architecture: A Tribute to Henry-Russell Hitchcock*, 150.

87. "Around the Bridge Approach," *Real Estate Record and Builders' Guide* 33 (May 3, 1884): 461–62. Also see "Buildings Projected," *Real Estate Record and Builders' Guide* 31 (June 2, 1883): 385; "Leather Warehouse, for G. B. Horton, Esq., New York, N.Y., Mr. Wm. B. Tubby, Architect, New York, N.Y.," *American Architect and Building News* 16 (October 4, 1884): 163, plate.

88. "Buildings Projected," *Real Estate Record and Builders' Guide* 35 (June 6, 1885): 669; White and Willensky, *AIA Guide* (1988), 34; Landmarks Preservation Commission of the City of New York, *South Street Seaport Historic District Designation Report* (New York, 1989), 5; Sarah Bradford Landau, *George B. Post, Architect: Picturesque Designer and Determined Realist*, Sources of American Architecture, ed. Robert A. M. Stern (New York: Monacelli Press, 1998), 67–69.

89. "Buildings Projected," *Real Estate Record and Builders' Guide* 36 (July 11, 1885): 802; White and Willensky, *AIA Guide* (1988), 34–35.

90. Montgomery Schuyler, "The Works of Francis H. Kimball and Kimball & Thompson," *Architectural Record* 7 (April–June 1898): 479–518. Also see "Buildings Projected," *Real Estate Record and Builders'*

Guide 37 (May 29, 1886): 731; "The New Mercantile District": 40–41; *A History of Real Estate, Building and Architecture in New York City During the Last Quarter of a Century*, 578; White and Willensky, *AIA Guide* (1988), 53; Andrew S. Dolkart, *The Texture of Tribeca* (New York: Tribeca Community Association, 1989), 52; *Tribeca West Historic District*, 118–19.

91. Schuyler, "The Works of Francis H. Kimball and Kimball & Thompson": 486–88.

92. "Out Among the Builders," *Real Estate Record and Builders' Guide* 35 (February 14, 1885): 163; "The 'Puck' Building to Be Extended," *Real Estate Record and Builders' Guide* 46 (August 16, 1890): 212; "Out Among the Builders," *Real Estate Record and Builders' Guide* 49 (April 2, 1892): 515; King, *King's Handbook of New York* (1893), 626, 638; Goldberger, *The City Observed*, 62–64; Landau, "The Tall Office Building Artistically Reconsidered: Arcaded Buildings of the New York School, 1870–1890," in Searing, ed., *In Search of Modern Architecture: A Tribute to Henry-Russell Hitchcock*, 154; Landmarks Preservation Commission of the City of New York, LP-1226 (April 12, 1983); White and Willensky, *AIA Guide* (1988), 80–81; Diamonstein, *The Landmarks of New York II*, 191.

93. "A New Brick Warehouse," *Real Estate Record and Builders' Guide* 41 (May 12, 1888): 598. Also see "Out Among the Builders," *Real Estate Record and Builders' Guide* 40 (September 10, 1887): 1154–55; Dolkart, *The Texture of Tribeca*, 43; *Tribeca West Historic District*, 65–66.

94. "Buildings Projected," *Real Estate Record and Builders' Guide* 39 (March 12, 1887): 351. Also see Winston R. Weisman, book review, *Journal of the Society of Architectural Historians* 26 (December 1967): 312–14; Weisman, "The Chicago School of Architecture: A Symposium—Part I": 23; *Soho—Cast-Iron Historic District*, 136; Landau, "The Tall Office Building Artistically Reconsidered: Arcaded Buildings of the New York School, 1870–1890," in Searing, ed., *In Search of Modern Architecture: A Tribute to Henry-Russell Hitchcock*, 155–56.

95. Landau, "The Tall Office Building Artistically Reconsidered: Arcaded Buildings of the New York School, 1870–1890," in Searing, ed., *In Search of Modern Architecture: A Tribute to Henry-Russell Hitchcock*, 155. Also see Weisman, book review, *Journal of the Society of Architectural Historians*: 313.

96. "A New Warehouse," *Real Estate Record and Builders' Guide* 43 (June 8, 1889): 794; A.D.F. Hamlin, "The Difficulties of Modern Architecture," *Architectural Record* 1 (October–December 1891): 137–50; Taylor, "The History of Terra Cotta in New York City": 148; Montgomery Schuyler, "The Works of Henry Janeway Hardenbergh," *Architectural Record* 6 (January–March 1897): 335–75; *A History of Real Estate, Building and Architecture in New York City During the Last Quarter of a Century*, 646; Goldberger, *The City Observed*, 66; White and Willensky, *AIA Guide* (1988), 152.

97. Schuyler, "The Works of Henry Janeway Hardenbergh": 343.

98. Schuyler, "The Works of Henry Janeway Hardenbergh": 345–46. Also see "Buildings Projected," *Real Estate Record and Builders' Guide* 47 (June 20, 1891): 1009; *A History of Real Estate, Building and Architecture in New York City During the Last Quarter of a Century*, 681; Dunlap, *On Broadway*, 187.

99. See Stroh, "The Commercial Architecture of Alfred Zucker in Manhattan": 6–9.

100. "Out Among the Builders," *Real Estate Record and Builders' Guide* 33 (January 5, 1884): 7; "Buildings Projected," *Real Estate Record and Builders' Guide* 33 (February 16, 1884): 173; "The Highest Building in the Dry-Goods District," *Real Estate Record and Builders' Guide* 36 (September 12, 1885): 996–97; "The New Mercantile District": 8–9; *Photographed from Designs for Buildings and from Buildings Erected by Alfred Zucker, Architect* (New York: National Chemigraph Co., 1894), n.p.; *A History of Real Estate, Building and Architecture in New York City During the Last Quarter of a Century*, 691; Stroh, "The Commercial Architecture of Alfred Zucker in Manhattan": 16–19, 94.

101. "The New Mercantile District": 9.

102. "The Highest Building in the Dry-Goods District": 996–97.

103. "Buildings Projected," *Real Estate Record and Builders' Guide* 46 (October 25, 1890): 53; "The New Mercantile District": 17, 35; *Photographed from Designs for Buildings and from Buildings Erected by Alfred Zucker, Architect*, n.p.; Stroh, "The Commercial Architecture of Alfred*

Zucker in Manhattan": 41–43, 105. Other Zucker buildings for Rachel Cohnfeld include the five-story 159–161 Greene Street (1887); two six-story buildings at 171–177 Greene Street (1888); and the six-story 98–100 Bleecker Street (1889). See "Buildings Projected," *Real Estate Record and Builders' Guide* 39 (January 17, 1887): 92; "Buildings Projected," *Real Estate Record and Builders' Guide* 41 (April 21, 1888): 515; "Important Buildings Projected and Under Way," *Real Estate Record and Builders' Guide* 41 (April 28, 1888): 529; "Buildings Projected," *Real Estate Record and Builders' Guide* 43 (April 27, 1889): 606; "The New Mercantile District": 11, 45; *A History of Real Estate, Building and Architecture in New York City During the Last Quarter of a Century*, 692; Stroh, "The Commercial Architecture of Alfred Zucker in Manhattan": 100, 102. Other warehouse buildings by Zucker include the six-story 127 West Broadway (1884); the six-story 102 Bleecker Street (1884); the six-story Meinhard Building (1889), at 97–99 Bleecker Street; and two six-story buildings of 1890 along Greene Street at numbers 190–192 and 200½–202. See "Out Among the Builders," *Real Estate Record and Builders' Guide* 34 (July 19, 1884): 768; "Buildings Projected," *Real Estate Record and Builders' Guide* 34 (August 2, 1884): 826; "Out Among the Builders," *Real Estate Record and Builders' Guide* 34 (August 23, 1884): 876; "Buildings Projected," *Real Estate Record and Builders' Guide* 34 (August 30, 1884): 901; "Out Among the Builders," *Real Estate Record and Builders' Guide* 43 (January 5, 1889): 8; "Buildings Projected," *Real Estate Record and Builders' Guide* 43 (January 12, 1889): 64; "Important Buildings Under Way: South of 14th Street," *Real Estate Record and Builders' Guide* 43 (May 25, 1889): 728–29; "Buildings Projected," *Real Estate Record and Builders' Guide* 46 (October 25, 1890): 53; "The New Mercantile District": 13, 21, 23, 26; *A History of Real Estate, Building and Architecture in New York City During the Last Quarter of a Century*, 692; Stroh, "The Commercial Architecture of Alfred Zucker in Manhattan": 95, 101, 103.

104. "Buildings Projected," *Real Estate Record and Builders' Guide* 46 (October 25, 1890): 53; "The New Mercantile District": 20, 29; *Photographed from Designs for Buildings and from Buildings Erected by Alfred Zucker, Architect*, n.p.; *A History of Real Estate, Building and Architecture in New York City During the Last Quarter of a Century*, 692; Stroh, "The Commercial Architecture of Alfred Zucker in Manhattan": 31, 34–36, 104.

105. "Buildings Projected," *Real Estate Record and Builders' Guide* 45 (January 18, 1890): 94; "The New Mercantile District": 20, 23; *A History of Real Estate, Building and Architecture in New York City During the Last Quarter of a Century*, 692; *Soho—Cast-Iron Historic District*, 64–65; Stroh, "The Commercial Architecture of Alfred Zucker in Manhattan": 22–31, 83–87, 103; Gayle and Gillon, *Cast-Iron Architecture in New York*, 172; White and Willensky, *AIA Guide* (1988), 101.

106. "Out Among the Builders," *Real Estate Record and Builders' Guide* 43 (January 10, 1889): 76; "Buildings Projected," *Real Estate Record and Builders' Guide* 43 (February 16, 1889): 231; "Important Buildings Under Way: South of 14th Street": 728–29; *Photographed from Designs for Buildings and from Buildings Erected by Alfred Zucker, Architect*, n.p.; *A History of Real Estate, Building and Architecture in New York City During the Last Quarter of a Century*, 692; Weisman, "The Chicago School of Architecture: A Symposium—Part I": 22–23; *Soho—Cast-Iron Historic District*, 44–45; Stroh, "The Commercial Architecture of Alfred Zucker in Manhattan": 19–22, 87, 101–2; Gayle and Gillon, *Cast-Iron Architecture in New York*, 146–47; White and Willensky, *AIA Guide* (1988), 93–94; Dunlap, *On Broadway*, 78.

107. "No Windows in Six Stories," *New York Times* (July 25, 1882): 8. Also see "Buildings Projected," *Real Estate Record and Builders' Guide* 30 (July 8, 1882): 677; "Brick Architecture in New York," *Building* 1 (May 1883): 105–6; "The Lincoln Safe Deposit Building," *New York Daily Graphic* (November 1, 1883): 4–5; *A History of Real Estate, Building and Architecture in New York City During the Last Quarter of a Century*, 635; Smith, "The Commercial Architecture of John Butler Snook": 225.

108. "New Storage Warehouse Company," *New York Times* (January 22, 1882): 10; "Fire-Proof Storage Warehouses," *New York Times* (January 24, 1882): 3; "Out Among the Builders," *Real Estate Record and Builders' Guide* 29 (February 18, 1882): 142–43; "A Warehouse Experiment," *New York Times* (April 24, 1882): 2; "Two Storage Warehouses,"

Real Estate Record and Builders' Guide 31 (March 17, 1883): 102–3; "Brick Architecture in New York": 105–6; "Manhattan Storage and Warehouse Building, New York, N.Y., Mr. James E. Ware, Architect, N.Y.," *American Architect and Building News* 15 (February 2, 1884): 54; Van Rensselaer, "Recent Work in America—III": 514–15; "The Manhattan Storage Warehouse, Forty-second Street, New York, N.Y., James E. Ware, Architect, New York, N.Y.," *American Architect and Building News* 20 (November 27, 1886): 254, plate; W. Claude Frederic, "The Manhattan Storage Warehouse Plate," letter to the editor, *American Architect and Building News* 20 (December 11, 1886): 283; "Manhattan Storage Warehouse," *New York Daily Graphic* (March 3, 1888): 28; King, *King's Handbook of New York* (1893), 810–11; *A History of Real Estate, Building and Architecture in New York City During the Last Quarter of a Century*, 635.

109. "Two Storage Warehouses": 102–3.

110. "Brick Architecture in New York": 106.

111. Van Rensselaer, "Recent Work in America—III": 514–15.

112. "To Build a Big Warehouse," *New York Times* (October 31, 1890): 9; "Buildings Projected," *Real Estate Record and Builders' Guide* 46 (November 1, 1890): 602; "The Manhattan Storage and Warehouse Co.'s New Storage Warehouse, Safe Deposit and Silver Vaults," *Real Estate Record and Builders' Guide* 49 (April 2, 1892): 510; King, *King's Handbook of New York* (1893), 810–11.

113. "Buildings Projected," *Real Estate Record and Builders' Guide* 40 (August 6, 1887): 1052; "Out Among the Builders," *Real Estate Record and Builders' Guide* 40 (August 6, 1887): 1037; "Buildings Projected," *Real Estate Record and Builders' Guide* 40 (October 15, 1887): 1309; "Gelatine Plate—The Buildings of the Edison Electric Light Company, New York City," *Building* 11 (August 24, 1889): 63, plate; King, *King's Handbook of New York* (1893), 202–4.

114. "Buildings Projected," *Real Estate Record and Builders' Guide* 29 (April 22, 1882): 406; *Where They Lit Up New York* (New York: Con Edison, 1987), 5–6; Andrew S. Dolkart, *Lower Manhattan Architectural Survey Report* (New York: Lower Manhattan Cultural Council, fall 1987), no. 103.

115. "Out Among the Builders," *Real Estate Record and Builders' Guide* 41 (April 7, 1888): 427; "Important Buildings Projected and Under Way," (April 28, 1888): 529; "Buildings Projected," *Real Estate Record and Builders' Guide* 41 (May 26, 1888): 690; "Important Buildings Under Way," (September 1, 1888): 1065; "The Western Electric Building," *Real Estate Record and Builders' Guide* 44 (July 13, 1889): 978–79; A. W. Ross, "Buttresses in Commercial Buildings," letter to the editor, *Real Estate Record and Builders' Guide* 44 (July 20, 1889): 1017; King, *King's Handbook of New York* (1893), 837; Montgomery Schuyler, "Cyrus L. W. Eidlitz," *Architectural Record* 5 (April–June 1896): 411–35; *A History of Real Estate, Building and Architecture in New York City During the Last Quarter of a Century*, 585; Dolkart, *Lower Manhattan Architectural Survey Report*, no. 33.

116. "The Western Electric Building": 978–79.

117. Schuyler, "Cyrus L. W. Eidlitz": 418.

CHAPTER 4
Places Called Home:
Tenements, Hotels, Apartment Houses, and Houses

1. James Richardson, "The New Homes of New York: A Study of Flats," *Scribner's Monthly* 8 (May 1874): 63–76.

2. "The Problem of Living in New York," *Harper's New Monthly Magazine* 65 (November 1882): 918–24.

3. See Richard A. Plunz, "On the Uses and Abuses of Air: Perfecting the New York Tenement, 1850–1901," in Josef Paul Kleihues and Christina Rathgeber, eds., *Berlin—New York: Like and Unlike* (New York: Rizzoli International Publications, 1993), 159–79. Also see Ira Rosenwaike, *Population History of New York City* (Syracuse, N.Y.: Syracuse University Press, 1972), 63; Edward K. Spann, *The New Metropolis: New York City, 1840–1857* (New York: Columbia University Press, 1981), chapter 15.

4. Philip Hone, *The Diary of Philip Hone, 1820–1851*, ed. Allan Nevins (New York: Dodd, Mead and Company, 1927), 785, quoted in

Richard Plunz, *A History of Housing in New York City* (New York: Columbia University Press, 1990), 4.

5. Junius Henri Browne, *The Great Metropolis; a Mirror of New York* (Hartford, Conn.: American Publishing Company, 1869), 272–79; I. N. Phelps Stokes, *The Iconography of Manhattan Island*, 6 vols. (New York: Robert H. Dodd, 1915–28; New York: Arno Press, 1967), vol. 3: 654, vol. 5: 1683–84, 1796; I. N. Phelps Stokes, "Appendix," in James Ford, *Slums and Housing, with Special References to New York City: History, Conditions, Policy*, 2 vols. (Cambridge, Mass.: Harvard University Press, 1936), vol. 2: 867; Anthony Jackson, *A Place Called Home* (Cambridge, Mass., and London: MIT Press, 1976), 4; Plunz, *A History of Housing in New York City*, 50–52.

6. James D. McCabe Jr., *Lights and Shadows of New York Life; or, The Sights and Sensations of the Great City* (Philadelphia: National Publishing, 1872; New York: Farrar, Straus & Giroux, 1970), 402.

7. Jackson, *A Place Called Home*, 68–69.

8. Jacob A. Riis, *How the Other Half Lives* (New York: Charles Scribner's Sons, 1890), chapter 6.

9. H. C. Bunner, *The Story of a New York House* (New York: Charles Scribner's Sons, 1887), esp. 111–12, 146–47. Also see Elizabeth Collins Cromley, *Alone Together: A History of New York's Early Apartments* (Ithaca, N.Y., and London: Cornell University Press, 1990), 14.

10. Stokes, *The Iconography of Manhattan Island*, vol. 3: 608–9, vol. 6: 593–94. Also see Henry Collins Brown, *Book of Old New-York* (New York, 1913), 95; M. Christine Boyer, *Manhattan Manners: Architecture and Style, 1850–1900* (New York: Rizzoli International Publications, 1985), 12.

11. Charles Dickens, *American Notes* (London: Chapman and Hall, 1842; London: Oxford University Press, 1959), 89.

12. Edward Crapsey, *The Nether Side of New York; or, the Vice, Crime and Poverty of the Great Metropolis* (New York: Sheldon & Co., 1872), 154–56.

13. "The Charter Election—A Crying Evil," *New York Times* (November 21, 1864): 4. Also see "The Squatter Population of New York City," *New York Times* (November 25, 1864): 4.

14. "The Charter Election—A Crying Evil": 4.

15. "Squatter Sovereignty," *New York Times* (July 12, 1865): 5.

16. "A Visit to Shantytown," *New York Times* (July 11, 1880): 5.

17. "New York Health Commissioners and the 'Shanty Towns,'" editorial, *American Architect and Building News* 8 (November 20, 1880): 242. Also see "A Scene in Shantytown, New York," *New York Daily Graphic* (March 4, 1880): 38; "Squatter Life in New York," *Harper's New Monthly Magazine* 61 (September 1880): 562–69.

18. Edward T. Potter, "Urban Housing in New York—I. The Influence of the Size of City Lots," *American Architect and Building News* 3 (March 16, 1878): 90–92.

19. Amy Kallman Epstein, "Multifamily Dwellings and the Search for Respectability: Origins of the New York Apartment House," *Urbanism Past & Present* 5 (summer 1980): 29–39.

20. Lawrence Veiller, "Tenement House Reform in New York City, 1834–1900," in Robert W. De Forest and Lawrence Veiller, eds., *The Tenement House Problem*, 2 vols. (New York: Macmillan, 1903), vol. 1: 71–108; Stokes, "Appendix," in Ford, *Slums and Housing*, vol. 2: 867, 878, plate 1F; Jackson, *A Place Called Home*, 6–10.

21. New York State, Select Committee Appointed to Examine into the Condition of Tenant Houses in New York and Brooklyn, *Report*, Assembly Document, vol. 3, no. 205 (Albany, 1857), 10–12, quoted in Jackson, *A Place Called Home*, 1–2.

22. Cromley, *Alone Together*, 52.

23. "The Tenement Museum: Now, Landmark Status," *New York Times* (September 20, 1992), X: 1.

24. Nathaniel P. Willis, quoted in Veiller, "Tenement House Reform in New York City, 1834–1900," in De Forest and Veiller, eds., *The Tenement House Problem*, vol. 1: 92. Also see Stephen Smith, *The City That Was* (New York: F. Allaben, 1911), 99–100; Jackson, *A Place Called Home*, 25; Plunz, *A History of Housing in New York City*, 167.

25. Quoted in "The Evolution of the Tenement House," *Real Estate Record and Builders' Guide* 44 (September 28, 1889): 1293–95. Also see "Our City's Condition," *New York Times* (June 12, 1865): 1–2.

26. George Templeton Strong, diary entry dated August 6, 1866, in *The Diary of George Templeton Strong*, eds. Allan Nevins and Milton Halsey Thomas, 4 vols. (New York: Macmillan, 1952), vol. 4: 96–97.

27. Quoted in "The Evolution of the Tenement House": 1293–95. Also see "Reform in Tenement-houses," editorial, *New York Times* (October 21, 1866): 4; Veiller, "Tenement House Reform in New York City, 1834–1900," in De Forest and Veiller, eds., *The Tenement House Problem*, vol. 1: 94–97; Ellen Kramer, "The Domestic Architecture of Detlef Lienau: A Conservative Victorian" (Ph.D. diss., New York University, 1957): 210; Jackson, *A Place Called Home*, 27.

28. Ford, *Slums and Housing*, vol. 1: 154–55; Stokes, "Appendix," in Ford, *Slums and Housing*, vol. 2: 877, plate 1E.

29. New York State Legislature, *Laws* (1867), chapter 98, section 17, 2265–73, quoted in Veiller, "Tenement House Reform in New York City, 1834–1900," in De Forest and Veiller, eds., *The Tenement House Problem*, vol. 1: 94.

30. Editorial, *New York Sun* (April 13, 1870): 2, quoted in Jackson, *A Place Called Home*, 37–38.

31. "Dwellings for the Poor," *Morning Courier and New-York Enquirer* (January 30, 1847): 2; Stokes, "Appendix," in Ford, *Slums and Housing*, vol. 2: 878–79; Plunz, *A History of Housing in New York City*, 7–8.

32. Sarah Bradford Landau, *Edward T. and William A. Potter: American Victorian Architects* (New York: Garland, 1979), 390–92.

33. *The Thirteenth Annual Report of the New York Association for Improving the Condition of the Poor* (New York, 1856): 45–58; Working Men's Home Association, *A Statement Relative to the Working Men's Home Association* (New York, December 31, 1857); "The 'Big Flat' Tenement House," *New York Daily Tribune* (November 8, 1879): 3; Frederick N. Owen, "The Story of the 'Big Flat,'" *The Forty-third Annual Report of the New York Association for Improving the Condition of the Poor* (New York, 1886): 43–73; Veiller, "Tenement House Reform in New York City, 1834–1900," in De Forest and Veiller, eds., *The Tenement House Problem*, vol. 1: 85–87; Ford, *Slums and Housing*, vol. 2: fig. 114A; Stokes, "Appendix," in Ford, *Slums and Housing*, vol. 2: 869, 871–72, 878, plates 1G–H; Robert H. Bremner, "The Big Flat: History of a New York Tenement House," *American Historical Review* 64 (October 1958): 54–62; Jackson, *A Place Called Home*, 10–16; Plunz, *A History of Housing in New York City*, 7–8.

34. Veiller, "Tenement House Reform in New York City, 1834–1900," in De Forest and Veiller, eds., *The Tenement House Problem*, vol. 1: 87.

35. Riis, *How the Other Half Lives*, 271.

36. "Improved Dwellings for the Poor," editorial, *New York Times* (July 16, 1877): 4; "The Improvement of Tenements," editorial, *New York Times* (December 16, 1877): 4; "Reducing Disease in Tenement-Houses," *New York Daily Tribune* (August 21, 1878): 8; "Our Bad Tenement Houses," *New York Times* (March 1, 1879): 8; "Our Bad Tenement Houses: Further Discussion on the Subject," *New York Times* (March 12, 1879): 2; "Wholesome Air and Light Needed," *New York Times* (March 14, 1879): 8; "Tenement Life in New York," *Harper's Weekly* 23 (March 22, 1879): 224, 226–27; "City Tenement Houses," *New York Times* (March 22, 1879): 3; "Tenement-House Reform," *New York Times* (March 28, 1879): 8; "Tenement Life in New York," *Harper's Weekly* 23 (April 5, 1879): 265–67; "Midsummer Nights among City Tenements," *Harper's Weekly* 27 (June 30, 1883): cover, 410.

37. "The Stewart Tenement Houses," *New York Daily Tribune* (December 3, 1866): 2; Landau, *Edward T. and William A. Potter*, 393–94.

38. "The Stewart Tenement Houses": 2.

39. "Evils of the 'Deep-Lot,'" editorial, *New York Times* (January 1, 1877): 4; Potter, "Urban Housing in New York. I": 90–92; E. T. Potter, "Urban Housing. III," *American Architect and Building News* 3 (May 18, 1878): 171–72; "New York Yards. I," *American Architect and Building News* 5 (May 24, 1879): 163–64; "New York Yards. II," *American Architect and Building News* 5 (May 31, 1879): 173–74; "Urban Housing. V," *American Architect and Building News* 6 (September 27, 1879): 98–99; Landau, *Edward T. and William A. Potter*, 390–409.

40. Potter, "Urban Housing in New York. I": 90–92.

41. Frederick Law Olmsted, "The Future of New York," *New York Daily Tribune* (December 28, 1879): 5.

42. W., "The Tenement House Problem," *American Architect and Building News* 5 (March 15, 1879): 85–86; George W. Dresser, "Plan for

a Colony of Tenements," *Plumber and Sanitary Engineer* 2 (April 1879): 124; Stokes, "Appendix," in Ford, *Slums and Housing*, vol. 2: 872, 881, plate 4; Sarah Bradford Landau, *George B. Post, Architect: Picturesque Designer and Determined Realist*, Sources of American Architecture, ed. Robert A. M. Stern (New York: Monacelli Press, 1998), 38–39.

43. Nelson L. Derby, "A Model Tenement House, a Paper Read before the Committee of the State Charities' Aid Association, by Nelson L. Derby, F.A.I.A., December 8, 1876," *American Architect and Building News* 2 (January 20, 1877): 19–21; Plunz, *A History of Housing in New York City*, 28–29.

44. "Improved Homes for Workingmen," *Plumber and Sanitary Engineer* 2 (December 1878): 1, 32. Also see Veiller, "Tenement House Reform in New York City, 1834–1900," in De Forest and Veiller, eds., *The Tenement House Problem*, vol. 1: 100–102.

45. W., "Model Tenement Competition," *American Architect and Building News* 4 (December 21, 1878): 208.

46. "Crime and Disease in Tenements," editorial, *New York Times* (February 24, 1879): 4; "The Main Source of Crime: Condemning the Tenement-House System," *New York Times* (February 24, 1879): 5; Harvey O'Connor, *The Astors* (New York: Alfred A. Knopf, 1941), 167–68; Paul R. Baker, *Richard Morris Hunt* (Cambridge, Mass.: MIT Press, 1980), 262.

47. "Report of the Committee," *Plumber and Sanitary Engineer* 2 (March 1879): 90; "Model House Competition: Prize Plans," *Plumber and Sanitary Engineer* 2 (March 1879): 103–6, (April 1879): 131–32, (May 1879): 158–59, (June 1, 1879): 180, (June 15, 1879): 212, and (July 1, 1879): 230. Also see Editorial, *American Architect and Building News* 5 (February 22, 1879): 57–58; B.W., "Correspondence," *American Architect and Building News* 5 (February 22, 1879): 61–62; B.W., "The Tenement House Competition," *American Architect and Building News* 5 (March 1, 1879): 69; "The Tenement-House Competition," *New York Daily Tribune* (March 7, 1879): 1; "Criticism of the Prize Plans: Opinions of Richard M. Hunt, E.D.E. Raht and Others Upon the New Designs for Homes for the Poor," *New York Daily Tribune* (March 7, 1879): 1; "Prize Tenements," editorial, *New York Times* (March 16, 1879): 6; "Prize Designs for a Tenement-House," *American Architect and Building News* 5 (March 22, 1879): 93, plates; "Three Plans for Tenement Houses Recently Submitted in the 'Plumber's' Competition," *American Architect and Building News* 5 (May 17, 1879): 156, plates; "The Tenement-House Problem—II," *American Architect and Building News* 8 (July 31, 1880): 53–54; "Apartment-House—III," *American Architect and Building News* 31 (January 10, 1891): 20–23; Marcus T. Reynolds, *The Housing of the Poor in American Cities* (Baltimore: American Economic Association, 1893), 68, 70; Veiller, "Tenement House Reform in New York City, 1834–1900," in De Forest and Veiller, eds., *The Tenement House Problem*, vol. 1: 101; Ford, *Slums and Housing*, vol. 1: 162–63, vol. 2: figs. 116A–C; Stokes, "Appendix," in Ford, *Slums and Housing*, vol. 2: 872, 880–81, 908–10, plates 3C–G; Jackson, *A Place Called Home*, 45–58; Cromley, *Alone Together*, 53–54; Plunz, *A History of Housing in New York City*, 24–27.

48. Veiller, "Tenement House Reform in New York City, 1834–1900," in De Forest and Veiller, eds., *The Tenement House Problem*, vol. 1: 101.

49. Veiller, "Tenement House Reform in New York City, 1834–1900," in De Forest and Veiller, eds., *The Tenement House Problem*, vol. 1: 101.

50. "Report of the Committee": 90.

51. "Prize Tenements": 6.

52. "Criticism of the Prize Plans: Opinions of Richard M. Hunt, E.D.E. Raht and Others Upon the New Designs for Homes for the Poor": 1.

53. W., "Correspondence. The Tenement-House Problem," *American Architect and Building News* 5 (March 15, 1879): 85–86; Editorial, *American Architect and Building News* 6 (July 19, 1879): 18; Veiller, "Tenement House Reform in New York City, 1834–1900," in De Forest and Veiller, eds., *The Tenement House Problem*, vol. 1: 99–100; Ford, *Slums and Housing*, vol. 1: 164–65; Plunz, *A History of Housing in New York City*, 24.

54. "Out Among the Builders," *Real Estate Record and Builders' Guide* 39 (March 26, 1887): 406–7; Veiller, "Tenement House Reform in New York City, 1834–1900," in De Forest and Veiller, eds., *The Tenement House Problem*, vol. 1: 102–4.

55. Montgomery Schuyler, "The Growth of the City," *New York Times* (July 2, 1883): 4.

56. "Tenement-Houses," editorial, *New York Times* (July 5, 1883): 4.

57. "A Model Tenement," *Real Estate Record and Builders' Guide* 24 (December 6, 1879): 981–82.

58. "New Apartment Houses," *American Architect and Building News* 5 (May 31, 1879): 175; "A Model Tenement House," *New York Evening Post* (August 5, 1879): 4; Editorial, *American Architect and Building News* 6 (August 16, 1879): 49; William P. Miller, *The Tenement House Committee and the Open Stair Tenements* (New York: American Institute of Architects, 1912); Jackson, *A Place Called Home*, 60–61; Plunz, *A History of Housing in New York City*, 96–97.

59. "A Model Tenement House": 4.

60. "New Apartment Houses": 175.

61. "Tenement House for Edward N. & James Murphy," *Building* 3 (January 1885): 48, plate.

62. "Tenement House, Northwest Corner Hubert and Greenwich Streets, New York, for W. S. Livingston," *Building* 6 (April 30, 1887): 161, plate.

63. "Buildings Projected," *Real Estate Record and Builders' Guide* 38 (July 24, 1886): 964; "Buildings Projected," *Real Estate Record and Builders' Guide* 38 (August 7, 1886): 1021; "Buildings Projected," *Real Estate Record and Builders' Guide* 39 (March 19, 1887): 387; "Buildings Projected," *Real Estate Record and Builders' Guide* 41 (March 24, 1888): 380; Baker, *Richard Morris Hunt*, 509 (n. 24), 542, 545–46.

64. "The Costly and Substantial Buildings of 1886," *Real Estate Record and Builders' Guide* 39 (January 1, 1887): 6–8; "Model Tenements," *Harper's Weekly* 32 (January 14, 1888): 31–32; Tenement House Building Company, *The Tenement Houses of New York City* (New York: Albert B. King Press, 1891); Reynolds, *The Housing of the Poor in American Cities*, 93–95, 97; Elgin R. L. Gould, *The Housing of the Working People: Eighth Special Report of the Commissioner of Labor* (Washington, D.C.: GPO, 1895), 196–200; Ford, *Slums and Housing*, vol. 1: 176–78, vol. 2: figs. 117A–B; Stokes, "Appendix," in Ford, *Slums and Housing*, vol. 2: 883, plate 6B; Jackson, *A Place Called Home*, 70–71; Plunz, *A History of Housing in New York City*, 96–97.

65. "The Costly and Substantial Buildings of 1886": 6–8.

66. Quoted in "The Tenement-House Question," editorial, *New York Daily Tribune* (February 6, 1884): 4.

67. "Tenement House Reform," *Real Estate Record and Builders' Guide* 23 (May 3, 1879): 349.

68. "Buildings Projected," *Real Estate Record and Builders' Guide* 23 (June 28, 1879): 537; Landau, *Edward T. and William A. Potter*, 427–28, 475, fig. 296.

69. "Model Tenement-House. Mr. G. W. DaCunha, Architect, New York City," *American Architect and Building News* 7 (April 17, 1880): 166; "Model Tenement Houses," *Carpentry and Building* 2 (October 1880): 191; "Model Tenement Houses," reprinted from *New York Evening Post* in *Building* 5 (October 2, 1886): 162; Elizabeth Bisland, "Co-operative Housekeeping in Tenements," *The Cosmopolitan* 8 (November 1889): 35–42; Reynolds, *The Housing of the Poor in American Cities*, 92; Ford, *Slums and Housing*, vol. 1: figs. 38A–B, vol. 2: fig. 116D; Stokes, "Appendix," in Ford, *Slums and Housing*, vol. 2: 882, plate 5H; Jackson, *A Place Called Home*, 59–61; Landau, *Edward T. and William A. Potter*, 399–400; Plunz, *A History of Housing in New York City*, 94–96; William Alex, *Calvert Vaux: Architect & Planner* (New York: Ink, 1994), 210–13; Francis R. Kowsky, *Country, Park and City: The Architecture and Life of Calvert Vaux* (New York: Oxford University Press, 1998), 268–71.

70. "Conveyances," *Real Estate Record and Builders' Guide* 38 (August 7, 1886): 1009; "Buildings Projected," *Real Estate Record and Builders' Guide* 38 (September 4, 1886): 1115; "Model Tenement Houses," reprinted from *New York Evening Post* in *Building*: 162.

71. H. W. Fabian, "Evolution of the New York Dwelling-House," *Building* 5 (August 14, 1886): 81–82, plates.

72. "Plans for Apartment-Houses. Mr. E. T. Potter, Architect, New York, N.Y.," *American Architect and Building News* 23 (May 5, 1888): 210, plate; Landau, *Edward T. and William A. Potter*, 400–408, figs. 272–73; Plunz, *A History of Housing in New York City*, 29–31.

73. "Healthful Homes for New York's Working Classes," *Real Estate Record and Builders' Guide* 39 (January 22, 1887): 104.

74. Riis, *How the Other Half Lives*. Also see Jacob A. Riis, "The Clearing of Mulberry Bend," *Review of Reviews* 12 (August 1895): 172–78; Jackson, *A Place Called Home*, 92–94.

75. Alfred T. White, quoted in Jacob A. Riis, *The Making of an American* (New York: Macmillan, 1902), 248, and Jackson, *A Place Called Home*, 92.

76. Riis, *The Making of an American*, 248, quoted in Jackson, *A Place Called Home*, 92.

77. Jacob A. Riis, "How the Other Half Lives," *Scribner's Magazine* 6 (December 1889): 643–62.

78. Jackson, *A Place Called Home*, 92–93.

79. Riis, *How the Other Half Lives*, 295–96, quoted in Jackson, *A Place Called Home*, 94.

80. McCabe, *Lights and Shadows of New York Life*, 304.

81. "Family-Houses for People of Small Incomes," *New York Times* (October 19, 1866): 4. Also see Cromley, *Alone Together*, 6.

82. Browne, *The Great Metropolis*, 205. Also see Louise E. Furniss, "New York Boarding-Houses," *Appletons' Journal* 5 (March 1871): 259–61; McCabe, *Lights and Shadows of New York Life*, 502–7.

83. Browne, *The Great Metropolis*, 391. Also see "How We Live," *New York Times* (November 22, 1873): 4; "Life in Hotels," *New York Times* (October 31, 1875): 5; "Family Hotels," *New York Times* (December 29, 1875): 5; "Apartment Hotels," *Real Estate Record and Builders' Guide* 19 (January 20, 1877): 42.

84. "French Apartment Houses," *New York Times* (April 16, 1871): 3; "The 'Flats' of the Future," *New York World* (October 8, 1871): 3; Lewis Leeds, "Parisian 'Flats,'" *Appletons' Journal* 6 (November 18, 1871): 561–62; Richardson, "The New Homes of New York": 68–69; "Obituary: David Henry Haight," *New York Daily Tribune* (May 1, 1876): 5; "Obituary Notes: David Henry Haight," *New York Times* (May 1, 1876): 4; "The Problem of Living in New York": 918–24; Stokes, *The Iconography of Manhattan Island*, vol. 5: 1795; Charles Lockwood, *Bricks and Brownstone: The New York Row House, 1783–1929, an Architectural and Social History* (New York: McGraw-Hill, 1972), 132, 135–37, 204–5; Baker, *Richard Morris Hunt*, 207; Epstein, "Multifamily Dwellings and the Search for Respectability: Origins of the New York Apartment House": 37–38; Stern, Gilmartin, and Massengale, *New York 1900*, 280; Sarah Bradford Landau, "Richard Morris Hunt: Architectural Innovator and Father of a 'Distinctive' American School," in Susan Stein, ed., *The Architecture of Richard Morris Hunt* (Chicago and London: University of Chicago Press, 1986), 76 (n. 48); Cromley, *Alone Together*, 74, 125; Plunz, *A History of Housing in New York City*, 66; Elizabeth Hawes, *New York, New York: How the Apartment House Transformed the Life of the City (1869–1930)* (New York: Alfred A. Knopf, 1993), 35–38.

85. Richardson, "The New Homes of New York": 68.

86. Richardson, "The New Homes of New York": 69.

87. "The 'Flats' of the Future": 3.

88. Richardson, "The New Homes of New York": 69.

89. "The Problem of Living in New York": 918–24.

90. Richardson, "The New Homes of New York": 69; Kramer, "The Domestic Architecture of Detlef Lienau: A Conservative Victorian": 211–16; Landau, "Richard Morris Hunt: Architectural Innovator and Father of a 'Distinctive' American School," in Stein, ed., *The Architecture of Richard Morris Hunt*, 63; Hawes, *New York, New York*, 45.

91. Richardson, "The New Homes of New York": 69.

92. Leeds, "Parisian 'Flats'": 561–62; Montgomery Schuyler, "Buildings on Broadway," *New York World* (September 24, 1871): 3; Arthur Gilman, "Family Hotels," letter to the editor, *New York Times* (November 19, 1871): 5; Montgomery Schuyler, "Improvements in New York Architecture," *New York World* (November 26, 1871): 3; O. B. Bunce, "The City of the Future," *Appletons' Journal* 7 (February 10, 1872): 156–58; Richardson, "The New Homes of New York": 69; "Model Building," *Real Estate Record and Builders' Guide* 18 (September 30, 1875): 724; "Apartment Hotels," *Real Estate Record and Builders' Guide* 19 (January 20, 1877): 42; Editorial, *American Architect and Building News* 3 (January 26, 1878): 25; Montgomery Schuyler, "The Works of the Late Richard M. Hunt," *Architectural Record* 5 (October–December 1895): 97–180; Brown, *Book of*

Old New-York*, 323; Baker, *Richard Morris Hunt*, 208–10, 212–13; Epstein, "Multifamily Dwellings and the Search for Respectability: Origins of the New York Apartment House": 38; Paul R. Baker, "Richard Morris Hunt: An Introduction," in Stein, ed., *The Architecture of Richard Morris Hunt*, 3–12; Landau, "Richard Morris Hunt: Architectural Innovator and Father of a 'Distinctive' American School," in Stein, ed., *The Architecture of Richard Morris Hunt*, 64–66; Cromley, *Alone Together*, 20, 64, 69, 74; David W. Dunlap, *On Broadway: A Journey Uptown Over Time* (New York: Rizzoli International Publications, 1990), 134–36, 138; Plunz, *A History of Housing in New York City*, 68–69; Hawes, *New York, New York*, 35–36.

93. McCabe, *Lights and Shadows of New York Life*, 128, quoted in Dunlap, *On Broadway*, 134.

94. "Death of Mr. Paran Stevens," *New York Times* (April 26, 1872): 1.

95. Schuyler, "Buildings on Broadway": 3.

96. Douglass Shand-Tucci, *Built in Boston: City and Suburb 1800–1950* (Amherst, Mass.: University of Massachusetts Press, 1978), 101–2.

97. Richardson, "The New Homes of New York": 69.

98. Bunce, "The City of the Future": 156–58.

99. Leeds, "Parisian 'Flats'": 562.

100. Schuyler, "Buildings on Broadway": 3.

101. Schuyler, "Improvements in New York Architecture": 3.

102. Schuyler, "Buildings on Broadway": 3.

103. Schuyler, "The Works of the Late Richard M. Hunt": 111.

104. "New York Daguerreotyped," *Putnam's Magazine* 1 (April 1853): 353–68.

105. "The Fifth Avenue Hotel, New York," *Harper's Weekly* 3 (October 1, 1859): 632–34; Browne, *The Great Metropolis*, 395–96; McCabe, *Lights and Shadows of New York Life*, 308–12; Montgomery Schuyler, "Architectural Aberrations: The New Hoffman House," *Architectural Record* 24 (October 1908): 303–5; James L. Ford, "Famous New York Hotels of the 'Seventies,'" in *Valentine's Manual of Old New York (1924)*, ed. Henry Collins Brown (New York: Valentine's Manual Inc., 1923), 153–73; Henry Collins Brown, *Fifth Avenue: Old and New, 1824–1924* (New York: The Fifth Avenue Association, 1924), 53–55, 59, 62, 64–65; Frederick S. Lightfoot, ed., *Nineteenth-Century New York in Rare Photographic Views* (New York: Dover, 1981), fig. 79.

106. Henry Irving Dodge, quoted in *Valentine's Manual of Old New York (1924)*, 84.

107. "Another Uptown Hotel," *New York Daily Tribune* (November 18, 1859): 7; Schuyler, "Architectural Aberrations: The New Hoffman House": 303–5; Ford, "Famous New York Hotels of the 'Seventies,'" in *Valentine's Manual of Old New York (1924)*, 162; Stokes, *The Iconography of Manhattan Island*, vol. 5: 1882; Boyer, *Manhattan Manners*, 56–57; Dunlap, *On Broadway*, 132–33.

108. Ford, "Famous New York Hotels of the 'Seventies,'" in *Valentine's Manual of Old New York (1924)*, 162–63. Also see "Hotel Life in New York," *New York Times* (April 15, 1883): 5; Schuyler, "Architectural Aberrations: The New Hoffman House": 303–5; Mary Ann Clegg Smith, "The Commercial Architecture of John Butler Snook" (Ph.D. diss., Pennsylvania State University, 1974): 74–75; Boyer, *Manhattan Manners*, 56–57; Dunlap, *On Broadway*, 133.

109. Schuyler, "Buildings on Broadway": 3.

110. Schuyler, "Buildings on Broadway": 3; Ford, "Famous New York Hotels of the 'Seventies,'" in *Valentine's Manual of Old New York (1924)*, 162, 164; Landmarks Preservation Commission of the City of New York, LP-1041 (September 11, 1979); White and Willensky, *AIA Guide* (1988), 193; Dunlap, *On Broadway*, 142; Barbaralee Diamonstein, *The Landmarks of New York II* (New York: Harry N. Abrams, 1993), 151; Jeff Hirsh, *Manhattan Hotels: 1880–1920* (Dover, N.H.: Arcadia Publishing, 1997), 72.

111. Schuyler, "Buildings on Broadway": 3.

112. "Gilsey's New Hotel," *Real Estate Record and Builders' Guide* 6 (November 26, 1870): 1; "Metropolitan Improvements," *New York Evening Post* (March 10, 1871): 1; "Opening of the Gilsey House," *New York Times* (April 16, 1871): 6; Schuyler, "Buildings on Broadway": 3; "Hotel Life in New York": 5; Moses King, *King's Handbook of New York* (Boston: Moses King, 1893), 226; Ford, "Famous New York Hotels of the

'Seventies,'" in *Valentine's Manual of Old New York (1924)*, 156, 164; Landmarks Preservation Commission of the City of New York, LP-1039 (September 11, 1979); Boyer, *Manhattan Manners*, 32; White and Willensky, *AIA Guide* (1988), 193; Cromley, *Alone Together*, 18; Dunlap, *On Broadway*, 133–34, 136–37, 139; Christopher Gray, "Streetscapes: The 1871 Gilsey House," *New York Times* (December 29, 1991), X: 5; Diamonstein, *The Landmarks of New York II*, 156.

113. Schuyler, "Buildings on Broadway": 3.

114. Elias S. Higgins, quoted in Fremont Rider, ed., *Rider's New York City*, 2nd ed. (New York: Henry Holt & Co., 1923), 204. Also see "A Monster Hotel," *New York Times* (August 26, 1870): 5; McCabe, *Lights and Shadows of New York Life*, 126, 308; King, *King's Handbook of New York* (1893), 235–36; William Hutchins, "New York Hotels: The Hotels of the Past. I," *Architectural Record* 12 (October 1902): 459–71; Ford, "Famous New York Hotels of the 'Seventies,'" in *Valentine's Manual of Old New York (1924)*, 157, 170; Lightfoot, ed., *Nineteenth-Century New York in Rare Photographic Views*, fig. 59; White and Willensky, *AIA Guide* (1988), 866–67; Cromley, *Alone Together*, 18–20; Dunlap, *On Broadway*, 93, 98–99; Hirsh, *Manhattan Hotels: 1880–1920*, 4, 102.

115. Robert Higginson Fuller, *Jubilee Jim: The Life of Colonel James Fisk, Jr.* (New York: Macmillan, 1928), 537–64; W. A. Swanberg, *Jim Fisk: The Career of an Improbable Rascal* (New York: Charles Scribner's Sons, 1959), 271–78.

116. "Boarding Out," *Harper's Weekly* 1 (March 7, 1857): 146.

117. Browne, *The Great Metropolis*, 548–53; "Mr. Stewart's Hotel for Working-People," *Appletons' Journal* 1 (July 3, 1869): 417–19; Cromley, *Alone Together*, 112.

118. "Mr. Stewart's Hotel for Working-People": 417–19. Also see "An Architectural Ramble," *Real Estate Record and Builders' Guide* 6 (September 17, 1870): 1–2; "Metropolitan Improvements": 1; "The Busy Builders," *New York Times* (September 3, 1871): 6; "A. T. Stewart as a Real Estate Operator," *Real Estate Record and Builders' Guide* 17 (April 1, 1876): 237; "Notes and Clippings," *American Architect and Building News* 1 (April 8, 1876): 120; H.W.C., "Alexander T. Stewart," letter to the editor, *New York Daily Tribune* (April 22, 1876): 2; "The Estate of A. T. Stewart," *Real Estate Record and Builders' Guide* 17 (April 22, 1876): 299; Peter B. Wight, "A Millionaire's Architectural Investment," *American Architect and Building News* 1 (May 6, 1876): 147–49; "Stewart's Working-Women's Hotel," *American Architect and Building News* 2 (December 1, 1877): 386–87; "The Working Women's Hotel," *New York Times* (March 24, 1878): 5; "Opening the Women's Hotel," *New York Daily Tribune* (March 25, 1878): 5; "The Women's Hotel Opened," *New York Daily Tribune* (April 3, 1878): 5; "The Women's Hotel Open," *New York Times* (April 3, 1878): 1–2; "The Women's Home," *Puck* 3 (April 3, 1878): 2; "A. T. Stewart's Women's Home, the True Inwardness Thereof," cartoon, *Puck* 3 (April 3, 1878): 8–9; T., "The Stewart Hotel," letter to the editor, *New York Daily Tribune* (April 6, 1878): 3; A Teacher, "The Women's Hotel," letter to the editor, *New York Times* (April 26, 1878): 3; "The Stewart Hotel," *New York Daily Tribune* (May 27, 1878): 4; Anna C. Brackett, "The Women's Hotel: Causes of Its Failure," letter to the editor, *New York Daily Tribune* (May 28, 1878): 5; "Judge Hilton and the Ladies," *New York Times* (June 2, 1878): 12; "A Protest by Women," *New York Daily Tribune* (June 5, 1878): 5; "Scolding Judge Hilton," *New York Times* (June 5, 1878): 5; "A Woman's Hotel No More," *New York Times* (June 9, 1878): 2; "Change of the Women's Hotel: Transforming It in Name and Purpose," *New York Daily Tribune* (June 10, 1878): 8; Calhoun, "Common Sense About the Women's Hotel," letter to the editor, *New York Times* (June 11, 1878): 8; "Spinsters' Apartment-House," *Building* 6 (May 14, 1887): 177; King, *King's Handbook of New York* (1893), 229–30; Deborah S. Gardner, "The Architecture of Commercial Capitalism: John Kellum and the Development of New York, 1840–1875" (Ph.D. diss., Columbia University, 1979): 230–60; Lightfoot, ed., *Nineteenth-Century New York in Rare Photographic Views*, fig. 106; Boyer, *Manhattan Manners*, 59, 61; Cromley, *Alone Together*, 112–14; James Trager, *Park Avenue: Street of Dreams* (New York: Atheneum, 1990), 39–40; Hirsh, *Manhattan Hotels: 1880–1920*, 63–65.

119. "Stewart's Working-Women's Hotel": 386–87.

120. Wight, "A Millionaire's Architectural Investment": 149.

121. "Stewart's Working-Women's Hotel": 386.

122. "The Women's Home," *Puck*: 2, quoted in Trager, *Park Avenue*, 40.

123. "The Workmanship on the Buckingham Hotel," *Real Estate Record and Builders' Guide* 17 (January 1, 1876): 14; "The Buckingham—Additional Notes," *Real Estate Record and Builders' Guide* 17 (January 29, 1876): 83–84; King, *King's Handbook of New York* (1893), 226; Brown, *Fifth Avenue: Old and New, 1824–1924*, 63, 94; Boyer, *Manhattan Manners*, 60–61.

124. "Buildings Projected," *Real Estate Record and Builders' Guide* 28 (July 23, 1881): 757; Montgomery Schuyler, "Henry Janeway Hardenbergh," *Architectural Record* 6 (January–March 1897): 335–75; White and Willensky, *AIA Guide* (1988), 126; Hirsh, *Manhattan Hotels: 1880–1920*, 98.

125. "A New Hotel," *Real Estate Record and Builders' Guide* 33 (March 22, 1884): 285–86; "Murray Hill Hotel, Park Avenue, New York, N.Y. Mr. Stephen D. Hatch, Architect, New York, N.Y.," *American Architect and Building News* 15 (May 31, 1884): 260, plate; "The New Murray Hill Hotel," *New York Times* (October 20, 1884): 2; King, *King's Handbook of New York* (1893), 230; Trager, *Park Avenue*, 40–42; Hirsh, *Manhattan Hotels: 1880–1920*, 28–29.

126. "Buildings Projected," *Real Estate Record and Builders' Guide* 9 (January 27, 1872): 44; King, *King's Handbook of New York* (1893), 231–32; "Grand Union Hotel to Close on May 2," *New York Times* (April 22, 1914): 8; Trager, *Park Avenue*, 42–43; Hirsh, *Manhattan Hotels: 1880–1920*, 26.

127. "A New Hotel": 285–86.

128. "Out Among the Builders," *Real Estate Record and Builders' Guide* 30 (December 23, 1882): 140; *Prospectus of the Fifth Avenue Plaza Apartments* (New York, 1883); "Out Among the Builders," *Real Estate Record and Builders' Guide* 31 (January 30, 1883): 28; "The Fifth Avenue Plaza Apartments," *Real Estate Record and Builders' Guide* 31 (March 10, 1883): 93–94; "Sale of Fifth-Avenue Plaza Lots," *New York Times* (October 30, 1883): 8; "Out Among the Builders," *Real Estate Record and Builders' Guide* 32 (November 3, 1883): 858; "A Grand Family Hotel," *New York Times* (November 4, 1883): 5; "Carl Pfeiffer on the Plaza Apartment House," *Real Estate Record and Builders' Guide* 32 (November 10, 1883): 880; Phyfe & Campbell, "A Correction," letter to the editor, *Real Estate Record and Builders' Guide* 32 (November 10, 1883): 883; "The 'Plaza' Apartment-House, New York, N.Y. Mr. Carl Pfeiffer, Architect, New York, N.Y.," *American Architect and Building News* 16 (July 5, 1884): 6, plates; Carl Pfeiffer, "The Plaza Hotel," letter to the editor, *Real Estate Record and Builders' Guide* 37 (February 27, 1886): 251; Carl Pfeiffer, "Not the Architect of the Plaza Apartment-House," letter to the editor, *American Architect and Building News* 19 (March 6, 1886): 119; "Prospect of a New Hotel," *New York Times* (February 28, 1888): 8; "Sale of the Plaza Hotel," *New York Times* (September 19, 1888): 3; "Must Be Reconstructed," *New York Times* (November 24, 1888): 8; "Building in Fifth Avenue," *Real Estate Record and Builders' Guide* 44 (August 24, 1889): 1159–60; "Apartment-Houses—IV," *American Architect and Building News* 31 (January 17, 1891): 37–39; King, *King's Handbook of New York* (1893), 222–23; Mary Black, *Old New York in Early Photographs* (New York: Dover, 1973), 180; Edward B. Watson, *New York Then and Now* (New York: Dover, 1976), 66; Landau, *Edward T. and William A Potter*, 428–29; Leland Roth, *The Architecture of McKim, Mead & White, 1870–1920: A Building List* (New York and London: Garland, 1978), nos. 665–66; Christopher Gray, "A Street Most Grand," *Avenue* (June–August 1983): 49, 51–57; Mardges Bacon, *Ernest Flagg: Beaux-Arts Architect and Urban Reformer* (New York: Architectural History Foundation; Cambridge, Mass.: MIT Press, 1986), 14–15; Hirsh, *Manhattan Hotels: 1880–1920*, 9, 12.

129. "A Revolution in Living," editorial, *New York Times* (June 3, 1878): 4.

130. Portions of this section were first developed in Robert A. M. Stern, "With Rhetoric: The New York Apartment House," *Via* 4 (1980): 78–111.

131. Sigfried Giedion, *Space, Time and Architecture* (Cambridge, Mass.: Harvard University Press, 1941), 493–95; David H. Pinckney, *Napoleon III and the Rebuilding of Paris* (Princeton, N.J.: Princeton University Press, 1958), 8–9; David P. Jordan, *Transforming Paris: The Life and Labors of Baron Haussmann* (New York: Free Press, 1995), 290–96.

132. "New York Daguerreotyped—Private Residences," *Putnam's Magazine* 3 (March 1854): 233.

133. Calvert Vaux, "Parisian Buildings for City Residents," *Crayon* 4 (July 1857): 218, reprinted in *Harper's Weekly* 1 (December 19, 1857): 809–10. Also see John David Sigle, "Calvert Vaux: An American Architect" (master's thesis, University of Virginia, 1967): 24–25, plates 13–14; Landau, "Richard Morris Hunt: Architectural Innovator and Father of a 'Distinctive' American School," in Stein, ed., *The Architecture of Richard Morris Hunt*, 63; Cromley, *Alone Together*, 28–31; Alex, *Calvert Vaux*, 92; Kowsky, *Country, Park and City*, 93–95.

134. Vaux, "Parisian Buildings for City Residents": 218.

135. Peter B. Wight, "Apartment Houses Practically Considered," *Putnam's Magazine* 16 (September 1870): 306–13.

136. "A Revolution in Living": 4.

137. Edith Wharton, *The Age of Innocence* (New York: D. Appleton & Co., 1920), 28–29. Also see Stern, Gilmartin, and Massengale, *New York 1900*, 279.

138. James McCabe Jr., *Paris by Sunlight and Gaslight* (Philadelphia: National Publishing, 1869), 653.

139. "Central Park," *Scribner's Monthly* 6 (September 1873): 523–39.

140. Sarah Gilman Young, *European Modes of Living; or the Question of Apartment Houses* (New York: Putnam, 1881), 26–27. Also see S. G. Young, "Foreign Modes of Living," *Galaxy* 14 (October 1872): 474–82; Charles F. Wingate, "Apartment Houses," *Building* 5 (September 25, 1886): 152–53; Plunz, *A History of Housing in New York City*, 62.

141. Editorial, *New York Times* (July 2, 1883): 4.

142. Everett N. Blanke, "The Cliff-Dwellers of New York," *The Cosmopolitan* 15 (July 1893): 354–62.

143. "French Houses," *Real Estate Record and Builders' Guide* 1 (August 1, 1868): 1.

144. Wight, "Apartment Houses Practically Considered": 306–13. Also see César Daly, *L'Architecture privée au XIX siècle sous Napoléon III* (Paris: A. Morel, 1864).

145. Richardson, "The New Homes of New York": 67. Also see Baker, *Richard Morris Hunt*, 499 (n. 2); Landau, "Richard Morris Hunt: Architectural Innovator and Father of a 'Distinctive' American School," in Stein, ed., *The Architecture of Richard Morris Hunt*, 61; Cromley, *Alone Together*, 63, 65, 69.

146. Leeds, "Parisian 'Flats'": 561–62. Also see Cromley, *Alone Together*, 63, 65.

147. "Notes and Comment," *Carpentry and Building* 3 (December 1881): 233; Landau, "Richard Morris Hunt: Architectural Innovator and Father of a 'Distinctive' American School," in Stein, ed., *The Architecture of Richard Morris Hunt*, 75.

148. "Thomas Kilpatrick Dead," *New York Times* (November 24, 1902): 5. Also see "Death of Thomas Kilpatrick," *Real Estate Record and Builders' Guide* 70 (November 29, 1902): 808–9; Landau, "Richard Morris Hunt: Architectural Innovator and Father of a 'Distinctive' American School," in Stein, ed., *The Architecture of Richard Morris Hunt*, 61.

149. Schuyler, "The Works of the Late Richard M. Hunt": 99; Alan Burnham, "The New York Architecture of Richard Morris Hunt," *Journal of the Society of Architectural Historians* 11 (May 1952): 9–14; John A. Kouwenhoven, *The Columbia Historical Portrait of New York* (Garden City, N.Y.: Doubleday, 1953), 373; Mary Sayre Haverstock, "The Tenth Street Studio," *Art in America* 54 (September 1966): 48–57; Nathan B. Silver, *Lost New York* (Boston: Houghton Mifflin, 1967), 142; *Architecture and Society: Selected Essays of Henry Van Brunt*, ed. William A. Coles (Cambridge, Mass.: Harvard University Press, Belknap Press, 1969), 328–41; Baker, *Richard Morris Hunt*, 93–107; Baker, "Richard Morris Hunt: An Introduction," in Stein, ed., *The Architecture of Richard Morris Hunt*, 4–5; Landau, "Richard Morris Hunt: Architectural Innovator and Father of a 'Distinctive' American School," in Stein, ed., *The Architecture of Richard Morris Hunt*, 46, 49–50; Andrew Alpern, *Luxury Apartment Houses of Manhattan* (New York: Dover, 1992), 39–40; Hawes, *New York, New York*, 17–19; Annette Blaugrund, *The Tenth Street Studio Building*, exhibition catalogue (Southampton, N.Y.: Parish Art Museum, 1997); Christopher Gray, "Streetscapes/10th Street Studio Building," *New York Times* (May 25, 1997), IX: 5; Alastair Gordon, "America's First Art Marketplace," *East Hampton Star* (July 3, 1997), III: 13; Holland Cotter,

"How a Proto-SoHo Thrived in Old New York," *New York Times* (July 13, 1997), II: 35; "Evoking the World of Winslow Homer," *New York Times* (August 17, 1997), IX: 1.

150. Landau, "Richard Morris Hunt: Architectural Innovator and Father of a 'Distinctive' American School," in Stein, ed., *The Architecture of Richard Morris Hunt*, 49.

151. *Architecture and Society: Selected Essays of Henry Van Brunt*, 333.

152. "A New and Noble Project," *New York Evening Post* (March 27, 1879): 2; "A Home for the Artists," *New York Times* (May 2, 1879): 8; John Davis, "Our United Happy Family: Artists in the Sherwood Studio Building, 1880–1900," *Archives of American Art Journal* 36 (Nos. 3–4, 1996): 2–19; Christopher Gray, "Streetscapes/The 1880 Sherwood Studios, Once at 57th and Sixth," *New York Times* (August 9, 1998), XI: 7.

153. "Apartment Houses," *Real Estate Record and Builders' Guide* 3 (July 17, 1869): 1; "A Parisian House in New York," *New York Sun* (November 4, 1869): 3; "Houses on the European Plan," *Real Estate Record and Builders' Guide* 4 (November 6, 1869): 1; "Mr. Stuyvesant's Experiment," *Real Estate Record and Builders' Guide* 4 (November 13, 1869): 1; James M. MacGregor, *Annual Report of the Superintendent of Buildings for the Year 1869* (New York, 1870), 570; "Houses on the European Plan," *Real Estate Record and Builders' Guide* 5 (March 26, 1870): 3; Wight, "Apartment Houses Practically Considered": 306–13; Leeds, "Parisian 'Flats'": 561–62; "French Flats and Apartment Houses in New York," *Carpentry and Building* 3 (June 1881): 107–8; "Notes and Comment," *Carpentry and Building* 3 (December 1881): 233–34; Blanke, "The Cliff-Dwellers of New York": 354–62; Charles Israels, "New York Apartment Houses," *Architectural Record* 11 (July 1901): 476–508; "The Apartment Houses of New York, with an Example from Berlin in Comparison," *Real Estate Record and Builders' Guide* 85 (March 26, 1910): 644–46; Stokes, *The Iconography of Manhattan Island*, vol. 5: 1333; R. W. Sexton, *American Apartment Houses, Hotels and Apartment Hotels of Today* (New York: Architectural Book Publishing Co., 1929), 3; Stokes, "Appendix," in Ford, *Slums and Housing*, 869; Lloyd Morris, *Incredible New York* (New York: Bonanza Books, 1951), 109; Burnham, "The New York Architecture of Richard Morris Hunt": 9–14; Sigle, "Calvert Vaux": 25–26, plate 15; Andrew Alpern, *New York's Fabulous Luxury Apartments* (New York: McGraw-Hill, 1975; New York: Dover, 1987), 12–13; Jackson, *A Place Called Home*, 86; Charles Lockwood, *Manhattan Moves Uptown* (Boston: Houghton Mifflin, 1976), 294; David G. De Long, ed., *Historic American Buildings, New York*, 8 vols. (New York and London: Garland, 1979), vol. 8: 199, 204; Baker, *Richard Morris Hunt*, 204–8; Stern, "With Rhetoric": 80; Epstein, "Multifamily Dwellings and the Search for Respectability: Origins of the New York Apartment House": 35–36; Stern, Gilmartin, and Massengale, *New York 1900*, 280; Stephen Garmey, *Gramercy Park: An Illustrated History of a New York Neighborhood* (New York: Balsam Press, 1984), 146–47; Boyer, *Manhattan Manners*, 153–54; Landau, "Richard Morris Hunt: Architectural Innovator and Father of a 'Distinctive' American School," in Stein, ed., *The Architecture of Richard Morris Hunt*, 61–64; Cromley, *Alone Together*, 72–73, 79, 83, 87–88, 97–98, 107; Hawes, *New York, New York*, 5–7, 19–20, 22–23, 26–28; Andrew Alpern, *Historic Manhattan Apartment Houses* (New York: Dover, 1996), 3, 5.

154. MacGregor, *Annual Report of the Superintendent of Buildings for the Year 1869*, 570, quoted in Epstein, "Multifamily Dwellings and the Search for Respectability: Origins of the New York Apartment House": 35.

155. "Houses on the European Plan," (November 6, 1869): 1.

156. Epstein, "Multifamily Dwellings and the Search for Respectability: Origins of the New York Apartment House": 36.

157. "Mr. Stuyvesant's Experiment": 1.

158. Vaux, "Parisian Buildings for City Residents": 218.

159. "Apartment Houses," *Real Estate Record and Builders' Guide*: 1.

160. "Houses on the European Plan," (November 6, 1869): 1.

161. "Houses on the European Plan," (March 26, 1870): 3.

162. "Houses on the European Plan," (November 6, 1869): 1.

163. Landau, "Richard Morris Hunt: Architectural Innovator and Father of a 'Distinctive' American School," in Stein, ed., *The Architecture of Richard Morris Hunt*, 62.

164. Vaux, "Parisian Buildings for City Residents": 218.

165. Strong, diary entry dated January 3, 1871, in *The Diary of George Templeton Strong*, vol. 4: 339.

166. Constance Gray Harrison, *Recollections Grave and Gay* (New York: Charles Scribner's Sons, 1911), 281. Also see Martha J. Lamb and Mrs. Burton Harrison, *History of the City of New York* (New York: A. S. Barnes & Co., 1896); Hawes, *New York, New York*, 26.

167. W. C. Church, "Nebulae," *Galaxy* 14 (April 1872): 579–80. Also see Young, "Foreign Modes of Living": 474–82.

168. Richardson, "The New Homes of New York": 68.

169. "Design for an Apartment House, New York. Potter & Robertson," *New-York Sketch-Book of Architecture* 2 (April 1875): 1, plate 13; Landau, *Edward T. and William A. Potter*, 412–13, fig. 276.

170. "Attention, Builders!" *Real Estate Record and Builders' Guide* 27 (April 2, 1881): 299; Boyer, *Manhattan Manners*, 36.

171. "The Knickerbocker," *Real Estate Record and Builders' Guide* 17 (January 22, 1876): 66. Also see Hawes, *New York, New York*, 43.

172. "The Osborne," *Real Estate Record and Builders' Guide* 17 (June 3, 1876): 428; "The Osborne," *Real Estate Record and Builders' Guide* 18 (September 23, 1876): 704–5; "Model Buildings," *Real Estate Record and Builders' Guide* 18 (September 30, 1876): 724; Boyer, *Manhattan Manners*, 156–57; Hawes, *New York, New York*, 43.

173. "French Flats," *Real Estate Record and Builders' Guide* 14 (April 27, 1872): 1. Also see "Apartment Houses," *New York Daily Tribune* (July 31, 1875): 3; D.M.D., "Faults of Apartment Houses," letter to the editor, *New York Daily Tribune* (March 25, 1876): 4; "French Flats," *New York Times* (December 26, 1876): 2; "French Apartment Houses," *New York Daily Tribune* (January 7, 1878): 2; "Apartment-Houses," editorial, *New York Times* (June 6, 1878): 6.

174. "Apartment Houses," *Real Estate Record and Builders' Guide* 17 (April 1, 1876): 237–38.

175. "Apartment Buildings," *Real Estate Record and Builders' Guide* 18 (December 16, 1876): 924–25.

176. B.W., "Correspondence," *American Architect and Building News* 5 (January 11, 1879): 12–13.

177. "A Revolution in Living": 4.

178. Kramer, "The Domestic Architecture of Detlef Lienau: A Conservative Victorian": 207–11.

179. Kramer, "The Domestic Architecture of Detlef Lienau: A Conservative Victorian": 208.

180. "Correspondence," *American Architect and Building News* 1 (April 8, 1876): 118–19.

181. "Buildings Projected," *Real Estate Record and Builders' Guide* 31 (June 16, 1883): 437; "Buildings Projected," *Real Estate Record and Builders' Guide* 31 (June 30, 1883): 469; "Buildings Projected," *Real Estate Record and Builders' Guide* 35 (January 31, 1885): 119; "Buildings Projected," *Real Estate Record and Builders' Guide* 38 (July 3, 1886): 876; Landau, *George B. Post, Architect*, 64, 66, plates 17–18.

182. "Buildings Projected," *Real Estate Record and Builders' Guide* 37 (March 6, 1886): 307; Roth, *The Architecture of McKim, Mead & White, 1870–1920: A Building List*, 95; Christopher Gray, "Streetscapes: Wanaque Apartments," *New York Times* (June 11, 1989), X: 10, reprinted in Christopher Gray, *Changing New York: The Architectural Scene* (New York: Dover, 1992), 88.

183. "A Revolution in Living": 4.

184. B.W., "Correspondence," *American Architect and Building News* 5 (January 11, 1879): 12–13. Also see "'The Florence,'" *Real Estate Record and Builders' Guide* 21 (April 6, 1878): 287; Boyer, *Manhattan Manners*, 51, 157; Cromley, *Alone Together*, 102–3.

185. "'The Florence'": 287.

186. "The 'Bella' Apartment House," *Real Estate Record and Builders' Guide* 21 (March 23, 1878): 243; Boyer, *Manhattan Manners*, 157.

187. John Moran, "New York Studios. III," *Art Journal* 6 (January 1880): 1–4; Ik Marvel [Donald G. Mitchell], "From Lobby to Peak: On the Threshold," *Our Continent* 1 (February 15, 1882): 5; Ik Marvel [Donald G. Mitchell], "From Lobby to Peak: A Lobby," *Our Continent* 1 (February 22, 1882): 21; Ik Marvel [Donald G. Mitchell], "From Lobby to Peak: Halls," *Our Continent* 1 (March 1, 1882): 37; Ik Marvel [Donald G. Mitchell], "From Lobby to Peak: An Early Breakfast," *Our Continent* 1 (March 15, 1882): 69; Ik Marvel [Donald G. Mitchell], "From Lobby to Peak: Round About the Room," *Our Continent* 1 (March 22, 1882): 85; Ik Marvel [Donald G. Mitchell], "From Lobby to Peak: Round About—Again," *Our Continent* 1 (March 29, 1882): 101; Ik Marvel [Donald G. Mitchell], "From Lobby to Peak: Over the Mantel," *Our Continent* 1 (April 5, 1882): 117–18; Ik Marvel [Donald G. Mitchell], "From Lobby to Peak: In the Library," *Our Continent* 1 (April 12, 1882): 132; Ik Marvel [Donald G. Mitchell], "From Lobby to Peak: Between Rooms," *Our Continent* 1 (April 19, 1882): 148; Ik Marvel [Donald G. Mitchell], "From Lobby to Peak: A Library Corner," *Our Continent* 1 (May 3, 1882): 185; Ik Marvel [Donald G. Mitchell], "From Lobby to Peak: A Rolling Screen," *Our Continent* 1 (May 17, 1882): 217; G. W. Sheldon, *Artistic Houses: Being a Series of Interior Views of a Number of the Most Beautiful and Celebrated Homes in the United States, with a Description of the Art Treasures Contained Therein*, 2 vols. (New York: D. Appleton, 1883–84; New York: Benjamin Blom, 1971), vol. 1, part 1: 1–6; Charles de Kay, *The Art Work of Louis C. Tiffany* (privately published, 1914; Poughkeepsie, N.Y.: Apollo, 1987), 55–57, plates 56A–B; Edgar Kaufmann Jr., "At Home with Louis C. Tiffany," *Interiors* 117 (December 1957): 118–25, 183; Edgar J. Kaufmann Jr., letter to the editor, *Interiors* 117 (February 1958): 16; Robert Koch, *Louis C. Tiffany: Rebel in Glass* (New York: Crown, 1964), 17–19, 40–41; Arnold Lewis, James Turner, and Steven McQuillen, *The Opulent Interiors of the Gilded Age* (New York: Dover, 1987), plates 13–16; Tessa Paul, *The Art of Louis Comfort Tiffany* (New York: Exeter Books, 1987), 40–41.

188. Moran, "New York Studios. III": 1–4.

189. De Kay, *The Art Work of Louis C. Tiffany*, 55.

190. Sheldon, *Artistic Houses*, vol. 1, part 1: 1–6.

191. Ik Marvel [Mitchell], "From Lobby to Peak: Over the Mantel": 118.

192. "Buildings Projected," *Real Estate Record and Builders' Guide* 29 (April 22, 1882): 406; "Buildings Projected," *Real Estate Record and Builders' Guide* 31 (March 3, 1883): 142; Landmarks Preservation Commission of the City of New York, *Greenwich Village Historic District Designation Report* (New York, 1969), 75; White and Willensky, *AIA Guide* (1988), 119.

193. "A Home for Bachelors," *New York Times* (June 29, 1879): 5; "The Benedick," *Real Estate Record and Builders' Guide* 24 (September 20, 1879): 740; "Correspondence: The Building Transactions of the Past Year," *American Architect and Building News* 7 (February 7, 1880): 47–48; Gordon Hendricks, *The Life and Work of Winslow Homer* (New York: Harry N. Abrams, 1979), 168–69; Leland M. Roth, *McKim, Mead & White, Architects* (New York: Harper & Row, 1983), 50–51; Hawes, *New York, New York*, 46; Christopher Gray, "Streetscapes/The Benedick, 80 Washington Square East," *New York Times* (April 27, 1997), X: 7.

194. "Correspondence: The Building Transactions of the Past Year": 47–48.

195. "A Home for Bachelors": 5.

196. "Accommodations for Bachelors," *Real Estate Record and Builders' Guide* 31 (February 10, 1883): 57; King, *King's Handbook of New York* (1893), 286; Roth, *McKim, Mead & White, Architects*, 84; Christopher Gray, "Streetscapes/230 West 42d Street," *New York Times* (June 16, 1996), IX: 7.

197. "The Washington Apartments, 29 Washington Square West, New York City," *Building* 4 (January 23, 1886): 42, plate; *Greenwich Village Historic District*, 148.

198. "Buildings Projected," *Real Estate Record and Builders' Guide* 40 (October 8, 1887): 1276; White and Willensky, *AIA Guide* (1988), 119.

199. "Buildings Projected," *Real Estate Record and Builders' Guide* 41 (April 7, 1888): 448; *Greenwich Village Historic District*, 42; White and Willensky, *AIA Guide* (1988), 119.

200. "Buildings Projected," *Real Estate Record and Builders' Guide* 24 (August 2, 1879): 631; White and Willensky, *AIA Guide* (1988), 408; Christopher Gray, "Streetscapes: The Manhattan Apartment House," *New York Times* (August 14, 1988), X: 10; Alpern, *Historic Manhattan Apartment Houses*, 3–4.

201. "Up-town 'French-Flats,'" *Real Estate Record and Builders' Guide* 31 (June 16, 1883): 235–36. Also see "Buildings Projected," *Real Estate Record and Builders' Guide* 27 (January 22, 1881): 86; "Buildings Projected," *Real Estate Record and Builders' Guide* 29 (February 4, 1882): 114; "Buildings Projected," *Real Estate Record and Builders' Guide* 31 (June 9, 1883): 421.

202. "Apartment-Houses and Tenement-Houses," editorial, *American Architect and Building News* 3 (February 9, 1878): 45. Also see "What a Tenement House Is?" *American Architect and Building News* 2 (September 8, 1877): 290; Cromley, *Alone Together*, 5–6.

203. Cromley, *Alone Together*, 129.

204. Wingate, "Apartment Houses": 152–53.

205. Quoted in "The Apartment House from a New Point of View," *Real Estate Record and Builders' Guide* 31 (April 7, 1883): 136.

206. "Central Park Lots," *Real Estate Record and Builders' Guide* 18 (November 18, 1876): 851–52; "The March of Improvement," *Real Estate Record and Builders' Guide* 20 (September 5, 1877): 709–11; "The Bradley Apartment House," *Real Estate Record and Builders' Guide* 20 (October 6, 1877): 766–67; Gray, "A Street Most Grand": 49, 51–57; Boyer, *Manhattan Manners*, 158; Hawes, *New York, New York*, 46–47.

207. "The Bradley Apartment House": 766–67.

208. Warrington, "Correspondence," *American Architect and Building News* 3 (March 16, 1878): 94; "Mr. Peters' Apartment House Facing the Park," *Real Estate Record and Builders' Guide* 21 (June 29, 1878): 557; Boyer, *Manhattan Manners*, 157.

209. Richardson, "The New Homes of New York": 64, 72–74.

210. "Another First Class Improvement," *Real Estate Record and Builders' Guide* 33 (March 29, 1884): 315. Also see "Buildings Projected," *Real Estate Record and Builders' Guide* 25 (June 26, 1880): 608; "The Problem of Living in New York": 920–21; "In West Fifty-seventh Street," *Real Estate Record and Builders' Guide* 36 (September 12, 1885): 992–93; Bacon, *Ernest Flagg*, 11–12; Alpern, *Luxury Apartment Houses in Manhattan*, 17–18.

211. "The Problem of Living in New York": 920–21.

212. "The Hawthorne," *Real Estate Record and Builders' Guide* 31 (February 24, 1883): 72.

213. "Buildings Projected," *Real Estate Record and Builders' Guide* 31 (February 10, 1883): 93; *The Dalhousie, Elegant Apartment House*, leasing brochure (New York, 1884); "Fifty-seven Years of Progress in Apartment Building," *New York Herald Tribune* (June 29, 1941): 1–2; Stern, "With Rhetoric": 81; Stern, Gilmartin, and Massengale, *New York 1900*, 469 (n. 107).

214. Hawes, *New York, New York*, 54.

215. "Buildings Projected," *Real Estate Record and Builders' Guide* 29 (May 13, 1882): 495; "Two Notable First Class Apartment Mansions," *Real Estate Record and Builders' Guide* 30 (November 4–11, 1882): 61; Hubert, Pirsson & Co., letter to the editor, *Real Estate Record and Builders' Guide* 30 (November 11–18, 1882): 73; "A New Apartment House," *Real Estate Record and Builders' Guide* 31 (February 17, 1883): 63–64; Schuyler, "The Growth of the City": 4; Alpern, *New York's Fabulous Luxury Apartments*, 14–15; Bacon, *Ernest Flagg*, 12; White and Willensky, *AIA Guide* (1988), 194; Christopher Gray, "Streetscapes: 121 Madison Avenue," *New York Times* (January 13, 1991), X: 4; Alpern, *Luxury Apartment Houses in Manhattan*, 17, 20; Sarah Bradford Landau and Carl W. Condit, *Rise of the New York Skyscraper, 1865–1913* (New Haven, Conn., and London: Yale University Press, 1996), 135.

216. "A New Apartment House": 63–64.

217. "A New Apartment House": 63–64.

218. "Buildings Projected," *Real Estate Record and Builders' Guide* 30 (July 22, 1882): 717; "Tall Houses vs. Narrow Streets," *Real Estate Record and Builders' Guide* 31 (March 3, 1883): 80; Schuyler, "The Growth of the City": 4; "Yellow Brick in Building," *Real Estate Record and Builders' Guide* 32 (October 13, 1883): 780; "Interesting Talks on High Apartment Houses," *Real Estate Record and Builders' Guide* 41 (March 17, 1888): 332–33; Russell Sturgis, "A Review of the Works of Clinton & Russell," *Architectural Record* 7 (October–December 1897): 1–61; Silver, *Lost New York*, 143; Bacon, *Ernest Flagg*, 14, fig. 1; Cromley, *Alone Together*, 166.

219. Schuyler, "The Growth of the City": 4.

220. "Tall Houses vs. Narrow Streets": 80.

221. "Out Among the Builders," *Real Estate Record and Builders' Guide* 31 (February 17, 1883): 69; Schuyler, "The Growth of the City": 4; "Another First-Class Apartment Improvement," *Real Estate Record and Builders' Guide* 33 (March 29, 1884): 315; Blanke, "The Cliff-Dwellers of New York": 354–62; Alpern, *New York's Fabulous Luxury Apartments*, 18–19; Boyer, *Manhattan Manners*, 162–63; White and Willensky, *AIA Guide* (1988), 172–73; Plunz, *A History of Housing in New York City*, 71;

Alpern, *Luxury Apartment Houses in Manhattan*, 17, 19; Hawes, *New York, New York*, 57–60; Landau and Condit, *Rise of the New York Skyscraper, 1865–1913*, 137; Hirsh, *Manhattan Hotels: 1880–1920*, 82–83; Christopher Gray, "Streetscapes/The Chelsea Hotel at 222 West 23d Street," *New York Times* (February 15, 1998), XI: 5.

222. Quoted in "Another First-Class Apartment Improvement": 315.

223. *The Central Park Apartments* (New York: American Banknote, 1881); "Vast Apartment Houses," *Real Estate Record and Builders' Guide* 29 (June 3, 1882): 550; "Buildings Projected," *Real Estate Record and Builders' Guide* 29 (June 17, 1882): 611; "The Navarro Apartment Houses," *Real Estate Record and Builders' Guide* 31 (April 14, 1883): 145–46; "Brick Architecture in New York," *Building* 1 (May 1883): 105–6; Schuyler, "The Growth of the City": 4; Editorial, *American Architect and Building News* 14 (October 27, 1883): 193; "The Central Park Apartments," *Building* 2 (December 1883): 32, plate; "Out Among the Builders," *Real Estate Record and Builders' Guide* 17 (December 22, 1883): 1030; "The Central Park Apartment Houses," *Real Estate Record and Builders' Guide* 37 (March 21, 1886): 350; Editorial, *American Architect and Building News* 20 (July 31, 1886): 45; "Homes of the Rich," editorial, *Building* 9 (November 17, 1888): 177–78; Editorial, *American Architect and Building News* 24 (December 8, 1888): 261–62; Blanke, "The Cliff-Dwellers of New York": 354–62; "The Duplex Apartment House: A Comparison of the Newest Buildings of this Type," *Architectural Record* 29 (March 1911): 326–34; C. Matlack Price, "A Pioneer in Apartment House Architecture: A Memoir on Philip G. Hubert's Work," *Architectural Record* 36 (July 1914): 74–76; "Street that Has Maintained Its Character. Central Park South, Where Some of the First Apartment Houses Were Erected, Still Retains Its Hold as a Residential Center," *Real Estate Record and Builders' Guide* 96 (August 7, 1915): 225; Silver, *Lost New York*, 138–39; Alpern, *New York's Fabulous Luxury Apartments*, 16–17; Stern, "With Rhetoric": 88; Stern, Gilmartin, and Massengale, *New York 1900*, 468–69 (n. 101); Gray, "A Street Most Grand": 49, 51–57; Boyer, *Manhattan Manners*, 159–60; Bacon, *Ernest Flagg*, 11–12; Cromley, *Alone Together*, 129–34, 146, 160; Plunz, *A History of Housing in New York City*, 75–77; Alpern, *Luxury Apartment Houses of Manhattan*, 20–23; Hawes, *New York, New York*, 60–62; Alpern, *Historic Manhattan Apartment Houses*, 53–54; Landau and Condit, *Rise of the New York Skyscraper, 1865–1913*, 135.

224. Schuyler, "The Growth of the City": 4.

225. Editorial, *American Architect and Building News* 24 (December 8, 1888): 261–62. Also see Boyer, *Manhattan Manners*, 163.

226. Editorial, *American Architect and Building News*: 262.

227. Editorial, *American Architect and Building News* 20 (July 3, 1886): 2.

228. "Homes of the Rich": 177–78.

229. "Another First-Class Apartment Improvement," *Real Estate Record and Builders' Guide* 33 (March 29, 1884): 315; "Out Among the Builders," *Real Estate Record and Builders' Guide* 33 (March 29, 1884): 319; "Out Among the Builders," *Real Estate Record and Builders' Guide* 33 (April 5, 1884): 343–44; Hubert, Pirsson & Hoddick, "New York Flats and French Flats," *Architectural Record* 2 (July–September 1892): 55–64; Plunz, *A History of Housing in New York City*, 110; Hawes, *New York, New York*, 62–63.

230. Hubert, Pirsson & Hoddick, "New York Flats and French Flats": 63.

231. Hawes, *New York, New York*, 63.

232. "'The Albany,' New York. Mr. John C. Babcock, Architect," *American Architect and Building News* 1 (December 23, 1876): 412–13, plates; Cromley, *Alone Together*, 73, 76–77, 80, 86, 90, 98, 101; Dunlap, *On Broadway*, 186.

233. "Buildings Projected," *Real Estate Record and Builders' Guide* 23 (May 24, 1879): 435; "The Windsor Apartment House," *Real Estate Record and Builders' Guide* 24 (November 8, 1879): 896; Boyer, *Manhattan Manners*, 159; Dunlap, *On Broadway*, 192; Hawes, *New York, New York*, 48.

234. "Buildings Projected," *Real Estate Record and Builders' Guide* 16 (October 30, 1875): 710; "Buildings Projected," *Real Estate Record and Builders' Guide* 32 (September 29, 1883): 750; Dunlap, *On Broadway*, 194; Christopher Gray, "Streetscapes: Readers' Questions," *New York Times* (March 17, 1991), X: 6.

235. "Buildings Projected," *Real Estate Record and Builders' Guide* 16 (August 14, 1875): 555.

236. "The Clermont," *Real Estate Record and Builders' Guide* 21 (May 4, 1878): 382; Dunlap, *On Broadway*, 192.

237. "About Some Large Buildings," *Real Estate Record and Builders' Guide* 27 (April 30, 1881): 425; Jackson, *A Place Called Home*, 78, 80; Boyer, *Manhattan Manners*, 159; Alpern, *Historic Manhattan Apartment Houses*, 3, 5; "Long Fall from Elegance," *New York Times* (January 25, 1998), XIV: 2.

238. "Apartment-Houses—IV": 37–39. Also see "'The Berkshire,' New York, N.Y.," *American Architect and Building News* 14 (August 4, 1883): 53–54, plates; "Entrance to the 'Berkshire' Apartment House, Madison Avenue, New York, N.Y. Mr. Carl Pfeiffer, Architect," *American Architect and Building News* 24 (December 22, 1888): 290, plate; Boyer, *Manhattan Manners*, 163; Cromley, *Alone Together*, 134, 138–39, 162, 165.

239. "One of New York's Palaces Described," *Real Estate Record and Builders' Guide* 33 (January 26, 1884): 85; Boyer, *Manhattan Manners*, 161.

240. "Buildings Projected," *Real Estate Record and Builders' Guide* 30 (July 15, 1882): 699; "Brick Architecture in New York": 105–6; "The Future of the American Apartment House," *Real Estate Record and Builders' Guide* 32 (November 10, 1883): 881–82; "The Success of the Apartment House," *Real Estate Record and Builders' Guide* 32 (November 17, 1883): 903; Garmey, *Gramercy Park*, 147–50; White and Willensky, *AIA Guide* (1988), 198; Alpern, *Luxury Apartment Houses of Manhattan*, 24–26; Christopher Gray, "The City's Oldest Elevator System Is Being Replaced," *New York Times* (August 14, 1994), IX: 7.

241. "Brick Architecture in New York": 105.

242. "Out Among the Builders," *Real Estate Record and Builders' Guide* 31 (April 26, 1883): 174; "A High House," *The Builder* [London] 44 (June 23, 1883): 867; Schuyler, "The Growth of the City": 4; "In West Fifty-seventh Street": 992–93; "Men and Things," *Real Estate Record and Builders' Guide* 43 (June 22, 1889): 872–73; Koch, *Louis C. Tiffany*, 71; Alpern, *New York's Fabulous Luxury Apartments*, 22–23; Boyer, *Manhattan Manners*, 160–61; Joseph Giovannini, "The Osborne: Now 100 Years Old and Still a Nice Place to Live," *New York Times* (November 21, 1985), C: 1; David T. Deutsch, "The Osborne, New York City," *Antiques* 130 (July 1986): 152–58; White and Willensky, *AIA Guide* (1988), 277; Cromley, *Alone Together*, 168, 170; Landmarks Preservation Commission of the City of New York, LP-1770 (August 13, 1991); Alpern, *Luxury Apartment Houses of Manhattan*, 27–32; Diamonstein, *The Landmarks of New York II*, 389; Hawes, *New York, New York*, 105–9; Christopher Gray, "Streetscapes/The Osborne," *New York Times* (January 6, 1994), X: 7; Landau and Condit, *Rise of the New York Skyscraper, 1865–1913*, 136–37.

243. Quoted in Hawes, *New York, New York*, 105.

244. "In West Fifty-seventh Street": 992–93.

245. "Men and Things," (June 22, 1889): 872–73.

246. W., "A New Apartment House Design," *American Architect and Building News* 3 (April 6, 1878): 123; "Mr. Clark's Mammoth Apartment House," *Real Estate Record and Builders' Guide* 21 (April 20, 1878): 337; "The Vancorlear," *Real Estate Record and Builders' Guide* 24 (August 30, 1879): 688–69; "'The Vancorlear,' New York, N.Y. Mr. H. J. Hardenbergh, Architect, New York, N.Y.," *American Architect and Building News* 7 (January 24, 1880): 28, plates; "Apartment Houses," *Real Estate Record and Builders' Guide* 27 (January 15, 1881): 46–47; "Apartment-Houses—IV": 37–39; Schuyler, "Henry Janeway Hardenbergh": 336; Stern, "With Rhetoric": 78–111; Boyer, *Manhattan Manners*, 158–59; Cromley, *Alone Together*, 103; Plunz, *A History of Housing in New York City*, 71; Hawes, *New York, New York*, 48, 51.

247. "The Vancorlear," *Real Estate Record and Builders' Guide*: 688–69.

248. "The Vancorlear," *Real Estate Record and Builders' Guide*: 688–89.

249. W., "A New Apartment House Design": 123.

250. Schuyler, "Henry Janeway Hardenbergh": 336.

251. "The Winter Review," *Real Estate Record and Builders' Guide* 21 (February 16, 1878): 131–32; "The City of the Future," *Real Estate Record and Builders' Guide* 24 (December 27, 1879): 1056–57; Schuyler, "The Growth of the City": 4; "Prominent Buildings Under Way," *Real Estate Record and Builders' Guide* 33 (April 5, 1884): 341; "The City Note-Book," *Building* 2 (August 1884): 125; "The Dakota," *Real Estate Record and Builders' Guide* 34 (September 20, 1884): 948; "The Dakota," *New York Daily Graphic* (September 30, 1884), reprinted in *New York Times*

(October 22, 1884): 5; "Our Special Illustration, the Dakota Apartment House," *Sanitary Engineer* 11 (February 1885): 271; "The Dakota Apartment House," *Real Estate Record and Builders' Guide* 35 (March 7, 1885): 232; M. G. Van Rensselaer, "Recent Architecture in America—VI," *Century Magazine* 31 (March 1886): 677–87; Henry Hardenbergh, "The Sub-surface Courtyard of the Dakota Apartment House," *American Architect and Building News* 31 (January 24, 1891): 63–64; "Apartment-Houses—IV": 37–39; Schuyler, "Henry Janeway Hardenbergh": 336–38, 340; Franz K. Winkler [Montgomery Schuyler], "Recent Apartment House Design," *Architectural Record* 11 (January 1902): 98–109; Landmarks Preservation Commission of the City of New York, LP-0280 (February 11, 1969); Alpern, *New York's Fabulous Luxury Apartments*, 20–21; Stephen Birmingham, *Life at the Dakota* (New York: Random House, 1979), 1–55; Stern, "With Rhetoric": 87–88; Lightfoot, ed., *Nineteenth-Century New York in Rare Photographic Views*, fig. 134; Stern, Gilmartin, and Massengale, *New York 1900*, 283–85; Christopher Gray, "Streetscapes: The Dakota," *New York Times* (August 15, 1983), X: 7; Donald Martin Reynolds, *The Architecture of New York City* (New York: Macmillan, 1984), 226–29; Boyer, *Manhattan Manners*, 161–62; John Tauranac, *Elegant New York* (New York: Abbeville Press, 1985), 228–30; Cromley, *Alone Together*, 134–37, 160; Plunz, *A History of Housing in New York City*, 71–73; Alpern, *Luxury Apartment Houses of Manhattan*, 57; Diamonstein, *The Landmarks of New York II*, 176–77; Hawes, *New York, New York*, 48–49, 93–104; Christopher Gray, "How the Dakota Got Its Name," letter to the editor, *New York Times* (May 16, 1993), VII: 30; Landau and Condit, *Rise of the New York Skyscraper, 1865–1913*, 134–35.

252. Edward Clark, quoted in "The City of the Future," *Real Estate Record and Builders' Guide*: 1056.

253. "The Dakota," (September 30, 1884), reprinted in *New York Times*: 5.

254. Hardenbergh, "The Sub-surface Courtyard of the Dakota Apartment House": 64.

255. "The Dakota Apartment House," *Real Estate Record and Builders' Guide*: 232.

256. "Apartment-Houses—IV": 37–39.

257. Schuyler, "The Growth of the City": 4.

258. Modeste Tchaikovsky, *The Life and Letters of Peter Ilich Tchaikovsky*, translated, edited, and abridged by Rosa Newmarch (London, 1906; New York: Dodd, Mead & Co., 1924), 643; Elkhonon Yoffe, *Tchaikovsky in America: The Composer's Visit in 1891*, trans. Lidya Yoffe (New York: Oxford University Press, 1986), 74–75. Stephen Birmingham, in his *Life at the Dakota*, offers an exaggerated version of Tchaikovsky's visit; see pp. 46–47.

259. Schuyler, "Henry Janeway Hardenbergh": 338.

260. "Buildings Projected," *Real Estate Record and Builders' Guide* 30 (November 4, 1882): 982; Landmarks Preservation Commission of the City of New York, LP-0964 (July 12, 1977), 3; Christopher Gray, "Streetscapes/The Ontiora," *New York Times* (March 9, 1997), IX: 5.

261. "Buildings Projected," *Real Estate Record and Builders' Guide* 24 (December 13, 1879): 1020; "The South Kensington," *Real Estate Record and Builders' Guide* 26 (August 7, 1880): 703.

262. "Buildings Projected," *Real Estate Record and Builders' Guide* 29 (April 1, 1882): 316; Christopher Gray, "Streetscapes: Readers' Questions: A Dakota Cousin Called the Imperial," *New York Times* (March 4, 1990), X: 6; Alpern, *Historic Manhattan Apartment Houses*, 2–5.

263. "Buildings Projected," *Real Estate Record and Builders' Guide* 35 (January 24, 1885): 97; "The Lenox Hill Apartment House," *Real Estate Record and Builders' Guide* 37 (March 6, 1886): 283; Boyer, *Manhattan Manners*, 163.

264. "Buildings Projected," *Real Estate Record and Builders' Guide* 38 (November 13, 1886): 1411; "The Costly and Substantial Buildings of 1886": 6–8; Schuyler, "Henry Janeway Hardenbergh": 358.

265. "Buildings Projected," *Real Estate Record and Builders' Guide* 41 (January 14, 1888): 67; "Out Among the Builders," *Real Estate Record and Builders' Guide* 41 (May 26, 1888): 672–73.

266. "Out Among the Builders," *Real Estate Record and Builders' Guide* 41 (February 11, 1888): 181; "Important Buildings Projected and Under Way," *Real Estate Record and Builders' Guide* 41 (April 28, 1888): 529; "The East Side—Its Streets and Buildings," supplement, *Real Estate*

Record and Builders' Guide 45 (May 3, 1890): 1–11; "'The Yosemite,' Park Ave., New York, N.Y. Mssrs. McKim, Mead & White, Architects, New York, N.Y.," *American Architect and Building News* 31 (February 21, 1891): 126, plate; "Entrance to the Yosemite, New York, N.Y. Mssrs. McKim, Mead & White, Architects, New York, N.Y.," *American Architect and Building News* 31 (February 28, 1891): 146, plate; Russell Sturgis, "The Works of McKim, Mead & White," *Architectural Record* 4 (May 1895): 1–111; Roth, *The Architecture of McKim, Mead & White, 1870–1920: A Building List*, 106; Roth, *McKim, Mead & White, Architects*, 138, 140; Christopher Gray, "Neighborhood/A History of Park Avenue, Part III," *Avenue* (December–January 1983): 116–24; Cromley, *Alone Together*, 205.

267. Sturgis, "The Works of McKim, Mead & White": 51.

268. "Apartment House on East 21st Street, New York. Mr. Bruce Price, Architect, New York," *American Architect and Building News* 3 (May 4, 1878): 157, plate; Montgomery Schuyler, "Recent Building in New York—IV," *American Architect and Building News* 9 (April 30, 1881): 207–8; Samuel H. Graybill Jr., "Bruce Price, American Architect, 1845–1903" (Ph. D. diss., Yale University, 1957): 8; Garmey, *Gramercy Park*, 144–45; White and Willensky, *AIA Guide* (1988), 189; Cromley, *Alone Together*, 73–75, 82, 85, 87–88, 98–99, 107; Alpern, *Historic Manhattan Apartment Houses*, 3.

269. Schuyler, "Recent Building in New York—IV": 208.

270. William Dean Howells, *A Hazard of New Fortunes* (New York: Harper & Brothers, 1890), 52.

271. Kenneth S. Lynn, *William Dean Howells: An American Life* (New York: Harcourt Brace Jovanovich, 1970), 6–11, 298–302; Hawes, *New York, New York*, 117–24.

272. Howells, *A Hazard of New Fortunes*, 67.

273. Howells, *A Hazard of New Fortunes*, 72.

274. Hubert, Pirsson & Hoddick, "New York Flats and French Flats": 56.

275. Moses King, *King's Handbook of New York* (Boston: Moses King, 1892), 242–43.

276. "The Problem of Living in New York": 918–24.

277. "Domestic Architecture," *Real Estate Record and Builders' Guide* 1 (April 4, 1868): 1.

278. See Lockwood, *Bricks and Brownstone*, 104–5, 139–43.

279. Quoted in Lockwood, *Bricks and Brownstone*, 139.

280. William Chambers, *Things As They Are in America* (London: W. and R. Chambers, 1854), quoted in Silver, *Lost New York*, 136.

281. Montgomery Schuyler, "The Churches of New York," *New York World* (October 22, 1871): 2.

282. Richardson, "The New Homes of New York": 63, 65.

283. See Robert Tomes, "The Houses We Live In," *Harper's New Monthly Magazine* 30 (May 1865): 735–41.

284. "A Successful Enterprise," *Real Estate Record and Builders' Guide* 19 (April 7, 1877): 259–60; Boyer, *Manhattan Manners*, 145.

285. Montgomery Schuyler, "Recent Building in New York—III," *American Architect and Building News* 9 (April 23, 1881): 196–97.

286. M. G. Van Rensselear, "Recent Architecture in America—V," *Century Magazine* 31 (February 1886): 548–58.

287. "Domestic Architecture": 1.

288. Anthony Trollope, *North America* (Philadelphia: J. B. Lippincott, 1862; New York: Alfred A. Knopf, 1951), 214.

289. Jacob Landy, "The Domestic Architecture of the 'Robber Barons' in New York City," *Marsyas* 5 (1947–49): 63–85; Jay E. Cantor, "A Monument to Trade: A. T. Stewart and the Rise of the Millionaire's Mansion in New York," *Winterthur Portfolio* 10 (1975): 165–97; Mosette Broderick, "Fifth Avenue," in Jan Cigliano and Sarah Bradford Landau, eds., *The Grand American Avenue 1850–1920* (San Francisco: Pomegranate Artbooks, 1994), 2–33.

290. Browne, *The Great Metropolis*, 221–22.

291. Matthew Hale Smith, *Sunshine and Shadow in New York* (Hartford, Conn.: J. B. Burr, 1868), 52–62; "Mr. Stewart's New Residence," *Harper's Weekly* 13 (August 14, 1869): 521, 525–26; "An Architectural Ramble": 1–2; McCabe, *Lights and Shadows of New York Life*, 468–69; "Death of A. T. Stewart," *New York Times* (April 11, 1876): 1; Wight, "A Millionaire's Architectural Investment": 147–49; Sheldon, *Artistic Houses*, vol. 1, part 1: 7–18; "Inside the Stewart Mansion," reprint from

Boston Courier of Miss Grundy's New York letter, *Real Estate Record and Builders' Guide* 36 (November 28, 1885): 1312; Van Rensselaer, "Recent Architecture in America—V": 548–58; Harry W. Desmond and Herbert Groly, *Stately Homes in America* (New York: D. Appleton, 1903), 43, 45, 49, 228, 231–32, 252; Arthur Bartlett Maurice, *Fifth Avenue* (New York: Dodd, Mead and Company, 1918), 245; Brown, *Fifth Avenue: Old and New, 1824–1924*, 78; Landy, "The Domestic Architecture of the 'Robber Barons' in New York City": 65, 70–71, fig. 7; Kouwenhoven, *The Columbia Historical Portrait of New York*, 372, 411; Wayne Andrews, *Architecture, Ambition and Americans* (New York: Harper & Brothers, 1954), 154; Silver, *Lost New York*, 123; Black, *Old New York in Early Photographs*, 132–33; Cantor, "A Monument to Trade: A. T. Stewart and the Rise of the Millionaire's Mansion in New York": 165–97; Lockwood, *Manhattan Moves Uptown*, 227–29, 299–301; Watson, *New York Then and Now*, 56–57; John Grafton, *New York in the Nineteenth Century* (New York: Dover, 1977), 78; Gardner, "The Architecture of Commercial Capitalism: John Kellum and the Development of New York, 1840–1875": 211–16; Lightfoot, ed., *Nineteenth-Century New York in Rare Photographic Views*, fig. 109; Stern, Gilmartin, and Massengale, *New York 1900*, 157, 184; Christopher Gray, "History of the Upper East Side," *Avenue* (September 1985): 98–191; Lewis, Turner, and McQuillen, *The Opulent Interiors of the Gilded Age*, 33–39; Christopher Gray, "Show-off Houses," *Avenue* (April 1989): 93–103; Ronda Wist, *On Fifth Avenue: Then and Now* (New York: Carol, 1992), 19; Broderick, "Fifth Avenue," in Cigliano and Landau, eds., *The Grand American Avenue 1850–1920*, 14–15.

292. Van Rensselaer, "Recent Architecture in America—V": 553.

293. Lockwood, *Manhattan Moves Uptown*, 227–28; Cantor, "A Monument to Trade: A. T. Stewart and the Rise of the Millionaire's Mansion in New York": 178; Wist, *On Fifth Avenue: Then and Now*, 19.

294. Strong, diary entry dated March 21, 1864, in *The Diary of George Templeton Strong*, vol. 3: 416.

295. Broderick, "Fifth Avenue," in Cigliano and Landau, eds., *The Grand American Avenue 1850–1920*, 14–15. Also see Landy, "The Domestic Architecture of the 'Robber Barons' in New York City": 64–65.

296. Wight, "A Millionaire's Architectural Investment": 147–49. For Fonthill Abbey, see Antony Dale, *James Wyatt, Architect, 1746–1813* (Oxford, England: Basil Blackwell, 1936), 76–82.

297. Richard Morris Hunt, quoted in Cantor, "A Monument to Trade: A. T. Stewart and the Rise of the Millionaire's Mansion in New York": 191.

298. "Mr. Stewart's New Residence," *Harper's Weekly*: 521, 525.

299. "An Architectural Ramble": 1–2.

300. Wight, "A Millionaire's Architectural Investment": 147–49.

301. Van Rensselaer, "Recent Architecture in America—V": 551–53.

302. Smith, *Sunshine and Shadow in New York*, frontispiece.

303. *Appleton's New York Illustrated* (New York: D. Appleton, 1869), 20–34. The opinions of the *New York Sun* are cited in Andy Logan, "That Was New York, Double Darkness and Worst of All," *New Yorker* 34 (February 22, 1958): 81–113.

304. "Mr. Stewart's New Residence," *Harper's Weekly*: 521, 525.

305. For McKim, Mead & White's building, see Stern, Gilmartin, and Massengale, *New York 1900*, 157, 184.

306. For both of Davis's projects, see Roger Hale Newton, *Town & Davis, Architects* (New York: Columbia University Press, 1942), 141, 145–47, 281–83, 314; William C. Shopsin and Mosette Glaser Broderick, *The Villard Houses: Life Story of a Landmark* (New York: Viking, in cooperation with the Municipal Art Society of New York, 1980), 14–15, 17; Jane B. Davies, "Alexander J. Davis, Creative American Architect," in Amelia Peck, ed., *Alexander Jackson Davis: American Architect 1803–1892* (New York: Rizzoli International Publications, 1992), 12, 21.

307. "Buildings Projected," *Real Estate Record and Builders' Guide* 3 (May 15, 1869): 13; "How We Grow and Spread," *Real Estate Record and Builders' Guide* 3 (July 17, 1869): 2; Kouwenhoven, *The Columbia Historical Portrait of New York*, 312; Silver, *Lost New York*, 124; Theodore James Jr., *Fifth Avenue* (New York: Walker, 1971), 132–33; Lockwood, *Manhattan Moves Uptown*, 259, 261; Shopsin and Broderick, *The Villard Houses*, 17; Stern, Gilmartin, and Massengale, *New York 1900*, 308; Christopher Gray, "The Most Gilded Street," *Avenue* (November 1984): 88–96; Boyer, *Manhattan Manners*, 24; Wist, *On Fifth Avenue: Then and*

Now, 26; Hawes, *New York, New York*, 39–41; Broderick, "Fifth Avenue," in Cigliano and Landau, eds., *The Grand American Avenue 1850–1920*, 15–17; Christopher Gray, "Streetscapes/Historical Panorama," *New York Times* (October 19, 1997), X: 5.

308. Wharton, *The Age of Innocence*, 24. Also see R.W.B. Lewis, *Edith Wharton* (New York: Fromm, 1985), 13; Shari Benstock, *No Gifts from Chance: A Biography of Edith Wharton* (New York: Charles Scribner's Sons, 1994), 358, 360.

309. "Projected Buildings," *Real Estate Record and Builders' Guide* 5 (July 30, 1870): 6; Christopher Gray, "Streetscapes/17 East 57th Street," *New York Times* (January 14, 1996), IX: 7; Gray, "Streetscapes/Historical Panorama": 5.

310. Kramer, "The Domestic Architecture of Detlef Lienau: A Conservative Victorian": 164–71; Silver, *Lost New York*, 136; Shopsin and Broderick, *The Villard Houses*, 17; Gray, "The Most Gilded Street": 88–96; Boyer, *Manhattan Manners*, 24; Wist, *On Fifth Avenue: Then and Now*, 26–27; Hawes, *New York, New York*, 39; Broderick, "Fifth Avenue," in Cigliano and Landau, eds., *The Grand American Avenue 1850–1920*, 15–17.

311. "The Vanderbilt Purchase," *Real Estate Record and Builders' Guide* 23 (January 18, 1879): 43; "Expensive Houses," *Real Estate Record and Builders' Guide* 23 (February 22, 1879): 145; "The New Vanderbilt Mansions," *New York Times* (December 9, 1879): 8; "New Buildings Going Up," *New York Times* (July 14, 1880): 2; Montgomery Schuyler, "Recent Building in New York—V," *American Architect and Building News* 9 (May 21, 1881): 243–44; "The Vanderbilt Palace," *New York Times* (August 25, 1881): 3; Montgomery Schuyler, "The Vanderbilt Houses," *Harper's Weekly* 26 (January 21, 1882): 42, reprinted in Montgomery Schuyler, *American Architecture and Other Writings*, eds. William H. Jordy and Ralph Coe, 2 vols. (Cambridge, Mass.: Harvard University Press, Belknap Press, 1961), vol. 2: 489–501; Clarence Cook, "Architecture in America," *North American Review* 135 (September 1882): 243–52; "Miscellaneous City News. Two Elegant Mansions," *New York Times* (October 3, 1882): 8; Sheldon, *Artistic Houses*, vol. 1, part 2: 110–27; Edward Strahan [Earl Shinn], *Mr. Vanderbilt's House and Collection* (Boston: G. Barrie, 1883–84); Montgomery Schuyler, "Some New Houses," letter to the editor, *Real Estate Record and Builders' Guide* 31 (February 3, 1883): 43–44; "Mr. Vanderbilt's Pleasures," *New York Times* (March 24, 1883): 8; Montgomery Schuyler, "Recent Building in New York," *Harper's New Monthly Magazine* 67 (September 1883): 557–78, reprinted as "Concerning Queen Anne," in Schuyler, *American Architecture and Other Writings*, vol. 2: 453–587; "More Vanderbilt Houses," *Real Estate Record and Builders' Guide* 32 (October 20, 1883): 804; "Mr. Vanderbilt's Art Levee," *New York Times* (December 21, 1883): 2; Herter Brothers, "The Architects of W. H. Vanderbilt's House," *American Architect and Building News* 17 (May 2, 1885): 214; "The Best Ten Buildings in the United States," *American Architect and Building News* 17 (June 13, 1885): 282–83; "Mr. Vanderbilt's Homes," *Harper's Weekly* 29 (December 19, 1885): 843–44; "William H. Vanderbilt," *Harper's Weekly* 29 (December 19, 1885): 843, 845; Karl Hinckeldeyn, "William H. Vanderbilt," *Centralblatt der Bauverwaltung* 6 (January 2, 1886): 4–5; "Houses of Mrs. W. H. Vanderbilt and Mrs. E. F. Shephard, Fifth Avenue, New York, Messrs. Atwood, Snook and Herter Bros., Architects, New York, N.Y.," *American Architect and Building News* 20 (July 31, 1886): 50, plate; Van Rensselaer, "Recent Architecture in America—V": 548–58; Desmond and Croly, *Stately Homes in America*, 51, 55, 59, 61, 255–56; Brown, *Fifth Avenue: Old and New, 1824–1924*, 92–93; G. H. Edgell, *The American Architecture of To-Day* (New York: Charles Scribner's Sons, 1928), 140; Wayne Andrews, *The Vanderbilt Legend* (New York: Harcourt, Brace, 1941), 218–39; Frank Crowninshield, "The House of Vanderbilt," *Vogue* 98 (November 15, 1941): 33–55; Landy, "The Domestic Architecture of the 'Robber Barons' in New York City": 71, fig. 8; Andrews, *Architecture, Ambition and Americans*, 157; Clay Lancaster, *The Japanese Influence in America* (New York: Walton H. Rawls, 1963), 53; James, *Fifth Avenue*, 72–73, 147–51; Smith, "The Commercial Architecture of John Butler Snook": 163–64, 260; James T. Maher, *The Twilight of Splendor: Chronicles of the Age of American Palaces* (Boston: Little Brown, 1975), xvi–xvii; Lockwood, *Manhattan Moves Uptown*, 301–3; Grafton, *New York in the Nineteenth Century*, 78–79; Dianne H. Pilgrim, "Decorative Art: The Domestic Environ-

ment," in *The American Renaissance, 1876–1917* (Brooklyn: Brooklyn Museum, 1979), 110–11, 118–27; Shopsin and Broderick, *The Villard Houses*, 46–47; Lightfoot, ed., *Nineteenth-Century New York in Rare Photographic Views*, fig. 116; Stern, Gilmartin, and Massengale, *New York 1900*, 309; Gray, "History of the Upper East Side": 124–25; Gray, "The Most Gilded Street": 88–96; Lewis, Turner, and McQuillen, *The Opulent Interiors of the Gilded Age*, 114–24; Louis Auchincloss, *The Vanderbilt Era* (New York: Collier Books, 1989), 31; Robert B. King with Charles O. McLean, *The Vanderbilt Homes* (New York: Rizzoli International Publications, 1989), 18–27; Gray, "Show-off Houses": 94–103; John Foreman and Robbe Pierce Stimson, *The Vanderbilts and the Gilded Age* (New York: St. Martin's Press, 1991), 308–23; Wist, *On Fifth Avenue: Then and Now*, 29–31; Broderick, "Fifth Avenue," in Cigliano and Landau, eds., *The Grand American Avenue 1850–1920*, 18; Katherine S. Howe et al., *Herter Brothers: Furniture and Interiors for a Gilded Age* (New York: Harry N. Abrams, 1994), 53–55, 79–80, 82, 87, 93, 99, 200–11, 232; Alice Cooney Frelinghuysen, "Christian Herter's Decoration of the William H. Vanderbilt House," *Antiques* 147 (March 1995): 406–17. Also see Arnold Lewis and Keith Morgan, *American Victorian Architecture* (New York: Dover, 1975), plates II: 1–2, which is a republication of *L'Architecture américaine* (Paris: André, Daly fils et Cie, 1886).

312. "Central Park Lots," (November 18, 1876): 851–52.

313. "Encroaching on Fifth Avenue," *Real Estate Record and Builders' Guide* 24 (September 20, 1879): 739; "Promising Retail Centers," *Real Estate Record and Builders' Guide* 27 (April 30, 1881): 420.

314. Strahan [Shinn], *Mr. Vanderbilt's House and Collection*, vol. 1: v–vi.

315. "Mr. Vanderbilt's Art Levee": 2.

316. Landy, "The Domestic Architecture of the 'Robber Barons' in New York City": 69; Stern, Gilmartin, and Massengale, *New York 1900*, 309; King with McLean, *The Vanderbilt Homes*, 11–13.

317. "Mr. Charles B. Atwood," *American Architect and Building News* 50 (December 28, 1895): 141; "Charles B. Atwood," in Bernard S. Myers, ed., *McGraw-Hill Dictionary of Art*, 5 vols. (New York: McGraw-Hill, 1969), vol. 1: 188.

318. William Baumgarten, quoted in Maher, *The Twilight of Splendor: Chronicles of the Age of American Palaces*, xvi–xvii.

319. Schuyler, "Recent Building in New York—V": 243–44.

320. Van Rensselaer, "Recent American Architecture—V": 554–55.

321. Schuyler, "Recent Building in New York": 560.

322. Schuyler, "Recent Building in New York—V": 243–44.

323. Sheldon, *Artistic Houses*, vol. 1, part 2: 113–15.

324. Two influential books on Japanese design were published in the 1880s: Christopher Dresser, *Japan: Its Architecture, Art, and Art Manufactures* (London: Longmans, Green & Co., 1882), republished as *Traditional Arts and Crafts of Japan* (New York: Dover, 1994); and Edward S. Morse, *Japanese Homes and Their Surroundings* (Boston: Ticknor & Co., 1886; New York: Dover, 1961).

325. "Miscellaneous City News. Two Elegant Mansions": 8; "More Vanderbilt Houses": 804; Smith, "The Commercial Architecture of John Butler Snook": 164, 260; Lewis and Morgan, *American Victorian Architecture*, plate II: 9; Wist, *On Fifth Avenue: Then and Now*, 31; Stern, Mellins, and Fishman, *New York 1960*, 380.

326. "More Vanderbilt Houses": 804.

327. "The New Vanderbilt Mansions," *New York Times*: 8; "New Buildings Going Up": 2; Schuyler, "Recent Buildings in New York—V": 243–44; Schuyler, "The Vanderbilt Houses": 42, reprinted in Schuyler, *American Architecture and Other Writings*, vol. 2: 489–501; Cook, "Architecture in America": 243–52; Schuyler, "Some New Houses": 43–44; "Like an Oriental Dream," *New York Herald* (March 27, 1883): 3; Schuyler, "Recent Building in New York": 557–78; "The Best Ten Buildings in the United States": 282–83; Van Rensselaer, "Recent Architecture in America—V": 548–58; "Mr. Wm. K. Vanderbilt's House. First Paper," *Real Estate Record and Builders' Guide* 37 (June 12, 1886): 770; "Architectural Notes," *Art Age* 3 (July 1886): 213; "Mr. Wm. K. Vanderbilt's House. Concluded," *Real Estate Record and Builders' Guide* 38 (July 3, 1886): 856–57; Arthur Alfred Cox, "American Construction Through English Eyes—III," *American Architect and Building News* 33 (August 29, 1891): 131–32; Adolphe Bocage, "L'Architecture aux Etats-Unis: La Maison moderne et la situation de l'architecte aux Etats-Unis," *L'Archi-

tecture 7 (October 13, 1894): 333; Henry Van Brunt, "Richard Morris Hunt," *Journal of the Proceedings of the American Institute of Architects* 23 (1895): 71–84, reprinted in *Architecture and Society: Selected Essays of Henry Van Brunt*, 318–41; Schuyler, "The Works of the Late Richard M. Hunt": 129–31; Royal Cortissoz, "Richard Morris Hunt," *New York Daily Tribune* (August 4, 1895): 23; Montgomery Schuyler, "Richard Morris Hunt," *Harper's Weekly* 39 (August 10, 1895): 749; Barr Ferree, "Richard Morris Hunt: His Art and Work," *Architecture and Building* 23 (December 7, 1895): 271–75; John B. Gass, "American Architecture and Architects, with Special Reference to the Late Richard Morris Hunt and Henry Hobson Richardson," *Royal Institute of British Architects* 3 (February 6, 1896): 231; Louis Sullivan, "Kindergarten Chats," *Interstate Architect and Builder* 2–3 (February 16, 1901–February 8, 1902), reprinted in Louis Sullivan, *Kindergarten Chats*, ed. Claude F. Bragdon (Lawrence, Kansas: Scarab Fraternity Press, 1934), 140; Desmond and Croly, *Stately Homes in America*, 362, 365, 490; Indiana Limestone Company, *The William K. Vanderbilt Home: An Example of Exquisitely Carved Gray Indiana Limestone*, Booklet Series C2, no. 1 (Detroit: Evans, Winter, Hebb, c. 1920), 2; Consolidated Gas Company, *Gas Logic* 36, no. 2 (August 1924): 4; John Vredenburgh Van Pelt, *A Monograph of the William K. Vanderbilt House, Richard Morris Hunt, Architect* (New York, 1925); Arthur W. Colton, "The Architect's Library: A Monograph of the William K. Vanderbilt House," *Architectural Record* 58 (September 1925): 295–99; Herbert Croly, "The Work of Richard Morris Hunt," *Architectural Record* 59 (January 1926): 88–89; Thomas E. Talmadge, *The Story of Architecture in America* (New York: W. W. Norton, 1927), 153–54; Lewis Mumford, *The Brown Decades: A Study of the Arts in America, 1865–1895* (New York: Harcourt, Brace & Co., 1931), 110; Andrews, *The Vanderbilt Legend*, 251–61; Landy, "The Domestic Architecture of the 'Robber Barons' in New York City": 67–68, 71, figs. 9–10; Consuelo Vanderbilt Balsan, *The Glitter and the Gold* (New York: Harper & Brothers, 1952), 10; Burnham, "The New York Architecture of Richard Morris Hunt": 9–14; Andrews, *Architecture, Ambition and Americans*, 178–79, 182–83, 185; Henry-Russell Hitchcock, *Architecture: Nineteenth and Twentieth Centuries* (Baltimore: Penguin, 1958), 455 (n. 11); Grace M. Mayer, *Once Upon a City* (New York: Macmillan, 1958), 30–31; James, *Fifth Avenue*, 72–73, 149–51, 154–55; Richard Guy Wilson, "Charles F. McKim and the Development of the American Renaissance: A Study in Architecture and Culture" (Ph.D. diss., University of Michigan, 1972): 241–42; Lewis and Morgan, *American Victorian Architecture*, plate II: 6; Lockwood, *Manhattan Moves Uptown*, 301–2; Pilgrim, "Decorative Art: The Domestic Environment," in *The American Renaissance, 1876–1917*, 120; Baker, *Richard Morris Hunt*, 274–87; Shopsin and Broderick, *The Villard Houses*, 18–19, 21, 46–49; Lightfoot, ed., *Nineteenth-Century New York in Rare Photographic Views*, fig. 116; Stern, Gilmartin, and Massengale, *New York 1900*, 309–11; Gray, "History of the Upper East Side": 123–24; Gray, "The Most Gilded Street": 88–96; David Chase, "Superb Privacies: The Later Domestic Commissions of Richard Morris Hunt, 1878–1895," in Stein, ed., *The Architecture of Richard Morris Hunt*, 150–71; Landau, "Richard Morris Hunt: Architectural Innovator and Father of a 'Distinctive' American School," in Stein, ed., *The Architecture of Richard Morris Hunt*, 46–77; Auchincloss, *The Vanderbilt Era*, 38, 45–47, 56–57; King with McLean, *The Vanderbilt Homes*, 46–55; Gray, "Show-off Houses": 94–103; Foreman and Stimson, *The Vanderbilts and the Gilded Age*, 22–45; Wist, *On Fifth Avenue: Then and Now*, 31–32; Hawes, *New York, New York*, 71–74, 76–78; Broderick, "Fifth Avenue," in Cigliano and Landau, eds., *The Grand American Avenue 1850–1920*, 18–20.

328. Baker, *Richard Morris Hunt*, 271, fig. 61.

329. Baker, *Richard Morris Hunt*, 274.

330. Landau, "Richard Morris Hunt: Architectural Innovator and Father of a 'Distinctive' American School," in Stein, ed., *The Architecture of Richard Morris Hunt*, 71.

331. Baker, *Richard Morris Hunt*, 541; Chase, "Superb Privacies: The Later Domestic Commissions of Richard Morris Hunt, 1878–1895," in Stein, ed., *The Architecture of Richard Morris Hunt*, 153–55; Broderick, "Fifth Avenue," in Cigliano and Landau, eds., *The Grand American Avenue 1850–1920*, 18.

332. Catherine Howland Hunt, quoted in Balsan, *The Glitter and the Gold*, 6, and Baker, *Richard Morris Hunt*, 275.

333. Schuyler, "Recent Building in New York—V": 243–44.

334. Schuyler, "The Vanderbilt Houses": 42.

335. Schuyler, "Some New Houses": 43–44.

336. Van Rensselaer, "Recent Architecture in America—V": 555.

337. Van Brunt, "Richard Morris Hunt": 83.

338. "Mr. Wm. K. Vanderbilt's House. First Paper": 770.

339. See Charles Moore, *Daniel H. Burnham, Architect, Planner of Cities* (Boston: Houghton Mifflin, 1921), vol. 1: 116.

340. Ferree, "Richard Morris Hunt: His Art and Work": 274.

341. W., "New Work," *American Architect and Building News* 5 (March 1, 1879): 69–70; W., "Correspondence," *American Architect and Building News* 5 (April 12, 1879): 117–18; "The Vanderbilt Method of Building," *Real Estate Record and Builders' Guide* (October 25, 1879): 848; "The New Vanderbilt Mansions," *New York Times*: 8; Schuyler, "Recent Building in New York—V": 243–44; "House of Cornelius Vanderbilt, Esq., New York, N.Y., Mr. George B. Post, Architect, New York, N.Y.," *American Architect and Building News* 9 (May 21, 1881): 247, plate; "Novelties in City Architecture," *Real Estate Record and Builders' Guide* 30 (July 8, 1882): 659; "More Fine Houses," *New York Sun* (January 14, 1883): 3; Mary Gay Humphreys, "The Cornelius Vanderbilt House," *Art Amateur* 8 (May 1883): 135–36; "The Best Ten Buildings in the United States": 282–83; "Entrance Porch, House of Cornelius Vanderbilt, New York City," *Building* 5 (August 28, 1886): 103, plate; "Past and Present," *The Illustrated American* 6 (March 28, 1891): 271–77; "Mr. Vanderbilt's New House," *The Illustrated American* 14 (July 8, 1893): 22; Banister F. Fletcher, "American Architecture Through English Spectacles," *Engineering Magazine* 7 (June 1894): 316; "House of Cornelius Vanderbilt, Esq., 58th St. and Fifth Ave., New York, N.Y., Mr. George B. Post, Architect, New York, N.Y.," *American Architect and Building News* 45 (August 4, 1894): plates; Schuyler, "The Works of the Late Richard M. Hunt": 165; Russell Sturgis, "A Review of the Work of George B. Post," *Architectural Record* 4 (June 1898): 1–102; Desmond and Croly, *Stately Homes in America*, 362, 365, 501, 503, 507, 511, 513; "Fifth Avenue, Fifty-seventh to Fifty-eighth Street," *Valentine's Manual of the City of New York*, ed. Henry Collins Brown (1917–18): 295; Andrews, *The Vanderbilt Legend*, 346–47; Landy, "The Domestic Architecture of the 'Robber Barons' in New York City": 71, fig. 11; Lewis and Morgan, *American Victorian Architecture*, plates II: 3–5; Lockwood, *Manhattan Moves Uptown*, 302; Pilgrim, "Decorative Art: The Domestic Environment," in *The American Renaissance, 1876–1917*, 120; Richard Guy Wilson, "The Great Civilization," in *The American Renaissance, 1876–1917*, figs. 24, 45; Baker, *Richard Morris Hunt*, 522–23 (n. 35), 548; Shopsin and Broderick, *The Villard Houses*, 46, 49, 68–69; Stern, Gilmartin, and Massengale, *New York 1900*, 309, 313; Christopher Gray, "Neighborhood/West Fifty-seventh Street," *Avenue* (March 1985): 79–91; Gray, "History of the Upper East Side": 122–24; Gray, "The Most Gilded Street": 88–96; Foreman and Stimson, *The Vanderbilts and the Gilded Age*, 46–69; Auchincloss, *The Vanderbilt Era*, 38–39; King with McLean, *The Vanderbilt Homes*, 28–37; Wist, *On Fifth Avenue: Then and Now*, 32–33; Landau, *George B. Post, Architect*, 40–51.

342. Schuyler, "Recent Building in New York—V": 243–44.

343. Schuyler, "The Works of the Late Richard M. Hunt": 165.

344. Sturgis, "A Review of the Work of George B. Post": 56.

345. Humphreys, "The Cornelius Vanderbilt House": 135.

346. "More Fine Houses": 3.

347. Bacon, *Ernest Flagg*, 15.

348. Baker, *Richard Morris Hunt*, 522–23 (n. 35), 548; Stern, Gilmartin, and Massengale, *New York 1900*, 313.

349. "Mr. Vanderbilt's New House," *The Illustrated American*: 22.

350. Sturgis, "A Review of the Work of George B. Post": 53, 55–56.

351. "Out Among the Builders," *Real Estate Record and Builders' Guide* 28 (November 19, 1881): 1075; "Gossip of the Week," *Real Estate Record and Builders' Guide* 28 (December 10, 1881): 1146; "The New York House of the Future," *Real Estate Record and Builders' Guide* 28 (December 31, 1881): 1208; Sheldon, *Artistic Houses*, vol. 2, part 2: 161–63; "Millionaire's Houses," *Real Estate Record and Builders' Guide* 32 (July 21, 1883): 521–22; "Mr. Villard's Italian Palace," *Building* 2 (December 1883): 38; "Some Up-Town Buildings," *Real Estate Record and Builders' Guide* 33 (January 5, 1884): 2–3; "A New York Palace," *The Architect*

(London) 31 (January 12, 1884): 34; George E. Waring Jr., "The Drainage of the Villard House in New York," *American Architect and Building News* 16 (August 16, 1884): 75–76, plates; "Villard's Houses," *Real Estate Record and Builders' Guide* 34 (September 6, 1884): 909; "Interior of the Villard House," *Real Estate Record and Builders' Guide* 36 (November 14, 1885): 1247–48; Van Rensselaer, "Recent American Architecture—V": 548–58; "Fireplace in House Built for Henry Villard, Esq., New York, N.Y., Messrs. McKim, Mead & White, Architects, New York, N.Y.," *American Architect and Building News* 22 (December 24, 1887): 302, plate; "Gelatine Print:—Entrance Court of the Villard Houses, Madison Avenue, Fiftieth and Fifty-first Streets, New York City," *Building* 8 (June 9, 1888): 185; "Two Dwellings," *Real Estate Record and Builders' Guide* 42 (July 28, 1888): 944–45; "Dining-Room in the House of Hon. Whitlaw Reid, Madison Avenue, New York, N.Y.," *American Architect and Building News* 26 (December 21, 1889): 290, plate; Sturgis, "The Works of McKim, Mead & White": 21–22, 24; Desmond and Croly, *Stately Homes in America*, 77, 79, 83; Edgell, *The American Architecture of To-Day*, 141–42; Charles Moore, *The Life and Times of Charles Follen McKim* (Boston: Houghton Mifflin, 1929; New York: Da Capo Press, 1970), 47–49, 319; C. Howard Walker, "Joseph Wells, Architect, 1853–1890," *Architectural Record* 66 (July 1929): 14–18; Charles C. Baldwin, *Stanford White* (New York: Dodd, Mead & Co., 1931), 357–58; Henry-Russell Hitchcock, *The Architecture of H. H. Richardson and His Times*, rev. ed. (New York: Museum of Modern Art, 1936; Cambridge, Mass.: MIT Press, 1966), 296–97; Henry-Russell Hitchcock, "Frank Lloyd Wright and the Academic Tradition of the Early Eighteen-Nineties," *Journal of the Warburg and Courtauld Institutes* 7 (1944): 46–63; Andrews, *Architecture, Ambition and Americans*, 186–88; Landy, "The Domestic Architecture of the 'Robber Barons' in New York City": 72, figs. 15–16; Hitchcock, *Architecture: Nineteenth and Twentieth Centuries*, 227–28, plate 109B; Landmarks Preservation Commission of the City of New York, LP-0268 (September 30, 1968); Wilson, "Charles F. McKim and the Development of the American Renaissance: A Study in Architecture and Culture": 244–62; Leland Roth, "McKim, Mead & White Reappraised," in *A Monograph of the Works of McKim, Mead & White, 1879–1915* (New York: Architectural Book Publishing Co., 1915; New York: Benjamin Blom, 1973), 11–12, 19, plates 7–11; Roth, *The Architecture of McKim, Mead & White, 1870–1920: A Building List*, 19, 57, 77, 130–31, 157, figs. 718, 869; Wilson, "The Great Civilization," in *The American Renaissance, 1876–1917*, 64, figs. 23, 43–44; Shopsin and Broderick, *The Villard Houses*; Roth, *McKim, Mead & White, Architects*, 86–90; Stern, Gilmartin, and Massengale, *New York 1900*, 311–12; Richard Guy Wilson, *McKim, Mead & White, Architects* (New York: Rizzoli International Publications, 1983), 16–18, 94–99; Reynolds, *The Architecture of New York City*, 188–92; Tauranac, *Elegant New York*, 117–21; Lewis, Turner, and McQuillen, *The Opulent Interiors of the Gilded Age*, 183–89; White and Willensky, *AIA Guide* (1988), 266; Lawrence Wodehouse, *White of McKim, Mead and White* (New York and London: Garland, 1988), 44–45, 144–49; Paul Baker, *Stanny: The Gilded Life of Stanford White* (New York: Macmillan, 1989), 105–11; David Garrard Lowe, *Stanford White's New York* (New York: Doubleday, 1992), 107–19; Diamonstein, *The Landmarks of New York II*, 180–81; Hawes, *New York, New York*, 85–91.

352. Stanford White to Mrs. Harrison, March 19, 1896, quoted in Baker, *Stanny*, 110.

353. "Millionaire's Houses": 521–22.

354. "Some Up-Town Buildings": 2–3.

355. "Interior of the Villard House": 1247–48.

356. Van Rensselaer, "Recent American Architecture—V": 557.

357. "Sketchings: Street Musings of Architecture," *Crayon* 6 (May 1859): 153–54; "Important Trial: Compensation of Architects," *Architects' and Mechanics' Journal* 3 (March 9, 1861): 222–26, (March 16, 1861): 231–34, (March 23, 1861): 242–45, (March 30, 1861): 252–55, vol. 4 (April 6, 1861): 4, 9; "Dwelling House in New York. Mr. R. M. Hunt, Architect," *American Architect and Building News* 3 (June 22, 1878): 216, plate; Schuyler, "The Works of the Late Richard M. Hunt": 99; Burnham, "The New York Architecture of Richard Morris Hunt": 9–14; John Burchard and Albert Bush-Brown, *The Architecture of America: A Social and Cultural History* (Boston: Little, Brown, 1961), 111; Baker, *Richard*

Morris Hunt, 80–87; "The Architect's Fee: R. M. Hunt versus E. Parmly," in Leland Roth, ed., *America Builds: Source Documents in American Architecture and Planning* (New York: Harper & Row, 1983), 216–31; Landau, "Richard Morris Hunt: Architectural Innovator and Father of a 'Distinctive' American School," in Stein, ed., *The Architecture of Richard Morris Hunt*, 66; Susan Stein, "Role and Reputation: The Architectural Practice of Richard Morris Hunt," in Stein, ed., *The Architecture of Richard Morris Hunt*, 110–11; Hawes, *New York, New York*, 78.

358. *Hunt v. Parmly*, Superior Court, New York (February 21, 22, 25, 26, 1861), quoted in "The Architect's Fee: R. M. Hunt versus E. Parmly," in Roth, ed., *America Builds: Source Documents in American Architecture and Planning*, 217.

359. *Hunt v. Parmly*, quoted in "The Architect's Fee: R. M. Hunt versus E. Parmly," in Roth, ed., *America Builds: Source Documents in American Architecture and Planning*, 220.

360. Schuyler, "The Works of the Late Richard M. Hunt": 99.

361. "Projected Buildings," *Real Estate Record and Builders' Guide* 1 (August 1, 1868): 12; Baker, *Richard Morris Hunt*, 228, 230; Lewis I. Sharp, *John Quincy Adams Ward, Dean of American Sculpture* (Newark, N.J.: University of Delaware Press; London: Associated University Presses, 1985), 24, 54–56; Landau, "Richard Morris Hunt: Architectural Innovator and Father of a 'Distinctive' American School," in Stein, ed., *The Architecture of Richard Morris Hunt*, 66–67.

362. "Buildings Projected," *Real Estate Record and Builders' Guide* 29 (April 29, 1882): 436; Baker, *Richard Morris Hunt*, 300, 504 (n. 9), 544; Sharp, *John Quincy Adams Ward, Dean of American Sculpture*, 63–65.

363. "New York Projected Buildings," *Real Estate Record and Builders' Guide* 3 (August 14, 1869): 7; Baker, *Richard Morris Hunt*, 230–31; Landau, "Richard Morris Hunt: Architectural Innovator and Father of a 'Distinctive' American School," in Stein, ed., *The Architecture of Richard Morris Hunt*, 66–67; Stein, "Role and Reputation: The Architectural Practice of Richard Morris Hunt," in Stein, ed., *The Architecture of Richard Morris Hunt*, 114; Hawes, *New York, New York*, 78.

364. Schuyler, "Recent Buildings in New York—III": 196. Also see "New York Projected Buildings," *Real Estate Record and Builders' Guide* 3 (August 21, 1869): 7; Jeffrey Karl Ochsner, *H. H. Richardson: Complete Architectural Works* (Cambridge, Mass.: MIT Press, 1982), 62–63. For Richardson's Hay-Adams houses, see Ochsner, 344–49.

365. "Buildings Projected," *Real Estate Record and Builders' Guide* 12 (September 6, 1873): 418; Landmarks Preservation Commission of the City of New York, *Treadwell Farms Historic District Designation Report* (New York, 1967), 5; Harmon H. Goldstone and Martha Dalrymple, *History Preserved: A Guide to New York City Landmarks and Historic Districts* (New York: Simon & Schuster, 1974), 285–87; Baker, *Richard Morris Hunt*, 230, 232.

366. "Projected Buildings," *Real Estate Record and Builders' Guide* 10 (October 19, 1872): 148; "Buildings Projected," *Real Estate Record and Builders' Guide* 11 (January 18, 1873): 30; Baker, *Richard Morris Hunt*, 504–5 (n. 12), 542–43.

367. W., "Correspondence," *American Architect and Building News* 4 (August 31, 1878): 77; B.W., "Correspondence," *American Architect and Building News* 5 (January 11, 1879): 12–13; "Back Buildings," *Real Estate Record and Builders' Guide* 23 (May 17, 1879): 397–98; Sheldon, *Artistic Houses*, vol. 1, part 2: 135; Schuyler, "The Works of the Late Richard M. Hunt": 112, 175; Edith Wharton, *A Backward Glance* (New York: D. Appleton, 1934), 92–94; Baker, *Richard Morris Hunt*, 230, 543–44; Lewis, Turner, and McQuillen, *The Opulent Interiors of the Gilded Age*, 70–71; Richard Guy Wilson, "Edith and Ogden: Writing, Decoration, and Architecture," in Pauline C. Metcalf, ed., *Ogden Codman and the Decoration of Houses* (Boston: Boston Atheneum and David R. Godine, 1988), 136–38.

368. W., "Correspondence," (August 31, 1878): 77.

369. "Back Buildings": 397–98.

370. B.W., "Correspondence," (January 11, 1879): 12–13.

371. Sheldon, *Artistic Houses*, vol. 1, part 2: 135.

372. Wharton, *A Backward Glance*, 92–94.

373. Schuyler, "Some New Houses": 43–44; "House of Mr. H. G. Marquand, Esq., New York, N.Y. Mr. R. M. Hunt, Architect, New York, N.Y.," *American Architect and Building News* 19 (June 26, 1886): 306,

plate; "The East Side—Its Streets and Buildings": 1–11; Cox, "American Construction Through English Eyes—III": 131–32; Schuyler, "The Works of the Late Richard M. Hunt": 131–33; Desmond and Croly, *Stately Homes in America*, 99, 103, 107; "The Splendid Marquand Mansion and Its Future," *New York Times* (April 16, 1905), second magazine sec., part 4: 8; Russell Sturgis, "The Famous Japanese Room in the Marquand House," *Architectural Record* 18 (September 1905): 192–201; Landy, "The Domestic Architecture of the 'Robber Barons' in New York City": 71–72; Lancaster, *The Japanese Influence in America*, 53; Calvin Tomkins, *Merchants and Masterpieces: The Story of the Metropolitan Museum of Art* (New York: E. P. Dutton, 1970), 73–75; Baker, *Richard Morris Hunt*, 293–96, 544; Landmarks Preservation Commission of the City of New York, *Upper East Side Historic District Designation Report* (New York, 1981), 360, 371; Christopher Gray, "The Still More Stately Mansions of Madison Avenue," *Avenue* (September 1983): 59–68; Chase, "Superb Privacies: The Later Domestic Commissions of Richard Morris Hunt, 1878–1895," in Stein, ed., *The Architecture of Richard Morris Hunt*, 154–55, 166. In 1883 Marquand commissioned Hunt to design a stable at 166 East Seventy-third Street, between Lexington and Third Avenues. See Baker, *Richard Morris Hunt*, 545; Christopher Gray, "Streetscapes/73d Street between Lexington and Third Avenues," *New York Times* (April 20, 1997), IX: 5.

374. Schuyler, "Some New Houses": 44.

375. For a discussion of Shaw, see Andrew Saint, *Richard Norman Shaw* (New Haven, Conn., and London: Yale University Press, 1976), esp. 130–42, 221–43.

376. H. Hudson Holly, *Modern Dwellings in Town and Country* (New York: Harper & Brothers, 1878; Watkins Glen, N.Y.: Library of Victorian Culture, 1977), 17–28. Also see William H. Jordy and Ralph Coe, "Editor's Introduction," in Schuyler, *American Architecture and Other Writings*, vol. 1: 73.

377. Schuyler, "Recent Building in New York—III": 196–97. Also see W., "Correspondence," *American Architect and Building News* 2 (December 8, 1877): 394; "Mr. Dickerson's New Residence," *Real Estate Record and Builders' Guide* 22 (August 24, 1878): 699; B.W., "Correspondence," (January 11, 1879): 12–13; "A Very Remarkable Building," *Real Estate Record and Builders' Guide* 24 (October 4, 1879): 781–82; M.E.W. Sherwood, "Certain New York Houses," *Harper's New Monthly Magazine* 65 (October 1882): 680–90; Sheldon, *Artistic Houses*, vol. 1, part 1: 81–85; Schuyler, "Recent Building in New York": 566; Wilson, "Charles F. McKim and the Development of the American Renaissance: A Study in Architecture and Culture": 227–29; Roth, *The Architecture of McKim, Mead & White, 1870–1920: A Building List*, 14, fig. 34; Roth, *McKim, Mead & White, Architects*, 50; Lewis, Turner, and McQuillen, *The Opulent Interiors of the Gilded Age*, 86–87.

378. Sherwood, "Certain New York Houses": 680–90.

379. Schuyler, "Recent Building in New York": 566.

380. Schuyler, "Recent Building in New York—III": 196.

381. *A History of Real Estate, Building and Architecture in New York City During the Last Quarter of a Century* (New York: Real Estate Record Association, 1898), 510, 514, 516. Also see B.W., "Correspondence," (January 11, 1879): 12–13; James Taylor, "The History of Terra Cotta in New York City," *Architectural Record* 2 (October–December 1892): 136–48; Landau and Condit, *Rise of the New York Skyscraper, 1865–1913*, 83; Landau, *George B. Post, Architect*, 35–36.

382. B.W., "Correspondence," (January 11, 1879): 12–13.

383. Sheldon, *Artistic Houses*, vol. 1, part 1: 47–52; Schuyler, "Recent Building in New York": 566; Van Rensselaer, "Recent Architecture in America—VI": 685; Lancaster, *The Japanese Influence in America*, 52; Wilson, "Charles F. McKim and the Development of the American Renaissance: A Study in Architecture and Culture": 229–31; Roth, *The Architecture of McKim, Mead & White, 1870–1920: A Building List*, 15, fig. 45; Roth, *McKim, Mead & White, Architects*, 50–51; Lewis, Turner, and McQuillen, *The Opulent Interiors of the Gilded Age*, 74–77.

384. Sheldon, *Artistic Houses*, vol. 2, part 1: 40–42; "More Fine Houses": 3; Schuyler, "Recent Building in New York": 566; Van Rensselaer, "Recent Architecture in America—V": 554; Van Rensselaer, "Recent Architecture in America—VI": 677; Sturgis, "The Works of McKim, Mead & White": 60–61; Hitchcock, "Frank Lloyd Wright and the Academic Tradition of the Early Eighteen-Nineties": 59; Wilson, "Charles F. McKim and the Development of the American Renaissance: A Study in Architecture and Culture": 234–35; Roth, *The Architecture of McKim, Mead & White, 1870–1920: A Building List*, 54, fig. 268; Roth, *McKim, Mead & White, Architects*, 80–81; Lewis, Turner, and McQuillen, *The Opulent Interiors of the Gilded Age*, 174; Baker, *Stanny*, 74.

385. Sturgis, "The Works of McKim, Mead & White": 61.

386. Schuyler, "Recent Building in New York": 566.

387. Sturgis, "The Works of McKim, Mead & White": 61.

388. Sturgis, "The Works of McKim, Mead & White": 61–62. Also see Schuyler, "Recent Building in New York—III": 197; "More Fine Houses": 3; Schuyler, "Recent Building in New York": 568–69; Van Rensselaer, "Recent Architecture in America—VI": 683–84; "Something About Side Stoops," *Real Estate Record and Builders' Guide* 38 (August 28, 1886): 1076; "House on Fifty-fifth Street, Near Fifth Avenue, New York City," *Building* 5 (October 9, 1886): 175, plate; Wilson, "Charles F. McKim and the Development of the American Renaissance: A Study in Architecture and Culture": 235–37; Roth, *The Architecture of McKim, Mead & White, 1870–1920: A Building List*, 26, fig. 97; Roth, *McKim, Mead & White, Architects*, 80; Baker, *Stanny*, 74–75.

389. Schuyler, "Recent Building in New York—III": 197. For Godwin, see Dudley Harbron, *The Conscious Stone: The Life of Edward William Godwin* (London: Latimer House, 1949).

390. Schuyler, "Recent Building in New York—III": 197.

391. "More Fine Houses": 3.

392. "Millionaire's Houses": 521–22; "Yellow Brick in Building": 780; "Upper Madison Avenue," *Real Estate Record and Builders' Guide* 33 (May 24, 1884): 560; "The Tiffany House," *Real Estate Record and Builders' Guide* 34 (July 26, 1884): 785–86; Edmund Gosse, "Mr. Gosse's Notes on America," *The Critic* 6 (January 24, 1885): 37–38; "Tiffany House," *Sanitary Engineer* 11 (April 9, 1885): 395; "A Modern Tile Roof," *Carpentry and Building* 7 (August 1885): 152–53; "Handsome East Side Residences Under Way," *Real Estate Record and Builders' Guide* 36 (October 24, 1885): 1159–60; Van Rensselaer, "Recent Architecture in America—V": 548–58; "House for Charles L. Tiffany, Esq., On Seventy-second, New York, N.Y.," *American Architect and Building News* 20 (July 17, 1886): 30, plate; "An Interior in the House of C. L. Tiffany, Esq., New York, N.Y. Messrs. McKim, Mead & White, Architects, New York, N.Y.," *American Architect and Building News* 22 (December 10, 1887): 278, plate; "Entrance to the House of C. L. Tiffany, Esq. New York, N.Y. Messrs. McKim, Mead & White, Architects, New York, N.Y.," *American Architect and Building News* 25 (January 19, 1889): 30, plate; "Residence of Charles L. Tiffany," *Carpentry and Building* 11 (November 1889): 220; Sturgis, "The Works of McKim, Mead & White": 54–55; "The Tiffany House," *Architectural Record* 10 (October 1900): 191–202; Desmond and Croly, *Stately Homes in America*, 445, 449, 451; De Kay, *The Art Work of Louis C. Tiffany*, 57–61, plates; *A Monograph of the Works of McKim, Mead & White, 1879–1915*, plates 5–5A; Baldwin, *Stanford White*, 122–23; Mumford, *The Brown Decades*, 127–28; Hitchcock, *The Architecture of H. H. Richardson and His Times*, 239; Landy, "The Domestic Architecture of the 'Robber Barons' in New York City": 72, fig. 14; Kaufmann, "At Home with Louis C. Tiffany": 118–25, 183; Hitchcock, *Architecture: Nineteenth and Twentieth Centuries*, 227; Mayer, *Once Upon a City*, 50–52; Koch, *Louis C. Tiffany: Rebel in Glass*, 62–64, 94–95; Wilson, "Charles F. McKim and the Development of the American Renaissance: A Study in Architecture and Culture": 242–44; Roth, "Urban Architecture of McKim, Mead & White, 1870–1910": 186–88; Watson, *New York Then and Now*, 94; Roth, *The Architecture of McKim, Mead & White, 1870–1920: A Building List*, 149, figs. 824; Shopsin and Broderick, *The Villard Houses*, 17, 44–45; Roth, *McKim, Mead & White, Architects*, 83–84; Stern, Gilmartin, and Massengale, *New York 1900*, 310–11; Gray, "The Still More Stately Mansions of Madison Avenue": 59–68; Boyer, *Manhattan Manners*, 179, 181; Baker, *Stanny*, 75–77; Lowe, *Stanford White's New York*, 85–89; Hawes, *New York, New York*, 82–85.

393. For Voysey, see Duncan Simpson, *C.F.A. Voysey: An Architect of Individuality* (London: Lund Humphries, 1979), esp. 116–27.

394. Van Rensselaer, "Recent Architecture in America—V": 553.

395. "Upper Madison Avenue": 560.

396. "The Tiffany House": 785–86.

397. "The Tiffany House": 785–86.

398. Van Rensselaer, "Recent Architecture in America—V": 556–57.

399. De Kay, *The Art Work of Louis C. Tiffany*, 57–61.

400. Gosse, "Mr. Gosse's Notes on America": 38.

401. "Alternate Designs for a City Home, New York, N.Y. Mr. Bruce Price, Architect, New York," *American Architect and Building News* 6 (November 1, 1879): 140, plate; Graybill, "Bruce Price, American Architect, 1845–1903": 29–30.

402. "Buildings Projected," *Real Estate Record and Builders' Guide* 28 (November 19, 1881): 1079; Schuyler, "Recent Building in New York": 564, 566; "House for Dr. Morton, New York, N.Y. Mr. Bruce Price, Architect, New York, N.Y.," *American Architect and Building News* 22 (December 17, 1887): 291, plate; Russell Sturgis, "The Works of Bruce Price," *Architectural Record* 5 (June 1899): 1–64; Graybill, "Bruce Price, American Architect, 1845–1903": 276.

403. Schuyler, "Recent Building in New York": 564, 566.

404. Sturgis, "The Works of Bruce Price": 38.

405. Sturgis, "The Works of Bruce Price": 37–38. Also see "Buildings Projected," *Real Estate Record and Builders' Guide* 34 (July 19, 1884): 782; "House of Dr. Thomas, Fifth Avenue [*sic*], New York, N.Y. Mr. Bruce Price, Architect, New York, N.Y.," *American Architect and Building News* 19 (March 13, 1886): 126, plate; "City News," *Building* 4 (February 13, 1886): 84; "Dr. Thomas's House," *Art Age* 3 (May 1886): 181; "The East Side—Its Streets and Buildings": 10; "House of Dr. C. [*sic*] G. Thomas, 600 Madison Avenue, New York, N.Y. Mr. Bruce Price, Architect, New York, N.Y.," *American Architect and Building News* 72 (May 4, 1901): 39, plate; Graybill, "Bruce Price, American Architect, 1845–1903": 276.

406. Vincent J. Scully Jr., *The Shingle Style and the Stick Style: Architectural Theory and Design from Richardson to the Origins of Wright*, rev. ed. (New Haven, Conn., and London: Yale University Press, 1955, 1971), 125.

407. "City News," *Building*: 84.

408. "House of Dr. Thomas, Fifth Avenue [*sic*], New York, N.Y. Mr. Bruce Price, Architect, New York, N.Y.," (March 13, 1886): 126.

409. "Building in Fifth Avenue," *Real Estate Record and Builders' Guide* 44 (August 24, 1889): 1159–60. Also see "Buildings Projected," *Real Estate Record and Builders' Guide* 41 (May 19, 1888): 661.

410. Schuyler, "Recent Building in New York—IV": 207–8.

411. "Buildings Projected," *Real Estate Record and Builders' Guide* 9 (April 27, 1872): 198; "Buildings Projected," *Real Estate Record and Builders' Guide* 9 (June 15, 1872): 282; Schuyler, "Recent Building in New York—IV": 207–8; "Russell Sturgis's Architecture," *Architectural Record* 25 (June 1909): 404–10; Edmund Morris, *The Rise of Theodore Roosevelt* (New York: Coward, McCann & Geoghegan, 1979), 74–75; David McCullough, *Mornings on Horseback* (New York: Simon & Schuster, 1981), 126–28, 131–36; Gray, "Neighborhood/West Fifty-seventh Street": 79; Karin May Elizabeth Alexis, "Russell Sturgis: Critic and Architect" (Ph.D. diss., University of Virginia, 1986): 98–103; George E. Thomas, Michael J. Lewis, and Jeffrey A. Cohen, *Frank Furness: The Complete Works* (New York: Princeton Architectural Press, 1991), 180–83.

412. Schuyler, "Recent Building in New York—IV": 207–8.

413. Theodore Roosevelt Sr. to Martha Bulloch Roosevelt, July 11, 1873, quoted in Morris, *The Rise of Theodore Roosevelt*, 74.

414. Schuyler, "Recent Building in New York—IV": 207–8. Also see "Buildings Projected," *Real Estate Record and Builders' Guide* 24 (September 13, 1879): 732; Sheldon, *Artistic Houses*, vol. 1, part 1: 97–99; Lewis, Turner, and McQuillen, *The Opulent Interiors of the Gilded Age*, 108–9.

415. Sheldon, *Artistic Houses*, vol. 1, part 1: 97–99.

416. Schuyler, "Recent Building in New York—IV": 207–8. Also see "Buildings Projected," *Real Estate Record and Builders' Guide* 24 (July 19, 1879): 595.

417. Schuyler, "Recent Building in New York—IV": 207–8. Also see "Buildings Projected," *Real Estate Record and Builders' Guide* 25 (March 13, 1880): 259.

418. Schuyler, "Recent Building in New York—IV": 207–8. Also see "Buildings Projected," *Real Estate Record and Builders' Guide* 24 (September 13, 1879): 732; Schuyler, "Recent Building in New York": 565; Gray, "Neighborhood/West Fifty-seventh Street": 82–83.

419. A. J. Bloor, "Annual Address," *Proceedings of the Tenth Annual Convention of the American Institute of Architects, 1876* (Boston, 1877): 15–34; Schuyler, "Recent Building in New York—IV": 207–8; Sherwood, "Certain New York Houses": 680–90; Sheldon, *Artistic Houses*, vol. 1, part 1: 101–9; Van Rensselaer, "Recent Architecture in America—V": 548–58; *Collins' Both Sides of Fifth Avenue* (New York: J.F.L. Collins, 1910), 26; Boyer, *Manhattan Manners*, 31, 38; Lewis, Turner, and McQuillen, *The Opulent Interiors of the Gilded Age*, 48–49.

420. Bloor, "Annual Address": 28.

421. Schuyler, "Recent Building in New York—IV": 207–8.

422. "Bay Windows in House in East Tenth Street, New York," *Building* 10 (January 26, 1889): 29, plate; *Greenwich Village Historic District*, 41–42; White and Willensky, *AIA Guide* (1988), 119; Christopher Gray, "Streetscapes/7 East 10th Street," *New York Times* (September 11, 1994), XIV: 7. Also see Lockwood de Forest, *Indian Domestic Architecture* (Boston: Heliotype Printing Co., 1885); Lockwood de Forest, *Indian Architecture and Ornament* (Boston: G. H. Polley & Co., 1887).

423. "Work on Mr. Tilden's House," *New York Daily Tribune* (January 29, 1882): 12; Sheldon, *Artistic Houses*, vol. 2, part 1: 61–65; Schuyler, "Recent Building in New York": 573; "House in Grammercy [*sic*] Park, New York, N.Y. Messrs. Vaux & Radford, Architects, New York, N.Y.," *American Architect and Buildings News* 33 (September 5, 1891): 155, plate; Landmarks Preservation Commission of the City of New York, LP-0223 (March 15, 1966); Sigle, "Calvert Vaux: An American Architect": 56–57; Lewis and Morgan, *American Victorian Architecture*, plate II: 7; Garmey, *Gramercy Park*, 98–103; Lewis, Turner, and McQuillen, *The Opulent Interiors of the Gilded Age*, 65, 147; White and Willensky, *AIA Guide* (1988), 197–98; Diamonstein, *The Landmarks of New York II*, 200; Alex, *Calvert Vaux*, 27–28, 100–5; Christopher Gray, "Streetscapes/National Arts Club, 15 Gramercy Park South," *New York Times* (September 21, 1997), IX: 5; Kowsky, *Country, Park and City*, 286–89.

424. Schuyler, "Recent Building in New York": 573.

425. Sheldon, *Artistic Houses*, vol. 2, part 1: 64–65.

426. For H.A.C. Taylor's New York house, see Stern, Gilmartin, and Massengale, *New York 1900*, 342. For the Newport house, see Scully, *The Shingle Style and the Stick Style*, 58.

427. Schuyler, "Recent Building in New York—III": 197. Also see "Buildings Projected," *Real Estate Record and Builders' Guide* 21 (May 25, 1878): 467; Schuyler, "Recent Building in New York": 564.

428. Schuyler, "Recent Building in New York": 564.

429. "Buildings Projected," *Real Estate Record and Builders' Guide* 30 (December 2, 1882): 1047; Russell Sturgis, "The City House: The East and South," *Scribner's Magazine* 7 (June 1890): 693–713; Russell Sturgis et al., *Homes in City and Country* (New York: Charles Scribner's Sons, 1893), 26–27; Sturgis, "The Works of McKim, Mead & White": 62–63; "Recent Brick and Terra-Cotta Work in American Cities," *Brickbuilder* 5 (January 1896): 16; "No. 21 East 33rd Street, New York, N.Y.," *American Architect and Building News* 87 (February 4, 1905): 40, plate; Hitchcock, "Frank Lloyd Wright and the Academic Tradition of the Early Eighteen-Nineties": 59, plate 16A; Vincent Scully, *Frank Lloyd Wright* (New York: George Braziller, 1960), 15, fig. 8; Wilson, "Charles F. McKim and the Development of the American Renaissance: A Study in Architecture and Culture": 263; Roth, "McKim, Mead & White Reappraised," in *A Monograph of the Works of McKim, Mead and White*, 33, 37, fig. 20; Roth, *The Architecture of McKim, Mead and White, 1870–1920: A Building List*, 121; Roth, *McKim, Mead & White, Architects*, 94–95; Baker, *Stanny*, 74.

430. Scully, *Frank Lloyd Wright*, 15. Also see Hitchcock, "Frank Lloyd Wright and the Academic Tradition of the Early Eighteen-Nineties": 59.

431. Schuyler, "Recent Building in New York": 578.

432. Sturgis, "The Works of McKim, Mead & White": 62.

433. Sturgis, "The Works of McKim, Mead & White": 62–63. Also see "Buildings Projected," *Real Estate Record and Builders' Guide* 38 (December 11, 1886): 1545; "Residence, No. 30 West [*sic*] Fifty-first Street, New York City," *Building* 10 (April 6, 1889): 113, plate; Wilson, "Charles F. McKim and the Development of the American Renaissance: A Study in Architecture and Culture": 263–64; Roth, *The Architecture of McKim, Mead & White, 1870–1920: A Building List*, 57; Roth, *McKim, Mead & White, Architects*, 95–96.

434. Dennis Steadman Francis and Joy M. Kestenbaum, "Jacob Wrey Mould," in *Macmillan Encyclopedia of Architects*, 4 vols. (New York: Free Press; London: Collier Macmillan, 1982), vol. 3: 246–47; Boyer, *Manhattan Manners*, 134; Gray, "History of the Upper East Side": 134.

435. Schuyler, "Recent Building in New York—IV": 207–8. Also see "Mr. Bostwick's Fifth Avenue Residence," *Real Estate Record and Builders' Guide* 22 (July 27, 1878): 628–29; *Collins' Both Sides of Fifth Avenue*, 30; Gray, "History of the Upper East Side": 148.

436. Schuyler, "Recent Building in New York—IV": 208. Also see "Buildings Projected," *Real Estate Record and Builders' Guide* 25 (April 10, 1880): 353; *Upper East Side Historic District*, 939.

437. Schuyler, "Recent Building in New York—IV": 207. Also see "Buildings Projected," *Real Estate Record and Builders' Guide* 23 (May 24, 1879): 435; Schuyler, "Some New Houses": 43–44; *Upper East Side Historic District*, 939.

438. Schuyler, "Some New Houses": 43–44.

439. "Buildings Projected," *Real Estate Record and Builders' Guide* 24 (August 30, 1879): 700; Schuyler, "Recent Building in New York—IV": 207; Schuyler, "Recent Building in New York": 565–66.

440. Schuyler, "Recent Building in New York—IV": 207–8.

441. "Houses in East 67th St. for I. E. Doying, Esq.," *American Architect and Building News* 8 (September 18, 1880): 138, plate; Herbert Croly, "The Renovation of the New York Brownstone District," *Architectural Record* 13 (June 1903): 555–71; *Upper East Side Historic District*, 312, 316; Boyer, *Manhattan Manners*, 173.

442. "Buildings Projected," *Real Estate Record and Builders' Guide* 27 (March 26, 1881): 293; Sheldon, *Artistic Houses*, vol. 2, part 2: 149–50; *Upper East Side Historic District*, 360–61; Lewis, Turner, and McQuillen, *The Opulent Interiors of the Gilded Age*, 158–59.

443. "Buildings Projected," *Real Estate Record and Builders' Guide* 27 (April 19, 1881): 383; Sheldon, *Artistic Houses*, vol. 2, part 1: 101–3; "Two New Houses," *Real Estate Record and Builders' Guide* 31 (June 23, 1883): 244; Christopher Gray, "The Street that Smelled of Beer," *Avenue* (November 1983): 94–101; Gray, "History of the Upper East Side": 140–41; Lewis, Turner, and McQuillen, *The Opulent Interiors of the Gilded Age*, 124–25.

444. "Two New Houses": 244.

445. "The Residence of Mr. A. J. White," *Real Estate Record and Builders' Guide* 36 (November 21, 1885): 1279–80.

446. Schuyler, "The Growth of the City": 4.

447. "Dwelling to Be Built on Fifth Avenue, New York, N.Y.—Mr. R. H. Robertson, Architect, New York, N.Y.," *American Architect and Building News* 9 (March 12, 1881): 127, plate; "Out Among the Builders," *Real Estate Record and Builders' Guide* 31 (May 17, 1883): 205; Schuyler, "Recent Building in New York": 566; Montgomery Schuyler, "The Works of R. H. Robertson," *Architectural Record* 6 (October–December 1896): 184–219.

448. Schuyler, "The Works of R. H. Robertson": 207.

449. "Buildings Projected," *Real Estate Record and Builders' Guide* 27 (March 19, 1881): 266–67; Sheldon, *Artistic Houses*, vol. 2, part 2: 115–16; Schuyler, "Some New Houses": 43–44; Schuyler, "Recent Building in New York": 569–70; Van Rensselaer, "Recent Architecture in America—V": 558; *Collins' Both Sides of Fifth Avenue*, 34; *Upper East Side Historic District*, 313; Lewis, Turner, and McQuillen, *The Opulent Interiors of the Gilded Age*, 128–29.

450. Schuyler, "Recent Building in New York": 569–70.

451. Sheldon, *Artistic Houses*, vol. 2, part 2: 115.

452. Van Rensselaer, "Recent Architecture in America—V": 558.

453. "Buildings Projected," *Real Estate Record and Builders' Guide* 28 (October 8, 1881): 958; "Buildings Projected," *Real Estate Record and Builders' Guide* 29 (May 6, 1882): 470; "An Experiment in Cottage Building," *Real Estate Record and Builders' Guide* 31 (April 21, 1883): 156–57; Stokes, *The Iconography of Manhattan Island*, vol. 3: 993; Landmarks Preservation Commission of the City of New York, LP-0454 (February 11, 1969); White and Willensky, *AIA Guide* (1988), 413; Diamonstein, *The Landmarks of New York II*, 444; Andrew Dolkart, *Touring the Upper East Side* (New York: New York Landmarks Conservancy, 1995), 109–13.

454. "An Experiment in Cottage Building": 156–57.

455. "Buildings Projected," *Real Estate Record and Builders' Guide* 37 (May 8, 1886): 630; Landmarks Preservation Commission of the City of New York, LP-1004-9 (March 13, 1979); White and Willensky, *AIA Guide* (1988), 409; Diamonstein, *The Landmarks of New York II*, 193.

456. "Buildings Projected," *Real Estate Record and Builders' Guide* 27 (April 19, 1881): 383; Sheldon, *Artistic Houses*, vol. 2, part 1: 87; "More Fifth Avenue Houses," *Real Estate Record and Builders' Guide* 32 (July 7, 1883): 473–74; *Collins' Both Sides of Fifth Avenue*, 38; Landy, "The Domestic Architecture of the 'Robber Barons' in New York City": 72; *Upper East Side Historic District*, 935–36; Lewis, Turner, and McQuillen, *The Opulent Interiors of the Gilded Age*, 103–5.

457. "More Fifth Avenue Houses": 473–74.

458. "More Fifth Avenue Houses": 473–74. Also see "Buildings Projected," *Real Estate Record and Builders' Guide* 30 (July 29, 1882): 732; *Upper East Side Historic District*, 933.

459. "More Fifth Avenue Houses": 473–74. Also see "Buildings Projected," *Real Estate Record and Builders' Guide* 30 (July 1, 1882): 655; "The Residence of Mr. A. J. White": 1279–80; "Mr. A. J. White's House," *Art Age* 3 (May 1886): 181; "Residence of Andrew J. White, Esq., Fifth Avenue and Sixty-sixth Street," *Building* 9 (December 22, 1888): 225, plate; *Upper East Side Historic District*, 928.

460. "Mr. A. J. White's House," *Art Age*: 181.

461. "Millionaires' Houses": 521–22; "Notes About Town," *Real Estate Record and Builders' Guide* 36 (November 7, 1885): 1223; "House of Henry H. Cook, Esq., Corner 78th St., and Fifth Ave., New York, N.Y. Mr. W. Wheeler Smith, Architect, New York, N.Y.," *American Architect and Building News* 24 (December 15, 1888): 276, plate; "East Side Architecture—Fifth Avenue," *Real Estate Record and Builders' Guide* 45 (May 3, 1890): 640–41; "The East Side—Its Streets and Buildings": 3; Landmarks Preservation Commission of the City of New York, *Metropolitan Museum Historic District Designation Report* (New York, 1977), 11; Boyer, *Manhattan Manners*, 189.

462. "Millionaires' Houses": 521–22.

463. "East Side Architecture—Fifth Avenue": 640–41.

464. "Upper Fifth Avenue," *Real Estate Record and Builders' Guide* 34 (August 16, 1884): 853–54. Also see "Buildings Projected," *Real Estate Record and Builders' Guide* 24 (June 10, 1882): 591; *Upper East Side Historic District*, 951–52.

465. "Houses East of Central Park," *Real Estate Record and Builders' Guide* 39 (January 29, 1887): 130–31.

466. "City News," *Building* 4 (February 13, 1886): 84; "Some New East Side Buildings," *Real Estate Record and Builders' Guide* 39 (January 1, 1887): 5–6; Schuyler, "The Works of the Late Richard M. Hunt": 173; Burnham, "The New York Architecture of Richard Morris Hunt": 14; Baker, *Richard Morris Hunt*, 295, 297–98; *Upper East Side Historic District*, 935, 937; Chase, "Superb Privacies: The Later Domestic Commissions of Richard Morris Hunt, 1878–1895," in Stein, ed., *The Architecture of Richard Morris Hunt*, 152, 154–55.

467. "Some New East Side Buildings": 5–6.

468. "Buildings Projected," *Real Estate Record and Builders' Guide* 34 (April 2, 1887): 465; Baker, *Richard Morris Hunt*, 546; *Upper East Side Historic District*, 937.

469. "Buildings Projected," *Real Estate Record and Builders' Guide* 34 (January 15, 1887): 92; "Buildings Projected," *Real Estate Record and Builders' Guide* 34 (June 25, 1887): 883; "Foyer and Music-Room for E. Lauterbach, Esq., New York, N.Y. Messrs. A. Zucker & Co., Architects, New York, N.Y.," *American Architect and Building News* 24 (July 7, 1888): 7, plate; "Dining Room and Reception-Room in House of L. M. Hornthal, Esq., New York, N.Y. Messrs. A Zucker & Co., Architects, New York, N.Y.," *American Architect and Building News* 24 (August 11, 1888): 63, plate; "The East Side—Its Streets and Buildings": 7; *Photographed from Designs for Buildings and from Buildings Erected by Alfred Zucker, Architect* (New York: National Chemigraph Co., 1894), n.p.; *Metropolitan Museum Historic District*, 11.

470. "A Fifth Avenue House," *Real Estate Record and Builders' Guide* 41 (April 7, 1888): 420–21; "East Side Architecture—Fifth Avenue": 640–41; "The East Side—Its Streets and Buildings": 2; "Modern American Residences, No. I: The Brokaw Residence, Rose & Stone, Architects," *Architectural Record* 1 (October–December 1891): plates; Landy,

"The Domestic Architecture of the 'Robber Barons' in New York City": 73; Silver, *Lost New York*, 127; *Metropolitan Museum Historic District*, 87; Stern, Mellins, and Fishman, *New York 1960*, 1098, 1100.

471. "East Side Architecture—Fifth Avenue": 640–41.

472. "A Fifth Avenue House": 420–21.

473. "East Side Architecture—Fifth Avenue": 640–41.

474. "Buildings Projected," *Real Estate Record and Builders' Guide* 46 (August 30, 1890): 290; *Metropolitan Museum Historic District*, 11; Baker, *Richard Morris Hunt*, 340, 342, 547; *Upper East Side Historic District*, 964, 967; Chase, "Superb Privacies: The Later Domestic Commissions of Richard Morris Hunt, 1878–1895," in Stein, ed., *The Architecture of Richard Morris Hunt*, 169 (n. 4).

475. "Out Among the Builders," *Real Estate Record and Builders' Guide* 43 (March 23, 1889): 392–94; "East Side Architecture—Fifth Avenue": 640–41; Montgomery Schuyler, "The Romanesque Revival in New York," *Architectural Record* 1 (July–September 1891): 7–38; "Modern American Residences, No. II: Residence of H. O. Havemeyer, Esq.," *Architectural Record* 1 (April–June 1892): plates; Landy, "The Domestic Architecture of the 'Robber Barons' in New York City": 72–73; Kaufmann, "At Home with Louis C. Tiffany": 118–25, 183; Aline B. Saarinen, *The Proud Possessors* (New York: Random House, 1958), 143–73; Louisine W. Havemeyer, *Sixteen to Sixty: Memoirs of a Collector* (New York: Metropolitan Museum of Art, 1961), 10–25; Koch, *Louis C. Tiffany: Rebel in Glass*, 72–73, 101; Samuel Bing, *Artistic America, Tiffany Glass, and Art Nouveau* (Cambridge, Mass.: MIT Press, 1970), 130–31; Hugh F. McKean, *The 'Lost' Treasures of Louis Comfort Tiffany* (Garden City, N.Y.: Doubleday & Co., 1980), 112–13, figs. 103–4; *Upper East Side Historic District*, 275; Frances Weitzenhoffer, *The Havemeyers: Impressionism Comes to America* (New York: Harry N. Abrams, 1986), 49–52, 59, 70–81, 100, 145–47, 197–98; Paul, *The Art of Louis Comfort Tiffany*, 57–59; Alice Cooney Frelinghuysen, "The Havemeyer House," in Alice Cooney Frelinghuysen et al., *Splendid Legacy: The Havemeyer Collection* (New York: Metropolitan Museum of Art, 1993), 173–98.

476. Schuyler, "The Romanesque Revival in New York": 35–36.

CHAPTER 5
Amusements

1. "Concerning Men and Things," *Real Estate Record and Builders' Guide* 32 (November 17, 1883): 903.

2. Moses King, *King's Handbook of New York* (Boston: Moses King, 1893), 575.

3. Michael Pye, *Maximum City: The Biography of New York* (London: Sinclair-Stevenson, 1991), 156.

4. For a brief, informative history of theater in New York, see John W. Frick and Martha S. LoMonaco, "Theater," in Kenneth T. Jackson, ed., *The Encyclopedia of New York City* (New Haven, Conn., and London: Yale University Press; New York: New-York Historical Society, 1995), 1165–76. Also see Thomas Allston Brown, *A History of the New York Stage*, 3 vols. (New York: Dodd, Mead, 1903); Mary C. Henderson, *The City and the Theatre: New York Playhouses from Bowling Green to Times Square* (Clifton, N.J.: James T. White, 1973); William C. Young, *Documents in American Theater History: Volume 1, Famous American Playhouses, 1716–1899* (Chicago: American Library Association, 1973). For an overview of New York theater architecture, see "Theater Architecture," in Jackson, ed., *The Encyclopedia of New York City*, 1176–77.

5. Samuel Osgood, *New York in the Nineteenth Century* (New York: New-York Historical Society, 1866), 51.

6. John W. Kennion, *Architects' and Builders' Guide* (New York: Fitzpatrick & Hunter, 1868), part 3: 45–47; King, *King's Handbook of New York* (1893), 576; Brown, *A History of the New York Stage*, vol. 2: 376–79; I. N. Phelps Stokes, *The Iconography of Manhattan Island*, 6 vols. (New York: Robert H. Dodd, 1915–28; New York: Arno Press, 1967), vol. 5: 984; John Cornwall Edwards, "A History of Nineteenth Century Theatre Architecture in the United States" (Ph.D. diss., Northwestern University, 1963): 232–35; Nathan Silver, *Lost New York* (Boston: Houghton Mifflin, 1967), 76; Henderson, *The City and the Theatre*, 117.

7. A. Oakey Hall, quoted in Brown, *A History of the New York Stage*, vol. 2: 376.

8. Kennion, *Architects' and Builders' Guide*, part 3: 46; "The New French Theater," *New York World* (May 25, 1866): 5; "The Theaters: The Opening of the New French Theater," *New York Daily Tribune* (May 28, 1866): 5, King, *King's Handbook of New York* (1893), 602; Brown, *A History of the New York Stage*, vol. 2: 447–75; Robert Grau, "New York Theatres Forty Odd Years Ago," *American Architect* 104 (1913), part 2: 280–82, 284; Stokes, *The Iconography of Manhattan Island*, vol. 5: 984; Mollie B. Steinberg, *The History of the Fourteenth Street Theater* (New York: Dial, 1931), 21–22; "Old Fourteenth Street Theatre to Go," *New York Sun* (October 19, 1936): 9; Silver, *Lost New York*, 76, 81; Henderson, *The City and the Theatre*, 139–40; Clarence P. Hornung, *New York, 1850–1890* (New York: Schocken, 1977), 197.

9. Kennion, *Architects' and Builders' Guide*, part 3: 46.

10. "The New French Theater": 5.

11. "The Theaters: The Opening of the New French Theater": 5.

12. "Union Square Theater," *New York Daily Tribune* (September 12, 1871): 5; "Music and the Drama: The Union Square Theatre," *New York Herald* (September 13, 1871): 4; King, *King's Handbook of New York* (1893), 602; A. E. Lancaster, "A. M. Palmer and the Union Square Theater," *Theatre* (March 1903): 62–65; "The Union Square Theater Takes a Very Final Curtain," *New York Herald Tribune* (September 6, 1936), VII: 4; Edwards, "A History of Nineteenth Century Theatre Architecture in the United States": 235; Donald C. King, "New York's Oldest Existing Theatre—The Union Square," *Marquee* 6 (1974): 18; John W. Frick, *New York's First Theatrical Center—The Rialto at Union Square* (Ann Arbor, Mich.: UMI Research Press, 1985), 50–55; John W. Frick and Carlton Ward, eds., *Directory of Historic American Theaters* (Westport, Conn.: Greenwood, 1987), 190–91; Christopher Gray, "The Ghost Behind a Huge Sign," *New York Times* (January 29, 1989), X: 12, reprinted in Christopher Gray, *Changing New York: The Architectural Scene* (New York: Dover, 1992), 77.

13. "Union Square Theater," *New York Daily Tribune*: 5.

14. "Music and the Drama: The Union Square Theater": 4.

15. "Music and the Drama: The Union Square Theater": 4.

16. Kennion, *Architects' and Builders' Guide*, part 2: 19–22; "Booth's New Theatre," *New York World* (April 9, 1868): 8; "Edwin Booth's Theatre," *New York Daily Tribune* (November 18, 1868): 5; "Booth's Theatre," *Harper's Weekly* 13 (January 9, 1869): 21–22, 29; "Opening of Booth's Theatre," *New York Times* (February 4, 1869): 5; Montgomery Schuyler, "Opening of Booth's Theatre," *New York World* (February 4, 1869): 5; George Templeton Strong, diary entry dated February 13, 1869, in *The Diary of George Templeton Strong*, eds. Allan Nevins and Milton Halsey Thomas, 4 vols. (New York: Macmillan, 1952), vol. 4: 241–43; "Booth's Theatre," *Building News* (London) 10 (April 16, 1869): 20; "New York Illustrated—No. 2," *Appletons' Journal* 1 (June 12, 1869): 1–8; Montgomery Schuyler, "Recent Building in New York—I," *American Architecture and Building News* 9 (April 9, 1881): 176–77; King, *King's Handbook of New York* (1893), 582; Charles Burnham, "New York's Historic Theatres—Booth's Theatre," *Theatre* (April 1918): 236; Brown, *A History of the New York Stage*, vol. 2: 94; George C. D. Odell, *Annals of the New York Stage*, 8 vols. (New York: Columbia University Press, 1936), vol. 7: 26–27, vol. 8: 423; Stanley Kimmel, *The Mad Booths of Maryland* (Indianapolis, Ind.: Bobbs-Merrill, 1940), 277–87, 310; Rosalie Thorne McKenna, "James Renwick, Jr., and the Second Empire Style in the United States," *Magazine of Art* 44 (March 1951): 97–101; Eleanor Ruggles, *Prince of Players* (New York: W. W. Norton, 1953), 212–22, 242–45, 310–12; Edwards, "A History of Nineteenth Century Theatre Architecture in the United States": 222–26; Henderson, *The City and the Theatre*, 144, 146–47; Loren Hufstetler, "A Physical Description of Booth's Theatre, New York, 1869–1883," *Theatre Design and Technology* 46 (winter 1976): 8–18, 38; John Grafton, *New York in the Nineteenth Century* (New York: Dover, 1977), 138–39; Gene Smith, *American Gothic: The Story of America's Legendary Theatrical Family—Junius, Edwin, and John Wilkes Booth* (New York: Simon & Schuster, 1992), 234–35, 242.

17. Schuyler, "Opening of Booth's Theatre": 5.

18. Strong, diary entry dated February 13, 1869, in *The Diary of George Templeton Strong*, vol. 4: 241.

19. King, *King's Handbook of New York* (1893), 600; Stokes, *The Iconography of Manhattan Island*, vol. 5: 982; Henderson, *The City and the Theatre*, 162, 164, 167.

20. "Opening of Booth's Theatre," *New York Times*: 5.

21. Schuyler, "Opening of Booth's Theatre": 5.

22. Schuyler, "Recent Building in New York—I": 176.

23. "New York Illustrated—No. 2": 6.

24. "The New Theatre," *New York Times* (May 31, 1873): 4; "The New Park Theatre," *New York Times* (September 28, 1873): 18; "The New Park Theatre," *New York Times* (March 30, 1874): 5; "The New Park Theatre," *New York Times* (April 15, 1874): 2; "Burned to the Ground," *New York Herald* (October 31, 1882): 5; "The Park Theatre Gone," *New York Times* (October 31, 1882): 1; Editorial, *New York Times* (November 2, 1882): 4; King, *King's Handbook of New York* (1893), 582; Brown, *A History of the New York Stage*, vol. 3: 190–95; Stokes, *The Iconography of Manhattan Island*, vol. 5: 982; Henderson, *The City and the Theatre*, 123, 143–45; M. Christine Boyer, *Manhattan Manners: Architecture and Style, 1850–1900* (New York: Rizzoli International Publications, 1985), 33.

25. "The New Park Theatre," (April 15, 1874): 2.

26. Croswell Bowen, *The Elegant Oakey* (New York: Oxford University Press, 1956), 198–210.

27. "Correspondence," *American Architect and Building News* 1 (March 18, 1876): 95; Editorial, *New York Times* (November 2, 1882): 4; King, *King's Handbook of New York* (1893), 600; Brown, *History of the New York Stage*, vol. 2: 235; Pierre Sichel, *The Jersey Lily: The Story of the Fabulous Mrs. Lantry* (Englewood Cliffs, N.J.: Prentice-Hall, 1958), 165–67; Mary Black, *Old New York in Early Photographs* (New York: Dover, 1973), 153; Henderson, *The City and the Theatre*, 162–63; Edward B. Watson, *New York Then and Now* (New York: Dover, 1976), 16.

28. King, *King's Handbook of New York* (1893), 600.

29. "Buildings Projected," *Real Estate Record and Builders' Guide* 27 (May 14, 1881): 415; "New Wallack's Theatre," *American Architect and Building News* 10 (October 29, 1881): 201; "Mr. Wallack's New Theatre," *American Architect and Building News* 10 (December 24, 1881): 297–98; "Pictures of the Day," *New York Daily Graphic* (January 5, 1882): 446, 448; "A Notable First Night," *New York Times* (January 5, 1882): 5; "Wallack's Theatre," *Harper's Weekly* 39 (January 7, 1882): 21; King, *King's Handbook of New York* (1893), 592–93; Brown, *A History of the New York Stage*, vol. 2: 299–303, 310; Charles Burnham, "The Passing of Wallack's," *Theatre* (February 1915): 72–76; "The Passing of Wallack's Theatre," *New York Times* (March 9, 1915), VII: 5; Edwards, "A History of Nineteenth Century Theatre Architecture in the United States": 235–41; Henderson, *The City and the Theatre*, 114, 158–61; Hornung, *New York, 1850–1890*, 202; David Dunlap, *On Broadway: A Journey Uptown Over Time* (New York: Rizzoli International Publications, 1990), 139.

30. King, *King's Handbook of New York* (1893), 600–602.

31. "Pictures of the Day": 446.

32. Horace Townsend, "American Theaters," *Journal of the Royal Institute of British Architects* 8 (December 1891): 65–90, reprinted in *American Architect and Building News* 32 (January 9, 1892): 29–32. Also see "Correspondence," *American Architect and Building News* 1 (April 8, 1876): 118; "The Madison-Square Theatre: Mr. MacKaye's Improvements in the Stage Mechanism," *New York Times* (February 1, 1880): 5; "The Madison-Square Theatre," *New York Times* (February 5, 1880): 5; "Madison-Square Theatre," *New York Times* (March 5, 1880): 5; "Madison-Square Theatre Concert," *New York Times* (April 2, 1880): 5; "Movable Theater Stages," *Scientific American* 50 (April 5, 1884): 207; King, *King's Handbook of New York* (1893), 597; Montgomery Schuyler, "The Works of Francis H. Kimball and Kimball & Thompson," *Architectural Record* 7 (April–June 1898): 479–518; Brown, *A History of the New York Stage*, vol. 2: 399; Stokes, *The Iconography of Manhattan Island*, vol. 5: 983; Edwards, "A History of Nineteenth Century Theatre Architecture in the United States": 213–22, 399–446; Boyer, *Manhattan Manners*, 72, 74–75; Landmarks Preservation Commission of the City of New York, LP-1352 (December 8, 1987); Landmarks Preservation Commission of the City of New York, *Ladies' Mile Historic District Designation Report* (New York, 1989), 314.

33. "The Madison-Square Theatre: Mr. MacKaye's Improvements in the Stage Mechanism": 5.

34. "A Model Theatre," *Art Journal* (n.d., Dartmouth College Library), quoted in Edwards, "A History of Nineteenth Century Theatre in the United States": 218. For further discussion of Steele MacKaye, see Percy MacKaye, "Epoch: The Life of Steele MacKaye: Producer and Director" (Ph.D. diss., University of Illinois, 1958). Also see the Steele MacKaye Collection, Dartmouth College Library, and the Percy MacKaye Collection, Harvard College Library.

35. "The Madison-Square Theatre: Mr. MacKaye's Improvements in the Stage Mechanism": 5.

36. "Brougham's Theatre," *New York Times* (January 25, 1869): 5. Also see "Correspondence," *American Architect and Building News* 1 (April 8, 1876): 118; Schuyler, "The Works of Francis H. Kimball and Kimball & Thompson": 503–4.

37. "The Fifth Avenue Theatre," *New York Daily Graphic* (September 10, 1878): 489, 494.

38. "The Madison-Square Theatre: Mr. MacKaye's Improvements in the Stage Mechanism": 5.

39. Schuyler, "The Works of Francis H. Kimball and Kimball & Thompson": 502.

40. "Out Among the Builders," *Real Estate Record and Builders' Guide* 28 (September 24, 1881): 903; "The Casino," *New York Daily Graphic* (October 21, 1882): 793; "The New Casino Opened," *New York Daily Tribune* (October 23, 1882): 2; "The Alcazar Casino," *Real Estate Record and Builders' Guide* 30 (November 18–25, 1882): 84–85; "The Casino Opened," *New York Times* (December 31, 1882): 3; "Brick Architecture in New York," *Building* 1 (May 1883): 105; Montgomery Schuyler, "The Metropolitan Opera House," *Harper's New Monthly Magazine* 67 (November 1883): 877–89; Editorial, *American Architect and Building News* 10 (August 9, 1884): 61; "The Casino Theatre, New York, N.Y. Messrs. Kimball & Wisedell, Architects, New York," *American Architect and Building News* 18 (August 29, 1885): 102, plate; C. Hinckeldeyn, "A Foreigner's View of American Architecture," *American Architect and Building News* 25 (May 25, 1889): 243–44; Townsend, "American Theatres": 77; "Entrance to Casino," *Architectural Record* 2 (October–December 1892): 154; James Taylor, "The History of Terra Cotta in New York City," *Architectural Record* 2 (October–December 1892): 136–48; King, *King's Handbook of New York* (1893), 591–92, 601; *A History of Real Estate, Building and Architecture in New York City During the Last Quarter of a Century* (New York: Real Estate Record Association, 1898), 520–21; Schuyler, "The Works of Francis H. Kimball and Kimball & Thompson": 494–96; Brown, *A History of the New York Stage*, vol. 3: 485; Edwards, "A History of Nineteenth Century Theatre Architecture in the United States": 243–46; Silver, *Lost New York*, 86; Henderson, *The City and the Theatre*, 168; Stern, Gilmartin, and Massengale, *New York 1900*, 206–7, 220–21.

41. "Out Among the Builders": 903.

42. "The New Casino Opened," *New York Daily Tribune*: 2.

43. "The Alcazar Casino": 84.

44. "The Alcazar Casino": 84.

45. Hinckeldeyn, "A Foreigner's View of American Architecture": 244.

46. Townsend, "American Theatres": 77.

47. King, *King's Handbook of New York* (1893), 591–92, 601.

48. Schuyler, "The Works of Francis H. Kimball and Kimball & Thompson": 494.

49. King, *King's Handbook of New York* (1893), 599; Brown, *A History of the New York Stage*, vol. 2: 507; Henderson, *The City and the Theater*, 147–49.

50. King, *King's Handbook of New York* (1893), 599.

51. "Out Among the Builders," *Real Estate Record and Builders' Guide* 33 (January 19, 1884): 59; "The Amusement Season," *New York Times* (April 7, 1885): 5; Townsend, "American Theatres": 77; King, *King's Handbook of New York* (1893), 596; Brown, *A History of the New York Stage*, vol. 3: 419–20; Edwards, "A History of Nineteenth Century Theatre Architecture in the United States": 241–43; Robert Koch, *Louis C. Tiffany: Rebel in Glass* (New York: Crown, 1964), 59–61, 92–93, 131, 134; Tessa Paul, *The Art of Louis Comfort Tiffany* (New York: Exeter, 1987), 40–41.

52. "The Amusement Season": 5.

53. "Broadway Theatre," *New York Times* (February 18, 1888): 5; "Finishing a New Theatre," *New York Times* (February 18, 1888): 8; "The New Play House," *New York Times* (February 25, 1888): 3; "'La Tosca' and the New Theatre," *New York Daily Graphic* (March 3, 1888): 19, 25; "Near the Opera House," *Real Estate Record and Builders' Guide* 41 (March 10, 1888): 294–95; King, *King's Handbook of New York* (1893), 598; Brown, *A History of the New York Stage*, vol. 2: 396; Stokes, *The Iconography of Manhattan Island*, vol. 5: 982; Henderson, *The City and the Theatre*, 216; Watson, *New York Then and Now*, 18.

54. "Broadway Theatre": 5.

55. "Near the Opera House": 294–95.

56. "'La Tosca' and the New Theatre": 25.

57. For discussions of the development and history of opera in New York, see Richard Grant White, "Opera in New York: I," *Century Magazine* 23 (March 1882): 686–703; Richard Grant White, "Opera in New York: II," *Century Magazine* 23 (April 1882): 865–81; Julius Mattfeld, "A Hundred Years of Grand Opera in New York 1825–1925," *New York Public Library Bulletin* 29 (October 1925): 695–702; Ann M. Lingg, "Great Opera Houses: Old New York," *Opera News* 50 (February 3, 1962): 8–12; John Dizikes, *Opera in America: A Cultural History* (New Haven, Conn.: Yale University Press, 1993); John W. Freeman, "Opera," in Jackson, ed., *The Encyclopedia of New York City*, 865–66.

58. White, "Opera in New York: I": 703.

59. White, "Opera in New York: II": 875.

60. "Opera's Northward March," *New York Times* (July 20, 1891): 4; Richard Moody, *The Astor Place Riot* (Bloomington, Ind.: University of Indiana Press, 1958); Dizikes, *Opera in America*, 159–62. Also see William Rounseville Alger, *Life of Edwin Forrest: The American Tragedian*, 2 vols. (Philadelphia: J. B. Lippincott, 1877), vol. 1: 430–32; Montrose J. Moses, *The Fabulous Forrest* (Boston: Little, Brown, 1929), 250–64; Charles H. Shattuck, *Bulwer and Macready: A Chronicle of the Early Victorian Theatre* (Urbana, Ill.: University of Illinois Press, 1958), 223–37; Richard Moody, *Edwin Forrest: First Star of the American Stage* (New York: Alfred A. Knopf, 1960), 267–81.

61. "The New Academy of Music," editorial, *New York Times* (June 22, 1866): 4; "The Academy of Music," *New York Times* (January 22, 1867): 2; "The New Academy," *New York World* (March 2, 1867): 5; Kennion, *Architects' and Builders' Guide*, part 2: 113–14; King, *King's Handbook of New York* (1893), 603–4; Brown, *A History of the New York Stage*, vol. 2: 49; Edith Wharton, *The Age of Innocence* (New York: D. Appleton, 1920), 3; "Academy of Music Closed Forever," *New York Times* (May 18, 1926): 3; James V. Kavenaugh, "Three American Opera Houses: The Boston Theatre, The New York Academy of Music, The Philadelphia American Academy of Music" (Ph.D. diss., University of Delaware, 1967); Silver, *Lost New York*, 78–79; Henderson, *The City and the Theatre*, 110–13; Grafton, *New York in the Nineteenth Century*, 137; Frederick S. Lightfoot, ed., *Nineteenth-Century New York in Rare Photographic Views* (New York: Dover, 1981), fig. 71; John Frederick Cone, *First Rival of the Metropolitan Opera* (New York: Columbia University Press, 1983); Stephen Garmey, *Gramercy Park: An Illustrated History of a New York Neighborhood* (New York: Balsam, 1984), 106; Dizikes, *Opera in America*, 166–67; Nancy Shear, "Academy of Music," in Jackson, ed., *The Encyclopedia of New York City*, 4.

62. Quoted in Silver, *Lost New York*, 79.

63. Wharton, *The Age of Innocence*, 3.

64. Kennion, *Architects' and Builders' Guide*, part 2: 23–24; "Pike's New Opera-House," *Harper's Weekly* 36 (January 25, 1868): 60; "New York Illustrated—No. 2": 6; "Cellar to Dome at the Grand Opera House," *The Manufacturer and Builder* 4 (February 1872); King, *King's Handbook of New York* (1893), 603; Brown, *A History of the New York Stage*, vol. 2: 599; Edwards, "A History of Nineteenth Century Theatre Architecture in the United States": 226–32; Silver, *Lost New York*, 79–80; Grafton, *New York in the Nineteenth Century*, 139–40; Lightfoot, ed., *Nineteenth-Century New York in Rare Photographic Views*, fig. 81.

65. Montgomery Schuyler, "Architecture of New York," *New York World* (December 17, 1871): 3. Also see Brown, *A History of the New York Stage*, vol. 2: 367; Henderson, *The City and the Theatre*, 147.

66. "What Our New Opera House Should Be," *New York Daily Graphic* (November 11, 1880): 82; "Competitive Design Prepared for the Metropolitan Opera House, New York, N.Y., Messrs. Potter and Robertson, Architects, New York, N.Y.," *American Architect and Building News* 9 (November 13, 1880): 234–35; "A Grand Opera House in Reservoir

Square," *Real Estate Record and Builders' Guide* 26 (December 4, 1880): 1057; "Magnificent Buildings," *Real Estate Record and Builders' Guide* 27 (March 19, 1881): 245; "The Coming Opera War," editorial, *New York Times* (July 11, 1883): 4; "The New Opera House, Thirty-ninth Street and Broadway," *New York Daily Graphic* (August 16, 1883): 310; "Opening Night at the Metropolitan," *New York Evening Telegram* (October 22, 1883): 29; "Record of Amusements: The Opening of the New Metropolitan Opera House Last Night," *New York Daily Graphic* (October 23, 1883): 829–30; Henry T. Finck, "The Metropolitan Opera House," *New York Evening Post* (October 23, 1883): 5; "The New Opera-House," editorial, *New York World* (October 28, 1883): 4; Schuyler, "The Metropolitan Opera House": 877–89; Josiah Cleaveland Cady, letter to the editor, *New York Daily Tribune* (November 12, 1883): 6; "Patti Did Catch a Cold," *New York Sun* (November 14, 1883): 3; Mariana Griswold Van Rensselaer, "The Metropolitan Opera-House, New York-I," *American Architect and Building News* 15 (February 16, 1884): 76–77, plates; Mariana Griswold Van Rensselaer, "Recent Architecture in America, II—Public Buildings," *Century Magazine* 28 (July 1884): 323–34; "Fate of the Opera House," *New York Times* (August 30, 1892): 8; Montgomery Schuyler, "The Works of Cady, Berg & See," *Architectural Record* 6 (April–June 1897): 517–53; Irving Kolodin, *The Metropolitan Opera: 1883–1935: A Candid History* (New York: Alfred A. Knopf, 1936), 1–12; Wayne Andrews, *The Vanderbilt Legend* (New York: Harcourt Brace, 1941), 262–64, 378–79; Editors of *Opera News*, *The Golden Horseshoe: The Life and Times of the Metropolitan Opera House* (New York: Viking, 1966); Stuart Preston, ed., *Farewell to the Old House: The Metropolitan Opera House, 1883–1966* (Garden City, N.Y.: Doubleday, 1966); Quaintance Eaton, *The Miracle of the Met: An Informal History of the Metropolitan Opera, 1883–1967* (New York: Meredith, 1968), 1–56; John Briggs, *Requiem for a Yellow Brick Brewery: A History of the Metropolitan Opera* (Boston: Little, Brown, 1969), 3–32; Cone, *First Rival of the Metropolitan Opera*; Stern, Gilmartin, and Massengale, *New York 1900*, 214–15; Paul E. Eisler, *The Metropolitan Opera: The First Twenty-five Years, 1883–1908* (Croton-on-Hudson, N.Y.: North River, 1984), 1–19; Kathleen A. Curran, *A Forgotten Architect of the Gilded Age: Josiah Cleaveland Cady's Legacy* (Hartford, Conn.: Trinity College, 1993), 16–20, figs. 11–15; Stern, Mellins, and Fishman, *New York 1960*, 1125–26.

67. "A Grand Opera House in Reservoir Square": 1057; "Magnificent Buildings": 245.

68. "Competitive Design Prepared for the Metropolitan Opera House, New York, N.Y., Messrs Potter and Robertson, Architects, New York, N.Y.": 234–35.

69. James H. Mapleson, quoted in "Patti Did Catch a Cold": 3.

70. Schuyler, "The Metropolitan Opera House": 889.

71. "The New Opera-House," *New York World*: 4.

72. Cady, letter to the editor, *New York Daily Tribune*: 6.

73. Schuyler, "The Metropolitan Opera House": 889.

74. Van Rensselaer, "The Metropolitan Opera-House, New York-I": 76–77.

75. Van Rensselaer, "Recent Architecture in America, II—Public Buildings": 327.

76. Schuyler, "The Works of Cady, Berg & See": 539.

77. Schuyler, "The Metropolitan Opera House": 877.

78. Finck, "The Metropolitan Opera House": 5.

79. "The Coming Opera War": 4.

80. "Opening Night at the Metropolitan," *New York Evening Telegram*: 29.

81. Quoted in Andrews, *The Vanderbilt Legend*, 263.

82. James H. Mapleson, quoted in "Opera at the Academy Closes," *New York World* (November 28, 1885): 7.

83. King, *King's Handbook of New York* (1893), 607. Also see "Interior Improvement of Steinway Hall—Outlay of Twenty-five Thousand Dollars in Decoration," *New York Times* (June 26, 1868): 8; Lightfoot, ed., *Nineteenth-Century New York in Rare Photographic Views*, fig. 70; Boyer, *Manhattan Manners*, 70–71, 73.

84. "Interior Improvement of Steinway Hall—Outlay of Twenty-five Thousand Dollars in Decoration": 8.

85. "A New Music Temple," *New York Times* (November 11, 1875): 2; "A Perfect Music Hall," *New York Times* (November 14, 1875): 7; "Chick-

ering Hall," *New York Daily Graphic* (November 18, 1875): 140; Schuyler, "Recent Building in New York—I": 176–77; "Chickering Hall, Fifth Avenue, New York, N.Y.," *American Architect and Building News* 20 (August 7, 1886): 62, plate; King, *King's Handbook of New York* (1893), 608; Brown, *A History of the New York Stage*, vol. 2: 591–92; Theodore James Jr., *Fifth Avenue* (New York: Walker, 1971), 120–21; Winston Weisman, "The Commercial Architecture of George B. Post," *Journal of the Society of Architectural Historians* 31 (December 1972): 176–203; Lisa B. Mausolf, "A Catalog of the Work of George B. Post, Architect" (master's thesis, Columbia University, 1983): 44, 49; Boyer, *Manhattan Manners*, 72–73; Diana Balmori, "George B. Post: The Process of Design and the New American Architectural Office (1868–1913)," *Journal of the Society of Architectural Historians* 46 (December 1987): 342–55; *Ladies' Mile Historic District*, 226; Sarah Bradford Landau, *George B. Post, Architect: Picturesque Designer and Determined Realist*, Sources of American Architecture, ed. Robert A. M. Stern (New York: Monacelli Press, 1998), 31–33.

86. "Out Among the Builders," *Real Estate Record and Builders' Guide* 43 (March 23, 1889): 392–94; Editorial, *American Architect and Building News* 25 (March 30, 1889): 145; "Men and Things," *Real Estate Record and Builders' Guide* 44 (July 20, 1889): 1016–17; "The New Music Hall," *Architecture and Building* 12 (May 17, 1890): 234; "Music Hall, 57th Street and Seventh Ave., New York City," *Architecture and Building* 12 (June 7, 1890): plates; "The Carnegie Music Hall," *Real Estate Record and Builders' Guide* 46 (December 27, 1890): 867–68; "Music Hall: 57th St. and Seventh Avenue. Entrance Vestibule," *Real Estate Record and Builders' Guide* 47 (January 3, 1891): 9; "The Music Hall Opened," *New York Daily Tribune* (May 6, 1891): 17; "Music Crowd in Its New Home," *New York Herald* (May 6, 1891): 7; "It Stood the Test Well: The First Concert in the New Music Hall," *New York Times* (May 6, 1891): 5; King, *King's Handbook of New York* (1893), 590; Ethel Peyser, *The House that Music Built: Carnegie Hall* (New York: Robert M. McBride, 1936); Richard Schickel, *The World of Carnegie Hall* (New York: Julian Messner, 1960), 3–55; Theodore O. Cron and Burt Goldblatt, *Portrait of Carnegie Hall: A Nostalgic Portrait in Pictures and Words* (New York: Macmillan, 1966); Landmarks Preservation Commission of the City of New York, LP-0278 (June 20, 1967); Hornung, *New York, 1850–1890*, 204; Stern, Gilmartin, and Massengale, *New York 1900*, 13, 15, 87; Andrew Porter, "House of Music," *New Yorker* 62 (December 29, 1986): 80–82; Elkhonon Yoffe, *Tchaikovsky in America: The Composer's Visit in 1891*, trans. Lidya Yoffe (New York: Oxford University Press, 1986), 3, 10, 56–57, 62, 83–87; Frick and Ward, *Directory of Historic American Theaters*, 178–80; Richard Schickel and Michael Walsh, *Carnegie Hall: The First One Hundred Years* (New York: Harry N. Abrams, 1987), 6–18; Rebecca Read Shanor, *The City That Never Was* (New York: Viking Penguin, 1988), 73–76; White and Willensky, *AIA Guide* (1988), 278; Barbaralee Diamonstein, *The Landmarks of New York II* (New York: Harry N. Abrams, 1993), 202–3; Gino Francesconi, "Carnegie Hall," in Jackson, ed., *The Encyclopedia of New York City*, 181; Stern, Mellins, and Fishman, *New York 1960*, 1112–13.

87. "Out Among the Builders," *Real Estate Record and Builders' Guide* 29 (January 7, 1882): 3.

88. Yoffe, *Tchaikovsky in America*, 83.

89. Yoffe, *Tchaikovsky in America*, 84.

90. "Music Crowd in Its New Home": 7.

91. "The Metropolitan Concert Hall, New York, N.Y. Mr. G.B. Post, Architect, New York, N.Y.," *American Architect and Building News* 6 (December 20, 1879): 196, plates; "The Metropolitan Concert Hall," *Real Estate Record and Builders' Guide* 25 (June 12, 1880): 556–57.

92. "The Metropolitan Concert Hall, New York, N.Y. Mr. G.B. Post, Architect, New York, N.Y.": 196.

93. Brown, *A History of New York Stage*, vol. 2: 595.

94. "The Costly and Substantial Buildings of 1888," *Real Estate Record and Builders' Guide* 39 (January 1, 1887): 6–8; White and Willensky, *AIA Guide* (1988), 159. For a discussion of dance halls in New York, see Mark Ferris, "Dance Halls and Discothèques," in Jackson, ed., *The Encyclopedia of New York City*, 315–16.

95. Martha J. Lamb and Mrs. Burton Harrison, *History of the City of New York* (New York: A. S. Barnes & Co., 1896), 854. Also see Editor-
ial, *American Architect and Building News* 9 (August 7, 1880): 61–62; "Architectural Competitions," *Building* 6 (November 5, 1886): 166; "Out Among the Builders," *Real Estate Record and Builders' Guide* 39 (March 19, 1887): 366–67; "The New Madison Square Garden," *Real Estate Record and Builders' Guide* 40 (July 2, 1887): 923; "The New Madison Square Garden," *Real Estate Record and Builders' Guide* 40 (July 9, 1887): 923; "A Chance for Architects," editorial, *New York Times* (July 18, 1887): 4; "Out Among the Builders," *Real Estate Record and Builders' Guide* 40 (September 17, 1887): 1179; "Out Among the Builders," *Real Estate Record and Builders' Guide* 40 (September 24, 1887): 1203; "Out Among the Builders," *Real Estate Record and Builders' Guide* 40 (October 1, 1887): 1231–32; "Our Future Buildings," *Building* 7 (November 12, 1887): 157; "Out Among the Builders," *Real Estate Record and Builders' Guide* 41 (February 18, 1888): 213; "The Madison Square Garden Project," *Real Estate Record and Builders' Guide* 41 (March 10, 1888): 297; "A Big Scheme in Jeopardy," *New York Times* (March 23, 1888): 2; "Objecting to the Tower," *New York Times* (March 27, 1888): 8; "Nothing Venture, Nothing Have," editorial, *New York Times* (April 15, 1888): 4; "Mr. Thurman in New York," *Harper's Weekly* 32 (September 15, 1888): 689–91; "Out Among the Builders," *Real Estate Record and Builders' Guide* 43 (January 19, 1889): 76–77; "The Plans Completed," *New York Times* (March 22, 1889): 3; "A Project that Still Lags," editorial, *New York Times* (June 26, 1889): 8; "Men and Things," *Real Estate Record and Builders' Guide* 43 (June 29, 1889): 908–9; "Men and Things," *Real Estate Record and Builders' Guide* 44 (August 24, 1889): 1160; "Notes and Items," *Real Estate Record and Builders' Guide* 44 (November 23, 1889): 1568; "The Big Garden Opened," *New York Daily Tribune* (June 17, 1890): 7; "A Brilliant Audience: Opening of the New Madison Square Garden," *New York Times* (June 17, 1890): 5; "Madison Square Garden Opened," *New York World* (June 17, 1890): 7; "The Madison Square Garden," *Real Estate Record and Builders' Guide* 45 (June 28, 1890): 944–45; Mariana Griswold Van Rensselaer, "Madison Square Garden," *Century Magazine* 47 (March 1894): 732–47; Paul Bourget, *Outre-Mer: Impressions of America* (New York: Charles Scribner's Sons, 1895), 21–23; Mariana Griswold van Rensselaer, "People in New York," *Century Magazine* 49 (February 1898): 534–48; Brown, *A History of the New York Stage*, vol. 2: 518; Homer Saint-Gaudens, ed., *The Reminiscences of Augustus Saint-Gaudens*, 2 vols. (New York: Century, 1913; New York: Garland, 1976), vol. 1: 393; *A Monograph of the Work of McKim, Mead & White, 1879–1915* (New York: Architectural Book Publishing Co., 1915), plates 30–37; Charles C. Baldwin, *Stanford White* (New York: Dodd, Mead, 1931; New York: Da Capo Press, 1970), 199–211; Frederick P. Hill, *Charles F. McKim, the Man* (Francestown, N.H.: M. Jones, 1950), 27–28; Silver, *Lost New York*, 50; Louise Hall Tharp, *Saint-Gaudens and the Gilded Era* (Boston: Little, Brown, 1969), 254–60; Richard Guy Wilson, "Charles F. McKim and the Development of the American Renaissance: A Study in Architecture and Culture" (Ph.D. diss., University of Michigan, 1972): 305–8; Henderson, *The City and the Theatre*, 153, 155; Leland M. Roth, "The Urban Architecture of McKim, Mead and White, 1870–1910" (Ph.D. diss., Yale University, 1973): 298–303; Joseph Durso, *Madison Square Garden: 100 Years of History* (New York: privately printed, 1979); Leland M. Roth, *McKim, Mead & White, Architects* (New York: Harper & Row, 1983), 158–65; Stern, Gilmartin, and Massengale, *New York 1900*, 10, 15, 64, 67, 71, 122, 171–72, 202–9, 212, 287; Richard Guy Wilson, *McKim, Mead & White, Architects* (New York: Rizzoli International Publications, 1983), 12–20; Christopher Gray, "Remembering Madison Square Garden," *Avenue* (February 1986): 102–10; Stern, Gilmartin, and Mellins, *New York 1930*, 19–20; Paul R. Baker, *Stanny: The Gilded Life of Stanford White* (New York: Macmillan, 1989), 149–66; David Garrard Lowe, *Stanford White's New York* (New York: Doubleday, 1992), 128–47, 236–37; Steven A. Riess, "Madison Square Garden," in Jackson, ed., *The Encyclopedia of New York City*, 712–13. Other highly valuable sources are contained in the Stanford White Papers, Avery Architectural and Fine Arts Library, Columbia University, and in the McKim, Mead & White Collection, New-York Historical Society.

96. Neil Harris, *Humbug: The Art of P. T. Barnum* (Boston: Little, Brown, 1973), 243–46; Philip B. Kunhardt Jr., Philip B. Kunhardt III, and Peter Kunhardt, *P. T. Barnum: America's Greatest Showman* (New York: Alfred A. Knopf, 1995), 242–43, 342–43.

97. Editorial, *American Architect and Building News* 8 (August 7, 1880): 61–62.

98. "Out Among the Builders," (March 19, 1887): 366–67.

99. "The New Madison Square Garden," (July 9, 1887): 923.

100. "Objecting to the Tower": 8.

101. "Nothing Venture, Nothing Have": 4.

102. Baldwin, *Stanford White*, 202.

103. "A Project that Still Lags": 8.

104. "Notes and Items": 1568.

105. "Madison Square Garden Opened," *New York World*: 7.

106. "The Big Garden Opened," *New York Daily Tribune*: 7.

107. Van Rensselaer, "Madison Square Garden": 741.

108. Quoted in Baldwin, *Stanford White*, 205.

109. Van Rensselaer, "Madison Square Garden": 741.

110. Kennion, *Architects' and Builders' Guide*, part 2: 86.

111. Van Rensselaer, "Madison Square Garden": 741.

112. Stanford White to Augustus Saint-Gaudens, October 3, 1891, Press Book 4: 263, Stanford White Papers, quoted in Baker, *Stanny*, 158.

113. Bourget, *Outre-Mer: Impressions of America*, 21.

114. Quoted in Baker, *Stanny*, 160.

115. Van Rensselaer, "Madison Square Garden": 744–45.

116. Stanford White to Homer Bradley, November 9, 1893, Press Book 4: 33, Stanford White Papers, quoted in Baker, *Stanny*, 160.

117. Charles F. McKim, quoted in Hill, *Charles F. McKim, the Man*, 27–28.

118. Quoted in Baldwin, *Stanford White*, 216.

119. Quoted in Baldwin, *Stanford White*, 210.

120. Van Rensselaer, "Madison Square Garden": 732.

121. King, *King's Handbook of New York* (1893), 843.

122. King, *King's Handbook of New York* (1893), 843.

123. "Editor's Easy Chair," *Harper's New Monthly Magazine* 9 (July 1854): 260–61; Peter B. Wight, "A Millionaire's Architectural Investment," *American Architect and Building News* 1 (May 6, 1876): 147–49; John Crawford Brown, "Early Days of the Department Stores," in *Valentine's Manual of Old New York* (New York: privately printed, 1921), 97–148; Harry E. Resseguie, "A. T. Stewart's Marble Palace—The Cradle of the Department Store," *New-York Historical Society Quarterly* 48 (April 1964): 131–62; Mary Ann Clegg Smith, "The Commercial Architecture of John Butler Snook" (Ph.D. diss., Pennsylvania State University, 1974): 22–38; Mary Ann Clegg Smith, "John Snook and the Design for A. T. Stewart's Store," *New-York Historical Society Quarterly* 58 (January 1974): 18–33; Mary Dierickx, *649–659 Broadway* (New York: Office of Joseph Pell Lombardi, Architect, 1978), 11; Robert Hendrickson, *The Grand Emporiums: The Illustrated History of America's Great Department Stores* (New York: Stern and Day, 1979), 35–40; Stephen N. Elias, *Alexander T. Stewart: Forgotten Merchant Prince* (Westport, Conn.: Praeger, 1992), 59–69; David B. Sicilia, "A(lexander) T(urney) Stewart," in Jackson, ed., *The Encyclopedia of New York City*, 1123–24. For a general discussion of the development of department stores in New York, see Elaine Abelson, "Department Stores," in Jackson, ed., *The Encyclopedia of New York City*, 327–28.

124. "Alexander T. Stewart," *Harper's New Monthly Magazine* 34 (March 1867): 522–24; "Stewart's New Store," *New York Daily Tribune* (September 18, 1868): 2; Junius Henri Browne, *The Great Metropolis; a Mirror of New York* (Hartford, Conn.: American Publishing Co., 1869), 290–92; William J. Fryer, with Messrs. James L. Jackson and Brothers, "Iron Stone Fronts," *Architectural Review and American Builders' Journal* 2 (April 1869): 581, 620–22; "Stewart's Store," *Appletons' Journal* 54 (April 9, 1870): 411–13; Montgomery Schuyler, "Our City Architecture," *New York World* (September 17, 1871): 3; Montgomery Schuyler, "Buildings on Broadway," *New York World* (September 24, 1871): 3; James D. McCabe Jr., *Lights and Shadows of New York Life; or, The Sights and Sensations of the Great City* (Philadelphia: National Publishing, 1872; New York: Farrar, Straus & Giroux, 1970), 378–83, 465–67; "A. T. Stewart as a Real Estate Operator," *Real Estate Record and Builders' Guide* 17 (April 1, 1876): 237; "The Estate of A. T. Stewart," *Real Estate Record and Builders' Guide* 17 (April 22, 1876): 299; Wight, "A Millionaire's Architectural Investment": 147–49; "The Retail Store of A.T. Stewart & Co.," *New York Daily Graphic* (January 31, 1878): 604; "Stewart's," *The Nation*

34 (April 20, 1882): 332; "Men Who Have Assisted in the Development of Architectural Resources, No. 1, John B. Cornell," *Architectural Record* 1 (October–December 1891): 244–47; William J. Fryer, "A Review of the Development of Structural Iron," in *A History of Real Estate, Building and Architecture in New York City During the Last Quarter of a Century*, 459, 462; Brown, "Early Days of the Department Stores," in *Valentine's Manual of Old New York*, 97–148; Stokes, *The Iconography of Manhattan Island*, vol. 3: 777; Winston Weisman, "Commercial Palaces of New York: 1845–1875," *Art Bulletin* 36 (December 1954): 285–302; Silver, *Lost New York*, 168; Cervin Robinson, "Late Cast Iron in New York," *Journal of the Society of Architectural Historians* 30 (May 1971): 164–69; Black, *Old New York in Early Photographs*, 103; Jay E. Cantor, "A Monument to Trade: A. T. Stewart and the Rise of the Millionaire's Mansion in New York," *Winterthur Portfolio* 10 (1975): 165–97; Deborah S. Gardner, "The Architecture of Commercial Capitalism: John Kellum and the Development of New York, 1840–1875" (Ph.D. diss., Columbia University, 1979): 55–86; Hendrickson, *The Grand Emporiums*, 40; William Leach, *True Love and Perfect Union: The Feminist Reform of Sex and Society* (New York: Basic Books, 1980), 222–27; Lightfoot, ed., *Nineteenth-Century New York in Rare Photographic Views*, fig. 62; Boyer, *Manhattan Manners*, 93–94; Robert A. M. Stern with Thomas Mellins and Raymond Gastil, *Pride of Place: Building the American Dream* (Boston: Houghton Mifflin; New York: American Heritage, 1986), 227; Joseph Devorkin, *Great Merchants of Early New York: "The Ladies' Mile"* (New York: The Society for the Architecture of the City, 1987), 44–50; Elias, *Alexander T. Stewart: Forgotten Merchant Prince*, 69–79; William Leach, *Land of Desire: Merchants, Power, and the Rise of a New American Culture* (New York: Pantheon, 1993), 21–22; Christopher Gray, "The A. T. Stewart Department Store," *New York Times* (March 29, 1994), X: 7; Sicilia, "A(lexander) T(urney) Stewart," in Jackson, ed., *The Encyclopedia of New York City*, 1123.

125. "Men Who Have Assisted in the Development of Architectural Resources": 245, also quoted in Fryer, "A Review of the Development of Structural Iron," in *A History of Real Estate, Building and Architecture in New York City During the Last Quarter of a Century*, 459.

126. McCabe, *Lights and Shadows of New York Life*, 379.

127. Schuyler, "Buildings on Broadway": 3.

128. Schuyler, "Our City Architecture": 3.

129. Fryer, with Messrs. James L. Jackson and Brothers, "Iron Store Fronts": 620.

130. "Stewart's New Store," *New York Daily Tribune*: 2.

131. Wight, "A Millionaire's Architectural Investment": 148.

132. Wight, "A Millionaire's Architectural Investment": 148. Also see Boyer, *Manhattan Manners*, 93–94.

133. Frances R. Sprague, "Stewart's Hotel for Women," *Cincinnati Commercial* (March 4, 1878), quoted in Leach, *True Love and Perfect Union*, 226.

134. Jane Croly, "New York and Paris Fashions for September," *Cincinnati Commercial* (September 1, 1878), quoted in Leach, *True Love and Perfect Union*, 226.

135. "Stewart's," *The Nation*: 332.

136. Fryer, with Messrs. James L. Jackson and Brothers, "Iron Store Fronts": 581; King, *King's Handbook of New York* (1893), 852–53; Brown, "Early Days of the Department Stores," in *Valentine's Manual of Old New York*, 132–33; Stokes, *The Iconography of Manhattan Island*, vol. 5: 1744–45; Maxwell F. Marcuse, *This Was New York!* (New York: Carlton, 1969), 307–10; Black, *Old New York in Early Photographs*, 104; Gardner, "The Architecture of Commercial Capitalism: John Kellum and the Development of New York, 1840–1875": 87–91; Hendrickson, *The Grand Emporiums*, 363–64; Boyer, *Manhattan Manners*, 98; Devorkin, *Great Merchants of Early New York*, 84–86; White and Willensky, *AIA Guide* (1988), 157–58.

137. Fryer, with Messrs. James L. Jackson and Brothers, "Iron Store Fronts": 581.

138. For discussions of Union Square's changing urban character during the 1860s, see "The Up-town Movement—Changes in Union Square, St. John's Park and Other Localities," *New York Times* (August 20, 1867): 6; "Local Intelligence: Street Changes—Concentration of the Retail Trade at Union Square," *New York Times* (November 21, 1867): 2; "The Business District," *Real Estate Record and Builders' Guide* 1 (May 9,

1868): 10; "The Growth of New York," *Architectural Review and American Builders' Journal* 2 (July 1869): 4; Jennifer Dunning, "Browsing in Phantom Emporiums Along Ladies' Mile," *New York Times* (November 5, 1976), C: 19; Christopher Gray, "Mile of Style," *Avenue* (September 1990): 107–12; Amanda Aaron, "Ladies' Mile," in Jackson, ed., *The Encyclopedia of New York City*, 650.

139. Strong, diary entries dated May 19, 1868, and November 10, 1870, in *The Diary of George Templeton Strong*, vol. 4: 211, 326; "The Past Building Season," *Architectural Review and American Builders' Journal* 2 (November 1869): 242; "A Jewel Palace," *New York Times* (November 12, 1870): 2; "Tiffany & Co.'s New Building," *Real Estate Record and Builders' Guide* 6 (November 5, 1870): 1; Schuyler, "Buildings on Broadway": 3; "The Attractions of New York," editorial, *New York Times* (November 24, 1872): 4; Benson J. Lossing, *History of New York City*, 2 vols. (New York: Perine, 1884), vol. 2: 797–99; Stokes, *The Iconography of Manhattan Island*, vol. 5: 1744; Lightfoot, ed., *Nineteenth Century New York in Rare Photographic Views*, fig. 73; Boyer, *Manhattan Manners*, 99; Margaret Moore, *End of the Road for Ladies' Mile?* (New York: Drive to Protect the Ladies' Mile District, with the cooperation of the Municipal Art Society and the Historic Districts Council, 1986), 31; Devorkin, *Great Merchants of Early New York*, 34–39; John Loring, *Tiffany's 150 Years*, with an introduction by Louis Auchincloss (Garden City, N.Y.: Doubleday, 1987), 10–11, 14, 16–18, 23–25, 30–31; Dunlap, *On Broadway*, 79; Gray, "Mile of Style": 108–9; Janet Zapata, "Tiffany," in Jackson, ed., *The Encyclopedia of New York City*, 1183. For George B. Post's competition entry, see Weisman, "The Commercial Architecture of George B. Post": 179.

140. Schuyler, "Buildings on Broadway": 3.

141. "Tiffany & Co.'s New Building": 1.

142. Schuyler, "Buildings on Broadway": 3.

143. "A Jewel Palace": 2.

144. "The Attractions of New York": 4.

145. Strong, diary entry dated May 19, 1868, in *The Diary of George Templeton Strong*, vol. 4: 211.

146. Strong, diary entry dated November 10, 1870, in *The Diary of George Templeton Strong*, vol. 4: 326.

147. Schuyler, "Our City Architecture": 3. Also see "Gothic Architecture," *Real Estate Record and Builders' Guide* 6 (December 3, 1870): 1; Schuyler, "Buildings on Broadway": 3; Montgomery Schuyler, "The Work of Leopold Eidlitz: II—Commercial and Public," *Architectural Record* 24 (October 1908): 277–92.

148. Schuyler, "Buildings on Broadway": 3.

149. "Gothic Architecture": 1.

150. "Wheeler & Wilson's New Industrial Palace," *New York Daily Graphic* (December 29, 1874): 427. Also see McKenna, "James Renwick, Jr., and the Second Empire Style in the United States": 97–101.

151. "Wheeler & Wilson's New Industrial Palace": 427.

152. Editorial, *Real Estate Record and Builders' Guide* 1 (May 2, 1868): 1–2; "Building in New York," *New York Times* (May 4, 1868): 4; Montgomery Schuyler, "A New Dry Goods Palace," *New York World* (March 28, 1869): 5; Schuyler, "Buildings on Broadway": 3; McCabe, *Lights and Shadows of New York Life*, 385; "Arnold & Constable's Magnificent Dry-Goods Palace," *New York Times* (October 2, 1872): 8; "Arnold, Constable & Co.'s New Building," *Real Estate Record and Builders' Guide* 17 (February 5, 1876): 107; "A New Palace of Trade," *New York Daily Graphic* (January 8, 1877): 464; "Out Among the Builders," *Real Estate Record and Builders' Guide* 31 (June 30, 1883): 255–56; King, *King's Handbook of New York* (1893), 843–45; Brown, "Early Days of the Department Stores," in *Valentine's Manual of Old New York*, 99–100; Stokes, *The Iconography of Manhattan Island*, vol. 5: 1664; Weisman, "Commercial Palaces of New York: 1845–1875": 299; Marcuse, *This Was New York!*, 215–21; Robinson, "Late Cast Iron in New York": 164–69; Margot Gayle and Edmund V. Gillon Jr., *Cast-Iron Architecture in New York* (New York: Dover, 1974), 164; Dierickx, *649–650 Broadway*, 19; Hendrickson, *The Grand Emporiums*, 154–55; Stern, Gilmartin, and Massengale, *New York 1900*, 68; Boyer, *Manhattan Manners*, 96, 100; Moore, *End of the Road for Ladies' Mile?*, 40, 46–47; William Conklin, "Ladies Mile: The Architecture of Commerce," *Village Views* 3 (summer 1986): 6; Devorkin, *Great Merchants of Early New York*, 58–60; White and Willensky, *AIA Guide* (1988), 187, 189; *Ladies' Mile Historic District*, 83–88; Dunlap, *On Broadway*,

115–16; Gray, "Mile of Style": 110, 112; Leslie Gourse, "Arnold Constable," in Jackson, ed., *The Encyclopedia of New York City*, 56.

153. Schuyler, "Buildings on Broadway": 3.

154. Schuyler, "A New Dry Goods Palace": 5.

155. Schuyler, "A New Dry Goods Palace": 5.

156. "Arnold, Constable & Co.'s New Building": 107.

157. "A New Palace of Trade": 464.

158. "Iron Buildings: Lord & Taylor's New Store," *Real Estate Record and Builders' Guide* 6 (October 15, 1870): 1; "A Modern Trade-Palace," *New York Times* (November 27, 1870): 5; "Tiffany & Co.'s New Building": 1; Schuyler, "Buildings on Broadway": 3; McCabe, *Lights and Shadows of New York Life*, 383, 385; "Our Illustrations," *New York Daily Graphic* (April 12, 1873): 2, 8; *Appleton's Dictionary of New York* (New York, 1889), 114; King, *King's Handbook of New York* (1893), 848–49; Brown, "Early Days of the Department Stores," in *Valentine's Manual of Old New York*, 98, 141–46; Stokes, *The Iconography of Manhattan Island*, vol. 3: 906; Marcus, *This Was New York!*, 213–15; Weisman, "Commercial Palaces of New York: 1845–1875": 299; Silver, *Lost New York*, 175; Winston Weisman, "A New View of Skyscraper History," in Edgar Kaufmann Jr., ed., *The Rise of an American Architecture* (New York: Praeger, 1970), 115–59; Robinson, "Late Cast Iron in New York": 165–66; Gayle and Gillon, *Cast-Iron Architecture in New York*, 165; *The History of Lord & Taylor* (New York: privately printed, 1976); Landmarks Preservation Commission of the City of New York, LP-0970 (November 15, 1977); Dierickx, *649–659 Broadway*, 10; Hendrickson, *The Grand Emporiums*, 155–58; Lightfoot, ed., *Nineteenth Century New York in Rare Photographic Views*, fig. 77; Boyer, *Manhattan Manners*, 97, 100; "The Ladies' Mile," *Village Views* 2 (summer 1985): 18–19; Moore, *End of the Road for Ladies' Mile?*, 40–41; Devorkin, *Great Merchants of Early New York*, 66–70; White and Willensky, *AIA Guide* (1988), 188; *Ladies' Mile Historic District*, 105–14; Dunlap, *On Broadway*, 116–18; Gray, "Mile of Style": 108, 110, 112; Diamonstein, *The Landmarks of New York II*, 154; Christopher Gray, "The Former Lord & Taylor Store," *New York Times* (May 7, 1995), IX: 7.

159. "A Modern Trade-Palace": 5.

160. For Lord & Taylor's 461–467 Broadway store, see Weisman, "Commercial Palaces of New York: 1845–1875": 295, fig. 16.

161. McCabe, *Lights and Shadows of New York Life*, 385.

162. "Iron Buildings: Lord & Taylor's New Store": 1.

163. "Our Illustrations," *New York Daily Graphic*: 2.

164. Schuyler, "Buildings on Broadway": 3.

165. Weisman, "The Commercial Architecture of George B. Post": 194; Paul R. Baker, *Richard Morris Hunt* (Cambridge, Mass.: MIT Press, 1980), 210–13.

166. Stokes, *The Iconography of Manhattan Island*, vol. 3: 705, vol. 5: 2023.

167. "West Side Improvements," *New York Daily Graphic* (October 21, 1878): 771.

168. "Out Among the Builders," *Real Estate Record and Builders' Guide* 31 (April 7, 1883): 142; "Middle Broadway," *Real Estate Record and Builders' Guide* 33 (February 3, 1884): 106; Ellen W. Kramer, "Detlef Lienau, an Architect of the Brown Decades," *Journal of the Society of Architectural Historians* 14 (March 1955): 18–25; Moore, *End of the Road for Ladies' Mile?*, 27, 32; *Ladies' Mile Historic District*, 31–35; Dunlap, *On Broadway*, 114.

169. "Middle Broadway": 106.

170. "The New Mercantile Building," *New York Times* (March 19, 1881): 8; "Important New Buildings," *New York Times* (May 13, 1881): 8; "Middle Broadway": 106; "Store of W. & J. Sloane," *American Architect and Building News* 18 (November 28, 1885): 258; Hinckeldeyn, "A Foreigner's View of American Architecture": 243–44; King, *King's Handbook of New York* (1893), 851; *The Story of Sloane's* (New York: W. & J. Sloane's, 1950); Marcus, *This Was New York!*, 221–24; Weisman, "The Commercial Architecture of George B. Post": 183; Gayle and Gillon, *Cast-Iron Architecture in New York*, 173; Arnold Lewis and Keith Morgan, *American Victorian Architecture* (New York: Dover, 1975), 47, 146; Stern, Gilmartin, and Massengale, *New York 1900*, 195; Boyer, *Manhattan Manners*, 108, 144; Moore, *End of the Road for Ladies' Mile?*, 10–11, 36–37, 40; Devorkin, *Great Merchants of Early New York*, 56–57; White

and Willensky, *AIA Guide* (1988), 187; *Ladies' Mile Historic District*, 73–78; Dunlap, *On Broadway*, 116, 118; "Of Fathers and Sons and Business Deals," *New York Times* (April 25, 1993), X: 1.

171. "Middle Broadway": 106.

172. Hinckeldeyn, "A Foreigner's View of American Architecture": 244.

173. "Buildings Projected," *Real Estate Record and Builders' Guide* 29 (April 15, 1882): 377; Boyer, *Manhattan Manners*, 123; Moore, *End of the Road for Ladies' Mile?*, 33; *Ladies' Mile Historic District*, 61–65; Dunlap, *On Broadway*, 114.

174. "Buildings Projected," *Real Estate Record and Builders' Guide* 31 (June 9, 1883): 421; Boyer, *Manhattan Manners*, 97, 113; *Ladies' Mile Historic District*, 70–72; Dunlap, *On Broadway*, 116.

175. "Out Among the Builders," *Real Estate Record and Builders' Guide* 31 (March 3, 1883): 88; "Buildings Projected," *Real Estate Record and Builders' Guide* 31 (April 7, 1883): 238; "Middle Broadway": 106; "A Large Stock of Silverware," *New York Times* (May 28, 1884): 8; M. G. Van Rensselaer, "Recent Architecture in America, III," *Century Magazine* 28 (August 1884): 511–23; "The Art of the Silversmith," *New York Times* (April 4, 1885): 5; King, *King's Views of New York* (1893), 846–47; Landmarks Preservation Commission of the City of New York, LP-1227 (June 19, 1984); Boyer, *Manhattan Manners*, 100, 119, 123–24, 229–30; Moore, *End of the Road for Ladies' Mile?*, 40; White and Willensky, *AIA Guide* (1988), 188; "As We Were: The Ladies Mile," *Village Views* 5 (winter 1988): 25; *Ladies' Mile Historic District*, 98–102; Dunlap, *On Broadway*, 118–19; Diamonstein, *The Landmarks of New York II*, 182; Deborah Dependahl Waters, "Gorham Manufacturing," in Jackson, ed., *The Encyclopedia of New York City*, 474. For a history of the Gorham Company, see Charles H. Carpenter Jr., *Gorham Silver 1831–1981* (New York: Dodd, Mead, 1982).

176. Van Rensselaer, "Recent Architecture in America, III": 511–23.

177. "Middle Broadway": 106.

178. Van Rensselaer, "Recent Architecture in America, III": 515. Also see Schuyler, "Buildings on Broadway": 3; "Buildings Projected," *Real Estate Record and Builders' Guide* 31 (June 16, 1883): 437; "Middle Broadway": 106; *Brooks Brothers Centenary 1818–1918* (New York: Brooks Brothers, 1918); Boyer, *Manhattan Manners*, 33, 56, 97, 108, 124; Devorkin, *Great Merchants of Early New York*, 62–65; White and Willensky, *AIA Guide* (1988), 188; Dunlap, *On Broadway*, 126; Eileen K. Cheng, "Brooks Brothers," in Jackson, ed., *The Encyclopedia of New York City*, 161.

179. Montgomery Schuyler, "The Romanesque Revival in New York," *Architectural Record* 1 (July–September 1891): 7–38. Also see "Brooks Brothers' New Building," *New York Times* (April 11, 1874): 12; White and Willensky, *AIA Guide* (1988), 151–52; Dunlap, *On Broadway*, 96–97.

180. "Sketch for Improvements at Broadway and Twenty-Second Street, New York, N.Y. Mr. Bruce Price, Architect, New York, N.Y.," *American Architect and Building News* 19 (February 20, 1886): 90, plate; Samuel H. Graybill Jr., "Bruce Price, American Architect, 1845–1903" (Ph.D. diss., Yale University, 1957): 43–44, 235.

181. "Middle Broadway": 106.

182. "The Old Delmonico Corner," *Real Estate Record and Builders' Guide* 24 (September 20, 1879): 740; Stokes, *The Iconography of Manhattan Island*, vol. 5: 1893, 1903, 1963.

183. "Something About Side Stoops," *Real Estate Record and Builders' Guide* 38 (August 28, 1886): 1076. Also see Leland Roth, *The Architecture of McKim, Mead & White, 1870–1920: A Building List* (New York: Garland, 1978), 170, fig. 941.

184. *Ladies' Mile Historic District*, 240–42.

185. "In West Twenty-third Street," *Real Estate Record and Builders' Guide* 33 (June 28, 1884): 93–94; Montgomery Schuyler, "The Works of Henry Janeway Hardenbergh," *Architectural Record* 6 (January–March 1897): 335–75; *A History of Real Estate, Building and Architecture in New York City During the Last Quarter of a Century*, 567, 572, 600–601; Boyer, *Manhattan Manners*, 125; Moore, *End of the Road for Ladies' Mile?*, 45, 48; White and Willensky, *AIA Guide* (1988), 189; *Ladies' Mile Historic District*, 309–12.

186. "In West Twenty-third Street": 93–94.

187. Schuyler, "The Works of Henry Janeway Hardenbergh": 341.

188. "The Old Delmonico Corner": 740; Editorial, *Real Estate Record and Builders' Guide* 27 (April 9, 1881): 331.

189. Quoted in "Sixth Avenue Not Yet Ruined," *Real Estate Record and Builders' Guide* 22 (November 23, 1878): 947.

190. "A Broadway Railroad," *Real Estate Record and Builders' Guide* 23 (January 4, 1879): 1–2; "Buildings Projected," *Real Estate Record and Builders' Guide* 23 (January 4, 1879): 14; "A New Dry Goods Palace," *New York Times* (April 22, 1879): 8; Brown, "Early Days of the Department Stores," in *Valentine's Manual of Old New York*, 137; Hendrickson, *The Grand Emporiums*, 351–52; Devorkin, *Great Merchants of Early New York*, 18–19; Leslie Gourse, "Hearn's," in Jackson, ed., *The Encyclopedia of New York City*, 535.

191. "A New Dry Goods Palace": 8.

192. "Dobson's New Carpet Warehouse," *New York Times* (April 1, 1879): 8; "J. & J. Dobson's New Building," *Real Estate Record and Builders' Guide* 23 (June 28, 1879): 524–25.

193. Brown, "Early Days of the Department Stores," in *Valentine's Manual of Old New York*, 136–37; Gayle and Gillon, *Cast-Iron Architecture in New York*, 104–5.

194. "Buildings Projected," *Real Estate Record and Builders' Guide* 26 (November 6, 1880): 978; White and Willensky, *AIA Guide* (1988), 184. For D. & J. Jardine's building for the dry-goods business of Owen Jones, completed in 1876 and located west of the city's principal commercial district at the southwest corner of Eighth Avenue and Nineteenth Street, see "An Architectural Ornament: The New Dry Goods Building of Owen Jones," *New York Daily Graphic* (April 12, 1876): 343.

195. "Macy's," *New York Times* (December 9, 1876): 5; "A Busy Scene," *New York Times* (December 18, 1877): 5; Brown, "Early Days of the Department Stores," in *Valentine's Manual of Old New York*, 105–6, 111–19; Ralph M. Hower, *History of Macy's of New York, 1858–1919: Chapters in the Evolution of the Department Store* (Cambridge, Mass.: Harvard University Press, 1943); Margaret Case Harriman, *And the Price Is Right* (Cleveland: World, 1958); Hendrickson, *The Grand Emporiums*, 61–66; Boyer, *Manhattan Manners*, 90–91; Devorkin, *Great Merchants of Early New York*, 12–17; Christopher Gray, "How a Thorn Got in a Lion's Paw," *New York Times* (November 21, 1993), X: 8; Elaine Abelson, "R. H. Macy," in Jackson, ed., *The Encyclopedia of New York City*, 1002–3.

196. "A Busy Scene": 5.

197. "A New Palace of Trade," *New York Daily Graphic* (April 17, 1877): 329; "Altman & Co.'s New Building," *New York Times* (April 18, 1877): 8; "Enlarged and Improved," *New York Times* (September 25, 1887): 5; Brown, "Early Days of the Department Stores," in *Valentine's Manual of Old New York*, 99, 125–26; Stokes, *The Iconography of Manhattan Island*, vol. 5: 1917; John S. Burke Jr., *100: The First Century* (New York: B. Altman & Co., 1965), n.p.; Marcus, *This Was New York!*, 291–96; Robinson, "Late Cast Iron in New York": 166–67; Gayle and Gillon, *Cast-Iron Architecture in New York*, 105–7; Hendrickson, *The Grand Emporiums*, 159–62; Boyer, *Manhattan Manners*, 97; Landmarks Preservation Commission of the City of New York, LP-1274 (March 12, 1985); Moore, *End of the Road for Ladies' Mile?*, 52–53; White and Willensky, *AIA Guide* (1988), 180; *Ladies' Mile Historic District*, 336–42.

198. Christopher Gray, "Sixth Avenue: A Shopper's Paradise Lost," *Avenue* (May 1986): 106–11.

199. "Richard Meares," *New York Times* (December 20, 1874): 5; Montgomery Schuyler, "Architecture and Dry Goods," *New York World* (October 19, 1879): 3; "Goods for the Ladies: Simpson, Crawford & Simpson's New Establishment," *New York Times* (October 23, 1879): 8; "The Big Department Store Structure," *New York Times* (August 5, 1889): 11; Brown, "Early Days of the Department Stores," in *Valentine's Manual of Old New York*, 126–28; Weisman, "Commercial Palaces in New York: 1845–1875": 285–302; Marcus, *This Was New York!*, 298–300; Boyer, *Manhattan Manners*, 97; Moore, *End of the Road for Ladies' Mile?*, 52; Devorkin, *Great Merchants of Early New York*, 80–81; *Ladies' Mile Historic District*, 348–54.

200. "O'Neill's & Co.'s New Building," *New York Daily Tribune* (May 22, 1887): 5; "Meeting Business Demands," *New York Times* (May 23, 1887): 8; "The New O'Neill's," *New York Times* (September 18, 1887): 9; Brown, "Early Days of the Department Stores," in *Valentine's Manual of Old New York*, 128–30; Marcus, *This Was New York!*, 300–303; Robinson,

"Late Cast Iron in New York": 167–68; Gayle and Gillon, *Cast-Iron Architecture in New York*, 108–11; Moore, *End of the Road for Ladies' Mile?*, 52; Devorkin, *Great Merchants of Early New York*, 78–79; White and Willensky, *AIA Guide* (1988), 179; *Ladies' Mile Historic District*, 366–70; Daniel B. Schneider, "F.Y.I.," *New York Times* (January 11, 1998), XIV: 2.

201. "O'Neill's & Co.'s New Building": 5.

202. "Ehrich Brothers' New Store," *New York Times* (September 8, 1889): 9; "Inspecting a New Store," *New York Times* (September 22, 1889): 2; "Great Changes in Retail District," *Real Estate Record and Builders' Guide* (December 13, 1913): 1077, 1084; Brown, "Early Days of the Department Stores," in *Valentine's Manual of Old New York*, 133–35; Marcus, *This Was New York!*, 305–7; Robinson, "Late Cast Iron in New York": 168; Gayle and Gillon, *Cast-Iron Architecture in New York*, 112–13; Boyer, *Manhattan Manners*, 98; Moore, *End of the Road for Ladies' Mile?*, 49; Gray, "Sixth Avenue: A Shopper's Paradise Lost": 107; Devorkin, *Great Merchants of Early New York*, 82–83; White and Willensky, *AIA Guide* (1988), 178; *Ladies' Mile Historic District*, 394–98; Christopher Gray, "The Ehrich Brothers Store," *New York Times* (February 12, 1995), IX: 7.

203. Gray, "The Ehrich Brothers Store": 7.

204. "Stern Brothers," *New York Times* (December 17, 1876): 7; "West Side Improvements": 771; "Stern Brothers' New Building," *New York Times* (October 22, 1878): 8; "Stern's Great Store in Twenty-third Street," *Real Estate Record and Builders' Guide* 22 (November 2, 1878): 886–87; "Stern Brothers," *Frank Leslie's Illustrated Weekly* (April 30, 1893): 258–59; Brown, "Early Days of the Department Stores," in *Valentine's Manual of Old New York*, 130–32; Isadore Barmash, "Stern's Will Shut 42d St. Store on May 1 as Result of Losses," *New York Times* (January 25, 1969): 1, 39; Gayle and Gillon, *Cast-Iron Architecture in New York*, 118–19; Hendrickson, *The Grand Emporiums*, 389–91 Boyer, *Manhattan Manners*, 98, 101–2; Moore, *End of the Road for Ladies' Mile?*, 49, 56–57; White and Willensky, *AIA Guide* (1988), 178; *Ladies' Mile Historic District*, 917–21; Leslie Gourse, "Stern's," in Jackson, ed., *The Encyclopedia of New York City*, 1122.

205. "Stern's Great Store in Twenty-third Street": 886.

206. Browne, *The Great Metropolis*, 261.

207. Browne, *The Great Metropolis*, 261–62.

208. "Our Restaurants," *Real Estate Record and Builders' Guide* 29 (June 3, 1882): 551.

209. Browne, *The Great Metropolis*, 262.

210. Browne, *The Great Metropolis*, 265.

211. For useful general discussions of the history of Delmonico's, including its numerous locations, see "Delmonico Family," vertical file, and "New York City Restaurants," vertical file, Local History and Genealogy Division, General Research Division, New York Public Library. Also see Captain Prescott Van Tuyl, "Ninety Years of Delmonico's," *Vanity Fair* 6 (June 1916): 62, 122, 124; Henry Collins Brown, *Delmonico's: A Story of Old New York* (New York: Valentine's Manual, 1928); Robert Shaplen, "That Was New York, Delmonico: I—The Rich New Gravy Faith," *New Yorker* 32 (November 10, 1956): 189–92, 197–204, 207–11; Robert Shaplen, "That Was New York, Delmonico: II—A Salon of Almost Saracenic Splendor," *New Yorker* 32 (November 17, 1956): 105–6, 108, 110–12, 116, 119–20, 125–26, 128–30, 132–37; Lately Thomas, *Delmonico's: A Century of Splendor* (Boston: Houghton Mifflin, 1967); Stern, Gilmartin, and Massengale, *New York 1900*, 223; Betty Kaplan Gubert, "Delmonico's," in Jackson, ed., *The Encyclopedia of New York City*, 325; John Mariani, "Restaurants," in Jackson, ed., *The Encyclopedia of New York City*, 1000; Landmarks Preservation Commission of the City of New York, LP-1944 (February 13, 1996); Christopher Gray, "On the Menu at 1891 Delmonico's: 40 Apartments," *New York Times* (April 14, 1996), IX: 7.

212. Mariani, "Restaurants," in Jackson, ed., *The Encyclopedia of New York City*, 1000.

213. Quoted in Van Tuyl, "Ninety Years of Delmonico's": 122.

214. "Delmonico's New Restaurant," *New York Times* (April 7, 1862): 5; "Delmonico's Old Corner," *New York Times* (March 25, 1879): 5; Ward McAllister, *Society As I Have Found It* (New York: Cassell, 1890), 166–70, 181–88; Brown, *Delmonico's*, 49.

215. Brown, *Delmonico's*, 49.

216. "Delmonico's New Restaurant": 5.

217. McAllister, *Society As I Have Found It*, 181–82.

218. "Correspondence," *American Architect and Building News* 1 (March 18, 1876): 95; "Correspondence," *American Architect and Building News* 1 (March 25, 1876): 102; George Augustus Sala, *America Revisited: From the Bay of New York to the Gulf of Mexico, and from Lake Michigan to the Pacific*, 2 vols. (London: Vizetelly & Co., 1882), vol. 1: 90–99; King, *King's Handbook of New York* (1893), 237–40; Mrs. John King Van Rensselaer, in collaboration with Frederic Van de Water, *The Social Ladder* (New York: Henry Holt, 1924), 54–55; Lloyd Morris, *Incredible New York* (New York: Bonanza, 1951), 111; James, *Fifth Avenue*, 100–101; Boyer, *Manhattan Manners*, 80–81.

219. Sala, *America Revisited*, vol. 1: 92.

220. "Architectural Notes," *Art Age* 3 (May 1886): 182; "The New Down-town Delmonico's," *Real Estate Record and Builders' Guide* 28 (July 17, 1886): 916; "Interior Fittings of Delmonico's Restaurant, New York, N.Y., Mr. J. B. Lord, Architect, New York, N.Y.," *American Architect and Building News* 21 (June 18, 1887): 295, plate.

221. "Out Among the Builders," *Real Estate Record and Builders' Guide* 44 (July 27, 1889): 1049–50; "A New Delmonico's," *New York Times* (May 18, 1890): 13; King, *King's Handbook of New York* (1893), 239–40; "Delmonico's Downtown Restaurant," *American Architect and Building News* 42 (November 1925): 419–21; Stern, Gilmartin, and Massengale, *New York 1900*, 223; White and Willensky, *AIA Guide* (1988), 15; Landmarks Preservation Commission of the City of New York, LP-1944 (February 13, 1996); Gray, "On the Menu at 1891 Delmonico's: 40 Apartments": 7.

222. "A New Delmonico's": 13.

223. Michael and Ariane Balterberry, *On the Town in New York* (New York: Charles Scribner's Sons, 1973), 160–62; Rohit T. Aggarwala, "Sherry's," in Jackson, ed., *The Encyclopedia of New York City*, 1066.

224. "Building in Fifth Avenue," *Real Estate Record and Builders' Guide* 44 (August 24, 1889): 1159–60; Roth, *The Architecture of McKim, Mead & White, 1870–1920: A Building List*, 142; Stern, Gilmartin, and Massengale, *New York 1900*, 223.

225. "A Corner of the Ball-Room: 'Sherry's,' New York, N.Y., Messrs. McKim, Mead & White, Architects, New York N.Y.," *American Architect and Building News* 62 (December 24, 1898): 107, plate; "A Corner of the Palm-Garden: 'Sherry's,' 44th St. and Fifth Ave., New York, N.Y., Messrs. McKim, Mead & White, Architects, New York, N.Y.," *American Architect and Building News* 63 (January 7, 1899): 7, plate; "'Sherry's,' Forty-fourth St. and Fifth Avenue, New York, N.Y., Messrs. McKim, Mead & White, Architects, New York, N.Y.," *American Architect and Building News* 63 (January 21, 1899): 22, plate; *A Monograph of the Works of McKim, Mead & White, 1879–1915*, 98–99; Roth, "The Urban Architecture of McKim, Mead & White, 1870–1910": 467–68; Roth, *McKim, Mead & White, Architects*, 223–24; Stern, Gilmartin, and Massengale, *New York 1900*, 223–25; Baker, *Stanny*, 223–24; Lowe, *Stanford White's New York*, 176–78.

CHAPTER 6
New Neighborhoods

West Side

1. Montgomery Schuyler, "The Romanesque Revival in New York," *Architectural Record* 1 (July–September 1891): 7–38.

2. For a good overall introduction to the West Side's early history, see "West Side Is Itself a Great City," *New York Times* (March 10, 1895): 21. Also see Emily Goldblatt, "Image and Reality in Patterns of Change on Manhattan's Upper West Side" (master's thesis, Columbia University, 1969); Solomon Asser and Hilary Roe, "The Development of the Upper West Side to 1925, Thomas Healy and Pomander Walk" (master's thesis, Columbia University, 1981); James Trager, *West of Fifth* (New York: Atheneum, 1987), 7–9; Peter Salwen, *Upper West Side Story* (New York: Abbeville Press, 1989), 13–52; David W. Dunlap, *On Broadway: A Journey Uptown Over Time* (New York: Rizzoli International Publications, 1990), 205–6, 233–34, 261–62.

3. Charles Lockwood, *Manhattan Moves Uptown* (Boston: Houghton Mifflin, 1976), 313–14.

4. Salwen, *Upper West Side Story*, 34, 43–44.

5. Montgomery Schuyler, "Cyrus L. W. Eidlitz," *Architectural Record* 5 (April–June 1896): 410–35; Salwen, *Upper West Side Story*, 43.

6. Salwen, *Upper West Side Story*, 73, 100.

7. Stern, Gilmartin, and Massengale, *New York 1900*, 361, 363.

8. Stan Fischler, *Uptown, Downtown: A Trip Through Time on New York's Subways* (New York: Hawthorn Books, 1976), 252.

9. *Proceedings of a Meeting of Property Holders of the West Side District of New York. Held at the Museum Building, Manhattan Square* (New York, October 3, 1878), n.p.

10. Michael R. Corbett, "Meatpacking," in Kenneth T. Jackson, ed., *The Encyclopedia of New York City* (New Haven, Conn., and London: Yale University Press; New York: New-York Historical Society, 1995), 745–46. For further discussion of stockyards and slaughterhouses in New York during the period, see Thomas F. DeVoe, *Abattoirs: A Paper Read Before the Polytechnic Branch of the American Institute, June 8, 1865* (Albany, N.Y.: Van Benthuysen and Sons, 1866); Christopher Gray, "The Riverside Drive that Almost Was," *Avenue* (June–August 1986): 103–9.

11. "West Side Is Itself a Great City": 21; Salwen, *Upper West Side Story*, 57.

12. Quoted in Lockwood, *Manhattan Moves Uptown*, 313. Also see "The West Side Squatters," *New York Daily Graphic* (November 29, 1879): 209; "Ten Thousand Squatters," *New York Times* (May 20, 1880): 8; "Squatter Life in New York," *Harper's New Monthly Magazine* 61 (September 1880): 562–69.

13. Salwen, *Upper West Side Story*, 56.

14. Salwen, *Upper West Side Story*, 73, 97.

15. "Opening of the Building Season," *Real Estate Record and Builders' Guide* 1 (March 28, 1868): 1.

16. *A History of Real Estate, Building and Architecture in New York City During the Last Quarter of a Century* (New York: Real Estate Record Association, 1898), 62; Lori Zabar, "The Influence of W.E.D. Stokes' Real Estate Career on West Side Development" (master's thesis, Columbia University, 1977): 11.

17. "Opening of the Building Season": 1.

18. "West Side Is Itself a Great City": 21.

19. "West Side Number," *Real Estate Record and Builders' Guide* 46 (December 20, 1890): 1–64.

20. Board of Commissioners of Central Park, *Eleventh Annual Report* (1867), 157–66; Board of Commissioners of Central Park, *Twelfth Annual Report* (1868), 59; Board of Commissioners of Central Park, *Thirteenth Annual Report* (1869), 64; I. N. Phelps Stokes, *The Iconography of Manhattan Island*, 6 vols. (New York: Robert H. Dodd, 1915–28; New York: Arno Press, 1967), vol. 5: 1929.

21. "The New Boulevard in Court," *Real Estate Record and Builders' Guide* 1 (May 23, 1868): 1; Stokes, *The Iconography of Manhattan Island*, vol. 5: 1926.

22. "Capabilities of the West Side," *Real Estate Record and Builders' Guide* 21 (January 12, 1878): 1–2.

23. "The Latest Municipal Job," editorial, *New York Times* (July 17, 1868): 4; "The Broadway Widening Job," editorial, *New York Times* (July 24, 1868): 4.

24. "The New Parks and Boulevards," *Real Estate Record and Builders' Guide* 2 (January 16, 1869): 1.

25. William R. Martin, *The Growth of New York* (New York: George W. Wood, 1865), 34.

26. Martin, *The Growth of New York*, 34.

27. "The West Side," *New York Times* (February 4, 1872): 6.

28. "Up-Town Improvements Again," editorial, *New York Times* (May 5, 1875): 6; Stokes, *The Iconography of Manhattan Island*, vol. 5: 1973.

29. "The Sale on Riverside Avenue," *Real Estate Record and Builders' Guide* 25 (June 5, 1880): 527. Also see Ann L. Buttenwieser, *Manhattan Water-Bound* (New York: New York University Press, 1987), 113.

30. "The West End Plateau," *Real Estate Record and Builders' Guide* 24 (November 29, 1879): 958.

31. "How Riverside Park Will Look," *New York Daily Graphic* (February 16, 1875): 777; Martha J. Lamb, "General Grant's Resting Place,"

Magazine of American History 14 (September 1885): 225–48; "The Riverside Drive and Future City Construction," *Building* 7 (August 27, 1887): 65; "West Side Is Itself a Great City": 21; Stokes, *The Iconography of Manhattan Island*, vol. 5: 1914, 1927, 1973; Albert Fein, ed., *Landscape into Cityscape: Frederick Law Olmsted's Plans for New York City* (Ithaca, N.Y.: Cornell University Press, 1967), 343–48; Elizabeth Barlow, *Frederick Law Olmsted's New York* (New York: Praeger, 1972), 116–19; Albert Fein, *Frederick Law Olmsted and the American Environmental Tradition* (New York: George Braziller, 1972), plate 77; Laura Wood Roper, *FLO: A Biography of Frederick Law Olmsted* (Baltimore and London: Johns Hopkins University Press, 1973), 348, 356; John Grafton, *New York in the Nineteenth Century* (New York: Dover, 1977), 123; Landmarks Preservation Commission of the City of New York, LP-2000 (February 19, 1980); John Emerson Todd, *Frederick Law Olmsted* (Boston: Thayne Publishers, 1982), 94; Stern, Gilmartin, and Massengale, *New York 1900*, 363–64, 373; Elizabeth Cromley, "Riverside Park and Issues of Historic Preservation," *Journal of the Society of Architectural Historians* 43 (October 1984): 238–49; Buttenwieser, *Manhattan Water-Bound*, 109–16; David Schuyler and Jane Turner Censer, eds., *The Papers of Frederick Law Olmsted* (Baltimore and London: Johns Hopkins University Press, 1992), vol. 6: 596–600; Barbaralee Diamonstein, *The Landmarks of New York II* (New York: Harry N. Abrams, 1993), 162–63; Jonathan Kuhn, "Riverside Park," in Jackson, ed., *The Encyclopedia of New York City*, 1009–10.

32. Stokes, *The Iconography of Manhattan Island*, vol. 5: 1914.

33. Frederick Law Olmsted, quoted in Barlow, *Frederick Law Olmsted's New York*, 116.

34. Frederick Law Olmsted, *Landscape Architects Report*, Document 70, Parks Department, 1875, quoted in Landmarks Preservation Commission of the City of New York, LP-2000 (February 19, 1980), 8.

35. Editorial, *New York Times* (October 14, 1875): 4; "The Riverside Drive," *New York Times* (October 14, 1875): 2; "Riverside Drive Again," editorial, *New York Times* (May 17, 1876): 4; Stokes, *The Iconography of Manhattan Island*, vol. 5: 1964.

36. Egbert L. Viele, quoted in Salwen, *Upper West Side Story*, 72.

37. "Tearing Down Barricades," *New York Times* (May 8, 1880): 8.

38. "Riverside Drive," *Real Estate Record and Builders' Guide* 34 (December 18, 1884): 1251.

39. *Phillip's Elite Directory of Private Families and Ladies Visiting and Shopping Guide for New York City* (New York, 1887), 96.

40. Andrew Alpern, *Luxury Apartment Houses of Manhattan* (New York: Dover, 1992), 83, 85–86.

41. "On the Riverside Drive," *Real Estate Record and Builders' Guide* 42 (October 6, 1888): 1188–89. Also see Moses King, *King's Handbook of New York* (Boston: Moses King, 1893), 743, 818; Stern, Gilmartin, and Massengale, *New York 1900*, 362–63; M. Christine Boyer, *Manhattan Manners: Architecture and Style, 1850–1900* (New York: Rizzoli International Publications, 1985), 210–11; Gray, "The Riverside Drive that Almost Was": 103–9.

42. Schuyler, "The Romanesque Revival in New York": 8, 36; Stern, Gilmartin, and Massengale, *New York 1900*, 479–80 (n. 290); Salwen, *Upper West Side Story*, 73.

43. Schuyler, "The Romanesque Revival in New York": 36.

44. "On the Riverside Drive": 1188–89; "Residence of Mr. Cyrus Clark," supplement, *Building* 11 (November 23, 1889): 175, plate; Stern, Gilmartin, and Massengale, *New York 1900*, 363.

45. "On the Riverside Drive": 1188–89.

46. Schuyler, "The Romanesque Revival in New York": 36.

47. King, *King's Handbook of New York* (1893), 567; Salwen, *Upper West Side Story*, 124.

48. "The West Side," *New York Times* (February 4, 1872): 6.

49. "West Side Names," *Real Estate Record and Builders' Guide* 25 (February 7, 1880): 126.

50. "'Columbus' and 'Amsterdam' Avenues," *Real Estate Record and Builders' Guide* 45 (March 29, 1890): 399; Stokes, *The Iconography of Manhattan Island*, vol. 5: 1973; Salwen, *Upper West Side Story*, 67.

51. "Central Park West," *Real Estate Record and Builders' Guide* 40 (December 17, 1887): 1574.

52. W., "Correspondence," *American Architect and Building News* 5 (April 12, 1879): 117–18. Also see "The West End Plateau": 958; "Fate of the West Side," *Real Estate Record and Builders' Guide* 24 (December 13, 1879): 1004; "The West Side of New York," *New York Times* (December 14, 1879): 5; "Our West Side," *Real Estate Record and Builders' Guide* 24 (December 27, 1879): 1055; "The City of the Future (Paper Read Before the West Side Association by Mr. Edward Clark)," *Real Estate Record and Builders' Guide* 24 (December 27, 1879): 1056–57; "A Treatise for Speculators," *Real Estate Record and Builders' Guide* 25 (January 15, 1880): 53–55.

53. Egbert Viele, *The West End Plateau of the City of New York* (New York: Johnson and Pratt, 1879). Also see Boyer, *Manhattan Manners*, 198.

54. Viele, *The West End Plateau of the City of New York*, 14, 17.

55. "Ten Thousand Squatters," *New York Times* (May 20, 1880): 8.

56. "The Growing West Side," *New York Times* (April 17, 1881): 14.

57. Editorial, *Building* 2 (November 1883): 13; "On the West Side," *Real Estate Record and Builders' Guide* 34 (August 30, 1884): 889; "The Great Building Movement on the West Side," *Real Estate Record and Builders' Guide* 36 (August 29, 1885): 951–52.

58. "West of the Park," *Real Estate Record and Builders' Guide* 36 (November 7, 1885): 1215–16. Also see Mitchell, "The New City on the West Side," *Real Estate Record and Builders' Guide* 38 (August 7, 1886): 999; Mitchell, "The New City on the West Side. II," *Real Estate Record and Builders' Guide* 38 (August 14, 1886): 1029–30; Mitchell, "The New City on the West Side. III," *Real Estate Record and Builders' Guide* 38 (September 4, 1886): 1099; Observer, "West Side Improvements," letter to the editor, *Real Estate Record and Builders' Guide* 38 (September 11, 1886): 1122; Observer, "West Side Improvements," letter to the editor, *Real Estate Record and Builders' Guide* 38 (September 25, 1886): 1173; "The Growth of the City Westward," *Real Estate Record and Builders' Guide* 38 (December 11, 1886): 1519.

59. "Settling the West Side: New Dwellings Springing Up by the Hundreds," *New York Times* (September 11, 1886): 8. Also see Stokes, *The Iconography of Manhattan Island*, vol. 5: 1991; Lockwood, *Manhattan Moves Uptown*, 317; White and Willensky, *AIA Guide* (1988), 289.

60. "The Architecture of the West Side," *Real Estate Record and Builders' Guide* 40 (September 10, 1887): 1150.

61. Sarah Bradford Landau, "The Row Houses of New York's West Side," *Journal of the Society of Architectural Historians* 34 (March 1975): 19–36; Donald G. Presa, "The Development and Demise of the Upper West Side Row Houses: 1880–1980" (Ph.D. diss., Columbia University, 1982). For Boston's Back Bay compared to New York's West End, see "Streets on the West Side," in "The 'West Side' Illustrated," supplement, *Real Estate Record and Builders' Guide* 44 (November 16, 1889): 1–16. Also see Bainbridge Bunting, "The Plan of the Back Bay Area in Boston," *Journal of the Society of Architectural Historians* 13 (1954): 19–24; Bainbridge Bunting, *Houses of Boston's Back Bay: An Architectural History, 1840–1917* (Cambridge, Mass.: Harvard University Press, 1967).

62. "West of the Park": 1215–16. Also see "The Architecture of the West Side": 1150.

63. Landau, "The Row Houses of New York's West Side": 19.

64. "The West Side Boomers," *New York Daily Tribune* (April 14, 1889): 6.

65. E. Idell Zeisloft, ed., *The New Metropolis* (New York: D. Appleton & Co, 1899), 272–73, 279; Stern, Gilmartin, and Massengale, *New York 1900*, 360–95.

66. *Block of Houses on West Side Plateau, Seventy-third Street between Ninth and Tenth Avenues* (New York, c. 1879); "The Clark Houses," *Real Estate Record and Builders' Guide* 34 (October 11, 1884): 1019–20; Montgomery Schuyler, "The Works of Henry Janeway Hardenbergh," *Architectural Record* 6 (January–March 1897): 335–75; Landau, "The Row Houses of New York's West Side": 20–21; Landmarks Preservation Commission of the City of New York, LP-0964 (July 12, 1977); Stephen Birmingham, *Life at the Dakota* (New York: Random House, 1979), 49–50; White and Willensky, *AIA Guide* (1988), 324; Diamonstein, *The Landmarks of New York II*, 453.

67. "Buildings Projected," *Real Estate Record and Builders' Guide* 23 (June 21, 1879): 519; Landmarks Preservation Commission of the City of New York, *Upper West Side—Central Park West Historic District Designation Report*, 4 vols. (New York, 1990), vol. 2: 323, vol. 4: 218.

68. "Buildings Projected," *Real Estate Record and Builders' Guide* 26 (August 21, 1880): 750; *Upper West Side—Central Park West Historic District*, vol. 2: 336, vol. 4: 225.

69. "The Clark Houses": 1019–20.

70. Schuyler, "The Works of Henry Janeway Hardenbergh": 355.

71. "Out Among the Builders," *Real Estate Record and Builders' Guide* 39 (March 5, 1887): 299–300; "Central Park West," *Real Estate Record and Builders' Guide*: 1574; Jean Schopfer, "American Architecture from a Foreign Point of View: New York City," *Architectural Review* (Boston) 7 (1900): 25–30; Landau, "The Row Houses of New York's West Side": 24–26; *Upper West Side—Central Park West Historic District*, vol. 2: 41, vol. 4: 20; Alpern, *Luxury Apartment Houses of Manhattan*, 68.

72. "Central Park West," *Real Estate Record and Builders' Guide*: 1574.

73. "Out Among the Builders," *Real Estate Record and Builders' Guide* 32 (July 14, 1883): 501; "The 'Dakota' Stable, New York City, Messrs. Charles W. Romeyn & Co., Architects," *American Architect and Building News* 17 (June 6, 1885): 270, plate.

74. Christopher Gray, "Streetscapes: The Dakota Stables," *New York Times* (May 24, 1987), VIII: 10, reprinted in Christopher Gray, *Changing New York: The Architectural Scene* (New York: Dover, 1992), 11.

75. "Buildings Projected," *Real Estate Record and Builders' Guide* 41 (March 24, 1888): 380; White and Willensky, *AIA Guide* (1988), 310.

76. "Out Among the Builders," *Real Estate Record and Builders' Guide* 35 (May 2, 1885): 495; *Upper West Side—Central Park West Historic District*, vol. 1: A56, vol. 3: 563, vol. 4: 396.

77. "Out Among the Builders," *Real Estate Record and Builders' Guide* 33 (April 12, 1884): 378–79; *Upper West Side—Central Park West Historic District*, vol. 3: 533.

78. "Buildings Projected," *Real Estate Record and Builders' Guide* 31 (April 21, 1883): 282; "Buildings Projected," *Real Estate Record and Builders' Guide* 37 (February 6, 1886): 181; Ellen Kramer, "The Domestic Architecture of Detlef Lienau: A Conservative Victorian" (Ph.D. diss., New York University, 1957): 242–48, figs. 104–6; Landau, "The Row Houses of New York's West Side": 21–22; *Upper West Side—Central Park West Historic District*, vol. 3: 505–8, vol. 4: 347–48.

79. "Out Among the Builders," *Real Estate Record and Builders' Guide* 33 (February 9, 1884): 134–35; "Out Among the Builders," *Real Estate Record and Builders' Guide* 33 (March 27, 1884): 292–93.

80. "Out Among the Builders," *Real Estate Record and Builders' Guide* 40 (November 19, 1887): 1445; "Buildings Projected," *Real Estate Record and Builders' Guide* 40 (December 8, 1887): 1532; "A Block of Houses, New York, N.Y. Messrs. Charles W. Romeyn & Co., Architects, New York, N.Y.," *American Architect and Building News* 26 (September 28, 1889): 146, plate; George W. and Walter S. Bromley, *Atlas of the City of New York, Borough of Manhattan*, 5 vols. (Philadelphia: Bromley, 1898–99), vol. 3: plate 4.

81. *Upper West Side—Central Park West Historic District*, vol. 2: 201, vol. 4: 129.

82. *Upper West Side—Central Park West Historic District*, vol. 2: 233, vol. 4: 152.

83. "The Great Building Movement on the West Side": 951–52.

84. *Upper West Side—Central Park West Historic District*, vol. 1: 145–47.

85. *Upper West Side—Central Park West Historic District*, vol. 2: 219, vol. 4: 142.

86. *Upper West Side—Central Park West Historic District*, vol. 2: 218, vol. 4: 142.

87. *Upper West Side—Central Park West Historic District*, vol. 2: 231, vol. 4: 151.

88. "Out Among the Builders," *Real Estate Record and Builders' Guide* 39 (February 12, 1887): 202–3; "Houses on West Seventy-first Street, New York, N.Y. Messrs. Lamb & Rich, Architects, New York, N.Y.," *American Architect and Building News* 22 (November 5, 1887): 219, plate; *Upper West Side—Central Park West Historic District*, vol. 2: 254, vol. 4: 167–68.

89. *Upper West Side—Central Park West Historic District*, vol. 2: 254, vol. 4: 167.

90. *Upper West Side—Central Park West Historic District*, vol. 2: 255, vol. 4: 168.

91. Observer, "West Seventy-second Street: The Parkway," *Real Estate Record and Builders' Guide* 44 (December 14, 1889): 1668. Also see Christopher Gray, "From Prestigious Parkway to Advertising Anarchy," *New York Times* (August 10, 1997), IX: 5.

92. Stern, Gilmartin, and Massengale, *New York 1900*, 365, 380–81.

93. "In West Seventy-second Street," *Real Estate Record and Builders' Guide* 40 (September 17, 1887): 1172–73.

94. "The Improvement of Seventy-second Street," *Real Estate Record and Builders' Guide* 38 (December 18, 1886): 1554.

95. "In West Seventy-second Street": 1172–73.

96. "In West Seventy-second Street": 1172–73; *Upper West Side—Central Park West Historic District*, vol. 2: 297–301, vol. 4: 198.

97. "In West Seventy-second Street": 1172–73. Also see *Upper West Side—Central Park West Historic District*, vol. 2: 309, vol. 4: 207.

98. "In West Seventy-second Street": 1172–73.

99. "The 'West Side' Illustrated": 2.

100. "Buildings Projected," *Real Estate Record and Builders' Guide* 41 (May 12, 1888): 627; "Buildings Projected," *Real Estate Record and Builders' Guide* 41 (June 9, 1888): 757; Bromley and Bromley, *Atlas of the City of New York, Borough of Manhattan*, vol. 3: plate 5.

101. "The 'West Side' Illustrated": 2.

102. "Fabled Racers, a Brearley Purchase and a Church," *New York Times* (December 3, 1989), X: 9; *Upper West Side—Central Park West Historic District*, vol. 2: 338, vol. 4: 212.

103. White and Willensky, *AIA Guide* (1988), 309; *Upper West Side—Central Park West Historic District*, vol. 2: 127, 355–57, vol. 4: 78, 239.

104. "Seven Houses on Seventy-fourth Street, for C.T. Barney, Esq.," *Building* 7 (September 17, 1887): 93, plate; *Upper West Side—Central Park West Historic District*, vol. 2: 354–55, vol. 4: 238.

105. *Upper West Side—Central Park West Historic District*, vol. 3: 391, vol. 4: 260.

106. Stern, Gilmartin, and Massengale, *New York 1900*, 348.

107. *Upper West Side—Central Park West Historic District*, vol. 2: 361, vol. 4: 241.

108. *Upper West Side—Central Park West Historic District*, vol. 2: 362, vol. 4: 242.

109. "Buildings Projected," *Real Estate Record and Builders' Guide* 37 (January 30, 1886): 149; Observer, "Houses with Novel Features," *Real Estate Record and Builders' Guide* 37 (May 22, 1886): 674; "Architectural Notes," *Art Age* 3 (June 1886): 198; Observer, "A Handsome Row on Seventy-eighth Street," *Real Estate Record and Builders' Guide* 39 (February 12, 1887): 196–97; "Model Flats," *Real Estate Record and Builders' Guide* 41 (January 14, 1888): 35; Peter B. Wight, "The Life and Works of Rafael Guastavino: Part IV," *Brickbuilder* 10 (October 1901): 211–14; George R. Collins, "The Transfer of Thin Masonry Vaulting from Spain to America," *Journal of the Society of Architectural Historians* 27 (October 1968): 176–201; Landau, "The Row Houses of New York's West Side": 22–25; White and Willensky, *AIA Guide* (1988), 312; *Upper West Side—Central Park West Historic District*, vol. 3: 433, 438, vol. 4: 289, 294; Christopher Gray, "1887 Property Restriction Gives Block a Rare Charm," *New York Times* (October 5, 1997), IX: 5.

110. "Out Among the Builders," *Real Estate Record and Builders' Guide* 39 (February 5, 1887): 166–67; Argus, "Mansions in Fact," *Real Estate Record and Builders' Guide* 40 (December 24, 1887): 1611; "West Side Number": 19.

111. "West Side Number": 51.

112. Observer, "Houses with Novel Features": 674.

113. Observer, "Houses with Novel Features": 674.

114. Argus, "Mansions in Fact": 1611.

115. Russell Sturgis, "The City House in the East and South," in Russell Sturgis et al., *Homes in City and Country* (New York: Charles Scribner's Sons, 1893), 25–26; Bromley and Bromley, *Atlas of the City of New York, Borough of Manhattan*, vol. 3: plate 8.

116. "Buildings Projected," *Real Estate Record and Builders' Guide* 33 (April 26, 1884): 456; *Upper West Side—Central Park West Historic District*, vol. 3: 486, vol. 4: 332.

117. "Buildings Projected," *Real Estate Record and Builders' Guide* 38 (November 27, 1886): 1473; *Upper West Side—Central Park West Historic District*, vol. 3: 484, vol. 4: 330.

118. *Upper West Side—Central Park West Historic District*, vol. 3: 484, vol. 4: 330.

119. "Out Among the Builders," *Real Estate Record and Builders' Guide* 32 (July 28, 1883): 545.

120. "The Hotel Beresford," *Real Estate Record and Builders' Guide* 44 (September 21, 1889): 1263; Alpern, *Luxury Apartment Houses of Manhattan*, 135–36; Christopher Gray, "Namesake Precursors of Central Park West's Towers," *New York Times* (September 14, 1997), IX: 7.

121. "The Bedford Apartment House," *Real Estate Record and Builders' Guide* 25 (January 24, 1880): 81; "The Growing West Side," *New York Times* (April 17, 1881): 14; Elizabeth Collins Cromley, *Alone Together: A History of New York's Early Apartments* (Ithaca, N.Y.: Cornell University Press, 1990), 101–2.

122. For Thom & Wilson's 190–198 Ninth Avenue (1885–86), between Sixty-eighth and Sixty-ninth Streets, see *Upper West Side—Central Park West Historic District*, vol. 2: 60, vol. 4: 34; for their 200–208 Ninth Avenue (1886–87), between Sixty-ninth and Seventieth Streets, see *Upper West Side—Central Park West Historic District*, vol. 2: 64, vol. 4: 36; for their 220–228 (1885–86), 230–238 (1885–86) and 241–247 (1887–88) Ninth Avenue, all built for John Farley & Son, see *Upper West Side—Central Park West Historic District*, vol. 2: 68–69, vol. 4: 39–40; for the Adrian (1888–89), 249–257 Ninth Avenue, see "Out Among the Builders," *Real Estate Record and Builders' Guide* 43 (April 27, 1889): 583–84; *Upper West Side—Central Park West Historic District*, vol. 2: 70, vol. 4: 40; for 240–242 Ninth Avenue (1883–84), between Seventy-first and Seventy-second Streets, see *Upper West Side—Central Park West Historic District*, vol. 2: 71, vol. 4: 41; for 270–276 Ninth Avenue (1884–85), see *Upper West Side—Central Park West Historic District*, vol. 2: 75, vol. 4: 44; for 376 Ninth Avenue (1886), see *Upper West Side—Central Park West Historic District*, vol. 2: 92, vol. 4: 55; for the Nebraska (1890–91), at 451–457 Ninth Avenue, see *Upper West Side—Central Park West Historic District*, vol. 2: 100, vol. 4: 62; for 481 Ninth Avenue (1885–86), see *Upper West Side—Central Park West Historic District*, vol. 2: 108, vol. 4: 67; for 501–503 Ninth Avenue (1886–87), see *Upper West Side—Central Park West Historic District*, vol. 2: 111–12, vol. 4: 69; for the Pomona (1887–88), at 505–507 Ninth Avenue, see *Upper West Side—Central Park West Historic District*, vol. 2: 112–13, vol. 4: 69; for 561–567 Ninth Avenue (1889–90), see *Upper West Side—Central Park West Historic District*, vol. 2: 121, vol. 4: 74.

123. *Upper West Side—Central Park West Historic District*, vol. 2: 78, vol. 4: 46.

124. "Out Among the Builders," *Real Estate Record and Builders' Guide* 41 (January 28, 1888): 115. Also see "West Side Number": 38–39; *Upper West Side—Central Park West Historic District*, vol. 2: 73–74, vol. 4: 42–43. For Charles Buek's six-story St. Charles (1887–88), at 260–268 Ninth Avenue, see *Upper West Side—Central Park West Historic District*, vol. 2: 74–75, vol. 4: 43.

125. For Schellenger's Plymouth (1890–91), at 305–307 Ninth Avenue, see *Upper West Side—Central Park West Historic District*, vol. 2: 79–80, vol. 4: 47; for the Del Monte (1891–92), at 306–316 Ninth Avenue, see *Upper West Side—Central Park West Historic District*, vol. 2: 84–85, vol. 4: 50. For his earlier, Neo-Grec 483–485 Ninth Avenue (1886–87), between Eighty-third and Eighty-fourth Streets, see *Upper West Side—Central Park West Historic District*, vol. 2: 109, vol. 4: 67.

126. *Upper West Side—Central Park West Historic District*, vol. 2: 79, vol. 4: 46.

127. *Upper West Side—Central Park West Historic District*, vol. 2: 83, vol. 4: 49.

128. *Upper West Side—Central Park West Historic District*, vol. 2: 89, vol. 4: 53.

129. "Out Among the Builders," *Real Estate Record and Builders' Guide* 43 (March 9, 1889): 315–17; "West Side Number": 43–45; White and Willensky, *AIA Guide* (1988), 314–15; *Upper West Side—Central Park West Historic District*, vol. 2: 101, vol. 4: 62.

130. "West Side Number": 20–26; White and Willensky, *AIA Guide* (1988), 316; *Upper West Side—Central Park West Historic District*, vol. 2: 117, vol. 4: 72.

131. *Upper West Side—Central Park West Historic District*, vol. 2: 118, vol. 4: 72; "Ending Years of Vacancy," *New York Times* (June 21, 1992), X: 1.

132. "Model Flats," *Real Estate Record and Builders' Guide* 41 (January 14, 1888): 35. Also see "Buildings Projected," *Real Estate Record and Builders' Guide* 40 (August 27, 1889): 1119.

133. "Buildings Projected," *Real Estate Record and Builders' Guide* 35 (May 2, 1885): 513; Christopher Gray, "Is the Perspective Changing on Old Middle-Class Housing?" *New York Times* (February 28, 1988), VIII: 14, reprinted in Gray, *Changing New York*, 41; *Upper West Side—Central Park West Historic District*, vol. 3: 543, vol. 4: 376.

134. "Buildings Projected," *Real Estate Record and Builders' Guide* 41 (April 26, 1888): 554; White and Willensky, *AIA Guide* (1988), 315; *Upper West Side—Central Park West Historic District*, vol. 3: 546, vol. 4: 379.

135. *Upper West Side—Central Park West Historic District*, vol. 3: 544, vol. 4: 377.

136. West End Association, *West End Avenue; Riverside Park in the City of New York* (New York, May 1888), 14.

137. For further discussion of the West End's development, see Stern, Gilmartin, and Massengale, *New York 1900*, 360–68.

138. "The Growth of the City Westward": 1519. Also see "Buildings Projected," *Real Estate Record and Builders' Guide* 37 (January 30, 1886): 149.

139. "Buildings Projected," *Real Estate Record and Builders' Guide* 37 (March 20, 1886): 372; White and Willensky, *AIA Guide* (1988), 307.

140. Observer, "A Row of Ornate Dwellings," *Real Estate Record and Builders' Guide* 41 (January 14, 1888): 38. Also see "Buildings Projected," *Real Estate Record and Builders' Guide* 37 (March 20, 1886): 372.

141. "Out Among the Builders," *Real Estate Record and Builders' Guide* 35 (May 9, 1885): 526.

142. "Buildings Projected," *Real Estate Record and Builders' Guide* 41 (March 31, 1888): 413; "Some Examples in Good Building," *Real Estate Record and Builders' Guide* 45 (May 10, 1890): 688–90.

143. "The 'West Side' Illustrated": 2. Also see "West Side Number": 8–9; Schuyler, "The Romanesque Revival in New York": 23, 36; Landau, "The Row Houses of New York's West Side": 26–27.

144. Schuyler, "The Romanesque Revival in New York": 36.

145. "The 'West Side' Illustrated": 2.

146. "The 'West Side' Illustrated": 2. Also see "Buildings Projected," *Real Estate Record and Builders' Guide* 38 (October 9, 1886): 1254.

147. "The 'West Side' Illustrated": 2. Also see "Buildings Projected," *Real Estate Record and Builders' Guide* 40 (July 2, 1887): 913.

148. "Out Among the Builders," *Real Estate Record and Builders' Guide* 35 (February 28, 1885): 213. Also see "Buildings Projected," *Real Estate Record and Builders' Guide* 35 (April 4, 1885): 382.

149. "The Great Building Movement on the West Side": 951–52. Also see "Buildings Projected," *Real Estate Record and Builders' Guide* 35 (May 9 1885): 551; "Architectural Notes": 198; "House on 11th Ave., near 75th Street, New York City," *Building* 5 (September 11, 1886): 127, plate; "House on 11th Ave., and 75th Street, New York City," *Building* 5 (September 18, 1886): 139, plate; "The 'West Side' Illustrated": 2.

150. "Architectural Notes": 198.

151. "The 'West Side' Illustrated": 2. Also see "Buildings Projected," *Real Estate Record and Builders' Guide* 37 (January 9, 1886): 58; "The West Side Illustrated," *Real Estate Record and Builders' Guide* 38 (November 20, 1886): 1418; Zeisloft, ed., *The New Metropolis*, 23; Montgomery Schuyler, "The Small City House in New York," *Architectural Record* 8 (April–June 1899): 357–88.

152. "The 'West Side' Illustrated": 1–3. Also see "Houses for Wm. J. Merritt & Co. Seventy-fifth Street and West End Avenue, New York," *Building* 7 (July 16, 1887): 21, plate.

153. "The 'West Side' Illustrated": 2.

154. Schuyler, "The Small City House in New York": 376.

155. "The West Side Illustrated," (November 20, 1886): 1418.

156. "Two Houses Cor. 75th Street West of Boulevard, New York City," *Building* 5 (November 13, 1886): 235, plate; "Dwelling Houses on Seventy-fourth and Seventy-fifth Streets, New York, N.Y.," *American Architect and Building News* 21 (May 21, 1887): 246, plate; Zeisloft, ed., *The New Metropolis*, 23; Zabar, "The Influence of W.E.D. Stokes' Real Estate Career on West Side Development": 15.

157. Sturgis, "The City House in the East and South": 24–25. Also see "Buildings Projected," *Real Estate Record and Builders' Guide* 37 (March 13, 1886): 340; "Out Among the Builders," *Real Estate Record and Builders' Guide* 39 (March 19, 1887): 366–67; Landmarks Preservation Commission of the City of New York, *West End—Collegiate Historic District Designation Report* (New York, 1984), 228.

158. "Out Among the Builders," *Real Estate Record and Builders' Guide* 41 (February 25, 1888): 243; "The 'West Side' Illustrated": 2–3; "West Side Number": 11; *West End—Collegiate Historic District*, 75, 77.

159. "The 'West Side' Illustrated": 2–3.

160. "Out Among the Builders," *Real Estate Record and Builders' Guide* 42 (July 14, 1888): 890–91; "Buildings Projected," *Real Estate Record and Builders' Guide* 42 (August 11, 1888): 1012–13; "The 'West Side' Illustrated": 3; "West Side Number": 10; "Houses for Charles Lowther, Esq., New York, N.Y., Messrs. Lamb & Rich, Architects, New York, N.Y.," *American Architect and Building News* 31 (February 14, 1891): 110, plate; "Four Houses on Riverside Drive," *Architecture and Building* 18 (April 1, 1893): plate; Landau, "The Row Houses of New York's West Side": 27–28; Stern, Gilmartin, and Massengale, *New York 1900*, 364.

161. "The 'West Side' Illustrated": 3.

162. "Buildings Projected," *Real Estate Record and Builders' Guide* 42 (August 25, 1888): 1057; Sturgis, "The City House in the East and South": 29–31; "House of Theodore L. De Vinne, W. 76th St. and West End Ave., New York, N.Y. Messrs. Babb, Cook & Willard, Architects, New York, N.Y.," *American Architect and Building News* 24 (June 1899): 103, plate; Landau, "The Row Houses of New York's West Side": 34–35; Irene Tichenor, "Theodore Low De Vinne (1828–1914), Dean of American Printers" (Ph.D. diss., Columbia University, 1983): 58–60.

163. Landau, "The Row Houses of New York's West Side": 33; *West End—Collegiate Historic District*, 215–17, 219–20.

164. Stern, Gilmartin, and Massengale, *New York 1900*, 364.

165. "The 'West Side' Illustrated": 2.

166. "Buildings Projected," *Real Estate Record and Builders' Guide* 35 (June 6, 1885): 669; "Dwellings that Combine Comfort with Style," *Real Estate Record and Builders' Guide* 38 (October 23, 1886): 1294; "A Block of Eight Houses, Corner Seventy-eighth Street and West End Avenue, New York City. By the Late Frederick B. White, Architect," *Building* 5 (November 27, 1886): 259, plate; "The 'West Side' Illustrated": 1–3; Landau, "The Row Houses of New York's West Side": 22; Stern, Gilmartin, and Massengale, *New York 1900*, 366; *West End—Collegiate Historic District*, 183–86; White and Willensky, *AIA Guide* (1988), 300.

167. "The 'West Side' Illustrated": 3.

168. "Dwellings that Combine Comfort with Style": 1294.

169. "The 'West Side' Illustrated": 3.

170. "Out Among the Builders," *Real Estate Record and Builders' Guide* 39 (January 8, 1887): 36–37; "Buildings Projected," *Real Estate Record and Builders' Guide* 39 (March 19, 1887): 387; "Corner Eighty-second St. and West End Avenue, Lamb and Rich, Architects," *Building* 6 (April 30, 1887): 161, plate.

171. "The 'West Side' Illustrated": 3. Also see "Out Among the Builders," *Real Estate Record and Builders' Guide* 40 (December 31, 1887): 1647; "Buildings Projected," *Real Estate Record and Builders' Guide* 41 (January 28, 1888): 131.

172. "The 'West Side' Illustrated": 3. Also see "Residences, New York City," *Brickbuilder* 7 (March 1898): 65; Schuyler, "The Small City House in New York": 383–85; Leland M. Roth, "The Urban Architecture of McKim, Mead & White, 1870–1910" (Ph.D. diss., Yale University, 1973): 190–91; Landau, "The Row Houses of New York's West Side": 22; Leland Roth, *The Architecture of McKim, Mead & White, 1870–1920: A Building List* (New York and London: Garland, 1978), 84; Leland M. Roth, *McKim, Mead & White, Architects* (New York: Harper & Row, 1983), 84. Also see Stern, Gilmartin, and Massengale, *New York 1900*, 365, 367, which incorrectly states the address in both the text and the illustration caption.

173. Schuyler, "The Small City House in New York": 383.

174. "The 'West Side' Illustrated": 3. Also see "Buildings Projected," *Real Estate Record and Builders' Guide* 43 (June 15, 1889): 859.

175. "Buildings Projected," *Real Estate Record and Builders' Guide* 43 (June 22, 1889): 897; "Important Buildings Under Way, Part VI: Between Fifty-ninth and One Hundred and Twenty-fifth Streets, West of Eighth Avenue," *Real Estate Record and Builders' Guide* 43 (June 29, 1889): 912.

176. "West Side Number": 53; Landmarks Preservation Commission of the City of New York, *Riverside—West End Historic District Designation Report* (New York, 1989), 185–86.

177. "Buildings Projected," *Real Estate Record and Builders' Guide* 41 (January 7, 1888): 27; "The 'West Side' Illustrated": 3; *Riverside—West End Historic District*, 82, 84.

178. Schuyler, "Cyrus L. W. Eidlitz": 435. Also see "Buildings Projected," *Real Estate Record and Builders' Guide* 45 (June 28, 1890): 971.

179. "House on 86th Street, New York, N.Y. Mr. J. G. Prague, Architect, New York, N.Y.," *American Architect and Building News* 30 (December 27, 1890): 199, plate. Also see "Buildings Projected," *Real Estate Record and Builders' Guide* 39 (April 9, 1887): 503. Engravings of two of the five houses were published as "113 and 115 W. 86 St." in Lynx, "Model Houses," *Real Estate Record and Builders' Guide* 40 (December 10, 1887): 1542.

180. "Correspondence," *American Architect and Building News* 1 (March 18, 1876): 95. Also see "Correspondence," *American Architect and Building News* 1 (June 24, 1876): 206–7; "Correspondence: New Churches," *American Architect and Building News* 2 (June 9, 1877): 182; "The Paulist Fathers' Church," *Real Estate Record and Builders' Guide* 34 (September 6, 1884): 906; M. G. Van Rensselaer, "Recent Architecture in America—IV," *Century Magazine* 29 (January 1885): 323–38; "A Great Church Dedicated," *New York Daily Tribune* (January 26, 1885): 3; "The Dedication of the Church of St. Paul the Apostle, in New York," *Catholic World* 40 (March 1885): 836–42; "Sketch of Baptistery, Church of St. Paul the Apostle, New York, N.Y., Messrs. Heins & LaFarge, Architects, New York, N.Y.," *American Architect and Building News* (June 14, 1890): 169, plate; King, *King's Handbook of New York* (1893), 397–99; Henry Hope Reed Jr., "In the Shadow of St. Barbara and St. Thomas," *Thought: Ford University Quarterly* 31 (autumn 1956): 341; White and Willensky, *AIA Guide*, (1988), 225; Paul Baker, *Stanny: The Gilded Life of Stanford White* (New York: Macmillan, 1989), 111; David J. O'Brien, *Isaac Hecker: An American Catholic* (New York: Paulist, 1992); Christopher Gray, "Renewal and Change, Esthetic and Liturgical," *New York Times* (December 20, 1992), X: 5.

181. "A Great Church Dedicated": 3.

182. "Out Among the Builders," *Real Estate Record and Builders' Guide* 39 (June 18, 1887): 837–38.

183. "Entrance Doors to Park Presbyterian Church, Corner of Amsterdam and 86th Street, New York, N.Y. Mr. H. F. Kilburn, Architect, New York, N.Y.," *American Architect and Building News* 33 (July 25, 1891): 58, plate; King, *King's Handbook of New York* (1893), 370–71; Stern, Gilmartin, and Massengale, *New York 1900*, 369–70; Christopher Gray, "Streetscapes: West-Park Presbyterian," *New York Times* (January 10, 1988), VIII: 11.

184. "The Great Building Movement on the West Side": 951–52; "Dedicating a New Church," *New York Times* (October 23, 1887): 2; Lynx, "An Important Church Building," *Real Estate Record and Builders' Guide* 40 (October 29, 1887): 352; "Churches on the West Side," *Real Estate Record and Builders' Guide* 41 (May 12, 1888): 599–600; King, *King's Handbook of New York* (1893), 341.

185. "Churches on the West Side": 599–600; White and Willensky, *AIA Guide* (1988), 295.

186. "Out Among the Builders," *Real Estate Record and Builders' Guide* 40 (July 16, 1887): 955; "Churches on the West Side": 599; "Out Among the Builders," *Real Estate Record and Builders' Guide* 43 (February 2, 1889): 142–43; "In the New Church," *New York Times* (January 20, 1890): 8; "West Side Churches: Part I," *Real Estate Record and Builders' Guide* 45 (April 19, 1890): 559–60; "West Side Churches: Part II," *Real Estate Record and Builders' Guide* 45 (May 17, 1890): 731; Schuyler, "The Romanesque Revival in New York": 21–22, 24; King, *King's Handbook of New York* (1893), 372–73; Montgomery Schuyler, "The Works of R. H. Robertson," *Architectural Record* 6 (October–December 1896): 184–219; Stokes, *The Iconography of Manhattan Island*, vol. 5: 2001; Stern, Gilmartin, and Massengale, *New York 1900*, 369.

187. Schuyler, "The Works of R. H. Robertson": 189–91.

188. "Churches on the West Side": 599; "Christ Church Sold," *Real Estate Record and Builders' Guide* 41 (June 9, 1888): 734–35; "Out Among the Builders," *Real Estate Record and Builders' Guide* 41 (June 30, 1888):

836–37; "Men and Things," *Real Estate Record and Builders' Guide* 43 (May 18, 1889): 691; "West Side Churches: Part 1": 559–60; "West Side Number": 40; Schuyler, "The Romanesque Revival in New York": 20–21; King, *King's Handbook of New York* (1893), 350–51; Stern, Gilmartin, and Massengale, *New York 1900*, 369; White and Willensky, *AIA Guide* (1988), 878.

189. Stokes, *The Iconography of Manhattan Island*, vol. 5: 1859, 1864, 1874, 1877–78.

190. Schuyler, "The Romanesque Revival in New York": 20.

191. "Churches on the West Side": 599; "Laying the Cornerstones," *New York Times* (September 15, 1889): 8; "St. Andrew's Methodist Episcopal Church, New York, N.Y. Messrs. J.C. Cady and Co., Architects, New York, N.Y.," *American Architect and Building News* 26 (December 28, 1889): 30, plate; "A Flourishing Church," *New York Times* (March 24, 1890): 8; "St. Andrew's Dedicated," *New York Times* (June 9, 1890): 8; King, *King's Handbook of New York* (1893), 350; White and Willensky, *AIA Guide* (1988), 310; *Upper West Side—Central Park West Historic District*, vol. 3: 413, vol. 4: 275.

192. "Churches on the West Side": 599; "Grace Methodist Episcopal Church, New York, N.Y. Messrs. J. C. Cady and Co., Architects, New York, N.Y.," *American Architect and Building News* 28 (April 5, 1890): 14, plate; "In Their New Home: The Grace Methodist Episcopal Chapel Dedicated," *New York Times* (October 13, 1890): 8.

193. "Out Among the Builders," *Real Estate Record and Builders' Guide* 41 (April 14, 1888): 461; "Out Among the Builders," *Real Estate Record and Builders' Guide* 41 (April 21, 1888): 496–97; "Churches on the West Side": 600; "All Angels' Church, Corner of West End Avenue and Eighty-first Street, New York City," *Architecture and Building* 12 (February 8, 1890): 67, plates; "All Angels' Church," *Real Estate Record and Builders' Guide* 46 (November 1, 1890): 576; King, *King's Handbook of New York* (1893), 361, 364; White and Willensky, *AIA Guide* (1988), 878.

194. "Out Among the Builders," *Real Estate Record and Builders' Guide* 41 (April 21, 1888): 496–97; "Churches on the West Side": 599; "Out Among the Builders," *Real Estate Record and Builders' Guide* 42 (July 14, 1888): 890–91; "Competitive Design for Church, Clergy-House and Schools for Trinity Corporation, New York, N.Y. Mr. W. Halsey Wood, Architect, Newark, N.J.," *American Architect and Building News* 25 (May 11, 1889): 223, plate; "Competitive Design for Church, Clergy-House and Schools for Trinity Corporation, New York, N.Y. Mr. R. M. Hunt, Architect, New York, N.Y.," *American Architect and Building News* 25 (May 25, 1889): 247, plate; "Competitive Design for Church, Clergy-House and Schools for Trinity Corporation, New York, N.Y., Mr. F. C. Withers, Architect, New York, N.Y.," *American Architect and Building News* 25 (June 8, 1889): 272, plate; "Competitive Design for Church, Clergy-House, and Schools for Trinity Corporation, New York, N.Y. Mr. H. M. Congdon, Architect, New York, N.Y.," *American Architect and Building News* 25 (June 29, 1889): 306, plate; "Men and Things," *Real Estate Record and Builders' Guide* 44 (July 6, 1889): 944–45; "To Lay the Cornerstone," *New York Times* (May 19, 1890): 8; "Impressive Ceremonies," *New York Times* (May 20, 1890): 8; Schuyler, "The Romanesque Revival in New York": 18–20; "St. Agnes Chapel," *New York Times* (October 19, 1891): 2; "A Fine Church Structure," *New York Times* (April 23, 1892): 8; "St. Agnes Bells Ring," *New York Times* (June 6, 1892): 9; King, *King's Handbook of New York* (1893), 347–48; "St. Agnes Chapel, 92nd St. Bet. Columbus & Amsterdam Avenues, New York," *Architecture and Building* 19 (October 21, 1893): plate; Montgomery Schuyler, "Trinity's Architecture," *Architectural Record* 25 (June 1909): 424–25; Montgomery Schuyler, "The Work of William A. Potter," *Architectural Record* 26 (September 1909): 176–96; Stokes, *The Iconography of Manhattan Island*, vol. 5: 2005, 2011; Sarah Bradford Landau, *Edward T. and William A. Potter: American Victorian Architects* (New York: Garland, 1979), 204–10; Paul R. Baker, *Richard Morris Hunt* (Cambridge, Mass.: MIT Press, 1980), 546; Francis R. Kowsky, *The Architecture of Frederick Clarke Withers* (Middletown, Conn.: Wesleyan University Press, 1980), 197; Stern, Gilmartin, and Massengale, *New York 1900*, 368–69; White and Willensky, *AIA Guide* (1988), 333; Landmarks Preservation Commission of the City of New York, LP-1659 (August 1, 1989); Diamonstein, *The Landmarks of New York II*, 397.

195. Schuyler, "The Romanesque Revival in New York": 19–20.

196. Schuyler, "Trinity's Architecture": 424–25. For Richardson's Albany City Hall, see Jeffrey Karl Ochsner, *H. H. Richardson: Complete Architectural Works* (Cambridge, Mass.: MIT Press, 1982), 235–39, 295, 439.

197. "A Fine Church Structure": 8.

198. "Two Institutions," *Real Estate Record and Builders' Guide* 39 (February 19, 1887): 224–25; King, *King's Handbook of New York* (1893), 441–42; Montgomery Schuyler, "The Works of the Late Richard M. Hunt," *Architectural Record* 5 (October–December 1895): 97–180; Baker, *Richard Morris Hunt*, 297–99, 515, 544; Landmarks Preservation Commission of the City of New York, LP-1280 (February 9, 1982); Stern, Gilmartin, and Massengale, *New York 1900*, 370; White and Willensky, *AIA Guide* (1988), 344; Diamonstein, *The Landmarks of New York II*, 181.

199. J. F. Richmond, *New York and Its Institutions, 1609–1871* (New York: E. B. Treat, 1871), 425, quoted in Landmarks Preservation Commission of the City of New York, LP-1280 (February 9, 1982), 1.

200. Association for Respectable and Indigent Females, *Sixty-Eighth Annual Report* (New York: Martin Roberts, 1881), 4, quoted in Landmarks Preservation Commission of the City of New York, LP-1280 (February 9, 1982), 1.

201. Schuyler, "The Works of the Late Richard M. Hunt": 173.

202. "Buildings Projected," *Real Estate Record and Builders' Guide* 36 (August 22, 1885): 944; "Two Institutions," (February 19, 1887): 224–25; King, *King's Handbook of New York* (1893), 440.

203. King, *King's Handbook of New York* (1893), 443–44.

204. James D. McCabe Jr., *Lights and Shadows of New York Life; or, The Sights and Sensations of the Great City* (Philadelphia: National Publishing, 1872; New York: Farrar, Straus & Giroux, 1970), 649; "Notes and Clippings," *American Architect and Building News* 2 (August 4, 1877): 252–53; "The Costly and Substantial Buildings of 1886," *Real Estate Record and Builders' Guide* 39 (January 1887): 6–8; "The Roosevelt Hospital," *New York Times* (December 6, 1891): 20; "Roosevelt Hospital," *Harper's Weekly* 37 (November 25, 1893): 187–88; Special Committee on the History of Roosevelt Hospital, *The Roosevelt Hospital, 1871–1957* (New York, 1957); Christopher Gray, "A Mildly Romanesque West Side Bargaining Chip," *New York Times* (October 25, 1987), VIII: 14; Landmarks Preservation Commission of the City of New York, LP-1578 (July 11, 1989); Diamonstein, *The Landmarks of New York II*, 392; Andrea Balis, "Roosevelt Hospital," in Jackson, ed., *The Encyclopedia of New York City*, 1020.

205. "The Roosevelt Hospital," *New York Times*: 20.

206. "The Roosevelt Hospital," *New York Times*: 20.

207. "Roosevelt Hospital," *Harper's Weekly*: 187–88.

208. "Out Among the Builders," *Real Estate Record and Builders' Guide* 33 (May 24, 1884): 566; "More Building in Harlem," *Real Estate Record and Builders' Guide* 36 (August 15, 1885): 907; "Notes About Town," *Real Estate Record and Builders' Guide* 36 (November 7, 1885): 1223; "The Skin and Cancer Hospital at 106th Street and Eighth Avenue to Be Opened This Week," *New York Daily Graphic* (November 28, 1887): 193; Editorial, *New York Times* (December 7, 1887): 4; "Central Park West," *Real Estate Record and Builders' Guide*: 1574; "The New York Cancer Hospital," supplement, *Building* 8 (March 31, 1888): 105, plate; "New York Cancer Hospital," *Building* 8 (April 7, 1888): 113; "Cancer Hospital, New York, N.Y. Mr. C. C. Haight, Architect, New York, N.Y.," *American Architect and Building News* 24 (December 22, 1888): 290, plate; "Out Among the Builders," *Real Estate Record and Builders' Guide* 43 (January 5, 1889): 8–9; "American Construction Through English Eyes—II: The 'Cancer Hospital,' New York," *American Architect and Building News* 33 (August 8, 1891): 86–87; King, *King's Handbook of New York* (1893), 485; Montgomery Schuyler, "The Works of Charles Coolidge Haight," *Architectural Record* 6 (July 1899): 1–102; Landmarks Preservation Commission of the City of New York, LP-0938 (August 17, 1976); White and Willensky, *AIA Guide* (1988), 335; Diamonstein, *The Landmarks of New York II*, 188. Also see Stern, Gilmartin, and Massengale, *New York 1900*, 370, which incorrectly states the beginning date of the building's design and the width of the towers.

209. "More Building in Harlem": 907.

Upper Manhattan

1. For Harlem's early development, see James Riker, *Revised History of Harlem (City of New York): Its Origin and Early Annals* (New York: New Harlem, 1904). Also see Reginald Pelham Bolton, *Washington Heights, Manhattan: Its Eventful Past* (New York: Reginald Pelham Bolton, 1924); Karen Wolfe, "Visible City," *Metropolis* 6 (March 1987): 70–73, 75; Jeffrey S. Gurock and Calvin B. Holder, "Harlem," in Kenneth T. Jackson, ed., *The Encyclopedia of New York City* (New Haven, Conn., and London: Yale University Press; New York: New-York Historical Society, 1995), 523–25; Andrew S. Dolkart and Gretchen S. Sorin, *Touring Historic Harlem: Four Walks in Northern Manhattan* (New York: New York Landmarks Conservancy, 1997), 7–16.

2. *New York Commercial Advertiser* (June 6, 1848), quoted in I. N. Phelps Stokes, *The Iconography of Manhattan Island*, 6 vols. (New York: Robert H. Dodd, 1915–28; New York: Arno Press, 1967), vol. 5: 1811.

3. Stokes, *The Iconography of Manhattan Island*, vol. 5: 1732, 1739, 1760; Barbaralee Diamonstein, *The Landmarks of New York II* (New York: Harry N. Abrams, 1993), 447.

4. Stokes, *The Iconography of Manhattan Island*, vol. 5: 1740.

5. Alan Burnham, ed., *New York Landmarks* (Middletown, Conn.: Wesleyan University Press, 1963), 120–21; David M. Kahn, "Bogardus, Fire, and the Iron Tower," *Journal of the Society of Architectural Historians* 35 (October 1976): 186–203; Dolkart and Sorin, *Touring Historic Harlem*, 44.

6. Stokes, *The Iconography of Manhattan Island*, vol. 5: 1900.

7. "The Fifth Avenue," *Real Estate Record and Builders' Guide* 21 (June 15, 1878): 515–16. Also see Moses King, *King's Handbook of New York* (Boston: Moses King, 1893), 152; Stokes, *The Iconography of Manhattan Island*, vol. 5: 1992.

8. Christopher Gray, "Changeling Resists Landmark Status," *New York Times* (July 14, 1991), X: 6; Landmarks Preservation Commission of the City of New York, LP-1845 (July 26, 1994).

9. White and Willensky, *AIA Guide* (1988), 457.

10. Unidentified health inspector, quoted in Dolkart and Sorin, *Touring Historic Harlem*, 9.

11. Stokes, *The Iconography of Manhattan Island*, vol. 3: 759.

12. "The Mount Morris Bank," *Real Estate Record and Builders' Guide* 32 (November 3, 1883): 851–52. Also see "New York's Grand West End," *Real Estate Record and Builders' Guide* 24 (November 1, 1879): 871–72.

13. Montgomery Schuyler, "Some Suburbs of New York, Part I: New Jersey," *Lippincott's Magazine* 8 (July 1884): 9–23.

14. "The Harlem Flats," *New York Daily Tribune* (March 31, 1876): 8. Also see "Dead Oil," *New York Daily Tribune* (June 24, 1875): 6; "The Harlem Flats," *New York Daily Graphic* (July 15, 1875): 103; "The Condition of the Harlem Flats," *New York Daily Tribune* (August 1, 1877): 2.

15. "Up in Busy Harlem," *New York Daily Tribune* (September 1, 1889): 1. Also see "Just Above Central Park," *Real Estate Record and Builders' Guide* 42 (December 15, 1888): 1476.

16. Montgomery Schuyler, "The Works of Cady, Berg & See," *Architectural Record* 6 (April–June 1897): 517–53.

17. "The Mount Morris Apartment House," *Building* 1 (July 1883): 131–32; E. Robinson, *Robinson's Atlas of the City of New York* (New York: Robinson, 1885), vol. 1: plate 20.

18. "More Building in Harlem," *Real Estate Record and Builders' Guide* 36 (August 15, 1885): 907; *Harlem of To-day Illustrated: A Glimpse at Its Past, Present and Future* (New York: Davison, 1893), n.p.; Landmarks Preservation Commission of the City of New York, LP-1842 (January 5, 1993); Dolkart and Sorin, *Touring Historic Harlem*, 52.

19. "More Building in Harlem," (August 15, 1885): 907.

20. Observer, "A Harlem Improvement," *Real Estate Record and Builders' Guide* 44 (August 10, 1889): 1104–5. Also see "West Side Number," *Real Estate Record and Builders' Guide* 46 (December 20, 1890): 1–64; George W. and Walter S. Bromley, *Atlas of the City of New York, Borough of Manhattan*, 5 vols. (Philadelphia: Bromley, 1898–99), vol. 4: plate 8.

21. Dolkart and Sorin, *Touring Historic Harlem*, 58–59.

22. "Apartment Houses, Seventh Avenue and 118th Street, New York City," *Building* 9 (July 28, 1888): 29, plate.

23. "The Transformation of a Beautiful District," *Real Estate Record and Builders' Guide* 39 (May 21, 1887): 696.

24. Simon Stern, "Knickerbocker Avenue Proposed," letter to the editor, *New York Times* (February 2, 1891): 8.

25. Christopher Gray, "The Days Dwindle for Victorian Vestiges," *New York Times* (August 25, 1991), X: 5.

26. New York City Department of Buildings, Manhattan Division, Plans, Permits and Dockets, 1886; "House of E. Aug. Neresheimer, Esq., New York, N.Y., Mr. A. B. Jennings, Architect, New York, N.Y.," *American Architect and Building News* 22 (November 12, 1887): 230, plate; Bromley and Bromley, *Atlas of the City of New York, Borough of Manhattan*, vol. 4: plate 10.

27. Lynx, "A Choice Harlem Section," *Real Estate Record and Builders' Guide* 42 (September 22, 1888): 1134; White and Willensky, *AIA Guide* (1988), 443; Dolkart and Sorin, *Touring Historic Harlem*, 41. For a general discussion of the Mount Morris Park area, see Landmarks Preservation Commission of the City of New York, *Mount Morris Park Historic District Designation Report* (New York, 1971), 1–6.

28. Dolkart and Sorin, *Touring Historic Harlem*, 50–51.

29. Dolkart and Sorin, *Touring Historic Harlem*, 40.

30. Dolkart and Sorin, *Touring Historic Harlem*, 40.

31. Dolkart and Sorin, *Touring Historic Harlem*, 40.

32. "Recent Building in Harlem," *Real Estate Record and Builders' Guide* 36 (July 25, 1885): 831–32.

33. Dolkart and Sorin, *Touring Historic Harlem*, 50–51. The row at 133–143 West 122nd Street very nearly incorporates the facade design illustrated in "House Near Fifth Avenue, Harlem, N.Y. Messrs. Kimball & Wisedell, Architects, New York, N.Y.," *American Architect and Building News* 8 (November 27, 1880): 258, plate.

34. Dolkart and Sorin, *Touring Historic Harlem*, 48.

35. Dolkart and Sorin, *Touring Historic Harlem*, 50.

36. Dolkart and Sorin, *Touring Historic Harlem*, 42–43.

37. Lynx, "A Lenox Avenue Improvement," *Real Estate Record and Builders' Guide* 44 (October 12, 1889): 1368–70; Dolkart and Sorin, *Touring Historic Harlem*, 48.

38. Leland Roth, *The Architecture of McKim, Mead & White, 1870–1920: A Building List* (New York and London: Garland, 1978), 95; Christopher Gray, "Streetscapes: Wanaque Apartments," *New York Times* (June 11, 1989), X: 10, reprinted in Christopher Gray, *Changing New York: The Architectural Scene* (New York: Dover, 1992), 88.

39. "Harlem Supplement," *Real Estate Record and Builders' Guide* 48 (November 7, 1891): 1–14.

40. "Harlem Supplement": 6; Dolkart and Sorin, *Touring Historic Harlem*, 43–44. For further description of 121st Street between Mount Morris Park West and Lenox Avenue, see Christopher Gray, "Streetscapes: 121st Street West of Mount Morris Park," *New York Times* (March 16, 1997), IX: 4.

41. Landmarks Preservation Commission of the City of New York, LP-1135 (August 11, 1981); Diamonstein, *The Landmarks of New York II*, 153.

42. Christopher Gray, "An 1871 Row House Co-Designed by Calvert Vaux," *New York Times* (February 8, 1988), X: 5.

43. "Out Among the Builders," *Real Estate Record and Builders' Guide* 31 (March 10, 1883): 98; New York City Department of Buildings, Manhattan Division, Plans, Permits and Dockets, 1889.

44. "Out Among the Builders," *Real Estate Record and Builders' Guide* 31 (March 17, 1883): 116; Bromley and Bromley, *Atlas of the City of New York, Borough of Manhattan*, vol. 4: plate 22.

45. "Five Houses—Cor. 130th St. & 7th Ave. For E. S. Higgins, Esq.," *Building* 7 (September 10, 1887): plate; Bromley and Bromley, *Atlas of the City of New York, Borough of Manhattan*, vol. 4: plate 21.

46. "Recent Building in Harlem": 831–32; Landmarks Preservation Commission of the City of New York, LP-1138 (August 11, 1981); White and Willensky, *AIA Guide* (1988), 447; Andrew Dolkart, *Guide to New York City Landmarks* (Washington, D.C.: Preservation Press, 1992), 138; Brendan Gill, "The Sky Line: On Astor Row," *New Yorker* 68 (November 2, 1992): 51–53; Diamonstein, *The Landmarks of New York II*, 176; Dolkart and Sorin, *Touring Historic Harlem*, 129.

47. "The 'Hall Mansion,' Harlem, N.Y. Sketched by Mr. C. W. Stoughton, New York, N.Y.," *American Architect and Building News* 19 (March 20, 1886): 188, plate.

48. "Recent Building in Harlem": 831–32.

49. "Out Among the Builders," *Real Estate Record and Builders' Guide* 31 (June 30, 1883): 255–56. Also see Bromley and Bromley, *Atlas of the City of New York, Borough of Manhattan*, vol. 4: plate 21.

50. *The King Model Houses* (New York: D. H. King, c. 1891), n.p.; King, *King's Handbook of New York* (1893), 382; "King Model Houses," *Brickbuilder* 2 (October 1893): plates 73–75, 78–79; Montgomery Schuyler, "The Small City House in New York," *Architectural Record* 8 (April–June 1899): 357–88; Carl Van Vechten, *Nigger Heaven* (New York: Alfred A. Knopf, 1926), 77–78; Landmarks Preservation Commission of the City of New York, LP-0322 (March 16, 1967); McCandlish Phillips, "City Seeks a Way to Save Harlem Enclave," *New York Times* (March 30, 1972): 39; Leland M. Roth, "The Urban Architecture of McKim, Mead & White, 1870–1910" (Ph.D. diss., Yale University, 1973): 277–82; Roth, *The Architecture of McKim, Mead & White, 1870–1920: A Building List*, 85; Paul Goldberger, *The City Observed: New York* (New York: Random House, 1979), 296–98; Paula Deitz, "In Harlem's Elegant Strivers' Row," *New York Times* (April 16, 1981), C: 1, 6; Leland M. Roth, *McKim, Mead & White, Architects* (New York: Harper & Row, 1983), 140–43; Dolkart, *Guide to New York City Landmarks*, 150; Diamonstein, *The Landmarks of New York II*, 440; Dolkart and Sorin, *Touring Historic Harlem*, 73–78, 81–85.

51. Daniel Garrison Brinton Thompson, *Ruggles of New York* (New York: Columbia University Press, 1946), 46, 56, 58, 61, 65, 71; Stephen Garmey, *Gramercy Park: An Illustrated History of a New York Neighborhood* (New York: Balsam Press, 1984), 22–39.

52. *The King Model Houses*, n.p.

53. Schuyler, "The Small City House in New York": 383.

54. David I. Stagg, "Annual Report of the Superintendent of School Buildings," *Thirty-Eighth Annual Report of the Board of Education of the City and County of New York for the Year Ending December 31, 1879* (New York: Hall of the Board of Education, 1880), 286–87; "For the School Children, Four New School Houses Now Being Built," *New York Times* (August 14, 1880): 8; Christopher Gray, "A Big, Solid Centenarian that Still Exudes Potential," *New York Times* (May 29, 1988), X: 9, reprinted in Gray, *Changing New York*, 52; Landmarks Preservation Commission of the City of New York, LP-1836 (June 25, 1996).

55. King, *King's Handbook of New York* (1893), 254; Landmarks Preservation Commission of the City of New York, LP-0297 (August 2, 1967); Dolkart, *Guide to New York City Landmarks*, 144; Diamonstein, *The Landmarks of New York II*, 208.

56. "Improvements in Harlem," *New York Times* (July 14, 1873): 2; Harry Miller Lydenberg, *History of the New York Public Library* (Boston: Gregg, 1972), 151–84.

57. "To Have a New Home," *New York Times* (April 2, 1891): 2; "The Harlem Library," *New York Times* (May 24, 1891): 9; White and Willensky, *AIA Guide* (1988), 443; Dolkart and Sorin, *Touring Historic Harlem*, 38–40.

58. "Out Among the Builders," *Real Estate Record and Builders' Guide* 41 (June 9, 1888): 736–37; "Out Among the Builders," *Real Estate Record and Builders' Guide* 42 (July 14, 1888): 890–91; "The New Building of the Harlem Club," *New York Daily Graphic* (March 14, 1889): 9–10; "The Harlem Club," *Real Estate Record and Builders' Guide* 43 (June 22, 1889): 870; "The Harlem Club House, Corner of 125th [*sic*] Street and Lenox Avenue, New York, N.Y., Messrs. Lamb & Rich, Architects, New York, N.Y.," *American Architect and Building News* 28 (June 21, 1890): 186, plate; Montgomery Schuyler, "The Romanesque Revival in New York," *Architectural Record* 1 (July–September 1891): 7–38; King, *King's Handbook of New York* (1893), 548–49; *Mount Morris Park Historic District*, 3; Goldberger, *The City Observed*, 292; White and Willensky, *AIA Guide* (1988), 443; Dolkart and Sorin, *Touring Historic Harlem*, 38.

59. Schuyler, "The Romanesque Revival in New York": 26.

60. "Improvements in Harlem": 2.

61. King, *King's Handbook of New York* (1893), 377; Christopher Gray, "Unchanging Facade, but Sweeping Changes Within," *New York Times* (January 26, 1997), IX: 5.

62. "St. Andrews Church, New York City," *New-York Sketch-Book of Architecture* 3 (April 1876): 2, plate 14.

63. "More Building in Harlem," (August 15, 1885): 907; "The New St. Andrew's Episcopal Church," *New York Daily Graphic* (July 21, 1888): 160; "Dedicating the New Church," *New York Times* (December 1, 1890): 8; King, *King's Handbook of New York* (1893), 356–57; Landmarks Preservation Commission of the City of New York, LP-0294 (April 12, 1967); White and Willensky, *AIA Guide* (1988), 444; Dolkart, *Guide to New York City Landmarks*, 149–50; Diamonstein, *The Landmarks of New York II*, 204.

64. King, *King's Handbook of New York* (1893), 371–72; White and Willensky, *AIA Guide* (1988), 445.

65. Effingham P. Humphrey, "The Churches of James Renwick, Jr." (master's thesis, New York University, 1942): 24–26, plate 3.

66. Henry F. Withey and Elsie Rathburn Withey, *Biographical Dictionary of American Architects* (Los Angeles: New Age, 1956), 595.

67. "The Costly and Substantial Buildings of 1886," *Real Estate Record and Builders' Guide* 39 (January 1, 1887): 6–8; "The West Harlem Methodist Church," *Real Estate Record and Builders' Guide* 39 (April 16, 1887): 511–12; "The Largest in the City," *New York Times* (December 17, 1890): 9; "A New Church Edifice," *New York Times* (December 22, 1890): 5; King, *King's Handbook of New York* (1893), 376–77.

68. "The West Harlem Methodist Church": 511–12.

69. King, *King's Handbook of New York* (1893), 339; White and Willensky, *AIA Guide* (1988), 442–43.

70. "More Building in Harlem," (August 15, 1885): 907; "Their Church Dedicated," *New York Times* (October 13, 1890): 2; "Recent Architecture—At Home," *Real Estate Record and Builders' Guide* 47 (February 14, 1891): 232, 234; Landmarks Preservation Commission of the City of New York, LP-1134 (February 3, 1981); White and Willensky, *AIA Guide* (1988), 447; Dolkart, *Guide to New York City Landmarks*, 146–47; Diamonstein, *The Landmarks of New York II*, 191.

71. "More Building in Harlem," (August 15, 1885): 907.

72. "Out Among the Builders," *Real Estate Record and Builders' Guide* 39 (February 12, 1887): 202–3; "The Cornerstone Laid," *New York Times* (May 27, 1887): 8; "The Mount Morris Baptist Church," *New York Daily Graphic* (March 30, 1888): 224, 226; "Dedicating a New Church," *New York Times* (April 2, 1888): 8; White and Willensky, *AIA Guide* (1988), 443.

73. "The New German First Baptist Church of Harlem," *New York Daily Graphic* (July 9, 1888): 52; White and Willensky, *AIA Guide* (1988), 457.

74. "In Their New Church Edifice," *New York Times* (April 15, 1889): 2; "The Church of the Holy Trinity, Harlem," *Real Estate Record and Builders' Guide* 44 (October 12, 1889): 1363–64; Schuyler, "The Romanesque Revival in New York": 16–18; King, *King's Handbook of New York* (1893), 361–62; "Holy Trinity Church," *Scientific American Architects and Builders Edition* 20 (August 1895): 30–31; Montgomery Schuyler, "The Work of William A. Potter," *Architectural Record* 26 (September 1909): 176–96; Burnham, ed., *New York Landmarks*, 160–61; Landmarks Preservation Commission of the City of New York, LP-0293 (July 19, 1966); Goldberger, *The City Observed*, 291–92; Sarah Bradford Landau, *Edward T. and William A. Potter: American Victorian Architects* (New York: Garland, 1979), 198–202, figs. 106–11; White and Willensky, *AIA Guide* (1988), 442–43; Dolkart, *Guide to New York City Landmarks*, 150; Diamonstein, *The Landmarks of New York II*, 196; Dolkart and Sorin, *Touring Historic Harlem*, 48–50.

75. Schuyler, "The Romanesque Revival in New York": 17–18.

76. "The Church of the Holy Trinity, Harlem," *Real Estate Record and Builders' Guide*: 1363.

77. "All Saints' Church Rectory, One Hundred and Twenty-fifth [*sic*] Street, New York," *Building* 10 (January 19, 1889): 21, plate; White and Willensky, *AIA Guide* (1988), 444–45.

78. *A History of Real Estate, Building and Architecture in New York City During the Last Quarter of a Century* (New York: Real Estate Record Association, 1898), 647; Montgomery Schuyler, "Italian Gothic in New York," *Architectural Record* 26 (July 1909): 47–48; Humphrey, "The Churches of James Renwick, Jr.": 73–75, plate 28; White and Willensky, *AIA Guide* (1988), 444–45.

79. Dolkart and Sorin, *Touring Historic Harlem*, 46.

80. "Out Among the Builders," *Real Estate Record and Builders' Guide* 31 (March 10, 1883): 98; King, *King's Handbook of New York* (1893),

398–99; Goldberger, *The City Observed*, 303; White and Willensky, *AIA Guide* (1988), 455.

81. White and Willensky, *AIA Guide* (1988), 451.

82. "A New Synagogue Dedicated," *New York Times* (August 18, 1890): 5.

83. "Out Among the Builders," *Real Estate Record and Builders' Guide* 31 (January 20, 1883): 28; "Mount Morris Bank-Building, New York, N.Y. Messrs. Lamb & Rich, Architects, New York, N.Y.," *American Architect and Building News* 13 (April 28, 1883): 201, plate; "The Mount Morris Bank": 851–52; "Mount Morris Safe Deposit Company," *New York Daily Graphic* (April 24, 1884): 405; "Recent Building in Harlem": 831; "Harlem Supplement": 7–8; King, *King's Handbook of New York* (1893), 742; Christopher Gray, "A Derelict Is Freshened Up, but Its Fate Is Still Uncertain," *New York Times* (August 30, 1987), VIII: 12, reprinted in Gray, *Changing New York*, 21; White and Willensky, *AIA Guide* (1988), 442, 444; Landmarks Preservation Commission of the City of New York, LP-1339 (January 5, 1993); "And a Bank in Harlem," *New York Times* (January 10, 1993), X: 1; Dolkart and Sorin, *Touring Historic Harlem*, 128.

84. "The Mount Morris Bank": 851–52.

85. "Harlem Supplement": 1, 3. Also see King, *King's Handbook of New York* (1893), 743–44.

86. "Harlem Supplement": 8–9.

87. "Harlem Supplement": 8; White and Willensky, *AIA Guide* (1988), 445; Dolkart and Sorin, *Touring Historic Harlem*, 128.

88. "Harlem Supplement": 10.

89. "Harlem's New Theatre," *New York Times* (June 11, 1889): 8; "The Theatres," *New York Times* (October 1, 1889): 4; King, *King's Handbook of New York* (1893), 605; Stokes, *The Iconography of Manhattan Island*, vol. 5: 2000; Mary C. Henderson, *The City and the Theatre* (Clifton, N.J.: James T. White, 1973), 182; Kathryn Shattuck, "Showtime Showdown," *New York Times* (February 25, 1996), IX: 2.

90. "The Theatres": 4.

91. "Out Among the Builders," *Real Estate Record and Builders' Guide* 44 (December 21, 1889): 1704–5; "The East Side—Its Streets and Buildings," supplement, *Real Estate Record and Builders' Guide* 45 (May 3, 1890): 1–11; King, *King's Handbook of New York* (1893), 605.

92. "The Costly and Substantial Buildings of 1886": 6–8; "The Cornerstone Laid," *New York Times* (April 28, 1887): 12; "Out Among the Builders," *Real Estate Record and Builders' Guide* 40 (September 24, 1887): 1203; "The Y.M.C.A. Convention," *New York Daily Graphic* (February 20, 1888): 809–10; "How the Money Was Raised," *New York Times* (May 5, 1888): 3; "In Process of Dedication," *New York Times* (September 25, 1888): 2; King, *King's Handbook of New York* (1893), 377, 908; *Book of Young Men's Christian Association Buildings* (Chicago: Young Men's Era, 1895), 7; Stokes, *The Iconography of Manhattan Island*, vol. 5: 1996.

93. Landmarks Preservation Commission of the City of New York, LP-1838 (June 17, 1997).

94. King, *King's Handbook of New York* (1893), 47, 137; Stokes, *The Iconography of Manhattan Island*, vol. 3: 615–16, 987, plate 112, vol. 5: 1448, 1454, 1461, 1473, 1495, 1638, 1740; Karen E. Markoe, "Manhattanville," in Jackson, ed., *The Encyclopedia of New York City*, 724.

95. *Public Advertiser* (June 9, 1807), quoted in Stokes, *The Iconography of Manhattan Island*, vol. 5: 1461.

96. *New York Gazette and General Advertiser* (February 4, 1807), quoted in Stokes, *The Iconography of Manhattan Island*, vol. 5: 1454.

97. "August 1880: Manhattan Street between Amsterdam and Morningside Avenues," unpublished text accompanying photographic collection, Schomburg Center for Research in Black Culture, New York Public Library. In the 1920s, Manhattan Street's name was changed to 125th Street; from the East River to Morningside Avenue, 125th Street conformed to the street grid, but west of Morningside Avenue ran diagonally with respect to the overall street pattern. At the same time that Manhattan Street's name was changed, what formerly had been 125th Street between Morningside and Claremont Avenues became LaSalle Street.

98. Robinson, *Robinson's Atlas of the City of New York*, vol. 1: plate 28; "St. Joseph's Roman Catholic Church," unpublished text accompanying photographic collection, Schomburg Center for Research in Black Culture, New York Public Library.

99. "St. Joseph's Roman Catholic Church," unpublished text accompanying photographic collection, Schomburg Center for Research in Black Culture, New York Public Library.

100. White and Willensky, *AIA Guide* (1988), 427.

101. King, *King's Handbook of New York* (1893), 284, 286; J. Stephen Sullivan, *Manhattan College* (New York: Newcomer Society in North America, 1978); Gabriel Costello, *The Arches of Manhattan College 1853–1979* (Riverdale, N.Y.: Manhattan College, 1980); Sepp Seitz, *Manhattan College: Then and Now* (Louisville, Ky.: Harmony House, 1991); Marc Ferris, "Manhattan College," in Jackson, ed., *The Encyclopedia of New York City*, 722.

102. *Catalogue of Manhattan College, 1863–1864*, 6, quoted in Costello, *The Arches of Manhattan College 1853–1979*, 1.

103. Brother John Chrysostom [Francis Bart], "The Beginnings of Manhattan College," *Manhattan Quarterly* (April 1913): 1–8, quoted in Costello, *The Arches of Manhattan College 1853–1979*, 4.

104. King, *King's Handbook of New York* (1893), 286; Thomas Sibyllic, *Manhattanville College* (Louisville, Ky.: Harmony House, 1992).

105. "Their Convent Is in Ruins," *New York World* (August 14, 1888): 5; "Amid the Convent Ruins," *New York World* (August 15, 1888): 6.

106. Stokes, *The Iconography of Manhattan Island*, vol. 5: 1016.

107. Michele Herman, "Morningside Heights," in Jackson, ed., *The Encyclopedia of New York City*, 771; Martin Stolz, "F.Y.I.: Wrong Side of the Sun," *New York Times* (August 10, 1997), XIII: 2; Andrew S. Dolkart, *Morningside Heights: A History of Its Architecture and Development* (New York: Columbia University Press, 1998).

108. "The West Side," *New York Times* (February 4, 1872): 6; "A New 'Ground-Picture,'" editorial, *New York Times* (November 2, 1873): 4; "Morningside Park," *New York Daily Graphic* (June 25, 1877): 806; "Morningside Park," *New York Times* (August 16, 1881): 8; "The Morningside Park," *Real Estate Record and Builders' Guide* 28 (August 20, 1881): 812; "Morningside Park," *Real Estate Record and Builders' Guide* 30 (October 14–21, 1882): 23–24; "A New Pleasure Ground," *New York Daily Tribune* (August 1, 1887): 8; "A Vigorous Onslaught," *New York Times* (August 3, 1887): 8; "Morningside Park," editorial, *New York Times* (August 4, 1887): 4; "Morningside Park," editorial, *New York Daily Tribune* (August 25, 1887): 4; "City and Suburban News," *New York Times* (August 25, 1887): 3; "The Morningside Reservation," editorial, *New York Daily Tribune* (October 16, 1887): 4; "Our Park System," editorial, *New York Times* (July 1, 1888): 4; J.N.N., "Unique Park Gardening," letter to the editor, *New York Times* (June 9, 1889): 16; King, *King's Handbook of New York* (1893), 166; Edward Hagaman Hall, "A Brief History of Morningside Park and Vicinity," *21st Annual Report of the American Scenic and Historic Preservation Society* (1916): 539–72; Stokes, *The Iconography of Manhattan Island*, vol. 5: 1931, 1955, 1974, 1999; Albert Fein, ed., *Landscape into Cityscape: Frederick Law Olmsted's Plans for a Greater New York City* (Ithaca, N.Y.: Cornell University Press, 1967), 441–57; Elizabeth Barlow, *Frederick Law Olmsted's New York* (New York: Praeger, 1972), 47–48, 114–15; Albert Fein, *Frederick Law Olmsted and the American Environmental Tradition* (New York: George Braziller, 1972), 50–51, fig. 79; Jeffrey Simpson, *Art of the Olmsted Landscape: His Works in New York City* (New York: New York City Landmarks Preservation Commission and The Arts Publisher, Inc., 1981), 10–11; John Emerson Todd, *Frederick Law Olmsted* (Boston: Twayne, 1982), 94, 100; *Friends of Morningside Park*, special edition (New York, 1983), n.p.; White and Willensky, *AIA Guide* (1988), 438; David Schuyler and Jane Turner Censer, eds., *The Papers of Frederick Law Olmsted, Vol. 6: The Years of Olmsted, Vaux & Company* (Baltimore: John Hopkins University Press, 1992), 651–60; William Alex, *Calvert Vaux: Architect and Planner* (New York: Ink, 1994), 24, 148–49.

109. "The West Side": 6.

110. Frederick Law Olmsted and Calvert Vaux, *General Plan for the Improvement of Morningside Park* (1887), reprinted in Fein, ed., *Landscape into Cityscape*, 441–42.

111. Frederick Law Olmsted and Calvert Vaux, *Document No. 50 of the Board of the Department of Public Parks: Preliminary Study by the Landscape Architect of a Design for the Laying Out of Morningside Park* (1873), reprinted in Fein, ed., *Landscape into Cityscape*, 334–35.

112. "Morningside Park," (August 20, 1881): 812.

113. "Morningside Park," (August 25, 1887): 4.

114. Olmsted and Vaux, *General Plan for the Improvement of Morningside Park* (1887), reprinted in Fein, ed., *Landscape into Cityscape*, 443.

115. Stokes, *The Iconography of Manhattan Island*, vol. 3: 986; James Bradley, "Carmansville," in Jackson, ed., *The Encyclopedia of New York City*, 179.

116. T. Addison Richards, "New York Circumnavigated," *Harper's New Monthly Magazine* 23 (July 1861): 165–83, quoted in Stokes, *The Iconography of Manhattan Island*, vol. 5: 1898. For discussion of Minnie's Land, see Francis Hobart Herrick, *Audubon the Naturalist*, 2 vols. (New York: D. Appleton-Century, 1938), vol. 2: 310–11; Alice Ford, *John James Audubon* (New York: Abbeville, 1988), 383–98.

117. "Homes of the Dead," *New York Times* (March 30, 1866): 2; White and Willensky, *AIA Guide* (1988), 459; Alex, *Calvert Vaux*, 28, 196–97.

118. King, *King's Handbook of New York* (1893), 527; Landmarks Preservation Commission of the City of New York, LP-1389 (July 15, 1986); Diamonstein, *The Landmarks of New York II*, 160.

119. King, *King's Handbook of New York* (1893), 974; White and Willensky, *AIA Guide* (1988), 435.

120. John W. Kennion, *Architects' and Builders' Guide* (New York: Fitzpatrick & Hunter, 1868), part 1: 12; King, *King's Handbook of New York* (1893), 413; Theodore James Jr., *Fifth Avenue* (New York: Walker, 1971), 62–63; David W. Dunlap, *On Broadway: A Journey Uptown Over Time* (New York: Rizzoli International Publications, 1990), 284–85; Mike Sappol, "Colored Orphan Asylum," in Jackson, ed., *The Encyclopedia of New York City*, 256–57.

121. "The Hebrew Orphan Asylum," *Real Estate Record and Builders' Guide* 27 (June 11, 1881): 600; "Laying a Cornerstone," *New York Evening Post* (May 16, 1883): 1; Carl Schurz, "Education of Orphan Children," *New York Evening Post* (May 17, 1883): 4; "Laying the Cornerstone of the New Hebrew Asylum, Tenth Avenue between 136th and 138th Streets, Last Wednesday," *New York Daily Graphic* (May 18, 1883): 551; "The New Hebrew Orphan Asylum, Tenth Avenue, 136th and 138th Street, to Be Dedicated To-day," *New York Daily Graphic* (October 27, 1884): 849; King, *King's Handbook of New York* (1893), 414; Stokes, *The Iconography of Manhattan Island*, vol. 5: 1981; Max J. Kohler, "New York," *The Jewish Encyclopedia*, 12 vols. (New York: Funk & Wagnalls, 1901–06; New York: Ktav, 1964), vol. 9: 259–91; "Alumni to Mark Centennial of Home," *New York Times* (October 21, 1984): 60; Dunlap, *On Broadway*, 285; Christopher Gray, "An Orphan Asylum and a Fifth Avenue 'Farmhouse,'" *New York Times* (August 31, 1997), IX: 5.

122. "Gelatine Print—Building for the Montefiore Home for Chronic Invalids, Eleventh Avenue, 129th to 130th Streets, New York City," *Building* 10 (May 25, 1889): 169, plate. Also see King, *King's Handbook of New York* (1893), 414.

123. King, *King's Handbook of New York* (1893), 396–97.

124. King, *King's Handbook of New York* (1893), 433; "The Sheltering Arms Area," unpublished text accompanying photographic collection, Schomburg Center for Research in Black Culture, New York Public Library.

125. "The Sheltering Arms Area," unpublished text accompanying photographic collection, Schomburg Center for Research in Black Culture, New York Public Library.

126. White and Willensky, *AIA Guide* (1988), 429.

127. Landmarks Preservation Commission of the City of New York, *Hamilton Heights Historic District Designation Report* (New York, 1974); Dolkart, *Guide to New York City Landmarks*, 143–46; Diamonstein, *The Landmarks of New York II*, 451; Lisa Gitelman, "Hamilton Heights," in Jackson, ed., *The Encyclopedia of New York City*, 519–20.

128. "Hamilton Grange," *Real Estate Record and Builders' Guide* 38 (December 4, 1886): 1483–84. Also see "Hamilton Grange, New York City," *Building* 7 (December 3, 1887): 9; "Hamilton's Trees," *New York Times* (July 2, 1889): 4; "In Danger," *Historic Preservation* 8 (fall–winter 1956): 8; "Preservation Notes: A Federal Tragedy in New York," *Antiques* 72 (July 1957): 54; Landmarks Preservation Commission of the City of New York, LP-0317 (August 2, 1967); *Hamilton Grange National Memorial: Report* (Washington, D.C.: U.S. Government Printing Office, 1988); Diamonstein, *The Landmarks of New York II*, 55, 451; Christopher Gray, "A Move to Move a Historic House," *New York Times* (March 21,

1993), X: 7; Jonathan Kuhn, "Hamilton Grange," in Jackson, ed., *The Encyclopedia of New York City*, 519; Dolkart and Sorin, *Touring Historic Harlem*, 93–94.

129. "The Ottendorfer Grounds," unpublished text accompanying photographic collection, Schomburg Center for Research in Black Culture, New York Public Library.

130. "Out Among the Builders," *Real Estate Record and Builders' Guide* 39 (April 9, 1887): 479–80; "One of the Six Houses to Be Built on Tenth Avenue, Near One Hundred and Fortieth Street, New York City," *Building* 7 (July 12, 1887): 5.

131. "Doorway for John Dwight, Esq., Mt. Morris Park, New York, N.Y., Mr. Frank Smith, Architect, Boston, Mass.," *American Architect and Building News* 28 (December 5, 1885): 29, plate; "House of Nathan Hobart, Esq., Northwest Corner of One Hundred and Forty-sixth Street and St. Nicholas Avenue," *Building* 5 (October 9, 1886): 175, plate.

132. "Houses on St. Nicholas Avenue, New York, N.Y. Mr. T. M. Clark, Architect, Boston, Mass.," *American Architect and Building News* 18 (December 5, 1885): 271, plate; Dolkart and Sorin, *Touring Historic Harlem*, 105.

133. "Hamilton Grange, New York City," *Building*: 9; "City Dwellings, Washington Heights [*sic*], New York City," *Scientific American Architects and Builders Edition* 16 (November 1893): 63, 69; *Hamilton Heights Historic District*, 14; Dolkart and Sorin, *Touring Historic Harlem*, 101–2.

134. *Hamilton Heights Historic District*, 16; Dolkart and Sorin, *Touring Historic Harlem*, 101–2.

135. *Hamilton Heights Historic District*, 19–20.

136. *Hamilton Heights Historic District*, 25.

137. "Houses at Hamilton Grange, One Hundred and Forty-fourth Street and Tenth Avenue, New York City," *Building* 7 (December 11, 1887): 205.

138. "Gelatine Print—Five Houses, Northeast Corner Convent Avenue and 144th Street," *Building* 9 (October 12, 1889): 121, plate; *Hamilton Heights Historic District*, 13.

139. "The Hamilton Grange District: New Dwellings and Public Improvements," *Real Estate Record and Builders' Guide* 51 (March 25, 1893): 444; Christopher Gray, "Mending an Unusual 19th Century Limestone Row," *New York Times* (June 26, 1994),VIII: 7; Dolkart and Sorin, *Touring Historic Harlem*, 104–5.

140. "The New St. Luke's," *New York Times* (December 19, 1892): 8; King, *King's Handbook of New York* (1893), 355; Montgomery Schuyler, "The Works of R. H. Robertson," *Architectural Record* 6 (October–December 1896): 184–219; Stokes, *The Iconography of Manhattan Island*, vol. 5: 2011; *Hamilton Heights Historic District*, 7, 18–19; White and Willensky, *AIA Guide* (1988), 433; Dolkart and Sorin, *Touring Historic Harlem*, 92–93.

141. Schuyler, "The Works of R. H. Robertson": 193.

142. "Out Among the Builders," *Real Estate Record and Builders' Guide* 34 (October 18, 1884): 1049; "House for M. Van Rensselaer, Washington Heights, New York," *Building* 3 (December 1884): 29, plate; "A Gable End," *Building* 3 (March 1885): 66, plate.

143. "House of F. W. Seagrist. 153 St. Near St. Nicholas Ave., New York City," *Building* 6 (June 4, 1887): 207, plate.

144. Landmarks Preservation Commission of the City of New York, LP-0845 (February 19, 1974); White and Willensky, *AIA Guide* (1988), 435; Diamonstein, *The Landmarks of New York II*, 195; Dolkart and Sorin, *Touring Historic Harlem*, 110–11; Janet Allon, "Thieves with Eyes for Detail," *New York Times* (November 9, 1997), XIII: 8.

145. *Photographic Views of New York City from the New York Public Library* (Ann Arbor, Mich.: University Microfilm International, 1981), plate 0812-E6.

146. "The Jumel Mansion Sold," *Real Estate Record and Builders' Guide* 39 (April 16, 1889): 514; William Henry Shelton, *The Jumel Mansion* (Boston: Houghton Mifflin, 1916); Landmarks Preservation Commission of the City of New York, LP-0308 (July 12, 1967); Diamonstein, *The Landmarks of New York II*, 96–97; Jonathan Kuhn, "Morris-Jumel Mansion," in Jackson, ed., *The Encyclopedia of New York City*, 773; Dolkart and Sorin, *Touring Historic Harlem*, 117–19.

147. "The Jumel Mansion Sold": 514.

148. Landmarks Preservation Commission of the City of New York, *Jumel Terrace Historic District Designation Report* (New York, 1970); George W. Goodman, "Historic Homes in Harlem Restored," *New York Times* (February 27, 1983), VIII: 6; White and Willensky, *AIA Guide* (1988), 461; Christopher Gray, "Restoration Leaves Lots of Unhappy Homeowners," *New York Times* (April 9, 1989), X: 12, reprinted in Gray, *Changing New York*, 85; Dolkart, *Guide to New York City Landmarks*, 146; Diamonstein, *The Landmarks of New York II*, 445; Dolkart and Sorin, *Touring Historic Harlem*, 119–20.

149. "Another Generous Gift," *Harper's Weekly* 32 (January 14, 1888): 31; King, *King's Handbook of New York* (1893), 408.

CHAPTER 7
Brooklyn

1. Walt Whitman, "Brooklyniana," *Brooklyn Standard* (1862), reprinted in Henry M. Christman, ed., *Walt Whitman's New York: From Manhattan to Montauk* (New York: Macmillan, 1963), 57.

2. *Brooklyn Daily Eagle* (February 16, 1869), quoted in Henry R. Stiles, *A History of the City of Brooklyn*, 3 vols. (Brooklyn, 1869; Bowie, Md.: Heritage Books, 1993), vol 2: 497.

3. Stiles, *A History of the City of Brooklyn*, vol. 2: 9–33; James G. Wilson, *The Memorial History of the City of New York*, 5 vols. (New York: New York History Company, 1892), vol. 4: 18; Landmarks Preservation Commission of the City of New York, LP-0956 (June 28, 1977); Barbaralee Diamonstein, *The Landmarks of New York II* (New York: Harry N. Abrams, 1993), 452; Elizabeth Reich Rawson, "Fulton Ferry [Fulton Landing]," in Kenneth T. Jackson, ed., *The Encyclopedia of New York City* (New Haven, Conn., and London: Yale University Press; New York: New-York Historical Society, 1995), 443–44.

4. Brooklyn Daily Eagle, *The Pictorial History of Brooklyn* (Brooklyn: Brooklyn Daily Eagle, 1916), 36.

5. For the Hamilton Ferry House, see Montgomery Schuyler, "A Great American Architect: Leopold Eidlitz. Part 1," *Architectural Record* 24 (September 1908): 163–79.

6. Landmarks Preservation Commission of the City of New York, *Fulton Ferry Historic District Designation Report* (New York, 1977); White and Willensky, *AIA Guide* (1988), 597–98.

7. Montgomery Schuyler, "A Great American Architect: Leopold Eidlitz. Part 2," *Architectural Record* 24 (October 1908): 277–92; William Lee Younger, *Old Brooklyn in Early Photographs* (New York: Dover, 1978), 56.

8. "Buildings Projected," *Real Estate Record and Builders' Guide* 34 (December 17, 1884): 1318; *Fulton Ferry Historic District*, 18–19; White and Willensky, *AIA Guide* (1988), 598–99.

9. "Buildings Projected," *Real Estate Record and Builders' Guide* 40 (December 10, 1887): 1568; White and Willensky, *AIA Guide* (1988), 599.

10. Brooklyn Daily Eagle, *The Pictorial History of Brooklyn*, 55; Cervin Robinson, "Bravura in Brooklyn," *Architectural Forum* 131 (November 1969): 42–47; *Fulton Ferry Historic District*, 8, 10–11; White and Willensky, *AIA Guide* (1988), 597–98; Christopher Gray, "Streetscapes/Frank Freeman, Architect," *New York Times* (February 26, 1995), IX: 7.

11. Landmarks Preservation Commission of the City of New York, LP-0147 (April 19, 1966); Deborah S. Gardner, "The Architecture of Commercial Capitalism: John Kellum and the Development of New York, 1840–1875" (Ph.D. diss., Columbia University, 1979): 27–30; William J. Conklin and Jeffrey Simpson, *Brooklyn's City Hall* (New York: Department of General Services, 1983); Andrew S. Dolkart, *Borough Hall, 1848–1949* (New York: Fund for the Borough of Brooklyn, 1989); Diamonstein, *The Landmarks of New York II*, 96–97; Andrew S. Dolkart, "Brooklyn Borough Hall," in Jackson, ed., *The Encyclopedia of New York City*, 114.

12. "The New Court-House," *New York Times* (March 1, 1865): 8; Younger, *Old Brooklyn in Early Photographs*, 48–49; Gardner, "The Architecture of Commercial Capitalism": 431; Ellen M. Snyder-Grenier, *Brooklyn!* (Philadelphia: Temple University Press, 1996), 96–97.

13. Sarah Bradford Landau, *Peter B. Wight: Architect, Contractor, and Critic, 1838–1925* (Chicago: Art Institute of Chicago, 1981), 15–16.

14. "Proposed New Public Building," *New York Times* (March 1, 1876): 8; "Brooklyn's New Municipal Building," *New York Times* (June 22, 1876): 8; "Notes and Clippings," *American Architect and Building News* 1 (July 1, 1876): 216; "Brooklyn," *New York Times* (August 15, 1876): 8; "Notes and Clippings," *American Architect and Building News* 1 (November 18, 1876): 376; "A Competitive Design for the Brooklyn Municipal Building. Messrs. Cornwall and Maynicke, Architects," *American Architect and Building News* 1 (December 2, 1876): 388, plate; "Notes and Clippings," *American Architect and Building News* 2 (January 13, 1877): 16; "Notes and Clippings," *American Architect and Building News* 2 (January 27, 1877): 32; "The New Municipal Building to Be Erected in Brooklyn," *New York Daily Graphic* (April 3, 1877): 233; "Bad Sewerage," *New York Times* (December 5, 1878): 2; Moses King, *King's Views of Brooklyn* (Boston: Moses King, 1904), 10.

15. "Uncertain Rumors of Bribery," *New York Times* (November 23, 1884): 7; "Buildings Projected," *Real Estate Record and Builders' Guide* 35 (February 14, 1885): 175; "The Brooklyn Hall of Records," *New York Daily Tribune* (July 1, 1885): 8; "Laying a Cornerstone," *New York Times* (July 1, 1885): 8; "Rather Expensive Building," *New York Times* (April 22, 1887): 2; "Brooklyn Hall of Records," *New York Daily Tribune* (August 2, 1887): 10; King, *King's Views of Brooklyn* (1904), 10.

16. "Brooklyn Hall of Records," (August 2, 1887): 10.

17. "Buildings Projected," *Real Estate Record and Builders' Guide* 23 (April 19, 1879): 322; "Local Miscellany: Brooklyn's New Jail," *New York Daily Tribune* (December 14, 1879): 5; Younger, *Old Brooklyn in Early Photographs*, 38.

18. "A New Post-Office in Brooklyn," editorial, *New York Times* (March 14, 1867): 4; "Brooklyn's Federal Building," *New York Times* (March 8, 1883): 3; "Brooklyn's Federal Building," *New York Times* (March 9, 1883): 3; "Brooklyn Federal Building," *New York Times* (May 2, 1883): 8; Editorial, *New York Times* (May 2, 1883): 4; "The New Government Building in Brooklyn," *New York Daily Graphic* (September 20, 1884): 600; "To Build Brooklyn's Post Office," *New York Times* (April 1, 1885): 5; "The Brooklyn Federal Building," editorial, *New York Daily Tribune* (July 12, 1886): 4; "The Federal Building: The New Post Office Approaching Completion," *New York Daily Tribune* (August 24, 1890): 20; King, *King's Views of Brooklyn* (1904), 14; Brooklyn Daily Eagle, *The Pictorial History of Brooklyn*, 49; Landmarks Preservation Commission of the City of New York, LP-0146 (July 19, 1966); White and Willensky, *AIA Guide* (1988), 567; Diamonstein, *The Landmarks of New York II*, 192.

19. "The 'Boss' Gets a Good Price," *New York Times* (November 27, 1890): 8; "Fighting for a Big Job," *New York Times* (March 20, 1891): 8; "Design for Fire Headquarters," *Architectural Record* 1 (October–December 1891): 179; "Fire Headquarters: The New Building in Jay St.," *New York Daily Tribune* (November 27, 1892): 20; King, *King's Views of Brooklyn* (1904), 11; Landmarks Preservation Commission of the City of New York, LP-0148 (April 19, 1966); Robinson, "Bravura in Brooklyn": 42–45; White and Willensky, *AIA Guide* (1988), 568; Andrew Dolkart, *This Is Brooklyn* (Brooklyn: Fund for the Borough of Brooklyn, 1990), 21; Diamonstein, *The Landmarks of New York II*, 214; Gray, "Streetscapes/Frank Freeman, Architect": 7.

20. "Brooklyn Democrats," *New York Times* (March 25, 1889): 2; "'The Thomas Jefferson,'" *New York Times* (November 12, 1889): 4; "Cleveland in Brooklyn," *New York Times* (November 14, 1889): 1; "The Thomas Jefferson Association Building, Brooklyn, N.Y. Mr. Frank Freeman, Architect, New York, N.Y.," *American Architect and Building News* 26 (November 30, 1889): 255, plate; "Brooklyn's New Democratic Club," *New York Times* (June 12, 1890): 1; King, *King's Views of Brooklyn* (1904), 15; Gray, "Streetscapes/Frank Freeman, Architect": 7.

21. "To Have a New Clubhouse," *New York Times* (January 5, 1889): 8; "The Germania's Home," *New York Times* (October 10, 1890): 2; King, *King's Views of Brooklyn* (1904), 60; Gray, "Streetscapes/Frank Freeman, Architect": 7.

22. Montgomery Schuyler, "Architectural Aberrations No. 3: The Brooklyn Real Estate Exchange," *Architectural Record* 1 (April–June 1892): 401–4.

23. Landmarks Preservation Commission of the City of New York, LP-0836 (November 12, 1974); Landmarks Preservation Commission of the City of New York, LP-0885 (March 25, 1975); David W. McCul-

lough, *Brooklyn . . . and How It Got That Way* (New York: Dial Press, 1983), 132–33; White and Willensky, *AIA Guide* (1988), 569–70; Diamonstein, *The Landmarks of New York II*, 169.

24. "The Ovington Building, Brooklyn," *Building* 2 (October 1883): 6. Also see "Buildings Projected," *Real Estate Record and Builders' Guide* 31 (April 14, 1883): 260; "A Dangerous-Looking Fire," *New York Times* (July 3, 1892): 16.

25. "Buildings Projected," *Real Estate Record and Builders' Guide* 35 (May 23, 1885): 612.

26. "Buildings Projected," *Real Estate Record and Builders' Guide* 41 (April 14, 1888): 480; White and Willensky, *AIA Guide* (1988), 570.

27. "Buildings Projected," *Real Estate Record and Builders' Guide* 33 (February 9, 1884): 150; "A Complete Establishment," *New York Times* (January 10, 1885): 8; Robert Hendrickson, *The Grand Emporiums* (New York: Stein and Day, 1979), 387; White and Willensky, *AIA Guide* (1988), 570.

28. "A Magnificent Store," *New York Times* (May 5, 1891): 8.

29. "Buildings Projected," *Real Estate Record and Builders' Guide* 41 (April 14, 1888): 480; "The Smith, Gray & Co. Building," *Real Estate Record and Builders' Guide* 43 (February 2, 1889): 135; "Big Blaze in Brooklyn," *New York Daily Tribune* (February 29, 1892): 1; "A Big Fire in Brooklyn," *New York Times* (February 29, 1892): 1.

30. Editorial, *New York Times* (April 5, 1879): 4.

31. Schuyler, "Architectural Aberrations No. 3: The Brooklyn Real Estate Exchange": 401–4. Also see Brooklyn Daily Eagle, *The Pictorial History of Brooklyn*, 39; Younger, *Old Brooklyn in Early Photographs*, 26–27.

32. "The New Academy of Music, Brooklyn," *Architects' and Mechanics' Journal* 2 (September 29, 1860): 252; "The New Academy of Music, Brooklyn," *Architects' and Mechanics' Journal* 2 (December 22, 1860): 114–15; "Brooklyn Academy of Music," *New York Times* (January 15, 1861): 2; "Brooklyn Progress," *New York Times* (December 9, 1865): 2; Montgomery Schuyler, "Improvements in New York Architecture," *New York World* (November 26, 1871): 3; Montgomery Schuyler, "The Metropolitan Opera House," *Harper's New Monthly Magazine* 67 (November 1883): 877–89; Gabriel Harrison, *A History of the Progress of the Drama, Music and the Fine Arts in the City of Brooklyn* (Brooklyn, 1884), 8–10; Schuyler, "A Great American Architect: Leopold Eidlitz. Part 2": 283, 287–88; Brooklyn Daily Eagle, *The Pictorial History of Brooklyn*, 27; Bruce C. MacIntyre, "Brooklyn Academy of Music," in Jackson, ed., *The Encyclopedia of New York City*, 153.

33. "Brooklyn Progress": 2.

34. Whitman, "Brooklyniana," *Brooklyn Standard* (1862), reprinted in Christman, ed., *Walt Whitman's New York*, 61.

35. Schuyler, "Improvements in New York Architecture": 3.

36. Schuyler, "The Metropolitan Opera House": 880.

37. Schuyler, "A Great American Architect: Leopold Eidlitz. Part 2": 287–88.

38. "Brooklyn Academy of Music," (January 15, 1861): 2.

39. "Brooklyn Mercantile Library Association—Annual Meeting," *New York Times* (March 26, 1869): 8; "Brooklyn Mercantile Library," *New York Times* (November 19, 1869): 8; Paul R. Baker, *Richard Morris Hunt* (Cambridge, Mass.: MIT Press, 1980), 539; Landau, *Peter B. Wight: Architect, Contractor, and Critic, 1838–1925*, 23–26, 88, 90–96, 101–2; Sarah Bradford Landau, "Richard Morris Hunt: Architectural Innovator and Father of a 'Distinctive' American School," in Susan Stein, ed., *The Architecture of Richard Morris Hunt* (Chicago: University of Chicago Press, 1986), 50–51.

40. "Brooklyn Art Association," *New York Times* (November 12, 1869): 2; Schuyler, "Improvements in New York Architecture": 3; "Reception by the Brooklyn Art Association," *New York Times* (December 10, 1872): 2; "Brooklyn Academy of Design," *American Architect and Building News* 1 (January 29, 1876): 40; Harrison, *A History of the Progress of the Drama, Music and the Fine Arts in the City of Brooklyn*, 32, 36–38; Montgomery Schuyler, "The Works of Cady, Berg & See," *Architectural Record* 6 (April–June 1897): 517–53; Younger, *Old Brooklyn in Early Photographs*, 40; Kathleen A. Curran, *A Forgotten Architect of the Gilded Age: Josiah Cleaveland Cady's Legacy* (Hartford, Conn.: Trinity College, 1993), 6–10, fig. 1.

41. See Henry-Russell Hitchcock, *Architecture: Nineteenth and Twentieth Centuries* (Baltimore: Penguin Books, 1958), 26, plate 10.

42. Schuyler, "The Works of Cady, Berg & See": 519–20.

43. Schuyler, "Improvements in New York Architecture": 3.

44. "Long Island Historical Society," *New York Times* (January 2, 1870): 6; "Long Island Historical Society," *New York Times* (November 14, 1877): 2; "A New Library Building," *New York Times* (November 18, 1877): 7; W., "Correspondence," *American Architect and Building News* 2 (December 8, 1877): 395; W. Ames Archibald, "Correspondence," *American Architect and Building News* 2 (December 15, 1877): 402; "Correspondence," *American Architect and Building News* 3 (January 26, 1878): 32–33; W., "Correspondence," *American Architect and Building News* 3 (April 20, 1878): 138; "Long Island Historical Society Building," *New York Times* (October 25, 1878): 2; "Design for the Long Island Historical Society's Building, Brooklyn, N.Y. Mr. J. P. Putnam, Architect, Boston," *American Architect and Building News* 5 (February 1, 1879): 37, plates; "Design for the Long Island Historical Society's Building, Brooklyn, N.Y. Parfitt Bros., Architects, Brooklyn," *American Architect and Buildings News* 5 (May 10, 1879): 148, plate; "Competitive Design for the Long Island Historical Society's Building, Brooklyn, N.Y. Mr. H. H. Holly, Architect, New York," *American Architect and Building News* 6 (November 29, 1879): 173, plates; "The New Building for the Long Island Historical Society," *Real Estate Record and Builders' Guide* 24 (October 25, 1879): 848; "Historia Testis Temporum," *New York Daily Graphic* (April 2, 1880): 289, 291; "The Archives of Long Island," *New York Daily Tribune* (May 2, 1880): 7; "A Building to Hold Books," *New York Times* (September 12, 1880): 10; "A Historical Society Building," *New York Times* (January 13, 1881): 5; "The Archives of Long Island," *New York Daily Tribune* (January 14, 1881): 8; Montgomery Schuyler, "Recent Building in New York—I," *American Architect and Building News* 9 (April 9, 1881): 176–77; Russell Sturgis, "The Works of George B. Post," *Architectural Record* 4 (June 1898): 1–102; Winston Weisman, "The Commercial Architecture of George B. Post," *Journal of the Society of Architectural Historians* 31 (December 1972): 176–203; Younger, *Old Brooklyn in Early Photographs*, 58–59; Sarah Bradford Landau, "The Tall Office Building Artistically Reconsidered: Arcaded Buildings of the New York School, 1870–1890," in Helen Searing, ed., *In Search of Modern Architecture: A Tribute to Henry-Russell Hitchcock* (New York: Architectural History Foundation; Cambridge, Mass.: MIT Press, 1982), 147–48; Landmarks Preservation Commission of the City of New York, LP-1131 (March 23, 1982); White and Willensky, *AIA Guide* (1988), 589; Diamonstein, *The Landmarks of New York II*, 174; Jan Hird Pokorny, *The Brooklyn Historical Society: Historic Structure Report* (New York, 1993); Ellen Marie Snyder-Grenier, "Brooklyn Historical Society," in Jackson, ed., *The Encyclopedia of New York City*, 157–58; Snyder-Grenier, *Brooklyn!*, 9, 36; Sarah Bradford Landau, *George B. Post, Architect: Picturesque Designer and Determined Realist*, Sources of American Architecture, ed. Robert A. M. Stern (New York: Monacelli Press, 1998), 36, 38, plates 10–13.

45. Schuyler, "Recent Building in New York—I": 176–77.

46. Sturgis, "The Works of George B. Post": 44.

47. Schuyler, "Architectural Aberrations No. 3: The Brooklyn Real Estate Exchange": 403. Also see "Buildings Projected," *Real Estate Record and Builders' Guide* 46 (August 2, 1890): 169; King, *King's Views of Brooklyn* (1904), 13.

48. "Buildings Projected," *Real Estate Record and Builders' Guide* 35 (March 21, 1885): 316; "Apartment House, Montague Street, Brooklyn, N.Y., for Mr. William Ziegler," *Building* 4 (January 9, 1886): 18, plate; King, *King's Views of Brooklyn* (1904), 48.

49. "Buildings Projected," *Real Estate Record and Builders' Guide* 35 (March 21, 1885): 316; White and Willensky, *AIA Guide* (1988), 583.

50. "Out Among the Builders: Brooklyn," *Real Estate Record and Builders' Guide* 40 (July 2, 1887): 896–97; "Buildings Projected," *Real Estate Record and Builders' Guide* 40 (July 16, 1887): 974; Andrew Dolkart, "Visible City: Many of Brooklyn's Lavish Romanesque Revival Brownstones Were Built by the Now-Forgotten Architect Montrose W. Morris," *Metropolis* 4 (September 1984): 26–27, 34.

51. "Out Among the Builders: Brooklyn," *Real Estate Record and Builders' Guide* 43 (April 6, 1889): 466; Brooklyn Daily Eagle, *The Pictorial History of Brooklyn*, 93; Robinson, "Bravura in Brooklyn": 42–43; White and Willensky, *AIA Guide* (1988), 884–85; Gray, "Streetscapes/Frank Freeman, Architect": 7.

52. "Buildings Projected," *Real Estate Record and Builders' Guide* 35 (May 16, 1885): 581; "Out Among the Builders: Brooklyn," *Real Estate Record and Builders' Guide* 43 (March 9, 1889): 315–17; White and Willensky, *AIA Guide* (1988), 590.

53. "Out Among the Builders: Brooklyn," *Real Estate Record and Builders' Guide* 42 (July 7, 1888): 862; "Buildings Projected," *Real Estate Record and Builders' Guide* 42 (August 4, 1888): 990; "Apartment House on Clark St., Near Fulton St., Brooklyn, N.Y.," *American Architect and Building News* 28 (May 31, 1890): 138, plate.

54. Elizabeth Bisland, "Co-operative Housekeeping in Tenements," *The Cosmopolitan* 8 (November 1889): 35–42; Jacob A. Riis, *How the Other Half Lives* (New York: Charles Scribner's Sons, 1890; New York: Dover, 1971), 227–29; Alfred T. White, *The Riverside Buildings of the Improved Model Dwelling Company* (New York: Improved Model Dwelling Co., 1890); Marcus T. Reynolds, *The Housing of the Poor in American Cities* (Baltimore: American Economic Association, 1893), 89–92, figs. 23–25; "The Housing of the Poor—I," *American Architect and Building News* 52 (April 18, 1896): 23–26; James Ford, *Slums and Housing, with Special References to New York City: History, Conditions, Policy*, 2 vols. (Cambridge, Mass.: Harvard University Press, 1936), vol. 1: 197–98, 202, vol. 2: figs. 114c, 115b, appendix plate 6c; Robert A. M. Stern, "With Rhetoric: The New York Apartment House," *Via* 4 (1980): 78–111; White and Willensky, *AIA Guide* (1988), 578; Elizabeth Collins Cromley, *Alone Together: A History of New York's Early Apartments* (Ithaca, N.Y., and London: Cornell University Press, 1990), 55, 57–58; Richard Plunz, *A History of Housing in New York City* (New York: Columbia University Press, 1990), 108–10; Christopher Gray, "Streetscapes: The Riverside Buildings," *New York Times* (August 23, 1992), X: 7; Snyder-Grenier, *Brooklyn!*, 156–57.

55. Riis, *How the Other Half Lives*, 228.

56. "Out Among the Builders: Brooklyn," *Real Estate Record and Builders' Guide* 31 (May 12, 1883): 195; "Buildings Projected," *Real Estate Record and Builders' Guide* 31 (May 26, 1883): 386; Clay Lancaster, *Old Brooklyn Heights* (Rutland, Vt., and Tokyo: Charles E. Tuttle Co., 1961), 59, fig. 57.

57. "Buildings Projected," *Real Estate Record and Builders' Guide* 39 (June 11, 1887): 823; Lancaster, *Old Brooklyn Heights*, 89; White and Willensky, *AIA Guide* (1988), 577.

58. Francis R. Kowsky, *The Architecture of Frederick Clarke Withers and the Progress of the Gothic Revival in America After 1850* (Middletown, Conn.: Wesleyan University Press, 1980), 69–71, 193.

59. "Buildings Projected," *Real Estate Record and Builders' Guide* 46 (July 26, 1890): 134; White and Willensky, *AIA Guide* (1988), 580.

60. Lancaster, *Old Brooklyn Heights*, 50, 128–29; White and Willensky, *AIA Guide* (1988), 584.

61. "Buildings Projected," *Real Estate Record and Builders' Guide* 41 (June 30, 1888): 852; "Mr. Behr's House, Brooklyn, N.Y. Mr. Frank Freeman, Architect, New York," *Architecture and Building* 14 (May 2, 1891): 215, plate; Lancaster, *Old Brooklyn Heights*, 50, 128–29, fig. 19; Robinson, "Bravura in Brooklyn": 42; White and Willensky, *AIA Guide* (1988), 587.

62. Everard M. Upjohn, *Richard Upjohn: Architect and Churchman* (New York: Columbia University Press, 1939), 72–77, 199.

63. Jacob Landy, *The Architecture of Minard Lafever* (New York and London: Columbia University Press, 1970), 87–131.

64. Francis W. Kervick, *Patrick Charles Keely, Architect: A Record of His Life and Work* (South Bend, Ind., 1953), 35; Lancaster, *Old Brooklyn Heights*, 108, fig. 71; White and Willensky, *AIA Guide* (1988), 580.

65. "St. Ann's Church, Brooklyn," *Architects' and Mechanics' Journal* 2 (October 27, 1860): 39; Kervick, *Patrick Charles Keely, Architect*, 34.

66. "Our Architectural Progress," *New York Times* (April 5, 1868): 3; "New Churches in Brooklyn," *New York Times* (August 9, 1869): 8; "St. Ann's Church," *New York Times* (October 21, 1869): 2; King, *King's Views of Brooklyn* (1904), 62; Lancaster, *Old Brooklyn Heights*, 58, fig. 73.

67. "Notes and Clippings: An Unusual Church Plan," *American Architect and Building News* 2 (June 2, 1877): 176; "A New Baptist Church," *New York Daily Tribune* (June 16, 1877): 5; "Tearing Down a Brooklyn

Church," *New York Times* (July 10, 1877): 8; "Buildings Projected," *Real Estate Record and Builders' Guide* 20 (July 21, 1877): 588.

68. "Out Among the Builders: Brooklyn," *Real Estate Record and Builders' Guide* 42 (July 21, 1888): 921; "Buildings Projected," *Real Estate Record and Builders' Guide* 42 (October 20, 1888): 1269; White and Willensky, *AIA Guide* (1988), 569.

69. "Buildings Projected," *Real Estate Record and Builders' Guide* 44 (September 28, 1889): 1316; "Laying a Church Cornerstone," *New York Times* (November 2, 1889): 9; "The New Sands Street Church," *New York Times* (June 30, 1890): 8; King, *King's Views of Brooklyn* (1904), 64; Landmarks Preservation Commission of the City of New York, LP-2014 (May 12, 1981).

70. Landmarks Preservation Commission of the City of New York, LP-0320 (December 30, 1969); Landmarks Preservation Commission of the City of New York, LP-1554 (June 7, 1988); Diamonstein, *The Landmarks of New York II*, 445, 463.

71. King, *King's Views of Brooklyn* (1904), 20; Landmarks Preservation Commission of the City of New York, LP-0320 (December 30, 1969), 16–17; White and Willensky, *AIA Guide* (1988), 627.

72. "Buildings Projected," *Real Estate Record and Builders' Guide* 23 (May 17, 1879): 413; Landmarks Preservation Commission of the City of New York, LP-0320 (December 30, 1969), 17, 62.

73. "Brooklyn Model Tenements," editorial, *New York Times* (March 18, 1877): 6; "Model Tenements as an Investment," editorial, *New York Times* (April 30, 1877): 4; "Improved Dwellings for the Poor," editorial, *New York Times* (July 16, 1877): 4; "Houses for the Poor," editorial, *New York Times* (November 5, 1877): 4; W., "Correspondence," *American Architect and Building News* 2 (December 8, 1877): 395; "Buildings Projected," *Real Estate Record and Builders' Guide* 20 (December 8, 1877): 960; Editorial, *American Architect and Building News* 3 (January 19, 1878): 17; "Buildings Projected," *Real Estate Record and Builders' Guide* 22 (October 12, 1878): 844; "General Notes," *New York Daily Tribune* (December 5, 1878): 4; Alfred Tredway White, *Improved Dwellings for the Laboring Classes*, rev. ed. (New York: Putnam, 1879); "Tenement-House Reform," editorial, *New York Times* (February 10, 1879): 4; "Prize Tenements," editorial, *New York Times* (March 16, 1879): 6; "Houses for the Poor," editorial, *New York Times* (March 25, 1879): 4; "A Model Tenement House," *New York Daily Tribune* (August 11, 1879): 8; "Reformed Dwellings for the Poor," editorial, *New York Times* (August 20, 1879): 4; "The Improvement of Tenements," editorial, *New York Times* (December 16, 1879): 6; "A Good Work Well Done," editorial, *New York Times* (June 6, 1880): 6; R. R. Bowker, "Working-Men's Homes," *Harper's New Monthly Magazine* 68 (April 1884): 769–84; Alfred Tredway White, *Better Homes for Workingmen* (New York: Putnam, 1885); Bisland, "Co-operative Housekeeping in Tenements": 35–42; Reynolds, *The Housing of the Poor in American Cities*, 85–89, 102–3; Lawrence Veiller, "Tenement Housing Reform in New York City, 1834–1900," in Robert W. De Forest and Lawrence Veiller, eds., *The Tenement House Problem*, 2 vols. (New York: Macmillan, 1903), vol. 1: 71–118; Ford, *Slums and Housing*, vol. 1: 160–61, 175, 202, vol. 2: figs. 114b, 115a, appendix plates 3a–b; Landmarks Preservation Commission of the City of New York, LP-0320 (December 30, 1969), 23, 53–54, 67; Anthony Jackson, *A Place Called Home* (Cambridge, Mass., and London: MIT Press, 1976), 40–41; Stern, "With Rhetoric": 84; McCullough, *Brooklyn . . . and How It Got That Way*, 42–43; White and Willensky, *AIA Guide* (1988), 603–4; Cromley, *Alone Together*, 55–56; Plunz, *A History of Housing in New York City*, 89–92.

74. Walt Whitman, *Brooklyn Times* (May 1, 1857), quoted in Landmarks Preservation Commission of the City of New York, LP-0320 (December 30, 1969), 53.

75. White, *Improved Dwellings for the Laboring Classes*, 8–9, quoted in Plunz, *A History of Housing in New York City*, 92.

76. W., "Correspondence," (December 8, 1877): 395.

77. "Brooklyn Model Tenements": 6.

78. "Houses for the Poor," (November 5, 1877): 4.

79. Bisland, "Co-operative Housekeeping in Tenements": 37.

80. "A Chapel for a Brooklyn Church," *New York Times* (April 19, 1878): 8; "Buildings Projected," *Real Estate Record and Builders' Guide* 21 (June 28, 1878): 569; "The Chapel of the Pilgrims," *New York Times* (July

11, 1878): 2; "The Pilgrim Chapel, Brooklyn, N.Y. Mr. J. Cleveland Cady, Architect, New York," *American Architect and Building News* 4 (November 2, 1878): 147, plate; "Local Miscellany: A Handsome New Church Building," *New York Daily Tribune* (December 16, 1878): 2; "A New Church in Brooklyn," *New York Times* (December 16, 1878): 2.

81. "A New Church in Brooklyn": 2.

82. "Green Wood Cemetery," *New York Times* (June 7, 1868): 8; Stiles, *A History of the City of Brooklyn*, vol. 3: 622–30; King, *King's Views of Brooklyn* (1904), 69; Upjohn, *Richard Upjohn: Architect and Churchman*, 199; Younger, *Old Brooklyn in Early Photographs*, 152–53; McCullough, *Brooklyn . . . and How It Got That Way*, 109–15; Robert A. M. Stern, *Pride of Place: Building the American Dream* (Boston: Houghton Mifflin; New York: American Heritage, 1986), 127–28; Judith Salisbury Hull, "Richard Upjohn: Professional Practice and Domestic Architecture" (Ph.D. diss., Columbia University, 1987): 332–36; Christopher Gray, "Streetscapes/The Green-Wood Cemetery Gatehouse," *New York Times* (December 31, 1995), IX: 5; Snyder-Grenier, *Brooklyn!*, 203–4.

83. Quoted in Younger, *Old Brooklyn in Early Photographs*, 152.

84. "Green Wood Cemetery," *New York Times*: 8.

85. "Lodges at the East Entrance to Greenwood Cemetery. Mr. R. M. Upjohn, Architect, New York," *American Architect and Building News* 4 (August 3, 1878): 40, plate; King, *King's Views of Brooklyn* (1904), 69; Upjohn, *Richard Upjohn: Architect and Churchman*, 199; Hull, "Richard Upjohn: Professional Practice and Domestic Architecture": 336.

86. "Plans for the Improvement of Fort Greene," *New York Times* (September 26, 1867): 8; King, *King's Views of Brooklyn* (1904), 24; Albert Fein, *Frederick Law Olmsted and the American Environmental Tradition* (New York: George Braziller, 1972), 31, figs. 48, 103; Landmarks Preservation Commission of the City of New York, LP-0973 (September 26, 1978), 6–13; McCullough, *Brooklyn . . . and How It Got That Way*, 106–9; David Schuyler and Jane Turner Censer, eds., *The Papers of Frederick Law Olmsted, vol. 6: The Years of Olmsted, Vaux & Company, 1865–1874* (Baltimore and London: Johns Hopkins University Press, 1992), 24, 202–7, 336–37 (n. 8), 670; William Alex, *Calvert Vaux: Architect & Planner* (New York: Ink, 1994), 24, 144–45; Judith Berck, "Fort Greene," in Jackson, ed., *The Encyclopedia of New York City*, 428–49; Francis R. Kowsky, *Country, Park and City: The Architecture and Life of Calvert Vaux* (New York: Oxford University Press, 1998), 195–96. For a general discussion of the Fort Greene area, see Barbara Habenstreit, *Fort Greene, U.S.A.* (Indianapolis, Ind.: Bobbs-Merrill, 1974).

87. "Buildings Projected," *Real Estate Record and Builders' Guide* 23 (March 29, 1879): 259; Landmarks Preservation Commission of the City of New York, LP-0973 (September 26, 1978), 53.

88. "Buildings Projected," *Real Estate Record and Builders' Guide* 28 (July 30, 1881): 797; Landmarks Preservation Commission of the City of New York, LP-0973 (September 26, 1978), 99.

89. Landmarks Preservation Commission of the City of New York, LP-0973 (September 26, 1978), 106.

90. "Buildings Projected," *Real Estate Record and Builders' Guide* 27 (February 26, 1881): 189; Landmarks Preservation Commission of the City of New York, LP-0973 (September 26, 1978), 135.

91. "Buildings Projected," *Real Estate Record and Builders' Guide* 18 (October 21, 1876): 794; Landmarks Preservation Commission of the City of New York, LP-0973 (September 26, 1978), 81.

92. "Buildings Projected," *Real Estate Record and Builders' Guide* 27 (May 21, 1881): 537; Landmarks Preservation Commission of the City of New York, LP-0973 (September 26, 1978), 100–1.

93. "Buildings Projected," *Real Estate Record and Builders' Guide* 36 (November 7, 1885): 1242; Landmarks Preservation Commission of the City of New York, LP-0973 (September 26, 1978), 103–4.

94. "Buildings Projected," *Real Estate Record and Builders' Guide* 45 (April 5, 1890): 503; Landmarks Preservation Commission of the City of New York, LP-0973 (September 26, 1978), 101–2, plate.

95. "Buildings Projected," *Real Estate Record and Builders' Guide* 46 (November 15, 1890): 674; Albert Fein, Lois Gilman, and Donald Simon, *The Neighborhood of Fort Greene in the City of New York: A Historic Perspective* (Long Island: Long Island University, 1973), 19; Landmarks Preservation Commission of the City of New York, LP-0973 (September 26, 1978), 114; Dolkart, "Visible City: Many of Brooklyn's Lavish

96. King, *King's Views of Brooklyn* (1904), 63; Landmarks Preservation Commission of the City of New York, LP-0973 (September 26, 1978), 89–91, plate; White and Willensky, *AIA Guide* (1988), 625.

97. "Church of the Messiah, Brooklyn, N.Y., Mr. R. H. Robertson, Architect, New York, N.Y.," *American Architect and Building News* 24 (November 17, 1888): 230, plate; "Buildings Projected," *Real Estate Record and Builders' Guide* 45 (May 17, 1890): 761; "New Church of the Messiah," *New York Times* (October 1, 1893): 12; "Church of the Messiah Chancel Dedicated," *New York Times* (October 9, 1893): 9; Montgomery Schuyler, "The Work of R. H. Robertson," *Architectural Record* 6 (October–December 1896): 184–219; Landmarks Preservation Commission of the City of New York, LP-0973 (September 26, 1978), 86; White and Willensky, *AIA Guide* (1988), 885.

98. Schuyler, "The Work of R. H. Robertson": 193.

99. "Buildings Projected," *Real Estate Record and Builders' Guide* 35 (May 9, 1885): 552; Landmarks Preservation Commission of the City of New York, LP-0973 (September 26, 1978), 22.

100. "Long Island," *The Churchman* 58 (July 14, 1888): 39.

101. "Long Island," *The Churchman*: 39; "Buildings Projected," *Real Estate Record and Builders' Guide* 42 (August 4, 1888): 990; "That Troublesome Rooster," *New York Times* (March 4, 1889): 8; "New Church Opened in Brooklyn," *New York Times* (April 22, 1889): 8; Landmarks Preservation Commission of the City of New York, LP-0973 (September 26, 1978), 22.

102. "That Troublesome Rooster": 8.

103. "A New Cathedral," *New York Times* (June 22, 1868): 8; Patrick Mulrenan, *A Brief Sketch of the Catholic Church on Long Island* (New York: P. O'Shea, 1871), 32–40; "Notes and Comments," *American Architect and Building News* 2 (March 10, 1877): 80; Kervick, *Patrick Charles Keely, Architect*, 16–17, 67; Fein, Gilman, and Simon, *The Neighborhood of Fort Greene in the City of New York*, 12; Landmarks Preservation Commission of the City of New York, LP-0973 (September 26, 1978), 57.

104. *Brooklyn Daily Eagle* (June 22, 1868): 2, quoted in Landmarks Preservation Commission of the City of New York, LP-0973 (September 26, 1978), 57.

105. Mulrenan, *A Brief Sketch of the Catholic Church on Long Island*, 35.

106. "Buildings Projected," *Real Estate Record and Builders' Guide* 31 (June 16, 1883): 438; "Bishop Loughlin's House," *New York Times* (October 26, 1887): 8; Landmarks Preservation Commission of the City of New York, LP-0973 (September 26, 1978), 57.

107. Winefride de l'Hôpital, *Westminster Cathedral and Its Architect*, 2 vols. (New York: Dodd, Mead & Co., 1919), vol. 2: 440, 673–74.

108. Andrew S. Dolkart, "Historical Introduction," in Landmarks Preservation Commission of the City of New York, LP-2017 (November 10, 1981), 1–7; Elizabeth Reich Rawson, "Clinton Hill," in Jackson, ed., *The Encyclopedia of New York City*, 245.

109. For Euclid, Delaware, and South Prairie Avenues, see Jan Cigliano and Sarah Bradford Landau, eds., *The Grand American Avenue 1850–1920* (San Francisco: Pomegranate Artbooks, 1994), 34–63, 92–151.

110. "Buildings Projected," *Real Estate Record and Builders' Guide* 14 (August 29, 1874): 147; King, *King's Views of Brooklyn* (1904), 42; Landmarks Preservation Commission of the City of New York, LP-2017 (November 10, 1981), 48–49; White and Willensky, *AIA Guide* (1988), 632.

111. "Buildings Projected," *Real Estate Record and Builders' Guide* 15 (March 20, 1875): 204; Landmarks Preservation Commission of the City of New York, LP-2017 (November 10, 1981), 56–57; White and Willensky, *AIA Guide* (1988), 631.

112. "Buildings Projected," *Real Estate Record and Builders' Guide* 30 (August 26, 1882): 797; Landmarks Preservation Commission of the City of New York, LP-2017 (November 10, 1981), 76–77; White and Willensky, *AIA Guide* (1988), 630. Parfitt Brothers also designed a similarly styled carriage house and coachman's residence for Hoagland in 1882, at 409–411 Vanderbilt Avenue. See Landmarks Preservation Commission of the City of New York, LP-2017 (November 10, 1981), 152.

113. "Buildings Projected," *Real Estate Record and Builders' Guide* 29 (May 6, 1882): 471; Landmarks Preservation Commission of the City of New York, LP-2017 (November 10, 1981), 54.

114. Landmarks Preservation Commission of the City of New York, LP-2017 (November 10, 1981), 62–63.

115. "Out Among the Builders: Brooklyn," *Real Estate Record and Builders' Guide* 40 (November 12, 1887): 1417; "Buildings Projected," *Real Estate Record and Builders' Guide* 40 (December 17, 1887): 1602; "Buildings Projected," *Real Estate Record and Builders' Guide* 41 (June 16, 1888): 790; Landmarks Preservation Commission of the City of New York, LP-2017 (November 10, 1981), 55–56, 189; White and Willensky, *AIA Guide* (1988), 631.

116. "Out Among the Builders: Brooklyn," *Real Estate Record and Builders' Guide* 43 (March 9, 1889): 315–17; "Buildings Projected," *Real Estate Record and Builders' Guide* 43 (May 25, 1889): 753; King, *King's Views of Brooklyn* (1904), 45; Landmarks Preservation Commission of the City of New York, LP-2017 (November 10, 1981), 69–70; White and Willensky, *AIA Guide* (1988), 630, 632.

117. "Buildings Projected," *Real Estate Record and Builders' Guide* 46 (November 8, 1890): 688; King, *King's Views of Brooklyn* (1904), 42; Landmarks Preservation Commission of the City of New York, LP-2017 (November 10, 1981), 44–45; White and Willensky, *AIA Guide* (1988), 632–33.

118. Landmarks Preservation Commission of the City of New York, LP-2017 (November 10, 1981), 43–46.

119. "Buildings Projected," *Real Estate Record and Builders' Guide* 22 (October 5, 1878): 825; Landmarks Preservation Commission of the City of New York, LP-2017 (November 10, 1981), 79.

120. "Buildings Projected," *Real Estate Record and Builders' Guide* 48 (September 26, 1891): 388; Landmarks Preservation Commission of the City of New York, LP-2017 (November 10, 1981), 42–43.

121. Landmarks Preservation Commission of the City of New York, LP-2017 (November 10, 1981), 80; White and Willensky, *AIA Guide* (1988), 630.

122. "Buildings Projected," *Real Estate Record and Builders' Guide* 24 (September 20, 1879): 753; Landmarks Preservation Commission of the City of New York, LP-2017 (November 10, 1981), 157–58.

123. "Buildings Projected," *Real Estate Record and Builders' Guide* 22 (December 7, 1878): 997; Landmarks Preservation Commission of the City of New York, LP-2017 (November 10, 1981), 169.

124. "Buildings Projected," *Real Estate Record and Builders' Guide* 23 (June 28, 1879): 537; Landmarks Preservation Commission of the City of New York, LP-2017 (November 10, 1981), 175.

125. "Buildings Projected," *Real Estate Record and Builders' Guide* 35 (May 23, 1885): 612; Landmarks Preservation Commission of the City of New York, LP-2017 (November 10, 1981), 168–69.

126. "Buildings Projected," *Real Estate Record and Builders' Guide* 25 (January 24, 1880): 95; Landmarks Preservation Commission of the City of New York, LP-2017 (November 10, 1981), 161–62.

127. "Buildings Projected," *Real Estate Record and Builders' Guide* 40 (November 26, 1887): 1496; Landmarks Preservation Commission of the City of New York, LP-2017 (November 10, 1981), 164.

128. "Buildings Projected," *Real Estate Record and Builders' Guide* 40 (October 8, 1887): 1276; Landmarks Preservation Commission of the City of New York, LP-2017 (November 10, 1981), 175–76.

129. "Buildings Projected," *Real Estate Record and Builders' Guide* 35 (June 27, 1885): 750; Landmarks Preservation Commission of the City of New York, LP-2017 (November 10, 1981), 176–77; White and Willensky, *AIA Guide* (1988), 637.

130. "Buildings Projected," *Real Estate Record and Builders' Guide* 49 (May 28, 1892): 872; Landmarks Preservation Commission of the City of New York, LP-2017 (November 10, 1981), 156.

131. "Buildings Projected," *Real Estate Record and Builders' Guide* 43 (May 18, 1889): 716; Landmarks Preservation Commission of the City of New York, LP-2017 (November 10, 1981), 178.

132. "Buildings Projected," *Real Estate Record and Builders' Guide* 46 (July 19, 1890): 101; Landmarks Preservation Commission of the City of New York, LP-2017 (November 10, 1981), 182.

133. Landmarks Preservation Commission of the City of New York, LP-2017 (November 10, 1981), 145.

134. "Buildings Projected," *Real Estate Record and Builders' Guide* 24 (August 9, 1879): 650; Landmarks Preservation Commission of the City of New York, LP-2017 (November 10, 1981), 146.

135. "Buildings Projected," *Real Estate Record and Builders' Guide* 42 (October 13, 1888): 1241; Landmarks Preservation Commission of the City of New York, LP-2017 (November 10, 1981), 144.

136. "Buildings Projected," *Real Estate Record and Builders' Guide* 43 (May 25, 1889): 752; Landmarks Preservation Commission of the City of New York, LP-2017 (November 10, 1981), 147.

137. "Buildings Projected," *Real Estate Record and Builders' Guide* 45 (May 31, 1890): 830; Landmarks Preservation Commission of the City of New York, LP-2017 (November 10, 1981), 147–48.

138. "Buildings Projected," *Real Estate Record and Builders' Guide* 49 (May 21, 1892): 835; Landmarks Preservation Commission of the City of New York, LP-2017 (November 10, 1981), 144–45.

139. "Out Among the Builders: Brooklyn," *Real Estate Record and Builders' Guide* 44 (October 19, 1889): 1409; "Buildings Projected," *Real Estate Record and Builders' Guide* 44 (November 30, 1889): 1620; Landmarks Preservation Commission of the City of New York, LP-2017 (November 10, 1981), 82–83; Dolkart, "Visible City: Many of Brooklyn's Lavish Romanesque Revival Brownstones Were Built by the Now-Forgotten Architect Montrose W. Morris": 26–27, 34; White and Willensky, *AIA Guide* (1988), 631.

140. "Buildings Projected," *Real Estate Record and Builders' Guide* 45 (March 22, 1890): 427; Landmarks Preservation Commission of the City of New York, LP-2017 (November 10, 1981), 82, 84; Dolkart, "Visible City: Many of Brooklyn's Lavish Romanesque Revival Brownstones Were Built by the Now-Forgotten Architect Montrose W. Morris": 26–27, 34; White and Willensky, *AIA Guide* (1988), 631.

141. Jeffrey Karl Ochsner, *H. H. Richardson: Complete Architectural Works* (Cambridge, Mass., and London: MIT Press, 1982), 344–49.

142. "Buildings Projected," *Real Estate Record and Builders' Guide* 45 (January 25, 1890): 139; Landmarks Preservation Commission of the City of New York, LP-2017 (November 10, 1981), 88–89. Also see "George Pool Chappell," *New York Times* (June 21, 1933): 17.

143. "New Adelphi Academy," *New York Times* (July 24, 1867): 8; Landmarks Preservation Commission of the City of New York, LP-2017 (November 10, 1981), 127; White and Willensky, *AIA Guide* (1988), 636.

144. "Mr. Pratt's Gift to the Adelphi Academy," *New York Daily Tribune* (March 3, 1886): 8; "The Adelphi's New Building," *New York Daily Tribune* (February 23, 1889): 7; "Mr. Pratt's Generous Gift," *New York Times* (February 23, 1889): 8; King, *King's Views of Brooklyn* (1904), 27; Landmarks Preservation Commission of the City of New York, LP-2017 (November 10, 1981), 127–28; White and Willensky, *AIA Guide* (1988), 636.

145. "Affairs in Brooklyn: Workings of the Pratt Institute," *New York Daily Tribune* (December 22, 1888): 3.

146. "Mr. Pratt Speaks," *New York Times* (October 3, 1889): 3.

147. "The Pratt Institute, Brooklyn, N.Y. Messrs. Lamb & Rich, Architects, New York, N.Y.," *American Architect and Building News* 22 (September 3, 1887): 112, plate; "The Pratt Industrial Institute," *New York Daily Graphic* (January 30, 1888): 650; "Charles Pratt's Gift," *New York Daily Tribune* (June 1, 1888): 6; "Affairs in Brooklyn: Workings of the Pratt Institute": 3; "Gaining Useful Knowledge," *New York Times* (December 22, 1888): 2; King, *King's Views of Brooklyn* (1904), 27; Landmarks Preservation Commission of the City of New York, LP-2010 (December 22, 1981); White and Willensky, *AIA Guide* (1988), 634–35; Diamonstein, *The Landmarks of New York II*, 190.

148. "Buildings Projected," *Real Estate Record and Builders' Guide* 48 (July 3, 1891): 25; King, *King's Views of Brooklyn* (1904), 27; Landmarks Preservation Commission of the City of New York, LP-2010 (December 22, 1981); Diamonstein, *The Landmarks of New York II*, 190.

149. "In Its New Home," *New York Times* (January 1, 1890): 2; "Home of the Lincoln Club," *New York Times* (February 11, 1890): 9; "The New Lincoln Club House, of Brooklyn," *Harper's Weekly* 34 (February 15, 1890): 131–32; King, *King's Views of Brooklyn* (1904), 60; Landmarks Preservation Commission of the City of New York, LP-2105 (May 12, 1981); White and Willensky, *AIA Guide* (1988), 657, 660; Diamonstein, *The Landmarks of New York II*, 200.

150. Landmarks Preservation Commission of the City of New York, LP-2014 (October 27, 1981); Diamonstein, *The Landmarks of New York II*, 125.

151. "Added to Brooklyn Churches," *New York Times* (April 18, 1887): 8; "Emmanuel Baptist Church, Brooklyn, N.Y., Mr. Francis H. Kimball, Architect, New York, N.Y.," *American Architect and Building News* 23 (April 28, 1888): 198, plate; Montgomery Schuyler, "The Works of Francis H. Kimball and Kimball & Thompson," *Architectural Record* 7 (April–June 1898): 479–518; Landmarks Preservation Commission of the City of New York, LP-0160 (November 12, 1968); Landmarks Preservation Commission of the City of New York, LP-2017 (November 10, 1981), 123–26; White and Willensky, *AIA Guide* (1988), 636; Diamonstein, *The Landmarks of New York II*, 194.

152. "Buildings Projected," *Real Estate Record and Builders' Guide* 30 (October 21, 1882): 947; "The Emmanuel Baptist Church," *New York Times* (November 24, 1882): 3; "A New Church in Brooklyn," *New York Times* (September 7, 1883): 8; Landmarks Preservation Commission of the City of New York, LP-0160 (November 12, 1968); Landmarks Preservation Commission of the City of New York, LP-2017 (November 10, 1981), 124.

153. Schuyler, "The Works of Francis H. Kimball and Kimball & Thompson": 490–91.

154. "Out Among the Builders: Brooklyn," *Real Estate Record and Builders' Guide* 41 (February 18, 1888): 213; "Buildings Projected," *Real Estate Record and Builders' Guide* 41 (June 16, 1888): 790; "St. Luke's Fine Church," *New York Daily Tribune* (April 14, 1889): 21; Rev. R. B. Snowden, "New St. Luke's, Brooklyn, L.I.," *The Churchman* 59 (June 29, 1889): 816–17; "Buildings Projected," *Real Estate Record and Builders' Guide* 45 (April 12, 1890): 547; "A Fine Brooklyn Church," *New York Daily Tribune* (November 9, 1890): 22; "St. Luke's Church, Brooklyn," *New York Times* (October 17, 1891): 8; "The New St. Luke's," *New York Times* (October 19, 1891): 2; Rev. R. B. Snowden, "St. Luke's Church, Brooklyn, N.Y.," *The Churchman* 74 (October 17, 1896): 476–78; King, *King's Views of Brooklyn* (1904), 62; Landmarks Preservation Commission of the City of New York, LP-2014 (May 12, 1981); White and Willensky, *AIA Guide* (1988), 629–30; Diamonstein, *The Landmarks of New York II*, 198.

155. Landmarks Preservation Commission of the City of New York, LP-0695 (September 14, 1971), 3–12.

156. White and Willensky, *AIA Guide* (1988), 672.

157. Landmarks Preservation Commission of the City of New York, LP-1964 (September 16, 1997); Barbara Whitaker, "A Landmark Facade, a Troubled Interior," *New York Times* (December 7, 1997), X: 4.

158. Landmarks Preservation Commission of the City of New York, LP-0695 (September 14, 1971), 8, 32, 37.

159. Landmarks Preservation Commission of the City of New York, LP-0695 (September 14, 1971), 40.

160. Dolkart, "Visible City: Many of Brooklyn's Lavish Romanesque Revival Brownstones Were Built by the Now-Forgotten Architect Montrose W. Morris": 26–27, 34.

161. "Buildings Projected," *Real Estate Record and Builders' Guide* 36 (November 14, 1885): 1273; "Reception Hall," *Architectural Record* 3 (January–March 1894): 367; Dolkart, "Visible City: Many of Brooklyn's Lavish Romanesque Revival Brownstones Were Built by the Now-Forgotten Architect Montrose W. Morris": 26–27.

162. *Brooklyn Daily Eagle*, quoted in Dolkart, "Visible City: Many of Brooklyn's Lavish Romanesque Revival Brownstones Were Built by the Now-Forgotten Architect Montrose W. Morris": 27.

163. "Buildings Projected," *Real Estate Record and Builders' Guide* 41 (April 14, 1888): 480; Dolkart, "Visible City: Many of Brooklyn's Lavish Romanesque Revival Brownstones Were Built by the Now-Forgotten Architect Montrose W. Morris": 26–27; White and Willensky, *AIA Guide* (1988), 664.

164. "Buildings Projected," *Real Estate Record and Builders' Guide* 43 (March 2, 1889): 301; Dolkart, "Visible City: Many of Brooklyn's Lavish Romanesque Revival Brownstones Were Built by the Now-Forgotten Architect Montrose W. Morris": 26–27; White and Willensky, *AIA Guide* (1988), 664.

165. "Buildings Projected," *Real Estate Record and Builders' Guide* 43 (March 9, 1889): 338; Dolkart, "Visible City: Many of Brooklyn's Lavish Romanesque Revival Brownstones Were Built by the Now-Forgotten Architect Montrose W. Morris": 26–27; White and Willensky, *AIA Guide* (1988), 664.

166. "Buildings Projected," *Real Estate Record and Builders' Guide* 48 (April 16, 1892): 627; White and Willensky, *AIA Guide* (1988), 672.

167. "Buildings Projected," *Real Estate Record and Builders' Guide* 41 (March 3, 1888): 288; White and Willensky, *AIA Guide* (1988), 671.

168. "Buildings Projected," *Real Estate Record and Builders' Guide* 41 (June 23, 1888): 825; Landmarks Preservation Commission of the City of New York, LP-0695 (September 14, 1971), 43.

169. "Buildings Projected," *Real Estate Record and Builders' Guide* 41 (March 3, 1888): 287; Landmarks Preservation Commission of the City of New York, LP-0695 (September 14, 1971), 38–39.

170. "Buildings Projected," *Real Estate Record and Builders' Guide* 47 (April 11, 1891): 591; Landmarks Preservation Commission of the City of New York, LP-0695 (September 14, 1971), 33.

171. "Buildings Projected," *Real Estate Record and Builders' Guide* 50 (July 2, 1892): 29; Landmarks Preservation Commission of the City of New York, LP-0695 (September 14, 1971), 20.

172. "Buildings Projected," *Real Estate Record and Builders' Guide* 45 (February 22, 1890): 282; Landmarks Preservation Commission of the City of New York, LP-0695 (September 14, 1971), 26.

173. "Buildings Projected," *Real Estate Record and Builders' Guide* 44 (December 7, 1889): 1657; White and Willensky, *AIA Guide* (1988), 670.

174. "Out Among the Builders: Brooklyn," *Real Estate Record and Builders' Guide* 43 (April 6, 1889): 466. Also see "Buildings Projected," *Real Estate Record and Builders' Guide* 43 (April 20, 1889): 571; King, *King's Views of Brooklyn* (1904), 47; Dolkart, "Visible City: Many of Brooklyn's Lavish Romanesque Revival Brownstones Were Built by the Now-Forgotten Architect Montrose W. Morris": 26–27, 34; Landmarks Preservation Commission of the City of New York, LP-1431 (March 18, 1986); White and Willensky, *AIA Guide* (1988), 665; Diamonstein, *The Landmarks of New York II*, 201; Christopher Gray, "Streetscapes: The Alhambra in Bedford-Stuyvesant," *New York Times* (January 5, 1997), IX: 5.

175. "Buildings Projected," *Real Estate Record and Builders' Guide* 48 (April 2, 1892): 535; Dolkart, "Visible City: Many of Brooklyn's Lavish Romanesque Revival Brownstones Were Built by the Now-Forgotten Architect Montrose W. Morris": 26–27, 34; Landmarks Preservation Commission of the City of New York, LP-1433 (March 18, 1986); White and Willensky, *AIA Guide* (1988), 665; Diamonstein, *The Landmarks of New York II*, 212; Gray, "Streetscapes: The Alhambra in Bedford-Stuyvesant": 5.

176. "Buildings Projected," *Real Estate Record and Builders' Guide* 48 (April 2, 1892): 535; King, *King's Views of Brooklyn* (1904), 47; Dolkart, "Visible City: Many of Brooklyn's Lavish Romanesque Revival Brownstones Were Built by the Now-Forgotten Architect Montrose W. Morris": 26–27, 34; Landmarks Preservation Commission of the City of New York, LP-1432 (March 18, 1986); White and Willensky, *AIA Guide* (1988), 670; Diamonstein, *The Landmarks of New York II*, 212; Gray, "Streetscapes: The Alhambra in Bedford-Stuyvesant": 5.

177. "Buildings Projected," *Real Estate Record and Builders' Guide* 45 (March 29, 1890): 463; Landmarks Preservation Commission of the City of New York, LP-0695 (September 14, 1971), 42.

178. Landmarks Preservation Commission of the City of New York, LP-0695 (September 14, 1971), 28.

179. Olmsted, Vaux & Co., "Report on Tompkins Park Improvement (1870)," in Brooklyn Park Commission, *Eleventh Annual Report* (Brooklyn, 1871), 33–35; Fein, *Frederick Law Olmsted and the American Environmental Tradition*, 31, fig. 49; Schuyler and Censer, eds., *The Papers of Frederick Law Olmsted, vol. 6: The Years of Olmsted, Vaux & Company, 1865–1874*, 24–25, 395–99, 457–60; Alex, *Calvert Vaux*, 24.

180. "A Prosperous Brooklyn Club," *New York Times* (January 28, 1889): 4; "Among the Club-Houses: The Union League's New Home," *New York Daily Tribune* (May 12, 1889): 3; "Buildings Projected," *Real Estate Record and Builders' Guide* 44 (July 27, 1889): 1066; "The Cornerstone Laid," *New York Daily Tribune* (October 6, 1889): 17; "Laying Its Cornerstone," *New York Times* (October 6, 1889): 16; "Competitive Design for Union League Club House, Brooklyn, N.Y., Henry F. Kilburn, Architect," *Building* 11 (November 23, 1889): 175, plate; "The Growth of Clubs in New York City," supplement, *Real Estate Record and Builders' Guide* 45 (March 8, 1890): 2–3, 12; "Among the Club-Houses: Preparing to Move into Their New Home," *New York Daily Tribune* (June 22, 1890): 20; "A Merry House-Warming," *New York Daily Tribune* (November 13, 1890): 7; King, *King's Views of Brooklyn* (1904), 60; Younger, *Old Brooklyn in Early Photographs*, 74–75; White and Willensky, *AIA Guide* (1988), 670–71.

181. For Kilburn's Colonial Club, see Stern, Gilmartin, and Massengale, *New York 1900*, 390–91.

182. "For the Twenty-third," *New York Times* (November 15, 1891): 5; "Marched to Its New Armory," *New York Times* (November 4, 1894): 12; "Some Sights of Brooklyn," *New York Daily Tribune* (July 18, 1897): 4; King, *King's Views of Brooklyn* (1904), 24; Landmarks Preservation Commission of the City of New York, LP-0950 (March 8, 1977); McCullough, *Brooklyn . . . and How It Got That Way*, 215–16; White and Willensky, *AIA Guide* (1988), 669; Diamonstein, *The Landmarks of New York II*, 210. For Richardson's Allegheny County Courthouse and Jail, see Ochsner, *H. H. Richardson: Complete Architectural Works*, 325–36.

183. "Some Sights of Brooklyn": 4.

184. "Buildings Projected," *Real Estate Record and Builders' Guide* 36 (July 11, 1885): 802; King, *King's Views of Brooklyn* (1904), 28; Landmarks Preservation Commission of the City of New York, LP-1246 (June 28, 1983); White and Willensky, *AIA Guide* (1988), 665; Diamonstein, *The Landmarks of New York II*, 188.

185. "Buildings Projected," *Real Estate Record and Builders' Guide* 42 (October 27, 1888): 1295; Landmarks Preservation Commission of the City of New York, LP-1289 (September 11, 1984); White and Willensky, *AIA Guide* (1988), 668; Diamonstein, *The Landmarks of New York II*, 199.

186. "Buildings Projected," *Real Estate Record and Builders' Guide* 43 (June 15, 1889): 860; White and Willensky, *AIA Guide* (1988), 668.

187. "Buildings Projected," *Real Estate Record and Builders' Guide* 47 (April 14, 1891): 542; King, *King's Views of Brooklyn* (1904), 28; Landmarks Preservation Commission of the City of New York, LP-0896 (September 23, 1975); White and Willensky, *AIA Guide* (1988), 663; Diamonstein, *The Landmarks of New York II*, 209.

188. "Out Among the Builders: Brooklyn," *Real Estate Record and Builders' Guide* 39 (February 5, 1887): 166–67; "Buildings Projected," *Real Estate Record and Builders' Guide* 39 (April 28, 1887): 577; Landmarks Preservation Commission of the City of New York, LP-0946 (January 11, 1977); White and Willensky, *AIA Guide* (1988), 663; Diamonstein, *The Landmarks of New York II*, 194.

189. "A Splendid Church for Brooklyn," *New York Times* (June 6, 1888): 3; "Buildings Projected," *Real Estate Record and Builders' Guide* 41 (June 23, 1888): 825; "A New Brooklyn Church," *New York Daily Tribune* (October 1, 1888): 2; "Pews in Brisk Demand," *New York Times* (January 4, 1889): 2; "To the Service of God," *New York Times* (January 7, 1890): 3; White and Willensky, *AIA Guide* (1988), 665.

190. "A New Congregational Church," *New York Times* (July 16, 1875): 2; Editorial, *American Architect and Building News* 1 (August 19, 1876): 265.

191. "Buildings Projected," *Real Estate Record and Builders' Guide* 45 (January 11, 1890): 60; Landmarks Preservation Commission of the City of New York, LP-0820 (March 19, 1974); White and Willensky, *AIA Guide* (1988), 670; Diamonstein, *The Landmarks of New York II*, 206.

192. "Buildings Projected," *Real Estate Record and Builders' Guide* 44 (October 12, 1889): 1390; "New Church in Brooklyn," *New York Times* (November 3, 1889): 16; "Throop Avenue Presbyterian Church, Brooklyn, N.Y., Messrs. Fowler & Hough, Architects, New York, N.Y.," *American Architect and Building News* 27 (March 15, 1890): 174, plate; "Dedicated Free of Debt," *New York Times* (April 3, 1893): 9.

193. "A Congregation's New Home," *New York Times* (May 23, 1889): 8; "Buildings Projected," *Real Estate Record and Builders' Guide* 44 (July 27, 1889): 1065; "A New Brooklyn Church," *New York Times* (October 19, 1890): 16; "A New House of Worship," *New York Times* (October 20, 1890): 8; Schuyler, "The Works of Cady, Berg & See": 545; White and

Willensky, *AIA Guide* (1988), 671; Curran, *A Forgotten Architect of the Gilded Age*, 29.

194. "Buildings Projected," *Real Estate Record and Builders' Guide* 46 (December 27, 1890): 890; "Interesting Ceremonies," *New York Times* (April 28, 1891): 9; "New Brooklyn Synagogue," *New York Times* (April 18, 1892): 9; White and Willensky, *AIA Guide* (1988), 886–87.

195. "New Brooklyn Synagogue": 9.

196. "Embury Chapel Cornerstone Laid," *New York Times* (July 13, 1894): 6; "Embury Chapel Dedication," *New York Times* (December 17, 1894): 2; Landmarks Preservation Commission of the City of New York, LP-0695 (September 14, 1971), 12, 23–24.

197. Frederick Law Olmsted and Calvert Vaux, *Preliminary Report to the Commissioners for Laying Out a Park in Brooklyn, New York: Being a Consideration of Circumstances of Site and Other Conditions Affecting the Design of Public Pleasure Grounds* (1866), reprinted in Albert Fein, ed., *Landscape into Cityscape: Frederick Law Olmsted's Plans for a Greater New York City* (Ithaca, N.Y.: Cornell University Press, 1967), 95–127; "Brooklyn Prospect Park," *New York Times* (April 12, 1866): 2; "Prospect Park and Brooklyn Improvements," editorial, *New York Times* (May 12, 1866): 4; "Brooklyn News," *New York Times* (March 6, 1867): 8; "Prospect Park, Brooklyn," *New York Times* (October 6, 1867): 8; John W. Kennion, *Architects' and Builders' Guide* (New York: Fitzpatrick & Hunter, 1868), part 3: 44–46; Frederick Law Olmsted and Calvert Vaux, *Report of the Landscape Architects and Superintendents to the President of the Board of Commissioners of Prospect Park, Brooklyn* (1868), reprinted in Fein, ed., *Landscape into Cityscape*, 129–64; "Prospect Park," *New York Times* (December 15, 1868): 11; "Prospect Park," *New York Times* (February 8, 1869): 8; "Our Great Parks," *New York Times* (June 20, 1869): 8; "Prospect Park," *New York Times* (August 6, 1869): 2; "Prospect Park Water Supply," *New York Times* (December 23, 1869): 2; "Prospect Park," *New York Times* (March 27, 1870): 6; "The Brooklyn Park," editorial, *New York Times* (July 2, 1871): 4; "Prospect Park Assessments," *New York Times* (October 18, 1873): 5; "Facts about Prospect Park," *New York Times* (June 3, 1881): 8; "Prospect Park's Decay," *New York Times* (April 20, 1888): 8; "Prospect Park," editorial, *Garden and Forest* 1 (July 4, 1888): 217–18; Fein, ed., *Landscape into Cityscape*, 91–93; Clay Lancaster, *Prospect Park Handbook* (New York: Walton H. Rawls, 1967); Julius Gy. Fabos, Gordon T. Milde, and V. Michael Weinmayr, *Frederick Law Olmsted, Sr.: Founder of Landscape Architecture in America* (Amherst, Mass.: University of Massachusetts Press, 1968), 30–31; Leonard Joseph Simutis, "Frederick Law Olmsted's Later Years: Landscape Architecture and the Spirit of Place" (Ph.D. diss., University of Minnesota, 1971): 120–31; Elizabeth Barlow, *Frederick Law Olmsted's New York* (New York: Praeger, 1972), 36–37; Fein, *Frederick Law Olmsted and the American Environmental Tradition*, 27, 30, figs. 46–47, 95–96; Laura Wood Roper, *FLO: A Biography of Frederick Law Olmsted* (Baltimore, Md., and London: Johns Hopkins University Press, 1973), 292–94, 299, 390, 403; Margaret Mitchell, "Frederick Law Olmsted's Park Aesthetic: As Seen in Prospect Park and Other Urban Parks" (senior project, Vassar College, April 26, 1974); Landmarks Preservation Commission of the City of New York, LP-0901 (November 25, 1975); Younger, *Old Brooklyn in Early Photographs*, figs. 131, 134–35; Bruce Kelly, "Art of the Olmsted Landscape," in Bruce Kelly, Gail Travis Guillet, and Mary Ellen W. Hern, eds., *Art of the Olmsted Landscape* (New York: New York City Landmarks Preservation Commission and The Arts Publisher, 1981), 4–71; McCullough, *Brooklyn . . . and How It Got That Way*, 99–104; M. M. Graff, *Central Park, Prospect Park: A New Perspective* (New York: Greensward Foundation, 1985), 107–78; White and Willensky, *AIA Guide* (1988), 653; Alex, *Calvert Vaux*, 130–41, 143; Christopher Gray, "Streetscapes/Prospect Park," *New York Times* (July 17, 1994), IX: 5; Charles C. Beveridge and Paul Rocheleau, *Frederick Law Olmsted: Designing the American Landscape* (New York: Rizzoli International Publications, 1995), 72–83; David Schuyler, "Prospect Park," in Jackson, ed., *The Encyclopedia of New York City*, 946; Snyder-Grenier, *Brooklyn!*, 204–9; Kowsky, *Country, Park and City*, 175–89, 216–21.

198. Olmsted and Vaux, *Preliminary Report to the Commissioners for Laying Out a Park in Brooklyn, New York: Being a Consideration of Circumstances of Site and Other Conditions Affecting the Design of Public Pleasure Grounds* (1866), reprinted in Fein, ed., *Landscape into Cityscape*, 105.

199. Egbert L. Viele, quoted in *First Annual Report of the Commissioners* (Brooklyn, 1861), quoted in Lancaster, *Prospect Park Handbook*, 24.

200. Egbert L. Viele, quoted in *First Annual Report of the Commissioners* (Brooklyn, 1861), quoted in Landmarks Preservation Commission of the City of New York, LP-0901 (November 25, 1975), 4.

201. In 1889 the eastern portion of the site was earmarked for the Brooklyn Institute of Arts and Sciences (McKim, Mead & White, 1895–1915). For the western end of the site, plans were drawn in 1908 by Raymond F. Admiral for a new headquarters for the Brooklyn Public Library. Foundations were laid for Admiral's design, but, as ultimately redesigned by Githens & Keally, the building was not realized until 1941. For the Brooklyn Institute of Arts and Sciences, see Stern, Gilmartin, and Massengale, *New York 1900*, 87–91. For the Brooklyn Public Library, see Stern, Gilmartin, and Massengale, *New York 1900*, 25, 88, 95–96; Stern, Gilmartin, and Mellins, *New York 1930*, 132–33, 139–40, 166.

202. Calvert Vaux to Frederick Law Olmsted, January 9, 1865, cited in Simutis, "Frederick Law Olmsted's Later Years": 120.

203. Calvert Vaux to Frederick Law Olmsted, 1865, quoted in Graff, *Central Park, Prospect Park: A New Perspective*, 118.

204. Olmsted and Vaux, *Report of the Landscape Architects and Superintendents to the President of the Board of Commissioners of Prospect Park, Brooklyn* (1868).

205. Olmsted and Vaux, *Preliminary Report to the Commissioners for Laying Out a Park in Brooklyn, New York: Being a Consideration of Circumstances of Site and Other Conditions Affecting the Design of Public Pleasure Grounds* (1866), summarized by the Board of Park Commissioners for the Brooklyn Common Council, quoted in Lancaster, *Prospect Park Handbook*, 28.

206. Olmsted and Vaux, *Preliminary Report to the Commissioners for Laying Out a Park in Brooklyn, New York: Being a Consideration of Circumstances of Site and Other Conditions Affecting the Design of Public Pleasure Grounds* (1866), quoted in Fein, ed., *Landscape into Cityscape*, 101.

207. George Templeton Strong, diary entry dated July 18, 1871, in *The Diary of George Templeton Strong*, eds. Allan Nevins and Milton Halsey Thomas, 4 vols. (New York: Macmillan, 1952), vol. 4: 374.

208. Kennion, *Architects' and Builders' Guide*, part 3: 45.

209. "Prospect Park," (August 6, 1869): 2.

210. "Prospect Park," *Garden and Forest*: 218.

211. *Brooklyn Daily Eagle* (1882), quoted in Landmarks Preservation Commission of the City of New York, LP-0901 (November 25, 1975), 4. Also see "A New Park Board in Brooklyn," *New York Daily Tribune* (June 16, 1882): 8; "Prospect Park Commission," *New York Times* (June 16, 1882): 3; "Prospect Park Commission," *New York Times* (June 18, 1882): 9; "The Prospect Park Commission," *New York Times* (July 28, 1882): 8; "A Deficit Promptly Made Good," *New York Daily Tribune* (December 15, 1882): 2.

212. Olmsted and Vaux, *Preliminary Report to the Commissioners for Laying Out a Park in Brooklyn, New York: Being a Consideration of Circumstances of Site and Other Conditions Affecting the Design of Public Pleasure Grounds* (1866), quoted in Fein, ed., *Landscape into Cityscape*, 126–27.

213. *The East Parkway and Boulevards, in the City of Brooklyn* (New York: Baker & Godwin, 1873); Barlow, *Frederick Law Olmsted's New York*, 148–51; Fein, *Frederick Law Olmsted and the American Environmental Tradition*, 31, fig. 50; Landmarks Preservation Commission of the City of New York, LP-0998 (August 22, 1978); McCullough, *Brooklyn . . . and How It Got That Way*, 118–19; Diamonstein, *The Landmarks of New York II*, 158; Alex, *Calvert Vaux*, 142; Kenneth T. Jackson, "Eastern Parkway," in Jackson, ed., *The Encyclopedia of New York City*, 356; Kowsky, *Country, Park and City*, 180–83.

214. "Cost of Extending Ocean Avenue," *New York Times* (July 18, 1875): 7; "The Finest Drive in America," *New York Daily Tribune* (October 18, 1876): 2; "Local Miscellany: Brooklyn's Ocean Avenue," *New York Daily Tribune* (November 18, 1876): 2; "Brooklyn's New Drive to the Sea," *New York Times* (November 18, 1876): 10; "An Ocean Parkway," *New York Times* (May 6, 1877): 10; King, *King's Views of Brooklyn* (1904), 56; Landmarks Preservation Commission of the City of New York, LP-0871 (January 28, 1975); Diamonstein, *The Landmarks of New York II*, 162; Alex, *Calvert Vaux*, 142; Ellen Marie Snyder-Grenier, "Ocean Parkway," in Jackson, ed., *The Encyclopedia of New York City*, 860; Kowsky, *Country, Park and City*, 102, 180–83.

215. "The Finest Drive in America": 2.

216. Board of Park Commissioners, *Twelfth Annual Report* (1872), quoted in Landmarks Preservation Commission of the City of New York, LP-0871 (January 28, 1975).

217. "An Ocean Parkway": 10.

218. For a brief overview of Park Slope's history, see John J. Gallagher, "Park Slope," in Jackson, ed., *The Encyclopedia of New York City*, 883.

219. Judith Berck, "Prospect Heights," in Jackson, ed., *The Encyclopedia of New York City*, 945.

220. Landmarks Preservation Commission of the City of New York, LP-0709 (July 17, 1973), 7.

221. "Buildings Projected," *Real Estate Record and Builders' Guide* 17 (May 20, 1876): 404; Landmarks Preservation Commission of the City of New York, LP-0709 (July 17, 1973), 3.

222. "Buildings Projected," *Real Estate Record and Builders' Guide* 19 (May 19, 1877): 413; Landmarks Preservation Commission of the City of New York, LP-0709 (July 17, 1973), 6.

223. "Buildings Projected," *Real Estate Record and Builders' Guide* 28 (July 23, 1881): 757; Landmarks Preservation Commission of the City of New York, LP-0709 (July 17, 1973), 9.

224. "Buildings Projected," *Real Estate Record and Builders' Guide* 29 (June 17, 1882): 611; Landmarks Preservation Commission of the City of New York, LP-0709 (July 17, 1973), 7.

225. "Buildings Projected," *Real Estate Record and Builders' Guide* 40 (July 16, 1887): 974; Landmarks Preservation Commission of the City of New York, LP-0709 (July 17, 1973), 8.

226. "Buildings Projected," *Real Estate Record and Builders' Guide* 43 (May 4, 1889): 637; Landmarks Preservation Commission of the City of New York, LP-0709 (July 17, 1973), 57.

227. "Buildings Projected," *Real Estate Record and Builders' Guide* 35 (June 6, 1885): 670; Landmarks Preservation Commission of the City of New York, LP-0709 (July 17, 1973), 85; White and Willensky, *AIA Guide* (1988), 642–43.

228. "Buildings Projected," *Real Estate Record and Builders' Guide* 40 (September 24, 1887): 1217; Landmarks Preservation Commission of the City of New York, LP-0709 (July 17, 1973), 89; White and Willensky, *AIA Guide* (1988), 646.

229. "Buildings Projected," *Real Estate Record and Builders' Guide* 44 (August 17, 1889): 1149; "Examples of Recent Architecture in Brooklyn," supplement, *Real Estate Record and Builders' Guide* 85 (July 26, 1890): 2; King, *King's Views of Brooklyn* (1904), 44; Landmarks Preservation Commission of the City of New York, LP-0709 (July 17, 1973), 33; Dolkart, "Visible City: Many of Brooklyn's Lavish Romanesque Revival Brownstones Were Built by the Now-Forgotten Architect Montrose W. Morris": 26–27, 34; White and Willensky, *AIA Guide* (1988), 644.

230. *Brooklyn Daily Eagle*, quoted in Dolkart, "Visible City: Many of Brooklyn's Lavish Romanesque Revival Brownstones Were Built by the Now-Forgotten Architect Montrose W. Morris": 34.

231. "Buildings Projected," *Real Estate Record and Builders' Guide* 39 (April 30, 1887): 612; Landmarks Preservation Commission of the City of New York, LP-0709 (July 17, 1973), 18.

232. "Buildings Projected," *Real Estate Record and Builders' Guide* 37 (March 27, 1886): 408; Landmarks Preservation Commission of the City of New York, LP-0709 (July 17, 1973), 17–18.

233. "Out Among the Builders: Brooklyn," *Real Estate Record and Builders' Guide* 40 (October 15, 1887): 1294; "Buildings Projected," *Real Estate Record and Builders' Guide* 40 (December 31, 1887): 1661; Landmarks Preservation Commission of the City of New York, LP-0709 (July 17, 1973), 46.

234. "Buildings Projected," *Real Estate Record and Builders' Guide* 37 (May 29, 1886): 732; "House for F. L. Babbott, Esq., Brooklyn, N.Y., Messrs. Lamb & Rich, Architects," *American Architect and Building News* 22 (July 9, 1887): 19, plate; Landmarks Preservation Commission of the City of New York, LP-0709 (July 17, 1973), 67; White and Willensky, *AIA Guide* (1988), 647.

235. "Buildings Projected," *Real Estate Record and Builders' Guide* 45 (May 17, 1890): 762; "Examples of Recent Architecture—At Home," *Real Estate Record and Builders' Guide* 47 (January 24, 1891): 120; "House of Tangermann [*sic*], Esq., No. 276 Berkeley Place, Brooklyn, N.Y.

Messrs. Lamb & Rich, Architects, New York, N.Y.," *American Architect and Building News* 35 (February 27, 1892): 142, plate; "The Tangeman House, Brooklyn," *Architectural Record* 3 (October–December 1893): 187; King, *King's Views of Brooklyn* (1904), 45; Landmarks Preservation Commission of the City of New York, LP-0709 (July 17, 1973), 47–48; White and Willensky, *AIA Guide* (1988), 640; Cara Greenberg, "A Pristine Victorian House Comes Out of the Cobwebs," *New York Times* (October 1, 1992), C: 1, 6.

236. "Buildings Projected," *Real Estate Record and Builders' Guide* 44 (October 26, 1889): 1459; "Residence of Guido Pleisner [*sic*], Plaza and Lincoln Place, Brooklyn, N.Y.," *Architecture and Building* 23 (August 10, 1895): 67, plate; Younger, *Old Brooklyn in Early Photographs*, 87.

237. Landmarks Preservation Commission of the City of New York, LP-0709 (July 17, 1973), 41; White and Willensky, *AIA Guide* (1988), 644.

238. "Out Among the Builders: Brooklyn," *Real Estate Record and Builders' Guide* 40 (August 13, 1887): 1062–63; "Out Among the Builders: Brooklyn," *Real Estate Record and Builders' Guide* 40 (October 15, 1887): 1293–94; "Out Among the Builders: Brooklyn," *Real Estate Record and Builders' Guide* 43 (May 18, 1889): 695; "House of H. Murdock, Esq., Brooklyn, N.Y., Mr. C.P.H. Gilbert, Architect, N.Y.," *American Architect and Building News* 26 (September 21, 1889): 135, plate; Landmarks Preservation Commission of the City of New York, LP-0709 (July 17, 1973), 71–72, 75–76; White and Willensky, *AIA Guide* (1988), 644.

239. "Out Among the Builders: Brooklyn," *Real Estate Record and Builders' Guide* 39 (June 4, 1887): 771; "Buildings Projected," *Real Estate Record and Builders' Guide* 39 (June 11, 1887): 822.

240. "Out Among the Builders: Brooklyn," *Real Estate Record and Builders' Guide* 41 (June 23, 1888): 897; "Examples of Recent Architecture—At Home," supplement, *Real Estate Record and Builders' Guide* 47 (May 2, 1891): 1; "Door in the Residence of Thomas Adams, Esq.," *Architectural Record* 1 (September 1891): 100; Landmarks Preservation Commission of the City of New York, LP-0709 (July 17, 1973), 21–22; White and Willensky, *AIA Guide* (1988), 642–43; *Carroll Street, Brooklyn* (New York: Historic Preservation Division, Graduate School of Architecture, Planning and Preservation, Columbia University, 1989–90), 62–64.

241. "Buildings Projected," *Real Estate Record and Builders' Guide* 45 (March 29, 1890): 463; "Examples of Recent Architecture in Brooklyn," supplement, *Real Estate Record and Builders' Guide* 45 (July 26, 1890): 3.

242. "Out Among the Builders: Brooklyn," *Real Estate Record and Builders' Guide* 40 (August 13, 1887): 1062–63; "Buildings Projected," *Real Estate Record and Builders' Guide* 40 (August 20, 1887): 1098; Landmarks Preservation Commission of the City of New York, LP-0709 (July 17, 1973), 51–52; White and Willensky, *AIA Guide* (1988), 642.

243. "Out Among the Builders: Brooklyn," *Real Estate Record and Builders' Guide* 40 (August 13, 1887): 1062–63; "Buildings Projected," *Real Estate Record and Builders' Guide* 40 (August 20, 1887): 1098; Landmarks Preservation Commission of the City of New York, LP-0709 (July 17, 1973), 51; White and Willensky, *AIA Guide* (1988), 642.

244. "Out Among the Builders: Brooklyn," *Real Estate Record and Builders' Guide* 40 (August 13, 1887): 1062–63; "Buildings Projected," *Real Estate Record and Builders' Guide* 40 (August 20, 1887): 1098; Landmarks Preservation Commission of the City of New York, LP-0709 (July 17, 1973), 51; White and Willensky, *AIA Guide* (1988), 642.

245. "Out Among the Builders: Brooklyn," *Real Estate Record and Builders' Guide* 44 (September 21, 1889): 1266; "Buildings Projected," *Real Estate Record and Builders' Guide* 44 (September 28, 1889): 1316; Landmarks Preservation Commission of the City of New York, LP-0709 (July 17, 1973), 63.

246. "Buildings Projected," *Real Estate Record and Builders' Guide* 43 (May 25, 1889): 752; "Hallway of R. A. Ward, Esq.," *Architectural Record* 1 (September 1891): 51; Landmarks Preservation Commission of the City of New York, LP-0709 (July 17, 1973), 63.

247. "Buildings Projected," *Real Estate Record and Builders' Guide* 44 (July 13, 1889): 1006; Landmarks Preservation Commission of the City of New York, LP-0709 (July 17, 1973), 62.

248. "Buildings Projected," *Real Estate Record and Builders' Guide* 40 (November 26, 1887): 1496; Landmarks Preservation Commission of the

City of New York, LP-0709 (July 17, 1973), 53–54; *Carroll Street, Brooklyn*, 68–71.

249. "Buildings Projected," *Real Estate Record and Builders' Guide* 44 (July 27, 1889): 1066; Landmarks Preservation Commission of the City of New York, LP-0709 (July 17, 1973), 69.

250. "Buildings Projected," *Real Estate Record and Builders' Guide* 46 (August 2, 1890): 169; Landmarks Preservation Commission of the City of New York, LP-0709 (July 17, 1973), 56.

251. Kervick, *Patrick Charles Keely, Architect*, 17, 65; White and Willensky, *AIA Guide* (1988), 620.

252. "Buildings Projected," *Real Estate Record and Builders' Guide* 25 (March 27, 1880): 303; Landmarks Preservation Commission of the City of New York, LP-0709 (July 17, 1973), 4.

253. "Buildings Projected," *Real Estate Record and Builders' Guide* 29 (April 1, 1882): 316; "A New Methodist Church in Brooklyn," *New York Daily Tribune* (January 21, 1883): 5; King, *King's Views of Brooklyn* (1904), 63; Landmarks Preservation Commission of the City of New York, LP-0709 (July 17, 1973), 9.

254. Landmarks Preservation Commission of the City of New York, LP-0709 (July 17, 1973), 90–91; Sarah Bradford Landau, *Edward T. and William A. Potter: American Victorian Architects* (New York: Garland, 1979), 131–32, 362–64; White and Willensky, *AIA Guide* (1988), 646.

255. "Out Among the Builders: Brooklyn," *Real Estate Record and Builders' Guide* 28 (December 3, 1881): 1120; "Buildings Projected," *Real Estate Record and Builders' Guide* 29 (March 25, 1882): 288; "The New Memorial Presbyterian Church, Brooklyn," *New York Daily Graphic* (February 19, 1883): 765, 767; Landmarks Preservation Commission of the City of New York, LP-0709 (July 17, 1973), 10; White and Willensky, *AIA Guide* (1988), 645.

256. "Buildings Projected," *Real Estate Record and Builders' Guide* 18 (November 25, 1876): 883; Landmarks Preservation Commission of the City of New York, LP-0952 (March 8, 1977); White and Willensky, *AIA Guide* (1988), 648; Diamonstein, *The Landmarks of New York II*, 170.

257. "Builders—Brooklyn," *Real Estate Record and Builders' Guide* 54 (November 24, 1894): 781; "Builders—Brooklyn," *Real Estate Record and Builders' Guide* 54 (December 15, 1894): 907; "New Buildings," *Real Estate Record and Builders' Guide* 54 (December 15, 1894): 913; Landmarks Preservation Commission of the City of New York, LP-0709 (July 17, 1973), 29–30.

258. "A New Club for Brooklyn," *New York Times* (February 3, 1889): 3; "No Name for the Club Yet," *New York Times* (February 26, 1889): 2; "Brooklyn," *New York Times* (March 7, 1889): 3; "A New Brooklyn Club," *New York Times* (March 16, 1889): 4; "Brooklyn," *New York Times* (March 21, 1889): 3; "Out Among the Builders: Brooklyn," *Real Estate Record and Builders' Guide* 44 (July 27, 1889): 1049–50; "For the Montauk Club," *New York Times* (September 30, 1889): 4; "Buildings Projected," *Real Estate Record and Builders' Guide* 44 (November 2, 1889): 1492; "Their Cornerstone Laid: Exercises of the Montauk Club," *New York Daily Tribune* (December 15, 1889): 8; "Its Cornerstone Laid: The New Home of the Montauk Club of Brooklyn," *New York Times* (December 15, 1889): 16; "A Home to Be Proud Of," *New York Daily Tribune* (July 6, 1890): 20; "The Montauk Club," *Architecture and Building* 16 (January 2, 1892): plate; James Taylor, "The History of Terra Cotta in New York City," *Architectural Record* 2 (October–December 1892): 136–48; "The Montauk Club, Brooklyn," *Brickbuilder* 3 (August 1894): 154, 156; Schuyler, "The Works of Francis H. Kimball and Kimball & Thompson": 497–99; King, *King's Views of Brooklyn* (1904), 60; Landmarks Preservation Commission of the City of New York, LP-0709 (July 17, 1973), 13–14; McCullough, *Brooklyn . . . and How It Got That Way*, 53; Stern, Gilmartin, and Massengale, *New York 1900*, 98, 231; White and Willensky, *AIA Guide* (1988), 640; Christopher Gray, "Streetscapes/The Montauk Club in Brooklyn," *New York Times* (April 28, 1996), IX: 7.

259. "Out Among the Builders: Brooklyn": 1049–50.

260. Schuyler, "The Works of Francis H. Kimball and Kimball & Thompson": 497.

261. For a brief discussion of Flatbush, see Elizabeth Reich Rawson, "Flatbush," in Jackson, ed., *The Encyclopedia of New York City*, 416.

262. Edmund Drew Fisher, *Flatbush, Past and Present* (Brooklyn: Flatbush Trust Co., 1902), 43, 45.

263. Montgomery Schuyler, "Some Suburbs of New York," *Lippincott's Magazine* 8 (August 1884): 113–26.

264. Landmarks Preservation Commission of the City of New York, LP-0770 (October 16, 1973); White and Willensky, *AIA Guide* (1988), 697; *Flatbush: Architecture and Urban Development from Dutch Settlement to Commercial Strip* (New York: Historic Preservation Division, Graduate School of Architecture, Planning and Preservation, Columbia University, 1990), 4; Diamonstein, *The Landmarks of New York II*, 168.

265. Fisher, *Flatbush, Past and Present*, 47, 84; Landmarks Preservation Commission of the City of New York, LP-0989 (July 11, 1978), 2.

266. Fisher, *Flatbush, Past and Present*, 84; Landmarks Preservation Commission of the City of New York, LP-0988 (July 11, 1978); White and Willensky, *AIA Guide* (1988), 698; Christopher Gray, "Fire-Damaged Flatbush Landmark May Be Razed," *New York Times* (April 3, 1988), X: 8; Diamonstein, *The Landmarks of New York II*, 214.

267. *Brooklyn Daily Eagle*, quoted in Gray, "Fire-Damaged Flatbush Landmark May Be Razed": 8.

268. "House at Flatbush, L.I. for W. A. Porter," *Building* 6 (April 16, 1887): 145, plate.

269. See "Coney Island Improvements," *New York Daily Tribune* (May 5, 1877): 4; "A Watering Place at Home," *New York Times* (August 13, 1877): 8; "Coney Island's Attractions," *New York Daily Tribune* (September 8, 1877): 2; "Coney Island's Prosperity," *New York Daily Tribune* (July 2, 1878): 1; "Local Miscellany: The Coming Season at Coney Island," *New York Daily Tribune* (March 12, 1879): 8; "Changes at Coney Island," *New York Daily Tribune* (May 19, 1879): 5; "The Season at Coney Island: More Visitors Than Ever Before," *New York Daily Tribune* (October 20, 1879): 2; "Business at the Sea-Side," *New York Times* (July 17, 1881): 12; "An Evident Want," editorial, *New York Daily Tribune* (July 18, 1881): 4. For further discussion of the development of Coney Island, see Lucy P. Gillman, "Coney Island," *New York History* 36 (July 1955): 255–90; Edo McCullough, *Good Old Coney Island: A Sentimental Journey into the Past* (New York: Charles Scribner's Sons, 1957); John F. Kasson, *Amusing the Million: Coney Island at the Turn of the Century* (New York: Hill and Wang, 1978); Stephen Weinstein, "The Nickel Empire: Coney Island and the Creation of Urban Seaside Resorts in the United States" (Ph.D. diss., Columbia University, 1984); Stephen Weinstein, "Coney Island," in Jackson, ed., *The Encyclopedia of New York City*, 272–74.

270. "A Watering Place at Home": 8.

271. "An Ocean Parkway": 10.

272. "A Ferry to Brighton Beach," *New York Times* (March 20, 1879): 3; "Coney Island's New Pier," *New York Times* (April 23, 1879): 2; "Coney Island's Pier," *New York Times* (June 24, 1879): 2; "The New Iron Pier at West Brighton Beach, Coney Island," *New York Daily Graphic* (August 29, 1879): 416; Frederick S. Lightfoot, ed., *Nineteenth-Century New York in Rare Photographic Views* (New York: Dover, 1981), fig. 147.

273. Frederick Law Olmsted, manuscript on tourism (no date), Olmsted Papers, box 22, quoted in Albert Fein, "Centennial New York, 1876," in Milton M. Klein, ed., *New York: The Centennial Years 1676–1976* (Port Washington, N.Y., and London: Kennikat Press, 1976), 105.

274. "Coney Island Improvements": 4; "Hotel and Restaurant for the N.Y. and Manhattan Beach Railway Company. J. Pickering Putnam, Architect," *American Architect and Building News* 2 (June 2, 1877): 174, plate; "On the Coney Island Beach," *New York Daily Graphic* (July 3, 1877): 11–13; "A Watering Place at Home": 8; "Coney Island's Attractions": 2; "Coney Island's Prosperity": 1; Nathan Silver, *Lost New York* (Boston: Houghton Mifflin, 1967), 64, 66–67; Younger, *Old Brooklyn in Early Photographs*, 130–31; Lightfoot, ed., *Nineteenth-Century New York in Rare Photographic Views*, fig. 146; Snyder-Grenier, *Brooklyn!*, 178–79.

275. J. Pickering Putnam, quoted in "Hotel and Restaurant for the N.Y. and Manhattan Beach Railway Company. J. Pickering Putnam, Architect": 174.

276. "Hotel and Restaurant for the N.Y. and Manhattan Beach Railway Company. J. Pickering Putnam, Architect": 174.

277. "Changes at Coney Island," (May 19, 1879): 5; "The Season at Coney Island: More Visitors Than Ever Before," (October 20, 1879): 2.

278. "Hotel Brighton, Coney Island, N.Y. Mr. John G. Prague, Architect, New York," *American Architect and Building News* 4 (September 7, 1878): 85, plate.

279. "The New Railroad and Hotel," *New York Daily Tribune* (July 2, 1878): 1.

280. "St. George's Inn, Coney Island, N.Y. Mr. Bruce Price, Architect, New York, N.Y.," *American Architect and Building News* 7 (June 26, 1880): 285, plate; Samuel H. Graybill Jr., "Bruce Price, American Architect, 1845–1903" (Ph.D. diss., Yale University, 1957): 37.

281. "A Jumbo House for Coney Island," *New York Times* (February 21, 1884): 8; "Coney Island's Big Elephant," *New York Times* (May 30, 1885): 8; "The Colossal Elephant of Coney Island," *Scientific American* 53 (July 11, 1885): 1, 21; Younger, *Old Brooklyn in Early Photographs*, 125; McCullough, *Brooklyn . . . and How It Got That Way*, 149–51; Snyder-Grenier, *Brooklyn!*, 182–85.

282. "Out Among the Builders: Brooklyn," *Real Estate Record and Builders' Guide* 32 (October 20, 1883): 610.

283. "To Be Moved To-Day," *New York Times* (April 3, 1888): 2; "Big Hotel on Wheels," *New York Daily Tribune* (April 4, 1888): 2; "Moving the Big Hotel," *New York Times* (April 4, 1888): 8; "More Progress Made," *New York Times* (April 5, 1888): 8; Editorial, *American Architect and Building News* 23 (April 14, 1888): 169; John Grafton, *New York in the Nineteenth Century* (New York: Dover, 1977), 129; Younger, *Old Brooklyn in Early Photographs*, 126–27; Snyder-Grenier, *Brooklyn!*, 176–77.

284. "Garbage at Coney Island," *New York Times* (August 4, 1886): 5; "Editorial Note and Comment," *Building* 6 (August 7, 1886): 61.

285. Schuyler, "The Works of Francis H. Kimball and Kimball & Thompson": 488–89. Also see "Out Among the Builders: Brooklyn," *Real Estate Record and Builders' Guide* 40 (October 15, 1887): 1293–94.

286. For general discussions of Bensonhurst, see "A Unique Suburb," *Real Estate Record and Builders' Guide* 44 (August 17, 1889): 1132–33; *Bensonhurst-by-the-Sea* (New York: New York Engraving and Printing, 1890); "Suburban New York, III—Bensonhurst-by-the-Sea," *Real Estate Record and Builders' Guide* 46 (August 23, 1890): 243–44; John A. Kouwenhoven, *The Columbia Historical Portrait of New York* (Garden City, N.Y.: Doubleday, 1953), 422; Nanette Rainone, ed., *Brooklyn Neighborhood Book* (Brooklyn: Fund for the Borough of Brooklyn, Inc., 1985), 10–12; Stephen Weinstein, "Bensonhurst," in Jackson, ed., *The Encyclopedia of New York City*, 102–3; Brian Merlis, *Brooklyn: The Way It Was* (Brooklyn: Israelowitz, 1995), 9. For Blythebourne, see James Bradley, "Blytheborne," in Jackson, ed., *The Encyclopedia of New York City*, 120–21. For Bath Beach, see Merlis, *Brooklyn: The Way It Was*, 17. For Bay Ridge, see City of New York, Department of City Planning, *Bay Ridge: Preserving Neighborhood Character and Scale Through Zoning* (New York, 1978), 8; Rainone, ed., *Brooklyn Neighborhood Book*, 3–5; Elizabeth Reich Rawson, "Bay Ridge," in Jackson, ed., *The Encyclopedia of New York City*, 90.

287. *Bensonhurst-by-the-Sea*, 16.

288. Silver, *Lost New York*, 65, 67; Younger, *Old Brooklyn in Early Photographs*, 105.

289. Younger, *Old Brooklyn in Early Photographs*, 101.

290. Younger, *Old Brooklyn in Early Photographs*, 108.

291. Christopher Gray, "Streetscapes/217 82d Street, Bay Ridge, Brooklyn," *New York Times* (July 5, 1998), IX: 5.

292. Martha J. Lamb and Mrs. Burton Harrison, *History of the City of New York* (New York: A. S. Barnes & Co., 1896).

293. *Bensonhurst-by-the-Sea*, 5–6.

294. *Bensonhurst-by-the-Sea*, 8, 15.

295. "House for D. W. Tallmadge, Esq., Bensonhurst-by-the-Sea. Stouly [*sic*] S. Covert, Architect," *Building* 11 (November 2, 1889): 145, plate. Also see "The Obituary Record: Daniel W. Tallmadge," *New York Times* (November 16, 1894): 5.

296. "Suburban New York, III—Bensonhurst-by-the-Sea": 243–44.

297. "To Help Poor Children," *New York Times* (June 13, 1884): 8; "Comfort for the Sick," *New York Times* (July 11, 1884): 5; Alex, *Calvert Vaux*, 230; Kowsky, *Country, Park and City*, 295–96.

298. Bonnie Yochelson, *Berenice Abbott: Changing New York* (New York: New Press and Museum of the City of New York, 1997), 313, 394.

299. Yochelson, *Berenice Abbott: Changing New York*, 314, 394.

300. For a brief discussion of Williamsburg, see Judith Berck, "Williamsburg(h)," in Jackson, ed., *The Encyclopedia of New York City*, 1263–64.

301. "Brooklyn Eastern District," *New York Times* (December 15, 1867): 8.

302. Landmarks Preservation Commission of the City of New York, LP-0165 (March 15, 1966); White and Willensky, *AIA Guide* (1988), 685; Diamonstein, *The Landmarks of New York II*, 152.

303. "The Williamsburgh Savings Bank," *New-York Sketch-Book of Architecture* 1 (February 1874): 1, plate v; A. J. Bloor, "Annual Address," *Proceedings of the Tenth Annual Convention of the American Institute of Architects, 1876* (Boston, 1877): 15–34; Henry-Russell Hitchcock, *The Architecture of H. H. Richardson and His Times*, rev. ed. (New York: Museum of Modern Art, 1936; Cambridge, Mass.: MIT Press, 1966), 152; Landmarks Preservation Commission of the City of New York, LP-0164 (May 17, 1966); Weisman, "The Commercial Architecture of George B. Post": 184; Landau, *P. B. Wight: Architect, Contractor, and Critic, 1838–1925*, 28–29; White and Willensky, *AIA Guide* (1988), 686; Diamonstein, *The Landmarks of New York II*, 168; Eve Kahn, "50-Year Dark Age Ends in Brooklyn," *New York Times* (May 4, 1995), C: 4; Landau, *George B. Post, Architect*, 18–23, plate 3.

304. "The Williamsburgh Savings Bank," *New-York Sketch-Book of Architecture*: 1.

305. Bloor, "Annual Address": 25.

306. "Buildings Projected," *Real Estate Record and Builders' Guide* 44 (October 12, 1889): 1389; White and Willensky, *AIA Guide* (1988), 687.

307. "Notes and Clippings," *American Architect and Building News* 1 (September 9, 1876): 296; "Synagogue Architecture in New York," *Village Views* 5 (1989): 61–62; Oscar Israelowitz, *Synagogues of the United States* (Brooklyn: Israelowitz Publishing, 1992), 54.

308. "Out Among the Builders: Brooklyn," *Real Estate Record and Builders' Guide* 34 (August 9, 1884): 835; "Dedicating a Church," *New York Times* (October 12, 1885): 2.

309. Landmarks Preservation Commission of the City of New York, LP-1977 (January 13, 1998); Barbara Whitaker, "Former 'Colored School' Houses Artist and Studio," *New York Times* (March 1, 1998), X: 4.

310. William Felter, *Historic Green Point* (New York: Green Point Savings Bank, 1918); Landmarks Preservation Commission of the City of New York, LP-1248 (September 14, 1982); Diamonstein, *The Landmarks of New York II*, 459.

311. "Buildings Projected," *Real Estate Record and Builders' Guide* 44 (August 10, 1889): 1121; Landmarks Preservation Commission of the City of New York, LP-1248 (September 14, 1982), 37.

312. Landmarks Preservation Commission of the City of New York, LP-1288 (April 12, 1983); White and Willensky, *AIA Guide* (1988), 692; Diamonstein, *The Landmarks of New York II*, 149.

313. Landmarks Preservation Commission of the City of New York, LP-1248 (September 14, 1982), 37–38; White and Willensky, *AIA Guide* (1988), 692–93.

314. Landmarks Preservation Commission of the City of New York, LP-1248 (September 14, 1982), 35–36; White and Willensky, *AIA Guide* (1988), 692.

315. "Dedication of St. Anthony's Roman Catholic Church of Brooklyn," *New York Times* (June 14, 1875): 8; Kervick, *Patrick Charles Keely, Architect*, 35; Landmarks Preservation Commission of the City of New York, LP-1248 (September 14, 1982), 45–46; White and Willensky, *AIA Guide* (1988), 694.

316. "Buildings Projected," *Real Estate Record and Builders' Guide* 40 (October 29, 1887): 1374; Landmarks Preservation Commission of the City of New York, LP-1248 (September 14, 1982), 77–78; White and Willensky, *AIA Guide* (1988), 694.

317. "The Astral Apartments, Greenpoint, N.Y., Messrs. Lamb & Rich, Architects, and Mr. E. L. Roberts, Consulting Architect, New York, N.Y.," *American Architect and Building News* 20 (November 13, 1886): 230–31, plate; Elgin R. L. Gould, *The Housing of the Working People: Eighth Special Report of the Commissioner of Labor* (Washington, D.C.: GPO, 1895), 788; Frederic B. Pratt, "Memories of My Father," in *Charles Pratt: An Interpretation, 1830–1930* (Brooklyn, 1930), 13–14; Ford, *Slums and Housing*, vol. 2: 883; McCullough, *Brooklyn . . . and How It Got That Way*, 42; Landmarks Preservation Commission of the City of New York, LP-1194 (June 28, 1983); White and Willensky, *AIA Guide* (1988), 692–93; Plunz, *A History of Housing in New York City*, 98; Diamonstein, *The Landmarks of New York II*, 189.

318. Elizabeth Reich Rawson, "Bushwick," in Jackson, ed., *The Encyclopedia of New York City*, 171–72. Also see Landmarks Preservation Commission of the City of New York, *Bushwick South and Bushwick Avenue*, undated report on proposed historic district.

319. "Buildings Projected," *Real Estate Record and Builders' Guide* 38 (August 7, 1886): 1021; White and Willensky, *AIA Guide* (1988), 677, 680.

320. White and Willensky, *AIA Guide* (1988), 677, 680.

321. "Buildings Projected," *Real Estate Record and Builders' Guide* 45 (March 15, 1890): 388; White and Willensky, *AIA Guide*, 680–81.

322. "Buildings Projected," *Real Estate Record and Builders' Guide* 42 (July 7, 1888): 880; White and Willensky, *AIA Guide* (1988), 680.

323. "Buildings Projected," *Real Estate Record and Builders' Guide* 39 (February 5, 1887): 186; White and Willensky, *AIA Guide* (1988), 680–81.

324. "Buildings Projected," *Real Estate Record and Builders' Guide* 35 (March 21, 1885): 316; White and Willensky, *AIA Guide* (1988), 681.

325. "Handsome New Church Building," *New York Times* (March 18, 1894): 16; "Laying of Cornerstone Stopped," *New York Times* (July 26, 1895): 3; "A Church Cornerstone Laid," *New York Daily Tribune* (September 13, 1895): 10; White and Willensky, *AIA Guide* (1988), 681–82.

326. "Buildings Projected," *Real Estate Record and Builders' Guide* 47 (May 30, 1891): 889; "Its Cornerstone Laid," *New York Times* (July 1, 1892): 1; "New Home of Democrats: Opening of the Bushwick Club's Fine Structure," *New York Times* (September 29, 1892): 1; Robinson, "Bravura in Brooklyn": 42–47; White and Willensky, *AIA Guide* (1988), 888; Gray, "Streetscapes/Frank Freeman, Architect": 7.

327. "Its Cornerstone Laid": 1.

328. "New Home of Democrats: Opening of the Bushwick Club's Fine Structure": 1.

329. "Fine Quarters for Police," *New York Daily Tribune* (September 22, 1895): 19; Landmarks Preservation Commission of the City of New York, LP-0951 (March 8, 1977); White and Willensky, *AIA Guide* (1988), 682; Diamonstein, *The Landmarks of New York II*, 219.

CHAPTER 8
The Suburban Ideal

1. Montgomery Schuyler, "Some Suburbs of New York: Part I—New Jersey," *Lippincott's Magazine* 8 (July 1884): 9–23.

2. Edward K. Spann, *The New Metropolis: New York City, 1840–1857* (New York: Columbia University Press, 1981), 176–204.

3. "Quick Travel," *Real Estate Record and Builders' Guide* 4 (January 1, 1870): 1.

4. James Richardson, "The New Homes of New York: A Study of Flats," *Scribner's Monthly* 8 (May 1874): 63–76.

5. "A Revolution in Living," editorial, *New York Times* (June 3, 1878): 4.

6. Raymond Westbrook, "Open Letters from New York," *Atlantic Monthly* 41 (January 1878): 91–99.

7. For discussions of commuting times, see F. A. Wright, "Suburban Houses of New York, Part I," *Building* 4 (February 20, 1886): 87; F. A. Wright, "Suburban Houses of New York, Part II," *Building* 4 (April 10, 1886): 172; "Suburban New York—I," *Real Estate Record and Builders' Guide* 40 (July 19, 1890): 73–76.

8. "The Problem of Living in New York," *Harper's New Monthly Magazine* 65 (November 1882): 918–24.

9. Westbrook, "Open Letters from New York": 93.

10. "Westchester Annexation," *Real Estate Record and Builders' Guide* 12 (November 1, 1873): 1; William Cauldwell, "Annexation," in *The Great North Side of the City of New York* (New York: North Side Board of Trade, 1897), 19–29. For general discussions of the development of the Bronx, see Stephen Jenkins, *The Story of the Bronx* (New York: G. P. Putnam's Sons, 1912); Gary D. Hermalyn and Lloyd Ultan, "Bronx," in Kenneth T. Jackson, ed., *The Encyclopedia of New York City* (New Haven, Conn., and London: Yale University Press; New York: New-York Historical Society, 1995), 142–46.

11. George M. Zoebelein, "Boundaries of the Bronx and Its Communities," *Journal of the Bronx County Historical Society* 3 (July 1966): 51–78.

12. "Give Us Room," editorial, *New York Times* (May 5, 1873): 4–5.

13. Andrew Wolf and Dita Mantegazza, "Transit Expansion and the Growth of the Bronx," *Journal of the Bronx County Historical Society* 7 (January 1970): 12–24.

14. Editorial, *Real Estate Record and Builders' Guide* 36 (August 22, 1885): 927; Editorial, *Real Estate Record and Builders' Guide* 36 (October 31, 1885): 1183–84; "The Mott Haven Station," *Real Estate Record and Builders' Guide* 39 (April 9, 1887): 472–73; "New Mott Haven Station of the New York Central and Hudson River Railroad at 138th Street," *New York Daily Graphic* (November 21, 1887): 149; "Supplement—New York Central and Hudson River Railroad Station at 138th Street, New York City," *Architecture and Building* 12 (February 1, 1890): 55, plate; "The East Side—Its Streets and Buildings," supplement, *Real Estate Record and Builders' Guide* 45 (May 3, 1890): 1–11; Montgomery Schuyler, "The Romanesque Revival in New York," *Architectural Record* 1 (July–September 1891): 7–38; Montgomery Schuyler, "The Works of R. H. Robertson," *Architectural Record* 6 (October–December 1896): 184–219; Edwin P. Alexander, *Down at the Depot* (New York: Clarkson N. Potter, 1970), 135; Carl W. Condit, *The Port of New York* (Chicago: University of Chicago Press, 1980), 113, 115.

15. "The Mott Haven Station," *Real Estate Record and Builders' Guide*: 472–73.

16. Schuyler, "The Romanesque Revival in New York": 24–26.

17. Schuyler, "The Works of R. H. Robertson": 193–94.

18. Albert E. Davis, "A Home Center," in *The Great North Side of the City of New York*, 118.

19. "Pleasant Homes Near at Hand: Working in the City and Living in the Country," *New York Times* (February 16, 1884): 7; "Uptown Improvements. What Is Being Done to Build Up and Beautify the Twenty-Fourth Ward," *New York Daily Graphic* (April 19, 1884): 370; Kathleen Whitney Bukofzer, "Bedford Park: A Victim of Its Own Success" (master's thesis, Columbia University, 1983); Gary D. Hermalyn, "Bedford Park," in Jackson, ed., *The Encyclopedia of New York City*, 94.

20. *Bedford Park* (London: Harrison and Sons, 1882); Margaret Jones Bolsterli, *The Early Community at Bedford Park* (Athens, Ohio: Ohio University Press, 1977); Robert A. M. Stern with John Montague Massengale, *The Anglo-American Suburb* (London: Architectural Design, 1981), 27.

21. "Pleasant Homes Near at Hand": 7.

22. "Uptown Improvements. What Is Being Done to Build Up and Beautify the Twenty-Fourth Ward": 370.

23. John W. Kennion, *Architects' and Builders' Guide* (New York: Fitzpatrick & Hunter, 1868), part 2: 104–5; Bukofzer, "Bedford Park: A Victim of Its Own Success": 14–15; Lloyd Ultan, "Jerome Park: The First Site of the Belmont Stakes," *Yankee Magazine* 50 (September 1, 1983): 31.

24. Landmarks Preservation Commission of the City of New York, LP-0917 (March 23, 1976); Barbaralee Diamonstein, *The Landmarks of New York II* (New York: Harry N. Abrams, 1993), 118.

25. "The Van Schaick Free Reading-Room, Westchester, N.Y. Mr. F. C. Withers, Architect, New York, N.Y.," *American Architect and Building News* 14 (October 20, 1883): 186, plate; Editorial, *New York Times* (August 30, 1885): 6; Editorial, *American Architect and Building News* 18 (September 5, 1885): 110; Francis R. Kowsky, "The Huntington Free Library and the Van Schaick Free Reading Room," *Journal of the Bronx County Historical Society* 7 (January 1970): 1–7; Francis R. Kowsky, *The Architecture of Frederick Clarke Withers and the Progress of the Gothic Revival in America After 1850* (Middletown, Conn.: Wesleyan University Press, 1980), 137–38; Landmarks Preservation Commission of the City of New York, LP-1886 (April 5, 1994).

26. White and Willensky, *AIA Guide* (1988), 527–34; Landmarks Preservation Commission of the City of New York, LP-1663 (October 16, 1990).

27. Effingham P. Humphrey, "The Churches of James Renwick, Jr." (master's thesis, New York University, 1942): 69; Landmarks Preservation Commission of the City of New York, LP-0128 (April 19, 1966); Diamonstein, *The Landmarks of New York II*, 142.

28. Landmarks Preservation Commission of the City of New York, LP-0126 (January 11, 1967); Diamonstein, *The Landmarks of New York II*, 148.

29. Landmarks Preservation Commission of the City of New York, LP-0672 (October 13, 1970); John Zukowsky and Robbe Pierce Stimson, *Hudson River Villas* (New York: Rizzoli International Publications, 1985), 24; White and Willensky, *AIA Guide* (1988), 530; Diamonstein, *The Landmarks of New York II*, 142.

30. Frederick Law Olmsted and J. James R. Croes, *Report of the Landscape Architect and the Civil and Topographical Engineer, Accompanying a Plan for Laying Out That Part of the Twenty-fourth Ward Lying West of the Riverdale Road*, Department of Parks, November 21, 1876, reprinted in Albert Fein, ed., *Landscape into Cityscape: Frederick Law Olmsted's Plans for a Greater New York City* (New York: Van Nostrand Reinhold, 1981), 360–61.

31. Frederick Law Olmsted et al., *Report to the Staten Island Improvement Commission of a Preliminary Scheme of Improvements* (1871), reprinted in Fein, ed., *Landscape into Cityscape*, 180.

32. Frederick Law Olmsted, quoted in Albert Fein, *Wave Hill, Riverdale and New York City: Legacy of a Hudson River Estate* (Bronx, N.Y.: Wave Hill, 1979), 6. Also see "The Future Suburbs of New York," editorial, *New York Times* (February 25, 1877): 6.

33. Olmsted and Croes, *Report of the Landscape Architect and the Civil and Topographical Engineer, Accompanying a Plan for Laying Out That Part of the Twenty-fourth Ward Lying West of the Riverdale Road*, reprinted in Fein, ed., *Landscape into Cityscape*, 352.

34. "Streets in the Annexed District," *New York Daily Tribune* (March 1, 1877): 3.

35. Landmarks Preservation Commission of the City of New York, LP-1086 (November 25, 1980); Diamonstein, *The Landmarks of New York II*, 198.

36. "Rochelle Park," *New York Daily Graphic* (May 14, 1887): 612; Wanderer, "New Rochelle," *Real Estate Record and Builders' Guide* 40 (December 17, 1887): 1582; "Proposed House at Rochelle Park, New Rochelle, N.Y. George Martin Huss, Architect, N.Y.," *Architecture and Building* 12 (March 1, 1890): plate; "Suburban New York, IV—New Rochelle," *Real Estate Record and Builders' Guide* 46 (August 30, 1890): 271–74; Samuel Swift, "Community Life at Rochelle Park, American Suburban Communities IV," *House and Garden* 4 (May 1904): 235–43; "Study of a New York Suburb, New Rochelle," *Architectural Record* 25 (April 1909): 235–48; Richard Schermerhorn Jr., "Nathan Franklin Barrett, Landscape Architect," *Landscape Architecture* 10 (April 1920): 108–13; Herbert B. Nichols, *Historic New Rochelle* (New Rochelle, N.Y.: Board of Education, 1938); David Finn, *New Rochelle: Portrait of a City*, with an introduction by Ruth Kitchen (New York: Abbeville, 1981); Stern with Massengale, *The Anglo-American Suburb*, 30, 95; Marilyn E. Weigold, ed., *Westchester County: The Past Hundred Years* (Valhalla, N.Y.: Westchester County Historical Society, 1984). For a description of New Rochelle prior to the Civil War, see Robert Bolton, *Guide to New Rochelle and Its Vicinity* (New Rochelle, N.Y.: A. Hanford, 1842).

37. Swift, "Community Life at Rochelle Park, American Suburban Communities IV": 235.

38. Swift, "Community Life at Rochelle Park, American Suburban Communities IV": 236.

39. "Rochelle Park," *New York Daily Graphic*: 612.

40. Wanderer, "New Rochelle": 1582.

41. "Rochelle Park," *New York Daily Graphic*: 612.

42. "Long Island," *New York Times* (June 24, 1875): 12; "The Long Island City Shore Railroad," *New York Times* (July 4, 1875): 12; "Population of Queen's [sic] County," *New York Times* (September 6, 1875): 8; "Long Island," *New York Times* (July 4, 1880): 12; "America, the Future Home of Music: Our Growing Taste for Good Music—Influence of the Pianoforte: Steinway & Sons," *New York Times* (January 1, 1886): 3; "William Steinway," *Magazine of Western History* 10 (October 1889): 665–70; "Busy Times for Croker," *New York Times* (June 8, 1890): 5; "Lessons in Rapid Transit: Mr. Steinway's Observations on a Trip Abroad," *New York Times* (November 1, 1890): 9; Moses King, *King's Handbook of New York* (Boston: Moses King, 1892), 942–43; "Steinway's Road Reorganized," *New York Times* (March 31, 1892): 8; "Why Foster Resigned," *New York Times* (April 16, 1892): 2; Julius Hoffman, "Evolution of the Piano," *National Magazine* 16 (October 1892): 701–10; "North Beach, Steinway, Long Island," *New York Times* (July 12, 1896):

25–28; "William Steinway Dead," *New York Daily Tribune* (December 1, 1896): 7; "William Steinway," editorial, *New York Times* (December 1, 1896): 4; "William Steinway Dead," *New York Times* (December 1, 1896): 9; "William Steinway," *Harper's Weekly* 40 (December 12, 1896): 1228; Landmarks Preservation Commission of the City of New York, *Steinway Historic District Designation Report* (New York, 1974); Aaron Singer, "Labor-Management Relations at Steinway & Sons, 1853–1896" (Ph. D. diss., Columbia University, 1977): 73–75, 87–105; Janet E. and Robert K. Lieberman, *City Limits: A Social History of Queens* (Dubuque, Iowa: Kendall/Hunt, 1983), 180–84; White and Willensky, *AIA Guide* (1988), 732–33; Ronald V. Ratcliffe, *Steinway & Sons* (San Francisco: Chronicle Books, 1989), 42, 48; Jeffrey A. Kroessler and Nina S. Rappaport, *Historic Preservation in Queens* (Flushing, N.Y.: Queensborough Preservation League, 1990), 33, 50; Richard Plunz, *A History of Housing in New York City* (New York: Columbia University Press, 1990), 114–16; Joann P. Krieg, ed., *Long Island Studies: Long Island Architecture* (Interlaken, N.Y.: Heart of the Lakes Publishing, 1991), n.p.; Jeffrey Andrew Kroessler, "Building Queens: The Urbanization of New York's Largest Borough" (Ph. D. diss., City University of New York, 1991): 180–84, 208–28; Vincent F. Seyfried and William Asadorian, *Old Queens, N.Y. in Early Photographs* (New York: Dover, 1991), 146–49; Christopher Gray, "Streetscapes: The Steinway Rowhouses," *New York Times* (March 3, 1991), X: 8; D. W. Fostle, *The Steinway Saga: An American Dynasty* (New York: Scribner, 1995), 278–85, 290–95, 304–9, 315–24; Richard K. Lieberman, *Steinway & Sons* (New Haven, Conn., and London: Yale University Press, 1995), 77–86.

43. William Steinway, quoted in "North Beach, Steinway, Long Island": 25.

44. William Steinway, quoted in "North Beach, Steinway, Long Island": 25.

45. William Steinway, diary entry dated July 11, 1870, quoted in Singer, "Labor-Management Relations at Steinway & Sons, 1853–1896": 89.

46. "Out Among the Builders," *Real Estate Record and Builders' Guide* 28 (July 16, 1881): 721.

47. "Out Among the Builders," *Real Estate Record and Builders' Guide* 28 (July 23, 1881): 744.

48. "Out Among the Builders," *Real Estate Record and Builders' Guide* 28 (October 1, 1881): 923.

49. "Out Among the Builders," *Real Estate Record and Builders' Guide* 33 (March 22, 1884): 292–93.

50. "House at Steinway, L.I. N. Gillesheimer, Architect, New York City," *Building* 7 (November 19, 1887): 169.

51. William Steinway, quoted in "North Beach, Steinway, Long Island": 25.

52. "Death in Dynamite," *New York World* (December 29, 1892): 1–2.

53. The tunnel was constructed for a streetcar line that was never built. It did not become operational until 1915, when the Interborough Rapid Transit Company extended service into Queens. See Condit, *The Port of New York*, 95.

54. "The Newtown Creek Ammonia Works," *New York Times* (August 1, 1879): 8. Also see "City and Suburban News," *New York Times* (July 8, 1878): 8; "A Newtown Creek Factory," *New York Times* (August 12, 1879): 8.

55. "Bowery Bay Beach," advertisement, *New York Sun* (June 18, 1886): 4.

56. "Bowery Bay Damage Suit," *New York Times* (August 5, 1887): 8.

57. *Long Island City Star* (July 21, 1882), quoted in Kroessler, "Building Queens: The Urbanization of New York's Largest Borough": 209–10.

58. "Bowery Bay Beach," *New York Times* (June 18, 1886): 5.

59. William Steinway, testimony before the United States Senate Committee on Education and Labor, 1883, quoted in Fostle, *The Steinway Saga*, 292.

60. "North Beach, Steinway, Long Island": 25.

61. King, *King's Handbook of New York* (1892), 942.

62. Landmarks Preservation Commission of the City of New York, LP-0826 (September 26, 1974); Diamonstein, *The Landmarks of New York II*, 141.

63. "Beauties of College Point," *New York Daily Graphic* (August 3, 1888): 263–66; Landmarks Preservation Commission of the City of New

York, LP-0662 (August 18, 1970); Diamonstein, *The Landmarks of New York II*, 152.

64. William Alex, *Calvert Vaux: Architect & Planner* (New York: Ink, 1994), 229.

65. Landmarks Preservation Commission of the City of New York, LP-0139 (July 30, 1968); White and Willensky, *AIA Guide* (1988), 769; Diamonstein, *The Landmarks of New York II*, 143.

66. "The New Queens County Court-House," *New York Times* (February 9, 1874): 3; "New Court House for Queens County, N.Y.," *New York Daily Graphic* (July 10, 1876): 59; White and Willensky, *AIA Guide* (1988), 737, 739; Seyfried and Asadorian, *Old Queens, N.Y. in Early Photographs*, 43.

67. M., "A Millionaire's Cathedral City—I," *American Architect and Building News* 6 (September 20, 1879): 91. Also see "Metropolitan Annexation and Consolidation," editorial, *New York Times* (July 20, 1869): 4; "The Hempstead Plains," *Harper's Weekly* 13 (August 7, 1869): 503; M., "A Millionaire's Cathedral City—II," *American Architect and Building News* 6 (September 27, 1879): 102–3; James C. Brierley, "A Millionaire's Cathedral," letter to the editor, *American Architect and Building News* 6 (October 25, 1879): 135; "Stewart's Garden City," *New York Herald* (January 20, 1880): 3; W. G. Marshall, *Through America; or Nine Months in the United States* (London: Sampson, Low, Marston, Searle & Rivington, 1881), 16–19; Montgomery Schuyler, "Some Suburbs of New York: Part II—Westchester and Long Island," *Lippincott's Magazine* 8 (August 1884): 113–26; M. H. Smith, *History of Garden City*, rev. ed. (Garden City, N.Y.: Garden City Historical Society, 1963, 1980); Vincent F. Seyfried, *The Founding of Garden City: 1869–1893* (Uniondale, N.Y.: published by the author, 1969); Deborah S. Gardner, "The Architecture of Commercial Capitalism: John Kellum and the Development of New York, 1840–1875" (Ph.D. diss., Columbia University, 1979): 261–313, figs. 114–34; Bette S. Weidman and Linda B. Martin, *Nassau County, Long Island in Early Photographs, 1869–1940* (New York: Dover, 1981), figs. 82–83; Kenneth T. Jackson, *Crabgrass Frontier: The Suburbanization of the United States* (New York: Oxford University Press, 1985), 81–84; M. H. Smith, *Garden City, Long Island, in Early Photographs, 1869–1919* (New York: Dover, 1987), esp. figs. 1–48; Plunz, *A History of Housing in New York City*, 113–14; Stephen N. Elias, *Alexander T. Stewart: The Forgotten Merchant Prince* (Westport, Conn.: Praeger, 1992), 177–88.

68. Alexander T. Stewart, quoted in "Stewart's Garden City": 3.

69. "Stewart's Garden City": 3.

70. M., "A Millionaire's Cathedral City—I": 91.

71. Alexander T. Stewart, quoted in "Stewart's Garden City": 3.

72. "Stewart's Garden City": 3.

73. M., "A Millionaire's Cathedral City—I": 91.

74. "The Hempstead Plains": 503.

75. Quoted in Smith, *History of Garden City*, 21.

76. Quoted in M., "A Millionaire's Cathedral City—I": 91.

77. M., "A Millionaire's Cathedral City—I": 91.

78. M., "A Millionaire's Cathedral City—II": 102.

79. Schuyler, "Some Suburbs of New York: Part II—Westchester and Long Island": 113–26.

80. Shirley Zavin, *Staten Island: An Architectural History*, exhibition catalogue (New York: Staten Island Institute for Arts and Sciences, 1979), 5; Stern with Massengale, *The Anglo-American Suburb*, 19; Shirley Zavin and Elsa Gilbertson, *Staten Island Walking Tours* (Staten Island, N.Y.: Preservation League of Staten Island, 1986), 8. For discussions of Staten Island's history and development, see Charles W. Leng and William T. Davis, *Staten Island and Its People: A History, 1609–1929* (New York: Lewis Historical Publishing, 1930); Dorothy Valentine Smith, *This Was Staten Island* (New York: Staten Island Historical Society, 1968); Charles L. Sachs, "Staten Island," in Jackson, ed., *The Encyclopedia of New York City*, 1112–18.

81. George A. Ward, *Description of New Brighton on Staten Island Opposite the City of New York* (New York: New Brighton Association, 1836), 6.

82. Haviland Papers, University of Pennsylvania, Book IV: 4–5; Ira K. Morris, "Historic Landmarks of Staten Island," *American Scenic and Historic Preservation Society, Tenth Annual Report* (1905), appendix B: 147;

83. Matthew Eli Baigell, "John Haviland" (Ph.D. diss., University of Pennsylvania, 1965): 187–88.

83. Zavin, *Staten Island: An Architectural History*, 5.

84. Frederick Law Olmsted Jr. and Theodora Kimball, eds., *Forty Years of Landscape Architecture: Frederick Law Olmsted, Senior*, 2 vols. (New York: G. P. Putnam's Sons, 1922, 1928), vol. 1: 85–86; Laura Wood Roper, *FLO: A Biography of Frederick Law Olmsted* (Baltimore: Johns Hopkins University Press, 1973), 56–65; Lee Hall, *Olmsted's America* (Boston: Little, Brown, 1995), 29–31, 47–48.

85. Zavin, *Staten Island: An Architectural History*, 5, 8.

86. Frederick Law Olmsted et al., *Report to the Staten Island Improvement Commission of a Preliminary Scheme of Improvements* (1871), reprinted in Fein, ed., *Landscape into Cityscape*, 173–299.

87. Christopher Gray, "The Old Yacht Club on Staten Island," *New York Times* (September 8, 1991), VIII: 6.

88. Zavin, *Staten Island: An Architectural History*, 6.

89. "The S. I. Athletic Club's New Boat House," *New York Daily Graphic* (July 12, 1887): 85; Smith, *This Was Staten Island*, 111; Zavin, *Staten Island: An Architectural History*, 6.

90. Smith, *This Was Staten Island*, 114.

91. "Hotel Castleton, Brighton Heights, New Brighton, Staten Island, N.Y.," *Building* 10 (February 16, 1889): 55, plate. Also see A Layman, "The Architectural League Exhibit," *Real Estate Record and Builders' Guide* 45 (January 11, 1890): 35–36; "Examples of Recent Architecture—At Home," *Real Estate Record and Builders' Guide* 46 (December 6, 1890): 758; "Hotel Castleton, New Brighton, Staten Island, N.Y. Mr. C.P.H. Gilbert, Architect, New York, N.Y.," *American Architect and Building News* 30 (December 13, 1890): 167, plate; Smith, *This Was Staten Island*, 70–71; Zavin, *Staten Island: An Architectural History*, 6.

92. "The Demand for Dwelling Houses," *Richmond County Gazette* (March 8, 1865), quoted in Landmarks Preservation Commission of the City of New York, LP-1883 (July 19, 1994), 12.

93. Zavin, *Staten Island: An Architectural History*, 8.

94. Landmarks Preservation Commission of the City of New York, LP-1883 (July 19, 1994).

95. White and Willensky, *AIA Guide* (1988), 810.

96. Henry-Russell Hitchcock, *The Architecture of H. H. Richardson and His Times*, rev. ed. (New York: Museum of Modern Art, 1936; Cambridge, Mass.: MIT Press, 1966), 310; Vincent J. Scully Jr., *The Shingle Style and the Stick Style* (New Haven, Conn.: Yale University Press, 1955), 4–5; Henry-Russell Hitchcock, *Henry Hobson Richardson as a Victorian Architect* (Baltimore: Smith College at the Barton-Gillett Company, 1966), 9; Lawrence Wodehouse, "Henry Hobson Richardson's Home at Arrochar," *Victorian Society in America Bulletin* 2 (September 1974): 6; Jeffrey Karl Ochsner, *H. H. Richardson: Complete Architectural Works* (Cambridge, Mass.: MIT Press, 1982), 46–47; White and Willensky, *AIA Guide* (1988), 833.

97. Ochsner, *H. H. Richardson: Complete Architectural Works*, 30.

98. Bruce Price, "The Suburban House," *Scribner's Magazine* 8 (July 1890): 3–19.

99. "Cottage at New Brighton, Staten Island, for Alexander J. Hamilton, Esq. Mr. Bassett Jones, Architect," *American Architect and Building News* 2 (May 5, 1877): 140, plate; Price, "The Suburban House": 18. For McKim, Mead & White's Fairchild stable, see Leland M. Roth, *McKim, Mead & White, Architects* (New York: Harper & Row, 1983), 38.

100. "Gardener's Cottage and Stable for William Krebs, Esq., Staten Island. Mr. Bassett Jones, Architect," *American Architect and Building News* 2 (May 5, 1877): 140, plate. Also see Price, "The Suburban House": 18; Sadayoshi Omoto, "The Queen Anne Style and Architectural Criticism," *Journal of the Society of Architectural Historians* 23 (March 1964): 29–37.

101. "Gardener's Cottage and Stable for William Krebs, Esq., Staten Island. Mr. Bassett Jones, Architect": 140.

102. "Some Suburban Architecture," *Real Estate Record and Builders' Guide* 33 (February 23, 1884): 181. For a discussion of John C. Henderson and Henderson Place, see chapter 4.

103. Landmarks Preservation Commission of the City of New York, LP-1883 (July 19, 1994); Christopher Gray, "78 Houses and a Church Overlooking the Harbor," *New York Times* (October 2, 1994), XIII: 7.

104. Landmarks Preservation Commission of the City of New York, LP-1883 (July 19, 1994), 33–34.

105. White and Willensky, *AIA Guide* (1988), 808; Landmarks Preservation Commission of the City of New York, LP-1883 (July 19, 1994), 51–52.

106. Landmarks Preservation Commission of the City of New York, LP-1883 (July 19, 1994), 54–55.

107. White and Willensky, *AIA Guide* (1988), 808; Landmarks Preservation Commission of the City of New York, LP-1883 (July 19, 1994), 56–57.

108. White and Willensky, *AIA Guide* (1988), 808. For the Francis L. Skinner house, see Roth, *McKim, Mead & White, Architects*, 77.

109. White and Willensky, *AIA Guide* (1988), 809; Landmarks Preservation Commission of the City of New York, LP-1883 (July 19, 1994), 19–23. For Bay Villa, see Smith, *This Was Staten Island*, 100–101.

110. Landmarks Preservation Commission of the City of New York, LP-1870–73 (July 26, 1994).

111. Landmarks Preservation Commission of the City of New York, LP-1875 (July 26, 1994).

112. Landmarks Preservation Commission of the City of New York, LP-0391 (February 20, 1968); Diamonstein, *The Landmarks of New York II*, 189.

113. Landmarks Preservation Commission of the City of New York, LP-1113 (September 9, 1980).

114. White and Willensky, *AIA Guide* (1988), 807–8.

115. Landmarks Preservation Commission of the City of New York, LP-0373 (February 19, 1974); White and Willensky, *AIA Guide* (1988), 830; Diamonstein, *The Landmarks of New York II*, 154.

116. Kennion, *Architects' and Builders' Guide*, part 2: 1–2; Sarah Bradford Landau, *Edward T. and William A. Potter: American Victorian Architects* (New York: Garland, 1979), 138–39, 457, fig. 37; White and Willensky, *AIA Guide* (1988), 825.

117. Landmarks Preservation Commission of the City of New York, LP-0399 (November 15, 1967); White and Willensky, *AIA Guide* (1988), 848; Diamonstein, *The Landmarks of New York II*, 158.

118. Zavin, *Staten Island: An Architectural History*, 11.

119. "The Tomb of the Vanderbilts," *New York Daily Tribune* (December 16, 1884): 2; Montgomery Schuyler, "The Works of the Late Richard M. Hunt," *Architectural Record* 5 (October–December 1895): 97–180; "How the Rich Are Buried," *Architectural Record* 10 (July 1900): 26; Wayne Andrews, *The Vanderbilt Legend* (New York: Harcourt, Brace, 1941), 232–33, 239; Wayne Andrews, *Architecture in New York* (New York: Atheneum, 1969), xii; Robert Miraldi, "The Vanderbilt Mausoleum," *Staten Island Advance* (September 24, 1978): 1, 12; Robert Miraldi, "The Vanderbilt Mausoleum," *Staten Island Advance* (September 25, 1978): 1, 8; Robert Miraldi, "The Vanderbilt Mausoleum," *Staten Island Advance* (September 26, 1978): 1, 8; Robert Miraldi, "The Vanderbilt Mausoleum," *Staten Island Advance* (April 15, 1979): 8; Paul R. Baker, *Richard Morris Hunt* (Cambridge, Mass.: MIT Press, 1980), 290–92; Paul R. Baker, "Richard Morris Hunt: An Introduction," in Susan R. Stein, ed., *The Architecture of Richard Morris Hunt* (Chicago: University of Chicago Press, 1986), 7; Francis R. Kowsky, "The Central Park Gateways: Harbingers of French Urbanism Confront the American Landscape Tradition," in Stein, ed., *The Architecture of Richard Morris Hunt*, 87; White and Willensky, *AIA Guide* (1988), 844–45.

120. Landmarks Preservation Commission of the City of New York, LP-1112 (November 25, 1980); White and Willensky, *AIA Guide* (1988), 807; Diamonstein, *The Landmarks of New York II*, 153.

121. White and Willensky, *AIA Guide* (1988), 825.

122. Zavin, *Staten Island: An Architectural History*, 5.

123. Zavin, *Staten Island: An Architectural History*, 5.

124. Christopher Gray, "The Samuel H. Smith Infirmary," *New York Times* (May 3, 1987), VIII: 5, reprinted in Christopher Gray, *Changing New York: The Architectural Scene* (New York: Dover, 1992), 8; White and Willensky, *AIA Guide* (1988), 826–27.

125. "Llewellyn Park: Country Homes for City People," undated promotional pamphlet; Henry Winthrop Sargent, supplement to Andrew Jackson Downing, *A Treatise on the Theory and Practice of Landscape Gardening, Adapted to North America; . . . with remarks on Rural Architecture*,

6th ed. (New York, 1859), 567–73; "Llewellyn Park," *Demorest's New York Illustrated News* 2 (May 12, 1860): 5; "Country Seats and Parks," *Demorest's New York Illustrated News* 2 (May 19, 1860): 20, 32; "Country Seats and Parks," *Demorest's New York Illustrated News* 2 (June 23, 1860): 100–101, 106; "Literature: The May Festival in Llewellyn Park," *Demorest's New York Illustrated News* 2 (June 23, 1860): 107; Theodore Tilton, "Llewellyn Park," *Independent* (May 26, 1864), reprinted in *New York Times* (April 23, 1865): 5; *Newark Daily Advertiser* (May 11, 1866), Newark Public Library Clipping Files; "Llewellyn Park," *Every Saturday* 3 (September 2, 1871): 227; Samuel Swift, "Llewellyn Park, West Orange, Essex Co., New Jersey: The First American Suburban Community," *House and Garden* 3 (June 1903): 327–35; Christopher Tunnard, "The Romantic Suburb in America," *Magazine of Art* 40 (May 1947): 184–87; Christopher Tunnard and Henry Hope Reed, *American Skyline* (New York: New American Library, 1953), 115; Richard Guy Wilson, "Charles F. McKim and the Development of the American Renaissance: A Study in Architecture and Culture" (Ph.D. diss., University of Michigan, 1972): 6; Wayne Andrews, *American Gothic: Its Origins, Its Trials, Its Triumphs* (New York: Random House, 1975), 43, 49; Jane B. Davies, "Llewellyn Park in West Orange, New Jersey," *Antiques* 107 (January 1975): 142–58; Michael Robinson, "The Suburban Ideal: 19th-Century Planned Communities," *Historic Preservation* 30 (April–June 1978): 24–29; Gardner, "The Architecture of Commercial Capitalism: John Kellum and the Development of New York, 1840–1875": 275–77, fig. 112; Leland M. Roth, *A Concise History of American Architecture* (New York: Harper & Row, 1979), 102–7; Richard Guy Wilson, "Idealism and the Origin of the First American Suburb, Llewellyn Park, New Jersey," *The American Art Journal* 11 (October 1979): 79–90; Stern with Massengale, *The Anglo-American Suburb*, 21; John Archer, "Country and City in the American Romantic Suburb," *Journal of the Society of Architectural Historians* 42 (May 1983): 139–56; Jackson, *Crabgrass Frontier*, 76–79; Robert A. M. Stern with Thomas Mellins and Raymond Gastil, *Pride of Place: Building the American Dream* (Boston: Houghton Mifflin; New York: American Heritage, 1986), 129, 132–33; Susan Henderson, "Llewellyn Park, Suburban Idyll," *Journal of Garden History* 7 (No. 3, 1987): 221–43; John R. Stilgoe, *Borderland: Origins of the American Suburb, 1820–1939* (New Haven, Conn., and London: Yale University Press, 1988), 52–55; Plunz, *A History of Housing in New York City*, 9–10.

126. "Llewellyn Park: Country Homes for City People," undated promotional pamphlet. Also see advertisements in the *Orange Journal*, May 16, 1857, to November 28, 1863, and March 24 to April 14, 1866.

127. Tilton, "Llewellyn Park," reprinted in *New York Times*: 5.

128. Sarah Allibone McKim to Charles Follen McKim, June 7, 1866, quoted in Charles Moore, *The Life and Times of Charles Follen McKim* (Boston: Houghton Mifflin, 1929; New York: Da Capo Press, 1970), 15.

129. Tilton, "Llewellyn Park," reprinted in *New York Times*: 5.

130. Letter of Edward D. Page, March 24, 1916, quoted in Wilson, "Idealism and the Origin of the First American Suburb, Llewellyn Park, New Jersey": 85.

131. Alexander Jackson Davis to Jas. Eddy and Mrs. H. M. Louvier, January 30, 1879, New York Public Library, Davis Collection, Letterbook, 266b–266e, quoted in Wilson, "Idealism and the Origin of the First American Suburb, Llewellyn Park, New Jersey": 89.

132. William T. Comstock, *Modern Architectural Designs and Details* (New York: William T. Comstock, 1881), reprinted as *Victorian Architectural Plans and Details* (New York: Dover, 1987), plate 45; "Cottage for A. B. Rich, D.D., Short Hills Park, N.J. Messers. Lamb & Rich, Architects, New York, N.Y.," *American Architect and Building News* 11 (January 7, 1882): 6, plate; "'Redstone,' Short Hills, N.J. Messrs. Lamb & Rich, Architects, New York, N.Y.," *American Architect and Building News* 12 (September 2, 1882): 110, plate; G. W. Sheldon, *Artistic Houses: Being a Series of Interior Views of a Number of the Most Beautiful and Celebrated Homes in the United States, with a Description of the Art Treasures Contained Therein*, 2 vols. (New York: D. Appleton, 1883–84; New York: Benjamin Blom, 1971), vol. 2, part 1: 76–78, vol. 2, part 2: 187–88; Schuyler, "Some Suburbs of New York: Part I—New Jersey": 21–23; "An American Park," *American Architect and Building News* 16 (July 12, 1884): 15–16, 19, plates; G. W. Sheldon, *Artistic Country-Seats*, 2 vols. (New York: D. Appleton, 1886; New York: Da Capo Press, 1979), vol. 1: 114–18, vol. 2:

132–35; "House at Short Hills, N.J., for Mr. A. Stewart, Jr. and Other Sketches," *Building* 7 (July 16, 1887): 21, plates; "Notice," *Building* 8 (February 23, 1888): 29; Cora L. Hartshorn, "A Little History of the Short Hills Section of Millburn Township, N.J., Developed by Stewart Hartshorn," unpublished manuscript dated July 31, 1946, Millburn Public Library; Scully, *The Shingle Style and the Stick Style*, 133; Marian Keefe Meisner, "A History of Millburn Township, N.J.," unpublished manuscript dated 1957, Millburn Public Library; *Millburn: 1857–1957* (Millburn, N.J.: Millburn Centennial Committee, 1957); Leland M. Roth, "The Urban Architecture of McKim, Mead and White, 1870–1910" (Ph.D. diss., Yale University, 1973): 333, 336–37; Leland Roth, *The Architecture of McKim, Mead & White, 1870–1920: A Building List* (New York and London: Garland, 1978), 14, 143; David Gibson and the Millburn-Short Hills Historical Society, "Survey for the National Register," unpublished manuscript dated 1980; Anne Klemme, ed., *Sticks, Shingles and Stones: The History and Architecture of Stewart Hartshorn's Ideal Community at Short Hills, New Jersey, 1878–1937* (Millburn, N.J.: Millburn-Short Hills Historical Society, 1980); Robert Philip Griter, "The New Jersey Commissions of McKim, Mead & White, 1874–1916" (master's thesis, Columbia University, 1981): 153–54; Stern with Massengale, *The Anglo-American Suburb*, 26; E. Richard McKinstry, book review, *Journal of the Society of Architectural Historians* 40 (December 1981): 344–46; Roth, *McKim, Mead & White, Architects*, 67–68; Jerry Cheslow, "If You're Thinking of Living In: Millburn," *New York Times* (April 5, 1992), X: 7.

133. Schuyler, "Some Suburbs of New York: Part I—New Jersey": 21.

134. Sheldon, *Artistic Country-Seats*, vol. 2: 133.

135. "An American Park": 16. For another house by Lamb & Rich in Short Hills, see "House at Short Hills, N.J., Messrs. Lamb & Rich, Architects, New York, N.Y.," *American Architect and Building News* 11 (May 13, 1882): 223, plate.

136. "An American Park": 16.

137. "An American Park": 16.

138. *The History of Essex County* (1884), quoted in Klemme, ed., *Sticks, Shingles and Stones*, 2–3.

139. "An American Park": 15.

140. Schuyler, "Some Suburbs of New York: Part I—New Jersey": 21–23.

Index